Pasquenoke

WEAPEMEOC

Trinety harbor

This engraving from deBry's *America*, published in 1590, shows a view of Sir Walter Raleigh's colony on Roanoke Island, near present-day North Carolina. Settled in 1587, it was the first English colony in the New World. When Raleigh returned to the colony in 1590, the settlers had disappeared, and their fate remains a mystery to this day.

THE
AMERICAN
PAST

A SURVEY OF AMERICAN HISTORY

THE
AMERICAN
PAST

A SURVEY OF AMERICAN HISTORY

JOSEPH R. CONLIN

Harcourt Brace Jovanovich, Publishers

San Diego   New York   Chicago   Atlanta   Washington, D.C.

London   Sydney   Toronto

Cover photo: Werner Kalber
Background photo: John G. Nemanich, Jr.
Window art: Diane Polster
Maps: Intergraphics

ISBN: 0-15-502309-8
Library of Congress Catalog Number: 83-81974
Printed in the United States of America

To J.R.C. and L.V.C.

Preface

No historian needs to be told that the past is worth knowing about. No teacher of United States history needs a reminder that the story of our people and our nation is a saga fascinating in itself, or that knowing how we got to where we are is essential to understanding the present and preparing for the future. But a great many students may not be so sure about such self-evident truths when they walk into their first university or college class in American history, especially when their attendance is dictated by state law or university requirement. As a professor of American history whose career has, over two decades, been devoted very largely to teaching a survey course to nonmajors, I have been painfully aware of these facts of life. It was the challenge of motivating indifferent and even hostile students in my classes that led me to write *The American Past*. As I worked and reworked each page of this book, I glanced up from time to time to see a message to myself that I had tacked to the wall behind my desk: GET THEM TO READ! For it seems to me the greatest challenge facing teachers of the American history survey course is not getting students to come to class or to bone up for quizzes and exams—the good old primal fear of flunking takes care of those—but to get them to read. Students must discover that learning about the past through books is *not* a useless, irrelevant, deadly dull, and depressing thing to do: they must realize that when that final clicking of the ball-point pens occurs at the end of the term, and the quiet collection of final examination papers takes place, books will still be available out there to be perused and read.

I hope I have written a *teacher's* textbook, one that will not simply lay out the information and perspective that make up a fundamental knowledge of American history but one that will help instructors in the U.S. history survey to arouse the minds of their students to the value of understanding the national heritage. My book is, first of all, a general history, comprehensive in its subject matter. I do not believe in ignoring or neglecting any of the subdivisions of historical inquiry—social, cultural, intellectual, economic, political, constitutional, diplomatic, or military—in order to concentrate exclusively on one or two of them as more important than the others.

The American Past is a social, cultural, intellectual, economic, political, constitutional, diplomatic, and military history of the American people. My own scholarly research and writing interests have been largely in the area of social history and popular culture. But the presidents and generals and thinkers, and the constitutional issues and impersonal economic forces are in these pages, as well as the story of the millions of ordinary and largely anonymous men, women, and children who have made our country and been formed by it. Indeed, if I were to make a claim for the uniqueness of *The American Past* among other general American history textbooks, it would be that the book integrates into a cohesive, flowing narrative subjects that are too often assigned to separate compartments as if the people involved had nothing to do with one another save for the fact that they lived on the same one thousand by three thousand mile tract of real estate. In *The American Past*, majorities, minorities, great men and women and common folk, rich and poor, priviliged and oppressed, factory workers and bosses, slaves and slave owners, women and men and children, blacks, whites, Native Americans, conquered peoples, and immigrants of every era are part of the same story, often at odds with each other, to be sure, but always interacting.

This textbook tells a compelling tale that I hope will grab and hold the interest of students whose personal and career interests may lie far in other fields. I strove for an easy writing style without trivializing the solemn, dodging controversial subjects, or ignoring subtle points of analysis. Always the goal has been: GET THEM TO READ!

The special features of the book were also designed with this goal in mind. The sidebars or boxed extracts elaborate on subjects mentioned in the text that students are likely to be unfamiliar with but at least casually interested in—why our money system deviated from the British model, for example, or the origin and historical meaning of popular catch-phrases. They also present humorous sidelights that vivify historical issues and personalities. These sidebars, it seems to me, make better use of valuable space in a teacher's textbook than, say, summarizing disputes among professional historians over their interpretations of this or that issue.

Toward the end of each chapter is a short essay entitled "How They Lived" or "Notable People."

These deal in some detail with an aspect of the daily life of ordinary people in the past—from women facing childbirth to soldiers facing battle—or with individuals whose lives had an influence on American development that was far from ordinary.

I am particularly pleased with the design, map, and illustration programs created by the excellent staff of my publisher, Harcourt Brace Jovanovich. I should like to thank those members of the production department—designer Don Fujimoto, production manager Diane Polster, and art editor Maggie Porter—for producing a book of such visual beauty.

Not so obvious but equally appreciated by the author are the contributions of those who poured over that pile of typescript and the galleys it turned into and improved the book with each pass. I am grateful beyond gracious expression to William J. Wisneski, Everett M. Sims, and Eben Ludlow, whose enthusiasm for the project from its inception made a long, arduous job seem more like an adventure. At different stages of development, Sidney Zimmerman and Irene Pavitt transformed ill-chosen words, awkward sentences, and rambling paragraphs into good and even fine English prose. During the latter part of the labor, Drake Bush and John Holland were generous and almost always on the nose with advice as to how to improve both the substance and form of *The American Past*. Where I balked and exercised an author's prerogative in ignoring their suggestions, I was probably mistaken. The many rewrites they sent back to me were typed several times over by Jean L. Harvey who, among flesh-and-blood typists, is the best I have ever seen.

I am told that because "they were just doing their job," it is not customary to cite by name the dozen people in Harcourt Brace Jovanovich's editorial, promotion, and marketing departments with whom I dealt at one time or another, not to mention those who had a hand in the book whose names I do not know. So be it. They did their jobs exceedingly well and, like true artisans, will take their acknowledgment in knowing that. I do insist, however, in singling out Sara J. Lowen, with whom I held daily, usually lengthy, phone conversations during the final harrowing months of bringing *The American Past* to realization. Not only were her insights and suggestions veritable revelations to an author who had been immersed in his own words so long he was groggy, but her kindness, equanimity, and tact in dealing with her bedraggled charge were far beyond the call of any artisan's job description.

A number of fellow historians read all or part of the typescript and provided valuable advice. They will hardly be pleased with every aspect of the final result, for historians are cantankerously individualistic in their interpretations of the past. I hope they will also be generous with my foolishness where I disagreed with them, for I am grateful for every word of their critiques. My thanks to Carol Berkin of Baruch College; Robert Calhoun of the University of North Carolina; Evan Coe of Miami-Dade Community College; Eli Faber of John Jay College of Criminal Justice; Jacob Needle of Brookdale Community College; C. H. Peterson and Dale Steiner of California State University, Chico; and Leroy T. Williams of the University of Arkansas at Little Rock.

Professors Steiner and B. Spencer Culbreth of Cleveland State Community College, Tennessee, with whom I collaborated on the Instructor's Manual and Study Guide respectively, have my appreciation and respect. And finally, although it appears to be going out of style to mention one's spouse and children in prefaces, thank you Deborah, Eamonn, and Ana for tolerating those thousands of hours when I neglected you in order to scribble on a yellow lined pad or peck at the typewriter or puzzle over the word processor or just stare at the wall. For my dedication of the book, I will neglect you for a few more moments and return to days before I was favored with your company; days themselves historical now, when I read my first books of history and indulged myself in other less wholesome activities and, through it all, was patiently tolerated by my parents, Joseph R. Conlin and Lenore V. Conlin.

J.R.C.

Contents

Maps

THE
AMERICAN
PAST
A SURVEY OF AMERICAN HISTORY

1

Old World, New World

The European Background and the Age of Discovery, 25,000 B.C.–1550

Twenty-five thousand or more years ago a band of Stone Age people crossed the Bering Strait from Siberia to Alaska, possibly over a land bridge that has since disappeared. These were the first people to set foot in the Western Hemisphere. We know very little about them or their culture. From scattered stone implements we know that later generations of migrants from Siberia moved southward to populate the two continents that are known today as the Americas.

Over the centuries these peoples divided into a wide variety of tribes speaking more than five hundred distinct languages. Some of these tribes remained primitive, barely surviving as hunters and gatherers of small game and wild berries and nuts. Others developed intensive agriculture, utilizing complex irrigation systems under the most severe desert conditions. Some tribes perfected the weaving of baskets, others the use of bow and arrow. Poetry was important to some tribes, religious piety to others. Many Native American peoples were nomadic, but not all.

Although we have studied Mayan hieroglyphics for many years, we have not yet been able to decipher them. To our knowledge, this is the only writing system developed in the Americas. Thus we must depend on archeologists and anthropologists, who study humanity through nonwritten sources, for everything we know about the American past before October 12, 1492.

A sixteenth-century sailing ship.

Christopher Columbus

On October 12, 1492, American history began. That day, under the curious gaze of native Arawaks, a group of haggard but exhilarated men waded ashore on a sunny Caribbean island they named San Salvador, or Holy Savior. Their leader, solemn and dressed for a ceremony, was a forty-year-old Italian navigator named Christopher Columbus. Driving a banner into the sand, he claimed that the land on which he stood belonged to the Spanish queen who had made possible his voyage across the Atlantic, Isabella of Castile, and her husband, Ferdinand of Aragon.

By no means was Columbus the first human being to link the two hemispheres since that early band crossed the Bering Strait. Migrations across the strait continued for centuries; and the Eskimos and Aleuts, who hunted the waters and ice floes of the Arctic Ocean, lived in Siberia as well as in Alaska. Some anthropologists believe that Polynesia, in the South Pacific, was settled from the west coast of South America after open-sea voyages longer than the one that Columbus made. Untold numbers of European, Japanese, and Chinese fishermen were probably blown off course over the centuries and made a landfall in the Western Hemisphere. Irish legends tell of St. Brendan, a monk who visited a country far to the west of his native island and returned to the Emerald Isle to speak of it; similar stories can be found in the folklore of other nations. And it is known that Norsemen, farmers from Iceland, attempted to found a colony in Newfoundland shortly after A.D. 1000.

But none of these things was known or taken seriously in Europe at the end of the fifteenth century. To Christopher Columbus and his contemporaries, the world consisted of Europe, Africa, and Asia. It was to the part of Asia called the Indies that Columbus was bound when he ran into San Salvador.

This watercolor of American Indians of the Atlantic coast was painted by John White, an artist and mapmaker who accompanied the first English colonists to Roanoke in 1585.

Why the Explorers Sailed

Believing that he had reached the Indies, Columbus called the people he greeted "Indians," reporting to Queen Isabella that "they are very gentle and do not know what it is to be wicked." He and the other great explorers of his time, sailing under the flags of Spain, Portugal, England, and France, were looking not for new lands—a New World—but for new routes to Cipango (Japan), Cathay (China), the Spice Islands (Indonesia), and India itself. These lands, with those of Asia Minor, were known as *the East.*

The object of exploration was to set up direct trade with the peoples of those places, buying jewels (particularly pearls), fine silk cloth, beautiful tapestries and carpets beyond the craft of European weavers, exotic drugs, dyes, and perfumes. The most desirable commodities were the spices that are cheap and taken for granted in the twentieth century, but at the time of Columbus were rare and valuable: cinnamon, nutmeg, allspice, clove, peppercorn.

None of these trade articles were necessities. Europeans did not need them in order to survive. They were luxury goods that made life more pleasant, more than a wan struggle for survival. Because they were very expensive, they were of interest only to the rich and powerful. However, it was the rich and powerful who, in fifteenth-century Europe, made great decisions, such as whether to support navigators who proposed risky overseas expeditions. The goods of the Indies were the keys that opened the door to exploration and discovery.

A Nasty and Brutish Life

Europe was economically self-sufficient. Temperate in climate and blessed with rich fisheries, fertile land, and broad forests, the continent provided its people with the basic necessities of life: food, clothing, and shelter. Everyone did not get an equal share of the wealth, of course. European society was marked by sharp class lines, with the wealthiest 2 to 4 percent of the population controlling and consuming far more than their share of goods and resources. The aristocrats, the bishops of the Roman Catholic Church, the large-scale landowners, and the wealthy urban merchants did not have to worry, as did the masses of peasants, about skimping at meals lest there not be enough food to get through the winter. The rich had more than enough warm clothing to ward off the elements, whereas the peasant or laborer made do with a single tattered tunic. The privileged classes had large, fortresslike dwellings in which to take shelter in troubled times, while the lower classes took their chances.

But the difference between daily life at the top of European society and daily life at the bottom was less a matter of quality than of quantity. The quality—the *kind*— of food, clothing, and shelter that Europe provided was much the same for people of all classes, and it was not, by our standards, very sumptuous. In medieval and early modern Europe, life was "nasty, brutish, and short" for the rich as well as the poor.

Diet was monotonous. The staple was grain porridge or coarse-ground bread. While the poor had little or no meat at most meals, stretching what they had in watery soups and gruels, the rich glutted on haunches of venison and whole hogs roasted on a spit. But the meats available to all were the same—mostly pork, mutton, fish, and game. Seasonings were few and plain—salt, honey, and a few herbs. Vegetables, fruits, and nuts were eaten in season, and all classes washed down their fare with beer in the north and wine in the south.

Clothing was made from leather, woven wool, or linen; colors were limited to a few generally drab native dyes. Housing consisted of a flimsy stick and mud (wattle and daub) hut for the rural poor, cramped and dim quarters for the city dweller, and a timber or stone castle for the rural gentry and nobility. None of it was preferable to a modest tract home in the United States today. One historian has written that if people who are accustomed to twentieth-century comforts were suddenly transported back to medieval Europe and given the choice of spending a winter night in the cold, damp, drafty castle of the local lord, or in the hut of one of his serfs snuggled next to a warm pig on the floor, they would be wise to select the serf's hut.

It would not even smell better in the lord's castle. Bathing was uncomfortable and generally thought to be unhealthy. Not even kings and queens submerged their bodies in tubs or creeks very often. Worst of all, excrement collected in the inefficient interior conduits of castles, whereas peasants used outside latrines. The daily life of even the most privileged Europeans was squalid.

What Asia Offered

It was because they aspired to a higher standard of living that wealthy Europeans were interested in the

With the royal buildings of the Île de la Cité in Paris at their backs, serfs labor in their lord's fields. This page from a fifteenth-century book of hours depicts peasant life in an idyllic light.

products of Asia. From the East came perfumes to mask odors. Oriental carpets and tapestries not only brightened castle walls, but they also insulated the cold floors and reduced the drafts and eternal damp of stone buildings. Although they did not much improve the barbaric medical practices of the time, drugs from the East relieved some of the pain that injury, disease, and doctors inflicted.

Rich Europeans also coveted what are now called "status symbols." The knights and ladies who sported gems not found in Europe were saying that they could afford to do so, that paying high prices for useless baubles caused them no inconvenience. When they wore expensive clothing made of silk or cotton imported from the East, especially when dyed in rare oriental hues, they announced by their appearance that they were of a higher order than the masses in their uniform, rough-woven, and less comfortable linsey-woolsey.

The Roman Catholic Church taught that it was an act of piety to adorn God's cathedrals and chapels with beautiful or valuable objects, such as pearls and rubies from the East and gold and silver mined in Europe. Incense, another import, played a prominent part in religious ritual. Burning such an expensive item was not only pleasing to the senses, but it was also thought of as pleasing to God.

The Importance of Spices

Of all the goods that aroused European interest in Asia, none was coveted more than spices. Spices enhanced

Caravans much like this one, rendered in a sixteenth-century engraving, carried precious spices overland from Asia to the Mediterranean ports.

the pleasure of eating. Their pungent flavors broke the monotony of a diet restricted to a few basic ingredients. Medical, sometimes magical, properties were ascribed to them. Most important of all, some spices like cloves and peppercorns were preservatives as effective as salt but with a more appealing taste.

The preservation of meat was vital all over Europe. While a surplus of grain could be stored for long periods of time and eaten when needed, meat could not. Animals kept for meat, milk, and work (plowing, pulling carts) competed for food with human beings. Even in the summer, when horses, cattle, and sheep could subsist on grass, every acre that was set aside as pasture was one less acre planted in wheat, rye, or oats. The allocation of land between farming and grazing had to be very closely watched.

In winter, however, the problem of keeping enough animals became acute. Then there was no pasture at all for beasts that grazed, and in countries that had heavy snowfalls there were not even wastelands where hogs could root. A few animals were kept as breeding stock, sharing the food saved for people. The rest of the animals were slaughtered in the fall, many of them eaten within a short period of time. If there was to be any meat available in winter and spring, it had to be preserved. Spices were a means of preserving meat and, consequently, were highly prized.

Indeed, wealthy Europeans valued some spices so highly that they stored them in fine silver or wooden caskets as we would store precious jewelry or a precision instrument. When Marco Polo, a Venetian merchant who traveled to China in the thirteenth century, wanted to impress Europeans with the fabulous wealth of the Great Khan, he did not dwell on the Chinese emperor's gold and silver. He spun a story of pepper-laden caravans stretching for miles entering the khan's capital in tribute. That was the sort of tale that quickened European pulses. A commodity that they paid exorbitant prices for in their own countries was as cheap as cabbage on the other side of the world.

The Trade with the Indies

The goods of the East had trickled into Europe since the time of Alexander the Great. The trade withered with the fall of the Roman Empire but revived as a result of the Crusades of the eleventh through the thirteenth centuries. The knights failed in their quest to win back the holy places of Christianity from Moslem "infidels" who had conquered them. But living among the Moslems for many years acquainted the Europeans with a living standard that was far superior to the one they knew at home. The Moslem upper classes enjoyed a gracious and comfortable mode of life, thanks to their

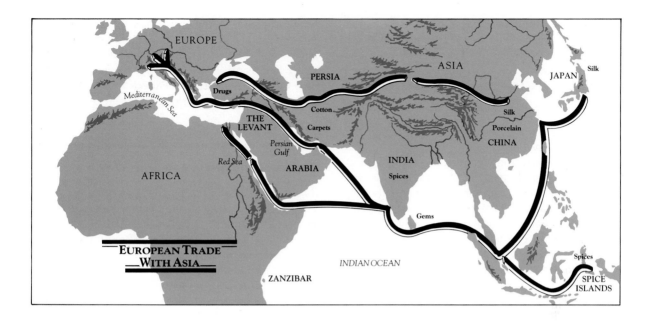

access to the products of the Middle and Far East. When the crusaders returned to their castles in the Italian states, France, the German lands, Scandinavia, and the British Isles, they brought back a taste for more comfortable living and formed a lucrative market for anyone who could supply them with Asian goods.

By the end of the Middle Ages, commerce was flourishing. The coveted products were brought from the farthest reaches of East Asia by ship through the Indian Ocean and the Persian Gulf or by overland caravan to Constantinople and the Levant at the eastern end of the Mediterranean Sea, what we know today as Istanbul and the nations of Syria, Lebanon, and Israel. From these Middle Eastern ports, the goods were carried across the Mediterranean by the fleets of Italian city-states—Venice, Pisa, Genoa—which jealously drove other countries' ships away from their routes. Acting as middlemen, the Italian merchants wholesaled the spices, tapestries, gems, and other commodities throughout Europe in the great market towns, and supplied wandering peddlers who sold them on the retail level.

By the time Eastern goods reached their final purchaser, they were extremely expensive. The costs of transportation were prodigious, for the pepper that enlivened a French or an English stew may have been borne as far as eight thousand miles on a donkey's back. To make matters worse, the trade routes passed through the lands of warlike tribes or, if by sea, through the haunts of pirates. Merchants added to their selling price by paying such bandits tribute, a "toll" for the

privilege of safe passage. If a caravan or a ship decided to fight its way through, that too cost money. Armed men who were rugged enough to stand up to Tartars or East African pirates had to be paid generously out of the retail price.

The Levantine traders took a large profit when they sold to the Italian merchants, who added their own handsome commission to the final cost. Today, the magnificent Renaissance cathedrals and palaces these great traders built with their profits are a source of pride to Italians and an artistic inspiration to all. At the time, the glories of Italy were more likely to cause resentment and envy among those Europeans whose expenditures made the construction possible.

Resentment and envy gave birth to the dream of finding a new route to the source of precious Eastern goods. The king or queen whose nation secured a way to bypass the Italian middlemen would not only stop the flow of that country's wealth to Italy, but he or she could expect to compete with or even displace the Italians as wholesalers. The navigator who found a new route to the Indies could expect a princely reward. There was nothing new about this reasoning in the final decades of the fifteenth century. Two developments, however, made the search more urgent.

The Turks and a Revolution in Agriculture

One development was the startling triumph of the Ottoman Turks. A tribe of central Anatolia, they swept into the Moslem world in the thirteenth century and, in a few decades, conquered most of it. Militarily, they were an awesome people. In 1453 they accomplished what no other Moslems had been able to do. They captured Constantinople, the great Christian city in the middle of the Islamic crescent and an important station in the Asian trade. Before the Ottomans halted their march, they would conquer southeastern Europe, reaching the gates of Vienna in 1529. The empire they created lasted until 1918.

Like other successful conquerors—the Germanic tribes that overran Rome, the Mongols and Manchus who took China—the Ottomans preferred living as victorious overlords to taking up agriculture and trade. While the Ottoman subjugation of the Levant did not completely choke off trade with the Indies, it reduced the supply of Eastern goods entering Europe, forcing prices even higher than they had been.

The Ottoman conquests coincided with the second historical development. The revolution in agriculture that had been underway in Europe for centuries was coming to a climax. Population, a source of labor and, therefore, of higher production, had recovered from the horrors of the Black Death (bubonic plague), which in the fourteenth century had killed about one-third of Europe's people. New farmlands, reclaimed from marshes and forests, were producing larger surpluses of food. Improved plows and the substitution of quick horses for slow oxen to pull them increased the acreage that each peasant could cultivate. The shift from farming to sheep raising by many landowners, particularly in England, provided greater incomes for the landed rich by reducing the number of people their estates supported. And the change from a barter to a money economy increased trade and the wealth of merchants and bankers. In brief, the rich were getting richer in fifteenth-century Europe; the monied classes, who were the market for the goods of the Indies, had more money to spend on them.

Portugal and Spain Lead the Way

The Portuguese and the Spanish pioneered the search for new routes. Portugal and Spain were not as rich as France, England, or the Italian and German states. But the Italians monopolized the traditional routes; they were uninterested in new ones. France and England either tended to look inward rather than abroad or were concerned with expansion on the continent of Europe. Germany did not exist; the German-language area of Europe was home to the Holy Roman Empire, which at first was preoccupied with Italy and afterward gained Spain by inheritance.

By way of contrast, Portugal and Spain were unified nations that had dynamic and decisive central governments. They were outgoing and ambitious countries as a consequence of their long, successful wars to drive the Moors of northern Africa from the Iberian Peninsula, a conflict that instilled in the Portuguese and Spanish a taste for aggressive action. Both countries had long coastlines on the Atlantic. They faced the west and the future, Portugal entirely so, rather than back toward Europe and the past.

Portugal's Route to the South

Portugal, independent and unified before Spain, began the quest for new routes early in the fifteenth century. Prince Henry the Navigator, a younger son of King John I, set up a kind of "explorers' institute" in southern Portugal where mariners studied geography and ship design, and made improvements in devices and methods. Putting their skills into practice, Prince Henry's bold sailors led expeditions down the coast of Africa, visiting and trading with lands that did not even appear on many European maps.

Portugal grew richer from this commerce and planted the beginnings of colonies in Africa. But the national purpose remained finding a way *around* Africa to Asia. Finally, in 1487, Bartholomew Diaz reached the Cape of Good Hope at the foot of the African continent. He returned to Lisbon with the news that the corner had been turned. There was clear sailing to the Indies by way of a southern and then northeastern route. In all

PRESTER JOHN

Troubled times often make for wishful thinking. In fifteenth-century Europe, fear of the military might of the Ottoman Turks, led to a revival of belief in the existence of Prester John—Priest John—a powerful Christian king who dwelled somewhere beyond the world of Islam and who, once Europeans made contact with him, would join with them to defeat the Moslem infidels.

Prester John seemed to be wherever he would be most useful. To central Europeans, he lived in central Asia. To southern Europeans like the Spanish and Portuguese, Prester John was a black African who lived to the south of their enemies, the Moors. The search for his kingdom contributed to the European explorations and discoveries of the 1400s and 1500s. Some scholars suggest that the existence of a Christian kingdom in Ethiopia was a basis for the belief in Prester John.

of Portugal there was probably only one man who was unhappy with such news. He was Christopher Columbus, who had spent much of his life in that country trying to convince the king that Asia could be reached by sailing *westward*. Diaz's accomplishment had the effect of killing Portuguese interest in Columbus's plan, even though it would be nine years, in 1498, before Vasco da Gama actually reached Calicut in India by the Diaz route.

Portugal's discovery of the African way to the Indies determined that nation's imperial history. Portugal's most highly prized possessions overseas were to be in Africa, India, southeast Asia, and as far as Macau in China. Its only American colony, Brazil, was settled as the result of a storm that struck a Portuguese captain on his way around Africa. In 1500, Pedro Cabral was blown far off course and landed on the bulge of the South American continent, establishing Portugal's sole claim in the New World.

Spain Looks West

In the meantime, Columbus had taken his plan to Spain. Much has been written of his "theory" that the earth was a sphere, of the difficulty he supposedly had convincing Isabella of this fact. A famous painting shows Columbus holding an orange and lecturing the queen and a skeptical court. In reality, the shape of the earth was never an issue in Columbus's long, frustrating campaign to find a financial backer. Only the uneducated and superstitious believed that the world was flat and that a ship would fall off its edge into a void or worse horrors. Isabella did not.

Columbus's chief problem was to get the queen's attention. Until she and her husband, Ferdinand of Aragon, drove the last of the Moors out of Spain, Isabella could think of little else. Finally, early in 1492, Granada, the last Moorish stronghold, collapsed. Columbus had the queen's ear and needed only to convince her that an investment of $14,000 was a bargain, considering the rewards that Spain would reap should he succeed.

Ironically, Columbus's plan for reaching the Indies by sailing west was based not on any pioneering breakthrough in geography, but on a major error. Columbus seriously underestimated the size of the globe. He thought that Japan lay about twenty-five hundred miles west of the Canary Islands, whereas it is much farther away. Had he known how large the earth actually is, Columbus might have abandoned his scheme: it is nine thousand miles from the Canaries to Japan; no ship of the time could have been provisioned for so long a voyage.

Christopher Columbus (1446–1506), as depicted in an oil portrait by Venetian artist Sebastiano del Piombo.

Dreams Die Hard

Until the day of his death, Columbus insisted that he had touched on the outlying shores of the Indies. Four times he had crossed the Atlantic bearing letters of introduction to the emperors of Japan and China, and it was too much to admit that he had failed to come close to delivering them.

But by 1506, the year Columbus died, other navigators were facing up to the fact that the Admiral of the Ocean Sea had stumbled on a previously unknown

WHY "AMERICA"? WHY NOT "COLUMBIA"?

Columbus is partly to blame for the fact that his great discovery was not named for him. He insisted until the day of his death in 1506 that he had touched the outskirts of the Indies.

The man for whom the two continents of the Western Hemisphere were named was a relative latecomer to the New World and was not even the leader of an expedition. Amerigo Vespucci (1451–1512), an Italian, accompanied at least two Spanish voyages to the coast of South America, the first in 1499. Without claiming to have discovered anything, Vespucci speculated in widely published letters that the lands he saw were not part of Asia but were previously unknown countries.

In 1507, a German mapmaker who knew of only a few of Spain's adventures published some of Vespucci's letters and suggested that the New World be named America in honor of his informant. It was all a mistake. But the German map became a standard, and the name stuck.

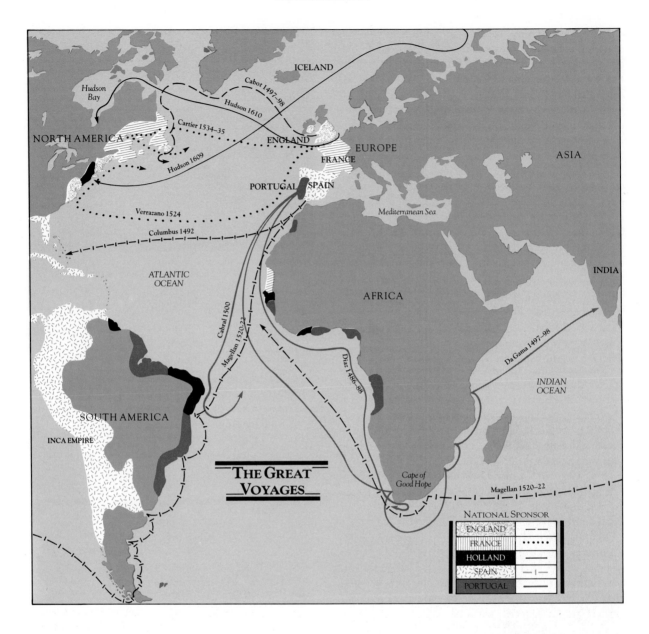

THE GREAT VOYAGES

NATIONAL SPONSOR	
ENGLAND	– – –
FRANCE	......
HOLLAND	——
SPAIN	–·–·–
PORTUGAL	——

"New World." Indeed, the Americas got their name from a comparatively minor figure in the explorations, Amerigo Vespucci, who cruised the South American coast and recognized this reality.

For the Spanish it was an unpleasant reality. In 1493, Spain had asked the pope to divide all the non-Christian lands of the world between Spain and Portugal. He did so, giving Portugal the African route, and Spain the Americas. By the early sixteenth century, the Portuguese were reaping rich rewards from their gift, while the Spanish found themselves in possession of nothing but a few tropical islands where there were no riches. The New World was no prize. It was an obstacle.

In 1513, Vasco Nuñez de Balboa discovered the shortest way over the obstacle, across the Isthmus of Panama. But it was useless as a trade route, since it was plagued by tropical diseases that would stifle any development until modern science found a way to exterminate the mosquitoes. In 1520, Ferdinand Magellan, a Portuguese mariner commanding five ships for Spain, found a way around the tip of South America. Although Magellan lost his life in the Philippines, one of his vessels returned to Spain, completing the first voyage around the world. Magellan had discovered a westerly route to Asia, but it was even less workable than Balboa's.

For three decades the New World was a profound

disappointment. On the island of Hispaniola, site of the largest Spanish settlement, the soldiers writhed in discomfort and frustration, brutalized the native people until they exterminated them, and fought viciously among themselves. The few, like Balboa, who ventured into the unknown returned with more bad news or, like Juan Ponce de León, who in 1513 searched Florida for a "fountain of youth," made fools of themselves.

Spain Wins an Empire

In 1519, acting on little more than rumor and dissatisfaction, one of those restless soldiers landed on the Mexican mainland with three hundred men and eighteen horses. Moving cautiously inland, Hernando Cortez first battled and then formed alliances with one native tribe after another. They told him about Tenochtitlán, present-day Mexico City, the capital city of the Aztecs, who dominated every other Mexican people and commanded great wealth in gold and silver.

Portuguese explorer Ferdinand Magellan discovered a route around the tip of South America.

Reaching the city on November 8, Cortez and his men were dazzled. The Aztecs were unlike any Native Americans they had met. Hardly a primitive people subsisting on fish and fruit, the Aztecs had created a sophisticated society, farmed intensively, built great pyramid-shaped temples, and boasted an island capital of tens of thousands of buildings that was protected by the huge lake in which it was situated. The marketplace alone held sixty thousand people. The Aztec Empire was larger than Spain itself.

Cortez was disgusted by the Aztec religion. The Mexicans worshiped more than a thousand gods and demigods and practiced human sacrifice, tearing and beating hearts out of victims and cooking them in meals "prepared with peppers and tomatoes." But the wily Spaniard also exploited Aztec beliefs to serve his own ends. For several centuries the Mexicans had taught that a white-skinned deity named Quetzalcoatl would come one day to rule them. The Aztec emperor, Montezuma, mistook Cortez to be this god just long enough for the Spaniards to gain his confidence and make him their prisoner. Once inside Montezuma's palace, they found a huge room filled with "jewels, precious stones, silver, and an astonishing amount of gold."

After a few months the Aztec nobles realized that the visitors were quite human, and dangerous humans at that. They rebelled and the Spaniards barely managed to fight their way out of Tenochtitlán. Their own greed nearly destroyed them; with their lives in danger, Cortez and his men insisted on carrying eight tons of gold with them. But it was the Aztecs who were doomed by the gold, not the Spaniards. Cortez easily gathered allies from Indian peoples resentful of Aztec domination, returned to Tenochtitlán, and destroyed the great city brick by brick—killing fifteen thousand people on the final day of the war, August 13, 1521.

Cortez not only won a battle; he gained a ready-made empire for Spain. He and his lieutenants simply inserted themselves at the top of Aztec society in place of the nobility they had massacred. They lived off the labor of the lower classes, as the Aztec nobles had done, and as the nobility did in Europe. Rarely has one people been able to set itself up over another with such ease. The centralized political structure of Mexico made it possible for the Spaniards to rule with a minimum of resistance from the common people.

Equally important, the conquest of Mexico breathed new enthusiasm into Spanish interest in the New World. There was a rush to the Americas, as thousands of Spaniards of all classes packed into ships to search for their own Mexicos. They called themselves *conquistadores*—conquerors—and in little more than a generation they subdued an area several times the size of Europe.

PROHIBITION AMONG THE AZTECS

The Indians had no distilled liquors, but some peoples fermented wines and beers. The drink in Mexico was *pulque*, made from the agave plant, which is the basis of tequila and is still drunk today. While weak, *pulque* was rigorously regulated by the Aztecs. Except on special occasions, only nursing mothers, victims of human sacrifice, very old people, and warriors were allowed to drink it. Commoners found guilty of drunkenness had their heads shaved after the first offense and were executed after the second. Members of the upper classes had no second chance. Caught drunk on *pulque*, they were beaten to death or strangled.

The Conquistadores

Perhaps no people were so well suited by their history for conquest of such heroic proportions. Because much of Spain is naturally poor—dry or mountainous or both—agriculture always had been unattractive to the ambitious. Because the Spanish associated trade with the Moors and Jews, whom they despised, the upper classes also shunned commerce. The aristocratic Spanish male's role in life was to fight. He was a soldier, a knight, a conqueror. This ideal had been nurtured and reinforced during Spain's long conflict with the Moors, when Spanish Christian culture depended on its fighting men for survival.

Another element of the Spanish character that contributed to the conquest of so much territory in so little time was the nation's zealous, even fanatical, devotion to Roman Catholicism. Because the national enemy had been Islamic, Spanish nationalism was inextricably intertwined with religion. Like some Moslems, the Spaniards felt that a war for the purpose of spreading their religion was holy, and that death in such a war was a guarantee of salvation. This feeling made for extremely brave soldiers who were unafraid to die and were willing to face appalling odds. The notion that nonbelievers who refused to submit to the one true faith lost their right to mercy made for ruthless ones.

These cultural traits would curse Spain in later centuries, a fact that was apparent to the great Spanish writer Miguel de Cervantes as early as 1605, when he wrote the first part of his satire, *Don Quixote*. By expelling the Moors and Jews in the name of religious uniformity, Spain deprived itself of an industrious middle class just as the middle class was becoming an important economic factor. The disdain felt by the Spanish *hidalgo*—that arrogant member of the lower nobility—for agriculture, trade, and other productive work contributed to the nation's increasing impoverishment over the centuries. In the sixteenth century, however, reckless Spanish bravery and ruthless religious fanaticism were excellently calculated to conquer a New World.

Far-Flung Adventures

After news of Mexican riches reached him, the Spanish king, and Holy Roman Emperor, Charles V, encouraged more expeditions by promising *conquistadores* 10 to 20 percent of all the gold and silver they won from the natives. He also granted them land in the New World and the right to put its inhabitants to work for them. The Church soothed the legalistic consciences of the *conquistadores* by means of a device called the *requerimento*, or "requirement." On confronting a native tribe, the priest who accompanied every expedition read from a document—usually in Spanish or Latin—that promised fair and generous treatment if the Indians submitted to the Spanish king and the Christian religion. If they resisted, however, the responsibility for what happened next rested on them. When Indians resisted, or simply sat confused at what they did not understand, the Spanish fell on them, almost inevitably winning and taking possession of their lands.

Few expeditions turned up gold and silver, especially those that ventured north of Mexico into what is now the United States. Between 1539 and 1542, Hernando De Soto explored the southeastern part of the United States in a fruitless search for riches. He was buried by

In this drawing from an Aztec manuscript, Hernando Cortez accepts the surrender of the last emperor of the Aztecs.

his soldiers in the Mississippi River. During the same years, Francisco Coronado trekked extraordinary distances in the arid Southwest in search of the Seven Cities of Cibola, said to be made of gold. He found only dusty pueblos of adobe brick, but was persuaded by a Plains Indian called the Turk that the golden city of Quivira lay farther on. Although he didn't find Quivira, Coronado explored New Mexico, Arizona, and parts of Texas.

But there was also an expedition that matched that of Cortez in valor and profit. In 1531, an aging former pig farmer named Francisco Pizarro led a small expedition high into the Andes mountains of South America and penetrated the empire of the Incas, another highly developed people with rich sources of gold and silver. Like the Aztec Empire in Mexico, the Inca Empire was highly centralized, and the person of the emperor, known as the Inca, was even more vital to the stability of the society than Montezuma had been. The Inca was considered a god.

There was little native resistance when Pizarro captured the Inca, held him for ransom, and then murdered him after it was delivered. The morale of the people collapsed, and Pizarro and his successors inserted themselves into the top of an already highly structured society.

Spanish America

For a century, Mexican and Peruvian gold and silver made Spain the richest and most powerful nation of Europe. American wealth financed the cultural blossoming of Spain as well as huge armies to enforce the will of Spain. Toward the end of the seventeenth century, Spain's empire stretched from Tierra del Fuego at the foot of South America to what is now northern Mexico. In the eighteenth century, Spain expanded into present-day Texas, New Mexico, and California.

Over such a huge area, economy and society varied immensely. But for the most part, the ownership of land in Spanish America was monopolized by a small group of privileged *encomenderos* who lived off the labor of Indians in peonage or black Africans in slavery. Government was centralized in the hands of viceroys (vice kings), and the Roman Catholic Church exerted great power, sometimes protecting those on the bottom from the greed of the upper clases but also maintaining the legitimacy of the Spaniards as a ruling class. Spanish America grew steadily. Before there was a single English or French settler in the New World, and when there were no more than a few hundred Portuguese, Spain boasted two hundred towns and cities, two universities, and a population of 5.5 million in the Western Hemisphere.

The Black Legend

Spanish American civilization was built on a foundation of ruthlessness and cruelty; the *conquistadores* destroyed several advanced cultures and innumerable lesser ones. Art works of unknown beauty were melted down into gold and silver ingots for shipment to Madrid. Tens of thousands of Indians were killed in the name of God, the Blessed Virgin, and the patron saint of Spain, Santiago (San Diego, or St. James). Hundreds of thousands of others were demoralized and destroyed gradually when they were put to work in a system foreign to them. The Arawaks of the Caribbean islands, for example, were a physically delicate people who literally died out under hard labor that was routine to other peoples. When monks like the great Bartolomé de Las Casas tried to save other Indians from this fate, their well-meaning solution resulted in cultural disruption on another continent. To end the enslavement of Indians, de Las Casas advocated the importation of black Africans to labor on the *haciendas* and in the mines. The Spanish king supported his plan, and the African slave trade started.

On balance, however, the Spaniards were no more brutal or ruthless than any conquering people would have been given the same opportunities. Had the English occupied a part of America where there was gold and silver and a dense native population, their record would have been much the same. Indeed, because the Spaniards were frankly conquerors and claimed to be nothing else, they contributed to a pattern of race relations that had happier consequences than did the English colonial model.

The Spaniards came as soldiers. They brought few Spanish women with them for many years. Instead, they took Indian women as their wives and mistresses, with the result that from its beginnings much of the ruling class was of mixed blood. Race was never so sure a guide to social class in Spanish America, and therefore was not a stigma, as it was among the English who emigrated as families, intermarried much less with the native peoples, and therefore came to identify race with social class.

The Columbian Exchange

Before examining the origin of the English colonies, it is important to understand that the discovery of America had even more fundamental consequences than the enrichment of Spain. Christopher Columbus's voyage not only opened a New World to exploitation by Europeans, but it also linked land masses that had drifted apart 150 million years before human beings appeared on earth. Not only was the existence of America unknown to Europeans, Africans, and Asians before 1492, and the existence of the Old World unknown to the Indians, but the biological systems of Old World and New World had developed independently.

Some species flourished everywhere. Some had been well developed by the time of the great continental drift, and thus were in Europe and Africa as well as in the Americas. Others, such as sea birds and plants that had air- or water-borne seeds, crossed the oceans long before Columbus and therefore were also familiar to European travelers. Nevertheless, there were a large number of strange animals and plants in the Americas. The first Europeans here filled their letters and journals with amazed reports about the strange flora and fauna they discovered. Moreover, these Europeans were themselves the instruments of a profound biological exchange.

The Impact on America

Because mammals in Spanish America were generally smaller and less suited for meat and draft than Old World livestock, hogs, cattle, and sheep were imported almost immediately with European grasses to feed them. This not only altered the ecology of parts of the New World, but the Indians exposed to the imported animals soon came to depend on them for their own survival. Even those native tribes that escaped Spanish political domination were glad to raid and adopt the enemy's flocks and herds as a step to a better standard of living. The magnificent wool-weaving art that is closely identified with the culture of the Navajo was not developed until the Navajo had domesticated sheep.

The impact of the horse was also dramatic. The people of Mexico were initially terrified by the sight of a mounted man, which reinforced their belief that the Spaniards were gods. Even after the Indians had come to realize that horses were simply beasts, Spanish monopoly of them gave the *conquistadores* an immense advantage in war.

Two centuries later, herds of wild horses wandered over the Great Plains of North America, where they became the basis of several cultures. The Sioux, Commanche, Pawnee, Apache, Nez Percé, Blackfeet, Crow, and other tribes of the plains, previously an agricultural people or simple gatherers who lived much like the Indians of the Eastern Woodlands, captured the mustangs and became peerless horsemen independent of European example. Their warlike, seminomadic way of life was built around the horse and the herds of bison they followed long before they had any

WHITE MEN'S FLIES

One item of the Columbian exchange that dates from the arrival of English colonists in the seventeenth century was the honeybee. Apparently the species was unknown in the New World, at least on the coast of North America. After the Pilgrims of Plymouth imported honeybees for honey, the Algonkian Indians named them "white men's flies."

social or cultural contacts with the white settlers. Ironically, it was the imported part of their culture—the horse—that enabled the Plains Indians to hold out longer against the whites than any other tribes.

Feeding the World

The American continents did not contribute many animals to be used for food in the Old World, although the American turkey was previously unknown in Europe. The plant foods of the New World, however, revolutionized life in Europe, Africa, and Asia. Maize (Indian corn), an American native, astonished Europeans by the size of its grains. Cultivation of the crop spread quickly on every continent, improving nutritional levels and contributing to the rapid increase in

A Spanish conquistador, *initially thought by the Indians to be a god, as represented in an Aztec drawing.*

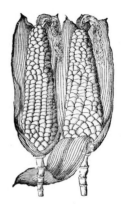

Native Americans: turkey and maize.

population that has characterized the last five hundred years of human history.

The potato and the sweet potato, two more Americans, were scarcely less important. The potato became a major staple in temperate climates from Ireland and England through Russia to northern China. The sweet potato flourished in warmer areas and became the fundamental food in West Africa, where it was introduced by slave traders. Beans, squashes and pumpkins, manioc, peppers, and tomatoes are other foods that were unknown in the Old World before Columbus and have become important throughout much of the world ever since. Many great cuisines are dependent on foods of American origin, particularly the tomato and the extraordinary variety of chili peppers that have been developed from a Mexican forebear. It has been estimated that of 640 food crops grown in Africa today, all but 50 originated in the Americas.

In return, Europeans brought to America numerous grasses (plus about 70 percent of what we call weeds), grains such as wheat and barley, citrus fruits, and sugar cane. It is difficult to imagine the Caribbean and Central America without cane. The profitability of growing sugar in the West Indies led to the development of slavery there. If the Europeans did a disservice to the New World with that contribution, the Indians got even by introducing the Old World to tobacco addiction.

New Diseases for Old

The most tragic exchange between the hemispheres was in microscopic forms of life. Diseases for which Europeans and Africans had developed immunities were unknown to American Indians, previously insulated from them by three thousand miles of open sea. Biologically, they had not "learned to live with" measles, smallpox, whooping cough, chicken pox, and even mild influenzas, as people of the Old World had done.

THE LOVE APPLE

The tomato, an important food in the European diet and vital to a number of great cuisines, originated in the Americas. But, curiously, it was not eaten for several centuries. Some Europeans believed that it was poisonous; others said that it was a morally dangerous aphrodisiac, a "love apple." It was grown only as an ornamental plant, in effect a flower. Only during the eighteenth century did Europeans begin to eat tomatoes. Appropriately, it was probably an Italian, like Columbus, who was the first to dare.

In the United States, the old myths survived somewhat longer. As late as the middle of the nineteenth century, a man in Newport, Rhode Island, caused a sensation when, in front of a crowd, he consumed a raw tomato.

COMMON SEAMEN IN THE AGE OF DISCOVERY

They were little people by today's standards. Few of the seamen who sailed the Spanish Main (the American mainland surrounding the Caribbean) and the seas of the world were taller than five and a half feet. But they were as tough as the oak planks they walked on, for they could not have otherwise survived to adulthood in the fifteenth and sixteenth centuries. Diseases that are now merely a nuisance carried off those children who were weak and sickly in the Age of Discovery.

Common seamen were often little more than children themselves: young teenagers or men in their early twenties. Reaching adulthood did not guarantee a long life, however. The odds were that a person who survived the childhood diseases of the sixteenth century would die before the age of thirty-five. The odds were even worse for the men who went to sea.

Ships were frequently wrecked when their wooden hulls faced the might and fury of the Atlantic. The rules governing ships meeting at sea were those of the jungle: do what you are strong enough to do. The men on a Spanish vessel were prepared to battle every Portuguese, Dutch, French, English, or freebooting pirate ship they encountered. Spanish ships sailing from the Americas were especially attractive prey—who knew what treasures might be stored in their leaky hulls?—and defeat in battle meant death, or enslavement and brutal treatment for the crew. Vasco da Gama once poured boiling oil on the belly of a prisoner in order to extract information from him.

If the sixteenth-century sailor survived the assaults from other ships, he then faced hazards on his own vessel. He might be killed by one of his own crewmates in a fight over a trivial matter. Or he might be executed for a petty offense as an object lesson to his fellows.

Discipline on the high seas consisted of quick, harsh punishment for the slightest transgressions. These were usually flogging, keelhauling (dragging a man underwater the length of the hull where, if he was not drowned, his body was shredded and broken by barnacles), or hanging from the yardarm. After a mutiny against him, Magellan decapitated one ringleader, quartered another alive, and marooned a third on a desert island. When he pardoned the rest, they were so grateful that they became Magellan's most loyal followers.

Finally, the common seaman not only continued to risk the diseases that plagued people on land, but he also ran a higher risk of scurvy. Scurvy is a vitamin C deficiency and was a very common disease in the centuries before our own. The disease can be completely reversed by a few days' crash diet of fresh fruits and vegetables. The island of Curaçao in the Caribbean got its name—curaçao is the Portuguese word for "cure"—when Columbus left several men nearly dead from scurvy there, later returning to find them fit and strong. They had fed on fresh fruits in his absence.

At sea, however, the men's daily diet did not contain fresh fruit and consisted of about one pound of salt beef, one and a half pounds of biscuit, two and a half pints of water, and one and a quarter pints of wine. The captain's larder served him and his officers scarcely better, although there might be onions, garlic, and dried fruits in it.

Sixteenth-century sailors relied on muscle power for work as few people do today. They loaded cargoes of a hundred tons with only the help of a winch or a windlass. At sea they hauled only with the aid of ropes heavy canvas fifty feet up and down the masts. Merely holding the ship on course in peaceful seas was heavy work. The crude tiller pitted the seaman's strength di-

The effect on them was devastating. While Europeans and Africans suffered badly enough from the epidemics that swept through the early colonies, the Indians died in extraordinary numbers. Invisible bacteria and viruses killed far more Native Americans than did Spanish swords or English muskets. Like wild horses out of Mexico, Old World diseases usually preceded the whites, brought home to isolated Indian villages by individuals who had visited the newcomers.

In return, the Indians probably made a gift of venereal disease to the Europeans and, through them, to Africans, and Asians. Medical historians disagree on the origins of syphilis, but it is a disease of which we have a complete history. We know that it first appeared in 1493 in Cádiz, Spain, shortly after Columbus returned to that port from his first voyage.

From Spain, syphilis traveled to Naples, where several of Columbus's crewmen are known to have served in the army. From there, it spread like wildfire throughout the world, following the trade routes, exactly where sailors, a notoriously promiscuous lot, would be expected to take it.

Europeans, Africans, and Asians reacted to syphilis as Indians reacted to measles and chicken pox. Symptoms were severe, and death came quickly. About 10 million people died of syphilis in the Old World within fifteen years of Columbus's voyage. Only later did the disease take on the slower-acting form in which it is known today. Adding to the case for an American origin, traces of syphilis have been found in pre-Columbian Indian bones but none in the Old World.

be rearranged, the seamen virtually rebuilt the ship above deck. Even when such special tasks were not needed, the crew was kept hopping every moment, repairing sails and lines, and scrubbing the decks with vinegar and salt water. Boredom was far more dangerous than overwork.

Why did someone choose such a life? The first answer is that *choose* is the wrong word. Most sailors were born and raised in seaports. They were literally bred to the life. Occupation, like social status, was not something about which a person of the sixteenth century had much choice. What else could a young man of Cádiz or Seville (or Le Havre or Bristol) do to make his way through life?

Then too, some portion of the crews of the sixteenth century were forced onto the ships. The crew for Columbus's momentous voyage, for example, was put together by drafting convicts. For several centuries to come, short-handed captains made up their crews by waylaying ("shanghaiing") young men.

Finally, for all its dangers and discomforts, the sea offered a remote but alluring chance for social and economic advancement. While some of the great captains of the era were, like Magellan, born into the upper classes, others, like Columbus, worked their way up. Columbus first shipped out as a boy, perhaps only ten years old, and was illiterate until he was thirty. Yet he became the adviser of royalty and, for what the title was worth, Admiral of the Ocean Sea. Quite a number of the *conquistadores*, who first came to the New World as common seamen, lived to become wealthy landowners.

Of course, such success stories tell us of only a tiny fraction of the whole. For most sailors, life was brutal and short. But, in the sixteenth century, these seamen, brutal or not, were the agents of the great adventure that revolutionized the world.

rectly against the forces of wind and ocean currents. Every ship leaked and had to be pumped by hand regularly, and constantly during storms.

On long voyages the ship had to be serviced and refitted regularly. When this was wanted, the ship was sailed onto a beach where it was "careened," turned on its side, and the barnacles covering its hull were scraped off. Then the hull was recaulked with pitch and tar. If the captain decided that the sails needed to

For Further Reading

The best single book for understanding the Europe that reached out to the Americas is an eighty-year-old classic, Edward Cheyney, *The European Background of American History* (1904). For the people who were already here, see A. M. Josephy, Jr., *The Indian Heritage of America* (1968), and Wilcomb E. Washburn, *The Indian in America* (1975).

The great voyages of exploration and discovery are ably discussed in J. H. Parry, *The Age of Reconnaissance* (1963), and in Samuel Eliot Morison's two-volume work, *The European Discovery of America* (1971, 1974). Morison's *Admiral of the Ocean Sea* (1942), about Columbus, is a masterpiece of biography. An enjoyable and profusely illustrated book on the period is Richard Humble, *The Explorers* (1979).

On the Spanish in the New World, see Charles Gibson, *Spain in America* (1966), and Carl Sauer, *The Early Spanish Main* (1966). For Spain's presence in lands that became part of the United States, see Sauer's *Spanish in Sixteenth-Century North America* (1971). J. H. Elliott, *The Old World and the New* (1970), deals with interactions between Europe and America. The question of the biological interaction between Europe and America is brilliantly treated by Alfred W. Crosby, *The Columbian Exchange: Biological and Cultural Consequences of 1492* (1972).

SECOTAN

Dasamonquepeuc

Roanoac

Hatorasck

Pasquenoke

Trinety harbor

2

England Goes to America
The Struggle to Found a Colony, 1550–1620

England's claim to the New World was almost as old as Spain's. In 1497, only five years after Columbus waded ashore on San Salvador, another Italian navigator, John Cabot (Giovanni Caboto), sailed to Newfoundland on behalf of King Henry VII and claimed the lands he touched for England.

France, by way of contrast, showed little interest in crossing the Atlantic until 1523, when a French privateer captured a Spanish ship carrying gold from Mexico. His curiosity piqued by so curious a cargo, King Francis I sent his Italian sailor, Giovanni Verrazano, to North America, where he claimed for France much of what is now the east coast of the United States. When the pope scolded Francis, reminding him that all non-Christian lands had been divided between Portugal and Spain, the king dipped his pen in sarcasm and responded that he would like to see the section of Adam's Last Will and Testament that gave the pope the right to dispose of such a prize.

Adam's Will or not, Spain enjoyed a monopoly in the New World for a hundred years. It was not that England and France were uninterested in Spain's empire. The stream of gold that flowed to Spain from Mexico and Peru aroused their greed too.

But through most of the 1500s—Spain's *siglo de oro*, or "golden century"—no nation was able or willing to challenge Spanish power. During

Sir Walter Raleigh's colony on Roanoke Island, at left. First settled in 1587, the colony had mysteriously disappeared when Raleigh's men returned with provisions in 1590.

the second half of the century, France was pre-occupied with a vicious civil war, as two and sometimes three great nobles fought for the right to wear the crown. Similar troubles in England had been resolved by Henry VII in 1485, but the Tudor dynasty he founded was vexed by the intertangled problems of succession, religion, and foreign relations. Only at the end of the century, under Elizabeth I, the last of the Tudors, did England rise to the status of a major power.

England's Problems

Religion played a large part in England's uncertain development under the Tudors. The early sixteenth century was not only the age of Spanish supremacy in European politics, but it was also a time of religious upheaval—the Protestant Reformation. During the same years that Cortez was shattering the Aztecs, a German monk named Martin Luther was shattering the unity of European Christendom.

The Protestant Reformation

Luther declared that some doctrines of the Roman Catholic Church were false. In 1517, Luther nailed to a church door ninety-five "theses" in which he attacked certain doctrines and practices of the Catholic Church. Called to account for his challenge by the Holy Roman Emperor, Luther denied the authority of the pope. Almost immediately, large parts of Germany and Scandinavia fell in behind the charismatic former monk. The common people had long been disgusted with the moral laxity of many priests and resented the fact that the Church owned about one-third of the land in Europe. These riches also attracted many princes, always in need of wealth, to Luther's new faith. If these great nobles broke with the pope, they could seize Church lands for their own.

Much of northern and central Europe was permanently lost to Roman Catholicism. A large minority of people in France also declared their acceptance of Protestant doctrines, as did many Scots. In Spain, however, the powerful monarchy stood by Rome and used the repressive Spanish Inquisition, previously directed against Moslems and Jews, to persecute anyone who was suspected of being a Protestant. In England, King Henry VIII also remained loyal to the Catholic Church and wrote a condemnation of Lutheran beliefs called *Defense of the Seven Sacraments*. For his services, the pope named him *Defensor Fides*, or "Defender of the Faith."

England Breaks with Rome

It proved to be an ironical title because, in 1527, Henry himself rejected the pope's authority. His quarrel with Rome had little to do with religious doctrine. Henry VIII wanted an annulment of his marriage to an aging Spanish princess, Catherine of Aragon, so that he could wed a young lady of the royal court, Anne Boleyn. Henry was infatuated with Anne, but, far more important, he believed that he must have a legitimate male heir to the throne if the Tudor dynasty were to survive. Catherine had borne a daughter, Mary, but suffered a series of miscarriages and was at the end of her childbearing years.

Popes tended to be sympathetic to royal problems of this sort, but Clement VII was under the thumb of the Spanish king, who happened to be Catherine's nephew and defender. Clement refused the divorce, and Henry responded by declaring the authority of the pope invalid in his kingdom. He stated that he was the head of the Church in England and saw to it that his annulment and remarriage were promptly approved. By breaking with Rome, Henry was also able to confiscate the rich lands owned by monasteries in England. These he sold to ambitious subjects, filling his treasury to bursting and ensuring a prosperous reign.

Henry ordered few changes in Church doctrine and structure in England. His "reformation" made little difference in the daily lives and Sunday worship of the common people. But the simple act of striking down an ancient and powerful authority liberated a spirit of religious debate and innovation. Slowly but steadily a true Protestantism grew up within the English Church, and during the short reign of Henry's son, Edward VI (1547–53), reformers held power and turned England in a Protestant direction.

Unfortunately for them, Edward was a sickly young man who died in 1553. He was succeeded by his older half-sister, Henry's daughter by Catherine of Aragon. Mary Tudor was a zealous Catholic. She married King Philip II of Spain, "His Most Catholic Majesty," and together they resolved to return England to the Roman Church. The queen systematically rooted out Protestants in the government and also among the common people, executing many and earning the unflattering nickname of "Bloody Mary." Nevertheless, had she lived a long life and borne a son or daughter by Philip of Spain, she might have brought England back to

Rome and forever changed that nation's history and the history of the Americas as well. But like her brother, Mary was on the throne for only a short time; she died in 1558.

The Elizabethan Age

England's new ruler was the shrewdest politician ever to wear the crown of St. George. Elizabeth I, Henry's daughter by Anne Boleyn, was a survivor. She had to be. Her mother was beheaded by her father because Henry tired of her charms. When Elizabeth was fourteen (an age considered adult in the sixteenth century), the English Church embraced Protestantism and English foreign policy turned against Spain. She went along. When Elizabeth was twenty, England went back to Rome under Bloody Mary and became an ally of Spain. Elizabeth went along. Now queen at twenty-five, she was well practiced in the arts of concealing her true sympathies, cajoling both sides on an issue, and biding her time.

When Philip II rushed to England to marry the new monarch and tie the country to his empire once again, Elizabeth told him neither yes nor no. To marry the zealously Roman Catholic ruler of Spain would frighten English Protestants and turn them against her, as they had turned against Mary. To reject Philip abruptly, however, would risk a war with Spain for which England was not then prepared. Flirtatiously when the occasion demanded, formally when it served her purpose, Elizabeth seemed to say yes to the proposal, then seemed to say no. In fact, she said nothing at all, and had her way, which was to win time.

Queen Elizabeth I (1533–1603), in the "Armada" portrait by Marc Geerarts.

The Sea Dogs

She pursued a similarly devious policy toward the New World. During the first two decades of Elizabeth's reign, England was officially at peace with Spain and, therefore, recognized Philip II's claim to all of the Americas. Beginning in 1577, however, Elizabeth quietly encouraged an ambitious, swashbuckling, Spaniard-hating fraternity of sea captains to chip away at Philip's American monopoly.

The most daring of these Sea Dogs, as these privateers were called, was Francis Drake. In 1577, with Elizabeth's secret approval, he set sail in the *Golden Hind*, rounded South America by the Straits of Magellan, and swooped down on the rich and completely unsuspecting Spanish ports on the Pacific. No ship of England or of any nation other than Spain had ever been seen in those waters. Drake guessed that Spanish warships were waiting in the Atlantic for him, so he sailed north as far as California, claiming it for England, and then struck west across the Pacific to home. His expedition was the second to circumnavigate the globe.

At about the same time that Drake departed for South America, Elizabeth authorized another Sea Dog, Martin Frobisher, to scout Newfoundland for a likely place to plant a colony. In 1578, again quietly, she granted two half-brothers, Humphrey Gilbert and Walter Raleigh, the right to establish an English settlement in any land "not in the actual possession of any Christian prince."

Elizabeth was up to her usual game. While appearing to recognize Spain's monopoly in the New World, she was in fact challenging it; although Philip II claimed all of North America for Spain, the northernmost "actual" Spanish outpost was a lonely fort at St. Augustine, Florida.

As it was, the game was nearly up. In 1580, Drake returned to England, his ship so overloaded with Spanish treasure that it could barely float. The profit on the voyage topped 4,000 percent, and Elizabeth ceremoniously boarded the *Golden Hind* and knighted Drake for his services. At about the same time, Sir John Hawkins carried out several daring raids in the Spanish West Indies with Elizabeth's open approval.

Unsuccessful Colonies

In 1578, Gilbert and Raleigh tried to plant a colony in North America, but bad weather forced them to return to England. In 1583, Gilbert briefly established an outpost in Newfoundland but decided that the climate was too rigorous there and turned south. His ship was wrecked in a storm, and he was drowned.

Undaunted, the next year Raleigh sent an exploration party. His men did careful work and recommended the shores of Chesapeake Bay as the best site for a colony. The climate was mild, and the soil was good. And it was far enough from the nearest Spanish outpost to be safe from that dreaded enemy. Raleigh named the country Virginia after Elizabeth (the "Virgin Queen") and, in 1587, shipped more than a hundred men and women across the Atlantic.

They did not, however, set ashore on Chesapeake Bay but, as a result of miscalculation and ill winds, on Roanoke Island, farther south in what is now North Carolina. This was not nearly so good a site as Raleigh had expected. Nevertheless, the Roanoke colony might have succeeded had it not been three long years before supplies and reinforcements arrived. When Raleigh's men finally did return to the Carolina coast in 1590, they found no people and a cryptic message, the word CROATOAN, carved on a tree. There was an island nearby that the Indians called Croatoan, but no trace of the colonists could be found either there or anywhere else that Raleigh's men looked. The first English in America, including Virginia Dare, the first English child born in the New World, simply vanished. Their fate remains a mystery to this day.

Sir Francis Drake (c. 1540–1596), English privateer who was the second man to circumnavigate the earth.

A Pomeiock Indian village, as depicted by John White during the Roanoke expedition of 1585.

The English Start an Empire

Raleigh was prevented from resupplying Roanoke on schedule in part because of financial problems chronic with him, but also because, in 1588, few Englishmen of wealth and power were interested in anything but a dark threat to the nation's very survival. Philip II, concluding that Elizabeth was Spain's mortal enemy, had mobilized his vast riches to construct and assemble a vast armada of 130 ships with which to invade England.

The Spanish (or "Invincible") Armada was a disaster. In the English Channel, the Sea Dogs met the powerful but clumsy Spanish galleys, galleasses, and galleons with daring tactics and small quick pinnaces, ships of the latest design. One destructive form of attack was to set old, unmanned vessels on fire, and then send them into the midst of Spanish transports in close formation, drowning hundreds of soldiers. The next year, trying to return home by rounding the British Isles to the north, the remnants of the Armada were further devastated by ferocious Atlantic storms. So crushing was the Spanish defeat that the English could be excused for claiming that God was on their side.

Spanish power did not collapse with the death of the Armada. Philip briefly considered assembling another great fleet and trying again; Spain's income from the Americas still topped $12 million a year. Nevertheless, the English had demonstrated that Spanish seapower was not invincible and, therefore, that Spain was unable to enforce its monopoly of the Americas. As the sixteenth century drew to a close, England (as well as France, Holland, and Sweden) were ready to create colonial empires.

Raleigh's Contribution

Sir Walter Raleigh did more than any other individual to stimulate English interest in the possibilities of colonization. Not only did he personally try to found colonies, but he also lobbied tirelessly for an overseas empire at the queen's court and among the wealthy English merchants whose financial backing was indispensable to such an expensive undertaking.

And yet, the flamboyant Raleigh, who was said to have spread his cloak over a mud puddle so that Elizabeth would not soil her shoes, was by 1603, the year Elizabeth died, a man of the past. He was closer in his attitudes to the Spanish *conquistadores*—to feudal knights—than to the sober-minded capitalists whom he endlessly badgered for money.

Raleigh thought of a colony as a kind of naval base for privateers, a safe haven from which English Sea Dogs could sally forth and raid Spanish treasure ships. Just as the Spanish took gold and silver from the Indians by force of arms, English buccaneers would take it from the Spanish by virtue of their prowess on the waves.

Sir Walter Raleigh (c. 1552–1618), English Sea Dog and colonizer.

TRAVELOGUES

In 1589, an Oxford clergyman named Richard Hakluyt collected descriptions of America that had been written by a number of English seamen and published them as *Navigations, Voiages, Traffiques and Discoveries of the English Nation.* No book did more to arouse interest in colonization until John Smith's *Historie of Virginia,* written to celebrate his own exploits but also filled with glowing descriptions of opportunities in the New World.

Title page of John Smith's Generall Historie of Virginia, New England and the Summer Isles *(1624).*

To Raleigh and many of his associates, economics was little more than a matter of *taking* gold and silver as best one could. Because the enemy was impregnable on the Spanish Main, England's economic health depended on winning the booty at sea. In essence, Raleigh and the Sea Dogs thought of economy as piracy and of colonies as pirate strongholds supplied by the mother country.

Hard Economic Facts

The merchants of the counting houses and ledger books, who were then rising to prominence in England, found such reasoning crude. They also realized that Sea Dog economics would fail in its purpose, the enrichment and strengthening of the nation. Although final proof would be half a century away, by 1600 there

were plenty of signs that Spain's American gold and silver mines were as much a curse as a blessing to that country.

It was true enough that because of its fabulous wealth, the Spanish ruling class was able to purchase whatever it desired, from an elegant style of life that was the envy of Europeans to the huge armies that terrorized the Continent. It was also true, however, that the Spanish ruling class assumed that its matchless bravery and sense of honor were quite enough on which to base an economy. In reality, of course, the mines of Mexico and Peru had bottoms; the gold and silver would run out. By acting as though this doleful truth were not so, the Spanish ensured that one day their country would be destitute.

Instead of using American gold and silver to improve Spanish agriculture, Spain purchased too much of its food abroad, impoverishing its own farmers. Fisheries were neglected in favor of buying fish from Dutch, English, and later American sources of supply. Instead of encouraging the manufacture of textiles, leather goods, and iron work at home, Spain imported these things from the Low Countries and England. Even the bulk of the vaunted Spanish army was imported from abroad— the soldiers were German mercenaries. Spain paid to have its naval and merchant fleets built in Italy and England rather than spend its gold and silver at home in its own shipyards. Thanks to the neglect of its own shipbuilding, much of Spain's cargoes were eventually carried by foreign vessels.

The result was that gold and silver dribbled out of Spain as quickly as they poured in. They went to countries with no gold mines but with a lively merchant class and enterprising manufacturers. Other nations did the final count of the Spanish doubloons, including enemies of Spain that were quite glad to sell whatever the Spanish would buy, to carry across the ocean whatever the Spanish would ship. Every transaction made Spain poorer and its enemies richer. England and Holland, Spain's bitterest foes, actually fought wars with each other to determine which country would bleed Spain of more loot. In the Treaty of Utrecht in 1713, England took as part of the spoils of victory the *Asiento,* the right to sell forty-eight hundred black slaves in the Spanish colonies annually for a period of thirty years. Even Spain's trade in human beings was in foreign hands.

Mercantilism

The realization that trading and manufacturing countries, including England, were getting richer at the expense of Spain, led to the formulation of a set of economic ideas that later became known as mercantilism. They were first systematized in a book of 1664, *England's Treasure by Foreign Trade*, by Thomas Mun. But the English (as well as the French and Dutch) governments began acting on mercantilistic principles at the beginning of the seventeenth century when they adopted policies and passed laws to encourage the development of manufacturing, to favor overseas merchants, and to establish colonies in North America.

The object of mercantilism was to increase the nation's store of gold and silver—not the government's but the entire nation's—and therefore to increase the nation's power. Manufacturing was vital to this scheme because manufacturing added to the value of a natural resource with no expense but time and labor. Thus long before 1600, the English learned that to ship raw wool abroad and to buy it back in the form of woven cloth was economic lunacy. The manufactured cloth cost more than the wool that went into it and drained money out of the realm.

Since the fourteenth century, the Crown had forbidden by law the export of raw wool and, through subsidies and favors, encouraged the carders, spinners, dyers, and weavers who added value to the wool at home. When English cloth was sold abroad, England reaped profits at the expense of those nations that purchased it. The policy did not have the name, but it was good mercantilism.

Overseas trade was even more valuable in mercantilist economics. The money made by transporting goods represented considerable gain for the nation. When a sea captain from Bristol or Plymouth carried a cargo of Dutch cloth to the Spanish colony at Santo Domingo and sugar back to Spain, the gold and silver that he charged the shippers and brought home enriched England at the expense of two rival nations. Mercantilist policy was to encourage England's merchant marine in every way possible.

The ideal was a self-sufficient England, an England that produced everything its people needed at home and bought nothing abroad. If that ideal were achieved, the gold and silver from sales abroad would roll in, while none would leave.

In practice, such perfect self-sufficiency was impossible. An island nation in a northern latitude, England had to purchase any number of tropical products as well as the spices and other goods of the Indies. The English people drank a great deal of wine but produced next to none; wine had to be imported from France and Portugal. England consumed large quantities of furs in the manufacture of clothing and felt. These had to be imported from Muscovy (Russia) and Scandinavia. As a maritime nation, England needed timber and naval stores in profusion (tar, pitch, fiber for rope), but the

country was largely deforested by the seventeenth century. These essentials also had to be imported from Muscovy and Scandinavia.

In the world as it was, then, the object of mercantilism was to minimize imports that cost money and maximize exports and the trade that brought money in. It was at this point that mercantilists thought of colonies.

Why England Wanted Colonies

First of all, colonies were a means of reducing the nation's dependence on foreign countries. By gaining control of the forests of North America, which teemed with fur-bearing animals and seemingly limitless timber and naval stores, England could stop the flow of gold and silver to Scandinavians and Russians. By seizing islands in the tropics, the English could produce their own tropical goods (sugar was most important) and stop paying money to the Spanish for them. And by settling loyal English colonists overseas, the Crown would create exclusive and dependable markets for English manufactures.

Another circumstance that tended to encourage the founding of colonies was the widespread recognition that there were simply too many people in the kingdom. Indeed, the population of the island jumped from 3 to 4 million during the sixteenth century, and employment and food production had not kept pace with this increase.

They had not kept pace because of the "enclosure movement," the tendency of wealthy English landowners during this period to turn formerly cultivated common lands into sheep runs by enclosing them with hedges. Not only was wool more profitable than wheat

---

HISTORICAL RHYMES

Almost every child in the English-speaking world hears the famous nursery rhyme:

> Hark, hark, the dogs do bark;
> The beggars are coming to town,
> Some in rags and some in tags
> And some in velvet gowns.

Like many seemingly meaningless rhymes, this one has historical significance. It refers to the important social phenomenon in England during the time of the enclosure movement, when people were forced off their lands to make way for sheep and took to wandering jobless over the countryside.

or other food crops, but sheep raising required the labor of a fraction of the population that tilling the land did.

Those small farmers and poor villagers who were sent packing were England's "surplus population." When they wandered the countryside, they worried villagers and gentry alike with their begging. Desperate to survive, they sometimes robbed isolated farms and travelers whom they caught on lonely stretches of road.

In the cities the problem was even more alarming. Many of the people who were displaced by enclosure gravitated to London and the seaports. Finding little employment, they formed a large, half-starved, and seemingly permanent underclass that was a source of disease and crime at all times and that periodically erupted in angry rebellion.

During the reign of Henry VIII, concerned humanists like Sir Thomas More realized what was happening and tried to halt the enclosure movement. But they were bucking powerful economic forces. The lure of the money to be made in wool was too great for the landowners to respond to calls for community responsibility.

NOVA BRITANNIA.

OFFERING MOST

Excellent fruites by Planting in
VIRGINIA.

Exciting all such as be well affected
to further the same.

LONDON
Printed for SAMVEL MACHAM, and are to be sold at
his Shop in Pauls Church-yard, at the
Signe of the Bul-head.
1 6 0 9.

Advertisement to encourage emigration to the
New World.

Instead, England tried to solve its population problem by enacting a chilling criminal code. In seventeenth- and eighteenth-century England, a person could be hanged for the pettiest thefts, for stealing as little as a loaf of bread. When there seemed to be "too many people," it was difficult to argue against hanging on humanitarian grounds. When the poor were so numerous as to be a source of worry and fear to the ruling class, it was easy to believe that only the constant threat of the gallows on London's Tyburn Hill or of the local squire's white oak kept them from running completely amok. The "bloody code" was a device designed to maintain social order. And so were colonies.

Colonies were seen by many as a safety valve by which the pressure of England's excess population could be relieved. People who were economically superfluous and socially dangerous in England could, by the alchemy of shipping them overseas, become valuable consumers of English goods and gatherers of the raw materials that England needed. Hence, many convicts were sent to the colonies as indentured servants. The wretchedness of the poor, whether in or out of prison, contributed to colonization by making a great many of them glad to go overseas.

The Lure of the New World

For the poorest English men and women, struggling for bread on the lanes and streets, America promised the simple possibility of a decent life. For people who were just scraping by in England on a small plot of land or in an artisan's shop, the New World offered the opportunity to live in comfort and security. For a few people of means in the old country, America offered the chance to become rich.

The Promoters

Once permanent settlements were actually established, invitations for more people fell on England like leaves in the autumn. Dozens of colonists published exaggerated accounts of the riches to be found; hundreds wrote letters to be circulated. Like advertisers of every era, they played down the dangers and risks, inflated the advantages, and simply lied through their teeth. Virginia rivaled "Tyrus for colours, Balsan for woods, Persia for oils, Arabia for spices, Spain for silks, Narcis for shipping, Netherlands for fish, Pomona for fruit and by tillage, Babylon for corn, besides the abundance of mulberries, minerals, rubies, pearls, gems, grapes, deer," and on and on. The playwrights Beaumont and Fletcher wrote of the place "Where every wind that rises blows perfume,/And every breath of air is like an incense."

But there was no distortion in the simple realities that one could *hope* to own land in America at a time when to do so in England was next to impossible for most people; that familiar English crops grew in America; that there was an abundance of game *and no game laws* (poaching was a capital offense in England); and, most remarkably, that a roaring fire was an everyday pleasure in a land of dense forests. England has a cold, damp climate, and the poor were frequently forbidden to cut wood; hence, it is perhaps not so strange that the simple image of a warm fire should have figured prominently in colonization propaganda.

Private Enterprise

Most of these propaganda efforts were made by individuals. Indeed, although the government was pleased to see colonization under way, the actual task was carried out by private companies that were forerunners of the modern corporation. These "Merchants-Adventurers Companies" had developed in response to the demands of international trade. It was an expensive and risky proposition to send out a big trading expedition. Few investors (the word *Adventurer* refers to "adventuring" capital) had the resources to finance such undertakings individually, and fewer yet wanted to risk their entire fortunes on one. Instead, they formed companies in which they took "shares" of the risks and of possible profits and secured charters from the Crown that gave them monopolies that protected their investments.

The Muscovy Company (founded in 1555) was empowered to trade with Russia, largely in furs and forest products. The Levant Company (chartered in 1581) had a monopoly of English imports from the Mediterranean. The Guinea Company (established in

A warning against skimping on provisions accompanies this "shopping list" for those bound for the New World.

1588) dealt in African goods, although not in slaves at this early date. The most famous and longest lasting of the trading companies was the East India Company (founded in 1600).

Gilbert's and Raleigh's personal losses in Newfoundland and Roanoke persuaded the merchants of London and the Channel ports that the joint-stock company was the medium for making money out of America too. In 1606, King James I granted charters to two groups, one centered in London and the other in Plymouth. The London Company was empowered to establish a settlement between 34° and 41° north latitude, the Plymouth group between 38° and 45°. Although these regions overlapped, the rival groups were required to settle at least one hundred miles from each other. One reason for this provision was the Spanish colonials' history of petty rivalries and battles between and even within their towns. More important, because the chief mission of English settlements was trade with the Indians, they were not to compete against each other.

The charters put a premium on being first to get the best site because the actual grant of land would be made only after a colony was established. Therefore, both groups dispatched ships almost immediately. The Plymouth Company tried to set up on the Kennebec River in Maine, but, as with Gilbert in Newfoundland, the cold climate sent the colonists scurrying home within a few months.

CHILD LABOR

In a subsistence economy, children began to work—to contribute to the survival of a household—as soon as they were able to perform simple tasks. In 1630, Francis Higginson wrote back to England from the newly founded town of Salem, Massachusetts, that "little children here by setting of corn may earn much more than their own maintenance." In other words, a child who was old enough to plant corn actually produced more than he or she consumed. Such productivity was a powerful inducement to emigrate to America among people for whom children were often an economic liability.

Jamestown, Virginia: Success at Last

The London Company had better luck in Raleigh's Virginia, if fifteen years of hardship and regular disasters can be called "better luck." In May 1607, Captain Christopher Newport brought three ships into Chesapeake Bay and decided on a peninsula on the James River (named for the king) as the location of the colony. Captain Newport had Roanoke on his mind. He would select no island that was exposed to the open sea and Spanish raiders, but he made sure to pick a peninsula site that could be defended from the natives almost as easily as an island. Unfortunately, he did not pay enough attention to the fact that Jamestown was low lying and surrounded by marshy scrub woods, little more than a malarial swamp.

Nor did Newport care that the peninsula was not particularly suitable for crops. The first settlers of Virginia were not expected to be self-supporting, growing their own food. Their assignment was to look for gold, to establish commercial contacts with the Indians, to buy pelts and other goods that would turn a profit in England, and—oddly—a group of Polish glassmakers among them was instructed to set up a workshop or factory for their trade.

The experience of this all-male expedition bore little relationship to the promotional literature that several of the first Virginians actually wrote. Of the one hundred men who built the log stockade that summer, only thirty-eight lived to hail the relief ship that arrived in January 1608. That expedition replenished the population of Virginia, but more people died over the winter of 1608/09. The following winter was the worst yet—the infamous "Starving Times." A population of five-hundred men and women disintegrated, so that in May 1610, only sixty wretched souls remained. They abandoned the stockade to move down to the bay, where they were living on oysters when a supply ship arrived in May. They begged to be taken back to England. Even a year later, when life in the colony had definitely improved, the new governor appointed by the London Company wrote that "everie man allmost laments himself of being here." At his wit's end, Governor Sir Thomas Dale suggested to his employers that they send convicts over. Only the doomed, he feared, would find Virginia preferable to the mother country.

The Problem of Survival

Why was survival so difficult? Basically, the design of the colony—as a trading post—was all wrong for a region that offered few valuable goods. Raw wilderness proved to be a more demanding host than the English were prepared for. Many of the settlers were soldiers and could have lived by raiding the Indians' lands. But the Eastern Woodlands Indians were, unlike the Aztecs and Incas, rather desultory farmers. They themselves barely scraped through the winter by hunting and gathering. There was little to be stolen from them.

If the native Indians found winter a challenge, the English were lost. They could not compete with these far more skillful foragers, even if the woods and waters were rich in game and fish. No ecology can support more than a sparse foraging population, and it is probable that the sudden introduction of hundreds of newcomers simply taxed the area around Jamestown beyond its capacity. Once their numbers declined to sixty, the English did survive. If they survived on such as oysters and snakes and toadstools, that is what foraging is all about.

The first turning point came with the arrival of Lord De La Warr in 1610. As governor for a year he directed the seizure of some Indian fields and established a rigorous program aimed at producing the colony's food needs. The colonists were marched to work in the fields like soldiers, and troublemakers were roughly dealt with. De La Warr and his successors, Thomas Dale and Thomas Gates, executed a number of people for little

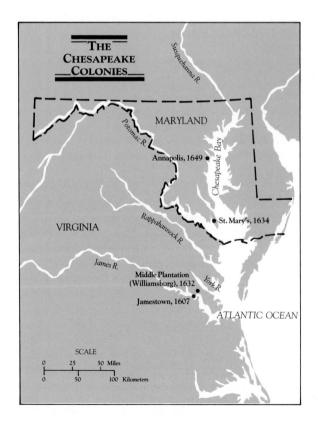

THE CHESAPEAKE COLONIES

Susquehanna R.

MARYLAND

Potomac R.

Annapolis, 1649

Chesapeake Bay

VIRGINIA

Rappahannock R.

St. Mary's, 1634

James R.

Middle Plantation (Williamsburg), 1632

York R.

Jamestown, 1607

ATLANTIC OCEAN

SCALE

0   25   50 Miles

0   50   100 Kilometers

The building of Jamestown, Virginia.

more than laziness. Under this authoritarian rule, however, more fields were cleared, better shelters were built, and settlement was expanded along the banks of the James.

De La Warr's system may have saved the colony. But it did not make money, a fact of increasing concern to the investors back in London. In the end, they never did realize a profit. But the settlers of Virginia found a reason to cease lamenting themselves of being there.

The "Stinking Custom"
The reason was tobacco, which already was well known in Europe. Columbus brought tobacco back on his first voyage, and the habit of "drinking" it spread steadily throughout Europe. Some physicians seized on it as a "miracle drug," prescribing it for any number of ailments. More than a few found smoking loathsome. In 1604, King James I wrote *A Counterblaste to Tabacco*, which described the habit as savage, "beastly," and "vile." He called tobacco a "noxious weed" and forbade smoking it in his presence. (An Ottoman emperor went further. He executed smokers!) But only as long as tobacco was a product of the Spanish West Indies, and its purchase therefore prohibited by mercantilist policies, was there significant resistance to the "noxious weed" in England. Once it was grown in an English colony, tobacco was acceptable, and smoking was a habit whose time had come.

John Rolfe, a Virginian usually remembered for his marriage to the Indian princess Pocahontas, began to experiment with West Indian tobacco in 1612. He succeeded in developing a product that turned into a boom. From a few barrels, exports jumped to ten tons in 1617 and twenty-five tons in 1618. From that point, the economy of Virginia soared. One industrious man could tend one thousand tobacco plants and four acres of maize, beans, and squash planted Indian style—enough to feed five people. Virginia never again wanted for food nor, before long, for luxuries imported from England. Nor did the colony lack immigrants.

The Headright System
Tobacco eventually became a crop raised largely by slave labor. Africans first made their appearance in English America in 1619, a year before the famous *Mayflower* in Massachusetts, when a Dutch ship weighed anchor in the James River and sold, among other commodities, about twenty blacks probably captured from a slave ship bound for Spanish America. These first black Americans were almost certainly not slaves but were sold into servitude for a specific term of years (probably seven), according to the system under which British laborers were imported.

In 1618, the London Company had devised the "headright system" to attract Englishmen to Virginia. Under it, each person or head of household who came to Virginia received fifty acres of land for himself and fifty for every other person whose passage he paid. This attractive law not only stimulated the emigration of women and children and the beginning of a self-perpetuating population, but it also led to the evolution of "indentured servitude."

People with cash could become large landowners instantly by recruiting "servants" from among the destitute masses of England, who were a ready-made labor force. In return for their transportation to Virginia, these poor people were bound by contract to labor for their master without pay for a number of years, after

KING JAMES I ON TOBACCO

"A custom loathesome to the eye, harmful to the brain, dangerous to the lungs, and in the black stinking fume thereof, nearest resembling the Stygian smoke of the pit that is bottomless."

MIRACLE DRUG

While James I loathed tobacco, many of his subjects regarded its use as not only pleasurable, but also as a health aid. In an essay about Virginia published in 1588, Thomas Hariot wrote that because the Indians smoked, they "know not many greevous diseases wherewithall wee in England are oftentimes afflicted."

H O W   T H E Y   L I V E D

How They Found Their Way

Sailors bound for Asia by rounding Africa found their way by the ancient and obvious method of keeping the coastline in sight. They needed more than their eyes and their maps only when adverse winds blew them off course to the west and when they made their final dash across the Indian Ocean. But when they crossed the Atlantic, they were out of sight of land from start to finish. Deep-water sailors of the sixteenth and seventeenth centuries depended on two navigational instruments—the compass and the astrolabe—in order to arrive at their destination in the Americas or in Europe. Just *when* they would arrive, however, remained a matter of dead reckoning—guesswork—until nearly the time of the American Revolution.

The instruments that were available to the shipmasters who took the English colonists to North America were more accurate than those Columbus had used on his voyage of discovery, but in principle they were the same as those aboard the *Santa Maria.* Indeed, by the time Columbus sailed to the New World, it was known that magnetic north differed from true north. By using the compass, sailors could determine, though with some margin of error, the direction in which they were sailing. By the seventeenth century, the ship's

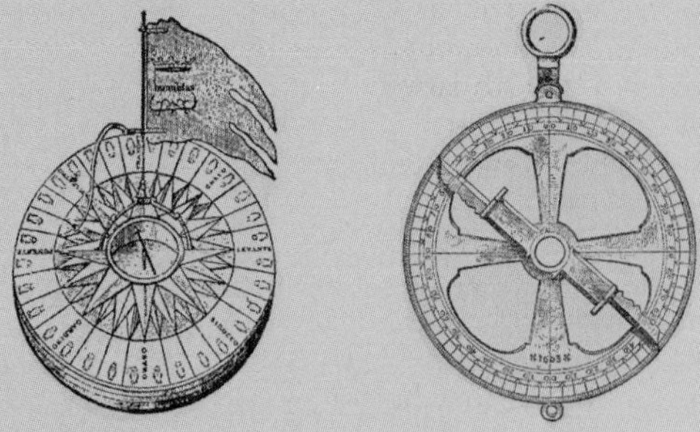

compass (left) consisted of a brass bowl marked with thirty-two directions in the center of which a magnetized needle was delicately balanced. It was positioned near the helmsman and mounted on pivots so that it remained level despite the pitching and rolling of the vessel.

The astrolabe (right), perfected in the century before Columbus, enabled navigators to measure the angle between the sun (or, at night, certain stars) and the horizon. From this information, they could determine their latitude—that is, the distance of their position from the equator. Using an astrolabe, a sailor knew on what east–west line he was sailing.

which time they were freed and provided with clothing, perhaps tools or a little money, and sometimes even land. It was an attractive prospect to many. Others were forced to go against their will: convicts, for

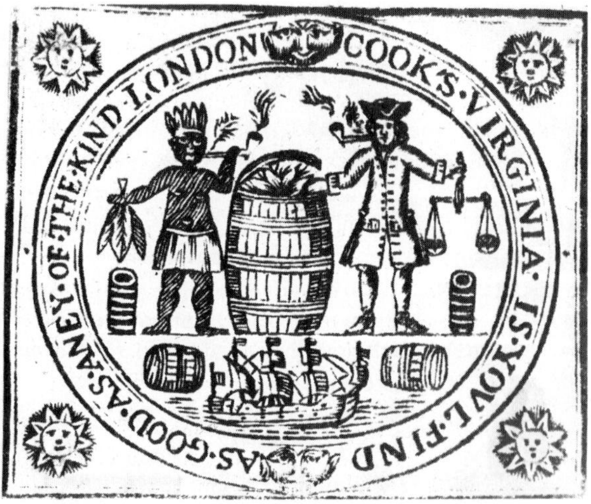

An early tobacco label, from the Imperial Tobacco Company in Bristol.

instance, and even children kidnapped off the streets of English cities by professional procurers.

High profits in tobacco and a work force of indentured servants formed the basis of the Virginia economy for a century. Although the institution of black slavery had emerged by 1650, and the importation of Africans increased dramatically after 1700, white indentured servants outnumbered black slaves until well into the eighteenth century.

The Massacre of 1622

For fifteen years the English coexisted reasonably well with the natives of the region, an Algonkian-speaking tribe called the Powhatans whose chief, when Jamestown was settled, was also named Powhatan. Red and white skirmished often enough, but few battles were serious. Powhatan did not view the tiny enclave as much of a threat, and he was fascinated by the wondrous goods that the newcomers offered him in trade, from firearms to woven cloth, pots, pans, and mirrors. In 1614, when John Rolfe married his daughter, Pocohantas, something of an alliance was formed.

Then Pocohantas died while in England, and shortly thereafter, Powhatan joined her. He was succeeded as

Thus, in order for an English captain to make a landfall at, say, Plymouth on Cape Cod, which he knew was located about 42° north latitude, he sailed in a southerly direction out of England until the ship arrived at 42° north latitude. Then completing the voyage was a simple matter of following the compass west—simple to the extent that winds and currents were cooperative.

What seventeenth-century sailors could not determine with any accuracy was longitude—their position on the imaginary lines that run north–south from pole to pole. In other words, they had no more than a vague notion of how far they had sailed from their port of departure and, therefore, how far they were from their destination. The log line was an "instrument" of sorts for gauging the speed of a ship. It was a rope knotted every forty-eight feet and tied to a wood float, which was heaved overboard. Measuring minutes with a sand-glass, the captain counted the number of knots that passed over the stern in a given period of time. Since the float was not blown, as the ship was, wind speed could thus be ascertained. However, ships were only occasionally blessed with a wind they could ride before in a straight line; usually, a ship tacked, or zigzagged against the wind. Moreover, the log line did not take account of the actions of ocean currents, which could radically increase or decrease a ship's progress: the float

was in the grip of currents, just as the ship was.

It was not until 1752 that a German astronomer named Tobias Mayer devised a set of tables and a mathematical formula for determining longitude from the position of the moon. But Mayer's system was not very practical. Even the most skilled mathematician could not complete the calculations in less than four hours—not the sort of exercise a hurried captain would want to do every day.

Later in the eighteenth century, an English watch-maker named Larcum Kendall devised a highly accurate clock, or chronometer. Such a clock would be set when a ship began its voyage; the captain would know the exact time back home and be able to compare it with the time aboard his ship (determined from the position of the sun), thus establishing his position on the globe in relation to his home port—longitude. A chronometer was first used by Captain James Cook on his second great voyage of exploration in the South Pacific in 1772.

Seventeenth-century ocean travelers arrived when they arrived. Depending on winds and currents, a sailing ship made the trip between England and the colonies in anywhere from six weeks to three months and sometimes even longer. The expedition that settled Jamestown took eighteen weeks to cross the Atlantic; the *Mayflower* took ten weeks.

---

chief by his brother Opecanough, who realized what many Indians after him were to realize: the little half-starved white enclave with interesting things to trade was growing in size and strength, taking over the tribe's ancestral lands by hook and by crook. In March 1622, Opecanough tried to turn the tide back by swooping down on Jamestown and killing 350 whites, perhaps one-quarter of Virginia's population.

It was not enough. The survivors regrouped, bandaged their wounds and retaliated with their superior weapons, driving the Powhatans far into the interior. The pattern of white–Indian relations that would be repeated time and again over two and a half centuries had been marked in the mud of Jamestown.

Of more pertinence to the settlers there, the massacre also wrote an end to the London Company. Although some individuals were already getting rich from tobacco, the company was not; it never recorded a profit. Using this failure and the massacre as excuses, James I revoked the company's charter and placed Virginia under his direct control. There would be a legislative assembly—the House of Burgesses—elected by men of property. But the king would appoint the governor. Virginia was the first royal colony. In the meantime, the Plymouth Company—the businessmen

who had been beaten to Virginia by the London Company—had finally found a way to plant their colony.

For Further Reading

Four excellent books provide a vivid and comprehensive picture of what England was like during the period of colonization. A. L. Rowse, *Elizabethans and America* (1959), looks at English society from the top. Wallace Notestein, *The English People on the Eve of Colonization, 1603–1630* (1954), and Carl Bridenbaugh, *Vexed and Troubled Englishmen, 1590–1642* (1968), survey the whole range of English society. Peter Laslett, *The World We Have Lost* (1965), provides a feel for the era.

The reigning classic about English colonization is still Charles M. Andrews, *The Colonial Period of American History* (1934–38). Designed as a textbook but also an authoritative history is Curtis P. Nettels, *The Roots of American Civilization* (1938). Clarence Ver Steeg, *The Formative Years* (1964), and Wesley F. Craven, *The Southern Colonies in the Seventeenth Century* (1949), are excellent brief accounts of Virginia and Maryland. Alden Vaughan, *Captain John Smith and the Founding of Virginia* (1975), provides illumination on the early history of the first successful colony. On white–Indian relations, see Gary Nash, *Red, White, and Black: The Peoples of Early America* (1974).

3

Puritans and Proprietors
The Growth of Colonial America, 1620–1732

In 1608, less than a year after Captain Newport discharged his passengers in Virginia, a small band of villagers from the English Midlands set out on a less adventurous journey. They traveled overland from Scrooby in Nottinghamshire to the North Sea and crossed by boat to the Dutch city of Leiden. The trip was not dangerous, but the manner of these men, women, and children was uneasy and furtive because what they were doing was illegal. No nation permitted subjects to travel abroad without permission.

The travelers were not overly concerned about breaking that particular law. They were fleeing their homeland because their religion, the most important thing in their lives, was illegal. They were members of a small Protestant sect known as Separatists because they believed that people who were saved—whom God had granted the gift of salvation—should separate from the mass of the population and worship only in the company of other Visible Saints. Because all English men and women were required to belong to the established church, the Church of England, the refusal of the Separatists to attend services was a crime.

The Mayflower in Plymouth harbor, in a later depiction by W. F. Halsall.

Unlike Queen Elizabeth, who paid little heed to her subjects' religious practices as long as they did not threaten her politically, her successor, James I, meant to enforce the authority of the Church of England in every particular. Religious dissenters were fined, imprisoned, and flogged during his reign, which began in 1603, and a few were executed for their beliefs. Fearing that the situation could only worsen, the Separatists fled to Holland, where all religions were tolerated.

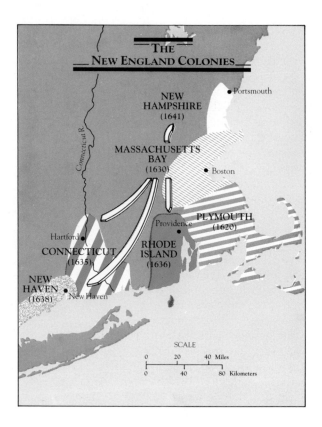

Pilgrims and Puritans

In American history, the Separatists are better known as Pilgrims, which means "travelers" or "wanderers." In Leiden, Holland, they found only menial, low-paying work. Dissatisfaction with Holland grew; they disliked the fact that their children were growing up as much Dutch as English, speaking the language of the country and behaving in ways they regarded as licentious. Although the Pilgrims disapproved of the Church of England and despised James I's oppression, they were nevertheless English to the core, and yearned for a place where they could speak their own language, follow their own ideas about how children should be reared, and worship God in their own way.

The seal of the colony of Massachusetts Bay (1676).

Plymouth

News of Virginia's success resolved their dilemma. It meant it was possible for the English to survive in the New World. When the sympathetic Sir Edwin Sandys, an influential shareholder in the Plymouth Company, assured the Pilgrims that King James would not molest them if they went to New England (as the region north of Virginia was now called), they returned to their homeland just long enough to sail for America in two small ships. The *Speedwell* leaked and rushed back to port before it was fairly started, but the *Mayflower*, although none too seaworthy a craft itself, made it across the Atlantic.

In November 1620 the Pilgrims found what they were looking for. At the lower end of Massachusetts Bay they picked a townsite where, they believed, they could preserve their English culture while worshiping God in the manner they chose. This was the Plymouth Colony, the second permanent English settlement in America.

In some ways the experience of the Pilgrims paralleled that of the first Virginians. There was a "starving time" that almost destroyed the colony. During the first winter, 44 of the 102 original colonists died of malnutrition or disease. Like Virginia, Plymouth experimented with a strictly regulated communal society.

The company owned everything; the colonists worked in supervised gangs and were allotted what they needed in order to live.

Also as in Virginia, this system did not work. It was difficult for people who awakened daily to the sight of broad lands for the taking to be content as employees who were regulated at every turn by the sound of a bell or the cry of an overseer. Married women grumbled because they had to cook and mend for bachelors who were assigned to their households. The bachelors, in turn, complained that they worked as hard and as long as the husbands but were paid less. (Each individual was allotted food, clothing, and shelter according to his or her needs, so married men with children who were too young to work received more than unmarried men.) It seemed to Governor William Bradford that everyone had a grievance against the communal character of Plymouth, and after little more than a year, he distributed farmland among the families.

In other ways, Plymouth was altogether different from Jamestown. Because the Pilgrims settled outside the boundaries specified in the company's charter, the leaders of the group feared that there was no legal basis for their authority. Of the 102 people who founded Plymouth, only 35 were church members, and many of the others aboard the *Mayflower* spoke openly of doing as they pleased once they set foot on shore.

THE MAYFLOWER COMPACT

IN THE NAME OF GOD, AMEN

We whose names are underwritten, the loyal subjects of our dread Sovereign Lord King James, by Grace of God of Great Britain, France, and Ireland King, Defender of the Faith, etc.

Having undertaken, for the glory of God and advancement of the Christian Faith and Honour of our King and Country, a Voyage to plant the First Colony in the Northern Parts of Virginia, do by these presents solemnly and mutually in the presence of God and one of another, Covenant and Combine ourselves together into a Civil Body Politic, for better ordering and preservation and furtherance of the ends aforesaid; and by virtue hereof to enact, constitute and frame such just and equal Laws, Ordinances, Acts, Constitutions and Offices from time to time, as shall be thought most meet and convenient for the general good of the Colony, unto which we promise all due submission and obedience. In witness whereof we have hereunder subscribed our names at Cape Cod, the 11th of November, in the year of the reign of our Sovereign Lord King James, of England, France and Ireland the eighteenth, and of Scotland the fifty-fourth, Anno Domini 1620.

THE FORGOTTEN COLONY

Many English settlements in North America have not been remembered because they were abandoned or absorbed by those that survived. The most interesting was "Merrymount," located near what is now Quincy, Massachusetts, a few miles from Plymouth.

In 1623, a curious character named William Morton arrived at Plymouth in a servant ship commanded by Captain Wollaston. The captain disliked the area and left for Virginia with most of his servants. He apparently intended to send for the rest, but Morton led a peaceful rebellion among them, persuading those who remained (in the words of Plymouth Governor Bradford) to join in a colony where they would be "free from service, and . . . trade, plante, & live togeather as equalls."

Morton presided over a riotous style of life that infuriated the austere Puritans. Like many pioneers after them, the Merrymounters were frequently drunk, and they "set up a May-pole, drinking and dancing aboute it many days togeather, inviting the Indean women, for their consorts, dancing and frisking togither, (like so many fairies, or furies rather,) and worse practices."

Worst of all, Morton seems to have stolen the Indian trade from Plymouth. He offered guns in return for furs and hides. This worried Govenor Bradford because the Indians were better hunters than the whites "by reason of ther swiftnes of foote, & nimblnes of body" and because he feared the firearms would be turned against his own people.

He resolved to break up the colony and sent Captain Miles Standish and a few other men to arrest Morton. There was no battle because, according to Bradford, Morton and his friends were too drunk to shoot. The only casualty was a Merrymounter who staggered into a sword and split his nose.

Morton was put on an uninhabited island to await the next ship bound for England. However, the Indians brought him food and liquor. He managed to slip away, returning on his own to England, where he denounced the Pilgrims in words as impassioned as Bradford's. Neither he nor Plymouth was punished, however, and Morton later returned to America to lead a quieter life. It is interesting to reflect on how differently New England might have developed had Morton's taste for the "high life" and anarchic attitude toward government and social class taken hold, as it might well have done. Morton seems to have been prospering, and Bradford tells us that when "the scume of the countrie, or any discontents" heard that Morton forbade the holding of servants, they "would flock to him from all places."

In order to save their religious refuge from chaos, the Pilgrims joined with others such as the military officer of the expedition, Captain Miles Standish, to sign a compact binding all the inhabitants of the colony to follow the will of a majority of freemen.

Because Plymouth was too far from England for the Crown to have much control over the colony, the Mayflower Compact served as Plymouth's constitution for seventy years. The government built on it was not democratic by modern standards. Only male heads of households who were church members were entitled to vote. But the document's fundamental assumption, that the authority of government derived from the consent of at least some of the people who were governed by it, and not from any outside source, was full of democratic potential.

Plymouth survived, but no one came up with a moneymaker like John Rolfe's tobacco plants. The colony produced foodstuffs of scant commercial value back home, harvesting the abundant codfish that fishermen back in England were able to catch for themselves. After a few years the shareholders in England came to despair of ever realizing a profit on their investment, and they sold the company to the settlers, thus transferring virtually all decision-making power to the colony itself. Plymouth remained a colony until 1691, when it was absorbed into its younger but larger neighbor, Massachusetts.

NO-NONSENSE EDUCATION

To the Puritans, once a child was old enough to learn to read, he or she was old enough to be confronted with the harsh realities of Calvinist theology. The *New England Primer,* from which several generations of Puritan children learned their ABC's, did not use light rhymes or cute pictures for each letter. The first thing a pupil learned was

*In Adam's fall
We sinned all.*

A	In *Adam's* Fall We sinned all.
B	Thy Life to mend, This *Book* attend.
C	The *Cat* doth play, And after flay.
D	A *Dog* will bite A Thief at Night.
E	An *Eagle's* Flight Is out of Sight.
F	The idle *Fool* Is whipt at School.

The Puritans of Massachusetts Bay

Self-government was half accidental in Plymouth. If a weary Pilgrim plowman had turned up a gold mine in his corn field, the English investors and king would have clamped on to the colony with a grip of iron. Plymouth's very lack of rich resources was the source of its independence, whereas in the most important colony of New England, self-government was the result of well-laid plans.

Massachusetts Bay was established in 1630, about forty miles up the coast from Plymouth. There were no starving times there. The founders of the Bay Colony had planned every detail of their Great Migration before they weighed anchor in England. Supplies were abundant, and about a thousand people formed the first wave, a cross section of age, sex, social class, and occupation that amounted to a ready-made city, which they promptly founded and called Boston. Because the founders intended to create a society such as the earth had never quite known—a Godly Commonwealth—they brought with them the charter of the Massachusetts Bay Company, the document that guaranteed their right to self-government in black and white.

These cautious, prudent people—calculating all contingencies, plotting how to meet them—were the Puritans. As was the Pilgrims', their religion was Calvinistic; they were disciples of the French lawyer and Protestant theologian John Calvin, who believed that human nature was inherently depraved, and that men and women still carried the burden of Adam and Eve's original sin. In the words of the Massachusetts poet Anne Bradstreet, man was a "lump of wretchedness, of sin and sorrow."

If God were merely just, every human being would deserve eternal damnation. Since God was all good, there was nothing that sin-stained men and women could do to *earn* salvation—no act of charity, no act of faith. All deserved to burn in hellfire.

The formidable character of the seventeenth-century Puritan of Massachusetts Bay is well depicted in this nineteenth-century bronze sculpture by Augustus Saint-Gaudens.

A PURITAN VIEW OF MAN

Raised by a Puritan father, married to a Puritan, Anne Bradstreet (1612–72) and her family joined John Winthrop on his voyage to Massachusetts Bay in 1630. The following lines from her long poem "Contemplations" express the Puritan's view of the frail human creature.

Man at the best a creature frail and vain,
In knowledge ignorant, in strength but weak,
Subject to sorrows, losses, sickness, pain,
Each storm his state, his mind, his body break,
From some of these he never finds cessation,
But day or night, within, without, vexation,
Troubles from foes, from friends, from dearest,
    near'st relation.

And yet this sinful creature, frail and vain,
This lump of wretchedness, of sin and sorrow,
This weatherbeaten vessel wracked with pain,
Joys not in hope of an eternal morrow;
Nor all his losses, crosses, and vexation,
In weight, in frequency and long duration
Can make him deeply groan for that divine
    translation.

A Mission in the Wilderness

The Puritans did not come to America in order "to worship as they pleased." They were a powerful minority in England, worshiping pretty much as they pleased there. They came to Massachusetts because they believed that King Charles I and the leaders of the Church of England were worshiping in an ungodly way, practicing old Roman Catholic forms and, therefore, committing the sin of blasphemy. "I am verily persuaded," wrote John Winthrop, the leader of the Puritans who left England, "God will bring some heavy affliction upon this land."

The Puritans hoped to establish a Godly Commonwealth in the wilderness of the New World that would stand as "a citty on a hill," beckoning to all saintly people. They had undertaken a sacred mission to show England and the rest of the world how to live. Life in Puritan Massachusetts was closely regulated because the Puritans believed that if they tolerated sin among themselves they would be punished.

This belief in their solemn covenant with God, not a kill-joy attitude toward the pleasures of life, explains why the Puritans punished what are today called "victimless crimes," such as fornication. As a girl named Tryal Pore confessed to the Middlesex County Court when she was tried for that offense in 1656, "by this my sinn I have not only done what I can to Poull Judge-

Was there then no hope? In fact there was, and in the Puritans' hope for the next world lies the key to understanding the kind of society they built in this one. God in his infinite love for his creatures granted the gift of grace to some, designating them the Elect, or the Visible Saints. They did not deserve the gift; like everyone around them they were lumps of wretchedness. But God had predestined them to live with him in paradise.

In return for God's awesome gift, the Visible Saints were bound by a covenant (or contract) with God to enforce divine law in the community in which they lived. If the Saints failed to keep their part of the bargain, if they sinned or tolerated sin within their community, God would punish them as severely as he had punished his chosen people of an earlier epoch, the ancient Hebrews.

JOHN COTTON ON DEMOCRACY

The Puritans did not believe in democracy. John Cotton (1584–1652), the most influential minister in the early years of Massachusetts Bay, put it this way in a letter to England: "Democracy I do not conceyve that ever God it ordeyne as a fitt government eyther for church or for commonwealth. If the people be governors, who shall be governed?"

The stocks, a common Puritan punishment, as depicted by a nineteenth-century artist.

ment from the Lord on my selve but allso upon the place there I live."

The same sense of community moved Puritans to point out to their neighbors that they might be committing sins. Judge Samuel Sewall of Massachusetts was not accused of being a busybody when he visited a wig-wearing relative to tell him that his practice was sinful. Sewall was looking after his kinsman's soul and the well-being of the community. Rather than telling Sewall to mind his own business, the man argued with the judge only as to whether wearing a wig really was a sin.

Puritan "Blue Laws"

The lawbooks of Massachusetts (and other New England colonies) were filled with regulations that, in the late twentieth century, would be considered outrageous or ridiculous. God commanded that the sabbath be devoted to him; therefore, the Puritans forbade on Sunday activities that on any other day were perfectly in order: working; playing games, such as was the custom in England; "idle chatter"; singing; whistling; breaking into a run; and "walking in a garden." Some things were permitted in private but not in public. For example, married couples were forbidden to embrace or kiss in public. A sea captain, returning home after a voyage of several years' duration, kissed his wife at the door of their cottage, and was fined.

Other minor offenders—for example, a woman who was "a scold" heard nagging too often in public—spent a few hours in the stocks or pillory on market day, subjected to ridicule. More serious crimes, such as wife beating, were punished by public flogging.

Lest the Puritans be thought unduly harsh, almost all the colonies had similar laws, and in one particular the Puritans were far more lenient than other Englishmen. Because the Bible was their guide in these, as in other, matters, the Puritans reserved capital punishment for those offenses that merited the death penalty in the Good Book: murder, treason, witchcraft, and several sexual offenses: (incest, homosexuality, and bestiality).

Adultery was also a capital crime, but the ultimate penalty was rarely exacted for it. In 1695, a law of Salem, Massachusetts, punished adulterers by requiring them to wear a cloth *A* on their clothing for life. Although the psychological consequences of this law provided the inspiration for Nathaniel Hawthorne's great novel *The Scarlet Letter*, written a century and a half later, the punishment was actually a liberalization of the practice of branding offenders with a hot iron.

The Puritans believed that social class and social distinctions were divinely decreed. "Some must be rich, some poore, some high and eminent in power and dignitie," said John Winthrop. Winthrop did not say

WERE THE PURITANS HYPOCRITES?

The fact that the Puritans of Massachusetts persecuted people who held religious views other than theirs has led some historians to call them hypocrites: they came to America because their form of worship was not tolerated in England, and once in control, they persecuted others.

The Puritans were intolerant. But they were not hypocrites. They came to America because they disapproved of the religious practices of the dominant Church of England, not because they were persecuted in any severe way. They never claimed that they would be tolerant of forms of worship that they regarded as sinful.

that some *are* rich but that some *must be* rich. It was a crime for people of lower class to imitate the fashions of those above them. In Connecticut in 1675, thirty-eight women were arrested for dressing in silks. Other laws forbade workingpeople to wear silver buckles on their shoes. Silver buckles were reserved for those of higher social class—magistrates, ministers, and so on.

The Expansion of New England

Between 1630 and 1640, ten thousand people left England for Massachusetts. Most of them formed townships and won grants of land from the colony's governing body. Others, however, moved beyond the boundaries of the Bay Colony. Puritan insistence that everyone in the community conform to God's law played a large part in this expansion. Religion was a factor in the founding of four New England colonies: Rhode Island, Connecticut, New Haven, and New Hampshire.

Rhode Island

Rhode Island and Providence Plantations, still the long official name of the smallest state, was founded by a brilliant, zealous, and cantankerous Puritan preacher named Roger Williams. In Massachusetts in 1630, he quarreled with his friend John Winthrop and with the colony's other leaders almost before he settled in. Not that Williams was anti-Puritan. He was the strictest sort of Puritan. It was his demanding conscience, more rigorous with himself than with others, that led to his banishment from Massachusetts Bay.

MARRIED LIFE

Because they believed that marriage was the only natural state of life for an adult, because the family unit was better suited to contend with the near-subsistence conditions of the early colonial economy, and because recently widowed or widowered people usually inherited property from their deceased spouses (thus making them desirable mates), men and women usually remarried very soon after their wives and husbands died. The first marriage performed in Plymouth matched Edward Winslow, whose first wife had been dead for a month and a half, with Susanna White, whose husband had died less than three months previously. One early governor of New Hampshire married a widow of ten days.

ESTABLISHMENT OF COLONIAL CHURCHES

1609 The Church of England was established in Virginia and later in New York, Maryland, the Carolinas, and Georgia. James Blair, Commissary of the Bishop of London, was particularly important in the Anglican Church in Virginia after 1689.

1620–1630 The Congregational Church was established in Plymouth and Massachusetts Bay. The power of the Church began to decline somewhat with the establishment of the Halfway Covenant, 1657–62. This doctrine permitted the baptism of the children of church members even though the children had not experienced conversion.

1628 The Dutch Reformed Church was started in New Amsterdam.

1634 The Roman Catholic Church was established in Maryland, where it was protected by the Toleration Act. The Act was later repealed, and Maryland passed anti-Catholic laws.

1636–1637 Roger Williams, Anne Hutchinson, and others left the Massachusetts Congregational Church and founded separate congregations. Williams founded the first Baptist Church, which stressed the separation of church and state, in Providence, R.I., 1639.

1640 The Lutheran Church was started in New Sweden under Rev. Reorus Torkillus.

1654 Jews first arrived in New Amsterdam.

1681 Quakers in large numbers settled in Pennsylvania.

1706 The Presbyterian Church was organized in Philadelphia. William Tennent's Log College in Neshaminy, Pa. (1736), and the College of New Jersey (1746) promoted Presbyterianism.

Williams believed that the English had no right to settle in America unless the Indians granted them title to the land. In sermon and pamphlet he attacked the Puritans' assumption that the king's charter gave them a legal and moral right to be there. This argument disturbed Winthrop and his allies, not because of the cost involved in buying land from the Indians (no one, including Williams, ever paid them very much for land), but because in denying the validity of the colony's charter in one particular, Williams was striking at the Puritans' most valued possession, the king's grant of their right to govern themselves.

Williams also came to believe in religious toleration. He did not think that one religion is as good as another. Far from it. Williams was convinced that the majority of people were damned and that all forms of worship other than the Puritan one were sinful. However, he maintained that no individual, no minister, no church body, and no civil government had the ability or the right to determine which person was a Saint and which was not. Only God and the individual concerned could know whether the gift of grace had

Roger Williams, who founded Rhode Island after being banished from Massachusetts Bay in 1635, believed in separation of church and state.

Anne Hutchinson

In 1638, another Massachusetts dissenter was banished to the shores of Narragansett Bay. Like Williams, Anne Hutchinson was an intensely committed Puritan. She took seriously the admonition that Saints should spend their time studying the word of God, and she began to invite people to her home after services in order to discuss the sermons they had heard. Unfortunately for Hutchinson, her own comments on the colony's leading preachers were brilliant and often critical. Her informal meetings became popular among some of the most serious believers in Boston and a source of resentment among preachers who were wounded by her sharp tongue.

It was bad enough that a woman should lead such discussions. Although women generally enjoyed a higher status in New England than in England, they were assigned a decidedly secondary place, particularly in religious matters. John Winthrop, who ruled on Hutchinson's fate, believed that women would jeopardize their mental balance by thinking too deeply about difficult theological questions! They were expected to listen and accept the preaching of learned ministers.

Anne Hutchinson not only dealt with theological fine points without going insane, but she repeatedly got the better of Winthrop when she was haled before the General Court to give an accounting of herself. Because she had influential supporters as well as critics, she might have gotten off with a scolding. But Hutchinson believed that the Holy Spirit directly motivated some persons, such as herself, to speak, and this tenet challenged the Puritans' political control of Massachusetts. Who was to say whom the Holy Spirit had touched? According to Hutchinson, certainly not the small groups of Saints who decided which persons would be admitted to church membership and, therefore, could vote.

It was a dangerous doctrine. Hutchinson's "Antinomianism" came close to the separation of church and state that Roger Williams preached. Like Williams, she moved to Rhode Island. With two such strong-minded founders, it was a quarrelsome place. In a few years, Hutchinson moved on to New York, where, in 1643, she and several of her children were killed by Indians.

been granted. Consequently, government could not interfere with anyone's religious convictions or base the right to vote on membership in an established church.

This idea struck at the Puritan belief that the Commonwealth must be governed by Saints in accordance with God's law. In 1635, Williams was ordered to return to England. Instead, he escaped into the forest, spent the winter with the Narragansett Indians, and in 1636 established a farm and townsite (Providence) on land that he had purchased from them.

During Rhode Island's first years, the governors of Massachusetts could have rooted out Williams and his followers with little difficulty. But Governor Winthrop respected Williams in spite of his dangerous beliefs and let him be. Now that Williams was outside the boundaries of Massachusetts, the Bay Colony would not suffer for his sins. In 1644, Williams traveled to London, where he secured a charter for his colony. He may have denied the right of king or Parliament to give away what did not belong to them, but he also knew how to play the game. The Puritans of Massachusetts, staking so much on their own royal charter, would not dare to violate another.

New Hampshire and Connecticut

New Hampshire's first settlers were followers of Anne Hutchinson who moved north from Massachusetts with a minister, John Wheelright. However, the colony never developed Rhode Island's reputation for eccentricity. New Hampshire was largely populated by orthodox Puritans who were looking for better lands than those that Massachusetts seemed to offer.

Connecticut was established in 1634 as a result of religious bickering of a sort different from that in Massachusetts. Thomas Hooker and his followers were not expelled from Massachusetts Bay. They fled for much the same reason the Puritans had left England; Hooker believed that the Massachusetts Puritans were too lax, that Winthrop and his associates were flirting with sin and God's vengeance as a result of lenient laws. No doubt the rich bottomlands of the Connecticut River Valley also played a part in the rapid peopling of the country.

In 1639, Theophilus Eaton and John Davenport, ministers who worried that Connecticut, in turn, was too soft, settled outside its boundaries at New Haven on Long Island Sound. New Haven Colony remained independent until 1662, when the Connecticut colony centered around Hartford gained authority over it.

Connecticut was generally stricter than Massachusetts. Yale University was founded at New Haven in 1701 by latter-day Puritans who thought that Harvard was not strict enough. One Connecticut blue law provided that "If any Childe or Children above fifteen years old, and of sufficient understanding, shall Curse or Smite their natural Father or Mother, he or they shall be put to death, unless it can be sufficiently testified, that the Parents have been unchristianly negligent in the education of such Children." There is no record of the law ever having been enforced, but it may well have helped form child-rearing practices in the colony.

The Proprietary Colonies

With the exception of New Hampshire, the New England colonies were *corporate colonies*. They were, in effect, self-governing commonwealths that recognized the English monarch. In practice, this fealty was little more than symbolic. In their charters, the corporate colonies were granted the right to elect their governor and to make such laws as they saw fit.

Virginia was a corporate colony until 1624, when King James I took it over. As a *royal colony*, Virginia was ruled directly by the king through his appointed governor. Royal colonies had elected assemblies, but the governors held a veto power over any laws they passed. By the time of the American Revolution in 1776, nine of the thirteen colonies were royal colonies.

Feudal Lords in a New World

The third kind of colony was the *proprietary colony*. Ironically for a system that worked very well, the principle underlying the proprietary colonies was antiquated, dating back to the Middle Ages. The proprietors—usually wealthy gentlemen and nobles who were "favorites" of the king—were vice kings, in effect, holding over the colonies given to them the same power the monarch held over the royal colonies. Their rights and privileges were the same as those that had been held by the bishop of Durham in the Middle Ages. The bishop was the king's vassal in the north of England who was allowed greater power than most nobles because he commanded the first line of defense against the hostile Scots.

Making Money from America

Even the proprietors' method of making money out of their colonies was feudal, although, once again, it worked quite well. Like the London Company and later the king in Virginia, they encouraged people to settle on their lands by granting headrights—so many acres per head (the amount varied from colony to colony) for every person who came or who paid the way of others.

In return, the settlers were required to pay the proprietor an annual quitrent. This was not rent in our sense of the word. The settlers owned their land; they were not tenants. The quitrent principle dated from the time when feudalism was breaking up in England (around 1300) and the lords freed their serfs. With little money in circulation, the serfs had owed their lords a number of days of labor each year or specified services such as repairing the castle moat or shearing sheep. When the lord came to prefer money to these services, he turned title to the land over to the peasants in return for an

---

SELECTED WRITINGS

1608   John Smith, *A True Relation of . . . Virginia.*
1644   Roger Williams' *The Bloudy Tenent of Persecution* attacked Congregational theology.
1647   William Bradford, *History of Plimoth Plantation* (published in 1856).
1649   John Winthrop's *Journal* (published in 1790).
1693   Cotton Mather's *The Wonders of the Invisible World* defended the witchcraft trials. His *Magnalia Christi Americana* (1702) provided a theological interpretation of New England's history.
1705   Robert Beverley, *The History . . . of Virginia.*
1710   John Wise, *The Churches' Quarrel Espoused,* supported democratic Congregationalism.

annual sum that they paid to be "quit" of the old obligations.

Quitrents were generally quite small in England, and the proprietors followed that practice in America: two pence an acre paid in overpriced tobacco in Maryland; a bushel of wheat for each hundred acres in New York; two shillings per fifty acres in Georgia.

But for the proprietor of a vast domain, these pittances added up to a handsome income, while the quitrents that the proprietors owed the king were purely symbolic: two arrowheads a year for Maryland; two beaver pelts for Pennsylvania. The kings did not give colonies to their favorites in order to make money themselves. They granted them as a favor to friends and to fill up North America with English subjects.

Maryland: A Refuge for Catholics

While making money was a major motive of every proprietor, some had other purposes to serve. Maryland, founded in 1631 (at about the same time as Massachusetts Bay), was intended by its proprietors, George Calvert and his son Cecilius, the first and second Lords Baltimore, to be a refuge for their coreligionists, English Catholics. The Calverts favored Catholics in making land grants, and they invited priests to the colony.

However, comparatively few Catholics took the

George Calvert, Lord Baltimore (c. 1580–1632).

Calverts up on their offer, and they were a minority of Maryland's population from the beginning. Because they were often the richest planters, Catholics were the targets of social resentment and distrust. In 1649, Cecilius Calvert feared for the future of the Catholics in Maryland and approved the Act of Toleration, which provided that "noe person or persons whatsoever within this Province . . . professing to believe in Jesus Christ, shall from henceforth bee any waies troubled, Molested or discountenanced for or in respect of his or her religion."

It was hardly complete toleration: Jews were not allowed to settle in Maryland, as they were in Rhode Island and Pennsylvania. But the act was too much for Maryland's Protestant majority, and they raised an armed revolt in 1654 and repealed the act.

Maryland's Catholics were too well established to be chased out. The colony remained a center of American Catholicism, and the first bishop appointed in the United States was seated in Baltimore.

New York: An English Conquest

In 1624, a Dutch trading company established the colony of New Netherland between the two English settlements that then existed: Virginia and Plymouth. The Dutch tried to encourage agriculture in the Hudson River Valley by granting patroonships, huge tracts of land, to any person who settled fifty families in the colony. Only one such domain actually succeeded, 700,000-acre Van Rensselaerwyck south of Fort Orange, present-day Albany in New York. New Netherland remained a thinly populated country; only seven thousand people lived in the whole province, with fifteen hundred in the principal city of New Amsterdam.

It was a prosperous colony, thanks to a flourishing trade in furs and deerskins with the Iroquois Indians. In 1655, Dutch ships sailed to the Delaware River to the south and took over a small Swedish and Finnish colony in what is now the state of Delaware.

What was fair for the Dutch was fair for the English. In 1664, the duke of York sailed into the harbor at New Amsterdam and demanded that the governor of New Netherland—a one-legged, foul-tempered old tyrant named Peter Stuyvesant—surrender to him. Stuyvesant wanted to fight. But he was so unpopular as a result of his arbitrary decisions and the price controls he slapped on most imported goods that he was just about the only New Netherlander who did. The colony became New York, the proprietorship of the duke. When he became King James II in 1685, he made his holding into a royal colony.

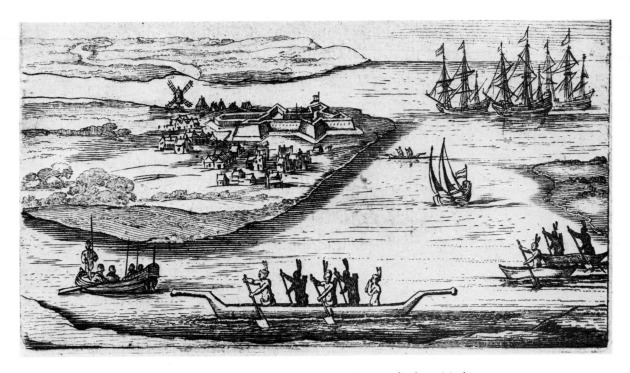

New Amsterdam, 1651: the earliest view of present-day lower Manhattan.

The duke of York was a popular proprietor because he ratified the Dutch land grants and tolerated the Dutch Reformed Church and use of the Dutch language. He also encouraged English settlement, so that when Holland briefly recaptured New York in 1673, it was already as much English as Dutch.

Dutch contributions to American culture survive in some foods (such as cole slaw), place names, and folklore. Some historians have suggested that the American inclination to coddle children is of Dutch origin. Certainly the Puritans in New England thought the Knickerbockers of New York were too indulgent, and several of the Dutch words that have been adopted into English seem to bear them out. *Fun* is of Dutch origin. So are *hooky, hanky-panky,* and that unsounded childish word that is spoken by putting one's thumb to one's nose, wiggling the fingers, and running away.

Pennsylvania, New Jersey, and Delaware: A Holy Experiment

In 1681, King Charles II gave a large tract of land including the present states of Pennsylvania and Delaware and parts of New Jersey to William Penn, the son of a man to whom the king owed £16,000. Charles was generally free with American land, but this grant was unusual because Penn was a member of an exotic religious sect, the Society of Friends, or, as they were called because they trembled with emotion at their religious services, "Quakers."

They were figures of scorn, amusement, and some worry in England. George Fox, the founder of the society, wandered about England in order to preach in village squares. On occasion, Quakers protested their persecution by taking off their clothes in public. Conventional people thought of them much as later generations would think of "Holy Rollers," "Moonies," or "Hare Krishnas."

However, the Quakers also worried the authorities. They preached an absolute Christian pacifism, forbidding society members to take up arms, even in self-defense. Seventeenth-century armies were not made up of draftees, but pacifism was still a worrisome doctrine for a country that was frequently at war.

More immediately, because the Quakers taught that every individual had the light of God within himself or herself, the society did away with the church hierarchy—priests, ministers, and bishops. In their early years, they denied the legitimacy of the civil authority and social class. When they were haled before magistrates, Quakers refused to remove their hats and to take oaths. Telling the truth was between the individual and God; it was none of the civil authority's business.

They addressed everyone, including nobles and the king himself, in the *thee, thy,* and *thou* form of the

This charcoal sketch by Francis Place is the only known authentic likeness of William Penn.

second-person pronoun. This seems merely quaint today, but in the seventeenth century it was highly insulting to address a social superior or even a stranger in that way. Finally, since they believed that all people were equal before God, Quaker women were as active as the men in preaching and testifying. This affronted the popular feeling that women should not play a role in public life, least of all in religious matters.

Religious Toleration

William Penn was the Quakers' savior. Whereas almost all Quakers were of the lower classes, he was a gentleman of wealth and education. Penn used his prestige to moderate some of the Quakers' more outrageous practices, and he gave them a refuge. Like other proprietors, he saw his Pennsylvania ("Penn's Woods") as a means of making money. But he also envisioned it as a Holy Experiment. All people who believed in One Almighty and Eternal God were welcome. Because the Quakers believed in an Inner Light, they would not impose their faith on any person.

Pennsylvania thrived from the start. Pietists from the German Rhineland and from Switzerland, whose ideas were much like the Quakers', settled there in great numbers and developed the fertile rolling land of south-

eastern Pennsylvania into model farms. They survive, many still loyal to seventeenth-century customs, as the Pennsylvania Dutch of Lancaster and York counties.

Philadelphia (and Charleston) were the colonies' first "planned cities." Laid out on the gridiron plan, Philadelphia, "A greene countrie towne," became the largest and most prosperous city in the colonies as an exporter of Pennsylvania's abundant foodstuffs. At the time of the American Revolution, it was "the second city of the British empire," smaller than only London in the English-speaking world.

Because the Quakers maintained control of the colonial assembly until after the age of religious fanaticism had passed, Pennsylvania remained a refuge for persecuted sects, the most cosmopolitan and liberal-minded colony in English America. New Jersey and Delaware developed as separate proprietary colonies. However, they too were heavily populated by Quakers and practiced much the same policies as Pennsylvania.

Indeed, it must be emphasized that even where there was an established church—that is, a church supported by taxes levied on everyone—the rule throughout English America was religious toleration. With the exception of Massachusetts and Connecticut in their zealous youth, colonial promoters were more interested in population than in religious conformity. Toleration was on the books only in Maryland (until 1654), Rhode Island, and the Quaker colonies. But it was quietly practiced almost everywhere.

The Carolinas: A Feudal Experiment

The proprietors of the Carolina Grant of 1663 (named after Charles II, *Carolus* in Latin) were a consortium of eight powerful gentlemen and nobles. In 1689, they attempted to fasten a completely artificial social structure on their holdings. Their plan was outlined in The Fundamental Constitutions of Carolina. This remarkable document was the brainchild of Anthony Ashley Cooper, one of the most active of the proprietors, but its 120 detailed articles were actually written by his secretary, the political philosopher John Locke. Locke's primary place in American history is as the author of principles of political liberty that were incorporated into the Declaration of Independence. It is difficult to imagine that in the Fundamental Constitutions he created a blueprint for a society that was even more rigidly structured than feudalism had been.

The grant was divided into square counties, in each of which the proprietors ("seigneurs") owned ninety-six thousand acres. Other contrived ranks of nobility called "caciques" and "landgraves" would have smaller but still vast tracts. The work would be done by humble "leetmen" and even humbler African slaves, over whom their owners were guaranteed "absolute power and authority."

Some historians think that this fantastic system was simply a promotional device designed to excite English land buyers with the promise of a puffed-up title. Certainly it was unworkable. A city might be laid out in squares, but not a country shaped by rivers, creeks, hills, swamps, and mountains. The mere abundance of land meant that development would be free and open, not a subject of strict regulation. Although the Fundamental Constitutions remained technically in effect for several decades, the document had little to do with the actual development of the Carolinas.

Northern and southern Carolina developed along different patterns. In the northern part of the grant, most settlers were small farmers who drifted down from Virginia and planted tobacco, as they had done at home. Centered on Albemarle Sound, northern Carolina was poor, fiercely democratic and independent, and isolated even from Virginia by the Great Dismal Swamp. In 1677, a Virginian named John Culpeper led a rebellion in northern Carolina that briefly defied all outside authority.

In the southern part of the grant, an entirely different kind of society developed. In 1680, the proprietors and early settlers from Barbados (an English sugar island) founded Charleston on the coast where the Ashley and Cooper rivers flowed into the Atlantic. At first, southern Carolina was a trading colony, tapping the interior as far as present-day Alabama for furs and hides and converting the vast pine forests into timber and naval stores. By 1700, however, the outline of a plantation system similar to that of tidewater Virginia took shape. Rice, a lucrative export crop, flourished in the easily flooded lowlands along the rivers; long-staple cotton, used in manufacturing fine textiles, was cultivated on the sea islands that fringed the coast. Indigo, a plant that produced a coveted blue dye, also grew well in South Carolina, and its cultivation and harvesting provided work for the colony's numerous slaves when rice was not in season. These crops lent themselves to being worked by large gangs of laborers, and by 1700, half the five thousand people in southern Carolina were slaves, by far the highest proportion of Africans in any mainland colony.

The slaveowners dominated society to an extent that even the tobacco grandees of Virginia and Maryland never managed. Because the "low country" that produced their wealth was so unhealthy, however, this small elite took to keeping town houses in Charleston, where they spent at least the malarial summer months and in some cases the better part of the year. It was a cultured and cosmopolitan society, quite obnoxious to the democratic small farmers of the north. In 1712, the proprietors, recognizing the different social bases of the northern and southern settlements, granted the two Carolinas separate assemblies and governors. When the proprietors sold their holdings to the king in 1729, he wisely established them as separate royal colonies: North Carolina and South Carolina.

Georgia: A Philanthropic Experiment

Georgia was the last of the thirteen colonies to be founded. It was chartered in 1732, with Savannah actually established the next year. The Crown's interest in this afterthought of a settlement was as a military buffer state protecting valuable South Carolina against the Spanish in Florida. Although Spain had recognized England's right to its colonies in 1676, ten years later an armed force destroyed a small English settlement on the Florida side of the boundary. During an English–Spanish war between 1702 and 1713, Charleston was threatened.

In Colonel James Oglethorpe, Parliament found the perfect man to develop a fortress colony. Oglethorpe was an experienced and successful soldier. He was also a philanthropist who was troubled by the misery of the English poor. At that time, a person could be imprisoned for debt and not released until his obligation was paid, a somewhat self-defeating provision since a man in jail could hardly earn money.

Oglethorpe and others conceived of the tract below South Carolina as a place to which such unfortunates might go to begin anew. They received the colony as a "trust"; that is, they were to make no profit from it.

Slaves in South Carolina harvest indigo, one of the colony's three major crops.

TWO WOMEN OF NEW ENGLAND

In the seventeenth century, a woman was superior in authority to every member of her household but her husband. Children and servants were expected to defer to her; she was obligated to obey her husband. Woman's world was centered around the hearth and the cradle. It was her husband's responsibility to deal with the world, to instruct children, servants, and wife in religion, and to represent the household in civil matters.

In a subsistence economy, of course, women were called on to work as hard as men and as grown children, and the records are full of widows operating town businesses efficiently and profitably. In the professions, in public life, and in matters of the soul and the intellect, however, women's names are hardly to be found. This, the people of the seventeenth century believed, was as it should be. John Winthrop liked to tell the story of a woman who tried to wrestle with difficult religious questions instead of just listening to what was told her. Her mind, Winthrop concluded, snapped under the strain.

That woman could not have been Anne Marbury Hutchinson (1591–1643) or Anne Dudley Bradstreet (1612–72), both of whom Winthrop knew. Hutchinson nearly toppled the Massachusetts theocracy within a decade of its founding, and Bradstreet became, anonymously in her lifetime, the first American poet of distinction.

Anne Marbury was born in Lincolnshire in 1591. At the age of twenty-one, she married a Puritan merchant named William Hutchinson. Little is known of her life in England. But she must have turned heads there, for shortly after she emigrated to Massachusetts in 1634 she began to turn the colony upside down.

Hutchinson was obsessed with the intricacies of theology, and she organized discussion groups at her home to meet after Sunday sermons. In principle, there was

Anne Hutchinson, Puritan dissident.

nothing amiss in this. Puritans were encouraged to discuss religion at every pass, and the meetings at the Hutchinson home attracted some of the colony's most distinguished leaders, including Henry Vane, the twenty-three-year-old governor of Massachusetts.

However, when Anne Hutchinson began to dominate the discussions—to deliver sermons of her own, in effect—she went to the brink of Puritan propriety. When she criticized John Cotton, the most distinguished preacher of Massachusetts, she went too far. Not only did Hutchinson have sharp words for every minister but two (who were her supporters), but she challenged the principles on which the government of Massachusetts was based. Antinomianism, the name

Landholdings were small, only fifty acres, both to discourage land speculators and to encourage the formation of a compact, easily mobilized defense force. Slavery was forbidden. Oglethorpe did not want to see the development of an elite such as dominated South Carolina. He also prohibited alcohol, believing that drunkenness was a major source of crime and poverty in England.

In all, the trustees sent about eighteen hundred debtors and paupers to Georgia, and about one thousand people came on their own. Unfortunately, among the latter were some slaveowners from South Carolina, and Oglethorpe, although inclined to be a tyrant, was unable either to keep them out or to keep the other Georgians independent of the bottle. He returned to England disgusted, and in 1752 the trustees returned control of the colony to the king. The experiment in social engineering was a failure, as others had been. The natural character of the region determined how it developed. Although still tiny at the time of independence, Georgia became a slavery-based agricultural colony much like South Carolina.

given to Hutchinson's teaching, held that an individual was raised above civil authority by God's grace. Not only did this justify her preaching—Anne believed she was inspired by God—but it challenged the firm hold of the religious leaders of Massachusetts on the colony. By determining who could preach and who was admitted to church membership and therefore could vote, a network of preachers like Cotton and officials like Winthrop kept Massachusetts society godly. Hutchinson denied their right to make these decisions.

In 1637, the Cotton–Winthrop group succeeded in removing Vane from the governorship and moved against Hutchinson. Although Anne more than held her own at her trials, she was found guilty of "traducing the ministers" and was excommunicated with the words, "I do deliver you up to Satan."

Instead of going to hell, Hutchinson, her family, and several loyal disciples went to Portsmouth, Rhode Island. Still tendentious, Hutchinson quarreled with other disciples. After the death of her husband in 1642, she moved to New Netherland to a farm in what is now the borough of the Bronx in New York City. The Bronx was frontier at that time, and, the next year, Hutchinson and all her children but one were killed by Indians.

Anne Bradstreet never challenged the authorities. On the contrary, all her connections were with the Massachusetts Establishment. She emigrated to Massachusetts from her native Northampton in the Winthrop expedition of 1630. Both her father, Thomas Dudley, and her husband, Simon Bradstreet, later served as governors of the colony, always choosing the right side in political disputes.

Bradstreet made her mark above the crowd with her pen. In 1650, a book of her poems was published in London as *The Tenth Muse Lately Sprung Up in America*. It was remarkable enough for a book written by a woman to be published in the seventeenth century. It would have been unacceptable to sign it with the au-

thor's name. Instead, Anne was identified on the title page as "A Gentlewoman in Those Parts."

The book was little noticed. While craftsmanlike, the poems in *The Tenth Muse* did not stand out in a literary age dominated in England by John Milton. Bradstreet was no revolutionary in literature as well as in politics. She imitated the forms of others and clung to standard classical and religious themes. Nevertheless, if unextraordinary when measured against the finest English poetry of the seventeenth century, Bradstreet's love lyrics, descriptions of the Massachusetts landscape, and variations on Puritan religious beliefs raise her far above any American contemporary.

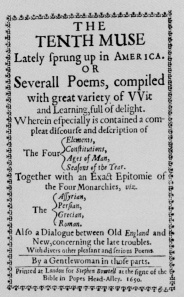

Title page of Anne Bradstreet's collection of poems, The Tenth Muse Lately Sprung Up in America (1650).

For Further Reading

Charles M. Andrews, *The Colonial Period of American History* (1934–38), and C. P. Nettels, *Roots of American Civilization* (1938), both of which are cited at the end of Chapter 2, are also relevant to this chapter. On the Puritans of old and New England, the historical literature is vast and contradictory. The classic critical history of the Saints is James Truslow Adams, *The Founding of New England* (1930). Published in the same year as an "answer" to Adams is Samuel Eliot Morison, *The Builders of the Bay Colony* (1930).

Largely inspired by Perry Miller of Harvard University, a revival of interest in the Puritans in the 1950s produced a number of worthwhile books. Perry Miller, *The New England Mind* (1939, 1953), is brilliant scholarship but not easy go-

ing, concentrating on Puritan thought, which Miller found very subtle. E. S. Morgan, *The Puritan Dilemma* (1958), is a biography of John Winthrop, but also provides an easily grasped understanding of Puritanism in general. Morgan's *Visible Saints* (1963) carries his account further. If it is convenient to read only one book on the subject, it should be the crystal-clear Larzer Ziff, *Puritanism in Old and New England* (1973).

On the Middle Colonies, see T. J. Wertenbaker, *The Founding of American Civilization: The Middle Colonies* (1938), and Gary Nash, *Quakers and Politics: Pennsylvania, 1681–1726* (1971). On Georgia, see Phinizy Spalding. *Oglethorpe in America* (1977).

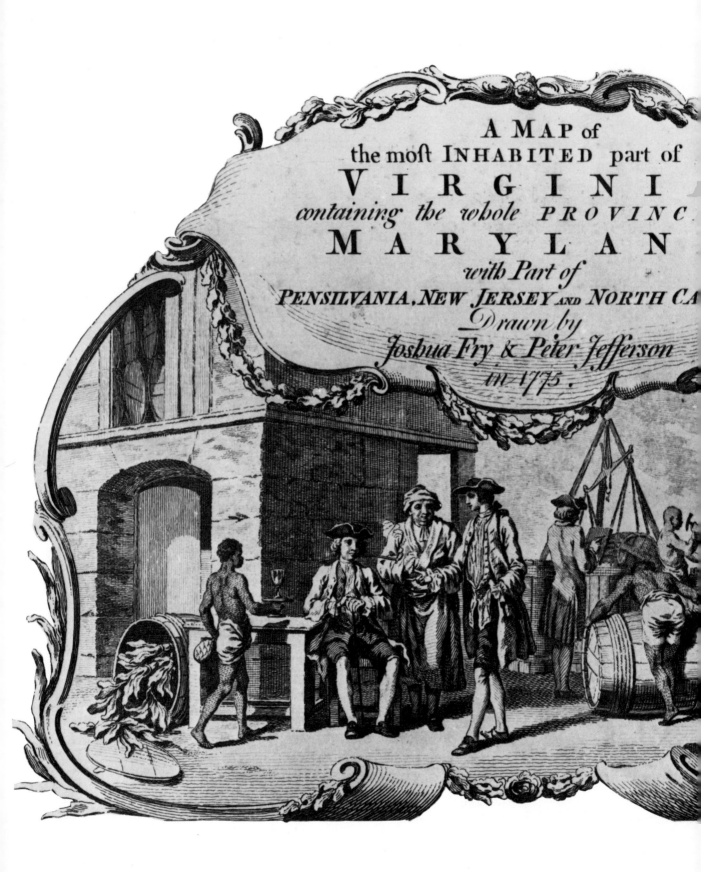

A MAP of
the most INHABITED part of
VIRGINIA
containing the whole PROVINCE
MARYLAND
with Part of
PENSILVANIA, NEW JERSEY AND NORTH CA
Drawn by
Joshua Fry & Peter Jefferson
in 1775.

4

From Survival to Society

The First Century of Colonial Development

There is some truth in the old saying that the British Empire was established in a fit of absent-mindedness. The approval of the Crown, in the form of a charter, was the necessary first step in the foundation of a colony. But neither king nor Parliament played an active role in setting up a single one of them. From Portsmouth in New Hampshire to Savannah in Georgia, every English settlement was funded and promoted by investors hoping to make money; by religious groups looking for a place where their beliefs could flourish; by courtiers making the most of their friendship with the king; or, in the belated case of Georgia, by philanthropists striving to make the world a better place.

So cavalier were the English kings toward their American property that the boundaries they drew for the colonies were vague and overlapping, breezy strokes of a pen on a map that were next to useless on the actual ground. Parliament's interest in formulating a uniform colonial policy was likewise fitful and half-hearted.

And yet there was an empire across the chill Atlantic. By 1702, when Queen Anne, the last of the Stuart monarchs, ascended the throne, her coronation was marked by three hundred thousand subjects in North America. They made

Workers at a Virginia wharf load tobacco into ships for export.

their homes in settlements that stretched a thousand miles north to south. Fewer than a hundred years after the Virginians fought off starvation by scraping oysters from the floor of the Chesapeake Bay, three distinct regional patterns of economy and society had evolved in the American colonies.

The South included Maryland, Virginia, North Carolina, South Carolina (and after 1732, Georgia). New England was made up of New Hampshire, Massachusetts, Rhode Island, Connecticut. In between lay the Middle Colonies: New York, New Jersey, Pennsylvania, Delaware. So distinct were the economies and social structures of the three regions that when the mother country did attempt to legislate a uniform colonial policy—to define the relationship of the colonies to England—the result was to promote their separate identities.

The Navigation Acts

England's colonial policy was clearly stated in the Navigation Acts of 1660 to 1663. Based on laws adopted by the revolutionary regime of Oliver Cromwell (1649–58), the acts put mercantilism into legal form. The Navigation Acts defined the purpose of the American colonies as the enrichment of the mother country and stated the colonists' economic responsibilities (in effect, economic subordination) to England.

The first of the laws stipulated that all colonial trade be carried in vessels built and owned by English or colonial merchants, and manned by crews in which at least three seamen in four were English or colonial. The purpose was to prevent any other nation from profiting by the colonies' busy import and export trade.

Second, the Navigation Acts required that all goods imported from Europe into the colonies be taken first to certain English ports—the entrepôts—unloaded there, and then reloaded for shipment to America. The purposes of this provision were to keep a precise record of colonial trade, to collect a tax on some cargoes, and, most important of all to the mercantilist, to ensure that English merchants and port workers benefited from every colonial overseas transaction, even if it involved no English-made goods. For example, wealthy colonists had a taste for Madeira and port wines. But they could not buy them directly from Portugal. First the casks, tuns, kegs, and barrels had to be shipped to the mother

country. If this raised the cost, that was the idea: the premium that colonial bibbers paid for their wines went into English purses.

According to the third provision of the Navigation Acts, certain colonial products, called the "enumerated articles" (because they were specifically listed), could be shipped only to England, even if they were destined for sale on the continent of Europe. Once again, the object was to guarantee that part of the profit on every colonial transaction went to the English merchants who handled the enumerated articles in the entrepôt ports. Enumerated goods included almost every colonial product that could be sold for cash in the world market: molasses, furs and hides, naval stores, cotton, rice, indigo, and tobacco—the prince of colonial exports from the time of John Rolfe until the Revolution.

The Southern Colonies

With good reason, English mercantilists smiled contentedly when they thought of the southern colonies. Although some merchant families, including a few of Sephardic Jewish origin, set up shop in Charleston, the southern colonies were overwhelmingly agricultural. Like England's sugar islands in the West Indies, the southern colonies produced crops that English farmers did not grow, but that were important in terms of world trade.

Also, like Jamaica and Barbados, these colonies were home to a large, bonded labor force of white servants and black slaves for whom cheap clothing, shoes, and tools had to be purchased, thereby profiting English manufacturers. And living off the labor of these workers was a rich and extravagant master class that learned to covet every luxury item a merchant ever thought to load on a sailing ship.

Tobacco: Blessing and Curse

Tobacco could be grown in England, but in order to encourage colonial exports of the golden leaf, Parliament forbade English farmers to plant it. Thus Maryland, Virginia, and, to some extent, North Carolina had a monopoly of the home market that, until the 1660s, was quite enough to keep the planters (as they called themselves) quite busy.

During the 1660s, however, the wholesale price of tobacco (the price at which the planters sold their crop) collapsed from two and a half pence a pound to a halfpenny. The Americans had expanded their

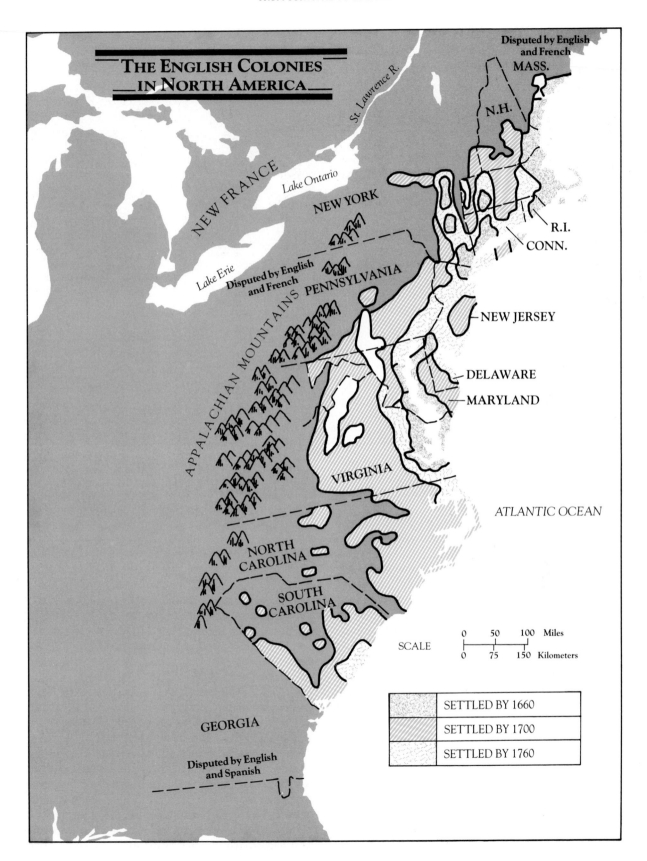

THE ENGLISH COLONIES IN NORTH AMERICA

Disputed by English and French

MASS.

N.H.

St. Lawrence R.

NEW FRANCE

Lake Ontario

NEW YORK

R.I.

CONN.

Lake Erie

Disputed by English and French

APPALACHIAN MOUNTAINS

PENNSYLVANIA

NEW JERSEY

DELAWARE

MARYLAND

VIRGINIA

ATLANTIC OCEAN

NORTH CAROLINA

SOUTH CAROLINA

SCALE

| 0 | 50 | 100 | Miles |
| 0 | 75 | 150 | Kilometers |

GEORGIA

Disputed by English and Spanish

	SETTLED BY 1660
	SETTLED BY 1700
	SETTLED BY 1760

Large plantations characterized seventeenth-century settlement in the tidewater region.

acreage so quickly that England was no longer able to absorb Chesapeake production.

From the planter's point of view, the solution to the problem of falling prices seemed obvious. Since no other European country had a source of the weed comparable to England's, tobacco could be sold elsewhere. But the Navigation Acts, which dictated that the interests of English merchants come first, made the opening of new markets very difficult. "If the Hollanders must not trade to Virginia," one group of colonists complained, "how shall the planters dispose of their tobacco? . . . The tobacco will not vend in England, the Hollanders will not fetch it from England." (The Dutch were mercantilists, too) "What must become thereof?"

The planters responded to their dilemma by using more black slaves, rather than white indentured servants, as the backbone of their labor force. Laborers who were bound to a master for life were cheaper than men and women who could leave after three, four, or seven years. They also engaged in a fair amount of illegal trade—smuggling. Dutch traders arrived at Virginia and Maryland wharves and had little difficulty persuading the planters to sell them their leaf. Evasion

of the Navigation Acts proved rather easy because of the peculiar topography of the Chesapeake country.

The Tidewater

The Chesapeake is one huge estuary made up of uncountable smaller ones. Among the hundreds of creeks and inlets, the larger rivers that flow into the great bay are broad and slow moving. They are also deep enough to have allowed the small sea-going vessels of the seventeenth and eighteenth centuries to float for as many miles inland as high tide pushed salt water. The country that bordered on these navigable rivers, a series of peninsulas called necks, was known as the tidewater. It was the first area of the tobacco colonies to be settled, and it became the home of an elite that dominated Virginia and Maryland society.

The tidewater aristocrats had not necessarily been wealthy before they settled in America. Some had been; but others simply had the good luck to be on the spot when tobacco boomed, and they grabbed as much of the choice land as they could. For about a generation there was plenty of land to go around, even to people who had arrived in the servant ships. In 1629, seven

THE OYSTER WAR

In 1632, when King Charles I drew the boundary between Virginia and Maryland, he did not, as was customary, set it at the *thalweg,* or deepest part of the Chesapeake Bay, but at the high-water mark on the Virginia side. This gave Maryland oystermen the right to harvest oysters up to the very shores of the Old Dominion. Virginia oystermen did not much approve of this state of affairs, and they periodically engaged in a shooting war that killed at least fifty men. The last known fatality was in 1959. Today, oystermen on the Chesapeake are forbidden to carry firearms.

members of the Virginia assembly—by definition the colony's elite—had been indentured servants only five years earlier.

The odds of getting rich quickly dwindled at mid-century. Not only was the land of the tidewater almost entirely taken up by then, but the collapse in the price of tobacco bankrupted hundreds of small farmers. The larger planters, who were less vulnerable to the depression, picked up the small holdings and became even more powerful in the economy of the colonies.

After 1660, even comparatively well-off immigrants to Virginia were forced to trek into the backcountry if they wanted to build their estates. There in the Piedmont, or foothills of the Appalachians, they found hundreds of small frontier farmers, some recently dispossessed in the tidewater, and a large floating population of unmarried, boisterous young men, former servants who lived by doing occasional work for wages or by attaching themselves to the Piedmont plantations. In 1676, differences between westerners on the one hand, and the tidewater planters, on the other, burst into an ugly demonstration that white colonists could fight among themselves as well as against the Indians.

Bacon's Rebellion

The governor of Virginia, appointed by the king, was Sir William Berkeley. He was a major landowner (Berkeley was one of the proprietors of the Carolinas) and the political and social leader of the tidewater aristocracy. Berkeley and his friends were involved in a prosperous trade with the Indians, selling them English goods in return for furs and deerskins. When the bottom dropped out of the tobacco market in the 1660s, this business became even more important to them than before, and it provided the Berkeley group with an interest in good relations with the Indians.

At the same time, however, the Piedmont settlers were encroaching on the hunting grounds of the Susquehannock Indians, and, as often before and for

two centuries to come, there were bloody clashes of white and red. The backcountry settlers complained of the effective Indian resistance, particularly hit-and-run raids on their farms, and Berkeley agreed to build a system of defensive stockades along the line of white settlement.

Berkeley's concession was not enough for the westerners on two counts. First, the forts were so far apart that Susquehannock war parties could easily slip between them and wreak their havoc. Second, the Piedmont settlers did not think in terms of a fixed boundary between white and Indian lands. They looked to the future and expansion. What they wanted from Berkeley was an aggressive policy that would not only tame the hostile tribes but would also push them back.

With the Indian trade so vital to his and his friends' income, Berkeley would not oblige the people of the Piedmont. As a result, when the death toll in the backcountry climbed to more than a hundred, the frontier blew up. Nathaniel Bacon, a gentleman and university graduate who had emigrated to Virginia and built a

This later depiction presents a romantic view of the conflict between Nathaniel Bacon, leader of the Piedmont rebels, and Sir William Berkeley, governor of Virginia.

Piedmont plantation, set himself up as the commander of a force that attacked the Oconeechee tribe. Ironically, the tribe had not been involved in the attacks on whites and had expressed some interest in an alliance with them against the Susquehannocks. Decimating the Oconeechee, Bacon turned his informal army toward the capital of Jamestown.

Berkeley arrested Bacon for rebellion, but when the angry frontiersmen who had followed Bacon to Jamestown showed that they were quite capable of taking over the little town, he set their leader free. After a period of uneasy stalemate between tidewater and Piedmont, Bacon returned to Jamestown and spoke of hanging the governor. Berkeley took him seriously. He fled across the Chesapeake to the Eastern shore, and, for several months, Nathaniel Bacon governed Virginia.

It will never be known how the English authorities would have dealt with the rebellion. In October 1676, Nathaniel Bacon fell ill with malaria, which was a constant plague of the American frontier, and died. His personality must have been compelling because without his leadership the rebels quickly lost heart and scattered into the forests. Berkeley returned, rounded up several dozen rebels, and hanged them.

The governor never regained his personal preeminence in Virginia. King Charles II lost confidence in him, remarking that "the old fool has hanged more men in that naked country than I have done for the murder of my father." However, the suspicion and ill feeling between tidewater and Piedmont that Bacon's Rebellion represented was to endure for over a century because the tidewater aristocracy continued to dominate the economy, government, and culture of the tobacco colonies.

A Land Without Cities

The great planters could dominate Virginia so thoroughly because, short of rebellion, no other social group was able to compete with them. There was no urban middle class of merchants, bankers, and manufacturers in Virginia because no center of commerce developed. The broad, deep rivers of the Chesapeake allowed ships from Europe to tie up at private wharves maintained by the great tidewater plantations. The planters sold their tobacco and received the goods that they had ordered the previous year in their own backyards. Planters and small farmers whose lands did not front on salt water used the great planters' facilities for their trade.

It was an exciting time when the ships arrived. Servants and slaves rolled great hogsheads of tobacco to the dock, enjoying the expansive hospitality of the master during those few heady days of celebration. Farmers and backcountry planters and their families gathered to dance, drink, race on foot and horseback, hunt deer, and shoot birds or targets. For women, who lived a far more isolated life than their menfolk, the arrival of a tobacco factor (agent) was a rare opportunity to enjoy one another's company. Everyone discussed the news of European battles and the machinations of kings, such as the shipmasters brought with them, and some received letters from old-country associates. The sailors enlivened the carnival with their giddiness at being ashore after weeks at sea, and they spent money on (or traded goods for) games and drink.

Most important was the receipt of the manufactured goods on which the isolated colonists depended in order to live in European style. A single ship would be loaded with spades, shovels, axes, and saws; household items such as kettles, pots, pans, sieves, funnels, pewter tankards, and tableware; such oddments as buttons, needles, thread, pins, and ribbons; textiles for both the planter families' fine clothing and rough wraps for servants and slaves; shoes and boots; bricks, nails, and paint; goods to trade with the Indians (which would include all of the above plus trinkets, mirrors, and the like); firearms, shot, and gunpowder. And for the wealthy few there were luxuries; silver candlesticks, chests and other fine furniture, wine, brandy, spices, books, and perhaps even violins and harpsichords.

All the business affairs that were carried out in cities elsewhere were transacted at the great plantations for a week or two a year. When the ships departed for London, Plymouth, Bristol, and perhaps Amsterdam, they took not only tobacco but also Virginia and Maryland's banks, factories, and commercial apparatus. The middle class of the tobacco colonies lived across the ocean; Virginia and Maryland's cities were afloat. Even the capitals of the tobacco colonies, Jamestown (Williamsburg after 1699) and Annapolis, were little more than ghost towns when the legislative assemblies were not in session. The county seats were clusters of buildings at the crossing of trails. Small farmers lived isolated from one another by forests; the great planters got together in one another's houses.

A Life of Elegance, A Habit of Debt

By the end of the seventeenth century, the great planters of Virginia and Maryland had created a gracious style of life patterned after that of the country gentry back home. They copied as best they could the manners, fashions, and quirks of the English squires and their wives. When tobacco returned a good price, they built mansions in the style of English manors and furnished them with the best goods that England had to offer. They stocked their cellars with expensive port and Madeira wine, hock from the Rhineland, claret from France, which they generously poured for one another at a round of dinners, parties, balls, and simple visits that marked the origins of "southern hospitality."

Tidewater families educated sons at Oxford, Cambridge, or the Inns of Court (the law schools of Great Britain). Or if they feared the effects of English diseases on less-immune American bodies (smallpox, nearly universal in England, was less common in the colonies) they schooled their heirs at the College of William and Mary, founded at Williamsburg in 1693 and staffed by Oxford and Cambridge graduates.

When the profits from tobacco dropped or disappeared, the planters found it difficult to break such pleasant habits, and they continued to order their luxurious goods, running up debts to the English merchants who handled their tobacco. In time, this indebtedness would make anti-British rebels of most southern aristocrats.

The earliest known view of the busy Charleston, South Carolina, harbor.

The Carolinas

The social structure of South Carolina was similar to that of Virginia and Maryland and yet different. The cash crops there were rice and indigo, which conveniently required intensive labor at different times of the year. Because the low-lying plantations were extremely unhealthy, flooded rice fields serving as rich breeding grounds for mosquitoes, the South Carolina

planters spent much of the year in Charleston, leaving the management of their plantations to hired overseers. By congregating in a real city, South Carolina's elite was all the more aware of its privileged position, all the more united in order to preserve it. No colony (or state) was dominated by so small an aristocracy as ran South Carolina for two hundred years.

North Carolina was an exception within the South. Although tobacco was grown there, the colony was largely a society of small farmers with very few servants and slaves and fewer very rich people. Quite the opposite of its neighbor to the south, North Carolina was never the province of a tiny elite.

The New England Colonies

North Carolina, however, was kith and kin to the other southern colonies compared with the radically different economy and society that evolved in the New England colonies. As in the South, geography was a determining force in the northernmost colonies. And there was that all-pervasive companion of all New Englanders, the shadow of the Puritan founders.

Geography and Economy

The preeminent facts of life in New England were the short growing season and the difficult rocky character of the soil. Geologically, New England is a huge glacial

---

EDUCATION

1635	Boston Latin School was founded.
1636	Harvard College.
1647	Massachusetts Bay passed an act that required towns to provide a teacher or a school. Other New England colonies followed this example.
1693	College of William and Mary.
1697	William Penn Charter School in Philadelphia was typical of church-supported schools in the Middle Colonies. In the South, the children of the planters were educated by tutors.
1701	Yale University.
1746	College of New Jersey (later Princeton).
1751	Franklin's Academy (later the University of Pennsylvania).
1754	King's College (later Columbia).
1764	Rhode Island College (later Brown).
1766	Queen's College (later Rutgers).
1769	Dartmouth College.
1769	American Philosophical Society was founded at Philadelphia.
1795	North Carolina opened the first state university.

YANKEE DOODLE

To foreigners, especially the British, all Americans are "Yanks." To southerners, a Yankee is a northerner. To most other Americans, a Yankee is a New Englander, a use of the word that dates back to colonial times. And then, of course, there is the New York Yankees baseball team.

Etymologists—people who study the origins of words—offer three explanations of the word *Yankee.* Some say it comes from a Cherokee word meaning "slave" or "coward" and was first applied to northern colonists by Virginians when the northerners refused to help them in a war against the Cherokees. Others say that *Yankee* was the Algonkian Indian mispronunciation of *English,* adopted by the white settlers.

However, most etymologists believe that *Yankee* has a Dutch origin. The Dutch equivalent of *Johnny* is *Janke,* which is more or less pronounced "Yankee." It was commonly applied to New Englanders by the Dutch of New York.

moraine. It was there that the glaciers of the last ice age stopped their advance. When they receded, they deposited the boulders and gravel that they had scooped from the earth on their trip from the Arctic.

Before the farmers of New England could plow, they had to clear thousands of rocks from every acre, breaking up the big boulders and piling the lot in the endless stone fences of the region that are so picturesque to those of us who did not have to build them. This back-breaking toil went on for decades, for each year's sub-zero winter heaved more boulders to the surface of the earth.

Rocky soil and a short growing season kept most New England farms small.

The intensive labor required to clear and plant the land reinforced the Puritans' commitment to a society of small family farms. The demanding New England countryside could and did produce food for a fairly dense population. But there were no plantations, no big commercial farms; each family grew its own sustenance and, at most, a small surplus for sale in the towns and cities.

New England's foodstuffs could not be sold in England. The crops that New England produced were much the same as those that flourished in abundance in the mother country: grain (mostly Indian corn in New England), squash, beans, orchard nuts and fruits (particularly apples), livestock of all sorts, and perishable vegetables.

Consequently, English mercantilists took less interest in the region than in the south and the West Indies. Indeed, English shipbuilders, merchants, and fishermen resented the competition of the New Englanders. Boston was sending ships down the ways before 1640. The shipwright's craft flourished in every town with a protected harbor.

Whaling, a calling that New Englanders would eventually dominate over all others, began as early as 1649. Fishermen sallied out of Portsmouth, Marblehead, New London, and dozens of towns to harvest more than their fair share of the codfish of the North Atlantic. In every port of the world open to commerce, the nickname "Yankee Trader" meant shrewdness at business. Newport, Rhode Island, was a center of the African slave trade, another pursuit that English shippers would have preferred to reserve for themselves.

But the New Englanders had no choice but to compete. It took money—gold and silver coin—to purchase English manufactures, and the country produced no cash crop. One of the most ingenious accommodations to this economic fact of life was a series of three-legged trading voyages.

The Triangular Trade

One sequence involved transporting blacks who were captured or purchased in West Africa to the West Indies, where they were enslaved. This human cargo was exchanged for molasses made from sugar cane; it was returned to New England, where it was distilled into rum. Resuming the cycle, the rum went to West Africa as one of the goods exchanged for slaves. Not only did the shippers in this trade profit from each exchange of cargoes, but the colonies improved their balance of payments by manufacturing cheap molasses into higher priced rum—a bit of home-grown mercantilism!

New Englanders dominated the whaling industry from its beginnings in the seventeenth century. This illustration is from Harper's Weekly, 1856.

There were other "triangles." The New Englanders carried provisions from home or from the Middle Colonies to the West Indies; sugar and molasses from there to England; and English manufactures back home. Or, reversing direction, they carried tobacco from Maryland and Virginia to England; manufactures to the

West Indies; and molasses back home or slaves to the southern colonies.

An Independent Spirit

To many English mercantilists, the Yankees were no better than common smugglers. Indeed, the most pious Puritan shipmasters saw no sin in dodging British trade laws. Because their charters gave them such extensive powers of self-government, the corporate colonies of Massachusetts, Plymouth, Rhode Island, and Connecticut functioned much like independent commonwealths. They acknowledged the king—technically, the Puritans claimed that they were members of the Church of England—but these were but polite formalities in a century when two kings were dethroned, one of them decapitated, and when it took at least a month for a ship to cross the Atlantic carrying new laws.

During the years when Oliver Cromwell ruled England as virtual dictator (1649–58), the New England colonies disregarded almost every directive that either he or Parliament issued. In 1652, Massachusetts minted its own money, the "Pine Tree Shilling," thus assuming a right reserved to independent sovereigns since antiquity.

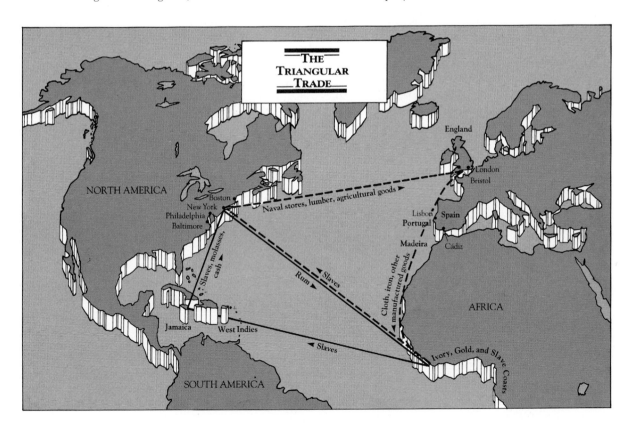

The "Pine Tree Shilling," the first colonial coin, was produced from 1652 to 1684, against royal orders.

Nor did Massachusetts retreat when Charles II became king in 1660. The colony continued to strike the shilling, to evade royal instructions, and to protect smugglers and even pirates. Charles was forced to sue to have the Massachusetts charter revoked. In 1684, he won his case.

The Dominion of New England

The next year, the new king, James II, combined all the New England colonies into a single "Dominion of New England." (New York and New Jersey were later added.) He abolished all local assemblies and gave what amounted to a dictator's power to his appointed governor, Sir Edmund Andros.

Andros never had a chance. Not only was he hated in New England, but James II's reign was short lived. In 1688, the king was forced to flee England during the "Glorious Revolution," and the news was the signal for popular uprisings in several colonies. In Maryland, John Coode seized power from the Catholic proprietors whom he assumed had fled England with the Catholic James II. In New York, a German immigrant named Jacob Leisler gained effective control, claiming that he acted in the name of the new English sovereigns, William and Mary. In New England, the merchant elite so briefly out of power simply resumed acting as it always had—independently—while Andros prudently put to sea.

However, the Calverts of Maryland had not supported James II, and they and the Penn family in Pennsylvania regained their proprietary rights under William and Mary. In New York, Leisler became overconfident by the ease with which he had taken control and rashly ordered a volley fired at arriving troops who really did act in the name of the new king and queen. He was hanged.

As for New England, William and Mary knew better than to revive the hated Dominion, but they had no intention of allowing Massachusetts to return to its semi-independent status. They restored the charters of Connecticut and Rhode Island (where there had been little tumult), but they made Massachusetts, with Plymouth incorporated into it, a royal colony. After 1691, the governor of the Bay Colony was no longer elected by freeholders who lived there but was appointed by the Crown.

This was not an easy pill for the latter-day Puritans to swallow. They had regarded their mission in America as divinely inspired. They expected to be at odds with the Crown. But for God to allow the Crown to take control—that was perplexing. Some historians suggest that the loss of its charter was a prime ingredient in the episode that convulsed Massachusetts beginning in January 1692.

Witchcraft

In January 1692, two young girls who lived in the village of Salem fell ill with fits of screaming and crawling about while making odd throaty sounds. The physician who examined them diagnosed their affliction as supernatural. They had no earthly disease, he said, but they had been bewitched by Satan or through spells cast on them by witches, sworn servants of the Devil.

Few were shocked and fewer laughed at the mention of witchcraft. Almost everyone in seventeenth-century Europe and America believed that people could strike a bargain with the Devil by which they traded their souls for the power of black magic. Witchcraft was mentioned in the Bible along with the admonition "thou shalt not suffer a witch to live." Since the Middle Ages, thousands of people had been executed for worshiping Satan, or for having sexual relations with him or female imps called succubi. Others had suffered lesser penalties for practicing minor magic. Just the year before the Salem excitement began, a witch had been hanged in Boston.

What was different about Salem was the fact that for nearly two years the fear of witches obsessed the community. Whatever the explanation for their behavior, the girls accused three women of bewitching them. Two of the women, fearing they would be executed, named others as responsible for their plight. People who expressed doubt about the existence of witchcraft, or who criticized the girls, were almost automatically added to the list of those tried for the crime.

Before the hysteria was played out, nineteen persons were hanged as witches, another was pressed to death (a plank was placed on his prostrate body and heaped with heavy boulders), and still others died while being held in jail.

What happened? To people who live in the twentieth century, when witchcraft is viewed as an absurd superstition, the Salem affair is puzzling. Some historians have suggested that the trying times the colony had undergone account for the panic. Puritans believed that they were God's chosen people; the only explanation for their misfortunes, such as the loss of their charter and the establishment of blasphemous churches in Massachusetts, was that someone had committed the very grave sin of practicing witchcraft.

Some historians have focused on the fact that most of Salem's victims were women, and women without friends at that. A black slave, a poverty-stricken hag who may have been mentally unbalanced, and a wealthy woman who had openly lived with a man who was not her husband were the first to be accused. Only when the girls and other bewitched people began to accuse influential persons of witchcraft—ministers, the wife of the governor, a respected soldier, and Boston's leading preacher and scholar, Cotton Mather—did the hysteria die out.

What of the people who were actually involved in the accusations and trials? Many of them later admitted that they had been wrong and publicly asked forgiveness of God and their community, accepting punishment for their real sin. They did not admit that they had been wrong in believing in witchcraft. But they did take responsibility for having falsely accused innocent people or, in the case of Judge Samuel Sewall, for having accepted inadequate evidence in reaching his decisions.

A nineteenth-century depiction of a Salem witchcraft trial by Augustus L. Mason.

POUNDS, SHILLINGS, AND PENCE

During the colonial period (and in Great Britain until 1970), money was not broken down into units of ten and one hundred, but according to a medieval system that was comparable to our system of measurement of inches, feet, yards, rods, and miles. A person who grew up using the system could easily understand it, but it was a source of perplexity for everyone else.

The basic unit of money was the pound sterling, symbolized £. There were twenty shillings (s) to the pound and twelve pence (d) to the shilling. (A farthing, as in the old saying "Not worth a farthing," was a quarter of a penny.)

Prices were written as 6d, 3/7 ½, and £5/4/7 and spoken as "sixpence," "three shillings, seven pence, ha'penny," and "five pounds, four and seven." Just to make things more confusing, there were also crowns (5s), half-crowns (2/6), florins (2s), and guineas (21s or £1/1).

The Middle Colonies

Not every person of the late seventeenth century believed in witchcraft. When at the height of the Salem hysteria, William Penn was asked if there might not be witches in Pennsylvania too, he replied sarcastically that the people of his colony were quite free to fly about on broomsticks. He had no laws forbidding it.

The liberality of the laws of the Middle Colonies, particularly those guaranteeing religious toleration and easy access to land, ensured that New York and the Quaker colonies of Pennsylvania, New Jersey, and Delaware would be contented, placid provinces. Between the time of Leisler's Rebellion in New York in 1689, and a split between Quakers and non-Quakers in Pennsylvania in the mid-1700s, the Middle Colonies grew faster than either New England or the South and generally prospered.

Balanced Economies

Except for the Hudson Valley of New York, where a few of the feudal Dutch patroonships survived into the eighteenth century, great landowners were rare in the Middle Colonies. As in New England, the agricultural pattern was a patchwork of small, family farms tilled by the landowners themselves with comparatively few servants and slaves. Unlike that of New England, the climate of the Middle Colonies provided a long growing season, and the soil in the alluvial valleys of the

A PURITAN FAMILY GOES TO MEETING

Early in the morning on Sunday, Thursday, and on special days of feasting and Thanksgiving, even before the sun rose in winter, the Puritan family bundled up in heavy woolen clothing and furs and walked to the meeting house. Few people skipped worship services, even during a blizzard. There was a fine for absenteeism, and if the weather could be withering, the distance to be traveled was short. Most New Englanders lived in villages, their houses clustered together with the meeting house near the center.

They went to a *meeting house,* not a church. To call the simple, unpainted clapboard structure a church would have been "popish," and the Puritans shunned every emblem that hinted of the Church of Rome. In the meeting house, there were no statues or other decoration, such as adorned Catholic and Anglican churches. The building was a place of preaching and worship, not an object for beautification. A weathercock rather than a cross sat atop the steeple, and was a good Calvinist symbol. It reminded the congregation that even St. Peter had sinned by denying that he knew Christ before the cock crowed three times after the Romans had seized the Lord. The sinfulness of humanity was a theme on which the Puritans constantly dwelled. In their churchyards, the tombstones were carved with death's heads—skulls.

Inside the building in winter, it was little warmer than the snow-swept fields that surrounded the village. There may have been a fireplace, but it had little effect more than ten feet from the flames. The congregation bundled in envelopes made of fur—*not* sleeping bags; there was a fine for nodding off!—and people rested their feet on brass or iron footwarmers that contained coals brought from home. In towns that prohibited the use of footwarmers—since they were a fire hazard—worshipers brought to meeting a large, well-trained dog to lie at their feet.

The women sat on the left side of the meeting house with their daughters. The men sat on the right side, but boys who were apt to be mischievous were placed around the pulpit where a churchwarden could lash out at them with a switch. He probably had his work cut out often enough, for the service went on and on, sermons alone running as long as three hours. If a sermon was shorter than two hours, there might well be gossip about the preacher's lack of zeal. And lest anyone wonder how long the sermon was lasting, an hourglass sat conspicuously on the preacher's pulpit; when the sand ran down, the hourglass was turned by the man who kept watch over the boys. Many people took notes—some out of piety; some, no doubt, to keep themselves awake.

Although the Puritans forbade organs in their meeting houses (organs were not mentioned in the scriptures), they loved to sing psalms, at home as well as at services. The *Bay Psalm Book,* from which they sang, was written with accuracy rather than poetry in mind.

The psalms, which are so beautiful in the King James Version of the Bible, sounded awkward and strained in Puritan voices. For example, in the Puritans' translation, the magnificent and touching Psalm 100 is barely comprehensible.

The rivers on of Babylon, there when we did sit downe;
Yes even then we mourned, when we remembered Sion.
Our harp we did hang it amid upon the willow tree,
Because there they thus away led in captivitie,
Required of us a song, thus asks mirth; us waste who laid
Sing us among a Sion's song unto us then they said.

Morning services ended around noon, and the family returned home for a meal that had been prepared the previous day. Like observant Jews, the Puritans observed their sabbath very strictly. There would be no work and certainly no play or sports, as in the Anglican England they had fled. Even conversation was spare on Sunday. It was no more proper to talk about workaday matters and tasks than to do them. At most, a pious family discussed the morning's sermon and other religious topics. In the afternoon, the family returned to the meeting house to hear secular announcements and another sermon and to sing psalms. Sunday was a day of rest only in one sense of the word! The solemnity of the Puritan sabbath and the earnestness with which the pious approached life did not mean that family life was without affection, laughter, and homely enjoyment. It was partly because of their love for their children that, in the Half-way Covenant of 1657, the Massachusetts Puritans eased the requirements of church membership and, according to some historians, fatally diluted the vitality of that remarkable people.

Hudson, Delaware, Schuylkill, Susquehanna, and other smaller rivers was deep and rich. The Middle Colonies produced a surplus in grains and livestock. Pennsylvania quickly earned the nickname "bread-basket of the colonies," and Delaware, New Jersey, and New York were scarcely less productive.

Because foodstuffs (with the exception of rice) were not enumerated under the Navigation Acts, they could be sold wherever the sellers could find a market, and a canny merchant class in the cities soon found one. They shipped grain and meat animals on the hoof to the sugar islands of the West Indies, where a small master class forced huge gangs of black slaves to grow cane and little else. Thanks to good soil, moderate climate, liberal laws, and shrewd merchants, the Middle Colonies found a comfortable niche for themselves within the imperial system.

Political Stability

The merchants of Philadelphia and New York governed those cities as though they were personal property. However, because landowning farmers (and therefore voters) were so numerous in the Middle Colonies, neither group was able to dominate the elected assemblies. Neither agricultural nor commercial interests were completely in charge. Instead, they cooperated to counterbalance the power of the proprietor's appointed governor in Pennsylvania and of the royal governors in Delaware, New Jersey, and New York.

Liberal Institutions

New Jersey and Delaware practiced toleration on the same Quaker grounds as did Pennsylvania. In New York, in theory, only the Church of England was legal. However, the laws were rarely enforced. For a time a Roman Catholic, Thomas Dongan, served as governor, and a Jewish synagogue was established as early as 1654. Indeed, once the Puritan grip was broken in Massachusetts, religious toleration was the rule in all the colonies. America was a young country in need of people. Whatever the law said, there were apt to be few serious attempts to discourage immigration.

Until about 1700, most colonists either had been born in England or had English-born parents. There were a few third-generation families in Virginia, Maryland, and New England. And there were some representatives of other nationalities: a handful of Sephardic Jews in Rhode Island, New York, and South Carolina; a contingent of French Protestants in South Carolina; and a growing community of German Pietists in Lancaster and York counties, Pennsylvania.

PENNSYLVANIA DUTCH

The "Plain People," the Amish and Mennonites of Lancaster and York counties in eastern Pennsylvania, who shun modern ways, frequently using horse and buggy rather than automobiles and plowing their fields behind mules, are called the "Pennsylvania Dutch." They are not Dutch but are descended from German immigrants who were attracted by the liberality of William Penn. They were called "Dutch" because the German word for "German" is *Deutsch*. In fact, calling Germans "Dutchmen" remained common practice in the United States until the end of the nineteenth century.

These people suffered little discrimination because of their origins, religion, and language. By no means, however, was America the land of opportunity for everyone. Equality was not extended to the two large groups of colonial people not of the dominant white race.

For Further Reading

Once again, see Charles M. Andrews, *The Colonial Period of American History* (1934–38), and Curtis P. Nettels, *The Roots of American Civilization* (1938), for an overview of colonial history. Most questions can be quickly answered by referring to these two books.

For the South, T. J. Wertenbaker, *The Planters of Colonial Virginia* (1927), concentrates on the first century of colonization, while L. B. Wright, *The First Gentlemen of Virginia* (1940), examines plantation society at its zenith. Students wishing to sample a primary source might look at any of the three secret diaries of William Byrd of Westover edited by Wright.

For New England, Sumner Powell, *Puritan Village* (1963), intensively examines a single community. So does K. A. Lockridge, *A New England Town* (1971), but with a larger focus. The witchcraft excitement has been interpreted in a bewildering variety of ways; the most recent persuasive book on the subject is Paul Boyer and Stephen Nissenbaum, *Salem Possessed* (1974).

On the Middle Colonies, see the works cited at the end of Chapter 3, as well as Michael Kammen, *Colonial New York* (1975).

5

The Red and the Black
Indians and Africans in the Colonies

When a statesman of the age of Queen Anne thought about the colonies in North America, he was likely to see one of two things. He might see precious national properties, nothing comparable to Spain's vaster empire to the south, but nevertheless English possessions that enriched the mother country at no appreciable expense. Or, if he was inclined to drollery in an era known for its wits, he might see ragged, rustic little congregations of his countrymen gone too far abroad for their own good. Provincials at a time when London was becoming the great metropolis of the Western world, the colonists were easy targets of scorn and ridicule.

Men and women of more modest station, the great mass of the English people, had to struggle to make a living. They had little time to think about such things as colonies. If they paused on the subject, they were likely to say that America was a place where poor people lived better than they did at home. It was this kind of thinking that fueled the steady immigration into the colonies.

In every case, the English perspective was European. English men and women thought of the North American colonies in terms of the relationship they bore to Europe, European institutions, European culture and conditions—to themselves.

But there were other perspectives from which the colonies might be viewed. To those North American Indians whose homelands bordered on

Settlers like these fur trappers on the Hudson Bay relied on Indian knowledge of the land to guide them in the New World.

the English settlements, the colonies were mere enclaves on the edge of the world. The colonists were one of many tribes—more numerous than any other, to be sure, and unique in more ways than the peculiar color of their skins. Nevertheless, to look at the colonists from the interior of North America, they were one people among others, a people with whom to fight, to trade, to compete for the means of living. England and Europe? They were just words, the names of the mysterious places from which the colonists received the goods that the Indians so desired.

From the perspective of West Africa, the low-lying lands around the Gulf of Guinea, America was the mysterious and fearful world. It was the place to which some people went in chains, never to return. To those Africans and their children who lived in the English colonies, North America was a place of heavy labor from dawn to dusk, of food just sufficient to live on, of fear of punishment by the whip or worse. America was the place where they were slaves, a condition that, they learned as quickly as they learned the English language, would not change as long as they lived.

The Red

The Native Americans who dealt with the English colonists had a different experience from those who knew Spanish invaders. There were not so many of them, first of all. No more than about 150,000 Indians lived in all the parts of the continent the English settled during their first century in America as compared with 100,000 Aztecs in Tenochtitlán alone.

Moreover, because the Indians of the Eastern Woodlands lacked the riches in gold and silver that Europeans coveted, the English had little interest in conquering, living among, exploiting, and governing the native peoples, as the Spaniards did in their part of the New World. The object of English colonization was to create Little Englands in America, replicas of the way of life the settlers knew back home; to do this, they had to take the land for themselves, and, peacefully or forcefully, push all others out of the way. The consuming passion of the English-speaking whites for land was to be the single most important fact of life for the Indians of North America for almost four hundred years after the settlement of Jamestown.

The Diversity of Native Americans

The most striking characteristic of the Native American world was diversity. The Indians' prehistory is a lesson in just how rapidly cultures diversify when population is small and scattered, and when people who hold different beliefs and practices are not constantly interacting. Although all Indians were descended from the few culturally similar bands of Asians who crossed the Bering Strait, in just a few thousand years they had divided and divided again into a great variety of linguistic and cultural groups and even markedly distinct physical types.

Native American political systems ran the gamut from totalitarianism (the Incas in Peru) to the absence of even an *idea* of government among some peoples of the American high desert (especially in what is now Nevada). Socially, there were caste systems so complicated that some tribes supported a distinct group of genealogists as the only means to keep track of them (in the southeastern United States). There were tribes in which men literally ignored the existence of every woman but their wives, others that required women to speak in a different language from men, and yet others that traced descent through the maternal line and consulted women in every important tribal decision. The variety of social relationships among the Indians at the time the whites arrived was more diverse than in seventeenth-century Europe.

Some Indians were warlike and aggressive, renowned for their cruelty towards enemies. Every tribe in the Northeast (and the colonists too) feared the Mohawks because they scalped their victims, sometimes alive. Others were extremely gentle people, pacifists who survived only because they lived in isolated or undesirable

The Mission San Diego de Alcalá. built in 1769. Father Junípero Serra used Indian labor in building the California missions.

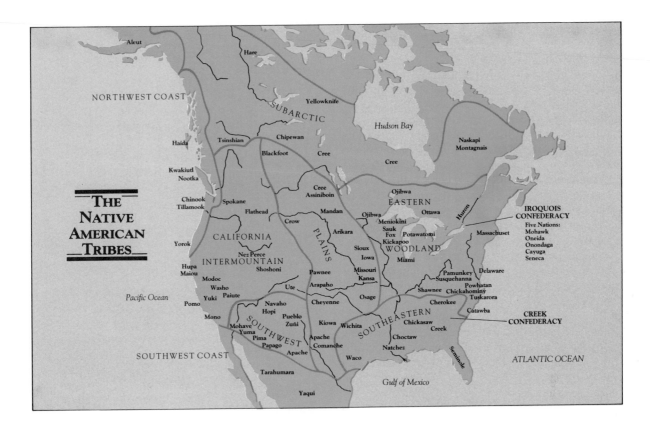

places. Many Indians were monotheists who worshiped a single manitou, or "Great Spirit." Others were simple fetishists. They worried about the supernatural powers in every stone, tree, bug, bird, and animal, and depended on magicians to cope with otherworldly powers. There was intense, sophisticated cultivation and an urban way of life among the Pueblo Indians of New Mexico and Arizona. There was the virtually complete ignorance of domesticated crops among some tribes that were stalled in a hunting and gathering economy. In California, whole peoples grubbed out the barest subsistence on little but acorns, a few roots and berries, and the odd small animal they were able to snare. In the Pacific Northwest, food was so abundant that the potlatch peoples expressed a disdain for material goods such as is associated with only very rich economies.

Language and Culture
The diversity of Native American cultures is best illustrated by the Indian languages. There are only the obscurest relationships between any North American tongue and the language of any Asian people. Among the Indians themselves, the linguistic differences were greater than they were among the various nationalities of Europe. During the colonial period, the Indians of the Americas spoke about five hundred mutually unintelligible languages. In one corner of North Carolina, several small tribes living within ten miles of one another for at least a century or two could not communicate except by sign language.

Fragmentation seems to be the natural tendency of language. Until it is written down and rules of expression (grammar) are devised, and when there is no pressing need to communicate with more than just a few daily associates, language changes very rapidly. This may be observed in the almost constant emergence of new slang words and expressions in American English. Today, however, new phrases are made immediately familiar to almost everyone through the newspapers, magazines, television, and cinema. They are either adopted by all or dropped and quickly forgotten. In a world that is constantly growing smaller, like our own, a common means of communication usually develops.

In the vast, thinly populated world of the Indians, however, in which large bands broke up into small groups in order to survive, distinct tongues developed and multiplied at an astonishing rate. This in itself served to divide the Indians. Almost every tribe's word for itself could be translated as something like "the people" or "the human beings," while those outside the tribe were called "the beasts" or "the other things."

The Indians of the Eastern Woodlands

It is possible that the process of fragmentation was being reversed on the Atlantic coast at the time the English settled there. While there were fifty language families in the whole of North America, there were only three significant linguistic groups in the territory of the thirteen English colonies. *Algonkians* (or Algonquins) controlled the coast from New England through the Chesapeake Bay, the St. Lawrence basin, and parts of New York and Pennsylvania. Tribes in this group (who were often hostile toward one another) included the Mohegans (or Mohicans), Abnaki, Lenni Lenape (Delawares), Pequots, Chippewas, and Powhatans. The Algonkians were the people with whom the English first made contact in both Virginia and Massachusetts and whom, by taking their lands, they made their enemies.

The second major linguistic group of the Eastern Woodlands was the *Iroquoian,* not so likely to be hostile among themselves except for the Hurons of the north, who had Algonkian allies. The Iroquois occupied a large wedge-shaped territory, running from the eastern Great Lakes through New York and into Pennsylvania, that split the Algonkians in two. The Conestogas and Eries were Iroquoian-speaking tribes, but the most important were the tribes that had joined together in a federation under the legendary figure Hiawatha a century before the arrival of Europeans. The Five Nations (or Iroquois Confederacy) were the Cayugas, Mohawks, Oneidas, Onandagas, and Senecas. Farther south, separated from the main group by Algonkian territory, were the Tuscarora of Virginia and North Carolina. During the 1710s they were defeated by colonial forces from South Carolina and moved north to become the sixth nation.

The English colonists had less contact at first with the third major linguistic group of the Eastern Woodlands, the *Muskogeans.* These tribes included the Apalachee, Chickasaw, Choctaw, Creek, Natchez, and Seminole. These agriculturally advanced and socially sophisticated tribes lived in what are now the southeastern states of Florida, Georgia, Alabama, Mississippi, and Tennessee. Few English settlers penetrated this country until late in the seventeenth century, when South Carolinians developed a hide and skin trade there.

Economy and Ecology

All three Eastern Woodlands groups practiced a similar economy. They cultivated corn, beans, pumpkins, and tobacco by the "slash and burn" method. This was an

Clearing land by the "slash and burn" method practiced in the Eastern Woodlands.

easy form of clearing land that suited the eastern tribes and was indispensable to each wave of white pioneers in forested country.

Slash and burn involved stripping a ring of bark from the trunks of trees, thus killing them. When the foliage fell, admitting sunlight into the woods, the women (who were the farmers in the East) burned the underbrush. In these ghostly forests, they planted corn, beans, and squash on hills dug up with a kind of spade roughed out of stone or wood. There were no plows or beasts of burden among the eastern tribes.

Such a primitive form of cultivation did not in itself provide sufficient food for a single people of the Eastern Woodlands. Every tribe looked more to the forests than to the fields for its survival, depending primarily on hunting, fishing, trapping, and gathering edible plants. Thus each tribe competed with its neighbors for hunting grounds, but because hunting and gathering do not require constant, absolute control over any specific plot of land, they provided the means of life for all.

Foraging for food makes for a precarious livelihood at best, and the Indians' communities inclined to be small. Some of the Powhatans whom the Virginians encountered lived in villages of five hundred people during the summer, but they broke up into smaller wandering bands in winter. Only with the introduction of European tools and, therefore, an increased food supply, were larger, more or less permanent communities established.

Culture Shock

The Eastern Woodlands Indians' first reaction to the colonists was curiosity. The white outposts were too small to be a threat, and the goods the English offered in trade intrigued the natives. During those few first years, when the Indians held the edge in numbers and might, it made no sense to destroy the source of such novel commodities as the famous glass beads and trinkets with which, for example, Peter Minuit purchased Manhattan Island in 1626. (It cost about $24.)

Much more important to a people who had no metals were the European commodities that improved their standard of living: brass and iron vessels; tools (spades, hatchets); woven blankets (which were much warmer than hides) and other textiles; and firearms, which allowed the Indians to hunt more efficiently and to turn on old tribal enemies. Finally, the Indians, who had known no alcoholic beverage except possibly a weak corn beer, took with tragic zest to liquor. "Firewater" devastated many of them physically and morally in a short period of time.

In return for these goods, the Indians provided foodstuffs to the first settlers, and, when the English became agriculturally self-sufficient, they supplied furs and hides for the European market.

The Fur and Hide Trade: A Suicidal Business

The English (and Dutch and French) desire for furs and hides altered Indian life as much as European manufactures did. Before the whites arrived, the Woodlands tribes hunted deer and trapped beaver and other fur-bearing animals only for their own use. Because the Indians were so few, their needs had little impact on the wildlife population.

However, Europeans could not get enough American skins and pelts. The upper classes coveted the lush furs of the beaver, otter, and weasel. Both furs and deerskin were made into felt, which was pressed into hats and served dozens of other purposes. In order to increase production, the tribes rapidly exterminated the valuable creatures in their ancestral hunting grounds.

It does not take very long to destroy a species when hunting is relentless and systematic. In only a couple of generations, nineteenth-century Americans annihilated a population of passenger pigeons that previously darkened the skies. The nearly total destruction of the North American bison after the construction of the transcontinental railroad took only ten years! Thus it happened in the Eastern Woodlands, as Indians and the odd white hunter and trapper set out after deer and beaver.

Unlike the case of passenger pigeon, very much like the case of the bison, the destruction of the animals of the eastern forests meant the destruction of the ecological system on which the native peoples' way of life depended. The short-term gains in trade goods from Europe led to the permanent loss of the traditional basis of life.

A New Kind of Warfare

The demands of the fur traders also introduced a new kind of warfare to the Indians. Not that war was new to them. On the contrary, enmity toward almost all other tribes was an integral part of Iroquois and Algonkian culture before the Europeans arrived.

Traditional Indian warfare was primarily a ritualistic demonstration of individual bravery. A warrior gained as much glory in "counting coup," giving an enemy a sound rap, as in taking his life. Women and children were rarely killed, and rape seems to have been unusual. A tribe that was short on wives kidnapped women of other tribes and adopted them. There was no glory in slaughtering or abusing the defenseless.

When they became part of an intercontinental economy, however, the Indians adopted a different concept of warfare. No longer was the main object glory, retribution, or thievery, but the takeover of other tribes' resources—their hunting grounds—and, if necessary, the total elimination of the competition.

The colonists tacitly encouraged this small-scale genocide by providing the weapons that made it possible. They also helped to spread the practice of scalping, which had been peculiar to the Mohawks, as a means of measuring a tribe's efficiency. In 1721, even Quaker Pennsylvania paid $140 for an Algonkian warrior's scalp and $50 for a squaw's. And to make the purpose of the bounty unmistakable, a live prisoner brought a paltry $30.

The gory practice eventually spread over much of the continent. Because tribes involved in the fur trade penetrated the West long before the whites dared to do so, Indians in the interior were introduced to European trade goods, European diseases, and the report of English and French muskets long before they saw their first paleface.

The French

The relationship between the Indians and the English colonists was complicated by the presence of another European people in North America. In 1608, a year after Jamestown was settled, the French explorer Samuel de Champlain established a trading post on the St. Lawrence River. He called it Quebec. Anxious to keep up with the English, the French kings, who were absolute monarchs, actually commanded some villagers of rugged Brittany to settle in Canada. When the population of New France still did not grow, the king ordered his troops to round up prostitutes from the streets of seaports and the daughters of impoverished peasants and ship them to New France to become wives of the soldiers there and mothers of a colonial population.

The drive for a large population was to no avail. The soil of the St. Lawrence basin was not inviting, and the Canadian winters were killing. Few French emigrated. The one group that showed some interest in settling North America, the Huguenots (Calvinists much like English Puritans), was forbidden to do so because Louis XIV was determined to keep New France Catholic.

The colony remained Catholic. Jesuit priests accompanied every explorer and ministered to spiritual needs in every settlement. But New France did not grow. By 1713, after a century, the French population in North America was twenty-five thousand, about the same number of people as lived in the single English colony of Pennsylvania, founded fewer than forty years earlier.

French Expansion

If their numbers were few, the boldness of the French Canadians was boundless. French traders and trappers fanned out throughout the Great Lakes region and beyond, while the English huddled within a few miles of ocean breakers. These *coureurs du bois*, or "runners of the woods," reverted more than halfway to savagery, as Europeans defined the Indians' way of life. In traveling through the Indians' forests, consorting with and marrying native women, and adopting a modification of Indian dress, the *coureurs du bois* renounced their European heritage in a way that was incomprehensible to the English. When a governor of Virginia reached the crest of the Appalachians, he celebrated by setting a table with pressed linen, fine china, and silver, and by pouring three kinds of wine into crystal glasses!

Spurred on by the tales of the *coureurs du bois*, intrepid French explorers charted what is now the central third of the United States. In 1673, Louis Joliet and Jacques Marquette, a Jesuit priest, descended the Mississippi to the mouth of the Arkansas River. In 1682, Robert Cavelier, the Sieur de La Salle, reached the mouth of the Father of Waters, which had not been discovered from the Gulf of Mexico because, at the end of its long journey, the great river divides into hundreds of muddy channels through forbidding swamps. In 1699, Pierre Le Moyne, the Sieur d'Iberville, began the series of settlements on the gulf that became New Orleans and the hub of the second French American province, Louisiana.

It was a flimsy empire by English standards, a string of lonely log forts and trading posts in the wilderness: Kaskaskia and Cahokia in the Illinois country; St. Louis where the Missouri flows into the Mississippi; dots on a map connected by lakes, rivers, creeks, and portages (a word that Americans learned from the Canadians).

But the French had one big edge on their rivals to the south. Most of the Algonkian-speaking people plus the Hurons, an independent Iroquoian tribe—a large majority of the Indians of the northeastern forests—were their friends and the sworn enemies of the English.

Contrasting Ways of Life

The French were better able to maintain amicable relations with these tribes for several reasons, none more important than the fewness of their numbers that King Louis so regretted. Not only were the French not a numerical threat to the Indians, but their economic interests in America seemed to favor the native peoples.

Both English and French wanted to trade European goods for furs and hides. But whereas New France was little more than trading posts and trappers, the English colonies were primarily agricultural settlements. The French glided silently through the forests, as the Indians did; the English chopped them down. Each acre of land put under cultivation meant one acre less in the hunting and gathering economy.

Moreover, intensive agriculture required exclusive use of land, and the very concept of owning the earth was foreign to the Indians. "Sell the land?" said the great nineteenth-century chief Tecumseh, echoing many before him. "Why not sell the air, the clouds, the great sea?" The French could accommodate themselves to this philosophy; the English could not.

The Role of Religion

The difference in religion between the Roman Catholic French and the Protestant English, particularly the Puritans of New England, also affected their respective relations with the tribes. Like every Christian people in the Americas, both English and French partly justified their presence in terms of winning the Indians to true faith. The intention to do so was mentioned more or less sincerely in every colonial charter. A few pious Englishmen, such as Roger Williams and John Eliot, the "Apostle of the Indians" who devoted his life to preaching among the tribes of the upper Connecticut Valley, took the mission seriously. Dartmouth College

*Louis Joliet and Jacques Marquette, early explorers of the Mississippi River, are pictured
here entering the upper Mississippi.*

in Hanover, New Hampshire, originated as a school for
Indians. When the College of William and Mary was
established in Virginia in 1693, provision was made for
Indian education. (Not one showed up to register.)

Whereas the French regarded the Roman Catholic
Church as a body to which everyone should belong
(the word *catholic* means "universal"), English Protestants, particularly the Puritans of the northern colonies, thought of church membership as a gift given to
very few people. Nothing intrinsic to Puritan doctrine
precluded Indian Visible Saints, but the intimate inter-
twining of Puritan religion with the New England way
of life—customs, prejudices, moral codes, manners,
even dress—made it extremely difficult for the colonists to think of Indians as acceptable to God.

By way of contrast, the Jesuits of New France were a
flexible lot who cared little for cultural differences.
When they preached to the Indians, they emphasized
the similarities between Christianity and the Indian
traditions. The French called for submission to a be-

lief, not a break with every custom that they did not
practice.

The Jesuits had another advantage over the Protestants in the competition for Native American loyalties.
The ornate Roman Catholic ritual—the mystery of the
Mass and other ceremonies, the vivid statues—
appealed to the Indians' aesthetic sense. The Puritans
remained a people of the word. Bible study and long,
learned sermons were the foundations of Protestant
worship services. Both were foreign to Indian culture.

The Five Nations

The English colonists had allies in the Five Nations,
whose hunting grounds centered in what is now New
York State. The Iroquois allied themselves with the
English because the English were the enemies of their
ancestral foes, the Algonkians and the Hurons.

It is not clear how long the Five Nations had warred
with the Algonkians, but their enmity started at least

a century before the whites arrived. The Iroquois were fewer in number than their foes, but because of the close alliance of their Five Nations, they seem to have held their own.

Until 1609. In that year, Samuel de Champlain and a party of Hurons stumbled across Iroquois hunters on the banks of what is now Lake Champlain. In order to please his companions, Champlain opened fire. It was the Iroquois' introduction to firearms, and they fled in terror.

Over the next several decades, the Algonkians and the Hurons used their French friends and gunpowder to whittle away at the Five Nations. The hardships and fears of this period guaranteed that when the Iroquois made contacts with other Europeans, first the Dutch in Fort Orange and then the English in Albany, they had a generation's worth of scores to settle.

Settle them they did. With their own firearms and white allies, the Iroquois took the offensive against the Algonkians, Hurons, and French with a frightening vengeance. The *coureurs du bois* so feared the Five Nations that they added as many as a thousand miles to their trek to the trapping grounds in the Illinois country rather than take the chance of running into a party of Cayugas, Oneidas, or Senecas.

They had good reason to be cautious, for the Iroquois tortured their captives. Several Jesuit priests were martyred when they attempted to preach to the Five Nations. Two of them, Isaac Jogues and Jean de Breboeuf, were canonized by the Catholic Church.

Black Americans

To most English colonists, who thought in agricultural terms, the Indians were as great an impediment to progress as the massive oaks and maples of the forests. The third great people of colonial America, on the contrary, were imported against their will in order to solve the problem of the chronic shortage of labor in the colonies.

POPULATION OF AMERICAN COLONIES
(thousands)

	Total	Negro
1630	5	0.1
1650	50	2
1670	112	5
1690	210	17
1710	332	45
1730	629	91
1750	1,171	236

Slavery in America

Black Africans were in the New World from the start. A black may have accompanied Columbus, and Estevan the Moor, an early explorer of the lands bordering the Gulf of Mexico, was probably from south of the Sahara. By the mid-1500s, before the English had a single toehold in the Western Hemisphere, blacks were the backbone of the labor force in the West Indies, on the Spanish Main, and in Portuguese Brazil. Some of these people, particularly those of mixed race, were free. A few exceptional individuals prospered as craftsmen, sailors, and even landowners. The vast majority, however, were slaves, the personal property of other people in accordance with Spanish laws that dated in part back to Roman times.

The English also needed cheap, dependable labor, particularly in the tobacco colonies. But they did not turn immediately to slavery to solve their problem. Unlike the Spanish and Portuguese, the English had

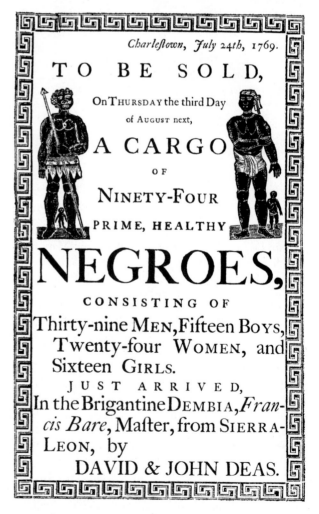

Poster announcing the sale of black slaves, 1769.

neither a long history of contact with black Africa nor a tradition of bondage for life. Even serfdom, the medieval institution that bound individuals to a piece of land—if the land was sold, they went with it—had died out in England centuries earlier.

When in 1620 a Gambian merchant offered slaves to an English shipmaster as payment for his trade goods, the captain replied indignantly that "we were a people who did not deal in any such commodities, neither did wee buy or sell one another, or any that had our owne shapes." The African was amazed and said that the other white men who came to his country wanted nothing but slaves. The captain answered that "they were another kinde of people different from us."

Had this goodly man's principles prevailed among his compatriots, North America would have been spared its greatest historical tragedy, the enslavement of millions of Africans and their descendants on the basis of their race. However, just a year before the incident on the Gambia River—and a year before the *Mayflower* anchored at Plymouth, Massachusetts—the history of black Americans had begun.

In 1619, a Dutch ship sailed up the Chesapeake to Jamestown and displayed a dozen black captives to the tobacco planters. Struggling to produce enough leaf to satisfy the English market, the planters bought them. Almost certainly, these first black Americans were not slaves. Not only were the Virginians unfamiliar with the idea of bondage *durante vita*—slavery for life—but the existence of a number of free blacks in Virginia in 1650 implies that the first Africans in the colonies were indentured servants, just like many whites, who were freed. By 1650, however, because of problems inherent in the institution of indentured servitude, the status of American blacks had begun to change for the worse.

Indentured Servants

People who were able to pay for their passage to the colonies and to secure land once there rarely went to work for others. Unable to hire workers, colonial landowners adapted the ancient system of apprenticeship to their situation.

Knowledge of the skilled trades was handed from one generation to the next by means of binding a boy as an apprentice to a master craftsman. In return for teaching a youth the skills of blacksmith, a cooper (barrelmaker), a wheelwright, a baker, the master was entitled to the use of the apprentice's labor and his complete obedience for a period of seven years, from age fourteen to age twenty-one.

Apprentices were not free to do as they pleased. The law enforced the master's authority over such servants. Similarly, communities cared for orphans—girls as well as boys—by binding them to a willing household. No craft was involved. The master of these orphans got a menial servant in return for sustaining her or him until adulthood.

Colonial farmers, planters, and merchants offered the price of passage to America (and sustenance) in return for such servitude for a period of years. Seven years was the most common term, but in times of grave labor shortage, a servant could strike a better bargain. Again, no craft was involved. The indentured servant exchanged a period of bondage for the chance of a fresh start in the New World.

Woman preparing tobacco for export.

More serious was the runaway problem. Throughout the colonies, including the most settled parts of the tidewater, America was densely forested. Farms and plantations were mere gaps in a wilderness. In Virginia and Maryland, the grandest plantations were separated from one another by belts of virgin hardwood or second-growth "pineys" (old fields gone to scrub). There were few towns. "Roads" were narrow tracks; most of them were not wide enough for two horsemen to pass without bumping.

Thus a servant could easily run away, hide, and elude capture. Planters' letters were filled with complaints of missing workers and lost investments. The recapture and return of runaways seems to have been the major activity of county sheriffs, the only law-enforcement officials in rural areas. Officials in cities like Baltimore and Philadelphia were flooded with descriptions of runaways, although, with hundreds of recent immigrants walking the streets of coastal cities, they probably caught very few. Punishment was harsh—a whipping and extra time in service. But the opportunities of freedom and the odds of success tempted many.

The most famous runaway was Benjamin Franklin. In 1723, at the age of seventeen, he walked out on his brother, to whom he was bound, and traveled from Boston to Philadelphia. Any number of people suspected him for what he was, a runaway, but no one tried to stop him.

Here lies the key to understanding why farmers and planters looked increasingly to the blacks as the solution to their labor problem. Their color was a handy, obvious badge. If it was assumed that a black person was a slave unless he or she could prove otherwise, the work

The system worked. Well into the 1700s, white indentured servants formed the majority of the labor force in every colony. However, it was in the South, with its commercial agriculture, where the system was most vital to the economy and where the weaknesses of indentured servitude were most keenly felt.

The Servant Problem

However cheap indentured servants were, the fact that they went free after a number of years added to the costs of cultivation, particularly because mortality among southerners of every class was high. (The master took a chance on every servant living to finish his or her term.) Moreover, although their rights were few, servants did have some and did know them. The instances of a servant taking a master to court and winning were few; but they occurred. The records are much more abundant in cases of masters complaining about stolen food and drink, rowdy parties, and pregnancies among the women, which exempted them from work for as long as a year.

THREE POUNDS REWARD.

RUN AWAY from the Subscriber, living at Warwick furnace, Minehole, on the 23d ult. an Irish servant man, named DENNIS M'CALLIN, about five feet eight inches high, nineteen years of age, has a freckled face, light coloured curly hair. Had on when he went away, an old felt hat, white and yellow striped jacket, a new blue cloth coat, and buckskin breeches ; also, he took with him a bundle of shirts and stockings, and a pocket pistol ; likewise, a box containing gold rings, &c. Whoever takes up said servant and secures him in any goal, so as his master may get him again, shall have the above reward and reasonable charges paid by   JAMES TODD.

N. B. All masters of vessels, and others, are forbid from harbouring or carrying him off, at their peril.

Planters offered rewards for the recapture of runaway indentured servants.

force was that much more controllable. Sheriffs and bailiffs (who were rewarded for the service) routinely detained blacks who were unknown to them without waiting for masters to announce a runaway. By 1670, there were two thousand blacks in Virginia, more than half of them slaves under a law passed in that year. After 1700, when the institution was universally accepted, the slave population grew rapidly until, by the time of the Revolution, there were about five hundred thousand slaves in the thirteen colonies, all but fifty thousand in the South.

The Slave Trade

This demand for black laborers completely changed the English and colonial attitude toward trading in "any that had our owne shapes." Not only did ships from England and New England, especially Newport, Rhode Island, sail annually to West Africa to capture or purchase slaves, but English negotiators at the Peace of Utrecht in 1713, which ended the War of the Spanish Succession, demanded and got as a fruit of English victory the *Asiento de negros*, or exclusive right to supply Spanish America with slaves. The *Asiento* was a richer prize than territory. Trade in human beings was an integral part of the mercantilist system.

The African slave trade was a sordid business in which African kings collaborated with European and American merchants. At first, African chiefs seem to have sold only their criminals and members of enemy tribes to the white-skinned strangers. As the European demand grew and the profits soared, some aggressive tribes began to build their economies on raids inland in search of fresh sources of supply.

COLONIAL SLAVERY: A NEGATIVE VIEW

Philip V. Fithian, tutor in a wealthy southern family, repeated what an overseer of slaves had told him:

For Sullennes, Obstinacy, or Idleness, . . . Take a Negro, strip him, tie him fast to a post, take then a sharp Curry-Comb, & curry him severely till he is well scrap'd; & call a Boy with some dry Hay, and make the boy rub him down for several minutes, then salt him and unlose him. He will attend to his Business (said the inhuman infidel) afterwards.

COLONIAL SLAVERY: A POSITIVE VIEW

Traveling from Boston to New York in 1704, a New England woman disapproved of familiarity between white and black:

They Generally lived very well and comfortably in their families. But too Indulgent (especially the farmers) to their slaves: suffering too great familiarity from them, permitting them to sit at Table and eat with them, (as they say to save time,) and into the dish goes the black hoof as freely as the white hand.

For the most part, the whites anchored their ships off the coast or fortified themselves in stockades at the mouths of rivers with the iron bars, brass, kettles, cloth, guns, powder, liquor, and tobacco that they traded for their human merchandise. Occasionally, however, some joined their African partners or ventured inland themselves. A trader of 1787 explained how the business worked: "In the daytime we called at

This cutaway view of a slave ship shows the crowded conditions in which slaves were brought to the New World.

the villages we passed, and purchased our slaves fairly; but in the night we . . . broke into the villages and, rushing into the huts of the inhabitants, seized men, women, and children promiscuously."

The cruelest part of the trade was the sea crossing, which was called the "middle passage" because it was flanked by overland marches at either end. Rather than providing the most healthful circumstances possible for their valuable cargo and keeping mortality low, the traders crammed the slaves in layers of low decks "like herrings in a barrel."

If only one in twenty captives died, the voyage was considered an extraordinary success. If one in five died, by no means unusual, the profits were still considerable. A slave who cost £5–10 in Africa in 1700 sold in the New World for £25. The Portuguese, who were reputed to be more humane than the English and New England traders, called their slave ships *tumbeiros*, or "coffins."

West African Roots

The Portuguese took their slaves principally in the southern part of Africa (Angola) and even on the east coast. English and American traders concentrated on the lands bordering the Gulf of Guinea, present-day Liberia, Ivory Coast, Ghana, Togo, Benin, and Nigeria.

Much of the coastline was mangrove swamp, but approximately a hundred miles inland the country pitched upward and provided a living that was rich enough to support a large population and a sophisticated culture. Until profits from the slave trade enabled the Ashanti Empire to extend its sway over a vast area in the late seventeenth century, there were few large domains in West Africa, but rather a great number of tribes speaking many languages and following a variety of customs. Most West Africans were polytheists who worshipped a complicated hierarchy of gods and spirits. Many tribes venerated the spirits of dead ancestors, and sacrifice was central to most religions. Islam and Christianity had made some headway, but since they were the faiths of the slavers, not very much.

West Africa was no Eden. The people who lived there were sophisticated agriculturists. Once the sweet potato was introduced in the sixteenth century, probably by Spanish or Portuguese slave traders, its cultivation spread so rapidly that it became the staple crop of much of the region. The West Africans' expe-

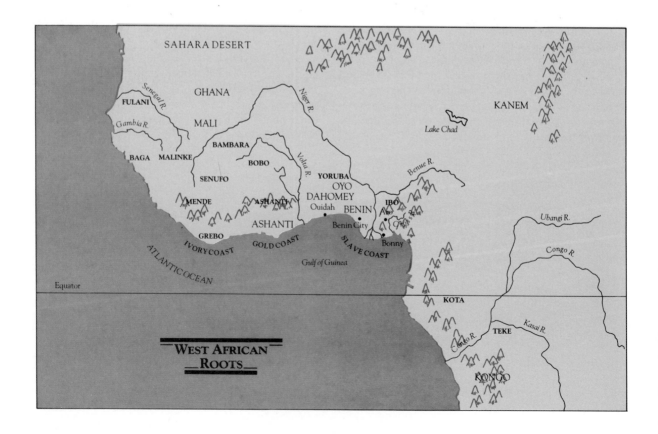

WEST AFRICAN ROOTS

Africans capture slaves for sale to whites, as represented in a nineteenth-century engraving.

rience with intensive farming, as well as their sturdy physique, made them all the more appealing to American planters.

There was no such person as a typical captive. Males might have been princes, priests, or criminals. Most likely, however, they were ordinary farmers who had the bad luck to cross the path of a raiding party. Most female slaves also came from the ordinary classes. Their status in Africa depended on the tribe to which they belonged. In most, women did a major part of the heavy labor. In other tribes, such as the Ashanti, descent was traced in the maternal line, and women were accorded high status.

Like the American Indians, the Africans were no technological match for Europeans. Superior weaponry and attractive trade goods made it easy for most slave traders to have their way. Also, as among the Indians, ancestral hatreds among African tribes made it easy for outsiders to manipulate the superior numbers of the natives. Not only was one tribe more than happy to sell its neighbors to the white men, but the divisions among the blacks were exploited to make them more manageable. "The safest way," wrote William Smith, who took part in an expedition of 1748, "is to trade with the different Nations, on either side of the River, and having some of every sort on board, there will be no more likelihood of their succeeding in a Plot, than of finishing the tower of Babel." Once in the colonies, these diverse peoples adopted English as the only means of communication among themselves. However, they were shut out of the mainstream of American development in virtually every other way.

TWO FRENCH PRIESTS

New France produced two kinds of colonists not to be found in the English settlements. One was the *coureur du bois*, the *trappeur*, the Frenchman who embraced the ways of the Eastern Woodlands Indians in order to hunt and trap with them far beyond the tiny white enclaves on the St. Lawrence River. Not until the nineteenth century would a noteworthy number of English-speaking Americans, the fabled mountain men of the Rockies, similarly abandon civilization for the wilderness. During the colonial period, the English settlers hoped to force the environment to conform to their way of life, rather than vice versa.

The second unique Canadian colonist was the Jesuit missionary, usually a well-born Frenchman who devoted his life—and frequently lost it—to the cause of converting the Indians to Christianity. While a few English colonists took an interest in winning the souls of the Native Americans—Roger Williams and John Eliot, for example—there was nothing in the English experience to compare with the single-minded sacrifices of the French Jesuits.

The Society of Jesus was an order of priests dedicated to spreading the Catholic faith to nonbelievers. Protestants despised them. Their vows of total obedience to their superiors (their founder had been a soldier) grated particularly on the English, who were jealous of their liberties. The Jesuits were also condemned for their brilliance in theological debate; critics called them sophists—deceivers who were willing to tell any lie, to use any means whatsoever, if it served their purpose. Finally, the Jesuits were criticized for concentrating their missionary work on politically powerful people— kings, princes, even the emperors of China and Japan—and then using force to convert ordinary souls.

Whatever truth there may have been to these accusations in Europe and Asia, they did not apply to the Jesuits in North America. The first member of the society arrived in Quebec in 1611, only three years after the city was founded, and there were never more than fifty in New France at any one time. While a few Jesuits stayed close to the military fortifications of New France, the vast majority struck out into the woods, enduring extreme hardship in their efforts to win the Indians to Roman Catholicism. Twenty-two of them would be killed for their beliefs.

One was Isaac Jogues (1607–46). Of a noble family, he was sent to Canada immediately after his ordination in 1636. He only paused in Quebec, then moved to the woods to live among the Hurons, the one Iroquois tribe that was cordial to the French, and he mastered their difficult language. In 1641 Jogues traveled three hundred miles to Sault Ste. Marie, where Lake Superior empties into Lake Michigan, paddling a canoe through fierce storms on the lakes, carrying back-breaking burdens over long portages, and risking attack by hostile Sioux or Mohawks and even betrayal by the Hurons

The martyrdom of Jesuit missionary Isaac Jogues at the hands of the Mohawks.

(who were by no means entirely Christianized).

Jogues was captured by the Mohawks, an Iroquois tribe that was loosely allied to the Dutch fur merchants in Fort Orange (Albany). For a year he lived among them as a slave, suffering repeated torture. He was tied to a stake while a fire was built around him, and most of his fingers were gnawed off joint by joint. Nevertheless, when physically able to do so, he preached the gospel to his tormentors and baptized Mohawk warriors who had been killed in battle.

Hearing of the white slave, the Dutch in New Netherlands more or less tricked the Mohawks into releasing Jogues to them. Although not Roman Catholics, they nursed him and, in 1643, sent him back to France. There he told of his experiences, exhibited his mutilated hands, and received special permission from the pope to celebrate Mass despite the loss of his fingers. He could have retired in France, teaching the Iroquoian language to other missionaries, but Jogues returned to Canada, where, in 1646, he acted as French ambassador to the Mohawks.

As ambassador he was unharmed—the Iroquois code was strict in such matters—but when he completed his negotiations, Jogues returned to the Mohawks as a missionary. He was immediately killed by a single blow from a tomahawk.

Jacques Marquette (1637–75) was a teacher in a Jesuit college in France when, on hearing tales of Isaac Jogues and other Jesuit martyrs, he resolved to go to Canada. He studied the language of the Ottawa Indians at Trois-Rivières and, in 1668, went to Sault Ste.

Marie, now a secure French base. In 1673, a *voyageur* whom he had met several years earlier, Louis Joliet, asked Marquette to accompany him on an expedition to look for a great southward-flowing river of which the Indians spoke.

Marquette jumped at the opportunity to preach to peoples whom no whites had ever met, and he and Joliet departed in May 1673, traveling by canoe on Lake Michigan and accompanied by five Ottawas. Paddling up the Fox River in present-day Wisconsin, Joliet and Marquette discovered the long portage, soon to become a veritable highway for *trappeurs*, to the Wisconsin River, which flows into the Mississippi. They continued down the Mississippi to the mouth of the Arkansas, where Indians told them of whites on the river to the south. Correctly surmising that the whites were Spaniards on the Gulf of Mexico, who would not be happy to see Frenchmen in their territory, Marquette and Joliet did not proceed to the mouth of the Mississippi. On their way back to New France, they blazed another route between the Mississippi Basin and the Great Lakes, via the site of present-day Chicago. His health ruined, Father Marquette died there in October 1675, not as a martyr for his faith but as one of the great explorers of the North American continent.

In order to appreciate the feats of Jogues and Marquette, it is necessary to remember that when Jogues was killed, New York was still Dutch, and the English in America were clustered in two small population centers on the Chesapeake and Massachusetts bays. No English explorer or settler had yet crossed the Appalachian crest.

When Marquette made his voyage, Pennsylvania, New Jersey, the Carolinas, and Georgia had not yet been founded, and little Massachusetts was about to suffer a devastating setback at the hands of the Wampanoag Indians under their chief, Philip, when one-third of its towns were wiped out.

Another Jesuit priest, Jacques Marquette, discovered the Mississippi River in 1673 with Louis Joliet.

For Further Reading

Gary Nash, *Red, White, and Black: The Peoples of Early America* (1974), deals with the three peoples who are the subject of this chapter. A. M. Josephy, Jr., *The Indian Heritage of America* (1968), and Wilcomb E. Washburn, *The Indian in America* (1975), treat the variety of Native American cultures. A. F. C. Wallace, *The Death and Rebirth of the Seneca* (1970), examines one of the most important tribes of the northern colonies. Wilcomb E. Washburn, *The Governor and the Rebel* (1957), and Douglas Leach, *Flintlock and Tomahawk* (1958), discuss white–Indian conflict in two theaters.

The classic treatment of the French in North America in the literary historical school of the nineteenth century is Francis Parkman, *Count Frontenac and New France* (1877). The first volume of G. M. Wrong, *The Rise and Fall of New France* (1928), and S. E. Morison, *Samuel B. Champlain: Father of New France* (1972), update Parkman without necessarily improving on him.

See E. S. Morgan, *American Slavery, American Freedom* (1966), for the various institutions of servitude in colonial America. Two different viewpoints on how black slavery developed in the colonies are offered by W. D. Jordan, *White over Black* (1968), and D. B. Davis, *The Problem of Slavery in Western Culture* (1966). Much criticized but still provocative is S. B. Elkins, *Slavery: A Problem in American Institutional and Intellectual Life* (1959).

A North East View of th

N° 1 Fort Hill, 2 South Battery, 3 Long wharf, 4 New South Meeting h

6

War, Peace, and Prosperity
The Colonies in the Eighteenth Century

In 1706, a male child was born into the household of a Boston tallowmaker, a craftsman who manufactured candles and soap from the fat of cattle and sheep. There would not have been much excitement about the arrival of Benjamin Franklin; he was the tenth child in the family.

Very large families were not rare in colonial America. In a place where labor was scarce, extra hands were needed on farm and in shop alike; in an age when cash expenditures on necessities were few, children were economic assets. Children grew up working and thus contributing far more to the economy of a household than they took from it.

Benjamin Franklin went to work full time in his father's business at the age of ten. Two years later he was bound as an apprentice to one of his brothers, a printer. Ben did not get along with James Franklin, who appears to have been no fraternal taskmaster. But he took exuberantly to printing, a trade that, in the eighteenth century, involved writing as much as setting type.

Franklin's pen was nimble, and he easily imitated the elegant style of the fashionable English essayists Joseph Addison and Richard Steele. No one faulted him for lack of originality. No one said, as Noah Webster and Ralph Waldo Emerson were to say a century later, that Americans should create a distinctively American literature from a distinctively American language. Bostonians (and New Yorkers and Baltimoreans

A northeast view of Boston, 1723–1728.

and Charlestonians) were content to be colonials; they were *proud* to be subjects of Queen Anne and the overseas population of the country that they believed to be the noblest on earth. They gladly took their culture as well as their manufactured goods—like the printing press, movable type, paper, and ink with which Ben Franklin set up shop in Philadelphia as a young man—from the mother country.

During Franklin's long life (he lived until 1790), the colonies outgrew their dependent status and mentality. Benjamin Franklin was never behind a trend. When the American population exploded, Franklin capitalized on it, investing in printers (his own apprentices) in several growing cities. Was the population growing heterogeneous, less English? Franklin knew what it meant; he lived in the colony with the most mixed population. Did the colonies become a force in international affairs because of their participation in the wars of the eighteenth century? Franklin was a major supporter of an aggressive foreign policy and several times went to Europe as a diplomat, lobbying on behalf of American interests.

Small wonder that he was the best-known American of his time—respected at home, lionized in Europe. He founded libraries, learned

societies, the first American hospital, and the first trained fire department. He was an internationally famous scientist, and a writer of charm and wit. There was scarcely a major event or trend in the eighteenth century in which Franklin's participation did not figure. He devised a plan to unite the colonies as early as 1754. He signed the Declaration of Independence and the Constitution. Slavery, which during his lifetime quietly evolved from a minor part of colonial life into a problem of grave concern, did not escape Franklin's notice. The last public act of his life was to petition the government to abolish the institution.

The Lineaments of Growth

Between 1700 and 1776, the population of the colonies increased eightfold, from about 350,000 people to about 2.8 million. Natural increase contributed to this astonishing growth. World population as a whole made a giant leap during the eighteenth century, and both family size and life expectancy at birth (thirty-four years for males, thirty-six for females) were greater in North America than on any other continent. But, for the most part, the colonies grew so dramatically because of a flood of newcomers. Immigrants from England, other parts of Europe, and West Africa crossed the Atlantic in numbers never dreamed of before 1700.

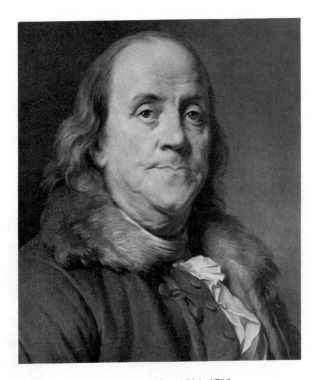

Benjamin Franklin, 1706–1790.

ESTIMATED POPULATIONS OF FIVE LEADING PORT CITIES: 1630–1775

Year	New York	Philadelphia	Boston	Charleston	Newport
1630	300	—	—	—	—
1640	400	—	1,200	—	96
1650	1,000	—	2,000	—	300
1660	2,400	—	3,000	—	700
1680	3,200	—	4,500	700	2,500
1690	3,900	4,000	7,000	1,100	2,600
1700	5,000	5,000	6,700	2,000	2,600
1710	5,700	6,500	9,000	3,000	2,800
1720	7,000	10,000	12,000	3,500	3,800
1730	8,622[a]	11,500	13,000	4,500	4,640[a]
1743	11,000	13,000	16,382[a]	6,800	6,200
1760	18,000	23,750	15,631[a]	8,000	7,500
1775	25,000	40,000	16,000	12,000	11,000

[a]Actual census.

POOR RICHARD'S ALMANACK

Benjamin Franklin first won fame among Americans
as the publisher of *Poor Richard's Almanack*, which he
began to publish annually in 1732. In addition to providing the useful information that is the staple of
almanacs—phases of the moon, dates of holidays, and
so on—Franklin charmed readers with his rendition
of homilies praising thrift, frugal living, hard work,
and other "bourgeois virtues." Among them:

Leisure is the time for doing something useful.
A ploughman on his legs is higher than a gentle-
man on his horse.
Handle your tools without mittens.
Time is money.

Poor Richard, **1733.**

A N

Almanack

For the Year of Chrift

1733,

Being the Firft after LEAP YEAR.

And makes fince the Creation	Years
By the Account of the Eaftern *Greeks*	7241
By the Latin Church, when ☉ ent. ♈	6932
By the Computation of *W.W.*	5742
By the *Roman* Chronology	5682
By the *Jewifh* Rabbies.	5494

Wherein is contained

The Lunations, Eclipfes, Judgment of
the Weather, Spring Tides, Planets Motions &
mutual Afpects, Sun and Moon's Rifing and Setting, Length of Days, Time of High Water,
Fairs, Courts, and obfervable Days.

Fitted to the Latitude of Forty Degrees,
and a Meridian of Five Hours Weft from *London,*
but may without fenfible Error, ferve all the adjacent Places, even from *Newfoundland* to *South-
Carolina*

By *RICHARD SAUNDERS,* Philom.

PHILADELPHIA:
Printed and fold by *B. FRANKLIN,* at the New
Printing-Office near the Market

Newcomers

The American population became less English in the
eighteenth century. Germans and German-speaking
Swiss swelled the size of the small central European
communities that William Penn had encouraged to
settle in Lancaster and York counties, Pennsylvania.
So numerous were the Germans by 1776 that some
Pennsylvanians suggested that German, not English,
should be the official language of the newly independent state.

Many of the German immigrants, members of the
plain-living Moravian, Amish, and Mennonite sects,
were pacifists like the Quakers. Having little interest in
active politics, they passively supported their benefactors and helped the Quakers maintain control of
Pennsylvania long after they had ceased to be the majority people. This meant that the Germans were in
opposition to another large group of newcomers, the
Scotch-Irish who emigrated to America in even larger
numbers than the Germans.

The Scotch-Irish were Scots whom William III had
settled in northern Ireland because they were Protestants and thus his allies against the Catholic Irish.
After William's death in 1702, the Scotch-Irish lost
favor in Westminster and suffered from steep increases
in rent and from a number of parliamentary acts that
undercut the weaving industry, on which many depended for their livelihood. About four thousand
Scotch-Irish a year gave up on the Emerald Isle and
emigrated to the colonies.

They were a combative people, and they did not
mellow in American air. James Logan, the agent of the
Penn family in Philadelphia, wrote to England in con-
sternation: "I must own, from my experience in the
land office, that the settlement of five families from
Ireland gives me more trouble than fifty of any other
people."

The Scotch-Irish wanted their own land, and to acquire it they moved to the backcountry in Virginia and
the Carolinas as well as in Pennsylvania. There they
came up against the Indians, with whom Quakers like
Logan tried to have amicable relations. On this issue,
these obstreperous frontiersmen helped drive the
Quakers from public life. Along with political allies
like Franklin, the Scotch-Irish lobbied relentlessly for
an aggressive, expansionist Indian policy—pushing the
tribes back, and crippling their power and that of their
French allies.

So great was the pressure on the Philadelphia Quakers that they were presented with a cruel dilemma. If
they clung to the principle that government should be
responsive to popular wishes, they would be party to
war, and that went against their pacifist ideals. If they
insisted on peace and fair dealings with the Indians,

A view of a Moravian settlement in Bethlehem, Pennsylvania, 1757. Pennsylvania was the home to a number of religious sects in the eighteenth century.

they would be denying the demands of the majority of Pennsylvanians.

The Quakers escaped between the horns of the dilemma. When England went to war with France in 1757, the Quakers retired wholesale from political life. Thus they preserved their personal scruples about war, while the backcountry settlers and the Crown got the war they wanted. While always numerous in Pennsylvania, Quakers remained a politically quiet people until the middle of the twentieth century.

The Growth of Slavery

By midcentury, some Quakers, such as John Woolman of New Jersey and Anthony Benezet of Pennsylvania, questioned the morality of holding blacks in slavery, but few listened. The institution was legal in every colony, and was supported by the assumption of most Americans that lifetime bondage was a perfectly legitimate condition of life.

Nevertheless, slavery steadily declined in the northern colonies during the eighteenth century, while it grew in importance below the Mason–Dixon line, the Pennsylvania–Maryland boundary surveyed by Charles Mason and Jeremiah Dixon between 1763 and 1767. For example, the number of blacks in Virginia, most of whom were slaves, grew from about four thousand in 1700 to twelve thousand in 1708, twenty thousand in 1715, forty-two thousand in 1743, and more than two hundred thousand at the time of the American Revolution.

Much of this increase, paralleled in other southern colonies and exceeded in South Carolina, was due to increased importation of captive West Africans. Between 1715 and 1750, about twenty-five hundred slaves were brought to the mainland each year. During the 1760s, the annual average tripled to seventy-five hundred, with South Carolinians alone buying twenty-eight hundred people. By the end of the colonial period, there were about five blacks to every seven whites in South Carolina. In some counties in South Carolina and in Virginia, black inhabitants outnumbered white inhabitants.

While natural increase among slaves lagged behind that of whites, a more equal balance of the sexes and a higher reproduction rate appear to have prevailed on the mainland than on the sugar islands of the West Indies. So high were the profits in sugar that West Indian planters preferred to import male slaves—field hands—almost to the exclusion of women. So killing was the pace of labor in Jamaica and Barbados that the few black women who did live there did not reproduce normally. Those who did give birth often practiced infanticide rather than raise children who would have to live the same dismal lives as their parents.

Growing Confidence

The productivity of both the slave and the free laboring classes and soaring population in every colony resulted in a more diversified economy and a more dynamic society. America remained a primarily agricultural country throughout the eighteenth century, a producer of raw materials and an importer of England's manufactured goods. But the demand for home-produced commodities, such as the candles that Benjamin Franklin's father made, and Franklin's own newspapers and almanacs, created a new class of craftsmen and merchants in America who made their homes in fast-growing cities.

The urban population represented only 2.5 percent of all colonists in 1710, 4.3 percent in 1740. By midcentury, Boston, Newport, New York, Baltimore, and Charleston were bustling centers of trade. Philadelphia, the greatest colonial city, was a metropolis of twenty-eight thousand by 1770, larger than any city in England except London. Indeed, the total colonial population of 2.8 million in 1776 was greater than the populations of several European countries.

By 1776, many Americans were ready to risk everything to win political independence. But the Revolution was not simply the offspring of tremendous growth. Between 1689 and 1763, the colonists participated in a series of wars that won for them a luxurious security known to no Europeans. And between 1713 and 1739, during one long period of peace, they got used to having their own way.

Neither development had its origins in the colonies. The peace was the accomplishment of a prime minister who was the eighteenth-century stereotype of an Englishman. The wars began a generation earlier, when a Dutchman with an ax to grind crossed the North Sea to wear the English crown.

English or British?

It is proper to speak of the *English* colonies if referring to the years before 1707, and the *British* colonies thereafter. Before the Act of Union in that year, England and Scotland shared the same monarch but were governed by separate parliaments and different codes of law. It was England that founded, financed, and claimed the North American colonies. After 1707, however, the colonies were part of a British empire ruled by a British queen and Parliament. Great Britain is the proper eighteenth-century name for those two large and many small islands off the northern coast of France. The people of the British Isles include not only the English and the Scots, but also the Welsh and the Irish. Indeed, some people from Cornwall in the southwest and Yorkshire in the north of England insist that they are not really English.

World Wars, Colonial War

The Dutchman was William of Orange, the no-nonsense, sour-humored ruler of Holland who became the king of England in 1689 by virtue of his marriage to Mary, the older daughter of James II, and James's flight to France in 1688. William was interested in English domestic politics only to the extent that they affected his wars against the French King, Louis XIV. Whereas James II had accommodated Louis in Europe and avoided conflict with New France in North America, William's whole life had been dedicated to combating the Sun King's campaign to win France's "natural boundaries," which brought French power deep into the Netherlands.

William was an excellent soldier. He had taken Louis to the mat with only the slender resources of Holland and a few German states. He could not wait to turn the greater wealth and power of England on the hated foe. He did not have to wait. In 1689, when the petty prince who ruled part of the Rhine River Valley died without an heir, Louis XIV claimed the right of France to take over. William said no.

Eighteenth-Century Warfare

Few colonists cared who ruled in the Rhineland or who became archbishop of Cologne (another matter over which Louis and William squabbled). Unconsciously, but with a certain elegance, they proclaimed their disdain for European affairs by ignoring the European name for the conflict, the War of the League of Augsburg, and calling it instead King William's War, as though it had been foisted on them.

The fighting that took place in North America represented a minor theater of the first of the world wars. William and his allies and his successors on the English throne fought France not only in Europe and North America, but also in the Caribbean, in South America, in India, and wherever ships flying belligerent flags met on the high seas.

In other ways, warfare in the eighteenth century was quite different from armed conflict in the twentieth century. War was considered an extension of diplomacy, the concern of rulers rather than of ordinary people. Wars were fought to win or to defend territory from rivals, or to avenge what one ruler regarded as the insult of another. There was no clash of ideologies, no claim that one social, economic, or political system was engaged in a life-or-death struggle with another. Armies were made up of professional soldiers, rough men who looked on fighting as a means of making a living, and not as a means of defending or furthering an abstract ideal. If they were attached to anything, it was the person of their commander.

What did ordinary farmers or merchants have to do with such business? As little as they could help. At best, war meant heavier taxation. At worst, people were unlucky enough to dwell where armies fought or marched. Then they suffered, no matter whose flag the fighting men were waving.

Otherwise, people went on as in peacetime. Because rulers neither expected nor won popular support for their wars, it was not a matter of treason in the modern sense of the word when, as in the world wars of 1689 to 1763, many Americans simply sat out the conflict or even continued trading with the French enemy.

King William's War, 1689–97

The French, Algonkians, and Hurons struck the first blow in the winter of 1689/90 with a series of raids on frontier settlements in New York, New Hampshire, and Maine (then part of Massachusetts). These were not great battles on the European pattern. Although often led by French officers, they were Indian-style attacks in which a few dozen braves hit without warning at isolated farms in the forest, killing or capturing the settlers and burning houses and fields. The French called it *la petite guerre,* or "little war," and viewed the raids as harassment and a warning.

It worked. Each successful *petite guerre* moved the unmarked boundary between New France and New England deeper into lands that the British colonies considered their own. Just as aggravating to commercial New England were attacks on New England merchant and fishing vessels by French ships out of Port Royal in Acadia (Nova Scotia).

On the sea, however, the more traditional fighting methods of the English were successful. An expedition from Massachusetts captured the French fortress of Port Royal in 1690. But it was returned to France at the Peace of Ryswick in 1697. The English armies had not fared well in the European theater, and the peacemakers used Port Royal as a way to limit concessions there. For New Englanders, the terms of the peace were a reminder that their interests were definitely subordinate to those of England in Europe, as interpreted, in this case, by a Dutchman.

Queen Anne's War, 1702–13

The French took North America more seriously. While King William's War was still in progress, they began to build a chain of forts in the backcountry. During the brief peace of 1699 to 1702, the Gulf of Mexico and Illinois country settlements were sketched in. Then, in

1700, the last Hapsburg king of Spain died without an heir, and Louis XIV moved to place his nephew on the throne of the declining but still powerful country. Austria, where Hapsburgs still ruled, joined England in an attempt to prevent the grab.

Again, the colonists named the war after the British sovereign, who was now Queen Anne, but this time the European maneuverings meant a great deal to the colonists in the far North and South. The same dynasty ruling in both Spain and France meant the union of neighbors who previously had sniped at each other. This time around, southerners, who had taken no part in King William's War, were in the thick of things.

THE COLONIAL WARS

	American Name	European Name
1689–97	King William's War	War of the League of Augsburg
1702–13	Queen Anne's War	War of the Spanish Succession
1740–48	King George's War	War of the Austrian Succession
1756–63	French and Indian War	Seven Years' War

Like the New Englanders, South Carolinians competed with the Spanish and French in the fur and hide trade. Beaver pelts were not so lush in the warm climate of South Carolina, but there were deer and bison, an important source of leather. The South Carolinian network of Indian contacts extended beyond the Mississippi River, well into territory that the French thought of as their own. However, the Carolinians had some formidable Indian enemies in what is now Georgia, Alabama, and Mississippi. Slave-catching expeditions among the Creek and Cherokee peoples kept the southwestern frontier in a state of chronic *petite guerre*.

In the North, the French and their Indian allies were more audacious than before, wiping out the substantial town of Deerfield, Massachusetts, in 1704. Once again, however, the New Englanders captured Port Royal. This time, at the Peace of Utrecht in 1713, the British kept it and the whole of Acadia. The war had gone well for England in Europe (the English took Gibraltar from

Spain at this time), and the French were content to retire to Cape Breton Island and build a new and stronger Atlantic fortress, Louisbourg.

In taking over the new province, which they renamed Nova Scotia (Latin for "New Scotland"), the English were responsible for one of the first tragic human deportations in American history. Just as in later years the United States government would force whole Indian tribes to abandon their ancestral lands and move elsewhere, the English expelled thousands of French from Acadia. The English feared that the Acadians, living so close to New France, would be a source of treachery. Their migration to Louisiana inspired Henry Wadsworth Longfellow's poem *Evangeline*, which was written 150 years later. The descendants of the Acadians are still a distinct ethnic and cultural group, the Cajuns of present-day Louisiana and eastern Texas.

In the South, the treaty resolved few difficulties for the simple reason that the European nations did not

A French and Indian raid wiped out the town of Deerfield, Massachusetts, in 1704.

hold the ultimate power there. The Creeks and Cherokees were numerous, confident, and proud peoples, less dependent on the Europeans than were the Algonkians and Hurons of the North. Curiously, they established their power by adopting the white settlers' ways. They took easily to European agricultural techniques and even to the slaveholding practices of the Spanish Floridians and the southern English colonists. Ultimately, they devised an alphabet and a system of writing for their languages, making communication easier. They would not finally fall before the whites' advance for two hundred years after Queen Anne's War.

In the Middle Colonies, there were no difficulties to be resolved by the negotiators at Utrecht. Virginia, Maryland, Delaware, New Jersey, and Pennsylvania had not taken part in Queen Anne's War. New York actually issued a formal declaration of neutrality and continued to trade with French Canada during the years in which the New England colonists were the victims of bloody raids.

Sugar plantations like this one in the French West Indies (1667) produced sugar and molasses for export to New England.

The Long Peace, 1713–39

For the next twenty-six years, North America was peaceful. During this period, Georgia was founded and the population steadily grew. These were generally prosperous years for the colonies, too. While tobacco never attained the bonanza prices of the mid-1600s, the weed returned a handsome enough profit to large planters. Indigo, rice, naval stores, and hides and furs were also lucrative, as were the various overseas trade routes plied by the merchant ships of New England and the Middle Colonies. Small wonder that, in later troubled times, colonists would look back on the long peace as a kind of golden age.

Salutary Neglect

The vision of a golden age was wrapped up in a parcel with the colonial policy of the first British prime minister, Robert Walpole. By disposition a lazy and easygoing fellow who liked his daily outsized bottle of port wine and idle gossip with other comfortable gentlemen, Walpole deduced that the best way to govern a country or an empire during good times was to govern as little as possible. Action could only disturb what was working quite well on its own. His policy toward the colonies came to be called "salutary neglect." If the colonists were content, bustling, and prosperous, thus enriching the English merchant class as it was their duty to do, it was then salutary—healthful—not to disturb such a pretty situation.

For the most part, Walpole winked at colonial violations of the Navigation Acts. He had to take some notice when representatives of special interest groups demanded that he enforce them, but Walpole's strategy was to pass a law—and immediately forget about it. For example, in 1733, sugar planters from the British West Indies demanded that Parliament tax sugar and molasses imported into the mainland colonies from outside the British Empire, specifically from the French sugar islands. They pointed out that the principles of mercantilism entitled them to a monopoly of the huge molasses market in New England, just as the tobacco growers of Virginia and Maryland had a monopoly in the sale of that product. (Rum, distilled from blackstrap, was the major liquor in the colonies and also was valuable in the slave trade.)

Such a law was bound to rile the New Englanders. They were accustomed to filling the holds of their ships with the cheaper French molasses. Walpole solved the problem by approving the Molasses Act of 1733 and promptly forgetting about it. The West Indian planters were placated, if not particularly helped; New England shipmasters were as content to buy French molasses illegally as legally. The bootleg product was either smuggled into Boston and other ports or provided with false invoices stating that the cargo came from Jamaica or Barbados. The customs officers in the colonies were not fooled. But they could be bribed, and if a penny or so on each barrel made them happy, too, that was the idea of salutary neglect.

Another law that was ignored in the interests of prosperity was passed in 1750 at the behest of English ironmakers, who wanted a monopoly of the colonial market in iron goods. The act forbade colonists to engage in most forms of iron manufacture. But not only did colonial forges operate with impunity, several colonial governments actually subsidized an infant iron industry within their borders. Salutary neglect was a wonderful way to run an empire—as long as there was no war and times were good.

Political Autonomy

An unintended consequence of Walpole's easy-going colonial policy was the steady erosion of the mother country's political control over her American daughters. In part, the seizure of the powers of governors by colonial assemblies merely reflected what was going on in England at the same time. During the eighteenth century, Parliament, particularly the elected House of Commons, pretty much completed the takeover of governmental functions formerly claimed by the kings and queens. In the colonies, elected assemblies took powers from the governors, who were appointed by either the monarchs or the proprietors.

The key to this important shift in the structure of government was the English political tradition that the people, through their elected representatives, had to agree to any taxation. In England, Parliament held the power of the purse; all money bills had to be approved by the House of Commons. In the colonies, the elected assemblies—whether called the House of Burgesses or the House of Delegates or whatever—assumed this prerogative.

Theoretically, the governor of a colony could veto any budget bill that he did not like. But to do so was a risky business. An assembly that was determined to have its way could retaliate by denying the governor the funds that he needed in order to operate his office and even his personal household, "starve him into compliance" as the royal governor of New York phrased it in 1741.

It was a formidable weapon. Few men who served as governors in America were fabulously wealthy before they took the job. Englishmen who were rich enough to maintain themselves opulently in London did not go to the colonies. For the most part, royal and proprietary governors were men on the make. And to make money in the colonies, they had to get along with powerful colonials, the sort of men who were elected to seats in the assemblies.

Of course, it was possible to yield too much in the interests of amity and to earn the displeasure of Crown or proprietor. But during the era of salutary neglect, it came easily to cooperate. As long as the quitrents flowed back to England, a governor was doing his job.

Religious Developments

Even the religious history of the colonies seems to have enjoyed the benefits of neglect. While toleration had been the rule in the colonies after the collapse of Puritan power in New England in the 1690s, religious regimentation of almost every sort disappeared during the Walpole era.

Except in Rhode Island and Pennsylvania, everyone was required to contribute to the support of the legally established church. In some colonies, members of other denominations were not allowed to vote, serve on juries, or exercise other civil rights. For example, Catholics were heavily penalized in Maryland.

But nowhere did the authorities seriously interfere with worship. In this atmosphere, one of the peculiarities of American life to this day took root—the bewildering multiplicity of denominations. Already by midcentury, it was not uncommon for modest villages to support two or three meeting houses within psalm-singing distance of one another. During the 1740s, religions divided along even finer lines, and that other distinctively American institution, the revival, was born.

The Great Awakening

The first American revival, the Great Awakening, broke out almost simultaneously in several colonies. The greatest figure in the movement and one of the intellectual giants of the age was the Reverend Jonathan Edwards of Northampton, Massachusetts. In 1734, Edwards began to preach sermons in the Connecticut River Valley that emphasized the sinfulness of humanity, the torment everyone deserved to suffer in hell, and the doctrine of salvation only through the grace of God. "The God who holds you over the pit of hell," Edwards preached in his most famous sermon, "much as one holds a spider or some loathesome insect over the fire, abhors you, and is dreadfully provoked."

This was all good Calvinist doctrine. However, whereas the Puritans of the 1600s insisted that members of the church closely scrutinize the claims of every man and woman who said they had been saved, Edwards was inclined to admit everyone who displayed the physical, highly emotional signs of being washed in the blood of the Lamb.

Revivals were aimed at stimulating the trauma of salvation. People broke down weeping, fainting, frothing at the mouth, shrieking Hallelujah!, and rolling about the floors. Many had to be restrained lest they injure themselves. Edwards himself was always careful not to inspire "false conversions" through theatrical arm waving and dancing about. It was said that he stared at the bellpull at the entrance to a church rather than incite ungodly hysteria.

SINNERS

In the Hands of an

Angry GOD.

A SERMON

Preached at *Enfield*, *July* 8th 1 7 4 1.

At a Time of great Awakenings ; and attended with remarkable Impreſſions on many of the Hearers.

By *Jonathan Edwards*, A.M.

Paſtor of the Church of CHRIST in *Northampton*.

Amos ix. 2, 3. *Though they dig into Hell, thence ſhall mine Hand take them ; though they climb up to Heaven, thence will I bring them down. And though they hide themſelves in the Top of Carmel, I will ſearch and take them out thence ; and though they be hid from my Sight in the Bottom of the Sea, thence I will command the Serpent, and he ſhall bite them.*

B O S T O N : Printed and Sold by S. KNEELAND and T. GREEN. in Queen-Street over againſt the Priſon. 1 7 4 1.

The sermons of Jonathan Edwards helped fuel the Great Awakening.

Others were less scrupulous. Whether for the money involved or simply to gratify their own psychological needs, charlatan preachers tore their clothes, rolled their eyes, pranced and danced about the pulpit or platform, and whooped and hollered. They collected a whole psychological bag of tricks to arouse their audiences to a state of high excitement.

Some historians have suggested that revivalism appealed to the poorest, least privileged people in a society. The high emotion of the revival meeting offered a brief release from the difficulties of life. The assurance of happiness in the hereafter compensated for deprivation in the here and now. The emphasis of the equality of all men and women before God made society's sexual and racial discriminations more bearable.

However that might be, equality was the message of the most successful of the Awakening's ministers, English-born George Whitefield. Ranging up and down the colonies, Whitefield often preached for forty hours a week. During one seventy-eight-day period, he delivered more than a hundred hellfire sermons exhorting people to accept God.

The teachings of the Great Awakening about salvation were not greatly different from those of Anne Hutchinson a hundred years earlier. But while the civil authority was ready and able to clamp down on her, the freer atmosphere of the eighteenth century permitted the revivalist message to burn over the colonies "like a prairie fire."

Paradoxically, given the anti-intellectual bias of revivalism, the Great Awakening led to the foundation of a number of "New Light" colleges. On the grounds that the established institutions of learning, such as Harvard and Yale, were dominated by "dry husks," the College of New Jersey (Princeton) was founded in 1746—Jonathan Edwards was its first president—and Dartmouth in New Hampshire in 1769. Other new colleges, such as Brown in Rhode Island, King's College (Columbia) in New York, and Queen's College (Rutgers) in New Jersey, were founded by the old denominations to defend against the new preaching. Of all the colonial-era colleges and universities, only the University of Pennsylvania, chartered at Benjamin Franklin's urging in 1751, was without a religious affiliation.

The Age of Enlightenment

Franklin was not a church member. Indeed, while Americans of modest means were turning to straightforward, emotional religion, Franklin and much of the educated upper class were adopting the world view of the European Enlightenment, the belief that human reason by itself, without any revelation from the heavens, could unlock the secrets of the universe and guide the improvement, even the perfection, of humanity and society.

The origins of eighteenth-century rationalism lay in the discoveries of the English scientist Sir Isaac Newton, especially those published in his *Principia Mathematica* (1687) and *Opticks* (1704). In these highly technical and difficult books, Newton showed that forces as mysterious as those that determine the paths of the planets and the properties of light and color work according to laws that can be reduced to mathematical equations.

Although Newton was a physicist and mathematician (and his personal religion was highly pious), the impact of his discoveries was felt in practically every field of human knowledge and art—other pure sciences, economics, music, politics, and religion.

The order and symmetry that Newton found in the universe were translated in architecture into strict laws of proportion and in literature into inflexible "classical" rules of style and design. Baroque music explored the variations that could be played on simple combinations of notes. Philosophers likened the universe to a clock, intricate but understandable when dismantled and its parts are examined rationally. God, according to deism, as the rationalists called their religious belief, did not intervene in the world of nature, but, like a clockmaker he had merely set the natural world in motion according to laws that human beings could discover and understand. The educated members of the last generation of colonial Americans were to some degree partisans of this rationalism.

ROLL CALL

Before the middle of the eighteenth century, students at Harvard and Yale colleges were listed on the class roll not in alphabetical or grade-level order, but according to their social standing. That is, the student whose father was highest in society (not necessarily richest) was listed first, and the young man who came from the humblest family was listed last. Others were listed in between with close attention to the fine points of status. A student was reminded daily of just where he stood.

Harvard abandoned this system in 1769. The youth who precipitated the change had demanded that he be moved up a notch because his father had been a justice of the peace for a month longer than the father of the student listed above him. When social status came to depend on such refinements, it became a useless and cumbersome principle.

Harvard College, 1726.

War Once More

The long peace ended in 1739, when Great Britain went to war against Spain over the right to trade in the Caribbean. The first of several conflicts involving the colonies much more deeply than King William's and Queen Anne's wars, it was called the War of Jenkins' Ear because Parliament was said to have been enraged when a shipmaster named Robert Jenkins arrived in London with his ear in a box. It had, Jenkins said, showing the souvenir to anyone who asked, been savagely separated from his head by Spanish customs officials.

The war involved Georgians and South Carolinians from the beginning. Coming increasingly into contact with the Spanish as their numbers grew, they made up the majority of the men who took part in an unsuccessful expedition against Florida in 1740 and, the next year, a disastrous attack on the Colombian port of Cartagena. Of the thirty-five hundred who set out with hopes of victory, only six hundred escaped the cutlasses of the Spanish, the incompetence of the British commanders, and the smallpox and tropical diseases of the Caribbean borderlands. One survivor was Lawrence Washington, the brother of nine-year-old George Washington. Not as bitter about the English commanders as were many of his fellows, Lawrence named his estate, Mount Vernon, after the defeated British admiral.

King George's War, 1740–48

In Europe, the world war of which this battle was an episode was called the War of the Austrian Succession. For the colonists once again, European dynastic intrigues meant little, even when the prize was the crown of the great Austrian Empire. They called the conflict King George's War.

Petite guerre flickered once more on the frontiers of New England, this time extending down into New York, but there was no repetition of the Deerfield disaster. Much better prepared than previously, a force of four thousand men, mostly from Massachusetts, besieged the great French fortress at Louisbourg. On June 17, 1745, the French commander surrendered.

This was a glorious victory. Louisbourg was considered impregnable, "the Gibraltar of North America." As the base from which French privateers operated, the fortress was particularly aggravating to New England merchants and fishermen. But the American celebration was short lived. Under the terms of the Treaty of Aix-la-Chapelle, Louisbourg was returned to the French. The British had lost Madras in India to a

French troops surrender to New England forces at Louisbourg, June 17, 1745.

French-led army and traded Louisbourg for its return.

Parliament reimbursed Massachusetts for the expense of the campaign, but this did not make up for the five hundred men who had been lost in the siege or for the fact that the French raiders were restored to their sanctuary. The protest was mild. The colonists were loyal British subjects. But the nullification of the greatest military victory that the Americans had ever won rankled in many breasts.

The Struggle for a Continent

The world war that broke out in 1756 was somewhat different from those that preceded it. There was a diplomatic revolution in Europe, with Prussia, previously England's ally, joining forces with France. England then formed an alliance with its old enemy, Austria. To the colonists, it made no difference who killed whom in the Old World, who got money from Great Britain. In North America, it was still England and its colonies versus France and its Indian allies. For the first time, the Middle Colonies participated in the struggle. (It was during this war that the Quakers turned over the government of Pennsylvania to the prowar party.) And once again, the colonists had their own name for it. What became known as the Seven Years' War in Europe was called the French and Indian War in America. This time, fortresses would not be exchanged for lost territory. This time, both France and England regarded the North American theater as the key to the struggle; from England's perspective what happened in the colonies was more important than what happened in Europe.

Despite the French success in *la petite guerre*, the French situation in North America was perilously weak. There were only about fifty thousand whites in all of French claimed territory, compared with 1.2 million in the thirteen English colonies plus Nova Scotia. The French still had the goodwill of the majority of Indians in the region, but even this advantage was partially nullified by the efficiency and fierceness of the pro-British Iroquois.

For the first time since the long series of wars began, the largest English colony, Virginia, took a serious interest in fighting. The Virginians, who were beginning to feel the effects of crowding east of the Appalachians, began looking beyond the Blue Ridge and north of the Ohio River to lands that were dominated by Algonkian Indians. This country was particularly attractive to the wealthy tobacco planters who dominated the Old Dominion because a combination of exhausted soil and a glut in the international tobacco market was undercutting their income. They saw speculation in Ohio Valley lands as the best way to restore their fortunes.

The French did not intend to settle the Ohio country, but it was of vital importance—life itself—to their Indian allies. As early as 1753, in order to placate them, the French began to lay out a string of forts in what is now western Pennsylvania.

Robert Dinwiddie, the governor of Virginia, responded by sending twenty-two-year-old George Washington to inform the French that they were trespassing on Virginian soil and to order them out. Accompanied by only 150 men, Washington, more realistically, was also instructed to construct a fort where the Allegheny and Monongahela rivers join to form the Ohio (the site of present-day Pittsburgh).

Washington never got that far. He was handily defeated by the French in an almost bloodless battle, and they seized the strategic site, calling the stockade they built Fort Duquesne.

Washington was released, and he returned to Virginia to accept a commission under the command of General Edward Braddock. From the first, things went poorly. Braddock, an arrogant, stubborn, and unimaginative soldier, was roundly defeated in the Pennsylvania forests. In retrospect, his reputation is even lower than it was at the time because, during the campaign, he engaged in germ warfare, seeing to it that blankets that had been used by smallpox sufferers fell into the hands of his Indian enemies.

The rout of Braddock's forces left the American frontier vulnerable to raiding fiercer than any since the destruction of Deerfield. The French were also winning in Europe and India. For the British, it was a dismal hour.

George Washington in a uniform of the French and Indian War, 1772.

The Glorious Victory

Then appeared two men who changed the course of history. William Pitt became prime minister of Britain in 1758, and he selected the young General James Wolfe to join Sir Jeffrey Amherst's army in North America. Pitt turned things around by leaving the fighting in Europe to Austria's armies while concentrating Britain's power overseas. Wolfe engineered one of the most astonishing campaigns in military history.

A nervous, frail-looking young man, so intense that his colleagues thought him insane, Wolfe looked at French Canada as a woodsman looked at a tree. Quebec City was the root structure that supported the whole. The St. Lawrence and Ohio-Mississippi rivers were trunks and branches. It was all very well to snip and hack at the leaves, as the previous captures of Port Royal and Louisbourg had done. The secret to a total victory over French Canada was to strike at the source of its life.

The theory was easier than its practical application. Quebec stood atop a steep rocky cliff. After leading several futile frontal attacks on this natural fortress (which lulled the French commander, Louis de Montcalm, into overconfidence), Wolfe quietly led four thousand troops up a steep, narrow trail under cover of night. When the sun rose over the Plains of Abraham, a broad prairie on the undefended landward side of Quebec, Montcalm saw a scarlet-coated army in full battle formation.

It was a risky as well as a daring gambit. The British had no avenue of retreat—a violation of military theory. Had the battle not ended in a total British victory (and few military victories were total in the eighteenth century), Wolfe's whole army would have been destroyed. But Montcalm was so unnerved by Wolfe's maneuver that, despite his superior position and artillery, he joined in battle with little preparation. After a single close-range exchange of musket fire, Montcalm lost his life and with it the French empire in America. Wolfe, unhappily, did not live to savor his triumph. He too died on the battlefield, only thirty-two years of age.

The war in Europe dragged on until 1763, but, as far as the colonists were concerned, it was over at Quebec. In the Peace of Paris, William Pitt redrew the map of North America. Great Britain took Florida from Spain as well as Canada from France. France, in order to compensate Spain for the loss of Florida, handed over Louisiana (the central third of what is now the United States).

England also drove France from India during the war. Indeed, 1763 marked the apex of the first British Empire. Britain had elected to find its future outside the European continent and had succeeded on every front. Unseen in the visions of a happy future was the fact

WILLIAM BYRD (1674–1744)

William Byrd of Westover was born in Virginia in 1674. He had the good luck to come into his maturity just as the plantation aristocracy was entering its golden age. Indeed, the historian Louis B. Wright called Byrd "the Great American Gentleman" because his life epitomized the elegance and culture of his class. In his famous portrait, Byrd looks more like a duke than a rude colonial.

Byrd loved the social whirl of London. He was educated in Holland and in England, at the Inns of Court, and, rather remarkable for the time, made several trips back to the mother country as a lobbyist for the Virginia colony. He appears to have been a bit bored by the quiet life of the New World.

Like most planters, Byrd chased after riches. During one long sojourn in London, he tried unsuccessfully to find a wealthy wife. One nobleman rejected his request to marry his daughter by sneering that her annual income was more than the Virginian's entire fortune. There was a big difference between being rich in England and rich in America.

And yet, few English owned the empire in land that Byrd amassed. He inherited 26,321 acres in 1704 and possessed 179,000 acres when he died in 1744. Most of this was wilderness, a speculation on the future, but huge tracts were planted in tobacco and food crops. William Byrd presided over a small kingdom of servants and slaves.

How did such a grandee spend his day? He awakened with the sun but stayed in bed to eat a small breakfast brought by a servant. Much more bookish than most planters, Byrd read for an hour or two in one of the six languages he knew (Hebrew, Greek, Latin, French, Dutch, and English). When he rose, he did some calisthenics ("I danced my dance"). Then his day varied according to circumstances and the season.

Byrd would often have guests to entertain. In a country with few towns and fewer inns, a gentleman like Byrd provided hospitality for travelers. Ordinary people were treated as such; they were provided some sort of roof and simple food for a day or two. Gentlemen and ladies, however, stayed in the plantation house and were feted at banquet-sized meals for as long as they chose. Living in isolation, cultured and sociable people like Byrd craved company. On a plantation that produced more than enough food for master and servant, the expense of wholesale entertainment was hardly noticed.

When there were no guests (and Byrd was not visiting someone else), there was plenty of work to be done. Although a grand gentleman did not labor in the fields, he was no idler. Managing thousands of acres and hundreds of people required nearly constant attention. A plantation was a delicately integrated community that was involved in the cultivating, processing, and storing of food, some manufacturing, blacksmith work, and barrelmaking, for example. Other planters of Byrd's class took greater interest than he did in account books and the mechanics of agriculture. But no one responsible for such an operation could escape endless duties.

Indeed, William Byrd had to oversee many of the household functions that usually kept the planter's wife busy from daybreak to long after dark. His first wife, Lucy Park, was a poor housekeeper. She and Byrd frequently quarreled about her management of the kitchen and larder, and he complained to his diary when he had to supervise the bottling of wine.

Byrd regularly rode and boated to Williamsburg. A gentleman in his position had interests to protect, and he was, at various times, a member of the House of Burgesses and the Governor's Council. In the capital, he roomed at a tavern. During the afternoon and early evening he conducted business, after which he and his cronies regularly got drunk. Every morning he vowed to break out of the cycle but only occasionally kept his word. There were few diversions in the sleepy town but dining, drinking, and chatting.

Byrd was something of a roué, but, oddly, otherwise practiced strict moderation. Virginia's abundance produced such a variety of fine foods that meals were huge, delicious, and long. Through most of his life, however, Byrd shunned gluttony. He practiced a strict regimen designed by a fashionable Scottish physician, George Cheyne, who made a handsome living by prescribing "fad diets" to the wealthy of London and of the resort city of Bath. Byrd adopted two of these regimens: the "milk diet" and the recommendation that a person eat only one dish at a meal. Thus, while his dinner companions were stuffing themselves with as many as seven or eight kinds of meat (the typical fare at a wealthy house), Byrd ate only one. Like a contemporary "Weight Watcher," he kept a written record of every morsel he consumed.

Life in London, in Williamsburg, and at Westover was comfortable, but no Virginian was ever far from the outdoors. In 1728, Byrd helped command an expedition that surveyed the "dividing line" between Virginia and North Carolina, a route which took him into the Great Dismal Swamp. There, without complaint, he slept on the sodden ground and lived off game like any pioneer. He described the expedition and the way of life of the occasional settler the surveyors met. He told of people ailing with malaria and other diseases, drinking themselves to death with cheap, sometimes poisonous rum, and scraping hour by hour for their food. It is difficult to imagine a more striking contrast with his own lot in life, but, while witty in depicting these early-day "poor whites," Byrd was never surprised. The grandest of the great American gentlemen were not insulated from the harsher realities of life.

Virginia planter William Byrd II.

that the Peace of Paris had created a situation in which the American colonies could think of going their own way.

For Further Reading

Francis Parkman, mentioned in the bibliography at the end of Chapter 5, continued his epic work on the French in North America with *A Half Century of Conflict* (1892), and his masterpiece, actually published earlier, *Montcalm and Wolfe* (1884). J. Henretta, *Salutary Neglect* (1972), is the best study of the manner in which Great Britain governed the colonies during the years of peace. An older but still worthwhile study of colonial administration before 1763 is G. L. Beer, *The Old Colonial System* (1912).

The best biography of Benjamin Franklin is C. Van Doren, *Benjamin Franklin* (1938), although students who are interested in the most famous colonial of all should read his own entertaining *Autobiography*, which is available in many editions.

Richard Hofstadter, *America at 1750* (1971), is a useful portrait of colonial society in maturity. One of the few historical works of the present era that can safely be pronounced a classic is D. Boorstin, *The Americans*, of which Volume 1 deals with *The Colonial Experience* (1958).

John Hancock Esq.

This Prospective View of part of the Commons & the encampment of the 29th Regiment & Field Pieces &c as taken from the grove on ye first of October 1768 is most humbly dedicated By his most Faithfull Servant Christian Remick

7

Years of Tumult and Trial

The Colonies Quarrel with Britain, 1763–1770

In the Peace of Paris of 1763, the British won an empire as far flung as Spain's and a good deal more valuable. But the addition of Canada to Britain's list of possessions complicated relations with the most valuable colonies of all, the thirteen "ancient provinces" to the south. Some British statesmen were aware of the problem; they suggested that the treatymakers return Canada to France and, as compensation, take the West Indian sugar islands of Martinique and Guadeloupe.

Canada was not so grand a prize, they argued. Its endless forests were home to Indians who had been hostile to the English for 150 years. Its fifty thousand white inhabitants were French, traditional enemies of the English, and mostly hard-bitten trappers and hard-scrabble farmers scratching out a meager living on soil that was as poor as New England's in a climate that was worse. The sugar islands, on the contrary, were small and manageable, dominated by wealthy planters who cared less for flags than for their fortunes, and produced a cash crop that could be sold anywhere in the world.

There was another troubling consideration. By 1763, the thirteen colonies comprised a substantial country in themselves. Was it not possible that they had remained loyal to Great Britain

British troops conduct a drill amidst strolling citizens on Boston Common, 1768.

LET THE FRENCH STAY

A Swedish naturalist, Peter Kalm, traveled through-out the colonies during the 1740s. He observed that the Americans depended on British armed might to protect their shores and to keep the French Canadians at bay. Kalm concluded with a word of advice: "The English government has therefore sufficient reason to consider the French in North America as the best means of keeping their colonies in due submission."

for so long only because they had lived in fear of the French? Remove that threat from their back-yard, and the Americans would no longer need British naval and military protection. Secure behind the broad Atlantic, they might unite and "shake off the yoke of the English monarchy."

This argument did not carry the day. British taxpayers were weary of war, and if Canada were still held by the French, there would be more fighting in North America sooner or later. Influential colonists such as Governor William Shirley of Massachusetts and reliable Benjamin Franklin, who was in England at the time as an agent for Pennsylvania, spoke rhapsodically of the future of the vast Canadian wilderness. The colonial lobbyists appealed to those lords and gentlemen who thought in terms of land specu-lation, and they found unexpected allies in the sugar planters of the British West Indies. This powerful group feared that raising the British flag over the rich islands of Martinique and Guadeloupe would glut the sugar market within the empire and drive down the price of their product. At the same time, they relished the idea of adding the Canadians to their list of sweet-toothed customers.

But, in the end, Britain kept Canada because few British seriously doubted the basic loyalty of the Americans, even though they could be cranky and troublesome when their interests were at issue. Even their good friend, Prime Minister William Pitt, had been disgusted when some American merchants had traded with the French during the bitterest years of the French and Indian War. But to a Briton of 1763, that glorious year when the churchbells tolled triumph from London to Land's End, it was diffi-cult to imagine that anyone who had the choice would choose to be anything but British.

The victory bells tolled in Boston and Savan-nah, too. It was difficult for an American to imagine choosing otherwise. Looking back to the days of 1763 after thirteen years had passed, Oliver Wolcott of Connecticut remembered a bottomless reservoir of goodwill toward the mother country. He wrote nostalgically that "the Abilities of a Child might have governed this Country, so strong had been the Attachment to Britain."

Wolcott was writing in the year of the Dec-laration of Independence. He was blaming the necessity for the Revolution on the gross incom-petence and tyranny of British rule in the mean-time. He had a point about incompetence. Blunder upon blunder characterized British rule between 1763 and 1776. But it would be a mis-take to accept at face value Oliver Wolcott's or John Adams's or Thomas Jefferson's or George Washington's words about tyranny. British colo-nial policy was never tyrannical. But it was *dif-ferent* after 1763, a new set of responses to a new kind of empire.

The Challenge of Canada

Canada presented British policymakers with two difficult problems. The first was the French population of Canada, foreign to the British in religion, language, culture, and his-tory. They, at least, were under the control of the British military. The Indian tribes, the second of the problems, were subjects of King George III only in name. The powerful former allies of New France had not been decisively defeated in the war. They were securely in possession of the forests west of the Appa-lachians that the mapmakers of Paris gave to the British.

Governing the Canadians
The Canadians were Roman Catholics, members of a faith that was disliked and discriminated against in eighteenth-century Britain. The colonists generally allowed people to worship as they pleased. But there was a big difference between tolerating small, quiet Roman Catholic minorities in Maryland and a few coastal cities, and coming to terms with a totally Cath-olic province. To eighteenth-century Protestants—particularly the descendants of the Puritans, who were Quebec's closest neighbors—Catholicism meant super-stition, blasphemy, and the reactionary political system of the pope.

Language was another problem. The French Canadians were as devoted to their culture as the English were to theirs. They could not be forced to abandon French and learn the language of their conquerors. But were the British overlords to learn French in order to govern their new subjects? To become French themselves? That was not why William Pitt had made the conquest of New France his major war aim or why General Wolfe had led an army up the cliffs of Quebec.

Finally, the Canadians had no experience with such fundamental British political institutions as representative government. The Estates General, the French equivalent of the British Parliament, had not met since 1614. At home, the king ruled as absolute monarch. In New France, a military officer had commanded the colony as though it were a regiment. What was to be done? The English colonists were bothersome enough with their periodic carping about their "rights as British subjects," but at least they voiced their complaints in terms rooted in British history and tradition.

Fortunately, the authoritarian character of Canadian society actually played into British hands. The inhabitants of the territory were accustomed to following orders. Command by red-coated victors was not much different in day-to-day terms from command by blue-uniformed French officers. Their country had been defeated in war, and they knew it. They would wait, and the British enjoyed a reprieve in finding a solution for the first Canadian problem. The second, however, would not wait. The Indians of the Great Lakes region had not been defeated, and they were quite accustomed to acting independently.

Pontiac's Conspiracy
and the Proclamation of 1763

In the summer of 1763, Sir Jeffrey Amherst, the commander of British troops in North America, informed the tribes of the Ohio Valley that he would not continue the French practice of presenting to them regular "gifts" of European goods: blankets, iron tools and vessels, firearms, liquor. Angered by the withdrawal of what they regarded as a right, several tribes united behind an Ottawa warrior named Pontiac. They overran most of the frontier forts and drove deep into Virginia and Pennsylvania, killing more than two thousand people—more than were lost in any battle of the French and Indian War. The British regulars and some colonial forces regrouped and defeated Pontiac at Bushy Run near Pittsburgh. But they knew that they had only stung the Indians, not destroyed their power.

No one wanted more war. The British restored the gifts, and, in October, in order to let tempers cool, the Privy Council drew an imaginary line on the Appa-

Major Rogers of the British forces meets the Ottawa warrior Pontiac.

lachian divide, between the sources of the rivers that emptied into the Atlantic and those that flowed into the Ohio-Mississippi river system. The council declared in the king's name, "we do strictly forbid, on pain of our displeasure, all our loving subjects from making any purchases or settlements whatever" west of the line. A few plucky frontiersmen who had already pushed into the closed zone were forced to return east, and there was a freeze on sales of tracts in the region.

No one considered the Proclamation Line as anything more than what one young land speculator, George Washington, called "a temporary expedient to quiet the minds of the Indians." Too many Virginia planters and powerful British politicians dreamed of riches from Ohio Valley land to consider the line permanent. Indeed, two newly appointed Superintendents of Indian Affairs immediately began to purchase territory from the western tribes. The southern part of the line was redrawn within a few months, and, regularly over the next decade, trans-Appalachian lands were opened to speculation and settlement.

But Americans were already an impatient people, and the West was already the place to which many looked for their fortunes. By interfering even temporarily with expansion, the Privy Council touched a tender nerve. Actual protest was quiet. Few were of a mind to belittle the power of the Indians after Pontiac's Conspiracy. Later, however, Americans would think of the Proclamation of 1763 as an early example of King George III's campaign to throttle their way of life.

The Redcoats

The Indian uprising also prompted General Amherst to ask Parliament for a permanent American garrison of five thousand to six thousand men. The troops would be stationed in Canada and in a string of frontier forts along the Great Lakes and the Ohio River. Parliament responded by voting Amherst ten thousand men, thereby putting more than twice as many troops in North America as had ever been stationed there during the years of the French menace.

A few years later, with many of these soldiers billeted in the coastal cities in order to police riotous colonial crowds, they became the "hated redcoats" and the "lobsters." When the force began to arrive, however, the Americans' biggest concern was the expense of maintaining them—£200,000 a year. The Quartering Act of 1765 charged the cost of the troops' shelter, food, and drink to the colony in which they were posted. Indeed, one of Parliament's motives in doubling General Amherst's request was to pension off crusty veterans of the French and Indian War at colonial expense. The men had some reward coming to them, and the English have never liked to keep large standing armies at home during peacetime. Unhappily, Parliament ignored the fact that Britain's loyal colonial subjects might have inherited this dislike.

Reorganizing the Empire

Whatever the motives, the flurry of activity in the wake of the war was a signal that the men who governed Great Britain were taking an unprecedented and keen interest in colonial matters. The change was basic, a fundamental reform. The empire had outgrown easygoing Robert Walpole's practice of winking at colonial violations of the law. Counting Canada, the West Indies, and British Honduras, twenty colonies in the Western Hemisphere flew the British flag. There would be chaos, not an empire, if each went about setting its own rules. During and immediately after the French and Indian War, "the king in Parliament" methodically scrapped the old tradition of salutary neglect and designed a centrally administered empire that was to be self-supporting.

Money Problems

Before the war, it had been enough that the colonies were profitable to the British economy. The prewar governments were not concerned that the administration of the colonies cost the Treasury money. And the colonies *were* profitable. In 1764, the cost of governing them was £350,000 a year, while the colonial trade annually brought at least £2 million into Great Britain.

But Britain faced a serious money problem. If £350,000 was a pittance compared with the economic worth of the colonies, it was still £350,000, and a steep increase over the £70,000 a year that colonial government had cost before the French and Indian War. Moreover, the expense of the fighting, a debt of £130 million, had England teetering on the edge of bankruptcy.

Higher taxes at home were out of the question. Each year, British landowners paid 20 percent of the value of their property into the Exchequer, and when Parliament tried to collect a small tax on cider, the daily drink of southwestern England, farmers rioted. Cutting costs was a possibility. British administration was shot through with graft and top-heavy with officials who lived off public funds without doing anything in particular. But such people are rarely apt to solve a problem by penalizing themselves. They prefer to find more money.

The Villain Grenville

The task of finding more money fell to George Grenville, who became prime minister in 1763. He was a talented man who was considered an expert on money matters. If the reforms he introduced had succeeded, history might well have ranked him as the architect of the British Empire. Instead, he is a fleeting figure in the English books and, to Americans, a villain.

Among his abilities, Grenville had a fatal limitation. Like too many English politicians of the era, he knew little about Americans and did not think it was worth his while to learn more. He was an imperialist who had a vision of worldwide British power, but he saw the vision through the half-closed eyes of the complacent upper class. To Grenville, Americans were half-civil-

EXPORTS TO AND IMPORTS FROM ENGLAND BY AMERICAN COLONIES
(thousands of £ Sterling)

	Total	
	Export	Import
1700	395	344
1710	250	294
1720	468	320
1730	573	537
1740	718	813
1750	815	1,313
1760	761	2,612
1770	1,016	1,926

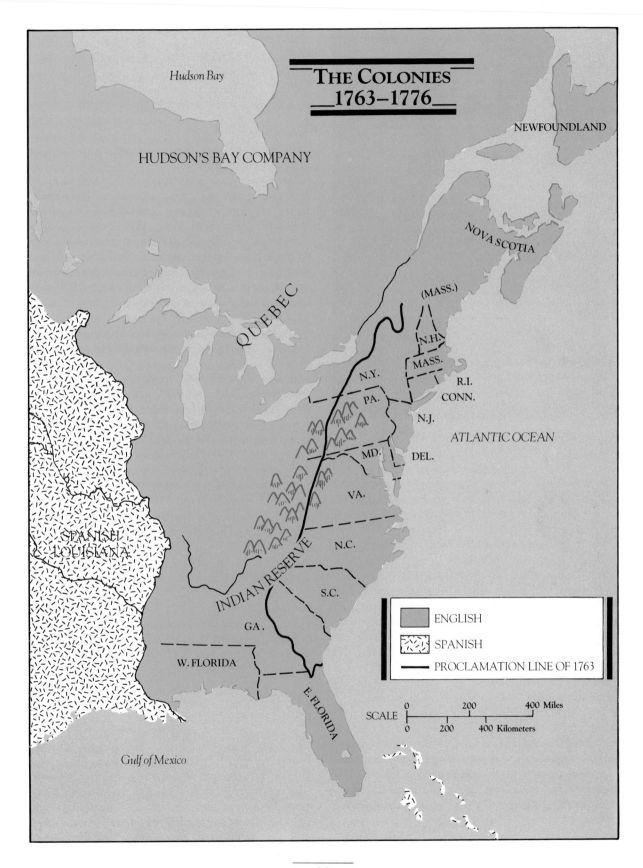

THE COLONIES
1763–1776

Hudson Bay

NEWFOUNDLAND

HUDSON'S BAY COMPANY

NOVA SCOTIA

QUEBEC

(MASS.)

N.H.

MASS.

N.Y.

R.I.

CONN.

PA.

N.J.

ATLANTIC OCEAN

MD.

DEL.

SPANISH
LOUISIANA

VA.

N.C.

INDIAN RESERVE

S.C.

GA.

W. FLORIDA

E. FLORIDA

Gulf of Mexico

ENGLISH

SPANISH

PROCLAMATION LINE OF 1763

SCALE

0   200   400 Miles

0   200   400 Kilometers

*Prime Minister George Grenville, author of the
unpopular Sugar and Stamp Acts.*

ized louts whose opinions did not have to be taken into account. He would have enjoyed Samuel Johnson's famous quip, "I am willing to love all mankind, except an American."

Grenville was particularly bothered because the colonials did not pay enough taxes. Using somewhat distorted figures, Grenville calculated that the average English taxpayer paid an annual tax of twenty-six shillings, while a British subject living in Massachusetts paid one shilling a year and the average Virginian only five pence. This was particularly intolerable, since the colonials had gained the most from the French and Indian War, which had been the cause of the debt that hung over England. They should therefore do their part in paying it off.

Few Americans publicly denied their obligation to help out with England's debt. Unfortunately, even if the thirteen assemblies had been willing to vote Grenville enough money to satisfy him, they did not get the chance to do so. Instead of requesting monies, as Pitt had done during the war, Grenville treated the financial question as part and parcel of his administrative reforms.

The Sugar Act of 1764

Grenville's first action was to overhaul the ineffective Sugar Act of 1733. Its sixpence a gallon tax on molasses imported into the colonies from non-British islands was so high that American merchants felt morally justified in ignoring it and paying a bribe of a penny or two to customs collectors. If they were arrested, they could usually count on local juries to acquit them regardless of the evidence—and then join them at the nearest inn for a drink of cheap rum.

Grenville's Sugar Act struck at both problems. It enlarged the customs service and removed enforcement of the law from local courts, transferring it to a new system of vice admiralty courts that would try violaters without juries. Grenville also slashed the molasses duty to threepence a gallon. He calculated that merchants would pay the lower rate rather than run the risk of sure conviction in courts they could not control. Grenville also extended the tax to molasses brought from British islands—the purpose of the act was to raise money, not to exclude French molasses—and he levied duties on imported wines, silks, tropical foods, and other luxury goods.

In New England, where molasses was a major trade item, protest was loud, fierce, and immediate. The powerful Boston town meeting declared that the city would import no British goods of any kind until Parliament repealed the obnoxious tax. Other cities, including New York, followed suit. Even "the young Gentlemen of Yale College" declared that they would not "make use of any foreign spirituous liquors until Grenville backed down." This painful sacrifice was eased by the fact that limitless quantities of domestic beer, cider, and fiery New England rum were still available to them.

When he heard news of the hubbub, Grenville was unmoved. He believed that the Americans simply did not want to pay any taxes; they wanted to enjoy the benefits of being a part of the British Empire at no cost. No doubt he was the better part of right. Importers of molasses, sippers of Madeira, and wearers of silk wanted the best bargains they could get. To this extent, the protest was sheer self-interest.

The Rights of British Subjects

Two principles were at stake, however. As a tax on foreign molasses, the act of 1733 had been designed to regulate trade. According to colonists like Daniel Dulany of Maryland, who wrote a widely distributed tract on the issue, this stipulation was perfectly legitimate. Parliament had the right and the obligation to control trade for the good of the empire. But the act of

1764 taxed British and foreign molasses equally. It did not regulate imports. It was explicitly designed to raise money. The official title of the law was the American Revenue Act.

This raised a ticklish constitutional question. It was a "sacred right" of British subjects that they *consented* to the taxes levied on them. By 1764, the House of Commons in England had nearly complete control over money matters. To many people, the whole meaning of English history was the struggle that won these liberties. But the Americans were not represented in Parliament. They had their own "parliaments," their elected assemblies, and according to the protesters, only these bodies could tax them. This arrangement had, in fact, been the unofficial custom for 150 years.

Just as important, the right of a British subject to be tried for a crime before a jury of his or her equals dated

New England town meetings were often the scene of lively debate.

A NEW KIND OF PEOPLE

Hector St. John de Crèvecoeur, a French essayist who lived in the Hudson Valley of New York, believed that a new race of people was emerging in North America. In 1770, he wrote that "I could point out to you a family whose grandfather was an Englishman, whose wife was Dutch, whose son married a French woman, and whose present four sons now have four wives of different nations."

back to Magna Carta of 1215. Such a right was what set the English and colonials apart from—and, in their own eyes, made them superior to—the French and Spanish and Poles and other nationalities. In denying this ancient right by establishing no-jury vice admiralty courts, Grenville seemed to be tampering with the very liberties that made being British a point of pride.

It is impossible to say what would have happened if Grenville's program had ended with the Sugar Act. The Americans were noisy, and some of their language was strong. But there was no violence. Protest began and ended with an annoying but perfectly legal boycott of imports. To the extent that colonial resentment was a matter of greed, it might well have died out. The duties seriously affected only wealthy consumers and a relatively small number of shippers and distillers. In the end, the Sugar Act was repealed. When, in 1766, the molasses duty was reduced to a penny a barrel (the level of the traditional bribe), it ceased to be a problem, although "the principle of the thing" remained intact.

But Grenville did not stop with the Sugar Act. Even before the protest against it peaked and fagged, he announced a new bill to raise money in America by means of a tax that could not easily be ducked because those who did not pay it could be identified on the spot.

The Stamp Act Crisis

The English had had a stamp tax since 1694. For documents such as wills, bills of sale, licenses, deeds, insurance policies, and other contracts to be legal and binding, a fee had to be paid into the Treasury. In countries that have a stamp tax today, payment is certified by buying and attaching an ordinary postage stamp to the document (some kinds of personal checks, for example). In the eighteenth century, before self-sticking stamps were invented, the taxable documents had to be printed or written on embossed paper that was sold only by the government and its agents. A will

A facsimile of the stamps required on all legal documents and printed material under the Stamp Act of 1765.

or marriage license or any document that was not on the stamped paper was simply not legal.

The Stamp Act of 1765

Grenville's act went somewhat further than the English stamp tax. The law required that in addition to the legal documents, newspapers, pamphlets, playing cards, and even handbills be printed on the special paper. The cost varied from a halfpenny on a handbill to £1 for a liquor license, quite a sum in both cases.

Again, enforcement of the law was given to the vice admiralty courts, but Grenville was careful to insert the provision that all money raised from the act would be used solely in "defending, protecting, and securing the colonies." None of it would go back to England.

This did not console the Americans. On the contrary, the stipulation that the revenues from the Stamp Act were to be raised and spent entirely within the colonies led some of them, such as Pennsylvania Quaker John Dickinson, to devise a detailed constitutional distinction between legitimate "external taxes"—duties placed on trade between the colonies and some other places—and unacceptable "internal taxes"—duties collected within the colonies. The Stamp Act was plainly internal, a direct tax on the people by a body in which they were not represented. Clearly, only a colonial assembly could enact such a tax within its boundaries. (Massachusetts had experimented with a stamp act in 1755.)

Grenville had no ear for such arguments. As far as he was concerned, Parliament was the supreme governing authority for the whole empire. Most members of Parliament agreed with him. After a dull debate, addressing few of the issues, they voted 204 to 49 to pass the bill. Many prominent Americans also failed to see the case against the Stamp Act. Richard Henry Lee of Virginia, who would introduce the independence resolution in 1776, applied for a job as a stamp tax collector in 1765.

A Stupid Law

Constitutional questions aside, the Stamp Act was politically stupid. Its taxes fell most heavily on those groups that were best able to stir up a fuss. Newspaper editors, who could influence public opinion, were hard hit. Advertisements, their bread and butter, were taxed two shillings, and every edition had to be printed on stamped paper. Printers, who depended to a large extent on putting out almanacs and broadsides (posters used for announcing goods for sale and public meetings—including protest meetings!), saw their business taxed at every turn of the press.

Lawyers, the single largest group in colonial public office and persuaders by profession, had to pay tax on every document with which they dealt. Tavernkeepers, saddled with more expensive licenses by the law, were key figures in every town and neighborhood. Their inns were the gathering places where, over rum or coffee, locals read newspapers and discussed politics.

What was worse for the British, most of these groups were concentrated in cities, where they could easily cooperate with one another and have an impact out of proportion to their numbers. It was one thing to upset them one time, as the Sugar Act had riled shippers and distillers. The Stamp Act affected all of them at once, and, possibly to everyone's surprise, they won the support of large numbers of ordinary workingpeople.

Riot and Rebellion

Parliament passed the Stamp Act at the end of February 1765; it was scheduled to go into effect in November. But as soon as the news of the law reached the colonies, they erupted in anger. Local associations called Sons of Liberty (a phrase used to describe Americans by one of their parliamentary friends, Isaac Barré) agitated against the law and called for a boycott of British goods.

Some of the Sons also took violent action. When the stamped paper was delivered to warehouses in port cities, mobs broke in and lit bonfires. Men who had accepted jobs as stamp masters were shunned, hanged in effigy, or roughed up in practically every important town. An official in Maryland was forced to flee for his

The burden of the stamp tax caused the Pennsylvania Journal *to announce on October 31, 1765 that it was ceasing publication.*

life to New York. That was a mistake. The New York Sons of Liberty were the most rambunctious of all. They located the Marylander and forced him to write a letter of resignation. Led by Isaac Sears, the captain of a merchant vessel, the New Yorkers frightened their own lieutenant governor (another future revolutionary named Cadwallader Colden), so that he went into hiding. As a consolation prize they burned his carriages. In Boston, the crowd looted and burned the homes of several officials of the Crown. Except in Georgia, not a penny was collected under the Stamp Act.

Rowdiness is rarely popular, but the Stamp Act riots were. When one governor was asked why he did not call out the militia to restore order, he pointed out that it would mean arming the very people who were wreaking havoc. The British had expected protests. Isaac Barré had warned of resistance. But they were caught short by what seemed the whole American people on a rampage.

The Stamp Act Congress

Many of the influential colonists who had started the protest were also surprised at its violence. In October 1765, thirty-seven delegates from nine colonies assembled in New York City and attempted to channel the uproar along peaceful, legal lines. They adopted fourteen resolutions criticizing the Stamp Act, Sugar Act, and other parliamentary policies, but they tactfully and prominently acknowledged "all due subordination" to the Crown. Although the congress had been the brainchild of one of the more volatile agitators, James Otis of Massachusetts, its "Declaration of Rights and Grievances" was principally the work of the conservative John Dickinson, who disapproved of mob action in any case.

Even to men as cautious as Dickinson, however, "due subordination" did not include obedience to laws passed by Parliament. All agreed that it was the constitutional right of British subjects to consent, through elected representatives, to all taxes imposed on them.

The Constitutional Debate

In the eighteenth century, Great Britain did not have a written constitution, as Great Britain does not have a written constitution today. However, both the colonial dissidents and their opponents, the leaders of Parliament, agreed that the actions of government were limited by a mixed collection of historic documents (Magna Carta, the Bill of Rights of 1688) and customs that had not been written down but were binding nonetheless. In that sense, the debate of the years preceding the American Revolution was a constitutional debate, with the antagonists offering decidedly different interpretations of what the English constitution meant.

Did Parliament, a legislative body to which the colonists elected no members, have the right to impose taxes on the colonists? No, said the colonists, only their own elected assemblies could do so. Nonsense, replied Parliament, including members such as Edmund Burke, who were friends of the Americans. Custom and usage in the colonies as well as in Great Britain said that the colonists were *virtually represented* in Parliament.

The Colonial Case

The colonists' point is easy for us to understand; it is the governing principle of representation in the United States today. In order for an individual to be represented in government, he or she must be entitled to vote for a city council member, county supervisor, state legislator, representative, or senator. The inhabitants of places like Puerto Rico, the Virgin Islands, and Samoa, which are territories of the United States but not states, are not represented in Congress. They elect no representatives or senators.

Likewise, a congressman from Kentucky does not represent an Iowa farmer. Only the representative for whom the farmer voted for or against does so. Reforms of voting laws throughout United States history—extending the vote to people who did not own property, to blacks, and to women—have been based on this concept of representation.

A REVOLUTION OF THE HEART

In 1818, looking back on the tumultuous years of his youth, John Adams wrote that "the Revolution was effected before the war commenced. The Revolution was in the minds and hearts of the people."

LONGING FOR THE GOOD OLD DAYS

Not until 1776 did more than a few colonials think of Great Britain's actions as meriting a fight for independence. On the contrary, most of them thought that the solution to the crisis was to go backward—to relations as they had existed before 1763. Benjamin Franklin's advice was to "*repeal* the laws, *renounce* the right, *recall* the troops, *refund* the money, and *return* to the old method of requisition."

James Otis spoke for this way of thinking at the Stamp Act Congress of 1765 when he suggested that Parliament end the dispute by allowing the colonists to elect members of Parliament. His colleagues ignored him. They did not want to elect members of Parliament; they wanted Parliament to recognize the authority of their own assemblies in taxation matters. The British might have confused and weakened the colonial protest by acting favorably on the Otis proposal. They did not because they held that the Americans were already represented in Parliament.

Virtual Representation

By eighteenth-century standards, the British were correct and the colonists were wrong. It was not necessary (and is not in Britain today) that a member of Parliament reside in the electoral district that sends him or her to the House of Commons. Indeed, a member of Parliament may never set foot in the district he or she represents. Each member is regarded as representing the entire nation. As Edmund Burke put it to his own constituents during the dispute with the colonies, "you choose a member . . . but when you have chosen him, he is not a member of Bristol, but he is a member of parliament."

Indeed, the colonists practiced virtual representation in their own elections. Washington and other Virginians were elected to the House of Burgesses from counties where they did not reside. Often, would-be burgesses stood for seats in more than one county, so they were covered in the event they were defeated in one. Few objected to this practice; it was assumed that those who were elected would act with the interests of all Virginians in mind.

The colonists also practiced virtual representation when they restricted the suffrage to free, white, adult male heads of household who possessed a certain minimum of property in land or money. These numbers amounted to only a small proportion of the inhabitants of any colony. Nevertheless, the colonists considered the vast majority of nonvoters to be virtually represented. The assumption was that elected assembly members acted on behalf of all, not just on behalf of the few freeholders who voted for them. This position was precisely the position that Parliament took.

The Mistakes of the British

But the Stamp Act crisis was not resolved by adding up the debaters' points. Few political battles are. If the colonists had a flimsy constitutional base on which to stand, they had the support of all sections and social classes of the colonies. No one spoke of independence. But Americans generally refused to be mere pawns of the mother country. They took their "rights as British subjects," as they stubbornly interpreted them, quite seriously.

A Breakdown in Parliamentary Leadership

Some members of Parliament appreciated the colonial position and supported the Americans. William Pitt, now the earl of Chatham, was idolized by the colonists for his words in defense of them. Colonel Isaac Barré, who had done military service in New England and (rare for a British officer) was fond of Americans, said that they were right. Edmund Burke, the father of modern conservatism, saw the colonists as the defenders of British tradition and the Grenville group as dangerous innovators. At the other extreme, English radicals like John Wilkes egged on the colonial agitators.

Unfortunately, except for a brief spell in 1766 and 1767 when the earl of Rockingham and Lord Chatham formed ministries, such men did not make colonial policy. For the most part, the leadership of Parliament was unable to see beyond constitutional fine points and their snobbish disdain for colonial rustics. This narrow-mindedness was the result of the way English politics functioned during this period and of the personal failing of King George III.

Members of Parliament used party names like Whig and Tory in the 1760s, but there were no political parties in any meaningful sense of the word. Parliament was a collection of at least half a dozen shifting factions. Some, such as Burke's Old Whigs—ever on the watch for violations of traditional liberties—were drawn together by agreement on a principle. Most were alliances of convenience, little cliques of men who supported one another for the purpose of serving their own immediate interests. In many cases, the men in a faction were related by blood or marriage.

There was money to be made in politics, not only through outright graft (which was not rare), but also through the distribution of public offices and government favors. The colonials played the game. One sure way for an American speculative venture to gain parliamentary approval was to cut in a parliamentary clique as stockholders. Benjamin Franklin named one land company after Robert Walpole.

King George III

It was an old system, tried and true. But a new wrinkle was added after 1760, when George III ascended the British throne at the age of twenty-two. His predecessors had used the royal favors at their disposal to reward military heroes, to support musicians and artists, or simply to keep congenial companions around the palace. The first two Georges were German. George I could not even speak English, and George II, who could, preferred French. Coming from the small state of Hanover, they were delighted merely to have the rich English income at their disposal and took no interest in government.

George III, however, had been raised as an Englishman. His mother had urged him to "be a king," and he

George III (1761), under whose reign British relations with the colonies worsened.

meant to have a hand in government. The days when the English monarch could issue decrees were long gone. But George could and did use the patronage he controlled to build his own parliamentary faction, the "king's friends."

George was not an evil man, and the "king's friends" were no more venal than the other Parliamentary groups. Nor was George a tyrant, as Americans came to see him. During his first ten years as king and politician, he several times used his faction to support conciliation with the colonies.

But he was not especially intelligent, and he was vain and stubborn. The king was uneasy with political allies whose abilities exceeded his own and with those who refused to flatter him. By keeping them out of office and raising up mediocrities and sycophants, he denied power to those who best understood the American situation. What was worse, the king was erratic. (Eventually he went insane, the victim of a mental disorder that is still not fully understood.) He dismissed even lackeys on the slightest pretext. So colonial policy was not only ill-advised, but it was also inconsistent. The effect was to worsen relations between the mother country and its colonies and to embolden the more radical American agitators.

A Mixed Victory

Thus, George Grenville, a hard-liner who always insisted that he could have solved the colonial problem in 1765 with the use of the army, was dismissed in July 1765 over an unrelated matter. Early the next year, during the short ministry of Lord Rockingham, Chatham moved the repeal of the Stamp Act, and it was passed. The colonial celebrations were so noisy that few paid much attention to the fact that king and Parliament had not yielded an inch on principle. Within a month of repeal, Parliament passed a Declaratory Act, which stated that Parliament "had, hath, and of right ought to have, full power and authority to make laws and statutes of sufficient force and validity to bind the colonies and people of *America*, subjects of the crown of Great Britain, in all cases whatsoever."

The wording was lifted from a law of 1719 that had made Ireland completely subject to Great Britain. The colonials might well have wondered if their rights as

A teapot commemorating the repeal of the Stamp Act of 1766.

A LIST of the Names of *thofe* who AUDACIOUSLY continue to counteract the UNITED SENTIMENTS of the BODY of Merchants thro'out NORTH-AMERICA; by importing Britifh Goods contrary to the Agreement.

John Bernard,
(In King-Street, almoft oppofite Vernon's Head.

James McMafters,
(On Treat's Wharf.

Patrick McMafters,
(Oppofite the Sign of the Lamb.

John Mein,
(Oppofite the White-Horfe, and in King-Street.

Nathaniel Rogers,
(Oppofite Mr. Henderfon Inches Store lower End King-Street.

William Jackfon,
At the BrazenHead, Cornhill, near the Town-Houfe

Theophilus Lillie,
(Near Mr. Pemberton's Meeting-Houfe, North-End.

John Taylor,
(Nearly oppofite the Heart and Crown in Cornhill.

Ame & Elizabeth Cummings,
(Oppofite the Old Brick Meeting Houfe, all of Bofton.

Ifrael Williams, Efq; *& Son,*
(Traders in the Town of Hatfield.

And, *Henry Barnes,*
(Trader in the Town of Marlboro.

A 1770 broadside announcing a boycott of merchants importing British goods.

English subjects were being restored or if they had been reduced to the degraded status of the Irish. But they did not. Chatham became prime minister a short time later, and he was known to have little sympathy for the Declaratory Act. In November, he eliminated another aggravation when he reduced the duty on molasses from threepence to a penny a gallon. What did a piece of paper mean when a good friend held power?

Then, in one of those accidents that change the course of events, Chatham was taken ill and dropped out of the government. From the perspective of the colonists, the man who stepped into the vacuum was even worse than George Grenville.

Townshend and His Duties

Charles Townshend, the Chancellor of the Exchequer, hoped to further his career by cutting taxes at home, thus winning favor with the landowning classes. In order to make up for the resulting loss in revenue, he would tax the colonies. He studied the American distinction between external taxes (those designed to regulate trade) and internal taxes (direct taxes like the Stamp Act) and designed duties that were undeniably "external." The Townshend Duties were imposed on paper, paint, lead, glass, and tea *imported into* the colonies.

It was an odd combination of goods. Although none of the taxed goods were produced in the colonies in quantity, all of them except tea could be made there. In failing to appreciate that the controversy was not an academic debate, Townshend invited a boycott. Trade fell off by 25 percent and then by 50 percent. Townshend had predicted that his duties would bring in £40,000 annually. The actual take was £13,000 in 1768 and under £3,000 the next year, hardly enough to operate a few frontier forts.

There was little violence. The boycott was organized by merchants, wealthy men who were still nervous about the Stamp Act riots. But it worked. English merchants felt the pinch and flooded Parliament with petitions for repeal. They pointed out that if Townshend had answered the colonial distinction between internal and external taxes, he had penalized goods that English manufacturers and merchants shipped abroad! In 1770, with the exception of the threepence a pound tax on tea, Parliament repealed the duties. The tea tax was kept in the spirit of the Declaratory Act. It was Parliament's statement that it retained the right to tax the colonies.

At Home Among the Iroquois

By the middle of the eighteenth century, the Iroquois Confederacy, consisting of the Cayuga, Seneca, Onondaga, Oneida, and Mohawk tribes, numbered about fifteen thousand people and securely controlled most of what is now New York State and much of western Pennsylvania. Iroquois hunters and war parties ranged even farther, over 1 million square miles as far west as the Mississippi River and as far north as Hudson's Bay.

The hunters and warriors were men, of course. Men also traveled to carry out the intricate and constant diplomatic negotiations that the confederacy depended on for its stability and to deal with non-Iroquois peoples, including the English and French. "It is not an exaggeration," Anthony F. C. Wallace wrote in the standard history of the Senecas, "to say that the full-time business of an Iroquois man was travel."

Iroquois women, on the contrary, stayed home in more or less fixed towns. They raised the corn that was the staple of the Iroquois diet. They cared for the children in the secure village, determining what values would be instilled into them. They kept the long houses in repair and maintained order in the towns, governing by social pressure—reputation was extremely important to the Iroquois—rather than by force. Finally, with their husbands absent much of the time, the women effectively decided whose children they would bear.

Descent, therefore, had to be traced through the maternal line. A typical Iroquois town consisted of about twelve to forty long houses in each of which dwelt fifty or sixty members of a clan. The clan (whose animal symbol was carved above the door of the long house and painted red) included its eldest female member and her daughters, immature male children, and sons-in-law. Because of a strict incest taboo, an Iroquois male left the clan into which he had been born and became a member of his wife's clan. Indeed, because marital relationships were fragile and transitory, an Iroquois man might drift from clan to clan throughout his life. At any given time, however, he was obligated to defend the honor of his wife's clan. For example, if a member

Iroquois warrior John Wolf Clan (1710) wearing European-style dress adopted by the Iroquois in the eighteenth century.

of her clan was killed and the matriarch insisted that revenge be taken, a warrior was required to do so, even if it was against the clan into which he had been born.

In addition to the authority to declare war between clans (which was not frequent and was governed by a complex set of rules), the elder women of the Iroquois selected each of the forty-nine delegates of the confederacy when death created a vacancy. They also participated, albeit more quietly than the orating men, in community decision making.

The system worked extremely well. Iroquois lands remained secure because the mobile men were such effective warriors and home life was placid and orderly. A Quaker wrote that the Senecas

appear to be naturally as well calculated for social and rational enjoyment, as any people. They frequently visit each other in their houses, and spend much of their time in friendly intercourse. They are also mild and hospitable, not only among themselves, but to strangers, and good-natured in the extreme, except when their natures are perverted by the inflammatory influence of spirituous liquors.

Alcohol was a serious problem. A good sale of pelts and hides to the whites inevitably led to the purchase of rum and wholesale drunkenness among men, women, and children. Although this was the most tragic element introduced into Iroquois life by the arrival of whites, it was not the only one. Contact with Europeans, into its fifth generation by the middle of the eighteenth century, also meant guns and metal tools ranging from scissors, knives, awls, kettles, and other household goods, to hatchets and axes. The latter influenced Iroquois building methods: by the mid-1700s long houses were made less often in the traditional way—sheets of elm bark lashed to bent saplings—and increasingly of logs.

Another interesting consequence of the mixing of cultures was the increased tendency of Iroquois to abandon living by clan in the long houses and to cluster in single-family log cabins. The white presence probably made for a more intensive agriculture by the end of the colonial era. Not only was game scarcer because of overtrapping, but European tools made it possible for the Seneca alone to produce as many as a million bushels of corn a year by 1750. It is difficult to imagine such a crop resulting from traditional slash and burn cultivation.

The appearance of the Iroquois also changed. European calico shirts, linen breechcloths, and woolen blankets characterized the Indians whom the Americans of the eighteenth century knew. Nevertheless, the Iroquois continued to shun Christian missionaries, and they "made obscene gestures" when anyone suggested that the white settlers' way of life was generally superior to their own.

For Further Reading

Bernard Donoughue, *British Politics and the American Revolution* (1965), provides an informative look at the deterioration of British–American relations from the other side of the Atlantic. J. R. Alden, *A History of the American Revolution* (1969); E. S. Morgan, *The Birth of the Republic* (1956); and Merrill Jensen, *The Founding of a Nation* (1968), provide accounts of the general events of the period in varying detail. See also E. S. Morgan, *The Stamp Act Crisis: Prologue to Revolution* (1953), and A. M. Schlesinger, *The Colonial Merchants and the American Revolution, 1763–1776* (1951), for two specialized studies that have greatly influenced historians of the period.

Carl Bridenbaugh, *Seat of Empire: The Political Role of Eighteenth-Century Williamsburg* (1950), and C. S. Sydnor, *Gentlemen Freeholders* (1952), discuss the nature of politics in the South.

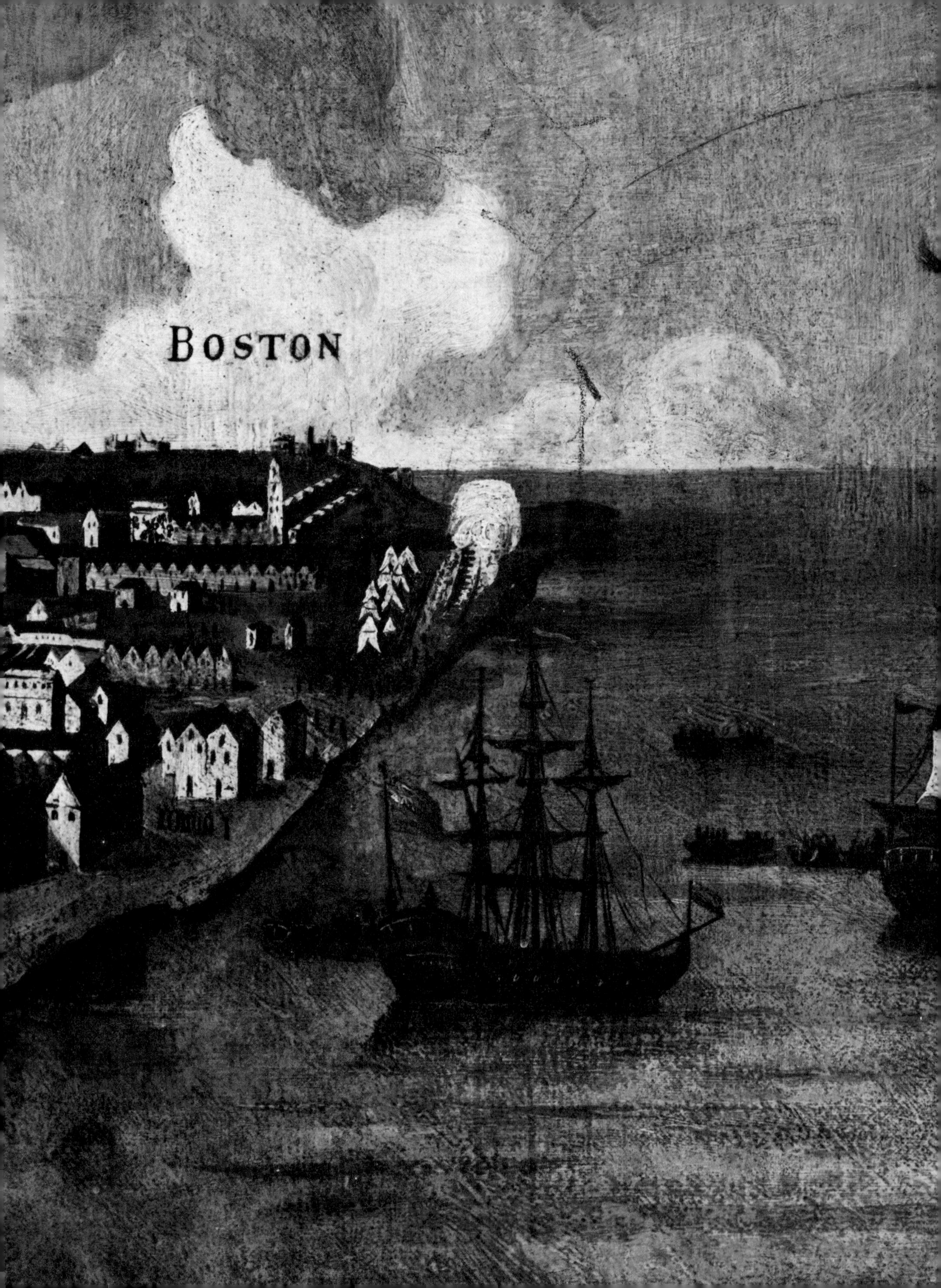
BOSTON

8

From Riot to Rebellion
The Road to Independence, 1770–1776

Nothing was settled by the repeal of Charles Townshend's duties. Neither Parliament nor the colonial protestors yielded an inch on the principle of taxation. In the Declaratory Act, Parliament asserted its right to raise money in the colonies in unequivocal, even belligerent language. For their part, no protest leader or colonial assembly offered a workable alternative by which Americans would contribute to the upkeep of the British Empire.

Nevertheless, both parties to the dispute were clearly happy to end the confrontation. For three years after 1770, Parliament passed no controversial colonial laws, and, as a people, the Americans were placid, loyal subjects. The colonists effectively had abandoned their boycott of British goods even before the Townshend Duties were repealed. In the first systematic public-opinion poll in American history, a door-to-door survey of New Yorkers revealed that a majority of households favored importing all the taxed items except tea (which they could buy more cheaply from Dutch smugglers). Beginning in early 1770, imports into the New England colonies, always the most obstreperous of Britain's possessions, increased from a low of £330,000 to £1.2 million, a higher total than ever before. Total colonial exports rose from £1.7 million in 1770 to £4.5 million in 1772. Quite clearly, the majority of Americans wanted calm, business as usual, a resumption of daily life unaggravated by the folderol of politics.

The Battle of Bunker Hill, first large-scale engagement of the Revolutionary War, 1775.

The Storms Within the Lull

While taxation questions lost their appeal during the quiet years of 1770 to 1773, other points of conflict indicated that not all was well. In Pennsylvania and the Carolinas, conflict between frontier settlers and the eastern elites erupted into actual warfare in 1771. On the streets of Boston, friction between working-people and British soldiers made for heat on the coolest days and boiled over into riot on several occasions. While neither dispute pitted all colonists against the British government, both helped to blaze the road to revolution.

The Paxton Boys and the Regulators

Hostility between the elites who controlled most colonial governments and frontier farmers closely resembled the conflict between Governor Berkeley and Nathaniel Bacon in seventeenth-century Virginia.

In 1764 a large group of Scotch-Irish frontiersmen in Pennsylvania massacred a settlement of Conestoga Indians who were entirely unprepared because they had a treaty with the Pennsylvania government. The armed band then moved against another tribe, which fled to Philadelphia for protection.

Over a thousand Paxton Boys, named for one of their leaders, pursued the tribe to the capital and demanded that the Indians be turned over to them. The people of the city were unnerved by this invasion. On the eve of the battle between white Pennsylvanians, Benjamin Franklin intervened. As prestigious among the crusty Scotch-Irish backwoodsmen as among the literati of Europe, Franklin persuaded the Paxton Boys to withdraw in return for his support of a more aggressive Indian policy.

In South Carolina, backcountry resentment boiled over as a result of the Charleston government's failure to organize county governments in the foothill lands. The frontiersmen rebelled, established their own counties, and paid taxes to them rather than to Charleston. The rebels were called Regulators because they said they would regulate their own affairs.

In North Carolina, a similar problem led to actual battle. A band of westerners rode east to demonstrate their resentment of the colony's penny-pinching policies. They were met and defeated by a smaller but better-trained militia at the Battle of Alamance. Only nine men were killed and six later hanged for rebellion, but the modesty of the clash did not sweeten the bitterness in the backcountry.

Some historians have suggested that the British missed a sterling opportunity to retain their colonies when they failed to exploit the hostility between western farmers and the eastern elites. To some extent, British imperial interests coincided with the demands of the frontiersmen: the Paxton Boys wanted an aggressive policy toward the Indians, which British soldiers could best effect; the Regulators wanted more government, not less, and their chief complaint was that not enough tax money was spent on maintaining law and order in their foothills homeland.

By wooing the backcountry farmers with policies that favored them, the British might have gained powerful allies in their developing conflict with the wealthy southern planters. Indeed, during the Revolution, many Regulators fought on the British side, while others pushed beyond the Appalachians so they could remain neutral. The British did not win more backwoods support than they did because their contempt for the lower classes was as strong as that of the colonial elite. It was impossible for British policymakers to regard the poor people of the frontier and the city streets as anything other than a "motley rabble" or, at best, a negligible political force.

The Boston Massacre

On March 5, 1770, the day the Townshend Duties were repealed, the weather in Boston was frigid. The streets were icy, and heaps of gritty snow blocked the cobbled gutters. No doubt aggravated by the prolonged winter, which brought unemployment as well as discomfort, a small group of local men and boys exchanged words with British troops who were patrolling the streets. From a handful of hecklers there grew a crowd, many cursing and throwing snowballs at the soldiers. A few dared the redcoats to use their muskets.

When the mob swelled in number and pressed close, the soldiers fired. Five in the crowd, including a boy and a black man named Crispus Attucks, fell dead. Boston was shocked. Samuel Adams, a fiery, eloquent former brewer and tax collector, tried to raise the anti-British feelings that were never buried deeply in New England. Adams described the incident as murder, and he distributed hundreds of woodcut prints showing aggressive soldiers shooting innocent Bostonians.

He did not convert many people to his version of the "Boston Massacre." His own cousin, John Adams, a hot-tempered fellow himself and no one's stooge—least of all a flunky of the British—rejected Samuel's charges. As defense attorney for the soldiers, he roundly criticized the British policy of stationing professional soldiers in cities like Boston. "Soldiers quar-

The Boston Massacre, as represented by Paul Revere in a 1770 engraving.

tered in a populous town will always occasion two mobs where they prevent one," he told the jury. "They are wretched conservators of the peace." But Adams argued that the mob was to blame for the tragedy. The hard-pressed soldiers were left no alternative but to fire on them. The jury agreed, acquitting several defendants and sentencing others to branding on the hand, a comparatively minor punishment as punishments went.

A number of colonial newspapers reported the affair, printing the story within a black border to represent mourning. But there was no massive protest, as there might have been. Most Americans seemed to agree with John Adams in apportioning blame.

THE GASPÉE

The Boston Massacre was not the only episode of violence during the period of peaceful relations between the colonies and the mother country after 1770. In June 1772, a British patrol boat, the *Gaspée,* ran aground in Rhode Island's Narragansett Bay while chasing smugglers. When night fell on the crippled vessel, a group of men descended on it and burned it to the waterline. Obviously, the work had been done by locals, but when the British investigated the episode, not a single person stepped forward to testify.

Colonists burn the British patrol boat, the Gaspée, *in Narragansett Bay, 1772.*

The Hated Redcoats

The Boston incident revealed a problem in colonial city life at least as serious as the sectional divisions in the countryside. People simply did not like the scarlet-uniformed soldiers in their midst. Wealthy taxpayers resented paying for their keep, and ordinary workingpeople disliked rubbing shoulders with men who commanded little respect in the eighteenth century.

The soldier of the period was not, like the soldier today, "the boy next door" in a uniform. First of all, few colonials signed up. The "lobsters" were almost all from Great Britain. Moreover, they were a rough and lusty lot, men sieved from the dregs of an unjust society. Some were convicted criminals who were in the army because it was offered to them as an alternative to prison or worse. Others, guilty of no crime, had been pressed (forced) into service simply because they were unable or unwilling to support themselves. If hardly appealing by contemporary standards, the bed and board these men found in the army was better than what most of them had ever known.

Stereotyped as undesirables, the soldiers were despised by people who regarded themselves as respectable. Their officers, who were gentlemen, looked down on them. They had few rights. They were regularly and frequently punished. If not slaves, they suffered a kind of bondage. There was no feeling among them of selfless service to king and country or of commitment to some other abstract national ideal.

At the cost of isolation from the larger society, they found fellowship with one another. So they clung together and regarded outsiders with suspicion or even hatred. When this hostility was returned by colonials who looked down on them and on what they stood for—British authority—it made for a tinder-box situation.

A Dangerous Relationship

The Crown made things worse by sending many troops to the colonies and, after the Stamp Act riots, moving a large number of them to the coastal cities. As long as soldiers lived in frontier forts or on the edge of towns away from the citizenry (Castle Island in Boston harbor, for example), there was a minimum of conflict. But under the terms of the Quartering Act of 1765, troops for whom there were no barracks available—or those who were moved into a city for the specific purpose of policing colonials—were quartered in vacant buildings and taverns in ordinary neighborhoods.

This brought the tightly knit group into intimate daily contact with working-class colonials. Like soldiers of all eras, they found girlfriends and stirred up resentment on that count. When off duty, they competed with locals for casual jobs and passed their idle hours in the inns and taverns where colonials gathered.

Inns and taverns were not merely hostels in which travelers bedded down. They were a central part of colonial social life. The tavern was the neighborhood social hall, more like a contemporary English pub, perhaps, than a modern American bar. Local workingmen popped in throughout the day for a cup of tea or coffee and, in the evening, for a shot of rum, a mug of mulled cider, a pipe of tobacco, and a chat about friends, work, business, and politics. Having more time on their hands, unemployed men and those between jobs (such as seamen) spent even more time at "the ordinary." The intrusion of scarlet-coated foreigners, laughing loudly and carrying on by themselves, kept resentments up even when, as between 1770 and 1773, general relations with Great Britain were good.

Street People

The redcoats had more to do with the anti-British feelings of lower-class colonials than the tax laws had. Poor people worried about the next day's meal, not about the price of suing a business rival or of a jeroboam of best Madeira wine. And these people were central to the protest that boiled over into the Revolution. The workingpeople, the unemployed, the boisterous street boys and apprentices, and the "disreputable" fringe elements did the dirty work in the Stamp Act crisis. They were also the ones who fought the soldiers in the streets and who were killed in the Boston Massacre.

Colonial crowds were made up overwhelmingly of poor or marginally employed young men, who had little to lose as a consequence of rash action. They were often social outcasts to some degree by virtue of class, occupation, or race. Seamen, suspect because they belonged to no community but merely came and went, were prominent in the riotous crowds; Crispus Attucks was an out-of-work sailor. John Adams described the mob at the State House as "Negroes and mulattoes, Irish teagues and outlandish jack-tars." He looked down on them, but the revolution he was to join with such enthusiasm owed much to their boldness.

Inns and taverns were places where colonists could socialize, exchange news.

Demon Rum

It is also worth noting the curious role of alcohol in the agitation. The soldiers were a bibulous lot. It was standard military practice to pass around strong drink before a battle, and the governor of New York dissolved the Assembly in 1766 when its members refused to provide the redcoats five pints of beer or four ounces of rum a day.

Moreover, Americans were a hard-drinking people, and the lower classes, less observant of social niceties and with more pain to forget, were the thirstiest of all. The crowd that set off the Boston Massacre had come out of the taverns. The Sons of Liberty, who ignited the last phase of the revolutionary movement with the Boston Tea Party of 1773, assembled over a barrel of rum.

The upper-class protest leaders had mixed feelings about this kind of support. They were willing to exploit the crowd, as they thought they were doing, by stirring up its anger at British policies and by winking at abuses of the law. But because, like the British, they looked down on "the rabble," the more conservative protesters expected the crowd to fade away after having played its role—after the Stamp Act was repealed, the Sugar Act duty reduced, the Townshend taxes eliminated.

But the masses did not disappear. The British concessions did not remedy *their* grievances. The redcoats continued to jostle them in the streets and to intrude on their lives. Their elemental economic problems were untouched by lighter taxation and parliamentary concessions. They remained anonymous, producing few individual leaders. But they continued to agitate, some of them realizing that they had as many complaints against the colonial elites as against the British.

The March Toward War

The quiet years, when conflict simmered rather than boiled, ended in the spring of 1773, when Parliament once again passed a law that angered the Americans. This time, however, instead of spontaneous protests under the control of no one in particular, resistance to British policy was organized by a number of able men.

Professional Agitators:
James Otis and Patrick Henry

The new leaders might best be described as professional agitators. Some of them were articulate speakers who aroused widespread hostility toward the British; others were organizers, people willing to search out issues and, as full-time politicians, devote their lives to turning protest into rebellion. There can be no revolutions without revolutionaries. Men such as James Otis of Massachusetts and Patrick Henry of Virginia made the difference between spontaneous outbursts like the Boston Massacre and calculated actions like the Boston Tea Party.

James Otis, a Boston lawyer, was a man of hot temper. He had been a prosecutor for the hated vice admiralty courts, and his contribution to the agitation of the 1760s may have had as much to do with personal political disappointments as with commitment to a principle.

Nevertheless, his was an exciting presence. He could whip up passions to the fighting point like few of his contemporaries. In 1761, Otis led Boston's fight against "writs of assistance." The "writs" were general search warrants that enabled customs collectors to enter any property to search for smuggled goods. Arguing the case, Otis appealed to the cause of the rights of British subjects, coining the phrase "taxation without representation is tyranny." John Adams later said that "then and there the Child Independence was born."

Curiously, Otis grew more moderate while men like John Adams grew more militant. By the time the spirit of revolution matured, Otis was no longer among its leaders. Indeed, he lived out his final years intermittently insane as the result of a brawl with a British official. In a horrible moment that seemed to symbolize his career, he was killed by a bolt of lightning in 1783.

Patrick Henry was his counterpart in the South. Not a deep thinker, Henry was a red-haired, sharp-tongued, Scotch-Irish shopkeeper who educated himself to become one of Virginia's most effective trial lawyers. He caused a furor in 1763 when, only twenty-seven years old, he denounced George III as a tyrant because the king reversed a law that had been passed by the Virginia House of Burgesses.

Two years later, Henry gained the attention of all the colonies as the center of the Stamp Act storm. Although only the more moderate of the resolutions he introduced were actually passed by the House of Burgesses, all of them were published throughout the colonies under his name. Henry became even more famous for a speech he delivered to the burgesses. "Caesar had his Brutus," he was quoted as shouting, "Charles I his Cromwell, and George III may profit by their example." Talking about the killing of rulers was heady stuff, and Henry was shouted down with cries of "Treason." He is supposed to have replied, "If this be treason, make the most of it."

Relentless in his attacks on the Crown (and on the tidewater planters), Patrick Henry spearheaded the final drive toward independence by calling for the establishment of an army in May 1775 with the famous words "Give me liberty or give me death."

Samuel Adams

More substantial than either Otis or Henry because more thoughtful and calculating was Samuel Adams of Massachusetts. He had been a tax collector until 1764, when he resigned to go into business and primarily, it seems, into agitation. Adams was active in every major protest in Boston. He led the battle against the Sugar Act, the Stamp Act, and the Townshend Duties.

Samuel Adams was no orator; he was nervous and stumbling on a platform. Nor was he impetuous like Otis. Adams was an organizer, the man who handled the undramatic but essential work that turns protest into politics. He may have been thinking in terms of independence as early as the mid-1760s, but, except for the ill-fated fuss over the Boston Massacre, he was careful never to get so far ahead of his supporters that they shouted him down. Most important, Adams was the link between wealthy opponents of British policy (he got considerable financial support from rich John Hancock) and the lower-class Sons of Liberty, whom he neither feared nor disdained.

Adams was a true revolutionary, and only during the quiet, prosperous years of 1770 to 1773 was he unable to rally the people of Boston to his side. Even then, however, Adams seems to have been waiting like a cat for an opportunity to pounce. He got it in May 1773, when Parliament obliged with an act that had far less sense behind it than had the Grenville and Townshend taxes.

The Tea Act of 1773

The purpose of the Tea Act of 1773 was to rescue the East India Company from bankruptcy. This company, one of the first modern corporations, was vital to England because it handled, along with its own business, many governmental functions in the eastern part of the British Empire, including the support and supervision of the army. (The Hudson's Bay Company did much the same in the wilderness north of Canada.)

But the company had fallen on evil times, due partly to mismanagement and partly to bad luck. One problem, which also seemed to be its own solution, was an inventory of 17 million pounds of tea stored in English warehouses. The home market was already glutted, so the directors of the company suggested to the new prime minister, Lord North, that they be allowed to sell their surplus as a monopoly in North America.

North liked the idea. Dutch smugglers had grabbed what was left of tea sales in the colonies, so no other British exporters would complain. The prime minister even agreed to remove a British tax from the tea so that the East India Company could actually undersell the Dutch. But he turned down a suggestion that he also repeal the Townshend tea duty. Part of his scheme was to win the principle of Parliament's right to tax Americans. What better way to do it than to offer taxed goods that were cheaper than anything else on the market!

The Tea Parties

Townshend was wrong. When a dozen East India Company ships carrying seventeen hundred chests of tea sailed into American ports, they were greeted by the angriest defiance of British authority since 1765. The Americans would not be bought. Tea Act tea may have been cheap, but the precedent was both dangerous and obvious. Parliament was not only taxing the colonies,

American revolutionary Samuel Adams, in a portrait by John Singleton Copley, 1771.

but it was also introducing a monopoly into their economy. If the Tea Act succeeded, who knew what controls would follow?

The company managed to land its tea in Charleston, where it was hastily locked up in a warehouse. In New York and Philadelphia, authorities ordered the ships to return to England for fear of a riot. In Annapolis, Maryland, a tea ship was burned. But it was a milder action in Boston that triggered the crisis.

American-born Thomas Hutchinson of Massachusetts, one of the most intelligent of the colonial governors, would not allow the tea ships to depart from Boston, as they had from Philadelphia and New York. He would handle the situation one step at a time, and the first step was to get the cargo ashore. Hutchinson decided to seize the tea for nonpayment of an obscure port tax; thus the royal government of Massachusetts rather than a more vulnerable private company would unload the tea.

It was a clever idea, but Samuel Adams was cleverer. Rather than allow Hutchinson to lock up the tea in a well-guarded warehouse, he assembled his Sons of Liberty on the evening of December 16, 1773, dressed them as Indians, filled them with rum (probably purchased by John Hancock), and led them to the wharf where they boarded the East India Company ships. To

> ## THE BOSTON TEA PARTY: THE MORNING AFTER
>
> If the men of Boston who dumped the tea into Boston harbor were in their cups, a few at least suffered no hangovers. One participant remembered what he did on the morning after:
>
> *The next morning, after we had cleared the ships of the tea, it was discovered that very considerable quantities of it were floating upon the surface of the water, and to prevent the possibility of any of its being saved for use, a number of small boats were manned by sailors and citizens, who rowed them into those parts of the harbor wherever the tea was visible, and by beating it with oars and paddles so thoroughly drenched it as to render its entire destruction inevitable.*

the rousing cheers of a large crowd, they dumped the tea chests into Boston harbor.

Adams knew what he was doing. He made an act of vandalism look like innocent fun by dubbing it the "Boston Tea Party." He also knew that Britain could not let the incident pass, and he gambled that Parliament would overreact. Parliament did. Instead of try-

The Boston Tea Party, 1773, was calculated to infuriate the British government.

ing to root out the perpetrators and treat the incident as a criminal matter, Lord North decided to punish Boston and the whole colony of Massachusetts.

The Intolerable Acts

With the "king's friends" comfortably in control of Parliament, the Coercive Acts of 1774 sailed through both Commons and Lords. As a result of these laws, two centuries of colonial loyalty and three years of increasing goodwill abruptly ended.

The first of what the colonials called the Intolerable Acts closed the port of Boston to all trade until such time as the city would pay for the spoiled tea. Second, the new governor (an army general, Thomas Gage) was empowered to transfer out of the colony the trials of soldiers or other British officials accused of killing protesters. This seemed to be an open invitation to the redcoats to shoot. Third, the entire structure of government in Massachusetts was overhauled, with elected bodies losing powers to the king's officials. Fourth, a new Quartering Act pushed civilian–soldier relations to the breaking point. It authorized the army to house redcoats in occupied private homes!

Finally, although it was not designed as a punishment, the Quebec Act of 1774 infuriated colonists by officially recognizing the French language and Catholic religion in the province of Quebec, by extending the boundaries of the province into the Ohio River Valley, and by providing for no elective assembly for the French Canadians.

There were a number of good reasons for the Quebec Act. Many historians have regarded it as a rare example of enlightened imperial government. Instead of oppressing its French subjects, the Crown respected and protected their institutions. As for the absence of an elected assembly, there never had been one in Quebec. That was all well and good for the French-Canadians. To English-speaking colonial Protestants whose own elected assemblies were under attack, the religious and political provisions of the Quebec Act were ominous, and land-hungry farmers and speculators did not like to see "their" western reserves given to Frenchmen.

Lord North hoped that the Coercive Acts would isolate Massachusetts and set an example. The Bay Colony always had been the most troublesome of the thirteen and was never popular with the other twelve. Instead, the Coercive Acts angered important groups in every colony. Several sent food to paralyzed Boston. More important than charity, when Massachusetts called for a "continental congress" to meet in Philadelphia in order to discuss a united retaliation, every colony except Georgia agreed to send delegates.

The Revolution Begins

This was the turning point. Before the summer of 1774, relations between Great Britain and America had been a series of scattered episodes—action, reaction, and accommodation. Only a handful of militants had continually pressed for an open break. Now, although most of the delegates who began to trickle into Philadelphia continued to speak and to think in terms of loyalty to the Crown, their actions pointed unmistakably toward a serious break with the mother country.

The First Continental Congress

The delegates to the Congress arrived in Philadelphia in early September and began their discussions on the fifth of the month. Some of them, such as Benjamin Franklin, were world famous; others, such as Sam Adams and Patrick Henry, had recently become notorious. But since each of the colonies had closer relations with England than with any other American province, few of the fifty-five men had ever met. The delegates themselves were different in many ways—in temperament, in their general attitude toward Great Britain, in their opinions as to what should, what could be done.

But they got along remarkably well. Ironically, the heritage they were soon to rebel against gave them something in common. They were all "gentlemen" in the English mold—merchants, planters, and professionals (especially lawyers). They prized education and cultivation. They knew how to keep debates decorous and impersonal. In the evening, they recessed to a round of festive dinners and parties with Philadelphia high society. George Washington (conspicuously dressed in military uniform) rarely dined in his own rooms. Dour John Adams gushed in letters to his wife, Abigail, about the lavishness of the meals. Only his cousin Samuel, wrapped up in his ideals of Roman republican frugality, shunned the social whirl. He had the reputation of being a grind.

The delegates also worked together so smoothly because most of them were uncertain about what to do. They were all angry, even those who would later remain loyal to King George, and they were determined to settle their squabble with Parliament. The Congress adopted a defiant set of declarations called the Suffolk Resolves, which had been rushed to Philadelphia from Suffolk, Massachusetts, by the rebellious silversmith Paul Revere. The resolutions stated that the Intolerable Acts were completely invalid, and called for a complete boycott of trade with Britain if the obnoxious laws were not repealed.

But the Congress also insisted on loyalty to the Crown. The delegates agreed to British regulation of colonial trade as a token of their goodwill, and they almost adopted a conciliatory plan designed by Joseph Galloway of Pennsylvania just a few days before they voted for the hard-line Suffolk resolutions. At their parties they self-consciously lifted their glasses to the health of the king and queen (colonials loved to drink toasts). They may have been angry, but the idea of war with their mother country was repugnant.

Unhappily, King George did not feel the same. He, too, was determined to stand firm, and, assuming that he wielded overwhelming power, he was more than willing to use force. "Blows must decide whether they are to be subject to the Country or independent," George told Lord North at a time when no colonial leader had publicly mentioned the possibility of independence.

Hearing of the king's intransigence, the delegates to the Congress could not ignore the likely consequence of their convention. One of their last actions before adjourning was to call on Americans to organize and train local military units.

Colonial Soldiers

Many Americans needed no encouragement. In the Massachusetts countryside, tempers were already burning. When a British spy, sent out from Boston to get a feel for the mood of the people, asked an old farmer why, at his age, he was cleaning his gun, the old man replied that "there was a flock of redcoats in Boston, which he expected would be here soon; he meant to try

The colonial army was a motley group, as these watercolors of American militia suggest.

and hit some of them." Did his neighbors feel the way he did? Yes, most of them. "There was one Tory house in sight," the old man said, "and he wished it was in flames."

Younger men oiled their muskets and rifles and met on village greens to elect officers and drill. Practically every adult colonial male was armed. Guns were as much tools as axes were. Farm families in the most settled regions still hunted for some of their food, and the day when they had to protect themselves from the Indians and the French was not long gone.

The Americans were said to be excellent marksmen. Their rifles were generally more accurate than the redcoats' muskets, and powder and shot were too expensive to waste. But the colonists were not soldiers. They had shunned British attempts to recruit them, and General Wolfe had called his American militia "the dirtiest, most contemptible cowardly dogs you can conceive." Considering the nature of eighteenth-century warfare, however, this was almost a compliment.

How Wars Were Fought

Like much in the Age of Enlightenment, eighteenth-century warfare was highly structured. In battle, two armies in close formation maneuvered to face one another from the best possible position, preferably high ground. After an exchange of artillery, the attacking army closed the gap to the oddly cheery music of fife and drum (or bagpipes if the soldiers were Scots). The armies exchanged musket fire in volleys. The men pointed rather than aimed their weapons, and the army that stood its ground amidst the horror of smoke, noise, and companions dropping to the sod defeated the one that panicked, broke ranks, and fled.

The key to winning such battles was long, hard, and tedious training according to manuals written by French and Prussian tacticians. These drills (and a dram of rum or gin before battle) were designed to make a machine of thousands of individual human beings. Marksmanship counted for little. Individual initiative was a curse, to be exorcised by brutal discipline. The goal was nothing less than unnatural behavior on a grand scale: not fleeing from a horrifying experience.

Lexington and Concord

And so, when General Gage decided to seize a rebel arsenal at Concord, Massachusetts, twenty-one miles from Boston, he did not worry about the Minutemen, plain farmers pledged to be ready to fight at a minute's notice. On April 19, 1775, he sent seven hundred well-drilled soldiers under Major John Pitcairn to seize

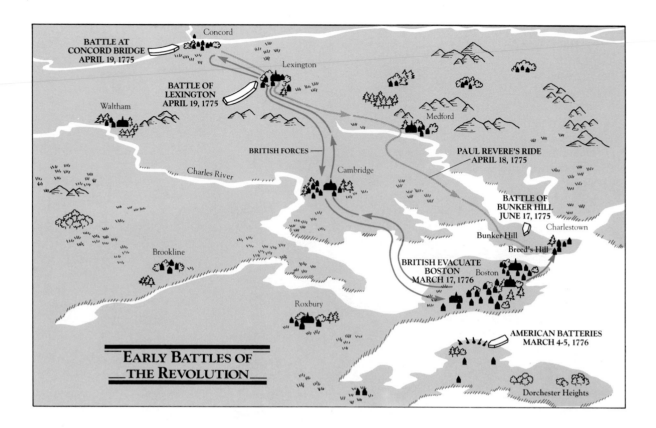

BATTLE AT CONCORD BRIDGE APRIL 19, 1775

Concord

BATTLE OF LEXINGTON APRIL 19, 1775

Lexington

Waltham

Medford

BRITISH FORCES —

PAUL REVERE'S RIDE APRIL 18, 1775

Charles River

Cambridge

BATTLE OF BUNKER HILL JUNE 17, 1775

Charlestown

Bunker Hill

Breed's Hill

Brookline

BRITISH EVACUATE BOSTON MARCH 17, 1776

Boston

Roxbury

AMERICAN BATTERIES MARCH 4-5, 1776

EARLY BATTLES OF THE REVOLUTION

Dorchester Heights

---

the munitions and, if possible, to arrest Samuel Adams and John Hancock, who were hiding in the area.

The Americans were warned by "the midnight ride of Paul Revere" and several other men, who actually got farther than Revere, bringing the news that "the British are coming" to crossroads and town commons. When Pitcairn arrived at Lexington, he discovered seventy nervous farmers drawn up in a semblance of battle formation. Their fate seemed to confirm British confidence. Indeed, what happened at Lexington Green encapsulated what was happening between Britain and its colonies all over North America.

The Americans were frightened and confused at the sight of the solid ranks of tough, grim men, who outnumbered them ten to one. They stood around uncertainly, murmuring among themselves while Pitcairn repeated his orders to disperse. Like many English, the major was not anxious to kill Americans.

Finally, giving in to the reality of the situation, the farmers began to shuffle off. Then "the shot heard 'round the world" rang out, setting off several volleys of British fire and a token American response. Eight lay dead, ten wounded.

Who fired the shot? A colonial militant who, like Sam Adams, was determined to force the issue? A British soldier, blundering as George III and Lord

North had blundered and would continue to do? Or was it an accident, the result of the tension that gripped the whole of Massachusetts? No one really knows, and it did not matter in the end. In London, on the same day as the Battle of Lexington, Parliament was passing another Intolerable Act, which banned Massachusetts fishermen from the Grand Banks of Newfoundland. When Americans heard of that act, which seemed designed to finish off the already crippled New England economy, it would surely have set off armed rebellion.

After clearing the Lexington green, the British detachment marched on to Concord, where a larger group of Americans met them at a bridge. Surprised and alarmed by the extent of resistance, Major Pitcairn ordered a retreat to Boston. All the way, Minutemen sniped at the British soldiers from behind trees and stone fences, inflicting serious casualties. When the redcoats reached the city, more than 250 of the expedition were dead or wounded. Minutemen, elated by their success, set up camp outside Boston.

Bunker Hill

Soon sixteen thousand Americans surrounded the city. In England, Edmund Burke pleaded with Parliament to

Unprepared Minutemen were outnumbered by British troops at the Battle of Lexington.

evacuate Boston and allow tempers to cool. As usual, the most thoughtful politician of the age was ignored. Lord North dispatched another one thousand troops to Boston along with three more generals—Henry Clinton, "Gentleman Johnny" Burgoyne, and William Howe. They argued Gage out of his reluctance to take action, and Howe took on the job of occupying a peninsula across the Charles River. The day before Howe moved, the Americans took the peninsula, including high ground on Bunker Hill and, nearer to Boston, Breed's Hill. When Howe began to move, sixteen hundred armed colonials were dug in on the summit of Breed's Hill.

Howe sent two thousand crack troops up the slopes. No one returned their shots. Then, when the Americans could "see the whites of their eyes" (in other

words, when they could aim), they let loose a murderous volley. The redcoats staggered and retreated. Again Howe sent up his troops, and again they were thrown back. Now, however, the British correctly calculated that the Americans were short of ammunition. Reinforcing his badly mauled front line with fresh troops, Howe took Breed's Hill with bayonets.

The British had won, or had they? Hearing that two hundred men had been killed and one thousand wounded, General Clinton remarked that too many such "victories" would destroy the British ability to fight. Clinton was right. The misnamed Battle of Bunker Hill was an American triumph. The British gained nothing. The colonial militia simply fell back to encircle Boston, while revolutionaries tightened their control of the countryside. Just as important, the

Americans had learned that it was possible to stand up to the well-trained British army in pitched conventional battle.

Ticonderoga

American morale had another boost in the spring of 1775. Soon after Lexington and Concord, a would-be revolutionary government, the Massachusetts Committee of Safety, instructed Benedict Arnold, scion of a wealthy Connecticut family and a proven soldier, to raise an army and attack Fort Ticonderoga, a small former French outpost on Lake Champlain in New York. Before he started, Arnold learned that a group of backwoodsmen from what is now Vermont, a kind of guerrilla group called the Green Mountain Boys, were prepared to march behind a cantankerous land speculator named Ethan Allen.

Arnold caught up with the Green Mountain Boys, but he was unable to get Allen to recognize his authority. Quarreling all the way to the remote fort, the two nevertheless captured Ticonderoga on May 10. When the British detachment, having heard of no revolution, asked in whose name they were supposed to surrender, Allen allegedly replied, "in the name of the great Jehovah and the Continental Congress." Since Allen was an atheist, however, he was unlikely to have spoken such words.

Over the next days, the Arnold–Allen group captured several other small forts. They were not big battles. They were hardly battles at all by European standards. The British garrisons were caught entirely by surprise. But along with "Bunker Hill," these triumphs established that a war had begun, and Americans began to take sides. Nowhere was the psychological impact of the northern victories greater than in Philadelphia, where the Second Continental Congress already was in session.

The Second Continental Congress

The delegates to the Second Continental Congress were less cautious than those to the First. Some conservatives, such as Joseph Galloway, were no longer present, and their places were taken by militants such as young Thomas Jefferson, a Virginian who had written a number of scorching anti-British polemics.

Even if the men who gathered in Philadelphia in May 1775 had been more cautious, events would have forced them to take drastic steps. War was a reality, and if the Congress was to retain the authority that Ethan Allen had ostensibly bestowed on it, it had to catch up with the New Englanders. In order to do so, the delegates sent George Washington, silently eloquent in his handsome uniform, to take command of the troops around Boston. The delegates mulled over the news of Bunker Hill, Ticonderoga, an unsuccessful attack on Canada led by Arnold, and the defeat of Governor Dinsmore of Virginia by Virginians and North Carolinians at the end of 1775. Even where there was no bloodshed, royal authority was disintegrating as governors fled to the safety of British warships and self-appointed rebel committees took over government functions. Only in far-off Georgia did a decisive royal governor hold fast to real authority. But even he could not prevent three Georgia delegates from making their way to Philadelphia.

Congress still shied away from independence. Their "Declaration of the Cause and Necessity of Taking up Arms," of July 1775 denied any motive but the defense of their liberties under the British flag. But the inconsistency of shooting at King George's soldiers while swearing undying love for him was preying on the minds of all. Throughout the autumn of 1775, more and more voices were raised for independence. With Lord North refusing to propose any kind of compromise, Congress held back purely because of a thread of sentiment—the ancestral tie with the mother country.

Breaking the Tie

The man who stepped forward to snip it was not even an American, but an Englishman. Thirty-nine years of age in 1775, Thomas Paine had been born into a family of artisans (as Benjamin Franklin had been); his father was a corsetmaker. Perhaps their common origins helped Franklin to see through Paine's record of failures in half a dozen occupations, his "loathesome" appearance, and his vainglorious opinion of his own talents. In 1774, Franklin urged Paine to go to America, and he provided him with valuable letters of introduction.

Paine's Common Sense

Egotistic Paine was, but his talents as a rouser of protest were unparalleled. In January 1776 he published a pamphlet that ranks with Luther's ninety-five theses and *The Communist Manifesto* as works that changed the course of history.

In *Common Sense*, Paine argued that it was foolish to risk everything for the purpose of British approval, and he shredded the Americans' sentimental attachment to King George III and to the very idea of monarchy. George was a tyrant, Paine said, a "Royal Brute." All kings were vile. With a genius for propaganda that would produce many stirring calls for democracy and liberty over the next twenty years, Paine made converts by the thousands. Within a few years, a country with a population of 2.5 million bought five hundred thousand copies of the pamphlet. Every American who could read must have at least skimmed through it.

Paine's depiction of the king seemed to come to life with every new dispatch from London. George refused even to listen to American suggestions for peace, and he backed Lord North's plan to hire German mercenaries to crush the rebellion. As the spring of 1776 wore on, colony after colony formally nullified the king's authority within its boundaries. Others, borrowing phrases from Tom Paine, instructed their delegates in Philadelphia to vote for independence.

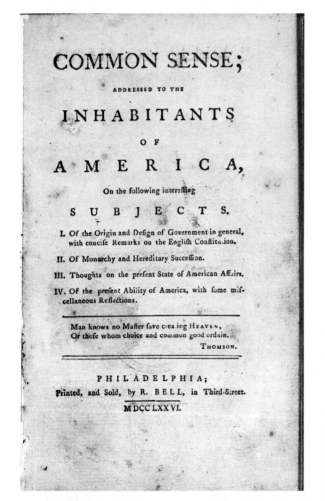

The title page of Thomas Paine's Common Sense, which argued for American political independence.

ROUSING REVOLUTION IN COMMON SENSE

"O! ye that love mankind! Ye that dare oppose not only the tyranny but the tyrant, stand forth! Every spot of the Old World is overrun with oppression. Freedom hath been hunted around the globe. Asia and Africa have long expelled her. Europe regards her as a stranger and England hath given her warning to depart. O! receive the fugitive and prepare in time an asylum for mankind."

Thomas Paine

Independence

On June 7, Richard Henry Lee of Virginia introduced the resolution that "these United Colonies are, and of right ought to be free and independent states." For three weeks the delegates debated and privately argued the issue. New England and the southern colonies were solidly for the resolution; the Middle Colonies were reluctant and divided. New York never did vote for independence, but Pennsylvania—the large, prosperous, and strategically located "keystone" state—gave in. The pacifistic John Dickinson (who was a Quaker) and the conservative Robert Morris agreed to absent themselves so that the deadlock in the delegation could be broken in favor of the resolution. (Both men later supported the patriot cause.)

Delaware swung to the side of independence when Caesar Rodney galloped full tilt to Philadelphia from Dover, casting the deciding vote in his delegation. On July 2, these maneuvers concluded, the Congress broke America's legal ties with England. "The second day of July 1776," an excited John Adams wrote home, "will be the most memorable epoch in the history of America." He was two days off. The "Glorious Fourth" became the national holiday when, on that day, the

WRITING THE DECLARATION

Thomas Jefferson did not try to be original in writing the Declaration of Independence, but to call on ideas that were in the air so that the American cause would be immediately accepted. His famous statement of the natural rights of man, for example, was taken from a speech that Samuel Adams had made in Boston in November 1772: "Among the natural rights of the colonists are these: first, a right to life; secondly, a right to liberty; thirdly, to property; together with the right to support and defend them in the best manner they can."

Congress gathered to adopt its official statement to Americans and to the world of why it chose "to dissolve the political bands" that tied America to Great Britain.

The Declaration of Independence

Officially, the Declaration of Independence was the work of a committee consisting of Thomas Jefferson, Roger Sherman of Connecticut, John Adams, Benjamin Franklin, and Robert Livingston of New York. In fact, appreciating that a committee cannot write anything readable, the actual work was assigned to Jefferson because of his "peculiar felicity of style." The Virginian, red-haired, lanky, almost as careless of his personal appearance as was Thomas Paine, holed up in his room and in two weeks emerged with a masterpiece. Franklin and Adams changed a few words, and the

Congress made some alterations, the most important of which was to delete an attack on the institution of slavery.

Then, on July 4, the signing began. John Hancock, the president of the Congress, wrote his name in flamboyant outsized script so that King George would not need his spectacles in order to read it. Hancock was risking little. Along with Samuel Adams, he already had a price on his head. Many of the others who affixed their names, some only months later, were taking a bold step. They were unknown to the king and his advisers.

And it was King George who bore the brunt of Jefferson's attack. He was blamed for practically everything that was wrong in the colonies but the weather. This was propaganda, of course. King George was beholden to Parliament for every colonial policy he tried to en-

The signing of the Declaration of Independence, July 4, 1776, portrayed by John Trumbull.

TWO BLACKS OF THE YOUNG REPUBLIC

Samuel Johnson, who was recognized during his own lifetime as one of the greatest figures of English literature, did not like Americans. Among their other unpleasant traits, Dr. Johnson said, they were shameless hypocrites. "Why is it," he wrote in 1775, "that we hear the loudest yelps for liberty among the drivers of negroes?" His point, of course, was painfully apparent to many of the people who subscribed to the phrase "all men are created equal," and then held one American in five in bondage for life.

Proslavery whites simply ignored the sentiments of the Declaration of Independence. Others, who disliked slavery, lived with the contradiction by consoling themselves that blacks were intellectually and morally inferior to whites, and so could not fulfill the duties of a citizen in a republic. In order to hold to this rationalization, however, they had to ignore the example of two remarkable individuals.

Phillis Wheatley (1755–84) was born in West Africa, probably in what is now Senegal. She was kidnapped when eight years of age by slavers bound for Boston. There, despite the girl's frail appearance, a successful tailor and merchant, John Wheatley, purchased her as a personal maid for his wife.

Phillis, as the Wheatleys named her, was lucky in her master and mistress. Had she been sold to work on a farm or plantation, her intelligence and charm would have gone unnoticed, as the abilities of other blacks were ignored. The Wheatleys recognized the girl's brilliance and treated her as they did their own children, providing her an education as well as decent food, clothing, and lodging. Wheatley was a prodigy, mastering the English language within sixteen months and astonishing visitors by reading and explaining the meaning of the most difficult sections of the Bible, Greek myths, and the poetry of Alexander Pope and Thomas Gray, then the most admired of the English poets.

At the age of thirteen, Phillis wrote her first poem, an ode "To the University of Cambridge in New England" (Harvard), and in the next years a salute to King George III (still immensely popular in America) and a eulogy to George Whitefield, the founder of American Methodism, a faith Phillis adopted.

Phillis Wheatley became a well-known poet in America.

In 1772 or 1773, John Wheatley freed the young woman, not an uncommon practice in Massachusetts during the decade of the Revolution, and helped pay her passage to England, where she hoped to recover her health and to meet the countess of Huntingdon, with whom she had corresponded. With the countess's help, Phillis published a book of her *Poems on Various Subjects, Religious and Moral,* but she soon returned to Boston when she heard that Mrs. Wheatley was dying.

In 1775, with the Revolution about to explode, Phillis wrote a letter to George Washington, who responded, expressing his interest in meeting her (they never met). Like many Virginia slaveowners, Washington worried about the wisdom and morality of slavery, and he looked on Wheatley as evidence that blacks were indeed capable of great attainments.

In 1778, Phillis alienated the Wheatley heirs by marrying John Peters, a free black who apparently was quite intelligent and was a writer of some ability. Peters, however, was a ne'er-do-well and a deserter. He stole a manuscript that Phillis was preparing for publication, lost it, and was jailed for bad debts. After bearing three children, all of whom were stillborn or died in infancy, Phillis Wheatley died in poverty in 1784.

force. But the propaganda worked; like Paine's *Common Sense,* Jefferson's essay focused American anger on a visible and vulnerable scapegoat.

The Declaration is not remembered for its catalog of English abuses. It is one of the great political documents in world history because, in the first part of it, Jefferson penned one of the most stirring statements of the rights of human beings that has been written to this day. He did not speak only of the rights of American colonials. He put the case for independence in terms of the rights of all human beings: *We hold these truths to be self-evident, that all men are created equal, that they are endowed by their Creator with certain unalienable Rights, that among these are Life, Liberty and the pursuit of Happiness.* And he codified the principles that government drew its authority only from the consent of the people to be governed and when the people withdrew that consent, they had the right to rebel.

Benjamin Banneker (1731–1806), who is known as the black Benjamin Franklin because of the breadth of his interests and the fact that he published a popular almanac, was the son of a free black mother and a slave father who, when Benjamin was still a child, prospered as a planter in Maryland. The elder Banneker educated his son at a Quaker school near Baltimore, one of very few in the colonies that accepted black students.

As a young man, Benjamin farmed his father's lands, which he inherited, but his heart was not in the life. Neighbors remembered him as a detached, dreamy man, given to eccentric dress and habits. On clear nights, Banneker lay outside on a blanket, studying the stars. In free moments during the day, he studied bees, on which he wrote a treatise, and worked difficult mathematical problems, at which he was a genius. Banneker constructed a wooden clock (said by some to be the first clock made wholly in North America) and was locally famed as an astronomer. His reputation spread in 1789, when he accurately predicted a solar eclipse. This led to the publication of *Banneker's Almanac* (1792–1802), a successor to *Poor Richard's* in popularity, and a correspondence with Thomas Jefferson, who secured from President Washington a position for Banneker on the commission that surveyed the District of Columbia.

Banneker was a natural scientist; politics were of no great interest to him. As a Quaker, he was a pacifist during the Revolutionary War. In 1791, he wrote a letter to Jefferson, which has since become famous, in which he offered his own example of proof that blacks were capable of citizenship and should be granted it:

I apprehend that you will embrace every opportunity to eradicate that train of absurd and false ideas and opinions, which so generally prevail with respect to us [black people]; and that your sentiments are concurrent with mine which are: that one universal Father hath given being to us all; that He not only made us all of one flesh, but that He hath also without partisanship afforded us all with the same faculties and that, however variable we may be in society or religion, however diversified in situation or color, we are all the same family and stand in the same relation to Him.

Banneker knew that only the most extraordinary individuals, such as Wheatley and himself, could hope to break through the prejudice against blacks. He hoped that political leaders like Jefferson would see in their accomplishments evidence that, given the opportunities of freedom, all blacks could earn places in society commensurate with their abilities. The existence of a Banneker did trouble Jefferson, who wanted to believe that blacks were not the intellectual and moral equals of whites and therefore were not entitled to the rights stated in his Declaration of Independence. Habit, self-interest (Jefferson's social position was built on slave ownership), and the death of the astronomer in 1806, when Jefferson was president, allowed him to ignore his doubts.

Benjamin Banneker, natural scientist and author of a popular almanac.

For Further Reading

Most of the books listed at the end of Chapter 7 also treat material covered in this chapter. In addition, see Carl Becker, *The Declaration of Independence* (1922), for an intensive study of the great document that is still revealing. B. W. Labaree, *The Boston Tea Party* (1964), and H. B. Zobel, *The Boston Massacre* (1970), provide detailed accounts of those two signal events. David Ammerman, *In the Common Cause* (1974), does the same for the Coercive, or Intolerable, Acts.

Garry Wills, *Inventing America* (1978), and Morton White, *The Philosophy of the American Revolution* (1978), are recent and very readable studies of the ideas that formed the consciousness of the revolutionary generation.

9

Fighting the War and Facing the Peace

The Independent Republic, 1776–1787

The signers of the Declaration pledged their lives, their fortunes, and their sacred honor to the cause of independence. This was no empty slogan. Had George III won the quick victory he expected, at least some of those men at Philadelphia would have been punished severely, even hanged. They called themselves patriots. From George's point of view they were traitors, and where the king was able to do so, as in Ireland, he dealt brutally with traitors both before and after the American Revolution.

Washington Crossing the Delaware by Emmanuel Leutze, 1851, presents an heroic image of General Washington and his men. In reality, Washington's troops were weary and desperate when they fled across the river in 1776.

The Balance of Power

Looked at without benefit of hindsight, the patriots' chances of succeeding were not, in 1776, very bright. Despite the military and moral victories of the preceding year, the Americans had challenged one of Europe's finest armies, commanded by experienced generals. Britain's great wealth enabled that nation to augment the regular army by hiring mercenaries from small German states whose rulers made a living by training and renting out soldiers. Six months before the signing of the Declaration, in January 1776, Lord North contracted for eighteen thousand (later thirty thousand) Hessians from the principality of Hesse-Anhalt. Against these professionals, the Americans could field only hastily organized militia. "To place any dependence on them," George Washington wrote, "is assuredly resting on a broken staff."

The British were handicapped by distance from the field. But the breadth of the Atlantic was not too important to a nation that fought battles in India. The size and efficiency of the Royal Navy balanced the colonists' edge in fighting on their home ground. By 1778, the British had fifty thousand troops in North America, while Washington considered it a good day when he could field five thousand.

The Loyalists

Nor must it be forgotten that a great many Americans remained fiercely loyal to King George, and bitterly hostile to the Revolution. There were probably very few Loyalists (or Tories, as the patriots called them) in rural New England and the coastal counties of the South. Nevertheless, in March 1776, when General William Howe evacuated Boston, a city of fewer than fifteen thousand people, one thousand Bostonians went with him rather than live under the rebels. When he set up his headquarters in New York in September, Howe was received more as a liberator than as a conqueror.

Perhaps fifty thousand Americans fought on the "British" side at one time or another, including black slaves to whom the British promised freedom, and made good on their word. At the end of the war, as many as one hundred thousand Americans (one in thirty!) left their native land for England or Nova Scotia. These immigrants were surely just a fraction of the losers. Records show many incidents of patriots harassing loyalists after the war, so plenty of pro-British people must have stayed.

John Adams estimated that one-third of the American population was Tory, another third patriot, and another third willing to hop either way, depending on which side was winning in their neighborhood. In a metaphorical version of the war between "birds" and "beasts," New Jersey poet Francis Hopkinson wrote that there were

'Mongst us too many, like the Bat,
Inclin'd to this side or that
As in'trest leads—or wait to see
Which party will the strongest be.

Adams probably overestimated the number of active Loyalists, and Hopkinson was too harsh on those who did not commit themselves decisively to one side or the other. As at all times in human history, including those later regarded as cataclysmic, many people wished only to be left alone to pursue their daily lives. During the Revolution, many Americans felt strongly on neither side and were no more villains or opportunistic "Bats" than they were heroes. About all that can be said for certain is that the militant revolutionaries were a minority, decidedly so at the beginning of the war.

Patriot Chances

Despite the obstacles, the Revolutionary cause was far from doomed. The rebels were fighting a defensive war

---

THE FEARS OF A LOYALIST

The Reverend Mather Byles (1706–88) was an oddity, a Massachusetts Congregational minister who opposed the Revolution. In a sermon of 1776 he expressed his fears of democracy: "Which is better, to be ruled by one tyrant three thousand miles away, or by three thousand tyrants not a mile away?"

A VISION OF THE FUTURE

John Adams understood that circumstances made him a politician and a revolutionary. But he envisioned another kind of future for his country:

I must study politics and war, that my sons may have liberty to study mathematics and philosophy, geography, natural history and naval architecture, navigation, commerce, and agriculture, in order to give their children a right to study painting, poetry, music, architecture, statuary, tapestry and porcelain.

in their homeland. As many twentieth-century "wars of liberation" have shown, such wars bestow a great many advantages on the defenders. Militarily, the patriots did not have to destroy or even decisively defeat the British. Rebels on their own ground have only to hold on and hold out in the hope that weariness, demoralization, and dissent take their toll on the enemy. There was a considerable pro-American, antiwar sentiment in England, even among powerful members of Parliament—Edmund Burke, the marquess of Rockingham, William Pitt, and the radical John Wilkes. A substantial minority in the House of Commons believed that the Americans were in the right, and they noisily sniped at Lord North's ministry from first to last.

Also like members of modern insurrectionary movements, the Americans hoped for foreign intervention. Since 1763, many European nations envied Great Britain its preeminence and wished it nothing but harm. No enemy of Britain was more powerful than France—which Britain had humiliated in North America, India, and Europe. And France was friendly to the American cause. In May 1776, the French government began to funnel money and arms to the rebels through a secret agent, Pierre de Beaumarchais. Over the next two years, the most critical part of the war, the Americans depended on France for 80 percent of their gunpowder and a large proportion of other material. In September 1776, recognizing the importance of foreign assistance, the Continental Congress sent Benjamin Franklin, seventy years old but far from creaky, to join two other American diplomats in Paris to work for a French alliance.

Franklin was a social sensation. The French aristocracy, in the last years of its glories, was enamored of him. The wigged and powdered ladies and lords of Louis XVI's court were in the midst of a "noble-savage" craze. They believed (rather naively for such a sophisticated group) that their own peasants and the "primitive" Americans led happy, wholesome lives because they were close to nature.

Queen Marie Antoinette had a "peasant village" built at Versailles, where she and her ladies-in-waiting dressed like shepherdesses and milked well-scrubbed cows. Aware of this fashion, Franklin, who preferred the elegant life when he could find it, made a point of appearing at court wearing homespun wool clothing, no wig, and rimless bifocal spectacles (which he had invented) on the end of his unpowdered nose. The French nobles were under the impression that Franklin was a Quaker; so, although he had been a lifelong enemy of the Quaker faction in Pennsylvania politics, he played the part.

Benjamin Franklin charmed French aristocrats at Versailles with his humble manner and homely dress.

French society loved the show, but the government of Count Vergennes was more cautious. Vergennes knew that open war with Great Britain was risky at any time, and France's important ally, Spain, which possessed a huge American empire, was understandably nervous about encouraging colonial rebellions. Franklin's mission was made even more difficult when news arrived in Versailles and Paris of a string of American defeats in the field.

"The Times That Try Men's Souls"

General William Howe, who took command of all British troops in North America after the Battle of Bunker Hill, was a skilled soldier of the traditional school. He prepared meticulously, thinking through every conceivable detail of his problem, and moved only when he was positive of success. Howe's caution sometimes caused him to miss opportunities. But early in 1776, when the American General Henry Knox arrived outside of Boston with forty-three cannon and sixteen big mortars, which George Washington placed on Dorchester Heights overlooking Boston, Howe correctly calculated that to remain in the city was suicidal.

Howe's Plan

Howe moved his headquarters to New York, where Loyalists were more numerous than in Boston. From there, Howe reasoned, he could move easily into the interior, defeat Washington on ground more favorable to the British and then turn north up the Hudson River, joining a British invasion from Canada. This pincers movement would isolate New England from the rest of the colonies. Then, with the help of the Royal Navy (commanded in American waters by his brother, Admiral Richard Howe), he could subdue troublesome Massachusetts at his leisure. If the colonies south of New York continued to hold out, Howe could then turn on them.

It was a sound plan that might easily have worked. On July 2, 1776, the same day that Congress voted for independence, Howe landed ten thousand men on Staten Island, just south of New York City. Within a few weeks, he tripled his numbers and moved to Long Island, where Washington had hurriedly dug in with a smaller force. Washington's maneuver was not well conceived. Fighting on islands such as surrounded New York harbor favors the side with naval power, and the Howes had more than two hundred ships in the area.

On August 27, Howe almost surrounded Washington at the Battle of Long Island, but the Americans slipped away to fortifications at Brooklyn Heights, across the East River from Manhattan. Again Howe's redcoats and Hessians punished the five thousand rebels to the breaking point, but, in one night, Washington managed to sneak the bulk of his army to Manhattan. Howe pursued him, capturing three thousand American troops at Fort Washington and forcing General Nathaniel Greene to abandon Fort Lee, across the Hudson River in New Jersey. Once again Washington led away his bedraggled army just hours shy of defeat, first north to White Plains and, when nearly surrounded there, across the Hudson River into New Jersey.

The Fox Turns on the Hounds

It was like the British aristocrats' favorite sport, the fox hunt. Indeed, Howe infuriated the dignified and self-conscious Washington by sounding the traditional bugle call of the chase when the Americans were on the run north of New York City. In truth, Washington's army was as desperate as a weary fox. Washington had to flee across New Jersey without a fight. When he crossed the Delaware River into Pennsylvania, his men were demoralized and ready to desert. In Philadelphia, one day's march to the south, Congress panicked and fled to Baltimore, effectively leaving the Virginian in complete control of what was left of the Revolution.

Washington's army at Valley Forge, 1777/78, as represented on a nineteenth-century bank note.

"These are the times that try men's souls," Thomas Paine wrote. There is no doubt that the American Revolution could have been snuffed out in December 1776, not six months after the Declaration of Independence. But William Howe soldiered by the book, and the book said that an army goes into winter quarters at the best convenient location. For Howe, the best location was New York, where his mistress and a lively social life beckoned him. He recalled his pack of hounds from Washington's heels, leaving small garrisons of Hessians to guard Trenton, Princeton, and several other New Jersey towns.

George Washington was not by nature an innovator. Had his army not been so near disintegration, he also might have followed the book into winter quarters. Instead, on Christmas night, his army rowed quietly across the Delaware into New Jersey, the boats dodging ice floes and, in the fog, one another. They marched nine miles to Trenton, the most isolated British out-

DESPAIR AT VALLEY FORGE

The winter of 1777/78 was extremely difficult for Washington's army. Inadequately fed, clothed, and sheltered at Valley Forge, while the British enjoyed comfortable quarters in Philadelphia, many fell to the depths of despair. Albigence Waldo, a surgeon with Connecticut troops, wrote this entry in his journal on December 14, 1777:

Poor food—hard lodging—cold weather—fatigue—nasty cloathes—nasty cookery—vomit half my time—smoaked out of my senses—the Devil's in't—I can't endure it—Why are we sent here to starve and freeze?—What sweet felicities have I left at home: A charming wife—pretty children—good beds—good food—good cookery—all agreeable—all harmonious! Here all confusion—smoke and cold—hunger and filthyness—a pox on my bad luck!

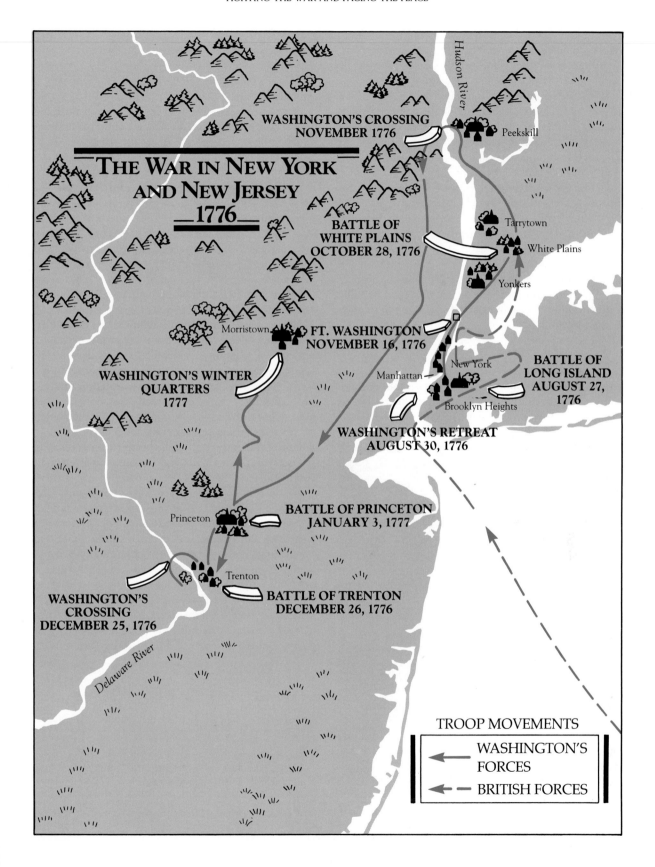

THE WAR IN NEW YORK AND NEW JERSEY 1776

WASHINGTON'S CROSSING
NOVEMBER 1776

Peekskill

Hudson River

Tarrytown

BATTLE OF
WHITE PLAINS
OCTOBER 28, 1776

White Plains

Yonkers

Morristown

FT. WASHINGTON
NOVEMBER 16, 1776

WASHINGTON'S WINTER
QUARTERS
1777

New York

BATTLE OF
LONG ISLAND
AUGUST 27,
1776

Manhattan

Brooklyn Heights

WASHINGTON'S RETREAT
AUGUST 30, 1776

BATTLE OF PRINCETON
JANUARY 3, 1777

Princeton

Trenton

WASHINGTON'S
CROSSING
DECEMBER 25, 1776

BATTLE OF TRENTON
DECEMBER 26, 1776

Delaware River

TROOP MOVEMENTS

WASHINGTON'S
FORCES

BRITISH FORCES

post and, at dawn, caught the Hessians asleep and, no doubt, none the better for their holiday celebrations. Washington captured almost the entire garrison, while suffering only five American casualties.

Howe was shaken and infuriated by his first defeat in America. He sent two detachments to battle Washington before the Americans could press closer to New York, cancelling half Washington's winnings. At Princeton, on January 3, 1777, General Charles Cornwallis was outsmarted by Washington, who avoided him and defeated another surprised force, this time British. Cornwallis had no choice but to withdraw to New Brunswick, within easy reinforcement range of New York. Finally, in the depths of a severe winter, Washington set up his quarters at Morristown. He had saved the patriot cause.

But Washington's victories at Trenton and Princeton did not significantly affect Howe's strategy. The British were still snug in New York, while a fresh army massed in Canada.

The Father of His Country

In every particular by which greatness is measured, the tall and solemn Washington comes up short. He lacked originality. He was no thinker, and seems to have read

George Washington in the famous Gilbert Stuart "Athenaeum" portrait, 1796.

few books. He contributed no document to the rich literature of colonial protest and rarely addressed the two Continental Congresses he attended. His personality was cool, quiet, dull. He excited none of his contemporaries.

Nor was Washington a successful field commander. His expeditions during the French and Indian War, which culminated in the disastrous Braddock campaign, were fiascos.

In the early years of the Revolutionary War, he won a few small battles, such as those at Trenton and Princeton, but never a big one; his defeats were legion. Most of his years in command were spent in retreat, a step ahead of annihilation. Any number of American commanders exceeded him as a tactician, and his strategy amounted to responding to the British generals' maneuvers.

But it would be difficult to overstate Washington's contribution to the establishment of the American republic, to deny him the honor bestowed on him during his lifetime—the Father of His Country. It was in retreat that his military contribution to independence lay. If he rarely won a battle, he kept an army in the field against overwhelming odds. Washington survived in the face of repeated defeats, superior British forces, inadequate provisions, disease, and almost no shelter for his men during several extremely cold winters. In order to explain this accomplishment, it is necessary to fall back on the intangibles that transfixed most of his contemporaries. Radicals like Samuel Adams, instinctive conservatives like Alexander Hamilton, intellectuals like Jefferson, warriors like Israel Putnam, cultivated European aristocrats like the Marquis de Lafayette—all idolized and deferred to the Virginian.

Washington's aristocratic bearing, integrity, sense of dignity, and aloofness from petty squabbles set him a head taller than the best of his contemporaries, just as his height of six feet two inches made him a physical giant of the time. Despite his setbacks and lack of flash, he held the cause together by that vague personal quality known as "character." The historian Garry Wills writes,

There would be no doomed romance of failure around him. He accomplished everything he set out to do, went home, and died prosaically in bed. He succeeded so well that he almost succeeds himself out of the hero business. He made his accomplishments look, in retrospect, almost inevitable. Heroism so quietly efficient dwindles to managerial skill.

Managerial success is not the stuff about which epic poems are written. But it was Washington's dogged grip on the reins of the war effort, while the British won the battles and Congress bickered, that kept alive the enthusiasm of 1776.

The Watershed Campaign of 1777

In the spring of 1777, Howe could have carried out his strategy of marching north, joining John Burgoyne's army from Canada and invading New England from the west. Washington would have had little choice but to try to catch up with the British forces. Instead, Howe hatched the plan of conquering Pennsylvania, where, as in New York, he counted on widespread Loyalist support. His decision proved to be a mistake, especially when, slow as ever, Howe did not get started until July.

Washington met him twice: first at Brandywine Creek, southwest of Philadelphia, on September 11; and then at Germantown, a suburb of the city, on October 4. Both times the Americans had to fall back and managed to escape only at the last moment. Howe easily occupied the largest city in the colonies, which was also, in theory, the American capital.

In the north, however, a more significant campaign was under way. In June, General Burgoyne left Canada with eight thousand men and more than a hundred cannon—a formidable force. Like Howe, he moved slowly. The Americans scoffed at his trivial baggage, including enough changes of clothing to outfit King George's court and a mistress who dined nightly with Gentleman Johnny off a table set with linen table-cloths, china, crystal, and silverware.

Such fripperies were not unusual, however, and could not have amounted to much in the equipment that was necessary to supply an army of eight thousand men. Burgoyne's real problem was that the Lake Champlain route was no route at all for a party larger than a band of traders. The British, Hessians, and Indians literally had to construct a road from narrow footpaths. Small groups of Americans, who felled large trees across the path of the advancing British army, did not make the job easier.

Saratoga

By July, Burgoyne retook Fort Ticonderoga, but he already was in trouble. Reinforcements due from the west were turned back by Benedict Arnold. A raiding party he sent east to seize supplies in Bennington, Vermont, was wiped out by local militia. In a series of skirmishes around Saratoga, another fort, Burgoyne lost hundreds more men.

Knowing by now that Howe was en route to Philadelphia, Burgoyne should have given up the expedition and backtracked to the safety of Canada. Even if he reached New York, he would accomplish little. His troops could be moved south more easily by sea from Montreal. But the charming and witty playboy (he was also a successful playwright) was an inexplicably foolish

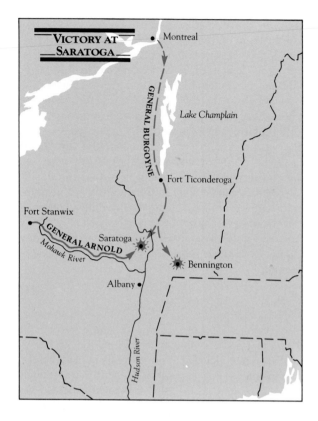

soldier. He decided to sit tight in the wilderness of New York and Vermont and wait for help from General Clinton in New York.

Burgoyne's blunder was a godsend to the Americans. On October 12, after yet another damaging battle, he surrendered five thousand soldiers to General Horatio Gates. The Battle of Saratoga was the most important event of the year, perhaps of the war. With it, New England was lost to the British. Except for Newport, Rhode Island, which they held only by tying down a large army and fleet, the British had no foothold north of New York. Indeed, the British tacitly wrote off New England and Howe's excellent strategy when they decided to transfer their main operations to the South.

The Tide Turns

Just as important, the news of Saratoga was exactly what Benjamin Franklin and his fellow American diplomats were waiting for in Paris. The victory allayed Vergennes's doubts about patriot chances. The defeat of an army of eight thousand crack redcoats was no skirmish even by French military standards.

Nor by British standards. When Lord North heard of the battle, he informed Franklin and Silas Deane that King George was willing to end the war on the basis of the terms demanded by Americans up to July 1776. That is, the Intolerable Acts and every other obnoxious law enacted between 1763 and 1775 would be repealed. Great Britain would guarantee colonial control of internal affairs in return for loyalty to the king.

It was an attractive offer; it amounted to an American victory. Essentially, what Lord North suggested was the commonwealth system by which Britain organized its second empire in the nineteenth and twentieth centuries. But the French counteroffer of a formal alliance was even more attractive. By the end of 1777, American enthusiasm for independence and animosity toward the British were too strong to permit backtracking.

Foreign Friends

On December 17, 1777, Count Vergennes recognized the United States as an independent nation. In February 1778, he concluded a formal treaty of alliance. To go into effect if France and Britain went to war (which they did in June 1778), the agreement provided for close commercial ties between France and the United States and stated that if the United States conquered Canada, France would assert no claims to its former colony. France's reward in the event of victory would be the British West Indies. Finally, both sides pledged not to make peace separately and to continue to fight until Britain returned Gibraltar to Spain, an ally of France.

The Revolutionary War could not have been won without French support. Not only did "America's oldest friend" pour money and men into the fray, but France also provided a fleet to make up for the Americans' nearly total lack of sea power. Although Americans relished the one-on-one victories over British warships by such captains as Scottish-born John Paul Jones ("I have not yet begun to fight") and John Barry, an Irishman, the American coastline was effectively at the mercy of the Royal Navy.

France's diplomatic influence was also critical to the American cause. Vergennes averted a war that was brewing between Prussia and Austria that would have tied down French troops in Europe (a traditional British objective), and he persuaded both of those countries as well as Russia to declare their neutrality in the American conflict. Vergennes's diplomatic maneuvers denied England a sorely needed ally against America, France, Spain, and, after 1780, the Netherlands, and paved the way for informal assistance to the patriots from all over Europe.

Mercenaries for America

The chronic warfare of eighteenth-century Europe had created a cadre of military professionals who, during times of peace, were literally unemployed. Volunteers of this stripe, aristocrats looking for a commission with a salary attached, poured into the infant United States.

There was plenty of deadwood in the lot. But others were able men who were motivated by more than money. They were professional officers who relished the idea of "twisting the lion's tail," striking a blow at mighty England. Or they sympathized with the principles of liberty expressed in the Declaration of Independence.

Such a figure was the Marquis de Lafayette, a nineteen-year-old aristocrat (the British called him "the boy") who proved an excellent field commander and a personal friend to Washington. Lafayette was no dilettante, dabbling in fashionable notions. After returning to France, he worked for social and political liberalization until his death in 1834.

Just as idealistic was Casimir Pulaski, a Polish noble who had fought unsuccessfully for his country's independence from Russia. Recruited in Paris by Benjamin

The Marquis de Lafayette, a French aristocrat, served as a field commander in Washington's army.

Franklin, Pulaski was a romantic figure, a cavalry commander in gaudy uniform and waxed mustache. He was killed leading a charge at the Battle of Savannah late in the war. Johann Kalb, a Prussian who took the title Baron de Kalb when he went to America (oddly, titles wore well in the United States), also lost his life during the war, at the Battle of Camden.

Probably more valuable than combat officers were military specialists like Tadeusz Kosciusko, an engineer who was expert in building fortifications, a military field in which few Americans were trained. Kosciusko returned to Europe to work for the independence of Poland, where he is a national hero.

Friedrich Wilhelm von Steuben, a Prussian who also named himself a baron, was an expert in drill. During the winter of 1777/78 he supervised the training program that turned Washington's soldiers from a ragtag crowd into a well-disciplined army.

The War Drags On

Steuben worked his wonders just in time. By the spring of 1778, it was obvious that the war would last for several years. The Americans could not hope to force the issue against the superior British. Their strategy was to hold on, fighting battles only when conditions were auspicious, and waiting for a golden opportunity to knock the British back across the Atlantic. Lord North and General Clinton (who took over from Howe in May 1778) planned to strangle the American economy through a naval blockade and to concentrate their major military effort in the South.

Beginning with the occupation of Savannah, Georgia, in December 1778, the redcoats won a series of victories, but they could not break the stalemate. For each British victory, the Americans won another, or, in losing ground, the rebels cost the British so heavily that they had to cling to the coast.

The war wore heavily on the American side too. Prices of necessities soared. Imports, with the exception of war materiel, were available only at exorbitant cost. When Congress failed to pay and provision troops during 1780 and 1781, mutinies erupted on the Connecticut, Pennsylvania, and New Jersey lines. On the frontier, British-backed Indians ravaged newly settled areas in Pennsylvania's Wyoming Valley and New York's Cherry Valley.

Then, in September 1780, Washington learned that Benedict Arnold, commander of the fortress at West Point, had agreed to sell the fort and his services to the British for £20,000. Disgruntled at what he considered shabby treatment, Arnold also was deeply in debt. He calculated that the British eventually would win, and so accepted a commission along with pensions for his

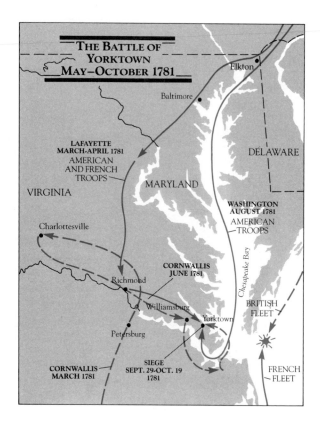

wife and children. It was an expensive proposition, but the British believed that betrayal by one of the Revolution's few heroes would demoralize the rebels.

It did. The campaign of 1781 opened with American hopes lower than they had been since the Battle of Trenton. Washington was idle outside New York. The most active British army, led by Lord Cornwallis, lost a battle at Cowpens, South Carolina, but then repeatedly pummeled Nathaniel Greene the width of North Carolina and joined with several other commanders (including Benedict Arnold) to mass seventy-five hundred men in Virginia.

The Sudden End

But Charles Cornwallis was in a delicate situation. In the South, anywhere away from navigable water was dangerous ground for the British troops, who depended on the Royal Navy to keep them supplied. So, on August 1, 1781, Cornwallis set up what he regarded as a routine encampment at Yorktown, Virginia, a little town on the same neck of land where the first permanent English settlement in America had been founded. Cornwallis then requested supplies and further orders from General Clinton in New York. Clinton, however, was no more decisive than his predecessors. His

The British army surrenders to American troops in Yorktown, Virginia, October 19, 1781.

dawdling set up the golden opportunity for which the Americans had been waiting.

In mid-August, Washington learned that a French admiral, Count François de Grasse, was sailing from the West Indies to the Chesapeake Bay with three thousand French troops and twenty-five warships. Washington had just completed a plan for an attack on New York, but he recognized a more attractive opportunity in the new combination of circumstances. Faking a maneuver around New York to keep Clinton sitting tight, he raced across New Jersey. In September, he joined his troops to those of Lafayette and de Grasse. This combined army of seventeen thousand outnumbered Cornwallis's eight thousand, almost the first time in the war that the rebels enjoyed numerical superiority.

Cornwallis did not panic. His men were well dug in, and he expected to move them out by sea and resume the war of attrition elsewhere. But between September 5 and 10, de Grasse, reinforced again, sent the British evacuation ships sailing off empty to New York. Cornwallis fought a futile defense for a few days. On October 19, he faced the inevitable and surrendered.

As if to provide one last symbol of the British arrogance that led to the nation's humiliation in North America, Cornwallis displayed his contempt for the Americans two final times. A British band played the hymn, "The World Turn'd Upside Down" during the surrender ceremonies, and Cornwallis refused to surrender personally his sword to Washington, as military etiquette required. He sent an inferior officer to the American camp with his blade. Washington refused to receive him, nodding that the symbol of capitulation should be given to General Benjamin Lincoln, whom the British had humiliated earlier in the war.

The British could have fought on. They still occupied New York and had fifty-four thousand troops in North America. But, except for King George, no one in power had the stomach for it. In February 1782, the House of Commons voted against continuing the war, and Lord North resigned. He was succeeded by Edmund Burke's patron, the earl of Rockingham, the same Whig peer who had repealed the Stamp Act in 1766. Although there were a few nasty skirmishes over the next year, mostly between Loyalists and patriots, the main armies were inactive, waiting for the results of the peace negotiations in Paris.

The Treaty of Paris

The Treaty of Paris was not signed until January 1783, because, once the war was won, the Americans and the French grew increasingly suspicious of each other.

Fearing that the other would betray it, each tried to move first. The Americans won the game. They agreed with the British on independence, the boundary between the United States and Canada, American fishing rights off Newfoundland and Nova Scotia, and a promise that Congress would urge the states not to molest Loyalists or seize Loyalist property. France had no choice but to give in and persuade Spain, the real loser, to concede British control of Gibraltar.

Across the English Channel, George III was less gracious about being stung by upstart colonials. He wrote of his former empire that "knavery seems to be so much the striking feature of its inhabitants that it may not in the end be an evil that they become aliens to this Kingdom."

Inventing a Country

The American Revolution was not the first successful war of independence. Peoples subject to other peoples had fought their masters since biblical times, and, more recently in Europe, the Dutch and the Swiss had established their independence by force of arms.

What was singular about the American case was the necessity of inventing a country from scratch. Before

George Washington addresses the Second Continental Congress.

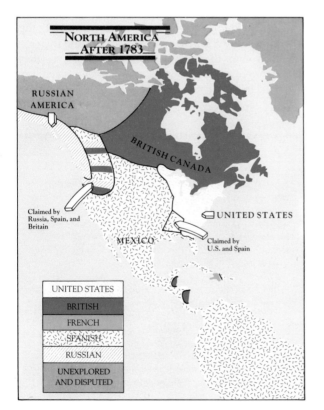

the Revolution, thirteen colonies had maintained relations with the mother country but no official connections among themselves. Establishing a union was the purpose of the first American constitution, the Articles of Confederation.

Written Constitutions

The Articles of Confederation were drawn up during the first year of independence. Consequently, that frame of government and most of the state constitutions that were adopted during the war years represented a conscious reaction to the colonial experi-

A REMARKABLE GENERATION

More than a century after the American Revolution, the historian Henry Adams (great-grandson of John Adams) looked back on the generation of Americans who declared independence, fought the war, and wrote the Articles of Confederation and the Constitution. Then he considered the caliber of political leadership in his own time. He concluded that American history was not a story of progress and evolution but of decline and decay.

ence and embodied the fears, ideals, and hopes of the Revolution.

In a notable break with British tradition, these frames of government were *written*. The British constitution is not a single supreme document but a collection of several (Magna Carta of 1215, the Bill of Rights of 1688) plus the unwritten customs and traditions of centuries.

This system has served Great Britain well to this day, but it had not served Americans well in the 1760s and 1770s. Parliament, insisting on its supremacy, had repeatedly overruled what Americans regarded as their unwritten constitutional rights. Only in Connecticut and Rhode Island, which possessed charters that set down their status, had liberties seemed relatively safe. Notably, these two new states merely changed the wording of their charters after independence and continued to use them satisfactorily as constitutions until 1818 (Connecticut) and 1842 (Rhode Island). The other states got the point. As the Virginian Thomas Jefferson put it, while written constitutions could be violated too, "they furnish a text to which those who are watchful may again rally and recall the people."

The new constitutions were written not by legislatures but by conventions elected specifically for that purpose. They were then ratified by a popular election. They could be changed only by a similar procedure and not by the legislature. The American tradition that "sovereignty" (ultimate governmental power) came from the people was institutionalized from the start.

Reaction to recent British rule took other forms. Because the patriots had resented the old officeholding elite, they guarded against a new one by holding annual elections for almost all offices and by limiting the number of years a person might serve.

The patriot constitution writers most feared executive power; the royal governors and governors' councils had been the strong arms of English power. So in order to prevent the development of an independent executive power, the new state constitutions stipulated that the governors would be weak, largely ceremonial figures. In Pennsylvania, which in 1776 adopted the most radical constitution of all the new states, there was no governor.

Other old resentments were voiced in the movement to separate church and state. Those favoring disestablishment were strongest in the former colonies where the Church of England had been the official church. There, especially in the southern states, the Anglican clergy had been pro-British and therefore an easy target. Thomas Jefferson wrote the Virginia law that struck down the privileges of the Church of England and made religion a private matter. He regarded it as one of the major accomplishments of his life.

Disestablishment moved more slowly in New England, where the ministers of the Congregational Church were generally pro-Revolutionary. There, churches continued to receive tax monies until well into the nineteenth century.

The Growth of Democracy

In every colony, the right to vote was extended to more people. In Pennsylvania and Vermont (an independent state in fact if not in name until it was formally admitted to the Union in 1791), every adult male taxpayer could vote. In most of the other states, the property qualification was so low that few free white males were excluded. Women who met the qualification could vote in New Jersey, and a few, willing to offend local sensibilities, exercised the right elsewhere. In some states, free blacks who met other tests were enfranchised.

There were limits to this democratic trend, however. Roman Catholics were not allowed to vote in North Carolina until 1835, and even democratic Pennsylvania required an officeholder to be a Christian. In a majority of the states, the man who could vote could not necessarily run for office. There still were strict property qualifications for that right, and the higher an office a man wished to hold, the more wealth he was required to have. The revolutionaries may have been radical by European standards, but they still held to the eighteenth-century idea that property alone gave a person a stake in society and therefore qualified him to govern it. In New Jersey, where women were allowed to vote, they as well as men were required to own land or money.

FOMENTING REBELLION

Abigail and John Adams were touchingly affectionate with each other, and, much rarer, they discussed the momentous issues of the Revolutionary era. Abigail was twitting John when she made her famous appeal for the rights of women in 1777, but it would be a mistake to think that her challenge was nothing more than a joke:

In the new code of laws . . . I desire you would remember the ladies and be more generous and more favorable to them than your ancestors. Do not put such unlimited power into the hands of husbands. Remember, all men would be tyrants if they could. If particular care and attention is not paid to the ladies, we are determined to foment a rebellion, and will not hold ourselves bound to any laws in which we have no choice or representation.

Abigail Adams urged her husband to consider women's rights.

Bills of Rights

Most of the states added a bill of rights to their constitutions, beginning with Virginia's in 1776 (also drafted by Thomas Jefferson). The revolutionaries were determined that there be no vagueness on the question of an individual's liberties. Most of the freedoms defined in the first ten amendments to the United States Constitution were listed in one or another of the state bills of rights that were written during the 1770s and early 1780s—freedom from cruel punishment; the right of counsel and trial by jury; the right to refuse to testify against oneself.

In 1777, when talk of these expanded liberties was much in the air, Abigail Adams wrote to her husband, John, who represented Massachusetts at the Continental Congress, to be sure to "remember the ladies and be more generous and favorable to them." But the time was not ripe for the legal redefinition of women's status, least of all in the matter of voting. In 1807, New Jersey rescinded the part of its constitution that enfranchised women because an increasing number of women were taking advantage of the right.

Massachusetts blacks benefited from the spirit of liberty. The supreme court of the Bay State ruled that slavery was unconstitutional there because the Massachusetts constitution stated that "all men are born free and equal." This principle also was stated in the Declaration of Independence, and many Confederation-era leaders were troubled by their own hypocrisy in speaking loudly for human liberty while, in every state but Massachusetts, continuing to hold men and women in bondage.

There was no escaping the contradiction between principle and practice. Later defenders of both slavery and the inferior civil status of women would recognize the contradiction and backtrack from the Declaration. The political leaders of the 1770s and 1780s simply lived with it.

The Articles of Confederation

The constitution that formed the first permanent union reflected the same trends as did the constitutions that the states wrote for themselves. Written and repeatedly changed during 1776 and 1777 (and not approved by Maryland, the last state to do so, until 1781), the Articles of Confederation provided for no president or other executive. Congress was the only organ of government. Members were elected annually and could serve only three years out of every six. That is, if a man were elected to Congress three years in a row, he was ineligible for reelection until three more years had passed.

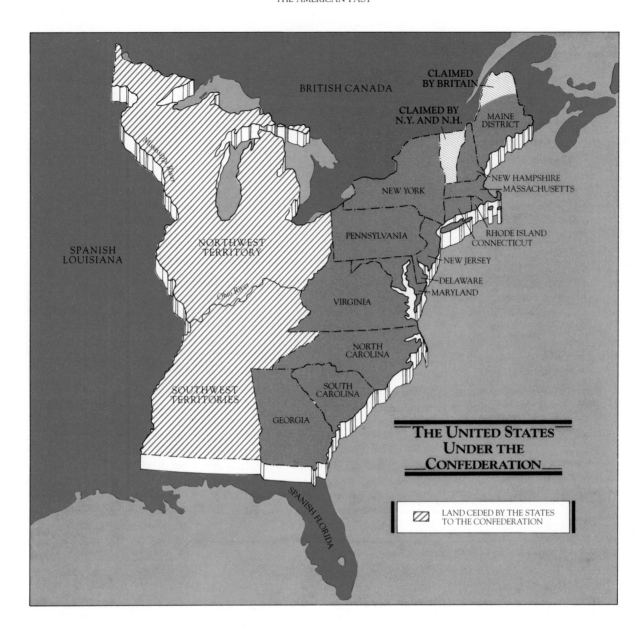

BRITISH CANADA

CLAIMED BY BRITAIN

CLAIMED BY N.Y. AND N.H.

MAINE DISTRICT

SPANISH LOUISIANA

NEW YORK

NEW HAMPSHIRE
MASSACHUSETTS

NORTHWEST TERRITORY

PENNSYLVANIA

RHODE ISLAND
CONNECTICUT

NEW JERSEY

DELAWARE
MARYLAND

VIRGINIA

NORTH CAROLINA

SOUTHWEST TERRITORIES

SOUTH CAROLINA

GEORGIA

SPANISH FLORIDA

THE UNITED STATES UNDER THE CONFEDERATION

LAND CEDED BY THE STATES TO THE CONFEDERATION

Under the Articles, the United States explicitly were not a nation like Britain or France, or, as Americans came to prefer, a "union." They formed a confederation, little more than an alliance of states that retained their "sovereignty, freedom, and independence." Congress could wage war and make peace, maintain an army and a navy, and supervise diplomatic relations with foreign countries and administer Indian affairs (viewed as much the same thing). Congress was also entrusted with maintaining a post office and setting uniform weights and measures, and it was given the power to coin money, issue paper money, and make loans.

But Congress could not regulate trade between individual states and foreign countries (an obvious reference to the experience with Parliament), or even among the states. The individual states also reserved the rights to make war (with the "consent" of Congress), coin money, and, if they chose, ignore the declarations of the confederation government on such matters as standards of measurement.

These "weaknesses" were deliberately built into the Confederation government. The framers of the Articles believed that freedom could best be preserved by hobbling that government that was farthest from the people. The generation that called King George a tyrant had no intention of creating a home-grown central government in his place. The price of their principles was some inefficiency in prosecuting the war. George Washington wrote dozens of letters to Congress begging for money over which the delegates bickered and connived, taking advantage of every limitation on power that the Articles provided. Congress was capable of devoting long hours to debating whether a man who claimed $222.60 for ferrying troops across a river should get it.

The Confederation's Problems

As it had been the center of the dispute with Great Britain, money was the Confederation's major problem. When states were slow to vote funds, Congress issued increasingly larger amounts of paper money, popularly called Continentals. From $6 million in paper money in 1775, Congress printed $63 million in 1778 and $90 million in 1779. Because the value of this currency depended on the people's faith in the ability of Congress to redeem it at face value, the Continentals depreciated rapidly. By 1781, it took almost 150 paper dollars to purchase what 1 dollar in gold would buy.

The Economy of the 1780s

The job of establishing financial stability on this shaky foundation fell to Robert Morris, a Philadelphia banker whom Congress named Superintendent of Finance. By floating loans at home and abroad, Morris managed to keep the Confederation solvent. But when the war ended, the government was faced with an enormous debt and a currency that few would accept. "Not worth a continental" was a popular catch phrase that meant "worthless."

The economy of the 1780s also suffered from the termination of privileges that Americans had enjoyed as British subjects. No longer did tobacco planters have their English market. Shipmasters from New England were now shut out of the imperial trade and had to look elsewhere for routes. And when the armies of both sides were suddenly disbanded between 1781 and 1783, farmers who had grown rich by provisioning them lost their ready-made markets. These problems would have tried whatever kind of government the revolutionaries adopted, but because of the particular weakness of the Confederation in financial matters, critics blamed Congress.

The Western Problem

Through a combination of wisdom and luck, Congress confronted and solved its most divisive problem—that of the western lands. Royal charters had been so careless in drawing colonial boundaries that the vast tract of land between the Appalachians and the Mississippi River was a tangle of conflicting claims. Seven states (Massachusetts, Connecticut, New York, Virginia, North Carolina, South Carolina, and Georgia) had overlapping claims. Virginia, for example, insisted that its boundaries fanned out like a funnel at the mountains, encompassing virtually the whole wilderness region.

The problem was complicated by the fears of the six states that did not claim western lands (New Hampshire, Rhode Island, New Jersey, Pennsylvania, Delaware, and Maryland). With good reason they worried that the landed states would be able to finance themselves indefinitely without taxation by the sale of trans-Appalachian farms, while they, the landless states, would drive their citizens out with high taxes. On these grounds, Maryland refused to sign the Articles of Confederation until 1781.

The solution was obvious. The landed states would have to grant their western territories to the Confederation government, so that all states could share in the wealth. Fortunately, Virginia—the state with the most to lose by doing so, and the one most able to defend its claims—had good reasons to cede its lands. Virginians played a prominent role in the Confederation government, and they did not want to see it fall apart. Moreover, many Virginians believed that free republican institutions could not survive in huge countries. For the sake of hard-won freedoms, such men preferred to see new states carved out of the West.

In January 1781, Virginia ceded to the Confederation Government the northern part of its western lands. Within a few years, one by one, all the states except Georgia followed suit, with Virginia adding its southern territories to the national domain in 1792. (Georgia held out until 1802.)

The Northwest Ordinances

This remarkable act—European nations went to war over lesser tracts of land—was followed in 1784 and 1787 by two congressional ordinances that were even more innovative. The Northwest Ordinances defined the status of the western lands as self-governing states in the making and set the basic pattern of settlement and statehood followed throughout American history. The acts applied to the Northwest Territory, the area that is today occupied by the states of Ohio, Indiana,

PAYING FOR THE WAR: TWO FINANCIERS

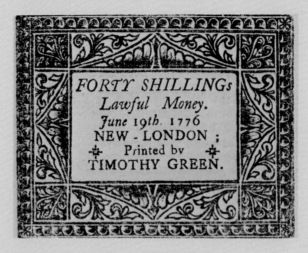

*Forty shillings in "continentals," the paper
currency of the Confederation.*

Although George Washington won few battles, his greatest frustrations were not military but financial. From Boston to Yorktown he rarely had enough money to feed, clothe, shoe, shelter, supply, and transport his soldiers. In part, the problem was the shortage of coin in America; the colonies were not a rich country. In part, the weak taxation powers and indecision of the Continental Congress was at fault. In any event, the money problem would have been much worse, perhaps bad enough to scuttle the cause of independence, had it not been for the financial wizardry of Haym Salomon and Robert Morris.

Haym Salomon (1740–84) was descended from the Sephardic Jews who were expelled from Spain and Portugal during the late 1400s. He was born in Poland, but apparently wandered over much of Europe as some sort of trader until he was thirty; he spoke several languages, including English and German. In 1770, Salomon returned to his native land, where he joined the Polish resistance movement then seeking to rid the country of Russian, Prussian, and Austrian rulers. When the Poles lost, Salomon fled for his life, a refugee like Pulaski and Kosciusko.

Salomon settled in New York in 1772. Although little is known of his life over the next four years, Salomon must have succeeded in business; in 1777, he was able to win the hand of the daughter of one of New York's wealthiest and most influential Jews. In the meantime, the liberal-minded Salomon had become a supporter of the patriots, and, for reasons that are not entirely clear, the British arrested him as a spy in

September 1776. Salomon escaped prison and the gallows because of his linguistic ability; on parole he became an interpreter for the Hessian troops who were then pouring into New York. Unrepentant, Salomon secretly urged the Germans to desert to the patriot side, and he was arrested again in August 1778. This time he was sentenced to death.

Prepared for this eventuality, Salomon bribed his jailer with some gold he had secreted on his person and made his way to Washington's lines. When the Continental Congress turned down his offer to take a post in the government, Salomon established himself as a supplier of provisions and liquor to Washington's army and as paymaster for the French troops in America. Dealing largely in promissory notes as payment for his goods, Salomon opened up a commission house that evolved into a bank, and he was one of the original shareholders in the Bank of North America, which was founded as a clearing house for the finances of the Revolutionary government.

On paper, Salomon made a great deal of money in a very short time. By the end of the war, the United States government owed him more than $650,000 for credit he had extended. He was also generous with officers and political leaders; James Madison, never a wealthy man, borrowed from Salomon in order to meet his expenses.

In actuality, Salomon was penniless when he died in 1784. Like others who lent the money that won the war, he was unable to collect a cent from the Confederation government. His estate, including the government notes, was valued at about $45,000, which was used to settle his own debts at face value. His children, still quite young, were taken into Jewish families in New York and later failed in several attempts to win compensation for their father's services.

Salomon was a close associate of Robert Morris (1734–1806), who also became rich during the war years only to die in poverty. Born in England, Morris emigrated to Maryland at the age of thirteen. Apprenticed to a shipping company in Philadelphia, he so impressed his employers that they made him a full partner in 1754, a year before his twenty-first birthday. Like many colonial merchants, Morris disliked British trade laws, and in 1765 he was one of the leaders of the anti-Stamp Act movement in Philadelphia.

But Morris was a wealthy man, a conservative who feared the effects of too much agitation. He was one of the most cautious members of the First Continental Congress, and he voted against the Declaration of Independence in July 1776. Within a month, however, he changed his mind and signed the document.

Like Salomon, Morris acted as an independent banker during the first years of the war, and, on paper, made a lot of money. In January 1779, Thomas Paine attacked him for profiteering while holding public office (as a member of Congress), and Morris retired from public life. However, exhorters like Paine were less valuable in the difficult days of 1780 and 1781 than hard-headed money men like Morris. In February 1781,

he was named Superintendent of Finance and given almost dictatorial powers over the money matters of the Revolutionary government. At Morris's insistence, Congress allowed him to continue to conduct his private business while in office.

Although Morris was criticized roundly for this conflict of interest and resigned as superintendent in January 1793, his actions are regarded as largely responsible for the financial stability of the patriot cause in its final phases.

Like most bankers, Morris was a federalist and supported the move toward a more centralized government in 1787. Washington offered him the post of Secretary of the Treasury, but Morris declined in order to devote himself to his own affairs. Unfortunately, although he was conservative with public monies, he plunged deeply into land speculation in western New York (then wilderness) and on the site where Washington, D.C., would eventually be built. He lost everything and, in 1798, was imprisoned for debt.

It was not unusual for even such a distinguished man as Morris to be held in debtor's prison. The impatient creditor usually was paid quite quickly. But Morris and his family were destitute, and old associates would not help him for fear of being held responsible for other of his debts. Morris remained in prison until 1801, when a new federal bankruptcy law enabled him to repudiate his obligations. Poor and obscure, the "Financier of the Revolution" died in 1806.

As Superintendent of Finance for the revolutionary government, Robert Morris kept the Confederation solvent.

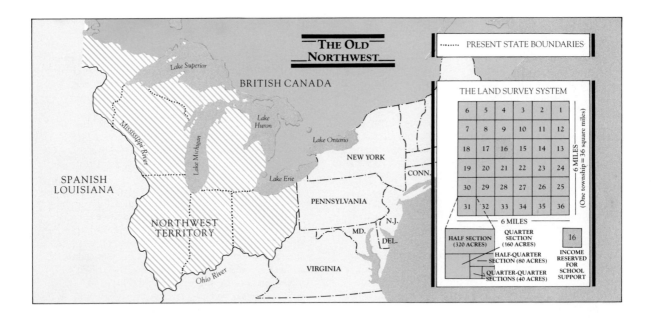

Michigan, Illinois, and Wisconsin. Congress drew boundaries for these future states and provided that as soon as the population in any of these districts equaled that of the smallest state within the Confederation, that territory would be admitted as an equal partner in the union. The United States would hold no colonies.

In 1785, Congress provided for a system of survey to prepare land for public sale in these territories. Townships six miles square were divided into thirty-six "sections" of one square mile (640 acres) each. At first, a section was the smallest plot that could be purchased. In time, the plot was reduced to a half-section, and then a quarter-section (160 acres). Eventually, a quarter-quarter-section could be purchased, the classic midwestern American farm of 40 acres.

The thinking behind the rectangular pattern was wise and fruitful. Had purchasers been able to enter public lands and map their own property, they would have carved out oddly shaped tracts of prime land. Hills, marshes, rocky ground, and the like would technically belong to the government. While no one would pay taxes on these scattered plots or be held accountable for their possible destruction, individuals would definitely use them for grazing livestock, cutting wood, digging gravel and stone, and extracting minerals.

The consequences of the rectangular system of land survey can be observed by anyone who travels through rural America. In the East, the former French parts of Louisiana, and some areas of the Southwest settled by the Spanish and Mexicans, farms are oddly shaped and roads trace the lay of the land. In the Midwest and much of the Far West, a somewhat sloppy checker-board pattern holds. Roads, on the boundaries of individual properties, are as straight as a surveyor's gaze.

Thomas Jefferson was the chief designer of the Northwest Ordinances. He included in it the slap at slavery he was denied in the Declaration of Independence. In the act of 1787, slavery was forbidden in the territories north of the Ohio River.

Discontent

Despite these successes, many political leaders, including members of Congress were unhappy with the Articles of Confederation. Indeed, with the exception of some Rhode Islanders who believed that only political independence guaranteed their little state's integrity against the power of larger neighbors, no one was delighted with the first American constitution.

Almost everyone active in politics agreed that changes were in order. The Articles had been improvised in the midst of war in order to prosecute that war. The Continental Congress that drafted them had not been elected to write a frame of government, but merely to respond to the Intolerable Acts. Scarcely a voice could be heard that did not admit that the power of Congress had to be increased.

When the changes came, however, they did not originate in Congress, nor did they take the form of amendments to the Articles of Confederation. Beginning in 1785, eight years after the Articles went into effect and only two years after the Revolutionary War was declared at an end, a small group of men started inventing a country from scratch.

For Further Reading

For the military history of the Revolutionary War, see D. Higginbotham, *The War of American Independence: Military Attitudes, Policies, and Practice* (1971), and Christopher Ward, *The War of the Revolution* (1952). A briefer account is Howard Peckham, *The War for Independence* (1952).

On the social aspect of the war, J. Franklin Jameson, *The American Revolution Considered as a Social Movement* (1926), has been corrected in many particulars but is still valuable reading. More recent studies are Merrill Jensen, *The American Revolution Within America* (1974), and John Shy, *A People Numerous and Armed* (1976). For the diplomatic history of the Revolution, S. F. Bemis, *The Diplomacy of the American Revolution* (1935), is still standard.

The classic account of the Confederation period as a dismal time for the young country is John Fiske, *The Critical Period of American History, 1783–1789* (1883). Fiske's interpretation is challenged by Merrill Jensen, *The Articles of Confederation* (1940), and Jensen in turn is challenged by J. N. Rakove, *The Beginnings of National Politics* (1979).

The definitive biography of George Washington is D. S. Freeman's seven-volume *George Washington* (1948–57). A more than adequate single-volume study is J. T. Flexner, *George Washington in the American Revolution* (1968).

On political "parties" during the Confederation period, see J. T. Main, *Political Parties Before the Constitution* (1973), and H. J. Henderson, *Party Politics in the Continental Congress* (1974).

We the People

of t...

insure domestic Tranquility, provide for the common defen...
and our Posterity, Do ordain and establish this Constitution...

Articl...

Section. 1. All legislative Powers herein granted shall be ...
of Representatives.

Section. 2. The House of Representatives shall be compose...
in each State shall have the Qualifications requisite for Electors of the m...

No Person shall be a Representative who shall not have a...
and who shall not, when elected, be an Inhabitant of that State in wh...

Representatives and direct Taxes shall be apportioned among...
Numbers, which shall be determined by adding to the whole Number...
not taxed, three fifths of all other Persons. The actual Enumeratio...
and within every subsequent Term of ten Years, in such Manner a...
thirty Thousand, but each State shall have at Least one Represent...
entitled to chuse three; Massachusetts eight; Rhode Island and ...
eight; Delaware one; Maryland six; Virginia ten; North Caroli...

When vacancies happen in the Representation from any ...

The House of Representatives shall chuse their Speaker an...

Section. 3. The Senate of the United States shall be composed of ...
Senator shall have one Vote.

Immediately after they shall be assembled in Consequence...
the Senators of the first Class shall be vacated at the Expiration ...
Class at the Expiration of the sixth Year, so that one third may be cho...
Recess of the Legislature of any State, the Executive thereof may make...

10

We the People
Making and Using the Constitution, 1785–1791

For two hundred years the American Constitution has been hailed with a reverence that can only be described as religious. Patriots, politicians, moralists, and historians—Americans and foreigners alike—have stood in awe of a legal document that could survive for two centuries during which technology, ideology, revolution, imperialism, and war have turned the world upside down. William E. Gladstone, prime minister of Great Britain in the midst of this tumultuous historical period, was neither alone nor excessive when he called the American Constitution "the most wonderful work ever struck off at a given time by the brain and purpose of man."

The men who struck it off in the summer of 1787 also have been heaped with honors. The "Founding Fathers" have been depicted as wise, selfless individuals who peered into their nation's future and designed for it a timeless gift. The Constitution was "intended to endure for ages to come," Chief Justice John Marshall proclaimed in 1819. On the floor of the Senate in 1850, a critical year for the union of states that the Constitution had created, Henry Clay of Kentucky went much further. "The Constitution of the United States," he said, "was not made merely for the generation that then existed but

Preamble to the U.S. Constitution, written in 1787.

for posterity—unlimited, undefined, and endless, perpetual posterity."

In truth, the Constitution has been a remarkably successful basic law, and the generation of political leaders who wrote and debated it was rich in talent and wisdom. But the Founding Fathers were not "demigods," as Thomas Jefferson feared Americans would make them out to be. They were decidedly human, with prosaic faults and very immediate purposes to serve. Indeed, the series of meetings that led to the writing of the Constitution began because of a squabble over oysters, crabs, and flounder.

Writing the Constitution

In March 1785, a small group of gentlemen from Maryland and Virginia gathered at Mount Vernon, George Washington's home on the Potomac River. Their purpose was to discuss the conflicting claims of Maryland and Virginia fishermen over rights to fish in the Chesapeake Bay. They never did determine the boundary between the fisheries of the two (Marylanders and Virginians still argue the point). They did, however, conclude that the Chesapeake problem was only one in a snarl of disputes among the states and between the states and the Confederation government. They decided to invite all thirteen states to send delegates to a meeting to be held the next year in Annapolis, Maryland, to discuss what might be done.

Only five states responded, so definitive action was out of the question. Undiscouraged, Washington's former aide-de-camp, Alexander Hamilton of New York, persuaded the small group to meet once again, this time in more centrally located Philadelphia, the capital of the Confederation. They should prepare, Hamilton told them, to discuss all the "defects in the System of the Federal Government."

Hamilton and some other delegates, such as James Madison of Virginia, had more than an academic debate in mind. They intended to plump for replacing the Articles of Confederation with a completely new frame of government, and rumors about their plan spread quickly. Patrick Henry, Madison's rival in Virginia politics, said that he "smelled a rat" and refused to attend. Rhode Island sent no delegates at all. Since the days of Roger Williams, Rhode Islanders had smelled a rat in any hint that their independence of action as a colony and state, which the articles of Confederation nicely guaranteed, might be impaired.

Elsewhere, however, unhappiness with the Confederation was rife. Early in 1787, Congress itself nervously approved the meeting "for the sole and express purpose of revising" the Articles.

The Convention

The delegates to the convention began their work on May 25. After only a few days, the fifty-five delegates from twelve states agreed that revision was not enough. They had little choice but to start from scratch.

Ironically, it was legally easier to effect a coup d'état, to create a new government without regard to the procedures of the one that existed, than to amend the Articles of Confederation, which required that every state agree to the change. It was clear that at least Rhode Island would oppose any revision the convention suggested.

The Constitutional Convention met in secret from first to last. For four months the delegates bolted the doors and sealed the windows of the Pennsylvania State House (Independence Hall), a heroic sacrifice of comfort in the humid Philadelphia summer. In addition, every member swore not to discuss the proceedings with outsiders.

There was nothing sinister in their secrecy. The purpose of the convention was common knowledge, but the delegates realized that they were performing a historic as well as a revolutionary act, and should proceed with the utmost caution and calm. As James Wilson, a

Independence Hall, Philadelphia, site of the 1787 Constitutional Convention.

Pennsylvania delegate, said, "America now presents the first instance of a people assembled to weigh deliberately and calmly, and to decide leisurely and peaceably, upon the form of government by which they will bind themselves, and their posterity." No small business that! Never had a nation been founded so methodically, and the delegates wished to voice their frankest opinions without fear of affecting their political careers back home.

Moreover, they knew there would be opposition to their constitution. Wilson said "the people" were assembled in Independence Hall. The document that the convention produced begins with the words "We the People of the United States." In reality, the men who drew up the Constitution represented just one political faction. They wanted their statement to be complete before they had to defend it against their rivals.

The Founding Fathers

The job was finished in September 1787. After a celebration at City Tavern, the delegates scattered north and south to lobby for their states' approval of their document.

They were a formidable lot to sally forth on such an errand. By virtue of wealth and education they were influential people back home. Of the fifty-five, only Roger Sherman of Connecticut, who had been a cobbler as a young man, could be said to have been weaned on anything less glittering than a silver spoon.

Lifetimes spent in justifying independence and creating state governments made close students of political philosophy of most of them. Just as important was their practical experience. Seven of the delegates had been state governors; thirty-nine had attended the Continental Congress. If they were revolutionaries, they were very well-established ones.

They were young. Only nine signers of the Declaration of Independence attended the convention of 1787 (and three of them refused to sign the Constitution). Only Benjamin Franklin, eighty-one years old in 1787, was truly ancient. The other Founding Fathers averaged just over forty years of age, and the two leading spirits of the meeting were only thirty-six (James Madison) and thirty-two (Alexander Hamilton). They had been in their twenties in 1776, just old enough to take an active role in the war. They had been adolescents at the time of the Stamp Act crisis. They were children of the Revolution rather than the creators of it.

This is of some importance in understanding the nature of the constitution they wrote. The delegates to the Constitutional Convention were never colonials;

they never thought of themselves as Virginians or New Yorkers before they decided to become Americans. Their vision of the United States was forged in the crucible of a *national* struggle, "these United States" versus a foreign power.

Unlike their more provincial forebears, these young men moved freely and often from one state to another. In the Continental Army (a third of them had been soldiers, mostly junior officers) and in Congress, they had met and mixed easily with men from other states and from Europe. They thought in terms of a continent rather than of coastal enclaves that looked back to a mother country for an identity. They wanted the United States to take its place in the world as an equal among nations.

Why the Constitution Was Written

Europe's refusal to recognize the United States as a nation was a major reason for the Founding Fathers' decision to redesign their government. France, the indispensable ally in war, would not lend money in peace because the Confederation government was unable to make good on earlier loans. Nor was credit the only problem. Virtually every European country regarded the United States as a collection of weak principalities, like Indian tribes or the petty states of Germany that occasionally formed a league but, more often, could be played off against one another.

A Diplomatic Joke

In 1784, a shrewd Spanish diplomat, Diego de Gardoqui, played on the commercial interests of the northern states in an effort to split the country in two. He offered to open Spanish trade to American ships (which meant northern ships) if Congress would give up its insistence on navigation of the Mississippi River for twenty-five years. The seven most northerly states cared little about the Mississippi and, ignoring the fact that the river was a vital artery to the tens of thousands of Virginians and North Carolinians who had moved to what are now Kentucky and Tennessee, tried to ram the treaty through. They failed, but only by a hair. Had the Gardoqui Treaty passed, the southern states would have had to go their own way, fulfilling the predictions of even friendly Europeans that the former English colonies were destined to remain weak and divided.

In the far north, England schemed to detach Vermont from the United States. Traditionally a part of New York, and claimed by New Hampshire, the isolated Green Mountain country actually functioned as an independent commonwealth under the leadership of Ethan and Levi Allen, two Revolutionary veterans who trusted no one but each other. The brothers attempted to make a treaty with the British that would have tied the area more closely to Canada than to the Confederation. Congress was powerless to stop them. Only because the British failed to act quickly did the venture fall through.

Britain's condescension was insulting and infuriating. The former mother country refused to turn over to the Confederation a string of Great Lakes forts that were American under the terms of the Treaty of Paris. Nor did the British send an ambassador to America. A British minister joked that it would be too expensive to outfit thirteen men with embassies and other accouterments of office. In London, American ambassador John Adams was ridiculed when he attempted to act with the dignity of a national legate.

It was the same elsewhere. A world-traveling American sea captain said that the United States was regarded "in the same light, by foreign nations, as a well-behaved negro is in a gentleman's family"; that is, as an inferior, scarcely to be noticed.

Even the venal Barbary States of northern Africa looked down on Americans. These little fortress countries lived by piracy, collecting tribute from nations whose ships traded in the Mediterranean. When American ships lost the protection that the British annually purchased for vessels flying the Union Jack, they were sunk or captured. The dey of Algiers sold several American crews into slavery, and Congress was unable either to ransom them or to launch a punitive expedition. It was a sorry state of affairs for proud young men who dreamed of national greatness and who were, many of them, involved in international trade.

Problems at Home

The Confederation's domestic weakness also mortified the young nationalists. The thirteen states squabbled among themselves like Barbary pirates. Because it was legally independent, each state could and did adopt tariffs that discriminated against the goods produced by the other states. New York was a major offender, and when New Jersey and Connecticut encouraged smuggling into their large neighbor's lands, New York actually took military action. New Jersey charged the New York Assembly for the cost of a lighthouse at Sandy Hook. Although the lighthouse was essential to New Jersey's shipping too, the state said that New York, as the major beneficiary should pay the bill.

These disputes, and the one between Maryland and Virginia over fishing in the Chesapeake, were more ludicrous than dangerous. Not so the actions of cantankerous Rhode Island. In 1781, Rhode Island almost canceled out the military victory at Yorktown when, alone of the thirteen states, it refused to approve Congress's request to levy a 5 percent tax on imports. Because the Articles of Confederation required unanimous state approval for tax bills, the government teetered on the brink of bankruptcy. On another occasion, New York alone vetoed a congressional tax bill.

Financial irresponsibility naturally worried wealthy people who dealt in money. They were particularly disturbed when, in 1786, the Rhode Island Assembly, under the control of farmers deep in debt, issued $100,000 in paper money. This currency was worth even less than the Continental notes, but the Assembly declared it legal tender for payment of debts at face value. Tales were told of bankers fleeing Rhode Island to avoid being paid back in the useless paper, with debtors, gleefully waving handfuls of it, in hot pursuit.

Whether they were true or not, such stories caused men of property to shudder. They yearned for a reliable currency that would be valid in every state. Only a strong central government could guarantee such a currency; Congress was unable even to maintain the value of the bonds and certificates it had issued during the Revolution. Tellingly, forty of the fifty-five men who drafted the Constitution owned portfolios of depreciated Continental currency and notes. They were badly stung as long as the government was unable to collect taxes and meet its financial obligations.

Shays's Rebellion

Then, as if to emphasize the fact that a complete overhaul was necessary, an epidemic of protest against taxes and strong government swept over western Massachusetts. Crowds of farmers held their own conventions at which they demanded that their state taxes be reduced and, in order to make up for the loss of revenue, that Boston abolish "aristocratic" branches of the government.

In several towns, angry crowds surrounded courthouses, harassed lawyers and judges, whom they considered to be unproductive parasites, and forcibly prevented the collection of debts. In the winter of 1786/87, a Revolutionary War veteran named Daniel Shays led two thousand armed men against the Springfield arsenal. His rebellion was put down fairly easily, but the bitter discontent of the Shaysites did not sweeten.

Shays and his followers did not regard themselves as a dangerous social force. They believed that they were the true Americans, carrying on the spirit and struggle of the Revolution against a privileged elite. Serving as ambassador to France, Thomas Jefferson agreed with

By his EXCELLENCY
George Clinton, Efq.

Governor of the STATE of NEW-YORK, General and Commander in Chief of all the Militia, and Admiral of the Navy of the fame.

A Proclamation.

WHEREAS His Excellency JAMES BOWDOIN, Efq; Governor of the Commonwealth of Maffachufetts, did iffue his proclamation, bearing date the ninth day of this inftant month of February, fetting forth, that the General Court of the faid Commonwealth had, on the fourth day of the faid month declared, that a horrid and unnatural rebellion had been openly and traiteroufly, raifed and levied againft the faid Commonwealth, with defign to fubvert and overthrow the conftitution and form of governnent thereof, and further fetting forth, that it appeared that Daniel Shays,

New York Governor George Clinton issued this denunciation of Shays's Rebellion in 1787.

them. "A little rebellion now and then is a good thing," he wrote to a friend. "The tree of liberty must be refreshed from time to time with the blood of patriots and tyrants."

To the men who were just beginning their work in Philadelphia, however, it was not the pine tree of liberty that needed attention. It was the ailing oak of stability and order. George Washington was said to have been deeply troubled by the news of the uprising of Daniel Shays and his followers. He feared that such disorder was the natural consequence of excessive democracy, and he was not alone in his fear.

A Conservative Movement

The men who drew up the Constitution were conservatives in the classic meaning of the word. Far from believing with Jefferson that human nature was essentially good, that people and human society were perfectible if left free, the Founding Fathers suspected the human race and feared its darker side.

Free of institutional restraints and given power, con-

CONSERVATIVES

In identifying men such as Washington, Hamilton, and Adams as conservatives, it is important not to confuse their political philosophy with that of the "conservatives" of the late twentieth century. Classical conservatives like these three Founding Fathers were suspicious of human nature and therefore inclined to cling to tried and true institutions rather than to experiment. Unlike conservatives of today, they believed that a strong central government that was active in the economic life of the nation was desirable and essential. They had no more tolerance for economic freedom than for excess of political freedom.

Present-day conservatives, by way of contrast, want a minimum of government interference in the economy. Implicitly, they say that in economic life, human nature should not be closely supervised.

servatives believed, the individual was selfish and trampled on the rights of others. To conservatives, democracy and liberty did not go hand in hand. On the contrary, people left to their own devices would destroy liberty. Uncontrolled democracy led to despotism.

Alexander Hamilton

The most pessimistic and therefore the most conservative of the lot was Alexander Hamilton, who was born in the West Indies in 1755 as the illegitimate son of a Scottish merchant. Sent to King's College in New York by friends who recognized his talents, Hamilton never returned to the islands. He joined the patriot movement and served George Washington as aide-de-camp during the Revolutionary War.

Hamilton impressed his superior with his intelligence and perhaps also with his conservatism. For Hamilton had no sympathy with democratic ideas. A few years after the adoption of the Constitution, he would listen to Thomas Jefferson expound on the wisdom and virtue

ALEXANDER HAMILTON ON DEMOCRACY

"All communities divide themselves into the few and the many. The first are the rich and the wellborn, the other the mass of the people. . . . The people are turbulent and changing; they seldom judge or determine right. Give therefore to the first class a distinct, permanent share in the government. They will check the unsteadiness of the second, and as they cannot receive any advantage by change, they therefore will ever maintain good government."

inherent in the people and snap back angrily, "Your people, sir, are a great beast."

Had Hamilton been an Englishman, he would have defended those institutions that conservatives believed helped to control the passions of the people: the ceremonial monarchy, the privileged aristocracy, the established church, the centuries-old accretion of law and custom that is the English constitution.

Indeed, Hamilton was an unabashed admirer of English culture and government. Like Edmund Burke, he thought of the American Revolution as a conservative movement. In rebelling, the Americans had defended tradition against a reckless, radical Parliament that had run roughshod over it.

In the Constitution, Hamilton wanted to recapture as much of tradition as he could. He suggested that president and senators be elected for life, thus creating a kind of monarch and a privileged elite with a kind of House of Lords as their exclusive property. But he was unable to sway his fellow delegates. Much as many of them, a privileged elite themselves, may have had conservative sentiments, they also understood that the "common run" of people would not accept such backsliding toward the old order. What the majority of delegates did approve, and Hamilton accepted, was a system of government that expressed democratic yearnings but placed effective checks on them.

Alexander Hamilton (1755–1804), advocate of a strong central government.

The Principles of the Constitution

The men who wrote the Constitution agreed that an excess of democracy was the chief weakness of government under the Articles of Confederation. The solution, they believed, was "mixed government," a balance of the three principles of democracy (power in the hands of the many), aristocracy (power in the hands of a few), and monocracy (power in the hands of one).

Mixed Government

The chief exponent of mixed government was John Adams of Massachusetts. He did not attend the convention. In 1787, Adams was serving an unhappy stint as ambassador to Great Britain, accomplishing little while suffering many British insults. Before he had gone abroad, however, Adams had stamped his ideas about government on the Massachusetts state constitution, which provided for a strong governor, a voice for the wealthy in the state senate, and a voice for the people in the state assembly.

James Madison pushed for a similar structure for the new national government. The key to preserving liberties, he argued, was a system that balanced the monocratic, aristocratic, and democratic principles. Madison—short of stature, sharp of mind, and softspoken in speech—had his way. The basic principle of the American Constitution is a complex arrangement of checks and balances.

Checks, Limits, and Balances

The House of Representatives was "democratic." Representatives were elected frequently (every two years) by a broad electorate—all free, white, adult males in many states; most free, white, adult males in others.

The Senate and the Supreme Court reflected the "aristocratic" principle. Senators were elected infrequently (every six years) by state legislatures. Senators were insulated from democracy by both time and a buffer of legislators. However, because state legislatures were elected by the same broad electorate that chose the House of Representatives, senators were not completely independent of the popular will.

The Supreme Court was. Justices were appointed by the president, but, once seated, they were immune to his influence. Justices served for life and could be removed only by a difficult impeachment process, which was full of pitfalls for those who tried to use it.

The "monocratic" principle was established in the presidency, the most dramatic break with government as established under the Confederation. The president alone represented the whole nation, but he owed his power neither to the people nor to Congress. He was put into offce by an electoral college that played no other role than selecting the president. Once the president was inaugurated, the electoral college disbanded.

An intricate system of checks and balances tied together the three branches of government. Only Congress could make law, and both democratic House and aristocratic Senate had to agree. The president could veto an act of Congress if he judged it adverse to the national interest. However, Congress could override his veto by a two-thirds majority of both houses.

Applying these laws was the job of the judiciary, with the Supreme Court the final court of appeal. In time (it was not written into the Constitution), the Supreme Court claimed a legislative role of its own in the principle of "judicial review." That is, in judging according to the law, the Supreme Court also interpreted the law. Implicit in this process was the power to declare a law unconstitutional. This proved to be a mighty power because, while there are checks on the Court, they are indirect and difficult to exercise.

John Jay (1745–1829), first Chief Justice of the U.S. Supreme Court.

Debate gives way to a battle in Congress, as portrayed in this 1798 cartoon.

Thus, the president can affect the Court's decisions by the character of the justices he appoints to it (and the Senate has the power to turn down his choices). Like all public officials, Supreme Court justices can be impeached and removed for "high crimes and misdemeanors," a phrase that in practice translates into any reason whatsoever. Finally, the Constitution can be amended by the states in order to make the Court conform to their wishes.

A Federal System

Another network of checks and balances defined the relationship between the central government and the states. Under the Articles of Confederation, the United States was not a nation. That frame of government created a confederation of independent states that retained virtually all the powers possessed by sovereign nations. The Constitution reversed this structure, giving preponderant powers to the central government and leaving the states relatively weak. The Constitution made the United States into a nation.

The states were not reduced to mere administrative divisions, like the counties of England and the provinces of France. Nationalistic thought may have been riding high in 1787, but local interests and jealousies were hardly dead. If the Constitution was to win popular support, the states had to be accommodated.

In order to ensure that the small states like New Jersey and Connecticut would not be bullied by their larger and wealthier neighbors, states rather than population were represented in the Senate. That is, each state elected two senators, no matter what its population. Virginia, the largest, was ten times as populous as Rhode Island, but had the same number of senators. Without this "Great Compromise," which was accomplished after a tense debate in July 1787, the Constitution would not have been completed.

The difference between North and South also was recognized in the constitutional compromises, particularly in the matter of America's seven hundred thousand slaves. Almost all of these people lived in the South. The institution of slavery had died or was obviously declining north of the Maryland–Pennsylvania boundary. With the exception of the delegates from South Carolina, few of the Founding Fathers regarded slavery as a blessing. Tellingly, the word *slave* does not appear in the Constitution, as though the framers were expressing their sense of shame that such an institution existed in a country consecrated to liberty. Rather, in the provision that prevents Congress from abolishing the African slave trade for twenty years (Article I, Section 9), slaves are referred to obliquely as "such

Persons as any of the States now existing think proper to admit," and elsewhere the euphemism is "all other Persons."

This nimble phrase was used in the "three-fifths compromise." Whereas the northern states wished to count slaves for purposes of taxation, the southern states insisted on counting slaves when seats in the House of Representatives were apportioned. Of course, both the North and the South opposed the other's plan. In the end, the convention agreed that three-fifths of the slaves would be counted for both purposes. That is, five slaves were considered the equivalent of three citizens; legally, each slave was defined as three-fifths of a person.

Ratifying the Constitution

The Constitution provided that it would go into effect when nine of the thirteen states ratified it. Three did so almost immediately—Delaware and Connecticut almost unanimously, Pennsylvania in a mannner that dramatized the widespread opposition to the new government and the determination of the supporters of the Constitution to have their way.

The Federalists

People who favored the Constitution called themselves Federalists. This was something of a misnomer, since the Federalists sought to replace a truly federated government with a highly centralized one. In Pennsylvania, the Federalists managed ratification only by physically forcing two anti-Federalist members of the state convention to remain in their seats when they tried to leave. This rather irregular maneuver guaranteed a quorum so that the Federalists could cast a legal pro-Constitution vote.

It was ony the first of a series of manipulations that has convinced some historians that a majority of Americans opposed the Constitution and preferred to keep the old Articles. In Massachusetts, ratification was voted in February 1788 by a very narrow margin, and then only because several anti-Federalist delegates voted against their announced position. Critics at the time argued that the midwinter date prevented many western farmers, who presumably were anti-Federalist, from getting to the polls.

In June, 1788, Edmund Randolph of Virginia, an anti-Federalist, changed his vote and took a coterie of followers with him. Even so, the Federalist victory was by a vote of only eighty-nine to seventy-nine. A switch of five or six people would have reversed the verdict of the largest state, and that, in turn, would have kept New York in the anti-Federalist camp.

In New York, a large anti-Federalist majority was elected to the ratifying convention. After voting at first to reject the Constitution, they reversed their decision when news of Virginia's approval reached them. Even then, the New Yorkers saddled ratification with the proviso that a convention be called to amend the Constitution. It never was. Technically, New York's vote was no.

North Carolina was decisively anti-Federalist. The state ratified the Constitution reluctantly and not until November 1789, a year after the new government had begun to function. Rhode Island held out even longer, until May 1790. Rhode Island became the thirteenth state to accept the Constitution only when Congress threatened to pass a tariff that would have kept its goods out of the other twelve states.

The Anti-Federalists

Today, now that the Constitution has worked successfully for almost two hundred years, it would be easy to ignore the anti-Federalists of 1787 and 1788 as an unimportant historical force, a collection of nonconstructive reactionaries and cranks. Actually, the

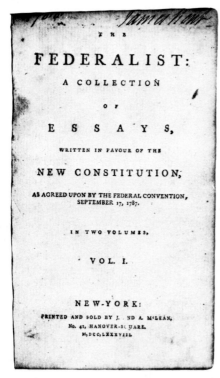

Title page from The Federalist (1787–1788), which urged support for the Constitution.

anti-Federalists may well have represented the views of the majority of the Americans, whose reasons for preferring the old Articles of Confederation were firmly within the democratic tradition.

Among the anti-Federalists were fiery old patriot leaders who feared that centralized power was an invitation to tyranny. Among those who preferred the Articles was Samuel Adams—still padding around the streets of Boston on the lookout for threats to liberty, still dressing in the fashions of 1776. Adams opposed the new government until Massachusetts Federalists, needing his support, agreed to press for a national bill of rights.

In Virginia, none other than Patrick Henry battled James Madison around the state. Some of Henry's arguments against the Constitution were foolish. At one point he concluded that the Constitution was an invitation to the pope to set up his court in the United States.

But Henry and other anti-Federalists also argued that free republican institutions could survive only in small countries such as Switzerland and ancient Greece, and they had the weight of historical evidence on their side. When Rome, the greatest republic of them all, grew large, it became despotic. Would the same thing happen to Rhode Island and Virginia and Georgia and the other small independent states when they were subsumed into a centralized United States?

Answering this objection to the Constitution was the Federalists' most difficult task. Madison, Hamilton, and John Jay of New York took it upon themselves to do so. In a number of treatises that, under the name The Federalist Papers, are still a basic textbook of political philosophy, they argued that a powerful United States would also guarantee liberty. These ingenious essays, however, were less important to the triumph of the Federalists than their agreement to add a bill of rights to their Constitution.

The Bill of Rights

The Constitutional Convention dedicated little time to debating the rights of citizens under the new government. The concern of the delegates was strengthening government, not putting limits on the powers that it was to exercise over individuals. The delegates, including even Hamilton, were not opposed to guaranteeing the civil liberties of citizens. They assumed that these were accounted for in the lists of rights most states included in their basic law.

Because the Constitution made the national government superior to those of the states, many powerful anti-Federalists such as Samuel Adams and Edmund

Randolph agreed to drop their opposition to the new document only when the various rights that had been adopted by the states since 1776 were guaranteed on a national level.

The first ten amendments to the Constitution were ratified in 1791. The First Amendment guaranteed the freedoms of religion, speech, the press, and peaceable assembly. The Second Amendment guaranteed the right to bear arms. The Third and Fourth Amendments guaranteed security against the quartering of troops in private homes (still a sore issue among Americans so soon after the Revolution) and against unreasonable search and seizure.

The famous Fifth Amendment is a guarantee against being tried twice for the same crime and, in effect, against torture; it is the basis of the citizen's right to refuse to testify in a trial in which he or she is a defendant. The Sixth Amendment also pertains to trials, ensuring the right to a speedy trial and the right to face accusers (no secret witnesses). The Seventh and Eighth Amendments likewise protect the rights of a person who is accused of committing a crime.

The Ninth and Tenth Amendments are catchalls. They state that simply because a right is not listed in the Constitution it does not mean that the right does not exist, and that any powers not explicitly granted to the federal government are reserved to the states.

The American Nation

With the new government approved, Americans once again looked to George Washington for leadership. There was never any question that he would be the first president. Washington alone commanded the respect of people of every religion, social class, and political inclination; the staunchest, most suspicious anti-Federalists admired him. He was elected unanimously by the electoral college.

President Washington

Washington was no more a political theorist than he was a military genius. He had little to say at the Constitutional Convention; he contributed none of the great ideas that were incorporated into the frame of government. But he possessed three virtues that are not only rare, but were indispensable to the extraordinary task of founding a government. He was committed to a republic and to the ideal of mixed government. He had an inbred sense of personal dignity and an awareness that he was setting precedents each time he addressed official guests or presided at a state dinner. And he was aware of his personal limitations. Far from jealous of the superior intellects of others, Washington

A triumphal arch erected in Philadelphia for George Washington's inauguration in 1789.

THE EMPEROR OF AMERICA

George Washington wanted a more exalted title than "Mr. President" for the nation's chief executive. President James Madison was perfectly happy with simplicity, but in one communiqué from the ruler of Algiers, he was addressed:

His Majesty, the Emperor of America, its adjacent and dependent provinces and coasts and wherever his government may extend, our noble friend, the support of the Kings of the nation of Jesus, the most glorious amongst the princes, elected among many lords and nobles, the happy, the great, the amiable, James Madison, Emperor of America.

took care to surround himself with and seek the advice of the best and the brightest of his time.

It was fortunate that Washington was a republican. With his great popularity, he could likely have been named a king. Hamilton and some members of the Order of Cincinnatus, an organization of Revolutionary War officers, wanted to crown him. But Washington knew that such an act would plunge the country into bloody civil war. Tom Paine had gone to France to take part in the revolution there. But the spirit of *Common Sense* lived on.

At the same time, Washington believed that the president occupied an exalted position and should therefore stand aloof and dignified. He would have preferred to be addressed as "Your Highness" or "Your Mightiness, the President of the United States" instead of the simple "Mr. President." He surrounded himself with servants in livery and powdered wigs, and he drove about the city of New York (which was the national capital) in a regal carriage drawn by matching cream-colored horses. He looked very much like the prince of a small European country. When on a bet the convivial Gouverneur Morris slapped Washington on the back at a social function, Morris was stared down with such icy disdain that he retreated stammering from the room and was never again able to address the president on cordial terms.

Washington and his cabinet, 1789.

In keeping his distance, in being more monument than man, Washington earned for the new government the respect of both foreigners and Americans that had been absent under the Confederation. Britain and France did not fear the power of the United States. But there was no mistaking George Washington for one of the uncultured bumpkins they liked to pretend Americans were.

The President's Advisers

In the workaday world of government, Washington took care to select good advisers—men whose opinions he trusted or, at least, thought it necessary he hear—rather than "yes men." In naming the members of his cabinet, he tried to balance both political philosophies and sectional and state interests.

From the South—from Washington's own Virginia—came Attorney General Edmund Randolph and Secretary of State Thomas Jefferson. Randolph had opposed the Constitution; by naming him to the cabinet, Washington extended a hand of reconciliation to the anti-Federalists. Jefferson had been abroad during the debate over the Constitution, but he was recognized as a spokesman for the democratically inclined farmers who were suspicious of the new government. His appointment helped to mollify them.

Balancing South with North, Washington named General Henry Knox of Massachusetts as Secretary of War. Knox was a personal friend and wartime crony of Washington's. Moreover, as the chief military official under the Confederation, he represented continuity. Finally, the ubiquitous and dynamic Hamilton was selected as Secretary of the Treasury. Partly because he was personally closer to Washington than were the others, partly because the most burning questions facing the new government were money questions, Hamilton soon emerged as the most powerful figure in the cabinet.

Hamilton Makes Policy

In order to pay the government's daily expenses, Hamilton proposed a 5 percent tariff on imports. Congress promptly agreed. The next priority, the secretary said, was to establish the government's credit; in times of trouble, it then would be possible to borrow money. In order to accomplish this, Hamilton proposed that Congress *fund* the United States' debt at face value—guarantee payment in full of the $11 million owed to foreign governments and banks and the $40 million owed to American citizens.

DOLLARS, NOT POUNDS

Why did the dollar, a Spanish monetary unit, become the basis of American currency rather than the British pound sterling, to which the Americans were accustomed? In part, it was a reaction against all things British. More important, there was more Spanish than British coin circulating in the colonies and states in the late eighteenth century. The British paid in trade goods for the American products they purchased, and they preferred British coin for what they sold to the colonies. Thus pounds tended to flow back to Great Britain. But the colonists had a favorable balance of trade with Spanish America—selling more than they bought—so Spanish coin was comparatively abundant.

BUCKS AND QUARTERS

The money slang word *buck* dates back to the eighteenth century, when the hide of a deer, a buckskin, was commonly used as a medium of exchange. Its value was approximately that of a dollar.

The American dollar eventually was divided into *quarters* of twenty-five cents each (quite an odd breakdown in a decimal system). Before coins valued at less than a dollar were common, it was customary to make change by sawing a Spanish dollar into eight wedge-shaped pieces. Two of them—two bits—equaled a quarter of a dollar. This is the origin of the now-dying custom of calling a quarter "two bits" and half a dollar "four bits."

No one objected to paying back loans. The government that does not pay its debts is a government that cannot borrow again. Because the United States was still a poor country by European standards, all agreed that the foreigners must receive their due. Nowhere was a good credit rating more necessary than in the financial centers of Europe.

But there was a catch to Hamilton's proposal to pay the domestic debt in full. Most of this debt dated back to the war years when, moved by patriotism, Americans lent money to the Continental Congress by buying Continental bonds. In the intervening ten or more years, as the weak Continental Congress repeatedly was unable to repay these people, many of them sold their notes to speculators at large discounts, sometimes just a few cents on the dollar. By 1789, most of the domestic debt was owed to such adventurers.

Nor were all of them so adventurous. As James Madison explained to the House of Representatives in opposing Hamilton's funding bill, some bankers and merchants, tipped off on Hamilton's proposal, had bought what public paper they could find in the months before the funding bill was introduced.

Should such profiteering be rewarded? Madison said no. As an alternative to Hamilton's plan, Madison argued that Congress pay the face value of the debts plus 4 percent interest only to original lenders who still held the notes. Speculators who had bought the notes at bargain rates should receive half of the face value, with the remainder going to the original lender. Morally, Madison's argument was impeccable: the government should reward those people who had stepped forward during the times that tried men's souls; it should not reward cynical and often corrupt speculators.

Hamilton met his former ally head-on. Credit, not morality, was the issue. By rewarding the speculators, the government would encourage them to be lenders in the future. Moreover, by enriching capitalists, the government would encourage investment in industry such as the United States sorely needed.

These practical arguments, plus the fact that several dozen congressmen stood to profit directly from funding, won the day. Hamilton's bill was passed.

Assumption

Next Hamilton proposed that the federal government *assume* responsibility for the debts of the states. By paying back loans that some states had ignored for more than a decade, he pointed out, the federal government would establish even better credit among money lenders. On the assumption issue, however, Hamilton ran into a split along sectional lines.

As Madison, again leading the opposition, pointed out, Virginia and most other southern states had retired most of their debt, while northern states, particularly Massachusetts, had been rather lax in the matter. If the national government now assumed these obligations, and paid them off through taxation, Virginians would pay twice. Some years before, Madison had anticipated and feared political splits along sectional lines. Now he found himself the leader of one.

As northerners and southerners would solve sectional disputes for more than a century, the assumption issue was settled by compromise. Hamilton got his bill by agreeing to persuade several New York congressmen to vote to locate the permanent national capital on land owned by Maryland and Virginia. Thus was the site of Washington, D.C., decided on.

The Bank of the United States

Hamilton's first two victories were accomplished by persuasion and compromise. His third was scored by going over Madison's (and Jefferson's) head to George Washington. The issue was whether to establish a national bank to handle the financial affairs of the government. Although chartered by the government, the Bank of the United States would be a private enterprise; the president would appoint only five of the twenty-five directors. Obviously, Hamilton's "people of wealth" would profit directly from such an institution. Private bankers would collect fees and interest as a result of handling public money.

The bill passed Congress over Madison's protests, but both he and Jefferson argued to President Washington that the Bank was unconstitutional. Nothing in the document gave the federal government the power to incorporate such an institution, and, therefore, that right was reserved to the states.

Washington was troubled. But in the end, Hamilton's pleas for tying the wealthy to the national government carried the day. Washington consoled Jefferson with the somewhat lame explanation that when opinions in his cabinet differed, he preferred to listen to the officer who was most closely involved in the matter.

At this point, Hamilton's magic touch failed him. His next program, presented in a lengthy "Report on Manufactures" in December 1791, called for a high protective tariff in order to encourage the development of American industry. For example, if British cloth were taxed and therefore priced so high that American investors were tempted to build their own textile mills, the nation would achieve a healthy balance of agriculture, trade, and industry.

But agricultural sections feared that foreign nations would respond to an American tariff by establishing tariffs against American agricultural exports. They preferred free trade both to encourage exports and to keep down the price of cloth and other manufactured goods, which they purchased in large quantities. On this issue, enough northern congressmen who represented rural districts joined Jefferson's and Madison's southern group to kill the bill.

By the summer of 1792, the hostility between Jefferson and Hamilton was common knowledge. Washington disliked factions and attempted, in a series of meetings and letters, to bring the men together. The president's efforts were unsuccessful, and Jefferson announced that he would leave the cabinet after the election of 1792. The stage was set for the emergence of full-blown political parties.

LIFE ON THE LOG-CABIN FRONTIER

*A view of Pittsburgh with Fort Pitt in 1790. The end of the Revolutionary War
opened up western Pennsylvania to settlers.*

The end of hostilities after the Battle of Yorktown led to the rapid settlement of western Pennsylvania, a land of ridges, rolling hills, and mixed hardwood and conifer forests. The American victory meant that the Proclamation of 1763, which forbade white settlement west of the Appalachians, was null and void. More important, when the fort at Pittsburgh was transferred from the redcoats to the Continental soldiers in their blue and buff, the power of the Indians of the region, who were British allies, was sharply reduced.

Perhaps the social disruptions that accompany every war also played a part in populating western Pennsylvania. In raising its armies, the Revolution wrenched thousands of young men from their homes and accustomed ways of life at a critical time in their lives. As young adults, they faced decisions about the future. When the war was over, many veterans found it impossible to return home and take up life where they had left off. In the United States, such people could head west, to the frontier as unsettled as themselves. During the 1780s (and for half a century to come), the West was centered in what is, geographically, the Eastern Woodlands.

The author of an article about the Pennsylvania frontier that appeared in *The Columbian Magazine* for November 1786 did not mention the recently concluded war. But "the first settler in the woods," whom the author describes as a kind of social misfit, sounds very much like a Revolutionary War veteran: the pioneer was "generally a man who has outlived his credit of fortune in the cultivated parts of the State." Not a very good citizen, he was an anarchic, irreligious, and hard-drinking individual who "cannot bear to surrender up a single natural right for all the benefits of government."

The pioneer moved on when too many people began to crowd into his neck of the woods—when he could hear the barking of his nearest neighbor's dogs, or see the curl of smoke from his nearest neighbor's fire. He sold out to a settler who improved the primitive farm and who, in turn, made way for the solid citizen whose habits obviously relieved the author of the *Columbian* article. In the third wave came the "settler who is commonly a man of property and good character."

"The *third* and last species of settler" meant the end of the log-cabin frontier literally as well as figuratively, for he built a solid house and barn of quarry stone. At last there could be schools, churches, law and order—a civilized town. The writer for the *Columbian* left no doubt as to where his hopes for the country lay. Nevertheless, he granted the obvious: that neither the third nor the second phase of settlement was possible without the pioneers who had been willing to face the hardships of the log cabin in return for freedom and independence.

Pioneers opening up forest land tried to arrive at their destination in April. Their first task was to build a cabin and stable in order to be sheltered by the third week of May, when, in Pennsylvania, the year's crop of corn, beans, and squash had to be planted. The pioneers' fields were not pretty; they were not even really fields. The pioneers adopted the Indian method of cultivation, killing the great oaks and maples by girdling their bark about two or three feet from the ground and planting wherever sun shone through the ghostlike trees. In the rich organic soil, created by the fallen leaves and toppled trees of centuries, even this primitive agriculture produced a crop of forty to fifty bushels an acre, harvested in October.

Cattle and horses—generally bony, unsavory-looking beasts—were allowed to roam, at most hobbled by the length of rope or leather thong that tied together two legs. There were no predators in the forests capable of bringing down such large animals, and the frontier family with the most casual work habits had little time for tending livestock.

Most families also owned hogs. They too ran loose and were hunted rather than rounded up when pork was needed. Indeed, with the forests teeming with game, meat shortage was less a problem than keeping domestic and wild animals out of the corn fields.

Toward this end, the log-cabin pioneer built a rude zigzag fence. It was a marvelous adaptation to the conditions of the forest frontier—abundant wood and land, scarce labor. Logs could be split into rails using one tool, and the zigzag pattern required no post holes. It was not a very good fence. The rails were toppled by hungry hogs and easily leapt by deer. But it sufficed, and sufficient was enough for a family struggling against the virgin forest.

The log cabin was another adaptation to forest conditions. Again, only one tool was required to build one. With their axes, the pioneers easily felled small trees, hewed (squared) them if they chose, and cut the notches that made it possible to build a cabin wall without an upright timber. In all but the rudest cabins—and many were but three-sided structures that faced an open fire—the only task requiring more than a single man's and woman's labor was raising the roof beam, itself a log. Other frontier families were called on to help, and the event became a social occasion. Even the sniffy author of the *Columbian* article, who had little good to say about the pioneer, was moved to admire the cooperation involved in performing such tasks "without any other pay than the pleasures which usually attend a country frolic." The roofing itself consisted of split rails or a thatch of rye straw.

Not only did the log cabin go up quickly, but it was a strong house. Its walls were thick and almost invulnerable to arrowhead, musket ball, or fire. (To burn a log cabin, it was necessary to set fire to the roof.) Finally, if the logs were well chinked with moss and mud, they provided better insulation against cold than sawn clapboards did.

The sturdiness of the well-built log cabin was attested to by the fact that the people who came in the second wave of settlement purchased the pioneer log cabin, added on to it, laid floor boards, and shingled the roof. Otherwise they found the pioneer's dwelling quite serviceable. Even the third settler, the permanently fixed farmer, often found a use for the cabin after building a stone house.

By the middle of the nineteenth century, the log cabin entered American folklore as a symbol of the opportunity the nation provided its citizens. A man who was born in a log cabin could hope to rise, as Abraham Lincoln had done and James A. Garfield would do, to the highest office in the land.

For Further Reading

The books dealing with the politics of the Confederation period listed at the end of Chapter 9 are also pertinent to this chapter.

A largely discredited work is still the first book to read about the writing of the Constitution. According to Charles A. Beard, *Economic Interpretation of the Constitution of the United States* (1913), the long-lived frame of government was written largely because men who held Confederation notes wanted to profit from their speculations. Forrest McDonald, *We the People: The Economic Origins of the Constitution* (1958), effectively disproves Beard's main points.

J. C. Miller, *Alexander Hamilton: Portrait in Paradox* (1959), is the best biography of Washington's principal adviser during the first years of his administration. J. T. Flexner focuses on the president himself in *George Washington and the New Nation* (1970). The best single volume about the 1790s is J. C. Miller, *The Federalist Era* (1960).

11

The Federalist Decade

Unity and Conflict in the American Republic, 1791–1801

George Washington was reelected in 1792 as resoundingly as he had been elected in 1788. No one was so audacious as to run against him. Only 3 electors out of 123 failed to write his name on their ballots.

On balance, Washington's eight years in office were successful. He managed to carry out most of the policies he felt strongly about and to establish sensible precedents for his successors to imitate. Most important, as Washington saw it, he presided over the establishment of a functioning, stable government for 4 million people and (on the map, at least) nine hundred thousand square miles of territory. The United States, which had appeared to be on the verge of splitting into a gaggle of small, quarrelsome principalities when the Constitution was adopted, was a single republic when, early in 1797, a sixty-five-year-old and none-too-healthy George Washington returned to Mount Vernon, the plantation home where he had spent so little of his life.

George Washington, shown here in a detail from Washington at Verplanck's Point *by John Trumbull (1790, oil on canvas, 30″ × 20⅛″ rectangular), helped the colonies become a unified republic during his presidency.*

The Problems of a Young Country

Washington's success did not come easily. His presidency was a time of grave challenges, and it is not clear that the first president was entirely satisfied with his responses to them. In his farewell address of September 1796, Washington devoted little time to crowing about accomplishments. Instead, he focused on four ongoing and related problems that caused him grave concern.

First, Washington urged—virtually begged—his countrymen not to form political parties. Washington regarded parties as combinations of selfish people who were willing to sacrifice the common good for their own narrow interests.

Second, Washington strongly admonished Americans to "discountenance irregular opposition" to the authority of their government. That is, they should voice their opposition to laws they did not like through peaceful and legal channels, rather than resort to resistance and rebellion. Third, he regretfully identified the beginnings of sectionalism in the United States. He feared that many Americans felt more a part of North, South, East, or West than of the nation. Division along geographical lines, fraught with the possibilities of civil war, must be nipped before it bloomed.

Finally, Washington warned against "the insidious wiles of foreign influence," the attempts by European diplomats to entangle the United States in their own chronic, tragic, wasteful wars. Honor alliances already in effect, Washington said, but make no new permanent commitments to other countries. Formulate foreign policy according to the interests of the United States, rather than those of England or France, the great world powers of the time, or some abstract principle.

Europe in Turmoil

There was nothing abstract about the turmoil in Europe during the 1790s. In 1789, France had erupted in a revolution that, within a few years, pushed far beyond what the Americans had done. At first rebelling against the extravagance and excesses of the French king and aristocracy, the French revolutionaries soon set about redesigning their society from bottom to top.

Americans and the French Revolution

At first, Americans rejoiced almost unanimously at the events in France. Their ally in the struggle against Great Britain was joining them as a land where liberty flourished. It became fashionable for Americans to

After his presidential term expired in 1797, George Washington retired to his Mount Vernon home.

wear a cockade of red, white, and blue—the badge of the revolutionaries in France. When the Marquis de Lafayette sent Washington the key to the Bastille, the gloomy fortress where Louis XVI had imprisoned political prisoners, the president displayed it proudly to his guests.

Nor were most Americans perturbed when the revolution turned on the institutions of monarchy and aristocracy. Had not the Americans themselves renounced kingship and forbidden citizens to accept titles of nobility?

Then the French Revolution moved beyond liberty to the principles of equality and fraternity. Conservative men such as Washington and Hamilton were not happy with talk about wiping out all social distinctions and privileges. Even Thomas Jefferson, who supported the revolutionaries, worried that the French were moving too far too fast. He doubted that a people accustomed to an all-powerful monarchy could create overnight a republic like the United States.

But found a republic the French did, and in January 1793, as Washington's first term of office was ending, King Louis XVI and his queen, Marie Antoinette, were beheaded. During the Reign of Terror that followed, French radicals called Jacobins guillotined or drowned thousands of nobles and political rivals. The virtual dictator of France during this period, Maximilien Robespierre, launched a campaign to wipe out religion in France. He transformed the Cathedral of Notre Dame in Paris into a Temple of Reason where politicians and actors performed rituals that struck many as ridiculous and others as blasphemous.

Very few Americans looked fondly on the Catholic Church. Many ministers realized, however, that Robespierre was attacking not just one church but all religion. They shuddered when they heard Americans expressing admiration for his campaign. William Cobbett, an Englishman who also was appalled by the events in France, observed with distaste that Americans guillotined King Louis in effigy "twenty or thirty times every day during one whole winter and part of the summer." He also reported seeing fist fights between gangs of pro-English "Anglomen" and pro-French "cutthroats."

Choosing Sides

Cobbett had hit one point of conflict that contributed to the birth of the political parties that Washington had warned against. Americans who supported the French were believers in democracy at home and critics of social privilege. Workingpeople in the cities, backcountry farmers who disliked institutionalized religion, small farmers generally, people (including some southern planters) who resented the favors that Hamilton's financial program gave to the rich merchants, looked increasingly to Thomas Jefferson as their spokesman on a national level and began to call themselves Republicans. Jefferson, who resigned from Washington's cabinet in 1793, was troubled by the bloodletting in the country where he had been ambassador, but he refused to desert what he regarded as the cause of democracy and human liberty.

Conservatives such as Washington, Hamilton, and Vice President John Adams, soon referred to as Federalists, were neither friendly to democracy nor hostile to privilege. Until 1793, they contented themselves with attacking the principles of the French Revolution on a philosophical level. After 1793, however, that was not enough. Great Britain declared war on France in that year, and, because of the alliance of 1778, the United States was technically obligated to join France in the fight.

No important government officials, not even Jefferson, wanted to go to war. Britannia ruled the waves of the Atlantic, and Washington's advisers feared that another war would prove too large a burden for the four-year-old government. Hamilton argued that the treaty of 1778 was invalid on two counts: it had been made with the French monarchy, which no longer existed; it provided that the United States must help France only if England were the aggressor, which England strongly denied.

Washington announced that the United States would be neutral, "impartial toward the belligerent powers." This might have averted crisis had it not been for the arrival in Charleston in April 1793 of the French ambassador, Edmond Charles Genêt, or, as this preposterous character styled himself, Citizen Genêt.

Citizen Genêt

The ambassador was young, bombastic, and utterly devoid of a sense of diplomacy. Soon after he stepped ashore, he began to commission American shipmasters as privateers in the service of France. Within a short time, a dozen of these raiders brought eighty British merchantmen into American ports, where Genêt presided over "trials" at which he awarded the prizes to the captors. Genêt also assigned several adventurers to organize an invasion of Spanish Louisiana. Amidst this busy schedule, he managed to attend dozens of dinners held in his honor, at which he spoke as though he were the governor of a French colony.

By the time the ambassador made his way to Philadelphia to present his credentials to the president, Washington was enraged by his behavior. Genêt's lack of diplomatic etiquette was bad enough to a man deter-

Edmond Charles "Citizen" Genêt, the colorful French ambassador to America.

PRIVATEERS

In order to expand their striking power beyond the number of warships in their navies, governments often commissioned "privateers." Captains of private vessels were given authority to wage war against the merchant ships of the enemy. Obviously, it was often not easy to distinguish between a legal privateer and a pirate, who preyed on any country's ships regardless of who was at war with whom. In fact, many privateers became pirates when the war was over, and governments frequently refused to accept their enemy's commissions as legal. Captured privateers often were hanged for piracy. It was a profitable, but dangerous, business.

CITIZEN GENÊT

The French revolutionaries hated the symbols of inequality as much as the reality of it. They tried to eliminate all titles, not only those of nobility (duke, countess, and marquis), but also *Monsieur* and *Madame*, forms of address that were then reserved for gentlemen and ladies. During the early stages of the French Revolution, it was declared that everyone was to be addressed as *Citoyen* and *Citoyenne*, or "Citizen" and "Citizeness." King Louis XVI was brought to trial as "Citizen Capet," and when Edmond Genêt arrived in the United States as ambassador, he called himself Citizen Genêt. His Jeffersonian friends briefly adopted the custom, referring to one another as "Citizen."

The Russian revolutionaries of 1917 did much the same thing when they abolished traditional Russian forms of address in favor of *Tovarich*, or "Comrade." In countries like the United States and Britain, the problem has been resolved by upgrading everyone to the level of "Mr." and "Mrs."—titles that previously were reserved to members of the gentry.

mined to establish the dignity of his government. Worse, Genêt's actions promised to drag the United States into a war with England that the president had determined to sit out. Washington received Genêt coldly, and ordered him to subdue his politicking and to cease bringing British prizes into neutral American ports.

Genêt did neither. He continued to appear at dinners and demonstrations, now adding criticism of the president to his speeches. When Genêt defied Washington by recommissioning a captured British vessel, the *Little Sarah,* as a privateer, it was too much. Washington ordered him to return to France.

Genêt did not go. He was a member of a political faction that had been ousted. The Reign of Terror was in full swing; to return to France meant facing the guillotine. Suddenly abject, he asked Washington for asylum, and the president granted it. More surprisingly, Genêt actually did quiet down. He married the daughter of New York governor George Clinton and settled down to a long, contented life as a gentleman farmer in the Hudson River Valley.

The British Flirt with War

Genêt's debacle served to cool pro-French feelings. But a British decision revived a much stronger passion in American breasts, hatred for the former mother country. Britain proclaimed that the war at sea would be fought under the rule of 1756, which provided that neutral countries could not trade in enemy ports from which they had been excluded before the war.

The principal target of this proclamation were those American overseas merchants who were enriching themselves by provisioning the French West Indies—the sugar islands of Martinique and Guadeloupe and the French half of Santo Domingo (present-day Haiti).

Before the war, ports in these colonies had been closed to all but French ships. Fearing that it would be unable to supply these valuable possessions with grain, livestock, and other foodstuffs, the French government invited the Americans in. In New England, New York, and Pennsylvania, merchants grew rich on the trade and moved from apartments in their warehouses to elegant town houses whose architectural style has come to be known as Federal Period. In sharp contrast to the ways of their dour Puritan and Quaker forebears, they hosted grand levees and balls and sponsored a sparkling social whirl in the coastal cities. They also expanded their fleets until the American merchant marine was at least as large as, if not larger than, the British.

The British were concerned. Would they defeat France again only to discover that their overseas trade had been stolen by upstart Yankees? The enforcement of the rule of 1756 was an attempt to prevent that

eventuality. During 1793 and 1794, British warships seized six hundred American vessels, about half of them in West Indian waters or within sight of American beaches.

American shipowners were not amused, but neither were they unduly disturbed. The overseas trade was a high-risk business in the best of times, and the trade with the West Indies was so lucrative that they were able to absorb the losses. Moreover, in New England (the leading mercantile section of the country), wealthy people were generally anti-French and pro-British. They were inclined to wink at whatever the British did.

But many of the pro-French party, the Jefferson Republicans, who were always keen to pick a fight with England, took the seizures as an affront to national honor. Workingpeople in seaports, many of them connected with the overseas commerce, were not so willing as their employers to shrug off the loss of ships. The shipowners lost only property; the sailors on seized ships sacrificed their freedom and sometimes their lives. Seamen and their families also resented the right of impressment on which the British insisted; that is, the right of a captain of a British warship to board an American vessel, whether or not involved in illegal trade, and remove sailors whom he thought to be British subjects for service in the Royal Navy.

Washington Saves the Peace—At a Price

Faced with a growing clamor for war and with James Madison's demand in Congress that the nation boycott all trade with Britain, Washington acted. In April 1794, he sent the Chief Justice of the Supreme Court, John Jay, to England to appeal for peace. This alone was enough to raise Republican hackles, especially when the news trickled back that Jay was hobnobbing happily in English high society and had kissed the hand of King George's queen.

That fuss was nothing compared with the reception given the treaty that Jay brought back. Although the English did not want a war with the United States, they made few concessions to the New Yorker. They agreed to evacuate the western forts, which should have been transferred to the Americans in 1783. The treaty stated that both British and American ships should be allowed to navigate the Mississippi River. Britain also agreed to compensate American shipowners £1.3 million for vessels seized in the West Indies and to make a few minor concessions regarding trade with British possessions. In return, the Americans pledged not to discriminate against British shipping (as Madison had proposed) and to pay about £600,000 in debts owing to British subjects from before the Revolution.

Chase Lloyd House in Maryland, a town house of the Federal Period.

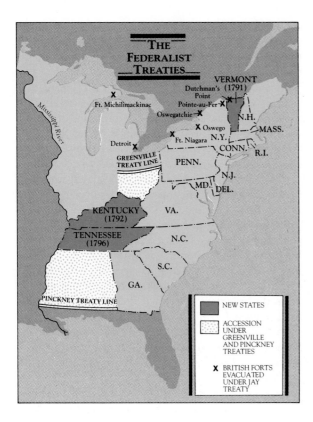

THE FEDERALIST TREATIES

Ft. Michilimackinac

Dutchman's Point (1791)

Pointe-au-Fer

Oswegatchie

VERMONT

N.H.

Oswego

MASS.

Detroit

Ft. Niagara

N.Y.

CONN.

R.I.

GREENVILLE TREATY LINE

PENN.

N.J.

MD.

DEL.

KENTUCKY (1792)

VA.

TENNESSEE (1796)

N.C.

S.C.

GA.

PINCKNEY TREATY LINE

Mississippi River

NEW STATES

ACCESSION UNDER GREENVILLE AND PINCKNEY TREATIES

X BRITISH FORTS EVACUATED UNDER JAY TREATY

Not a word was said about impressment. Nothing was conceded on the question of the Royal Navy's future treatment of American shipping. Like Hamilton's fiscal policy, Jay's Treaty seemed to benefit only the wealthy. As for the British evacuation of the western forts, the fulfillment of a promise that had been made and broken a decade before hardly soothed the wounded pride of Republican patriots.

Protest swept the country. When Washington submitted the treaty to Congress, he was attacked more bitterly than at any other time during his administration. Jay had to resign from the Supreme Court, and he joked uneasily that he could travel the length of the country by the light of the effigies of him that were burned by furious Republican crowds who shouted: "Damn John Jay! Damn every one that won't put lights in his windows and sit up all night damning John Jay!"

It was, to say the least, an expression of party spirit. Moreover, Washington, Adams, Hamilton, and others calling themselves Federalists did not damn John Jay. They believed that however imperfect his treaty, he had done the country a service by preserving the peace. They too were taking sides. Not as a party; with Washington as their leader, they dared not call themselves a party. But the beginnings of a political party they

were. Nothing was more important in the evolution of the first American party system—Federalists versus Jefferson Republicans—than the well-damned treaty of John Jay.

Pinckney's Treaty

Another consequence of Jay's Treaty was a very advantageous agreement with Spain. Like the English, the Spanish had been warring with France. By the end of 1794, however, weak and unstable Spain wanted to end the conflict. France, fighting practically the whole of Europe, was willing to come to terms. But the clause about the navigation of the Mississippi in the agreement between England and the United States led Spain to fear that those two countries might form an alliance to invade Louisiana. Not two years before, Citizen Genêt had proposed such an expedition to Americans.

The best way to ward off the danger was to placate the United States. Meeting with Thomas Pinckney, the ambassador to Madrid, the Spanish acquiesced to practically every demand that the Americans had made on them since 1783. In Pinckney's Treaty (officially the Treaty of San Lorenzo), Spain agreed to the American version of the boundary between the United States and Louisiana; to open the Mississippi River to American navigation (the Spanish owned the western bank); and to grant Americans the "right of deposit" in New Orleans. That is, Americans could store their exports (mostly foodstuffs and timber), and carry on commercial transactions in the Spanish city at the mouth of the river.

These concessions were of vital importance to the first "westerners," the more than one hundred thousand people who, by 1795, had settled in Kentucky (admitted to the Union in 1792) and Tennessee (admitted in 1796), and the several thousand who lived in what is now Ohio.

The First American West

Life on the frontier contrasted sharply with the elegance, comfort, and security of Federalist society in the East. The killing labor involved in wrenching a farm out of dense forest combined with infectious disease and sometimes malnutrition to make the death rate west of the Appalachians as high as it had been in seventeenth-century Virginia and Maryland. Isolation from the eastern states meant that manufactured commodities were expensive when they were available at all. Atop these hardships was the determination of the

Indians who lived between the Appalachians and the Mississippi to hold their ancestral lands.

President Washington was as eager as any log-cabin pioneer to clear the western lands of Indians. Not only was it a matter of national pride that the federal government actually govern all its territories, but Washington himself and many of the wealthy planters and northern merchants with whom he associated were deeply involved in land speculation in the Northwest Territory. They owned thousands of acres of virgin forest that they found difficult to sell to settlers as long as the native peoples, particularly the well-led Miamis and Shawnees of present-day Ohio and Indiana, maintained independence of action.

In 1790, Washington sent Josiah Harmer to find and defeat the Miamis and Shawnees, who were led by the war chieftain Little Turtle. Poorly supplied, wracked by dysentery and malaria, and handicapped by unfamiliarity with the country, Harmer and his men were trounced near the site of present-day Fort Wayne, Indiana. The next year, a better-prepared expedition was mounted under Arthur St. Clair, but he met the same fate as Harmer.

The Miamis and Shawnees, with their loose ties with the British in Canada, remained supreme in the Northwest Territory until August 1794, when General Anthony Wayne defeated them at the Battle of Fallen Timbers in northwestern Ohio. In the meantime, whereas the Federalist government seemed ineffective

The Battle of Fallen Timbers in Ohio, where General Anthony Wayne defeated the Miami and the Shawnee Indians in 1794.

in dealing with Indians, Washington had moved with dispatch and armed force against backcountry farmers in western Pennsylvania.

Of Pioneers and Whiskey

The men and women of the frontier were known to be heavy drinkers. Future president William Henry Harrison said that he "saw more drunk men in forty-eight hours succeeding my arrival in Cincinnati than I had in my previous life." One reason behind this weakness for the jug was, no doubt, disease. Settlers in the woodlands frontier suffered miserably from the alternating chills and fevers of malaria, which they called the "ague," and the first medicine for which they reached was alcohol.

The isolation of western life was another reason for settlers' heavy drinking. It was easy to grow corn, even in freshly cleared forest; when a farm was a few years old, pioneers turned to wheat and rye, which also flourished. But where were they to sell it? The Mississippi River was not opened to them until 1795. The costs involved in transporting a low-value bulk commodity like grain eastward over the Appalachians were prohibitive.

By comparison, it was cheap to bring distilling equipment west. Not only did many family farmers keep a small still percolating day and night, turning their grain into raw white whiskey, but commercial distillers established large operations on major waterways throughout the Ohio Valley.

Everyone drank. A jug sat on every shop counter; every general store doubled as a saloon. People swigged corn or rye whiskey like wine with their meals and like water with their work. The image of the hillbilly asleep next to his jug of moonshine was not invented by cartoonists. In time, the backcountry's love of whiskey would lead to religious crusades against it among the people there. In the 1790s, however, the local preacher was more likely to match his flock shot for shot.

Of Whiskey and Rebellion

Whiskey served the westerners as money. If it was too expensive to transport grain any distance and make a profit, the brown jugs traveled well. A horse that could carry only four bushels of grain could carry the equivalent of twenty-four bushels if it had been transformed into liquor. A gallon of whiskey, which weighed less than six bushels of corn and took up far less space, could be sold for twenty-five cents or more.

Even then the profit was small. Hamilton's excise tax of 1791 (seven cents on the gallon!) wiped it out, destroying the modest cash income of farmers in western Pennsylvania. Just as Daniel Shays's men had done in Massachusetts in 1787, the Pennsylvania farmers roughed up tax collectors and rioted in river towns.

Washington and Hamilton, who had been disgusted by the disorder represented by the Shaysites, saw a grand opportunity to demonstrate the authority of the new government. The president himself set out at the head of fifteen thousand troops to suppress the "rebellion." He left the expedition when the rebels scattered. But Hamilton, who had a never-sated yen for military glory, pushed on and arrested a few men who were tried, convicted of treason, and sentenced to death. Washington pardoned them, calling them mental defectives. Perhaps they were; perhaps it was just Washington's way of showing his contempt for rebels of every kind.

In one sense, the venture was a farce. An army as large as the one that had defeated the British—and far larger than those sent against the Indians—was organized to crush a rebellion that it could not even find. But the political significance of the episode was profound. The Federalist Hamilton was delighted simply to establish the national government's right to enforce order in a state. The resentment of the westerners, however, ensured that when political parties emerged full-blown, the people of the frontier would be overwhelmingly in opposition to the Federalists. Almost to a man, they were Jefferson Republicans.

Angry westerners tar and feather an excise officer during the Whiskey Rebellion of 1791.

Federalists Versus Republicans

By the summer of 1796, when Washington announced that he was retiring and warned Americans against forming political parties, two parties existed in everything but name. On every controversy that arose during Washington's presidency, Americans not only disagreed, but they also divided along pretty much the same lines.

Party Lines

The Federalists supported Hamilton's financial policy; feared the French Revolution as a source of atheism and social disorder; were friendly to England and its policies; accepted, even if they did not much like, Jay's Treaty; and believed that the national government should act decisively and powerfully to maintain internal order, as Washington had done in western Pennsylvania.

Vice President John Adams and Alexander Hamilton were the chief spokesmen for the Federalist group, which also included John Jay, the wealthy Pinckneys of South Carolina, and—because no matter what he said, he agreed with the policies of the Federalists—George Washington himself.

Wealthy people were inclined to be Federalists. In the North (especially New England), where money had been made in trade and speculation, the urban rich were almost unanimously Federalists. In the South, where money had been made in agriculture, support for the Federalists was not so overwhelming. People who lived in coastal areas were heavily Federalist, believing that that party—especially as John Adams of Massachusetts and Alexander Hamilton of New York would run it—was favorable to the interest of the overseas trade on which they depended.

The Jefferson Republicans generally opposed Hamilton's financial policy, at least those provisions that enriched speculators. Farmers (and great planters) believed that they paid the taxes that financed funding and assumption. Republicans were friendly to the ideals of the French Revolution, although they were by no means uncritical of excesses like the Reign of Terror. Republicans were generally suspicious of England, as both the former oppressor and, in the West, the tacit ally of the Indians. The Republicans despised Jay's Treaty; they were the damners. With an affection for democratic values that the Federalists spurned, the Republicans worried about an overly powerful national government quick to use soldiers against protestors like the Whiskey Rebels.

Thomas Jefferson was unmistakably the Republican leader, although Congressman James Madison's energy and wise counsel were indispensable to their cause. The Republicans were supreme in the West and held the edge in the South, but, as the election of 1796 showed, they were a significant minority elsewhere.

A New President

Vice President John Adams won the election of 1796. He won all the states of New England plus New York, New Jersey, Delaware, and scattered electoral votes elsewhere, compiling seventy-one electoral votes to Thomas Jefferson's sixty-eight. Because, until 1804, the runner-up in the electoral college became vice president, Adams found himself in the awkward situation of seeing his chief rival in the second highest office in the land.

Adams was a hearty, healthy sixty-two year old (he would live to be ninety-two), and the vice president, then as now, had little real power. Much more a threat to Adams was fellow Federalist Alexander Hamilton. Holding no public office himself, Hamilton was nonetheless the acknowledged leader of perhaps half the Federalists in Congress, and he neither liked nor much respected Adams. Indeed, Jefferson's electoral-vote total was only three fewer than Adams's because Hamilton had devised a scheme to elect Thomas Pinckney, officially the Federalist vice-presidential candidate, in Adams's place.

Only six states selected presidential electors by pop-ular vote in 1796. Nine states gave this power to their legislatures, and one, Massachusetts, used a complicated combination of the two methods. There was much room for manipulation. Unlike electors today, only a few eighteenth-century electors committed themselves to support a candidate.

Working his considerable talents for persuasion, Hamilton secretly urged some Federalist electors to withhold votes from Adams, to cast one of their two votes for Pinckney, and to waste the other on a man who was not a candidate. Hamilton hoped that some southern Republicans would cast votes for Pinckney because he was from South Carolina, and he would edge out Adams in the final tally.

It might have worked except that Adams's supporters got wind of the plot, and the fifteen electors from Connecticut and New Hampshire withheld their votes from Pinckney! So the hated Jefferson was only a beat of Adams's heart away from the presidency. Adams blamed the results on the Hamilton people. He actually began his administration by warming up to the Republicans.

"His Rotundity"

Such a flirtation could not last. Jefferson was wedded to radical democratic and agrarian ideals, and Adams, for all his personal dislike of Hamilton, was a conservative. Like Hamilton, he feared and distrusted "the mob," more so as president than during the Revolution.

In retrospect, it is easy to admire John Adams. He was a moderate man who acted according to stern and steadfast principles. He was "always honest and often great," in Benjamin Franklin's words. But, as Franklin added, he was "sometimes mad." John Adams was extremely unpleasant to know and to work with. He had a furious temper, a bottomless capacity for intolerance, and an absurdly pompous manner. When elegant Federalist socialites sniggered at his short, dumpy physique ("His Rotundity," they whispered) and gossiped about his wife, Abigail (who was his principal adviser), Adams withdrew peevishly into himself. Adams spent astonishingly little time in the national capital (Philadelphia until the last year of his presidency). During his four years as president, he passed more than a quarter of his time at the Adams home in Quincy, Massachusetts. (By comparison, Washington was absent fewer than one day in eight.) His absence and his inheritance of Washington's last cabinet, which was as bumbling a group as the first had been brilliant and which reported every bit of business to Hamilton, made the president a man with only half a party behind him.

WASHINGTON THE VILLAIN

Although no one dared oppose him in the election of 1792, Washington was not universally worshiped. Indeed, the invective heaped on him by editor Benjamin Bache (who was Benjamin Franklin's nephew) exceeds anything to be found in newspapers today. In December 1796, Bache wrote, "If ever a nation was debauched by a man, the American nation has been debauched by Washington." When Washington turned over the presidency to John Adams in March 1797, Bache exulted, "If ever there were a period for rejoicing, it is this moment. Every heart, in unison with the freedom and happiness of the people, ought to beat high in exultation, that the name of Washington ceases from this day to give a currency to political iniquity and to legalize corruption." In another place, Bache warned, "The American people, Sir, will look to death the man who assumes the character of a usurper."

John Adams, second U.S. president.

Another War Scare

Like Washington in his second term, Adams was preoccupied with the war in Europe and the danger that the United States would be sucked into it, this time against France. Angered by Jay's Treaty, the French government known as the Directory ordered its navy to treat American ships as fair game. By the time Adams took the oath of office, three hundred American vessels had been seized. Americans whom the French captured off British ships (many of whom had been pressed involuntarily into service) were defined as pirates and were therefore liable to be hanged. In Paris, the French ignored the existence of the American ambassador, Charles Cotesworth Pinckney, except when they threatened to arrest him. In the United States, the French minister, Pierre Adet, railed publicly against Adams almost as intemperately as Genêt had attacked Washington.

Hamilton's supporters, so-called High Federalists who had reacted so calmly to British seizures of American ships, demanded war with France. Determined to keep the peace, as Washington had done, Adams dispatched to Paris two special ambassadors, John Marshall and Elbridge Gerry, to join Pinckney in asking for negotiations.

The XYZ Affair

They were shunned. Weeks passed, and they could not get near the French foreign minister, Charles Maurice de Talleyrand. Then that randy old rogue, who not only survived half a dozen changes of politics under the French Republic, but would serve Napoleon and his successor, Louis XVIII, sent word to the Americans through three henchmen, discreetly identified as X, Y, and Z. Talleyrand would receive the Americans if they would agree in advance to lend the French government $12 million and to pay Talleyrand $250,000 under the table.

Bribery of this sort was routine in diplomacy; but the amount was excessive, and the tempers of the Americans were worn thin by waiting. "Not a sixpence," Pinckney snapped to X, Y, and Z. His reply was dressed up back in the United States as "millions for defense but not one cent for tribute" and carved on Pinckney's tombstone.

The High Federalists greeted the news of Talleyrand's insult with joy. Hamilton pressured Adams to mobilize an army of ten thousand men, and Washington agreed to become its titular commander on the condition that Hamilton be second in command. Not only did this mean jumping rank over several Revolutionary War officers, but it humiliated Adams and caused him to worry about a military coup.

Adams was more comfortable with the navy. He came from a shipbuilding state, and sea power posed no threat to the domestic peace. Moreover, while it was difficult to say where France and America could fight on land, an undeclared war already raged on the seas. Adams authorized the construction of forty frigates and lesser warships, a huge jump from the three naval vessels that he had inherited from Washington.

Domestic Repression

Because the Jefferson Republicans remained sympathetic to France, they spoke loudly and fiercely against these preparations for war. They were egged on in their anger by French diplomats and by a group of Irishmen who had fled to America after the failure of their rebellion against England. Both Adams Federalists and Hamiltonian High Federalists responded to this protest with a series of laws called the Alien and Sedition Acts of 1798.

One act extended the period of residence required for American citizenship from five to fourteen years. This was a tacit admission that few newcomers to the United States supported the Federalists.

A second law gave the government authority to move expeditiously against enemy aliens (meaning the French and the Irish) in the event of war. The third Alien Act allowed the president to deport any foreigner whom he deemed "dangerous to the peace and safety of the United States." It was a dangerously vague law.

Indeed, because it was to expire after two years (just when Adams's term would end), the Republicans calculated that it was aimed at winning the president's reelection.

None of the three Alien Acts were ever enforced, although many foreigners fled the United States for fear that they would be. The Sedition Act was. This law was aimed not at foreigners but at American citizens. It called for stiff fines and prison sentences for persons who published statements that held the United States government in "contempt or disrepute." Twenty-five cases were brought to trial, and ten people were convicted. Two of them, Jefferson men in Newark, New Jersey, were imprisoned under the act. When John Adams passed through the city and the militia provided the usual salute of gunfire, one said, "There goes the president and they are shooting at his ass," and the other responded, "I don't care if they fire through his ass." A court presided over by George Washington's nephew, Bushrod Washington, ruled that these were seditious words.

Other prosecutions under the Sedition Act were not so comical. In a palpable effort to crush the political opposition, Federalists indicated and convicted four important Republican newspaper editors for the same crime. Thomas Jefferson, in very active retirement at his home, Monticello, received alarmed and angry letters from his supporters in every part of the country. He feared that the Bill of Rights and the ideals of the Declaration of Independence were in danger.

The Virginia and Kentucky Resolutions

Out of Jefferson's and Madison's response to the Alien and Sedition Acts came a constitutional theory that haunted American history for half a century and contributed to the tragic Civil War of 1861 to 1865. Jefferson and Madison aimed to determine how the unconstitutional actions of Congress could be overruled. In a series of resolutions adopted by the Virginia and Kentucky legislatures in late 1798 and early 1799, Madison and Jefferson declared that the states possessed this power. They said that the federal government was a voluntary compact of sovereign states. When Congress, the creation of the states, enacted a law that was obnoxious to one of them, that state had the right to nullify the law within its boundaries. Madison and Jefferson were declaring that the Alien and Sedition Acts did not apply in Virginia and Kentucky.

Nothing came of this challenge to the authority of the national government. No other state assemblies adopted the Virginia and Kentucky Resolutions, and the death of George Washington in December 1799 briefly brought together all political factions in mourning.

Moreover, as the election of 1800 drew closer, it became increasingly obvious to Jefferson and Madison (and Adams) that instead of serving as Federalist tools, the Alien and Sedition Acts were so unpopular that they improved the chances of a Republican victory whence they would be allowed to expire.

The Very Peculiar Election of 1800

As it happened, Jefferson's victory over Adams was nearly as close as Adams's victory over Jefferson in 1796. Jefferson won seventy-three electoral votes to Adams's sixty-five; the only significant change in how the states voted was the switch of New York from the Federalist to the Jefferson Republican column. This neat trick—with nineteen electoral votes, New York was the third biggest prize—was the handiwork of a man who was Hamilton's rival for control of the state and his equal in political scheming.

Aaron Burr, only forty-four years old, brilliant and imaginative, was the Republican vice-presidential candidate. However, because the Constitution held that the candidate who received the most votes became president, the runner-up became vice president, and each elector was to vote for two men, it was necessary for one of the seventy-three Republican electors to drop Burr's name from his ballot. Otherwise, Burr would be tied with Jefferson for the presidency.

That is precisely what happened. No Republican elector threw away a vote, so neither Jefferson nor Burr had the majority. The task of choosing the next president fell to the House of Representatives, where members would vote not as individuals but as states.

As third-place finisher, Adams was disqualified; the House was permitted to choose between only the top two candidates. The Federalist congressmen held the balance of power; nine states were needed for election, and the Republicans controlled only eight.

When the first ballot was taken, Jefferson received eight votes to Burr's six; two states were evenly divided. The Federalists voted mainly for Burr, some because they believed that Jefferson was a dangerous radical, others because they hoped to throw their Republican rivals into disarray. To his credit, Burr refused to urge on his supporters. But he also did not ask his few Republican supporters to change their votes to Jefferson. He remained in seclusion.

After thirty-five deadlocked ballots, a Delaware Federalist named James A. Bayard, fearing that the crisis would destroy the national government his party had toiled to build, announced that he would change his

H O W   T H E Y   L I V E D

GIVING BIRTH

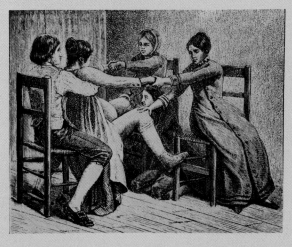

Women provided assistance and comfort for each other during childbirth.

A woman who married during the Federalist period could expect to be pregnant about seven times during her life—if she did not die as a young woman, in childbirth or otherwise. During the 1790s, there were almost three hundred live births for each one thousand women between the ages of fifteen and forty-four—more than one woman in four delivered each year—as compared with eighty-four pregnancies for each one thousand women in 1970. Pregnancy, childbirth, and the nursing of infants were a far more important part of a woman's existence then they are in the late twentieth century. Indeed, giving birth to children was generally considered to be the chief reason for a woman's existence.

Almost every child was delivered at home. The few hospitals that existed were reserved for the seriously ill or injured, and childbirth was eminently normal. Most children were delivered by female midwives (the word means "*with* a woman") and in the company of the mother-to-be's own mother, sisters, neighbors, friends, and even older daughters. Historian Catherine M. Scholten has shown that childbirth was a communal event, the climactic shared experience of women. Except during the early stages of labor, when the husband might be called in to pray with or comfort his wife, men were excluded.

The midwife might have served an apprenticeship, or she might have slipped into the job as a consequence of accidentally getting "catched" in a number of childbirths and therefore developing a reputation as someone who knew what to do. In any event, while midwifery lacked the formal recognition in the United States that it had in England, it was very definitely a profession. The tombstone of one Boston woman says that she "by the Blessing of God has brought into this world above 3,000 Children."

In part, the presence of other women was a practical matter. Water had to be heated, and linens washed. In the event of a prolonged labor, food had to be prepared. Because in the eighteenth century few women gave birth lying on their backs in bed but, instead, squatting or standing, the mother depended on other women for physical support. Moreover, it was common practice for a recent mother to remain in bed for at least four weeks after childbirth. Her friends performed her household duties during this final phase of confinement.

But the attendants also served important cultural, social, and psychological purposes. By their presence and the exclusion of men, they emphasized the uniquely feminine character of the suffering involved in childbirth at a time when liquor was the only anesthetic available. The pains of bearing children were still generally thought of as God's punishment for the sin of Eve. By their presence—because they too had undergone childbirth or could expect to do so—the attendants were sharing in the travail.

Moreover, as Scholten discovered, they cheered the mother-to-be by distracting her with gossip, comparing her labor with more difficult labors they had witnessed (or suffered), and even making her laugh by telling bawdy jokes.

Already in the 1790s, however, the supervision of childbirth was being taken away from women by male physicians who had been trained in obstetrics. This trend began in England during the 1740s and 1750s, when Dr. William Smellie was appalled by the incompetence of many midwives. "We ought to be ashamed of ourselves," he told physicians, "for the little improvement we have made in so many centuries." Smellie invented the forceps used for assisting difficult births.

The development of obstetrics as a branch of medicine also reflected society's general drift away from literally interpreted religion. In 1804, Peter Miller, a student at the University of Pennsylvania, home of the country's best medical school, wrote that the dangers of pregnancy and the death of so many infants involved enough sorrow for women. It was absurd to cling to the belief that the moment of birth should also be a travail. Dr. William Dewees, a pioneer of medical obstetrics in the United States, asked, "Why should the female alone incur the penalty of God?"

In the cities and particularly among the upper and middle classes, male physicians supplanted female midwives in a surprisingly short period of time. In Boston and Philadelphia (and probably in other large cities) during the Federalist period, physicians were called into childbirth cases only when there were serious difficulties. By the 1820s, doctors virtually monopolized the delivery of children in urban areas.

The survival rate among both mothers and newborns improved with the triumph of medical obstetrics. (Although the significant advance took place only later in the nineteenth century, when the Hungarian Ignaz Semmelweiss and the English surgeon Joseph Lister discovered that "childbirth fever" [puerperal fever] was caused by the failure of most physicians even to wash their hands.) However, the triumph was not entirely progressive. The demands of a sexual modesty that was in fact prudery, which was strongest among the upper and middle classes, forced doctors to ask questions of "a delicate nature"—just about all questions about childbirth—through another woman. It was an unwieldy procedure at best, and in emergencies it was potentially dangerous.

In addition, the birth had to be carried out under covers, with the physician working entirely by touch. Indeed, even such an awkward process offended some people. In *Letters to Ladies, Detailing Important Information Concerning Themselves and Infants*, published in 1817, Dr. Thomas Ewell told of a husband who "very solemnly . . . declared to the doctor, he would demolish him if he touched or looked at his wife." Finally, as is common with scientific advances, there was a human cost. Transforming childbirth from a communal event into a private medical operation destroyed an important social relationship among women.

vote to Jefferson on the next ballot. In the end, he did not have to do so. Hamilton's agents had indirectly contacted Jefferson and extracted vague commitments that he would continue Federalist foreign policy and maintain the Hamiltonian financial apparatus. Moreover, Hamilton despised Burr. If president, Hamilton said, Burr would form an administration made up of "the rogues of all parties to overrule the good men."

Although he feared Jefferson's democratic ideas, Hamilton conceded that the Virginian had at least a "pretension to character." It was not much of a compliment, but it was enough. Hamilton pressured a few Federalist congressmen from key states to abstain. This enabled Jefferson to be elected on the thirty-sixth ballot on February 17, 1801.

The crisis proved that parties were a fact of American life. The Constitution had to be amended to avoid a repetition of the election of 1800. In 1804, the Twelfth Amendment was ratified. It provided that electors would vote separately for president and vice president, the system that prevails today.

For Further Reading

J. C. Miller, *The Federalist Era* (1960), is the standard study of the 1790s. J. T. Flexner, *George Washington: Anguish and Farewell* (1972), deals with the first president's less-than-happy second term. For the foreign events that vexed Washington's final years, see Harry Ammon, *The Genêt Mission* (1973).

On John Adams, Stephen Kurtz, *The Presidency of John Adams* (1957), and Manning Dauer, *The Adams Federalists* (1953), approach their subject from two different perspectives. J. R. Howe, *The Changing Political Thought of John Adams* (1966), also provides excellent insights into the too-often-neglected second president.

Samuel F. Bemis is the authority on the two important foreign treaties of the 1790s: *Jay's Treaty* (1923), and *Pinckney's Treaty* (1926). J. A. Combs, *The Jay Treaty* (1970), updates Bemis in some respects.

On the development of the Jeffersonian ideology and political party, see Daniel Boorstin, *The Lost World of Thomas Jefferson* (1948), and Noble Cunningham, *The Jeffersonian Republicans* (1957).

A Declaration by the Represen

OF AMERICA, in General Con

When in the course of human
dissolve the political bands which have
~~   ~~
~sume, among the powers of the earth
which the laws of nature & of nature
to the opinions of mankind require
which impel them to ~~the~~ the

We hold these truths to be,
created equal ~~& independent~~ the
~~   ~~
~~rights~~ inherent & inalienable
life, & liberty, & the pursuit of h

12

The Age of Thomas Jefferson
Successes at Home, Setbacks Abroad, 1800–1815

In April 1962, President John F. Kennedy told an assembly of Nobel Prize winners that "this is the most extraordinary collection of talent, of human knowledge, that has been gathered at the White House, with the possible exception of when Thomas Jefferson dined here alone." It was more than a witty remark. Few human beings have been so broadly learned, so versatile in their skills, and so successful in what they set out to do as was Thomas Jefferson, the tall, slightly stooped man with graying red hair who took the presidential oath of office in March 1801.

As president, Thomas Jefferson (shown here in a portrait by Rembrandt Peale, 1805) defended the republican principles he expressed in the Declaration of Independence. This is a copy of his handwritten draft.

The Sage of Monticello

Jefferson is best known as a political figure: author of the nation's birth certificate, the Declaration of Independence; wartime governor of Virginia; ambassador to France during the Confederation period; first Secretary of State under the Constitution; and political strategist who created the party machine that made him president in 1800.

But Jefferson was also a philosopher, happy when he could sit quietly in his study and think. He read and spoke several foreign languages. He wrote better English than any American president but Abraham Lincoln, precise in its vocabulary and mellifluous in its rhythms. He maintained a correspondence with dozens of people on dozens of subjects; in book form his letters fill a library shelf. He founded the University of Virginia, designing not only its curriculum but also its buildings (as well as his own home, Monticello).

He dabbled in natural science. He invented the dumbwaiter, the swivel chair, and perhaps the decimal system of coinage. He was a gourmet who introduced pasta to the United States; spent up to $2,800 a year on wines for his table; kept a French chef, probably the first American to do so; and once risked his life in order to smuggle out of Italy a variety of rice that he fancied.

Jefferson was not, however, universally admired. John Adams envied him and rarely missed an opportunity to snipe at his reputation. Alexander Hamilton thought him intellectually soft-headed and frivolous. Many other Federalists believed that he was an immoral "voluptuary" and a dangerous, even insane radical. They spread the rumor that Jefferson, whose wife had died when he was a young man, kept a slave, Sally Hemmings, as his concubine. A writer in the *Connecticut Courant* in September 1800 echoed what many other New Englanders believed when he warned that Jefferson's election would mean "your dwellings in flames, hoary hairs bathed in blood, female chastity violated, children writhing on the pike and the halberd." The anti-Republican message concluded: "GREAT GOD OF COMPASSION AND JUSTICE, SHIELD MY COUNTRY FROM DESTRUCTION."

Jefferson as President

Jefferson was well aware of these fears, and he attempted to allay them in his eloquent inaugural address. "Every difference of opinion is not a difference in principle," he said. "We have called by different names brethren of the same principle. We are all Republicans, we are all Federalists."

Continuities

Unlike Hamilton, Jefferson believed in the democratic principle that, on balance and in the end, the majority of the people would choose to do the correct thing; if they did not, their will should be followed nevertheless. But it was Hamilton more than any other who, in 1800, made possible the peaceful transference of power from Federalists to Republicans.

Jefferson believed that all people had the same rights—"all men are created equal"—but he did not believe that all possessed equal abilities. He thought that a "natural aristocracy" of virtue and talent should rise to the top and govern the society, and in his old age, Jefferson discovered in a long correspondence with John Adams, his old rival, that they agreed in the matter.

Once in the presidency, Jefferson maintained some Federalist policies that, as a private citizen, he had condemned. He honored most of Hamilton's fiscal policies, including the Bank of the United States, which earlier he had considered unconstitutional. He appointed as Secretary of the Treasury the Swiss-born Albert Gallatin, who also had been denounced as a reckless revolutionary but who, once in office, proved

---

REPUBLICANS AND DEMOCRATS

Thomas Jefferson's Republicans were not the ancestors of the present-day Republican party. On the contrary, they were the direct forebears of today's Democrats. During the 1810s, the old Federalist party simply ceased to exist, and every politician called himself a Republican. When the party split into several factions in 1824, one group, later headed by John Quincy Adams and Henry Clay, called itself National-Republicans to emphasize its commitment to economic policies that would benefit the nation as a whole. The followers of Andrew Jackson, who considered their leader the choice of the people, called themselves Democratic-Republicans. Later they simply dropped the tag "Republican." Claiming that Jackson acted as though he were a king, the National-Republicans renamed themselves Whigs after the British political party that was opposed to leaving broad powers in the hands of the king.

The name "Republican" vanished from American politics until 1854, when it was adopted by the antislavery Republican party, ancestor of today's Republicans.

to be as conservative as his predecessors, Hamilton and two Hamilton disciples.

While in the opposition, Jefferson had called for sharp limitations on federal authority (the Virginia and Kentucky Resolutions). He had insisted on a strict construction of the Constitution, according to which the government's powers were limited to those explicitly spelled out in the document. As president, Jefferson proved even more willing than Washington and Adams to stretch his powers beyond the letter of the law. In fact, if not in name, he adopted the broad construction views of Hamilton, according to which the government possessed all powers not strictly forbidden it in the Constitution.

A New Style

But Jefferson was not a third Federalist president. He disliked the pomp that had surrounded the presidencies of Washington and Adams. He abolished the practice of holding formal levees, and, much to the annoyance of some officials and European diplomats, he ignored the rules of protocol that assigned a rank of dignity to every senator, congressman, cabinet member, and ambassador. Not even at Jefferson's state dinners were seats assigned; guests scrambled for their places. The president preferred small parties at which he wore bedroom slippers and served the meal himself.

Jefferson's taste for this "republican simplicity" was made easier by the move of the capital, the summer before his inauguration, from sophisticated Philadelphia to new, raw "Federal City," as Washington, D.C., was called. It was really not even a city in 1800, but a bizarre combination of unfinished white marble public buildings, ramshackle boarding houses, and wilderness.

Abigail Adams had to do her laundry in the "ballroom" of the White House. Jefferson spent the night before he was inaugurated in a drafty rooming house, taking his breakfast with other boarders at a long table. For years, there would be no room in the city for con-

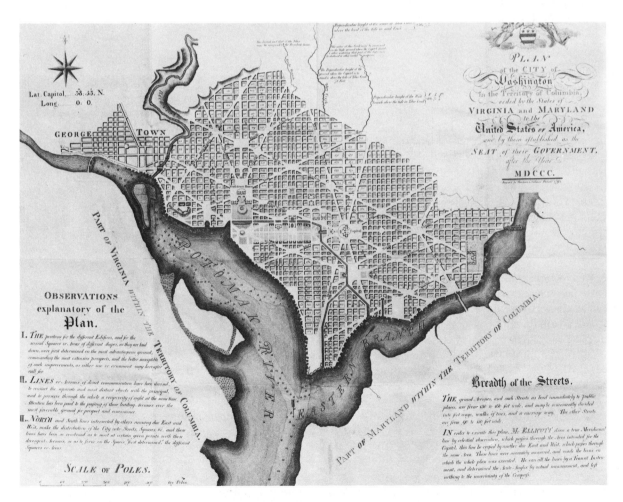

Plan for the construction of Washington, D.C., 1792.

gressmen's families and, therefore, no social life except for smoky card games and whiskey drinking around the fire.

Strangers got lost trying to find their way from the president's mansion to the Capitol, not in a warren of streets and alleys but on muddy, narrow wagon trails that cut through the woods. The place suited Jefferson's style.

Jefferson's innovations were not exclusively stylistic. He pardoned the people who were still imprisoned under the Sedition Act (all of them his supporters, of course); changed the residency requirement for citizenship back to five years; and slashed government expenditures, mostly by reducing the budgets of the army and navy. Within two years, Jefferson and Gallatin paid off half the national debt.

But these actions hardly comprised the "Revolution of 1800," as Jefferson once styled his election. Indeed, the only development in government that qualified as revolutionary during Jefferson's presidency was effected by one of his most bitter enemies (and a distant cousin), the Federalist Chief Justice of the Supreme Court, John Marshall.

Marbury v. Madison

On the day before he had left office, John Adams had appointed forty-two Federalists to the federal judiciary. Federal judges were appointed for life, even "Midnight Judges," as Adams' last-minute appointees were called. Jefferson was apparently stuck with a judiciary packed with members of the opposing party.

The commission of one of the Midnight Judges, William Marbury, had not been delivered to him in time. Jefferson's Secretary of State, James Madison, refused to order that it be delivered. Marbury petitioned the Supreme Court for a writ of mandamus, a legal order that means "we compel" a government official to perform the duties of his office. To the surprise of many, who expected the Federalist Supreme Court to act on behalf of the loyal Federalist Marbury, the Court turned him down. Dominating the other justices by the force of his personality and the excellence of his legal mind, John Marshall ruled that the law under which Marbury had sued was unconstitutional—that Congress did not have the power to give the Supreme Court the authority it had given it.

Jefferson and Madison soon understood what Marshall had done. By sacrificing the paycheck of one Federalist and canceling part of a Federalist law, Marshall had asserted the right of the Supreme Court to decide which acts of Congress were constitutional and which unconstitutional. In Marbury v. Madison, John Marshall ruled that the Supreme Court not only judged cases according to the law, but judged the law itself. There was nothing in the Constitution that granted the Court this power. Jefferson had tried to reserve it for the states in the Kentucky Resolutions. But John Marshall won it for the Court. In order to rub a little salt in the wound, Marshall ruled at the same session that the Republican Circuit Court Act of 1802 could remain on the books—because the Supreme Court, he, John Marshall, had decided it was constitutional.

The Jefferson Republicans tried to retaliate. Through the impeachment process they removed a Federalist judge, John Pickering. That was easy, since Pickering was given to drunken tirades in court and was probably quite insane.

They next moved against Supreme Court Justice Samuel Chase as a means of getting closer to Marshall. Everyone agreed that Chase was a poor judge, openly prejudiced in his rulings. But the Senate refused to find him guilty of the "high crimes and misdemeanors" that are the constitutional bases of impeachment. Marshall's "Revolution of 1803," the principle of judicial review, was secured.

The Expansion of the Nation

If Marshall stretched the Constitution in Marbury v. Madison, Jefferson gave it a twist of his own in the most important action of his first term, the purchase of Louisiana from France for $15 million. French Louisiana was not merely the present-day state of Louisiana. The province included the better part of thirteen states, about one-third of the continental United States as it is known today. The Louisiana Purchase was the greatest real-estate deal of all time. The United States bought 828,000 square miles of land—more than 500 million acres—at a cost of less than three cents an acre!

Napoleon Makes an Offer

This bargain came to pass because Napoleon Bonaparte, who rose from captain of artillery to dictator of France in fewer than ten years (and emperor in 1804) briefly toyed with and then abruptly canceled a plan to reestablish French power in North America.

In 1801, Napoleon forced Spain to return Louisiana to France. There were only about fifty thousand Creoles (people of French and Spanish ancestry born in Louisiana) in the province, but its agricultural potential was obvious. Napoleon hoped to develop Louisiana into the supplier of grain and livestock to the French West Indies.

In the meantime, the most important of France's Caribbean holdings, Santo Domingo (Haiti), had virtually established its independence under the leadership of a former black slave, Toussaint L'Ouverture. Although the French tricked and put L'Ouverture into prison (where he died), the black rebels fought on and defeated more than twenty thousand crack French soldiers under General Charles Le Clerc. When, by April 1803, Napoleon realized that Santo Domingo was gone for good ("Damn sugar," he said. "Damn colonies!"), he found he had no use for Louisiana. In fact, in case of war with Great Britain, which Napoleon was already planning, the colony would be wide open to British naval attack.

Talleyrand, back in power, summoned American ambassador Robert Livingston to tell him that the United States could purchase all of Louisiana for $15 million. Livingston was stunned. For a year he had been trying unsuccessfully to purchase the city of New Orleans.

Sacrificing Principle for a Prize

The swampy port was vital to the United States. By 1800, almost four hundred thousand Americans lived in the western states of Ohio, Kentucky, and Tennessee, and each year they shipped twenty thousand tons of produce down the Mississippi. As Madison put it, for the people beyond the mountains, the Mississippi was "the Hudson, the Delaware, the Potomac, and all the navigable rivers of the Atlantic States formed into one stream."

As long as New Orleans was in the hands of feeble Spain and Pinckney's Treaty guaranteed Americans free navigation and the right of deposit, the westerners were content. But in October 1802, the Spanish suspended both rights, and Jefferson believed that Spain's action was instigated by Napoleon. If France held on to Louisiana under these conditions, the United States would have no choice but to "marry the British fleet," a repugnant thought to the author of the Declaration of Independence. Jefferson therefore sent James Monroe

New Orleans at the time of the Louisiana Purchase, 1803.

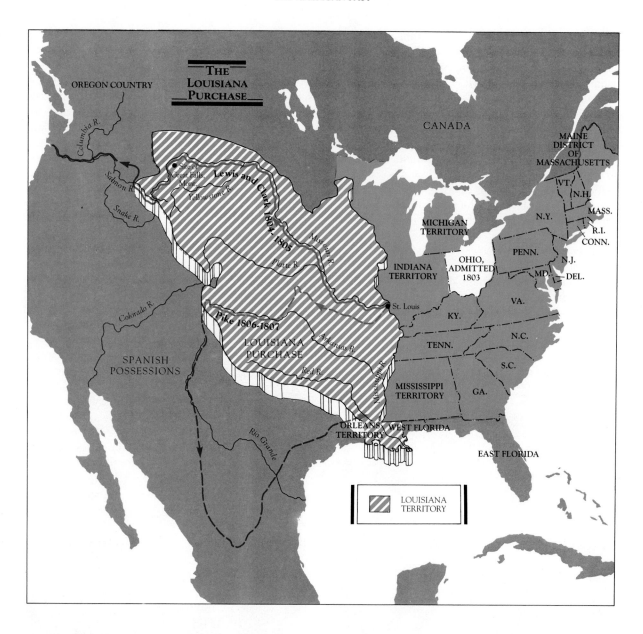

THE LOUISIANA PURCHASE

OREGON COUNTRY

CANADA

MAINE DISTRICT OF MASSACHUSETTS

Columbia R.

Salmon R.

Snake R.

Site of Great Falls Mont.

Lewis and Clark 1804-1805

Tellowstone R.

Missouri R.

Platte R.

VT.

N.H.

N.Y.

MASS.

R.I.

CONN.

MICHIGAN TERRITORY

PENN.

N.J.

OHIO, ADMITTED 1803

MD.

DEL.

INDIANA TERRITORY

St. Louis

VA.

Colorado R.

Pike 1806-1807

KY.

LOUISIANA PURCHASE

Arkansas R.

TENN.

N.C.

S.C.

SPANISH POSSESSIONS

Red R.

Mississippi R.

MISSISSIPPI TERRITORY

GA.

Rio Grande

ORLEANS TERRITORY

WEST FLORIDA

EAST FLORIDA

LOUISIANA TERRITORY

to join Livingston in Paris and push for the sale of New Orleans. As it happened, Talleyrand made his offer a day or two before Monroe arrived, and, although neither he nor Livingston was authorized to make such a deal, they agreed. In one swoop the United States doubled the size of its territory.

There were obstacles. There were no constitutional provisions for such an acquisition or for conferring immediate citizenship on the Creoles who lived in the province, as the treaty required.

Jefferson was the leading spokesman for sticking to the letter of the law, but, as frequently happens in politics, the ideal was sacrificed to the main chance.

Jefferson wrote privately that "what is practicable must often control what is pure theory." He instructed his supporters in Congress that "the less we say about constitutional difficulties respecting Louisiana the better."

They had little to fear. The Federalists enjoyed calling Jefferson a hypocrite, but they had no intention of passing up such a bargain. Even members of Jefferson's own party, states'-rights and strict-construction zealots like John Randolph and John Taylor, who would later attack the president, objected little to the purchase of Louisiana. They were Virginians and North Carolinians who were closely tied to Kentucky and Tennessee.

The Magnificent Journey

The acquisition of Louisiana revived Jefferson's long-standing curiosity about the interior of the continent. Even before the treaty was approved, he persuaded Congress to appropriate $2,500 for an expedition across the continent for the purposes of looking for a feasible overland trade route (the "Northwest Passage" again) and of gathering scientific data.

The mission was put under the command of Meriwether Lewis, Jefferson's Virginia neighbor, and William Clark, Lewis's friend and former commanding officer. No doubt wishing he could go himself, Jefferson attended to the smallest details of preparation, even listing in his own hand the provisions that the explorers should carry with them.

The trek of Lewis and Clark exceeded anything ventured by the old *voyageurs*. Poling, pulling, and rowing their way up the Missouri to the river's spectacular falls (present-day Great Falls, Montana), they portaged sixteen miles. With the help of various Indian tribes—especially the Mandan, Shoshone, and Nez Percé—they found a tributary of the Columbia River. Following the great drainage, they reached the Pacific in October 1805. There they spent four and a half months, during which time, as residents of Oregon and Washington can believe, it rained every day but twelve.

National heroes, Lewis and Clark arrived back in St. Louis in September 1806. Not only was their trip a prodigious feat of exploration, but they collected a large body of information about the plant and animal

THE NORTHWEST PASSAGE

The dream of finding a "Northwest Passage" to Asia never did die. When President Thomas Jefferson sent Meriwether Lewis and William Clark across North America in 1804, there was still a wan hope that a workable passage to the Pacific was possible. Throughout the nineteenth century, intrepid sailors attempted to trace an all-water route around the top of North America. Several expeditions spent years locked in polar ice. When, in 1958, the nuclear submarine *Nautilus* circled the continent by cruising under the ice of the North Pole, commentators implied that there was a Northwest Passage after all.

life of the region and put to rest dreams of an easy route across the continent.

Lewis and Clark were among the last white people to deal with Indians unaffected by civilization. While they had a few close scrapes, they engaged in no real battle with the dozens of tribes they met. Virtually all the native peoples of the interior were curious, hospitable, and helpful. The Shoshone, with whom the expedition could communicate in detail through a female Indian interpreter, Sacajawea, gave key advice toward finding the Pacific, which they themselves had never seen. The Indians of the Northwest coast, of course, had long dealt with American and European seamen, whalers, and fur traders. As a result, one of their favorite expressions was "son of a beech."

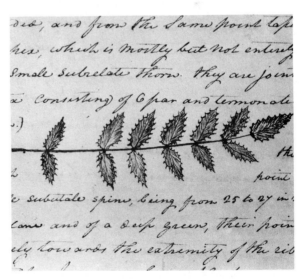

William Clark's sketches of new flora and fauna discovered during his exploration of the Louisiana Territory.

A BLACK EXPLORER

William Clark took one of his slaves on his famous trek. York was Clark's personal servant, and, in the informality the wilderness made necessary, he contributed to the expedition as an equal. Meriwether Lewis recorded that when many Indians first saw York, they believed he was a white man wearing paint. Only after trying to rub his color from him did they accept York's explanation of himself. Lewis noted that "instead of inspiring any prejudice, his color served to procure him additional advantages from the Indians."

Jefferson thought that the country traversed by Lewis and Clark would provide land for expansion-minded Americans for a thousand years. His estimate was off by 915 years, for the frontier was declared closed in 1890. But the West served his Republican party very well. Ohio became the seventeenth state in 1803 and, voting Republican like Kentucky and Tennessee, enabled Jefferson to win reelection easily in 1804. The Federalists carried only fourteen electoral votes—Connecticut and Delaware. The quirks of fate had made them the provincials and Mad Tom's Jefferson Republicans the national party.

The Adventures of Aaron Burr

Quirks of fate and the Louisiana Purchase also figured prominently in the simultaneously tragic and comic career of Aaron Burr. He was replaced on the 1804 Republican ticket by George Clinton, but his fortunes had begun to tumble downhill immediately after his near elevation to the presidency in 1801.

Convinced (unfairly) that Burr had schemed to steal the presidency from him, Jefferson denied him access to the patronage—appointive offices to reward political allies, government contracts that profited supporters—that greases the political machine. The master politician found himself in an office that provided him with nothing to do—except to scheme and plot.

There is some evidence that Burr, while still vice president, formed an understanding with a group of New England Federalists called the Essex Junto to detach New York from the United States. However, the plan depended on Burr's winning control of New York, which he tried to do by running for governor in 1804.

He was defeated when Hamilton threw his support to Burr's opponent. The two old enemies traded insults. An old and well-known adultery of Hamilton was bandied about, and when Hamilton responded with a slur on Burr's integrity, Burr challenged him to a duel.

Hamilton did not believe in dueling, but the feud had gotten out of hand. On July 11, 1804, the two men and their seconds rowed across the Hudson River to Weehawken, high on the New Jersey Palisades, where they fired at each other from twenty paces. Hamilton's bullet went astray—some would say he deliberately shot high—and Burr's pierced Hamilton's heart.

The first Secretary of the Treasury was never a beloved man, but his death shocked the nation. Burr had to flee. Dueling was illegal in both New York and New Jersey, and both states handed down indictments for murder. After a few weeks in seclusion in the South, while friends ironed out the legal difficulties, Burr returned to Washington, where he presided over the impeachment trial of Justice Chase. But he knew his career was finished in New York as well as in Washington. Not yet fifty years of age and possessed of manic energy and keen imagination, Burr turned his gaze toward Louisiana.

The "Conspiracy"

Although it is not known just what they were, Burr had plans. He struck up a friendship with James Wilkinson, the territorial governor of Louisiana Territory, and, in April 1805, set out for Pittsburgh. There Burr fell in with Harman Blennerhasset, a wealthy Irish refugee who lived on an island in the Ohio River. The two men supervised the construction of a flotilla of thirteen flatboats, including a fabulously outfitted barge for Burr with glass windows, a fireplace, and a promenade deck. With sixty men, they meandered down the Ohio and

THE VICE PRESIDENCY

The vice president's only constitutional function is to preside over the Senate, and on the very rare occasions a vote is tied, to cast the deciding ballot. No ambitious politician has ever been happy in the post. John Adams called it "the most insignificant office that ever the invention of man contrived." When Theodore Roosevelt was nominated for the job in 1900, he believed that his political career had come to an end. John Nance Garner, vice president between 1933 and 1941, said the job wasn't "worth a pitcher of warm spit." Finley Peter Dunne, who wrote a popular newspaper column in Irish-American dialect around the turn of the twentieth century, summed it up: "Th' prisidency is th' highest office in th' gift iv th' people. Th' vice-prisidincy is th' next highest an' the lowest. It isn't a crime exactly. Ye can't be sint to jail f-r it, but it's a kind iv a disgrace."

Aaron Burr's career declined rapidly after he killed Alexander Hamilton in a duel.

the Mississippi, recruiting more followers and speaking secretly with regional leaders such as Andrew Jackson of Tennessee.

Burr, Blennerhasset, and Wilkinson planned either to invade Spanish Mexico, or to lead a secession of the western states and territories from the United States. Or both, depending on what circumstances allowed and whose word is to be believed. No one really knows what was afoot, but Jefferson was prepared to believe the worst. When Wilkinson, an unsavory character who had none of Burr's redeeming charm, told the president that Burr was plotting treason, Jefferson had the New Yorker arrested and returned to Richmond, where he was tried before the Supreme Court.

Chief Justice Marshall presided, obviously prejudiced against Jefferson. He need not have been. The case against Burr was sloppy; nothing of substance was proved against him. Nevertheless, Marshall took special pleasure in subpoenaing the president to present evidence. Standing on the independence of the executive branch (which he had denigrated before his election), Jefferson refused to comply.

Burr was acquitted and went abroad. A few years later, he returned to New York and got into trouble again. This time, however, it was entirely personal. He wed an extraordinary woman who publicly claimed that she had slept with both George Washington and Napoleon Bonaparte. The marriage ended in a scandalous divorce. Burr has never since been highly thought of by his countrymen, although the only crime ever proved against him was his killing of Hamilton at a time when many Americans considered dueling a legitimate means of asserting personal honor.

Foreign Woes

Like those of Washington and Adams, Jefferson's record was blemished by his inability to deal constructively with foreign nations. In order to save money, and thus keep taxes at a minimum, Jefferson allowed the Adams navy to dwindle. However, he learned as early as 1801 that a country with important interests in international trade had to be able to protect its traders.

The Barbary Pirates

In 1801, Jefferson approved a punitive expedition against the pasha of Tripoli (present-day Libya) in order to free a number of American seamen held hostage there. Like Morocco, Algiers, and Tunis, Tripoli was a Barbary State whose economy was based on extorting a kind of "protection money" from seafaring nations. Even mighty England paid, considering it cheaper to buy free passage for merchant vessels than to make war against the corrupt but effective pirate states. Before Jefferson became president, the United States paid too. Through the 1790s, the price of sailing in Barbary waters cost the American Treasury about $2 million.

The indignity of it rankled on Jefferson. Like John Adams, he abhorred sordid bargaining. But four years of naval bombardment and even an amphibious attack ("To the shores of Tripoli," in the Marine Corps hymn) were indecisive. Americans got a popular hero in Stephen Decatur, who led a daring raid in Tripoli harbor. But the English decision was proved right; the Barbary States could not be subdued at a cost that made

TRIBUTE TO THE PASHA

The annual payment to the pasha of Tripoli, which Jefferson attempted to cancel in 1801, consisted of $40,000 in gold and silver, $12,000 in Spanish money, and an odd assortment of diamond rings, watches, and fine cloth and brocade. The rulers of the Barbary States sincerely thought of these as gifts of friendship rather than as extortion. For example, in 1806 the bey of Tunis, who also received tribute, sent Jefferson a gift of four Arabian horses.

The bombardment of Tripoli, one of repeated American attempts during 1801–1805 to subdue the Barbary States.

the effort worthwhile. In 1805, Jefferson gave up and paid Tripoli $60,000 in return for the release of captive Americans.

Caught in the Middle Again

The great powers of Europe were even more difficult than the Barbary pirates. France and England went to war shortly after the purchase of Louisiana, and, at first, American shipowners once again reaped huge profits by trading with both sides. Between 1803 and 1806, the value of foreign products reexported from the United States (goods bought in the West Indies and then shipped to Europe) quadrupled from $13 million to $60 million.

Then, in 1805, the European war took a fatal turn. At the Battle of Trafalgar, Lord Horatio Nelson destroyed the French fleet, establishing British supremacy on the seas that would last for a hundred years. Retaliating on land in one of the most ambitious military campaigns of all time, Napoleon defeated the armies of Austria, Prussia, and Russia in rapid succession. France was supreme on the continent of Europe.

The two powers settled down into a kind of cold war, each trying to cripple the economy of the other. The British government issued Orders in Council that forbade neutrals to trade in European ports unless they first stopped in England to purchase a "license." The Americans gladly would have come to terms with this restriction. New England, where the overseas trade was centered, was inclined to be friendly to Britain.

Napoleon retaliated with his Continental System, promulgated in the Berlin and Milan decrees of 1806 and 1807. These declared that neutral ships that observed the British Orders in Council would be seized by the French.

While caught in the middle, American merchants continued to prosper. Although within a year the British seized one thousand American ships and the French about five hundred, profits poured in from those that completed their voyages. One Massachusetts senator calculated that if a shipowner sent three vessels out and two were seized—dead losses—the profits from the third made him a richer man than he had been. Statistics bear him out. In 1807, at the height of the commerce raiding, Massachusetts merchants earned $15 million in freight charges alone. Profits from American goods sold abroad must have multiplied this tidy sum.

Impressment

How Jefferson would have reacted to this curious situation cannot be known, for the crisis was complicated by British insistence on the right to impress crewmen off American ships.

Impressment was an ancient practice, the means by which the Royal Navy replaced seamen lost in battle, to disease, or to desertion. Captains were authorized to send "press gangs" into British ports. The gangs forced able-bodied young men to return with them to their vessels. It was a highly unpopular form of draft. News of a press gang in town sent men scurrying into cellars or to the countryside. Equally resented was impressment on the high seas. Commanders of warships were legally empowered to order British merchantmen to heave to. Officers could then board the hapless ship and, within limits, draft what men were needed.

If the English hated impressment, Americans were infuriated when men-of-war flying the Union Jack took crewmen from their ships. Britain claimed the right to impress only British subjects from American ships. There were plenty of these. Because conditions were far superior in the American merchant marine and the pay was as much as triple that on British ships, desertion was common. Some estimates have about ten thousand British seamen serving on American ships, about half the total crews during the first decade of the nineteenth century.

The issue was complicated by the two countries' conflicting definitions of citizenship. Britain claimed that British birth made a person a lifelong British subject. The United States insisted that an immigrant could become a naturalized American citizen after five years of residence in the United States. Whenever British captains impressed men caught in the middle, the sensitive issue of national independence was revived. To make matters worse, many captains routinely seized any American seaman, even one of proved American birth. About ten thousand native-born Americans were forced into the Royal Navy during the Napoleonic Wars. The British government did not approve of this practice, and released almost four thousand sailors who had been illegally impressed. But as quickly as these lucky men were surrendered to American consuls in England, arrogant or perhaps just desperate naval captains were grabbing more on the seas.

The crisis came to a head in June 1807, when H.M.S. *Leopard* ordered the American naval frigate *Chesapeake* to stand by for boarding within swimming distance of the Virginia coastline. The American captain refused the importunate command, but he was unprepared to fight. After the *Leopard* fired three broadsides into the *Chesapeake* that killed several sailors, the press gang boarded and removed four men, including two American blacks, who had served in the Royal Navy.

The uproar, even in Anglophile New England, was deafening. The *Chesapeake* was no merchantman taking a chance on an illegal expedition, but a naval vessel in American waters. Jefferson had to act, and he elected to employ what he called "peaceable coercion" rather than war.

The Embargo

Under the Embargo Act of 1807, American ships in port were forbidden to leave and foreign vessels were required to depart in ballast, that is, carrying boulders or other worthless bulk in the hull. No further imports or exports were permitted. The United States halted its purchases of European manufactures, exports of food, and carrying services in an effort to force the British (who also had profited from the American trade) to come to terms.

It was a logical action for Jefferson, who in his revolutionary youth had seen nonimportation bring Parliament around. In 1807, however, it was a failure. Farmers throughout the country suffered from the closure of their foreign markets. New England nearly perished when its ships were forced to ride at anchor, generating no profit and literally rotting in harbor. The Federalist party, crippled in 1804, began to make a comeback with a new, younger generation of leaders.

By the end of 1808, Jefferson ruefully admitted that the embargo policy was a failure. It had cost the economy at least three times what a war would have cost. In order to spare his hand-picked successor the burden of his mistake, Jefferson approved the repeal of the embargo a few days before he left office.

Little Jemmy Applejohn and More Trade War

James Madison, political philosopher and Jefferson's faithful aide for fifteen years, was the new president. He was elected easily, winning 122 electoral votes to 53 for Federalist Charles Cotesworth Pinckney and Jefferson's vice president, George Clinton. Madison was physically unimpressive. Short of stature, he struck writer Washington Irving as a "withered applejohn," a kind of apple that is best eaten after it has dried for two years.

In fact, Madison was as personable privately as he was intelligent. His vivacious and fashionably buxom wife, Dolley Payne Todd Madison, introduced a spar-

---

A BOSTONIAN ON THE EMBARGO

In July 1808, an anonymous Boston versifier summed up how New England felt about the embargo:

Our ships all in motion,
Once whitened the ocean,
    They sail'd and return'd with a cargo.
Now, doom'd to decay
They have fallen a prey
    To Jefferson, worms, and Embargo.

Jefferson's successor James Madison and his vivacious wife, Dolley.

kling social scene to a Washington that had been somewhat subdued under the widower Jefferson.

Unfortunately, Madison was no better able than his predecessor to cope with the international crisis. His first attempt took the form of the Nonintercourse Act, which opened trade with all nations except England and France and provided that the United States would resume trading with whichever of those two belligerents agreed to respect the rights of American shipping. David Erskine, the pro-American British ambassador to Washington, negotiated a favorable treaty, and Madison renewed trade with Britain. Then the British Foreign Office repudiated the agreement, and, sheepishly, Madison had to resume nonintercourse.

In May 1810, the Republicans tried a new twist. Under Macon's Bill No. 2, they reopened commerce with both England and France, with the condition that as soon as either agreed to American terms, the United States would cut off trade with the other. This was asking for trouble from a trickster like Napoleon. With no intention of ceasing his seizures of American cargoes, Napoleon abrogated the Continental System, and Madison again declared an end to commerce with England. Through all these gyrations, as before, New England prospered. While some shipowners went

bankrupt or quit in disgust, others found that trade under any conditions meant money.

Macon's Bill No. 2 actually worked. On June 16, 1812, feeling the pinch, the British canceled their Orders in Council. Unhappily, despite American enquiries, Prime Minister Castlereagh had given no hint of his intentions. On June 18, 1812, bowing to pressure that his three predecessors had resisted, Madison declared war.

The War of 1812

On the face of it, the War of 1812, like the attack on Tripoli, was fought to defend the rights of neutral Americans on the seas as Jefferson and Madison defined those rights. But mercantile New England was largely hostile to the war. Antiwar Federalists, some of them hinting at secession from the United States, won election to Congress in numbers unprecedented since 1800. In 1814, several Federalists sponsored a convention at Hartford, Connecticut, that denounced the war in stinging terms.

The support for "Mr. Madison's War," as New Englanders called it, came from the solidly Republican parts of the country, the South and the West. A new, younger generation of congressmen, called the "War Hawks" by their critics, gave Madison the votes necessary to get his declaration approved. Whereas the Federalist and mercantile states of New England, New York, and New Jersey voted thirty-four to fourteen against war, Pennsylvania, the South, and the West voted sixty-five to fifteen in favor. Not a single Federalist congressman voted for war.

Agricultural sections suffered from British depredations too, in one way worse than did the mercantile regions. Once unsold, their crops were useless, whereas trade could always be resumed. More important, however, was the War Hawks' outrage at "the injuries and indignities" heaped on the United States by British arrogance. The War Hawks were children of the nation rather than its founders, and thus were intensely nationalistic. Moreover, westerners felt a special grievance because the British supported the Indians of the Northwest, with whom they were chronically in competition. The more exuberant of them spoke of invading and easily capturing Canada.

Stalemate

On the face of it, Canada should have been easy pickings. The Indians of the Great Lakes basin had been crippled before the war began by the defeat in Novem-

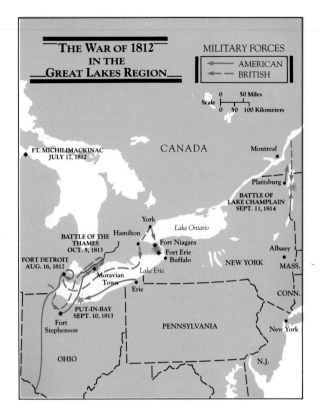

"THE STAR-SPANGLED BANNER"

It is to the War of 1812 that Americans owe their national anthem. On the night of September 13/14, 1814, a lawyer named Francis Scott Key was being detained on a British ship, which he had boarded in order to arrange for the release of a prisoner. While he was aboard, the British shelled Fort McHenry, the chief defense for the city of Baltimore. Fort McHenry resisted capture, and the sight of the American flag waving atop it on the morning of September 14 inspired Key's lyrics, which he wrote while being rowed back to shore.

Most singers have said that Key did the nation no favor by choosing as his music a popular English song, "To Anacreon in Heaven." Perhaps because it was a drinking song, sung and heard by people who did not care, "Anacreon" resisted (and still resists) attractive voicing.

Curiously, "The Star-Spangled Banner" has not been the national anthem for very long. Although unofficially sung since Key published it on September 20, 1814, the song was not officially adopted by Congress until 1931.

ber 1811 of a confederacy led by the Shawnee Tecumseh and his brother Tenskwatawa, who was known as "The Prophet." Because of the war in Europe, Britain had withdrawn all but twenty-two hundred redcoats from the Canadian garrison, and the Canadian militia was as undependable as American irregulars.

But a three-pronged American invasion of Canada ended in a fiasco on every front. One army was led by a general who was so fat that he could not ride a horse. He had to be hauled about in a special cart. On the Niagara River, New York militia refused to advance and delayed their return home only long enough to watch a duel between two American commanders (which the Canadians across the river also enjoyed). Surprised at American ineffectiveness, the Canadians counterattacked and captured Detroit, while their Indian allies destroyed the stockade at Chicago, then called Fort Dearborn.

The Northwest would have been laid wide open to further British advance if it had not been for the seamanship of Captain Oliver Hazard Perry on Lake Erie. He nullified the impact of American defeat on land by establishing his control of that fresh-water lake. Curiously, for Britain was undoubtedly the world's premier sea power, American vessels won a number of one-to-one confrontations on the ocean.

TECUMSEH AND THE PROPHET

The Shawano, or Shawnee, Indians, an Algonkian-speaking tribe of the Eastern Woodlands, were fierce warriors. But the tribe was small, numbering only about fifteen hundred people as late as 1750. As a result, the Shawnee had been wanderers as far back in time as their legends reached.

They were in the Ohio River Valley during the early 1600s, but, perhaps pushed by tribes armed with European weapons, they migrated south as far as Florida. About 1750, the tribe returned to the north and carved out hunting grounds on both banks of the Ohio River.

They planned to stay; they planted crops and built towns that were intended to be permanent. It was in one of these settlements, Old Piqua near the present site of Dayton, Ohio, that Tecumseh was born in 1768, followed in 1775 by his brother Laulewasika. Their lives would run in different directions for thirty years. Then, in the first years of the nineteenth century, they would join hands to inspire and mobilize a spirit of resistance among the Indians of the Northwest Territory that briefly threatened the expansion of the United States.

Tecumseh ("Panther Lying in Wait") was the warrior, the politician, the practical organizer. He knew little but war when he was growing up. In 1774, when Tecumseh was six, the Shawnee were defeated by a force of Virginians and Iroquois, losing their hunting grounds in Kentucky. During the American Revolution, when Laulewasika was born, the tribe formed an alliance with the British and fought the Americans to a standstill.

During the 1780s, Tecumseh's people regularly skirmished with whites who illegally entered their lands, but there were no full-scale battles until 1790, when a Shawnee–Miami alliance led by Little Turtle defeated an American force under Colonel Josiah Harmer. Tecumseh established his reputation as a peerless warrior in that battle and enhanced it the next year in the much greater victory over General Arthur St. Clair. The Revolutionary War veteran lost six hundred men in one of the bloodiest defeats ever sustained by white soldiers at the hand of Indians.

Valor in battle earned status among Indians, and Tecumseh increased the range of his fame in 1792 when he traveled south to fight on behalf of the Cherokees. Then, however, came the crushing defeat of the northwestern Indians at the Battle of Fallen Timbers. For a decade after that battle, and the Treaty of Greenville that followed, Tecumseh's people lost the heart to resist.

One group of Shawnees, including Tecumseh's mother, fled to Missouri, which was outside the borders of the United States. Others remained among the

Shawnee warrior Tecumseh.

whites to cope as best they could. Legally landless and increasingly dependent on their conquerors for food and clothing, many became wretched beggars debauched by liquor. Their dissipation seemed to confirm the prejudice of the whites that Indians were a depraved race, destined to destroy themselves with their own immorality.

One of the most pathetic was Laulewasika, who lost an eye in a drunken accident. Filthy handkerchief covering his disability, he loitered about farms, towns, and military outposts, and in exchange for whiskey told stories of his brother's feats.

Tecumseh, instead, tried to come to terms with the new way of life by learning about it. In 1798, he formed a warm friendship with the family of James Galloway of Chillicothe, Ohio. He continued to visit other tribes, but he regularly returned to the Galloway homestead and lived there for months at a time. Galloway owned a library of three hundred books, quite unusual for the frontier, and—even more unusual—he encouraged Tecumseh to delve into them.

In 1808, Tecumseh asked to marry Galloway's daughter, Rebecca. She agreed, but only on condition that they live as Americans. Tecumseh refused to give up his culture. He might have agreed just a few years earlier, but in 1808 a great stirring was under way among the native peoples of the Northwest Territory. It had been inaugurated three years before by none other than Tecumseh's brother.

In 1805, Laulewasika had undergone a profound mystical experience. Influenced by the revivalism that periodically swept the frontier—some said that he had attended the famous camp meeting at Cane Ridge, Kentucky, in 1801 when twenty thousand people gathered to hear impassioned preachers tell them they must be born again—Laulewasika reformed and changed his name to Tenskwatawa, meaning "Open Door." Because he announced that he was the way to Jesus Christ, he was known among the whites as The Prophet.

Tenskwatawa's Christianity was not the white's version of Christianity. On the contrary, he preached that the whites were Christ's enemies—they had killed him, or tried to kill him. The Prophet preached that the Indians must reject white ways, particularly alcohol, and return to the old traditions. In 1806, The Prophet's fame spread as far south as Georgia when he predicted an eclipse of the sun, which he may have known of from Tecumseh.

The Prophet also demanded an end to tribalism and urged all native peoples to join him in Tippecanoe, a town where a creek of that name joins the Wabash. Tecumseh visited only briefly. He traveled constantly, urging Indians of every tribe not only to embrace the new religion, but also to form a military alliance to halt the advance of the whites. Territorial Governor William Henry Harrison grew concerned. A religious revival was one thing, united Indian tribes quite another.

Tecumseh did not conceal his intentions. At Vincennes, Indiana, in August, 1810, he said within earshot of the governor:

The way, and the only way, to check and stop this evil is for all the Redmen to unite in claiming a common and equal right in the land, as it was and should be yet; for it was never divided, but belongs to all for the use of each.

When Harrison spoke of paying for the land that the whites wanted, Tecumseh replied, "Sell the land? Why not sell the air, the clouds, the great sea?"

Just as The Prophet grafted Christianity onto the yearnings of the Indians, Tecumseh used the knowledge he had acquired in Galloway's library. His appeals to tribes were based on history as well as logic and his brother's religion. He told them of tribes of which they never heard, Pequots and Narragansetts and Mohicans, whom the whites had divided and conquered.

In November 1811, when Tecumseh was away from Tippecanoe, Harrison swooped down on the town and destroyed it. The Prophet, whom Harrison had hoodwinked by telling him he wanted to talk, was discredited. Tecumseh's dream of a grand alliance was shattered. With bitterness but probably few hopes, he joined the British in the War of 1812. On October 5, 1813, he was killed at the Battle of the Thames. Richard M. Johnson, who claimed to have fired the fatal shot, parlayed his fame into the vice presidency. William Henry Harrison did even better. As the hero of Tippecanoe, he was elected president in 1840.

The Prophet lived on—in Canada on a British pension. In 1826 he returned to the United States and a new humiliation. In that year the Shawnees were removed as a people to Missouri. Tenskwatawa died in 1837 in Kansas, where the Shawnees had been shunted once again. Nor was that their final exile. Today the Shawnee people live in Oklahoma, and the boundaries of their lands are plainly marked, as Tecumseh said they never should be.

His brother Tenskwatawa, also known as The Prophet.

*Led by General Andrew Jackson, American troops defeated the British
at the Battle of New Orleans, 1815.*

These were largely symbolic victories, and the British had their own share of those. In August 1814, an amphibious raid on Washington, D.C., led to the burning of the Capitol and the White House. British officers claimed that they ate a dinner, still warm, that had been set for the president and his wife. Indeed, Madison narrowly escaped capture when, at a battle he drove out to view, the American army fled without fighting.

The British had not wanted the war. But when Napoleon abdicated in the spring of 1814 and a large army thus became available for American service, Britain combined the beginning of peace talks at Ghent in Belgium with a plan to seize lower Louisiana from the United States. An army of eleven thousand excellent troops supported by as many sailors was dispatched under General Sir Edward Pakenham to attack New Orleans from the south. What augured to be a disaster turned out to be a most amazing victory and the making

of a most remarkable national hero, Andrew Jackson of Tennessee.

The Battle of New Orleans

Assembling a force of two thousand Kentucky and Tennessee volunteers, New Orleans businessmen, two battalions of free blacks, some Choctaw Indians, and artillerymen in the employ of the pirate-businessman Jean Lafitte, Jackson threw up earthworks five miles south of Louisiana's great port. The Mississippi River was on his right, a nearly impenetrable mangrove swamp on his left. In front of the motley army was an open field.

Too confident, Pakenham sent his men through the morning fog. Lafitte's cannoneers raked them with grapeshot. When the redcoats were two hundred yards from the earthworks, riflemen opened up with "a leaden torrent no man on earth could face." More than two thousand Britons fell dead. The army that had helped defeat Napoleon broke and ran. Only seven Americans were killed, four of them when they ran after and directly into the retreating enemy army. (After the battle, Jackson hanged as many American soldiers for desertion as were killed during it.)

The Treaty of Ghent was signed before the Battle of New Orleans was fought. Nevertheless, the news of the astonishing victory had an electrifying effect. Such a glorious end to a war of disasters was like a reaffirmation of the nation's destiny. When, within three years, Jackson crushed the powerful Creek tribe in the Southeast and Stephen Decatur returned to the Barbary Coast to sting the Algerians, Americans could feel that they had taken their rightful place in a world where armed might meant greatness.

For Further Reading

The definitive biography of the man whose person looms over the early nineteenth century is Dumas Malone's five-volume *Jefferson and His Time* (1948–74). A good single-volume study is Merrill Peterson, *Thomas Jefferson and the New Nation: A Biography* (1970). See Daniel Boorstin, *The Lost World of Thomas Jefferson* (1948), for a thoughtful and engagingly written study of what and how Jefferson thought. Dumas Malone has written intensive studies of each of Jefferson's terms in office: *Jefferson the President: First Term, 1801–1805* (1970) and *Jefferson the President: Second Term, 1805–1809* (1974).

On the Louisiana Purchase, see Alexander De Conde, *The Affair of Louisiana* (1976). Nor should the student who is interested in the Louisiana Territory fail to look at the *Journals* of Meriwether Lewis and William Clark which are available in several editions. This is one subject on which the primary sources are as good an introduction as are books by historians.

On the War of 1812, see Bradford Perkins, *Prologue to War: England and the United States, 1805–1812* (1961), and Reginald Horsman, *The Causes of the War of 1812* (1962). Horsman is also the author of a narrative history of the war itself, *The War of 1812* (1969).

13

Imperfect Nationalism
Political, Diplomatic, and Economic Developments in the Era of Good Feelings, 1815–1824

The discharging of muskets and pistols, the flag-waving, the shouting and singing, and the patriotic oratory that greeted the news of Jackson's and Decatur's victories were not isolated events. Intense and vocal nationalism flavored the American mood for a decade after the War of 1812. Americans in every section of the country embraced an image of themselves as a new chosen people—unique and blessed on the face of the earth, unsullied by the corruptions of Europe, nurtured by their closeness to nature, committed in the marrow of their bones to liberty, democracy, and progress.

It was during this period that the Fourth of July became a day of raucous popular celebration. Formerly reserved for religious services and decorous promenades in city squares, the Glorious Fourth burst into prominence as a day when everyone paid noisy homage to the nation with games, informal feasting, overdrinking, and boisterous gaiety.

It was an era of patriotism in popular art. Woodcarvers and decorative painters trimmed sailing ships and stagecoaches with patriotic motifs: screaming eagles clutching a brace of arrows;

A woven coverlet (1842) incorporates patriotic slogans and eagle emblems into its design.

the idealized, intrepid, and vigilant female figure that represented liberty; and the flag, the only national ensign in the world that had progress sewn into its design. Between 1816 and 1820, six new stars were added to Old Glory as six new states entered the Union.

Even needlepoint samplers began to depict patriotic rather than religious themes: the Stars and Stripes, or the saying of some national hero like John Paul Jones's "I have not yet begun to fight." Newspapers published exuberant verses that touted the glories of the United States. Songwriters churned out lyrics that celebrated American grandeur.

In 1817, William Wirt wrote a biography of Patrick Henry that implied that Virginians had led the movement for independence and had fought the war single handed. Patriots from other states were sufficiently offended that they looked for and dependably found patriotic demigods of their own.

Less controversial because of its singular subject was Mason Locke Weems's book, *The Life and Memorable Actions of George Washington.* Although originally published in 1800, Parson Weems's unblushing avowal of hero worship peaked in popularity during the 1810s and 1820s, running through fifty-nine large editions. It was Weems who originated the story of the boy Washington and the cherry tree and the tale of an older Washington throwing a silver dollar the width of the Rappahannock River. So perfect was the Father of His Country that even as a child he could not fib; so far above other humans was he that even in physical strength he was a superman.

A YANKEE-DOODLE SONG

One of the most joyously patriotic songs to come out of the War of 1812 was "The *Constitution* and the *Guerrière*," about a two-ship battle that ended in an American victory:

> It oft-times has been told
> How the British seamen bold
> Could flog the tars of France so neat
>   and handy, O!
> But they never found their match
> Till the Yankees did them catch.
> Oh the Yankee boys for fighting are
>   the dandy, O!

The Era of Good Feelings

The gentleman who presided over this outpouring of national pride was, like three of the four presidents before him, a Virginian—James Monroe of Westmoreland County. He is a blurred figure in the history books, a personality with no clear, hard edges. Even James Madison, by no means a scintillating character and not a successful president, glows in comparison.

Monroe's accomplishments can be listed. It can be noted that people thought his wife one of the most beautiful women in the country. Portraits and diaries reveal that Monroe was eccentric in his dress; he wore the old-fashioned knee breeches of the Revolutionary era, while his contemporaries pulled on utilitarian trousers.

But it is not easy to determine what kind of person James Monroe was. Perhaps it is because he was so very successful as president, calmly meeting and promptly dispatching every problem that rose to face him. History, like the audience at a play, thrives on conflict and grows dull and torpid in times of stability.

Political Stability

The Founding Fathers' hopes for a government without political parties came to pass under Monroe. The Federalists, revived by the War of 1812, completely collapsed when the shooting was over. After General Andrew Jackson's great victory at New Orleans, their opposition to the war seemed more like treason than good sense.

The number of congressmen styling themselves Federalists declined from 68 during the war to 42 in 1817 and 25 in 1821 (as compared with 158 Democratic-Republicans). By 1821, there were only 4 Federalists in a Senate of 48 members. Old John Adams, in retirement in Quincy, Massachusetts, took scant interest in the evaporation of the party that he had helped to found. His son, John Quincy Adams, joined the Democratic-Republican party of Thomas Jefferson and became Monroe's Secretary of State.

During the 1810s, a caucus of Democratic-Republican congressmen and senators chose presidential candidates and therefore, in effect, the president. Monroe handily defeated Federalist Rufus King in 1816. King won the electoral votes of only Delaware, Connecticut, and Massachusetts. The next year, when Monroe visited Boston, where Jefferson had been despised, he was received as a hero. A Boston newspaper

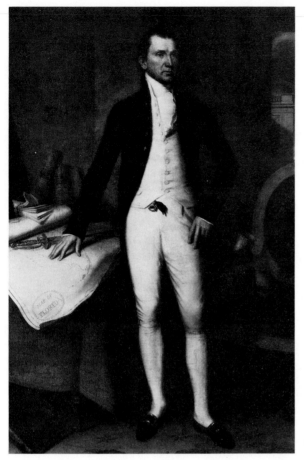

James Monroe's term as president was marked by prosperity and political apathy.

congratulated him for inaugurating an "era of good feelings."

In 1820, Monroe was unopposed in the presidential election, although one member of the electoral college cast his vote for John Quincy Adams so that no president but Washington would have the distinction of being his country's unanimous choice. With only one political party, the United States had no parties at all.

Political Apathy

But there was another side to the consensus of the era, an indifference toward politics and particularly the presidency. In 1816, William Crawford of Georgia actually had more support for the Democratic-Republican nomination than did Monroe, but Crawford would not take the trouble to ensure that his supporters showed up at the party caucus.

Nor was there much popular interest in general elections. In 1816, only six of nineteen states chose presidential electors by statewide popular vote; in 1820, only seven of twenty-four states did. In most of the others, the state legislatures made the choice, and they treated the chore as though it were of no more importance than a proclamation of the Thanksgiving holiday. In 1820, the returns from Richmond, Virginia, a city of twelve thosand people, revealed that only seventeen men had bothered to vote.

Monroe's Accomplishments

There is nothing intrinsically wrong in a subdued presidency and popular indifference to politics. One of the gospels of the Jeffersonian faith, to which James Monroe subscribed, was that the government that governed least governed best. The absence of a deeply divisive domestic issue during Monroe's eight years in office reflected the relative prosperity of the times and the American people's concern with other matters.

Not that Monroe simply lived in the White House. On the contrary, he was presented with a number of foreign challenges, and he became the first president to meet them successfully.

Two Favorable Treaties

In the Rush-Bagot Agreement of 1817, the United States and Britain agreed to limit the number of armed vessels on the Great Lakes. It was the first major concession that the former mother country had made to the upstart Americans since the Revolution. The treaty set the pattern for what became a permanent policy between neighbors who share the world's longest unfortified international boundary.

In 1818, Britain and the United States established the southern boundary of British Canada at 49° north latitude, a line that now runs from west of Lake Superior to Puget Sound. Although American claims in the Pacific Northwest were pretty flimsy, the British conceded that Americans should have equal rights with them in what was called the Oregon country: present-day Oregon, Washington, the Idaho panhandle, and British Columbia.

With Spain, Monroe's diplomacy reaped even greater rewards. By 1819, the Spanish Empire was in tatters. Rebellions had broken out in practically every province, and rebel armies won most of the battles with demoralized Spanish troops. The leaders of the independence movement—Simón Bolívar, José de San Martín, and Bernardo O'Higgins—paid homage to the example set by the United States. Their praises of the United States as the beacon light of their own freedom provided more justification for the Americans' bumptious national pride.

The disintegration of the Spanish Empire also gave Florida to the United States. The peninsula never had been a very secure part of New Spain. The British held it for twenty years after 1763. In 1818, Andrew Jackson brazenly crossed the border and did pretty much as he pleased, including hanging two British subjects for treason.

When the Spanish ambassador to Washington protested Jackson's invasion of Spanish territory, Secretary of State John Quincy Adams responded by offering to buy Florida. For $5 million, Spain agreed. Adams had only to confirm Spain's version of the disputed boundary between American Louisiana and Spanish Texas (at the present eastern border of the state of Texas). It was no concession at all. In the Adams-Onís Treaty, the United States was guaranteed every acre to which the country had a reasonable claim.

The Monroe Doctrine

John Quincy Adams was also the author of the American statement of policy that has immortalized Monroe's name. In December 1823, the president declared to Congress (and to Europe) that the United States was no longer to be considered an appendage of the Old World. With an "essentially different" destiny, the United States pledged not to dabble or intervene in European affairs. In return, Europe was to consider the Western Hemisphere closed to further colonization. Monroe said that any such attempts would be defined in Washington as "an unfriendly disposition." In other words, he threatened war.

The proclamation was prompted by rumblings in Austria and France that they would send armies to Spanish America to help Spain regain control of its lost colonies. Just how much the American threat influenced these two powerful countries in their decision to abandon the project is difficult to determine. They had other problems, and the United States was probably neither able nor willing to send an army to South America. Moreover, Great Britain quietly seconded Monroe's statement. (It was not called the "Doctrine" until many years later.)

In fact, the British had been the chief beneficiaries of Spanish American independence. Previously restricted in the extent of their trade with the rich markets of South and Central America, British merchants now had a free hand there. Indeed, the British foreign minister, George Canning, had suggested a joint statement guaranteeing the independence of the Latin American republics. Adams decided to act alone so that the United States would not appear to be "a cock-boat in the wake of the British man-of-war." Nevertheless, it was the powerful Royal Navy that enforced the Monroe Doctrine until the end of the century.

John Marshall's Court

While John Quincy Adams proclaimed the national dignity of the United States to the world, Chief Justice John Marshall worked for the primacy of the national government at home. He never again led the Court in overturning a law of Congress. Instead, Marshall devoted his long career to asserting the supremacy of the federal government over the states.

In *Fletcher* v. *Peck* (1810), the Marshall Court declared a state law unconstitutional, thus establishing the right of the Supreme Court to act in matters that concerned one state alone. In *Martin* v. *Hunter's Lessee* (1816), Marshall established the Court's authority to reverse the decision of a state court. In *McCulloch* v. *Maryland* (1819), Marshall prevented the state of Maryland (and all states) from taxing the nationally chartered Bank of the United States. "The power to tax is the power to destroy," the Court declared. The right of the national government to charter institutions for the public good took precedence over state authority.

In *McCulloch*, Marshall also propounded his views on the extent of governmental power. If the goal was legitimate and the law did not run counter to the Constitution, Congress and president had the power to enact whatever legislation they chose to enact. It did not matter that the government in Washington was not specifically authorized by the Constitution to take a certain action (such as the establishment of a national bank).

This was the issue that had led to the original split between Hamilton and Jefferson. Now with Hamilton and Hamilton's party both dead, John Marshall made "broad construction" of the Constitution the prevailing law of the land.

The Industrial Revolution

Another of Hamilton's dreams—and one of Jefferson's nightmares—headed for fulfillment during the early nineteenth century. Particularly in New England and the Middle Atlantic states, manufacturing came to rival agriculture in economic importance, and population began a significant shift from farms and villages to industrial towns and cities. In this process, the people of the northeastern states were early participants in the Industrial Revolution—the greatest worldwide upheaval since the one that Christopher Columbus had inaugurated.

What Industrialization Means

Machine technology, the factory system of making goods, and the rapid growth of industrial cities were not revolutionary in the sense that people's lives were changed overnight. But the consequences of machines that made goods quickly and cheaply changed the terms of human existence far more profoundly than did any battle, or the beheading of any king or queen.

For example, in the United States today, less than 8 percent of the population lives on farms, and virtually no people produce more than a tiny fraction of the food they consume and the goods they use. They buy the things they need in order to live with money received for performing very specialized jobs. Even the typical farm family raises only one or two crops for market and purchases the same necessities and luxuries that the city dwellers do.

Before industrialization, in colonial and early national America, the situation was reversed. Roughly 90 percent of the population (the proportion was constantly declining, of course) lived on farms, and most of them purchased very little that was grown or made by others: shoes; some clothing; tools such as axes and guns; some services such as transportation, milling flour, shoeing horses; and things of that sort. As for

other necessities (luxuries were genuinely luxurious and therefore for the rich alone) people improvised them from materials on hand.

Everyone had to be "handy." A man who had to hang a door made the hinges himself; a woman who wanted a tidy house made the broom with which she swept it. In all but the half dozen largest cities, townspeople kept gardens of an acre or so, a dairy cow, a hog, and a spinning wheel. The Industrial Revolution changed that kind of unspecialized, largely self-sufficient life into the specialized, interdependent economy we know today.

It Started with Cloth

The first industrial machines were devised for the manufacture of textiles, and, even in the late twentieth century, a newly developing nation is likely to industrialize its cloth manufacture before anything else. This is because cloth is a universal need, but its manufacture is tedious, complicated, and time consuming.

In the United States, as in most of the Western world, clothmaking was largely woman's work, and the process took up much of the spare time of that half of the population. On poor and even prosperous American farms, cloth was made at home from scratch. Natural fiber from animals (wool) or plants (cotton and flax for linen) had to be gathered, cleaned, carded (untangled, combed), spun into thread or yarn, dyed, and

Modern urban areas such as Brooklyn were more like villages in the early nineteenth century, as this painting illustrates.

FORTUNETELLING

In the early nineteenth century, some upper-class families amused themselves on a boy's fourth birthday by putting him in front of a pair of dice, a piece of fruit, a purse, and a silver knife. It was prophesied that if he picked up the knife, he would become a gentleman of leisure; the purse, a businessman; and the fruit, a farmer. If he picked up the dice, everyone had a good laugh.

A REVOLUTION IN LANGUAGE

Industrialization changed the way people spoke as well as the way they lived. Today, for example, the word *manufacture* conjures up images of factories and assembly lines. But, strictly speaking, *manufacture* means the same thing as *handicraft*, a term that would never be confused with it. *Manufacture* comes from the Latin words for "hand" and "to make," just as *handicraft* is a compound of the Anglo-Saxon equivalents.

Industry was also redefined by the Industrial Revolution. The word now brings to mind factories belching smoke and producing anything from automobiles to cocktail napkins printed with witless jokes. Before there were factories, *industry* simply meant "diligence in attention to business." Benjamin Franklin used the word in that way, and we still say that a person who works hard at anything is *industrious*.

Factory originally referred to any place of business, particularly a place of trade, and businessmen were often known as factors. A seventeenth-century poem about Maryland, "The Sot-Weed Factor," refers to a dealer in tobacco. Slave-trading stations on the African coast were called *factories*. Today, it would almost be incorrect to attach the word to anything but a place of manufacture.

then woven or knitted by hand into a fabric that could warm a body, cover a bed, protect a wagonload, or propel a ship.

Because the process was so lengthy and required hard-learned skills at every turn, clothes were expensive. Americans of modest means rarely owned more than two changes, one for everyday use and a better garment for "Sunday-go-to-meeting" and other special occasions.

The wealthy did not make their own cloth, of course, nor did quite "everyone" among the middle and lower classes. Before industrialization, their needs were met by "cottage industries," or what was sometimes called "the putting-out system."

Farm wives and daughters arranged with a merchant to receive fiber from him and spin it into yarn or thread in their homes. Working in odd, snatched moments, they were paid by the piece. The women (and sometimes men) in another family might weave cloth under the same system, again in their spare time.

This system of production did not disturb the traditional social structure in any significant way. Households involved in cottage industry were able to participate in the money economy to the extent of what the women earned. Socially, these people remained farm women. They were not "textile workers." Their values and the rhythm of their life were essentially the same as those of their neighbors who did not spin or weave.

In the middle of the eighteenth century, this system began to change. English inventors devised water-powered machines that spun thread and wove cloth at many times the speed that hand spinners and weavers could do it, and, as a result, at a fraction of the cost. With a monopoly of this technology, Britain prospered, supplying the world with cheap fabric. Not only were most women delighted to be spared the tedium of spinning and weaving, but the machine-made cloth was cheap enough for almost all to buy, and it was of better quality than home-made cloth. England found a market for its cheap cloth everywhere in the world.

In the southern United States, owners of slaves leapt at the possibility of clothing their bondservants so cheaply. Comparable machines were rapidly developed for other forms of manufacture.

The Importance of Power

The key to exploiting James Kay's flying shuttle, James Hargreaves's spinning jenny, and Richard Arkwright's water frame was power—a fast-moving river, or somewhat later, a noisy steam engine. A geared water wheel or steam boiler could turn hundreds of machines much faster than any foot-driven spinning wheel. However, this meant that the process of making cloth had to be centralized, brought under one roof, and that machines had to be run for as long as there was light by which to see. In other words, industrialization created the factory.

Industrialization also created a class of workers who did nothing but tend machines. No longer was thread spun by a farm wife in odd moments. The industrial textile worker spent six days a week, from dawn to dusk, at the factory. Because she had to live close to the factory, the mill hand had to live in a town and socially, was no longer the farmer's daughter. A new social class emerged—the urban, industrial working class that Karl Marx called the proletariat. Fortunately

Women tend the spinning machines in this early cotton factory, 1839.

for the English, the "surplus population" that had provided so many people for North America also made up a readily available supply of factory hands.

The First American Factories

The British tried to protect their monopoly of industrial technology, as a magician guards a bag of tricks. Not only was it illegal to export the magical machines, but the complicated plans for them were closely guarded. The small number of men who were expert in building or repairing them were forbidden to leave the country.

One of these was Samuel Slater, twenty-three years old in 1790. He was a protégé of the Arkwright group and, realizing the opportunities that were open to him in the United States, committed to memory several long and intricate lists of machine specifications. He slipped away from his home and shipped off to America, where he struck a bargain with a Rhode Island merchant, Moses Brown.

Brown, who had tried without success to build spinning machines, put up the money, and Slater contributed the expertise. In 1790, they opened a small water-powered spinning mill in Pawtucket, Rhode Island. The little factory housed only seventy-two spindles, a picayune operation compared with what was to come. Still, they were the equivalent of seventy-two spinning wheels in seventy-two cottages, and each of the Slater devices turned many times faster and spun much longer than any farm wife could manage. The whole place was run by one supervisor and nine children between the ages of seven and twelve. Their labor cost Slater and Brown thirty-three to sixty-seven cents per worker per week. Within a few years, both men became quite rich. Slater, a young man at the time, lived to become one of New England's leading industrialists, owning mills in three states.

There were other such acts of technological piracy. In 1793, two brothers from Yorkshire, John and Arthur Schofield, came to Byfield, Massachusetts, and estab-

Slater Mill, established in Rhode Island in 1790, was the first successful cotton spinning factory in the United States.

lished the first American woolens mill. Francis Cabot Lowell smuggled out of England plans for a power loom. Throughout the nineteenth century, Englishmen would bring valuable technological advances in their sea trunks.

Yankee Ingenuity

Once aroused, however, Americans proved more than able to advance the Industrial Revolution on their own. Alexander Hamilton had observed "a peculiar aptitude for mechanical improvements" in the American people. In the 1820s, a foreign observer marveled that "everything new is quickly introduced here. There is no clinging to old ways; the moment an American hears the word 'invention' he pricks up his ears."

One reason for the American infatuation with the machine was the labor shortage that had vexed employers since the earliest colonial days. Land was abundant and cheap in the United States. Opportunities for an independent life were so great that it was difficult to find people who would work for wages. Those who did demanded and usually got premium pay. In the early nineteenth century, an American carpenter made about three times as much money as his European counterpart. Even an unskilled worker in the United States could live considerably better than the laborers of the Old World. What was sauce for the worker, however, was poison to the men who hired help. The machine, which did the job of many handworkers, was inevitably attractive to them.

Thus, Oliver Evans of Philadelphia earned a national reputation when he contrived a continuous-operation flour mill. One man was needed to dump grain into one end of an ingenious complex of machinery. Without further human attention, the grain was weighed, cleaned, ground, and packed in barrels. Only at this point was a second man needed to pound a lid on the keg. Evans had saved millers half their payroll.

In 1800, Eli Whitney announced a system for casting small iron parts that promised to displace gunsmiths, one of the most skilled of preindustrial craftsmen. Muskets and other firearms were expensive because the lock (firing device) was made up of a dozen or more moving parts, several of which were quite tiny. These were individually fashioned by hand so that no two guns were the same; in modern language, every one was "custom made." Not only was this procedure time consuming and therefore expensive, but repairs required the attention of an artisan who was as skilled as the man who made the gun. He had to fashion the replacement part from scratch.

Whitney's innovation was to make the molds for the parts of a gun so precise that one component cast in them was enough like every other that they could be used interchangeably. He appeared before a congressional committee with ten functional muskets constructed from interchangeable parts, took them apart, shuffled the components, and reassembled ten working muskets. His dramatic little show won him a government contract to make ten thousand more.

A Country Made for Industry

Many cultures produce inventors. The United States was unique in raising the inventor to the status of a hero, quite the equivalent of a conquering general or a great artist. Even bastions of tradition embraced practical science. In 1814, Harvard College instituted a course called "Elements of Technology." In 1825, Rensselaer Polytechnic Institute, a college devoted entirely to the new learning, was founded at Troy, New York, a center of the iron-molding industry. Others followed in quick succession because Americans found nothing odd in teaching engineering side by side with Greek and Latin. Indeed, they were more likely to be suspicious of those who studied the "useless" classics.

The United States was also endowed with the other prerequisites of an industrial society: resources necessary to feed the new machines; capital, surplus money to finance the building of factories; and labor, people to work them.

It was as though the northern states had been created with water-driven mills in mind. From New England to New Jersey, the country was traversed with fast-running streams that, dammed and channeled, provided power for factories. When steam power proved superior to water power, the dense forests and rich deposits of coal could be exploited to stoke the boilers. America's forests and strong agricultural base produced what raw materials the new industry required, from lumber to leather to hemp for rope. At the same time the textile industry was growing in New England, cotton cultivation expanded throughout the South to pro-

POPULATION OF TEN LARGEST AMERICAN CITIES—1820

Philadelphia	137,000
New York	135,000
Baltimore	63,000
Boston	44,000
New Orleans	27,000
Charleston	25,000
Washington	13,000
Albany	13,000
Richmond	12,000
Salem, Mass.	11,000

vide enough of the snowy fiber for both England and America.

Capital

Money free for investment came from the merchants and shippers of the Northeast. Ironically, many of these capitalists were practically forced to convert their wealth from ships to mills by the restrictions on trade that they thought would be the ruin of them. In 1800, at the beginning of the Napoleonic Wars, there were only seven mills in New England, with a total of 290 spindles. After Jefferson's embargo, Madison's Non-intercourse Acts, and the War of 1812 had disrupted shipping for fifteen years, there were 130,000 spindles in 213 factories in Massachusetts, Connecticut, and Rhode Island alone. Aware of a good thing once they saw it, northern industrialists continued to expand. By 1840, there were two million spindles in the United States.

Banks, a new phenomenon in the early nineteenth century, made it easier to channel capital where it was needed. Not everyone was pleased at the multiplication of lending institutions from thirty in 1801 to eighty-eight in 1811. A bank issued more money in paper certificates than it actually had on hand in gold and silver. In 1809, John Adams growled that "every dollar of a bank bill that is issued beyond the quantity of gold and silver in the vaults represents nothing and is therefore a cheat upon somebody."

In time, events would prove how right his simple economics could be. However, as long as the people who built a mill, supplied it with fiber, and worked the machines accepted the paper dollars lent by a bank to the millowner, and as long as their grocers, landlords, and other business contacts accepted the paper money from them, it did not matter that the bank owned only $100,000 in gold and issued $1 million in paper. As long as the people who traded in the bills believed that they could present the paper to the bank and receive gold, capital was increased tenfold. As long as confidence and optimism were in rich supply, banks were a source of energy as powerful as the thirty-two-foot falls of the Merrimack River.

Industry and Politics

With the increasing importance of industrial interests in the Northeast, the section's political interests shifted. Traditionally, New England shipowners had been suspicious of a high tariff on imported goods. If taxes were high on foreign goods, fewer Americans bought them and thus merchants got less business carrying manufactures across the ocean. Alexander Hamilton failed to get the tariff he wanted partly because New England merchants, his strongest supporters in other matters, joined with farmers (who were consumers of manufactured goods and wanted the lowest prices possible) to defeat the bill.

As late as 1816, many New England congressmen voted against high tariffs. One of them was Daniel Webster, a thirty-four-year-old representative from New Hampshire who numbered Portsmouth shipmasters among his legal clients.

By 1823, when Webster returned to Congress, he had moved to Massachusetts and become counsel and confidant to several manufacturers. Now he was a strong and eloquent supporter of a high tariff. If "infant industries" were to be established, they had to be protected from the cheaper goods that the older and better-developed British manufacturers could produce. The idea of "protection" was to tax foreign goods so high that the domestic competition could undersell them.

The Working Class

Industrialization eventually undercut and almost destroyed handicraft. Many people were needed to tend the machines in the new mills, and the United States

The Lowell Offering (1845) was a literary magazine produced by women who worked in the Lowell, Massachusetts, mills.

lacked England's surplus of "sturdy beggars" roaming the countryside and overcrowding the cities. Few Americans who could choose among farming profitably, moving west, or working in small independent shops, were attracted to low-paying, highly disciplined factory work.

The difficulty of recruiting labor from traditional sources was revealed in the failure of the "Fall River system." In Fall River, Massachusetts, the millowners attempted to hire whole families to work in the mills. It was an honest mistake. The family was the unit of production on the traditional farm and in the artisan's shop. But the system did not work very well in the factories.

Much more successful, because it found a niche within traditional social structures, was the system developed by Francis Cabot Lowell, who, with several partners, established a series of large mills at Waltham, Massachusetts, in 1813 and a whole town at Lowell in 1826. Lowell dispatched recruiters all over rural New England. They persuaded farmers to send their young daughters to work in the mills. For a seventy-hour week, they would earn $3 and pay half of that for room and board at company-supervised lodging houses.

The long workweek put no one off in the early nineteenth century; it was a normal schedule for a farm family. The money was attractive, too. Farming the rocky New England soil never made anyone rich. And Yankee farmers burdened with large families inevitably liked the idea of subtracting one diner from the table, especially if that diner was a daughter who, by going to Waltham or Lowell for a few years, could save a dowry large enough to attract a suitable husband. The "Waltham system" was successful precisely because it drew on a body of people for whom there were few other opportunities.

In order to persuade strait-laced New Englanders to allow girls of sixteen and seventeen to leave home (and in order to satisfy his own Puritan scruples), Lowell provided a closely regulated life during off-hours as well as working hours. The "Lowell girls" lived in company-run dormitories, were watched closely, and were disciplined without ceremony for moral lapses. They were required to attend church services, and were kept busy (as if seventy hours at work were not enough!) with a variety of educational and cultural programs.

Thus, the first American industrial workers were women—and children! In 1820, about half the factory

Winslow Homer's Morning Bell *portrays girls on their way to a day's work at a factory. By 1866, when the painting was made, the rustic wholesomeness of factory life depicted here had given way to unhealthy conditions.*

hands in Massachusetts mills were under sixteen years of age. A society of farmers, in which everyone down to six years of age had assigned chores, did not find this inhumane. And the pace of the early factory was slow. In some mills, girls were permitted to have company while they watched their spindles. Most English visitors commented that American factories were idyllic compared with England's "dark, satanic mills."

In time, the American factory, too, would become a place of stultifying, killing toil. But it is difficult to find many horrors in the first phase of industrialization. Artists depicted mills as objects of beauty and town pride. By way of contrast with what later builders would create, those structures that have survived are regarded as architectural gems.

The South at the Crossroads

While the people of the North were building an urban, capitalist society, those of the South were reaffirming their section's agrarian heritage. There were those who would have had it otherwise. In 1816, when Daniel Webster was still speaking for the shipping interests of old New England, John C. Calhoun of South Carolina dreamed of cotton factories in his own state.

But Calhoun's attraction to industrialization, like his shrill nationalism during the War of 1812, was already doomed. His future lay in defending the plantation system and the institution of slavery on which it rested. Ironically, this brilliant thinker (and somewhat less able politician) was chained to these anachronistic, semifeudal institutions because of one of the most dramatic technological breakthroughs of the new era.

The Decline of Slavery

When John C. Calhoun was born in 1782, black slavery appeared to be dying out. The northern states took steps to abolish human bondage during the last years of the eighteenth century. Slavery was never vital to their economy, and they could afford to practice the Revolutionary principle of equality of rights.

Slavery was also declining in the South. The world price of tobacco, one of the few crops for which slave labor was profitable, collapsed, and the old Chesapeake and North Carolina lands were exhausted. Other slave-raised crops, such as South Carolina's rice and indigo, lost their appeal when British subsidies were lost following independence. Southerners, as well as northerners, were moved by the ideals of the Declaration of Independence. Thomas Jefferson, its author, agonized throughout his life over the injustice of the institution. In their wills, George Washington and many other planters freed at least some of their slaves. Few people spoke of slavery as anything better than a tragic social burden, a necessary evil. As late as 1808, only a few southerners objected when Congress (as the Constitution allowed) outlawed further importation of blacks from Africa.

It would be a mistake to think that the slaveowners of the 1780s and 1790s did not free their slaves only because they worried about how well a biracial society would work. If not excessively profitable, slave labor still made it possible for wealthy planters like Washington and Jefferson to live leisured, cultivated lives. Nevertheless, it is reasonable to suggest the gradual, peaceful disappearance of the institution. That is, if it had not been for Eli Whitney's "absurdly simple contrivance."

The Cotton Gin

In 1793, seven years before his demonstration of interchangeable parts to the congressmen, Eli Whitney visited a plantation near Savannah, Georgia. There he saw his first cotton plant and learned from a friend that it grew all over the upland South. Cotton fiber was worth thirty to forty cents a pound—a good price—but the upland cotton was commercially useless because of the expense involved in separating the precious fiber from the plant's sticky green seeds. This job could be done only by hand, and the most nimble-fingered of people could process no more than about a pound of fluff a day. Given the high price of hired labor and even the costs of feeding and clothing slaves, it was not economical to set them to work at the task.

On the frost-free sea islands off the coast of South Carolina and Georgia, cotton had been cultivated profitably since 1786. But the cotton grown there was another variety, "long-staple." The fibers were long, and the shiny, smooth black seeds could be popped out of the fiber by running the bolls between two rollers. When this method was tried with the cotton of the uplands, unfortunately, the sticky green seeds were crushed, fouling the fiber with oil.

Whitney's device was so simple that a planter who had a decent collection of junk in the yard could make a workable version. Indeed, the ease of constructing the "gin" (short for *engine*) denied Whitney the fortune he deserved for inventing it. His patents were simply ignored.

Essentially, the bolls were dumped into a box at the bottom of which were slots too small for the seeds to pass through. A drum studded with wire hooks revolved so that the hooks caught the fibers and pulled them through the slots, leaving behind the seeds without crushing them. Another drum, revolving in the

Eli Whitney's cotton gin provided a simple, inexpensive means to process upland cotton.

opposite direction, brushed the fiber from the wire hooks.

It was a magnificent device. A single slave cranking a small gin could clean ten pounds of cotton a day ($3 to $4 at 1790 prices!). A somewhat larger machine tended by several people and turned by a horse and windlass could clean fifty pounds a day ($15 to $20!). Once steam-powered gins were introduced, the capacity for producing cotton was limited not by any processing, but by the number of acres that a planter could cultivate. Technology had come to the South.

The Revival of Slavery

But not industry. The effect of Eli Whitney's machine was to revive the pattern of a one-crop economy, the domination of southern society by large planters, and the reinvigoration of slavery. Like tobacco, cotton was

well adapted to gang-cultivation. The crop required plenty of unskilled labor: plowing, planting, "chopping" (weeding, an endless process in the hot, wet, fertile South), ditch digging, picking, ginning, baling, and shipping.

Moreover, the fertile upland "black belt" that extends from South Carolina and Georgia through eastern Texas was natural cotton country. Spurred by the dreams of a fortune, small farmers, southeastern planters with their slaves, and land speculators alike streamed into the Old Southwest (Alabama, Mississippi, and northern Louisiana) and eventually into Arkansas across the Mississippi River. In 1800, excluding Indians, there were about one thousand people in what is now Alabama. In 1810, there were nine thousand; in 1820, one hundred twenty-eight thousand! The growth of Mississippi was a little less dramatic but not exactly lethargic: 1800, eight thousand; 1810, thirty-one thousand; 1820, seventy-five thousand. Nor was this an emigration of buckskin-clad frontiersmen with no more baggage than a long rifle and a frying pan. In 1800, there were four thousand blacks in Alabama and Mississippi. In 1810, there were seventeen thousand blacks, virtually all of whom were slaves; in 1820, there were seventy-five thousand. Almost half the population of Mississippi was black and in bondage.

The price of slaves soared, doubling between 1795 and 1804. Blacks who had been financial burdens in Maryland and Virginia became valuable commodities in the new cotton South. The most humane masters could not resist the temptation of the high prices offered for their "prime field hands," males between eighteen and thirty years of age, and slaveowners from as far north as New Jersey liquidated their human holdings to cotton planters.

There were still slaves in the North to be sold. Most states had adopted a gradualist approach to emancipation, by which no person born or brought into the state after a certain date could be enslaved. (There were a handful of aged slaves in New Jersey as late as the Civil War.)

But there was, almost by accident, a clear-cut line between the "slave states" and the "free states." North of the Mason-Dixon line (the Maryland–Pennsylvania border) and the Ohio River, slavery was forbidden. South of it, the institution had survived and was quite profitable. The tragically precise division broke into the open in 1819, right in the middle of Monroe's "era of good feelings."

The president was not unduly disturbed. He was sure that the issue raised by Missouri's application to join the Union could be easily compromised. One of his principal advisers, John Quincy Adams, was not so sure. Nor was old Thomas Jefferson. Hearing of the congressional debate, he said that he was startled as though he had heard "a firebell in the night." What awakened him with a sense of danger was the introduction of the moral issue into discussions of slavery. Moral conflict, Jefferson knew, was not easily settled.

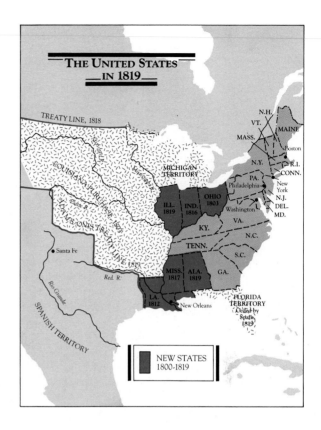

The Missouri Compromise

There were twenty-two states in 1819. Although there had been nothing deliberate about it, free and slave states were balanced. There were eleven of each. Indeed, there had been little thought on the matter until, when Missouri applied for admission as the twenty-third state, the House of Representatives voted to approve on condition that Missouri immediately abolish slavery. The Senate rejected this Tallmadge Amendment, and a debate ensued in which a number of northern congressmen condemned slavery as immoral, "a sin which sits heavy on the soul of every one of us."

Quakers and other religious groups had used even stronger words for more than fifty years. But this was the United States Congress, and a majority of the lower house at that. Even in the Northwest Ordinance, which forbade slavery north of the Ohio River, Jefferson had focused on the social and economic ill effects of the institution, which many southerners were willing to concede.

Shocked and angered, southern congressmen and senators replied in equally righteous tones. Only after the bitterness had dragged on for months did Henry Clay of Kentucky, beginning his career as "The Great Compromiser," work out a scheme to please both sides.

Missouri was admitted as a slave state. In order to maintain the balance of free states and slave states, the Maine District was detached from Massachusetts and admitted as a free state. In what seemed to close the issue for good, the southern boundary of Missouri (36° 30′ north latitude) was extended through the remainder of American territory. When the Arkansas Territory, south of the line, was prepared to enter the

WORKING AND PLAYING IN FRONTIER OHIO

When Europeans traveled through newly opened parts of the United States, like much of Ohio during the 1820s, they were impressed by the feats of labor necessary to make a home in raw wilderness. They invariably complained about the food of the frontier—greasy fried pork and corn-meal mush or fire-roasted corn bread. And they were shocked by the heavy drinking in which everyone seemed to indulge.

But most of all they shuddered at the isolation of those who were building a life in a new country. The Europeans who wrote books about their American experiences were sophisticated and literate; they were accustomed to a full and stimulating social life. So they were disturbed by the loneliness endured by American westerners, particularly the women whose daily chores centered around solitary cabins in the woods.

Mrs. Frances Trollope, an English woman who wrote a celebrated book on *The Domestic Manners of the Americans,* blamed the emotional excesses of revivalist religion on the absence of any form of recreation, of release from daily toil and tedium, even in the comparatively large river port of Cincinnati. "It is thus," she wrote, in the shrieking, howling, and rolling about the floor she witnessed at churches, "that the ladies of Cincinnati amuse themselves; to attend the theatre is forbidden; to play cards is unlawful; but they work hard in their families and must have some relaxation."

Just a few miles outside of Cincinnati, Mrs. Trollope met a hard-bitten frontier woman who showed off her farm and boasted that it produced almost everything the household needed. Economically, the family was self-sufficient but for tea, sugar, and whiskey. Socially, the situation was somewhat different. When Mrs. Trollope prepared to leave, her hostess sighed and said, "Tis strange for us to see company; I expect the sun may rise and set a hundred times before I shall see another *human* that does not belong to the family."

There is no distortion in this picture. Frontier life was extremely lonely for a great many pioneers. But not for all. During the 1820s, people in northern Ohio, an even newer region than the neighborhood of Cincinnati, managed to have a rich social life. William Cooper Howells, a printer who saw Ohio develop from wild forest into a populous industrial state, looked back on the parties of his youth with fond nostalgia. The point Howells made in his memoirs, *Recollections of Life*

in Ohio from 1813 to 1840, was that Ohio pioneers combined amusement and diversion with work.

The raising of a family's log cabin or barn was done collectively by the people who lived within a radius of a few miles. The host had cut all the logs in advance and brought them to the site; sometimes, though, this job too was done by means of a community "log-roll." The men who best handled an ax took charge of notching the logs at each end and raising them into position by hand. With a team for each of the four walls, the job went quickly. When the walls rose too high for the men to reach, the logs were lifted by means of young, forked trees to men straddling the tops of the walls. "The men understood handling timber," Howells wrote, "and accidents seldom happened, unless the logs were icy or wet or the whisky had gone around too often." Howells himself, still quite a young man in Ohio's early years, took pride in taking on the job of "cornerman." While others built the walls, he "dressed up" the corners with an ax and guided the final logs into place. "It was a post of honor." The job was less laborious than that of raising the walls, but it took a head that "was steady when high up from the ground."

When a gathering of men for such a purpose took place there was commonly some sort of mutual job laid out for women, such as quilting, sewing, or spinning up a lot of thread for some poor neighbor. This would bring together a mixed party, and it was usually arranged that after supper there should be a dance or at least plays which would occupy a good part of the night and wind up with the young fellows seeing the girls home in the short hours or, if they went home early, sitting with them by the fire in that kind of interesting chat known as sparking.

In addition to log-rolling and barn- and cabin-raisings, "grubbing out underbrush" and the tedious task of processing flax (for linen and oil) were often done in conjunction with a community party. Other tasks—splitting logs into rails for fences, for example—were spiced up by holding a competition. Abraham Lincoln first ran for political office on his reputation as a champion rail-splitter. But by far the most enjoyable kind of work party, remembered wistfully in practically every reminiscence of the frontier, was the husking bee. Not only was the job less laborious than most, and

Community projects like this flax scutching bee provided the occasion for socializing on the frontier.

the occasion of a contest and a party, but husking bees took place in the autumn, when the harvest was done. It was the season when good food was most abundant on the frontier and spirits were highest.

The ears of corn to be husked were divided into two piles. Two captains chose up sides, alternately selecting their teams from among the young men and boys and sometimes also from among the women and girls. Then

the two parties fell to husking, all standing with the heap in front of them, and throwing the husked corn to a clear space over the heap, and the husks (for animal fodder) behind them. From the time they begin till the corn was all husked at one end, there would be steady work, each man

husking all the corn he could, never stopping except to take a pull at the stone jug of inspiration that passed occasionally along the line.

When one team had finished husking, they let out a great shout (which was the signal to lay a community dinner on the table), briefly exchanged taunts for the excuses of the losers, and then finished the husking along with them. Another "rule of the game" that increased interest was the provision that a boy who husked a red ear could claim a kiss from one of the girls at the party. But Howells concluded: "I never knew it necessary to produce a red ear to secure a kiss when there was a disposition to give or take one."

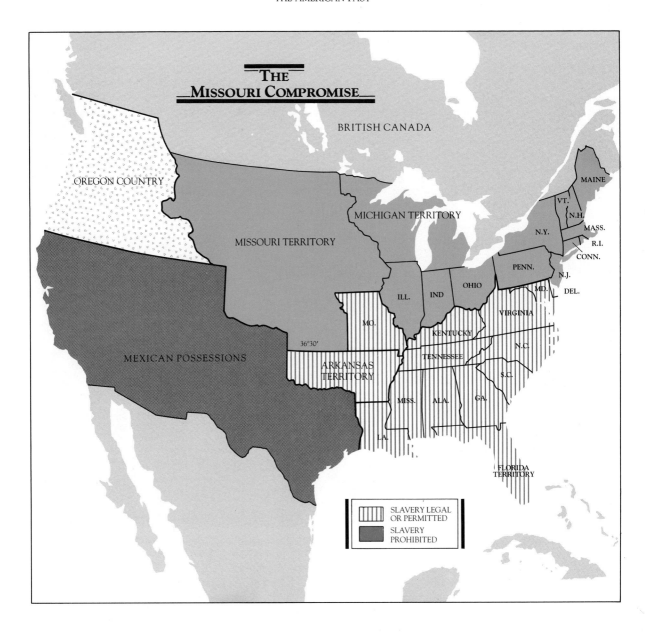

Union, the citizens there could decide whether the state would be slave or free. The same applied to the Florida Territory. North of 36° 30′, slavery was "forever prohibited."

The issue faded. Congressmen who had denounced one another shook hands and turned to other business. But Jefferson's firebell continued to echo, however faintly. Moral questions are not resolved by drawing lines on maps.

The institutionalization of the idea that there should be a balance of free and slave states was also fraught with danger. Even without the addition of more territory, which was an abstract possibility at best in 1820, one glance at a map showed that someday a territory would apply for admission as a free state with no slave territory left to balance it.

Not only was the part of the old Louisiana Territory from which slavery was prohibited vastly larger than the potential slave territory, but the North was growing more quickly than the South. Until 1810, the two sections had grown at an uncannily similar rate. In 1820, however, despite the extraordinary increase of population in Alabama and Mississippi, there were nearly 1 million more people in the North than in the South, 5,219,000 to 4,419,000. The difference was more than made up by the third American section, the only one in which further growth was inevitable— the West.

For Further Reading

An English historian, George Dangerfield, is the reigning authority on this period. See his *Era of Good Feelings* (1952) and *The Awakening of American Nationalism, 1815–1828* (1965). A more detailed examination of the decay of the Federalist party is Shaw Livermore, Jr., *The Twilight of Federalism* (1962). On the development of the Supreme Court under John Marshall, see R. K. Faulkner, *The Jurisprudence of John Marshall* (1968).

Otherwise, biography may be the best means of reading further into the history of this period. See Leonard Baker, *John Marshall: A Life in Law* (1974); William P. Cresson, *James Monroe* (1971); and Harry Amon, *James Monroe: The Quest for National Identity* (1971).

S. F. Bemis, *John Quincy Adams and the Foundations of American Foreign Policy* (1949), and Dexter Perkins, *The Monroe Doctrine* (1927), deal with the successful foreign policy of the Monroe administration. Students who are interested in the subsequent history of the Monroe Doctrine should read William A. Williams, *The Tragedy of American Diplomacy* (1972).

14

Beyond the Appalachian Ridge
The West in the Early Nineteenth Century

In 1790, when the first federal census was taken, only a few thousand white people lived west of the Appalachian Ridge. Virtually the whole population of the United States was concentrated in the thirteen original states. The Atlantic Ocean was a highway to Americans, not a barrier. One reason the government was so preoccupied with European politics and maritime rights during the first decades under the Constitution was that historical roots, habit, and geography faced the United States to the east.

By 1830, fully one-quarter of the American people lived west of the Appalachians, between the Blue Ridge and the Mississippi River and even beyond. These "westerners" had not necessarily been born in the Mississippi Valley—in 1830, few adults had been born there—but their outlook on matters of society, economy, and politics had been formed by the experience of cutting ties in the East, turning a back to the ocean, packing up what possessions could be carried, and striking off to the frontier where land was cheap and therefore, as Americans saw it, opportunities abounded. Inasmuch as opportunity was synonymous in many minds with America, the West had become the symbol of the United States.

Conestoga wagons became a familiar sight on American roads as settlers traveled westward in the nineteenth century.

The West always has been as much an idea as a place. The frontier, where white settlement and institutions ended and the open wilderness began, moved farther west every few years. By 1850, for example, half the American people lived beyond the Appalachian Divide. By mid-century, Americans no longer thought of the former Northwest Territory (Ohio, Indiana, Illinois, Michigan) or the Old Southwest (Tennessee, Alabama, Mississippi) as the "West." In the first decades of the nineteenth century, however, it was in these states and in Kentucky, Missouri, and Arkansas that the idea of the West made its impact on the American experience.

The Growth of the West

Between 1800 and 1820, the population of Mississippi grew from eight thousand to seventy-five thousand. Alabama, with about one thousand whites and blacks in 1800, was home to one hundred twenty-eight thousand people in 1820. The states north of the Ohio River were populated even more rapidly. In 1800, there were forty-five thousand white people in Ohio. Ten years later, the population was two hundred thirty thousand. By 1820, Ohio was the fifth largest state in the Union. By 1840, there were 1.5 million Ohioans; only New York, Pennsylvania, and Virginia were larger. Indeed, this rich, green country, only a generation old, was home to more people than were any of the Scandinavian nations except Sweden.

During the same years, the population of Indiana grew from almost nil to 685,856; Illinois, from a few

hundred whites to 476,183. In 1800, what is now Michigan consisted of one tiny, muddy lakefront fort that had been inherited from the French and English. In the 1830s, New Englanders flocked to Michigan's "oak openings," small fertile prairies in the midst of the hardwood forests, and brought them under the plow.

A People on the Move

To outsiders and sometimes to themselves, Americans seemed to be a people who were incapable of putting down roots. The young couple repeating their marriage vows and promptly climbing atop a wagon to head west was as familiar a sight in New England as was that of people mending stone fences. During the first decades of the nineteenth century, Virginians headed across the mountains as rapidly as a high birth rate could replace them. In central and western Pennsylvania, where one of the most popular wagon roads wended west, the economy was closely tied to emigration. Inns and the stables of horse traders lined the highway. A small Pennsylvania valley lent its name to the heavy-wheeled vehicles made there that proved so well suited to overland travel—the Conestoga wagons.

Europeans, who were more familiar with a world in which people died within a few miles of where they had been born, found the motion dizzying. "In the United States," Alexis de Tocqueville marveled, "a man builds a house in which to spend his old age, and he sells it before the roof is on." An Englishman looking over lands in the Ohio Valley was astonished to discover that if he paused to admire the work that a

The log cabin in the wilderness was a symbol of the primitive life on the American frontier.

MICHIGAN BOUND

As they sang of military victories and political candidates, Americans also sang of the experience of going west. There were dozens of songs about every destination that promised a better life. This one celebrated Michigan:

> Come all ye Yankee farmers who wish to
>   change your lot,
> Who've spunk enough to travel beyond your
>   native spot,
> And leave behind the village where Pa
>   and Ma do stay,
> Come follow me and settle in Mich-i-gan-i-ay.

ABRAHAM LINCOLN AND JEFFERSON DAVIS

Both Abraham Lincoln and Jefferson Davis, opposing presidents during the Civil War, were born in log cabins on the Kentucky frontier. Lincoln's parents migrated there from Virginia in 1782, Davis's from Virginia in 1793. The two men were born within a year of each other.

In 1810, like many restless Kentuckians, the Davis family moved southwest to the rich cotton lands of Mississippi, where they became one of the richest slaveowning families in the state. Other Kentuckians went northwest, and Lincoln's father, a ne'er-do-well named Tom Lincoln, was among them. When Abraham was seven his family moved to Indiana and, when he was eleven, to Illinois. There, in Salem and Springfield, he became a successful attorney.

Perhaps because he realized that it was only a quirk of fate—the direction that their families had chosen when, with so many Americans, they "moved on"—that had made Davis the slaveowner and himself the antislavery politician, Lincoln refused to take a self-righteous attitude toward southern slaveowners. "They are just what we would be in their situation," he said.

recent settler had done on his house and fields, the man was likely to propose selling everything on the spot so that he could try his luck farther west. Americans joked that the chickens crossed their legs in the spring, in anticipation of being tied up for the inevitable trip farther west.

A few of these restless people were simply antisocial. Others wanted as much company as they could persuade to follow them. They were promoters, developers, ambitious men who sometimes had a little money and always had big ideas. The people who made a profession of clearing a few acres of land and building a cabin, then selling out to a newcomer, were promoters of a sort. Bigger operators bought large tracts, advertised them, and sold subdivided plots at a profit.

There were town boosters who laid out marketing centers complete with street names before a single tree had been felled. Some of them were businessmen, merchants, or even manufacturers who planned to stay and prosper as the country grew. Others were professional boomers who made money by selling lots and then moved on as easily as hunters and trappers, never giving their creation another thought.

The Problem of Isolation

Whatever the westerner's intention, "growing up with the country" meant overcoming the problem of isolation from the eastern and foreign markets, and from the factories that manufactured all but the westerners'

simplest needs. Isolation was not a matter of mere loneliness. In order to get to new homes beyond the Appalachians, the earliest emigrants had to walk. So-called roads were not much more than narrow tracks that were hardly up to carrying much baggage, let alone a commerce.

Difficulties in transportation were not unique to the West. The entire country was notorious for the problems involved in traveling and in shipping goods. The tidewater South still depended on waterways. The few roads there were abominable, even in country that had been settled for two hundred years. In the Northeast, beginning about 1790, the demands of regional business prompted some improvement in highways. States and counties graded and graveled old animal tracks that followed the land's natural contours. The Old Post Road between Boston and New York provided the possibility of year-round long-distance travel on that important route, albeit an uncomfortable trip.

In areas with large populations, entrepreneurs constructed toll roads ("turnpikes"). On one of the most famous, the Lancaster Pike, a farmer from the rich farm town of Lancaster, Pennsylvania, could cart his produce to Philadelphia, the country's largest city. He paid a toll at the entrance to the road. A bar that looked like a pike (a medieval weapon), which had been suspended across the way, was "turned" to let him pass, and he could count on a relatively smooth, quick trip to market, sixty miles distant.

By 1820, there were four thousand miles of such toll roads in the United States. Some were surfaced with crushed rock, or macadam, a British import that was the ancestor of blacktop paving. A cheaper surfacing was made of planks laid parallel like railroad tracks, or even of logs laid crosswise. For the obvious reason, the

Though plank roads provided a bumpy ride for travelers, they were an improvement over muddy, rutted trails.

latter were called corduroy roads. The ride they provided was bumpy, but they kept a narrow, spoked wagon wheel out of the mud.

Most toll roads were in the East. Even corduroy roads cost money, and few investors would risk their capital in the thinly settled West. Young and ambitious state and county governments in the West were anxious to encourage such "internal improvements." But they could not afford the cost. They were caught in the vicious circle of needing good roads in order to attract population, while lacking the population—the tax base—necessary to finance them.

Handsome Harry Clay and the Building of the West

The solution, or so it seemed to many westerners, lay in the national Treasury. Only the federal government could afford the huge monetary outlays that were necessary to build the roads, with no expectation of immediate return. To the man who built a long and distinguished political career on calling for federally financed internal improvements, easterners and southerners also had a vital interest in promoting the West.

Henry Clay was born in Virginia in 1777. As a young lawyer he moved to Kentucky and prospered as a planter, land speculator, and politician. Elected to

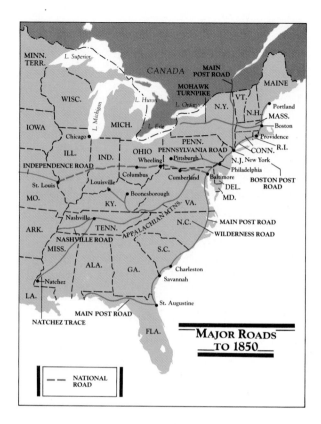

Henry Clay promoted continentalism by supporting federal financing of internal improvements.

Congress in 1810, Clay first won national fame as one of the most exuberant of the War Hawks of 1812. When the war with England bogged down, he went to Ghent, Belgium, as one of the commissioners who drew up the peace treaty.

Both in Europe and at home, Henry Clay liked to have a good time. An outgoing, personable, and handsome man, he charmed women with his good looks and wit, and appealed to men with his willingness to sit down to a game of cards, share a bottle of whiskey, and, if necessary, defend his honor with a dueling pistol. Like many prominent politicians of the day, Henry Clay fought several duels. Although he was a poor shot (and killed no one), he was not afraid to face a loaded, large-bore pistol at short range. This was the kind of bravado that commanded respect in the rambunctious West.

Clay was not simply a *bon vivant*. He viewed his job as a congressman and senator as building the West. He worked tirelessly on behalf of the first federal construction project in the West—the National Road that connected Cumberland, Maryland, on the Potomac River, with Wheeling on the Ohio River. It cost $13,000 per mile to build and was completed in 1818. Delighted by what this access to ocean-going commerce meant for Kentucky, Clay worked to have the National Road extended to Vandalia, Illinois. Handsome Harry was always interested when fellow westerners proposed new internal improvements to benefit their section.

Clay usually was successful. But not always. Many southerners, nationally minded before the War of 1812, began to worry about the cost of internal improvements—and the taxation needed to pay for laying roads, dredging rivers, and the like. Even some westerners, such as Andrew Jackson, Clay's arch rival for leadership of the section, feared that government finance of improvements was unconstitutional. Moreover, while Clay was personally uncorrupt, many unscrupulous manipulators made fortunes on unnecessary or wasteful "improvements." These crimes increased the opposition toward improvements.

Until the 1820s, the northeastern states inclined to oppose spending federal money on internal improvements. Their own road system was adequate. Although little federal money would be spent in the old states, the Northeast, as the richest section, would pick up the biggest part of the bill in taxes. In addition, until the War of 1812 disrupted their shipping business, New Englanders tended to look abroad, rather than to the far-off West, for their economic life. Nor did the increasingly powerful factory owners of the Northeast wish to encourage any more westward emigration than already existed. Better for them that the West remain "at the end of the world," a wilderness that offered none of the security and society of life in a mill town. The more New Englanders who went west, the higher wages rose at home.

Thinking Continentally

But there was another spirit at work, the gospel of "continentalism." Since the days of Alexander Hamilton, some political leaders had urged Americans to cease thinking in terms of Europe and the high seas and to find their future on the North American continent. Henry Clay tried to translate this sentiment into a concrete legislative program that he called the American System.

Clay attempted to convince northeastern industrialists not to fear the consequences of internal improvements in the West. A populous West, connected to the Northeast by good roads, would be a huge market for the manufactured goods of New England and the Middle-Atlantic states. The improvements would be financed by the sale of the federal government's western lands and by the proceeds from a high tariff that would protect northeastern factories from foreign competition.

To westerners, largely farmers who would be likely to oppose a high tariff, Clay pointed out that a flourishing industry would lead to large urban populations of work-

ers who would buy western food products. Higher prices for manufactures—the consequence of the high tariff—were a small price to pay for such markets. To complete the circular movement of products among the regions, the South would supply the mills of New England with cotton. The capstone of this nationalistic program that promised something to every section was the Second Bank of the United States. Chartered in 1816, it would regulate the money supply for this delicately integrated economy.

The weak link in Clay's American System was the South, to which it did not offer very much. Southerners needed no help in finding very profitable markets for their cotton. The mills of Manchester and Leeds and Bradford in England gobbled up almost all the fiber that southern planters could grow. With the exception of a few special interest groups like Louisiana sugar planters, who wanted tariff protection against the West Indian sugar growers, southerners opposed Clay's program. The American System would result in higher price tags on the manufactured goods that they, as agriculturists, had to buy. When they bought English cloth and shoes and tools and luxuries, they paid a large tax—the tariff. When these commodities came from American mills and factories, they carried an artificially high price because northern manufacturers did not have to compete with Europeans on an equal basis.

The Transportation Revolution

In the end, the American economy was integrated less by congressional legislation than by a revolution in transportation that conquered seasons, leveled mountains, and diverted the course of rivers.

The Erie Canal

New York showed the way. In 1817, after years of prodding by De Witt Clinton, the mayor of New York City who became state governor in 1816, the state legislature voted funds to dig a canal from the Hudson River to Lake Erie, from Albany to Buffalo.

With picks, shovels, mules, and wagons to haul the dirt, gangs of rough, muscular laborers excavated a ditch 4 feet deep, 40 feet wide, and, when it was completed in 1825, 364 miles long. (The canal was later enlarged to 7 feet deep and 70 feet wide.) It was expensive—$7 million, or almost $20,000 per mile. Skeptical outsiders waited for the state of New York to buckle under such a financial burden and declare bankruptcy. But when the Erie Canal was finished, it opened up the Great Lakes basin to New York City's merchants and shippers by the cheapest means of trans-

The Erie Canal made possible the cheap overland transportation of goods.

portation, water. Both city and state boomed, and New York outstripped Philadelphia to become the country's biggest city.

Travel on the Erie Canal was slow. Mules on towpaths pulled the long, flat-bottomed canal boats at a lazy four miles an hour. But it made the risky adventure of emigrating to the West into an almost pleasant excursion. For one cent a mile, a traveler could put himself into Buffalo and the Great Lakes basin. For five cents a mile, a man with capital and ambition could travel to the land of opportunity in comfort. Far more important, it cost only $8 a ton to move factory goods west or western agricultural products east. That was a 90 percent cut in the cost of overland transport!

The Canal Craze

Before the Erie Canal was dug, there were only about one hundred miles of canal in the United States. (The longest one ran twenty-eight miles.) Now, those who

had laughed at "Clinton's Folly" went berserk in their rush to imitate it. They were the real fools. They laid out canals where none should have been built.

The most preposterous was the Mainline Canal in Pennsylvania. Feeling the loss of business to New York City, Philadelphia merchants pressured the state legislature into pumping millions into an ill-advised venture. The Mainline Canal was actually shorter than the Erie. But whereas the New York route rose only 650 feet above sea level at its highest point and required 84 locks to control the muddy water, the Mainline Canal rose 2,200 feet and took 174 locks to make it operable. At several points, boats had to be hauled out of the water and over ridges on fantastic inclined planes. The Mainline Canal was completed, but it was a bust: too slow, too expensive, too many disruptive bottlenecks at the mountains.

Most of the four thousand miles of ditch that were dug in imitation of the Erie Canal were similarly ill advised. (Another seven thousand miles were on the

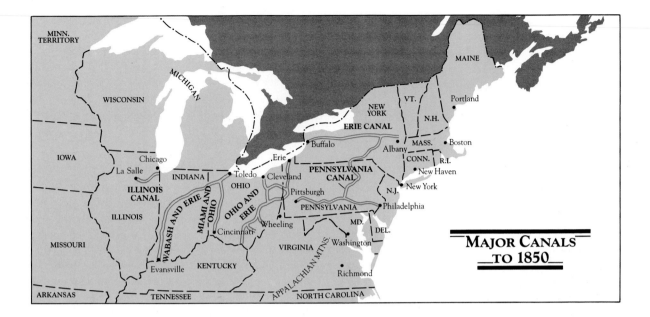

Major Canals to 1850

drawing boards when the bubble burst.) So many states came close to bankruptcy in their attempts to fund poorly advised projects with tax money that many politicians, including westerners, swore never again to finance internal improvements. As late as 1848, the new state of Wisconsin forbade in its constitution the expenditure of tax money on such ventures.

Railroads

The canal craze was also brought to an end by the appearance of an even better means of overland transportation, the railroad. As Pennsylvania's venture showed, canals were feasible only where the terrain was comparatively flat and a constant source of water was available. Even the best canals, like the Erie, were out of commission during the winter months, when they froze. The railroad, while never providing as cheap transportation as did the canal boats, could go anywhere faster and, barring exceptional blizzards, at any time of the year.

The first commercial lines in the United States were constructed in 1827, just two years after the first railroad in the world (in England) proved itself. One connected the granite quarries of Quincy, Massachusetts, with the Neponset River. The other carried coal from Carbondale, Pennsylvania, to the Lehigh River. Both were only a few miles long and served business enterprises exclusively, supplementing existing commercial routes and modes of transportation.

Some entrepreneurs immediately recognized that the railroad, like the Erie Canal, would be most valuable as

the "trunk" of a completely new transportation system, competing with old routes and even opening up new markets. In 1828, work began on the Baltimore and Ohio, which was designed to put Baltimore back into the race with New York City for the western trade. Construction repeatedly was stalled by financial difficulties, but, by 1853, the B & O was completed to Wheeling on the Ohio River. In the meantime, dozens of less ambitious projects were completed. By 1848, there were more than six thousand miles of railroad in the United States, more than double the total of tracks in all other countries combined.

The United States and particularly the West had found the key to the future. At the end of the War of 1812, it took more than seven weeks to ship a cargo from Cincinnati to New York (by keelboat, wagon, and river boat). In 1852, when the two cities were connected by rail, it took six to eight days.

The expense of constructing a railroad was immense. In addition to securing right of way and hiring armies of laborers, a railroad company had to buy its own rolling stock. (A canal or turnpike company simply collected tolls from users.) As a result, despite the total mileage of American railroads, few lines went very far. Indeed, competitive jealousies among the companies worked against a true system that connected distant points. Railway entrepreneurs built their short lines in different gauges (the distance between the tracks), so that the cars of competing lines could not run on connecting tracks.

The canals and railroads inclined to link the West with the Northeast. There remained, however the great natural north—south artery, the Mississippi River, which was not slighted during the revolution in transportation.

"Old Man River"

It could not have been otherwise. With its great tributaries, the Ohio and the Missouri, and dozens of smaller but navigable waterways, the Father of Waters tapped the central third of the continent. Westerners who lived on the Mississippi system could easily ship their corn or livestock to New Orleans on large log rafts that, broken up and sawed into lumber, were themselves a source of income.

The problem was the difficulty of bringing goods back upstream. Sailing ships could not do the job. Channels made narrow by sand bars and high riverbanks that stole the wind from their sails prevented such vessels from bucking the current much beyond New Orleans. Bringing a cargo upriver involved rowing or poling small skiffs a distance of thousands of miles. Or, tough keelboatmen, such as the Ohio River's legendary Mike Fink, literally pulled their vessels upstream by tying lines to trees, heaving from the deck of their boats, and then repeating the process.

It took about six weeks for a huge raft to float pleasantly downstream from Pittsburgh, where the Ohio River begins, to New Orleans. It took four to five months to bring a much smaller tonnage back. It was more expensive to ship a cargo of English cloth or furniture from New Orleans to Illinois than to sail it from England to New Orleans.

Steamboat A-Coming

The technical (and romantic) marvel that resolved this dilemma was the flat-bottomed steamboat. Unlike the cotton gin, which was invented by a single remarkable person in a few days, the steamboat was a long time coming. James Watt, the Scotsman who first harnessed steam power for the purpose of pumping water out of mines, regarded ships as the second most important application of his discovery. In 1787, a Connecticut Yankee named James Fitch succeeded in making a practical steamboat. During the summer of the Constitutional Convention in Philadelphia, with several

The voyage of Robert Fulton's steamboat, the Clermont, *from New York City to Albany proved that steamboats were well-suited to river travel.*

delegates witnessing the spectacle, he ran his forty-five-foot steamer down *and up* the Delaware River.

But Fitch was a crank, a demanding and difficult man to work with; those who might have put up with his temperament and financed his experiments, the great merchants of the eastern seaboard, were not interested. They still thought in terms of the sea and could not imagine how a steamship, which had to carry its own fuel, could be superior to a sleek sailing ship, which could be loaded entirely with salable merchandise.

Indeed, the age of sail was far from over. For more than a century after the perfection of the steamship, clipper ships and great steel-hulled windjammers dominated many world trade routes, especially the long ones around Cape Horn.

Clipper ships reigned on the ocean. Workable steamboats would rule on the rivers. Robert Fulton understood this. In 1807, his *Clermont* wheezed and chugged up the Hudson River from New York City to Albany at five miles per hour. The *Clermont* was three times as long as John Fitch's boat, but the dimension that thoughtful people noticed was that it drew only seven feet of water. The boat thus was able to clear obstacles that would have upended a sailing ship with a similar capacity.

The steamboat paid its way on eastern rivers like the Hudson. (Fulton's success helped to inspire the campaign to dig the Erie Canal.) But it was in the West that it found its natural home. In 1817, only ten years after the *Clermont's* maiden voyage, there were 17 steamboats on the Mississippi. By 1830, there were 187 of them, and new ones were constructed far more quickly than they blew up.

Boiler explosions were no small problem. In order to save weight, boilers were constructed more flimsily than they should have been, and Mississippi captains found it difficult to resist a race. Speed sold tickets and attracted shippers, so despite the opulence of some river boats, a trip on one was always a bit of a gamble.

Designers competed just as frantically to adapt boats to the western rivers. The greatest natural obstacles were the shifting sand bars of the Mississippi and "snags," whole fallen trees that were to the river what icebergs were to the North Atlantic, quiet predators capable of tearing a gaping hole in a wooden hull.

In 1841, the *Orphan Boy* was completed and eased on to the water. It could carry forty tons of freight plus passengers. But even when fully loaded, it skimmed through water only two feet deep! That was the ultimate, but a good many paddle-wheelers needed only three or four feet. Not only was this quality necessary to navigate the Father of Waters, but it enabled the boats to tie up at remote riverbanks in order to take on the cordwood they burned in prodigious quantities.

Westerners

The National Road, the Erie Canal, the railroads, and the river boats often carried people through country that was still wilderness. Sooner or later, however, travelers in the West came upon a sizable bustling city in which they could find most of the goods and services that they would expect to find in the East. As early as 1820, the Old Northwest was more urbanized than the Old South. The popular image of the Ohio and Mississippi Valley frontier as a land of snaggle-toothed frontiersmen in ragged buckskin shirts and coontail caps can distort the facts of pioneering experience.

Patterns of Settlement

Some areas were opened by families of this kind, who wrested a farm out of the wilderness on the power of muscle, blood, sweat, tears, and white whiskey.

The military was the cutting edge on some frontiers. Soldiers who were posted to keep an eye on Indians had to be fed, clothed, and entertained. Shopkeepers, saloon keepers, even prostitutes clustered around lonely military installations. The security of a fort encouraged trappers and hunters and others who tramped the unsettled land to gather there in winter and during times of Indian trouble. Their trade stimulated an urban business community before there was much tillage in the neighborhood. Detroit and the other French and English military installations that had been taken over by the United States developed in this way.

In other parts of the West, cities came first. Only after a fairly refined urban life had evolved did the

---

THE LONG RIFLE

The gun that won the trans-Appalachian West was the Kentucky long rifle. It had a forty-four-inch barrel and enough maple stock to make it the height of an average man. It weighed only about eight pounds, however, and was a muzzle loader. To load it, the butt was placed on the ground, a light charge of coarse black powder (measured by dead reckoning) was poured down the muzzle into the breech, and a ball wrapped in greased linen or leather patch was rammed home. (The patch was to seal the compression of the explosion and to ensure that the bullet "took" the rifling, the spiraling grooves that gave it spin and therefore accuracy.) Even in the most practiced hands, the long rifle fired only about three times in four. Our phrase "flash in the pan" came from the all-too-common phenomenon of a charge that flashed without sending the ball on its way.

Four engravings from O. Turner's History of the Holland Purchase *show how a New York farm is developed from wilderness over a forty-year period.*

engines in the whole of France, a major nation of 20 million people, while Kentucky could boast six steam mills that turned out cloth and even paper. Before the War of 1812, St. Louis had a steam mill that was six stories high. Like a medieval town determined to construct a cathedral higher than that in the next town, Cincinnati built a mill that was nine stories high. These cities were no mere clearings in the wilderness.

Speculation as a Way of Life

Such rapid development led to heated financial speculation. Many people went to Ohio or Michigan or Alabama neither to farm, run a shop, salt and pack pork in barrels, nor invest in a factory. They were the speculators who had some money and planned to grow rich by the timeless, if risky, game of buying land cheap and selling it dear. Although many were "sharpers," who were interested in nothing but lining their pockets and moving on to another likely spot, it was inevitable in a country where growth was a way of life that everyone who had some money to spare was attracted to the "inevitability" of rising values.

This made the price of the government's land (*all* western land, except for a few old French grants) a matter of considerable political interest. Under an ordinance of 1785, the federal government required buyers to purchase at least 640 acres at a minimum price of $1 an acre. Farmers protested that 640 acres was more than a typical family could work, and $640 was far more than ordinary people could raise in cash.

From the point of view of the Federalists, the farmers' criticisms were unimportant. The sale of western lands paid the government's bills. As always, Federalist policy was to favor speculators who could afford to buy

hinterland fill in with farmers to feed the bustling town. In such places, there never was a subsistence agriculture and a self-sufficient economy. The first farmers in such regions found a market ready made and a broad range of suppliers and services hungry for their business.

Places like Cincinnati, Louisville, Henry Clay's Lexington, and Andrew Jackson's Nashville were true, if small, cities before agriculture developed fully in the surrounding country. Occupying good locations for shippers to tie up their keelboats and rafts, these cities began as jumping-off points for emigrants. When the cotton states of the lower Mississippi Valley began to boom, sending out calls for provisions for their slaves, cities like Cincinnati responded with shipments of grain and livestock. Cincinnati, "the Queen City of the West," already was famous for its slaughterhouses and packing plants, yet ten miles away, the great hardwood forests blocked the sun from the earth and lonely hard-bitten men and women chewed on homemade pipes and fought against malnutrition and malaria.

Not far from this wilderness, steam engines were being manufactured—in Pittsburgh and Lexington, towns of five thousand and eight thousand, respectively. In 1815, there were no more than fifteen steam

land at the government's prices, and then sell sub-divided plots at a higher price per acre.

The Jeffersonian program was to serve the interests of "the cultivators" over those of the speculators. In 1804, after several modifications of the original law, the Jefferson administration allowed the purchase of tracts as small as 160 acres for a down payment as small as $80. The minimum price was now $2 an acre, so that a buyer on such terms owed the government $240, which was payable over four years.

This reform neither shut out the speculator nor satisfied the small western farmer. The credit provision actually worked to the advantage of speculators because they had no compunctions about borrowing heavily from banks and putting down the minimum payment on as much land as possible. The idea was to sell to a later comer before the second installment came due. Irresponsible "wildcat banks" in the West, fired up with dreams of quick profits, were more than willing to make such loans, churning out paper money to pay the government land office and counting on a rise in values. After the War of 1812, land sales soared. In 1815, the government sold about 1 million acres; in 1819, more than 5 million.

Moreover, much land went for higher than the minimum price. Before land was let go at $2 an acre, it was offered at auction. Settlers found themselves priced out of the market by speculators who did not care how much they spent, so sure were they that in a few months someone, maybe another speculator, would be willing to pay a higher price. Some government lands in the cotton belt sold for more than $100 an acre—on paper.

The Panic of 1819

The speculative boom in western lands depended, as does all speculation, on human dreams and gullibility. Some economists call it the "greater fool" principle: one person pays an irrationally high price for a commodity—stocks or gold or land—in the belief that there is a "greater fool" who will pay him even more. However, when there are no more buyers and a part of the fraternity of speculators decides that prices have hit the top and can only decline, there is a crash. Because the speculator deals in borrowed money, there is a "panic" to sell in order to pay off loans. Indeed, if the lenders are the first to decide that there is going to be a decline in values, they can start the panic by calling in their loans and thus forcing speculators to sell at whatever price they can get.

This is what happened in 1819. The Second Bank of the United States began to call in its loans to western banks. Having themselves lent out their slim resources to speculators, the wildcat banks called in their notes. When the speculators were unable to pay their debts because no "greater fool" would buy their land, the whole paper structure came tumbling down. The Bank of the United States lost money. The wildcat banks closed by dozens, leaving those who had deposited money in them flat broke. The speculators, rich as kings in acres, could not meet their installment payments, and the land reverted to government ownership.

Stunned by the Panic of 1819, Congress abolished credit purchases in 1820 and reduced the minimum tract for sale to eighty acres and the minimum price per acre to $1.25. With financial recovery, speculation resumed, but, in the meantime, western farmers had devised extralegal techniques to deal with it.

The key figure in this movement was the "squatter," the man and his family who began to develop a farm before they bought the land on which it was built. Such improved property was especially attractive to speculators, since its cabin and clearings increased its value. Frequently, a farmer saw his own home purchased at auction by a newcomer from the East who had no calluses on his hands but did have a wad of borrowed bank notes in his pocket.

In some areas, squatters combated these speculators by vigilante action. They banded together into "land clubs" and threatened physical reprisals on those who bid against them, not uncommonly making good on their talk. Such clashes have made for exciting books and films and, no doubt, saved many a family farm. It was inevitable, however, that highly political Americans should turn to government for a more dependable solution.

Old Bullion Benton

A westerner who was as well loved in his day as was Henry Clay arose to speak for the small farmers' cause. Thomas Hart Benton had gone to Missouri from North Carolina by way of Nashville. Like Clay, he was a boisterous, imperfectly polished character, but more a blusterer than a charmer. Short-tempered and eloquent, Benton was inclined to form an opinion and hold fast to it like a bulldog, which he slightly resembled.

After the Panic of 1819, Benton's strongest opinion was his hatred of banks and paper money. Having seen many people ruined by speculation based on paper money, he became the West's leading voice calling for hard money. Benton won the nickname "Old Bullion" because of his crusade on behalf of gold and silver

NOTABLE PEOPLE

THOMAS HART BENTON (1782–1858)

Thomas Hart Benton was a prime exemplar of that generation of Americans who went west not once but several times. Like the families of Jefferson Davis and of Abraham Lincoln, Benton made two major relocations before he was thirty years old.

Born in North Carolina in 1782, he crossed the Appalachians in 1801, settling in Tennessee, where he practiced law and served as a state senator. Benton was well-educated—with himself his teacher—in the classics, literature, and history as well as in the law. But he was also capable of throwing a punch, grappling with a rival, pulling a knife, or aiming a pistol. In 1813, he was involved in a scrape with fellow Tennessean Andrew Jackson and shot the future president, seriously wounding him in the arm.

Two years later, Benton crossed the Mississippi River into Missouri Territory, where he edited a newspaper in St. Louis and got back into politics. When Missouri applied for admission to the Union in 1820, Benton was one of those who insisted that it be admitted as a slave state. When his side prevailed, he was rewarded by election as one of Missouri's first two senators. He was reelected four times, serving until 1851.

In 1824, letting bygones be bygones, Benton became one of Andrew Jackson's strongest supporters. Despite Benton's efforts, Missouri voted for Henry Clay in that election; when Jackson took over the White House four years later, Benton served as his chief spokesman in the Senate. Throughout his career, he championed the cause of gold and silver coin over paper money and a federal land policy that favored settlers over speculators.

He generally favored expanding the territory of the United States. When his daughter, Jesse, on whom he doted, married John C. Frémont, Benton used his influence to get the young army officer commissioned to lead several exploration parties in the Far West.

In an age of political wits and eloquent orators, Benton gave ground to no one. He could bully his political

As a senator, Thomas Hart Benton promoted development of the West.

opponents, reminding them of his youthful reputation for rough-and-tumble. "Mr. President, sir," he said in the Senate, "I never quarrel, sir. But sometimes I fight, sir; and whenever I fight, sir, a funeral follows, sir."

In fact, Benton fought well enough with his tongue. On one occasion, Senator Henry S. Foote of Mississippi, who had a knack for setting himself up as a tar-

coin—bullion—as the common man's currency.

Elected one of Missouri's first senators in 1820, Benton also fought for a land policy that would shut out speculators. His pet project was *preemption,* or, as it was popularly called, "squatter's rights." Under this principle, the man who actually settled on and improved land before the government officially offered it for sale would be permitted to purchase it at the minimum price. He would not have to bid against speculators.

Another Benton program was graduation. Land that remained unsold after auction would be offered at one-half the government minimum, and after a passage of

time, at one-quarter. In other words, the price of the land would be graduated downward. Eventually, the land would be given away to settlers.

Benton's program was firmly within the Jeffersonian tradition. He argued that his policies would not only promote the development of the West, but also would get land on the tax rolls, thus making the western states less dependent on the federal government.

Like Henry Clay, however, whom he did not much like, Benton found that his program was intertwined with other national questions, such as the tariff and, in time, slavery. Just as they remained wary of expensive

get, said he planned to write a little book in which Benton would figure very prominently. Benton replied that he intended to write a big book in which Foote would not figure at all.

As he grew older, Benton changed his mind about slavery. He was not overly concerned about the morality of human bondage. He shared in the prejudice of most whites against blacks. But Benton came to believe that their ownership of slaves allowed the great planters of the South to dominate the small, self-supporting farmers who, as a good Jeffersonian, Benton believed were the "bone and sinew" of the republic. Moreover, he feared that the increasing arrogance and belligerence of slaveowners in defense of their institution threatened the dissolution of the Union that, as a good Jacksonian, Benton prized.

In 1848, disgusted by the introduction of the slavery question into every issue that came up in the Senate, Benton's eloquence again shone. He drew his imagery from the plagues visited on Egypt in the Old Testament:

You could not look upon the table but there were frogs. You could not sit down at the banquet table but there were frogs, you could not go to the bridal couch and lift the sheets but there were frogs! We can see nothing, touch nothing, have no measures proposed, without having this pestilence thrust before us.

Although there were few great planters in Missouri, it was nevertheless a slave state. In the crisis year of 1850, Benton lost his Senate seat. He won election to the House of Representatives in 1854, but was defeated two years later. Then he ran for governor, and again Missouri's voters rejected him. There was no place for a critic of slavery in a slave state during the years that the Union was splitting on the issue. Mercifully, Benton died in 1858, three years before the start of the Civil War that he feared.

But the demands of the West could not be ignored. Each census revealed that the balance of political power was shifting to the West as the trans-Appalachian population grew. In 1815, when Andrew Jackson was victorious at New Orleans, there were eighteen states, only four of which were beyond the Appalachian Ridge. In 1824, when Jackson had his name entered as a candidate for the presidency, there were twenty-four states, nine of which were in the West.

For Further Reading

Essential background for understanding the significance of every "West" in American history is F. J. Turner, *The Frontier in American History* (1920). Although many of Turner's main points have been corrected by later historians, no other historian or idea has had such an influence on writing about the American past. For a comprehensive study of the West written by a disciple of Turner, see Ray A. Billington, *America's Frontier Heritage* (1967).

Two more specifically focused studies of the West during this period are Dale Van Every, *The Final Challenge: The American Frontier, 1804–1845* (1964), and F. S. Philbrick, *The Rise of the West, 1754–1830* (1965).

R. M. Robbins, *Our Landed Heritage: The Public Domain* (1942), is the standard study of the national domain. P. W. Gates, *The Farmer's Age: Agriculture, 1815–1860* (1960), and G. R. Taylor, *The Transportation Revolution, 1815–1860* (1951), play a similar part for their respective subjects.

R. E. Shaw, *Erie Water West: A History of the Erie Canal, 1792–1854* (1966), and L. C. Hunter, *Steamboats on the Western Rivers* (1949), treat in detail two aspects of the revolution in transportation. Also see G. G. Van Deusen, *The Life of Henry Clay* (1937).

internal improvements, southern congressmen worried about Benton's plan to sell western lands cheaply. The less income that the federal government received from the sale of lands, the more dependent it would be on the tariff. The low tariff was the cornerstone of southern agrarian politics.

Northern congressmen, on the contrary, worried about the magnetic attraction of the West. If it was too easy for the people of the northeastern states to move west, the North would be left with a smaller population and, as a result, higher individual taxes and higher costs in the mills and factories.

15

The People and Their Hero

Andrew Jackson Ushers in a New Era, 1824–1830

The "era of good feelings" was bound to end. Senators and congressmen and other elected officials did not need more than one party in order to debate. In some ways, public discussion of issues was as candid and eloquent during the Monroe administration as ever before or since for the very reason that political leaders could take a position on an issue uncomplicated by concern for the party line.

A single party could not contain the personal ambitions of every prominent politician, however, particularly when capable and strong-willed men were as numerous as they were in the 1820s; there simply were not enough nominations to high office to go around. Nowhere was this more obvious than in the collapse of the caucus system, by which presidential and vice-presidential nominations were made, and in the abandonment of the unwritten law of presidential succession that the Jefferson Republicans had evolved.

Andrew Jackson's rise from humble roots and his military feats made him a popular hero.

The Fateful Election of 1824

Between 1800 and 1824, nominations for president and vice president were made by a caucus of the party's senators and congressmen. That is, they assembled as members of the Jefferson Republican party and decided by vote whom they would support in the election. Unsuccessful candidates accepted the proclamation of "King Caucus"; so did party members in the states.

Somewhat by accident, an unwritten rule of succession had emerged. After Jefferson served two terms (1801–09), he was succeeded by his Secretary of State, James Madison. After Madison served two terms (1809–17), he was succeeded by his Secretary of State, James Monroe. Heading the State Department became an informal apprenticeship for the presidency.

According to this rule, the Jefferson Republican caucus of 1824 should have selected Monroe's Secretary of State, John Quincy Adams. But many southern Republicans were suspicious of the New Englander because of his Federalist background. Moreover, both Monroe and old Jefferson himself, who was still interested in politics in his retirement, preferred the Secretary of the Treasury, William H. Crawford of Georgia. Crawford was more in line than Adams with the party's agrarian origins (favoring agricultural interests over commercial and industrial interests) and strict construction of the Constitution. And he was a southerner, Virginia born like four of the first five presidents. King Caucus nominated him.

Unhappily for Crawford, the age of Jefferson, the Virginia Dynasty, and King Caucus was drawing to a close. Too many of his colleagues and rivals had presidential ambitions of their own. Indeed, only Crawford supporters attended the caucus. Others returned to their states to make their nominations.

Too Many Candidates Spoil the Stew

For a while it appeared that Senator John C. Calhoun of South Carolina and Governor De Witt Clinton of New York would put their names in nomination. Both dropped out, however, when the field filled up with men who had larger followings.

One of these was John Quincy Adams. His supporters rallied around the tradition that the Secretary of State should step up to the presidency. They also liked Adams because of his assertive foreign policy, his support of a high tariff to protect young industries, and his belief that the federal government should take an active role in promoting economic prosperity, including the financing of internal improvements.

Adams's stand on improvements might have won him the votes of western states, except that the legislatures of Kentucky and Tennessee nominated their own favorite sons, Henry Clay and Andrew Jackson.

PRESIDENTIAL ELECTION OF 1824

CANDIDATE	POPULAR	ELECTORAL
JACKSON	153,544	99
ADAMS	108,740	84
CLAY	47,136	37
CRAWFORD	46,618	41

REMEMBERING 1824

Andrew Jackson never forgot his rejection by the House of Representatives in the presidential election of 1824. In his first address to Congress in 1829, he made harsh and unsubtle references to the "corrupt bargain" and proposed a constitutional amendment that would abolish the electoral college. The president would be chosen by majority electoral vote (each state would have the same weight as in the electoral-college system), and if no one in a race among three or more candidates won a majority, a runoff would be held between the two top vote getters. Jackson also proposed that the president be restricted to one term of office.

Congress did not act on his proposal. The electoral college still survives, and if no presidential candidate wins a majority in it, the House of Representatives still does the choosing, just as it did in 1824.

Clay's principles were much the same as those of Adams: nation above state and section, high tariff, federally financed internal improvements—the American System. Clay hoped for eastern votes, but his principal appeal was that he was a man of the growing, progressive West.

So was Andrew Jackson, however, and a military hero as well, the conqueror of the British and of the Indian tribes of the Southeast. His political views were something of a mystery. Indeed, it is easy to see in retrospect that Jackson's political principles were not well formed in 1824. He resembled Crawford in looking back wistfully to an agrarian past that had never quite existed. Jackson never had a real understanding of the needs of an industrial capitalist economy. He disliked banks and paper money, in part because he had been ruined by a financial panic during the 1790s, in part because, like many Americans, he did not believe that paper money issued by a bank was as valid as gold and silver. Like Thomas Hart Benton, Jackson was a hard-money man.

He was also a rich man, the wealthiest in the West at the time—a land speculator, a planter, and a slave-owner. In Tennessee politics, when there had been conflicts between the rich and the not so rich, Jackson always had lined up with his own kind.

And yet, even in 1824, he was spoken of as a hero of the common man. His great victory at New Orleans nine years before had electrified a demoralized country. In addition, Jackson was a symbol of the American quest for riches. He had settled in Tennessee as a poor man and had grown up with the country. No matter what his political ideas, Jackson was an embodiment of the American success story.

An Indecisive Tally

This sentimental appeal was enough to win "the Ginral" more popular and electoral votes than any of his three opponents, each of whom had clear-cut stands on the issues. But Jackson fell short of a majority in the electoral college. As in 1800, the House of Representatives, voting by state rather than by congressman, was given the responsibility of electing the next president.

Unlike in 1800, because of the Twelfth Amendment to the Constitution (1804), the House was required to choose from among the top three candidates. Clay, who was fourth, was disqualified. William Crawford also seemed to be out of the running. He had suffered a stroke that left him bedridden and unable to speak. His supporters insisted that he would recover, and, in time, he did. But they were unable to arouse any enthusiasm outside the southern states that he had carried in the general election.

Jackson's followers had a good argument. They insisted that the House ratify what a plurality of voters wanted, the general's election. But they did not have their way, either because of the impulsive decision of an elderly congressman from New York, Steven Van Rensselaer, or, more likely, because of the personal ambitions and political influence of Henry Clay.

Rensselaer, who cast the vote that threw the New York delegation and the election to John Quincy Adams, later said that while he was praying for guidance, he glanced at the floor, saw a piece of paper on which was written "Adams," and took it as a sign from on high. But Clay, the Speaker of the House, had decided long before that moment to throw his influence behind the New Englander. Not that they were friends. The strait-laced Adams did not approve of Clay's looser views on drinking, gambling, and womanizing. But their sense of nationalism and their economic policies were almost identical. Jackson, on the contrary, while vague on most issues, had gone on record as opposing one of Clay's pet projects, the congressionally chartered Bank of the United States.

Equally important, Jackson was Clay's greatest rival as the spokesman of the West, and the two men detested each other. Moreover, Clay sorely wanted to be president, and Jackson already was surrounded by would-be successors: the vice president under Adams, John C. Calhoun of South Carolina; John Eaton of Tennessee; and Richard M. Johnson of Clay's own Kentucky. There was no room in this crowd for Handsome Harry of the West.

Adams, however, was a cranky, solitary man who had few close friends. Because he had spent much of his life abroad, Adams was not surrounded by a circle of political associates to whom he owed anything. With him, Clay could hope to make an arrangement involving the next presidential election.

"Corrupt Bargain"

It is unlikely that there was a tit-for-tat understanding between Clay and Adams. Clay was certainly a man for a deal, but Adams disliked political manipulations with a righteousness that was self-destructive. Nevertheless, when Clay threw his influence in the House of Representatives to Adams and Adams later appointed Clay Secretary of State, the Jackson men were sure that they had been cheated by two cynical schemers.

John Randolph of Roanoke (a Crawford supporter) sneered at the union of "the puritan and the blackleg," an insult that led Clay to challenge him to a duel. (No one was hit.) The Jacksonians settled for shouting about the "corrupt bargain," obstructing the Adams presidency, and planning for revenge.

Between 1824 and 1828, they created a new political party, the Democratic-Republicans, which came to be called the Democrats. As an alliance, the organization consisted of Jackson's western following and southerners led by John C. Calhoun. The key to putting together a *national* majority, however, was in breaking the grip of the Adams and Clay forces in the populous Northeast. The way to accomplish this was offered by a young New Yorker, only forty-two years old in 1824, Martin Van Buren. He called on Jackson at his Tennessee home, the Hermitage, and offered his support.

The South, the West, and New York—this was the same combination that had allowed Jefferson and Aaron Burr to throw the first Adams out of office in 1800. The party's leaders came from the same generally privileged classes as did the Jeffersonians and the group around John Quincy Adams. But in the "corrupt bargain" controversy, the Jacksonians found themselves on the side of democracy. Enough of sinister elites deciding great questions behind closed doors, they cried, let the people rule! Let the common man have the president whom he chose in 1824!

John Quincy Adams was a well-qualified but unpopular president.

The Age of the Common Man

Like his father, John Quincy Adams brought impressive credentials to the White House. On paper, no one—surely not General Jackson—was better qualified for the job. While Jackson could claim to have been slashed in the face by a British officer at the age of fourteen (for refusing to shine the soldier's shoes), John Quincy Adams had been in high government service at that age, as secretary to the American ambassador in Russia. He had been a diplomat in several European countries. He also had been congressman, senator from Massachusetts, and a consistently successful Secretary of State.

Another Unhappy Adams

Also like his father, Adams's qualifications ended with the long list of his accomplishments. Temperamentally, he was out of tune with his times, unable to provide what Americans of the 1820s demanded in a leader. In an age of magnetic political personalities—of Clay and Jackson and Calhoun—no one loved John Quincy Adams. In an age that was beginning to prize equality and easy, informal society, Adams was standoffish, pompous, and sniffily self-conscious of his abilities, his learning, his ancestry, and his record, which he felt earned him the *right* to be president. He found it difficult to accept the point of view that high office should be awarded on any other basis; he never doubted

for a moment that he was the best that his generation had to offer.

Most damaging of all in an age when political horse-trading was rank, fast, and furious, John Quincy Adams tried to stand above partisan politics. He allowed avowed enemies to hold office under him. To have removed them and filled the posts with his supporters, he felt, would have been to stoop to the shabby party politics of which—unjustly in his opinion—he had been accused in the "corrupt bargain" controversy.

But Adams also was thin-skinned and short-tempered. He took every criticism and sometimes mere suggestions as unforgivable affronts to his office and his person. He cut himself off from possible allies who had honest, minor disagreements with him. By the end of his term, he had a smaller political base in Washington than had any previous president, including his unhappy father.

INTERVIEWING THE PRESIDENT

John Quincy Adams may have been aloof, but he certainly was not more distant from the people than are presidents of the late twentieth century. On the contrary, it was his custom to rise early, walk alone to the Potomac River, shed his clothes, and take a swim. A woman journalist, who had attempted for weeks to get an interview with the president, hit on the idea of following him on one of those expeditions. While he was in the water, she sat on his clothes and refused to budge until Adams answered all of her questions! He did, while treading water.

A Democratic Upheaval

If Adams's personality was unique, his attitudes did not differ appreciably from those of his five predecessors. Even the staunchest Jeffersonians, despite their democratic talk, had been self-conscious members of an elite of wealth, education, manners, and talent.

During the 1820s, however, it was outdated to think in terms of a "natural aristocracy" (or at least to speak of it in public). During the 1820s and 1830s, politics ceased to be the exclusive concern of the leisured classes and came to preoccupy much of the white male population. The foremost commentator on American attitudes, Alexis de Tocqueville, wrote that "almost the only pleasure which an American knows is to take part in government." A less sympathetic foreign visitor, Mrs. Frances Trollope, was appalled that American men would rather talk politics than mend their fences and tend their crops.

In part, this great outpouring was the natural fruit of half a century of democratic rhetoric. Whatever the Jeffersonians had thought, they had *said* that the people should rule, and the idea caught up with them.

The democratic upheaval was also the consequence of the extraordinary growth and energy of the young republic. An increasingly prosperous people needed to struggle less in order to survive and had more time to think about public affairs. With issues like the tariff, land policy, and internal improvements bearing heavily on individual fortunes, the people had good reason to do so.

Finally, the wave of democratic spirit that swept Andrew Jackson on its crest had some peculiarly western sources. In attempting to attract population, the young western states led the way in extending the vote to all free, adult white males and in enacting reforms that were popular among lower-class people. Kentucky, for example, abolished imprisonment for debt in 1821.

Democratization was an eastern and urban movement, too. Fearful of losing their population to the West, the eastern states quickly responded to the lib-

Stump speaking became popular in the nineteenth century as interest in politics spread among the public.

eral western voting laws by adopting universal manhood suffrage. In 1824, about half the states still insisted on some property qualifications in order to vote. By 1830, only North Carolina, Virginia, and Rhode Island retained such laws on their books, and Rhode Island's official conservatism on the matter was deceptive. Still governed under the state's seventeenth-century colonial charter, which could not be easily amended, Rhode Islanders finally erupted in an armed uprising in 1842, Dorr's Rebellion, which resulted in extending the vote to all adult white males.

In 1824, one-quarter of the states chose presidential electors in the state legislatures; the others chose electors by popular vote in one form or another. By 1832, only planter-dominated South Carolina still clung to the less democratic method. Moreover, given the right to vote, people did. In 1824, the first presidential election in which there was widespread participation, about one-quarter of the country's adult white males cast ballots. In 1828, one-half did. In 1840, more than three-quarters of the eligible voters participated in the national election.

The "Workies"

Some of these new voters built parties around social issues. During the 1820s, a number of workingmen's parties sprang up in the eastern cities. Called the "Workies" and supported largely by skilled artisans, these organizations pushed for a variety of reforms to protect mechanics, as all skilled craftsmen were called:

Nineteenth-century politicians rejected Frances Wright's demands for female equality.

the abolition of imprisonment for debt, which hit the independent artisan hard; mechanics' lien laws, which prevented creditors from seizing a worker's tools; and free public education for all children.

The workingmen's parties had their local victories, especially in New York. But they dwindled when visionaries, such as Scottish-born reformer Frances Wright, tried to convert them to their demands. Wright, for example, fought for female equality and—always a volatile issue in the nineteenth century—freedom of married persons to take sexual partners who were not their spouses, which became known as "free love." Mainstream politicians of every persuasion had little interest in modifying the legal status of women or in tampering with the sanctity of the home and family, institutions that they believed depended on the supremacy of the male head of household. Far more disastrous for the short-lived Workies was the fact that the Jacksonian Democratic party was friendly to their more moderate demands, and it possessed real power.

The Anti-Masons

A more curious expression of the democratic upheaval of the 1820s and 1830s was the Anti-Masonic party, which was born in upstate New York when a bricklayer from Batavia named William Morgan wrote an exposé of the Society of Freemasons. Morgan did not have so very much to say. Originally an association of freethinkers who were skeptical of revealed religion (many of the Founding Fathers, including George Washington, had been members), the Freemasons had become, like most fraternal organizations, a social club for well-to-do men.

Most of Morgan's revelations had to do with rituals, secret handshakes, and other hocus-pocus. For example, he quoted the order's initiation ceremony, in which a new member swore "to keep all Masonic secrets under the penalty of having his throat cut, his tongue torn out, and his body buried in the ocean," not exactly the sort of thing to take too seriously.

But some Masons took it very seriously, or so it seemed. Morgan disappeared, and, a short time later, a corpse that may have been mutilated according to regulations was dragged out of the Niagara River. The alleged murder inspired an extraordinary movement.

According to politicians who pointed out that Morgan was a bricklayer and that most Masons were prosperous farmers, merchants, bankers, and the like, the order was a conspiracy aimed at keeping the common man down.

Secrecy, they added, had no place in a free, open society. It was through their handshakes and other signs exposed by Morgan that Masons recognized one another, favored brother Masons in business to the disadvantage of truly free men, and schemed to control the economy and the government. Ironically, the Anti-Masons benefited from the traditional views about the sanctity of the family that militated against the Workies. That is, by maintaining that some secrets must be shared only with brother Masons, the order was insinuating itself between the special relation that bound husband and wife. If a husband were required to keep secrets from his own spouse, he was violating the marriage contract as surely as would Fanny Wright's "free love."

The Anti-Masonic movement spread, especially in the Northeast. A brace of leaders who would later play an important part in national politics came to the fore as Anti-Masons. Among them were Thaddeus Stevens, Thurlow Weed, William H. Seward, and Millard Fillmore. In 1832, the party's candidate for president, William Wirt, won thirty-three thousand votes and carried the state of Vermont. In the same year, the party elected fifty-three men to Congress.

Because Jackson was a Mason, and the ruling party in New York State was headed by Jackson's chief political strategist, Martin Van Buren, the Anti-Masons were hostile to the Democrats; most of them remained in opposition when their party faded.

The Paranoid Streak

The Anti-Masons provide an example of the streak of paranoia that is periodically important in American politics. While the Society of Freemasons was not blameless of everything of which it was accused, and Masonic true believers very likely did murder Morgan, it was far from being the dangerous, virtually diabolic force that the Anti-Masons depicted.

From time to time in American political history, movements based on a hysterical fear of conspiracy win large numbers of voters. During the 1790s, many New Englanders sincerely believed that Thomas Jefferson was an agent of French radicalism and that he would introduce a reign of terror in the United States. Following quickly on the Anti-Masonic furor, many Americans came to fear that the pope was scheming to subvert the republic through Roman Catholic immigrants.

Some Populists of the late nineteenth century drifted here and there into anti-Semitism. In the twentieth century, the paranoid streak has taken the form of irrational anti-Communism, not open opposition to Communist ideology and practice, but the conviction that spies and subversives are slowly taking over the nation. The common denominator in all these phenomena is the belief in a conspiracy that is designed to subvert democratic institutions.

A rather more positive contribution of the Anti-Masonic party was the national party convention. It held the first in 1831. With the caucus system already dead, the major parties adopted the convention procedure as the method for selecting presidential candidates.

Like the workingmen's parties, however, the Anti-Masonic party was short lived. The principal beneficiary of the upheaval in democratic sentiments was the Democratic-Republican party, which formed around the person of Andrew Jackson. Between 1824 and 1828, Jackson's supporters perfected a nationwide organization whose sole purpose was to win the presidential election. Their work paid off. In a two-man race with John Quincy Adams (whose supporters, not nearly so well organized, called themselves National-Republicans), Jackson swept to victory with 56 percent of a total vote that was more than three times as large as the vote in 1824.

The Revolution of 1828

Thomas Jefferson had called the election of 1800 the "Revolution of 1800." But in 1800, there had been not nearly so great a break with what had gone before as there was in Andrew Jackson's victory in 1828. His

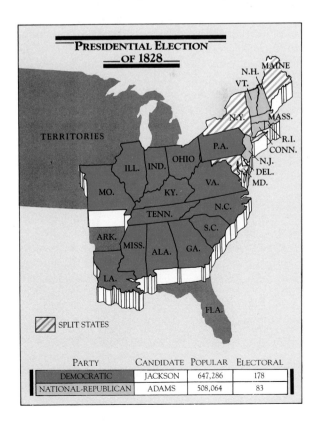

PRESIDENTIAL ELECTION OF 1828

SPLIT STATES

PARTY	CANDIDATE	POPULAR	ELECTORAL
DEMOCRATIC	JACKSON	647,286	178
NATIONAL-REPUBLICAN	ADAMS	508,064	83

election ended the era of sedate transfers of power from incumbent president to Secretary of State. Jackson was the first chief executive to come from a western state. Indeed, he was the first president who was not from Virginia or Massachusetts. And the campaign that led to his election was noisier, harder fought, and "dirtier" than any the United States or, indeed, any nation ever had experienced.

Slinging Mud

Jackson himself followed precedent by taking no part in the campaign. He sat in his Tennessee mansion while his supporters fired searing personal salvos at President Adams. They depicted the incumbent as a usurper, an elitist, a man with effete European tastes who squandered money by filling the White House with elegant furniture and its cellar with European wines. The Democrats made a great fuss over Adams's purchase of a billiard table—billiards was then a game for aristocrats—although Adams had paid for his toy out of his own pocket.

Alarmed by the popularity of these attacks, the Adams men replied in kind. Jackson was a savage, a murderer. The National-Republicans reminded voters that Jackson had hanged two British subjects in Spanish Florida in 1818 (conveniently forgetting that Adams had supported him after the fact). They printed broadsides that listed the men whom Jackson had killed in duels and the soldiers whom he had ordered shot during military campaigns.

The assault that stung Jackson most was the claim that he and his beloved wife were adulterers. Years before, they had married before Rachel Jackson's divorce was final, thus requiring them to go through a

The "Coffin Handbill," published by pro-Adams forces, presented Andrew Jackson's war deeds and duels as evidence of his barbarism.

mortifying second ceremony, and they may have lived together before the first wedding. Such laxity in marriage customs was not rare on the frontier. Whatever her attitudes as a young woman, Rachel Jackson had become a prim and proper old lady by 1828, and she was tortured by the ugly gossip. When his wife died shortly after the election, Jackson blamed Adams and his supporters for his deeply felt loss.

In response, Jackson's party gave as viciously as it took. The Democrats dug up an old tale that, as ambassador to Russia, Adams had procured the sexual services of a young American girl for the dissolute czar. (Not likely.) There were whispers of bizarre perversions in the Adams household. (Less likely yet.) Mudslinging had come to American politics with a vengeance. Everything was fair game for discussion—except public issues.

The Symbol of His Age

On Inauguration Day 1829, ten thousand people crowded the streets of Washington. They shocked genteel society with their drinking, coarse shouting, and boisterous invasion of the White House. Invited there by the new president, the mob muddied the carpets, broke crystal stemware, and stood on expensive upholstered sofas and chairs in order to catch a glimpse of their gaunt, white-haired hero.

Adoring as it was, the mob was so unruly that Jackson's friends feared that he might be injured. They spirited him away through a low window, and he spent his first night in office at a hotel. Back at the executive mansion, worried servants lured the crowd outside to the broad lawn by setting up bowls of lemonade and whiskey punch and tables heaped with food.

The man whom these people worshiped was by no sensible definition a common man. Jackson's talents were exceptional, and his will and integrity extraordinary. Nor was he the vicious desperado whom the Adams forces depicted. Jackson was a gracious, courtly gentleman whose public manners, as more than one person announced with an air of surprise, were the equal of royalty's.

It was also said of Jackson, however, that he was entirely comfortable sitting on a stump and conversing with the most rugged, plain-spoken and poor men of the frontier. If he had become wealthy and ready to defend to the death every last cent and slave's straw hat that he owned, he never forgot his humble origins. Jackson was the first of the log-cabin presidents, the first to reap the rewards of his countrymen's respect for self-made men.

Jackson believed that his success was due to the openness of American society. All people were not

A huge crowd turned out for Andrew Jackson's inauguration in 1829, as represented in Robert Cruikshank's lithograph, The President's Levee, or All Creation Going to the White House.

equally talented, in his view, but the good, free society provided everyone an equal opportunity to demonstrate his abilities. It was the task of government to preserve this opportunity by striking down artificial obstacles to improvement, such as the laws that benefited some while handicapping others.

Jackson's view of government was essentially negative. He was a laissez-faire man. He believed that government should leave people, society, and the economy alone so that natural social and economic laws could operate freely.

Attitudes of a Popular Hero

Jackson's vision of equal opportunity extended to only white males. But in this, as in his attitudes toward others—women, children, blacks, and Indians—he also represented the dominant opinion of his era.

Jackson believed that women lived in a different "sphere" from males. While their menfolk struggled in an often brutal world, women guarded home and hearth. They were superior to men in religious sense

and morality; indeed, it was because of these faculties that they had to be sheltered. Jackson and most Americans, including women, agreed with the clergyman who preached the "Gospel of Pure Womanhood." Woman's "chastity is her tower of strength, her modesty and gentleness are her charm, and her ability to meet the high claims of her family and dependents the noblest power she can exhibit to the world."

The reward for playing this private, inactive role in life was the right to be treated with deference, and Jackson was famous for his chivalry. Rough as the old soldier's life had been, he was properly prudish in mixed company. Even in the absence of the ladies, he referred to them as "the fair." Adding the word *sex* would have violated his sense of delicacy.

Toward children, visitors were amazed to discover, Jackson was indulgent. The man who had aroused armies to bloodlust and had slaughtered hundreds without wincing, and the man who as president periodically exploded in frightening rages, beamed quietly as young children virtually destroyed rooms in the White House before his very eyes. The British ambassador wrote that he could not hear the president's conversation because the two men were surrounded by screaming children. Jackson smiled absent-mindedly and nodded all the while. At the table, the president fed children first, saying that they had the best appetites and the least patience.

Such indulgence was not universal in the United States. Many New Englanders tried to raise children strictly by the Puritan book. But Europeans commented in horror that American children generally had the manners of "wild Indians." Some also noticed that American children were more self-reliant than European children because of the freedom that was allowed them. It was this quality—"standing on your own two feet"—that Jackson and his countrymen valued in their heirs.

Democracy and Race

Toward the real Indians and toward blacks, Jackson also shared the prejudices of his age. Blacks were doomed to be subject to whites by Bible or Mother Nature or both. Blacks *were* slaves. As a southerner, Jackson did not think much, if at all, about equal rights.

As a westerner, Jackson thought a great deal about Indians. He spent much of his life fighting them and taking their land. More than any single person, he was responsible for crushing the military power of the great southeastern tribes—the Creeks, Choctaws, Cherokees, Chickasaws, and Seminoles. Although in these wars he was ruthless and brutal, Jackson was not the simple "Indian-hater" whom enemies like Clay portrayed. He found much to admire in Native Americans, their closeness to nature and their courage in resisting their conquerors. There was an unmistakable tinge of tragic regret in his statement to Congress that the white and red races could not live side by side and, therefore, the Indians would simply die out.

Government by Party

Attitudes are not policies, but President Jackson lost no time in establishing the latter. He was the first president to represent a political party frankly and without apologies. As soon as he took office, he made it clear that he would replace those federal officeholders who had opposed him with his own supporters. One of Jackson's men, William Marcy of New York, phrased the practice of rewarding supporters as "to the victor belong the spoils. . . ."

There were about twenty thousand federal jobs in 1829, and Jackson eventually dismissed about one-fifth

of those who held them, not really a clean sweep. His view of the "spoils system" was not so cynical as Marcy's. When critics claimed that the men who were best qualified by education and training should be appointed to government jobs, Jackson replied that no one had a right to an appointment. A government job was not the property of an individual, but of all the people. Therefore, they should be designed so that *any* intelligent man could perform them.

The debate over the "spoils system" was noisy but brief. John Quincy Adams, who never dismissed anyone, privately admitted that many of the people whom Jackson fired were incompetent. When the anti-Jackson forces finally came to power in 1840, they carved up the spoils far more lustily than had Jackson.

Momentous Issues of the Jackson Years

The partisan spirit also informed Jackson's approach to the great political issues of the day. He did not have particularly strong opinions on the questions of the tariff and of internal improvements when he became president. In his first address to Congress, he called for a protective tariff, but he later leaned (again without passion) to the southern position of a tariff for revenue only.

Internal Improvements

As a westerner, Jackson understood the need for good roads and other internal improvements. But, as an advocate of laissez faire and of strict construction of the Constitution, he worried that it was not constitutional for the federal government to finance them. When, in 1830, he vetoed a bill to construct a road between Maysville and Lexington, Kentucky, he told Congress that if the Constitution was amended to authorize such projects, he would approve them.

In the Maysville Road veto, Jackson seems to have been as interested in taking a slap at Henry Clay as in protecting constitutional niceties. The projected road would have been completely within Clay's home state of Kentucky, adding immeasurably to Clay's popularity. Later, Jackson quietly approved other internal-improvement bills when the expenditures promised to win votes for his own party.

On the rising constitutional issue of the day, the division of power between the federal government and the states (which was so touchy that even the Founding Fathers had skirted it with generalities), Jackson was inconsistent, again according to how his personal and party interests were involved. When the issue was

Georgia's attempt to ignore the federally guaranteed rights of Indians, Jackson allowed the state to have its way. But when South Carolina attempted to defy his presidential power, he moved quickly and decisively to crush the challenge—coming close to pulling his old uniform and sword out of the closet and personally leading an army south.

Indian Removal

The rapid settlement of the trans-Appalachian West once again brought whites into close contact with large Indian tribes. Congress and Presidents Monroe and Adams agreed that this situation was unworkable. They advocated a policy of "Indian removal," the relocation of all tribes to an Indian Territory west of the Mississippi River that would be guaranteed to them "forever."

To implement this policy, the terms of old treaties had to be changed. The original agreements had given the Indians land east of the Mississippi "as long as the water runs and the grass grows." Given the choice of accepting the new rules or fighting a losing battle, most tribes agreed. Others rebelled. The Sac and the Fox of Illinois and Wisconsin rose up under Chief Black Hawk, but were defeated. The Seminoles of Florida,

allied with a large number of runaway slaves, also fought back. They were never defeated, but escaped into the swamplands, from where, between 1835 and 1842, they fought an effective holding action against the army.

Still other tribes, such as the Choctaws of the Old Southwest, were defrauded. Federal officials bribed some chiefs to sign removal treaties that were then applied to the entire people. But it was another of the "civilized tribes," the Cherokees, that seemed to win their fight to remain in their ancestral homeland.

Like the Creeks, Choctaws, and Chickasaws, the Cherokees had adopted white culture. They gave up their seminomadic hunting and gathering economy and developed intensive agriculture, raising crops for sale as well as for use. They kept black slaves, lived in houses, operated a school system (one of the better ones in the South), and printed newspapers and books in their own language. (A Cherokee-white silversmith named Sequoyah had developed an eighty-six-character alphabet that was formally adopted in 1821.) Ironically, they were good Jacksonians in everything but their color.

According to their treaty with the United States government, the Cherokees were entitled to remain where they were. They were recognized as a semi-

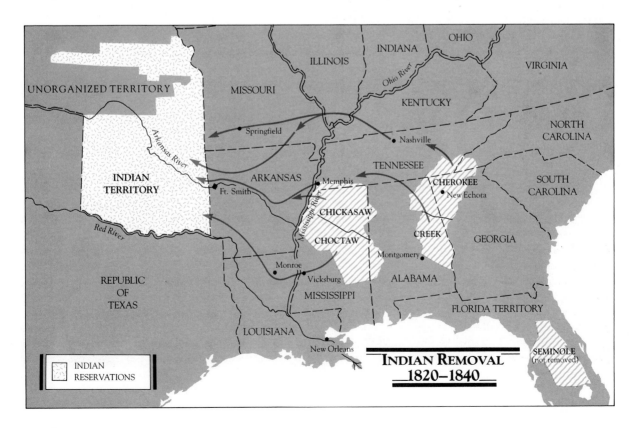

INDIAN RESERVATIONS

INDIAN REMOVAL 1820–1840

sovereign "nation" within the United States. Therefore, they refused every attempt of the federal government to alter their treaty.

The state of Georgia was determined to have Cherokee lands and convicted a white missionary for a "crime" committed in Cherokee territory according to Georgia law. The legal issue of *Worcester* v. *Georgia*, which came before the Supreme Court in 1832, was Georgia's right to ignore a federal treaty.

Chief Justice John Marshall had no more confidence in the ability of whites and Indians to live side by side than did Andrew Jackson. He had waffled on an earlier dispute between the Cherokees and Georgia. But Marshall was a staunch defender of the sanctity of a contract, which is precisely what the treaty with the Cherokees was. He ruled that the state of Georgia had no authority over the Cherokee territory, threw out the state's conviction of Worcester, and made it clear that Georgia could not force the Cherokees to give up their land.

That seemed to settle the matter, and the Cherokee nation celebrated. But Georgia gambled. The state had

The journey of Cherokee and other southeastern Indian tribes to Oklahoma is portrayed in Robert Lindneux's Trail of Tears.

voted for Jackson in 1828, and the president was a lifelong Indian fighter. Georgia defied the Supreme Court, held on to its prisoner, engineered some fraudulent agreements with renegade Cherokees, and began the forcible removal of the tribe.

Georgia won the bet. "John Marshall has made his decision," Jackson said. "Let him enforce it." Thus began the Trail of Tears, the twelve-hundred-mile trek of the Cherokees and other southeastern tribes to what is now Oklahoma. The thousands of deaths from hunger, disease, and exposure left some tribes permanently scarred and demoralized. For others, such as the Cherokees, it would take two or even three generations to recover. They would never forget the betrayal both of themselves and of its own constitutional principles by the white nation that had robbed them of their homeland.

Nullification

If Georgia succeeded in defying the federal government, neighboring South Carolina did not. The issue that brought Jackson into conflict with the Palmetto State and his own vice president, John C. Calhoun, was the tariff.

In 1828, Congress passed an extremely high protective tariff, which no one completely liked, but which a majority accepted and the president signed. While most southern planters hated this "Tariff of Abominations," South Carolina's cotton planters were enraged. They believed that their snowy crop was paying the whole country's bills and underwriting industrial investment.

They had a point. Cotton accounted for fully half of the wealth that poured into the United States from abroad. This income was diverted in part to the North by the tariff that required everyone, including southern cotton planters, to pay higher prices for manufactured goods. South Carolina's problem was political. The will of the majority of Americans (as voted in Congress) was that the national wealth should be employed to promote industrial development. The free traders, who wanted cheap prices and had no interest in an industrial future, were in the minority.

Despairing of altering this political situation, South Carolina's leading politician, John C. Calhoun, looked to the Constitution for an escape. In 1829, while serving as Jackson's vice president, he secretly penned *The South Carolina Exposition and Protest*, a logically brilliant and politically mischievous interpretation of the Constitution.

The *Exposition* took up where Jefferson's and Madison's Virginia and Kentucky Resolutions had left off.

Following Jefferson and Madison, Calhoun claimed that the Union had not been formed by the people of America as a whole, but by the people acting *through* the individual states of which they were citizens. The states were sovereign, not the federal government. That is, the states were the fundamental, indivisible units of government, and the Union was merely a compact, a kind of alliance for mutual benefit.

When this "alliance" passed a law to which a state objected, as South Carolina objected to the Tariff of Abominations, that state had the right to nullify that law (say that it would not be enforced) within its borders until such time as two-thirds of the other states overruled its decision. Calhoun was here referring to the amendment process of the Constitution, which requires the ratification of two-thirds of the states.

In such an event, Calhoun concluded, the nullifying state could choose between capitulation to the decision of the other states or secession from the Union.

Nullification in Practice

Jefferson and Madison had allowed their theory to remain a theory. When they had written the Virginia and Kentucky Resolutions they had had hopes of winning control of the federal government, which they did, and they subsequently lost interest in their abstract doctrine of state sovereignty.

Calhoun and South Carolina had their own hopes that the Tariff of Abominations would be repealed in 1829. Andrew Jackson was now president. However, in 1832, Congress adopted another high protective tariff, which had all the earmarks of permanence, and Jackson signed it into law. The great planters of the Palmetto State blew up, and elected a convention that declared the law "null and void" in their state.

Jackson said privately that South Carolinians could do whatever they chose on paper, but if they refused to comply with the tariff, he personally would lead an army into the state. Congress responded to his request for authority to do so with a "force bill."

The crisis was averted because, while several southern states disliked the tariff as much as South Carolina did, they would not support the doctrine of nullification. Standing alone, John C. Calhoun met with Henry Clay, "The Great Compromiser," to work out a tariff low enough that South Carolina could save face. In 1833, the state rescinded its nullification of the tariff. But two cries of defiance remained: South Carolina did not repudiate the principle of nullification, and the convention of 1832 nullified the force bill.

Jackson let it ride. He had had his way, and he had identified a new enemy—his own vice president.

DUELING AND BRAWLING THE AMERICAN WAY

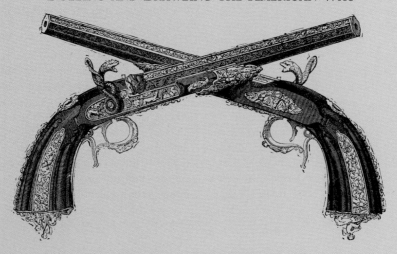

As these silver-inlaid pistols suggest, dueling was a sport of gentlemen.

The duel—a prearranged fight with deadly weapons between gentlemen—originated in the medieval practice of the Wager of Battle. A form of ordeal, the Wager pitted a person accused of a crime against his accuser. If the accused won, he was declared innocent.

Although condemned by religious leaders, the Wager of Battle survived in France until the 1500s, when it was abolished and effectively wiped out. However, the duel rose in fashion to take its place. A duel was not concerned with guilt or innocence of a crime; it had no standing in the law. The issue in dueling was a gentleman's honor. A man who thought himself or a woman under his protection insulted challenged the defamer to meet on the field of honor. It was not necessary to fight to the death, as it had been in the Wager. Merely following the intricate code of manners that governed dueling established one's honor. A majority of duels ended when blood was drawn or, if by pistols, when each party discharged his weapon in the general direction of the other. The point was good manners. Only gentlemen dueled. The vulgar multitude brawled.

Colonial Americans did not duel. Careful scholars have found records of only a dozen such fights between 1607 and 1776. Then, during the Revolutionary War, French officers such as Lafayette, Rochambeau, and de Grasse introduced the Code Duello to their American friends. A decade later, when French aristocrats fled the revolution in their country and settled in Louisiana, they made New Orleans the dueling capital of America. (On one Sunday in 1839, ten duels were fought in the Crescent City. A woman wrote that the young men of society kept score of their duels, as a young lady kept score of proposals of marriage.)

Dueling spread as rapidly as sudden wealth created self-made men (particularly southerners) who were in a hurry to prove their gentility. Librarian of Congress Daniel Boorstin has written that "of southern statesmen who rose to prominence after 1790, hardly one can be mentioned who was not involved in a duel."

It is only a slight exaggeration. Button Gwinnet, signer of the Declaration of Independence from Georgia, was killed in a duel in 1777. James Madison fought a duel in 1797. Maryland-born Commodore Stephen Decatur fought one duel in 1801 and was killed in another in 1820. William H. Crawford, Secretary of the Treasury under Monroe and presidental candidate in 1824, fought a duel. John Randolph of Roanoke fought two, the second in 1826 with Henry Clay of Kentucky, who also fought other men. Hero of the common man Senator Thomas Hart Benton of Missouri fought a number of duels and killed at least one of his opponents. Sam Houston of Texas fought a duel. A great many southerners who were prominent in the Confederacy were involved in duels; among them were William L. Yancey, Vice President Alexander H. Stephens, and General John C. Breckinridge. Confederate president Jefferson Davis was challenged to a duel by Judah P. Benjamin, who later became a fast friend and served in three cabinet positions. Romantic legend has it that duels were fought over ladies. In fact, as implied in this list, most of them were fought over politics.

The most famous American duelist was Andrew Jackson, seventh president of the United States, who did fight over insults to his wife. Some of his enemies said that Jackson was involved in a hundred duels. That is unlikely. Even Old Hickory was not so tough or so lucky as to survive that many confrontations.

However, the written terms of one of Jackson's duels have survived. In 1806, Jackson faced Charles Dickinson, a Nashville lawyer:

It is agreed that the distance shall be 24 feet, the parties to stand facing each other, with their pistols drawn perpendicularly. When they are ready the single word fire to be given at which they are to fire as soon as they please. Should either fire before the word is given, we [the seconds of both parties] pledge ourselves to shoot him down instantly. The person to give the word to be determined by lot, as also the choice of position.

Neither Dickinson nor Jackson fired before the word was given, but Dickinson fired first, gravely wounding but not felling Jackson. "Back to the mark, sir," Jackson said when Dickinson staggered in fear of what was to come. Then, according to Jackson's enemies, Jackson's pistol misfired, and in violation of the Code Duello, he pulled the hammer back and fired again. This breach of honor haunted Jackson for the rest of his life, for Dickinson died from the dubious shot.

Perhaps it was because of this slur on his character that when a man whom Jackson considered no gentleman challenged him some years later, Jackson refused to duel. But he offered to shoot it out in some "sequestered grove" as long as both parties understood that it was not an affair between social equals.

Actually, according to *The Code of Honor, or Rules . . . . in Dueling,* written by a governor of South Carolina, a gentleman who had been insulted by a social inferior was to cane him. But Jackson's action points up the fact that in the West, dueling merged undetectably into plain brawling. An Alabama law of 1837 that outlawed dueling also forbade the carrying of the decidedly ungentlemanly weapons "known as Bowie knives or Arkansas Tooth-picks." The people who carried bowie knives were not likely to have read the "Twenty-eight Commandments of the Duel."

Of course, dueling was by no means an exclusively southern and western practice. Alexander Hamilton and Aaron Burr were not southerners. Benedict Arnold was from Connecticut; De Witt Clinton, from New York; and Nathaniel Greene, from Rhode Island—they all fought duels. Moreover, the practice was just as illegal in the South as it was in the North. Killing a person in a duel was murder, punishable by death. South Carolina imposed a fine of $2,000 and a year in prison for seconds as well as duelists. Officeholders in Alabama were required to take an oath that they never had dueled or acted as seconds.

But Daniel Boorstin is certainly correct to say that the prevalence of dueling in the South up to the Civil War reflected the peculiar, tragic, and fatal propensity of upper-class southerners to regard the unwritten laws of honor, manliness, decency, and courage as more important than the laws of legislatures.

For Further Reading

The age of Jackson is one of the most controversial subjects in the study of American history. Disputes rage over both the personality of Old Hickory and the meaning of "Jacksonian Democracy." On Jackson's luckless predecessor, see S. F. Bemis, *John Quincy Adams and the Union* (1956).

Sympathetic to Jackson are Marquis James, *Andrew Jackson, Vol. 2: Portrait of a President* (1937), and, a briefer book, Robert V. Remini, *Andrew Jackson* (1966). Also see Remini, *The Election of Andrew Jackson* (1963), for the election that brought him into power.

Hostile to Jackson are J. C. Curtis, *Andrew Jackson and the Search for Vindication* (1976), and Edward Pessen, *Jacksonian America* (1978). A fascinating, if not altogether convincing, psychohistory of Jackson is M. P. Rogin, *Fathers and Children: Andrew Jackson and the Destruction of American Indians* (1975). Any standard history of Indians in North America will deal in detail with the policy of removal. A good special study is Angie Debo, *The Road to Disappearance: A History of the Creek Indians* (1941).

On the meaning of Jacksonian Democracy in general, the following books offer starkly contradictory interpretations: A. M. Schlesinger, Jr., *The Age of Jackson* (1945); J. W. Ward, *Andrew Jackson: Symbol for an Age* (1955); Marvin Meyers, *The Jacksonian Persuasion* (1957); Bray Hammond, *Bank and Politics in America from the Revolution to the Civil War* (1957).

16

Personalities and Politics
The Age of Jackson in Full Flower, 1830–1842

When Andrew Jackson became president in 1829, few of the people who knew him expected that he would serve for more than one term—if he lived to finish that. To his supporters around the country, Jackson might have been Old Hickory—a tough and timeless frontiersman who stood as straight as a long rifle. In truth, he was a frail, sixty-two-year-old wisp of a man who often looked to be a day away from death.

Over 6 feet tall, Jackson weighed only 145 pounds. No other president was as frequently ill as he was. Jackson suffered from lead poisoning (the consequence of two bullets that he carried in his body), headaches, diarrhea, coughing fits, kidney disease, and edema (a painful swelling of the legs). During his White House years, he suffered two serious hemorrhages of the lungs.

An election day as depicted in 1851 in George Caleb Bingham's painting The County Election.

The Contest to Succeed Jackson

Jackson's choice of a vice president, therefore, was a matter of some political importance. In giving his approval to John C. Calhoun, Jackson was not simply pocketing South Carolina's electoral votes. He was naming his successor as president and leader of the Democratic party.

John C. Calhoun

In terms of concentrated intelligence and Jacksonian will power, he could scarcely have chosen better. Of Scotch-Irish descent, as was the president, Calhoun was possessed of the keen, logical mind that the impulsive and emotional Jackson lacked. He was a humorless man. Portrait painters depicted him with a piercing, burning gaze just an eyelash short of open rage, never with the slightest hint of a smile, never in a posture that would indicate that Calhoun knew even odd moments of peace of mind.

By 1828, in fact, Calhoun was the captive of an obsession. He feared that the basic social institutions of

John C. Calhoun, Andrew Jackson's first vice president, as photographed by Mathew Brady.

South Carolina and much of the South—black slavery and the plantation aristocracy that owed its eminence and privileges to slavery—were mortally threatened by northern industrial interests and an increasingly powerful national government.

As a young man, ironically, Calhoun had been both a nationalist and an exponent of industrialization, urging South Carolinians to build steam-powered cotton mills in the midst of their cotton fields. But when the South did not industrialize and the North did, thenceforth demanding a high protective tariff that would raise the prices of the goods that southern agriculturalists had to purchase, Calhoun changed his mind. He became one of the most eloquent defenders of the plantation system, including slavery. Jackson did not necessarily disagree with Calhoun's social sentiments. But the president was wedded to the idea of a supreme national government, and Calhoun had defended state sovereignty in *The South Carolina Exposition and Protest.*

This document, with its doctrine of nullification, would have been quite enough to anger Jackson. As it was, at about the same time that Jackson learned that his own vice president was the author of the *Exposition,* a tempest on the Washington social scene further alienated the two men. Few incidents better illustrate how the direction of history can turn on trivial incidents than the Peggy Eaton affair.

Floride Calhoun and Peggy Eaton

Peggy O'Neill, the winsome daughter of a Washington hotelkeeper, was the wife of a sailor who, as seamen are inclined, was rarely at home. In her husband's absence, Peggy found company in the person of one of her father's boarders, Tennessee congressman John Eaton, who fathered several of her children. Eaton was a Jackson supporter, and, in 1829, the new president named him Secretary of War.

Eaton's affair made for a tasty scandal, but his behavior was by no means unheard-of in the capital. Washington was no longer the largely male city that it had been when it was first constructed and there were no living quarters for families. But many congressmen continued to leave their wives at home, and some consorted with ladies of shady reputation. It had been hot rumor that President Jefferson himself kept a black mistress, and Henry Clay was said to be a satyr. Richard M. Johnson, vice president between 1837 and 1841, lived openly with a black woman who was also his slave.

Johnson did not introduce his mistress into Washington high society. But Eaton did exactly that when Peggy's husband died at sea and he married her.

Peggy Eaton is introduced to President Jackson and his cabinet in this 1836 caricature entitled The Celestial Cabinet. *The "Eaton Affair" rocked the Jackson administration and caused a split between Jackson and Vice President Calhoun.*

A great fuss ensued. Irregular affairs were one thing. It was quite another to expect women who were faithful to the gospel of chaste true womanhood to mix socially with a fallen sister. Peggy O'Neill Eaton was roundly and brusquely snubbed.

The leader of the snubbers appeared to be Floride Calhoun, as sternly moralistic a Presbyterian as her husband. The wives of the other cabinet members followed her example, and Jackson steamed. When his own niece, who served as his official hostess, refused to receive Peggy Eaton, Jackson told her to move out of the White House. Still mourning the death of his wife, which he blamed on scandalmongers, Jackson also was charmed by the vivacious Peggy. He summoned a cabinet meeting on the subject (as he hardly ever did on political and economic issues), and pronounced her "as chaste as a virgin." He told his advisers to command their wives to receive her socially.

This was too big an order. If they were excluded from politics and the professions, women wrote and enforced the rules of morality and social life. While the president raged, Peggy Eaton continued to stand alone at social functions. Almost alone. Secretary of State Martin Van Buren, who as a widower, had no wife to placate,

dared to be seen speaking with Peggy and fetching her refreshments.

The Rise of the Sly Fox

Van Buren was an old hand at charm and chitchat. His worst enemies conceded that he was gracious and witty. But he was much more than a social lion. Van Buren was the shrewdest and most successful political organizer of his time. Indeed, his shrewdness earned him the nickname Sly Fox of Kinderhook (his New York hometown). He owed his position in Jackson's cabinet to his having delivered the votes of New York in 1828, and no other individual was more important than he in constructing the Democratic machine—ensuring votes in the future by rewarding those who delivered them with government jobs. Van Buren's sensitivity to the feelings of Peggy Eaton may have been quite sincere. It was also calculated to win Jackson's favor and thus further his own career.

Van Buren admired the president, and he understood his crotchets better than any other member of the administration. He knew that Jackson was a creature of impulse who, once having made up his mind, never looked back. Van Buren did not always agree with Jackson's decisions. But he knew when to keep his mouth shut and when the president was open to suggestion.

When hard feelings over the Eaton affair threatened to paralyze the administration, it was Van Buren who showed Jackson the way out. He would resign as Secretary of State, and Eaton would give up his post as Secretary of War. The other members of the cabinet, whose wives were causing the president so much anxiety, would have no choice but to follow their example. Jackson would be rid of the lot, without having offended any particular wing of the Democratic party.

Jackson appreciated both the strategy and Van Buren's willingness to sacrifice his own position in order to help him. He rewarded Van Buren by naming him ambassador to England.

Calhoun Seals His Doom

The Sly Fox of Kinderhook was lucky, too. He was helped in his ascent by Calhoun's own blunders. While the Eaton affair was still rankling him, the president discovered in some old cabinet reports that, ten years before, Secretary of War Calhoun had favored punishing General Jackson for his unauthorized invasion of Florida. Confronted with the evidence, Calhoun tried to lie his way out of his fix, but the president cut him off by writing, "Understanding you now, no further communication with you on this subject is necessary."

Nor, it turned out, was there much further communication between Jackson and his vice president on any subject. In April 1830, Jackson and Calhoun attended a formal dinner during which more than twenty of Calhoun's cronies offered toasts in favor of states' rights and nullification. When it was the president's turn to lift a glass, he rose, stared at Calhoun, and toasted, "Our Union: It must be preserved." Calhoun got the last word. He replied, "The Union, next to our liberty, the most dear." But Jackson took satisfaction from the fact that, as he told the story, Calhoun was trembling as he spoke.

The old duelist delighted in such confrontations. Van Buren took pleasure in his wiles and good luck. He was in England during the nastiest period of the split between Jackson and Calhoun, when even the Sly Fox might easily have made a slip.

Then Calhoun, whose political sense was no match for his intelligence, guaranteed that Van Buren would succeed Jackson. Seeking revenge, Calhoun cast the deciding vote in the Senate's refusal to confirm Van Buren's diplomatic appointment. This brought the New Yorker back to the United States, but hardly in disgrace. Completely in Jackson's good graces by

this time, Van Buren was named vice-presidential candidate in the election of 1832, an assignment he would not likely have received had Calhoun left him in London.

The War with the Bank

Unlike his campaign in 1828, Jackson's bid for reelection in 1832 was fought over a real issue—the future of the Bank of the United States, or, as it was commonly known, the B.U.S. The Bank had been chartered in 1816 for a term of twenty years. After a shaky start, it fell under the control of Nicholas Biddle, a courtly Philadelphian who administered its affairs cautiously, conservatively, and profitably.

The Powers of the Bank

And, so it seemed, to the benefit of the federal government and the national economy. The B.U.S. acted as the government's financial agent, providing vaults for its gold and silver, paying its bills out of its accounts, investing deposits, and selling national bonds (borrowing money for the government when it was needed).

Every cent that the government collected in taxes and from the sale of land flowed into the B.U.S. It was a large and fabulously rich institution; its twenty-nine strategically located branches controlled about one-third of all bank deposits in the United States and did some $70 million in transactions each year.

With wealth and size came power over the nation's money supply and, therefore, its economy. In a foolish but revealing moment, Nicholas Biddle told congressmen that the B.U.S. was capable of destroying any other bank in the country.

What he meant was that at any moment the B.U.S. was likely to have in its possession more paper money issued by a state bank than that state bank had specie (gold and silver) in its vaults. If the B.U.S. were to present these bills for redemption in specie, the issuing bank would be bankrupt and the savings and investments in it wiped out.

On a day he was more tactful, Biddle said that his bank exercised "a mild and gentle but efficient control" over the economy. That is, because the state banks were aware of the power that the B.U.S. held over them, they maintained larger reserves of gold and silver than they might otherwise have done, considering the possibility of reaping large profits from speculation. Rather than ruining banks, the B.U.S. ensured that they acted conservatively.

GENERAL JACKSON SLAYING THE MANY HEADED MONSTER.

This 1836 cartoon shows Andrew Jackson attacking the "many-headed monster," the second Bank of the United States.

Biddle was as proud of the public service he rendered as of the Bank's annual profits. Nevertheless, the fact remained that the Bank was powerful because of its control of the people's money, but its policies remained in the hands of individuals who were responsible not to the people, as were elected officials, but to shareholders.

This was enough in itself to earn Jackson's suspicions, and he resisted Biddle's attempts to make a friend of him. Biddle lent money to several of Jackson's supporters, and he designed a plan to retire the national debt—a goal dear to Jackson's heart—by timing the final installments to coincide with the anniversary of the Battle of New Orleans. But Jackson shook his head and explained to Biddle that it was not a matter of disliking the B.U.S. more than he disliked other banks;

Jackson did not trust any of them. Faced with such hostility in the White House, Biddle turned to Congress for support.

The Enemies of the Bank

Biddle needed friends. The Bank had many enemies who, except for their opposition, had little else in common.

First there was the growing financial community of New York City—the bankers and brokers who became known collectively as "Wall Street." Grown wealthy from the Erie Canal and from New York's sudden surge as the nation's leading port, they resented the Philadelphia financier's continuing control of the ultimate money power.

251

Second, the freewheeling bankers of the West disliked Biddle's restraints on them. Caught up in the optimism of the growing region, these bankers wanted a free hand to take advantage of soaring land values.

Ironically, the third group that hated the Bank was even more conservative in money matters than was Biddle. Hard-money people like Jackson distrusted all banks and opposed the very idea of an institution that issued paper money in quantities greater than it had gold and silver on hand. Eastern workingmen had had good reason to support the hard-money position. They were often paid in bank notes that proved to be worth less than their face value because of irresponsible banking practices. Before the Bank war, the B.U.S. was not guilty of such practices. Nevertheless, the working-class wing of the Democratic party, called "Locofocos" in New York, lumped Biddle along with the rest and inveighed against his monopolistic powers.

Biddle and Clay Fire the First Shot

Jackson did not start the Bank war. Henry Clay and a somewhat reluctant Nicholas Biddle did. In January 1832, Henry Clay was nominated for the presidency by his and John Quincy Adams's supporters, who still called themselves National-Republicans. Clay persuaded Biddle to apply for a new Bank charter, although the present one would not expire until 1836. Clay had the votes to ensure that Congress approved the charter because some Democrats (including some Calhoun supporters) would vote for it. Jackson was put on the spot. If he signed the bill for fear of losing the election, all well and good; the Bank was one of the foundation stones of Clay's American System. If he vetoed the bill, Clay would run against him on that issue and, because the Bank had proved its worth, defeat him.

Jackson did veto the bill, and Clay did run on the issue. But he did not win the election. However irreconcilable the various anti-Bank forces, Jackson was once again the man in tune with the popular spirit. He won 55 percent of the popular vote and 219 electoral votes to Clay's 49. (Anti-Masonic candidate William Wirt won 7 electoral votes, and South Carolina gave its 11 votes to John Floyd.)

In September 1833, for the first time, Jackson took the offensive. He ceased to deposit government monies in the Bank, putting them instead into what were called his "pet banks." The Bank of the United States, however, continued to pay the government's bills out of its accounts. As a result, government deposits sank from $10 million to $4 million within three months. Biddle had no choice but to reduce the scope of his

LOCOFOCOS

Members of the Democratic party who strongly opposed special privilege and were hostile to banks were called Locofocos. They got their unusual name in New York City in 1835, when conservative Democrats tried to drive them out of a meeting by turning off the gas lights. The rebels relit the lamps with self-igniting matches, which at that time were called locofocos (from the words *locomotive* and the Italian *fuoco*, or "self-moving fire"). Adopted by both the Locofocos and those who opposed them, the name stuck.

operations and begin to call in debts that were owed the Bank by state institutions. The result was a wave of bank failures that wiped out the savings of thousands of people, just what Jackson had feared Biddle's actions would lead to.

Under pressure from the business community, Biddle relented and increased the supply of money, thus feeding a new speculative boom. To Jackson's chagrin, many of the eighty-nine state banks to which he had entrusted the federal Treasury proved to be irresponsible in using it. They, too, fed the speculation.

Then, in 1836, Henry Clay made his contribution to what would be the most serious depression since the time of Jefferson's embargo. He convinced Congress to pass a distribution bill under the terms of which $37 million was distributed to the states for expenditure on internal improvements. Presented with this windfall, the states spent freely. Values in land, both in the undeveloped West and in eastern cities, soared. Federal land sales rose to $25 million in 1836. Seeking to get a share of the freely circulating cash, new banks were chartered at a dizzying rate. There had been 330 state banks in 1830; there were almost 800 in 1837.

There was no Bank of the United States to cool things down gradually. Alarmed by this activity, Jackson did the only thing within his power. He slammed a lid on the sale of federal lands, which was the most important commodity in the boom. In July 1836, he issued the Specie Circular, which required that government lands be paid for in gold and silver coin; paper money was no longer acceptable.

Jackson's action slowed down runaway speculation, but with a foot on the brakes rather than the tug on the reins that the B.U.S. might have used. Western speculators who were unable to pay their debts to the government went bankrupt. Moreover, gold and silver were drained from the East, which contributed to a panic and depression there too.

By the time the economy hit bottom, however, Jackson had returned to Tennessee. Seventy years old now, the man who many thought would be lucky to live through one term, "an easy and dignified retirement" of a presidency, had cut and chopped his way through eight pivotal years in the history of the nation.

The Giant of His Age

Indeed, though aching and coughing, Jackson would live for nine more years, observing from his mansion home an era that unfolded in his shadow. He was the symbol of a democratic upheaval that changed the character of American politics. He presided over a time of ferment in nearly every facet of American life. He set a pattern of presidential behavior. He took the initiative in making policy. He used the veto more often than had all his six predecessors put together.

Jackson also impressed his personality on a political party and on an era that would end only when the slavery issue tore it and the whole country apart. Even the party that his enemies formed during his second term was held together, to a large extent, by hostility toward him and his memory. And his political foes managed to succeed only when they followed his example.

Jackson was not a wise man. His intelligence was

Andrew Jackson became a symbol of a democratic upheaval that changed the character of American politics.

limited; his education, spotty. He was easily ruled by his passions. He confused his interests with those of his country. But the majority of his countrymen saw nothing wrong in this, since Jackson seemed to be the embodiment of the aspirations of his age.

Whigs and Democrats

By 1834, the realignment of politics that had been forced by Jackson's triumph was complete. In the congressional elections that year, the old National-Republicans joined with former Jackson supporters who objected to one or another of the president's actions—his promiscuous use of the veto, his high-handed treatment of the Indians, his blow against South Carolina, his war against the Bank—and called themselves the Whigs.

They were a mixed lot. In addition to the National-Republicans, the Whig party (particularly in the North) included most men of education and some means; supporters of Henry Clay's American System who believed that the federal government should take a hand in shaping economic development; southern high-tariff advocates, such as Louisiana sugar planters and Charleston financiers; and (nominally) strict states'-rights advocates like John Tyler of Virginia and, for a short time, even the great nullifier, John C. Calhoun.

During the 1830s, Anti-Masons drifted into the Whig party. New Englanders, suspicious as ever of any movement like the Democratic party that was attractive to southerners, inclined to Whiggery. So did those few blacks who were permitted to vote, and the upper and middle classes of city and town who found Democratic vulgarity offensive to the old ideals. In 1834, this patchwork alliance was enough to win ninety-eight seats in the House of Representatives and almost half the Senate, twenty-five seats to the Democrats' twenty-seven.

"The Godlike Daniel"

Except for Henry Clay, the greatest of the Whigs was Daniel Webster of Massachusetts. Until the end of his life, he was idolized as a demigod, particularly in New England. It was more for his presence and his peerless oratorical powers than for anything for which Webster stood. With a great face that glowered darkly when he spoke, and eyes that burned like "anthracite furnaces," Webster was, according to one admirer, "a living lie because no man on earth could be so great as he looked."

Daniel Webster was idolized for his presence and his peerless oratorical powers.

One of his looks, it was said, was enough to win most debates. Admirers described him as "a steam engine in trousers" and "a small cathedral in himself." A cathedral dedicated to nationalism, for it was on the majesty of the federal government as a moral force that Webster spoke his greatest words.

In 1830, Webster replied to a Calhoun supporter, Robert Hayne of South Carolina, who identified the doctrine of nullification with liberty. He declared that, on the contrary, the Constitution was the wellspring of American liberty, and the indissoluble union of the states was its greatest defense. "It is, Sir, the people's Constitution, the people's government, made for the people, made by the people, and answerable to the people." Knowing well to end a speech with an easily remembered slogan, Webster coined one of the classics: "Liberty and Union, now and for ever, one and inseparable." The speech turned a political abstraction (the Union) into an object for which some people would be willing to die. (It also provided three generations of schoolchildren with a memorization piece.)

Webster was capable of hard work; he was an able administrator and an excellent diplomat. But Webster had his problems. Of humble origin, he took too zestfully to the good life of the eminent man. He dressed grandly, loved good food, and sought the company of the wealthy. He was an alcoholic. He invested his money as foolishly as he spent it and was constantly in debt. This tied him closely to the New England indus-

trialists who regularly sent him money. During the Bank war, Webster indirectly threatened to end his services as legal counsel to the Bank unless Nicholas Biddle paid him off. (Biddle did.) He came to expect money in the mail after every speech on behalf of the tariff or even the ideal of the Union. As a result, while Webster remained popular in New England, his corrupt practices provided an easy target for the Democrats and made him an object of suspicion among fellow Whigs who took personal integrity as seriously as they took public virtue.

The Election of 1836

Differences within the Whig party prevented its convention of 1836 from agreeing on a platform. The party could not even agree on a single candidate to oppose Martin Van Buren. Instead, the convention tried to throw the election into the House of Representatives, as had happened in 1824. The Whigs named three candidates to run against Van Buren in those parts of the country where they were most popular. Webster ran in lower New England. Hugh Lawson White of Tennessee was the candidate in the South. In the Northwest and upper New England, the Whigs' man was William Henry Harrison, the hero of the Battle of Tippecanoe. Although the battle was now a quarter of a century in the past, the party hoped that the memory was still strong among a people ever hungry for new lands.

This peculiar strategy failed. While all three Whigs (and cantankerous South Carolina's candidate, Willie P. Mangum) won some electoral votes, Van Buren carried states in every section and a comfortable 170 to

---

CHEWING TOBACCO

Chewing tobacco was a widespread custom in the early nineteenth century. It was practiced by poor farmers and, it seems, senators and congressmen too. These remarks, both by British visitors, indicate the disgust with which at least they (and probably other foreigners) viewed the habit.

Harriet Martineau: "If the floors of boarding houses and the decks of steamboats, and the carpets of the Capitol, do not sicken the Americans into a reform; if the warnings of physicians are of no avail, what remains to be said?"

Charles Dickens: "I was surprised to observe that even steady old chewers of great experience are not always good marksmen, which has rather inclined me to doubt that general proficiency with the rifle, of which we have heard so much in England."

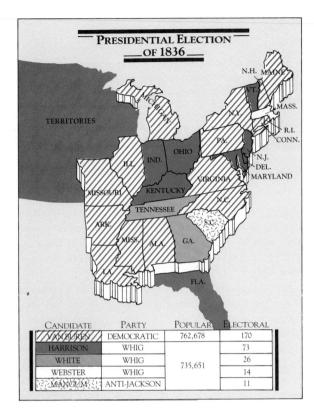

PRESIDENTIAL ELECTION OF 1836

CANDIDATE	PARTY	POPULAR	ELECTORAL
VAN BUREN	DEMOCRATIC	762,678	170
HARRISON	WHIG		73
WHITE	WHIG	735,651	26
WEBSTER	WHIG		14
MANGUM	ANTI-JACKSON		11

124 majority in the electoral college. The Whigs held their own in Congress, still the minority but, with South Carolina unpredictable, in a strategic position.

Panic and Depression

Election to the presidency was just about the last good thing that happened to Martin Van Buren. When his administration was just a few months old, the country reaped the whirlwind of wild speculation and Jackson's Specie Circular. Drained of their gold and silver, several big New York banks announced in May that they would no longer redeem their notes in specie. Speculators and honest workingmen found themselves holding paper money that even its issuers would not accept as valid.

After a brief recovery in 1838, the country plummeted into depression. In 1841 alone, twenty-eight thousand people declared bankruptcy. Factories closed because their products did not sell. Several cities were unsettled by riots of unemployed workers. Eight western state governments defaulted on their debts.

Van Buren tried to meet the fiscal part of the crisis. A good Jacksonian, he attempted to "divorce" the government from the banks (which he blamed for the disaster). He established the subtreasury system, by which, in effect, the government would keep its funds

in its own vaults. The Clay and Webster Whigs replied that what was needed was an infusion of money into the economy, not a withdrawal. But they could not carry the issue.

Van Buren also maintained the Jacksonian faith in laissez faire by refusing to take any measures to alleviate popular suffering. The Founding Fathers, he said (in fact voicing Jackson's sentiments), had "wisely judged that the less government interfered with private pursuits the better for the general prosperity."

Whatever the virtues of Van Buren's position and the convictions of most Americans on the question of government intervention in the economy, it is difficult for any administration to survive a depression. The man in the White House gets blamed. By early 1840, the Whigs were sure that hard times would give their candidate the White House.

"Tippecanoe and Tyler Too"

But who was to be the candidate? In that year of likely victory, Henry Clay believed that he deserved the nomination. For twenty-five years, through the American System, he had offered a coherent national eco-

Martin Van Buren faced four opponents in his 1836 bid for the presidency.

nomic policy that was, in effect, the Whig platform. For half that time he had led the fight against the Jacksonians. More than any other man, he had founded the Whig party. Never once had he failed to stand up to King Andrew and Van Buren.

Clay's great strength was also his great weakness. In taking strong stands on so many issues for more than a quarter of a century, Clay inevitably had made enemies. Victory-hungry young Whigs like Thurlow Weed of New York thought it better to choose a candidate who had no political record, but who, like Jackson in 1824, could run for office as a symbol. Taking a leaf from Van Buren's political book, Weed said that the object of politics was neither to honor heroes nor further ideas nor cling to abstract principle; it was to win elections.

Weed's candidate was William Henry Harrison, a western war-horse like Jackson. Descended from an old Virginia family—his father had signed the Declaration of Independence—Harrison had run stronger than any other Whig in the peculiar election of 1836. Identified with the West, he would undercut the popularity of the Jacksonians there on the basis of his residence alone. With New England already firm in the Whig column, the vice president should be a man from the South. The party chose John Tyler of Virginia.

At first the Whigs planned to campaign simply by talking about Harrison's military record. But then a Democratic newspaper editor made a slip that opened up a whole new world in American politics. Trying to argue that Harrison was incompetent, he sneered that the old man would be happy with an annual pension of $2,000, a jug of hard cider, and a bench on which to sit and doze at the door of his log cabin.

Such snobbery toward simple tastes and the humble life were ill suited to a party that had come to power as the mouthpiece of the common man. The Whigs, who had suffered Democratic taunts that *they* were the elitists, charged into the breach. They hauled out miniature log cabins at city rallies and at country bonfires. They bought and tapped thousands of barrels of hard cider. They sang raucous songs like

> Farewell, dear Van,
> You're not our man,
> To guide our ship,
> We'll try old Tip.

Stealing another leaf from the Jacksonian campaign book of 1828, the Whigs depicted Van Buren as an effeminate fop who sipped champagne, ate fancy French food, perfumed his whiskers, and flounced about in silks and satins.

It was all nonsense. Harrison lived in no log cabin but in a large and comfortable mansion. He was no

A WHIG MARCHING SONG

Let Van from his coolers of silver drink wine,
*   And lounge on his cushioned settee;*
Our man on his buckeye bench can recline,
*   Content with hard cider is he.*
Then a shout from each freeman—a shout from each State,
*   To the plain, honest husbandman true,*
And this to be our motto—the motto of Fate—
*   "Hurrah for Old Tippecanoe!"*

simple country bumpkin but something of a pedant. Van Buren, while quite the dandy, was also an earthy man who held much more democratic ideas than did old Tip and who was closely tied to the Locofocos of New York.

But it worked. Although Van Buren won 47 percent of the popular vote, he was trounced in the electoral college by a vote of 60 to 234. Jacksonian chickens had come home to roost. Rarely again would a presidential election be contested without great fussing about irrelevancies and at least an attempt to avoid concrete issues. Moreover, with their successful appeal to the sentiments of the "common man," the Whigs of 1840 demonstrated that the democratic upheaval of the pre-

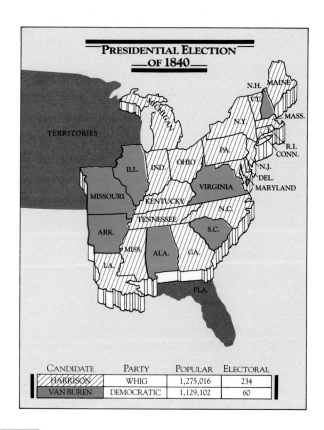

CANDIDATE	PARTY	POPULAR	ELECTORAL
HARRISON	WHIG	1,275,016	234
VAN BUREN	DEMOCRATIC	1,129,102	60

This 1840 campaign banner shows William Henry Harrison walking from a humble log cabin to greet a wounded soldier. In fact, Harrison lived in a fine house, but chose to present himself to voters as a simple man.

ceding two decades was complete. Never again would there be political profit in appealing to the superior qualifications of "the better sort" in the egalitarian United States.

Fate's Cruel Joke

However William Henry Harrison felt about specific issues, he agreed with one of the few principles that held the Whig party together—that Congress should make the laws and the president execute them. He apparently was willing to defer to the party professionals, including Clay. He did annoy Webster by rejecting an inaugural address that the great orator wrote for him, delivering instead a turgid treatise on Roman history that still stands as the longest inauguration speech ever given. But he also named Webster to be his Secretary of State, and the position was still considered a stepping stone to the White House.

Clay did not want a post in the administration. With large Whig majorities in both houses of Congress, he preferred to stay in the Senate. But he was pleased

GOING TO COLLEGE

Mary Lyon founded Mount Holyoke College as the first women's college in the United States in 1837.

A student of today would have difficulty recognizing the colleges of the early nineteenth century. Indeed, a student's life during the Jacksonian era more closely resembled college life in the Middle Ages than in the late twentieth century.

For example, all but a few colleges and universities were private institutions; as late as 1860, only 17 of the 246 colleges and universities in the United States were state institutions. Rather, most were maintained by one or another Protestant denomination in order to train ministers and to indoctrinate other young men in their principles, and they were funded by student tuition and by the subsidies that were granted by their affiliated churches. This was particularly true of the colleges that were founded during the Jacksonian era, many of which were inspired by the evangelical commitment to reform society.

Colleges were all-male institutions. Higher education was still regarded as the final polishing of a cultivated man, the foundation for public life and for the practice of the professions, particularly the ministry. Women, whose social role most people perceived as domestic and private, had no need for formal learning.

This attitude was beginning to change, however. In 1833, Ohio's Oberlin College, a hotbed of reformism, began to admit women students. A few colleges and universities followed suit, but the real expansion of educational opportunities for women came not with coeducation but with all-female institutions. The first of these was Mount Holyoke College in South Hadley, Massachusetts, founded by Mary Lyon in 1837.

College was not vocationally oriented, as it is today. That is, students were not taught the specific skills involved in the career they had selected. The young man who wanted to become an accountant, an engineer, an architect, or a businessman in the early nineteenth century apprenticed himself to someone skilled in those callings and learned "on the job." Although some universities had established medical and law schools, apprenticeship was also the most common means of preparing for those professions.

At college the curriculum remained much as it had been for centuries, a strictly prescribed course of study in the liberal arts and sciences (*liberal* in this case meaning "suitable to a free man"). Students learned the ancient languages (Latin, Greek, sometimes Hebrew), literature, natural science, mathematics, and political and moral philosophy—according to the beliefs of the church that supported the institution. Some colleges had added modern languages and history by the Jacksonian period, but there were no "electives"; every student took the same courses.

The colleges were small. Except for the very oldest, such as Harvard and Yale universities, and for some public institutions, such as Thomas Jefferson's University of Virginia, the typical student body numbered only a few dozen and the typical faculty perhaps three or four professors and an equal number of tutors. While faculty members and students came to know one another by sight and name, relations between them were not informal and chummy. On the contrary, professors erected a high wall of formality and ritual between themselves and those whom they taught, both out of the belief in the principle of hierarchy and out of the fear that too much friendliness would lead to a breakdown in discipline. Historian Joseph F. Kett has pointed out that stiff-necked behavior by instructors often owed to the fact that many of them were little older and sometimes even younger than most of their students. For example, Joseph Caldwell became *president* of the University of North Carolina when he was only twenty-four years old.

Student behavior was regulated by long lists of detailed rules. Students were expected to toe the line not only in class but also in their private lives. Attendance at religious services was mandatory at most private institutions. Strict curfews determined when students living in dormitories turned out their lamps. Even impoliteness might be punished by a fine or suspension. Students were expected to be deferential at all times.

This was the theory, at any rate. In practice, college students were at least as rambunctious as students of every era and more rebellious than any, save the generation of the 1960s. They defied their professors by day—the distinguished political philosopher Francis Lieber had to tackle students he wanted to discipline—and they taunted them by night. A favorite prank was stealing into the college chapel and ringing the college bell until dawn. They threw snowballs and rocks through the windows of their tutors' quarters. They led the president's horse to the roof of three- and four-story buildings. Students at Dickinson College in Pennsylvania sent a note to authorities at Staunton, Virginia, where the college president was visiting, informing them that an escaped lunatic headed their way would probably claim to be a college president and should be returned under guard.

Other student actions were rebellions and not just pranks. Professors were attacked by mobs angry at strict rules or poor food. Professors sometimes were stoned, horsewhipped, and fired on with shotguns. At the University of Virginia in 1840, Professor Nathaniel Davis was murdered. Writing to his own son at college in 1843, Princeton professor Samuel Miller warned against so much as sympathizing with potential rebels. Miller lived in fear of student uprisings, perhaps because one rebellion at Princeton was so serious that the faculty had to call in club-wielding townspeople to help put it down.

Why so much discontent? One reason is that the rules of college life had been written at a time when most college students were fourteen to eighteen years old, while, by the early nineteenth century, college students were often in their mid-twenties. Adults simply were not inclined to conform to behavior appropriate to adolescents, and in a society that took pride in individual freedom, they were quite capable of reacting violently to constraint.

Moreover, many college students lived not in dormitories but in their own lodgings in nearby towns. They fraternized largely with other students and developed a kind of defiant camaraderie directed against all outsiders. Enjoying broad freedoms in their off-campus lives, they were unlikely to conform to strict rules of behavior when they were at the college.

Finally, while the rules were strict, enforcement was often inconsistent. "There were too many colleges," writes Joseph F. Kett, "and they needed students more than students needed them." Faculty members who were nervous for their jobs would overlook minor offenses until they led to greater ones, at which point, suddenly, they drew the line. Inconsistency, as ever, led to contempt for would-be authority.

Colleges might expel or suspend the entire student body for "great rebellion." However, financial pressures apparently resulted in their readmission for the price of a written apology. Samuel Miller described student rebels as "unworthy, profligate, degraded, and miserable villains," but if they had the tuition, there was always a place for them somewhere.

when Harrison dutifully named four of his supporters to his cabinet. At last, Henry Clay could smell real power.

Then, before the celebrations had quite died down, the unthinkable happened. Harrison died. The old soldier caught a cold on a wet and windy Inauguration Day, grappled with it for several weeks while receiving Whig office seekers as greedy as the Democrats of 1828, and then took to his bed with pneumonia. On April 4, 1841, exactly one month after lecturing the country on republican virtue, he passed away.

John Tyler

At first the Whigs did not miss a stride. Clay lectured "Tyler Too" that he should consider himself an acting president, presiding over the formalities of government while a committee of Whigs chaired by Clay made the real decisions. Tyler would have none of it. A nondescript man who had little imagination and a provincial view of national problems, Tyler did know his Constitution. It provided that he exercise the same full presidential powers that he would have had if elected to the office.

John Tyler became president when Harrison died shortly after taking office.

POPULATION OF TEN LARGEST AMERICAN CITIES—1840	
New York	349,000
Philadelphia	258,000
New Orleans	102,000
Baltimore	102,000
Boston	93,000
Cincinnati	46,000
Albany	34,000
Charleston	29,000
Washington	23,000
Providence	23,000

Nevertheless, he tried hard to get along with Clay. He went along with the abolition of the subtreasury system, and, although a low-tariff man, he agreed to an increase of rates in 1842 as long as the rise was tied to ending federal finance of internal improvements. Tyler also supported Clay's attempt to woo western voters from the Democrats with his Preemption Act of 1841. This law provided that a family that had "squatted" on up to 160 acres of public land could purchase it at the minimum price of $1.25 per acre without having to bid against others.

A President Without a Party

But Tyler was no real Whig. He had split with Jackson over King Andrew's arrogant use of presidential power. As a southern planter, his views on other issues were closer to those of John C. Calhoun (and Jackson!) than to those of the northern and western Whigs. Most important, Tyler disliked the idea of a national bank and warned Clay not to try to force one on him.

Clay did try, and Tyler vetoed one bank bill after another. Furious, the majority Whigs expelled the president from the party, and Tyler's cabinet resigned (except Webster, who wanted to complete some touchy negotiations with Great Britain). Clay left the Senate in order to prepare for the presidential campaign of 1844.

Tyler's new cabinet was made up of nominal southern Whigs much like Tyler himself. He hoped to piece together a new party of states'-rights Whigs and Democrats for the contest of 1844. Toward this end, he named John C. Calhoun Secretary of State.

But party loyalty was too strong among both Whigs and Democrats for Tyler's scheme to work. He was, in effect, a president without a party. The major political consequence of his presidency was to begin the destruction of the Whig party in the South. Aristocratic states'-righters like himself (and Calhoun) went back to the Democratic party. In time, the great planters would not only return to the party of Jackson, but they would take it over.

The Webster-Ashburton Treaty

The major accomplishment of the Tyler administration was in the area of foreign affairs: solving a series of potentially dangerous disputes with Great Britain, and paving the way for the annexation of the Republic of Texas.

The first was a Whiggish goal that was engineered by Daniel Webster. One of the problems was a boundary dispute between Maine and New Brunswick. According to the Treaty of 1783, the line ran between the watersheds of the Atlantic and the St. Lawrence River. And both sides had agreed to the boundary as shown by a red line that Benjamin Franklin had drawn on a map. The map disappeared, however, and in 1838, Canadian lumberjacks began cutting timber in the Aroostook Valley, which the United States claimed. A brief "war" between the Maine and New Brunswick militias ended with no deaths, and Van Buren managed to cool things down. But he could not resolve the boundary dispute.

The Canadian-American line immediately west of Lake Superior was also in question, and two other points of friction developed over American assistance to Canadian rebels and over the illegal but still flourishing slave trade. The slavery issue waxed hotter late in 1841, when a group of blacks on the American brig *Creole* mutinied, killed the crew, and sailed to Nassau in the British Bahamas. The British hanged the leaders of the mutiny but freed the other slaves, enraging sensitive southerners.

Neither England nor the United States wanted war, but the old rancor and the British determination to build a road through the disputed Aroostook country repeatedly stalled a settlement. Fortuitously, Webster found a kindred spirit in the high-living British negotiator, Lord Ashburton, and over brandy and port wine they worked out a compromise. Webster made a big concession to the British, too much as far as New Englanders were concerned. But never above a little chicanery, Webster actually forged Franklin's map to show a "red line" that gave Maine less territory than he had negotiated, and he warned that the United States had better take what it could get. (The real map surfaced many years later, and showed that the United States was shorted.)

Ashburton was generous, too. He ceded a strip of territory in northern New York and Vermont to which the United States had no claim, and also about sixty-five hundred square miles at the tip of Lake Superior. While wilderness at the time, the area around Lake Superior later became known as the Mesabi Range, one of the world's richest iron-ore deposits.

When the Senate ratified the treaty in 1842, every outstanding issue between the United States and Britain was settled, except the two nations' joint occupation of Oregon on the Pacific coast. Webster had good reason to be pleased with himself, and he joined his fellow Whigs in leaving John Tyler's cabinet.

For Further Reading

G. G. Van Deusen, *The Jacksonian Era, 1828–1848* (1959), is still the best general history of the Jacksonian period. J. W. Ward, *Andrew Jackson: Symbol for an Age* (1955), is a fascinating explanation of how the personality and image of Old Hickory came to merge with the values of the period in which he lived. A psychohistorical study of the president that is probably excessive but nevertheless enjoyable reading is M. P. Rogin, *Fathers and Children: Andrew Jackson and the Destruction of American Indians* (1975). On the eastern and urban component of the Jacksonian movement, see A. M. Schlesinger, Jr., *The Age of Jackson* (1945).

For the Bank war, the appropriate sections of Bray Hammond, *Banks and Politics in America from the Revolution to the Civil War* (1957), are still the standard work. On nullification and its author, see W. W. Freehling, *Prelude to Civil War: The Nullification Controversy in South Carolina* (1966), and M. L. Coit, *John C. Calhoun: American Portrait* (1950). Students should read the essay on Calhoun in Richard Hofstadter, *The American Political Tradition* (1948) and also Hofstadter's look at Jackson in the same book.

Perhaps the most enjoyable biography of Martin Van Buren is fifty years old but readily available: Holmes Alexander, *The American Talleyrand* (1935). R. G. Gunderson, *The Log-Cabin Campaign* (1957), explains the election of 1840, and O. D. Lambert follows the aftermath in *Presidential Politics in the United States, 1841–1844* (1936). The best short biography of Daniel Webster is R. N. Current, *Daniel Webster and the Rise of National Conservatism* (1955).

17

Ideas in Ferment

Religious Sects, Utopian Communities, Bold Thinkers

Before the 1820s, literate Europeans thought of the United States as little more than a rook's pawn in the game of power politics. America was a remote, semicivilized place. It was a factor in world trade, to be sure, but culturally it was a backwater, of little more interest to cultivated people than were the Indians with whom the Americans fought and the Africans whom they enslaved.

Sydney Smith summed up the contempt of Great Britain's intelligentsia in 1820:

> In the four quarters of the globe, who reads an American book? or goes to an American play? or looks at an American picture or statue? What does the world yet owe to American physicians or surgeons? What new substances have their chemists discovered? or what old ones have they analyzed? What new constellations have been discovered by the telescopes of Americans?—what have they done in the mathematics?

Few of Smith's readers would have disagreed, including those Americans who imported the magazine for which he wrote. There was no mistaking the fact that culturally the Americans were still a colonial people. Only in their political thought and writings had Americans made a

Frontier settlers found respite from their lonely lives by attending outdoor religious revival meetings.

mark worth noticing. It was European interest in American political practices, and in the quaint everyday lives of ordinary Americans, that, about the time Andrew Jackson was elected president, began to compel the interest of reading Europeans and soon became something of a mania.

As Others Saw Us

Before 1828, about forty books about the United States were published in Europe. After 1828, when the election of Andrew Jackson seemed to roll in an era dominated by the common man—a droll notion in European countries—a kind of America craze swept literate European circles.

Hundreds of books about Americans were published in little more than a decade, most of them in English but a considerable number in French and German and a few in Spanish, Italian, Polish, and the Scandinavian languages. To sate the appetite of European readers (and their own curiosity) successful authors such as Frederick Marryat and Charles Dickens crossed the Atlantic to describe the scenery, wonder over the curiosities, explain the political institutions, and scrutinize the manners, morals, and crotchets of the American people. The best of them were *Democracy in America* by a French aristocrat, Alexis de Tocqueville, and *Domestic Manners of the Americans* by an English gentlewoman, Frances Trollope.

Alexis de Tocqueville

In his first volume, published in 1835, Tocqueville explained the workings of American political institutions, emphasizing their democratic character. In the second volume, published in 1840, he commented on the social attitudes and customs of Americans.

Tocqueville found much to admire in the United States. Because he was a conservative, he was surprised to discover how well democratic government worked, and he admitted it. He had no trouble liking Americans as individuals. However, because Tocqueville believed that spiritual values, tradition, a sense of security, and continuity in human relationships were essential to a healthy society, he was concerned that Americans seemed always to be on the move. Tocqueville saw in them a love of the new and contempt for the old, and most of all the relentless pursuit of money. In one of his most disturbing passages, Tocqueville wrote that the American way of life not only makes "every man forget his ancestors, but it hides his de-

scendants, and separates his contemporaries from him; it throws him back for ever upon himself alone, and threatens in the end to confine him entirely within the solitude of his own heart."

Frances Trollope

The subject of Mrs. Trollope's book, published in 1832, was "domestic manners," everyday life. With an eye as keen as an eagle's and a wit as sharp as talons poised for the kill, she swooped through American parlors, dining rooms, kitchens, drawing rooms, cabins, steamboats, theaters, churches, and houses of business—and liked very little of what she found. Like Tocqueville, Mrs. Trollope was disturbed by the materialism and the instability of American society. On the former, she cited an Englishman who had lived in the United States for a long time who told her "that in following, in meeting, or in overtaking, in the street, on the road, or in the field, at the theatre, the coffee house, or at home, he had never overheard Americans conversing without the word DOLLAR being pronounced between them."

She had a terrible time in Jacksonian America. Mrs. Trollope observed (and was far from alone in her observations) that Americans rushed through hastily prepared meals. They trotted rather than walked down the street. They fidgeted when detained by some obligation lest they miss something in another part of town. When they did bring themselves to sit down, they whittled a piece of wood, so unable were they to be still.

"The Very Houses Move"

More than one commentator remembered as a symbol of their American experiences the spectacle of a team of sweating horses pulling a house on rollers from one

---

MISS MARTINEAU

While Americans execrated Mrs. Trollope, they rather liked the book written about them by another English visitor, Harriet Martineau. Miss Martineau was disturbed by many of the things that had bothered Mrs. Trollope. But it was obvious from her *Society in America* (1837) that she personally liked Americans and thoroughly enjoyed her lightning-fast trips throughout the United States. While traveling through the country, the rather deaf Miss Martineau thrust a huge ear-horn into the faces of everyone she met and shouted questions at them.

*This domestic scene is typical of what Mrs. Trollope might have seen during her visit
to America.*

site to another. Nothing, it seemed, was rooted in the United States, neither the homes nor the mighty oak trees that westerners mowed down as though they were hay nor customs nor social relationships nor religious beliefs that had served people well for a century.

Such instability was not without its casualties, and dollar worship was not without its native as well as foreign critics. Many people failed through no fault of their own in the first frantic decades of the nineteenth century. The topsy-turvy, boom-and-bust financial cycle turned rich men into debtors overnight and threw workers out of jobs that barely kept their families fed.

In the older agricultural regions of the eastern states, people who had once been secure on little farms found that they were impoverished, as foodstuffs cheaper than those they produced were transported from western

farms by new canals and, later, railroads. They felt manipulated by bankers and cheated by businessmen. Townspeople became disoriented as canals and railroads integrated them into an impersonal national economy and exposed them daily to a more diverse world than that their parents had been confronted with in a lifetime: strangers passing through, some of them to pluck the locals as they went; immigrants from abroad coming to work in the new factories; people urging their children to strike for the West, where they would prosper.

The westerners, of course, were displaced by definition. They were separated from the restraints but also from the comforts of family connections, tightly knit insular communities, and institutions that were not so mobile as individuals. Small wonder, then, that in addition to being a time of extraordinary economic growth, the age of Jackson was one when people groped for explanations of change and attempted, in their spiritual lives, to come to terms with it.

Religion in the Early Nineteenth Century

During the last two decades of the eighteenth century, organized religion had declined both in the numbers of church members and in influence. The Anglican Church had suffered because it was so closely tied to England. The Congregationalists had supported the war for independence, but, in the 1790s, they had bitterly opposed Thomas Jefferson. When he triumphed in 1800 and blood did not run in the gutters, as many ministers had predicted, Congregationalism became discredited in the opinion of many rural New Englanders.

The educated middle and upper classes abandoned old-time Calvinism because its overriding doctrine of predestination no longer accorded with the benign world they saw around them. Oliver Wendell Holmes wrote a light-spirited poem about one-doctrine religion called "The Deacon's Masterpiece":

> Have you heard of the wonderful
>   one-hoss shay,
> That was built in such a logical way
> It ran a hundred years to a day?

And then suddenly collapsed.

In the same years that the Jacksonians came to power, Massachusetts and Connecticut, the last states to pay ministers out of tax monies, ceased to do so. It was a sharp break with the Puritan past.

The Second Great Awakening

If the old churches suffered, old-time religion did not disappear so much as it changed form, adapting to the democratic spirit of the new era. In the Second Great Awakening, as in the First of the mid-eighteenth century, eloquent preachers such as Charles Grandison Finney crisscrossed New England and New York with the message that human nature was tainted, just as the Puritans had preached. Unlike the Puritans, however, Finney and others said that not just a few "Elect" were saved through God's grace; everyone who repented and prayed for deliverance from their sinful natures would be blessed.

A well-turned revivalist sermon began with an emotional description of the sinfulness of human beings, of

---

UNITARIANS

Unitarianism originated in 1785 when a Boston church struck from its services all references to the Trinity because the notion seemed idolatrous as well as superstitious. The denomination spread rapidly throughout New England as the church of enlightened, generally well-to-do people. (A working-class equivalent of Unitarianism was Universalism.)

The Unitarian God was tailored to fit the worldly optimism of a comfortable people. He was not a distributor of justice and retribution but a kindly, well-wishing father. In the words of William Ellery Channing, the most famous early-nineteenth-century Unitarian preacher, God had "a father's concern for his creatures, a father's desire for their improvement, a father's equity in proportioning his commands to their powers, a father's joy in their progress, a father's readiness to receive the penitent, and a father's justice for the incorrigible." He was not the God of John Winthrop and Jonathan Edwards.

---

which few ordinary people needed proof. The second part of the sermon gruesomely detailed the sufferings of hell, for which all sinners were destined. Again, it was not a difficult message to put across to people who suffered abundantly in the material world. Like good politicians, however, the revivalists concluded on a note of hope. Any person, in this religion of equal opportunity, could be saved if he or she repented and declared faith in Jesus Christ.

While the revivalism of the Second Great Awakening spread through every state to some extent, and some people of every social class were converted, revival fires burned hottest in rural New England and in New York, long-settled regions that seemed to be left behind by the nineteenth century, and on the frontier, where life was equally hard and uncertain.

Tenting on the Old Camp Ground

It was the frontier camp meeting that particularly attracted European tourists. Because few frontier settlements had buildings that were large enough to hold a crowd, the revivalists held their meetings in openings in the forest, which sometimes were cleared especially for the purpose. Beginning at Cane Ridge and Gasper River, Kentucky, at the turn of the century, the people who lived isolated, lonely lives responded to the calls by the thousands—more than twenty thousand in one instance—and came to the camp meeting from as far away as two hundred miles.

Such a concentration of people was itself exciting in

A Methodist camp meeting, as depicted in a detail from an 1836 lithograph by E. W. Clay.

the sparsely populated region. But there was something else. The atmosphere of the camp meeting was electrifying. As many as forty preachers simultaneously harangued the crowd. Some spoke from well-constructed platforms; others, from atop stumps. The meeting went on day and night for a week or more. When the final appeals tailed off in the early morning hours, the moans of excited people could be heard from every direction as the thousands fell asleep in tents or under their wagons.

Conversions were passionate. Some people fell to their hands and knees, weeping uncontrollably. Others scampered around on all fours, barking like dogs. A common manifestation was the "jerks." Caught up in the mass hysteria, people lurched about, their limbs jerking quite beyond their control.

Small wonder that European tourists listed the camp meeting as one of the two peculiarly American sights that they insisted on seeing. (The other was the slave auction.) Indeed, many Americans went just for the show and the chance to take advantage of the crowd by thieving, heckling preachers, heavy drinking, and sexual philandering.

Circuit Riders

The excesses of the camp meeting eventually led to a reaction. Even the Methodists, who were among the earliest organizers of religious revival on the frontier, drew back from sponsoring meetings. In place of the periodic revival they offered the circuit rider, a minister who was assigned to visit ten or twenty little western settlements that were too poor to support a permanent parson. Intensely devoted, poorly paid, and usually unmarried, the circuit riders rode through slashes in the woods in all weather. They preached, performed marriages and baptisms, took their rest and meals in the cabins of the faithful, and rode on. The most famous were Finis Ewing and Peter Cartwright, both of whom were rarely off their horses for more than two or three days at a time in more than three decades.

Other denominations imitated the Methodists because, when towns grew to more than half a dozen cabins, individualistic Americans were rarely able to agree on one denomination to serve the whole community. Unlike the situation today, the theological differences among most American denominations were profoundly important during the nineteenth century. A town of one thousand or two thousand people might support half a dozen churches: Methodist (or Free Methodist, for the churches divided and multiplied like bacteria); Baptist (or Primitive Baptist or Free Will Baptist); Presbyterian; Disciples of Christ; Christian; and so on.

Nor were all the denominations offshoots of the older churches. New religions sprouted and grew in Jacksonian America, and most of them withered and died. But others have survived to this day. The two most important survivors originated in a part of rural new York State that was called "the burned-over district" because fiery revivals flared up there so often.

The Adventist Episode

Sometime before 1831, a Baptist named William Miller calculated that Christ's Second Coming—the end of the world—would occur between March 21, 1843, and March 21, 1844. He began to preach his message throughout the northeastern states. Most listeners hooted him, but Miller convinced tens of thousands with the complex mathematical formula by which he had come to his conclusion.

Along with an energetic disciple, Joshua V. Himes of Boston, Miller published a newspaper and regularly preached two or even three long sermons a day. At the beginning of the fateful year, a magnificent comet appeared in the sky for a month, and converts flocked to join Miller's Adventists (*advent* means "coming" or "arrival"). Many sold their possessions and contributed the proceeds to the sect, which led many critics to accuse Miller and Himes of conscious fraud.

On March 21, 1844, in order to be first to greet the Lord, several thousand people throughout New York and New England climbed hills in their "Ascension Robes" (sold by Himes).

When Christ did not come, Miller discovered an error in his computations and set the date of the Second Coming at no later than October 22, 1844. Again there was hysteria in some towns as the day approached, and an even greater disappointment when Christ still did not appear. Miller himself was bewildered and broken-hearted. He returned to his home in upstate New York, where he died in 1849. A disciple named Hiram Edson eventually reorganized some of the Millerites around the vaguer belief that Christ would return *soon*. Because Edson observed the Jewish sabbath, Saturday rather than Sunday, this remnant of the Millerite excitement became known as Seventh-Day Adventists.

The Mormons

The Church of Jesus Christ of the Latter-Day Saints, or Mormons, another distinctively American religion, also came out of the burned-over district. The founder of the church was Joseph Smith, a farm boy from Vermont whose family could barely scrape by. Smith had a reputation for being a solitary daydreamer who preferred wandering the rolling hills of the region to the tedious chores of farm life. When he was only twenty, he announced to his family and a few friends that he had been visited on one of these hikes by the angel Moroni, who had shown him where some mysterious gold plates were buried. Somewhat later, Moroni provided Smith with spectacles called Urim and Thummim, through which he could read the strange inscriptions on the plates.

The story he translated was *The Book of Mormon*, a Bible of the New World that told of a lost tribe of Israel in America, the Nephites, and the history of their wars with the Lamanites, or Indians. Christ had founded Christianity in America, as he had done in Palestine. In A.D. 384, the Lamanites wiped out all Nephites, sparing only the prophet Mormon, who wrote the book that Smith published in 1830.

Tales similar to this one had long circulated in the folklore of the burned-over district, and a novel that incorporated some of the details of *The Book of Mormon* was written about the same time as Smith's revelations. To many Americans, told from childhood that their country was a new Eden, there was nothing preposterous in the idea that Christ should have visited the New World. To those who were impoverished and displaced by the frenzied pace of the age of Jackson, it was not surprising that God should make his truth known in upstate New York in 1830. It was a time, as one of Smith's early converts, Orson Pratt, wrote,

when "wickedness keeps pace with the hurried revolutions of the age."

Smith offered a way out of the era, but he was also its child. He extended the priesthood of his new religion to all males, thus appealing to the Jacksonian yearning for equality, and he tapped the mystique of the West by taking his congregation first to Ohio, then to Missouri, and finally, in 1840, to Nauvoo, Illinois. There they prospered, and by 1844, Nauvoo was the largest city in the state.

There, they were resented and harassed, both because of their prosperity and because of their defensive attitude toward outsiders, whom they called Gentiles. The resentment and fear of secret societies that had led to the Anti-Masonic movement also vexed the Mormons. But the crisis came only when Smith fell prey to political ambition. Both Whigs and Democrats courted Nauvoo's votes because they were cast as a bloc, but in 1844, Smith spurned both parties and announced that he would be a candidate for the presidency. This news, added to rumors that Smith commanded a well-armed private militia of two thousand, the Nauvoo Legion, led to his arrest. On June 27, with the complicity of officials, he and his brother were taken from the jailhouse and murdered. Without their extraordinary leader, the Mormons might well have foundered, had not an even more remarkable (and politically more able) man grappled his way to the top of the organization.

Safe in the Desert

Brigham Young, a Vermonter like Smith, also had received revelations directly from God. The most important of these was the command that the Latter-Day Saints move beyond the boundaries of the sinful country that oppressed them. Young organized the great migration of the Mormons down to the last detail. Advance parties planted crops that would be ready for harvesting when the thousands, pushing and pulling their few possessions in handcarts, arrived on the trail. For his Zion, Young chose the most isolated and inhospitable region he could find, the basin of the Great Salt Lake. "This is the place," he said, looking down from the Ouachita Mountains, and there the Mormons laid out a neat city with broad avenues and irrigation ditches that were fed with water from the surrounding peaks. They made the desert bloom. By 1847, Salt Lake City had a population of eleven thousand.

In one respect, Young was frustrated. At the same time that the Mormons were constructing their Zion, American victory in a war with Mexico brought them back under the American flag. Young did not fight the

Brigham Young organized the great migration of the Mormons to Utah.

people who were distressed by the fruits of a wide-open economy. Some of the communities, like the Mormon, had a religious foundation. Others were based on secular social theories.

Religious Communities

The Rappites were an import, six hundred German followers of George Rapp who came to the United States in 1803 and founded communities—Harmony, Pennsylvania; New Harmony, Indiana; and Economy, Pennsylvania—whose members held property in common and practiced celibacy.

The Rappites died out quickly because of their celibacy and because they discouraged non-Germans from joining their communities. A similar group, the Shakers, had a longer history, since they courted converts and adopted children out of orphanages. Founded and brought to the United States by an English woman, Mother Ann Lee, the movement flourished as a refuge for people who sought stability in the tumultuous Jacksonian period. During the 1830s, they maintained more than twenty neat and comfortable communities in the eastern and midwestern states.

Like the Millerites, the Shakers believed that Christ would return to earth at any time. Because there was, therefore, no need to perpetuate the human race, they practiced celibacy. Men and women lived in different parts of their towns. Property was communal, and people who joined the Shakers turned over what they owned to the whole.

The Shakers were neither persecuted nor much ridiculed. Celibacy was considered peculiar, but it did not offend conventional morality, as did Mormon polygamy. Indeed, as a group that needed converts in order to survive, the Shakers were unfailingly polite, cooperative, and fair in their dealings with outsiders. They lived very simply, exciting no resentment of their prosperity.

troops who arrived to raise the flag, but he made it clear that real federal control of Utah, then called the State of Deseret, depended on his cooperation. The president wisely gave in and named Young territorial governor. Despite its large population, however, Utah was not admitted to the Union until 1890. The Mormons practiced "celestial marriage" (polygamy); Young himself had twenty-seven wives and fifty-six children. Congress refused to grant statehood until that institution was declared illegal.

Utopian Communities

Unlike members of traditional churches, Mormons lived in highly regulated communities in which individual rights and an individual's freedom to accumulate private riches were subordinated to the good of the whole. The institution of private property developed fully in Utah only because of the necessity of conforming to American law. Other early-nineteenth-century advocates of communal living insisted that private property was a gross evil because it set people in competition with one another, and they practiced a form of communism. These experiments appealed to

Shakers gathered in simple meeting houses to perform the rhythmic dances that were part of their religion.

Indeed, the Shaker communities were popular tourist attractions because of the fine workmanship and elegant simplicity of their crafts, which they sold in order to support themselves.

Setting an Example: The Utopians

The religious communities had two purposes in withdrawing from society: to live in what they believed was the godly way in order to save their own souls, and to set an example that others might follow. Other utopians, although by no means irreligious, were primarily interested in the social aspect of their communities. They had theories about what was wrong with the larger society (which almost always included its material preoccupations and commitment to private property) and sought to show the world, by the contentment of their alternative way of life, how the whole society should be organized.

The most famous of these utopian communities was also one of the first to come to grief. New Harmony, Indiana, was purchased from the Rappites in 1825 by Robert Owen, a British industrialist who, in an age of "dark, satanic mills," had made a model of paternalism of his textile mill in New Lanark, Scotland. About a thousand people responded to Owen's call to build a community at New Harmony in which all property was to be held in common, and life was to consist not of drudgery for the enrichment of others but of joyous work for the good of all. Unfortunately, the idealists at New Harmony were joined by many who looked forward to only the weekly philosophic discussions and, in the meantime, an easy life financed by Owen's fortune. An idealist who believed in the goodness of human nature, Owen was incapable of throwing out the freeloaders. In 1827, disillusioned and a good deal poorer, he returned to Scotland. Within a short time, New Harmony broke up, and the old Rappite fields, orchards, and vineyards went to seed and weeds.

The Icarians, who followed the teachings of the Frenchman Étienne Cabet, also believed in the common ownership of property. In 1848, they established communities in Texas, and, in 1849, on the site of the abandoned Mormon settlement at Nauvoo, Illinois. One faction of the movement survived until 1895. Another Frenchman, Charles Fourier, founded a larger utopian movement that established more than twenty "phalanxes," or cooperative associations, throughout the North and Midwest. Most of them lasted only a few months; again, bickering and laziness were their undoing.

A similarly doomed colony was Fruitlands, the project of Bronson Alcott, a magnificent eccentric who is best remembered as the father of the author Louisa May Alcott. Lovable and a daydreamer, the friend of most of the important writers and thinkers of the period, Alcott was also totally incapable of coping with the facts of workaday life. He inaugurated his communal lesson to the world by planting several trees—about a foot or two from the front door of the community house—and dropping the shovel when he was done. Alcott returned to his meditations and his endless discussions with the extraordinary collection of crackpots who gathered at Fruitlands.

One, whose name was Abram Wood, announced his defiance of the world by deciding that his name was really Wood Abram. Another would not weed the garden because he insisted that weeds had as much right to grow as did vegetables. Samuel Larned lived for one year on nothing but crackers (so he said) and the next on apples. Another Fruitlander said that the way to break loose from empty social conventions was to greet people, "Good morning, God damn you!"

Through it all, Mrs. Alcott kept the community afloat by doing most of the work. It is not clear if the sturdy, stoical woman ever took seriously a word her husband said.

Oneida: A Success Story

Most of the utopias were based on the belief that private property is the source of injustice and human unhappiness. In this, they were rebelling against the most conspicuous phenomenon of the period—the helter-skelter competition for riches. To this, John Humphrey Noyes added the institution of marriage. Marriage, he said, was itself a form of property: under American laws and customs, the husband effectively owned his wife, and, therefore, both were miserable.

Instead of preaching celibacy as an alternative, Noyes devised the concept of "complex marriage." In the community he founded at Oneida, New York, in 1847, every man was married to every woman. Couples who chose to have sexual relations for pleasure could do so, but not for the purpose of procreation. Noyes was a believer in eugenics, improving the human race (and therefore society) by allowing only those who were superior in health, constitution, and intellect to have children. (His method of birth control was male continence.)

Oneida's practice of "free love," like the Mormons' polygamy, enraged the community's neighbors, and Noyes had to flee to Canada to escape arrest. Oneida, however, enjoyed a long life. The community prospered from its manufacture of silverware, silks, and a superior trap for fur-bearing animals. Finally abandoning complex marriage in 1879 and communal property in 1881, the surviving Oneidans reorganized as a corporation.

Transcendentalism

Noyes was what students of philosophy call a Perfectionist. He believed that Christ's redemption of humanity was complete. Individuals had it within themselves to be perfect—that is, without sin—and therefore above rules that were written for the imperfect. People only had to face up to their own perfection, and it would be so.

Members of the Oneida community founded by John Humphrey Noyes believed that every man was married to every woman, a concept they called "complex marriage." They abandoned the concept in 1879, thirty-two years after the group's founding.

Perfectionism was not so very far out of step with the spirit of the Jacksonian era. It was a time when, figuratively speaking, Americans believed that everything was within human competence. Noyes's mistake was to take the implications of his philosophy literally. When he put sinlessness into practice at Oneida by approving behavior that more conventional Americans were quite sure was sinful, he suffered their censure. Ralph Waldo Emerson, on the contrary, by calling Perfectionism by another name—Transcendentalism—and by avoiding its implications in the way he led his life, became America's favorite philosopher.

The Sage of Concord

Emerson was the Unitarian pastor of the same church in Boston where Cotton Mather had preached gloom and doom more than a century before. Emerson's own view of human nature glowed with warmth and love, but, despite his congregation's approval, he found the pulpit constraining. In 1832, he announced that he could no longer accept the Unitarian practice of celebrating the Lord's Supper, resigned, and moved to Concord, Massachusetts (then well outside Boston).

"The profession is antiquated," Emerson said of preaching. But within a few years he was preaching again, albeit from a lectern rather than a pulpit, and his message was a welter of notions far more mystical than the Christian sacrament.

Emerson's philosophy of Transcendentalism explicitly defied criticism that it was vague or contradictory. Based on feelings rather than reason, Transcendentalism exalted a vague concept of nature over civilization, personal morality over laws, and the individual's capacity within himself to be happy, or sinless. When his ideas were attacked, Emerson responded that the critic was not morally capable of understanding that "consistency is the hobgoblin of little minds" and that the truly enlightened human being could dispose "very easily of the most disagreeable facts."

The word *transcend* means "to go beyond, to rise above." As used by Emerson and his disciples, it meant to go above reason and beyond the material world. God was not a being, but a force. God was the "oversoul," which was within all men and women because it was in nature. "Standing on the bare ground," Emerson wrote, "my head bathed by the blithe air and uplifted into infinite space—all mean egotism vanishes. I become a transparent eyeball; I am nothing; I see all; the currents of the Universal being circulate through me."

The writer Herman Melville, a contemporary of Emerson, called this sort of thing "gibberish." But while Melville remained an obscure author, barely able to eke out a living by writing what were thought of as mere sea stories, Emerson was lionized as the greatest American philosopher. While Melville scrutinized the problem of evil in the world, Emerson ignored that "disagreeable" fact. His buoyant, bubbly optimism was brilliantly tailored to his times.

PANTHEISM

Fuzzy in philosophic prose, Ralph Waldo Emerson's pantheism—the belief that nature is divinity—made for beautiful lyric poetry. In "The Rhodora," he reflected on the purple flower of that name that grows only in obscure nooks of the woods:

> Rhodora! If the sages ask thee why
> This charm is wasted on the earth and sky,
> Tell them, dear, that if eyes were made for
> seeing,
> Then beauty is its own excuse for being;
> Why thou wert there, O rival of the rose!
> I never thought to ask, I never knew:
> But, in my simple ignorance, suppose
> The self-same power that brought me there,
> brought you.

Other Transcendentalists

Emerson's close friend Henry David Thoreau was the introspective son of a Concord pencil manufacturer. Less sociable than the strait-laced Emerson, Thoreau flaunted his eccentricity. In 1845, Thoreau constructed a hut in the woods near Walden pond, just outside Concord. There he wrote *A Week on the Concord and Merrimack Rivers* (published in 1849) and *Walden* (1854), an account of his reflections while sitting by the pond.

Although *Walden* is surely the masterpiece of Transcendentalism—Thoreau was an elegant stylist—it is marred by the same half-baked dilettantism that robs Emerson's works of lasting value. Thoreau wrote as though he had seceded from civilization and struck off into the wilderness:

> I wanted to live deep and suck out all the marrow of life, to live so sturdily and Spartan-like as to put to rout all that was not life, to cut a broad swath and shave close, to drive life into a corner, and reduce it to its lowest terms.

But Walden was no Rocky Mountain fastness. It was a short walk to Concord, a walk that Thoreau took often when he needed a decent meal or a keg of nails. Living deep and sucking the marrow out of life was rather like camping in the backyard. There was a sense of having things both ways—the mystical perception of being above the tawdry materialism of the United States, while enjoying its benefits—about much of what the Transcendentalists did.

Bronson Alcott was a frequent visitor to the Emerson home. So were the Unitarian ministers William Ellery Channing and George Ripley. (In 1841, Ripley founded a Transcendentalist utopia, Brook Farm, at

American philosopher Ralph Waldo Emerson as portrayed in a daguerreotype by J. J. Hawes.

AUTHORS

"The Americans have no national literature," sniffed a writer for the *British Critic* in 1819. And the next year, Sydney Smith framed his derisive question for the *Edinburgh Review:* "In the four quarters of the globe, who reads an American book?" At the time, even Americans seemed to respond, "No one." Well into the nineteenth century, it was a sign of high discernment in many parts of society to read only English and French authors. In 1837, in an address to the Phi Beta Kappa Society at Harvard College, Ralph Waldo Emerson called for an end to this "long apprenticeship to the learning of other lands," for a declaration of independence from European literary themes and styles.

In fact, two New Yorkers (albeit New Yorkers living in Europe) were creating a distinctly American literature at the very time that the *British Critic* and the *Edinburgh Review* were passing their judgment. By the time Emerson gave his famous lecture in 1837, the literary "flowering of New England" was already in bloom.

Washington Irving (1783–1839) wrote the hilarious *Diedrich Knickerbocker's History of New York* before he went to England in 1815 as an agent of his father's trading company. There, in 1820, he published *The Sketch Book,* a collection of tales based on the Dutch folklore of his native Hudson Valley. Two of the stories, "Rip Van Winkle" and "The Legend of Sleepy Hollow," were immediately recognized as classics.

Even then, however, Irving was uncertain of his literary standing as long as he employed American themes. He was fully accepted by the English literary establishment only with the publication in 1832 of *The Alhambra.* Centered on the magnificent Moorish palace in Granada, Spain, where Irving lived while serving in the American diplomatic service, the book aroused interest in the priceless monument and played a major part in saving the Alhambra from destruction or at least steady decay during the nineteenth century.

James Fenimore Cooper (1789–1851) spent most of his literary years in England and France, where he was recognized and even lionized for his novels. His first successful book was *The Spy* (1821), an adventure story set against the American Revolution. His masterpiece is *The Leather-stocking Tales,* five novels published between 1823 and 1841. The hero is Natty Bumppo, a buckskin-clad frontiersman who, with his Indian friends, Uncas and Chingachgook ("the last of the Mohicans"), served as vehicles for Cooper's study of what Emerson called "the great moment in history." Emerson was referring to the point at which civilization confronted savagery, the decency of the former enhanced by, all the while it moderated, the vitality of

A card from the nineteenth century parlor game "Authors" featured writer Washington Irving.

the latter. It was a peculiarly American moment; Cooper's great theme was the most American theme of all—the frontier.

Most of the writers of the ante-bellum period whom Americans came to worship, putting their portraits on playing cards that were used in the parlor game "Authors," were New Englanders. In addition to Emerson, Thoreau, Hawthorne, and Fuller, four Massachusettsmen were honored for their poetry. Another Massachusettsman and a New Yorker, both of whom were not honored in their lifetimes, are now considered to be among the greatest nineteenth-century authors.

Oliver Wendell Holmes (1809–94) wrote for *The Atlantic Monthly,* the magazine that became the unofficial organ of the "flowering of New England." His friends—for Massachusetts was a small place—William Cullen Bryant (1794–1878) and John Greenleaf Whittier (1807–92) were also popular. Indeed, Bryant's "Thanatopsis," a lyric poem, was not only written in 1810, ten years before the pronouncements of the *British Critic* and the *Edinburgh Review,* but it was written when Bryant was only sixteen years of age.

Whittier's nostalgic, romantic poems, such as "Barefoot Boy with Cheek of Tan," were second in popularity only to the works of Henry Wadsworth Longfellow (1807–82), a professor of modern languages at Harvard. His verses on homey themes ("The Village Blacksmith") and long narratives of American history (*The Song of Hiawatha, The Midnight Ride of Paul Revere, Evangeline*) made him the nation's favorite poet. He wrote without profundity, but also without pretension. A good-natured man, Longfellow undoubtedly delighted in the silly rhyme memorized by generations of American children: "He don't know it but he's a poet 'cause his feet are long fellows."

A writer who did tackle profound subjects was New York-born Herman Melville (1819–91), whose study of evil against the backdrop of a whaling voyage, *Moby Dick* (1851), was recognized as a milestone in world literature only decades after his death. His second finest book, *Billy Budd,* was not even published until 1924.

Finally, Edgar Allan Poe (1809–49), Boston-born but southern by adoption, was regarded during his life as little more than an ill-tempered literary critic, an author of spooky stories, and an obnoxious drunk. Poe was capable of prodigious feats of self-destruction, but he was also frustrated by the short-sighted provincialism of the New England writers who believed, as Holmes put it sarcastically, that Boston was "the hub of the solar system." It was not until the twentieth century that Poe was recognized as a prolific author of deep thought and graceful style. Some critics have ranked him above all his contemporaries.

James Fenimore Cooper, best known for The Leatherstocking Tales, *also appeared on an* "Authors" *card.*

Henry David Thoreau, author of Walden, *the master-piece of Transcendentalism.*

of the Seven Gables (1851). In *The Blithedale Romance* (1852), Hawthorne roundly satirized the Transcendentalist utopian community at Brook Farm.

Just as he disagreed with the Transcendentalists' belief in human perfectability, Hawthorne disagreed with their politics. Whereas his New England friends were usually Whigs, Hawthorne was a Democrat. When his college crony Franklin Pierce became president in 1853, Hawthorne was named American consul in England.

Margaret Fuller lived and died a romantic's life. She married a vapid Italian aristocrat in 1847, participated in the rebellion of Giuseppe Garibaldi, and committed suicide by leaping from a ship while returning to the United States. But she was also a hard-headed thinker and a political activist, a radical where Hawthorne was a conservative. In 1845, fully three years before the

West Roxbury, Massachusetts.) Other visitors included authors James Russell Lowell and Nathaniel Hawthorne, and Margaret Fuller, a prolific writer who was the first literary critic for the New York *Tribune*.

Dissenters

Hawthorne and Fuller were never fully sympathetic with the Transcendentalist euphoria. Both were romantics, like Emerson and his circle. But when Hawthorne looked into the human heart, he found evil rather than the divinity perceived by Emerson's transparent eyeball; and Fuller was impatient with the Transcendentalists' contentment to issue broad political pronouncements instead of cutting a broad swath and shaving close in real political action.

"The heart, the heart," Hawthorne wrote, "there was the little yet boundless sphere wherein existed the original wrong of which the crime and misery of the outward world were merely types." He made guilt, sin, and moral decay the themes of *Twice-Told Tales* (1837), the classic *Scarlet Letter* (1850), and *The House*

Political activist Margaret Fuller published a scathing indictment of the arguments against female equality in 1845, three years before the emergence of an organized feminist movement in America.

emergence of feminism as a social and political movement, Fuller published *Woman in the Nineteenth Century,* a scathing indictment of the arguments against female equality.

Fuller died too soon to participate in the organized feminist movement or in the even greater reform movement of the nineteenth century, the fight against slavery. But she was, in her writings, a bridge between the reflective thought of her age and its busy devotion to practical social action.

For Further Reading

S. E. Ahlstrom, *A Religious History of the American People* (1972), relates religious ideas to events in the larger society. I. H. Bartlett, *The American Mind in the Mid-Nineteenth Century* (1967), is the most readable of the shorter books. On revivalism, see W. R. Cross, *The Burned-Over District* (1950), and C. A. Johnson, *The Frontier Camp Meeting* (1955). But if only one book on the subject is to be consulted, it should be B. A. Weisberger, *They Gathered at the River* (1958). Gilbert Seldes, *The Stammering Century* (1928), is old but an eternally delightful, if waspish, look at American sects in the nineteenth century.

F. M. Brody, *No Man Knows My History: The Life of Joseph Smith* (1945), deals with the early years of Mormonism and is excellent reading. On the utopias, see A. E. Bestor, *Backwoods Utopias* (1950), which is the standard work.

The best way to approach the Transcendentalists is through their own writings; an excellent selection is in Perry Miller, ed., *The Transcendentalists* (1950). Most students enjoy and benefit from Thoreau's *Walden,* available in a number of inexpensive editions. In the same vein, there are two or three abridged versions of De Tocqueville's *Democracy in America,* the continued relevance of which is always enlightening. Mrs. Trollope's *Domestic Manners of the Americans* is available in a 1949 edition.

18

Fighting Evil, Solving Social Problems
America's First Age of Reform

In Jacksonian America, democracy, individualism, and the competition for riches were the dominant gods. But the country was also home to a great many people who rejected these deities as false idols. The utopians withdrew from a society that they found bewildering and sinful and founded small, closed communities whose members lived according to simple, forthright principles. The Mormons rejected the tensions of individualism and competition and attempted to leave the United States.

In their own way, the Millerites on the hills hoped to get out, as did the tens of thousands of people who found God's blessing through revivalist preachers. In their conversion experiences, they were saying, in effect, that they would merely tolerate this world and fight its sinfulness to a draw, reserving the pursuit of happiness for the next life.

Even the Transcendentalists, who lived within and enjoyed the material benefits that the expansive society offered, insisted that in their spiritual lives they were above it all.

Yet other Americans, while sharing the belief that individuals need not be swept up in the whirl of their times, chose not to withdraw from the world in body or soul, but to stay and fight. They would not be satisfied with only their own redemption, but would reform society according to the lights within them.

Some early organizers and leaders of the women's suffrage movement.

Lighting One Candle: The Practical Reformers

The evangelical reformers believed that it was the moral duty of Christians to bear witness against the evil they found around them. Most of them sympathized with the goals of other reformers. The most effective, however, concentrated their energies on a specific reform, lighting a candle in one corner of the darkness. Some devoted their lives to helping the neglected and disadvantaged people for whom busy America seemed to have no time: the physically handicapped, the insane, the prisoners. Others were concerned with uplifting the behavior of people they saw as benighted: the lower classes, particularly recent immigrants and people plagued by drunkenness. The most important of the evangelical reform movements were those devoted to righting the wrongs suffered by the slaves of the South and by women. The goal in every case was to do good.

The Blind and the Deaf

In a traditional society, blindness and deafness were thought to be the concern of no one but the unfortunate sufferers and their families; the blind or deaf person was cared for by his or her family or, when the victim had no relatives able to do so, by the community. Blindness and deafness were not considered disabilities, but conditions of life for which no one was "responsible."

In the early nineteenth century, however, the spirit of individualism and the disintegration of old communities led to the gross neglect of disabled people. Their plight offended the moral sensibilities of people who continued to believe that everyone was his brother's keeper.

Thomas Gallaudet was such a person. Shocked by the fact that the deaf were simply shunted aside and often written off as mental defectives who had no place in society, he crossed the Atlantic in 1815 to study the techniques that an English physician had developed for teaching the deaf to read lips and to communicate by sign language. But he was disgusted to learn that the methods were considered trade secrets, an article of commerce to be guarded as closely as a textile manufacturer guarded the plans for his weaving machines. To Gallaudet, the means of doing good was not a commodity to be bought and sold.

In France, fortunately he found a teacher of the deaf whose views on helping the afflicted accorded with his own. The two men returned to the United States and,

Laura Bridgman, who was both deaf and blind, toured the country with Samuel Gridley Howe to demonstrate that physically disabled people could be capable, productive members of society.

in 1817, founded the American Asylum, a free school for the deaf in Hartford, Connecticut. True to his ideals, Gallaudet demonstrated his methods to every interested party and encouraged others to establish institutions like the American Asylum in other cities.

Samuel Gridley Howe was a physician who, after fighting in the Greek rebellion against the Turks, returned to Boston with a comrade-in-arms who shared his interest in educating the blind. Howe organized the Perkins Institute for the Blind in Boston. Not only did he publicize his techniques, but, being a bit of a showman, Howe toured the country with a young girl named Laura Bridgman who was both deaf and blind. Howe had established communication with her, laying to rest the widespread belief that such people were mentally deficient and forever helpless. Even the most serious impediments to human fulfillment, Howe said, could be overcome if men and women were willing to make an effort to overcome them.

Dorothea Dix

The plight of the insane was understood even more poorly than that of the deaf and blind. The insane also had been considered the responsibility of their families

REFORMERS AND PERFECTIONISM

John Humphrey Noyes tried to make the connection between Perfectionism and the reform movements of the day explicit when he wrote: "As the doctrine of temperance is total abstinence from alcoholic drinks, and the doctrine of antislavery is immediate abolition of human bondage, so the doctrine of perfectionism is the immediate and total cessation from sin." However, very few of the reformers supported him because they either failed to see the connection or feared what might happen to their movements if they associated their ideals with the unpopular apostle of "free love."

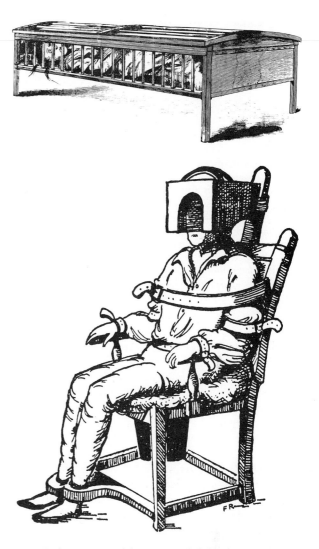

Early treatment of the insane included locking them in cages or strapping them into tranquillizing chairs. Dorothea Dix denounced such inhumane treatment and prompted reforms.

or, if they were dangerous to others, of the legal authorities. The line between insanity and criminality was blurred. People who were not responsible for their actions were often confined in prisons. Where there were asylums (the word means "refuge"), they were poorly financed and were operated much like prisons. It was not uncommon for guards to charge admission to fashionable people and goad the inmates into performing antics for the visitors' amusement.

In 1841, Dorothea Lynde Dix, a teacher at a school for wealthy girls in Massachusetts, discovered that insane people were kept in an unheated room in the Cambridge House of Correction, even in the depths of the Massachusetts winter. Thirty-three years old, pious, and shy, Dorothea Dix had lived a genteel, sheltered life. But her discovery was as shocking as any religious experience, and it galvanized her into becoming one of the most effective reformers of the century. She investigated conditions at other Massachusetts institutions, including the single state asylum at Worcester, and, in 1843, she drafted a memorial on the subject that she presented to the state legislature.

Dix passionately denounced the inhumane treatment of the insane. Harmless, sweet-natured imbeciles were confined with dangerous lunatics in "cages, closets, cellars, stalls, pens!" They were fed slops and "chained, naked, beaten with rods, and lashed into obedience!"

Dix's revelations did not square with Massachusetts's proud self-image as the nation's most progressive state. The legislature hurriedly passed a bill to enlarge the state asylum and improve conditions elsewhere. Dix then set out to carry her message throughout the nation and the world. Self-effacing and saintly in her demeanor, she persuaded Congress to establish St. Elizabeth's Hospital for the insane. She traveled to Europe, where she moved both Queen Victoria and the pope to improve treatment of the mentally deficient in their realms.

Changing Views of Crime and Punishment

Another institution that attracted the notice of reformers was the penitentiary. Large prisons for long-term convicts were themselves new to the United States. Before the late eighteenth century, lawbreakers were rarely given long prison terms. The most serious crimes were punished by hanging; there were as many as sixteen capital offenses in some states: rape and homosexuality as well as murder and treason. Other major felonies merited a public flogging or physical mutilation; arsonists, wife beaters, and thieves were whipped or had their ears cropped or their cheeks branded with a hot iron. Petty offenders—drunk and disorderly people and disturbers of the peace—were

SOCIAL RIDICULE AS PUNISHMENT

The stocks and the pillory were devices for punishing minor criminal offenses from the seventeenth century until, in some places, well into the nineteenth century. A person who was sentenced to the stocks sat on a stool, his or her legs locked by two blocks of wood into each of which semicircles had been sawed. The pillory had three such holes, one for each wrist and the other for the miscreant's neck.

While neither punishment was comfortable, discomfort and pain were not the idea. The offenders were punished by being ridiculed in front of people among whom they lived. The man or woman was helpless in an awkward, ridiculous position, and subjected to jesting in which, within limits, everyone was encouraged. A latter-day survival of social ridicule as a punishment was the dunce cap that a mischievous or a poor student was forced to wear.

fined or humiliated, sentenced to the stocks or the pillory for a few hours or days.

During the 1790s, influenced by the theories of the Italian criminologist Cesare Beccaria, the states reduced the number of capital offenses, eliminated mutilation, largely abandoned whipping, and turned instead to prison sentences as a means of punishing serious crime. Unfortunately, legislatures were rarely as generous in appropriating funds for maintaining penal institutions as they were in reforming the criminal code. Conditions of confinement were generally execrable. Connecticut, for example, used an abandoned mine shaft as its state penitentiary.

Prison Reform

It was universally agreed that the purposes of prison were the punishment of the wrongdoer and the protection of society. As reformers pointed out, however, the security of society was not served if prison sentences transformed petty offenders into hardened criminals. In jailing those who committed minor crimes with habitual and serious offenders, the penitentiaries acted as schools of criminality. This observation led to the idea of the prison as a correctional institution, as a place for rehabilitation.

A lively controversy developed between exponents of what was called the Pennsylvania System and those of the Auburn System, which was named after the town in which New York's state prison was located. Pennsylvania kept its convicts in solitary confinement; they rarely left their tiny, individual cells. The theory behind this practice was that the inmates would meditate

on their crimes and leave prison determined not to offend again.

The flaws of the system were twofold: it was extremely expensive, and it produced as many cases of insanity as of personal redemption. In order to combat both problems, Pennsylvania provided its inmates with productive work such as weaving, which was regarded as morally uplifting.

At New York's Auburn Penitentiary, prisoners slept in individual cells, but during the day they were marched silently to large workrooms and a common dining hall. Conversation was absolutely forbidden, both to prevent education in crime and to keep order. The Auburn System was more economical than the Pennsylvania System because the prisoners were able to work more productively in groups and thus pay the expenses of housing them. Through the efforts of the Prison Discipline Society, the Auburn System was adopted by other states, including Pennsylvania.

Another innovation of the period was the "house of refuge," in which juveniles were kept isolated from adult criminals. By 1830, New York City, Philadelphia, and Boston maintained such facilities. After 1830, the practice of public executions declined. Reformers rejected the ancient belief that the sight of a man hanging provided a grim lesson for onlookers when as many as ten thousand people eagerly flocked to witness an execution in New Jersey. It was obvious from the spectators' ribald behavior that they were there not to absorb a moral lesson but to enjoy a good show.

Moral Uplift

It was toward this kind of undesirable behavior on the part of the great masses of people that a second kind of evangelical reform was directed. Instead of attracting the attention of the many to the misfortunes of a few—as Gallaudet, Howe, and Dix tried to do—the advocates of temperance, Protestant nativism, and missionary work addressed problems that affected the whole of society. Unfortunately, their work amounted to the imposition of the moral code of a few upon the many.

Demon Rum

Americans drank heavily and always had. In part because grains were abundant and cheap, the consumption of alcohol in Jacksonian America probably was higher than in any country before or since. Ales, beers, and ciders were the everyday beverages of common people in the East. In the West, the daily tonic was whiskey made from corn or rye. Wine and brandy were fixtures of middle-class and upper-class life.

Few social occasions lacked alcohol. The hospitable family's first act upon receiving a guest was to uncork a bottle or to tap a barrel. Urban workingmen insisted that they needed liquor for strength, and employers of both craftsmen and unskilled laborers provided a ration as part of the day's pay. Farmers, especially in the West, were famous for the "little brown jugs" that accompanied them wherever they went.

By 1820, the annual consumption of hard spirits (not including beer, cider, and wine) was more than seven and one-half gallons for each man, woman, and child. There were about fifteen thousand licensed distilleries in the country, and private stills were as common as chicken coops on backcountry farms.

Nevertheless, drunkenness was universally regarded as sinful and, obviously, as socially unacceptable. Cotton Mather had preached temperance for moral reasons in the early eighteenth century, and during the 1780s, Dr. Benjamin Rush, a Philadelphia physician, described the physically destructive effects of excessive bibbing. With the rush of the moral-betterment campaigns of the 1830s, reformers added two more arrows to their quiver. First, they published statistics showing that a substantial number of crimes were committed by people who were drunk. Second, they draw a connection between poverty and drinking. A few said that the miseries of poverty led to drunkenness. Most, steeped in moralism, believed that drunkenness was the reason for poverty.

Once evangelicals took up the theme of temperance, the movement spread rapidly. By 1835, there were five thousand temperance societies in the United States with a membership of more than 1 million people. In 1840, six reformed sots founded a national organization, the Washington Temperance Society. Two years later, a much more militant association, the Sons of Temperance, began to promote sobriety as a basic religious duty. One of the Sons' most effective lecturers

By 1835, there were five thousand temperance societies in the United States. This 1846 lithograph was used to encourage prohibition of alcohol.

was John B. Gough, another former drunk. He rallied audiences with the lurid language of the fire-and-brimstone revivalist: "Crawl from the slimy ooze, ye drowned drunkards, and with suffocation's blue and livid lips speak out against the drink." Wherever Gough and others appeared, men and women tearfully swore off the bottle.

Prohibition

Temperance reformers quarreled and split as promiscuously as did utopians and religious fundamentalists. One line of division ran between the advocates of temperance in the use of alcohol and the complete abstainers. The former argued that drunkenness was the evil, and not alcohol itself. The latter said that alcohol was addictive and, therefore, inherently sinful. It was necessary to swear off drink completely in order to live morally.

This split took on political significance when the teetotalers divided between moral suasionists, who regarded temperance or abstinence as an individual decision, and legal suasionists, who considered the prohibition of the manufacture and sale of liquor as a means of reforming society.

ON THE WAGON

The phrase *on the wagon*, which means "no longer drinking alcoholic liquor," dates from the 1840s. To publicize their cause, temperance groups hauled a water wagon through the streets of towns and cities and urged people to climb aboard. This vehicle—like a float in a parade—was so common that "going on the wagon" became a universally understood saying. Another catch phrase of the temperance movement has been lost: *cold-water man*, which meant "a person who did not drink."

THE PLEDGE

Although it did not ease the fears of Protestant nativists, there was a temperance movement among Irish Catholics in the United States. In 1840, an Irish priest, Theobald Mathew, toured the United States and administered "The Pledge" to more than half a million Irish Catholic immigrants and their children, swearing them into the Teetotal Abstinence Society.

In 1838, Massachusetts experimented with an act that was designed to cut down consumption among the poor, who, the reformers believed, were the chief sufferers from strong waters. The Fifteen Gallon Law prohibited the sale of whiskey or rum in quantities smaller than fifteen gallons. However, the whole temper of the age of the common man ran against a device that gave new privileges to the rich, and the law was repealed within two years.

In 1845, New York adopted a more democratic law, which authorized local governments to forbid the sale of alcohol within their jurisdictions. Within a few years, five-sixths of the state was dry. In 1846, led by Neal Dow, a public-spirited Portland businessman, Maine adopted the first statewide prohibition law. By 1860, thirteen states had followed suit. But the custom of drinking was too strong to be abolished by mere ordinances. The prohibition laws were flagrantly ignored, and, by 1868, they had been repealed in every state but Maine.

Temperance and prohibition were, for the most part, native Protestant movements that were supported by evangelical reformers and largely directed toward native-born Protestant Americans. In the 1830s and 1840s, however, the crusade against alcohol took on a new dimension because of the huge influx of immigrants who had different customs, among which was a seemingly inordinate devotion to beer and whiskey.

The Stresses of Immigration

Only 8,400 Europeans came to the United States in 1820, hardly enough to excite notice. More than 23,000 arrived in 1830, however, and 84,000 in 1840.

The sudden flood of immigrants into the United States created a period of social turmoil, as reflected in this lithograph of an 1844 anti-Irish riot in Philadelphia.

In the midcentury year, at least 370,000 people stepped from crowded immigrant ships onto wharves in the eastern seaports.

Not only were the numbers larger than could have been imagined, but the great immigration of the mid-nineteenth century consisted mainly of people who followed religions that were rare in the United States and, in many cases, who spoke languages other than English.

Thus, while 3,600 Irish came to the United States in 1820, most of them Protestant, 164,000 arrived in 1850, most of them Roman Catholic. Immigration authorities counted only 23 Scandinavian immigrants in 1820 and 1,600 in 1850, a number that would nearly triple within two years. In 1820, 968 Germans entered the United States; in 1850, 79,000 arrived.

Because the many Scandinavian and German immigrants formed large communities that retained the native languages and preserved Old-World customs, including the convivial musical beer garden, they aroused the suspicion of Americans who had been influenced by the temperance movement. The Irish were worse. They spoke English, but they were also notoriously given to whiskey drinking and they were Roman Catholic, as were at least half of the Germans. Between 1830 and 1860, the Roman Catholic population of the United States increased tenfold—from 300,000 to more than 3 million, or from 3 percent to 13 percent.

The Whore of Babylon

The growth of Catholicism in the United States was difficult for many Americans to accept. Since the days of the Puritans they had been taught that the Church of Rome was the Bible's Whore of Babylon, not merely another Christian denomination but a fount of evil.

This prejudice took on new life in the second quarter of the nineteenth century because the pope was considered not only the spiritual leader of the world's Catholics but also the political head of a reactionary and repressive state. In the Papal States of central Italy, dissidents were jailed and, it was believed, tortured. The political principles of Catholicism seemed to be the very antithesis of American traditions of democracy and liberty. Because the Irish immigrants were devoted to the religion, many Protestants feared that they were shock troops for political reaction.

Moreover, the vast majority of the Irish immigrants were destitute. They had been forced to leave Ireland because the failure of the island's potato crop was literally starving them to death. Once in the United States, they were willing to accept work at any rate of pay. Protestant workingmen regarded them as a threat

to their own standard of living, believing they pulled all wages down.

When economic uneasiness combined with the evangelical crusade against the new immigrants' religious beliefs and their apparently heavy drinking, the result was social movement.

Anti-Catholicism and the Know-Nothings

The famous painter and inventor of the telegraph, Samuel F. B. Morse, urged political action against Catholics. Street wars between Protestant and Irish Catholic workingmen regularly erupted in northeastern cities. In 1834, a mob, angered by stories that Catholic priests kept nuns in convents for their sexual use, burned an Ursuline convent in Charlestown, Massachusetts.

Anti-Catholicism eventually took on political form with the founding of the Order of the Star-Spangled Banner, a secret organization that was dedicated to shutting off further immigration. The order's members came to be known as "Know-Nothings" because, when asked by outsiders about the organization, they replied, "I know nothing."

After 1850, the order came above ground as the American party. Capitalizing on the disintegration of the Whigs, the anti-Catholic, anti-immigrant group swept to power in several states, and to complete control of Massachusetts. At its peak, the American party elected seventy-five congressmen, and a former Whig president, Millard Fillmore of New York, ran as its presidential nominee in 1856.

Anti-Catholicism took on political form with the founding of a secret organization known as "Know-Nothings." This caricature shows Know-Nothings campaigning on election day.

An illustration from a membership certificate for the New York City Tract Society, a group organized to disseminate religious literature.

Missionaries

Only a minority of Protestants believed in taking political action against Roman Catholics. The majority was indifferent or continued to stand by the guarantees of religious freedom in the First Amendment to the Constitution. Even these people, however, approved of the attempts by various missionary societies to convert Catholics and other peoples to a more acceptable religion.

The American Tract Society (founded in 1814) and the American Bible Society (1816) distributed literature among the Catholic population. By 1836, the Tract Society estimated that it had sold or given more than 3 million publications that explained Protestant beliefs.

Another small group concentrated on converting the few Jews in the United States, but most of the missionaries' energies were directed overseas. Partly because the numerous denominational colleges of the United States turned out many more ministers than there were pulpits to fill, and partly because evangelicals felt responsible for the wrongs wreaked by Americans around the world, groups such as the American Board of Foreign Missions raised money to send zealous young men and women to preach the gospel far beyond the boundaries of the United States.

Hawaii

American missionaries worked among the Indians of the West and traveled as far as Africa, India, and China. It was, however, the Sandwich, or Hawaiian, Islands that exercised the greatest attraction after 1819 when a young Hawaiian Christian told recent graduates

of Andover Theological Seminary of the harm done to his homeland by American seafarers.

Whalers from New Bedford and Nantucket had been calling at the islands for decades in order to refit their vessels, replenish their provisions, recover from scurvy on island fruits, and, not incidentally, introduce diseases unknown to Hawaiians that devasted the population. Because they also brought fascinating modern goods to a people who had lived simply from the sea, the visitors irrevocably corrupted Hawaiian culture. Back in New England, evangelicals who felt responsible for their own deaf, blind, and insane found it easy to consider the sins visited on the Hawaiians a burden upon themselves.

As early as 1820, young ministers and their wives, sisters, and mothers shipped out to Hawaii. They met with a mixed reception. While they made many converts and had some success protecting the native people from the depredations of their less moral countrymen, they were greeted with some resistance when they forced proper Boston manners on the natives as though manners were part of religion. The most famous example of their failure to separate theology from custom was their insistence that in the warm, humid climate of the Islands, Christian girls and women dress in full-length calico and flannel "Mother Hubbard" dresses.

Women were the backbone of missionary efforts in Hawaii and elsewhere. In part this reflected the consequences of the westward movement back home. Because young men were freer than young women to break old ties and strike off on their own, New England was left with a surplus of women of marriageable age for whom there were no spouses. Single women were prominent in every reform movement from temperance to abolitionism.

But there was more to the flowering of social activism among American women than statistics. In devoting themselves to missions and participating in other reform movements, women were evincing their restlessness in the private, domestic, and dependent role that society assigned them. This discontent was made explicit in the emergence of feminism as a social movement.

The Birth of the Women's Movement

In the summer of 1848, a group of women called for a convention to be held at Seneca Falls, New York, to consider the "Declaration of Sentiments and Resolutions" they had drafted. The declaration was a deadly serious parody of the Declaration of Independence. "When in the course of human events," it began,

it becomes necessary for one portion of the family of man to assume among the people of the earth a position different from that which they have hitherto occupied, but one to which the laws of nature and nature's God entitle them, a decent respect to the opinions of mankind requires that they should declare the causes that impel them to such a course.

The injustices suffered by women included the denial of the right to vote even when it was extended to "the most ignorant and degraded men"; the forfeiture by a married woman of control over her own property; the nearly absolute control of the husband over a wife's behavior, which "made her, morally, an irresponsible being"; and the exclusion of women from the professions and other gainful employment.

Only sixty-eight women and thirty-two men signed the document, but the Seneca Falls Declaration got national attention—sympathetic in reform newspapers, scornful and taunting in more conventional publications. Among the organizers of the conference were Lucretia Coffin Mott and Elizabeth Cady Stanton, who continued to play an important part in the

Elizabeth Cady Stanton was one of the original participants in the 1848 Seneca Falls convention for women's rights.

feminist movement for a generation. Among the spectators was Amelia Jenks Bloomer, who was soon to become famous as the advocate of a new style of dress that bore her name. But the expectations of 1848, that equal rights for women was a demand whose time had come, were soon dashed to pieces. Americans, including most women, were not ready to think seriously about the civil equality of women. Even the vote, only one of the Seneca Falls demands, was fully seventy years in the future.

The community of evangelical reformers, while generally sympathetic to women's rights in theory, urged the feminists to set their problems aside until a reform that they considered far more important was carried out. This was the abolition of slavery, a cause that was entering its final phase when the first women's rights convention was called. Stanton and Mott, who had been abolitionists before they became feminists, tacitly agreed. They never silenced the call for women's rights, but they stepped to the side in the belief that when the slaves were freed, woman's cause would have its day. Indeed, the over-arching evil of slavery seemed, by 1850, to absorb the energies of every other reform movement.

Lucretia Coffin Mott played an important part in the feminist movement for a generation.

THE FOUNDING MOTHERS

While individuals such as Fanny Wright and Margaret Fuller raised eloquent objections to the inequality of the sexes before 1848, that year marks the beginning of feminism as a social and political movement in the United States. Three of the four women who can be called the Founding Mothers of American feminism were present in the little town of Seneca Falls, New York, during the second week of July 1848 when the "Declaration of Sentiments and Resolutions," a biting parody of the Declaration of Independence, was presented to the country.

Lucretia Coffin Mott (1793–1880) and Elizabeth Cady Stanton (1815–1902) had been friends for a number of years by virtue of their participation in the cause of abolition. In 1840, they tried to register as delegates to an international antislavery convention in London (it was Stanton's wedding trip), but they were refused admission because they were women. The injustice and the absurdity of it—people committed to the equal rights of the races defending the inequality of the sexes—rankled on them. But not until eight years later did they conclude that the rights of women deserved the same kind of fight as did the rights of blacks. Mott and Stanton were principal authors of the declaration "that all men and women are created equal" and the demand for "immediate admission of all to the rights and privileges which belong to them as citizens of the United States."

Both remained active in the long and mostly frustrating battle for female equality until their deaths at ripe ages. They were good-humored people—Stanton, a portly mother of seven, could be downright garrulous—living disproof of the sour-faced fanatics that enemies of the women's movement liked to depict feminists as being. However, they were not afraid to defy the powerful social convention that women should take no part in public life. In 1861, Stanton addressed the New York state legislature; she called for a reform of divorce laws, which, like those in other states, discriminated against and even sealed the social exorcism of divorced women.

Amelia Jenks Bloomer (1818–94), by way of contrast, was a shy, retiring woman who was more comfortable alone with a pen than at the speaker's lectern. Ironically, her name was affixed to what was, at midcentury, considered the ultimate proof that the women's movement was ridiculous—the reform costume known as "bloomers."

Mrs. Bloomer attended the Seneca Falls convention but did not sign the declaration. Over the next several years, she drew closer to Stanton and increasingly devoted her temperance newspaper, *The Lily*, to questions of sexual inequality. In 1851, Bloomer began to advocate reform in women's dress. Female fashion at the time consisted of tightly laced corsets, layers of petticoats, and floor-length dresses that had to be held up

Susan B. Anthony, *pictured here at her desk surrounded by photographs of other feminists.*

in the dusty, muddy, or garbage-strewn streets. The corset was dangerous—literally maiming vital organs—and a kind of shackle. It was difficult to do much of anything in the constrictive garb but to wear it.

The bloomer costume dispensed with the corset in favor of a loose bodice, substituted ankle-length pantaloons for the petticoats, and cut the outer skirt to above the knee. It was, in fact, not new in 1851, when Elizabeth Smith Miller, not Amelia Bloomer, dared to wear it in public. Women at the utopian colony of New Harmony had worn something like the reform costume, as had otherwise quite conventional women at lake and seaside resorts. But Miller and Bloomer wanted to make it standard wear. Because Mrs. Bloomer was its best-known exponent in the pages of the widely circulated *Lily* (and because her name suggested the billowing pantaloons), bloomers they came to be called.

Mrs. Bloomer wore the reform costume for about ten years. However, Stanton and her principal associate after 1852, Susan B. Anthony, gave up on it after only one year. Like many reformers before and since, they discovered that when they tried to emphasize issues that lay close to the heart of women's inferior status, enemies and journalists were more interested in the highly eccentric dress they wore.

As the century progressed, the most important feminist issue became the vote, woman suffrage, and the name of Susan B. Anthony (1820–1906) became synonymous with it. Ironically, like her friend Mrs. Stanton, Anthony considered the woman's plight as much broader than mere disenfranchisement. But as the vote alone was regarded by otherwise conservative women as a "respectable" demand they would support, Anthony went along for the sake of unity.

An unmarried woman, Susan B. Anthony was able to devote all her time to the movement. The other Founding Mothers, burdened with the duties of marriage and motherhood, were unable to do so. For more than half a century—from 1852, when she was refused permission to speak at a temperance convention, until her death in 1906—she labored tirelessly for the cause that was still unfulfilled at the time of her death. Not until the Nineteenth Amendment to the Constitution was ratified in 1920 was the right of women to vote guaranteed.

All four of the Founding Mothers had connections with the Quakers, a sect that almost alone in the United States took the education of girls seriously. All but Bloomer had some formal schooling, which was very unusual in early-nineteenth-century America. Every one of them was also interested in other reform movements: temperance, peace, costume, abolitionism (and some trivial quackeries). And all believed in principle that the emancipation of women depended on more than gaining the right to vote.

For Further Reading

To begin to understand the reform impulse in American history, one could not do better than to read A. M. Schlesinger, *The American as Reformer* (1950). On the reform movements of the first half of the nineteenth century, the classic study is A. F. Tyler, *Freedom's Ferment: Phases of American Social History to 1860* (1944). A more recent analysis of the reformers is C. S. Griffin, *Their Brothers' Keepers: Moral Stewardship in the United States, 1800–1865* (1960).

On the reformers who dedicated themselves to a special cause, see three books: Blake McKelvey, *American Prisons: A Study in American Social History Prior to 1915* (1936); H. E. Marshall, *Dorothea Dix: Forgotten Samaritan* (1937); and F. L. Byrne, *Prophet of Prohibition: Neal Dow and His Crusade* (1961). On anti-Catholicism, see Ray A. Billington, *The Protestant Crusade, 1800–1860* (1936).

In recent years there has been a burst of writing about feminism that explores every aspect of the movement. The best general studies are Page Smith, *Daughters of the Promised Land* (1970); W. L. O'Neill, *Everyone Was Brave: The Rise and Fall of Feminism in America* (1970); and Eleanor Flexner, *Century of Struggle: The Woman's Rights Movement in the United States* (1975). A representative list of feminist writings can be found in A. S. Kraditor, *Up from the Pedestal: Selected Writings in the History of American Feminism* (1968).

19

A Different Country
The Evolution of the South

Doodling at his desk one day, Thomas Jefferson drew up a list of character traits in which, he observed, northerners and southerners differed. Northerners were cool and sober; southerners, fiery and voluptuary. Northerners were self-interested and chicaning (devious); southerners, generous and candid. Northerners were hard-working; southerners, lazy. Northerners were "jealous of their own liberties, and just to those of others"; southerners, "zealous for their own liberties, but trampling on those of others."

No doubt he had a point. Jefferson usually did. But to emphasize differences between the people of the North and the people of the South before the 1830s would be to distort the facts. They were much more alike than not. South-erners and northerners shared not only a linguistic, religious, cultural, and political heritage, but also, by 1826, the year of Jefferson's death, fifty years of national history.

They were shaped by the same social forces. The people of both sections were profoundly moved by the Second Great Awakening and by the outpouring of nationalism that followed the War of 1812. Both southerners and northerners looked to the West for their future. Southerners were not averse to the frantic pursuit of wealth that sometimes was described as a Yankee characteristic: the wildest land speculations of the early nineteenth century took place in Alabama and Mississippi.

Some political issues, particularly financial ones, several times threatened to divide Americans

The New Orleans cotton market as seen by French painter Edgar Degas.

along sectional lines, but, in the end, failed to do so. If the Jefferson Republican party was strongest in the south, Jefferson won the presidency only because he attracted northern votes too. If the Whig party was sometimes associated with the New England conscience and northern reformism, southern Whigs were the equal of southern Democrats well into the 1840s.

The South at the Crossroads

Until the 1830s, not even the survival of slavery in the South was a divisive issue between the people of the two sections. Involuntary servitude was not abolished in most northern states until the nineteenth century; as late as 1827 it was still legal in New York. The institution was a living memory everywhere, and if few northerners regretted having done away with it at home, equally few found anything grossly offensive in the idea of human bondage.

Moreover, the future of slavery was still an open question in the South. It was not common, but it was not unheard of for slaveowners to free their slaves in their wills. As late as 1833, Virginian John Randolph freed four hundred blacks with a stroke of his pen, the largest single manumission in American history. The possibility of legally abolishing the institution was peri-

> ### SOUTHERN SUCCESS STORY
>
> In 1841, John Hampden Randolph purchased a plantation in Iberville Parish (county), Louisiana. The price was astronomical, $30,000, but the down payment was only $863, the odd amount implying that Randolph was not cash rich. He paid off the mortgage by planting cotton, but then switched to sugar. Before the outbreak of the Civil War, Randolph owned several thousand acres and 195 slaves. His sons were university educated, and he sent his daughters to an upper-class finishing school in Baltimore. In 1858, he built a fifty-one-room mansion, Nottoway, which survives.

odically raised by southern politicians. Indeed, the most important antislavery organization of the 1820s drew much of its support from the southern states.

Why Southerners Feared Abolition

The chief reason that southerners did not voluntarily do away with slavery was the obvious one: the wealth and privileged position of the South's dominant political group, the great planters, depended on the forced labor of the blacks. Nevertheless, many southerners, including great planters, agreed that the system of slave labor had more drawbacks than it had advantages. They conceded that the South would be better off economically with free workers who were paid in

The privileged position of the South's plantation owners depended on the forced labor of blacks.

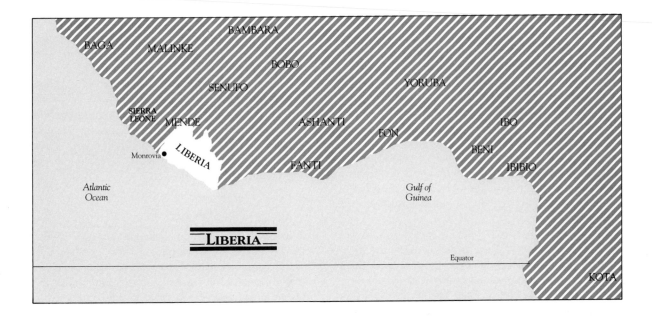

BAGA
MALINKE
BAMBARA
BOBO
SENUFO
YORUBA
SIERRA LEONE
MENDE
ASHANTI
IBO
FON
BENI
LIBERIA
Monrovia
FANTI
IBIBIO
Atlantic Ocean
Gulf of Guinea
LIBERIA
Equator
KOTA

wages, the system that northerners and the rest of the Western world had adopted.

The catch was the race of the South's laboring people. White southerners sincerely believed that blacks were innately inferior to whites. They were not capable of competing with whites for land and for jobs on an equal basis. Or, if by some chance they could compete in a free economy, the antipathy between the races would result in chronic racial war. Next to sex, race was the fundamental division of humanity; the two peoples of the South could not or would not live side by side as equals.

In continuing to hold the blacks as slaves, therefore, the planters believed that they were shouldering a tragic burden that had been heaped on them by history. They were protecting the blacks in return for using their labor; they were saving their society from anarchy and violence.

The Failure of "Colonization"

The American Colonization Society was founded in 1817 to provide slaveowners with an alternative. With the active support of such distinguished southerners as Madison, Monroe, Marshall, and Clay, the society proposed to raise money with which free American blacks would be transported to and set up in West Africa. By ridding the South of free blacks, the advocates of colonization believed, they would encourage slaveowners to free their people and state legislatures to adopt laws abolishing slavery.

In 1821, the society provided money to send a few former slaves to Sierra Leone. The next year, it pur-

chased a part of the area and helped establish the Republic of Liberia, with its capital at Monrovia (named for President Monroe). Overall, about eleven thousand American blacks settled in Liberia under the auspices of various colonization groups. They established a government patterned on the American model and, less happily, reduced the native people of the region to a kind of servitude with themselves on top.

But colonization was not realistic. There were 1.5 million slaves in the United States in 1820, and 2 million in 1830. This was far more people than could be colonized on a small strip of African seacoast. Moreover, few free blacks were willing to go to Africa. Most were several generations removed from their Old-World roots and felt no attraction to an unknown land. Surely most slaves wanted to be free. But they thought of the southern United States as their home.

Finally, the more the price of cotton boomed on the world market, returning huge profits to planters, the less was heard about the antislavery aspects of colonization. When the Mississippi Colonization Society was founded in 1829, its explicit purpose was to rid the state of free blacks, not to encourage planters to free those they held as slaves. Even in the upper South, where little cotton was grown, it became profitable to sell surplus slaves "down the river," and the colonization impulse waned. Except for one last debate, the southern antislavery movement was dead.

The Last Debate

In December 1831, Governor John Floyd of Virginia asked the state legislature to consider a plan to phase out slavery over a period of years, with cash compensation for planters who lost their property. For three weeks in January 1832, the delegates debated the proposal moderately and intelligently.

Even the staunchest proslavery men were defensive. Their speeches typically opened with the express wish that blacks had never been introduced into Virginia, that the state would be a better place if it had been developed by free white labor. However, they concluded, blacks constituted about half of Virginia's population, the colonization movement was obviously a failure, and a large population of free blacks was out of the question. However sadly, Virginia must continue to be a slave state.

The assumption that a biracial society would not work carried the day. At the end of January, the legislature rejected the Floyd plan by a vote of seventy-three to fifty-eight. A switch of only eight votes would have changed the course of American history, for the other states of the upper South—Delaware, Maryland, Kentucky—often followed Virginia's lead. Had they abolished slavery in the 1830s, it would not have continued as an institution of a whole section but of a few, generally lightly populated states of the Deep South. As it was, once the Virginia debate was over, no powerful party of southern whites ever again considered the possibility of abolishing the tragic institution until the Civil War.

Threats to Southern Order

Both Floyd's proposal and the Virginia legislature's rejection of it were profoundly influenced by two events that had alarmed the South in 1831: the appearance in the North of a new kind of antislavery movement, and an uprising of slaves in Southampton County, Virginia, under the leadership of Nat Turner.

The Early Abolitionists

While the mainstream debate over slavery revolved around its political justice, economic wisdom, and social consequences, there always had been a few voices raised about the morality of human bondage. Many eighteenth-century Quakers, such as John Woolman of New Jersey and Anthony Benezet of Philadelphia, had spoken publicly of the sinfulness of slavery. During the 1820s, Benjamin Lundy continued this tradition, calling for gradual abolition and the colonization of blacks in Haiti, Canada, or Texas (then a part of Mexico).

Some blacks, notably the mathematician and astronomer Benjamin Banneker, also published moral argu-

ments against slavery and drew support from white religious groups and most communities of free blacks in both North and South. With few exceptions they treated the subject as one to be discussed calmly and moderately, in terms of one Christian concerned about the soul of another. Their fraternal attitude toward slaveowners was typified by the Boston Unitarian William Ellery Channing, who told southerners, "We consider slavery your calamity and not your curse." None of them used language as harsh as had Thomas Jefferson in his denunciations of slavery.

David Walker and William Lloyd Garrison

But in 1829, the language began to change. In that year, a free black artisan named David Walker published a pamphlet called *The Appeal.* After reviewing the traditional arguments about the immorality and injustice of slavery, Walker stated that unless whites abolished the institution, blacks had a moral duty to rise up in violent rebellion.

William Lloyd Garrison, a spare, intense young man of twenty-four who was working for Benjamin Lundy in Baltimore, did not believe in violent rebellion. Among the reforms he supported was the peace movement. And yet, when he founded his own antislavery newspaper in Boston in January 1831, *The Liberator,* he took an aggressive and uncompromising approach toward both the institution of slavery and the slaveowners. "I am aware," Garrison wrote in the first issue of his paper,

that many object to the severity of my language; but is there not cause for severity? I *will be* as harsh as truth, and as uncompromising as justice. On this subject I do not wish to

SOUTHERN ANXIETIES

Both antislavery and proslavery southerners feared slave rebellion. The chief difference between them was in the tone in which they spoke of blacks.

Thomas Ritchie, an antislavery Virginian: "To attempt to excite discontent and revolt, or publish writings having this tendency, obstinately and perversely, among us, is outrageous—it ought not to be passed over with indifference. Our own safety—the good and happiness of our slaves, requires it."

Edward D. Holland, a proslavery South Carolinian: "Let it never be forgotten that our NEGROES are truly the *Jacobins* of the country; that they are the *anarchists* and the *domestic enemy,* the *common enemy of civilized society,* and the barbarians who would, IF THEY COULD, become the DESTROYERS of our race."

THE LIBERATOR.

VOL. I.] WILLIAM LLOYD GARRISON AND ISAAC KNAPP, PUBLISHERS. **[NO. 33.**

BOSTON, MASSACHUSETTS.] OUR COUNTRY IS THE WORLD—OUR COUNTRYMEN ARE MANKIND. [SATURDAY, AUGUST 13, 1831.

The masthead of William Lloyd Garrison's antislavery newspaper.

think, or speak, or write, with moderation. No! no! Tell a man whose house is on fire to give a moderate alarm; tell him to moderately rescue his wife from the hands of the ravisher; tell the mother to gradually extricate her babe from the fire into which it has fallen;—but urge me not to use moderation in a cause like the present.

It was the ultimate statement of the evangelical reformer's approach to social questions. There was no more compromising with an evil institution than there was discussing sin with Satan. In order to avoid defilement, it was necessary to break off all association with the enemy. Rejecting the traditional Christian ideal of distinguishing the sinner from the sin, Garrison described the slaveowner's life as "one of unbridled lust, of filthy amalgamation, of swaggering braggadocio, of haughty domination, of cowardly ruffianism, of boundless dissipation, of matchless insolence, of infinite self-conceit, of unequalled oppression, of more than savage cruelty."

He was never a popular man, as, indeed, he did not wish to be. Even in Boston, a center of antislavery sentiment, Garrison was sometimes hooted at and pelted with stones when he delivered public speeches. On one occasion a mob threw a noose around his neck and dragged him through the streets. Garrison was saved by a group of abolitionist women whose boldness shocked the mob. (Garrison was also a supporter of women's rights.)

In the South, Garrison was regarded as a monster. Not because he was against slavery, at least not at first; antislavery southerners loathed him as intensely as did proslavery southerners. Garrison and other extremist abolitionists were hated in the South because they were believed to be inciting bloody slave rebellion, and in 1831, the fear of slave rebellion in the South was no abstract speculation.

Nat Turner

Nat Turner, a slave of Southampton County, Virginia, was a queer amalgam of mystic dreamer and hard-headed realist. Literate—unusual among slaves—he pored over the Bible, drawing his own interpretations of its meaning. The rebellion he led in August and September 1831 was triggered by a solar eclipse that he took as a sign from God.

If mystically inspired, Turner's revolt had a very practical goal—personal liberty—and Turner had a realistic conception of the odds against his succeeding. He planned with care, divulging his scheme to only a few trusted friends who swore with him to fight to the death. On the night of August 21, 1831, armed with farm tools, the little group moved like lightning. They swept across Southampton County, killing sixty whites and recruiting more supporters from among the slaves. Before they were rounded up, an event that Turner regarded as inevitable, there were seventy in the band. Forty, including Nat Turner, were hanged. Rebels who were not directly responsible for spilling blood were sold out of state. Undoubtedly other blacks, including

---

WANTED: NAT TURNER

Five feet 6 or 8 inches high, weighs between 150 and 160 pounds, rather bright complexion, but not a mulatto. Broad shoulders, large flat nose, large eyes. Broad flat feet, rather knock-kneed, walks brisk and active. Hair on the top of the head very thin, no beard, except on the upper lip and at the top of the chin. A scar on one of his temples, also one at the back of his neck. A large knot on one of the bones of his right arm, near his wrist, produced [by] a blow.

With a handful of trusted friends, Nat Turner, a Virginia slave, led an unsuccessful revolt designed to win freedom for the slaves.

the innocent, were quietly murdered in retaliation by angry or frightened whites.

The Fear of Rebellion

Turner's rising was not the first in the United States. In 1800, an obscure black named Gabriel Prosser had led an uprising in Richmond that may have involved as many as one thousand slaves. In 1822, a free black in Charleston, Denmark Vesey, had been accused of organizing a conspiracy to murder whites. Runaway slaves in Georgia joined with Seminole Indians to raid outlying plantations and free the slaves there. At one time or another, planters in every part of the South suspected slaves of planning to rebel.

No doubt many of these plots were figments of overwrought imaginations; but there was nothing imaginary about Nat Turner's rebellion, and a shiver of fear ran through the white South. In large parts of Louisiana, Mississippi, and South Carolina, blacks outnumbered whites by twenty to one. Mary Boykin Chesnut, a South Carolinian of the planter class, revealed the dark thoughts that plagued many southerners when she de-

scribed her family's plantation at Mulberry as "half a dozen whites and sixty or seventy Negroes, miles away from the rest of the world."

The Peculiar Institution

If many southerners shared such anxieties, their belief in black inferiority meant that few were willing to admit that blacks, left to their own devices, were capable of mounting a rebellion or, indeed, were interested in changing their status. To white southerners, it was no coincidence that Turner's uprising followed the belligerent first issue of *The Liberator* by only eight months. They took wry note of the fact that Turner knew how to read. They blamed the extreme abolitionists like Garrison for the tragedy.

Once Virginia made its landmark decision to remain a slave state, the South stood almost alone in the Western world. The northern states had abolished the institution; the Spanish-speaking republics of the Americas had done so; Great Britain was in the process of freeing the slaves in its empire. Alone of Western nations, Brazil still recognized slavery, and the Brazilian institution was considerably different from the slavery of the southern states.

The South Closes Ranks

After 1832, southerners faced up to the fact that slavery was a "peculiar institution," a way of life unique to them, and they moved on three fronts to protect it. First, they insulated the South from ideas from outside that threatened slavery, and they suppressed dissent at home. Second, southerners ceased to apologize to themselves and others for slavery. Instead of calling it a historical tragedy or a necessary evil, they devised the argument that slavery was "a positive good" that benefited slaveowner, slave, and southern society as a whole. Third, they reformed the state slave codes (the laws that governed the peculiar institution), both improving the material conditions under which slaves lived and instituting stricter, often harsh controls over the black population.

Suppression of Dissent

Most southern states passed laws that forbade the distribution of abolitionist literature within their borders. They screened the federal mails and seized copies of *The Liberator,* other antislavery newspapers, and books. Georgia's legislature offered a reward of $5,000 to any person who would kidnap William Lloyd Garrison and bring him into the state to stand trial for inciting rebellion.

Even if the resolution was meant to be symbolic, a state legislature's willingness to sanction a felony illustrates the depth of bitterness toward abolitionists in the South. In border states like Kentucky, abolitionists such as John Gregg Fee and the politician Cassius Marcellus Clay (a relative of Henry) were generally unmolested, but they were the exception. Antislavery opinions were no longer acceptable below the Mason-Dixon line.

Not even in Washington. Beginning in 1836, southern congressmen annually nagged the House of Representatives to adopt a gag rule. The gag rule provided that every petition dealing with slavery that the House received would be tabled (set aside) with no discussion whatsoever. Former president John Quincy Adams, now a member of Congress, argued that the rule violated the right to free speech. He was no abolitionist; indeed, Adams considered men like Garrison to be dangerous and irresponsible. But he insisted on their constitutional right to be heard, and because he criticized southerners for quashing the right of petition, he came to be lumped with the abolitionists as an enemy.

A Positive Good

Shortly after Virginia's debate on the future of slavery, a professor of economics at the College of William and Mary, Thomas Roderick Dew, published a ringing defense of the slave system as a better way to organize and control labor than the wage system of the North. By 1837, John C. Calhoun and most southern political leaders were repeating and embroidering on Dew's theories. In the Senate, Calhoun declared that compared with other systems by which racial and class relationships were governed, "the relation now existing in the slaveholding states is, instead of an evil, a good—a positive good."

The proslavery argument included religious, historical, cultural, and social proofs. The Bible, the positive-good theorists argued, sanctioned slavery. Not only did the ancient Hebrews own slaves with God's blessing, but Christ had told a servant who wanted to be his disciple to return to his master.

Dew and others argued that the great civilizations of antiquity, Greece and Rome, were slaveholding societies. Hardly barbaric, slavery had served as the foundation of high culture since the beginning of recorded time. Slavery made possible the existence of a gracious and cultured upper class that, with its leisure, guarded the highest refinements of human society. Southern planters took pride in the fact that, although elementary and secondary education in the South was vastly inferior to that provided by the public-school systems of the North, they were far better educated than the northern elite. In 1860, eleven thousand students attended southern colleges and universities. In New England, which had about the same population as the South, there were fewer than four thousand college students.

As an aristocracy, southerners said, the planters were closer to the tradition of the gentlemanly Founding Fathers than were the vulgar, money-hungry capitalists of the North. Because gentlemen dominated politics in the South, the section was far better governed than was the North, where demagogues from the dregs of society could win election by playing on the whims of the mob. The planters liked to think of themselves as descended from the Cavaliers of sixteenth- and seventeenth-century England. Their favorite author was Sir Walter Scott, who spun tales of flowering knighthood and chivalry.

George Fitzhugh and Sociology

But did all these proofs justify denying freedom to men and women? Yes, answered George Fitzhugh, a Virginia lawyer, in two influential books: *A Sociology for the South* (1854) and *Cannibals All* (1857). He amassed

CALHOUN'S CONSISTENCY

When abolitionists quoted the Declaration of Independence to proslavery southerners—"all men are created equal"—the southerners were generally forced to make convoluted interpretations of the phrase in order to excuse slavery. John C. Calhoun, at least, was consistent. "Taking the proposition literally," he said, "there is not a word of truth in it."

This invoice from 1835 shows that a buyer purchased ten slaves for $5,351, a substantial amount of money at that time.

statistics and other evidence with which he argued that the southern slave lived a better life than did the northern wageworker or the European peasant.

Fitzhugh argued that someone had to perform the drudgery in every society. In the South, menial work was done by slaves who were cared for from cradle to grave. Not only did the slaveowner feed, clothe, and house his workers, but he also supported slave children, the injured and the disabled, and the elderly—all of whom were nonproductive people. Fitzhugh delighted to point out that by comparison, the northern wageworker was paid only as long as there was work to be done and the worker was fit to do it. The worker who was injured was cut loose to fend for himself in an uncaring world. His children, the elderly, and the incompetent were no responsibility of the employer.

Consequently, the North was plagued with social problems that were unknown in the South. The section teemed with obnoxious, disruptive reformers; the lower classes were irreligious and, in their misery, tumultuous. The free working class was tempted by socialistic, communistic, and other dangerous doctrines that threatened the social order. By comparison, the slaves were happy and contented. "A merrier being does not exist on the face of the globe," wrote George Fitzhugh, "than the Negro slave of the United States."

Slave Management

Fitzhugh equated "happiness" with the material conditions of slave life—housing, clothing, diet—and compared them favorably with the conditions under which the poorest wageworkers of the North lived. By the 1850s, when he wrote, most southern state legislatures had adopted minimum living standards as part of their slave codes, and magazines like the *Southern Agriculturalist* regularly featured lively exchanges among slaveowners about how they treated "their people."

The most commonly stated reason for keeping slaves adequately housed, clothed, and fed was practical: a healthy slave worked more efficiently and was less likely to rebel or run away. Underlying the trend

toward improvement in the conditions of slave life after the 1830s, however, was the South's determination to give the lie to the abolitionists' depiction of slavery as a life of unremitting horror. Planters who did provide decent accommodations for their slaves took pleasure in showing slave quarters to northern or foreign visitors. Indeed, they needed to reassure themselves that they were the generous patriarchs that the positive-good writers described. Less often talked about were the measures of control that were devised in the wake of the Turner rebellion.

Controlling the Slaves

By 1840, the states of the Deep South had adopted laws that made it virtually impossible for a slaveowner to free his slaves. Virginia forced recently freed blacks to leave the state. It was a crime in some southern states to teach a slave to read.

County governments were required to fund and maintain slave patrols. These mounted posses of armed whites policed the roads and plantations, particularly at night. They had the legal right to break into slave cabins or demand at gunpoint that any black (or white) account for himself or herself.

Usually rough, hard-bitten men who were so poor

Louisiana slaves cut sugar cane under the threat of an overseer's whip.

that they needed the undesirable job, the "pad-dyrollers" were brutal even with unoffending slaves. The blacks hated and feared them. Their mere presence and arrogance lent an atmosphere of repression to the plantation regions that few outsiders failed to notice.

Blacks who were not under the direct supervision of their masters or overseers were required by law to carry written passes that gave them permission to be abroad, even just a mile or two from their cabins. Free blacks—there were about 250,000 in the South by 1860, 1 to every 15 slaves—also had to protect carefully the legal document that guaranteed their status.

The presence of free blacks presented a problem for slaveowners. One of the most effective means of controlling the slaves was to convince them that God and nature intended them to be slaves because of their race, and that they should be thankful to be under the care of their masters. Religion was an effective means of control, and careful masters paid close attention to the kind of preaching their slaves heard.

Some owners took their slaves to their own churches, where the ministers delivered sermons based on biblical stories such as that of Hagar: "the angel of the Lord said unto her, return to Thy mistress, and submit thyself under her hands." Other masters permitted the blacks, who preferred an emotional Christianity mixed with a strong dose of African tradition, to have preachers of their own race. But these often eloquent men were instructed—specifically or indirectly—to steer clear of any topics that might cast doubt on the justice of slavery. Some toed the line. Others developed coded language and song by which they conveyed their protest. The idealized institution of John C. Calhoun and George Fitzhugh bore only an accidental relationship to slavery as it actually existed.

ABOLITIONISTS

Sojourner Truth was a freed slave who devoted her-self to the abolition and women's rights movements.

William Lloyd Garrison was the most famous of the abolitionists—and the one most hated by slaveowners. But he was only one of dozens of people who made a profession of antislavery, devoting their lives to fighting the hated institution. Indeed, some historians have suggested that Garrison was the least effective of the abolitionists because he alienated more people with his intemperate language and self-righteous demeanor than ever he converted.

Theodore Dwight Weld (1803–95), who devoted himself to the antislavery cause from 1830, found slavery as morally repugnant as did Garrison. Unlike Garrison, he shunned publicity, refused even to use his real name when he published his arguments, and concentrated on converting the people of the rural Midwest, rather than remaining in Boston and writing for those who already agreed with him. "Eloquent as an angel and powerful as thunder" on the speaker's platform, Weld was also able to speak rationally with people who disagreed with him.

Two of his converts were probably indispensable to the antislavery cause. Arthur Tappan (1786–1865) and Lewis Tappan (1788–1873) were wealthy New York merchants who generously financed a number of abolitionist institutions, including Garrison's *Liberator,* Kenyon and Oberlin colleges in Ohio, and the American Anti-Slavery Society, which they founded with Weld in 1833.

Another Weld convert was southerner James G. Birney (1792–1857), who, under Weld's influence, freed his own slaves and founded a newspaper in Cincinnati, *The Philanthropist.* Birney carried on even after his presses and offices were destroyed by a proslavery mob in 1836. (Another proslavery mob in Illinois not only destroyed Elijah Lovejoy's abolitionist newspaper in 1837, but it killed Lovejoy.) Unlike Garrison, who regarded political action as beneath him and who called the Constitution "a covenant with hell," Birney believed in fighting slavery at the polls. In 1840 and 1844, he was the presidential nominee of the antislavery Liberty party.

In 1838, Weld married Angelina Grimké (1805–79). She and her sister, Sarah (1792–1873), had been born into a wealthy slaveowning family in South Carolina. Convinced from their association with Quakers that slavery was morally wrong, the sisters shocked public opinion by speaking publicly on behalf of abolition and women's rights.

A black woman who devoted herself to both of these causes was Sojourner Truth (1797–1893). Born Isabella, a slave in New York, she was freed under the state emancipation law of 1827, worked as a domestic servant for several years, and then burst on the abolitionist scene as one of the most powerful orators of her age. Sojourner Truth remained illiterate to the end of her days, but, reminiscent of more recent reformers, she was popular because she accompanied her speeches with songs she had written herself.

The most famous black abolitionist was Frederick Douglass (1817–95), who had been born a slave in Maryland. After one unsuccessful attempt that landed him in jail, Douglass escaped to Massachusetts. There he studied (he had taught himself to read while still a slave) and was regarded as one of the most learned of the antislavery activists. In 1845, he wrote his *Autobiography*, which is still valuable for its insights into the realities of slavery as well as the fight against it. Because Douglass revealed factual details of his life as a slave in the book, he feared that he would be arrested as a runaway and returned to Maryland. He moved to England, where he continued to work in the antislavery cause and made enough money by writing and lecturing to buy his freedom from his former master.

No other abolitionist was quite so good-humored and humane as Frederick Douglass. He had few illusions about himself or his fellow abolitionists, many of whom, he realized, disliked blacks as deeply as did many white southerners. When some erstwhile friends criticized him in 1884 for marrying a white woman, he replied sardonically that he was trying to demonstrate his impartiality. His first wife, Douglass said, "was the color of my mother, and the second the color of my father."

Harriet Tubman (1821–1913) was less a propagandist than a guerrilla. After escaping from slavery in 1849, she returned to the South nineteen times to lead other runaways to freedom. Because her name was soon known to southern authorities, she was risking not only her freedom but also her life. During the Civil War, Tubman served as a Union spy behind Confederate lines.

Frederick Douglass was one of the most learned of the antislavery activists.

For Further Reading

On the abolitionist movement in general, see Louis Filler, *The Crusade Against Slavery* (1960), and Gerald Sorin, *Abolitionism: A New Perspective* (1972). A. S. Kraditor, *Means and Ends in American Abolitionism: Garrison and His Critics on Strategy and Tactics, 1834–1850* (1967), deals with the heated question that frequently split the abolitionists. The neglected prominence of blacks in the antislavery movement is remedied in J. H. and W. H. Pease, *They Who Would be Free: Blacks' Search for Freedom, 1830–1861* (1974). For a biography of each of the two best-known abolitionists, see B. P. Thomas, *Theodore Weld: Crusader for Freedom* (1950), and J. L. Thomas, *The Liberator: William Lloyd Garrison* (1963).

W. S. Jenkins, *Pro-Slavery Thought in the Old South* (1935), is comprehensive. In addition, the works of the leading proslavery apologist, George Fitzhugh, are available in inexpensive editions. For the racism on which proslavery thought was eventually based, see William Stanton, *The Leopard's Spots: Scientific Attitudes Toward Race in America, 1815–1859* (1960).

On the institution itself, the literature is vast. For an introduction, students should see K. M. Stampp, *The Peculiar Institution* (1956), and Eugene Genovese, *Roll, Jordan, Roll* (1974). Those desiring to pursue the matter might wish to look at the book that Stampp's set out specifically to answer, U. B. Phillips, *American Negro Slavery* (1919).

20

The Great Exception
Slavery as it Was

In December 1865, news reached Washington, D.C., that the Thirteenth Amendment had been ratified and was a part of the Constitution. The Thirteenth is one of the shortest amendments; but in terms of what it did, it was the most momentous. In providing that "neither slavery nor involuntary servitude . . . shall exist within the United States," the Thirteenth wrote an end to the Great Exception, a legal and social institution that flew in the face of the ideals that Americans believed gave their nation special meaning to the world: the freedom of the individual, impartial justice, equality of opportunity, and government by the people.

Adults and children gathered beside a row of slave quarters in South Carolina in 1863.

Images of Slavery

Since 1865, two images of slavery have competed for the American mind. One is rich in romance; the other is rife with misery. Actually, both visions evolved while slavery was still a living institution: the first by the positive-good theorists with the assistance of a Pennsylvania-born songwriter who spent only a few months of his life in the South; the latter by abolitionists who also, for the most part, had little firsthand knowledge of what life was like in the slave states.

Stephen Foster and the Sweet Magnolia

Stephen Foster was born in Pittsburgh in 1826. Musically minded, he was one of the first Americans able to support himself as a composer of popular songs. He wrote for traveling minstrel shows and made his living from the sale of sheet music.

Foster's first successful song was "Oh! Susannah," a whimsical nonsense piece about the California gold rush of 1849 that is still popular with children. Then, perhaps because the minstrel show was "set" in the South, with white (and some black) performers blacking their faces and singing grotesque dialect, Foster turned to sentimental depictions of plantation life from the slave's perspective. In the world of "Old Folks at Home" and "Swanee River" (1851), "Massa's in de Cold, Cold Ground" (1852), "My Old Kentucky Home" (1853), and "Old Black Joe" (1860), slaves were represented as uncomplicated, loving creatures who enjoyed a secure, satisfying life attached to a kindly master whose first concern was their well-being.

Contented slaves, grand houses, Spanish moss, the scent of magnolia blossoms, and easygoing, gracious, cultured people were the ingredients of Foster's South. Within a generation of the abolition of slavery, this

Slaves at rest, romantically depicted in this 1859 painting by Eastman Johnson.

vision of ante-bellum southern life was embraced by most Americans, particularly middle- and upper-class northerners. In the industrial age, goaded along by the relentless pace of the machine, it was not difficult to dream nostalgically of a South that had never been. The tradition culminated in Margaret Mitchell's classic novel of 1936, *Gone with the Wind,* and the Hollywood film of 1939.

Harriet Beecher Stowe and the Sting of the Lash

The contrasting image of life under slavery is that depicted by the abolitionists. It was a world of black-snake whips, brutal slave catchers following packs of bloodhounds, children torn away from their mothers, squalor, disease, and half-starvation under callous masters.

It made no difference to thoughtful abolitionists that proslavery people could describe hundreds of kind and generous masters. Their hatred of slavery was based not on how it worked in practice, but on the moral belief that it was a sin for one human being to hold another in bondage. Nevertheless, in their books, pamphlets, and lectures, abolitionists found it most effective to emphasize the physical deprivation and cruelty suffered by slaves. Some antislavery lecturers traveled with runaway blacks whose backs were disfigured from brutal beatings.

The most important single shot in the abolitionist campaign was a novel, *Uncle Tom's Cabin,* published by Harriet Beecher Stowe in 1852. Not only did the book sell an astonishing three hundred thousand copies within a few years (the equivalent of 3 million copies today), but it was adapted into a play that was performed by dozens of professional and amateur troupes in small town and city alike. So influential was the tale of Uncle Tom, a submissive and loyal old slave, that when Abraham Lincoln met Mrs. Stowe during the Civil War, he said, "So you are the lady whose book started this great war."

The underlying theme of *Uncle Tom's Cabin* is a subtle abstract point: no matter how decent and well-intentioned the individual slaveowner, he does wrong by subscribing to an inherently evil institution. In the story, Uncle Tom's original owner is the epitome of the paternalistic planter who genuinely loves his old slave. But when financial troubles require him to raise money quickly, he is forced to sell Tom. Heartbroken, the planter promises Tom that he will find him and buy him back as soon as he is able. (The book ends with Tom dying in his arms.)

It was not, however, this insight into the institution that made *Uncle Tom's Cabin* so popular. Rather, the book was so effective because of its graphic, lurid scenes

Harriet Beecher Stowe (1811–1896) helped the abolitionists' campaign with her novel, Uncle Tom's Cabin.

Published in 1853, Uncle Tom's Cabin *was widely read, selling 300,000 copies within a few years.*

of cruelty that Tom witnesses and suffers in the course of the story. Mrs. Stowe herself accepted this as the book's contribution. When southerners angrily complained that she had distorted the realities of slave life, she responded in 1853 with *A Key to Uncle Tom's Cabin,* which set out the documentary basis of most of her accusations, much of it quotations from southern newspapers.

Blacks never forgot this side of slavery, but with the ascendancy of the romantic vision in the late nineteenth century, most white Americans did. Not until the civil-rights movement of the 1950s awakened the country to the tragic history of American blacks did the ugly face of the peculiar institution again impress itself on the popular consciousness. With the great success of Alex Haley's *Roots* as a book and television series in the 1970s, the popular vision of slavery came full circle—from Uncle Tom through Scarlett O'Hara and Mammy to Kunta Kinte.

What Slavery Was Like

Which image is correct? Both and neither. Although proslavery and antislavery people dealt with the peculiar institution as though it were the same in Virginia and Texas, on cotton plantation and New Orleans riverfront, on giant plantation and frontier farm, for field hand and butler, the reality of slavery was as diverse as the South itself.

The Structure of the Institution
The census of 1860, the last census that was taken while slavery was legal, revealed that nearly 4 million people lived in bondage. They were equally divided between males and females. All but a few lived in the fifteen states south of the Mason-Dixon line and the Ohio River. West of the Mississippi River, Missouri, Arkansas, Louisiana, and Texas were slave states.

Only one white southern family in four owned slaves. Even when those whose jobs involved dealing directly with the institution—overseers, slave traders, patrollers—are added to this number, it is clear that only a minority of white southerners had a direct material stake in slavery.

Those who were very rich and politically powerful because they owned slaves were extremely few. In 1860, only 2,200 great planters, less than 1 percent of the southern population, owned 100 or more slaves. Only 254 persons owned 200 or more. Nathaniel Heyward of South Carolina was at the top of this pyramid; he owned 2,000 slaves on seventeen plantations.

More typical of the southern slaveowner was Jacob Eaton of neighboring North Carolina. On his 160-acre farm he worked side by side with the slave family he owned. Eaton's yeoman class—small independent farmers who owned two to nine slaves—was the backbone of both the South and the slavery system. About 40 percent of southern slaveowners fell into this category.

Another 45 percent owned ten to twenty slaves, still not enough to support the grand plantation style. Very few slaves knew what life was like on the large plantation that was featured in the legends.

First Light to Sundown
What all slaves did know was work. For a slaveowner to justify investing capital in a labor force rather than hiring free laborers and investing his capital elsewhere, it was necessary to get the maximum labor from a slave. Few blacks enjoyed the comforts and privileges of being domestic servants; cooks and maids made life more pleasant for those who owned them, but they did not make money for them. The vast majority of slaves were field hands who raised a cash crop by means of heavy labor from first light to sundown the year round.

Cotton was by far the most important southern product. Indeed, it was the most important American product! During the 1850s, an average annual crop of 4 million bales brought more than $190 million into the American economy from abroad. Cotton represented two-thirds of the nation's total exports. Other cash crops that slaves raised were sugar (mostly in Louisiana), rice (mostly in the Carolinas), tobacco (in the upper South), and hemp, from which rope was manufactured (in Kentucky).

Since southern farmers and planters strived to be self-sufficient and, therefore, raised corn, vegetables,

---

KING COTTON

Southern politicians repeatedly lectured northerners that the South supported the national economy. That is, the money that cotton brought in from abroad provided most of the surplus capital that paid for the industrialization of the nation. This transaction was direct when protective tariffs on English-made goods forced southerners to buy American-made goods.

The politicians were right. Cotton did industrialize the United States before the Civil War. However, northern antislavery people had another way of considering this economic fact of life. Who, they asked, really produced the cotton? To a large extent, slaves did. And to that extent, the United States was industrialized by the forced labor of the blacks.

Most slaves were used as field hands and performed the heavy labor needed to raise such cash crops as cotton.

and hogs for food, and hay for fodder, as well as their cash crop, there was plenty of work to be done on farm or plantation the year round. The calendar of a cotton plantation was full of both major and odd jobs to be done every week except for a short period around Christmas, to which the slaves looked forward as "laying-by time."

Curiously, however, because slaves were expensive—up to $1,800 for a first-rate field hand, a healthy man in the prime of life—planters preferred to hire free black or Irish workers to perform unhealthy and dangerous tasks. Few would risk their human property on the jobs of draining swamps or working at the bottom of chutes down which six-hundred-pound bales of cotton came hurtling at high speeds, sometimes flipping end over end.

The Rhythms of Labor

By the 1850s, a slave produced from $80 to $120 in value each year and cost from $30 to $50 to feed, clothe, and shelter. The margin of profit was not large enough to allow the small-scale slaveowner to live without working in the fields along with his slaves.

Planters who owned up to about twenty slaves were less likely to perform menial tasks. But because slaves rarely worked any more than they were forced to work (their master, not they, enjoyed the fruits of their labor) the owner of twenty slaves had to supervise them—bribing, cajoling, threatening, or whipping them to move along. With more than twenty slaves, a planter could afford to hire a professional overseer or to put a slave driver (himself a slave) in charge of supervision. On the very large plantations, masters had little direct contact with their slaves, all of whom were supervised by overseers and drivers.

Slaves on larger plantations worked according to the task system or the gang system. Under the task system, a specific job was assigned each day. When it was done, the slave's time was his or her own. Under the gang system, slaves worked in groups under a white overseer or black driver. It is impossible to know how frequently they felt the sting of the blacksnake. The lash was always in evidence, however, in black hand as well as white. Frederick Douglass wryly remarked that "everybody in the South wants the privilege of whipping someone else."

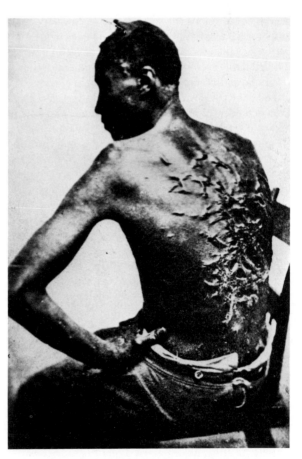

A slave displays scars from a brutal whipping. Such extreme cruelty was unusual, but many, perhaps most, slaves were whipped at one time or another.

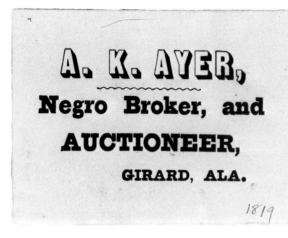

A. K. AYER,
Negro Broker, and
AUCTIONEER,
GIRARD, ALA.

1879

Slaves were regarded as property and were bought and sold by brokers who carried such business cards as this one.

The Slave Trade

Slaves were defined in law as chattel property, personal movable possessions the same as cattle, hogs, a cotton gin, or a piece of furniture. They could be bought, sold, bartered, willed, or given away as a present. In practice in the volatile cotton economy, the commerce in slaves was brisk and potentially quite profitable.

The slave trade was also the ugliest face of slavery, as even defenders of the institution admitted. The general flow of it was "down the river"—the Mississippi—from the older tobacco states to the cotton states of the Deep South. Professional slave traders bought blacks in Virginia and Maryland and shipped them or marched them in coffles (groups chained together in a line) to New Orleans, where as many as two hundred companies were in the business.

The slave auction was, in effect, an auction of human livestock. Foreigners and northerners were simultaneously disgusted and fascinated by them, much as American tourists in Mexico or Spain today react to bullfights. Prospective buyers crowded around the auction block, examining the teeth of the slaves in which they were interested, much as they would examine those of horses; running them around to test their wind; wiping handkerchiefs over their bodies to determine if the auctioneer had dyed gray hairs black or had oiled old dry skin; and then raucously entering their bids.

Some abolitionists claimed that slaves were methodically bred like animals. It is true that women were rewarded for bearing children, thus increasing their owners' wealth, and were described in auction advertisements as "good breeders." In Maryland, census takers discovered "plantations" on which the slave force consisted of one adult male, half a dozen young

women, and about the same number of children—not an efficient work force if agriculture was the idea. But because the gospel of the positive good required that a slaveowner be a model of moral rectitude, explicit breeding of slaves was surely not widespread.

Indeed, model masters usually disapproved of everything about the slave trade, describing slave traders as base, crude, unworthy men. Nevertheless, as Harriet Beecher Stowe and others pointed out, without the slave trade there could be no slavery. If some humans were to be property, others had to have the right to buy and sell them.

The Foreign Slave Trade

After 1808, it was a violation of federal law to import slaves. But when the price of slaves was high, some buccaneers were willing to try to bring in blacks from West Africa or Cuba.

It was a risky business. The Royal Navy patrolled the African coast, and American naval vessels cruised the Atlantic and Gulf coasts. Nevertheless, an estimated fifty thousand to fifty-five thousand Africans and Cubans were smuggled into the United States between 1808 and 1861. During the 1850s, several travelers in the South reported seeing a number of black men and women with filed teeth, tattoos, and ritual mutilations that were practiced only in Africa. On the eve of the Civil War, a slave vessel successfully sneaked into Charleston harbor.

In the late 1850s, the price of slaves soared beyond the reach of all but the very wealthy. A group of southern politicians met at Vicksburg, Mississippi, and formally demanded the reopening of the African slave trade. Such a law would never have passed Congress, but the Vicksburg Convention alarmed many northerners and contributed to the hardening of sectional hostilities that contributed to the Civil War.

Life in the Quarters

The slave codes of the southern states provided that slaves had no civil rights whatsoever. They could not own property in the law. They could not buy and sell goods. They could not make contracts. They could not marry legally. They could not testify in court against any white person. They could not leave the plantation without their owners' written permission.

It was a crime for a slave to strike a white person under any circumstances, even self-defense. Slaves could not carry firearms. They could not congregate in more than small groups except at religious services under white supervision. They could not be abroad at night. In most southern states, it was a crime for a white or another black to teach a slave to read.

The slaves' rights were those to life and, under most slave codes, a minimum standard of food, clothing, and shelter.

Humans Without Human Rights

The actual experience of slave life had little to do with the letter of the slave codes. For example, because it was not accounted murder when a master killed a slave during punishment, the legal right to life was almost unenforceable. Whipping was the most common means of corporal punishment, and fifty and more lashes—quite enough to kill a man—was not an uncommon sentence. In the end, the slaves' only real guarantee against death or brutal mistreatment at the hands of their masters was their cash value.

There are few better guarantees, but the masters' self-interest was not foolproof. Slaveowners and overseers did fly into uncontrolled rages and kill slaves. Because their property rights in their slaves inevitably took precedence over the slaves' human rights, owners were rarely punished. After an incident of hideous torture in Virginia in 1858, with the slave victim dying after twenty-four hours of beating and burning, the law punished the sadistic master by imprisoning him. But he was not required to forfeit ownership of several other blacks.

A black nursemaid poses with the white child for whom she cares.

A Diverse Institution

If the laws protecting slaves were not effective, it was also true that many slaveowners were moved by personal decency and by their determination to live up to the ideal of the benevolent patriarch to care for their slaves far better than the law required and sometimes in violation of the slave codes.

A family that owned only one or two slaves sometimes developed a relationship much like partnership with them. White owners and black slaves ate the same food, slept in the same cabin, and worked together intimately.

The slave's lot on the large plantations was also diverse. After about 1840, large-scale slaveowners generally provided simple but adequate rations. It was common to allow slaves to keep their own vegetable plots and even chickens; the masters often did not keep their own gardens and coops but bought vegetables and eggs from their slaves. Here and there was a master who allowed the blacks to raise hogs for their own use, but the master could not always be sure if the pork chop on the slave's table was the slave's own or stolen from him.

Some slaves were permitted to buy and sell outside the boundaries of the plantation and to keep the money. Along the Mississippi River, slaves working on their own time cut wood for the steamboats. They sold chickens and eggs in nearby towns, and some slaves even kept shotguns for hunting. One remarkable character was Simon Gray, a skilled flatboatman who was paid $8 a month to haul lumber to New Orleans. Gray commanded crews of up to twenty men, including free whites, and kept detailed accounts for his owner. He eventually bought his own freedom.

RACISM IN THE BIBLE

Defenders of slavery were hard pressed when abolitionists quoted the Bible on the equality of all men and women before God. A few went so far as to answer that blacks were a different species from whites, even though it was known that mating between species produces sterile offspring and the children of mixed parents in the South were both numerous and fertile.

Southerners were more comfortable when they went to the Bible. They quoted the story of Noah's son Ham, who had humiliated his father and was therefore cursed when Noah said, "a servant of servants shall he be unto his brethren." Blacks were human beings, proslavery southerners agreed, but their race was "the mark of Ham." As Ham's descendants, they were doomed by God to be (borrowing from another source) "hewers of wood and drawers of water."

Many slaves observed an emotional brand of Christianity in which services were led by charismatic preachers and included lively singing of spirituals.

A few masters permitted their slaves to save money in order to purchase their own, their spouse's, or their children's freedom. In at least one instance, a Kentucky judge actually enforced an agreement on a purchase price between a master and slave as a valid contract.

Another example of open violation of the slave code was on the model plantation of Joseph Davis, brother of Jefferson Davis, the future president of the Confederate States of America. While the family was among the most respected in Mississippi, the state with the strictest of the laws forbidding the education of blacks, Joseph Davis maintained a school and teacher for the children of the quarters.

It is important to recall, however, that for every such master there was another who kept his slaves just sound enough to work and who agreed with the man who wrote without embarrassment to a magazine that "Afri-

cans are nothing but brutes, and they will love you better for whipping, whether they deserve it or not."

Modes of Protest

Whether their master was kindly or cruel and their material circumstances comfortable or wretched, the blacks hated their lot in life. While some, particularly domestic servants, were deeply and sincerely attached to their masters, and while slave rebellion was unknown after Nat Turner, the blacks demonstrated in other ways that they hated slavery. When freedom became a real possibility during the Civil War, slaves deserted their homes by the thousands to flee to Union lines and, in the case of the young men, to enlist in the Union Army. As a South Carolina planter wrote candidly after the war, "I believed these people were content, happy, and attached to their masters." That, he concluded sadly, was a "delusion."

Malingering and Thieving

This honest man might have been spared his disappointment had he given deeper consideration to white people's stereotypes of the blacks under slavery. It was commonly held that blacks were inherently lazy and irresponsible and would not work except under close supervision. In fact, free blacks generally worked quite hard, and the same slaves whose laziness was a "constant aggravation" in the cotton fields, toiled in their own gardens from dawn to dusk on Sundays and often, by moonlight, during the week. In slavery, the only incentive to work hard for the master was negative—the threat of punishment—and that incentive was rarely enough to cause men and women to ignore the blazing southern sun. When the overseer or driver was over the hill, it was nap time.

Theft was so common on plantations that whites believed blacks to be congenital thieves. Again, the only incentive not to steal a chicken, a suckling pig, or a berry pie from the big-house kitchen was fear of punishment. If a slave was not caught, he had no reason to believe he had done wrong.

One chicken thief who was caught in the act of eating his prize explained this point trenchantly to his master: if the chicken was master's property and he was master's property, then master had not lost anything because the chicken was in his belly instead of scratching around the henyard. It is not known if this meditation saved the philosopher from a whipping.

Running Away

The most direct testimony of slave discontent was the prevalence of runaways. Only blacks who lived in the states that bordered the free states—Delaware, Maryland, Kentucky—had a reasonable chance of escaping to permanent freedom. A great many were successful. In calling for a stricter Fugitive Slave Act in 1850 (a law that gave the federal government the responsibility of returning slaves), southerners estimated that as many as one hundred thousand blacks had escaped to the free states. Several times that number tried and failed.

Far more common was running away in the full knowledge that capture and punishment were inevitable. Nevertheless, the appeal of a few days or weeks of freedom, or the chance to visit a spouse or a friend on another plantation, was worth the risk to so many

blacks that runaway slaves were a vexation in every part of the South.

Runaways in hiding relied on other blacks to conceal and feed them. The fact that they were hidden and fed at the risk to their benefactors of corporal punishment reveals the existence of a sense of solidarity among the slaves that can never be fully understood by historians because the slaves kept no written records. But some indication of the quality of life in the slave quarters "from sundown to first light" can be conjectured from what is known of black religion and folklore.

Let My People Go

By the 1850s, most slaves had warmly embraced an emotional brand of Protestant Christianity that was basically Baptist and Methodist in outline. Religious services were replete with animated sermons by unlettered but charismatic preachers and bumptious rhythmic singing, the "Negro spirituals" loved by whites as well as blacks.

In the sermons and spirituals, hymns that combined biblical themes with African musical forms, the slaves explicitly identified with the ancient Hebrews. While in bondage in Babylonia and Egypt, the Hebrews had

---

UNCLE REMUS EXPLAINS

Many historians of slavery believe that because violent resistance by blacks was suicidal, many slaves (and post-Civil War southern blacks) devised the technique of "playing Uncle Tom," that is, playing a docile role in front of whites in order to survive. Uncle Remus describes this behavior in "Why Br'er Possum Loves Peace." Mr. Dog attacks Br'er Coon and Br'er Possum. Br'er Coon fights back and drives Mr. Dog away, but at the price of taking some damage himself. In the meantime, Br'er Possum plays possum, plays dead.

Later, representing blacks who want to fight back, Br'er Coon berates Br'er Possum for cowardice. "'I ain't runnin' wid cowerds deze days,' sez Br'er Coon." Br'er Possum replies that just because he did not fight does not mean that he is a coward:

I want no mo' skeer'd dan you is right now . . . but I'm de most ticklish chap w'at you ever laid eyes on, en no sooner did Mr. Dog put his nose down yer 'mong my ribs dan I got ter laffin. . . . I don't mine fightin', Br'er Coon, no mo' dan you duz . . . but I declar' ter grashus ef I kin stan' ticklin.

Wit, not violence, was the way to deal with vicious whites. Note that it is Mr. Dog, not Br'er—Brother.

MARY BOYKIN CHESNUT (1823–1886)

She was part of the elegant aristocracy at the pinnacle of southern society. Her father and her husband were United States senators. Her relatives owned dozens of large plantations and hundreds of slaves. She associated with only the rich and cultivated. She was waited on by slaves, and her days were filled with parties, dances, and receptions in big houses. Mary Boykin Chesnut was a southern belle and a grand lady who was expected to do little with her life but serve as her husband's hostess and as her elegant society's ornament. If she had not kept a diary during the Civil War years, we would know nothing but her name. Because she did keep one of the most revealing documents of the era, we know her as one of the South's most perceptive critics.

Mary Boykin was born on March 31, 1823. She attended Madame Talvande's School in Charleston, more a finishing school than an academy. Upper-class southern girls were expected to learn little but gracious manners. In 1840, seventeen years of age, she married James Chesnut, Jr., who was of the same social standing as herself. They honeymooned in Europe.

Mary Chesnut enjoyed the idle social whirl of the southern elite. Even when she was more than forty years old, her enthusiasm for gossip about belles and their beaus and hints of sexual scandal continued, and her reports of it have the ring of girlishness. She spent endless hours with other women simply sitting and talking. But Mary Chesnut did not quite fit in. She was an avid reader who devoured classical and contemporary authors alike. On more than one occasion, she breached the etiquette of her class by making it clear that she knew more about literature and even politics than did the gentlemen in her company.

Mary Chesnut never had children, an even more basic violation of the code of her class. Before she was married, a wealthy southern woman was expected to be beautiful and flirtatious but shy. After marriage, she was expected to be the mother of her husband's children, the means by which his line as an aristocrat was preserved. The failure of the Chesnuts to have children sorrowed Mary, but the distance it put between her and the ideal of southern womanhood probably contributed to her ability to dissect so shrewdly the society in which she moved.

Mary Chesnut hated slavery, but not for the same reasons that northern abolitionists did. In fact, she condemned them on the grounds that they did not know anything about the institution as it actually functioned, but spoke and wrote on the basis of abstract principles from ivory towers in New England. Like other white southerners, Mary did not believe that blacks were the equals of whites, but she felt that slav-

Mary Boykin Chesnut (1823–1886), a plantation owner's wife, kept a candid diary during the Civil War years that historians regard as one of the most revealing documents of the era.

ery corrupted the integrity and morals of her own people. She wrote of a relative who praised her slaves in extravagant terms when they were nearby. When the blacks left, the woman fearfully told friends that they were trying to poison her.

According to Mary Chesnut, a plantation was a house of concubines, with the men of the planter class abusing their authority over the young female slaves and making prostitutes of them. Mary's friends must have talked a great deal about this, for she wrote acerbically that women knew the identities of the fathers of every light-skinned black except those on their own plantations. The pain in her comments implies that she may have suffered from sexual humiliation.

After the war, the Chesnuts' wealth declined, but was not destroyed. Mary and James lived out their final years in comfortable obscurity in South Carolina. James died in 1885. Mary followed him the next year.

been, in their simplicity and poverty, God's chosen people. In the afterlife, all human beings would be equal and happy.

This cry of protest was not lost on the whites. But as long as the slaves associated freedom with the next life, there was no reason to stifle the cry. What the black preachers told their congregations out of earshot of the master and mistress may well have been more worldly.

"Bred en Bawn in a Brier-Patch"

Another thinly masked form of protest was the folk tales for which black storytellers became famous, particularly the Br'er Rabbit stories that were collected after the Civil War as *Uncle Remus: His Songs and Sayings* by Georgia journalist Joel Chandler Harris. In these yarns, which have been traced back to West African folklore, the rabbit, the weakest of animals and unable to defend himself by force, survives and flourishes through the use of trickery and complex deceits.

In the most famous of the Uncle Remus stories, "How Mr. Rabbit Was Too Sharp for Mr. Fox," Br'er Fox has the rabbit in his hands and is debating with himself whether to barbecue him, hang him, drown him, or skin him. Br'er Rabbit assures the fox that he will be happy with any of these fates as long as the fox does not fling him into a nearby brier-patch, which he fears more than anything. Of course, that is exactly what Br'er Fox does, whence Br'er Rabbit is home free. "Bred en bawn in a brier-patch, Br'er Fox," Br'er Rabbit shouts back tauntingly, "bred en bawn in a brier-patch." The slaves, unable to taunt their masters so bluntly, satisfied themselves with quiet trickery and coded tales about it.

It is worth noting that in the Uncle Remus stories, Br'er Rabbit now and then outsmarts himself and suffers for it. As in all social commentary of substance, the slaves were as sensitive to their own foibles as to those of their masters.

For Further Reading

The best kind of reading program on the subject of slavery is one that traces how historians have changed their minds on the subject. Begin with two books by U. B. Phillips, *American Negro Slavery* (1919) and *Life and Labor in the Old South* (1929). While hardly an advocate of slavery, Phillips describes a basically beneficent institution, a view that most white Americans of his time probably shared. Kenneth Stampp, *The Peculiar Institution* (1956), uses the structure of Phillips' books and comes up with the diametrically opposed view: that slavery was essentially a harsh, cruel institution.

Stanley Elkins, *Slavery* (2nd ed., 1968), is even harsher. Elkins sees the peculiar institution as warping the personalities of the slaves. More recently, John Blassingame, *The Slave Community* (1972), contradicts this, depicting a vital if surreptitious community life in "the quarters."

R. Fogel and Stanley Engermann present an economic study of slavery in *Time on the Cross* (1974), but are contradicted in many of their findings by Herbert Gutman and Richard Sutch, *Slavery and the Numbers Game* (1975). See Leon Litwack, *North of Slavery: The Negro in the Free States, 1790–1860* (1961), for the history of free blacks, and R. Starobin, *Industrial Slavery in the Old South* (1970), for slaves who worked outside agriculture. If students are to read only one book on slavery, it ought to be Eugene Genovese, *Roll, Jordan, Roll* (1975), or William Styron, *The Confessions of Nat Turner* (1967), a novel of profound value to historians.

21

From Sea to Shining Sea

American Expansion to the Pacific, 1820–1848

With the acquisition of Louisiana in 1803, the boundaries of the United States appeared to be complete. Thomas Jefferson, who was far more given to thinking about the future than were most of his contemporaries, was confident that the land he purchased from France would provide farms for sons and daughters of his American yeomanry for several centuries. After Lewis and Clark returned with the news that there was no easy route across the North American continent to the Pacific, killing hopes of a direct trade with the Far East, the United States had no interest in expansion farther west.

The Atlantic Ocean was still America's avenue to the rest of the world. The Rocky Mountains, imagined more than known, provided the most formidable of natural boundaries. Indeed, the American slope of the mountains was an obstacle. The rolling arid plains were considered fit for only the herds of bison that wandered them and the mounted Indians who pursued the great beasts.

Only in the South did Americans settle on land that abutted the territory of a foreign nation—Spain and, by the 1820s, the Republic of Mexico. In the Adams-Onís Treaty of 1819, the possibility of conflict was solved forever, so it seemed, by friendly agreement on a border.

The Sweetwater River at Devil's Gate by W. H. Jackson depicts a wagon train moving westward through Wyoming.

The early leaders of the Mexican Republic were cordial toward the *norteamericanos*. The American Revolution was their inspiration, and they wrote many features of the Constitution into their own frame of government. After only a few decades, however, they came to a different conclusion, which was nicely phrased later in the century by President Porfirio Díaz. "Poor Mexico," he said. "So far from God and so close to the United States."

Mexico: So Close to the United States

Even after Cortez and his successors had looted the riches of the native Mexican cultures, the Viceroyalty of New Spain remained the jewel of the Spanish Empire. Spanish-born *gachupines* or *peninsolares* and Mexican-born white *criollos* monopolized the best lands and lived fat off the labor and skills of the Indians and mixed-blood *mestizos*. Mexico became home to the greatest of the indigenous New World cultures, the fruit of the interactions between the Spanish and the Indians. When the English settlers at Jamestown were fighting off starvation, three hundred poets competed for a prize in Mexico City. When Sydney Smith was mocking the absence of high culture in the United States, an intellectual and literary life rivaling that in the capitals of Europe flourished in Mexico.

Mexico Expands North

Indeed, Spanish adventurers and friars were planting colonies deep in the North American continent before Americans penetrated the Appalachians. The most secure of them, Santa Fe in the Sangre de Cristo Mountains of present-day New Mexico, was established in 1609. Although its existence was threatened several times by Indian rebellions, Santa Fe survived and is now the oldest seat of government in the United States.

During the first years of American independence, a Franciscan priest named Junípero Serra established a string of missions in California, the farthest north at Sonoma above San Francisco. His plan, which eventually was fulfilled, was to make it possible for a foot traveler along the *Camino Real* (or Royal Highway) to spend every night in a secure, hospitable mission compound. As in New Mexico, a simple and gracious style of life developed among the small numbers of *californios* who lived in the northernmost Mexican province. Today, their culture has been swallowed up, and their only legacy is the Spanish-language place-names of the American Southwest.

The Santa Fe Trade

In 1821, the Mexican government abandoned the Spanish restrictions on trade with the United States. William Becknell, an alert and enterprising businessman in Independence, Missouri, immediately set off in a wagon packed with American manufactures: cloth, shoes, tools, luxury goods. Feeling his way by compass and dead reckoning across what is now Kansas, he blazed an eight-hundred-mile trail to Sante Fe. The seven thousand inhabitants of the beautiful mountain community were so remote from the centers of Mexican population that they were starved for goods from outside, and Becknell made a huge profit from the furs and gold that he took back to Missouri.

For fourteen years, a convoy of wagons annually retraced Becknell's route. Only a few Missourians, such as the famous scout Kit Carson, actually settled in Santa Fe or nearby Taos, and those who did were happy to settle into the gracious Spanish-Indian culture of the region. Nevertheless, the fatal link was forged between energetic *gringos* and an attractive country that was only nominally under the flag of Mexico.

As for the American territory that the traders crossed, they believed it was worthless. Beginning in what is now central Nebraska and Kansas, at about 100° west longitude, the land rises gradually from an elevation of about two thousand feet to, at the base of the Rockies, six thousand to seven thousand feet. Rainfall was sparse in this country compared with that in the East the Americans knew. Few trees grew except along the rivers, and the vastness of the landscape unnerved a people who were accustomed to dense forests.

When Americans gazed over the rolling plains, the short buffalo grass rustling in the wind, they were re-

---

GRINGO

Mexicans began to use the derogatory word *gringo* to refer to Americans in the first half of the nineteenth century. Like many slang terms that one people uses to disparage another, it reflects how American English sounded to Mexicans: *gringo* means "gibberish." A late-twentieth-century equivalent is the word *honky*, which was used by blacks to describe the sound of white inflections.

A ranch foreman meets with the owner of the hacienda in this painting by Julio Michaud.

minded of the ocean. Traders called their wagons prairie schooners. Less romantic military mapmakers labeled the country the Great American Desert. It was, of course, a mistake to believe that only land that grew trees naturally would support crops. However, it was true enough that the tough sod of the plains was more than a cast-iron or a fire-tempered wood plowshare could break and turn over.

The grass was worth notice. Even the most pessimistic army scouts had to admit that if more than 10 million bison grazed on the prairie, cattle would fatten too. But in the days before the railroad, it was impossible to imagine how hypothetical steers might be transported to eastern markets. All agreed that the Indians of the plains, who were satisfied to trade with or charge "tolls" to the Santa Fe trekkers, were welcome to what they had.

The Texans

To the south, the Great Plains extended into the Mexican province of Texas. There cattle could be grazed within easy driving distance of the Gulf of Mexico and shipped by water to New Orleans. As early as 1819, a Connecticut Yankee named Moses Austin was attracted by the possibilities of a grazing economy there, and he also noted the suitability of eastern Texas to cotton cultivation.

He died before he was able to implement his idea, but in 1821, his son Stephen Austin made a deal with the Mexican government. In return for the license to settle 300 American families in Texas, each household to receive 177 acres of farmland and 13,000 acres of pastureland, Austin promised that his people would abide by Mexican law, learn the Spanish language, and observe the Roman Catholic religion.

The earliest settlers meant to keep their part of the bargain, but Texas was so far from the centers of Mexican power and culture, and the immigrants were so numerous (twenty thousand whites and two thousand slaves by 1834), that Texas was inevitably American in culture and customs. Even so, because the province was prosperous and produced some tax revenues, there might have been no trouble. But in 1831, Mexico abolished slavery, and in 1833, General Antonio López de Santa Anna seized power. Slavery was vital to the

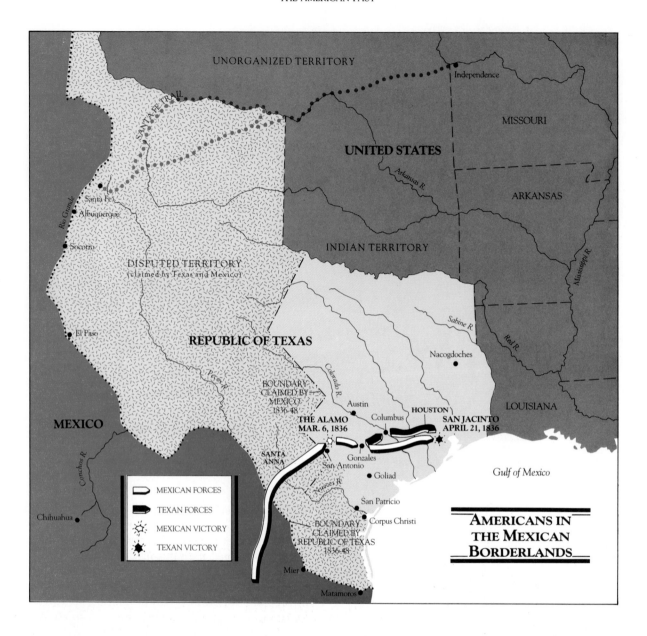

Legend:
- MEXICAN FORCES
- TEXAN FORCES
- MEXICAN VICTORY
- TEXAN VICTORY

AMERICANS IN THE MEXICAN BORDERLANDS

Texans, and Santa Anna proved to be inept both as a politician and as a soldier.

His goal was unexceptional. Santa Anna wanted to overcome the internal squabbling that had plagued Mexico since independence, and toward that end he promulgated a new constitution in 1835. It centralized the Mexican government, canceled American trading rights in Santa Fe, and forbade the Texans to exercise the considerable autonomy they had enjoyed.

A number of them rebelled and seized the only military garrison in Texas, at San Antonio. At first, like the American rebels of 1775, the Texans claimed that they were fighting only for the rights they had traditionally exercised as Mexican citizens. Having far less in common with their mother country than the Americans of 1775, however, they talked of independence from the outset.

The Alamo and San Jacinto

Like King George III, Santa Anna had no intention of negotiating with his troublesome subjects. Indeed, he welcomed the uprising as an opportunity to rally the divided Mexican people around a national cause. In early 1836, he led an army of six thousand to San Antonio, where his calculations that he could easily defeat the Texans seemed to be confirmed. Only about two hundred Texans and Americans were holed up in the former mission compound, the Alamo.

Among them were men who were already famous in the United States. The garrison was commanded by William Travis, one of the most prominent Texans. Second in command was James Bowie, inventor of the long knife that many westerners carried as a weapon and that now bears his name. Best known was the anti-Jackson Whig politician and humorist, David Crockett of Tennessee.

Santa Anna could have passed them by, leaving a small detachment to contain the garrison. The real threat lay farther east, where Sam Houston was frantically trying to organize an army out of frontier farmers. Not every Texan supported Houston, and, moving quickly, Santa Anna might have snuffed out the resisters.

To his sorrow he stayed put for ten days, unable to comprehend why the doomed defenders of the makeshift fort would not surrender. When he realized that they were buying time for Sam Houston, he attacked the Alamo at tremendous cost to his army and ordered all prisoners executed. That was his second mistake. The atrocity (only a few women were spared) rallied virtually all Texans, including many of Mexican blood and culture, to the fight against the General.

On the banks of the Rio San Jacinto on April 21,

Sam Houston fell on Santa Anna and not only routed his army but captured the president. In order to secure his own release, Santa Anna agreed to the independence of Texas with a southern boundary at the Rio Grande rather than at the Rio Nueces, which had been the boundary of the Mexican state of Texas. As soon as he was free, Santa Anna repudiated the agreement and refused to recognize the Republic of Texas. But the demoralized Mexican army was in no condition to mount another campaign, and the Texans discreetly remained north of the Nueces.

In October 1836, Sam Houston was inaugurated president of a republic that had a constitution patterned after that of the United States. Texas legalized slavery and dispatched an envoy to Washington. Houston hoped that his old friend Andrew Jackson would favor annexation. In his nationalistic heart, Jackson liked the idea of sewing the Lone Star on the American flag. However, Congress was embroiled in a hot debate in which the question of slavery repeatedly figured, and Jackson did not want to complicate matters by proposing the admission of a new slave state. In order to avoid trouble for both himself and his successor, he delayed diplomatic recognition of the Republic of Texas until his last day in office.

Martin Van Buren opposed annexation, and he was spared a debate on admission when the depression of

This 1885 painting of the storming of the Alamo, done after a study of available sources, provides what is probably the most accurate view of the event.

the late 1830s distracted Americans from all but economic questions. The Texans, disappointed and still worried about Mexico, looked to Europe for an ally.

Great Britain was glad to oblige them. The British coveted Texas cotton and always welcomed opportunities to limit American expansion. Had it not been for the Texans' intense commitment to slavery, which the British just as intensely opposed, there might have been more than a commercial connection between the old monarchy and the new republic.

The Oregon Country

The American government was uneasy about British influence in Texas. Britons and Americans also stepped warily around one another on the western coast of North America in what was known as the Oregon country. This land of prosperous Indians, sheltered harbors, spruce and fir forests, and rich valley farmland was not considered the property of any single nation. The Oregon country had been created when two empires with claims to it had withdrawn, one to the south and one to the north.

Too Distant a Place

Spain's claim to Oregon was never more than nominal. Spanish and Mexican influence ended at Sonoma in California. So after 1819, when the boundary of Spanish America was set at 42° north latitude, the present southern line of the state of Oregon, the claim was itself overreaching.

The Russians had established a string of forts, timbering outposts, and fur-trapping stations on the Pacific coast from present-day Alaska to Fort Ross, less than a hundred miles from San Francisco Bay. However, few Russians were interested in removing to permanent settlements so far from home, and, by the 1820s, the trappers had looted the coastal waters of the sea otters whose lush, warm furs had brought them there. Rather than get involved in a competition for territory that they could not defend, the Russians withdrew northward in 1825 and set the boundary of Russian America at 54° 40′ north latitude, the present southern boundary of the state of Alaska.

Between 42° and 54° 40′ lay Oregon. Because the country was also far from their centers of power, the British and Americans agreed to what they called a joint occupation, which was in truth very little occupation at all.

The Mountain Men

The Americans and British in Oregon were few in number and not the sort to put down roots. They were fur trappers after the pelt of the North American beaver, which teemed in the chill creeks of the Rocky Mountains and farther west. Furriers in New York, London, and Paris paid high prices for beaver; they sewed the pelts into plush coats for the wealthy, and chopped, steamed, and pressed the fur into felt, a versatile fabric with a worldwide market.

Even before William Becknell set out for Santa Fe, American and Canadian adventurers were disappearing into the northern Rockies with large-bore rifles, iron traps, and a sense of relief at leaving civilization behind for eleven months a year.

These were the mountain men, who never numbered more than a few hundred at any one time. They took Indian wives; they adopted those Indian ways that were calculated to help them survive in remote, rugged wilderness; and they sometimes lived with, sometimes battled against the native peoples of the region. Other whites who dealt with the mountain men considered them to be savages.

Jeremiah "Liver-Eatin'" Johnson waged a ten-year vendetta with the Crow tribe. He earned his nickname because he regularly cut out and ate the livers of the Crow warriors whom he killed. (Toward the end, Johnson said, he just cut them out.) Jim Beckwourth, a black man, discovered the pass through the Sierra Nevadas that rose to the lowest elevation. New York–born Jedediah Smith opened South Pass in Wyoming, the route that would be followed by most of the overland emigrants. Jim Bridger explored almost every nook of the Rockies. He was the first white or black man to see the Great Salt Lake.

Each year, in late summer or early fall, the trappers brought their furs to arranged locations on the Platte, Sweetwater, or Big Horn rivers. For a few weeks, the motley group of buyers from the British Hudson's Bay Company and John Jacob Astor's American firm, mountain men, and Indians of many tribes traded goods and enjoyed a riotous orgy. Of more lasting significance than their revelry was the knowledge of geography that was imparted to the folks back home, particularly the fact that while it was a long hard trip, it was possible to cross overland to Oregon.

The Oregon Trail

Among the first to make the six-month journey were missionaries. In 1834, the Methodists sent Jason Lee to preach the gospel to the Indians of Oregon. In 1835,

Fur trappers and explorers steered canoes along the rivers of America's western frontier, as shown in The Voyageurs, *an 1846 painting by Charles Deas.*

four Flatheads visited the American Board of Foreign Missions and, so the board said, persuaded them that Presbyterian was the gospel that they really wanted to hear. In 1836, Marcus and Narcissa Whitman carried it to them on foot. A few years later, the Catholic University at St. Louis sent Father Pierre-Jean de Smet to the Oregon country.

The trek began at Independence, Missouri. In that town also, in 1843, was organized the first great wagon train. A thousand Oregon-or-Busters outfitted and provisioned themselves, often packing oddly chosen mementos of home: cumbersome furniture and fragile china gewgaws. They swore to observe strict rules of behavior and cooperation for the duration of the crossing, and hired mountain men as guides.

The Oregon Trail crossed Kansas to the Platte River and followed that broad, shallow course to Fort Laramie, the last army outpost. Then, the emigrants and their famous covered wagons crossed the Continental Divide at South Pass and struggled through the Rockies to near the source of the Snake River, which flows into the great Columbia and the Pacific.

A wagon train made up to twenty miles a day (or as few as none at all) depending on the terrain and the weather. At night, exhausted by the tremendous labor of moving a hundred wagons and several hundred head of cattle, horses, and mules, the emigrants drew their prairie schooners into a hollow square or circle.

The Indians of the plains and mountains were not a serious threat to large, well-organized expeditions. While the Indians were hardly delighted to see large numbers of strangers crossing their ancestral lands (three thousand in 1845 alone), the whites at least were crossing it and disappearing into the sunset. Although they warred constantly with one another, the tribes had few firearms and were, therefore, no match for the pale-skinned strangers.

For their part, the Oregon-bound travelers worried less about Indian attack than about theft. The Indians made a game of stealing horses that strayed too far from the emigrant parties. They also traded with the whites and picked up the discarded goods that littered the trail. Even before the stream of wagons wore deep ruts into the sod—which can still be seen today here and

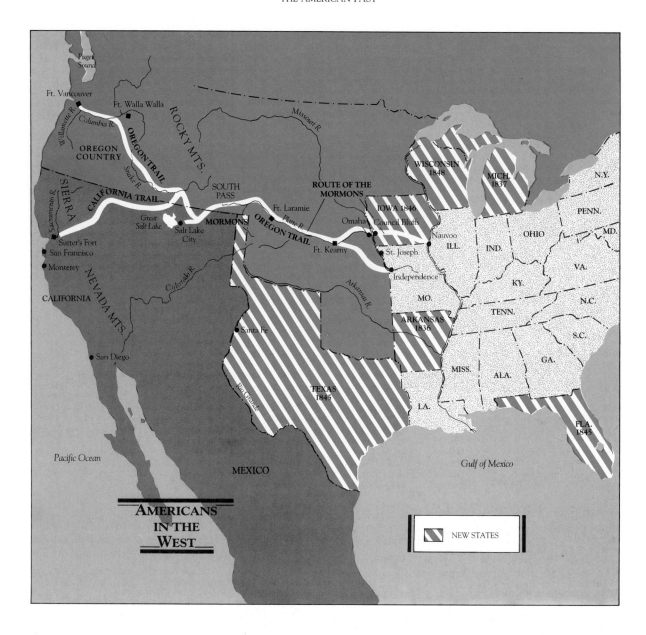

AMERICANS IN THE WEST

NEW STATES

there—the Oregon Trail was marked like a highway with broken furniture, empty barrels, incapacitated wagons, the skeletons of worn-out cattle and horses, and simple grave markers that signaled the end of someone's dream. Death from accident or disease, particularly cholera, was common, but it was virtually impossible to lose the way.

Joint Occupation

By 1845, the American population of the Columbia and Willamette valleys had grown to seven thousand. South of the Columbia River there were few British and Canadian settlers, so the Hudson's Bay Company prudently moved its headquarters from the mouth of the Columbia to Vancouver Island. Nevertheless, despite the vast forested buffer zone between the two nationalities, occasional clashes threatened to sabotage the Anglo-American settlement that Daniel Webster and Lord Ashburton had worked out in 1842.

The Americans wanted to end the joint occupation and annex Oregon to the United States. In July 1843, a group met at Champoeg and established a provisional territorial government under the American flag. A few politicians back east supported them, as much to taunt the British as for any realistic hope of affecting policy. The idea of territorial expansion, previously something of a dirty concept because it involved seizing land that belonged to someone else, had taken on positive dignity. Expansion became a sacred duty for Americans; they had an obligation to increase the domain over which democracy and liberty held sway.

Expanding to the Pacific

This was the doctrine of Manifest Destiny. Dazzled by the nation's energy and progress, politicians and newspaper editors, mostly Democratic and mostly southern and western, began to speak of the "right" of Americans to seize lands that were being wasted under the backward Mexicans or corrupted by the decadent British.

Legal claims, however universally recognized, were less important than the obvious mission of the United States to plant free, democratic institutions in Oregon and in the northern reaches of Mexico. It remained for a New York journalist, John O'Sullivan, to coin the phrase. It was, he said, the "manifest destiny" of the United States to expand from sea to sea. God and nature intended Americans to possess the North American continent.

The First Step

In 1843, the debate began in earnest. The Texans renewed their request for annexation, and they were supported by a number of prominent Americans. Many northern Democrats such as Lewis Cass of Michigan, James Buchanan of Pennsylvania, and Stephen Douglas of Illinois were enraptured by the idea of territorial expansion. They and others also feared that if Texas were not admitted, Great Britain might be tempted to seize the Lone Star Republic.

Southern Democrats such as Calhoun and his new ally, President John Tyler, had an added reason for favoring annexation. Slavery was legal in Texas. If Texas were brought into the Union, the power of the proslavery forces would increase.

For the same reason, many political and cultural leaders of New England strenuously opposed annexation. Northern Whigs and some northern Democrats were determined that slavery not expand beyond the states where it was already legal. Less Anglophobic (hostile toward England) than people of other sections, New Englanders did not object to the possibility of Great Britain's taking Texas. The British, at least, would abolish slavery there. Finally, the anti-Texas

A rare photo of a wagon train moving west.

forces pointed out that admitting Texas would almost certainly lead to a war with Mexico in which the Mexicans, not the Americans, would be in the right. The issue pitted the moral consciousness of Jacksonian-era reformers against the ambition (and interest in slavery) of Jacksonian Democracy.

The Very Important Election of 1844

Both of the likely presidential nominees of 1844 were unhappy to see the question of the annexation of Texas shaping up as the principal issue. Henry Clay knew that his Whig party, which was divided along sectional lines between southern Cotton Whigs (proslavery) and northern Conscience Whigs (antislavery), could split in two on the issue. Like Clay, Martin Van Buren, who commanded a safe majority of delegates to the Democratic nominating convention, opposed annexation, but did not wish to alienate the members of his party in the South. The solution to their common problem was obvious: the two old rogues quietly met and agreed that they would oppose annexation, thus eliminating it as an issue.

Their bargain presented the lame-duck Tyler with an opportunity. He would run as the third candidate, the only one in favor of taking Texas. Tyler had no political machine behind him, so his announcement disturbed neither Clay nor Van Buren. Then occurred one of those unlikely events that change the course of history. Manifest Destiny Democrats revived a neglected party rule that a presidential nominee receive the support of two-thirds instead of a simple majority of the delegates to the convention. With his anti-Texas platform, Van Buren was stymied. After eight ballots ended in a deadlock, the convention turned to a "dark-horse candidate," that is, a person who was not considered a candidate at the beginning of the race. He was James Knox Polk of Tennessee, a young (under fifty years old) Jackson protégé (he was called "Young Hickory") who was nominally a supporter of Martin Van Buren.

Henry Clay Blunders

"Who," the Whigs asked scornfully when they learned who was running against their hero, Clay, "is James K. Polk?" He was a moderately successful politician who had been defeated twice in attempts to be governor of Tennessee. He was a frail, small man with a look of melancholy and timidity about him. He was pious; Polk disapproved of alcohol, dancing, and card playing. And he was also an unblushing expansionist who believed that the United States would have all of Oregon, Texas, and maybe more.

FIVE STATES OF TEXAS?

Texas is unique among the states not only because it was an independent republic before it became a state. By the joint resolution of the American and Texan congresses that brought Texas into the Union, Texas reserved the right to divide into five states without further congressional approval. The advisability of splitting arose periodically in Texas politics because collectively, the states carved out of Texas would have ten United States senators rather than two.

At first, Henry Clay was overjoyed to be running against a political nobody. He would be president at last! The unpopular Tyler and the obscure Polk would divide the pro-Texas vote; the anti-Texas vote, including the large number of antislavery Democrats who would have voted for Van Buren, was his alone. Then the sky fell. Tyler withdrew from the race, and every dispatch seemed to say that Manifest Destiny was carrying the day. Clay began to waffle on the expansion issue, but his vagueness only alienated enough Conscience Whigs to cost him the election. In New York State, which Polk carried by a scant five thousand votes (and with New York, the election), Whig districts gave sixteen thousand votes to James G. Birney's abolitionist Liberty party.

Encouraged by the result of the election and egged on by Secretary of State Calhoun, Tyler moved on the Texas question. He could not muster the two-thirds vote in the Senate that a treaty required, but he had a simple majority of both houses of Congress, which was enough to pass a "joint resolution" with the Texas Congress. On March 1, 1845, three days before Polk's inauguration, Texas became the twenty-eighth state.

A Successful President

Polk was a master politician, a shrewd diplomat, and, in terms of accomplishing what he set out to do, one of the most successful presidents. When he was sworn in, Polk intended to serve only one term and during those four years to secure Texas, acquire New Mexico and California from Mexico, and annex as much of the Oregon country as circumstances permitted.

Texas was a state on Inauguration Day. The hard-working president immediately went to work on Oregon. Taking his cue from a chauvinistic slogan, "Fifty-four Forty or Fight!" (seizing all of Oregon for the United States up to the southern boundary of Russian America at 54° 40′ north latitude) Polk alarmed the British by hinting of a war they did not want. He then

James J. Polk was a hardworking man who promoted the notion of Manifest Destiny.

made it look like a concession that he was willing to settle for an extension of the Webster–Ashburton line, at 49° north latitude, as the northern boundary of Oregon. The Oregon country would be cut in half, with England retaining all of Vancouver Island.

Britain got no more than it occupied, and the United States got no less than it could reasonably defend. Except for a minor adjustment of the line in the Strait of Juan de Fuca, worked out in 1872, the permanent northern boundary of the continental United States was final in 1846.

Polk was no less agreeable or candid about his designs on California and New Mexico. The United States had no legal claim in either province or the excuse that, as in Texas and Oregon, California and New Mexico were already peopled by Americans. Unassimilated *gringos* were few in New Mexico, and there were only about seven hundred Americans in California compared with six thousand *californios*. In 1842, an American naval officer, Thomas ap Catesby Jones, somehow got it into his head that the United States was at war with Mexico, and he seized the provincial capital of California at Monterey. When he learned that he was mistaken, he had to run down the flag and sail off, rather the fool. But, embarrassed as Jones might have been, he was merely a few years ahead of his time. When Polk was unable to buy California and New Mexico for $30 million, he decided to take them by force.

War with Mexico

The hapless General Santa Anna was back in power in Mexico City. This time, however, while he refused even to discuss the sale of the two provinces, he acted quite sensibly in ordering Mexican troops not to provoke the Americans. However, Polk was determined to have war. He prepared to ask Congress for a declaration on the basis of the Mexican government's debts with some American banks. In the meantime, he ordered General Zachary Taylor of Louisiana to take fifteen hundred men from the Nueces River in Texas to the Rio Grande. In April 1846, sixteen American soldiers were killed in a skirmish between Mexican and American patrols in the disputed region.

Feigning moral outrage, Polk rewrote his speech and declared that because of this battle, a state of war already existed. Such a proclamation was entirely unjustified under the Constitution, which gives Congress alone the right to declare war. But patriotic danders were up, and despite the opposition of some Whigs, including a young congressman from Illinois named Abraham Lincoln, both Houses of Congress approved Polk's action.

The Mexican army was actually larger than the American and, on the face of it, more professional. But the Mexican troops were ill equipped, demoralized by incessant civil wars, and commanded by officers who owed their commissions to social status. In less than two years, the Americans conquered most of the country.

In the summer of 1846, Stephen W. Kearny occupied Santa Fe without resistance. Then he marched

An 1846 daguerreotype of United States General John Wool and his troops in Saltillo, Mexico.

DINNERTIME ON THE TRAIL

The business of a wagon train was movement. Ideally, the people who were bound for Oregon and California wanted to make twenty miles a day. Few companies maintained that pace. Some observed the sabbath, camping all day Sunday. Severe storms, unseasonably swollen rivers, injury, illness, and the call to make repairs on the sturdy canvas-topped wagons all caused delays. Nevertheless, because the object was to keep the big wheels turning, overland travelers soon learned to adjust the rhythms of their lives to the demands of the trail. Among the habits that had to be left behind was a familiar, varied diet and old patterns of preparing and taking meals.

Independence, Missouri, was the most important jumping-off point for the emigrants to the West. Living at the head of the trail that the Santa Fe traders had used for twenty years before the Oregon emigration be-

gan, the people of Independence understood what it took to make long overland journeys on the North American continent. The city's economy was geared to outfitting and provisioning "pilgrims." A family bound for Oregon could purchase from the dozens of Independence merchants anything that was needed (and a good deal that was not needed) to make the crossing.

The busiest season was late winter and early spring, when the migrants gathered in vast camps on the outskirts of Independence to await the first signs of green grass on the Great Plains. A wagon train could not set out until there was dependable pasture for the animals on whose strength the company moved.

The emigrants did not lack for advice during the weeks that they waited impatiently in Independence. They swapped opinions and read and reread guidebooks to the trail that they had bought at home or borrowed

Wagon train pioneers break for lunch in a Kansas field.

from their temporary neighbors. Historian John Mack Faragher has drawn up a composite larder as recommended in the guidebooks he studied. Four people were advised to pack 600 pounds of flour, 120 pounds of biscuit, 400 pounds of bacon, 60 pounds of coffee, 4 pounds of tea, 100 pounds of sugar, 200 pounds of lard, 200 pounds of beans, 120 pounds of dried fruit, 50 pounds of salt, 8 pounds of pepper, 8 pounds of saleratus (for making soda-raised bread), and 1 keg of whiskey.

According to modern nutritional standards, this was an adequate diet in every particular but one: it did not provide enough vitamin C to ward off scurvy indefinitely. The emigrants had their own name for the dread disease, "the black canker of the plains," and it is not uncommon to come upon grave markers like W. Brown's in western Nevada:

> *W. Brown*
> *of the Rough and Ready Company*
> *of Platte Co. Mo.*
> *Died with the skervy Sept. 19, 1849*
> *Aged 35 years*

Scurvy could be avoided. If a family left Independence in good health, after some weeks of a diet rich in fresh vegetables, and took advantage of every opportunity to eat berries or wild greens found along the trail or were able to purchase vegetables in Salt Lake City (where the Mormons maintained lush gardens), they were likely to reach Oregon or California in good shape. Indeed, many emigrants wrote in their diaries that the adventure was a tonic; never had their physical condition been sounder, their sleep deeper, or their appetites keener.

A good appetite was a blessing. The only universal complaint about the food on the trail concerned the monotony of biscuit and salt pork. When emigrants broke out a jar of preserves brought from home for a special occasion—all tried to celebrate the Fourth of July—they remembered the sheer pleasure of their treat as the best part of the day.

On the plains, the luckier pilgrims were able to shoot and feast on bison or prairie hens, but the responsible guidebook writers warned travelers not to count on game as a part of their diet. Few overland companies were truly alone on the trail. Most traveled within sight of another company ahead and another behind. In effect, the westward migration was a city— a moving, oddly shaped, long narrow city that was thickly populated nonetheless. And game is not attracted to congregations of people.

The Oregon emigration was a family affair. The pilgrims banded together in companies of fifty to a hundred people for protection and mutual assistance, but at mealtime they withdrew into their familiar family circle.

Even when gold became the magnet that drew Americans west, and the emigrant trains were made up largely of men, the trekkers continued to break up into family-sized messes at mealtime.

The reason was movement. If a wagon train were to be forging ahead every available moment of the day, little time was left in the evening for cooking, let alone preparing a meal for fifty to a hundred people. Whereas the professional cook on a cattle drive could travel ahead of the slow-moving herd and set up his chuck wagon where he chose and begin to prepare a meal, the overland wagon master never knew where he would halt his people for the night. Not only did daily mileage vary, but the presence of other companies meant that the wagon train that was late in stopping had to take whatever ground was available for a campsite.

The preparation of a meal, therefore, could not begin until everyone had stopped. The cook had only an hour or two—the time it took others to unyoke the oxen and put them out to graze—to get a fire lit and a meal ready. Through experimentation, the emigrants learned that nine was the ideal number for a mess. Fewer than nine and there was too much work to do; more than nine and the cook would not be ready.

When there were women in a party, they did the cooking. During the gold rush, men learned at least the rudiments of the craft. The experience of John A. Johnson of Tennessee is instructive. When his party started out, he wrote to his wife that "all of us seem to understand cooking as well as our wives and are anxious to try our hands." At first they intended to rotate the job of cook because they believed that it was the easiest duty. After only a few weeks, however, the other men decided to let Johnson take over as full-time cook in return for exempting him from all other jobs, including guard duty at night, which everyone hated. He wrote to his wife that he was delighted. The job "will not be burdensome because I have a natural taste for that kind of work and they all think so."

Johnson lasted a week:

> I have given up the office of chief cook and take my turn with the rest and my portion of the other duties. I had rather do so as [cooking] is more slavish work than I had anticipated and by far the hardest post to occupy. I found I was working all the time during our halts while others were at least a portion of the time resting.

John A. Johnson probably did not get rich in California. He did, however, gain a greater appreciation for what he and probably most midcentury American men scorned as "woman's work."

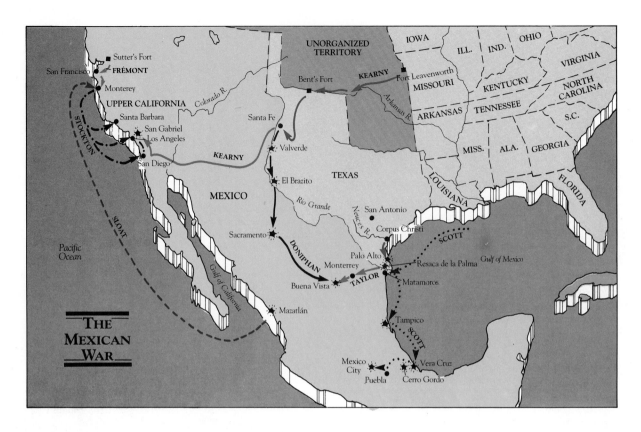

THE
MEXICAN
WAR

his troops to California, where he found that the Americans and some *californio* allies already had won a nearly bloodless revolution and had established the Bear Flag Republic. Kearny had only to raise the American flag and mop up a few scattered Mexican garrisons.

In September, Zachary Taylor took the offensive in northern Mexico, defeating Mexican armies at Matamoros and Nuevo León (also known as Monterrey). Although Old Rough and Ready, as his men called him, showed shrewd tactical judgment, the Nuevo León garrison escaped. Polk disliked Taylor, and he used this mistake as an excuse to divert some of his troops to a command under General Winfield Scott. Nevertheless, in February 1847, Taylor became a national hero when, with his shrunken army, he was attacked at Buena Vista by Santa Anna himself and won a total victory.

The next month, March 1847, General Winfield Scott landed at Vera Cruz and fought his way toward Mexico City along the ancient route of Hernando Cortez. He won a great victory at Cerro Gordo and an even bigger one at Chapultepec, where he captured three thousand men and eight generals. On September 14, 1847, Scott donned one of the gaudy uniforms he loved (his men called him Old Fuss and Feathers) and occupied Mexico City, "the Halls of Montezuma."

By the Treaty of Guadalupe Hidalgo, which was signed in February 1848, Mexico ceded to the United States the Rio Grande boundary, California, and the province of New Mexico (which included the Mormon Zion in Utah and the present states of Arizona and Nevada). The United States paid Mexico $15 million and assumed responsibility for about $3 million that the Mexican government owed Americans.

Mexico was dismembered like a carcass of beef. One-third of its territory was taken from it largely because the United States was strong enough to do so. While the ineptitude of the Mexican military played a part in the national disaster, the partition of the country could

OPPOSITION TO THE MEXICAN WAR

One of the strongest voices against the Mexican War was that of Whig congressman Thomas Corwin of Ohio. "If I were a Mexican," he shouted during the debate, "I would tell you, 'Have you not room in your country to bury your dead men? If you come into mine, we will greet you with bloody hands, and welcome you to hospitable graves!'"

General Zachary Taylor of Louisiana became an American war hero during battles against Mexico.

not help but leave a bitterness in the historical memory of the Mexican people.

Expansionism Run Amok

Cynical as the Mexican acquisition was, it was moderate compared with the suggestions of some American expansionists. Some southerners wanted Polk to seize even more of Mexico, and he was leaning in that direction when the signed Treaty of Guadalupe Hidalgo arrived in Washington. When a rebellion broke out in the Yucatán Peninsula in 1848, Polk asked Congress to authorize the army, which was still in Mexico, to take over the tropical province. Curiously, some antislavery northerners suggested the same thing. Because slavery was illegal in Mexico and the Mexicans were opposed to the institution, they believed, new American states carved from the country would come into the Union as free states.

The president also had designs on Cuba, where 350,000 slaves had long excited the imagination of

proslavery southerners. Polk wanted to present the Spanish government there with a choice between selling the rich sugar island or running the risk of a rebellion fomented by the United States, followed by military intervention.

This was the most bizarre suggestion that was offered in the flush of victory, but not the most grandiose. J. D. B. De Bow, an influential southern editor and publisher, wrote that it was the American destiny to absorb not only all of Mexico, but also the West Indies, all of Canada, and Hawaii. Really taking off, De Bow said that

> the gates of the Chinese empire must be thrown down by the men from the Sacramento and the Oregon, and the haughty Japanese tramplers upon the cross be enlightened in the doctrines of republicanism and the ballot box. The eagle of the republic shall poise itself over the field of Waterloo, after tracing its flight among the gorges of the Himalaya or the Ural mountains, and a successor of Washington ascend the chair of universal empire.

No such golden age of empire followed the Mexican War. On the contrary, the incorporation of so much new land into the United States poisoned American politics by reintroducing questions that had been solved in 1820: Were citizens who owned slaves permitted to settle in the territories and take their human property with them? Would the new states carved from the Mexican acquisition be permitted to enter the Union as slave states?

It was the stormy debate over these questions—and not over slavery itself—that in an eventful, unlucky thirteen years would lead to civil war.

For Further Reading

Frederick Merk, *Manifest Destiny and Mission in American History: A Reinterpretation* (1963), provides an excellent conceptual framework for the study of American expansionism. Merk's *The Oregon Question* (1967) and *Slavery and the Annexation of Texas* (1972) are good special studies. D. M. Pletcher takes up both subjects in *The Diplomacy of Annexation: Texas, Oregon, and the Mexican War* (1973). However, the best single book that brings the many aspects of expansion together is still Ray A. Billington, *The Far Western Frontier, 1830–1860* (1956). Also see the literary classic, Bernard De Voto, *The Year of Decision, 1846* (1943).

On special subjects covered in this chapter, see L. R. Duffus, *The Santa Fe Trail* (1930); D. L. Morgan, *Jedediah Smith and the Opening of the West* (1953); P. C. Phillips, *The Fur Trade* (1961); Jay Monaghan, *The Overland Trail* (1937); and Wallace Stegner, *The Gathering of Zion: The Story of the Mormon Trail* (1964). On James K. Polk, the standard work is Charles Sellers, *James K. Polk, Continentalist, 1843–1846* (1966).

STATISTICS: MEXICAN WAR, 1846–48	
Numbers engaged	78,718
Battle deaths	1,733
Wounds not mortal	4,152
Total casualties	Not available

22

Apples of Discord
The New Territories Divide the Old States, 1848–1856

The bitter fruits of the victory over Mexico were not immediately apparent to Americans. On the contrary, the ill-feeling between those who had favored the war and those who had opposed it seemed to disappear once the fighting was over—for the briefest of historical moments.

Then two events of 1848 that promised to usher in an era of harmony between the North and the South—the election of Zachary Taylor to the presidency and the discovery of gold in California—proved instead to be the first in a series of incidents that tore the Union apart.

A gun crew armed with a cannon protects Topeka, Kansas, capital of the Free-Soilers, in this 1856 daguerreotype.

The Sectional Split Takes Shape

Abolitionists, particularly reformers and intellectuals in New England, had hated the Mexican War from the start. They believed that it had been foisted on Mexicans and Americans alike by southern slaveowners for the callous and cynical purpose of expanding the area in which slavery would be legal.

In Concord, Massachusetts, Henry David Thoreau refused to pay a tax as a protest against the immoral war. When he was arrested, his friend Ralph Waldo Emerson visited him in jail and asked, "Henry, what are you doing in here?"

"Waldo," Thoreau replied, "what are you doing out there?" As he explained in his essay "Civil Disobedience," published in 1849, Thoreau believed that it was the moral person's *duty* to refuse to collaborate with an immoral government and to disobey immoral laws.

During the 1850s, many New England abolitionists, including Emerson, swung over to Thoreau's position. Nevertheless, they remained a small minority of the population of the North. The issue of the introduction of slavery into the territories acquired from Mexico, however, soon became important closer to home: Should slavery be permitted in lands from which it had long been banned, the unorganized part of the old Louisiana Purchase? In this matter, not only abolitionists but also the majority of Americans were intensely interested.

The Wilmot Proviso

As soon as it became obvious that the United States was going to annex millions of acres of Mexican land, Congressman David Wilmot of Pennsylvania attached a rider to an appropriations bill declaring that slavery would be forbidden in the new territories. The Wilmot Proviso passed the House of Representatives in both 1846 and 1847. A clear majority of the nation's congressmen did not want slavery to spread beyond those states in which it already existed.

In the Senate, however, where half the seats were held by men from the slave states, the Wilmot Proviso was defeated. The anti-Wilmot argument, devised by John C. Calhoun, was that the Constitution forbade Congress to discriminate against the citizens of any of the states. Citizens in fifteen of the thirty states had the legal right to own slaves, and Congress could not prevent them from moving to the territories accompanied by their legal property.

Although the argument was not up to Calhoun's

NONVIOLENT CIVIL DISOBEDIENCE

Henry David Thoreau's preachment that a person was morally obligated to disobey an immoral law was given effective political form in the twentieth century by the leader of the Indian independence movement, Mohandas Gandhi, and by the leader of the American civil-rights movement, Martin Luther King, Jr. Both insisted on defying unjust laws. With those who said that their principle would lead to anarchy if everyone accepted it, Gandhi and King disagreed. Because they would not use violence and they would passively accept the punishment that the established government inflicted on them—in other words, go to jail—the majority of people would recognize the justice of their cause and change the law.

---

logical standards, many northern Democrats supported it for the sake of party harmony. Not all, however. A vocal minority withdrew from the Democratic party in protest and formed a new organization, the Free Soil party.

The Free Soil party was not an abolitionist party. If the southern states chose to cling to slavery, the Free-Soilers said, it was their constitutional right to do so. As intellectual heirs of Thomas Jefferson, however, the Free-Soilers believed that small family farmers were the backbone of the country. The public domain, the new western lands that were owned by all the people through the federal government, should be dedicated to the prosperity of that most valuable social class. Slavery must be kept out. Where there were slaves, there were slaveowners. And slaveowners, as the example of the southern states amply demonstrated, used their economic edge over small farmers to stifle democracy.

RIDERS

In the process of lawmaking, a *rider* is a clause, usually dealing with an unrelated matter, that is attached to a bill that is already under consideration in Congress or in a state assembly. The strategy of those who propose riders is to turn them into law despite considerable opposition. Opponents will so badly want the bill under consideration that they will pass it even with the objectionable rider. Thus Wilmot tried to attach his antislavery measure to an appropriations bill that was desperately needed. Only because the anti-Wilmot forces in the Senate were strong enough to vote it down did the Wilmot Proviso not cause a major crisis.

Free Soil! Free Speech! Free Men!—this line of reasoning appealed to midwesterners who were proud of their independence. Some of them, though not many, were also abolitionists. Most Free-Soilers cared little about the plight of the blacks. There was, in fact, a streak of racism in the Free Soil party. Some members made it clear that they wanted not only slaves and slaveowners but also free black family farmers banned from the territories. As late as 1857, an Oregon law forbade both slaves and free blacks to enter the territory.

The Election of 1848

Polk did not run for reelection in 1848. A hard worker, he literally wore himself out as president and died only four months after leaving the White House. In his place, the Democrats nominated one of his northern supporters, the competent but gloriously dull Lewis Cass of Michigan. The Whigs, having lost with their elder statesman Clay in 1844, returned to the winning formula of 1840—a popular general. They nominated the hero of the Battle of Buena Vista, Zachary Taylor of Louisiana. Because Taylor was a slaveowner as well as a southerner, Whig strategists hoped that he would carry southern states that were otherwise lost to the Democrats.

Taylor was no politician. A coarse, cranky, and stubborn old geezer of sixty-four years, he admitted (almost boasted) that he had never bothered to cast a vote in his life. When the letter from the Whig party announcing his nomination arrived, he refused to pay the postage due on it. When the news of the honor finally broke through his indifference, he responded: "I will not say I will not serve if the good people were imprudent enough to elect me."

As in 1844, the electoral votes of New York were the key to the election, and a third party—the Free Soil party led by Martin Van Buren—provided the hand that turned it in the lock. Van Buren's stand against the expansion of slavery won him more votes in New York than Lewis Cass and threw the state's thirty-six electoral votes to General Taylor. Because Taylor also carried all of New England but New Hampshire and Maine, and more than half of the southern states, there was good reason to believe that his presidency would be a time of reconciliation.

Gold in Them Thar' Hills

It might have been just that, had it not been for the discovery of gold in newly acquired California in January 1848. On the face of it, this event also promised to bring North and South together. News of the discovery reached the East in the autumn of 1848 and caused, in the spring of 1849, one of the most extraordinary population movements in the history of the human race.

There were five hundred people living in San Francisco, fifteen thousand in all of California, on the day that James Marshall, a carpenter, took a walk along the tailrace of a sawmill that he was building and returned to tell his workers, "Boys, I believe I have found a gold mine." Within a year, the port of San Francisco was flooded by gold seekers, and the town had swelled into a shanty and tent city of five thousand. Within two years, it was a bustling metropolis, the capital of the gold country. The population of all of California increased to one hundred thousand by the end of 1849.

Some got there by sailing ship around the bottom of South America. Other easterners steamed to Panama, crossed the isthmus on foot, and booked passage—sometimes after waiting many months—on vessels bound for San Francisco. Foreigners from almost every country in the world flocked to California by sea. The majority of the American gold seekers, however, crossed the continent on the trails that had been blazed by the Oregon-or-Busters a few years earlier.

Artist William Sidney Mount provided a glimpse of how easterners reacted to news of the California gold rush in his painting, California News.

INVENTIONS

Between 1790 and 1800, 306 patents on new inventions were registered with the federal government. Between 1850 and 1860, the United States Patent Office cleared more than 28,000. In 1849, Abraham Lincoln patented a device for floating steamboats over shoals, but it was in another line of work that he was to make his mark.

There were both southerners and northerners in the endless wagon trains, but sectional suspicions seemed insignificant compared with the common profound experience of negotiating a continent and the shared dreams of riches to come. While there was ill-feeling between northerners and southerners in the gold fields, it was only back home that talk of California meant talk of sectional crisis.

The California Crisis

California grew so quickly that Congress did not have time to establish it as a territory of the United States. In principle, California was a conquered land under military occupation; in practice, law and order were maintained by each community, including the little camps of miners that dotted the western slope of the Sierra Nevada.

Because California was so valuable, producing $10 million in gold in 1849, and its population was more than adequate to support a state government, President Taylor advised skipping the territorial stage and admitting California as a state. Californians agreed, and in November 1849, they sent their state constitution to Congress for approval. Its most important provision was the prohibition of slavery in the Golden State.

None were so stunned by the rapidity of events as the senators and congressmen of the South. They had taken it for granted that slavery would expand westward into the Mexican acquisition. After all, the new lands abutted on Texas, a slave state. Now, practically before the ink was dry on the peace treaty, the best part of the acquisition was applying for admission to the Union as a free state. It was not an easy morsel to digest.

What was worse, if California were admitted, the South would lose its equity in the United States Senate. Southerners were already a minority in the House of Representatives, where seats are apportioned according to population. In 1850, there were 9 million people in the South and 14 million in the North.

In the Senate, on the contrary, where each state is represented by two members, there were fifteen slave states and fifteen free states. However, with no potential slave state on the horizon, and with two potential free states in Minnesota and Oregon, the application of California for admission to the Union took on the shape of a calamity. Most southern congressmen declared their opposition to California statehood. The North's toleration of abolitionists made it impossible for them to trust to the goodwill of free-states senators. They needed their equity in the Senate in order to protect southern interests.

The southerners soon discovered that President Taylor was not their friend. He had nothing against slavery. Indeed, Taylor owned more than a hundred blacks and did not mind saying that he would fight in a civil war to protect his right to keep them. But Old Rough and Ready was a nationalist above all else. For reasons of national pride and security, he insisted that California be admitted immediately. If it must be as a free state, so be it. He further angered southern congressmen with his decision that a boundary dispute between Texas and what was slated to become New Mexico Territory be resolved in favor of New Mexico.

Tempers were already boiling when Congress con-

A miner searches for wealth in the streams of California by patiently panning for gold.

vened in December 1849. The House of Representatives went through sixty-three ballots just to elect a Speaker, usually a ceremonial affair. The next month, Henry Clay, seventy-two years old now and beyond all hopes of becoming president, attempted to cap his career as the Great Compromiser by offering a solution to the crisis.

Clay's Plan

Clay's Omnibus Bill was a compromise in the old tradition; it required both sides to make concessions in the interests of the common good. The bill provided that California be admitted as a free state and that the rest of the Mexican acquisition be organized as territories with no reference to slavery. This pleased Taylor, but also held out the possibility of future slave states in territory that is now Utah, Nevada, New Mexico, and Arizona. The Texas land dispute was resolved in favor of the federal government but with face-saving concessions to Texas, including a provision that Congress assume the large debt of the former Republic of Texas.

Clay ignored abolitionist demands that slavery be banned in the District of Columbia. The South had a strong constitutional point on that matter, and the mere suggestion of abolition in the national capital angered those southern moderates whom Clay was counting on to push through his Omnibus Bill. However, he tried to mollify northern antislavery congressmen by proposing the abolition of the slave trade in the national capital.

To compensate slaveowners for this symbolic rebuff, Clay included a new, stronger Fugitive Slave Act in his package. Until 1850, it was not difficult for antislavery officials in the North to protect runaway slaves within their jurisdictions. Clay's bill allowed federal provost marshals to circumvent local courts, arrest fugitive slaves in the North, and return them to their owners.

Failure

Not too many years earlier, the Omnibus Bill would have sailed through Congress amidst cheers, tossed hats, and invitations to share a bottle after adjournment. But times and tempers had changed. Extremists from both sections and congressmen who had been regarded as moderates refused to accept the Omnibus Bill because it contained concessions to the other section. Northerners particularly disliked the Fugitive Slave Act; it made slavery quasi-legal in the free states. Southern extremists could not bring themselves to vote for the abolition of the slave trade in the District of Columbia. Texans and their allies opposed taking lands

PUBLIC RELATIONS

Although few said so publicly, many southern leaders privately admitted that they were glad to see the slave trade abolished in Washington, D.C. It was not a major market town, and everyone admitted that the auction block was slavery's ugliest face. With a large foreign population, which inclined to be antislavery, in the national capital at all times, the disappearance of the auction block in Washington could be considered a kind of public-relations measure, hiding an unpleasant reality from visitors.

The ending of the slave trade in Washington did not have that effect, however. There were slave auctions in both Arlington and Alexandria, Virginia, across the Potomac River, and diplomats and tourists found it quite easy to cross over to see them.

from that slave state and putting them into a territory where slavery was not guaranteed. Friends of President Taylor resented compensating Texas in any way.

The spirit of compromise was dead. New York's William H. Seward called the idea of compromise "radically wrong and essentially vicious." John C. Calhoun, once a master of cool reason and cold logic, was reduced to appealing to a gaggle of romantic young southerners who thought they were knights in a Sir Walter Scott story. Calhoun sponsored the preposterous plan whereby there would be two presidents, one from the North and one from the South, each of whom would have a veto over all acts of Congress.

Even if Clay's bill had cleared Congress, Taylor would have vetoed it. The Texans and the southern extremists had enraged him with their defiance. California should be a state; it was as simple as that. And Texas would come to heel. If not, Taylor announced, he would lead an army into the Lone Star State.

1850: A Year for Anger

Depressed by his failure, Clay left Washington. Into his place stepped young Stephen A. Douglas of Illinois, a brilliant lawyer who sized up the crisis as a tactical problem. Instead of presenting the deeply divided Congress with a single Omnibus Bill, parts of which offended nearly everyone, Douglas separated Clay's package into six components. These he maneuvered through Congress by patching together a different majority for each part.

Douglas could count on northern senators and representatives to support California statehood and the abolition of the slave trade in the District of Columbia. To these votes he managed to add those of just enough southern moderates, mostly from the border states, to push the laws through. He could count on a solid southern bloc for the Fugitive Slave Act and the Texas bill. To this group he added just enough northern moderates like himself to make a majority.

Thus the "Compromise of 1850" was not really a compromise in the sense that both sides gave a little and took a little. A majority of both northern and southern congressmen refused to give an inch. Only 4 of 60 senators voted for all six of Douglas's bills, and only 11 for five of the six. Only 28 of 240 representatives voted for all of them. Douglas's manipulations were brilliant. They were also popular in the nation at large, where moderation appeared to be stronger than it was under the Capitol Dome. But Douglas did nothing to extinguish the fires of hostility that were smoldering in Congress.

Fate Lends a Hand

Because Douglas's plan included a Texas boundary and financial settlement that was unacceptable to Taylor, the scheme would have failed without the help of fate. On July 4, 1850, Taylor attended a ceremony on the Capitol Mall, where he stood for several hours under a merciless Washington sun. Returning to the White House, he wolfed down a large bowl of cucumbers and drank several quarts of iced milk.

A few hours later the old man took to bed with severe stomach cramps, not surprising under the circumstances. Instead of leaving him alone, his doctors bled him and administered one powerful medicine after another—ipecac to make him vomit, quinine for his fever, calomel as a laxative, and opium for the pain they were causing him. Old Rough and Ready could not handle nineteenth-century medicine, and he died on July 9. His successor, an easy-going New York Whig named Millard Fillmore, signed every one of the Douglas bills.

The Passing of the Old Guard

In the Thirty-first Congress, the generation of leaders who had governed the country since the 1820s rubbed elbows with the new and very different group of men who would guide the nation through its next era.

Andrew Jackson was already gone, dead in 1845. Henry Clay and Daniel Webster, who delivered one of his most eloquent speeches on behalf of the Omnibus Bill, both died in 1852. Thomas Hart Benton survived until 1858, but only to discover that the new era had no place for him. Old-fashioned Jacksonian nationalists had nothing to say to a nation that was splitting in two.

John C. Calhoun would have won election after election had he lived. Alone of the giants of the age of Jackson, he had made the transition—indeed, had led the transition—from devotion to the Union to extreme southern sectionalism. But Calhoun did not survive to see the results of his unhappy career. On March 4, 1850, too ill to deliver his last speech to the Senate, an uncompromising attack on the North, he had to listen while it was read for him, his glazed eyes burning with defiance and hatred. Less than a month later Calhoun was dead.

The New Breed

Shortly before his death, Calhoun croaked to one of his disciples that it was up to the young to save "the South, the poor South." With each year of the 1850s, these fire-eaters, so-called because of the invective with which they spoke of northerners, displaced moderates in state legislatures, governorships, the House of Representatives, and the Senate.

Congressman Thaddeus Stevens, a staunch abolitionist, as photographed by Mathew Brady.

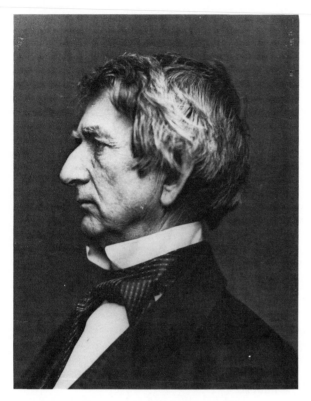

William H. Seward, a congressman from New York who held militant antislavery views.

anyone else; Salmon P. Chase of Ohio; and Charles Sumner of Massachusetts.

Chase was a Free-Soiler. The others were Whigs who, after 1854, joined with the Free-Soilers to form the Republican party. Rivaling them in numbers were the regular Democrats of the North, led by such men as Lewis Cass of Michigan; Franklin Pierce of New Hampshire; James Buchanan of Pennsylvania; and the ablest of them all, Stephen Douglas of Illinois, who was called the Little Giant in recognition of his contradictory physical and political stature.

None of them regarded slavery as a positive good. Most of them found the idea of human bondage distasteful. However, their moral sensibilities were not offended by the peculiar institution, and their principal political goal was conciliation of North and South under the leadership of the Democratic party. As a result, they were inclined to make concessions to southern fellow Democrats that offended both abolitionists and Free-Soilers.

The regular Democrats of the North considered themselves to be moderates, as indeed they were in the sense that they were flanked by antislavery Whigs and southern fire-eaters. But during the 1850s, moderation contributed as generously as extremism to the crisis of the Union. The issue on which the northern Democrats worked their mischief was the status of slavery in the territories.

The Whig party of the South, a refuge for moderates, dwindled. John Tyler had already led the states'-rights Whigs back to the Democrats. After 1854, most of the compromise-minded followers of Henry Clay either left politics or embraced southern extremism. Robert Toombs of Georgia, for example, supported the Compromise of 1850, but within a few years he was baiting the North in language as torrid as any fire-eater's.

In the North, the abolitionists, the fire-eaters' opposite numbers, were proportionately less powerful. Abolitionism remained unpopular with the majority of northerners, in part because most northern whites could no more imagine accepting blacks as equals than could most southern whites, and in part because of the self-righteousness of evangelical reformers like William Lloyd Garrison.

Nevertheless, there was a solid core of militant antislavery feeling in the Congress that included men whose abilities were rivaled only by their own taste for antagonistic rhetoric. Among them were William H. Seward of New York, a confederate of President Taylor; Thaddeus Stevens of Pennsylvania, a staunch believer in racial equality whom southerners hated more than

Slavery in the Territories

Except for California and Texas, the westernmost states were Iowa, Missouri, and Arkansas, stretching a little more than 250 miles from the Mississippi River. Most of the remainder of what is today the continental United States was organized into five territories, districts in which the people elected a legislature, while the governor, who exercised a veto power, was appointed by the president. North of Indian Territory (present-day Oklahoma), and including the major part of Wyoming, Montana, the Dakotas, Nebraska, and Kansas, was officially "unorganized territory." It had no territorial government at all. Here alone did the Indians of the Great Plains range free without having to answer to the United States government.

Here, too, slavery was forbidden under the Missouri Compromise of 1820. In that year, Congress had declared that any states entering the Union from territory north of 36° 30′ north latitude, the southern boundary of the state of Missouri, must be free states. The slavery question was settled in the Louisiana Purchase lands. In all the debate over the Mexican acquisition, unorganized territory was scarcely mentioned. In 1854, that was to change.

A Railroad to California

The reason it changed was the necessity of binding California to the other states by means of a transcontinental railroad. The route that railroad would follow was undetermined. Both southerners and northerners wanted the eastern terminus of the line to be located in their sections. The city that handled the California trade would profit richly from it.

Jefferson Davis of Mississippi, the Secretary of War, wanted the railroad to begin in the South. From a construction engineer's point of view, the route that he sketched through Texas was by far the best; it crossed no mountain ranges of consequence until it reached the southern part of New Mexico Territory, just above the Gila River. But the plan had a single handicap—the railroad line probably would have to pass through land that Mexico owned south of the river. Davis asked President Franklin Pierce to send James Gadsden, a railroad agent, to Mexico, where for $10 million, Gadsden purchased a thirty-thousand-square-mile triangular tract of arid but level land. (Today the Gadsden Purchase comprises the southernmost parts of New Mexico and Arizona.) Davis, it appeared, had plucked a juicy plum for the South. None of the four other routes that had been suggested for the railroad was nearly so attractive.

But Stephen A. Douglas of Illinois had an idea. The central route that he favored, with Chicago as the eastern terminus, had two serious drawbacks. First, it climbed over both the Rockies and the Sierra Nevada, the latter at more than eight thousand feet above sea level. Second, the central route ran through the unorganized part of the Louisiana Purchase lands. Congress would never authorize a multimillion-dollar investment in country where there was no governmental authority, particularly since the proud and powerful Plains Indians were in control of the land. Southern congressmen, convinced that their own route was nearly a sure thing, would never make things easier for Chicago by organizing territorial governments in areas where slavery was forbidden by law.

Never, that is, unless Douglas baited his hook with a concession on the matter of slavery, which, to southerners, had come to be a more important issue than all others combined.

The Kansas-Nebraska Act

In his Kansas-Nebraska bill of May 1854, that is what Douglas did. His bill explicitly repealed the Missouri Compromise by providing that the people who actually settled in the Kansas and Nebraska territories would decide for themselves whether they would have slavery there. Popular sovereignty, Douglas argued, was the democratic solution to the problem of slavery in the territories.

The southern congressmen jumped like trout after a cold winter. The Kansas-Nebraska Act opened to slavery land where it had been outlawed for thirty-four years. The congressmen had no illusions about Nebraska. It bordered on the free state of Iowa and would be populated by antislavery northerners. Kansas, however, abutted on Missouri, where slavery was not very important economically but where, curiously, the majority of people was fiercely in favor of it.

Douglas's popularity soared in the South, another development that he had anticipated. He hoped to win the Democratic party's presidential nomination in 1856 as a conciliator, the hero of both sections. To the South, he would be the man who opened Kansas to slavery. To the North, he would be the man who got the railroad.

To those who protested that he got the railroad by selling out to slaveowners, Douglas replied that in reality he had given up nothing. If Kansas was now legally open to slavery, the institution would never take root there because no crops that could be grown in Kansas were suited to a slave-labor system. It would become a state of small family farmers who would vote against slavery.

Thus did Stephen A. Douglas become the first "Doughface," a northern Democrat who took one line with the North and another with the South, kneading his face into different shapes according to whom he was addressing.

The Republican Party

The Kansas-Nebraska Act killed the Whig party. When the few remaining Cotton Whigs of the South voted for it along with the southern Democrats, they abandoned any reason for remaining in opposition; most of them joined the Democratic party. The Conscience Whigs of the North, who were strongly opposed to the expansion of slavery (and many of whom were abolitionists as well), joined with the Free-Soilers, some Democrats who opposed the Kansas-

Nebraska Act, and a few Know-Nothings to form the Republican party.

The Republicans were held together by the principle that no slavery be allowed in the territories. Their overarching legislative demand was that the Kansas-Nebraska Act must be repealed. As repeal was a very urgent matter, the Republicans campaigned hard in the elections of 1854 and won an astonishing victory, actually capturing the House of Representatives.

The Republican party was not just the Free Soil party under a different name; it was not a single-issue party. The Republicans stole some of Douglas's thunder in the North by enthusiastically supporting the transcontinental railroad. They appealed to farmers who were uninterested in the slavery issue by sponsoring a Homestead Act which provided that land would be given to families that would actually settle and farm it. From the Whigs, the Republicans inherited the demand for a high protective tariff, thus winning manufacturing interests to their side. Also appealing to industrial capitalists was the Republican demand for a liberal immigration policy, which would attract cheap European labor to the United States.

It was a comprehensive program, but the Republicans were not a national party, as the Whigs had been. They appealed only to northerners. They did not even put up candidates for office in the slave states. Their hopes of victory lay in a sweep of the free states.

"Bleeding Kansas"

While the Republicans operated on the political front to overturn the Kansas-Nebraska Act, New England reformers worked to keep slavery out of Kansas under the rule laid down in the principle of popular sovereignty: the majority governs. Groups such as Eli Thayer's New England Emigrant Aid Company raised money to finance the settlement of antislavery northerners in Kansas Territory. Within two years, Thayer's group sent two thousand people to Kansas and no doubt encouraged many other northerners to go on their own.

This painting, entitled Bloody Kansas, *suggests the violence that erupted in Kansas after passage of the Kansas-Nebraska Act in 1854.*

Southerners were shocked to discover that Douglas's Doughface message to the North—slavery would not take root in Kansas no matter what the law said—appeared to be true. The population of the free states was so much greater than that of the slave states that more people from Massachusetts than from Missouri were breaking the Kansas sod.

Few responded with more anger than those Missourians who lived on the Kansas border. They were a frontier people, generally poor and struggling, who owned comparatively few slaves. However, they were fiercely antiblack and understood that a free state of Kansas would be an attractive destination for runaway slaves. Those who took up Kansas homesteads or who merely rode across the state line to vote illegally in Kansas elections and to harass northern settlers became known as Border Ruffians.

Kansas was a lawless place. It is impossible to determine how many murders, beatings, and robberies were associated with the slavery controversy and how many reflected the disorder that was common to all American frontiers. Nevertheless, two incidents were clearly motivated by the slavery issue and represented the first acts of violence in the sectional conflict.

BORDER RUFFIANS

The western counties of Missouri would have become breeding grounds for violence even if, after 1856, the slavery issue had not been injected to agitate the settlers there. Western Missouri was still raw frontier, an extremely poor farming and grazing country where reigned the lawless instability of America's move west. With the slavery issue added to this dangerous mix, the border counties produced a disproportionate number of dubious characters in the years immediately before, during, and after the Civil War. In addition to the sacking of Lawrence, Kansas, and John Brown's action on Pottawatomie Creek, western Missouri was the recruiting ground for William C. Quantrill's notorious raiders, a Civil War unit given more to terroristic attacks on civilians than to fighting the Union Army. Quantrill's right-hand man, Bloody Bill Anderson, scalped the northerners whom he killed. Future outlaws Jesse and Frank James and the Younger brothers came from this country, as did the "bandit queen," Myre Belle Shirley, or Belle Starr.

Fervent abolitionist John Brown led the execution of five proslavery Kansans.

John Brown and Lawrence

On May 21, 1856, a gang of border ruffians rode into the antislavery town of Lawrence, Kansas, set it afire, and killed several people. Three days later, in an act that he announced was retribution, a fanatical abolitionist named John Brown swooped down on a small settlement on the banks of Pottawatomie Creek and ordered five proslavery Kansans executed with a farmer's scythe. Southern politicians, who had treated the violence in Kansas as something of a joke, screamed in anguish. Northern abolitionists, who had condemned the border ruffians for their barbarity, were suddenly silent. A few actually praised John Brown as a hero of the antislavery cause.

That a man who practiced ritual murder should be praised by people who were proud of their moral righteousness indicates to what an extent the hatred between antislavery northerners and proslavery southerners had reached. Extremists on both sides no longer spoke and acted according to rational principles; they were in favor of any act done in the name of "the South, the poor South" or of the godly cause of antislavery.

Charles Sumner and Preston Brooks

Another illustration of how bitter sectional politics had become was the Sumner–Brooks affair, which also oc-

An 1856 lithograph shows Congressman Preston Brooks beating Senator Charles Sumner into unconsciousness.

curred in May 1856. Charles Sumner, the prototype of the New England reformer, combined a commitment to pacifism with a weakness for vituperative oratory. At about the same time as the Lawrence and Pottawatomie incidents, he delivered a speech on the floor of the Senate called "The Crime Against Kansas."

For the most part it was standard antisouthern fare, spoken more for the folks back home than for Sumner's fellow senators. But Sumner also aimed some personal insults at an elderly senator from South Carolina, Andrew P. Butler. Butler suffered from a physical defect that caused him to drool when he spoke, and Sumner made some coarse allusions to this defect in connection with the barbarity of slaveowners.

Two days later, Butler's nephew, a congressman named Preston Brooks, walked into the Senate, found Sumner seated at his desk, and proceeded to beat him into unconsciousness with a heavy cane. Brooks said that he was merely putting into practice the Code Duello, which held that in the event of personal insult a gentleman challenged a social equal to a duel but "caned" a social inferior.

In fact, Brooks's action made a mockery of chivalry since instead of merely humiliating Sumner with a few sharp raps, he bludgeoned the senator to near death while Sumner, his legs tangled in his fallen desk, lay helpless to defend himself.

Instead of condemning Brooks as a bully and coward, southerners feted him at banquets and made him gifts of dozens of gold-headed canes to replace the one that he had broken. At the same time, northerners forgot that Sumner had stepped far beyond the bounds of common decency in his attack on Senator Butler, and made him a martyr. While Sumner recovered—it would be several years before he returned to the Senate—Massachusetts reelected him so that his empty desk would stand as rebuke to the South.

In normal times, politicians who argue violently in Congress socialize quite cordially outside the Capitol. Even Andrew Jackson and Nicholas Biddle had been capable of a few civil words at parties and balls. After the Sumner–Brooks affair, this ceased to be true. Both northerners and southerners carried firearms into the congressional chambers and ceased to speak even on informal occasions. It was a situation that called for strong leadership in the presidency. During the 1850s, however, the presidents proved to be among the weakest in the history of the office.

IN THE DIGGINGS

Very few of the forty-niners knew even the rudiments of how gold was mined. Only the Mexicans, who generally were called Sonorans in California after the Mexican state from which many came, and the Cornish from southwestern England had been miners before they came to the gold fields.

However, technological innocence was no great handicap in California in 1849 and the early 1850s because placer mining—recovering pure gold from the sands and gravels of creekbeds—required very little expertise. What placer mining required was back-breaking toil, which the forty-niners were ready to invest.

Placer mining is a mechanical process. In order to ascertain whether there was gold in a creek, a miner "panned" it. That is, he scooped up a pound or so of silt, sand, and pebbles in a sturdy, shallow pan; removed the stones by hand (making certain he did not discard any nuggets, chunks of gold); and then agitated the finer contents, constantly replenishing the water in the pan so that the lighter mud and sand washed over the sides while the heavier gold remained.

When miners (who usually worked in partnerships of two, three, or sometimes more) discovered enough "color" in a pan to warrant systematic mining of a placer, they staked a claim and built a "rocker" or a "long tom," two easily constructed devices that performed the washing process on a larger scale.

The rocker was a water-tight wooden box, three to five feet long and a foot or so across, that was built on a base such as that of a rocking chair so that it could be tipped from side to side. On the bottom were a series of riffles made of wood or in the form of corrugated metal, and sometimes a sheet of fine wire mesh. These simulated the crevices in a creekbed, where the gold naturally collected. Into the rocker, by means of a sluice, ran a constant stream of water. While one "pard" shoveled gravel and sand into the box, another rocked it and agitated the contents with a spade or a pitchfork. As with panning, the lighter worthless mineral washed out (stones, again, were manually discarded), and the gold remained at the bottom to be retrieved at the end of the day, weighed, divided and cached.

The long tom took more time to build but was easier to work and more productive. In effect, the water-bearing sluice was extended into a long, high-sided, water-tight box with a series of riffles built into the bottom. Using the long tom, all the partners could shovel gravel almost continuously. It was not necessary for one to agitate the contents. The long tom was also better adapted to "dry mining" than was the rocker. That is, in order to wash gold anywhere but in a creek,

it was necessary to transport water to the site by means of a sluice. Having invested that much labor, few dry miners were willing to be satisfied with the modest productivity of the rocker.

The placer mines were known as the "poor man's diggings" because placer mining neither required much money nor gave the man with capital any advantage. The placer miner had to buy comparatively few tools and materials. At the same time, because just about everyone was dreaming of striking it rich, few were willing to work for wages, no matter how high they were. The lucky discoverer of a valuable deposit had to take on partners. Gold mining became an industry with an employer–employee relationship only when the placers were exhausted and attention shifted to the mountains from which the gold had been extracted through erosion. In order to win gold that was still locked in the earth, it became necessary to introduce hydraulic mining—bringing a mountain down with high-pressure water cannons, thence retrieving the gold by washing—or quartz (hard-rock) mining—tunneling into the earth to dig out gold ore, gold compounded with quartz or other worthless rock. Very little hard-rock gold was pure element. The ore had to be milled (crushed) and then smelted (melted to separate the gold from the other elements). Obviously, both hydraulic and hard-rock mining called for capital, and lots of it.

As long as the "poor man's diggings" held out, mining life was highly democratic and egalitarian. No one was allowed to stake a claim larger than he and his partners were able to mine within a season or two. Law and order in the mining camps was maintained by the informal common consent of the men who lived and worked in them. There was no formal legal authority in California until late 1850, and no estimable governmental presence over much of the gold fields for several years thereafter.

All the fruits of this democracy were not sweet. A man with the majority of a camp behind him could "get away with murder" or, at least, lesser crimes. The justice brought to others was frequently brutal. Miner democracy did not extend to other than native-born Americans and immigrants from Western Europe. Despite the fact that the forty-niners learned what they knew of mining from the Sonorans, they expelled them from all but the southern gold fields within a year. As Spanish-speaking people also, Chileans came up against prejudice.

Worst-treated of all were the Chinese. Because their culture was so alien and because they worked in very large groups, thus spending less to live, the Chinese frightened the Californians; they feared that the

"Celestials," as the Chinese were sometimes called, would drag down the standard of living for all. Very few Chinese managed to remain in mining and then only on deposits that had been abandoned by whites as too poor. For the most part they were forced to take less desirable jobs in town and cities.

There were few blacks in the diggings; the few photographs of black miners that survive show them in apparently equal partnership with whites. The white miners must have been northerners, and, indeed, there was something of a sectional split among California's miners, especially during the crisis of 1850. Nowhere did the split take more theatrical form than in the mining camp of Rough and Ready, at the northern end of the Mother Lode. Populated largely by southerners, Rough and Ready (ironically named for President Zachary Taylor, an enemy of sectionalism) seceded from the Union in 1850.

Black and white miners dug for gold in California.

For Further Reading

The names of a few historians dominate any list of books about the breakup of the Union during the 1850s. Avery Craven, *The Coming of the Civil War* (1957) and *Civil War in the Making* (1959), presents the picture of a crisis that was unavoidable because of the nature of political leadership in the United States—both North and South. David Potter, *The Impending Crisis, 1848–1861* (1976) and *The South and Sectional Conflict* (1968), are essential. Allan Nevins, *Ordeal of the Union* (1947), is a highly readable two-volume work. Another comprehensive and judicious account is to be found in the early chapters of John G. Randall and David Donald, *The Civil War and Reconstruction* (1969).

On the Compromise of 1850, see Holman Hamilton, *Prologue to Conflict: The Crisis and Compromise of 1850* (1964). On the Free-Soilers, whose emergence caused such panic in the South, the best book is Eric Foner, *Free Soil, Free Labor, Free Men* (1970).

Useful biographies are Richard N. Current, *Daniel Webster and the Rise of National Conservatism* (1955); G. Van Deusen, *The Life of Henry Clay* (1937); F. B. Woodward, *Lewis Cass: The Last Jeffersonian* (1950); and G. M. Capers, *Stephen A. Douglas: Defender of the Union* (1959).

23

The End of the Old Union

The Secession of the Southern States, 1856–1861

Franklin Pierce was a handsome and amiable man, quick with a smile and a handshake, entirely lacking in malice—until he served four unhappy, unsuccessful years in the White House.

Pierce thought that he was out of politics when he was nominated. Several years before 1852, he had resigned from the Senate and had returned to New Hampshire to practice law. Then the Democratic convention deadlocked through forty-eight ballots and turned to him in desperation. He was one of the few northerners who were acceptable to the South.

Pierce was easily elected over Whig candidate Winfield Scott, but it was a terrible mistake from first to last. As a fellow New Hampshire-man explained, "Up here, where everybody knows Frank Pierce, he's a pretty considerable fellow. But come to spread him out over the whole country, I'm afraid he'll be dreadful thin in some places."

Pierce's term began with a personal tragedy and ended with the vicious violence in Kansas and on the Senate floor. Just before Inauguration Day his son was killed in a railroad accident, and Pierce's wife never quite recovered from her

The Confederate attack on Fort Sumter in Charleston harbor marked the beginning of the Civil War.

grief. She was a virtual recluse in the White House, and, preoccupied with her distraction, Pierce leaned heavily on his old friend and Secretary of War, Jefferson Davis of Mississippi, in making policy.

They were concerned with little more than Kansas after 1854, and the president flatly backed the proslavery government of the territory despite persuasive evidence that it represented only a minority of Kansans and sanctioned violence against Free-Soilers. To antislavery northerners, he was the ultimate Doughface, a northern man with southern principles. In fact, Pierce believed that the Union could be saved only if northern Democrats like himself stood as buffers between slavery and the abolitionists of their own section; thus they might convince white southerners that the threat to their institution could be contained. His sweet intentions turned to ashes in his mouth, and Pierce was as glad as any other president before or since to get out of the White House. By 1861, he was so embittered that when the Civil War broke out, he effectively announced that he hoped for a southern victory.

As president, Franklin Pierce tried to placate proslavery factions.

Overture to a Rebellion

The man who succeeded Pierce was also a Doughface, but he was not Stephen A. Douglas. A hero in the South in 1854, by 1856 the Little Giant was anathema to southern extremists; his doctrine of popular sovereignty had proved not to open Kansas and the West to slavery but to pit the slave states against the free states in a contest that the South could not win because the North was so much more populous.

Douglas lost the nomination to James Buchanan of Pennsylvania, a man of pedestrian talents but profound discretion and good luck. Buchanan had been out of the country as ambassador to Great Britain between 1853 and 1856 and was therefore not associated with the disappointments of popular sovereignty. He had, however, joined with two other diplomats in 1854 in writing the Ostend Manifesto, which called for the United States to buy Cuba from Spain (slavery was legal in Cuba) or if Spain refused to sell, to take the island by force.

The Republicans chose John C. Frémont, famous as the Pathfinder, the dashing leader of two exploration parties that had helped map the way to Oregon and California. Frémont was the husband of Jessie Benton, a beautiful and intellectually formidable woman with politics in her blood. She was the daughter of Old Bullion, Thomas Hart Benton.

Like his father-in-law, Frémont believed that the western lands should be reserved for family farmers. This was a popular position, but the Pathfinder suffered from two serious handicaps: he was not merely a free-soil man but had made abolitionist statements that worried many northerners; and he was a bastard at a time when illegitimacy carried a stain of shame.

Despite these burdens and despite his not being on the ballot in a single slave state, Frémont won a third of the total popular vote and might have defeated Buchanan had not former president Millard Fillmore been in the race on the Native American, or Know-Nothing, ticket. Fillmore actually outpolled Frémont in California and probably took enough votes from him in Pennsylvania and Illinois to throw those states and the election to the Democrats.

Dred Scott

Buchanan's presidency began with a bang. In his inaugural address he hinted that the issue of slavery in the territories would shortly be settled for all time. Two days later, on March 6, 1857, Americans learned what

Dred Scott went to the Supreme Court to win freedom and lost.

he meant when the Supreme Court handed down its decision in the case of *Dred Scott* v. *Sandford.*

Dred Scott was a slave in Missouri. In 1834, he had accompanied his army-officer owner to Illinois, where slavery was prohibited under the Northwest Ordinance of 1787, and, briefly, to a part of the Louisiana Purchase where slavery was illegal under the Missouri Compromise. For four years, Scott had lived on free soil before returning to Missouri. In 1846, he had sued for his freedom on these grounds. For a decade, financed by abolitionists, his case bounced around the lower courts.

Ironically, Missouri courts had released slaves with cases similar to Scott's, but that was before sectional animosity cut so deep. Scott lost his case on the grounds that whatever his status may have been in Illinois, he became a slave again when he returned to Missouri.

Chief Justice Taney: The Southern Solution

Although every justice wrote his own opinion in the complicated case, Chief Justice Roger B. Taney, an old Jacksonian from Maryland, spoke for the majority when he declared that as a slave, Scott was not a citizen and could not, therefore, sue in the state courts. In-

stead of leaving the decision at that, Taney continued. He believed that he had discovered the constitutional solution to the question that was tearing the country apart. In fact, what Taney propounded was the doctrine of John C. Calhoun, the extreme southern position on slavery in the territories.

Taney declared that the Missouri Compromise had been unconstitutional in prohibiting slavery in the territories because Congress was forbidden to discriminate against the citizens of any of the states. State legislatures could outlaw slavery. But territorial legislatures could not do so because they were created by Congress and were subject to the Constitution's restraints on Congress.

The Republicans Panic

Republicans, including moderates who had urged some degree of compromise with the South, were enraged. As they saw the history of the question, between 1820 and 1854, under the Missouri Compromise, slavery had been illegal in all territories north of 36° 30′. With the Kansas-Nebraska Act of 1854, slavery could be legalized in those territories if the settlers chose to do so. With the Dred Scott decision of 1857, there was no way that even the majority of settlers could prevent a slaveowner from moving to their territory with his human property. As far as the Republicans were concerned, the Senate, the presidency, and now the Supreme Court were all part of a slaveowners' con-

---

THE RACE ISSUE

Because few American whites believed in racial equality, it was to the interest of northern Democrats to accuse the Republicans of advocating race mixture. "I am opposed to Negro equality," Stephen A. Douglas said in his debate with Abraham Lincoln in Chicago. "I am in favor of preserving, not only the purity of the blood, but the purity of the government from any mixture or amalgamation with inferior races."

The Democrats' line forced Republicans to reassure their constituents that opposition to slavery did not necessarily mean a belief in the equality of the races. Lincoln replied to Douglas: "I protest, now and forever, against that counterfeit logic which presumes that because I do not want a Negro woman for a slave, I do necessarily want her for a wife. . . . As God made us separate, we can leave one another alone, and do one another much good thereby."

Lincoln shrewdly took the debate back to the territorial question by saying, "Why, Judge, if we do not let them get together in the Territories, they won't mix there."

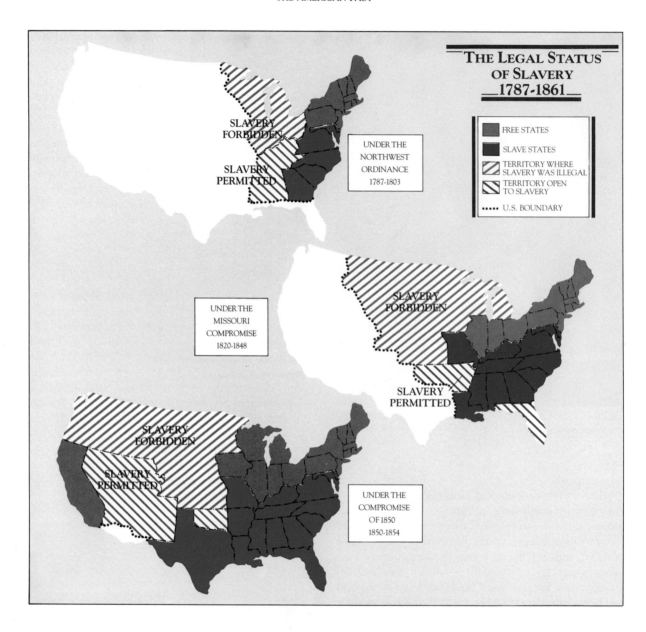

THE LEGAL STATUS
OF SLAVERY
1787-1861

FREE STATES

SLAVE STATES

TERRITORY WHERE
SLAVERY WAS ILLEGAL

TERRITORY OPEN
TO SLAVERY

U.S. BOUNDARY

SLAVERY
FORBIDDEN

SLAVERY
PERMITTED

UNDER THE
NORTHWEST
ORDINANCE
1787-1803

UNDER THE
MISSOURI
COMPROMISE
1820-1848

SLAVERY
FORBIDDEN

SLAVERY
PERMITTED

SLAVERY
FORBIDDEN

SLAVERY
PERMITTED

UNDER THE
COMPROMISE
OF 1850
1850-1854

spiracy that was determined to defy the will of the majority of the American people.

Their fury was fanned by the enthusiasm with which federal marshals enforced the Fugitive Slave Act, seizing runaway slaves in free states and returning them to their masters in the South. In one case, a fugitive was pursued and caught at the cost of $40,000. In Milwaukee, an antislavery mob stormed a jail where a runaway slave had been taken and set him free. Other abolitionists, particularly free blacks in the North, organized the "underground railroad," a constantly shifting network of households that began at the Ohio River and the Mason-Dixon line and extended to the Canadian border. Hiding by day, sometimes in secret cellars, runaway slaves moved by night, led by professional "conductors" such as Harriet Tubman.

Lincoln and Douglas: Two Northern Answers
Responding to Taney in a series of debates in Illinois in 1858, Stephen A. Douglas and a Springfield Republican who wanted Douglas's seat in the Senate, Abraham Lincoln, proposed two northern solutions to the question of slavery in the territories.

"A house divided against itself cannot stand," Lincoln said in June 1858. "I believe that this government cannot endure half slave and half free." He meant that southerners would not be satisfied with keeping

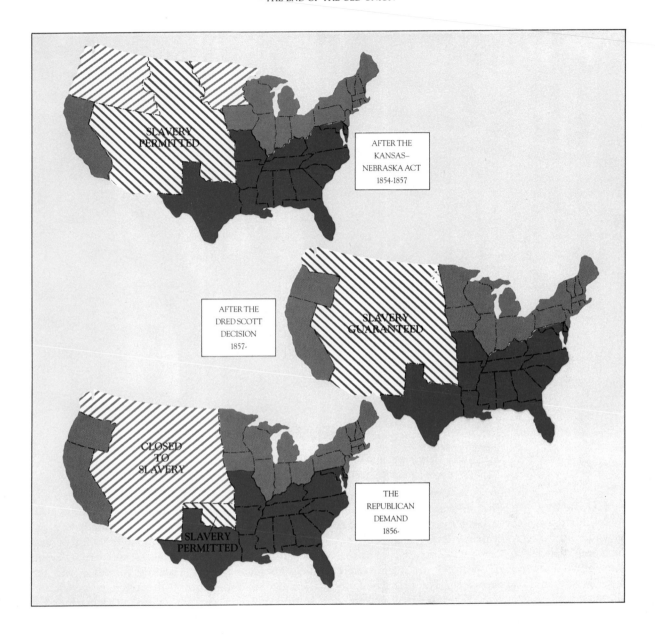

AFTER THE
KANSAS–
NEBRASKA ACT
1854-1857

SLAVERY
PERMITTED

AFTER THE
DRED SCOTT
DECISION
1857-

SLAVERY
GUARANTEED

CLOSED
TO
SLAVERY

THE
REPUBLICAN
DEMAND
1856-

SLAVERY
PERMITTED

slavery where it already existed. Since they had insisted in the Dred Scott decision and in the Fugitive Slave Act on imposing the institution on people who did not want it, the southerners were forcing a showdown that, in the long run, would result in sectional conflict.

Douglas argued that popular sovereignty was still the best solution to the problem. When Lincoln reminded him that the South had not accepted his doctrine but had ruled it unconstitutional in the Scott decision, Douglas replied at Freeport, Illinois, in August 1858 that a territorial legislature could keep slavery out by failing to enact a slave code. No slaveowner would dare take his human property to a country where there were no laws to protect his rights. The Supreme Court might

be able to overturn a territorial law; the Court could not force a territorial legislature to enact a law.

As usual, the ingenious Douglas was right. But events proved that Lincoln was too. When southerners were presented with the logic of the "Freeport Doctrine," they went on the attack again. They demanded that Congress pass a *national* slave code that would protect slavery in all the territories.

John Brown: Another Solution Yet
John Brown had dropped out of sight after he had murdered the proslavery Kansans on Pottawatomie Creek. But he was busy. Moving about New England

Harriet Tubman (left) stands with a group of slaves she helped escape to freedom.

behind a newly grown beard, he persuaded several well-to-do abolitionists that the time had come to strike violently at slavery. With their financial support, he organized a small band of insurrectionists, including some blacks and several of his own sons, at an isolated farm in Maryland. Just across the Potomac River, at the mouth of the Shenandoah, was Harper's Ferry, Virginia, site of one of the federal government's two major arsenals. Brown's plan was to seize the arsenal, capture guns and ammunition, and escape into the Appalachians, which rose steeply around Harper's Ferry.

From the mountains this guerrilla army would swoop down on plantations, free a few slaves at a time, and enlarge their corps. Soon, Brown predicted, black rebellions would erupt all over the South, resolving for all time the great moral and political problem of slavery.

Brown's critics later said that the scheme proved that the old man was out of his mind. He may have been insane, but there was nothing crazy about John Brown's military thinking. Essentially, he outlined the theory of guerrilla warfare that twentieth-century national-liberation movements have put into practice with great success: operate from a remote and shifting base; avoid big battles in which conventional military forces have the advantage; fight only small surprise actions when the odds favor the freewheeling guerrillas; win the friendship and support of the ordinary people, in Brown's case the slaves. The odds were against him, but they were not prohibitive.

JOHN BROWN'S MOUNTAINS

The Appalachians, to which John Brown planned to escape and failed to do, were nearly impenetrable in places. During the Civil War, gangs of Confederate draft dodgers and deserters roamed them without fear of the authorities. So isolated are some hollows in the Appalachians that patterns of speech and folk ballads of Elizabethan England and Scotland survived there unchanged into the twentieth century, while they had long since disappeared elsewhere in the Englsih-speaking world.

The Raid and the Reaction

Brown's mistake was to abandon his plan as soon as he got started. On October 16, 1859, his little band hit and easily captured the arsenal. Then, however, he either lost his nerve or fooled himself into believing that the slaves nearby were on the verge of joining him. He holed up in the roundhouse of the arsenal, where he was promptly surrounded by United States marines under the command of Colonel Robert E. Lee. In two days Lee's professionals killed most of Brown's followers and captured Brown. He was tried for treason in November, found guilty, and hanged in December.

Most northerners responded to the incident as southerners did. They had been shocked by the raid, and they grimly applauded the government's speedy trial and execution of the old man. However, many prominent abolitionists were ominously silent, and a few openly praised Brown as a hero and a martyr. Ralph Waldo Emerson said that Brown's death made the gallows as holy as the Christian cross.

There was just enough of this kind of talk to arouse the southern fire-eaters. Brown's raid revived deep fears of slave rebellion, and here were northerners praising a lunatic who had tried to start one. Southern editors and politicians wondered how they could continue to re-

Thomas Hovenden's painting, The Last Moments of John Brown, *is a sentimental interpretation of the abolitionist's final moments before execution.*

JOHN BROWN AS MARTYR

John Brown understood that while he was doomed, his death would ultimately serve the antislavery cause. Shortly before his execution, he wrote to his wife, "I have been whipped but am sure I can recover all the lost capital occasioned by that disaster; by only hanging a few minutes by the neck."

main under the same government as people who encouraged their massacre.

It was true that the federal government had moved quickly and efficiently to crush Brown. Southerners had few complaints with Washington. But 1860 was an election year. What would happen if the Republicans won the presidency, thus taking control of the federal police powers? Could the South still depend on protection against John Browns and Nat Turners?

The Election of 1860

The southern extremists declared that if the Republicans won the election, the southern states would secede from the Union. The Yankees should be aware of that possibility before they voted. Then, however, having delivered a threat to northern voters, the same extremists not only failed to work against a Republican victory, but they practically guaranteed it. They split their own Democratic party along sectional lines.

The Democrats Split

The Democratic party was the last national institution in the United States. The Whigs were long gone, buried by the slavery issue. The large Protestant churches had broken into northern and southern

TOTAL POPULATION—1860	
Urban	6,216,518
Rural	24,226,803
White, total	26,922,537
White, native	22,825,784
White, foreign-born	4,096,753
Black, total	4,441,830
Black, slave	3,953,760
Black, free	488,070
Other races	78,954
Grand total	31,443,321

branches. So had most men's fraternal lodges and commercial associations. The Republican party, of course, had an exclusively northern membership. Only within the Democratic party did men from both sections still come together to try to settle their differences.

Then, in April 1860, with the excitement of the Brown affair still hanging heavily in the air, the Democratic convention met in Charleston. The majority of the delegates, including some southern moderates, supported the nomination of Stephen A. Douglas. But the southern extremists withheld their votes. The delegations of eight southern states announced that they would support Douglas only if he repudiated his Freeport Doctrine and supported their demand for a federal slave code.

The Douglas forces pointed out that to do this would be to drive northern Democrats into the Republican party. Unmoved, the eight hard-line delegations walked out of the convention.

Hoping to woo them back, the Douglas delegates recessed without nominating their leader. When the Democrats reassembled in Baltimore in June, the southern extremists still refused to budge. Disgusted by what they considered political suicide, the regular Democrats nominated Douglas for president and chose a southern moderate, Herschel V. Johnson of Georgia, as his running mate. The southern Democrats then nominated John C. Breckinridge of Kentucky to represent them in the election. In an attempt to give the ticket a semblance of national support, the southerners chose a Doughface from Oregon, Joseph Lane, as their vice-presidential candidate.

The Republican Opportunity

Meanwhile, the Republicans met in Chicago. They were optimistic but cautious. With the Democrats split, they smelled victory; but they also knew that if they ran on too extreme an antislavery platform, many northern voters would scurry back to Douglas. Even worse would be winning on too radical a platform: southerners would make good on their threat to secede.

Consequently, the Republican convention retreated from the rhetoric of previous years, and the delegates rejected stalwarts such as William H. Seward and Salmon P. Chase. Both men were on the record with fierce antisouthern statements. Seward had spoken of "a higher law than the Constitution" in condemning slavery and of an "irrepressible conflict" between North and South, precisely the sort of words that the Republicans of 1860 wished to avoid. Chase had been a militant abolitionist in Ohio politics for more than a decade.

A photograph of Abraham Lincoln, taken about the time he became the Republican candidate for president.

Instead, the Republicans picked a comparatively obscure midwesterner, Abraham Lincoln of Illinois. Lincoln was rock solid on the fundamental Republican principle: slavery must be banned from the territories. But he was no abolitionist, and far from uncompromising in his manner. In his famous debates with Douglas in 1858 and in a speech introducing himself to eastern Republicans in New York City in February 1860, he struck a note of humility and caution. Not only was slavery protected by the Constitution in those states where it existed, he said, but northerners ought to sympathize with slaveowners rather than attack them. Lincoln had been born in Kentucky, a slave state. He knew that a quirk of fate would have made him a slaveowner, so he found it easy to preach the golden rule. By choosing him, the Republicans believed that they were accommodating southern sensibilities.

The party also stuck by the comprehensive platform of 1856: a high protective tariff; a liberal immigration policy; the construction of a transcontinental railway; and a homestead act. In part, this platform was designed to win the votes of rather different economic groups: eastern industrial capitalists and workers, and midwestern farmers. In addition, by avoiding a single-issue campaign, the Republicans hoped to signal the South that they were not, as a party, antislavery fanatics.

The Old Man's Party

A fourth party entered the race, drawing its strength from the states of the upper South: Maryland, Virginia, Kentucky, and Tennessee. Henry Clay's conciliatory brand of Whiggery—an inclination toward compromise and a deep attachment to the Union—survived in the border states. The platform of the Constitutional Union party consisted, in effect, of stalling: it was a mistake to force any kind of sectional confrontation

while tempers were up; put off the difficult problem of slavery in the territories to a later day. For president the Constitutional Unionists nominated John Bell of Tennessee, a protégé of Clay, and for vice president they chose the distinguished Whig orator Edward Everett of Massachusetts. But they found little support outside the border states. Republicans and both northern and southern Democrats sneered at them as "the old man's party."

The Republicans Win

Abraham Lincoln won 40 percent of the popular vote, not much more than Frémont had drawn in 1856. But

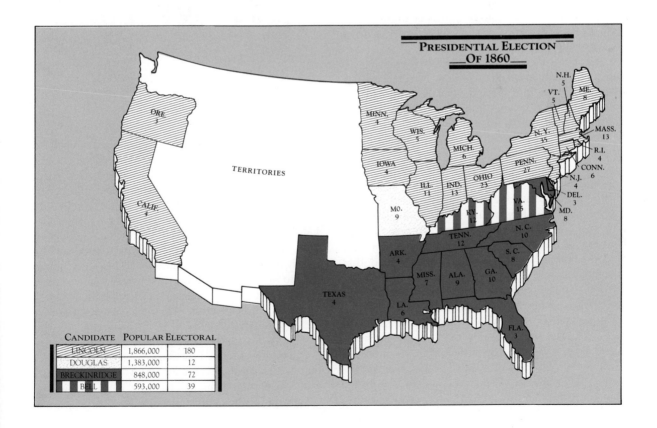

PRESIDENTIAL ELECTION OF 1860

CANDIDATE	POPULAR	ELECTORAL
LINCOLN	1,866,000	180
DOUGLAS	1,383,000	12
BRECKINRIDGE	848,000	72
BELL	593,000	39

POPULATION OF TEN LARGEST AMERICAN CITIES—1860

New York	1,072,000
Philadelphia	585,000
Baltimore	212,000
Boston	178,000
New Orleans	169,000
Cincinnati	161,000
St. Louis	161,000
Chicago	109,000
Buffalo	81,000
Newark	72,000

he carried every free state except New Jersey, which he split with Douglas, and therefore won a clear majority in the electoral college. Breckinridge was the overwhelming choice of the South. He won a plurality in eleven of the fifteen slave states and a popular vote of 18 percent. The voters preferred the candidates who appealed to strong sectional feelings and rejected the candidates who appealed to a spirit of nationalism, Douglas and Bell.

But not by much. Douglas won a mere twelve electoral votes (Missouri's nine and three from New Jersey), but he ran second, often a close second, to Lincoln in the North and to Breckinridge in the South. John Bell carried three of the border states and was strong in the others.

Even if the Douglas and the Bell votes had been combined, Lincoln would have won. Nevertheless, inasmuch as many Lincoln and some Breckinridge supporters were by no means itching for a fight, it seems clear that the majority of the American people preferred some kind of settlement to the breakup of the Union.

South Carolina Leads the Way

They did not get their wish. Having announced that Lincoln's election would lead to secession, the fire-eaters of South Carolina called a convention that, on December 20, 1860, unanimously declared that "the union now subsisting between South Carolina and the other States, under the name of the 'United States of America,' is hereby dissolved."

During January 1861 the six other states of the Deep South followed suit, declaring that a Republican administration threatened their "domestic institutions." Then came a glimmer of hope. The secession movement stalled when conventions in Virginia, Kentucky, Tennessee, and North Carolina voted against leaving

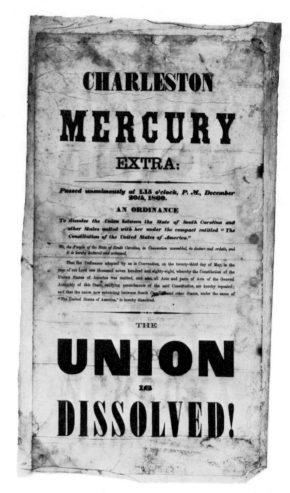

An edition of the Charleston Mercury *announces the South's decision to secede from the Union.*

the Union. At the same time, these states declared their opposition to any attempt by the federal government to use force against the states that had seceded. By rebuffing the tough talkers on both sides, the leaders of the border states hoped to force a compromise.

The outgoing president was not the man for this job. James Buchanan was dignified, proper, personally popular. But no one had much respect for Old Buck. The North repudiated him because he had deferred for so long to his southern advisers. Now those very advisers betrayed him. His Secretary of War, John Floyd of Virginia, transferred tons of war materiel to states that either had left the Union or were on the verge of leaving it. Floyd's act skirted close to treason.

Other allies resigned their offices and left Washington, hardly pausing to remember the president who had worked on their behalf. The only bachelor ever to occupy the White House was quite alone, and he knew it. After a pathetic hand-wringing speech in which he declared that while secession was illegal, he as president was powerless to do anything about it, Buchanan sat back to wait for the day he could go home.

How the Union Broke

As Buchanan slumped, Senator John J. Crittenden stood up. Like many Kentuckians, Crittenden had devoted his career to mediating between the North and the Deep South. Now he proposed a solution to the problem of slavery in the territories that was simultaneously as old as King Solomon and dramatically new. Rather than divide the Union, Crittenden argued, divide the territories. Extend the Missouri Compromise line to the California border; guarantee slavery to the south of it, and forbid slavery to the north.

The Compromisers Fail

Because of the Dred Scott decision, Crittenden's plan could not be put into effect by congressional action; it was necessary to divide the territories by constitutional amendment. Crittenden hoped that the spectre of civil

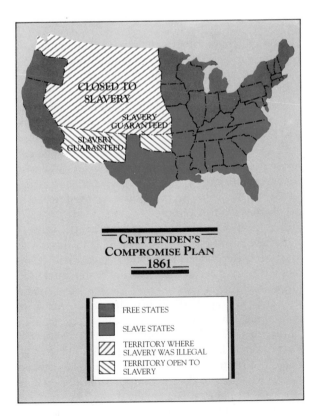

CRITTENDEN'S
COMPROMISE PLAN
1861

FREE STATES

SLAVE STATES

TERRITORY WHERE
SLAVERY WAS ILLEGAL

TERRITORY OPEN TO
SLAVERY

war, now chillingly real as military companies began to drill in cities and towns, would prompt both northern and southern states to act in haste.

With some encouragement they might have done so. There was a flurry of enthusiasm for Crittenden's compromise on both sides of the Mason-Dixon line. But before the southern extremists were forced to take a stand, President-elect Lincoln quashed the plan. His reasons were political but nonetheless compelling. His Republican party was a diverse alliance of people who disagreed with one another on many issues. The one adhesive that bound them together was the principle that slavery must not expand into the territories. If Lincoln gave in on this point, he would take office with a divided party behind him and be as impotent as James Buchanan.

Lincoln also discouraged a second attempt at compromise, a peace conference that was held in Washington during February. It was a distinguished assembly, chaired by former president John Tyler. Tyler had been a southern extremist, and, a few months later, he would support the secession of Virginia. But he worked hard for a settlement in February, proposing a series of constitutional amendments along the same lines as Crittenden's.

Once again, Lincoln drew the line on allowing slavery in the southern territories. He offered to sponsor an amendment that would forever guarantee slavery in the states where it already existed; as he well knew, this was a purely symbolic gesture that granted nothing the South did not already possess. By February, in fact, the secessionists had lost interest in preserving the Union. They were caught up in the excitement of inventing a new American nation.

The Confederate States of America

According to secessionist theory, the seven states that left the Union were now independent republics. However, no southern leader intended his state to go it alone. Although they were disappointed that eight of the fifteen slave states still refused to join them, they met in Montgomery, Alabama, shortly before Lincoln's inauguration and established their own "Confederacy."

The government that the southerners created differed little from the one that they had rejected. The Confederates declared that all United States laws were to remain in effect until amended or repealed, and they copied the Constitution of 1787 almost word for word. The few changes they made reflected the South's obsession with slavery and with Calhoun's political theories, and resulted in a series of curious contradictions. Thus, the Confederates defined the states as "sovereign and

LEE'S LOYALTY TO VIRGINIA

Robert E. Lee, perhaps the most respected active soldier in the army in 1861, was asked what he would do if there was a Civil War. Would he support the North or the South? In effect, Lee replied neither; he would support his native state, Virginia:

"If Virginia stands by the old Union, so will I. But if she secedes (though I do not believe in secession as a constitutional right, nor that there is sufficient cause for revolution) then I will follow my native state with my sword and, if need be, with my life."

Jefferson Davis, president of the Confederacy.

independent" but called their new government "permanent." Even more oddly, the Confederates declared that individual states might not interfere with slavery, a restriction on states' rights that no prominent Republican had suggested.

The Confederates also modified the presidency. The chief executive was to be elected for a term of six years rather than four, but he was not permitted to run for a second term. While this seemed to weaken the office, the Confederates allowed the president to veto parts of congressional bills rather than, as in the Union, requiring him to accept all or nothing.

Jeff Davis and Abe Lincoln

As their first president, the Confederates selected Jefferson Davis. On the face of it, he was a superb choice. A man of regal bearing and dignity, Davis was a generous and paternalistic slaveholder. He was the benign patriarch other slaveowners claimed to be. Davis seemed to be a wise choice politically because he was not closely associated with the secessionist movement. Indeed, Davis had asked his fellow Mississippians to delay secession until Lincoln had a chance to prove himself; when his state overruled him, Davis delivered a moderate, eloquent, and affectionate farewell speech in the Senate. By choosing such a man, rather than a fire-eater, the Confederates demonstrated their willingness to work with southerners who opposed secession. With Davis, the Confederacy could also appeal to the eight slave states that remained within the Union.

In other ways, the choice of Jefferson Davis was disastrous. It was not so much the unattractive coldness of his personality. George Washington had been icier. Davis's weakness was that despite his bearing, he lacked true confidence in himself and was, as a result, outwardly vain and inflexible. He proved incapable of cooperating with critics, even those who differed with

him on only minor matters. He needed sycophants—yes men—in order to function, and, therefore, he denied his administration the services of some of the South's ablest statesmen.

Worse, Davis was a dabbler. Instead of delegating authority and presiding over the government, Davis repeatedly interfered in the pettiest details of administration—peering over his subordinates' shoulders, arousing personal resentments among even those who put up with his peevishness. He had been a good senator, but the last thing that Davis was qualified to be was the "Father of His Country."

By comparison, Abraham Lincoln knew the value of competent assistants. Rather than shun his rivals within the Republican party, he named them to his cabinet. Seward became Secretary of State. Salmon P. Chase was Lincoln's Secretary of the Treasury. After a brief misadventure with an incompetent Secretary of War, Simon Cameron, Lincoln appointed a Democrat, Edwin Stanton, to that post because he was the best the country offered. Lincoln wanted talent, not pals or toadies. Within their departments, Lincoln's cabinet officers were free to do anything that did not conflict with general policy. As a result, a cantankerous and headstrong group of men remained loyal to him to the

A crowd gathered in front of the unfinished Capitol Building to hear Abraham Lincoln's first inaugural address on March 4, 1861.

end of his life without challenging his control of basic policy.

Lincoln differed from Davis in other ways. Far from regal, he was an awkward, plain, even ugly man. Tall and gangling, with oversize hands and feet, he impressed those who met him for the first time as a frontier oaf. His enemies called him the baboon, the ape. Some of his supporters snickered at his clumsiness and were appalled by his weakness for vulgar, knee-slapping jokes.

But both friends and enemies soon discovered that the president was no yokel. Lincoln had honed a sharp native intelligence on a whetstone of lifelong study, and proved to be the most eloquent man to occupy the White House since Thomas Jefferson. And yet, behind his brilliance was a humility born of modest background that can be found in no other American president.

Lincoln needed all his abilities. On March 4, 1861, when Lincoln was sworn in before a glum Washington crowd, the Union was in tatters. During the previous two months, the Stars and Stripes had been hauled down from every flagstaff in the South except for one at Fort Pickens in Pensacola, Florida, and another at Fort Sumter, a rocky island in the harbor of Charleston, South Carolina.

A War of Nerves

Neither of the forts threatened the security of the Confederacy. They were old installations that had been designed for defense. They big guns pointed toward the sea, not the land, and they were manned by token garrisons. But symbols take on profound importance in uneasy times, and the southern fire-eaters, itching for a fight, ranted about the insulting occupation of their country by a "foreign power."

Davis was willing to live with the Union forts for the time being. Unlike the hotheads, he understood that the seven-state Confederacy was too weak to survive on its own. His policy was to delay a confrontation with the North until he could make a foreign alliance or induce the eight slave states that remained in the Union to join the Confederacy. He feared that if he fired the first shot, the states of the upper South might support the Union.

The southern extremists disagreed. They believed that a battle, no matter who started it, would bring the other slave states to their side. Nevertheless, when the commander at Sumter announced that he would soon have to surrender the fort for lack of provisions, Davis had his way.

Within limits, Lincoln also favored delaying a confrontation. He believed that the longer the states of the upper South postponed their decision to secede, the less likely they were to go. Moreover, the leaders of Virginia, Kentucky, Tennessee, and Arkansas had formally warned him against using force against the Confederacy. If the Union fired the first shot, they would secede.

Finally, Lincoln did not have the people of the North solidly behind him. Northern Democrats would not support an act of aggression. Winfield Scott, Lincoln's chief military adviser, told him that the army was not up to a war of conquest. Some abolitionists who were also pacifists, such as Horace Greeley and William Lloyd Garrison, urged the president to "let the wayward sisters depart in peace."

Lincoln had no intention of doing that. He was determined to save the Union by peaceful means if possible, by force if necessary. He reasoned that if the Confederates fired the first shot, the border states might secede anyway, but at least the act of rebellion would unite northerners behind him. If he delayed a confrontation indefinitely, he still might lose the border states and still have a divided, uncertain North.

This was the reasoning behind Lincoln's decision to resupply Fort Sumter. He announced that the ship he dispatched carried no military materiel, only food and medicine. He was not, he stated, using force against the state of South Carolina. He repeated his wish that the crisis be resolved peacefully, but he insisted on his presidential obligation to maintain the government's authority in Charleston harbor.

And so the war came. When the relief ship approached the sand bar that guarded Charleston harbor, the Confederacy attacked. On the morning of April 12, 1861, artillery under the command of General P. G. T. Beauregard opened up. The next day, Sumter surrendered. Davis was reluctant until the end. In a way, he lost control of South Carolina. His inability to control the Confederate states would haunt his administration for four years.

The Border States Take Sides

The Battle of Fort Sumter served Confederate as well as Union purposes. While Lincoln was able to call for seventy-five thousand volunteers and to get them, his action pushed four more states into the Confederacy. Virginia, North Carolina, Tennessee, and Arkansas seceded from the Union, and in deference to Virginia's importance, the capital of the new nation was moved from Montgomery to Richmond.

Secessionist feeling was also strong in the slave states of Maryland, Kentucky, and Missouri. Lincoln was able to prevent them from seceding by a combination of shrewd political maneuvers and the tactful deployment

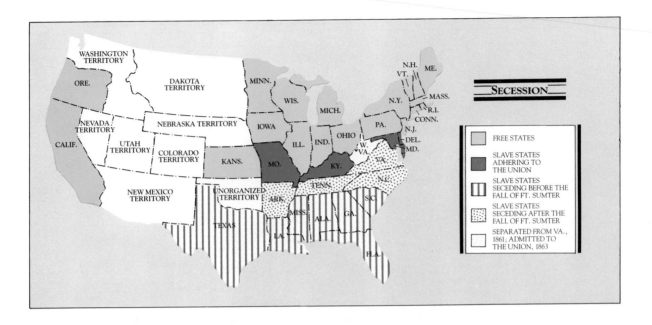

ATTENTION, TO SAVE YOUR BOUNTY!

SECOND REGIMENT

EMPIRE BRIGADE!

Col. P. J. CLAASSEN, Commanding.

FIRST REGIMENT IN THE FIELD UNDER THE NEW CALL.

WANTED, 25 MEN

Between the ages of 18 and 45 years, to fill up one of the best Companies now forming, under officers who have seen active service.

Clothing, Subsistence and Comfortable Quarters provided on enlistment.

PAY FROM $13 TO $23 PER MONTH, TO DATE FROM DAY OF ENLISTMENT.

$50 BOUNTY GIVEN BY THE STATE.

$25 BOUNTY GIVEN BY THE U. S. GOVERNMENT. TO BE PAID AS SOON AS MUSTERED INTO SERVICE

$100 BOUNTY WHEN THE WAR IS OVER!

It is intended to make this one of the best Companies in the Brigade or service, and no labor will be spared to do so. The Officers are experienced men, having been over one year in one of the First Regiments in the service.

CAPTAIN J. H. STINER, LATE OF HAWKINS ZOUAVES.

A recruiting poster calling for volunteers to fight for the Union.

of troops. Delaware, the fifteenth slave state, never seriously considered secession.

Then, in the contest for the border states, the North won a bonus. The mountainous western part of Virginia was peopled by farmers who owned few slaves and who traditionally resented the planter aristocracy that dominated Virginia politics and was now in favor of secession. The westerners had no interest in fighting and dying to protect the human property of the rich. In effect, the fifty western counties of Virginia seceded from the Old Dominion. By an irregular constitutional process, the Republicans provided the means for West Virginia to become a Union state in June 1863.

In these border states, the Civil War was literally a war between brothers. Henry Clay's grandsons fought on both sides. Several of President Lincoln's brothers-in-law fought for the South, and Jefferson Davis had cousins in the Union Army. The most poignant case was that of Senator Crittenden of Kentucky, who had tried to head off war with a compromise. One of his sons became a general in the Union Army and another a general in the Confederate Army.

The Irony of Secession

However much the people of the border states disliked secession, they were not against slavery. In order to reassure them, Lincoln issued several pronouncements that the purpose of the war was to preserve the Union and not to abolish slavery. In emphasizing his war aim, he pointed up the irony of secession. While southerners claimed that they had gone their own way in order to protect their peculiar institution, they actually had

[]

THE AGONY OF THE SOUTHERN WHIGS

Alexander Stephens of Georgia fought secession until the issue was decided. Then he served as the Confederacy's vice president as a show of unity, only to find himself at odds with Jefferson Davis.

Strictly speaking, there were no southern Whigs in 1861 because there was no Whig party. It had ceased to exist after the passage of the Kansas-Nebraska Act when the northern Conscience Whigs gave up in disgust on their proslavery fellows and joined with the Free-Soil Democrats to form the Republican party. The southern Cotton Whigs, now only a minority party in a minority section, either joined the Democratic party or, if they had a strong enough electoral base to do so, continued in politics as independents.

But Democrat or independent in 1861, they were still Whigs at heart, disciples of Henry Clay with a strong sense of the glory of the united American nation and a tradition of distrust for Democrats. The secession crisis—the handiwork of southern Democrats—and the Civil War that followed it were therefore an agony for them that no two faced in quite the same way.

Alexander Stephens (1812–83) fought secessionists in his home state of Georgia down to the hour that the state left the Union. Then, however, sadly loyal to his state, much like Robert E. Lee of Virginia, he pledged allegiance to the Confederacy, even allowing himself to be named vice president in what was viewed as a gesture of unity. Within a year, however, Stephens was at odds with Jefferson Davis. He began to spend less time in Richmond and more in Georgia, where he found himself, a former nationalist, in the unlikely position of fighting for states' rights against the former states'-rights Democrat, Davis.

In February 1865, Stephens took on a job more congenial to a Whig. He led a Confederate delegation to Hampton Roads, Virginia, where he met with Lincoln and tried to arrange a compromise peace. The mission failed because Stephens had been instructed to insist on Confederate independence, and, with Union troops on the verge of striking a deathblow to Lee's Army of Northern Virginia, Lincoln refused even to discuss that possibility. Immediately after the war, Georgians elected Stephens to the Senate, but he was refused his seat by former Whig comrades who were now members of the Union's Republican party. Eight years later, now a Democrat like most southern whites, he entered Congress, where he served for ten years without the distinction for which the Whig Stephens had been known.

Senator John J. Crittenden of Kentucky (1787–1863), a protégé and personal friend of Henry Clay, believed in sectional compromise as intensely as did his teacher. The plan he devised early in 1861 appealed to a good many moderates who, like himself, did not think slavery an issue important enough to destroy the Union. Split the difference, Crittenden said; divide the territories between slave territories and free territories. But Lincoln could not agree; he had run on a platform that had promised no slavery in the territories, and the Crittenden Compromise provided for a similar division of all territories "hereafter acquired." To Lincoln, who had been opposed to the Mexican War, this seemed an open invitation to proslavery southerners to provoke a

*Kentucky senator John J. Crittenden attempted to set-
tle the slave issue through a legislative compromise in
hopes of averting southern secession.*

war with Mexico or with Spain over Cuba in order to
grab land suitable to the raising of those crops that
were most profitably farmed by slaves.

Crittenden lived only to 1863, just long enough to
suffer the personal tragedy of seeing one son fight for
the Union and another for the Confederacy, not an
uncommon occurrence in border states like Kentucky
and in former Whig families like Crittenden's.

John Bell of Tennessee (1797–1869) was a slaveholder who agreed with the Republicans that slavery
should *not* be allowed in the territories. Like Crittenden, he did not believe that the question was worth
a war. Unlike Crittenden, he thought that the best way
to avoid one was to follow the wishes of the majority
and keep slavery restricted to the area where it was already established.

Curiously, Bell made few friends among the Republicans. The abolitionists among them saw Bell only as a
slaveowner, and therefore an immoral man. But his
position was by no means unattractive to southerners,
particularly those of the border states. Running for
president in 1860 on the Constitutional Union ticket,
Bell carried Virginia, Kentucky, and Tennessee and
ran strong in Delaware, Maryland, and Missouri.

More than a few southerners were satisfied with the
status quo or actually opposed slavery. Robert E. Lee
was one who probably wished John Bell had won.

Robert Toombs (1810–85) was the least predictable
of the southern Whigs. Capable of antinorthern language as scorching as any Democrat's, he nevertheless
opted for sectional compromise each time it was offered. Toombs supported the Compromise of 1850 and,
in 1861, backed Crittenden's plan to head off secession. Unlike his fellow Georgian Alexander Stephens,
however, Toombs actually helped to engineer Georgia's
secession when the Republicans refused to meet the
South halfway.

Named Confederate Secretary of State by Davis,
Toombs quit after a few months in order to get into
the fighting. He headed a brigade and fought bravely
if without particular distinction. A wound at Antietam
sent him home. When the war ended, he fled to England for fear of reprisals.

In 1867, Toombs returned to Georgia, where he
refused to apply for a pardon, as many extreme secessionists had quickly done. Nevertheless, while taking
this defiant stand, he stood up for compromise one
more time in 1877 when the Republican party promised
to withdraw all troops from the South if their dubiously
elected presidential candidate, Rutherford B. Hayes,
were permitted to take office without incident. The erratic course of Toombs's life may reflect nothing more
than a mercurial personality; or it may illustrate the
terrible strain placed on southern Whigs who loved
both the South and the United States.

thrown away the legal and constitutional guarantees that they had had as citizens of the United States.

Under the Fugitive Slave Act, slaves who ran away to the northern states were returned to their owners by federal marshals. In order to escape, slaves had to get to Canada, out of the country. With secession, however, "out of the country" was hundreds of miles closer—over the Tennessee–Kentucky or the Virginia–Maryland line. This fact was dramatized early in the war when several Union generals declared that slaves who had fled to Union lines were "contraband of war," subject to confiscation and therefore free. At first Lincoln countermanded these orders so as not to antagonize the loyal border states, especially Kentucky. But it was obvious that the South had made it easier for slaves to get away than it had been before secession.

In leaving the Union as individual states, the southerners had waived all legal rights to the territories, which were federal property. Their action was the most effective guarantee, short of a constitutional amendment, that slavery would be banned from the territories.

Some southerners had no intention of giving up the territories, of course. The "civilized tribes" that occupied Oklahoma, for example, were generally pro-Confederate. But in order to win the Indian lands and, perhaps, New Mexico, meant the very war that Davis hoped to avoid. Secession was less a rational political act than it was the fruit of passion, suspicion, and sectional hatred that blinded southern extremists to reality.

The Odds Against the South

Prudent southerners hoped to avoid war, or at least a long war, because the material superiority of the Union was overwhelming. Even after Virginia and the other three states of the upper South joined the Confederacy, the population of the country was 9 million as compared with 22 million in the North. Of these 9 million, more than 3 million were slaves. Although slaves contributed to the war effort by working the fields and building fortifications, the Confederacy dared not put guns in their hands. Consequently, the Confederates could draw on a manpower pool that was a quarter the size of the North's.

There were thirty thousand miles of railroad in the North, three times the mileage in the South. Moreover, the southern system was poorly integrated. Six lines ran into Richmond, an industrial center as well as the capital of the Confederacy, but none of them linked up with any of the others. Goods and men moving through Richmond had to be unloaded and marched or hauled across town.

SHERMAN'S PREDICTION

On Christmas Eve 1860, after South Carolina had seceded and talk of war was already in the air, William Tecumseh Sherman, soon to be fighting for the Union, told a southern friend in New Orleans that the South should not fight: "The North can make a steam engine, locomotive, or railway car; hardly a yard of cloth can you make. You are rushing into war with one of the most powerful, ingeniously mechanical and determined people on earth—right at your doors. You are bound to fail."

In industrial capacity, the imbalance between the sections was monumental. There were literally more factories in the North than factory workers in the South, 120,000 Union "industrial establishments" to 110,000 Confederate industrial laborers. Northern industry was also more efficient. According to the census of 1860, 90 percent of American manufactured goods was produced in northern factories. Even this overwhelming advantage is deceptive because several important manufacturing centers in the South, like New Orleans, fell into Union hands early in the war, subtracting their potential from the Confederate cause and adding it to that of the Union.

Finally, while the Confederacy controlled all the federal property within its boundaries, including military materiel that had been hurriedly transferred south by Secretary Floyd, the forty-ship navy remained loyal to the Union. This was an ominous sign. The Confederacy depended on exporting its cotton for its economic health. Its nearly total lack of sea power to protect this commerce was an almost insurmountable handicap.

The Southern Hope

How, then, did the Confederates think they could win? The southerners needed only to defend themselves. Militarily, defense is an easier assignment than conquest. It requires fewer men, and relies on internal lines. Since distances in the Confederacy were shorter and routes more direct, the South's advantage in internal lines somewhat counterbalanced the North's advantage in transportation.

The defensive nature of the war also meant familiarity with the battleground. The United States army had never planned on a war at home. Throughout the war, Union commanders were plagued by poor maps of the South or by no maps at all, while Confederate generals fought in their own backyards. Then, defense gave the southern soldiers an edge in morale. They were fighting for their independence in the American revolutionary tradition, while the northerners were cast in the role of George III and his hated redcoats, alien oppressors trying to force a government on a people who did not want it.

Many southerners also believed that they were better fighting men than were northerners. They were a rural people and thus better able to withstand the rigors of outdoor life than were hollow-chested Yankee peddlers. This was an illusion, of course, based on southern mythology. Most northerners were rural, and, in time, city-bred soldiers—as well as the recent immigrants from Ireland and Germany who formed entire brigades of Union volunteers—proved as tough as Alabama plowboys.

However, there was a great deal of truth in the southern claim that their commanders were superior. The military life was a highly honorable calling among southern planters. Southerners made up a disproportionate number of army officers, especially at the ranks of major and colonel, those men who became the commanding generals of the Civil War. Some of them remained loyal to the Union. The Union Army's ranking officer, Winfield Scott, was a Virginian who never considered joining the Confederacy. George H. Thomas, who proved himself one of the three or four best Union field commanders, also came from the Old Dominion.

But most military men went the way their states did. About a third of the American officer corps discarded their Union blue and donned the Confederate gray. The best of them, and also the great tragic figure of the war, was Colonel Robert E. Lee. "Marse Robert" disliked slavery and opposed secession. He had little in common with the fire-eaters and much with the American national tradition.

But Lee weighed his options carefully from the fort in Texas where he was stationed during the secession crisis and decided that his devotion to the state of Virginia was stronger than his loyalty to the Union. While Virginia was still on the fence, he accepted appointment as Superintendent of West Point, the United States Military Academy. When Virginia seceded, however, he turned down Lincoln's offer of overall command of active troops and rode south.

For Further Reading

David M. Potter, *The Impending Crisis, 1848–1861* (1976), and Avery O. Craven, *The Civil War in the Making* (1959), both continue the story of the sectional split up to 1861. On the Kansas question, see R. W. Johannsen, *Stephen A. Douglas* (1973), and J. C. Malin, *The Nebraska Question, 1852–1854* (1953) and *John Brown and the Legend of Fifty-Six* (1942). H. V. Jaffa, *Crisis of the House Divided* (1959), examines the Lincoln–Douglas debates, and it is also worthwhile to read what these two eloquent men had to say in R. W.

Johannsen, *The Lincoln–Douglas Debates* (1965).

There are competent biographies of the principal actors in the drama of the 1850s, among them R. F. Nichols, *Young Hickory of the Granite Hills* (1931), about Franklin Pierce; P. S. Klein, *President James Buchanan* (1962); C. B. Swisher, *Roger B. Taney* (1935); and S. B. Oates, *To Purge This Land with Blood* (1970), about John Brown.

A fascinating analysis of the final crisis over Fort Sumter is Richard N. Current, *Lincoln and the First Shot* (1963).

24

Tidy Plans, Harsh Realities
The Civil War Through 1862

The attack on Fort Sumter answered the first big question: there would be a shooting war. When Lincoln called for volunteers to preserve the Union, and Davis summoned the young men of the South to defend the honor and independence of the Confederacy, both were flooded with enthusiastic recruits. By the summer of 1861, the Union had 186,000 soldiers in uniform and the Confederacy, 112,000.

But what kind of war would it be? What would battle be like? Nowhere in the world had armies of such size clashed since the Napoleonic Wars in Europe half a century earlier. During the Mexican War, the United States had fielded no more than 10,000 men at one time. Now, just fifteen years later, two American armies were faced with the challenge of feeding, clothing, sheltering, transporting, and controlling a mass of humanity ten and twenty times that size.

The significance of numbers was not lost on the European nations. They quickly dispatched high-ranking officers to the United States to observe how the Americans managed their Civil War. The lessons they took back with them would inform military thinking for a full fifty years.

Union soldiers view their encampment from a nearby bluff.

The Arts and Science of War

The American Civil War took up where Napoleon and Wellington had left off. American military men had been trained according to the theories of battle devised by Antoine Henri Jomini, a Swiss officer who had fought for both the French and the Russian armies. Although Jomini's *Art of War* was not translated into English until 1862, a textbook based on his theories that had been written by an American disciple was the standard authority on tactics at West Point, where virtually all the generals of the Civil War had learned their craft.

Position, Maneuver, and Concentration

Jomini emphasized the importance of position and maneuver in winning battles or, preferably, in making battle unnecessary. The goal of the commanding general was to capture important points, occupy high ground, and, when a battle threatened, ascertain the weakest point in the enemy's lines and concentrate power there. The commander who prepared more thoroughly, better exploited the terrain, and moved his troops more skillfully during the fighting would break through the opposing line and force the enemy from the field.

Because Jomini reduced all battle situations to twelve models, commanders trained in his school knew pretty much what their adversaries had in mind at all times. As long as both sides observed the "rules," there would be no long casualty lists. The general who was outfoxed knew that his duty was to disengage so that his men would be able to fight on another day under more favorable circumstances. Retreat was itself a form of maneuver because it preserved an army as a functioning machine.

LINCOLN'S MILITARY CAREER

Abraham Lincoln, who came to understand military strategy better than most civilian leaders of nations at war, actually had some military experience. During the Black Hawk War against Indians in Wisconsin and Iowa in 1832, Lincoln was a captain of Illinois volunteers. His unit saw no action in the conflict (in which Jefferson Davis also served), but Lincoln remembered parading his men past a reviewing platform and then forgetting the command that would halt them. They marched directly into a creek.

The Armies

The armies of the Civil War were divided into cavalry, artillery, and infantry with support units such as the Corps of Engineers (which constructed fortifications) and the Quartermaster Corps (which was entrusted with supply).

The cavalry's principal task was reconnaissance. Horse soldiers were the eyes of an army on whose information battle plans were based. It was the glamorous service because cavalry was mobile and fast, striking suddenly and by surprise. In actual battle, cavalry was used to reinforce weak points and, if enemy troops were in retreat, to harass them as they went. Cavalry was lightly armed by definition. For all the dash and flash, it played a subsidiary and indecisive role in most battles.

The artillery was slow to move and notoriously unglamorous. But, as Napoleon had proved, the big guns were critical to both attack and defense. Before an attacking army moved, the artillery slugged away at enemy fortifications with exploding shells, "softening them up" for the foot soldiers. In defense, the artillery greeted attackers with grapeshot (a charge of small iron balls) and canister (projectiles that exploded and filled the air with a screen of metal). Systematic examinations of dead soldiers after Civil War battles revealed that an attacking army suffered more from cannon than from small-arms fire.

As always before the nuclear age, the infantry was the backbone of the army. The cavalry might worry the enemy and the artillery weaken him, but it was the foot soldiers who slogged it out face to face.

The Face of Battle

The basic infantry unit was the brigade. Between two thousand and three thousand men under the command of a brigadier general formed double lines in defense or advanced over a front of about one thousand yards, again in two ranks. During the first campaigns of the Civil War, captains in the front lines tried to march the men in step, as had been the rule in Napoleonic times. But with the far greater firepower of the Civil War, this formality was abandoned. It was enough that the men continued to run, trot, or simply walk into oncoming grapeshot, Minié balls (conical bullets), noise like a thunderstorm in hell, and clouds of sulfurous smoke. Junior officers led the charge; lieutenants and captains suffered high casualties. Others walked behind the lines in order to discourage stragglers. They were authorized to shoot men who panicked.

If the advancing army was not forced to turn back, the final phase of battle was hand-to-hand combat. The

A Union battery at the battle of Seven Pines, one of the major Civil War campaigns in Virginia, as photographed by Mathew Brady.

attackers clambered over the enemy's fortifications of earth and lumber. Attackers and defenders swung their muskets at one another until the defenders broke and ran or until the attackers were killed or captured. The men had bayonets, but during the Civil War neither side succeeded in training soldiers to use them very well. The importance of mastering this difficult and deadly skill was one lesson that the European observers took home with them.

There was plenty of shooting but not much aiming. Except for special units of sharpshooters, foot soldiers were not marksmen. There was little sense in taking on the big and expensive job of training large numbers of men in the skill of hitting small targets. With a few important exceptions (Shiloh, Antietam, Gettysburg),

Civil War battles were not fought in open country. The men confronted one another in dense woods on terrain broken by hills, stone fences, and ditches. They often could not see one another until they were almost close enough to touch.

Even in open country, hundreds of cannon and tens of thousands of muskets and rifles filled the air with a dense, acrid smog that, on a windless day, shrouded the battlefield. (Smokeless powder was still in the future.) If a soldier knew how to shoot well, there was little he could aim at in order to prove it.

Billy Yank and Johnny Reb

As in all wars, the men who fought it were quite young, most between the ages of seventeen and twenty-five with drummer boys as young as twelve. They came from every state and social class, although when both sides adopted draft laws (the Confederacy in April 1862, the Union in March 1863), the Civil War became the proverbial poor man's fight.

The Confederate draft law exempted men who owned twenty or more blacks. It was sorely resented by Johnny Reb, the common soldier, who rarely owned even one slave. Both Confederate and Union draft laws allowed a man who was called to service to pay for a substitute at a price that was beyond the means of the average man. In the North, a draftee could hire another to take his place or simply pay the government $300 for an exemption. In July 1863, lower-class resentment of this form of discrimination led to a week-

NORTH AND SOUTH: OUTBREAK OF WAR, 1861		
	North	South
Population	23,000,000	9,000,000*
Manufacturing establishments	110,000	18,000
Industrial workers	1,300,000	110,000
Value of firearms produced in 1860 (in dollars)	2,270,000	73,000
Locomotives built in 1860	451	19
Horses and mules	4,600,000	2,600,000
Railroad mileage	22,000	9,000

*including 3.7 million slaves

ADS FOR SUBSTITUTES

The following two advertisements ran in the Richmond *Dispatch*:

Wanted—Immediately, a SUBSTITUTE. A man over 35 years old, or under 18, can get a good price by making immediate application.

Wanted—two substitutes—one for artillery, the other for infantry or cavalry service. Also, to sell, a trained thoroughbred cavalry HORSE.

The Civil War was fought in large part by boys and young men like Private Edwin Francis Jennison, a Confederate soldier.

long riot in New York City. Mobs of Irish workingmen sacked draft offices, attacked rich men, and harassed and lynched blacks, whom they considered the cause of the war and a threat to their jobs.

In the South, resistance to the draft was less dramatic. Nevertheless, thousands of Confederate draft dodgers headed west or into the Appalachians and the Ozarks, where they formed outlaw gangs. They raided farms and occasionally skirmished with Confederate troops. As in West Virginia, most southern opposition to the war centered in the poorer mountain counties. Both Union and Confederate armies were plagued by a high desertion rate, about 10 percent through most of the war.

One kind of deserter who was peculiar to the Civil War was the bounty jumper. Because some states and cities paid cash bonuses, or bounties, to men who signed up, a few made a lucrative small business of enlisting, deserting at first opportunity, and looking for another unit that offered cash. In March 1865, Union military police arrested one John O'Connor. He confessed to enlisting, collecting a bounty, and deserting thirty-two times.

Nevertheless, such shirking was not typical of either army. Over the course of the war, 1.5 million young men served in the Union Army, and more than 1 million, from a much smaller population, with the Confederates. Whatever their resentments, ordinary people thought they had something at stake in the conflict.

Army Life

The war they knew was not much like what people back home imagined. In the artists' paintings and drawings in newspapers, masses of blue- and gray-clad men moved in an orderly way across open fields amidst waving flags and pretty puffs of white smoke. In reality, battle was a tiny part of military experience. Mostly,

In July 1863, anger about inequities in the draft system that allowed the rich to escape service led to a week-long riot in New York.

the war involved waiting, digging trenches, building breastworks, marching, and being carted from one place to another in crowded trains.

The war meant poor food and shelter. In the South, the administration of supply was rarely efficient. Even when the Confederacy had enough uniforms, shoes, and food—which was not always—there were problems in bringing them and the soldiers together. In the North, corrupt profiteers sold the government tainted beef and shoddy blankets that fell apart in the rain. On both sides, physicians were unprepared to cope with so many people in one place; dysentery, typhoid, influenza, and other epidemic illnesses killed more soldiers than did enemy guns.

The Sobering Campaign of 1861

Army life also involved drilling day in and day out. But those who rallied to the colors in the spring of 1861 thought of the war as an adventure, a vacation from the plow, the hog trough, and the pick and shovel that would be over all too soon for their taste. They trimmed themselves in gaudy uniforms. Some, influenced by pictures from the Crimean War, called themselves "Zouaves" and donned Turkish fezzes and baggy scarlet pantaloons. Other units adopted names that would have been more appropriate to a boys' club. One Confederate regiment was called "The Lincoln Killers."

BULL RUN OR MANASSAS?

The Confederacy named battles after the town nearest to the battlefield and armies after the state or part of a state where they were organized. The Union named both battles and armies after waterways. Thus, the Battle of Bull Run was known in the South as the Battle of Manassas. Bull Run is a creek; Manassas, a railroad town. The Battle of Antietam (Creek) was called the Battle of Sharpsburg in the South.

The two best-known armies of the war were the Union Army of the Potomac and the Confederate Army of Northern Virginia. In the western theater, the Confederacy had an Army of Tennessee, while the Union had an Army of *the* Tennessee (River).

On to Richmond

Abraham Lincoln shared the illusion that the war would be short and relatively painless. He shrugged off Winfield Scott's prediction that it would take three years and three hundred thousand men to crush the rebellion. Lincoln asked the first volunteers, mostly members of state militias, to enlist for only ninety days. That would be enough. In the South too, people spoke of "our battle summer." The soldiers and civilians on the two sides disagreed only as to who would be celebrating when the leaves fell in the autumn of 1861.

These pleasant illusions were blown away on a fine July day about twenty miles outside Washington. Be-

This pencil sketch, Panic on the Road Between Bull Run and Centreville, *illustrates the retreat of Union troops at the first battle of Bull Run.*

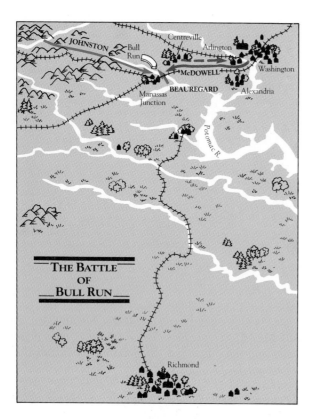

THE BATTLE
OF
BULL RUN

J. Jackson, a thirty-seven-year-old mathematics in-structor at Virginia Military Academy, shored up the sagging Confederate left. The union soldiers fell back and then broke in hysteria, fleeing for Washington along with the panicked would-be spectators.

Celebrations and Recriminations in the South

The South had a victory and a hero. At the peak of the battle for the left flank, a South Carolinian rallied his men by shouting, "There stands Jackson like a stone wall." The name stuck, for it seemed appropriate to more than Thomas J. Jackson's performance on the battlefield. He was an introspective, humorless, even dull man—somewhat a figure of ridicule to his students before the war—a stern Scots-Irish Presbyterian who lacked the human touch and was never loved by his men, as many generals are.

But his men stood in awe of him because Jackson came to life when the bullets whistled. He never

lieving that his volunteers could take Richmond before their short enlistments expired, Lincoln sent General Irvin McDowell marching directly toward the Confederate capital with thirty thousand troops. Laughing and joking as they went, sometimes shooting at targets, the boys from Ohio and Massachusetts were accompanied by a parade of carriages filled with congressmen, social-ites, newspaper reporters, and curiosity seekers. The crowd carried picnic lunches and bickered as to where in Richmond they would enjoy a late supper.

They were met by a Confederate force of about twenty-two thousand under the command of General Beauregard. The rebels had hastily dug in on high ground behind a creek called Bull Run, near a railroad crossing named Manassas Junction. McDowell at-tacked immediately, guessing the Confederate left flank to be the weakest point in the line. He was right about that. Although his troops were shocked by the ferocity of the musket fire that greeted them, they al-most cracked the southern line.

Had they succeeded, the war would likely have been over, at least in the upper South. Behind Beauregard's men, the road to Richmond lay open. At the critical moment, however, nine thousand Virginians arrived on the field after a frantic train ride from the Shenan-doah Valley. A brigade under the command of Thomas

Confederate General Thomas J. Jackson's reputation for refusing to yield to the enemy earned him the nickname "Stonewall."

yielded a line to the enemy, and he was a genius at maneuvering troops. For two years Jackson would do what the South needed done, insert his men in critical positions and stand like a stone wall against Union assaults.

By way of contrast, General Beauregard's reputation suffered at Bull Run because he failed to follow up his victory by marching on Washington. Within a few months he was replaced as Confederate commander in Virginia by Joseph E. Johnston, who had brought the troops and Stonewall Jackson from the Shenandoah Valley.

Johnston was the superior soldier, but neither Beauregard nor anyone else was to blame for the South's failure to capture Washington. As Johnston himself put it, "The Confederate Army was more disorganized by victory than that of the United States by defeat"; and a disorganized army is no army at all. All the better generals at Bull Run emphasized the need for regrouping and hard training.

The Summer Lull

President Davis agreed, and he cautioned Richmond society that there was more fighting to come. But few seemed to listen. The common soldiers were cocky and overconfident as a result of their victory and minor casualties. Southern politicians spoke as though the war were over. Volunteer officers nagged their tailors to finish sewing gold braid on dress uniforms, so that they could show them off once or twice before the Union capitulated. And then they bickered. At a round of lavish parties in Richmond, old personal jealousies erupted as blustering colonels and generals blamed one another for blunders real and imaginary.

In the North, however, the defeat at Manassas taught a sorely needed lesson. The spectacle of McDowell's troops throwing down their guns and trotting wild-eyed into Washington, where they lay down to sleep in doorways and on the sidewalks, alarmed Lincoln and brought him around to Winfield Scott's way of thinking. The war would be no summer's pastime but a long, hard fight. Now when Lincoln asked Congress for troops he wanted three hundred thousand men under three-year enlistments.

He also relieved Irvin McDowell from command of what was now called the Army of the Potomac, and appointed George B. McClellan. The former president of the Illinois Central Railroad, McClellan had a reputation as an organizer and administrator. In November 1861, Winfield Scott retired, and McClellan also took charge of the Union armies that were being drilled throughout the Midwest.

Northern Strategy

Though Scott was gone, the three-pronged strategy that he had outlined to Lincoln before the war began was now adopted. First it was necessary to defend Washington with the Army of the Potomac and to maintain constant pressure on Richmond in the hope of capturing the city. This was important because Richmond was not only the seat of the Confederate government (and only seventy miles from Washington), but also a major southern industrial center.

Second, because the Ohio-Mississippi waterway was vital to the economic life of the midwestern states, Union armies would strike down the great valley. Their object was to gain complete control of the Mississippi as soon as possible in order to permit western farmers to resume the export of foodstuffs, by which they lived, and to split the Confederacy in two. Then the western front could be neglected while the Union concentrated its force in the East.

Third, the Union would use its overwhelming naval superiority to blockade the South and thus strangle its export economy. If the Confederacy were unable to sell cotton abroad, it would be unable to buy the manufactures, particularly the munitions, that were essential in a lengthy war. Scott called this strategy the "Anaconda Plan" after the South American snake that slowly crushes its prey.

On the face of it, an effective blockade was out of the question. The Confederate coastline on both the Atlantic and the Gulf of Mexico was a tangle of coves, bays, bayous, salt marshes, and lonely broad beaches. It was impossible to prevent every vessel from reaching land or from making a successful break for Europe. Nevertheless, an effective commerce could not be rowed through the surf or unloaded in swamps, and the Union Navy felt confident that with time its vessels could bottle up the Confederate ports.

The South's Problem

Southern strategy had a simpler design but a flimsier foundation. In order to attain its basic goal—independence—the Confederacy needed only to turn back every Union advance until the British or French, who were friendly to the South, came to its assistance, or until the people of the North grew weary of fighting and forced Lincoln to negotiate. In the broadest sense, the story of the Civil War tells how this strategy was dashed and how, although long delayed, the Union strategy succeeded.

The Confederacy's hope of foreign intervention died first. In the case of France, it was doomed from the beginning by the personality of the French emperor,

Napoleon III. On one day a scheming power politician who realized that an independent Confederacy might be molded into a valuable French protectorate, Napoleon was, on the next, a flighty romantic.

After leading the southerners on, he lost interest in their cause when he was approached by a group of Mexican aristocrats who, in order to defeat a revolution of Indians and *mestizo* peons, offered to make an emperor of one of Napoleon's generals, Maximilian of Austria. Who wanted a dependency of quarrelsome, headstrong cotton growers when he could tread in the footsteps of Cortez? Not Napoleon III. By the end of 1862, he scarcely noticed the southern diplomats who continued to court him.

The pro-Confederate sentiments of the British government were more solidly based. The South was the principal source of cotton for the British textile industry, the owners of which were supporters of William E. Gladstone's Liberal government. Moreover, many in the English aristocracy regarded the southern planters, as rough-cut kinsmen. However rude, they were country gentlemen like themselves. Finally, a great many British politicians relished the opportunity to shatter the growing power of the American upstart.

However, whereas Napoleon III was impulsive, the British leaders were cautious. They would not throw in with the Confederacy until the rebels demonstrated that they had a real chance of winning. A combination of southern blunders in export policy, bad luck, Union diplomatic skill, and a key Union victory at the Confederacy's brightest hour dashed the Confederate (and British) dream of redrawing the map of North America.

King Cotton Is Dethroned

The first Confederate blunder was Jefferson Davis's decision to blackmail England into supporting the southern cause. He prevailed on cotton shippers to keep the crop of 1861 at home, stored on wharves and in warehouses. The object was to put the pinch on British millowners so that they would set up a cry for war.

It did not work, largely because English millowners had anticipated the problem and had stockpiled huge reserves of fiber. By the time these supplies ran out in 1862, cotton growers in Egypt and the Middle East were bringing in crops that were large enough to satisfy most English needs. To make matters worse, Union troops captured enough southern cotton by 1862 to keep the mills of New England humming and even to sell some to Great Britain.

As the war dragged on, the South's Cotton Diplomacy was further frustrated by the failure of two successive grain crops in Western Europe. Fearing food short-ages, monarchist England discovered that Union wheat was more royal than Confederate cotton. Blessed with bumper crops, northern farmers shipped unprecedented tonnages of grain and byproducts to Europe at both financial and diplomatic profit.

The Diplomatic War

In November, 1861, a zealous Union naval officer almost scuttled the northern effort to keep England neutral. The captain of the U.S.S. *San Jacinto* stopped a British steamer, the *Trent,* and seized two Confederate diplomats who were aboard, James M. Mason and John Slidell. Northern public opinion was delighted. It was refreshing to hear for a change of an American man-of-war bullying a British vessel. But Lincoln took a dimmer view of the incident. The British ambassador came close to threatening war. To the president, Mason and Slidell were two hot potatoes, and he took advantage of the first lull in the public celebrations to toss them aboard a British warship.

No harm was done. In England, Mason and Slidell proved no match for the Union ambassador, Charles Francis Adams, in the delicate game of diplomacy. They did manage to see two commerce-raiders, the *Florida* and the *Alabama,* constructed for the Confederacy and put to sea. But Adams, as irascible as his presidential father and grandfather, cajoled and threatened the British government into preventing a sister ship from leaving port. He moved with great skill and energy through the salons of London, and kept Great Britain out of the war until the North turned the tide of war in its direction.

1862 and Stalemate

As its chances of bringing England into the war grew fainter, the Confederate government increasingly pegged its hopes on northern sympathizers, defeatists, and antiwar activists. Many northerners frankly favored the South, particularly people in the Union slave states and in the lower counties of Ohio, Indiana, and Illinois, a region with a strong southern heritage. However, these "Copperheads," as northerners who sympathized with the South were called, were never able to mount a serious threat to the Union war effort. They were a minority, and Lincoln played free with their civil liberties in order to silence them.

Lincoln and the Copperheads

One of the president's most controversial moves against the opponents of the war was his suspension of the ancient legal right of habeas corpus, a protection against arbitrary arrest that is held sacred in English and American law. At one time or another, thirteen thousand people were jailed because of alleged anti-war activity. Lincoln also used his control of the post office to penalize and even suppress antiadministration newspapers.

The noisiest and most dangerous Copperhead was Clement L. Vallandigham, a popular Democratic congressman from Ohio. His attacks on the war effort were so unsettling that Lincoln jailed him and later passed him through the Confederate lines as though he were their agent. Identifying Vallandigham with treason was unfair but shrewd. In 1863, Vallandigham was forced to run for governor of Ohio from exile in Canada. At home, or even in prison, he might have won. But he was defeated, and when he returned to the United States the next year, he was harmless enough that Lincoln was able to ignore him.

More worrisome to Lincoln than pro-Confederate northerners was defeatism, the belief that the war was not worth the expense in blood and money. Each time Union armies lost a battle, more and more northerners wondered if it would not be wiser to let the southern states go. Or, they asked, was it really impossible to negotiate a reunion on the basis of some kind of compromise? Was Lincoln's Republican administration,

rather than the southern states, the obstacle to a negotiated peace?

It was impossible for Lincoln to secure reunion on any other basis than military victory. Even at the bitter end of the war, when the Confederacy was not only defeated but devastated, Jefferson Davis insisted on southern independence as a condition of peace. When the South was winning the battles, negotiation was out of the question.

And the South did win most of the battles in 1861 and 1862. The show belonged to Stonewall Jackson and General Robert E. Lee, who succeeded Joseph Johnston as commander of the Army of Northern Virginia. Time after time, they halted or drubbed the Army of the Potomac. Nevertheless, even in his most triumphant hour in the summer of 1862, Lee revealed that his military genius was limited by his virtues as a proud Virginia gentleman. Devoted to his native state rather than to the Confederacy, Lee never fully appreciated the fact that while he was defending the Old Dominion with such mastery, the southern cause was being slowly throttled in coastal waters and in the Mississippi Valley.

The Campaign in the West

"We must have Kentucky," Lincoln told his cabinet. Without Kentucky, the war would be lost. Even before the Union recovered from the defeat at Manassas, Lincoln approved the military occupation of the state by an army under General Ulysses S. Grant. From this base, Grant moved into Tennessee in early 1862, quickly capturing two important forts, Donelson and Henry. These guarded the mouths of the Tennessee and Cumberland rivers, two waterways of far greater strategic value than muddy Bull Run. Then, continuing to drive deep into the South, General Grant fought the battle that taught both sides that they were not playing chess.

Moving up the Tennessee River unopposed, Grant intended to attack Corinth, Mississippi, in the northern part of the state. He knew that Confederate General Albert Sidney Johnston planned to defend the town, but had no idea that Johnston was also prepared to attack. On April 6, 1862, while camped at Shiloh, Tennessee, Grant's armies were caught in their bedrolls by four thousand rebel troops. Many were killed before they awoke. The boys in blue held on, but just barely. Only when, during the night, Union reinforcements arrived under General Don Carlos Buell, did the Confederates withdraw.

A. S. Johnston, regarded by many military historians as one of the Confederacy's best field commanders, was killed at Shiloh. Much more important, however, were

THE WAR
IN THE WEST
1862

UNION FORCES
CONFEDERATE
FORCES

the total casualty lists. Southern losses numbered eleven thousand of forty thousand troops engaged. The Union lost thirteen thousand of sixty thousand men. Bodies were heaped like firewood while massive graves were dug. Acres of ground were reddened with blood, and the stench of death sickened the survivors. Compared with the minor casualties at Bull Run—compared with the losses in most battles in any war—Shiloh was appalling.

Grant was temporarily discredited, accused of having been drunk on the morning of the attack. Soldiers of the two armies ceased to fraternize between battles, as they had done in the woods of Tennessee, where Confederate and Union guards had conversed in the night, traded tobacco for coffee, and, on at least one occasion, played a Sunday baseball game. Bull Run showed that there would be a long war; Shiloh showed that it would be bloody. Not even the victory of naval officer David G. Farragut a short time after Shiloh, which put the Union in control of New Orleans, could erase the melancholy bitterness of the great battle.

The War at Sea

There never was fraternization on the seas. For the Union sailors assigned to the blockade, days were long and boring, spent slowly patrolling the waters outside southern ports. The Confederate seamen on the commerce-raiders *Florida* and *Alabama* got to see the world, however. These fast, heavily armed ships destroyed or captured more than 250 northern merchantmen ($15 million in ships and cargo) in every corner of the world.

The Confederates almost destroyed the blockade in March 1862. Out to the mouth of the Chesapeake steamed an old warship, the *Merrimack*, covered over with iron plates forming the shape of a tent. The *Merrimack* was a ram, outfitted on its bow with a sharp iron blade like a plowshare that could slice through a wooden hull. Cannonballs bounced off its sloping armor as though they were made of rubber, and within a few hours the *Merrimack* sank several proud Union warships.

Left to itself for a few weeks, this single ship might have broken the blockade. But the *Merrimack* did not have even a few days. The Union had an experimental vessel of its own, the even odder-looking *Monitor*. It was also an ironclad and resembled a cake tin on a platter barely riding above the waterline. For five hours on March 9, 1862, the two ships had at each other. The battle was technically a draw, but strategically an important Union victory. The *Merrimack* had to retreat for repairs, and, in May, the Confederates destroyed the vessel so that it would not fall into Union hands.

Once again, the material disparity between the two nations told in the long run. The South never could build another *Merrimack*. The *Monitor* proved to be just a prototype for others like it.

McClellan and "the Slows"

In creating the Army of the Potomac, George McClellan made an invaluable contribution to the Union cause. Not only were his men better trained than most southern troops, but they usually were better armed. While the Confederates had to import or capture most of their guns, McClellan and his successors had a limitless supply of munitions and constantly improved firearms. The Springfield repeating rifle, introduced toward the end of the war, allowed Union soldiers to fire six times a minute instead of once or twice.

The trouble with McClellan was that he would not exploit his edge. He was a man of contradictions. On the one hand, he loved to pose, strut, and issue bombastic proclamations in the style of Napoleon and Wellington. On the other, when it came time to fight, he froze as though he were one of their statues. His problem was not entirely a matter of personality. McClellan was a Democrat. He did not want to crush the South.

Abraham Lincoln and General George McClellan confer at Antietam.

He believed that merely by creating an awesome military force, the Union could persuade the Confederacy to give in without a bloody battle.

Moreover, McClellan was sincerely devoted to his men. He could not bring himself to fight a battle in which the dead bodies would pile up as they had at Shiloh. Finally, he was a traditionalist. If there had to be a battle, he wanted overwhelming superiority. He could never get enough men to suit his conservative nature. To Lincoln, who did not like McClellan any more than the general liked him, it was a simpler matter. Lincoln said that McClellan was ill. He had a bad case of "the slows."

The Peninsula Campaign

When McClellan finally did move in June 1862, he came up with a brilliant plan. Instead of driving directly toward Richmond and running up against well-prepared rebel fortifications, he transported 110,000 men by ship to the peninsula between the York and James rivers. The plan was to take Richmond from the south, bypassing the entrenchments.

It could have worked. General Joseph Johnston, then commanding the Confederate Army of Northern Virginia, was surprised and outnumbered. Instead of moving quickly, McClellan sat and fiddled. He over-

estimated Johnston's numbers and demanded more troops of Lincoln, who refused to send reinforcements because Washington seemed to be in danger of attack. In reality, Lee had set one of the traps that fooled the northerners time and again. He had sent Stonewall Jackson on a diversionary mission to feign an attack on Washington that Jackson did not have the strength to bring off. The ruse was successful, and Jackson then sped east to reinforce the Confederate armies that were defending Richmond. By the time McClellan gave in to the president's impatient demand for action, Johnston, Lee, and Jackson had brought down eighty-five thousand men to hold him.

Seven days of nearly constant battle followed between June 26 and July 2, 1862. Again overly cautious and outsmarted on the field, McClellan was fought to a standstill. Nevertheless, he retained a favorable position. His supply lines were intact. Confederate morale was badly shaken by the twenty thousand casualties that the South had suffered, and Richmond was only a few miles away, nearly within range of bombardment. A final Union push in the summer of 1862 might have carried the day and ended the war.

But then Lincoln blundered. He called off the Peninsula Campaign, ordering the troops back to Washington by ship, and he replaced McClellan with General John Pope, who was to take the old Manassas route to Richmond.

Pope had won several victories in the West and was a favorite with the abolitionists in Congress because of his opposition to slavery. But he was an unimaginative general who was no match for the wily Lee and Jackson. At the end of August, Lee met him on the same ground as the first Battle of Manassas and beat him back much more easily than the Confederates had defeated McDowell.

The Battle of Antietam

Lincoln had no choice but to recall McClellan to command, and the eastern theater bogged down into a stalemate that began to worry Jefferson Davis as much as Lincoln. Davis's critics were not satisfied with Lee's brilliant defenses and wanted the war carried into the North. Indeed, with the chances of British intervention rapidly fading, a major victory on Union soil seemed to be the only way that Britain might be brought into the war.

Unfortunately, while Lee worked defensive miracles with inferior numbers, his army of forty thousand was not up to an attack when the enemy had seventy thousand. Moreover, he suffered a fatal stroke of bad luck when his plans, wrapped around a pack of cigars, fell into McClellan's hands. The Union commander

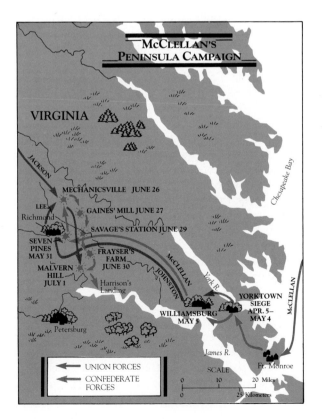

McCLELLAN'S PENINSULA CAMPAIGN

VIRGINIA

JACKSON

MECHANICSVILLE JUNE 26

LEE
Richmond

GAINES' MILL JUNE 27

SAVAGE'S STATION JUNE 29

SEVEN
PINES
MAY 31

FRAYSER'S
FARM
JUNE 30

MALVERN
HILL
JULY 1

Harrison's
Landing

JOHNSTON

York R.

Chesapeake Bay

McCLELLAN

Petersburg

WILLIAMSBURG
MAY 5

YORKTOWN
SIEGE
APR. 5–
MAY 4

James R.

Ft. Monroe

UNION FORCES
CONFEDERATE
FORCES

SCALE

0   10   20 Miles

0   25 Kilometers

About 10,000 Confederate soldiers were killed at the battle of Antietam. This photograph, entitled Harvest of Death, *was taken shortly after that battle in September 1862.*

caught Lee when he was least prepared for it, at Sharpsburg, Maryland, near Antietam Creek.

The fighting was as vicious as at Shiloh. Lee lost a quarter of his army, and he was in no position to retreat safely back across the Potomac into Virginia. Stoically, he waited for the counterattack that could destroy his army. To Lee's surprise, McClellan did not pounce. He was down with "the slows" again. On the second night, Lee slipped back to the safety of Virginia.

Emancipation: A Political Masterstroke

During the first year of the war, Lincoln continued to insist that his object was not the destruction of slavery but the preservation of the Union. As late as August 1862, when the antislavery editor Horace Greeley demanded that Lincoln move against the hated institution, the president responded, "If I could save the Union without freeing any slave, I would do it; and if I could save it by freeing all the slaves, I would do it; and if I could do it by freeing some and leaving others alone, I would also do it."

After Antietam, Lincoln decided that he could best save the Union by freeing some of the slaves. In the Emancipation Proclamation Lincoln declared that, as of January 1, 1863, all slaves held in territory that was still under the control of rebel forces were henceforth free. Slaves in Union slave states and in Confederate

territory that already was occupied by the Union would remain slaves.

Lincoln was roundly criticized for a proclamation that did not free a single slave. In fact, his action was a political masterstroke. The Emancipation Proclamation reassured loyal slaveowners by allowing them to keep their slaves. It also served as an inducement to Confederate slaveowners to make peace before January in order to save their human property.

At the same time, the Emancipation Proclamation permitted northern commanders to make use of the blacks who, once Union armies were nearby, fled to freedom by the thousands. Many of the young black men wanted to join the army, but, as long as they were legally slaves, they could not be enlisted. The Emancipation Proclamation paved the way for the recruitment of blacks, and, by the end of the war, 150,000 had served in Union blue. One Billy Yank in eight was black, a fact that was revealed in few pictorial representations of the troops.

Black units were usually assigned the dirtiest and most dangerous duty, for example, mining tunnels under Confederate fortifications. They were paid only half a white soldier's wages, about $7 a month. And yet, because they believed that they were fighting for freedom rather than for an abstraction such as the Union, black soldiers were said to bicker and gripe far less than whites did.

Following Lincoln's Emancipation Proclamation, blacks were recruited to fight in the Union army.

The Emancipation Proclamation also served Lincoln as a trial balloon. Without committing himself either way, he was able to test northern opinion on the subject of freeing the slaves. When Union soldiers adopted Julia Ward Howe's "Battle Hymn of the Republic"— "let us fight to make men free"—as their anthem, Lincoln learned that by striking at slavery, he had improved northern morale.

He also had ensured British neutrality. Dismayed by the Confederate defeat at Antietam, the pro-Confederate British government was almost completely silenced by the popularity of the Emancipation Proclamation among the ordinary people. Long hostile to the institution of slavery, British public opinion slowly but unmistakably drifted to the side of the Union.

Finally, Lincoln mollified his critics within the Republican party. Called the Radicals because they wanted an all-out conquest of the South and a radical remaking of its social institutions, this group controlled the Joint Committee on the Conduct of the War, which frequently criticized Lincoln's policies. The Radical leaders, Thaddeus Stevens in the House of Representatives and Charles Sumner in the Senate, were not satisfied with the Emancipation Proclamation. They wanted a constitutional amendment that would abolish slavery in the Union as well as in the Confederacy. But Lincoln's action did quiet them, since a congressional election was coming up. Lincoln also played for their support by once again dismissing the Democrat McClellan, and appointing another antislavery general, Ambrose E. Burnside, as commander of Union forces in the East.

Stalemate

Burnside did not want the job. An able corps commander like McDowell and Pope, he knew that he was not fit to direct an army. However, he was too good a soldier to turn Lincoln down and, on December 13, led a tragic attack against an impregnable southern position on high ground near Fredericksburg, Virginia. Watching the slaughter of thirteen hundred Union soldiers (plus ninety-six hundred wounded), General Lee remarked to an aide that "it is well that war is so terrible or we would grow too fond of it." Burnside retreated, in tears and broken. And the Union and Confederate armies settled down to winter quarters on either side of the Rappahannock River.

The war also bogged down in the West. After Shiloh, a Confederate force under General Braxton Bragg moved across eastern Tennessee into Kentucky in order to recapture the state. At Perryville on October 8, he fought to a draw against General Don Carlos Buell, decided his supply lines were overextended, and moved back into Tennessee. On the last day of 1862, Bragg fought another standoff with the Union Army at Murfreesboro. Both sides went into winter quarters— neither beaten, neither within sight of victory.

FACING BATTLE

The Civil War battle experience was much the same whether the soldier wore Union blue or Confederate gray—except that the troops of the North were almost always better supplied with shelter, clothing, shoes, medicines, food, and arms and ammunition. It is difficult to say how much this meant to the final outcome of the war. Cold, wet, tired, and ill soldiers are surely less effective than well-equipped ones, and Confederate troops without shoes—not an uncommon sight—were usually, but not always, exempt from charging enemy lines, a further depletion of the outnumbered southern force. Nevertheless, Johnny Reb, the Confederate foot soldier, won the respect of both his officers and his enemies as a formidable fighting man. As early as the second Battle of Bull Run in 1862, the commander of a unit called Toombs's Georgians told of leading so many barefoot men against the Yankees that they "left bloody footprints among the thorns and briars." Nevertheless, they followed him. Johnny Reb and his Union counterpart, Billy Yank, knew when they were going to fight. In only a few large-scale battles was an army caught by surprise. Jomini's "rules" were well-known by the generals on both sides, and preparations for massive attack were so extensive that getting caught napping, as Grant's men were at Shiloh, was rarely repeated. In fact, the men who would be *defending* a position were generally prepared for battle with extra rations and ammunition earlier than the attackers, who knew when they would be moving.

Two or three days' supply of food was distributed before a battle. A historian of the common soldier, Bell I. Wiley, suggests that in the Confederate ranks

this judicious measure generally fell short of its object because of Johnny Reb's own characteristics: he was always hungry, he had a definite prejudice against baggage, and he was the soul of improvidence. Sometimes, the whole of the extra rations would be consumed as soon as it was cooked, and rarely did any part of it last for the full period intended.

This carelessness could have serious consequences because fighting was heavy toil; tales of units that were incapacitated by hunger at the end of a day's battle were common. Wiley points out that after Bull Run in the East and Shiloh in the West, however, few soldiers took other than close care of their canteens. Waiting, marching, and running in the heat, cold, and rain, and the grime and dust of battle made everyone intolerably thirsty.

As short a time as possible before the ensuing battle, each infantryman was given forty to sixty rounds of ammunition to stash in the cartridge box he wore on a strap slung over a shoulder. (Soldiers rarely carried more than a few rounds of ammunition at other times because the powder got damp without meticulous care.) The Springfield repeating rifles took a round that looked like any modern cartridge. The muzzle-loading musket—which was used by all the Confederates and most of the Yankees—took a round that consisted of a ball and a charge of powder wrapped together in a piece of paper that was twisted closed at the powder end. To load the musket, a soldier bit off the twist so that the powder was exposed, pushed the cartridge into the muzzle of his gun, inserted the paper he held in his teeth to keep the ball from rolling out, and rammed a rod (fixed to his gun) into the barrel to the breech. Each time he fired, he had to fall to one knee in order to reload. That moment, and when men were retreating, were considered far more dangerous than when troops were advancing.

On the eve or morning of a battle, the commanding general addressed his troops either personally or in written orations read by line officers. George McClellan was noted among Union commanders for his stirring orations in the tradition of Napoleon and Wellington.

This soldier is one of the 620,000 men who died in the Civil War.

Confederate General Albert Sidney Johnston also took the high road in his speech before Shiloh:

The eyes and the hopes of eight millions of people rest upon you. You are expected to show yourselves worthy of your race and lineage; worthy of the women of the South, whose noble devotion in this war has never been exceeded in any time. With such incentives to brave deeds and with the trust that God is with us, your general will lead you confidently to the combat, assured of success.

Because the Confederate cause was defense of a homeland, it could easily be put in such noble terms. The Union Army, however, had something of a morale problem during the early stages of the war because "the Union" was so abstract and Billy Yank was, after all, invading someone else's land.

After the Emancipation Proclamation, the morale of the Union soldiers improved, while that of the Confederates declined. Now, Billy Yank was fighting "to make men free"—a line from the favorite Union song— while some southern commanders were reduced to appealing to base instincts. For example, General T. C. Hindman exhorted in December 1862:

Remember that the enemy you engage has no feeling of mercy. His ranks are made up of Pin Indians, Free Negroes, Southern Tories, Kansas Jayhawkers, and hired Dutch cutthroats. These bloody ruffians have invaded your country, stolen and destroyed your property, murdered your neighbors, outraged your women, driven your children from their homes, and defiled the graves of your kindred.

Bell I. Wiley points out that toward the end of the war, Confederate soldiers fought most grimly and intensely when they were up against a black detachment on the Union line.

Grimness was lacking before the earliest battles. The men were high spirited on both sides. As the war ground on, the experienced soldiers tended to grow quiet and reflective before the fighting started. Some read their Bibles. Others—but not many, it seems— took a few quick pulls of whiskey. Friends made and re-made promises to look for one another when the battle was over, to help those too seriously wounded to move, and to gather personal belongings to return to a friend's family if he was killed. During the final, brutal battles before Richmond, soldiers wrote their names and addresses on pieces of paper that they pinned to their clothing on the assumption that there would be no friends alive to care for their bodies. The waiting was usually over about dawn. The command to charge was given. And with a yell, the repeated "hoorays" of the Union troops, and the eerie "rebel yell" of the Confederates, the simultaneous excitement and dread of battle began.

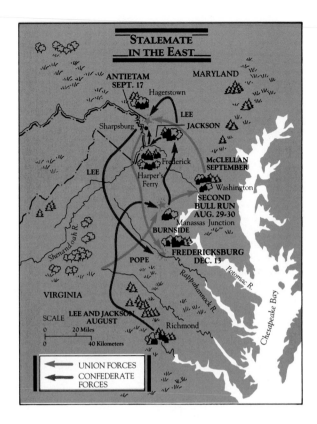

For Further Reading

The most comprehensive account of the first half of the Civil War is Allan Nevins, *Ordeal of the Union* (1947). The best single-volume history of the war is John G. Randall and David Donald, *The Civil War and Reconstruction* (1969). On military history, Bruce Catton's three volumes, *Mr. Lincoln's Army* (1951), *Glory Road* (1952), and *A Stillness at Appomattox* (1953), are the classic accounts of the eastern theater. See also T. Harry Williams, *Lincoln and His Generals* (1952), and, for the common soldier, Bell I. Wiley, *The Life of Johnny Reb* (1943) and *The Life of Billy Yank* (1952).

On the Confederacy, Clement Eaton, *A History of the Southern Confederacy* (1954), is the standard account, and Frank Vandiver, *Rebel Brass* (1956), looks at military history from the southern side.

Frank L. Klement, *The Copperheads in the Middle West* (1960), and Wood Gray, *The Hidden Civil War: The Story of the Copperheads* (1942), deal with antiwar opinion in the North from two different perspectives. Benjamin Quarles, *The Negro in the Civil War* (1969), is the standard account of black participation in the national tragedy, and Hans L. Trefousse, *The Radical Republicans* (1969), offers the best understanding of the most dynamic members of the party that fought the war. Biographies of interest are J. F. C. Fuller, *Grant and Lee* (1957), and W. W. Hassley, *General George B. McClellan* (1957).

25

Driving Old Dixie Down
General Grant's War of Attrition, 1863–1865

There was no celebrating the war's second anniversary. By the spring of 1863, the Confederacy was suffering severe shortages of men and materiel, and runaway inflation. In the Union, frustration smothered every encouraging word. Lincoln had men, money, and a strategy. He knew what needed to be done. But he could not find a general to do it. In the East, the Confederates had defeated or stymied four of his commanders.

In the West, the situation was no more encouraging. Kentucky was finally secure. Southern Louisiana and western Tennessee were under Union control. But elsewhere the smaller Confederate armies had, like Lee in Virginia, fought Union troops to a standstill.

The Georgia Central Railroad was systematically destroyed by General William T. Sherman's troops.

The Campaigns of 1863

Beginning in 1863, the tide began to turn in favor of the Union. In the three major campaigns of that year, Union armies broke the stalemate in the West and cut the Confederacy in two, and Lee carried the war in the East north of the Mason-Dixon line.

Chancellorsville: First Break in the Stalemate

The first months of the year, however, did not prove very auspicious for the Union.

Among the harshest critics of Ambrose Burnside—especially after Burnside's defeat at Fredericksburg at the end of 1862—was General Joseph Hooker. As extravagant in his speeches as was McClellan, but lacking half of McClellan's abilities, "Fighting Joe" Hooker had said that the country needed a dictator. In one of the most unusual commissions ever given a military officer, Lincoln told Hooker that only victorious generals could set up dictatorships. If Hooker could win the victory that the North needed, Lincoln would run that risk.

Hooker proved to be no more capable than Burnside. After several months' preparation, in early May he crossed the Rappahannock River with more than twice as many soldiers as Lee's sixty thousand. Lee knew that he faced a bungler. He divided his army, left his fortifications, and hit Hooker from two directions near the town of Chancellorsville. The Army of the Potomac suffered eleven thousand casualties, and Hooker's defeat seemed to confirm that Richmond, the goal of the Army of the Potomac, could not be taken. However, the Battle of Chancellorsville exposed yet another mortal weakness in the South's fighting ability. Lee's losses were even larger than Hooker's, and whereas the North had a large population base from which to replace the fallen men, the Confederacy did not.

Moreover, Lee's losses at Chancellorsville included his "right arm," Stonewall Jackson. Returning from a reconnaissance mission, Jackson was accidentally shot and killed by his own troops. Lee said he could never replace his favorite general, and he was correct. Never again would the Army of Northern Virginia be so daring and so successful as it had been in 1862.

Grant Takes Vicksburg

In the West, the Union had not yet succeeded in accomplishing its major goal—control of the Mississippi River. By holding fast to a 150-mile stretch of the river between Vicksburg, Mississippi, and Port Hudson, Louisiana, the rebels were able to shuttle goods and men freely from one end of their country to the other. Lincoln's own Midwest, on the contrary, was unable to use the great river that was its traditional life line.

The key to the impasse was Vicksburg. The city sat on high cliffs at a bend in the river. A Confederate force commanded by a renegade Pennsylvania Quaker, John C. Pemberton, manned heavy artillery on the top of the bluffs. No vessels could pass underneath save small, fast craft under cover of night. No army could approach the town. To the north and east, Vicksburg was insulated by rugged woodland laced by creeks and bayous—a tangle of earth, brush, and water. Pemberton's Mississippians had learned to flourish there like Br'er Rabbit. Union attackers found it difficult to move. Vicksburg was as near and as far from the Union western armies as Richmond was from the Army of the Potomac.

Then, within a few short weeks, an unlikely candidate for hero status broke the western stalemate wide

Ulysses S. Grant's unimpressive past made him an unlikely war hero.

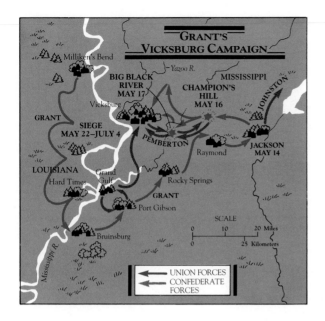

GRANT'S
VICKSBURG CAMPAIGN

Milliken's Bend

Yazoo R.

BIG BLACK
RIVER
MAY 17

MISSISSIPPI

CHAMPION'S
HILL
MAY 16

JOHNSTON

Vicksburg

GRANT

SIEGE
MAY 22–JULY 4

PEMBERTON

Raymond

JACKSON
MAY 14

LOUISIANA

Hard Times

Grand
Gulf

Rocky Springs

GRANT

Port Gibson

SCALE

0   10   20 Miles

0   25 Kilometers

Bruinsburg

Mississippi R.

UNION FORCES
CONFEDERATE
FORCES

to a few miles below Vicksburg, and then recrossed the river, ferried by gunboats that had raced by night under the Confederate guns.

Having flanked the rough country where Pemberton was so comfortable, Grant abandoned his lines of supply, a risky maneuver but one that confused the rebels. He charged to the east and forced a small Confederate force under Joseph E. Johnston to withdraw from the area. Grant attacked Jackson, the capital of Mississippi, and then, before the Confederates had quite grasped his intentions, he reversed direction, turning back toward Vicksburg. The befuddled Pemberton was trounced in a series of brief battles. In a little more than two weeks, Grant won half a dozen confrontations and captured eight thousand southern troops. On May 19, with Pemberton still reeling from the turnaround and penned up in Vicksburg, Grant sat his men down to besiege the city. Nothing was settled yet. But the Union had something to cheer about, and the Confederate government had cause for alarm.

open. He was General Ulysses S. Grant, whose life so far had been a study in mediocrity. A West Point graduate, Grant had served without distinction or shame in the Mexican War. After the peace, he had been shunted off to duty at a lonely desert fort and then to a cold, wet, and even lonelier outpost on the northern California coast. Grant had taken to the whiskey bottle and, under none too favorable circumstances, resigned from the army. In business back in Illinois, he had scraped by, never far from bankruptcy.

The Civil War was a godsend. Critically short of officers, the Union Army paid little attention to the past records of professional soldiers who were willing to volunteer. Grant was given the command that won the first Union victory of the war, the capture of Forts Donelson and Henry in Tennessee. Then, however, came Shiloh and stalemate. Lincoln was on the verge of giving up on Grant when the general hatched his plan to take Vicksburg.

Everyone who knew Grant commented on his unimpressive presence. He was a short, dumpy man with a carelessly trimmed beard. His uniform was plain, perpetually rumpled, and usually stained. From a distance, he could be mistaken for an aging corporal who was about to be demoted. Even up close he seemed listless and stupid. But he was neither. If he did not look the part, Grant was capable of boldness equal to that of Stonewall Jackson, and he had Lee's easy confidence with large commands.

At Vicksburg, Grant scored a feat of old-fashioned military derring-do. He transferred his troops to the western bank of the Mississippi, marched them speedily

The Gettysburg Campaign

Back in Richmond, some of Lee's advisers urged him to send part of the Army of Northern Virginia west to attack Grant from the rear and regain Vicksburg. Lee decided instead to invade Pennsylvania. If he could threaten Washington, Lincoln would be forced to recall Grant's troops to the East. In the meantime, there was a good chance that by moving quickly, Lee could catch the Army of the Potomac offguard and give it a drubbing.

It was a bold gamble. If Lee had succeeded, his reputation as a strategist would be as great as his reputation as a battlefield tactician. But he failed, ironically because in the midst of the most important battle of the war, Lee made the most serious tactical mistake of his career.

At first, Lee had everything his way. He caught the Union Army by surprise, and Lincoln, having lost faith in Hooker, changed commanders yet again. With Lee's troops somewhere on northern soil—exactly where, no Union commander knew—the president appointed a colorless but methodical general, George Gordon Meade, to find them and fight. Almost by accident, forward units of Meade's and Lee's armies bumped into each other on July 1, 1863, in the little town of Gettysburg, Pennsylvania. The Union soldiers were looking for Lee. The Confederate soldiers were looking for shoes.

Both armies descended on the rolling countryside south of Gettysburg. Curiously, the Confederates occupied the battlefield from the north, the Yankees from the south. Both established strong positions on parallel

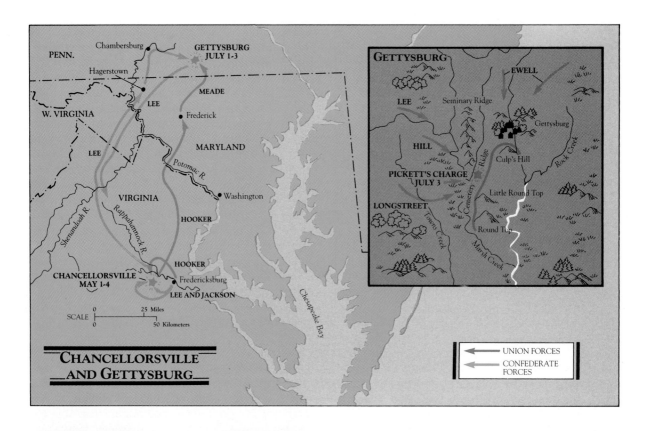

CHANCELLORSVILLE AND GETTYSBURG

Confederate General Robert E. Lee.

ridges about half a mile apart, the rebels on Seminary Ridge, the Union troops on Cemetery Ridge. Deciding to move before his enemy's entrenchments were complete, Lee attacked with his left flank and almost won the battle on the first day. His men pushed Meade's line back until it was curled into the shape of a fishhook. But the line held.

On July 2, Lee attacked at the other end of the Union line, at the "eye" of the fishhook. Once again, the rebels came within a few yards and a few hundred men of breaking through. But when the sun set on the second day, Union troops still held a steep bulbous knoll called Little Round Top. It was a valuable position. The troops who occupied Little Round Top could enfilade the open fields that separated the two armies.

That night, Lee's imagination failed him. Although outnumbered now, he decided on a mass frontal attack against the Union center. One of his generals, James Longstreet, argued long and loudly against a move that was chillingly reminiscent of Burnside's at Fredericksburg. He pointed out that after two days the Union troops would be well entrenched on Cemetery Ridge. Better that the Confederates sit tight and force Meade to attack them. The advantage always rests with the defensive position, and Meade could not ignore invaders with good lines of supply.

The Tide Turns

Stonewall Jackson might have persuaded Lee to defend or, alternatively, to try to turn the Union's right flank. James Longstreet could not. But he was dead right. General Meade gambled on an assault to his center—he outfoxed Lee—and he was ready for it. He concentrated every available man there, and, on the afternoon of July 3, he watched the tide of the war turn. Between one and two o'clock, howling the eerie "rebel yell," fifteen thousand men in gray uniforms began to trot across the no man's land. This was Pickett's Charge, somewhat of a misnomer because the angry Longstreet was actually in command of it. The attack was a nightmare. The men were slaughtered first by artillery and then by Minié balls. The worst of the fire came from Little Round Top, which had been reinforced during the night.

About a hundred Virginians actually reached the Union lines. There was a split second of glory, but it lasted no more than that. They were immediately surrounded by a thousand Union soldiers and killed or captured.

Pickett's Charge lasted less than an hour. When the Confederate survivors dragged themselves back to Seminary Ridge, twenty-five thousand men were dead, wounded, or missing. Five of twenty regimental commanders involved in the massive assault were wounded. The other fifteen were dead. So were two Confederate brigadier generals.

On July 4, a somber Robert E. Lee waited for the Union counterattack. It never came. Meade had learned the bloody lesson of Pickett's Charge. He would not expose his men to the horrors of crossing an open field into the mouths of cannon. By nightfall, a drizzle had become a downpour, making the Potomac impassable and setting up Lee's army for plucking. Defeated and huddled together, the Confederates were in an impossible position. But the rain also prevented Meade from launching an attack. When Lincoln got the news he fumed: "We had them within our grasp. We had only to stretch forth our hands and they were

ours. And nothing I could say or do could make the Army move."

The president was still without his general. But Gettysburg was undeniably the turning point of the war. Never again would the Confederates be up to an offensive campaign. Just as important as Lee's defeat on July 4, 1863, the day he withdrew from the field, was John C. Pemberton's surrender of starving Vicksburg to Grant. Five days later, Port Hudson, Louisiana, the last Confederate base on the Mississippi, gave up without a battle. General Nathaniel Banks took thirty thousand prisoners there. Within a few days, the Confederacy lost several times more men than it had put in the field at the first Battle of Bull Run.

The Tennessee Campaign

Worse was to come. In September, a previously cautious Union general, William S. Rosecrans, attacked the one remaining Confederate army in the West. Rosecrans pushed Braxton Bragg out of Tennessee and into northern Georgia. Union troops then occupied Chattanooga, an important railroad center on the Tennessee River.

Like Grant at Shiloh, however, Rosecrans was surprised by a counterattack. On September 19, reinforced by grim Confederate veterans of Gettysburg, Bragg hit him at Chickamauga Creek. It was one of the few battles of the war in which the Confederates had more men, seventy thousand to Rosecrans's fifty-six thousand, and numbers told. The rebels smashed through the Union right, scattering the defenders and making Chickamauga one of the bloodiest battles of the war. It would have been a total rout but for the stand on the Union left by a Virginian who had remained loyal to the North, George H. Thomas, the "Rock of Chickamauga." Thanks to Thomas's stand, the Union troops were able to retire in good order to the fortifications of Chattanooga.

Wisely, Bragg decided to besiege the city rather than attack it. But unlike Grant at Vicksburg, Bragg had other enemies than the army that he had trapped inside the town. Grant himself marched his men to Chattanooga and brought twenty-three thousand troops from the East by rail. Late in November, he drove Bragg's Confederates from their strongholds on Missionary Ridge and Lookout Mountain and back into Georgia.

The long campaign for Tennessee was over. It had taken two years longer than Lincoln had expected. But at last the Confederacy was severed in two, and the stage was set for the final Union offensive. After Vicksburg and Chattanooga, there was no doubt about who was the man to lead it. Early in 1864, Lincoln pro-

LOADED GUNS

Some twenty-four thousand of thirty-seven thousand muskets and rifles that were collected from the battlefield at Gettysburg were still loaded, never fired that day. About six thousand had between three and ten charges in them. The soldiers were so excited that they continued to reload without discharging their weapons.

moted U. S. Grant to the rank of lieutenant general and gave him command of all Union forces.

Total War

Grant had proved that he was a daring tactician of the old school. At Vicksburg, with dash and flash, he had outsmarted and outmaneuvered the enemy. Now he demonstrated his understanding that the nature of war had changed. He informed Lincoln that his object was not the capture of Confederate flags, commanders, cities, and territory, but the total destruction of the enemy's ability to fight.

The Union's superiority in numbers was overwhelming, and Grant intended to put his edge to work. He would force the Confederates to fight constant bloody battles on all fronts, trading casualties that the South could not afford and the North could. At the same time, he would destroy the Confederacy's capacity to feed, shoe, and arm its soldiers. He would complete on land what the naval blockade had begun. He would strangle the southern economy.

Grant called off the gentleman's war. His kind of battle was not chivalrous. It involved making war not only on soldiers but on a society. It was left to Grant's best general, the blunt-spoken William Tecumseh Sherman, to give it a name. "War is hell," Sherman said. He was a no-nonsense man. He would not dress up dirty work with fuss, feathers, and pretty words.

Sherman's assignment was to move from his base in Chattanooga toward Atlanta, laying waste the rich agriculture of the black belt. Grant, with General Meade as his field commander, would personally direct the onslaught against Richmond.

Grant Before Richmond

The war of attrition—the war of grinding down the Confederacy—began in May 1864. With one hundred thousand men, Grant and Meade marched into the Wilderness, wooded country near Fredericksburg where Burnside had been defeated. There Grant discovered that Lee was several cuts above any commander he had yet faced. Although outnumbered, Lee outmaneuvered Grant and actually attacked. While Grant's men suf-

The ruins of Richmond, Virginia, as photographed by Mathew Brady following the city's fall to Union troops led by General Grant in 1865.

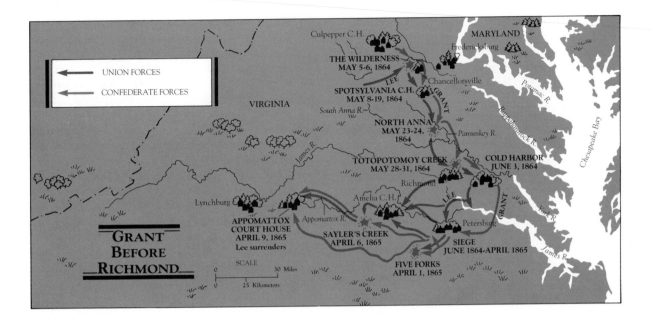

UNION FORCES

CONFEDERATE FORCES

VIRGINIA

GRANT BEFORE RICHMOND

Culpepper C.H.

MARYLAND

Fredericksburg

THE WILDERNESS
MAY 5-6, 1864

LEE

Chancellorsville

SPOTSYLVANIA C.H.
MAY 8-19, 1864

GRANT

Potomac R.

South Anna R.

NORTH ANNA
MAY 23-24, 1864

Pamunkey R.

TOTOPOTOMOY CREEK
MAY 28-31, 1864

COLD HARBOR
JUNE 3, 1864

Chesapeake Bay

Richmond

Lynchburg

James R.

Amelia C.H.

LEE

GRANT

York R.

APPOMATTOX
COURT HOUSE
APRIL 9, 1865
Lee surrenders

Appomattox R.

SAYLER'S CREEK
APRIL 6, 1865

Petersburg

SIEGE
JUNE 1864-APRIL 1865

James R.

SCALE

0   30 Miles

FIVE FORKS
APRIL 1, 1865

0   25 Kilometers

fered almost twice as many casualties as the southerners, replacements rushed to the Union front. On the southern side, however, Lee just counted losses and bade wounded men goodbye.

Now it was Lee's turn to discover that he too was up against a new kind of rival. When he earlier had defeated Union generals before Richmond, they had withdrawn to Washington to lick their wounds and regroup. This was standard military procedure, and it had given Lee time to reorganize too. But Grant broke the rules: he shifted his men to the south and attacked again, at Spotsylvania Court House. For five days, spearheaded in places by black troops, the Army of the Potomac assaulted the southern trenches. Grant lost twelve thousand men, again almost twice Lee's casualties. Northern congressmen and editors howled. The man was a butcher! But Grant was unmoved. He sent a curt message to Washington: "I intend to fight it out on this line if it takes all summer."

It took even longer. Time after time, Lee rallied his shrinking army and somehow managed to scratch to-gether enough munitions and provisions to keep his men in the field. Time after time, he threw Grant back. At Cold Harbor, south of Spotsylvania, the two fought another gory battle. Before they charged, Union troops wrote their names on scraps of paper and pinned the tags to their uniforms. When the fight was over, Grant had lost more men than Lee had under arms.

But still Grant came on, always swinging to the south. On June 15, Grant attempted to capture Petersburg, a rail center that was the key to Richmond's survival. He might have succeeded immediately but for the failure of General Benjamin Butler, a political general in charge of thirty thousand reinforcements, to join him in time. A little shaken, Grant finally paused and sat down to besiege Petersburg.

The Early Raid and the Loss of the Shenandoah

In July, Lee took advantage of the quiet to send General Jubal Early on a cavalry raid toward Washington. It was the kind of maneuver that, early in the war, had caused the union to call off its offensives. Early was remarkably successful. His men actually rode to within sight of the Capitol dome. But Early's raid was the Confederacy's last hurrah. Grant did not panic, and, this time, neither did Lincoln. They kept their men at Petersburg and sent a Union cavalry commander, Philip Sheridan, to prevent Early from joining Lee.

Sheridan chased Early into the Shenandoah Valley, the fertile country to the west of Richmond that had served as a Confederate sanctuary and as Richmond's breadbasket for three years. Sheridan defeated Early three times. More important, he laid waste to the val-

---

UNSUNG CONFEDERATE HERO

Joseph Reid Anderson is only occasionally mentioned in the histories of the Civil War, but he was second only to Robert E. Lee in allowing the Confederacy to fight as long as it did. Anderson was the owner and manager of the Tredregar Iron Works of Richmond, Virginia, and he kept the huge factory running until April 1865, when the Confederacy itself fell.

ley, burning houses, barns, and crops, and slaughtering what livestock his men did not eat. He reported that when he was done, a crow flying over the Shenandoah Valley would have to carry its own provisions.

Sherman in Georgia

General Sherman was even more thorough in his scouring of Georgia. He moved into the state at the same time that Grant entered the Wilderness. At first he met brilliant resistance from Joseph Johnston. Then Jefferson Davis replaced Johnston with the courageous but foolish John B. Hood, whom Sherman defeated. On September 2, 1864, Union troops occupied Atlanta. The loss of this major rail center was a devastating blow to Confederate morale.

Sherman's position was delicate. His supply lines ran to Chattanooga, more than one hundred miles away over an easily raided single-track railroad. A bold move by the Confederates would have isolated him in the middle of hostile territory with little chance of support. Once again, however, the new Union leadership turned difficulty into triumph. Sherman ordered the people of Atlanta to evacuate the city, and he put it to the torch. He then set out to the southeast, moving quickly in order to avoid a major battle that he could

not afford to fight but destroying everything of use to the Confederacy in a swath sixty miles wide. So thorough were Sherman's men that they not only tore up the railroad between Atlanta and Savannah, but they burned the ties and twisted the iron rails around telegraph poles. "Sherman bow ties," they called them.

Sherman's purpose was twofold. First, he wanted to make it difficult for the southern army that was chasing him (under Johnston's command once again) to feed itself. Second, he wanted to punish the people of Georgia. Those who had caused and supported the war would suffer for it.

Sherman reached Savannah on December 10 and captured it two weeks later. Resupplied from the sea, Sherman then turned north to join Grant. He would continue to scorch the southern earth and join Grant at Petersburg for the final battle of the war.

The Sudden End

That final battle was never fought. In February 1865, Jefferson Davis tried to make peace by sending the Confederate vice president, Alexander H. Stephens, and two other men to meet with Lincoln and Secretary of State Seward on a ship off Hampton Roads, Virginia. The South was reeling, but, absurdly, Davis insisted

General Robert E. Lee surrendered to General Ulysses S. Grant at the Appomattox Court House in Virginia, April 9, 1865.

on Confederate independence as a condition of peace. The conference broke up.

Late in March, Lee tried to draw Grant into a battle in open country. By this time he had 54,000 men to Grant's 115,000, and he was easily pushed back. On April 2, Lee abandoned Petersburg (and therefore Richmond) and made a dash to the west, hoping to link up with Johnston for a last stand.

With help from Sheridan, Grant cut him off. Desertions had reduced Lee's proud army to 30,000 men, and some of them were shoeless. On April 7, Grant called for a surrender, and, two days later, he met Lee at Appomattox Court House in Virginia. The terms were simple and generous. The Confederates surrendered all equipment and arms except for the officers' revolvers and swords. Grant permitted both officers and enlisted men to keep their horses for plowing. After taking an oath of loyalty to the Union, the southern troops could go home.

Jefferson Davis, who seemed to have lost his sense of reality, ordered Johnston to fight on. The veteran soldier knew better than to obey. On April 18, he surrendered to Sherman at Durham, North Carolina. The ragged remnants of two other Confederate armies gave up over the next several weeks.

The American Tragedy

The United States had never fought a more destructive war. More than one-third of the men who served in the opposing armies died in action or of disease, were wounded, maimed permanently, or captured by the enemy. In some southern states, more than one-quarter of all the men of military age lay in cemeteries. The depth of the gore can best be understood by comparing the 620,000 dead (360,000 Union, 260,000 Confederate) with the population of the United States in

1860, about 30 million. Considering that half the population was female and 7 or 8 million males were either too old or too young for military service, more than one out of every twenty-five men who were "eligible" to die in the war did lose their lives.

Assassination

There was one more casualty to be recorded just a few days after the fall of Richmond. On April 14, Good Friday, President Lincoln, his wife, and a few friends attended a play at Washington's Ford's Theater. Shortly after ten o'clock, he was shot point blank in the head by a pro-Confederate fanatic, John Wilkes Booth. Lincoln died early the next morning.

Booth was one of those unbalanced characters who pop up periodically to remind us of the role of the irrational in history. An actor who had delusions of grandeur, Booth had organized a cabal including at

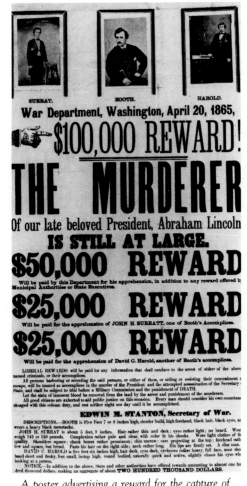

A poster advertising a reward for the capture of Lincoln's assassin, John Wilkes Booth, and his accomplices.

WAR ENLISTMENTS AND CASUALTIES: 1861–65		
	North	South
Enlistments[a]	1,556,678	1,082,119
Total deaths[b]	360,222	258,000
Battle deaths	110,070	94,000
Total wounded	275,175	125,000
Total casualties[c]	635,397	383,000

[a]Reduced by Livermore to the equivalent for three-year terms and taking desertion into account; the Union figure includes 178,895 Negro troops. T. L. Livermore, *Numbers and Losses in the Civil War* (Bloomington: Indiana University Press, 1958).

[b]Total for all U.S. wars before 1860 was 8,428.

[c]Total for both sides combined was almost 40% of the forces.

least one mental defective to revenge the Confederacy by wiping out the leading officials of the Union government. Only he succeeded in his mission, although one of his co-conspirators seriously wounded Secretary of State Seward with a knife.

As he escaped, Booth shouted, *"Sic semper tyrannis,"* which means "thus always to tyrants" and was the motto of the state of Virginia. Booth fled into Virginia; on April 26, he was cornered and killed at Bowling Green. In July, four others were hanged for Lincoln's murder. But vengeance did not bring the president back, and his loss proved to be inestimable, perhaps more for the South than for the North.

Father Abraham

To this day, Lincoln remains the central figure of American history. More books have been written about him than about any other person and, perhaps, any other event. He was the epitome of the American Dream. He rose from a destitute childhood to become the leader of the nation in its greatest crisis.

DON'T SWAP HORSES

Until the end of the nineteenth century, candidates for the presidency did not actively campaign. They did, however, urge on their supporters. In the wartime election of 1864, Lincoln himself provided his party's slogan by telling a leading supporter the story of the Dutch farmer who said he never swapped horses in the middle of a stream. Indeed, Americans never have changed presidents voluntarily during a war. Even during the unpopular war in Vietnam, it took the retirement of Lyndon B. Johnson in 1968 to put Republican Richard M. Nixon in the White House. With the war still on in 1972, Nixon won relection by a landslide.

Lincoln was not a popular president. The Radicals of his own party assailed him because of his reluctance to make war on slavery. Northern Democrats vilified him because the war dragged on and the casualties mounted to no avail. Editors and people of all points of view mocked his ungainly appearance and bemoaned his

Within five years, burdened by a nation split by war, President Abraham Lincoln aged dramatically. Left, a youthful Abraham Lincoln, as he was photographed June 3, 1860, by Alexander Hesler. On April 9, 1865, five days before his death, a weary-looking Lincoln (right) was photographed by Alexander and James Gardner.

lack of dignity. As late as September 1864, Lincoln expected to lose his bid for reelection to the Democratic party candidate, General George McClellan.

Lincoln weathered McClellan's threat thanks to Grant's victories and his own political manipulations. He made Nevada a state, although it consisted of little more than half a dozen mining camps of uncertain future. By pushing through admission, he gained three electoral votes for his party. He directed his generals to put Republican troops on furlough on election day so that they could vote for him, while he kept units that were favorable to McClellan on isolated duty. Lincoln also appealed to prowar Democrats by dropping the name "Republican" and calling himself the Union party candidate. For vice president he chose a Democrat from Tennessee, Andrew Johnson.

But Lincoln did not win the election of 1864 on the basis of political ploys. He won because he had quietly gained the respect of the majority of the people of the North by the example of his dogged will, personal humility, and eloquent humanitarianism. In a speech dedicating a national cemetery at Gettysburg in November 1863, he stated American ideals more beautifully (and succinctly) than anyone had done since Jefferson's preamble to the Declaration of Independence. His second inaugural address, delivered in Washington a month before Lee's surrender, was simultaneously a literary masterpiece—a signal to southerners that they could lay down their arms without fear of retribution, and a plea to northerners for a compassionate settlement of the national trauma. "With malice toward none," he concluded "with charity for all; with firmness in the right, as God gives us to see the right, let us strive on to finish the work we are in."

Consequences of the Civil War

The military triumph of the union guaranteed several fundamental changes in the nature of the American republic. Once and for all, the constitutional unity of the states was defined beyond argument. The states'-rights theories of John C. Calhoun, so compelling in the abstract, were buried without honor at Appomattox. The United States was *not* a federation of independent and sovereign states. It was a nation, one and indivisible. Politicians have described themselves as states' righters since the Civil War. To some extent, the line between state and national jurisdiction remains unsettled to this day. But never again after 1865 would anyone suggest that a state could leave the Union if its people disapproved of some national policy.

A New Political Majority

The political dominance of the South was destroyed by the Civil War. Since the founding of the republic, southerners had played a role in the government of the country out of all proportion to their numbers. Eight of the fifteen presidents who preceded Lincoln came from slave states. At least two of the seven northerners who had held the office were aggressively prosouthern. After Lincoln and Andrew Johnson, however, no resident of a former Confederate state would occupy the White House until Lyndon B. Johnson in 1963, and he was more westerner than southerner. Only in 1976, with the election of Jimmy Carter of Georgia, was a self-acknowledged southerner accepted by the American people as their leader.

Since the time of Andrew Jackson, southerners had dominated Congress through a combination of political skill, agrarian alliance with western farmers, and threat of secession. In making good on its threat, the southern bloc destroyed this alliance. The Democratic party remained a major force in the agricultural states of the North. But the Republicans held the edge above the Mason-Dixon line, and never again would a coalition of farmers dominate the government in Washington.

In its place, northeastern industrial and financial interests came to the fore. Businessmen had been late in joining the antislavery coalition. To bankers, great merchants, and factory owners, the Republican party was of interest more because of its economic policies than because of its hostility to slavery. With the war concluded, however, these forces held a strong position and could exploit the sentimental attachment of many voters to the "Grand Old Party," the party of liberty and union.

New Economic Policies

During the war, the Republican Congress passed a number of bills that would have been defeated had southerners been in their seats and voting. In July 1862, about the time of Antietam, both houses approved the Pacific Railways Act. As modified later in the war, this act gave sixty-four hundred square miles of the public domain to two private companies, the Union Pacific and the Central Pacific railroads. These corporations were authorized to sell the land and use the proceeds to construct a transcontinental railway, the ultimate internal improvement. In 1864, while Grant slogged it out with Lee before Richmond, Congress gave the Northern Pacific Railroad an even more generous subsidy. These acts revolutionized the traditional relationship between private enterprise and the federal government.

The tariff was another issue on which southern agricultural interests had repeatedly frustrated the manufacturers of the Northeast. Since 1832, with few exceptions, the Democratic party had driven the taxes on imported goods ever downward. The last tariff before the war, passed in 1857 with the support of southern congressmen, had set rates lower than they had been since the War of 1812.

In March 1861, even before secession was complete, the Republican Congress rushed through the Morrill Tariff, which pushed up the taxes. In 1862 and 1864, rates went even higher. By 1867, the average tax on imported goods stood at 47 percent, about the same as it had been under the act of 1828 that the southerners had called the Tariff of Abominations and that Calhoun had called fit grounds for secession.

The South had long frustrated the desire of northern financial interests for a centralized banking system. Hostility to a national bank was one of the foundation stones of the old Democratic party. During the war, with no southern congressmen in Washington and with the necessity of financing the Union Army looming over Congress, New York's bankers finally got their way.

The Union financed the war in three ways: by taxing heavily, by printing paper money, and by borrowing, that is, selling bonds abroad and to private investors within the United States. The principal taxes were an excise tax on luxury goods and an income tax. By the end of the war, the income tax provided about 20 percent of the government's revenue.

The government also authorized the printing of $450 million in paper money. These bills were not redeemable in gold. Called "greenbacks" because they were printed on one side in a special green ink, they had value only because the federal government declared they must be accepted in the payment of debts. When the fighting went badly for the North, they were traded at a discount. By 1865, a greenback with a face value of $1 was worth only sixty-seven cents in gold. This inflation was miniscule compared with that in the Confederacy, where government printing presses ran amok. By 1864, a citizen of Richmond paid $25 for a pound of butter and $50 for a breakfast. By 1865, prices were even higher, and some southern merchants would accept only gold or Union currency, including greenbacks!

The banking interests of the North were uncomfortable with the greenbacks. However, they profited from the government's large-scale borrowing. By the end of the war, the federal government owed its own citizens and some foreigners almost $3 billion, about $75 for every person in the country. Much of this debt was held by the banks. Moreover, big financial houses like Jay Cooke's in Philadelphia reaped huge profits in commissions for their part in selling the bonds.

Free Land

Another momentous innovation of the Civil War years was the Homestead Act. Before the war, southern fear of encouraging the formation of more free states in the

Black homesteaders pose in front of their houses near Westerville, Nebraska, in 1887.

territories had effectively paralyzed any attempt to liberalize the means by which the federal government disposed of its western lands. In May 1862, the system was overhauled. The Homestead Act provided that every head of family who was a citizen or who intended to become a citizen could receive 160 acres of public domain. There was a small filing fee, and homesteaders were required to live for five years on the land that the government gave them. Or, after six months on the land, they could buy it outright for $1.25 per acre.

A few months after approving the Homestead Act, Congress passed the Morrill Act. This law granted each loyal state thirty thousand acres for each member whom that state sent to Congress. The states were to use the money that they made from the sale of these lands to found agricultural colleges. In subsequent years, the founding of sixty-nine land-grant colleges greatly expanded educational opportunities, particularly in the West.

Again, it was a free-spending policy of which the South never would have approved, and the revolutionary infusion of government wealth into the economy spawned an age of unduplicated expansion—and corruption. But the consequences of the war that first preoccupied the nation had to do with people.

"DIXIE" AND "THE BATTLE HYMN"

The unofficial anthems of the Confederate and Union soldiers, "Dixie" and "The Battle Hymn of the Republic," were each stolen from the other side. "Dixie" had been written for a minstrel show by Dan Emmett, the Ohio-born son of an abolitionist. The music to "The Battle Hymn of the Republic" (and its predecessor, "John Brown's Body") was an anonymous southern gospel song, which first had been heard in Charleston, South Carolina, during the 1850s.

They were less interested in preserving the Union than in freeing their fellows. Their bravery won the admiration of a great many northerners. President Lincoln, for example, confessed that he was surprised that blacks made such excellent soldiers, and he revised the racist views that he formerly shared with most white Americans.

Temporarily, at least, so did many Union soldiers. Fighting to free human beings, a positive goal, was better for morale than fighting to prevent secession, a negative aim at best. By 1864, as they marched into battle, Union regiments sang "John Brown's Body," an

Free at Last

No consequence of the Civil War was so basic as the final and irrevocable abolition of slavery in the United States. In a sense, the peculiar institution was doomed when the first shell exploded over Fort Sumter. Slavery was not only an immoral institution, but by the middle of the nineteenth century, it was archaic. It is the ultimate irony of wars that are fought to preserve outdated institutions that war itself is a revolutionary force. Precariously balanced institutions such as slavery cannot survive the disruptions of warfare. Once hundreds of thousands of blacks had left their masters to flee to Union lines, once virtually all the slaves had learned of the war, it was ridiculous to imagine returning to the old ways. Even if the South had eked out a negotiated peace, even if the North had not elected to make emancipation one of its war aims, the Civil War would have killed slavery.

And yet, many southerners refused to recognize this reality until the end. Several times the Confederate Congress turned down suggestions, including one from General Lee, that slaves be granted their freedom if they enlisted in the Confederate Army. Only during the last two months of the conflict did any blacks don Confederate uniforms, and those few never saw action.

On the other side of the lines, 150,000 blacks, most of them runaway slaves, served in the Union Army.

The Thirteenth Amendment guaranteed the end of slavery in the United States. This photograph shows a freed slave couple in Savannah, Georgia.

N O T A B L E   P E O P L E

WILLIAM TECUMSEH SHERMAN (1820–1891)

A war hero second only to Grant in the eyes of northerners, a savage sadist to southerners, William Tecumseh Sherman is probably best described as having had fewer illusions about the nature of war than any other Civil War general.

Although born in Ohio, Sherman spent much of his life in the South, first as a junior officer at remote Texas forts (which he loathed) and then between 1859 and 1861 as head of a military academy in New Orleans (which he liked very much). Sherman was comfortable with southerners and the southern way of life, and he shared the views of white southerners (and most white northerners) toward blacks. Shortly before the war began, he told a group of New Orleanians that "Negroes in the great numbers that exist here must of necessity be slaves."

But Sherman was also a keen nationalist. When he went to New Orleans in 1859, he told his patrons that if Louisiana seceded, he would fight against them.

Beginning as a colonel under Grant, he advanced in rank and command each time Grant did. He was a gruff soldier, as was Grant, and almost as indifferent to the condition of his uniform.

Sherman took over as commander in the West when Grant went east to press the fight against Lee. He led his troops from Chattanooga to Atlanta, the last important southern railroad center that was still functioning normally. After winning several hard-fought battles, he finally broke out of Tennessee, which half a dozen Union commanders had been unable to do.

However, occupation of Atlanta put Sherman in a dangerous position. The single-track railroad to Chattanooga on which his sixty-two thousand men depended for their supplies was vulnerable to Confederate raids, as General John B. Hood, in command of the southern army, promptly demonstrated. Sherman's options were two: retreat to Chattanooga, leaving the southeastern quarter of the Confederacy free from war; or, in violation of standard military procedure, cut loose of supply lines and march three hundred miles through hostile country to the sea, where the Union navy could provision his army.

With Grant's approval (telegraphed to him), Sherman decided to march.

Giving up communications as well as supplies, his men would move in four columns on parallel routes, make ten miles a day, and live off what the land, sometimes called the "breadbasket of the Confederacy," had to offer. What they did not eat, Sherman ordered, they should destroy.

They did. By the time they entered the port city of Savannah, which was defended by only boys and old men, Sherman's troops had cut a swath of destruction forty to sixty miles wide. In a letter to his father,

Union General William Tecumseh Sherman, as photographed in 1865 by Mathew Brady. He is wearing a mourning sash on his left arm for Abraham Lincoln.

W. F. Saylor, a Union soldier, described the kind of havoc they wreaked:

You can form no idea of the amount of property destroyed by us on this raid. All the roads in the state are torn up and the whole tract of country over which we passed is little better than a wilderness. I can't for the life of me think of what the people that are left there are to live on. We have all their Cattle, Horses, Mules, Sheep, Hogs, Sweet Potatoes and Molasses and nearly everything else. We burnt all the Cotton we met which was millions of pounds. . . . A tornado 60 miles in width from Chattanooga to this place 290 miles could not have done half the damage we did.

Saylor said that his detachment never lost pace because they were constantly replacing their tired mules with fresh ones, killing those they no longer needed to deny their use to the Georgians. The same went for cattle. Sherman's army left Atlanta with five thousand head and entered Savannah with ten thousand. They killed so many along the way that the stench of death hung over north Georgia.

They created "Sherman sentinels," charred chimneys that stood where once a house had been, and tied "Sherman bow ties," iron rails torn up from the Atlanta–Savannah railroad that were heated and then twisted around telegraph poles and trees. They looted large plantations so thoroughly that the occupants had little choice but to leave or starve. One household, consisting of two white women and their slaves, rose early in the morning to eat what they could scrape up before the Yankees came, which they did every day for two weeks. On another plantation, the soldiers discovered that the owner, who had fled, had hidden his valuables in a cabbage patch and had replanted the garden. They admired his cleverness, but took or destroyed everything.

Sherman had three reasons for his scorched-earth policy. First, he had to feed his men, who were completely separated from other Union forces. Second, he did not want to fight the pursuing Confederate Army until he had reestablished supply lines, so he had to destroy *their* sources of supply. Finally, and most important, Sherman wanted to punish the South and southerners for causing what he regarded as an unnecessary as well as a costly war. "We are not only fighting hostile armies, but a hostile people," Sherman had said. "We must make old and young, rich and poor, feel the hand of war."

Southerners believed that he went too far, inflicting suffering on defenseless women and children. "I almost felt as if I should like to hang a Yankee myself," wrote Georgian Eliza Frances Andrews in her diary when she saw the "burnt country" around Milledgeville, then the state capital.

In fact, Sherman had ordered his men not to enter private homes; they were to burn only public buildings and railroad properties and bridges. And he made it clear that he would enforce the military penalty for rape and murder, which was death.

Sherman was no sadist, motivated by pleasure in causing suffering. He approached the job of the March to the Sea with a sense of grim necessity. Once in Savannah, with no sound military reason for burning the town or mistreating the people, he administered a liberal truce. When General Johnston surrendered to him in April, Sherman allowed him terms far more generous than Grant had allowed Lee.

By then, of course, the war was over. While it was still on, however, Sherman insisted on facing up to the fact that it was a dirty business and there was no way it could be made mannerly and clean. "Its glory is all moonshine," Sherman said in 1879. "It is only those who have neither fired a shot, nor heard the shrieks and groans of the wounded who cry aloud for blood, more vengeance, more desolation. War is hell." Sherman's real crime was that he refused to encourage the illusion that war could possibly be anything else.

abolitionist hymn, and Julia Ward Howe's more poetic "Battle Hymn of the Republic:"

> *As He died to make men holy,*
> *Let us die to make men free.*

Because the Emancipation Proclamation did not free all slaves, Radical Republicans in Congress proposed the Thirteenth Amendment to the Constitution in February 1865. It provided that "neither slavery nor involuntary servitude, except as a punishment for crime . . . shall exist within the United States." Most of the northern states ratified it within a few months. Once the peculiar institution was destroyed in the United States, only Brazil, the Moslem countries, and backward parts of the world continued to condone the holding of human beings in bondage. It is presumptuous to say that any object is worth six hundred thousand lives, but if one is, it was the destruction of slavery, which required a tragic war to accomplish.

For Further Reading

The titles listed at the end of Chapter 24 are also relevant to this chapter. In addition, J. G. Randall and Richard N. Current, *Lincoln the President* (1945–55), and two collections of essays edited by David Donald, *Lincoln Reconsidered* (1956) and *Why the North Won the Civil War* (1960), are recommended.

26

Bringing the South Back In

The Reconstruction of the Union

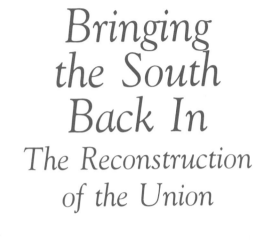

When the guns fell silent in 1865, the people of the South looked about them to see a society, an economy, and a land in tatters. Some southern cities, such as Vicksburg, Atlanta, and Richmond, were flattened, eerie wastelands of charred timber, rubble, and free-standing chimneys. Not many of the South's railroads were operable for more than a few miles. Bridges were gone. River-borne commerce, the lifeblood of the states beyond the Appalachians, had dwindled to a trickle. Old commercial ties with Europe and the North had been snapped clean. All the South's banks were ruined.

Even the cultivation of the soil had been disrupted. The small farms of the men who had served in the ranks lay fallow by the thousands, many of them never to be claimed by their former owners. Great planters who had abandoned their fields to advancing Union armies discovered that weeds and scrub pine were far more ruthless conquerors. The people who had toiled in them, the one-time slaves, were often gone, looking elsewhere for a place to start new lives.

There was little starvation. But many people who once enjoyed lives of ease had to scratch for a living. The poor, white as well as black, were destitute and often dependent on the Union Army's Freedmen's Bureau, a kind of relief agency, for short-term survival.

Freedmen in Richmond, Virginia, in 1865, the year the Civil War ended.

The Reconstruction Debate

In view of the widespread desolation, the word *reconstruction* appears to be an appropriate description of the twelve-year period following the Civil War. But the word does not refer to the literal rebuilding of the South, the laying of bricks and the reclaiming of the land. *Reconstruction* refers to the political process by which the eleven rebel states were restored to a normal constitutional relationship with the twenty-five loyal states and their national government. It was the Union, that great abstraction over which so many had died, that was to be reconstructed.

The Tragic Era

People who lived through both the Civil War and Reconstruction often remembered the postwar period as the unhappier time. White southerners came to think of Reconstruction as an era when they were bullied by northern soldiers, exploited by carpetbaggers (northerners who went south to take advantage of the peculiar economic and political opportunities there) and scalawags (white southern Republicans), and lorded over by ignorant former slaves. Southern blacks remembered Reconstruction as an interlude between slavery and ruthless repression when they had enjoyed full civil equality. It was a brief interlude because they believed that they had been abandoned by their erstwhile northern friends. Northern whites came to look on Reconstruction as a tragic mistake, well-meaning and idealistic but also doomed because of what they saw as the incapacity of the blacks to act as citizens. Attempting to guarantee black equality in the face of southern white resistance was, in the words of Albion W. Tourgee, "a fool's errand."

Perhaps the nearly general sense of disappointment that people felt in looking back was due to the fact that, unlike in the Civil War, for all its gore, there was little glory to be gained in fighting the battles of Reconstruction. Few reputations—northern or southern, white or black, Republican or Democratic—emerged unstained from Reconstruction. More than one historian has suggested that Abraham Lincoln comes down to us as a heroic and sainted figure only because he did not survive the Civil War.

Two False Starts

Actually, Lincoln was on record with having proposed a plan for reconstructing the Union. By the end of 1863, Union armies controlled large parts of the Confederacy, and ultimate victory was reasonable to suppose. To provide for a rapid reconciliation of the sections, Lincoln declared on December 8, 1863, that as soon as 10 percent of the voters in any Confederate state took an oath of allegiance to the Union, the people of that state could organize a government and elect representatives to Congress. Moving quickly, three occupied rebel states complied.

Congress refused to recognize them. Motives for doing so varied as widely as the styles of chin whiskers that politicians were sporting, but two were repeatedly voiced. First, almost all Republican congressmen were alarmed by the broad expansion of presidential powers during the war. No president since Andrew Jackson (still a villain to those Republicans who had been Whigs) had assumed as much authority as Lincoln had—at the expense of Congress. Few congressmen wished to see this trend continue during peacetime, as Lincoln's plan for Reconstruction promised to do.

In addition, Radical Republicans, abolitionists who frequently had been at odds with Lincoln over his reluctance to move against slavery, were alarmed that Lincoln's plan made no allowances whatsoever for the status of the freedmen, as the former slaves were called. They took the lead in framing the Wade-Davis bill of July 1864, which provided that only after 50 percent of the citizens of a state swore an oath of loyalty to the Union could the Reconstruction process begin. And then, the Wade-Davis bill insisted, Congress and not the president would decide when the process was complete.

Lincoln's own party, led by the Radicals, had snuffed out the presidential plan. Lincoln canceled the congressional plan with a pocket veto. When Lee surrendered at Appomattox and Lincoln was assassinated in Washington, no Reconstruction policy existed. Into this void stepped a man who was ill equipped to fill it, Vice President Andrew Johnson of Tennessee.

POCKET VETO

Section 7 of Article I of the Constitution provides that if a president vetoes an act of Congress, he shall return the act to Congress within ten days "with his Objections." If he fails to do so, the act becomes law without his signature.

However, if Congress passes a bill and then adjourns before ten days have passed, as was the case with the Wade-Davis bill, the president can veto it without explanation simply by pocketing it, or failing to sign it. Thus, the pocket veto.

Stubborn Andy Johnson

However Abraham Lincoln might have handled his standoff with Congress, it is difficult to imagine him blundering as badly as his successor did. Like Lincoln, Johnson grew up in stultifying frontier poverty. Unlike Lincoln, who taught himself to read as a boy and was ambitious from the start, Johnson was illiterate as an adult when he swallowed his pride and asked a schoolteacher in Greenville, Tennessee, to teach him to read and write. She did, and later married him, encouraging Johnson's keen political ambitions. Indeed, Andrew Johnson had more political experience than Lincoln or, for that matter, most presidents. Johnson held elective office on every level, from town councilman to congressman to senator and, during the war, governor.

Experience, however, is not the same thing as aptitude. Whereas Lincoln was an instinctive politician who was sensitive to the realities of what he could and could not do, a wizard at reading the characters of his friends and enemies, Johnson was unsubtle, willful, stubborn, and blind to circumstances and personalities.

His administration started badly for him. It was said that Johnson was tipsy when the presidential oath was administered. (He had been taking whiskey for a severe cold, his friends insisted.) In any case, Johnson was sober enough when he laid down a defiant challenge to Congress on the same question that had caused Lincoln to pause: whether the president or the Congress would decide when the southern states were reconstructed.

Andrew Johnson, Lincoln's successor to the presidency, as photographed in 1865 by Mathew Brady.

THE RADICALS' THEORY

In reply to President Johnson's insistence that the Confederate states had never legally seceded and were therefore entitled to representation in Congress, Radical Republicans responded, through the Joint Committee on Reconstruction, that "the States lately in rebellion were, at the close of the war, disorganized communities, without civil government, and without constitutions or other forms, by virtue of which political relations could legally exist between them and the federal government."

Some Radicals spoke of "state suicide." Others bluntly declared the southern states to be "conquered provinces."

Johnson: They Are Already States

Johnson based his case for presidential supervision on the assumption that the southern states had never left the Union because it was constitutionally impossible to do so: the Union could not be dissolved. Johnson and the entire Republican party and most northern Democrats had held to that principle in 1861. He would stick by it in 1865.

There had indeed been a war and an entity known as the Confederate States of America. But individuals had fought the one and created the other; states had not. Punish the rebels, Johnson said—he already was famous for having said that Jefferson Davis should be hanged for treason—but not Virginia, Alabama, and the rest. They were still states in the *United* States of America. Seating their duly elected representatives in the Congress was a purely administrative matter. The president, the nation's chief administrator, would decide how and when to do it.

The reasoning was neat: the constitutional theory was sound. Johnson's trouble was that he could not see beyond neatness and soundness to the world of flesh, blood, and human feelings. For the sake of principled consistency he was willing to make light of the fact that a bloody war had just been concluded. Most northerners blamed that war on the southerners, particularly the arrogant, antagonistic, rich slaveowners who, when Johnson announced that he would adopt Lincoln's plan of Reconstruction (with some minor changes), began to assume the leadership that they always had held in their states.

In the summer of 1865, the president began to pardon prominent Confederates, thus making them eligible to hold public office. In the elections held in the fall, the voters of the South sent many of these very people to Congress. Among the men who arrived in

Washington to claim their seats were four former Confederate generals and, as senator from Georgia, former Confederate vice president, Alexander F. Stephens.

The Radicals and Their Goals

Once again, the Republicans in Congress, led by the Radicals, said no to a president. The southern senators and representatives were turned away at the door. Angrily the Radicals informed Johnson that they would not welcome traitors into their midst.

None were more disappointed in Johnson than the Radicals. Because of Johnson's many vilifications of the southern planter class, the Radicals had thought that the president was one of them.

But he was not and never had been. Johnson was not even a Republican. He was a traditional southern Jacksonian Democrat who had run with Lincoln in 1864 on the *Union* party ticket. He had scant sympathy for Republican policies such as the protective tariff, the Homestead Act and other land-grant bills, and the central route of the transcontinental railroad (which was then under construction).

Nor did Johnson share the Radicals' views on the place of the blacks in the postwar South. He was on record as having said, "Damn the negroes. I am fighting these traitorous aristocrats, their masters." He fully shared the racial prejudice of most poor southern whites. He hated the slaveowners and was glad that slavery was dead; but he did not regard blacks as the equals of whites, citizens with full and equal rights.

A few Radical Republicans shared his prejudice. They were not in favor of blacks voting in their own states. But they realized that if the Republican party was to remain in power, it was necessary to guarantee

---

OLD THAD STEVENS

Few Radical Republicans were as sincerely committed to racial equality as Thaddeus Stevens of Pennsylvania. In his will he insisted on being buried in a black cemetery because blacks were banned from the one where he normally would have been interred.

Nevertheless, even Stevens came to terms with the racism of those northern whites who refused the vote to the blacks in their own states. In order to win their support for black suffrage in the South, Stevens argued that the situation was different in the South because blacks made up the majority of loyal Union men there. "I am for negro suffrage in every rebel state," he said. "If it be just, it should not be denied; if it be necessary, it should be adopted; if it be a punishment to traitors, they deserve it."

---

black civil rights in the South; blacks were the only southerners who would dependably vote Republican.

Other Radical Republicans, such as Thaddeus Stevens and George W. Julian in the House and Charles Sumner and Benjamin F. Wade in the Senate, were sincerely committed to the principle and practice of racial equality. They were offended not only by slavery, but by the degraded status accorded the blacks. Early in 1866, when Johnson made it clear that he was opposed to black equality in his veto of the Freedmen's Bureau bill, and the Johnsonian southern states defined an inferior civil status for blacks, the Radicals took the offensive.

Dealing with Disorder: The Freedmen's Bureau

The reaction of most blacks to the news of their freedom was to test it by leaving the plantations and farms on which they had lived as slaves.

Many congregated in cities that were traditionally associated with free blacks. Others, after a period of wandering, gathered in ramshackle camps in the countryside.

In order to cope with the potential social disorder created by this situation, Congress had established the Freedmen's Bureau, under the command of General O. O. Howard, and administered by the army. The Bureau provided relief for the freedmen (and some whites) in the form of food, clothing, and shelter; attempted to find jobs for them; set up hospitals and schools run by idealistic New England women, often at the risk of their lives; and otherwise tried to ease the transition from slavery to freedom for the South as well as the former slaves. When the Freedmen's Bureau bill was first passed, Congress had assumed that properly established state governments would be able to carry out these services within a year after the end of the hostilities, so the Bureau was scheduled to expire in March 1866.

But Congress did not recognize the Johnsonian state governments, and, in the meantime, those governments had adopted their own policy for adjusting to social conditions in a South without slavery.

Dealing with Disorder: The Black Codes

Because blacks as slaves had been the backbone of the southern labor force, the southern legislatures naturally expected the blacks to continue to bring in the crops after the war. And the blacks wanted the work. Far from providing the forty-acre farms that blacks thought they were going to be granted, however, the Johnsonian state governments did not even establish a sys-

The Freedmen's Bureau established schools to help former slaves and their children adjust to freedom.

tem of employment that treated the blacks as free men and women. On the contrary, the black codes defined a form of second-class citizenship that looked to the blacks like a step or two back into slavery.

In some states, blacks were permitted to work only as domestic servants or in agriculture, just what they had done as slaves. Other states made it illegal for blacks to live in towns and cities. In no state were blacks allowed to vote or to bear arms. In fact, few of the civil liberties listed in the Bill of Rights were accorded them.

Mississippi required freedmen to sign twelve-month labor contracts before January 10 of each year. Those who failed to do so could be arrested, and their labor sold to the highest bidder in a manner that was strongly reminiscent of the detested slave auction. Those blacks who reneged on their contracts were not to be paid for the work that they already had performed.

Not surprisingly, the Radicals were infuriated. There was little doubt in their minds that the southerners were trying to undo the consequences of the war.

Ten Critical Months

In February 1866, Congress passed a bill to extend the life of the Freedmen's Bureau pending a solution of the stalemate with the president on Reconstruction policy. Johnson vetoed it on the grounds that military government was unconstitutional in states of the Union, which he insisted the southern states were.

In March 1866, Congress passed a bill to grant full citizenship to the freedmen, and once again Johnson vetoed it on the grounds that the Constitution provided that each state defined the terms of citizenship within its borders.

Once again the president's interpretation of the Constitution was reasonable enough. Once again, however, he refused to recognize political realities. In the summer of 1866, when white mobs in several southern cities attacked black communities and killed more than a hundred people, more and more northerners began to ask themselves who had won the war—the antislavery North, or the southern slaveowners? Resentment of

Johnson was so high in Congress that the Radicals picked up enough support to pass both the Freedmen's Bureau bill and the Civil Rights bill over his veto.

More was needed, however, because enforcement of both laws was entrusted to the army, and in the case of *Ex parte Milligan* (1866), the Supreme Court declared that the military had no power in areas free from hostilities.

The only alternative to the collapse of the Radical cause was a constitutional amendment. The Fourteenth, proposed in June 1866, stipulated that high-ranking Confederate leaders—the men who headed many of the Johnson state governments—could not vote or hold public office until pardoned by *Congress*. More important, the Fourteenth Amendment provided that no state could deny the rights of state citizenship to any United States citizens (the freedmen).

If ratified, the Fourteenth would, of course, preclude

DISCOURAGING REBELLION

Among other provisions of the Fourteenth Amendment, the former Confederate states were forbidden to repay "any debt or obligation incurred in aid of insurrection or rebellion against the United States." By stinging foreign and domestic individuals and banks that had lent money to the rebel states, the amendment was putting future supporters of rebellion on notice of the consequences of their actions.

southern states from passing any more laws like the black codes. However, it also promised to cancel northern state laws that forbade blacks to vote, and in that aspect of the amendment Johnson saw an opportunity. Calculating that many northerners, particularly in the Midwest, would rather have Confederates in the gov-

Entered according to act of Congress in the year 1872 by Currier & Ives, in the Office of the Librarian of Congress at Washington.

ROBERT C. DE LARGE, M.C. of S. Carolina   JEFFERSON H. LONG, M.C. of Georgia

U.S. Senator H.R. REVELS, of Mississippi   BENJ. S. TURNER, M.C. of Alabama.   JOSIAH T. WALLS, M.C. of Florida.   JOSEPH H. RAINY, M.C. of S. Carolina.   R. BROWN ELLIOT, M.C. of S. Carolina.

A Currier and Ives print of the first black United States senator and black members of the House of Representatives in the 41st and 42nd congresses.

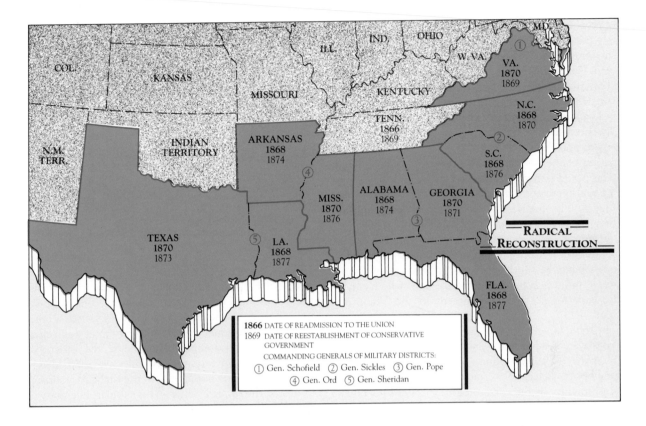

1866 DATE OF READMISSION TO THE UNION
1869 DATE OF REESTABLISHMENT OF CONSERVATIVE GOVERNMENT
COMMANDING GENERALS OF MILITARY DISTRICTS:
① Gen. Schofield ② Gen. Sickles ③ Gen. Pope
④ Gen. Ord ⑤ Gen. Sheridan

ernment than grant full civil equality to blacks, Johnson decided to campaign against the Radicals on the amendment issue in the 1866 congressional election.

The Radical Triumph

The first step was the formal organization of a political party. Johnson, Republican allies such as Secretary of State Seward and a few senators, and some Democrats therefore called a convention of the National Union party in Philadelphia. The message of the convention was sectional reconciliation; to symbolize it, the meeting was opened by a procession of northern and southern Johnson supporters in which couples made up of one southerner and one northerner marched arm in arm down the center aisle of the hall.

Unhappily for Johnson, the first couple was South Carolina governor James L. Orr, a huge, fleshy mountain of a man, and Massachusetts governor John A. Andrew, a little fellow with a way of looking intimidated. When Orr seemed to drag the mousy Andrew down the length of the hall, Radical politicians and cartoonists had a field day. Johnson's National Union movement, they said, was dominated by rebels and preached in the North by cowardly stooges.

In the fall, Johnson sealed his own doom. He toured the Midwest seeking support—he called it his "swing around the circle"—and from the start discredited himself. Johnson had learned his oratorical skills in the rough-and-tumble, stump-speaking tradition of eastern Tennessee. There, voters liked a red-hot debate between politicians who scorched each other and the hecklers that challenged them.

Midwesterners also liked that kind of ruckus, but not, it turned out, from their president. When Radical hecklers taunted Johnson and he responded gibe for gibe, Radicals shook their heads sadly that a man of so little dignity should be sitting in the seat of Washington and Lincoln. Drunk again, they supposed.

The result was a landslide. Most of Johnson's candidates were defeated. The Republican party, now led by the Radicals, controlled more than two-thirds of the seats in both houses of Congress, enough to override every veto that Johnson dared to make.

The Radical Experiment

The Radical Republicans' Reconstruction program was adopted in a series of laws that were passed by the Fortieth Congress in 1867. These dissolved the southern state governments that had been organized under

Johnson and partitioned the Confederacy into five military provinces, each commanded by a major general. The army would enforce order while voters were registered, blacks and those whites who were not specifically disenfranchised under the terms of the Fourteenth Amendment. The constitutional conventions that these voters elected were required to abolish slavery, give the vote to adult black males, and ratify the Thirteenth and Fourteenth Amendments. After examination of their work by Congress, the reconstructed states would be admitted to the Union, and their senators and representatives could take their seats in the Capitol. The Radicals assumed that at least some of these congressmen would be Republicans.

Tennessee complied immediately with these terms and was never really affected by the Radical experiment in remaking the South. Ironically, it was Andrew Johnson, as military governor during the war, who had laid the basis for a stable government in the Volunteer State.

In 1868, largely as a result of the black vote, six more states were readmitted. Alabama, Arkansas, Florida, Louisiana, North Carolina, and South Carolina sent Republican delegations, including some blacks, to Washington. In the remaining four states—Georgia, Mississippi, Texas, and Virginia—because some whites obstructed every attempt to set up a government in which blacks would participate, the military continued to govern until 1870.

In the meantime, with Congress more firmly under Radical control, Thaddeus Stevens, Charles Sumner, and other Radicals attempted to establish the supremacy of the legislative over the judicial and executive branches of the government. With the Supreme Court they were immediately successful. By threatening to reduce the size of the Court or even to try to abolish it, the Radicals intimidated the justices. Chief Justice Salmon P. Chase decided to ride out the difficult era by ignoring all cases that dealt with Reconstruction issues, just what the Radicals wanted.

As for the presidency, Congress took partial control of the army away from Johnson and then struck at his right to choose his own cabinet. The Tenure of Office Act forbade the president to remove any appointed official who had been confirmed by the Senate without first getting the Senate's approval of the dismissal.

The Impeachment of Andrew Johnson

Although Johnson had attempted to obstruct Radical Reconstruction politically—by urging southern whites not to cooperate—he had come to terms with the constitutional facts of the Radicals' control of the gov-

A ticket of admission to the Senate gallery to witness the impeachment of Andrew Johnson.

ernment. He had little choice. But he refused to obey the Tenure of Office Act on the same constitutional basis. To allow Congress to decide if and when a president could fire a member of his own cabinet was a clear infringement of the independence of the executive branch of the government. In February 1868, determined to have one last fight with the Radicals, Johnson dismissed the single Radical in his cabinet, Secretary of War Edwin Stanton.

Strictly speaking, it could be argued that the Tenure of Office Act did not apply to Stanton's dismissal because he had been appointed by Lincoln, not by Johnson. Nevertheless, Congress moved ahead. As the Constitution required, the House of Representatives drew up articles of impeachment, passed them, and appointed a committee to serve as Johnson's prosecutors. The Senate acted as the jury in the trial, and the chief justice as presiding judge.

All but two of the eleven articles of impeachment dealt with the Tenure of Office Act. As expected, Johnson's defenders in the Senate argued that it did not apply to the Stanton case, and, in any event, its constitutionality was highly unlikely. The other two articles condemned Johnson for disrespect of Congress. These charges were undeniably true; Johnson had spared few bitter words in describing the Radicals who dominated both houses. But the president's defenders argued that sharp and vulgar language did not qualify as the "high crimes and misdemeanors" that the Constitution stipulates as the reason for impeachment.

After two tense months, the Senate voted thirty-five to nineteen for conviction. Because the Constitution requires a two-thirds majority to convict (thirty-six to eighteen minimum in this case), Johnson remained in office by a single vote.

In fact, it was not so close. About six Republican senators had agreed privately that if their votes were

WAS JOHNSON IMPEACHED?

Andrew Johnson *was* impeached, the only American president to be so. *Impeachment* is not removal from office but the bringing of charges, the equivalent of indictment in a criminal trial. The official who is found guilty of the articles of impeachment is convicted and removed from office (and may be sent to prison or otherwise penalized if convicted in a subsequent criminal trial). Johnson was *not* convicted of the charges brought against him.

WHAT IF JOHNSON HAD BEEN CONVICTED?

What would it have meant for the structure of American government if Andrew Johnson had been removed from office for, in effect, disagreeing with Congress? It might have been a major step toward the parliamentary form of government that is practiced in most representative democracies. Whereas in the United States the executive branch of government is separate from the legislative branch, in parliamentary systems like that of Canada and Great Britain, the prime minister, the head of government, must be a member of Parliament and supported by a majority of the members of Parliament. If the prime minister loses that support, he or she loses the office and Parliament elects a new prime minister or is dissolved for new elections. The American presidency would still have been constitutionally independent had Johnson been removed, but the precedent probably would have emboldened later Congresses to remove presidents they disliked. As it was, Johnson's acquittal and, in 1973, Richard Nixon's resignation before he was impeached, have helped to preserve the independence of the executive branch.

essential to acquit the president, they would vote for him. They were practical men. They knew that an anti-Johnson vote was the popular vote back home. But they did not believe that the president should be removed from office. In addition to their constitutional compunctions, they simply did not share the extreme Radicals' intense personal loathing for Johnson. Moreover, they were content to wait for the autumn of 1868, when the voters would elect a new president. He would almost certainly be the Republican nominee and the choice of the Radicals, war hero Ulysses S. Grant.

Grant and the Fifteenth Amendment

Grant easily defeated New York governor Horatio Seymour in the electoral college by a vote of 214 to 80. However, the popular vote was much closer, a hair's

breadth in some states. Nationwide, Grant won by 300,000 votes, and, some rudimentary arithmetic showed, he got 500,000 black votes in the southern states. Grant lost New York, the largest state, by a very thin margin. Had blacks been able to vote in that northern state, Grant would have carried the state easily. In Indiana, Grant won by a razor-thin margin. Had blacks been able to vote in that northern state, it would not have been close.

In other words, the future of the Republican party seemed to depend on the black man's right to vote in the northern as well as the southern states. Consequently, the Radical Congress drafted a third "Civil War Amendment." The Fifteenth forbade the states of both the North and the South to deny the vote to any person on the basis of "race, color, or previous condition of servitude." Because Republican governments favorable to blacks still controlled most of the southern states, the amendment was easily ratified. The Radical Reconstruction program was complete.

Reconstruction Legends

By the end of the nineteenth century and increasingly after 1900, a legend of Reconstruction emerged in

This photograph of Ulysses S. Grant is a print from a restored glass plate negative.

American popular consciousness. According to widespread belief among white people, Reconstruction was a time of degradation and humiliation for white southerners. Soldiers bullied them, and they languished under the political domination of ignorant former slaves who were incapable of good citizenship, carpetbaggers, and scalawags.

The "Black Reconstruction" governments, the legend continued, were hopelessly corrupt as well as unjust. The blacks, carpetbaggers, and scalawags looted the treasuries and demeaned the honor of the southern states. Only by heroic efforts did the whites, through the Democratic party, *redeem* the southern states once they had retaken control of them. Some versions of the legend glamorized the role of secret organizations, such as the Ku Klux Klan, in redeeming the South.

The Legend in Perspective

As in all legends, there was a kernel of truth in this view of Reconstruction. The Radical governments did spend freely. There was plenty of corruption in south-

This cartoon from the British magazine Puck *illustrates the view many southerners held of Reconstruction as ordered by Ulysses S. Grant and the Republicans. It was, the southerners believed, a harsh and heavy burden forced upon a weary but solid South.*

ern government; for example, the Republican governor of Louisiana, Henry C. Warmoth, banked $100,000 during a year when his salary was $8,000.

Sometimes the theft was open and ludicrous. Former slaves in control of South Carolina's lower house voted a payment of $1,000 to one of their number who had lost that amount in a bet on a horse race. Self-serving carpetbaggers were numerous, as were vindictive scalawags and incompetent black officials.

Large governmental expenditures were unavoidable in the postwar South, however. Southern society was being built from scratch—an expensive proposition. Moreover, it was the lot of the Radical state governments to provide social services—for white as well as blacks—that had simply been ignored in the southern states before the Civil War. The modern public-school systems in some southern states were not founded until Reconstruction.

Corruption is probably inevitable in times of massive government spending, no matter who is in charge, and shady deals were not unique to southern Republican governments during the 1860s and 1870s. The most flagrant theft from public treasuries during the period was the work of Democrats in New York, members of the same party as the Redeemers. In fact, the champion southern thief of the era was not a Radical but a Redeemer, the first post-Reconstruction treasurer of Mississippi, who absconded with $415,000.

As for the carpetbaggers, many of them brought much-needed capital to the South. They were interested in making money, to be sure, but in the process of developing the South, not as mere exploiters. Many of the scalawags were by no means unlettered "poor white trash," as the legend had it, but southern Whigs who had never been happy with secession and who, after the war, drifted naturally, if briefly, into the Republican party that their northern fellow Whigs had joined.

The blacks who rose to high office in the Reconstruction governments were rarely ignorant former field hands, but well-educated, refined, even rather conservative men. Moreover, whatever the malfeasances of Reconstruction, the blacks could not be blamed; they never controlled the government of any southern state. For a short time, they were the majority in the legislatures of South Carolina and Mississippi (where blacks were the majority of the population), but there were only two black senators, Blanche K. Bruce and Hiram Revels, both cultivated men from Mississippi. And no black ever served as a governor, although Lieutenant Governor P. B. S. Pinchback of Louisiana briefly acted in that capacity when the white governor was out of the state.

Hiram Revels (left) and Blanche K. Bruce (right), both of Mississippi, were elected to the United States Congress during Reconstruction.

Redemption

For all this, Reconstruction was probably doomed from the day Congress rejected proposals to provide—"forty acres and a mule"—for each family of freedmen. With no economic foundation for their civil equality, the blacks of the South remained abysmally poor and therefore dependent on landowners—the former great planters—for their sustenance. When southern landowners concluded that it was to their interest to eliminate the blacks from political life, they could do so by threatening unemployment.

Unpropertied former slaves could not command the respect of poorer whites, who provided most of the members of terrorist organizations like the Ku Klux Klan, which was founded in 1868 by former slave trader and Confederate general Nathan Bedford Forrest. For several years these nightriders, identities concealed from authorities by masks, frightened, beat, and even murdered blacks who insisted on voting. Congress outlawed and, within a few years, effectively suppressed the Klan and similar organizations, but in many areas the damage was already done: blacks were no longer voting.

Congress was unable to counter the conviction of increasing numbers of white southerners that only through "white supremacy," the slogan of the southern Democratic parties, could the South be redeemed. In most southern states, where whites were the majority, an overwhelming white vote on this issue alone was enough to install legislators and governors who promptly found effective ways to disenfranchise the blacks.

Disillusionment in the North

Northern Democrats opposed Radical Reconstruction from the start, in part because of their traditional dislike for blacks, in part because Radical Republican control of the southern states reduced the Democrats to minority status. In 1872, however, Grant and the Radicals ran into opposition from another direction.

Led by former Radicals like Charles Sumner, Senator Carl Schurz of Missouri, and the influential editors E. L. Godkin of *The Nation* and Horace Greeley of the New York *Tribune*, the self-styled Liberal Republicans proclaimed Radical Reconstruction a failure. The ideal of black equality was noble but misguided, they said. Blacks voted unthinkingly, as a mass, much like the Irish immigrants of the North. They were unfit citizens who were not really capable of exercising political power in a virtuous republic.

The Liberal Republicans did not much like the southern Redeemers. But they preferred them, as white men, in control of the southern states to the continuing

VICTORIA WOODHULL: CRUSADER OR CHARLATAN? (1838–1927)

Presidential candidate and publisher of a feminist newspaper, Victoria Claflin Woodhull.

After the flurry of attention given the Seneca Falls conference of 1848 and the reform costume—bloomers—Americans came to pay less attention to the feminist movement. Elizabeth Cady Stanton, Susan B. Anthony, and other leaders continued to write and speak for the cause of equal rights for women, but slavery was the issue that riveted American reformers during the 1850s and the Civil War. Indeed, Stanton and Anthony tacitly agreed that the condition of the blacks needed attention more urgently than did the problems of women. At the end of the war, however, with voting rights for blacks on the agenda in Washington, feminists renewed their campaign for a constitutional amendment that would guarantee women's right to vote. They saw no reason why

that reform should not be written into the Fourteenth and Fifteenth Amendments, which guaranteed civil equality for blacks.

Many of the Radical Republicans agreed with them: Bluff Ben Wade and Charles Sumner in the Senate; Thaddeus Stevens and others in the House; Horace Greeley, editor of the New York *Tribune;* abolitionists like William Lloyd Garrison and Theodore Dwight Weld. The majority of the Republican party, however, found it easier to transcend racism than the conviction that women were intended to occupy the "domestic sphere." Least of all, they thought, should women dirty their hands in the world of politics. No mention was made of sex in the Reconstruction amendments.

In the meantime, a most remarkable pair of feminists

burst on the scene and, for a few years, seemed to have taken the leadership of the women's movement away from the generation of Seneca Falls.

Tennessee Claflin and Victoria Claflin Woodhull had been raised by parents who ran a traveling snake-oil show in the Midwest. While Father and Mother Claflin mesmerized the audiences of small-town and country folk into believing that the family's Elixir of Life (with Vicky's picture on the label) would solve all their problems, Victoria and Tennessee and their eight brothers and sisters circulated through the crowd selling the concoction at $1 a bottle.

In 1853, when she was fifteen years old, Victoria married a physician (possibly a quack) named Channing Woodhull. With her sister and a brother named Hebron in tow, she made a modest living as a spiritualist medium, communicating with the dead for a price.

Victoria divorced Woodhull in 1864, apparently dumped Hebron, and moved to New York City with Tennessee. There they had the good fortune to meet Cornelius Vanderbilt. The Commodore was swept off his feet by the bold and beautiful sisters with the silver tongues. He set them up in a stockbrokerage house, Woodhull and Claflin. It was unheard-of for women to operate such a business, but the sisters prospered, taking clients recommended by Vanderbilt and probably getting tips from the Commodore on likely investments.

By 1870, they had made enough money to found a feminist newspaper, *Woodhull and Claflin's Weekly*. It is difficult to say why they should have taken an interest in the women's cause if they were not sincerely dedicated to it. If money was their object, they did not need it; they were doing quite well as stockbrokers. And yet, it is also difficult to explain them as altruistic crusaders. Not only did the *Weekly* campaign for sexual equality, but Victoria and Tennessee dabbled in class revolution (they published Karl Marx's *Communist Manifesto*) and free love—two ideas that were offensive to the conventional middle-class Americans whom Stanton and Anthony were trying to reach.

But Victoria sometimes seemed to be more avid for free love than for votes for women. Free love was one of the planks in Victoria's platform when she announced that she would run for the presidency in 1872. Sharing the Equal Rights party nomination with her was Frederick Douglass, who refused to dignify the farce by withdrawing his name. The ticket received few votes, but, in the meantime, the *Weekly* had begun to prosper anew through a novel editorial policy.

Campaigning against the hypocrisy of conventional sexual morals, the sisters announced that they had acquired the books of a famous brothel that catered to New York's upper classes. Whether they really had such information, their announcement seems to have triggered a minor panic, and money flowed into the *Weekly* offices. The books were never published.

Also in 1872, the sisters made a serious miscalculation. In the *Weekly*, they accused the Reverend Henry Ward Beecher, New York's most famous preacher, of carrying on an adulterous affair with one of his parishioners, Mrs. Theodore Tilton. (Tennessee was probably carrying on an affair with Mrs. Tilton's husband at the same time.)

Although clearly guilty as charged, Beecher managed to weather the storm and to have his revenge. Victoria and Tennessee were indicted and tried on obscenity charges.

The trial dragged on for several years and ruined the sisters financially, but they were irrepressible. In 1877, they moved to England, where Victoria married a wealthy banker. She subdued herself somewhat, but, now protected by the custom that allowed the upper-class English to be eccentric, she never gave up her public lecturing. It was as though she never quite got the thrill of show business out of her blood.

Was Woodhull simply a charlatan who latched on to feminism simply because it drew a crowd even bigger than that drawn by the Elixir of Life? More conventional feminists like Stanton and Anthony thought so. They blamed the sluggishness of the equal-rights movement during the 1870s and 1880s on Victoria's mischief. Many historians have agreed, considering the sisters a diverting phenomenon but not true reformers. Since the 1960s, however, as the women's movement successfully expanded beyond civil issues to the social side of women's status in the United States, many have come to regard Victoria Woodhull as a crusader who was ahead of her time. Charlatan or crusader, she was a woman of extraordinary independence.

The Ku Klux Klan, an organization calling for white supremacy, terrorized blacks who tried to exercise their newly won right to vote.

ferment and conflict that seemed inevitable as long as the Grant administration used the army to enforce the civil rights of the blacks.

The Liberals failed to defeat Grant. By 1876, however, many more northerners shared their disillusionment with the Radical experiment, and there was little protest when, early in that year, Democrats took control of Mississippi. Only three southern states remained Republican: South Carolina, Florida, and Louisiana.

The Disputed Election

The Democratic candidate in 1876, New York governor Samuel J. Tilden, called for the removal of troops from these three states, which would bring the white-supremacy Democrats to power. The Republican candidate, Governor Rutherford B. Hayes of Ohio, ran on a platform that guaranteed black rights in the

South, but Hayes was known to be skeptical of black capabilities and a personal friend of a number of white southern politicians.

When the votes were counted, Hayes's opinions seemed to be beside the point. Tilden won a close popular vote, and he appeared to sweep the electoral college by a vote of 204 to 165. However, Tilden's margin of victory included the electoral votes of South Carolina, Florida, and Louisiana, where Republicans still controlled the state governments. After receiving telegrams from party leaders in New York, officials there declared that in reality Hayes had carried their states. According to these returns, Hayes had eked out a 185 to 184 electoral vote victory.

It was not that easy. When official returns reached Washington, there were two sets from each of the three disputed states—one set for Tilden, and one for Hayes. Because the Constitution did not provide for such an occurrence, a special commission was established to decide which set of returns was valid. Five members of each house of Congress and five members of the Supreme Court sat on this panel. Seven of them were Republicans; seven were Democrats; and one, David Davis of Illinois, a Supreme Court justice and Abraham Lincoln's former law partner, was known as an independent. Because no one was interested in determining the case on its merits, each commissioner fully intending to vote for his party's candidate, the burden of naming the next president of the United States fell on Davis's shoulders.

He did not like it. No matter how honestly he came to his decision, half the voters in the country would call for his scalp because their candidate had lost. Davis prevailed on friends in Illinois to get him off the hook by naming him to an empty Senate seat. He thus was able to resign from the Court and, therefore, the special commission. His replacement was a Republican, and the stage was set for the Republicans to "steal" the election.

The commission voted on strict party lines, eight to seven, to accept the Hayes returns from Louisiana, Florida, and South Carolina—thus giving Rutherford B. Hayes the presidency by a single electoral vote. Had that been all there was to it, there might have been further trouble. At a series of meetings, however, a group of prominent northern and southern politicians and businessmen came to an informal agreement that was satisfactory to the political leaders of both sections.

The End of Reconstruction

The "Compromise of 1877" involved several commitments, not all of them honored, for northern investment in the South. Also not honored was a vague agreement on the part of some conservative southerners to build a "lily-white" Republican party in the South based on economic and social views that they shared with northern conservatives.

As to the disputed election, Hayes would be permitted to move into the White House without resistance by either northern or southern Democrats. In return, he would withdraw the last troops from South Carolina, Florida, and Louisiana, thus allowing the Democratic party in these states to oust the Republicans and destroy the political power of the blacks.

Despite the proclamations before Inauguration Day that Democrats would fight if Tilden were not elected, there was no trouble. This was not because the men who hammered out the Compromise of 1877 were so very powerful. It merely reflected the growing disinterest of Americans in the issues of the Civil War and Reconstruction and their increasing preoccupation with the fabulous economic growth of the country. The southern blacks, of course, were the casualties of this watershed year, but since the price they paid was suppression, few whites heard their complaints and fewer were interested.

For Further Reading

As is the case with the Civil War, J. G. Randall and David Donald, *The Civil War and Reconstruction* (1961), is the standard one-volume account. It can be worthwhile to go back to W. A. Dunning, *Reconstruction: Political and Economic* (1907), which is the classic depiction of Reconstruction as a time when the South was brutally oppressed. By way of contrast, see W. E. B. DuBois, *Black Reconstruction* (1935), which set out to answer Dunning by showing how the period was one of justice to southern blacks and by no means repressive of whites.

Richard N. Current, *Three Carpetbag Governors* (1967), gives a balanced view of northerners in the South. A. W. Trelease has the most informative book on the KKK, *White Terror: The Ku Klux Klan Conspiracy and Southern Reconstruction* (1971).

On the Johnson crisis, the most sympathetic book is Howard K. Beale, *The Critical Year* (1930). Richard N. Current, *Old Thad Stevens* (1942), and Fawn Brodie, *Thaddeus Stevens: Scourge of the South* (1959), approach the issue somewhat differently. On Grant, see William B. Hesseltine's biography, *U. S. Grant, Politician* (1935). On the election of 1876, see C. Vann Woodward, *Reunion and Reaction: The Compromise of 1877 and the End of Reconstruction* (1951).

27

Laying the Foundations of Modern America

The Development of Railroads to 1900

In 1876, the American people celebrated their nation's centennial. It was a hundred years since the Founding Fathers had pledged their lives, their fortunes, and their sacred honor to the causes of liberty and independence. The party was held in Philadelphia, where the Declaration had been written, signed, and proclaimed. And it was a splendid show, the first of the great world's fairs to be held in the United States. Sprawling over the hills of Fairmount Park, housed in more than two hundred buildings, the Centennial Exposition remained open for half the year and dazzled 10 million visitors with its displays of American history, ways of life, and products.

The emphasis was on the products of the present and future rather than on the ideals of the past. The center of the fair was not the Declaration of Independence or any other statement of political principle. It was in Machinery Hall, a building that covered twenty acres and in which were arrayed the latest inventions and technological improvements: from typewriters

A view of Chicago in 1866 shows the proliferation of railroad tracks around Lake Michigan.

and the telephone through new kinds of looms and lathes for factories to a variety of agricultural machines.

Towering above all the pulleys and belts, five times the height of a man, was the largest steam engine ever built, the giant Corliss. Hissing, rumbling, chugging, and gleaming in enamel, nickel plate, brass, and copper, the monster powered every other machine in the building and was unequivocally the heart of the exposition. It was to the giant Corliss engine that President Ulysses S. Grant came in order to open the fair. When he threw the switch that set Machinery Hall in motion, he silently proclaimed that Americans were not just free and independent, but they were hitching their future to machines that made and moved things more quickly, more cheaply, and in far greater quantities than, just a few years earlier, the most visionary inventor could have imagined.

The Corliss steam engine, displayed at the Philadelphia Centennial Exposition in 1876, was one of many machines that brought about American industrialization.

An Era of Unparalleled Growth

There seemed to be few limits on American dreams in 1876. With the memories of the Civil War fading and Reconstruction unmistakably in its death throes, a new era of movement, growth, and progress was in full swing. Immigrants poured into the United States from all over Europe. Both immigrants and native-born Americans fanned out over the West to tame more land in one generation than had been settled during all the years since 1607. Between 1865 and 1900, the population of the United States more than doubled, from fewer than 36 million to 76 million people. Including the former Confederacy, there were thirty-six states in 1865. By 1900, there were forty-five.

The wealth of the American people grew even more rapidly than population. At the end of the Civil War, the annual production of goods was valued at $2 billion. It increased more than six times in thirty-five years, to $13 billion in 1900. At the center of this upheaval, as at the center of the Centennial Exposition, was the machine—industrialization.

The Emergence of an Industrial Nation

Even in 1860, the United States had been a major industrial power, the fourth largest in the world with more than one hundred thousand factories capitalized at $1 billion. But before the Civil War there was no doubt that the United States was primarily a farmer's country. Not only did more than 70 percent of the population live on farms or in small farm towns, but an even greater proportion of the population thought in agrarian terms and the majority of politicians catered to their point of view. In 1860, scarcely more than 1 million people worked in industrial jobs. Because many of them were women and children who did not vote, factory workers were an insignificant political force, scarcely more important to policy makers than were blacks or Indians.

By 1876, this was rapidly changing. Only the next year, a nationwide strike by railway workers would shake the nation to its foundations, and more upheavals were to come. By 1900, $10 billion was invested in American factories, and 5 million people worked in industrial jobs. During the first years of the 1890s, the industrial production of the United States surpassed that of Great Britain to put the United States in first place in the world, a position it has not yet relinquished.

Most important of all, by 1900 the American people understood that, for good or ill, they lived in an industrial capitalist nation and no longer in an agrarian republic. Their fate was rooted more deeply in black coal and red iron than in the soil.

A Country Made for Industry

Now that the preconditions of industrial development are understood, it can be seen that the United States was virtually destined to undergo this transformation. Unlike in the underdeveloped countries today, both foreign and domestic capital was readily available to Americans. Because of the western lands, America's agricultural base was constantly expanding, producing cheap food, and freeing capital for industrial investment.

Foreign capitalists found American opportunities irresistible once the Union victory in the Civil War ensured a stable national government that was committed to protecting private property. Foreign money was indispensable to the industrial development of the United States. By 1900, over $3.4 billion in foreign wealth, much of it from England, fueled the American economy. Thanks to investors from abroad, Americans had to divert only 11 to 14 percent of their national income into industrial growth, compared with 20 percent in Great Britain half a century earlier and in the Soviet Union some decades later. As a result, the experience of industrialization was far less painful in the New World than in the Old. Americans had to suffer less on behalf of the future.

Factories need people to work them, and in its labor supply, too, America was peculiarly blessed. The fecund and adaptable farm population provided a large pool of literate and mechanically inclined people to fill the skilled jobs created by the new order. American farmers were an odd breed. They were not peasants, attached to a particular plot of earth, timid before the seasons, and suspicious of any way of life but the one they knew. On the contrary, American farmers had always been quick to move on at the call of opportunity, not just to new homes but to new farming methods and even new occupations. They regarded their mission as the conquest of nature rather than submission to it. Moreover, the new farm machinery that was developed during the nineteenth century made it possible for each family still on the land to produce more food for those who left it.

During these same years, Europe's population underwent a spurt of growth with which the European economy could not keep pace. Cheap American food products undersold crops grown at home, and European peasants found it necessary to emigrate in order to survive. When they arrived in the United States by the hundreds of thousands each year, the European immigrants filled the low-paying, unskilled jobs that native

Americans found unattractive. At every level in the process of industrialization, the United States was provided a plenitude of clever hands and strong backs.

A Land of Plenty

No country has been so blessed with such varied and abundant natural resources as the United States. There was the rich agricultural land producing cheap food; seemingly inexhaustible forests supplying lumber; prosperous fisheries; deposits of gold, silver, semiprecious metals, and dross such as phosphates and gravel. Most important of all in the industrial age were huge stores of coal and iron.

The gray-green mountains of Pennsylvania, West Virginia, and Kentucky seemed to be made of coal, the indispensable fuel of the age of steam. In the Mesabi Range of Minnesota, just west of the birdlike beak of Lake Superior, the low hills literally were made of iron ore. A man could sink his pick through the flaky sod and bare the tell-tale rusty red of the mineral.

The United States had a huge, ready-made market for mass-produced goods in its constantly growing population. And with the growth of industry (and the growing political influence of the industrial capitalist class), government in the United States proved quick to respond to the needs of manufacturers.

In only one respect was the United States handicapped in the drive toward massive industrial development. The very vastness of the country, the very reason for its bountiful supply of resources, was an impediment. In England, the first industrial nation, a manufacturer could easily assemble raw materials, and the market for everything from heavy machinery to hairpins was concentrated. But the United States spanned a continent and was divided by rivers, mountains, and deserts into regions as large as some countries. If nature had had the last word, the United States would have remained a patchwork of self-dependent manufacturing areas, in which small local factories produced goods only for the people of the vicinity. Indeed, this is a fair description of manufacturing in the United States through the period of the Civil War.

The Railroad Ignites a Revolution

The steam railroad conquered America's awesome geography. With its funnel-shape smokestack, piercing whistle, and tracks that could go almost anywhere—"two streaks of rust and a right of way"—the steam-powered locomotive made it possible for Pittsburgh steelmakers to bring together the coal of Scranton and the iron of the Mesabi as though the mines of both regions were just across the county line. Thanks to the railroad, the great steam-powered flour mills of Minneapolis were able to scoop up the cheap spring wheat of the distant Northwest, grind it into flour, and put their trademarked sacks into every cupboard in the country.

Because most western railroads found their way into Chicago (the legacy of Stephen A. Douglas's Kansas-Nebraska Act), the Windy City quickly eclipsed river-based (and river-bound) Cincinnati as "hog butcher to the world" and the nation's dresser of beef. Livestock fattened on a range a thousand miles away rolled bawling into Chicago in rickety railroad cars and then rolled out—packed in cans, barrels, and refrigerator cars—to the east coast and from there around the world.

Railroads in 1865

The railroad had to be properly employed in order to serve this function in the national economy. By 1865, the United States already was the world's premier railway country, with about thirty-five thousand miles of track. But there were few "systems," integrated lines that tied together distant regions. With the exception of the Baltimore and Ohio and the Erie railroads, American lines had been built by entrepreneurs who thought in regional terms. They had constructed their lines to connect two nearby cities, or they had run

Chicago's proximity to major railroads helped make it the beef capital of the U.S.

tracks from a city into the surrounding countryside. While useful, such "feeder" lines reinforced the traditional local patterns of commerce rather than encouraging the development of factories with a national and international market.

Thus the older, more populous regions, where immediate profits were to be had, were overbuilt, while newly settled country had little, if any, trackage. The result was continued isolation in the hinterland, and fierce, often destructive competition in the densely populated Northeast and South.

In the former Confederacy, there were four hundred railroad companies with an average track length of only forty miles each. It was possible to ship a cargo between St. Louis and Atlanta by any of twenty routes. Forced to compete for the limited business in cutthroat rate wars, not a single southern line was financially secure. In the Northeast, few railroad companies were able even to entertain the idea of expanding their trackage.

Finally, the first generation of American railroads was inefficient because few independent companies linked up with one another. Goods to be shipped over long distances, and therefore on several lines, had to be unloaded (hand labor added to costs), carted across terminal towns by horse and wagon (another bottleneck), and reloaded onto another train. None of the six railroads that ran into Richmond shared a depot. Before the Civil War, Chicago and New York were linked by rail on the map, but a cargo going the entire distance had to be unloaded and reloaded as many as six times.

Ante-bellum railroaders actually encouraged inefficiency of this sort in order to survive as independent companies. Fearing that they would be gobbled up by more powerful competitors if their routes were too attractive, they deliberately built in a variety of gauges (the distance between rails) so that only their own locomotives and rolling stock could run on their tracks. As little as two feet in mountainous areas, the distance between rails ran to five feet in the South. Until 1880, the important Erie Railroad clung to a monstrous six-foot gauge. The Illinois Central, third largest railroad in the country, employed two different gauges.

The Consolidators

Because the advantages of long consolidated lines were obvious, such tactics proved only temporarily successful. Emerging in the years just before the Civil War, rapidly triumphing during and after the conflict, the first American big businessmen, the great railroaders, swept just about everything before them. Their object was to bring technological and economic order to transportation, to turn a patchwork of remnants into a finely woven system. In the South and the East, where the railroads already existed, these men were organizers and manipulators of ownership.

J. Edgar Thompson pieced together the Pennsylvania Railroad by secretly purchasing stock in small lines in Pennsylvania and Ohio and, once in a commanding position, by declaring all-out rate wars against the companies that resisted his takeover. With the help of able associates like Thomas A. Scott, who eventually became president of the Pennsylvania and Texas Pacific railroads, Thompson created a trunk line that reached to New York in the East and to Pittsburgh and Wheeling in the West. Ultimately, "the Pennsy" entered Chicago, where it connected with railroads that ran to the Pacific. All along the main line, feeders tapped the traffic of the surrounding countryside.

Thompson was all business, a no-nonsense efficiency expert with little celebrity outside his offices. The founder of New York Central, the Pennsylvania's chief rival in the Northeast, was a more colorful man. Born in 1794, Cornelius Vanderbilt began his working life as a ferryman in New York City's crowded harbor. It was a rough business, no place for a milquetoast. Driven to destroy his competitors, the Commodore, as Vanderbilt styled himself (even dressing in a mock naval uniform), fired the cannon that sank more than one competitor's Hudson River barge and negotiated many a contract with a stout club.

Vanderbilt gave up brawling as his shipping empire and responsibilities grew, but he was as tough and unscrupulous behind a broad oak desk as he had been at the tiller of a ferry. Once, when a reporter suggested that he had broken the law in a conflict with a rival, Vanderbilt snapped back gruffly, "What do I care about the law. Hain't I got the power?"

He had, and he used it masterfully to crush competition. By the time of the Civil War, Vanderbilt had a near-monopoly of New York harbor commerce. He even controlled the business that hauled New York City's monumental daily production of horse manure to farms in Staten Island and New Jersey. He also owned a trans-Atlantic steamship line that competed with the older British companies, and a passenger service around Cape Horn to California.

The Commodore was never quite respectable. His humble, rough-and-tumble origins echoed in his voice and wharf-rat language, rendering him unacceptable to the genteel society circles of New York. His readiness to say out loud what other businessmen kept to themselves—that ethics and social responsibility had no place in the counting room—made him an easy target for reformers and unpopular with his more image-conscious fellow businessmen. Vanderbilt could not have cared less. Like many of the great capitalists of the era, he regarded his fortune—$100 million when he died—as adequate justification for what he did.

Robber Barons

But there was more justification for builders such as Vanderbilt and J. Edgar Thompson than simply money, if their records are set beside those business buccaneers with whom they regularly did battle. If Vanderbilt cared little for ethics, he did build. Another breed of

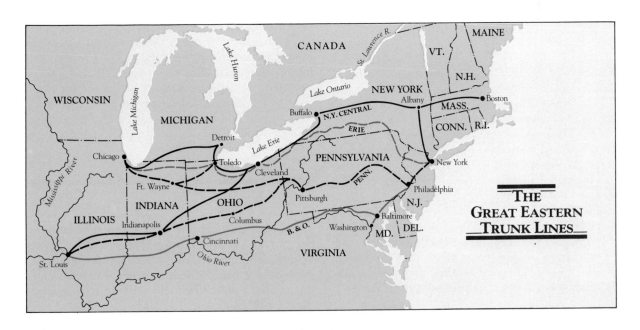

entrepreneur, represented by the three men of the Erie Gang—Daniel Drew, James Fisk, and Jay Gould—made their millions through destroying what others had created.

They were an odd trio. Drew, the eldest, a lifelong harbor-front rival of Vanderbilt, was a pious Methodist. He knew much of the Bible by heart and sprinkled his conversation with quotations for every occasion. But Drew apparently put a very liberal interpretation on the verse in Exodus that said "Thou shalt not steal." He was reputed to have cheated everyone with whom he had ever done business, customer and partner alike. It was said that Daniel Drew was incapable of an honest bargain.

James Fisk, only thirty-three years old in 1867, was another sort altogether. No Bible for Jubilee Jim; he was a stout, jolly extrovert who fancied gaudy clothes and jewelry, tossed silver dollars at street urchins, and caroused openly in New York's gaslit restaurants and cabarets with showgirls from the vaudeville stage (who were then considered little better than prostitutes). Rumor had it that Fisk had made his first fortune by buying cotton from Confederates and smuggling it into the North. (Like many other rich men of the era, Fisk had bought his way out of the draft.)

Jay Gould was a man of the shadows. When Drew went to church and Fisk stepped out, Gould slipped home to his respectable Victorian family. Furtive in appearance as in fact, tight fisted, and close mouthed, Gould was probably the brains of the Erie Ring. Certainly he lasted the longest, becoming almost respectable and marrying a daughter to a European nobleman. But when it came to making money, Gould was at one with his partners in the Erie Gang: consequences of their piracy were beside the point.

The Erie War

In control of the Erie Railroad, the three men knew that Vanderbilt wanted their property and was secretly making large purchases of Erie stock. In order to separate him from as much of his fortune as possible, they watered Erie's stock; that is, they marketed shares in the dilapidated railroad far in excess of the Erie's real assets. As Vanderbilt bought and bought, they pocketed the money that should have gone into expanding the Erie's potential earning power.

The Commodore eventually woke up to what was happening and went to judges, whom he regularly bribed, to indict the trio. Forewarned, Drew, Fisk, and Gould escaped to New Jersey, where they owned the judges. (It was said in the streets that they rowed across the Hudson River in a boat filled with paper money.)

WATERING STOCK

Daniel Drew was notorious for watering the stock in companies he owned. A popular story about him had it that he had started young. As a young drover, Drew would bring his cattle to the New York market, where he would pen them up with salt and no water. The next morning, before he sold them, he would drive them into a creek, where the groaning beasts bloated themselves. At market, they were fat, sleek, and largely phony.

A settlement reimbursing Vanderbilt most of his losses finally was pieced together. "Nothing is lost save honor," Jim Fisk joked.

Vanderbilt was no more squeamish about the methods he used than was the Erie Ring. But whereas Drew, Fisk, and Gould bled the company and let equipment and roadbed deteriorate so that the Erie had the worst accident record in the world and did not declare a dividend until the 1940s, Vanderbilt created a transportation system that was a vital artery of the national economy.

His New York Central ran on the newest steel rails (which lasted twenty times as long as iron). It was equipped with the life-saving Westinghouse air brake, while Erie trains were stopped (or not stopped) by manually operated chocks on the wheels of the locomotives. And the New York Central ran on a schedule between Boston and Chicago that was reliable to nearly the minute.

The Commodore's son and heir, William Vanderbilt, was as arrogant as the old man. (His motto was "The public be damned!") He was also as successful a businessman, doubling the $100 million Cornelius left him in only eight years. He played a leading part in standardizing the American gauge (at the present 4 feet, 8 1/2 inches), double-tracking (so that trains could run in both directions simultaneously), and, in 1883, adopting the four time zones by which the entire country now sets its clocks.

The Transcontinental Lines

In the Northeast and South, the creation of a railroad system required consolidating short lines that already existed. This movement peaked during the 1880s, when the names of 540 independent railway companies disappeared from the business registers. They were ab-

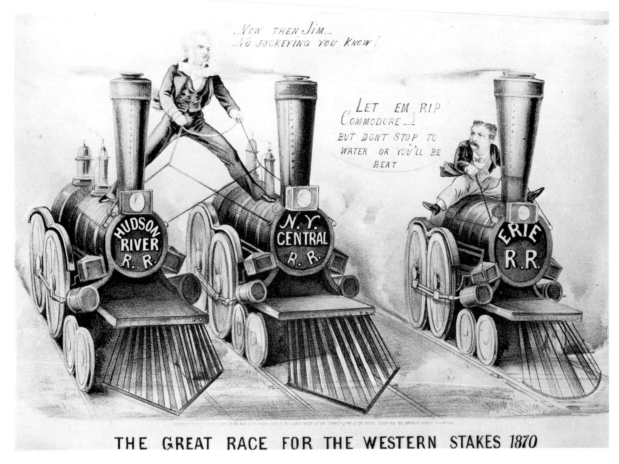

THE GREAT RACE FOR THE WESTERN STAKES 1870

*Cornelius Vanderbilt, transportation baron and owner of the New York Central Railway,
races James Fisk, a partner in the Erie Railway, for control of the rail route west
in this 1870 cartoon.*

sorbed by giants like the Pennsylvania, New York Central, and Baltimore and Ohio.

In the West, railroad lines were extensive, integrated transportation systems from the start. There, making railroad systems was a matter of new construction.

Public Finance

The lack of population between eastern Kansas and California made it impossible to attract private investment to railroad construction. To lay a mile of track required bedding more than three thousand ties in gravel and attaching four hundred rails to them by driving twelve thousand spikes. Having built that mile in Utah or Nevada at considerable expense, a railroader had nothing to look forward to but hundreds more miles of arid desert and uninhabited mountains.

With no customers along the way, there would be no profits and, without profits, no investors. However, because the federal government had political and military interests in binding California and Oregon to the rest of the Union, there was a way out of this dilemma. In its land, the public domain, the government had the means with which to subsidize railroad construction. In 1862, Congress committed the American people to underwriting the construction of a transcontinental line by giving away this land.

The Pacific Railway Act granted to two companies, the Union Pacific and the Central Pacific, a right of way of two hundred feet between Omaha, Nebraska, and Sacramento, California. For each mile of track that the companies built, they were to receive, on either side of the tracks, ten alternate sections (square miles) of the public domain. The result was a checkerboard-pattern belt forty miles wide, of which the U.P. and C.P. owned half the territory. (The rest

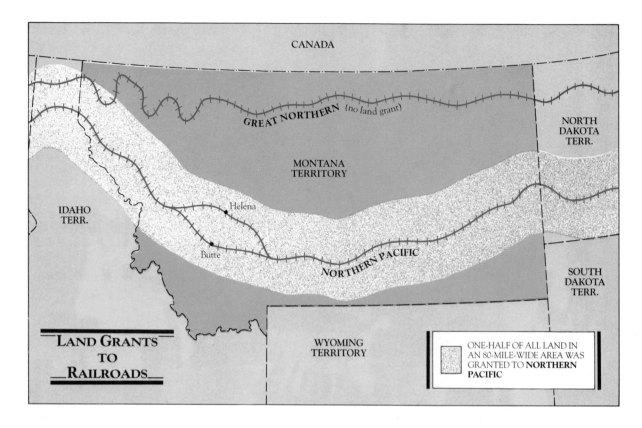

LAND GRANTS TO RAILROADS

CANADA

GREAT NORTHERN (no land grant)

MONTANA TERRITORY

NORTH DAKOTA TERR.

IDAHO TERR.

Helena

Butte

NORTHERN PACIFIC

SOUTH DAKOTA TERR.

WYOMING TERRITORY

ONE-HALF OF ALL LAND IN AN 80-MILE-WIDE AREA WAS GRANTED TO **NORTHERN PACIFIC**

was reserved for disposition under the Homestead Act or by direct government sale.)

This land the railroads could sell, simultaneously raising money for construction and creating customers. Or, just as important, they could use it as collateral to borrow cash from banks. In addition, the government lent the two companies $16,000 per mile of track at bargain interest rates (and up to $48,000 in mountainous country).

The Romance of the Rails

As in the consolidation of eastern trunk lines, the business end of the transcontinental railroad was marred by gross corruption. However, the actual construction of the line was a heroic and glorious feat. The Union Pacific, employing thousands of Civil War veterans and newly immigrated Irish pick-and-shovel men, the "Paddies," laid over a thousand miles of track. The workers lived in shifting cities of tents and freight cars built like dormitories. They toiled by day, and bickered and brawled with gamblers, saloon keepers, and whores by night. Until the company realized that it was more efficient to hire professional gunmen as guards, the workers kept firearms with their tools in order to fight off the Indians who sensed that the iron horse meant the end of their way of life.

The builders of the Central Pacific had no trouble with Indians, but a great deal with terrain. Just outside Sacramento rose the majestic Sierra Nevada. There were passes in the mountains through which the line could snake, but they were narrow and steep. The workmen—ten thousand Chinese organized in highly disciplined gangs—had to chip ledges into the slopes, build roadbeds of rubble in deep canyons, construct trestles of timbers two feet square, and mine their way through granite when there was no way around.

The snows of the Sierra proved to be the most difficult problem, not only for the builders but for the eventual operation of the line. To solve it, the workers constructed snowsheds miles long. In effect, the trans-

LAND FOR SALE

In order to promote land that it owned in Nebraska, the Burlington and Missouri River Railroad offered a number of come-ons. A would-be purchaser had to pay his own fare to go out to look at the land, but the railroad would refund his fare if he bought. Once a landowner, he would receive a free railroad pass, as well as "long credit, low interest, and a twenty percent rebate for improvements."

continental railroad crossed part of the Sierra Nevada indoors. Once on the Nevada plateau, the experienced C.P. crews built at a rate of a mile a day for an entire year.

The U.P. and C.P. joined at Promontory Point, Utah, on May 10, 1869. The final days were hectic. Because the total mileage that each company constructed determined the extent of its land grants, the two companies raced around the clock. The record was set by the crews of the Central Pacific. They built 10.6 miles of more-or-less functional railroad in one day. That involved bedding 31,000 ties, and connecting 4,037 iron rails to them with 120,000 spikes!

Four More Pacific Lines

Having made instant multimillionaires of its owners, the land grant to the first transcontinental railroad encouraged other groups to seek similar subsidies. In 1864, Congress authorized the construction of the Northern Pacific from Lake Superior to Puget Sound. The N.P.'s grant was doubly generous. In the territories, the N.P. received forty alternate sections for every mile built. By the 1870s, under the control of a German immigrant, Henry Villard, the Northern Pacific owned half the acreage in a belt eighty miles wide! It was completed in 1883, connecting Duluth, Minnesota, to Portland, Oregon, and Tacoma, Washington.

The next year, two more flimsy iron ribbons joined the two coasts, and a third was completed just across the Canadian border. The Atchison, Topeka, and Santa Fe ran from Kansas to Los Angeles. Also completed in 1884, the Texas Pacific and the Southern Pacific came to an arrangement in El Paso that made it

Ten thousand immigrant Chinese laborers built the Central Pacific Railway across the West. Here workers complete the Secrettown Trestle in the Sierra Nevada.

TRANSCONTINENTAL RAILROADS

possible to ship through from New Orleans to San Francisco. In the same year, the Canadians (who were even more generous with government land) completed the first of their two transcontinental lines, the Canadian Pacific. Never before had there been such an expenditure of effort and wealth to accomplish the same purpose in so short a time.

The costs were considerable. The federal government gave the land-grant railroads a total of 131 million acres. To this, the state governments added 45 million acres. Toted up, an area larger than France and Belgium combined was given to a handful of capi-

talists. In addition, towns along the proposed routes enticed the builders to choose them as sites for depots by offering town lots, cash bounties, and exemption from taxes.

These gifts were not always offered with a glad hand. If a railroad bypassed a town, that town frequently died. Aware of this, railroaders did not hesitate to set communities against one another like roosters in a cock fight. The Atchison, Topeka, and Santa Fe, popularly known as "the Santa Fe," did not enter that city at all. Nearby Albuquerque offered the better deal and got the depot.

BUILDING THE RAILROADS

"Track-laying is a science. A light car, drawn by a single horse, gallops up to the front with its load of rails. Two men seize the end of a rail and start forward, the rest of the gang taking hold by twos. They come forward at a run. At a word of command the rail is dropped in its place, less than thirty seconds to a rail for each gang, and so four rails go down to the minute: Close behind come the gangers, spikers, and a lovely time they make of it."

William Bell

A construction crew in the Montana Territory in 1887 is shown laying track for the Manitoba Railway which ran between Seattle, Washington and St. Paul, Minnesota.

Disillusionment with Railroads

Some Americans greeted the coming of the railroad with fear and anger. Nature-loving poets and philosophers saw "the machine in the garden" as a defilement of what was good and vital in American life. In some cities, people banded together to fight plans to run tracks down their streets. Unlike today, many railways ran into city centers on residential streets, and the wood-burning locomotives were noisy, dirty, and dangerous, throwing sparks and running over people and animals.

But the nay-sayers were in the minority. Most Americans welcomed the iron horse, especially those who lived in previously isolated rural areas. To them the railroad offered the possibility of shipping their produce to lucrative markets, thereby earning money with which to enjoy a fuller life.

A Short Honeymoon

But even in areas that actually were opened up by railroads, the honeymoon was very short lived. It was not difficult to see that pirates like Drew, Fisk, and Gould made money only to the extent that they stole from the railroad as a means of transportation. Town dwellers discovered that the railway barons' arrogance did not end with their demands for depot sites. Along the transcontinental lines, virtually every important piece of business had to be "cleared" with the local railway manager. Farmers learned that the railroads were less their servants, carting their produce to market, than the masters of their fate.

The Big Four of California were the most powerful of the railroad barons. Collis P. Huntington, Leland Stanford, Mark Hopkins, and Charles Crocker had been well-to-do merchants in California when, in 1862, partly through luck and partly because Huntington was a quick man with a payoff, they won the concession for the Central Pacific. Almost overnight, the four became the bosses of the growing state of California.

The Southern Pacific, which absorbed the Central Pacific, was the most lucrative of their properties. Whereas the bulk of the land that had been given to the transcontinental lines was sold quite cheaply, at $3 to $5 per acre, the S.P.'s land grants in the fertile central valley of California were worth tens and sometimes a hundred times that much. Instead of disposing of its California holdings, the S.P. held tight, driving up the value of the real estate. By the end of the nineteenth century, the railroad was the single biggest landowner in California.

LELAND STANFORD

When he was president of the Southern Pacific Railroad, Leland Stanford ordered that all employees of the company stand at attention in a line along the track when his private trains passed through. All Southern Pacific locomotives traveling in the other direction were to blow their whistles in salute.

The successors of the Big Four sometimes used the railroad's leverage to drive small farmers and ranchers out of business. The line's political officer at the turn of the century, William F. Herrin, was widely considered to be the boss of the state legislature, monitoring every law that was passed in the interests of the S.P. Novelist Frank Norris characterized the Southern Pacific for many Californians when he called it *The Octopus* (1901), its tentacles reaching into and gripping every aspect of life in the Golden State.

The Farmers' Grievances

In the Mississippi Valley, farmers also discovered that the coming of the railroad did not necessarily mean prosperity. In most parts of the West, there was no competition among railroads; one line handled all the traffic. As a result, the rates at which farmers shipped their wheat, corn, or livestock to markets in the city were at the mercy of the shippers. All too often, farmers saw their margin of profit consumed to the penny in transportation costs.

Most infuriating was the railroads' control of storage facilities, the grain elevators that stood close to the depot in every railway town. The farmer had to pay the company storage fees until such time as the railroad sent a train to haul away his grain. Obviously, it was often to the railroad's interests to delay scheduling a train as long as possible. The company determined how long a farmer had to store his products and, thus, how large his fee was. Within a few weeks, a railroad could gobble up a whole year's income.

Attempts to Regulate

In the early 1870s, an organization of farmers, the Patrons of Husbandry (or Grangers, as members were called) won control of the state legislature of Illinois and considerable influence in adjoining states. They passed a series of "Granger laws" that set maximum rates that railroad companies could charge both for hauling and storing. Convinced that the railroad industry had no interest in regulating itself, and that the federal government was not yet ready to control the railroads, other state governments followed Illinois's lead and passed regulatory laws. Immediately, the railroad barons launched a legal counterattack, hiring high-powered corporation lawyers like Richard B. Olney and Roscoe Conkling to take the regulatory legislation to the Supreme Court.

At first the Grangers prevailed. In the case of *Munn v. Illinois* (1877), a Supreme Court comprised of old-

Gift for the Grangers, *a lithograph made in 1873 celebrates the Patrons of Husbandry, a farmers' organization.*

fashioned midwestern agrarians and Whiggish Republicans declared that when a private company's business affected the public interest, the public had the right to regulate that business.

Nine years later, however, times and the membership of the Supreme Court had changed. In 1886, the justices wrote several prorailroad doctrines into the law of the land. In the Wabash case (*Wabash, St. Louis, and Pacific Railway Co.* v. *Illinois*), the Court broadly extended the interstate-commerce clause of the Constitution to protect the railroads. That is, the Constitution provides that only Congress can regulate commerce between the states. The Court ruled that because the Wabash, St. Louis, and Pacific Railroad ran through Illinois into other states, the state of Illinois could not legally regulate freight rates even between points within the state! In the age of consolidation, when a handful of syndicates controlled all important American railroads, this decision left state governments with authority over only those short, generally insignificant local lines (at most, a quarter of the track in the United States) that were rarely exploitative in the first place.

The Interstate Commerce Commission

There was an uproar. Rural politicians and urban reformers condemned the Court as the tool of the railway barons. If only Congress could bridle the iron horse, they shouted from Grange halls and from the stages of city auditoriums, let Congress do so. In 1888, Congress did, enacting the Interstate Commerce Act. But the consequences of that law showed that the legislative branch was as responsive as the judicial to the demands of the railways.

On the face of it, the law brought the national railroads under control. Excessive rates were outlawed, and Congress created an independent regulatory commission, the Interstate Commerce Commission, to keep an eye on railroad charges. Ostensibly, railroads were to publish their rates and were not to discriminate against small shippers by giving rebates (under-the-table-kickbacks) to the larger ones. They were not to charge less for long hauls along routes where there was competition than for short hauls in areas where a railroad had a monopoly. The act also outlawed the pooling of business by railroads, a practice by which, shippers believed, they were controlled and fleeced.

However, the Interstate Commerce Act did not forbid mergers or interlocking directorates, both of which were far more effective means of avoiding competition than were the informal pools. Moreover, the Commission was given little real power; it had to take its decisions to the same courts that had favored the railroads over the state legislatures, and within a few years railroaders and lawyers friendly to them held a majority of seats on the I.C.C.

Indeed, the principal effect of the landmark law was to silence the antirailroad movement by creating the illusion of government control. Its secondary effect was to provide, through the auspices of the federal government, the means for the further consolidation of power by an even smaller group of men than the eastern consolidators and the western railway builders.

The Money Power

By the early 1890s, the trunk lines of the country had been consolidated into five great systems. By 1900, even these had fallen under the effective control of two large New York investment banks, J. P. Morgan and Company and Kuhn, Loeb and Company, the latter in partnership with Union Pacific president, Edward H. Harriman.

When the government ceased to subsidize railway construction, the railroads had to look to other sources in order to mobilize the huge amounts of capital needed to lay second tracks, modernize equipment, and buy up competitors. The companies often needed more money than their profits provided. Capital was even more serious a problem during the recurrent business depressions of the period when income sank, while fixed costs (such as maintenance) remained the same.

The traditional means of raising capital—offering shares of stock to the public—was simply not up to these needs, particularly during depressions. Into the gap stepped the investment bank. These institutions served both as sales agents, finding moneyed buyers for railway stock at a commission, and as buyers themselves. In return for these services, men like John Pierpont Morgan insisted on a say in the formation of railroad policy, placing a representative of the bank on the client's board of directors.

Because every large railroad needed financial help at one time or another—every transcontinental but the Great Northern went bankrupt during the depression of 1893 to 1897—Morgan's and Kuhn and Loeb's men soon sat on every major corporate board, creating an interlocking directorate. Like all bankers, their goal was a steady, dependable flow of profit, and their means to that end was to eliminate wasteful competition. They called a halt to the periodic rate wars among the New York Central, Pennsylvania, and Baltimore and

Banker John Pierpont Morgan, as photographed by Edward Steichen in 1906.

INDUSTRY AT THE DINNER TABLE

Technology and the entrepreneurial spirit reached into the American home with more than the telephone during the latter part of the nineteenth century. Several inventors and business organizers devised new ways to process food that scrambled ancient patterns of marketing and cooking and, within a generation, changed the way Americans ate.

The first of these remakers of food was Gail Borden (1801–74). Living on the Texas frontier, Borden was aware of the monotony of the diets of overland travelers, and he began to experiment with ways to preserve and make more portable one of the most perishable and bulkiest of foods, milk. Borden's solution was condensation and canning. In 1856, he took out a patent on a process for evaporating milk in a vacuum and preserving the product in cans. Union soldiers in the Civil War did not find Borden's "Condensed Milk" particularly tasty, but it was milk and healthful too, as many military rations were not. Back home again, they continued to use it because, except on the farm where cows could be milked daily, that perishable food was risky eating. Before the pasteurization process, which came to the United States only at the end of the century, fresh milk was the source of numerous serious diseases.

Condensation became an obsession with Borden. "I mean to put a potato into a pill box," he said, "a pumpkin into a tablespoon, the biggest sort of watermelon into a saucer. . . . The Turks made acres of roses into attar of roses. . . . I intend to make attar of everything." He never had a success to rival his milk, but did condense fruit and vegetable juices with his process.

H. J. Heinz of Pittsburgh calculated that by using industrial methods, he could sell preserved foods such as were put up in many American homes at a price that would tempt buyers, particularly in the cities, to forgo that tedious task. He went bankrupt once but stuck by his idea, canning and bottling pickles, vegetables, fruits, and the mainstay of his prosperous company, ketchup or catsup. Before Heinz, the work *ketchup* referred to any number of sauces and relishes. Only after the success of Heinz's *tomato* ketchup did Americans forget how to make the others.

Much more fundamental was the revolution in processing America's staples, wheat flour and meat. The bread and fresh meat that Americans ate always had come from the region in which they lived. Local or regional millers gathered in the grain and ground it into flour, returning some to the grower and selling the rest. The butcher shops in every town and city were also slaughterhouses. Without refrigeration, the only fresh meat was meat that had been on the hoof a day or two earlier in the butcher's backyard.

A smartly-dressed working girl weighs a container of raspberry preserves, one of H. J. Heinz's fifty-seven varieties of canned and bottled foods.

The railroad was the key to changing this. Reaching westward into lands where wheat and livestock could be grown on a larger scale and, therefore, much more cheaply than in the East, the trains funneled grain and cattle into Minneapolis-St. Paul, Chicago, St. Louis, and other cities that had railroad connections with the east coast. In the transfer cities, gigantic processing companies such as General Mills, Ralston, Purina, Swift, Armour, Wilson, and Cudahy turned the raw materials into consumer goods.

Using huge steam-driven steel rollers instead of the slow and cumbersome water-powered grindstones, the great milling corporations were able to undersell and quickly destroy local millers almost everywhere in the country. Their flour did not spoil because the living germ had been refined out of it. Although refined flour was fine and white, therefore a much more elegant baking ingredient than previously had been available to ordinary people, it was, as numerous critics pointed out then and in the twentieth century, far less nutritious than unrefined flour.

Chicago was the center of the new meatpacking industry. From vast corrals in the yards of the western railroads, cattle and hogs were processed by applying industrial methods to slaughtering and butchering. The mass-produced meat sold so cheaply in the East that the combination slaughterhouse-butcher shop became a thing of the past.

The pioneers of centralized meatpacking were Gustavus Swift (1839–1903) and Philip D. Armour (1832–1901). Armour perfected the "disassembly line," a continuously moving chain in which hogs ran in one end under their own power, and pork packed for retailing came out the other. Armour kept his prices down by using what previously had been waste: bones, blood, hides, and even bristle (which was made into hairbrushes). It was said that he made money on every part of the pig but its squeal, and he was working on that.

Gustavus Swift pioneered the use of ice and, later, refrigerator cars to ship fresh sides of beef from Chicago to the east coast. He had to overcome popular suspicions of any meat from animals that had been slaughtered more than a few days before it was set on the table and the resistance of local butchers. By opening his own shops in the major cities of the East and underselling even locally raised steers with his Texas, Wyoming, and Montana beef, Swift had his way.

By the end of the nineteenth century, a middle-class family in Portland, Maine, would likely sit down to a loaf of bread baked with flour from Minneapolis, a beefsteak from Chicago seasoned with Heinz catsup from Pittsburgh, and oranges from Florida or California for dessert. Vegetables alone were local. Maine produced plenty of potatoes, and it was only in the twentieth century that the food revolutionaries shipped greens any considerable distance.

Ohio in the eastern states. In 1903, J. P. Morgan tried to merge the Northern Pacific and the Great Northern, two systems with essentially parallel lines between the Great Lakes and the Pacific Northwest. Competing for traffic, he believed, hurt them both.

Banker control had its beneficial side. No more did unscrupulous pirates like the Erie Gang ruin great transportation systems for the sake of short-term killings. The integration of the nation's railways resulted in a gradual but significant lowering of fares and freight rates. Between 1866 and 1897, the cost of shipping a hundred pounds of grain from Chicago to New York dropped from sixty-five cents to twenty cents, and the rate for shipping beef from ninety cents per hundred weight to forty cents.

But the control of so important a part of the economy by a few men with offices on Wall Street called into question some very basic American ideals. Where was individual freedom and opportunity, many people asked, when a sinister "money power" headed by the imperious J. P. Morgan could decide on a whim the fate of millions of farmers and workingpeople?

A resplendent and cultivated man who owned yachts that were larger than the ships in most countries' navies and collections of rare books and art that were superior to those in most countries' national museums, Morgan never attempted to disguise his power or his contempt for ordinary mortals. In return he was feared, held in awe, and hated.

Morgan shook off all those reactions. In the end, he was vulnerable only to ridicule. An affliction of the skin had given him a large, bulbous nose that swelled and glowed like a circus clown's when he was angry. Making fun of it, however, was the only foolproof way to make it light up, and Morgan rarely mixed with the kind of people who would notice his single human weakness. During the late nineteenth century, he had no difficulty in finding a congenial circle of friends, for it was the golden age of the big businessman.

For Further Reading

To understand the significance of the railroad, it is necessary to start by reading one of the great books of American economic history, George R. Taylor, *The Transportation Revolution* (1951). J. F. Stover, *American Railroads* (1961), is also valuable. For an approach from the top, see Thomas C. Cochran, *Railroad Leaders, 1845–1890* (1953).

Most comprehensive is E. C. Kirkland, *Men, Cities, and Transportation* (1948). Focusing specifically on the second half of the nineteenth century are G. R. Taylor and I. D. Neu, *The American Railroad Network, 1861–1900* (1956), and E. G. Campbell, *The Reorganization of the American Railroad System, 1893–1900* (1938). For the transcontinental lines, see James McCague, *Moguls and Iron Men* (1964).

28

Forces of Material Progress
Technology and Business to 1900

Railroads remained America's biggest and most important business, the linchpin of the industrial economy, well into the twentieth century. Building them—157,000 miles of track between 1865 and 1900—accounted for more construction than any other enterprise. Railroads were a major consumer of lumber and the chief consumer of coal, iron, and steel. The nation's machine and machine-tool industries became the best in the world in meeting the needs of the trains. Next to the federal government, railroads were the biggest proprietors of lands west of the Mississippi.

The national transportation system made it possible for entrepreneurs of every stripe to draw on the resources of the entire country and to market their products in Maine, California, and points in between. Perhaps as important as anything else, the example of the railroad barons—their vast wealth, power, and prestige—served as inspiration for ambitious men who were engaged in other endeavors, models to emulate both in methods and goals.

Inventor Thomas A. Edison at work in his Menlo Park, New Jersey, laboratory.

Fondness for wealth was hardly new with the American people in the final third of the nineteenth century. But the new industrial society offered so many opportunities for making so very much money that material success moved ever closer to the center of American culture. No longer simply a means to an end—whether a life of comfort, cultivation, and leisure, or a life of study, public service, or socially useful work— money became almost an end in itself.

Technology and American Society

The difference that this important half century made in American culture is nicely illustrated by the contrasting careers of two dedicated men who labored in the same field, teaching deaf mutes to cope in a world of silence. In 1815, Thomas Gallaudet had traveled to England to study new methods of communicating with the deaf. He was enraged to learn that a successful new technique for helping deaf mutes was closely guarded as a trade secret. To Gallaudet, moneymaking and philanthropy did not mix; he chose philanthropy. Highly respected, no richer than the day he was born, Gallaudet died in 1851.

Alexander Graham Bell was born in Scotland in 1847, son of a man who was as famous a teacher of the deaf as Gallaudet. Bell took up his father's work and was instructing teachers of the deaf in Boston in the mid-1870s when he had an idea for a device that would enable some people to hear: a mechanical eardrum made of paper and metal, and powered by low-voltage electricity.

No sooner had Bell completed his instrument than he recognized other possibilities for it. If two of the hearing aids were connected by wire, voices could be transmitted over long distances. Bell successfully tested the telephone early in 1876 and immediately bundled it off to the Centennial Exposition in Philadelphia.

The Telephone: A Success Story with Bells On

Bell's invention was one of the hits of the show. Millions of people picked up the odd-looking receivers and, alternately giggling and awed, chatted with companions across the room. Young men at the fair dropped a hint of what was to come by "ringing up" young ladies standing across from them, respectably striking up conversations that would have been unacceptable face to face without proper introductions.

Alexander Graham Bell demonstrating his invention, the telephone, in 1892.

Scarcely a report on the fair did not dwell on Bell's marvelous toy.

But he could not sell it. Western Union, the telegraph company and most likely buyer of a new means of communication, showed no interest whatsoever. Other investors enjoyed the phone well enough, but wrote it off as a plaything, not a businessman's business. J. P. Morgan took an immediate aversion to it, and his judgment deterred others. No one seemed to recognize the enormity of Bell's accomplishment, particularly for businessmen. The telephone made it possible to communicate with no delay and (important for dubious transactions) with no written records. Obviously, no one could foresee the time when the telephone would be considered a household essential.

Bell's disappointment proved to be a blessing in disguise. Had the "money power" been interested in his invention, they could have exploited it without him. As it was, Bell was forced to set up his own pilot company in New York, and he saw his "toy" quickly seize on the American imagination. President Rutherford B. Hayes put a phone in the White House in 1878. By 1880, only four years after they first had heard of the thing, fifty thousand Americans were paying monthly fees to hear it jangle on their walls. By 1890, there were eight hundred thousand in the United States; by 1900, 1.5 million. People in the tiniest hamlets knew all about "exchanges," "party lines," and nasal-voiced "operators."

Many systems were useful only locally. But as early as 1892, the eastern and midwestern cities were connected by a long-distance network, and rambunctious little western desert communities noted in their directories that "you can now talk to San Francisco with ease from our downtown office."

To J. P. Morgan's credit, he never changed his mind about the telephone. To the end of his life, he picked one up only when millions of dollars rode on the call, and then he shouted at the thing as though it had challenged his authority. But he was the exception. Bell's invention became the nervous system of American business, as the railroad was its circulatory system.

Bell lived until 1922, and he never lost his interest in the deaf. Both during his life and in his will, he gave millions to the cause of teaching them. Nevertheless, the philanthropist was as ruthless a businessman as Cornelius Vanderbilt. He moved against all would-be competitors, crushing or taming them. His American Telephone and Telegraph Company became the most thorough monopoly in American industry.

How Technology Changed Women's Lives

The story of the telephone is also a story of social behavior and even morality. The telephone permitted a familiarity between strangers that was impossible, in genteel society, face to face, a fact of particular importance in courtship practices. The rapid spread of the phone was significant in women's lives in two other ways.

First, by making it possible to converse over a distance in an instant, the home telephone chipped away at the isolation of the married woman, especially in rural areas. Shackled to the home by domestic chores

Telephone operators at work at early switchboards in Oregon.

and by the strict code of conduct enforced on the respectable, women were able through the phone to involve themselves in the world beyond the front door. It was a small, but important tear in the web of domesticity.

Much more noticeable to people of the time was Bell's American Telephone and Telegraph Company turning to young ladies to handle the job of connecting callers to each other. The company fired the young men whom it originally had hired because their conversation on the wires was flippant and occasionally obscene; also anticipating the future, they took advantage of anonymity to shock or insult proper middle-class subscribers.

Unlike factory work, which was menial and "dirty," a job as an operator was socially acceptable for middle-class girls. In addition to finding an escape from the plush and velvet prison of the parlor, thousands of women earned an income independent of their parents' or husbands'. Alexander Graham Bell, unknown to both parties, was a partner with American feminists in their movement to emancipate women.

The Changing Office

Another invention that created jobs for women was the typewriter. Because handwriting was often illegible, and potentially costly in business, dozens of inventors had taken a stab at creating a "writing machine." But the first practical—easily manufactured and reliable—typewriter was perfected only in 1867 by Christopher Latham Sholes, and first marketed in 1874 by the Remington Arms Company, a firearms manufacturer in search of a product with which to diversify its interests.

Before the use of the machine became standard in business, almost all secretaries were men. They not

The first typewriter manufactured by Remington Arms Company in 1874.

only wrote letters for their employers, but they ran various errands and sometimes represented the boss. The typewriter made it possible for businessmen to split the secretarial profession into assistant and typist. Men continued to perform the more responsible and better-paid job, rising to a status that would be described as "junior executive" today. The mechanical task of transcribing letters and business records into type went to women.

Like the job of telephone operator, that of typist did not require the general education that was available to only the wealthiest women. It was not heavy labor, an important consideration in an age that defined respectable young ladies as "delicate." And the job did not usually involve much responsibility, which nineteenth-century men were disinclined to allot to women.

The All-American Wizard of Menlo Park

Ranking above Sholes and perhaps Bell as a technological revolutionary was Thomas Alva Edison, whose success story was all the more remarkable because, as a boy, he could have qualified as any school's candidate for least likely to succeed. His teachers concluded that he was so dim that they urged him to quit school and go to work. Indeed, throughout his life, Edison was befuddled by books and incredulous that

---

DAMN TELEPHONE!

Bell's telephone company quickly opted for young ladies as operators because it was assumed that they would be more refined and less mischievous than the boys whom Bell first hired for the job. Soon, the burden for polite language was on the customer. On December 26, 1882, A. H. Pugh of Cincinnati was angered by his inability to get a connection and told the operator, "If you can't get the party I want you to, you may shut up your damn telephone." The company canceled Pugh's service and took his phone. He sued to get it back, but the court ruled that it was reasonable and legal to penalize a man who said "damn" to a young lady on the phone.

---

anyone could pursue knowledge for its own sake.

But Edison was the ultimate American tinkerer, attuned in his soul with the practical, and a genius at making, fixing, and remaking things with his hands. He became the greatest of American inventors, recognized as a wizard even in his very inventive era.

Edison did not come upon his creations as the result of other interests, as Bell did. Nor were his inventions lucky accidents such as Harvey Firestone's discovery of the vulcanization process, by which rubber, previously a curiosity, could be made into a stable, versatile material that was essential to the development of the bicycle, the automobile, and numerous other twentieth-century products. Nor did Edison's breakthroughs come about in a miraculous flash of insight, as Eli Whitney had invented the cotton gin only a day and a half after being presented with the problem that his machine solved.

Edison became a folk hero as well as a very rich man because he approached invention in a gruff, nononsense, all-American way. Invention was just another kind of hard work. Edison once said that his genius was "one percent inspiration and ninety-nine percent perspiration." He took up problems on assignment and, with a large corps of assistants, attacked them in the first research and development laboratory, at Menlo Park, New Jersey. His and his assistants' resourcefulness are still unparalleled. Between 1876 and 1900, Edison took out more than a thousand patents.

Electric Light

Most of these patents were for improvements in existing processes. (He perfected a transmitter for Bell.) However, a few of Edison's inventions were seedbeds for wholly new industries: the storage battery, the motion-picture projector, and the phonograph. The most important of his inventions was the incandescent light bulb, a means of converting electricity into stable, controllable light.

Edison solved the theoretical principle of the electric bulb—the 1 percent inspiration—almost immediately. Within a vacuum in a translucent glass ball an electrically charged filament or thread should burn (that is, glow) indefinitely. The perspiration part was discovering the fiber that would do the job. In 1879, after testing 6,000 materials, Edison came up with one that burned for 40 hours, enough to make it practical. Before he patented the incandescent light bulb early the next year, Edison improved the filament enough to make it work for 170 hours.

While he continued to scorn the telephone, J. P. Morgan backed Edison. Fascinated by the phenom-

enon of electrical illumination (his house and bank were among Edison's first customers), Morgan also realized that many people disliked gas, the principal source of nighttime light. Although clean enough (unlike kerosene), gas could be dangerous. Hundreds of fires were caused when, in a moment of ignorance, forgetfulness, or drunkenness, people blew out the flame instead of turning off the lamp. Hotel managers nervously plastered the walls of rooms with reminders that the lights were gas.

The incandescent bulb succeeded as dramatically as the telephone. From a modest start in New York in 1882 (about eighty customers), Edison's invention spread so quickly that by 1900, more than three thousand towns and cities were electrically illuminated. Within a few more years, the gaslight disappeared, and the kerosene lantern survived only on farms and in the poorer sections of the cities.

No single electric company dominated the industry, as American Telephone and Telegraph controlled Bell's patents. Nevertheless, like the railroads, the great regional companies were loosely associated by interlocking directorates and the influence of the investment banks. Edison, a worse businessman than scholar, saw most of his profit go to backers like Morgan. He ended his working life as an employee of mammoth General Electric, the corporate issue of his inventive genius.

Thomas A. Edison demonstrating an early movie projector in 1905.

Some Other Inventions

George Westinghouse became a multimillionaire from his invention of the air brake for railroad trains. By equipping every car in a train with brakes, operated from a central point by pneumatic pressure, Westinghouse solved the problem of stopping long strings of cars. Not only did his air brake save thousands of lives, but it led to bigger profits for railroads by making longer trains possible.

Well established, Westinghouse turned his inventive genius to electricity and capitalized on Edison's stubborn resistance to alternating current. Direct current served very well over small areas. (It is still the common kind of power in Europe.) But direct current could not be transmitted over long distances. By perfecting a means to transmit AC, Westinghouse leapt ahead of his competitor by fully utilizing massive natural sources of power at places like Niagara Falls. He also cornered the contracts for illuminating the streets of cities with his cheaper current. Unlike Edison, he was comfortable enough with the intricacies of business to retain control of the Westinghouse Electric Corporation and to see it

expand its operations into the industry's hundreds of possibilities. If it plugged into a socket, George Westinghouse made it.

Cyrus Hall McCormick was a carry-over from the previous age. He invented his first reaper for harvesting grain mechanically in 1831. He proved to be an even better businessman than inventor. For two decades he battled other inventors of farm machines in the courts, and by the time of the Civil War he had bought out or driven out of business virtually every important competitor. He was quick to purchase the inventions of younger men, and by the time of McCormick's death in 1884, the International Harvester Company owned hundreds of valuable patents. Headquartered in Chicago, the McCormick works manufactured more agricultural machines than every other company in the world combined. McCormick harvesters found their way to even the steppes of Russia and western China.

As the railroad harnessed steam to move heavy burdens across the land, Elisha Otis devised an elevator to move them up and down. His first safe elevator—stopping a load, not raising it, was the big problem with

An advertisement for a McCormick reaper, invented in 1831 to harvest grain.

earlier hoists—went on the market in 1853. Through the rest of the nineteenth century, his company (with competition from Westinghouse) regularly improved the device, converting to electric power and making possible both the digging of deeper mines and the constructing of taller buildings. In their turn, the tall office buildings, soon known as skyscrapers, encouraged the centralization of business administration. It was now possible for the nation's corporations to huddle together in New York, Chicago, and San Francisco. Thanks to the telephone, a capitalist did not have to be on the scene of his enterprises. Thanks to the elevator, he could afford to keep in constant close contact with other businessmen. Technology and the consolidation of economic power played leapfrog, each advancing the other by turns.

The Organizers

For all the accomplishments of America's inventors, the most successful businessmen of the late nineteenth century were neither engineers nor tinkerers. Indeed, most were not even informed in technological matters. They were organizers, manipulators of money and builders of business enterprises. Morgan was the greatest of them, but he was rivaled by the Scottish immigrant Andrew Carnegie, who took great pride in telling people that he knew less than the typical schoolchild about making steel. And yet (which was the point of his boast), he built the world's greatest steel company, which was producing half the nation's output by 1900, the year of Carnegie's retirement.

Steel: The Bones of the Economy

Steel is the element iron, purified by burning out at extreme temperatures the carbon and other "impurities" with which, in nature, iron is wed. Although the means of producing this super iron was known for centuries, the difficulty involved was so great that steel was used to make only small, expensive specialty items: knives, other cutting tools, and precision instruments. Nevertheless, iron manufacturers were aware of its potential. Steel is much stronger than iron per unit of weight. Produced in quantity, steel could be used in buildings, bridges, and, of particular interest in the late nineteenth century, superior rails for trains.

By the time of the Civil War, working independently of each other, two ironmakers, Henry Bessemer of England and William "Pig Iron" Kelly, of Kentucky, developed a method by which steel could be made in quantity at a reasonable price. Andrew Carnegie, then just a telegrapher for the Pennsylvania Railroad, one of the first lines to install steel rails, mused over the possibilities.

During the war, Carnegie organized telegraph resources for the government. In 1865, he left the Pennsy to become a manufacturer of structural iron bridges. Prospering because of his railway contacts, he began the construction of the largest steel factory in the world. Carnegie knew that in business one must polish an apple. He named his plant the J. Edgar Thompson Works after the president of the Pennsylvania Railroad, Carnegie's inevitable first customer.

Carnegie also knew better than to stake his future on a smile and a handshake. Instead of building his factory in Pittsburgh, which was then the center of steel manufacture in the United States, he located it just outside the city limits in a small town called Homestead. Thompson's Pennsy was the only railroad in Pittsburgh. With this monopoly, the company imperiously set the rates by which Pittsburgh businessmen shipped their goods. Homestead, however, was also served by a spur of the Baltimore and Ohio, a line that was noted for its cutthroat rate wars. Located there, Carnegie could force the two great lines to compete for his business and thus cut his own transportation costs.

Vertical Integration

Cutting costs was the heart of Carnegie's method. He told friends that he never looked at a profit sheet. Instead, he pored over the cost sheets, searching for places in the complex business where expenses might be shaved in acquiring materials, in transporting them, in actually making the steel, and in shipping it to his customers. Slash expenses, Carnegie said, and profits take care of themselves. And they did. Carnegie's personal income climbed to $25 million per year; his

---

STEEL AT ONE CENT A POUND

Just as John D. Rockefeller liked to point out that kerosene was cheaper after Standard Oil came to monopolize the refining industry, Andrew Carnegie had a neat justification of his organization of the steel industry:

Two pounds of ironstone mined upon Lake Superior and transported nine hundred miles to Pittsburgh; one pound and one half of coal, mined and manufactured into coke, and transported to Pittsburgh; a small amount of manganese ore mined in Virginia and brought to Pittsburgh— and these four pounds of materials manufactured into one pound of steel, for which the customer pays one cent.

A ladle used in a nineteenth-century steel mill dwarfs the men standing nearby.

several partners—including right-hand man Henry Clay Frick and Charles Schwab, later the head of United States Steel—also made huge sums.

Cost cutting could be as simple as paring down the wages of workers to the least they would accept without rebelling, or increasing the hours of work. Or it could be as complicated as replacing a whole factory with an improved, cheaper technology. Carnegie was aware of the importance of new inventions. He waited for depressions, when the cost of everything was down, to make his improvements.

Carnegie's fundamental means of reducing costs, however, was the vertical integration of the steel-making business. Instead of buying iron and coal from independent mining companies, which were often inefficient and, in any case, had to take their own profit, Carnegie purchased his own iron and coal mines, often taking advantage of bankruptcies. Although he was never completely independent of the trunk-line railways, Carnegie assumed control of as much of his own shipping as he could. He owned the barges that carried Mesabi iron ore from Minnesota to his own port facilities in Erie, Pennsylvania. He even owned the short-line railroad that brought the ore from Erie to Homestead. By eliminating from his final product price the profits of independent suppliers, distributors, and carriers, Carnegie was able to undersell competing companies that were not vertically integrated and, therefore, had to include the profits of independent suppliers in their final product price.

In 1901, sixty-six years old and bored with business, Carnegie sold his half interest in the company to the ubiquitous Morgan. His price was $.5 billion—cash—and he let it be known that if it was not forthcoming, he might amuse himself by competing directly with some steel interests that Morgan already controlled. Morgan paid, and, as he had done with the railroads, he combined Carnegie's properties with other steel companies to form the great United States Steel Corporation, the first corporation capitalized at more than $1 billion.

The Corporation

Although a pioneer in many ways, Andrew Carnegie was curiously old fashioned in that he organized his company as a partnership. The chief agency of business consolidation in the late nineteenth century was not the partnership or individual ownership but the corporation.

Corporate organization was not in itself a new idea. It had originated in early modern times as a means of financing business ventures that were too expensive or too risky to be undertaken by individuals. The first American colonies had been founded by corporate companies that had persuaded financiers to buy "shares" in them. If the project busted (as, financially, most of the colonies did), no individual lost more than an expendable fraction of his capital. If the venture succeeded, the investors took their profits in proportion to the number of shares they owned.

The corporation remained a popular way of financing large undertakings in the United States. In the late colonial and early national periods, it was customary

Andrew Carnegie, steel manufacturer and master of vertical integration.

for a merchant who could afford to own one ship outright to buy one-tenth shares in ten ships instead. That way, his income was the same, and he could not be wiped out by bad weather, pirates, mutiny, or war. In the expansive Jacksonian era, corporations became even more popular, and some state governments abandoned the old practice of chartering corporations individually (closely examining the intentions of each new company) and introduced standard corporation laws under which businessmen could incorporate at will.

The corporate structure accommodated the ambitious entrepreneur in other ways. By the post-Civil War period, courts usually guaranteed the privilege of *limited liability*. Before limited liability was recognized, if an individual's business went bankrupt, everything that person owned, even home and personal possessions, could be seized and sold by creditors, those people to whom the business owed money. The new principle limited a corporation's liability to the corporation's assets. Once creditors had seized these, they had to stop. They could not touch the personal property of the shareholders or their shares in other corporations.

This privilege not only made it easier for entrepreneurs to raise capital for high-risk ventures, but it could serve as an inducement to crooked business dealings. Pirates like the Erie Gang could drain a corporation of its assets, enrich themselves personally through their control of corporate policy, allow the company to go bankrupt (as the Erie did), and still hold on to their misbegotten personal fortunes.

The Fourteenth Amendment also served the interests of corporate manipulators. After ducking the question for several years, the Supreme Court ruled in *Santa Clara County v. The Southern Pacific Railroad* (1886) that a corporation was a "person" under the meaning of the Fourteenth Amendment. The states were forbidden to pass laws that applied specifically to corporations and not to flesh-and-blood persons because those laws would deny the corporate person the civil rights that were granted to others.

While a corporation could legally be granted the civil rights of a human being, it was difficult to exact the same responsibilities of it. A walking and talking man or woman could be sent to jail for violating the law. A corporation could not. Indeed, because corporate directors acted as employees of a corporation, and not as its owners, it was difficult to punish them legally for corporate policies that they themselves might have formulated. In the freewheeling business atmosphere of the late nineteenth century, it is not surprising that entrepreneurs found this kind of organization to their liking.

Perfecting the Corporation

While thousands of businessmen organized corporations during the final decades of the nineteenth century, every one of them disappears in the shadow of one somber, muscular, and deeply religious Sunday-school teacher.

John D. Rockefeller was the virtuoso of the corporate structure; he used it as the famous Niccolò Paganini used the violin. It was said that when the great musician broke a string on his instrument during a concert, he played on, finding every note he needed on the three strings that remained. That was what Rockefeller did. When protesters, reformers, and lawmakers tried to stop his drive toward monopoly, frequently directing general laws at him alone, Rockefeller found a way to play on. At one point he controlled more than 90 percent of his chosen business.

Like Carnegie, Rockefeller was no technologist. He probably could have done very much what he did in any business he chose. But the one he chose offered splendid opportunities for monopoly making because it was new.

Black Gold

Crude oil has been known since prehistoric times. Here and there, as in western Pennsylvania, it seeped to the surface. The Indians native to the region used it as a medicine, and that classical American huckster, the snake-oil salesman, sometimes bottled the stuff, flavoring it with sugar and spices and tossing in a healthy shot of alcohol, thence claiming it cured everything from smallpox to a rainy day.

The farmers of western Pennsylvania were more likely to hate the gunk. If fouled the soil, polluted the waterways, and, if it caught fire, filled the air with billows of noxious smoke.

It was the flammability of oil that attracted the attenion of the chemist Benjamin Silliman. With the world population of whales declining in the 1850s because of thoughtless overharvesting, he and others were looking for an illuminant to replace whale oil.

As it turned out, natural gas was to play that role in the cities. But during his experiments with crude oil, Silliman isolated kerosene, or, as it was sometimes misnamed, "coal oil." It was a more than adequate illuminant in places where the gas lines did not reach as well as an excellent heating fuel. Moreover, it was cheap—much cheaper than whale oil—or at least promised to be.

As Silliman showed how to use oil, a former military engineer, Edwin Drake, showed how to get it in quantities large enough for commerce. At Titusville, Pennsylvania, he perfected a drill and pump system in 1859 that made it possible to bring seemingly infinite quantities of crude from deep within the earth. Drake's breakthrough caused a rush to Titusville much like the gold rush of 1849. The town was wide open, new home to ambitious and cantankerous speculators. One who visited the first oil fields, saw the possibilities in the industry, but shuddered at the competition to drill it, was John D. Rockefeller, then just old enough to vote.

John D. Rockefeller

Rockefeller came from a middle-class family of rural New York that seems in the folklore to have eaten and slept moneymaking. It was said that his father deliberately cheated his sons in order to train them for business careers. An accountant by trade, Rockefeller remained so single minded in the pursuit of wealth that as a young man in Cleveland, he kept flawless records of every cent he spent on himself, shoelaces as well as rent.

Strait-laced and dignified to the point of priggishness, he sighed disapprovingly when associates lit a cigar or paused after a day's work for a drink and a chat. It was not primarily because Rockefeller thought such practices sinful (although, as a pious Baptist, he was apt to feel that way), but because smoking and drinking were a waste of money that could be used to make more money. Even idle chatter was entered as a loss on the ledgers in Rockefeller's head. Time really was money.

Buying a good suit was not a waste. It was important in business to make a good impression, and the tall, well-turned Rockefeller always looked as though he had stepped from a fashion plate. But he had no patience for expenditure for pleasure or recreation. One lifelong business associate remembered the young Rockefeller having cracked a smile only once: after having swung a particularly profitable deal, Rockefeller had left the board room and danced a two-step jig in the corridor, murmuring in a singsong, "I'm bound to be rich! Bound to be rich!"

DOING BUSINESS

John D. Rockefeller was all business. "Don't let good fellowship get the least hold on you," he advised those who would succeed in business. As for foolish expenditures, he said, "I never had a craving for tobacco, or tea or coffee. I never had a craving for anything."

*John D. Rockefeller, flanked by attorneys, on his way to court where the gigantic
Standard Oil Trust was on trial.*

Horizontal Integration

He became very rich indeed, in part because, like
Carnegie, he integrated his oil business from top to
bottom. His creations, especially the first million-
dollar corporation, the Standard Oil Company, controlled oil wells, refineries, pipelines, and even retail
sales. By the end of the century, the horse-drawn Standard wagon, which sold kerosene from block to block
and farm to farm, was a daily sight in most American
communities. Refinery control of most gas stations is a
legacy of the vertical integration of John D. Rockefeller. But his distinctive innovation in the movement
to consolidate American industry was horizontal integration, controlling an industry by dominating the strategic stage, or "narrows," in the flow of manufacture.

In the infant oil industry, the "narrows" was the
refining process. By its very nature, drilling was risky.
It required some capital to sink a drill, but not enough
to keep a horde of modestly fixed speculators from descending on the Titusville area. Refining the oil, on the
contrary, was a field open to far fewer people because of
the large investment required. Although a wealthy
man by the end of the Civil War, Rockefeller was only
part owner of one of Cleveland's refineries.

The Trust

What Rockefeller wanted was to control it all, and his
means of doing so was the trust, the first of which
he organized in 1867 as the South Improvement
Company.

Assembling other refiners, most of whom he knew

personally, Rockefeller pointed out that all of them flirted constantly with bankruptcy for two reasons. First, they competed fiercely with one another, often cutting their prices at the break-even point or below in an attempt to gain an edge in the market. Second, they were at the mercy of the railroads in transporting their product to its major markets, the large cities of the Northeast and the ports from which kerosene was shipped abroad.

Rockefeller proposed to the refiners that they overcome both of these problems by surrendering the controlling interest in their companies to a board of trustees led by him, his brother William, and a close associate named Samuel Flagler. In return, they would receive trust certificates (shares), claims on the profits of the new consolidated company. The Standard Oil Trust—Standard of Ohio was formed in 1870—would stabilize the price of kerosene and drive uncooperative competitors out of business.

It worked. In order to crush refiners who refused to join the trust, Rockefeller forced the railroads to grant rebates (kickbacks) on every barrel of oil that his huge combination shipped. Although hardly delighted with the situation, the railroads complied because they were in competition with one another; if one line turned down Standard's offer, another won the contract. Because transportation costs were a big part of the retail price of kerosene, Rockefeller delivered a much cheaper product in Boston, New York, Philadelphia,

and Baltimore than did Standard's smaller competitors. Only when, in the 1890s, the Pure Oil Company pioneered in the construction of long pipelines to move its oil, thus matching Rockefeller's prices, did Standard lose its near monopoly.

An Age of Trusts

The trust structure was most useful in industries in which there was a single critical stage of manufacture that involved relatively few companies. Some of Rockefeller's most successful imitators were in sugar refining (the sugar trust controlled about 95 percent of the nation's facilities) and whiskey distilling. In 1890, James Buchanan Duke of Durham, North Carolina, founded the American Tobacco Company, which coordinated the activities of practically every cigarette manufacturer in the United States. Duke even came to an agreement with a similar cartel in England.

By 1890, many Americans had become convinced that when a few men could control a whole industry, the principle of economic opportunity was mocked and the very foundations of American democracy were jeopardized.

The Sherman Antitrust Act

Responding to public pressure in that year, Congress passed the Sherman Antitrust Act, which declared that "every contract, combination, in the form of trust

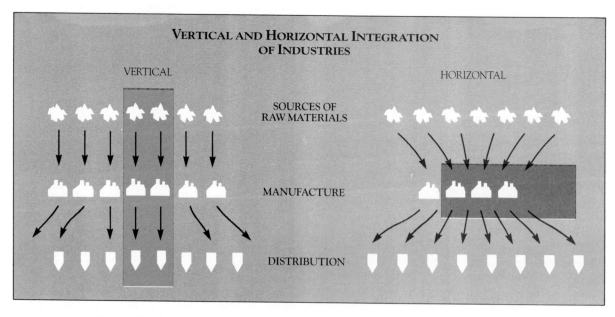

In controlling the manufacturing process from raw materials to final product, vertical integration permitted control of the price structure. In nearly monopolizing one stage of the manufacturing process, horizontal integration permitted control of the price structure.

An overfed monopoly demands tribute from workers, farmers, and merchants in the cartoon from the British magazine Puck.

or otherwise, or conspiracy, in restraint of trade or commerce among the several states, or with foreign nations, is hereby declared to be illegal." The Sherman Act authorized the Attorney General to move against such combinations and force them to dissolve into smaller businesses.

The law was no more successful in ending the consolidation movement than the Interstate Commerce Act was in controlling the power of the railroads. Critics said that the Sherman Act was a sham from the beginning, designed to quiet unease but not to hurt big business. In fact, the weakness of the law lay in the inability of congressmen to comprehend this new economic phenomenon. Real monopoly was so unfamiliar to the lawmakers that they were unable to draft a law that was worded well enough to be effective. The language of the Sherman Act was so ambivalent that a shrewd lawyer—and the trusts had the best—could always find a loophole.

Moreover, while congressmen could take fright at a popular uproar, the courts were immune to it. The Santa Clara County and Wabash cases were only the first of a whole string of probusiness decisions by the Supreme Court that ensured the supremacy of big business. In 1895, in *United States* v. *E. C. Knight Company*, the Court found that the most perfect monopoly in the nation, the sugar trust, could not be forced to disband because all its manufacturing facilities were within a single state, Pennsylvania. Although the refined sugar was sold in every state, the Court ruled that "commerce succeeds to manufacture and is not a part of it." Because the sugar trust was ostensibly a manufacturing concern, it was protected by the interstate-commerce clause of the Constitution.

Nor was the executive branch enthusiastic about attacking big business. President Grover Cleveland's Attorney General, Richard B. Olney, was a former corporation lawyer. Under Benjamin Harrison and William McKinley, the other presidents of the 1890s, the Justice Department was similarly probusiness. During the first ten years of the Sherman Act, only eighteen cases were instituted and four of these were aimed at labor unions, also "conspiracies in restraint of trade."

Consequently, rather than heralding doomsday for the trusts, the years between 1890 and 1901 were a

ENGINEERING PEOPLE: FREDERICK WINSLOW TAYLOR (1856–1915)

He was a slightly built, mild-looking, bespectacled man, but his impact on modern American industrial methods was colossal. Frederick Winslow Taylor was born into a comfortable and respectable family in Germantown, Pennsylvania, now a neighborhood of Philadelphia. Almost as a reflex for a young man of his class and time, he enrolled at prestigious Phillips Exeter Academy to prepare for a liberal arts education at Harvard. However, Taylor had scarcely begun college when he had to drop out because of extremely poor eyesight.

It was a blessing in disguise, for the young Philadelphian's interests and genius lay in the area of practical engineering, which in the nineteenth century was not an academic course of study.

Returning to Philadelphia, Taylor first apprenticed himself to a patternmaker (a craftsman who makes the wooden dummies from which molds for iron castings are constructed). Then, in 1878, no doubt to the dismay of his family, for such jobs were associated with immigrants and second-generation Americans, he went to work as a common laborer at nearby Midvale Steel.

Taylor did not remain a common laborer for long. His talents were recognized, and he moved into successively better jobs while studying mechanical engineering at Stevens Technological Institute, which granted him a Master of Science degree in 1883.

Stevens never had another student the likes of Taylor. In 1896, in collaboration with J. Maunsel White of Bethlehem Steel, Taylor invented a process for tempering the steel edges that are used in cutting other metals. Previously, the speed of metal-cutting machines had been limited because of the propensity of the steel to break or dull in a short period of time. The Taylor-White process allowed factories to speed up their production several times over and is still the basis of producing machinist's steel today. But Frederick Winslow Taylor's immortality rests in his engineering of workers to match his and others' improvements in industrial techniques.

His inventions in this realm were the "time-and-motion study" and "scientific management," phrases that spelled progress and bigger profits to most industrialists, lower wages to some workers, and dehumanization to many social critics.

Taylor's first time-and-motion study was made on men shoveling the coal at the Bethlehem Steel Works. With a stopwatch in his hand, Taylor intently watched every move the muckers made, how long it took them to make a forward thrust with the shovel, how long it took them to turn, how long to deposit the cargo in a furnace. He broke down the process into minuscule steps, just as one would approach a problem in mechanical engineering, and then redesigned the operation to get better production, that is, more coal shoveled in the same period of time.

Through experimentation Taylor discovered the maximum size and shape shovel for getting the job done. That is, at what point did the shovel become too big, draining the worker's strength by its load? At what point was the shovel too small to make the most of the worker's strength? His colleagues laughed at him, but not at the results. When Taylor was done, he had cut the number of men shoveling at Bethlehem Steel from 600 to 140.

Taylor believed that he was a benefactor of workers. For example, the adaptable and efficient shovelers who remained at Bethlehem were paid considerably more for their work than shovelers before Taylor went to work. The object of scientific management, Taylor told employers, was "lower labor costs, higher wages." Taylor believed that his invention not only would get jobs done more efficiently, but would solve the chronic and often violent conflict between workers and their employers by making them partners in efficiency.

It did not work out quite that way. The firms that purchased Taylor's services—he set up a consulting company in 1906—usually followed his advice to the letter in increasing worker productivity. Instead of paying the more efficient workers higher wages, however, companies adopted a "piecework" wage system with the rate tied to a worker's maximum efficiency. For example, when Taylor showed the managers of a New York sweatshop that women could, following his instructions, hem one hundred skirts during a ten-hour day, twenty or thirty more than they had sewed previously, the company promptly pegged the daily wage to which the women were accustomed to a production of one hundred pieces. That is, for each skirt they hemmed, the women received one-hundredth of a day's pay.

The woman who fell below this level, for whatever reason, took home less pay—often, as investigations showed, less than subsistence.

If, on the contrary, workers regularly increased their production to more than one hundred pieces a day, the common employer response was to cut the pay per piece. To workers, "Taylorism" was nothing but the old-fashioned speed-up, only more ruthless. Rather than making them partners in efficiency with employers, scientific management encouraged workers to soldier it, to work well below capacity, when a time-and-motion study was under way. Otherwise they would be driven to endurance to make their accustomed wage.

To some extent, it was unfair of labor leaders to heap the blame for worsening conditions on Taylor himself. Personally, he disapproved of sweating workers and undoubtedly would have applauded, in the year of his death, automobile manufacturer Henry Ford's introduction in his factories of the $5 day, then a handsome wage. But the principal purpose of scientific management was higher profits, and one of Taylor's leading disciples, Frank Gilbreth, was quoted as saying, "It is the aim of Scientific Management to induce men to act as nearly like machines as possible." Taylor was a villain to those who sympathized with the industrial worker. In his trilogy of novels, *U.S.A.*, John Dos Passos wrote that the father of scientific management died with his stopwatch in his hand.

Efficiency expert Frederick Winslow Taylor.

golden age. The number of state chartered trusts actually grew from 251 to 290. More telling, the amount of money invested in trusts rose from $192 million to $326 million. By the end of the century, there was no doubt that the demands of modern manufacturing meant that massive organizations were here to stay. But whether they would continue to be the private possessions of a few Bells, Morgans, Carnegies, and Rockefellers was still open to debate.

For Further Reading

For a general discussion of technology and inventors, see Roger Burlingame, *Engines of Democracy: Inventions and Society in Mature America* (1940). Some special studies in the history of technology that, untypically, make for engaging reading include Matthew Josephson, *Edison* (1959); H. C. Passer, *The Electrical Manufacturers, 1875–1900* (1953); Richard N. Current, *The Typewriter and the Men Who Made It* (1954); C. B. Kuhlman, *The Development of the Flour Milling Industry in the United States* (1929); and R. A. Clemens, *The American Livestock and Meat Industry* (1932).

On business itself, Edward C. Kirkland, *Dream and Thought in the Business Community, 1860–1900* (1956), and Sidney Fine, *Laissez Faire and the Welfare State: A Study of Conflict in American Thought, 1865–1901* (1956), are good to establish a conceptual framework. On the businessmen, Matthew Josephson, *The Robber Barons* (1934), provides a harshly critical analysis. Dissenting from him in the case of John D. Rockefeller is Allan Nevins, *Study in Power: John D. Rockefeller* (1953). The best single-volume study of Carnegie is J. F. Wall, *Andrew Carnegie* (1971).

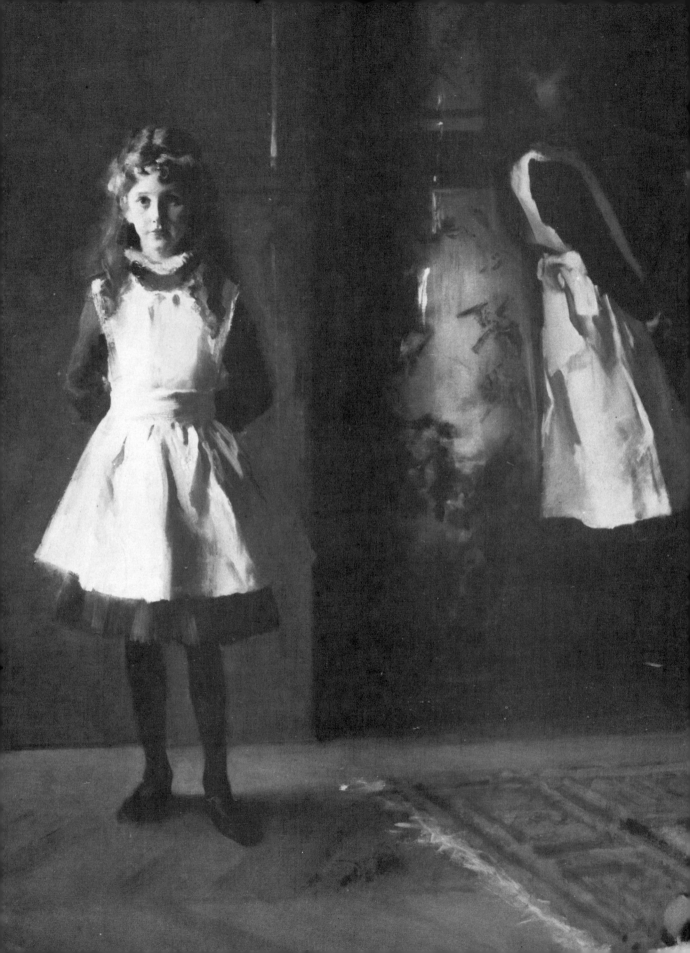

Great Wealth, Its Critics and Defenders

Americans React to Their Industrial Aristocracy

In *Democracy in America*, written more than twenty years before the Civil War, Alexis de Tocqueville admired the equity with which wealth was distributed in the United States. Except for the slaves of the South, no Americans seemed so poor that they could not hope to improve their situation. Perhaps more important, no Americans *believed* that they were destined to remain at the economic level at which they had been born.

At the same time, no Americans were so rich that they formed an aristocracy, a distinct social class permanently established above the mass of the population that enjoyed special privileges denied to the rest. Indeed, the wealthy people whom Tocqueville met or observed seemed to feel that a single stroke of bad luck would send them tumbling down into the world of hard work, sore backs, and calloused hands. In the land of opportunity, it was as easy to fail as to succeed. American society was as fluid as it was egalitarian.

Nevertheless, Tocqueville detected the beginnings of an American aristocracy in the owners

Members of America's leisure class flaunted their wealth and devoted themselves to idle pursuits. This detail from John Singer Sargent's painting, The Daughters of Edward Darley Boit, *portrays some young members of this privileged class.*

of factories who were first making their wealth, power, and interests known during the time he visited the United States. This new class worried him because its riches were quite different from traditional wealth. Unlike wealth derived from land, wealth derived from industry was potentially infinite because a capitalist's property could be expanded indefinitely. Should industrialization triumph in the United States, Tocqueville speculated, the nation that so highly prized the ideal of equal opportunity for all would find itself saddled and driven by a small class of people who were so rich and powerful that their privileged status was permanent.

What worried Tocqueville most about this eventuality was that industrial wealth was derived from an impersonal exploitation of workingpeople. Unlike agricultural grandees, who lived on their lands in frequent contact with those whose labor enriched them, industrial barons could live far from their factories, immune to feeling personal responsibility for their employees' welfare. The industrial aristocracy, Tocqueville suggested, would be "one of the harshest which ever existed in the world." It would treat workers not as people but as commodities to be bought and sold. Such dehumanization, as a nobleman from France knew better than anyone else, would produce social discontent, even revolution. Tocqueville warned that "the friends of democracy should keep their eyes anxiously fixed" on the people who owned the nation's factories.

The lavish interior of The Breakers, *a Newport, Rhode Island, mansion.*

How the Very Rich Lived

Much of what Tocqueville foresaw came to pass very suddenly during the years after the Civil War. The tremendous expansion of industry created an upper class with greater fortunes than could have been imagined in the age of Jackson. So rich that they could move far from the sources of their wealth and grow richer with no attention to business, the "filthy rich," particularly the second generation (which inherited its fortunes), cultivated idleness and leisure as a way of life. Tocqueville's "friends of democracy" did not keep so close an eye on this class that they prevented its rise. But they were quick to criticize America's new elite and to offer alternatives to the kind of society that produced them.

As Rich as Rockefeller

When Tocqueville visited the United States, the country's richest man was a Philadelphia merchant, Stephen Girard. When Girard died in 1837, his estate of $7 million awed Americans. They heaped praise on him not so much for having amassed such a treasure, but for what he did with it. Girard left his money to various philanthropic societies and to the city of Philadelphia. He reaffirmed America's belief in equality of opportunity by showing what a man could do in the United States and by plowing his fortune back into the society where new generations could compete for it on an equal basis.

Just a decade later, John Jacob Astor died and left $40 million to his son. The same press and pulpits that had lauded Girard vilified him. America wanted no aristocrats, Astor's critics said, no heirs and heiresses who had done nothing to earn their fortunes. That was Europe's way, not America's. Astor had mocked the ideal of equality and the gospel of hard work.

After the Civil War, the bequests of fortunes from one generation to the next had become so common that comment was superfluous. Moreover, the fortunes

YOU CAN TAKE IT WITH YOU

At the Vanderbilt family tomb on Staten Island, watchmen punched a time clock every hour on the hour around the clock. William Vanderbilt, son of the Commodore, had a deathly fear of graverobbers.

that were made in the new industry grew larger, as did the size of the millionaire class. In 1892, there were more than four thousand millionaires in the United States, most of them richer than Girard had been. The size of the fortune that it took to perch at the top of the pyramid grew greater too. Cornelius Vanderbilt left $100 million when he died in 1877. His son, William, doubled that amount in only eight years. By 1900, Andrew Carnegie pocketed $500 million in a single transaction. John D. Rockefeller gave that much away within a few years; all the while, his family continued to grow richer.

This phenomenon grated on traditional American sensibilities in two ways. First, fortunes of such size were effectively permanent. Capital of $5 million returning profits of 10 percent annually—modest in the late nineteenth century—provided the family that possessed the fortune with an annual income of $500,000, several million dollars by today's measure. And yet, without income tax, the fortune on which such an income was based grew larger. The very idea that someone could grow richer while not working mocked the deeply ingrained American value of hard work as the source of rewards.

Conspicuous Consumption

What was worse, the new industrial millionaires flaunted their wealth in ways that offended the traditional teaching that frugality was a virtue. As Thorstein Veblen, an eccentric sociologist of Norwegian origin, observed in several books written at the end of the century, the very wealthy literally lived to spend money for the sake of proving that they had money.

BELMONT'S WINE CELLAR

While many millionaires outspent August Belmont, New York associate of the Rothschild banking interests, few of them spent their money as gracefully as did the European-born banker. It was said of Belmont that his monthly wine budget was $20,000.

Veblen called this showy extravagance "conspicuous consumption," and the propensity to practically throw it away, "conspicuous waste."

Having much more money than they could possibly put to good use, the very rich competed in spending it by hosting lavish parties for one another, by building extravagant palaces, by purchasing huge yachts that were good for little but show, by adorning themselves with costly clothing and jewelry, and by buying European titles for their daughters.

Some high-society parties lasting but a few hours cost more than $100,000. At one, hosted by the self-proclaimed prince of spenders, Harry Lehr, one hundred dogs dined on "fricassee of bones" and gulped down shredded dog biscuit prepared by a French chef. The guests at one New York banquet ate their meal while mounted on horses (trays balanced on the animals' withers); the horses simultaneously munched oats out of sterling-silver feedbags. At a costume affair, guests boasted that they had spent more than $10,000 each on their fancy dress.

It was the golden age of yachting. Cornelius Vanderbilt's *North Star* was 250 feet long. Albert C. Burrage's *Aztec* carried 270 tons of coal; it could steam 5,500 miles without calling at a port for fuel. As on land, J. P. Morgan was champion at sea. He owned three successively larger, faster, and more opulent yachts called *Corsair*. (Morgan had a sense of humor;

Guests attending a horseback banquet at Sherry's Ballroom in New York in 1903.

PRIVATE CARS

Partial to yachts, J. P. Morgan never owned a private railroad car, which was one of the status symbols of the late nineteenth century. In George Gould's, guests for dinner were expected to dress formally; Gould's liveried waiters served the food on solid gold plates. The Vanderbilt family's car, called the "Vanderbilt," could not accommodate all the guests whom they wished to entertain, so they had a new one built and called it "Duchess" after Consuelo. At Palm Beach, a favorite pleasuring ground of the rich, twenty to thirty private cars were sometimes parked in a special section of the train yard. When Morgan wished to go to a place he could not reach by water, he had to rent an opulent private car. On one occasion, he rented a whole train of private cars to transport east coast Episcopalian bishops to a conference in San Francisco.

Consuelo Vanderbilt, the Duchess of Marlborough, was the most famous of the wealthy American women who married European nobles in the late nineteenth century.

corsair means "pirate.") At least Morgan used his—at every opportunity. Other millionaires bought yachts simply so they could say that they owned one.

Nowhere was consumption more conspicuous and lavish than at upper-class resorts such as Newport, Rhode Island. A summer "cottage" of thirty rooms, used for only three months a year, cost $1 million. Coal baron E. J. Berwind spent $1.5 million to build "The Elms." William K. Vanderbilt outdid everyone with "Marble House." That cottage cost $2 million; the furniture inside, $9 million.

Those places were for vacations. At home in the cities, the millionaires created neighborhoods of mansions such as New York's Fifth Avenue, a thoroughfare given over to grand houses for twenty blocks; Chicago's Gold Coast, which loomed over the city's lakeshore; and San Francisco's Nob Hill, from which palaces looked down on the city like the castles of medieval barons.

A Lord in the Family

A fad of the very rich that aggravated many Americans was the rush during the 1880s and 1890s to marry daughters to European nobles. Nothing more clearly dramatized the aristocratic pretensions of the new elite. Wealthy families took pride in the price that they paid for an earl or a prince.

It was a two-way bargain. An American daughter got a title to wear to Newport along with her diamonds. An impoverished European aristocrat got money with which to maintain himself in his life of fine wines and fox hunts.

Thus, heiress Alice Thaw was embarrassed on her honeymoon as countess of Yarmouth when creditors seized her husband's luggage. She had to wire her father for money to get it out of hock. Helena Zimmerman, the daughter of a coal and iron millionaire from Cincinnati, married the duke of Manchester. For twenty years their bills were paid by the father of the duchess out of the labor of workers living on subsistence wages.

The most famous American aristocrats were the heiresses of two of the original robber barons, Jay Gould and Cornelius Vanderbilt. Anna Gould became the Countess Boni de Castellane. Before she divorced the count so that she could marry his cousin, the higher-ranking Prince de Sagan, the count extracted more than $5 million from Jay Gould's fortune. Consuelo Vanderbilt was married against her wishes into the proudest family in England. Both when Consuelo married the duke of Marlborough and when she divorced him, the payoff ran to several million. The duke may have been the only individual ever to get the better of the Vanderbilt family. American businessmen could handle their own kind easily enough, but they had trouble with their status-symbol sons-in-law.

Women as Decor

The role of young heiresses as pawns in the game of conspicuous waste helps to illustrate the curious role of women in the new social class. They were, of course, more idle than the men; denied an active role in business and public life, they were spared the homemaking duties of the middle-class wife and daughter.

Mrs. George Gould, wearing the half-million dollar pearl necklace for which she gained fame.

They were, in effect, their families' chief consumers. Woman's role was to reflect her husband's accomplishment in amassing wealth; she was a glittering display piece for costly clothing and jewelry. Mrs. George Gould, daughter-in-law of the crusty Jay, went through life known exclusively as the owner of a single pearl necklace that was worth $500,000. No one ever mentioned Mrs. Gould in any other context. Her life revolved around the moments when she entered ballrooms, all eyes on her pearls.

Women's fashions were designed to emphasize their wearers' complete idleness. Fashion, by its very nature, is conspicuously wasteful. In keeping up with changes, the whole point of fashion, the wealthy woman was demonstrating that it made no dent in her husband's fortune if she annually discarded last year's expensive clothing to make room in her closet for the latest from Paris.

Fashion reflects social status in other ways. When wealthy women laced themselves up in crippling steel and bone corsets, which made it difficult for them to move, let alone perform any physical work, they were making it clear that they did not have to do such work and were purely decorative. They had servants to care for every petty detail of their lives.

Men's clothing reflected social status, too. The tall silk hat, the badge of the capitalist, was a completely useless headgear. It offered neither protection nor warmth. But it did prevent a man from so much as bending down to dust his patent-leather shoes. "White collar," displaying clean linen at wrist and neck, made it clear that the wearer did no work that would soil his clothing.

Unlikely Neighbors

For the most part, ordinary Americans knew of the shenanigans of the very rich only through hearsay and the popular press. Farmers and factory workers did not vacation at Newport or attend costume balls and ducal weddings. The nature of urban life in the late nineteenth century was such, however, that the idle rich could not completely conceal their extravagance from the middle and lower classes.

The rich employed legions of servants to maintain their mansions. The grandeur and waste of upper-class life was well known to these poorly paid people. (Two million women worked in domestic service at the end of the century.) More important, because it was impossible to commute long distances in the congested cities, whether for business or social life, the wealthy lived not in isolated suburbs but close to the centers of New York, Boston, Philadelphia, Chicago, and other great cities.

The tradesmen who made daily deliveries of groceries, meat, vegetables and fruit, ice, coal (for heating), and other necessities, not to mention repairmen and those who delivered durable goods, were intimately familiar with the kind of wealth that their customers enjoyed. Marginal workers who were employed by the service and the light manufacturing industries of the center city walked daily past palaces and saw the rich come and go in lacquered carriages tended by flunkies in livery.

Popular Sentiments

In newspapers aimed at a mass readership, in popular songs, and in the melodramas favored by working-people, the idleness and extravagance of the "filthy rich" were favorite themes. The wealthy were depicted with a mixture of envy and resentment. New York's Tin Pan Alley, the center of the sheet-music industry, preached a combination of pity for the "bird in a gilded cage," the wealthy woman, and the traditional moral that because poor people worked, they were more virtuous.

In the popular melodramas of the day, simple plays with no subtlety of character and a completely predictable plot, right-living poor people were pitted against an unscrupulous rich villain. "You are only a shopgirl," said the high-society lady in a typical play. "An honest shopgirl," replied the heroine in stilted language, "as far above a fashionable idler as heaven is above earth!" (The poor but virtuous shopgirl was often rewarded in the final act by marriage to a rich young man; she consequently took up the life of idleness that she had condemned through two and a half acts.)

Ordinary people studiously followed the scandals that periodically rocked high society. In 1872, "Jubilee Jim" Fisk was shot to death by a rival for the affections of his showgirl mistress, Josie Mansfield. Newspaper readers took satisfaction in the fact that Fisk's great wealth and power could not save him from a violent death at the comparatively young age of thirty-eight. Nevertheless, a good part of the story's appeal were the details of Fisk's sumptuous personal life, on which the newspapers lovingly dwelled.

Even more sensational was the 1906 murder of architect Stanford White by millionaire Harry Thaw. During his trial, Thaw accused White of having seduced his beautiful fiancée, Evelyn Nisbet. Her testimony concerning the famous White's peculiarities behind closed doors simultaneously titillated the public and served as a moral justification for the murder. (Thaw went free.) Such scandals were the stock in trade of nationally circulated periodicals, such as *Police Gazette* and *Frank Leslie's Illustrated Newspaper*, that appealed to the work-

Evelyn Nesbit, as photographed by Gertrude Kasebier around 1903.

ing classes. By the end of the century, many large daily papers also took to bumping conventional news to the back pages when an upper-class scandal came up in the courts.

The Critics of the New Order

While the popular media treated the idle rich with a mixture of titillation and resentment, America also produced a number of deadly serious social critics who attracted large followings with their explanations of how the land of equality had produced an aristocracy and their suggestions for getting rid of it.

Henry George and the Single Tax

A lively writing style and a knack for simplifying difficult economic ideas made journalist Henry George and his single tax the center of a briefly momentous social movement. In *Progress and Poverty*, which was published in 1879, George observed the obvious. Instead of freeing people from onerous labor, as it had promised to do, the machine had put millions to work under killing conditions for long hours. Instead of making life easier and fuller, the mass-production of goods had enriched the few in the House of Have, and had impoverished the millions in the House of Want.

George did not blame either industrialization or capitalism as such for the misery he saw around him. Like most Americans, he believed that the competition for comfort and security was a wellspring of the nation's energy. The trouble began only when those who were successful in the race grew so wealthy that they could live off the "rents" from their property.

George called income derived from mere ownership of property "unearned increment" because it required no work, effort, or ingenuity of its possessors; the property grew more valuable and its owners richer only because other people needed access to it in order to survive. Such value was spurious, George said. Government had every right to levy a 100 percent tax on it. Because the revenues from this tax would be quite enough to pay all the expenses of government, George called it the single tax. All other taxes would be abolished. The idle rich would be destroyed as a social class. The competition that made the country great would take place without the handicaps of taxation. Everyone would compete on an equal basis.

George's theory was both easy to grasp and firmly within American traditional attitudes. It made him immensely popular among ordinary people, who resented the power and life style of the very rich. In 1886, George narrowly missed election as mayor of New York, a city where real-estate values and "unearned increment" from land were higher than anywhere in the world. Within a few years, however, the single-tax movement lost ground to other ideas for reform.

Edward Bellamy and Looking Backward

One of these new movements was the Nationalism inspired by Edward Bellamy's novel of 1888, *Looking Backward, 2000–1887*. Within two years of publication, the book sold 200,000 copies (the equivalent of about 1 million in the 1980s) and led to the founding of about 150 "Nationalist clubs," made up of people who shared Bellamy's vision of the future.

The story that moved them so is rather simple. A proper young Bostonian of the 1880s succumbs to a mysterious sleep and awakes in the United States of the twenty-first century. There he discovers that technology has produced not a world of sharp class divisions and widespread misery (as in 1887), but a utopia that

American writer Edward Bellamy, author of the widely-read novel, Looking Backward.

provides abundance for all. Like George, Bellamy was not opposed to industrial development in itself.

Capitalism no longer exists in the world of *Looking Backward*. Through a peaceful democratic revolution—won at the polls—the American people have abolished competitive greed and idle unproductive living because they had become at odds with true American ideals. Instead of private ownership of land and industry, the state owns the means of production and administers them for the good of all. Everyone contributes to the common wealth. Everyone lives decently, and none wastefully, on its fruits.

Bellamy's vision was socialistic. Because he rooted it in American values rather than in the internationalism of the Marxists, he called it "Nationalism." The patriotic quality of his message made his gospel more palatable to middle-class Americans who, while troubled by the growth of fantastic fortunes and of wretched poverty, found foreign ideologies and talk of class warfare obnoxious and frightening.

After the 1890s, Bellamy's influence declined as rapidly as George's. In making socialistic ideas respectable, however, he too paved the way for the reform movements of the twentieth century.

Henry Demarest Lloyd

Henry Demarest Lloyd was not so much the dreamer as George and Bellamy were. His influential book, *Wealth Against Commonwealth* (1894), was an exposé of only one corporation, Standard Oil. (In 1904, Ida M. Tarbell wrote an even more thorough indictment.) In the book, by painstakingly detailing the morally dubious business practices of John D. Rockefeller, Lloyd called into question the desirability of the fundamental institution of the new American economy, the privately owned corporation.

Urban in his world view, well educated, and sophisticated, Lloyd embraced a Jeffersonian ideal of society. No socialist, he believed simply that no one should be so rich as to be able to tyrannize others and no one so poor as to be at the mercy of the rich. He envisioned not a socialist system, in which the state owns the means of production, but a society of independent, property-owning individuals who were more or less equally well fixed. During the 1890s, he joined the farmers' Populist party and worked to spread its Jeffersonian message among industrial workers. Workers and farmers, he argued, were producers. Powerful capitalists and bankers were parasites who, by virtue of their great economic power, threatened the good society. Because, in the final analysis, few Americans wanted to change the basic structure of society, especially private property, Lloyd may have struck closer than George or Bellamy to the national unease.

The Social Gospel

Taking a more moralistic approach to the tensions of the late nineteenth century were a number of influential Protestant clergymen. Troubled by the callousness of big business, preachers of the "Social Gospel" emphasized the Christian's social obligations, his duty to be his brother's keeper.

Walter Rauschenbusch began his ministerial career on the edge of Hell's Kitchen, one of New York City's worst slums. "One could hear human virtue cracking and crushing all around," he wrote in later years. Pov-

A photograph of Hell's Kitchen, a slum in New York, as shown in Jacob Riis's How the Other Half Lives.

erty was the cause of crime and sin, and mass poverty was the result of allowing great capitalists a free hand in enriching themselves. Later, as a professor at Rochester Theological Seminary, Rauschenbusch taught the obligation of the churches to work for both the relief of the poor and a more equitable distribution of wealth.

Washington Gladden, a Congregationalist, called unrestricted competition "antisocial and anti-Christian." He did not propose the abolition of capitalism, but he did call for regulation of its grossest immoralities. He was highly moralistic. Late in life, Gladden described John D. Rockefeller's fortune as "tainted money" and urged his church not to accept contributions from the millionaire.

The Social Gospel appealed to many middle-class people, often modestly well-to-do themselves, who did not suffer directly from the power of the very wealthy but who were offended by the extravagance and idleness of their life. William Dean Howells, the editor of the *Atlantic Monthly*, wrote a novel about a successful industrialist (*The Rise of Silas Lapham*, 1885) who finds the idleness of his new life discomfiting. He "rises," finds purpose and happiness again, only when he loses his fortune and is forced to return to productive work. Howells even convinced an old friend from Ohio, former president Rutherford B. Hayes, to go on record late in his life as an advocate of the peaceful abolition of capitalism.

The Defenders of the System

Such an array of criticism did not, of course, go unanswered. At the same time that great wealth was taking its knocks, it was reaping the praise of defenders. In part, like the critics, they drew on traditional American values to justify the new social system. In part, also like the critics, the defenders created new philosophies, original with the era of industrial capitalism.

The Success Gospel

The defenders' strongest argument touched the heart of the American Dream. The United States had been built on the desire to prosper. Therefore, if competition for riches was a virtue, what was wrong with winning? Far from a source of anxiety, as the critics said, or evidence of social immorality, the fabulous fortunes of America's wealthy families were an index of their virtue. The Rockefellers, Carnegies, and Morgans deserved their money.

Success manuals, books that purported to show how anyone could become a millionaire, were read as avidly

> ## HONEST MEN
>
> "Ninety-eight out of one hundred of the rich men of America are honest. That is why they are rich. That is why they are trusted with money. That is why they carry on great enterprises and find plenty of people to work with them. It is because they are honest men."
> Russell B. Conwell

as the books of George and Bellamy and the sidelong swipes of the scandal sheets. All pretty much the same, the manuals drew on the widespread assumptions that hard work, honesty, frugality, loyalty to employers and partners, and other "bourgeois virtues" drawn from Benjamin Franklin inevitably led to success. Having succeeded, American's millionaires deserved not resentment but admiration and imitation.

Shrugging off his enemies, John D. Rockefeller said flatly, "God gave me my money." A Baptist minister from Philadelphia, Russell B. Conwell, made a fortune delivering a lecture on the same theme. In "Acres of Diamonds," which the eloquent preacher delivered to paying audiences more than six thousand times, Conwell said that great wealth was a great blessing. Not only could every American be rich, but every American *should* be rich.

If a person failed, it was his own fault. "There is not a poor person in the United States," Conwell said, "who was not made poor by his own shortcomings." The opportunities, the "acres of diamonds," were everywhere, waiting to be collected.

Conversely, those who already were rich were by definition virtuous. "Ninety-eight out of one hundred of the rich men of America are honest. That is why they are rich." Conwell's own extraordinary success indicated that many Americans believed what he said.

Horatio Alger and "Ragged Dick"

Through the 130 boys' novels written by another minister, Horatio Alger, the Success Gospel was conveyed to the younger generation. Alger's books sold 20 million copies between 1867 and 1899, and a battallion of imitators doubtless accounted for millions more.

Alger was no writer. His prose was wooden, and his characters were snipped from cardboard. The plots of all the short novels are variations on two or three simple themes. Based on the assumption that the purpose of life is to get money, the most popular plot tells of a poor lad who is honest, hard working, loyal to his employer, and clean living. "Ragged Dick," Alger's first

The cover from one of Horatio Alger's 130 novels for boys.

hero and the prototype for "Tattered Tom," "Lucky Luke Larkin," and dozens of others, is insufferably courteous and always goes to church.

Curiously, the hero does not get rich slowly through hard work. At the beginning of the final chapter, he usually is as badly off as on page one. Then, however, Ragged Dick is presented with what amounts to a visitation of grace, a divine gift that rewards his virtues. The daughter of a rich industrialist falls off the Staten Island Ferry; or she stumbles into the path of a runaway brewery wagon drawn by panicked horses; or she slips into the Niagara River just above the falls. Because he acts quickly, rescuing her, the heroic lad is rewarded with a job, marriage to the daughter, and eventually the grateful father's fortune. While appealing to the adolescent boy's yen for adventure, the novels also touched the American evangelical belief in divine grace. Just as he did with Rockefeller, God gave Ragged Dick his money as reward for his virtues.

Philanthropy

The flaw in the Success Gospel as a justification of great fortunes was the obvious fact that many rich men got their money by practicing the opposite of the touted virtues: dishonesty, betrayal of partners and employers, reckless speculation rather than thrift; and they grew richer while living a life of sumptuous ease. Rockefeller's unethical practices were probably exaggerated, but there was no question that he cut corners. Similar suspicions surrounded practically every rich family in the country.

To compensate for the negative marks on their reputations, wealthy businessmen turned to philanthropy as a kind of retroactive justification of their fortunes. Horatio Alger supported institutions that housed homeless boys in New York City. Russell B. Conwell founded Temple University, where poor young men could study very cheaply and improve themselves. Rockefeller and other industrial millionaires gave huge sums to their churches and to universities. Leland Stanford built a wholly new "Harvard of the West" in California. In retirement, Rockefeller took particular interest in helping American blacks to break out of the prison that their race had built around them.

Andrew Carnegie devised a coherent theory that harked back to Stephen Girard and justified fabulous fortunes on the basis of stewardship. In a widely publicized essay entitled "Wealth," he argued that the unrestricted pursuit of riches made American society vital and strong. The man who succeeded became a steward, or trustee. He had an obligation to distribute his money where it would provide opportunities for poor people to join the competition of the next generation. Indeed, Carnegie said that the rich man who died rich, died a failure. He retired in 1901 and devoted the rest of his life to granting money to libraries, schools, and useful social institutions. He was so rich, however, that despite extraordinary generosity, he died a multimillionaire.

Social Darwinism

Carnegie was the most thoughtful of the Gilded Age millionaires. He was one of the few who understood and openly preached the justification of great wealth that was propounded in a series of books, essays, and lectures by the British philosopher Herbert Spencer.

Because Spencer seemed to apply Charles Darwin's biological theory of evolution to human society, his theory is known as "Social Darwinism." According to Spencer, as in the world of animals and plants, where species compete for life and those best adapted survive ("natural selection"), the "fittest" people rise to the top in the social competition for riches. Eventually, in the dog-eat-dog world, they alone survive. "If they are sufficiently complete to live," Spencer wrote, "they do live, and it is well that they should live. If they are not sufficiently complete to live, they die and it is best they should die."

The intellectual toughness of Social Darwinism made Spencer immensely popular among American businessmen who were proud of their practicality. The Englishman was never so celebrated in his own country as he was in the United States. Although a vain man, Spencer was frequently embarrassed by the adulation heaped on him at banquets sponsored by American academics and rich businessmen. Unlike the Success Gospel, Social Darwinism accounted for brutal business practices and underhand methods, justifying them as the natural "law of the jungle."

The language of Social Darwinism crept into the vocabulary of both businessmen and politicians who represented business interests. They argued against government relief of the plight of the poor not simply because they would have to pay higher taxes, but because such welfare policies would interfere with natural processes.

But few American millionaires were true Social Darwinists. The very ruthlessness of the theory, which made it more consistent than the Success Gospel, also made it unpalatable to rich families who, in their personal lives, were committed to traditional religious values. Moreover, businessmen are rarely intellectuals, and Spencer's philosophy and writing style were as

After he gave $10 million to four Scottish universities, Andrew Carnegie was dubbed "The MacMillion" by cartoonist Bernard Partridge in Punch *magazine, 1901.*

thick as crude oil. Understanding him demanded careful study, such as businessmen rarely had the time to do. As a result, his explanation of the new society was more influential among scholars.

William Graham Sumner

The most important American disciple of Herbert Spencer was a Yale professor, William Graham Sumner, and he was as uncompromising as his master in his opposition to aiding the poor, putting government restrictions on business practices, and interfering in any way whatsoever with the law of the jungle.

Sumner's consistency also led him to oppose the high protective tariff and government intervention in labor disputes. To protect and even to subsidize American industry by taxing imports was just as unnatural to him as was regulating the growth of trusts. If American manufacturers were not fit to compete with European manufacturers in a free market, Sumner said, they were not fit to survive. Likewise, Sumner opposed government intervention in strikes on behalf of employers. He believed that the strike was a natural test of the fitness of the employers' and the workers' causes. The outcome of a strike determined which side was "right." To businessmen who used government trade policy and courts to their own purposes, Sumner's applications of "natural law" were going too far.

After the turn of the century, the principles of Social Darwinism were turned on their head by the sociologist Lester Frank Ward of Brown University. Whereas Sumner argued that nature must be allowed to work without restraint, Ward suggested that human society had evolved to a point where natural evolution could be guided by government policy. Just as farmers improved fruit trees and ranchers improved livestock through selective breeding, government could improve society by intervening in the naturally slow evolutionary process. Ward's Social Darwinism influenced two generations of American reformers: the progressives of the early twentieth century, and the New Deal liberals of the 1930s.

Pragmatism

Equally durable was the influence of a peculiarly American philosophy, pragmatism. Both Charles Pierce and William James were influenced by evolutionary theories, and they carried them beyond human society to the nature of truth. They argued that just as species and societies evolve, truth evolves.

There was no single everlasting truth, only many truths that were always changing to adapt to reality. The test of what was true for a particular moment was

THE LAST DANCE OF THE IDLE RICH:
THE BRADLEY MARTIN BALL OF 1897

The Waldorf-Astoria Hotel was decorated to resemble the palace at Versailles for the Bradley Martin Costume Ball in 1897.

In the winter of 1896/97, Americans were languishing in the depths of the greatest depression that the nation had ever experienced, bad times that would be exceeded only during the Great Depression of the 1930s. Businesses had failed by the thousands. Several million people were out of work. People had been evicted from farms and homes by the hundreds of thousands. Charitable organizations were strained to the breaking point; some had given up in despair and closed their doors. Jobless people had marched on Washington; others had rioted; yet others coped in a stupor day by day—gathering coal along railroad tracks, or picking through the garbage pails behind expensive restaurants. In November 1896, a presidential candidate who was called the Great Commoner, William Jennings Bryan, was defeated by William McKinley, who, fairly or not, was widely described as a tool of the moneyed interests. It was an unhappy time, with class sensibilities at their keenest.

Sometime during that winter, at breakfast in his Fifth Avenue mansion, Bradley Martin, one of high society's grandest adornments, had an idea. "I think it would be a good thing if we got up something," he told his wife and brother, Frederick. "There seems to be a great deal of depression in trade; suppose we send out invitations to a concert."

Mrs. Martin complained that a concert would benefit only foreigners. Most professional musicians in the country at that time were German and Italian, and she wanted to do something for Americans. "I've got a far better idea," she said. "Let us give a costume ball at so short notice that our guests won't have time to get their dresses from Paris. That will give an impetus to trade that nothing else will."

The conversation was recorded by Frederick Townshend Martin with no intention of making his brother and sister-in-law look either vicious or ridiculous. In fact, he justified their economic theories, explaining that "many New York shops sold out brocades and silks which had been lying in their stockrooms for years."

The ball was held on February 10, 1897, in the ballroom of the Waldorf-Astoria Hotel, which had been decorated to resemble the palace of the French kings at Versailles. To the Martins' set, it was a glorious success. According to experts, there was never such a display of jewels in New York. Financier August Belmont came in gold-inlaid armor that cost him $10,000. The costumes of others were inferior only by comparison.

One woman said that in order to help the particularly hard-pressed Indians, she had had Native Americans make her Pocohontas costume. Bradley Martin himself made a curious selection. As the host at Versailles, he had first claim to be Louis XIV, the Sun King, who had built the great palace and was universally conceded to be the most glorious of the French monarchs. But Bradley chose to be his great-grandson, Louis XV. He would not have wanted to be Louis XVI, who had been beheaded because of his and his predecessors' extravagance in a country where the poor suffered wretched misery.

"Everyone said it was the most brilliant of the kind ever seen in America."

Not quite everyone. Even before the first waltz, Martin and his "idle rich" friends were being vilified from pulpit, editorial desk, and political platform for their callous decadence in a difficult time. Much more significant, the ball was criticized by more than one business leader. If idle heirs such as the vapid Martin did not know that such affairs caused resentment, class hatred, and (in more than one instance in the past) social revolution, sensible businessmen such as Mark Hanna did. Two years after the ball, in his book *The Theory of the Leisure Class*, sociologist Thorstein Veblen would give a name to Bradley Martin's life style, "conspicuous consumption." However, already by that time, America's wealthy were learning to enjoy their riches quietly. Indeed, looking back after several decades, two distinguished historians, Charles and Mary Beard, called the Bradley Martin ball of 1897 the "climax of lavish expenditure" in the United States. "This grand ball of the plutocrats astounded the country, then in the grip of a prolonged business depression with its attendant unemployment, misery, and starvation."

It was not only the fear of social upheaval that wrote an end to conspicuous consumption on a grand scale. To a large extent, high-society affairs like the ball were the doings of women, the wives and daughters of rich businessmen. After the turn of the century, many of them rebelled against their enforced idleness and frivolity and began to take an interest, even a leading role, in social and political causes: votes for women, of course, but also prohibition, suppression of the white-slave racket (prostitution), amelioration of lower-class suffering, and other social programs of the Progressive era.

Not Mrs. Bradley Martin and her husband, of course. Unreconstructable denizens of the ballroom, they carried on as before. But not in New York. The ball was so unpopular there that city hall slapped a large tax increase on the Martin mansion on Fifth Avenue. In a huff, the Martins moved to London. Brother Frederick Townshend Martin wrote of this relocation with an air of despondency, as though the United States had lost two valuable citizens.

the consequence of a belief. What worked? What got results? What, in James's phrase, so characteristic of the late nineteenth century, had "cash value"?

Dealing in even more abstruse matters than Sumner and Ward, the pragmatists were not easy to understand. However, their thought struck a chord deep within the American character. A practical people who were never comfortable with absolutes, Americans easily absorbed a philosophy that justified what had gone before and what was going on at the moment. Through pragmatism, the very rich could comfort themselves that their success justified the means by which they came by their money. The "truth" of their fortunes lay in their existence. There was no doubt that their methods worked.

By the end of the century, the rich dominated American society as never before. Ironically, a philosophical school that had seemed revolutionary when it was promulgated during the 1880s proved to be the essence of conservatism. But pragmatism was more than that. The philosophy seeped into every aspect of American thought and action. The reform movements of the twentieth century took pride in their pragmatic approach. So did the great institution of the American working class that emerged during the 1880s, the union movement.

For Further Reading

Any study of the very rich in the late nineteenth century will do well to begin with the virtually contemporary works of Thorstein Veblen, particularly *The Theory of the Leisure Class* (1899). It is available in several paperback editions with illuminating introductions. Edward Pessen, *Riches, Class, and Power Before the Civil War* (1973), provides a backdrop for the era, and Sigmund Diamond, *The Reputation of the American Businessman* (1955), spans both pre- and post-Civil War periods.

On the critics, see C. A. Barker, *Henry George* (1955), and A. E. Morgan, *Edward Bellamy* (1944). Both George's *Progress and Poverty* and Bellamy's *Looking Backward, 2000–1887*, are available in cheap editions.

On justifications of business methods, see Richard Hofstadter, *Social Darwinism in American Thought* (1944); Irwin F. Wylie, *The Self-Made Man in America* (1954); and John G. Cawelti, *Apostles of the Self-Made Man in America* (1966). The titles by Kirkland and Fine listed at the end of Chapter 28 are also relevant.

Workingpeople
The Bone and Sinew of the Industrial Republic

Leland Stanford and James J. Hill thought of themselves as the men who had built the railroads. So did most Americans. John D. Rockefeller took pride in the majesty of the Standard Oil Company as his personal creation, and, whether they liked the results or not, Americans agreed with him. Newspapers and magazines referred to Andrew Carnegie as the nation's greatest steelmaker. In the popular mind, vast industries were associated with powerful individuals, just as battles were identified with generals: Sherman had marched across Georgia; Grant had taken Richmond. J. P. Morgan even spoke of his hobby, yachting, in personal terms. "You can do business with anyone," he huffed, "but you can only sail a boat with a gentleman."

In reality, Morgan and his friends merely decided when and where the boat was to go. It took eighty-five grimy stokers and hard-handed sailors to get Morgan's *Corsair* out of New York harbor and safely into Newport. In the same way, Stanford, Hill, Rockefeller, Carnegie, and other great businessmen supervised the creation of industrial America, but the edifice was built by anonymous millions of men and women who wielded the shovels and needles and tended the machines that whirred and whined in the factories and mills.

Young boys at work in a Georgia cotton mill, as photographed by Lewis W. Hine.

A New Way of Life

America's workingpeople could not be kept below decks like the crew of the *Corsair*. While the population of the United States rose rapidly during the last part of the nineteenth century, more than doubling between 1860 and 1900, the size of the working class soared. In 1860, 1.5 million Americans made their living in workshops and mills, and another seven hundred thousand in mining and construction. By 1900, 6 million people worked in manufacturing and 2.3 million in mining and construction, increases of four times and 3.3 times respectively. Wageworkers, previously a minor part of the American population, now comprised a distinct and significant social class.

Bigger Factories, Better Technology

The size of the work place also grew, a fact of profound importance for the quality of workingpeople's lives. In 1870, the average workshop in the United States employed eight people and was owned by an individual or by partners who lived nearby and who personally supervised the business, sometimes working at the bench side by side with their employees. Like it or not, generous or cruel, such bosses were personally involved in the lives of their workers. They heard of events in their lives ranging from the birth of a child to the death of a parent, and they discussed matters such as wages, hours, and shop conditions face to face with the people who were affected by them.

By 1900, the average industrial worker labored in a shop with twenty-five employees, and many worked in large factories with hundreds of co-workers. In 1870, not one American factory employed as many as a thousand men and women. By 1900, such gigantic plants were common, and a few companies listed ten thousand people on the payroll. The typical employer of 1900 was a large company that was directed by men who rarely stepped onto the floor of a shop. They were interested in wages, hours, and conditions only insofar as these figures were entered in the ledgers that lined the walls of their offices.

The increased application of steam power—few mills were still water driven by 1900—and constantly improved machinery affected workers in other ways. The highly skilled craftsman, trained for years in the use of hand tools, ceased to be the principal factor in the manufacturing process. Not many crafts actually disappeared (as they would in the twentieth century), and some, like the machinist's trade, increased in im-

JOHN HENRY

Ironically, considering that few blacks held industrial jobs in the nineteenth century, a black man became the symbol of the decline of the skilled worker in the face of the new machines. "The Ballad of John Henry," written about 1872 and immediately popular among workingpeople, told the story of a black miner's contest with the newly introduced steam drill. There are several versions. Most of them end in tragedy for the human being. John Henry might defeat the steam drill in a contest to sink steel in rock, but he dies from the pace, "with his hammer in his hand."

portance. But in almost every area, steam-powered machines took over from artisans and "mechanics," performing their jobs more quickly and sometimes better.

Into their places came the unskilled or semiskilled machine tenders—men, women, and children who merely guided the device at its task. Unlike craftsmen, these workers were interchangeable, easily replaced because their jobs required little training. For this reason, they were poorly paid, and they commanded scant respect from employers, small businessmen, professionals, politicians, and skilled workers.

Girls work at a thread-winding machine at the Loudon Hosiery Mill in Loudon, Tennessee, in 1910.

Wages

The cash wages of workingpeople remained the same or declined during the final decades of the nineteenth century. However, *real wages,* or purchasing power, actually rose, at least statistically. The cost of food, clothing, and housing dropped more radically than did hourly pay during the deflationary final decades of the nineteenth century. So, starting in 1860 or 1870, with a higher standard of living than that of European workers, American workers at the end of the century were even better off than ever before. Taken as a whole, the industrial working class enjoyed almost 50 percent more purchasing power in 1900 than in 1860.

But this statistic can be misleading because the skilled "aristocracy of labor"—locomotive engineers, machinists, master carpenters, printers, and other highly trained craftsmen—improved their earnings much more than did the unskilled workers at the bottom of the pyramid. The average annual wage for manufacturing workers in 1900 was only $435, or $8.37 a week. Unskilled workers were paid about ten cents an hour on the average, about $5.50 a week. A girl of twelve or thirteen, tending a loom in a textile factory, might take home as little as $2 a week after various fines (for being late to work, for example) were deducted from her pay. As late as 1904, sociologist Robert

AVERAGE ANNUAL EARNINGS FOR SELECTED OCCUPATIONS—1890	
Farm laborers	$233
Public school teachers	256
Bituminous coal miners	406
Manufacturing employees	439
Street railway employees	557
Steam railroad employees	560
Gas & electricity workers	687
Ministers	794
Clerical workers in manufacturing & Steam RR	848
Postal employees	878

Hunter estimated that one American in eight lived in poverty, and he almost certainly hit below the true figure.

Hours and Conditions

Hours on the job varied as widely as wages. Most government employees had enjoyed an eight-hour day since 1840. Skilled workers, especially in the building trades (bricklayers, carpenters, plumbers), generally worked ten. Elsewhere, such short hours were virtually

A boy runs from the Amoskeog Manufacturing Company at quitting time in this photo taken in 1909 by Lewis W. Hine.

unknown. A factory worker was accounted lucky if he or she worked a twelve-hour day. During the summer months, many mills ran from sunup to sundown, as long as sixteen hours in some parts of the country—with only one shift.

The average workweek was sixty-six hours in 1860, and fifty-five hours in 1910. It was usually five and a half or six days long. (Half-day Saturday was considered a holiday.) In industries that were required to run around the clock, such as steel (the furnaces could not be shut down), laborers were divided into two shifts on seven-day schedules. Each shift worked for twelve hours. At the end of a two-week period, the day workers switched shifts with the night workers. This meant a "holiday" of twenty-four hours once a month. The price of this luxury was working for twenty-four hours two weeks later while the other shift enjoyed its vacation.

Except to skilled workers, real holidays were virtually unknown. Because of the erratic swings in the business cycle of the period, however, factory workers had plenty of unwanted time off. Some industries were highly seasonal. Coal miners, for example, could expect to be without wages for weeks or even months during the summer, when city people did not heat their homes. In times of depression, of course, unemployment was worse. During the depressions of the 1870s and 1890s, about 12 percent of the working population was jobless.

While some employers attended carefully to safety conditions, a safe work place was by no means the rule. Liability law provided that an employer could be sued by an injured worker only if the worker was not responsible for an accident. Short of the collapse of a factory roof, this was rarely the case. If a worker was hurt because his machine was dangerous, the employer was not liable, even if the worker could prove that he would have been fired had he refused to tend the machine. Railroads had a particularly horrid record. Every year, one railroad worker in twenty-six was injured seriously, and one in four hundred was killed. Textile workers without some fingers and ex-textile workers without hands were fixtures in every mill town.

Between 1880 and 1900, thirty-five thousand American workers were killed on the job, an average of one about every two days. In many cases, their wives or dependents received nothing. In most, employer compensation amounted to little more than burial expenses. In the coal fields, the mine owners thought themselves generous if they allowed a dead miner's teenage son, who was younger than the regulation age, to take a job in the mines in order to support his family. Turn-of-the-century America did not hold society responsible for such misfortunes.

What compensation there was applied only to accidents. Occupational diseases—the coal miner's "black lung," the cotton-mill worker's "white lung," and the hard-rock miner's silicosis—were not recognized as the employer's responsibility. Poisoning resulting from work with chemicals was rarely identified as related to the job.

The Company Town

Some of the worst conditions of labor were found in the company towns, in which employers owned not only the factory, but the houses in which workers lived, the stores at which they shopped, the utilities, the schools, even in some cases the land on which churches sat or the church buildings themselves.

Some company towns originally were forced on employers because there were no residential settlements near where their businesses were established—in the isolated Pennsylvania coal fields, for example, and in logging and lumbermill towns. Others were built because an idealistic industrialist wanted his employees to live *better than* workers elsewhere—as was Pullman, Illinois, site of the factory that built sleeping and dining cars for railroads. The company town soon came to appeal to factory owners as an almost foolproof means of controlling their employees. Thus when the textile industry began to move from New England and New Jersey to the southern states late in the nineteenth

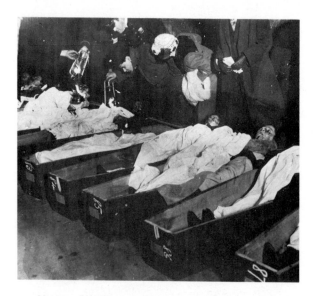

Victims of the Triangle Shirtwaist Factory fire of 1911 are lined up in coffins. The fire, which killed 146 women and girls, strengthened public opinion in favor of the movement to improve factory conditions, wages, and working hours.

century, its owners deliberately built in the pine woods rather than near established towns. They wanted to control their workers' lives so that they could not organize and push up wages, as workers had done in the North.

When the company owned the store at which food was purchased, workers could be paid in scrip rather than in money. Scrip was redeemable only at the company store; thus the factory owner could take profits by charging higher prices than did independent merchants who had to compete, or, in any case, he could keep his capital free for business purposes. Moreover, when employees went into debt at the company store, they gave the bosses additional leverage against them in case of a dispute over wages or conditions. Finally, if workers went on strike in a company town, they risked not only losing a job, but being evicted from a company-owned house.

Who Were the Workers?

In addition to their material problems, the unskilled workers suffered social ostracism as the inconsequential dregs of society. Their low status contrasted sharply with the respect accorded the skilled "aristocracy of labor." Often paid enough to be homeowners, craftsmen felt little common interest with machine tenders, but, instead, associated after hours with other skilled workers, small independent businessmen, and even professionals. One of the principal reasons for this division between one part of the working class and the other was ethnic. As the nineteenth century came to a close, the unskilled working class was increasingly an immigrant or a second-generation population, while skilled workers were overwhelmingly of old American stock or of British or Irish origin. The big-city building trades, for example, were dominated by Irishmen and the sons of Irish immigrants, and they were inclined to look down on more recent immigrants.

The skilled worker lived under the constant threat of losing his relatively favorable status. The thrust of technology was to replace hand skills with more efficient machines. Testifying in 1899, a Massachusetts shoemaker told a Congressional committee about former days when craftsmen like him

sat down and made shoes right in their laps and there was no machinery. . . . Of course, under these conditions, there was absolute freedom and exchange of ideas, they naturally would become more intelligent than shoe workers can at the present time when they are driving each man to see how many shoes he can handle, and where he is surrounded by noisy machinery.

Many other tradesmen worried that new inventions doomed them to the same fate.

Child Labor

In 1900, the socialist writer John Spargo estimated that 1,752,187 children under sixteen years of age were employed full time. They did all but the heaviest kinds of work. Girls as young as twelve tended dangerous looms and spinning machines in textile mills. "Bobbin boys" of ten hauled heavy wooden boxes filled with spindles from spinning rooms to weaving rooms and back again. Children swept filings in machine shops. Boys as young as eight were found working the "breakers" at coal mines, hand picking slate from anthracite in filthy, frigid wooden sheds.

In city tenement "sweat shops," whole families and their boarders sewed clothing or rolled cigars by hand, and children worked as soon as they were able to master the simplest tasks. In cities, children practically monopolized messenger-service work, light delivery, and

A newsboy peddles papers in St. Louis, Missouri.

some kinds of huckstering. Apprenticeship in some skilled trades largely amounted to low-paying menial labor for long hours.

In part, child labor was the fruit of greed. On the grounds that children had no nonworking dependents to support, employers paid them less than adults. The justification was not always convincing, however. In southern textile towns, the "Mill Daddy" became a familiar figure. Unable to find work because his own children could be hired for less, the Mill Daddy was reduced to carrying lunches to the factory and tossing them over the fence each noon.

But the widespread character of child labor also provides an example of "cultural lag." It took time for society to face up to the reality that industrial life was something new in the world; factory work was different from work on a family farm or in a small workshop. Children always had worked. But where relations in the work place were personal, as in the small shop, the limited capacity of the immature person, especially a child's fatigue when set to tedious, repetitive tasks, was easy to recognize and take into account. Placed in a niche in a massive factory, the child laborer became nothing but a number on an accountant's sheet.

Women Workers

Cultural lag also played a part in the large numbers of women in industry. The *first* industrial workers had been female, partly because the founders of the first American textile mills had not been able to imagine factory work as a suitable lifetime career for the head of a family. Instead of recruiting men to work in their mills, the early cloth manufacturers had persuaded New England farmers to send their unmarried daughters to towns like Lowell, Massachusetts. The plan had been that they would work for a few years, save their money, and return to the farm to take up their true calling as wives of farmers, with a dowry that their fathers could not afford.

A girl making a shoe in 1895 in a Lynn, Massachusetts, factory.

In devising the "Lowell system," the well-meaning pioneers of the factory system had believed that they had reconciled industrialization with the old way of life. But the increasing demands of growing industry, and the heavy nature of much factory work, soon resulted in a work force that was predominantly male. Nevertheless, Lowell paternalism survived here and there into the twentieth century. And the difficulty of supporting a family on one person's income forced working-class women to continue to labor for wages even after they married. In 1900, almost 20 percent of the total work force was female. About half the workers in textiles were women, and the percentage in the needle trades and other home manufactures was much higher.

With very few exceptions, women were paid less than men, sometimes half as much for performing the same tasks for the same number of hours. Abysmally low pay was particularly characteristic of the largest female occupation. In 1900, 2 million women were employed for subsistence wages or less in domestic service: cooking, cleaning, and tending the vanities and children of the well-to-do.

WOMEN IN THE WORK FORCE

There was at least one woman in each occupation listed by the Census Bureau in 1890. More than 225,000 were running farms, and 1,143 listed their occupation as clergyman. Women outnumbered men as teachers and as waiters (the latter by five to one). There were 28 female lumberjacks. In all the United States, however, out of 12,856 wheelwrights (makers and repairers of wagon wheels) there was only one woman.

Moving to Town

Like the Lowell girls, many male workers came from the farm. In the best of times, farm work was arduous and often enough unrewarding. By comparison, the social and cultural life in a manufacturing town or city looked good. Precise figures on the movement of people from the farm to the "bright lights" cannot be cited, but the almost hysterical appeals in rural newspapers and magazines for farmers' children to stay at home indicates that the emigration was considerable.

The city might be a dangerous, unholy place, but the lure of joining the money economy was too enticing for such propaganda to succeed. Well-known people as diverse as Henry Ford and the pessimistic novelists Hamlin Garland and Ole Rolvaag (who wrote in Norwegian) related their loathing for lonely, stultifying farm life.

Because the majority of white Americans were literate, thanks to a large public-school system, and farmers' sons were mechanically inclined, they got the best factory jobs, and rose to be foremen and supervisors far more easily than did women or immigrants.

Very few industrial jobs were open to blacks. While a few carved out places for themselves in the lowest-paying jobs, the prejudice of white workers as well as employers kept blacks concentrated in agriculture and in low-paying service occupations: domestic servants, waiters, porters, and the like. In 1900, more than 80 percent of the black population lived in the South, most of them on the land.

The industrial color line was just as distinct in the South as in the North. When the cotton textile industry moved south at the end of the century, the mill-owners drew on the poor white population for its work force. Implicitly, and sometimes explicitly, employees were informed that if they proved troublesome (that is, if they complained about wages, hours, and conditions), the companies could always tap the huge and poor black population. Racism served to keep southern workers the poorest in the country. Rather than risk the loss of poorly paid jobs, they accepted their low wages and standard of living. Except among machinists, labor unionism made virtually no headway in the South during the nineteenth century.

Conflict in Industrial America

Sociologists, psychologists, and physiologists still argue about the unnaturalness of the rhythms of life in the industrial age—living by the clock, working many hours at a stretch, performing the same monotonous task over and over. These social scientists do not yet know whether men and women are biologically suited to doing factory work without also doing harm to their well-being. In any case, whether the cause was biological or cultural, American workers resisted the new discipline in a number of ways.

Informal Protest

Despite the penalties, absenteeism plagued the factories of the late nineteenth century, especially during good times when a "vacationing" or tardy worker was less likely to be fired. "Blue Monday" was common enough to get its name. On Mondays, when workers were still recovering from a beery Sunday celebration, production at mills dropped as much as half from the level of other days. Also in good times, workers quit their jobs frequently, since they were confident that they could find another spot when they needed to do so.

Employers of immigrant work forces had to contend with ethnic or religious holidays that were of no meaning to American Protestants: the many holy days celebrated in the Catholic Church; the even more numerous saints' days observed in the Eastern Orthodox churches and the Yom Kippur, Rosh Hashanah, and Saturday sabbath of the Jews. Indeed, because factories operated according to the Christian week, Jews tended to shun factory work, even if the pay was better, in favor of home sweatshops, independent peddling, or employment with a Jewish boss.

Sabotage was a chronic problem, especially because workers found it easy to damage a machine so that it appeared to be an accident. When the pace became too taxing, it was easy enough to "throw a monkey wrench into the works" or to slash a leather power belt for the sake of a few moments' respite.

Employers never ceased to complain about the "inefficiency" and "irresponsibility" of their workers, rarely considering that the demands of industrial discipline were excessive or that monotony and low wages and poor conditions were not conducive to maximum productivity.

A Heritage of Violence

Violence was another characteristic of labor relations in the early phases of industrialization. Desperate and denied any means to discuss and resolve the conditions under which they worked and lived, workers turned to the riot, the gun, and the deftly placed stick of dynamite to wake up their bosses. During the nationwide railroad strike of 1877, an unorganized, spontaneous outbreak that was caused by depression, workers did not merely walk off the job, but they stormed in mobs into railroad yards and set trains and buildings on fire. In a few places they fought pitched gun battles with company guards and, toward the end of the unsuccessful strike, with troops who had been called out to put them down.

At Andrew Carnegie's Homestead Works in 1892, a strike led by the Amalgamated Association of Iron and Steel Workers actually besieged the giant factory and forced the withdrawal of a barge bringing three hundred armed guards into the town. Similar conflicts characterized labor disputes in many industries; they were nowhere more bloody and bitter than in the coal mines of Pennsylvania and in the hard-rock gold and silver mines of the mountain West.

The Molly Maguires

During the early 1870s, an indeterminate number of Irish coal miners in northeastern Pennsylvania gave up on the possibility of improving the conditions of their unhealthful and dangerous work through peaceful means. Within the semisecret atmosphere of a fraternal lodge, the Ancient Order of Hibernians, they formed a totally secret society called the Molly Maguires. The Mollys then launched an effective campaign of terrorism against the mine owners and particularly the supervisors. They systematically destroyed mine property and murdered loyal company men rather than merely beating them up. (In which case, the victims could have identified their attackers.)

Because of the ethnic dimension of the conflict— almost all the miners were Irish; almost all the bosses were American or Cornish—the Molly Maguires were

Members of the Molly Maguires, a secret organization launched to terrorize owners of dangerous mines, march to the gallows in Pottsville, Pennsylvania, in 1877.

able to maintain a secrecy that was more effective than that managed by any other terroristic group before or since. Their enemies did not know who they were, how numerous they were, how much support they had in the community. To this day, historians are unable to discuss the Mollys in other than general terms, and some believe that the organization was largely a figment of the mine owners' imagination, created in order to provide an excuse for demoralizing the mining community as a whole.

In any event, the mine owners brought in an Irish-American undercover detective, James McParland. He was an employee of the Pinkerton Agency, which specialized in breaking up unions. McParland infiltrated the Mollys and gathered evidence that led to the hanging of several men and the destruction of the organization.

Labor War in the West

In the gold and silver mines of the West, violence was chronic and on a much grander scale than that managed by the Molly Maguires. Wherever the Western Federation of Miners, the union of the hard-rock men, was weak and therefore vulnerable to company attack, violence was the rule. Mine owners employed Pinkertons (including McParland, who became head of the Denver division of the agency), who provoked workers into fracases that were more like small battles than industrial disputes. Miners and company guards shot it out from behind barricades in "territories" that were clearly identified as worker or company controlled.

Where the mine owners controlled local law enforcement, beatings and arbitrary arrests of strikers were common. In 1890, authorities in northern Idaho built a bull pen, a ramshackle wooden structure in which virtually every striking miner was confined under wretched conditions.

The miners, as well as the owners, were capable of initiating violence. An independent breed, imbued with the culture of the frontier, they "deported" workers who were unfriendly to them; after beating them, they walked them to the county line and warned them not to return. Resentful of absentee mine owners who lived in San Francisco, New York, and England, they regularly dynamited company property—mills, mine shafts, even private homes—during labor disputes.

Western labor relations were peaceful only in those mining towns—Virginia City and Gold Hill in Nevada, Butte in Montana, Silver City in southern Idaho—where the union was established and therefore was able to bargain with employers from a position of strength.

The Union Makes Us Strong

This lesson, that by uniting, workers could have a say in the conditions of labor, was not new with the industrial age. Before 1800, shoemakers in Philadelphia had banded together for mutual protection in the Knights of St. Crispin. Workingmen's associations had been the backbone of the Jacksonian political movement in the eastern states. By the early 1870s, skilled workers such as machinists, iron molders, carpenters, and locomotive engineers and firemen had formed thousands of local trade groups that totaled about three hundred thousand members.

For the most part, these scattered organizations had little to do with one another. Developing at a time when industry was decentralized, the unions inevitably lagged behind the employers in recognizing the need for national organization. But with the emergence from obscurity of a solemn, visionary iron puddler from Philadelphia, William Sylvis, the campaign to form a national labor union was launched.

The National Labor Union

Sylvis called his organization the National Labor Union (NLU). The charismatic and indispensable force behind its founding in 1866, he devoted his life to its cause, traveling around the eastern states and speaking to workers of every occupation in churches, fraternal lodges, or under the stars. People who never had seen his face recognized him immediately when he entered their drab factory town, often on foot. His trademark was the long, heavy overcoat flecked with tiny burns that was the emblem of his craft. Iron puddlers supervised the pouring of the molten metal into forms for casting, and they wore overcoats, even on the

hottest days, to protect themselves from flying sparks and glowing droplets of melted iron.

Sylvis believed that the workers' future depended on political involvement. He formed alliances with a number of reform groups, including the woman-suffrage movement and farmers' organizations that were lobbying for a cheap currency. Although Sylvis died in 1869, his National Labor party put up candidates in the presidential election of 1872. So poor was their showing, however, that the party and the NLU itself broke up, its members demoralized. From a membership of four hundred thousand in 1872, the NLU completely disappeared within two years.

The Knights of Labor

A different kind of national labor organization already had emerged to take the place of the National Labor Union. Organized in 1869 by a group of tailors led by Uriah P. Stephens, the Noble and Holy Order of the Knights of Labor spread its message much more quietly than Sylvis had done. Indeed the Knights spread it *secretly*. Stephens was aware that an employer's usual reaction, when he discovered a union man in his midst, was to fire him. When the Knights announced meetings in newspaper advertisements, they did not even reveal their name but identified the group as ******.

The Knights of Labor also differed from the NLU in their disinterest in political action as an organization. Members were urged to vote, but Stephens believed that the interests of workingpeople would ultimately be served by solidarity in the work place in opposition to their enemies. Who those enemies were, however, was never clearly defined. Sometimes the Knights spoke of a conflict between producers and parasites—workers and farmers, on the one hand; capitalists, on the other—but they barred membership to only saloon-keepers, lawyers, and gamblers, hardly professions that included all the bosses of industrial America. In fact, Stephens disliked the idea of class conflict and looked forward to a day when men and women of good will in all social classes would abolish the wage system and establish a cooperative commonwealth. Women were welcome in the Knights; so were blacks and unskilled workers, who usually were overlooked as union material in the nineteenth century. However, the Knights failed to appeal to one group that was essential to the success of any labor organization; Roman Catholics, particularly Irish-Americans, were the single largest ethnic group in the working class.

As the name of his organization implies, Stephens surrounded the Knights of Labor with the mystery, symbolism, ritual, secret handshakes, and other rig-

---

THE YELLOW-DOG CONTRACT

Yellow-dog contracts, which were forced on employees by some companies, were meant to intimidate as much as anything else. The penalty for violating such a contract was dismissal, which employers did often enough without such documents. Employees had to agree that "in consideration of my present employment I hereby promise and agree that I will forthwith abandon any and all membership, connection, or affiliation with any organization or society, whether secret or open, which in any way attempts to regulate the conditions of my services or the payment therefor."

Women delegates to a Knights of Labor convention held in 1886.

amarole that was common to American fraternal organizations. A lifelong Freemason, Stephens based the Knights' ritual on that of his own lodge.

The trouble was that in Europe, the Masons were an anti-Catholic organization, and the pope forbade members of the Church to join secret societies of any sort. The Catholic suspicion of the Knights was a serious drawback. Without Catholic support, no labor organization could prosper.

Enter Terence Powderly

In 1879, Stephens was succeeded as Grand Master Workman by Terence V. Powderly, a deceptively mild-looking man with a handlebar moustache. Himself a Roman Catholic, albeit not strictly observant, Powderly brought the Knights into the open and toned down the Masonic flavor of the ritual. He persuaded an influential Catholic bishop, Janes Gibbons, to prevail on the pope to approve Catholic membership in the union.

Then the Knights grew at a dazzling rate. By 1885, there were 110,000 members, and in only one year, the union grew to 700,000. Powderly disliked strikes, so it was ironic that the major impetus of this increase was a remarkable victory over Jay Gould's Missouri Pacific Railroad. Gould had vowed to destroy the union. "I can hire half the working class to kill the other half," he growled. But when he tried to cut wages, the Knights closed down his line and forced him to meet with their leaders and agree to their terms.

The easy victory and the explosive growth of the union proved to be a curse as well as a blessing. Powderly and the union's general assembly were unable to control the new members. Instead of working together according to a national policy, which was the rationale of a national labor organization, local leaders, who were often new to the concept of unionism, were encouraged by the victory in the Missouri Pacific strike to go it alone in a dozen unrelated directions. Powderly fumed and sputtered and refused to back the rash of strikes in 1885 and 1886. But he could not stop them.

Jay Gould got his revenge, completely crushing a strike against the Texas Pacific Railroad, another of his many properties. Then in 1886, after an incident for which the Knights were not responsible, the "Noble and Holy" experiment fell to pieces.

Haymarket

Defying Powderly, and demanding an eight-hour day, Chicago Knights called a strike against the McCormick International Harvester Company, the world's largest manufacturer of farm machinery. Almost immediately, everything went wrong. The Chicago police were blatantly on the side of the employers, and over several days, they killed four workers. On May 4, a group of anarchists (who advocated the ultimate destruction of the political state) called a rally in support of the strikers at Haymarket Square, just south of the city center.

The oratory was red-hot; but the speakers broke no laws, and the crowd was cool and orderly. Indeed, the rally was about to break up when a platoon of police entered the square and demanded that the people disperse. At that instant, someone threw a bomb into their midst, killing seven people and wounding sixty-seven officers. The police fired a volley, and four workers fell dead.

News of the incident fed an antianarchist hysteria in Chicago. Authorities rounded up several dozen individuals who were known to have attended anarchist meetings, and authorities brought eight to trial for the murder of the officers. Among them were a Confederate Army veteran from an old Virginia family, Albert Parsons, and a prominent German agitator, August Spies.

The trial was a farce. No one on the prosecution team knew or even claimed to know who had thrown the bomb. (His or her identity is still unknown.) Nor did the prosecution present evidence to tie any of the eight to the bombing. One, a deranged young German named Louis Lingg, was a bomb maker, although, ironically, he had a plausible alibi. Several of the defendants had not been at the rally. Parsons had been ill

The Haymarket Riot of 1886, depicted in an illustration from Harper's Weekly.

in bed that evening and, indeed, had been ill since before the rally was called.

All these facts were irrelevant. Chicago was determined to have scapegoats, and, although the charge was murder, the Haymarket anarchists were tried for their ideas and associations. Four were hanged. Lingg committed suicide in his cell. Three were sentenced to long prison terms.

In the meantime, despite the shabbiness of the trial and the fact that the defendants were not official representatives of the Knights of Labor, the organization fell to pieces. The majority of American workers were not interested in violence and shied away from even the unfair hint of it. Within four years, membership in the union plummeted from seven hundred thousand to one hundred thousand. In this emasculated form, the organization dragged on until almost 1900. By then even Powderly had quit to become a functionary of the Republican party.

The Birth of the Modern Labor Movement

Only with the founding of the American Federation of Labor in 1886 did a nationwide labor organization establish itself permanently in the United States. It was nationwide—and in Canada too—but not national. The AFL was put together by several dozen existing local associations of skilled workers whose "Internationals," unions of workers who practiced the same trade, retained considerable freedom of action independent of the federation's central office.

Samuel Gompers

Craft autonomy was one of the principles of labor organization on which the guiding spirit of the AFL insisted. Samuel Gompers was a cigarmaker, the practitioner of a skilled (and dying) craft. Born in London

OFF THE RACK, OUT OF THE SWEATSHOPS

In the early nineteenth century, four Americans in five wore clothing that had been made to order. The wealthy took their wants to the little shops in every town and city where fine garments were expertly made by hand from fabric to finished product. With great skill, tailors and seamstresses worked not from patterns, as someone interested in sewing would do today, but from fashion plates, carefully drawn pictures in magazines of people dressed in the latest styles. By the early nineteenth century, Paris already was considered the authority in such matters.

The middle classes, which began to pay more attention to "fashion" in the nineteenth century, depended on their womenfolk for their garb. That is why needlecraft learned at a mother's knee was such an important part of a young girl's education; clothing her family would be one of her most important duties as a wife and mother.

As for the poor, they made do with castoffs either scavenged or purchased from merchants who specialized in buying and reconditioning used clothing. The fact that most garments were made to fit an individual did not mean that any particular item had been made to fit the person who, at a given time, was wearing it.

Only sailors, slaves, and—after 1849—miners in the West were likely to wear clothing such as virtually everyone does today, ready-made in quantity to standard sizes and sold "off the rack." Sailors were not generally in a port long enough to be fitted and a garment sewn. (The first ready-made clothing stores were called "sailors' shops.") The slaves had no choice in the matter of what they put on their backs, and their owners, wanting to provide them some protection from the elements at a minimum cost, became an attractive market for enterprising tailors who abandoned the custom trade and took to producing rough, cheap garments in quantity. Miners, like sailors, were in a hurry, and they lived in an almost entirely masculine society. Their demand for sturdy, ready-made clothing provided the impetus for the founding in 1850 of the Levi Strauss Company of San Francisco, today perhaps the best-known manufacturer of ready-made clothing in the world.

By 1900, things had changed. Nine Americans in ten were wearing ready-made togs. A "Clothing Revolution," as historian Daniel Boorstin has called it, had

Workers make neckties in a crowded and gloomy sweatshop.
The photograph is by Jacob Riis.

taken place as a consequence of technology with, curiously, a boost from the American Civil War.

The technology was supplied by inventions such as the sewing machine, patented by Elias Howe in 1846, and powered scissors that could cut through eighteen pieces of fabric at once, thus making the parts for eighteen garments of exactly the same size. The standard sizes were provided by the United States government when the Civil War made it necessary to buy uniforms for hundreds of thousands of men. The army's Quartermaster Corps measured hundreds of recruits and arrived at sets of proportions that provided a fit for almost all. It was a simple step to do the same for women's sizes after the war ended, and ready-made-clothing shops began to displace tailors and seamstresses. The department store, which appeared at the end of the century, was built around its selection of every kind of clothing. The great mail-order houses such as Montgomery Ward and Sears Roebuck were able, with everyone knowing his or her size, to sell garments by mail.

How were the new ready-made clothes manufactured? Not, ironically, in factories. There was little outsize machinery involved in the making of garments (sewing machines were treadle- or electrically powered) and a great deal of handwork (finishing buttonholes, installing linings). Thus it was possible to farm out the work to people in their homes, just as, before the invention of cloth-making machinery, spinning and weaving had been farmed out.

Whereas the old putting-out system usually had involved the wives and daughters of farmers, leaving people on the land, the new putting-out system engaged people who lived in city slums and who depended exclusively on needlework for their livelihood.

The system was called "sweating," and the places in which the garmentmakers worked were called "sweatshops" because of the peculiarly exploitative character of the system. A manufacturer of clothing kept a small headquarters; at the most, the material was cut to pattern in his "factory." Then, the pieces of a garment were handed out on a weekly or daily basis to people, usually Jewish or Italian immigrants, who took them home to their tenement apartments. There the whole family—perhaps some boarders, perhaps even some neighbors—sat down during all the daylight hours to make up the garments. Sometimes a household saw a coat (usually called a cloak in the nineteenth century) or a gown through from components to completion. Other households specialized in different phases of the process, such as roughing the garment in, or finishing work. Some sweatshops made buttonholes, others sewed pockets, and so on.

The key to the system was that everyone involved was paid by the piece—so much per jacket, so much per lining. A complex hierarchy of subcontracting developed in which it was to the interest of all to pay those below them in the chain as little for their work as possible. That is, a man who provided finished cloaks to the manufacturer received a fixed rate for each garment that he delivered. In order to make a profit, he had to pay less than that rate to those households that had done the work. If the head of a household sweatshop had boarders or neighbors sewing, he had to pay them even less. Everybody was "sweating" their income out of somebody else.

Moreover, just as in "Taylorized" factories, employers were inclined to cut the piece rate as a worker's productivity increased or when someone else told the manufacturer whom he supplied (who sweated him) that others were willing to work for less. In order to compete, he sweated the people under him.

In turn, everyone in the chain had to take less for their work. The operator of a Chicago sweatshop explained the results to a Congressional committee in 1893:

Q. *In what condition do you get the garments?*
A. *They come here already cut and I make them up.*

Q. *What is the average wage of the men per week?*
A. *About $15 a week.*

Q. *How much do the women get?*
A. *About $6. They get paid for extra hours. . . .*

Q. *Are wages higher or lower than they were two years ago?*
A. *Lower. There are so many who want to work.*

Q. *How much do you get for making this garment?*
A. *Eighty cents.*

Q. *How much did you get for making it two years ago?*
A. *About $1.25.*

Q. *Is the help paid less now?*
A. *Yes, sir.*

A cloakmaker, Abraham Bisno, told the same panel that he had earned about $20 a week in 1885 for completing fewer garments than he had sewn in 1890, when he had made $13 to $14 a week. In 1893, he was being paid $11 a week for even greater productivity.

As the rate per piece fell, sweatshop workers increased their hours in the unhealthful, poorly ventilated tenements. Only when urban states such as New York and Illinois passed laws that forbade such work in residences was there any improvement in conditions. But, often as not, the driving exploitation of the sweat system was merely transferred to an unhealthful, poorly ventilated factory that was little different from a tenement flat.

of Dutch Jewish parents, he had emigrated to New York as a boy, and, while still in his teens, had astonished his fellow workers (and their employers) with his intelligence, learning, toughness in bargaining, and oratorical eloquence. He was a homely, even ugly man, squat and thick of body with a broad, coarse-featured face. But this uncomely character had very definite ideas about how organizations of labor could not only survive in the United States, but become a part of the interlocking forces that governed the country.

No Unskilled Workers or Dreamers Need Apply

First of all, Gompers believed that only skilled craftsmen could effectively force employers to negotiate with them. When bricklayers refused to work, and all the bricklayers in a locality stuck together, the employer who wanted bricks laid had no choice but to talk. When the unskilled hod carriers (workers who carried the bricks to the bricklayers) went out, however, employers had no difficulty in finding other men with strong backs and empty stomachs to take their place. Therefore, Gompers concluded, the AFL would admit only skilled workers.

Second, the goal of the AFL unions was "bread and butter," higher wages, shorter hours, better working conditions. Gompers had no patience with socialistic or other utopian dreamers. What counted was the here and now, not "pie in the sky." Unions with utopian programs not only distracted workers from the concrete issues that counted, but were easy targets for suppression by the bosses who were able (as in the Haymarket incident) to convince Americans that labor organizations threatened the very stability of their society.

Third, while Gompers believed that the strike, as peaceful coercion, was the union's best weapon, he made it clear that AFL unions would cooperate with employers who recognized and bargained with them. Make union partners in industry, especially AFL unions that supported the capitalist system, and radical anticapitalist organizations would wither and die.

Conservative Unionism

Gompers, who lived until 1924, served as president of the AFL every year but one (when AFL socialists defeated him). He did not see his hopes come to fruition, but he made a start. With his carrot-and-stick approach to dealing with employers—striking against those who refused to deal with the AFL, cooperating with those who accepted unions—he saw the AFL grow from 150,000 members in 1888 to more than 1 million shortly after the turn of the century.

Most employers continued to hate him and the AFL as dearly as they hated socialists and revolutionary labor unions. "Can't I do what I want with my own?" Cornelius Vanderbilt had asked years before about his company's policies. The majority of American industrialists continued to believe that the wages they paid and the hours their employees worked were no one's business but their own. Their argument was that the worker who did not like his pay had the right to quit. In 1893, hard-nosed antilabor employers formed the National Association of Manufacturers to destroy unionism wherever it appeared. The NAM remained the most important antiunion organization into the twentieth century.

In 1900, a more enlightened group of manufacturers led by Frank Easley and Marcus A. Hanna, a former Rockefeller associate, came to the conclusion that labor unions were a permanent part of the American industrial scene. The choice was not between unions and no unions. The choice was between conservative, procapitalist unions that were willing to cooperate with employers and desperate, revolutionary unions that were determined to destroy capitalism. They chose Gompers's AFL and joined with him in 1900 to form the National Civic Federation, which was to work for industrial peace through employer–union cooperation.

By 1900, there was no doubt that the AFL would survive. Nevertheless, and as much due to Gompers as were the successes of the AFL, the conservative trade-union movement failed to recognize some of the most serious questions that would face workingpeople in the twentieth century. The AFL remained inflexible in its opposition to organizing unskilled workers. On more than one occasion, Gompers used AFL unions to destroy unions that had been formed by the unskilled.

By the turn of the century, this policy was not so much a tough practical decision as it was a reflection of the labor aristocracy's prejudice against the new immigrants who made up the mass of the unskilled work force. In part, the AFL wanted immigration restricted on economic grounds. By cutting off the supply of cheap labor from abroad, American workers would be better able to improve their own situation. However, Gompers and many of his strongest supporters also harbored a racial dislike for the newcomers. Curiously, though of Jewish background (although personally irreligious), Gompers was able to denounce Jewish immigrants from Eastern Europe as being incapable of becoming good American citizens. His views concerning the Japanese and Chinese on the west coast were frankly racist.

The AFL unions also generally opposed the organization of women (20 percent of the work force) and blacks, who were not numerically important outside of agriculture but were potentially of supreme interest to any working-class movement because they could be used as strikebreakers. The result was that while the lot of the skilled workers steadily improved in the late nineteenth and early twentieth centuries, only 3 percent of "gainfully employed" Americans were members of labor organizations. A union movement, the AFL was; a working-class organization, it was not.

For Further Reading

There are any number of good histories of the organized-labor movement. See Henry Pelling. *American Labor* (1960), and Foster R. Dulles, *Labor in America* (1968).

For the late nineteenth century, see Norman J. Ware, *The Labor Movement in the United States, 1860–1893* (1929), and Philip Taft, *The A.F. of L. in the Time of Gompers* (1957). Gompers's own autobiography, *Seventy Years of Life and Labour* (1924), is an excellent source, except when his subject is his enemies.

On special subjects, see Robert V. Bruce, *1877: Year of Violence* (1959); Henry David, *History of the Haymarket Affair* (1936); A. L. Lindsay, *The Pullman Strike* (1942); and Ray Ginger, *Altgeld's America: The Lincoln Ideal versus Changing Realities* (1958).

The Nation of Immigrants
A Flood of Newcomers Changes the United States

"So at last I was going to America! Really, really going at last!" These words were written by Mary Antin, recalling her feelings as a girl in a *shtetl*, a Jewish village in the Russian Empire, when her family decided that their future lay in the United States. "The boundaries burst!" she went on. "The arch of heaven soared! A million suns shone out for every star. The winds rushed in from outer space, roaring in my ears, 'America! America!'"

No one ever caught the thrill of moving to the New World with such exuberance. It may have been Mary Antin's genius with her adopted language. Americans thought so: they bought eighty-five thousand copies of *The Promised Land* when it was published in 1912. Or her joy may have been because, as Jews, her mother and father had come to the United States not merely to improve their standard of living, but to survive.

In 1881, Alexander II, a liberal-minded czar who had relaxed laws that discriminated against Jews, was assassinated. Regularly thereafter, with the tacit approval of the new regime, peasants rampaged through the *shtetls* on bloody pogroms (from the Russian word meaning "riot" or "devastation"). Frustrated by the poverty and desperation of their own lives in that oppressive and poor country, they beat and killed Jews with no

Immigrants laden with baggage arriving at Ellis Island in 1907.

fear of the law. As they had before and would again, the Jews moved on. Between about 1881 and 1914, fully one-third of the Jewish population of Russia left the country, most of them for the United States. It was one of the greatest relocations of a people in such a short period in the history of the world.

And the Jews were not the largest group of people to come to the United States during the late nineteenth and early twentieth centuries. Between 1890 and 1914 (when the outbreak of the First World War choked off immigration), some 3.6 million Italians cleared the Immigration Service. And there were others: Irish, Scots, Welsh, English, Scandinavians, Germans—the so-called "Old Immigration" that continued in large numbers through the late nineteenth century—and Poles, Lithuanians, Ukrainians, Russians, Serbians, Croatians, Slovenes, Armenians, Greeks, and, from Asia, Chinese and Japanese. Indeed, if all the fine lines of cultural and linguistic divisions were drawn, the list of the kinds of people who emigrated to the United States during the generation that spanned the turn of the century would run for pages.

Immigrants: An Old American Tradition

Immigration was essential to the American experience, of course. Not even the Indians, the Native Americans, had originated in the Western Hemisphere. Throughout most of the colonial period, immigrants were as important to American growth as the natural increase of population. The Revolution and the uncertain period that followed slowed down the flow of newcomers, but not even the dangers of sea travel during the War of 1812 could quite close it down. After 1815, Europeans came over in numbers that increased almost annually. Only during serious depressions, when jobs were scarce, and during the Civil War, when a young man might be drafted before he shook down his sea legs, did the influx slow down.

The Old Immigration and the New

From 10,000 in 1825, immigration topped 100,000 in 1845. Except for the first two years of the Civil War, the annual total never dipped below that figure. In 1854, a record 428,000 foreigners stepped ashore. It was broken in 1880, when 457,000 immigrants made

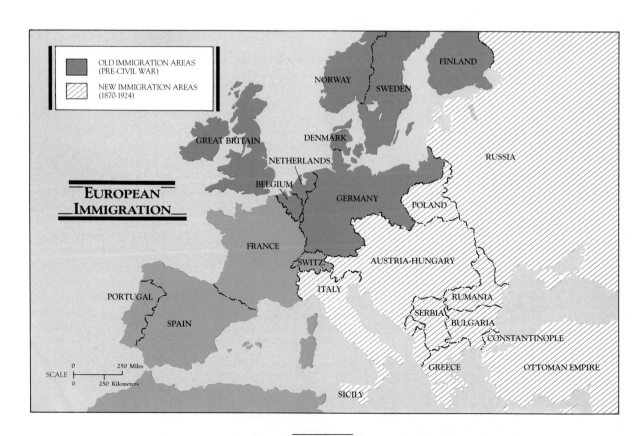

landfalls in Boston, New York, Philadelphia, Baltimore, New Orleans, and dozens of smaller ports. Only a crippling depression during the 1890s pushed the total below 300,000. After the turn of the century, during each of six years, more than 1 million people arrived to make homes in the United States. Always an abundant stream, sometimes swollen, immigration had become a flood.

But there was more to the immigration after 1880 than a mere increase in numbers. Before 1880, a large majority of immigrants listed the British Isles (including Ireland), Germany, or Scandinavia as their place of birth. While these northern and Western Europeans continued to arrive in large numbers after 1880, an annually larger proportion of newcomers after that year originated in Italy (especially the southern regions of Sicily, Campania, Calabria, Abruzzo, and Lucania; the Ottoman (Turkish) Empire; Greece; and the Slavic, Magyar (Hungarian), and Rumanian parts of the Austro-Hungarian Empire. And from Russia, which then included much of Poland, came Russians, Poles, Lithuanians, Latvians, Estonians, Finns, and Jews.

Before 1880, only about 200,000 people of southern and Eastern European origin *lived in* the United States. Between 1880 and 1910, about 8.4 million *arrived.* In 1896, this New Immigration exceeded the Old for the first time. By 1907, New Immigrants were almost the whole of the influx. Of 1,285,349 legal immigrants who were registered that year, just about 1 million began their long, difficult journey in Southern and Eastern Europe.

The difference between the experiences of the New Immigrants and those of the Old can be overstated. They did exist. But to a large extent the same forces compelled both pre- and post-Civil War newcomers to look to the United States for a home, and similar receptions awaited them when they arrived.

Birth Pains of the World Economy

Although only parts of Europe, North America, and Japan may be described as having been "industrialized" in the nineteenth century, the effects of this economic revolution were felt everywhere save the most remote jungles and mountain valleys in places like the Amazon, the African interior, New Guinea, and Tibet. A decline in infant mortality and an increase in life expectancy, side effects of the new technology, resulted in a giant leap in population in agricultural lands as well as in the industrial countries. The world production of foodstuffs soared too, but unequally. The biggest gains were made where agriculture itself was becoming mechanized, as in the United States. In those parts of the world where peasants remained the

agricultural work force, food production did not keep up with population growth, let alone produce a surplus to feed the burgeoning cities. Thus, the grain from the broad American prairies and increasingly from Canada undersold grain raised on small plots by peasants in countries such as Italy and Poland, the granary of Eastern Europe. Indeed, even in Italy and Poland, American and Canadian grain was cheaper than the home-grown product.

This and the increasing European population knocked the bottom out of the standard of living in the hinterlands. During the latter decades of the nineteenth century, southern Italian farm workers made between $40 and $60 a year, Polish farm workers about the same. The cash income of peasants in southern China was too small to be calculated.

When large landowners in Europe attempted to consolidate and modernize their holdings, the result was to push people off the land even more efficiently than declining incomes had.

The Jews of Russia felt the effects of the worldwide Industrial Revolution in their own way. Generally forbidden by Russian law to own land, most of them were old-style artisans who handcrafted goods. Others were peddlers, some fixed in one place, others wanderers. Both craftsmen and peddlers found that their way of life was undercut by modernization. The shoes made by a Warsaw cobbler could not compete with cheap, machine-made shoes from England. The peddler who wandered around Russian Poland trying to sell shoes learned the same lesson.

One way out for this "surplus population" was to find seasonal jobs abroad, work created by the Industrial Revolution. By the middle of the century, Italian "birds of passage" already were traveling annually to northern Europe in search of seasonal work, and returning home when they had earned enough money to live through the rest of the year.

Another option was to emigrate to the cities, as the people displaced by the enclosure movement in England had done centuries before. Liverpool, a modern English port that faces Ireland to the west, became as much Irish as English during the nineteenth century. Naples, in the midst of poverty-stricken southern Italy, grew in size until only London and St. Petersburg (Leningrad) were bigger. Everywhere in Europe, the metropolises doubled and tripled in size.

Once again, however, this escape was closed to Russian Jews. Over most of Russia, they were forbidden to live in cities; they were forced to slip into an increasingly difficult economic situation between agriculture and urban life.

The situation was aggravated because most European governments favored industry over agriculture in their

Hundreds of immigrants wait in the main hall at Ellis Island to be admitted to the United States.

tax policies. Even in the cities, competition was so great that life was no easier than in rural areas.

Finally, people on the bottom in Germany, in the Austro-Hungarian, Russian, and Ottoman empires, and in some smaller nations were cursed by the drive to build up modern military forces. In the period before the First World War, conscription into the army could mean a life sentence. Terms were ten to twelve years in Austria-Hungary, and sometimes twenty-five years in Russia. Even when the term of service was just a few years, army life was brutalizing. For generations, peasants and immigrants to the United States related chilling tales of self-mutilation by young men who were trying to escape the press gangs; they chopped off their toes or fingers, or blinded an eye.

Clearly it was better to go to South America, which became home to many Germans and Italians; to Australia, which soon had a huge Irish population; to Canada, which boasts a population as ethnically mixed as that of the United States. But most of all they emigrated to the United States, where the opportunities were greatest.

Promoting Immigration

For the most part, American industrialists welcomed immigration and actively courted it. Until the Foran Act of 1885 made it illegal to do so, some companies paid immigrants' fares if they signed contracts agreeing to work for their patrons when they arrived in the United States. James J. Hill plastered every sizable town in Sweden and Norway with posters that described the richness of the soil along his Great Northern Railroad. (South Dakota was nicknamed the "Sunshine State" in a promotional campaign; some advertisements had palm trees swaying in the balmy Dakotan breezes.) The American Woolens Company circulated handbills in southern Italy that showed an immigrant worker with a sleek, obviously perfumed handlebar moustache carrying a heavy sack of money from a mill to a *banco* across the street. In the West, railroaders and other employers encouraged Cantonese labor recruiters to import gangs of Chinese coolies to do heavy, low-paying construction work.

Employers liked immigrant labor because it was invariably cheaper than American labor; because immi-

---

HOLD FAST!

Some immigrants may have believed that the streets of the United States were paved with gold, but there is no sign of that fantasy in an immigrants' manual of 1891 that advised:

Hold fast, this is most necessary in America. Forget your past, your customs, and your ideals. Select a goal and pursue it with all your might. No matter what happens to you, hold on. You will experience a bad time, but sooner or later you will achieve your goal.

---

grants would take menial, dirty jobs that Americans shunned; and because the newcomers were almost always more docile than old-stock Americans. So far from familiar surroundings and customs, they hesitated to complain. Since many intended to work in America only temporarily, a few months or a few years, and then return to their homelands, they were likely to accept very low wages, live on next to nothing, and take no interest in joining a union or going on strike.

From the national perspective, immigrant labor was pure asset. On the average, more than 60 percent of the arrivals on late-nineteenth-century immigrant ships were able-bodied males; the percentage was higher among Italians and Greeks. The "old country" had borne the expense of supporting them during their unproductive childhood years and was still, in part, supporting their women and children. In the United States, they were producers and consumed little. It was a very profitable arrangement.

Ethnics

In addition to the general push and pull that affected all immigrants to some degree, each ethnic group had its unique experience that strongly influenced both the decision to make a home in a new land and the reception that greeted them.

The Easy Road of the British

It is easy to forget that people from England, Scotland, Wales, and the Protestant north of Ireland continued to be among the major immigrant groups of the nineteenth century. Between the Civil War and the turn of the century, 1.9 million Britons came to the United States. They were almost immediately at home among a people who derived primarily from their stock: they

looked the same as the majority of Americans, practiced the religious faiths that were most common in the United States, were familiar with the basic culture and folkways, and spoke the language.

To be sure, they spoke with identifiable accents that distinguished them from native-born Americans. But those accents are so rarely mentioned in the historical sources that the conclusion is inescapable: the foreign birth of English, Scottish, and Welsh immigrants separated them in no meaningful way from the mainstream of American society. For example, Andrew Carnegie, Alexander Graham Bell, and James J. Hill were all foreign-born, but their places of birth were of no consequence to their careers or historical images. This would not have been the case if the country's greatest steel baron had been Polish-born, the inventor of the telephone had been Jewish, or the greatest railroader had been Italian-born. Indeed, it can be wondered if people of such backgrounds would have found the opportunities to do what Carnegie, Bell, and Hill did.

Among the most significant as a group in the building of the American economy were the Cornish "Cousin Jacks." Miners in their homeland, the Cornish brought skills that were indispensable to the development of American mining: coal, iron, lead, and precious metals. The English and Scots and Welsh eased into positions at every level in every occupation and industry.

The Catholic Irish

The story is a little different for the people of southern Ireland, then officially a part of Great Britain but far from it in sentiment. Almost all of the 3.4 million Irish who came to the United States between 1845 and 1900 spoke English (the Irish Gaelic language survived only in outlying regions), and they too were familiar with the rudiments of Anglo-American culture. However, they differed from the British in two important ways. First, they were members of the Roman Catholic Church, which many nineteenth-century American Protestants feared and hated out of historical memory.

SUI GENERIS

The population of Ireland in 1840 was estimated to have been 8 million. In 1980, the population of the country was a bit less than 4 million. Surely the Emerald Isle is the only part of the world with fewer people today than 140 years ago, let alone less than half the number. Leaving is, perhaps, the central fact of Irish culture.

Indeed, in 1887 the institutionalized anti-Catholic prejudice of the Know-Nothing party that had declined during the Civil War was revived with the formation of the American Protective Association, which was especially strong in the Midwest. Members of the APA took an oath to "strike the shackles and chains of blind obedience" to the Roman Catholic Church from the minds of communicants, but their chief activity seemed to be discrimination against ordinary Catholics.

Second, the Irish arrived not only much poorer than most Britons, but practically starved. Their land had been exploited by England for centuries. Brutalized by poverty, the Irish were considered by their English lords to be semibarbaric, stupid, and given to drunken riot as their recreation. Many Americans, especially the WASPs (white Anglo-Saxon Protestants) who dominated American society, culture and economy, adopted the common English prejudice. Although Irish behavior was little different from the behavior of any people ground down by poverty, many of the idealistic Republicans who had fought against similar stereotypes when they had been applied to blacks were the most extreme Irish-baiters. Employers hung the sign "NINA" (No Irish Need Apply) on their gates and in their shop windows. Since they competed with blacks for the jobs at the bottom of the social pyramid, Irish-Americans were often in the front line of antiblack agitation. The most notable example is the New York City draft riots of July 1863, when white mobs attacked individual blacks and burned down the city's Colored Orphanage.

The Great Famine

The massive Irish emigration began in the 1840s when the Emerald Isle was hit by one of the greatest natural disasters in modern history. The Great Famine of the 1840s and early 1850s occurred because the Irish people were almost completely dependent on the potato for their food. The easily grown potato is one of the richest sources of energy and nutrition; if eaten in large enough quantities, it is almost enough in itself to support life, albeit not the pink of health. The typical Irish heavy laborer in the first half of the nineteenth century ate about ten pounds of potatoes a day.

Then, during the 1840s, the potato crop began to be killed by a blight that had spread slowly across Europe in a northwesterly direction, causing privation everywhere the tuber was important. In Ireland, the result was catastrophic. Within a few years, as many as 1 million people, out of a population of 8 million, died of starvation or nutrition-related diseases. People dropped dead on the roadsides and at work in the fields, digging up the black, gelatinous mass into which the blight turned potatoes.

People dropped dead while loading grain and livestock on ships bound for England. Ireland continued to *export* other foodstuffs all through the famine because most of the land was owned by Anglo-Irish landlords who made their money by selling agricultural products to England. The memory of the Great Famine, more than anything else, accounts for the enduring hatred of many Irish for Great Britain.

During the 1840s and 1850s, the Great Famine decimated the Irish population. In addition to the deaths, about 3 million people left Ireland for good, emigrating all over the world but particularly to the United States. In no other country was emigration so central to the people's culture.

Because life in the United States was infinitely more comfortable than in Ireland, even though the Irish began with the most menial jobs, Irish-Americans took with enthusiasm and patriotism to their adopted home. Numerous enough that they could insulate their personal lives from anti-Catholic prejudice, the Irish parlayed their cohesiveness and natural bent for oratory into a formidable political force. By the time of the Civil War, the Democratic party organizations in heavily Irish cities such as Boston and New York were catering to the interests of the Irish community and reaping rewards in an almost unanimous Irish vote. By the 1880s, Irish immigrants and Irish-Americans domi-

---

PADDY'S LETTER

A favorite Irish-American story that reflects the abundance that Irish immigrants found in the United States concerned "Paddy," who was writing to relatives back in Ireland with the help of his parish priest. (Most Irish immigrants were illiterate.)

"Why do you say you have meat on the table twice a week, Paddy," the priest asks, "when you know very well you have it twice a day."

"Because," Paddy replies, "if I said twice a day no one would believe me."

IRISH-AMERICAN PATRIOTISM

In 1835, John England, the Roman Catholic bishop of Charleston, provided an explanation of why the Irish took so adeptly to politics: "The Irish are largely amalgamated with the Americans, their dispositions, their politics, their notions of government; their language and their appearance become American very quickly, and they praise and prefer America to their oppressors at home."

nated urban politics in much of the East and Midwest, and in San Francisco. Ironically, it was their considerable power on the west coast that led to the first legislation to restrict immigration.

The Chinese and the Golden Mountain

In 1849, seamen brought the news to the Chinese port of Canton that a "Mountain of Gold" had been discovered in California. In a country plagued by overpopulation, flood, famine, epidemic disease, and civil warfare, the people of southern China listened avidly to the usual distortions of life across the ocean. "Americans are a very rich people," one promoter explained. "They want the Chinaman to come and will make him welcome. . . . It will not be strange company."

By the time the Chinese arrived in any numbers, the rich mines had been exhausted. Accustomed to work-

ing communally, they often made a living taking over diggings that Caucasians had abandoned and found employment in the menial jobs that whites disdained: cook, laundryman, farm worker, domestic servant. By 1860, there were thirty-five thousand Chinese immigrants in California. Most of them were young men who hoped to return home after they had made their fortune; there were only eighteen hundred Chinese women in the state, a good many of them prostitutes. In San Francisco, Sacramento, Marysville, and most mining camps of any size, lively Chinatowns flourished.

Race and a radically different culture kept the Chinese separate. "When I got to San Francisco," wrote Lee Chew, later a wealthy businessman, "I was half-starved because I was afraid to eat the provisions of the barbarians. But a few days living in the Chinese Quarter and I was happy again."

Leaders of the Gum Shan Hok—the Guests of the Golden Mountain—also encouraged the immigrants to stick to themselves. "We are accustomed to an orderly society," explained a leader of the San Francisco Chinatown, "but it seems as if the Americans are not bound by rules of conduct. It is best, if possible, to avoid any contact with them."

After the construction of the transcontinental railroad began in 1864, Chinese immigration stepped up. Previously about three thousand to six thousand a year had come to California; after 1868, the annual number jumped to twelve thousand to twenty thousand, peaking at twenty-three thousand in 1872. As long as there was plenty of work, hostility to the Chinese

A Chinese immigrant posed with his possessions to prove to relatives back home that he had been successful in America.

Chinese immigrants were subjected to stringent medical examinations by immigration officials at Angel Island near San Francisco.

was restrained. But in 1873, the country lapsed into a depression.

In 1877, when the Chinese represented 17 percent of California's population, a San Francisco teamster named Denis Kearney began to speak to white workingpeople at open-air rallies in the city's sandlots (empty lots), blaming their joblessness on the willingness of the Chinese to work for less than an American's living wage. Kearney led several rampages through Chinatown, but, much more important, the anti-Chinese movement inspired politicians to choke off the Asian immigration. In 1882, Congress enacted the Exclusion Act, which forbade the Chinese to come. A few hundred continued to enter legally every year (mostly women to become wives of Gum Shan Hok already here), and illegal immigration via Canada helped somewhat to augment the Chinese-American population.

To some extent, Filipinos and Japanese replaced the Chinese in the Asian immigration. Filipinos had free access to the United States after their country was made an American colony in 1898. Japanese began to trickle in, usually via Hawaii, where they were an important part of the agricultural labor force. Caucasians resented them as much as they had disliked the Chinese, but because Japan had a strong government that was sensitive to racial slights, the U.S. Congress never adopted a Japanese exclusion law.

The Germans and the Political Motive

In general, the large German immigration to the United States owed to the same worldwide economic forces that displaced other peasant peoples. After 1848, however, there was also a strong political dimension to the German removal. The failure of a series of liberal revolutions in several German states—revolutions aimed at establishing a democratic system and individual rights much like those that existed in the United States—forced the exile of many leading German liberals. The most famous German exile in the United States was Carl Schurz, who became a senator from Missouri and who was briefly a member of Grant's cabinet.

Many of the 4.4 million ordinary Germans who came to the United States between 1850 and 1900, an average of about one hundred thousand a year, were also influenced by fears that life would be intolerable under the new reactionary governments in their homeland.

Because many of them had been landowners in Europe, albeit not rich ones, German immigrants generally had enough money when they reached the United States to move west and take up free or cheap land. Wisconsin became heavily German in the last

half of the nineteenth century. By 1900, more Milwaukeeans spoke German, at least as their first language, than spoke English. There were other heavily German areas in Missouri and Texas.

Adapting to America

Like the Germans, Scandinavians inclined to become farmers in the United States. Norwegians predominated in whole counties in Wisconsin and Minnesota. Swedes were numerous in other parts of Minnesota and in the Pacific Northwest. Finns, who speak an entirely different language from the Swedes but are historically tied to them in many respects, were important in yet other regions, particularly in logging country and in the iron mines of the Mesabi Range.

Ethnic groups that predominated over large areas found adaptation to the New World comparatively easy since they could approximate familiar Old-World ways of life. They founded schools taught in their native languages, newspapers and other periodicals, European-style fraternal organizations (the Germans' athletically oriented *Turnverein*, or the Norwegians' musical Grieg Societies, named after their national composer), and so on. They continued to eat familiar food and raise their children by traditional rules. They were numerous enough to deal with "Americans" from a position of strength.

The problems that such immigrants faced were common to all settlers of a new land. Ole Rolvaag, a gloomy Norwegian-American writer, focused on the loneliness of life on the northern prairies, an experience that was shared by all pioneers there regardless of ethnic background; he did not write about cultural alienation. Indeed, he wrote in Norwegian and, like Isaac Bashevis Singer in the late twentieth century, became known as an American novelist only in translation.

Other immigrant groups had a comparatively easy time adapting because they were few and cosmopolitan. The best example is the Sephardic Jews (Jews descended from and still somewhat influenced by the customs of Spanish and Portuguese forebears.) Small in numbers, generally well educated and well fixed, they eased into middle- and upper-class society even before the Civil War, particularly in Rhode Island, New York, Charleston, and New Orleans. Considering the fewness of their numbers, they contributed a remarkable number of prominent citizens. Jefferson Davis's strongest supporter in the Confederacy was Judah P. Benjamin, a Sephardic Jew who served in three cabinet posts. Two Supreme Court justices, Benjamin Cardozo of New York and Louis Brandeis of Louisville, had Sephardic backgrounds. So did the twentieth-century

Scandinavian settlers in front of their sod house in Nebraska, 1887.

financier and presidential adviser, Bernard Baruch of South Carolina.

By 1880, there was also a small but flourishing German Jewish community in the United States, perhaps 150,000 people. The majority were small-scale tradesmen or businessmen—rare was the southern town without its Jewish-owned drygoods store. Some German Jews pioneered in the founding of the ready-made clothing industry (Levi Strauss is a prime example); others carved out places for themselves in finance, usually independent of the long-established American banking community, which was WASP and generally closed to outsiders. The Guggenheim syndicate was one of the nation's leading owners of metal mines by the turn of the century.

The German Jews clung to their religious heritage, but otherwise quickly adopted American mores and customs. Indeed, led by Rabbi Stephen Wise of Cincinnati, German Jews in the United States preferred Reform religious observance, which is highly secular and closely equivalent to liberal Protestantism, to the Orthodox, fundamentalist Judaism of the Jews of the New Immigration.

The Trauma of the New Immigration

Adapting to their new homes was not so easy for most of the New Immigrants. Very few of the newcomers after 1880 had much money when they arrived. Most were illiterate, and their Old-World experience in peasant village and *shtetl* did not prepare them for life in the world's greatest industrial nation during its era of most rapid development.

The Uprooting

However serious the immigrants' reasons for leaving ancestral homes, the homes were still ancestral, the rhythms of life familiar, the customs second nature. Wherever their origins, the New Immigrants had been accustomed to a rural and traditional way of life that was the very antithesis of life in the United States, whether on a commercial farm or in the crowded streets of the big city.

Not only was the circle of friends and acquaintances small in the Old World, but the number of people with whom the peasant or Jewish shopkeeper dealt in the course of life was limited to a comparatively few who, in any case, spoke a familiar language and thought according to similar (or, at least, well-understood) values.

In the United States, however, particularly in the big cities and industrial towns of the East and Midwest where most New Immigrants settled, all but a very few *Landsmen* or *campagni* were alien, and they spoke incomprehensible languages. The immigrants, at home for better or for worse in Europe or Asia, were foreigners, a *minority* in the United States.

Strangest of all for people who came from traditional, preindustrial cultures where life was regulated and slowed by the seasons, the weather, the use of hand tools, American life was regulated and rushed by the tyrannical clock and powered by the relentless churning of the dynamo. In the industrial society of the late nineteenth century, Americans were even more self-driven than they had been when Alexis de Tocqueville's head had been set spinning by the American pace.

Exotica

Once in the United States, the New Immigrants discovered that their most ordinary practices—even the way they looked!—were not only foreign but exotic. Americans who had grown accustomed to the restrained Roman Catholic worship of the Irish and the Germans found themselves faced with the mysticism of the Poles and the demonstrative emotionalism of the Italians. Indeed, Irish bishops joined Methodists in worrying about the paganism that was implied in the magnificently bedecked statues of the Madonna and the gory, surrealistic depictions of the crucified Christ that peasants from Sicily and the Campania carried through the streets of San Francisco, Chicago, and New York accompanied by the music of brass bands.

A Russian immigrant in native dress, photographed by R. F. Turnbull in 1900.

The Orthodox religion of the Greeks, Russians, some Ukrainians, Serbians, and other Slavic peoples featured even more ornate vestments and rituals than did the Catholicism of the Poles and Italians. The Jews and the Chinese, of course, were not even Christian and therefore seemed more exotic to Americans.

The newcomers looked different from Americans. The Greeks, Armenians, Assyrians, Lebanese, and Italians were swarthy in complexion, a formidable handicap in a nation that had long since drawn a sharp color line. Polish women often arrived clad in colorful babushkas, aprons, and the billowing ground-length skirts of the Eastern European peasant.

The poverty-stricken Jews dressed drably enough for late-nineteenth-century American taste, but the men, if religious, wore full beards and never removed their hats. Their Saturday sabbath attracted attention principally because the Jews then turned Sunday into a combination holiday and major market day, which offended the sabbatarian sensibilities of some Protestants.

Americans who visited immigrant neighborhoods were unsettled because the smells in the air were alien. Clinging to their traditional diets, which were often based on pungent seasonings and the use of much more onion and garlic than old-stock Americans deemed humane, the immigrants seemed determined to resist American ways all the while they lived in the country.

New-World Ghettos

Most of the New Immigrants clustered in the northeastern quarter of the United States, where they were soon an important part of the overall population. Eighty percent lived in the Middle Atlantic and Great Lakes states.

The newcomers were especially conspicuous in the cities, where most of them congregated. By 1890, one-

MELTING POT OR VEGETABLE SOUP?

Israel Zangwill, 1908: "There she lies, the great Melting Pot—listen! Can't you hear the roaring and the bubbling? . . . Celt and Latin, Slav and Teuton. Greek and Syrian—black and yellow—Jew and Gentile . . . how the great Alchemist melts and fuses them with his purging flame! Here shall they unite to build the Republic of Man and the Kingdom of God."

Jesse Jackson, 1969: "There is talk about [America] being a melting pot. But it is really more like vegetable soup. There are separate pieces of corn, meat, and so on, each with its own identity."

Early Chinese immigrants to San Francisco, most of them men, lived in a segregated section of town dubbed Chinatown, shown here in a photograph by Arnold Genthe.

third of the population of Boston and Chicago had been born abroad, and one-quarter of Philadelphia's people. When their children, who seemed to old-stock Americans as foreign as their parents, were added to this total, it was not unreasonable to think of the cities as bastions of the New Immigration.

Within the cities, members of each ethnic group clustered together into "ghettos" that were exclusively their own. A map of New York, wrote journalist and photographer Jacob Riis, himself a Danish immigrant, "colored to designate nationalities, would show more stripes than the skin of a zebra and more colors than the rainbow." Jane Addams sketched a similar patchwork in the poor part of Chicago, where she established one of the first American settlement houses, Hull House. The same was true of most large eastern and midwestern cities and of many smaller industrial towns. In Lawrence, Massachusetts, a woolens manufacturing

town, more than twenty languages and probably twice that many distinctive dialects were spoken.

Within each "Little Italy," "Jewville," and "Polack Town," immigrants found solace in a familiar language, familiar customs, and familiar foods. The ghetto was a buffer against the prejudice of old-stock Americans, and frequently, the hostility of other ethnic groups with whom its inhabitants competed for the lowest-level jobs.

Indeed, there were ghettos within ghettos. In New York City's Greenwich Village, an Italian community, people from the region of Calabria effectively controlled housing on some streets, immigrants from Sicily on others. On such regional blocks, Italians from a specific village would sometimes be the sole occupants of an "Agrigento tenement," and so on. Grocery stores and restaurants advertised themselves not as Italian but as purveyors of Campanian or Tuscan food. Priests fre-

THE IMMIGRATION EXPERIENCE

The immigrants' trek began with a walk. Most of the people who came to the United States after 1880 were peasants, from rural villages that were far from a seaport or a railroad line. So they walked, a circumstance that put a stricter limit on the amount of baggage they could carry to America than did the rules of the steamship companies. Some might fill a handcart and sell it in a buyer's market when they reached their port of embarkation. More commonly, they carried a cheap suitcase or a bundle filled with their few possessions: clothing; a down-filled pillow or comforter; perhaps a favored cooking pot; a treasured keepsake; sometimes a vial of the soil of the native land that they would never see again.

In Italy, they usually walked all the way to the seacoast, to Genoa in the north or to Naples in the south. In Greece, which is made up of peninsulas and islands, there would usually be a ferry ride to Piraeus, the port of Athens. From deep within Russia, Lithuania, Poland, and Germany, there would be a train ride—more likely in boxcars than in passenger wagons. Even the Russians and Poles headed for a German port, Bremen or Hamburg, because while the czarist government provided both Christian peasants and Jews with excellent reasons to leave, the absence of a first-class commercial port in Russia prevented exploitation of the emigrant trade at home. Indeed, despite the threat of persecution, Russian and Polish Jews often had to enter Germany illegally, paying people who lived on the frontier to smuggle them across and secure a semblance of legal passports and exit visas.

Tickets, at least, were cheap. By the 1890s, heated competition among steamship companies in both northern and southern Europe pushed the price of transatlantic passage in steerage (the lowest class) below $20 and sometimes as low as $10. There were humiliating but important ceremonies on departure day: a rude bath and fumigation for lice on the docks, and a more than casual examination by company doctors for contagious diseases (especially tuberculosis), insanity, feeblemindedness, and trachoma (an inflammation of the eye that leads to blindness and was common in Italy and Greece at the time). On the other side of the Atlantic, United States immigration authorities would refuse entry to anyone who suffered from these diseases, and the company that had brought them over was required to take them back. With paying passengers waiting in New York for passage home—there was a reverse migration too—captains were careful to make sure that they would not lose money on the return voyage. Moreover, while the horrors of shipboard epidemic were considerably reduced from what they had been in the age of sail, highly contagious diseases were not to be taken lightly.

The immigrants were crowded together. Immigrant ships held as many as a thousand people in steerage. There were no cabins, only large compartments formed by bulkheads in the hull. The only privacy was the minimum that could be created by hanging blankets around the few square feet of deck to which a family could enforce its claim. Bickering was constant, and fist fights were common. Except when the weather was bad, almost everyone preferred sitting on the open deck to huddling in the hold.

Most captains prohibited cooking of any kind, except perhaps the brewing of tea on the open deck. Meals were included in the price of passage and were taken in shifts; the last breakfast ran into the first dinner, and so on. Despite the efforts of the German and Italian governments to regulate the quality of food and cookery, the ship at sea was pretty much on its own, and emigrants were unlikely to complain about the quality of service once they arrived in America. Food was cheap, and the cause of constant complaint. Even when meals were good and prepared in sanitary galleys, the ship's cook could not please every passenger; the immigrants tended to be conservative in their culinary tastes, and devoted to a regional or village cuisine. Immigrant manuals recommended the smuggling on board of a sausage or two, or some fruit and vegetables, in order to escape from the poor fare.

Between meals the travelers chatted, sewed, played games, sang, danced, studied English in small groups, read and reread manuals and letters from friends and relatives who were already in the United States, exchanged information and misinformation about their new home, and worried that they might have made a mistake. Days could be interminable, but the voyage was not a long one by steamship. Depending on the port of embarkation and the size of the ship, it took from eight days to two weeks to arrive in New York harbor.

Indeed, an immigrant steamer that arrived at the same time as many others might lie at anchor in lower New York harbor for almost as long as it had taken to cross the Atlantic. In 1892, the United States Immigration Service opened a facility designed specifically for the "processing" of newcomers on Ellis Island, a landfill site in New York harbor that had served as an arsenal. Laid out so that a stream of immigrants would flow in controlled lines through corridors and examination rooms to be inspected by physicians, nurses, and officials, Ellis Island, its architects boasted, could handle eight thousand people a day. Fifteen thousand immigrants passed through on some days, and thousands more had to wait before they could be checked.

Processing at Ellis Island was an experience that few immigrants ever forgot. Crowds milled and shoved for

Immigrants huddled on the steerage deck of the S.S. Pennland, bound for the United States in 1893.

position before they entered the maze of pipe railings that took them from station to station. Instructions boomed over loudspeakers in half a dozen languages; children wailed; and anxious parents called for their lost children.

The first person to examine the immigrants was a doctor who was expected to make an instant diagnosis of afflictions for which the newcomers might be denied entry. If he saw a facial rash, he marked a large F on the immigrant's clothing with a piece of soft white chalk. People so marked were cut out of the herd and examined more closely. H meant suspected heart disease; L meant limp and examination for rickets (children were made to do a little dance); and a circle around a cross meant feeble-mindedness and thus immediate return to the ship. Thousands of families were faced with the awful decision, which had to be made within moments, whether to return to Europe with a relative who had been forbidden entry or to push on.

Those who pushed on were quickly examined for trachoma and other eye diseases and brusquely interviewed by an immigration officer. Everyone was prepared for the trick question: "Do you have a job waiting for you?" Immigrant manuals cautioned readers in capital letters *NOT* to reply in the affirmative. The Contract Labor Law of 1885 forbade the making of pre-arrival agreements to work. Previously—and surreptitiously after 1885—labor jobbers had impressed immigrants into jobs under virtually slavelike conditions, or, at least, many immigrants believed that they had no choice but to work for what the Italians called the *padrone,* or "master."

About 80 percent of those who had entered the building were given landing cards that enabled them to board ferries to the Battery, the southern tip of Manhattan Island. The United States government was through with them, and the horde of agents who made their living by offering "services" now took charge. Again in a babel of languages, previously arrived countrymen shouted that they could offer jobs, provide train tickets, change currency, recommend an excellent boarding house. Some, but not many, were honest. Every large ethnic group in the United States eventually founded aid societies to provide newcomers such services and to protect them from being swindled within hours of their arrival in the land of opportunity.

Hester Street in New York City was home to a large community of Jewish immigrants in the early 1890s.

quently ministered to the same people whom they had known back in Italy; lawyers often represented the same clients.

The same held true for Jewish neighborhoods, where Galician Jews (Galicia was a province of Poland) looked with suspicion on Jews from Russian-speaking areas. Rumanian Jews fastidiously set up their own communities, and the better established and more assimilated German Jews wondered what the world was coming to.

Germans divided on the basis of religion (Lutheran or Catholic). Serbians and Croatians (from what is now Yugoslavia), while never a large immigrant group, nevertheless separated according to their faiths (Orthodox or Catholic) and to whether they wrote their identical language in the Latin or the Cyrillic alphabet.

Nativist Fears

On the face of it, the ethnic ghetto served as an impediment to assimilation by permitting immigrants to cling to old ways and not come to terms with the culture and customs of their adopted country. Many WASP Americans thought so. They looked on the miniature Polands, Chinas, and Greeces in their midst as subversive of a culture they loved. Unlike older immigrants, including the once-despised Irish, the New Immigrants seemed determined not to become Americans.

Around the turn of the century, this cultural anxiety took on racist overtones. Writers who claimed to be social scientists described significant racial divisions among Europeans. The most important of these writers was William Z. Ripley, whose *Races of Man* was published in 1899. Ripley divided Caucasians into the

Teutonic, Alpine, and Mediterranean races. While all three had their redeeming traits (the Mediterranean Italians, for example, were credited with a finely developed artistic sense), there was no question that Teutons—Britons, Germans, northern Europeans generally—were the ones who were committed to liberty and to the American way of life.

In 1882, the Chinese were excluded from further immigration. In that same year, Congress determined that criminals, idiots, lunatics, and those likely to become a public charge (people with glaucoma, tuberculosis, and venereal disease were the chief targets) could no longer enter the United States. By 1900, pressure groups such as the Immigration Restriction League began to call for an immigration law that would discriminate against genetic inferiors—southern and Eastern Europeans, in brief, the New Immigrants.

The demand of a still expanding industry for cheap labor stymied the restrictionists for a quarter of a century. Not until 1921, in the wake of the First World War, was the first National Origins Act passed; it limited annual immigration from any country to 3 percent of the number of people of that nationality who were living in the United States in 1910. In 1924, Congress changed the measure to 2 percent and the base year to 1890, before the New Immigration had fairly begun. This legislation was the most frankly racist act by the federal government since the Fugitive Slave Acts.

Settling In

The restrictionists not only were mistaken about the racial propensities of the New Immigrants, but they mistook the short-term consequences of the ethnic ghetto to be permanent. The ghetto did help immigrants to resist assimilation, of course. In small western mining towns, where immigrants often were the majority of the population but any one nationality was rarely numerous enough to form a community, adoption of American ways came much more quickly than in Chicago or New York.

But, precisely because ethnics preferred religious leaders, merchants, doctors, lawyers, and other professionals of their own kind, they immediately created a middle class in the ghetto that was interested in getting ahead in the larger society. Often mediating between their own people and American businessmen, police, courts, and other institutions, the new professionals became a part of American society at the same time that they remained the elite of the ethnic ghetto. In doing so, they created gateways into the United States through which the second generation would pass. As if to give the lie to nativist fears for American political institutions, it was in politics—the politics of the city—that this process was most apparent.

For Further Reading

For an introduction to the immigrant experience, see Maldwyn A. Jones, *American Immigration* (1960). M. L. Hansen, *The Immigrant in American History* (1940), is still valuable, and John Higham, *Send These to Me: Jews and Other Immigrants in Urban America* (1975), helps to update Jones. On anti-immigrant spirit, see Higham, *Strangers in the Land* (1955), the classic study of American nativism. For a feeling of what immigrating was like, Oscar Handlin, *The Uprooted* (1951), is the classic literary work. However, many of its interpretations have to be modified in light of the findings of Nathan Glazer and Daniel P. Moynihan, *Beyond the Melting Pot* (1970).

There are many books that deal with the histories of specific immigrant groups in the United States. To name only a very few: Moses Rischin, *The Promised City: New York's Jews* (1962); Irving Howe, *World of Our Fathers* (1976); Humbert Nelli, *The Italians of Chicago* (1970); Virginia Yans-McLaughlin, *Family and Community: Italian Immigrants in Buffalo* (1977); Rowland T. Berthoff, *British Immigrants in Industrial America* (1953); and Thomas N. Brown, *Irish-American Nationalism* (1966).

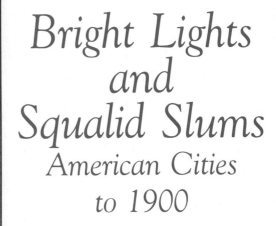

32

Bright Lights and Squalid Slums
American Cities to 1900

"Be a little careful, please! The hall is dark and you might stumble." A journalist, Jacob Riis, was taking the readers of his book of 1890, *How the Other Half Lives*, on a literary tour through parts of New York City that they had never visited and, Riis suspected, did not know existed. "You can feel your way, if you cannot see it," he continued. "Close? Yes! What would you have? All the fresh air that enters these stairs comes from the hall-door that is forever slamming." He paused at the entrance to a windowless apartment. "Listen! That short, hacking cough, that tiny, helpless wail. . . . The child is dying of measles. With half a chance it might have lived; but it had none. That dark bedroom killed it."

The Mulberry Bend, *a photograph by Jacob Riis, shows a New York neighborhood around 1888.*

Of the Growth of Great Cities

Piling one ghastly detail atop another, Riis described the miseries of life in New York's slums and, by extension, the slums of other American cities: the crowding, filth, disease, crime, immorality, and death against which the urban poor fought every day. *How the Other Half Lives* shocked its readers, particularly so because for them, the educated middle and upper classes, city life had become much more pleasant and stimulating in the late nineteenth century.

In another sense, however, Riis's readers were prepared to hear the worst. The slums that the reporter described and photographed were the immigrant quarters of New York, and it was the immigrants whom many Americans blamed for those urban problems of which they were aware. The more generous minded pointed to the destitution of the newcomers when they arrived: what else could they do but drag down the standard of living? Others wrote them off as riffraff, the offscourings of Eastern and southern Europe who, in their self-created ghettos, resisted American ways of life that could raise them out of squalor. By the 1890s, theories of race that held Jews, Slavs, Greeks, Italians, and other New Immigrants to be genetically inferior to old-stock Americans gained in popularity as an explanation of the troubles of the city's poor. Even Riis, himself an immigrant, albeit from racially acceptable Denmark, attributed a fair share of the urban poor's miseries to their own failings.

In fact, the immigrants did contribute to the profound social evils that cursed the late-nineteenth-century American city. They contributed in their numbers. Runaway growth—the dizzying rate at which cities expanded in the United States in the decades following the Civil War—was the fount of a sea of evils.

The courtyard of a New York slum, photographed by Jacob Riis around 1888.

Population Explosion

Americans had an ingrained prejudice against cities, but they were also, by the late nineteenth century, the world's most urbanized people. The proportion of city dwellers in the total population, the number of cities, and the size of cities all increased at a faster rate in the United States than in any other country in the world.

In 1790, when the first national census was taken, only 3.4 percent of Americans lived in towns of 8,000 people or more. By 1860, the eve of the Civil War, 16 percent of the population was urban, and by 1900, 33 percent.

The increase in the number of cities is rather more striking. In 1790, only 6 American cities boasted populations of 8,000 or more. The largest of them, Philadelphia, was home to 42,000 people. In 1860, 141 municipalities had at least 8,000 people within their limits; by 1890, 448 did (and by 1910, 778!). Fully 26 cities were larger than 100,000 in 1900, and 6 of them

POPULATION OF TEN LARGEST AMERICAN CITIES—1880

New York	1,773,000
Philadelphia	847,000
Chicago	503,000
Boston	363,000
St. Louis	351,000
Baltimore	332,000
Cincinnati	255,000
Pittsburgh	235,000
San Francisco	234,000
New Orleans	216,000

POPULATION OF TEN LARGEST AMERICAN CITIES—1900

New York	3,437,000
Chicago	1,699,000
Philadelphia	1,294,000
St. Louis	575,000
Boston	561,000
Baltimore	509,000
Pittsburgh	452,000
Cleveland	382,000
Buffalo	352,000
San Francisco	343,000

U.S. POPULATION: 1860–1900

	1860	1880	1900
Population (in millions)	32	50	76
Urban population (% of total)	20	28	40

From Country to City

Important as it was, however, the influx of foreigners alone was not responsible for the explosive growth of urban America. Throughout the nineteenth century, men and women from American farmsteads flowed into the cities in a steady stream. Dismayed by the isolation of farm life, ground down by the heavy tedious labor, and often as not reaping few rewards for their toil, they heard of well-paying jobs for literate, mechanically inclined people. Or they visited cities and were dazzled by the bright lights, the abundance of company, the stimulation of a world in constant motion, and the stories of the fortunes that might be made in business.

Parents, rural ministers, and editors of farm magazines begged, threatened, and cajoled in an effort to keep the children of the soil at home, but their efforts met with limited success. While the total number of farm families grew during the late nineteenth century, the proportion of farmers in the total population declined, and in some regions, with a nearby city beckoning, even the numbers dropped. During the 1880s, more than half the rural townships of Iowa and Illinois declined in population, while Chicago underwent its miraculous growth. In New England, while the overall population of the region increased by 20 percent, three rural townships in five lost people to the dozens of bustling mill towns that lined the fast-moving rivers and to the metropolises of Boston and New York.

For the most part, the American migration from farm to city was a white migration. Only 12 percent of the 5 million blacks in the United States in 1890 lived in cities. Nevertheless, about five hundred thousand moved from the rural South to the urban North during the final decade of the century, foreshadowing one of the most significant population movements of the next century.

The Walking City

While rapid growth was the rule in cities large and small, the most dramatic phenomenon of American urbanization in the late nineteenth century was the emergence of the gigantic metropolises, the six cities of more than five hundred thousand people that dominated the regions in which they sat like imperial capitals. Philadelphia doubled in size between 1860 and

topped 500,000. Philadelphia counted 1.5 million people at the turn of the century and, at that, had slipped to third place behind New York and Chicago.

Massive immigration, as old-stock Americans were painfully aware, had a lot to do with the growth of the urban population. If the native-born children of the New Immigrants are counted, most big cities were largely foreign in complexion by the end of the century. When the novelist William Dean Howells walked the streets, he wrote, he had to remind himself that he was in his own country, so little English did he hear spoken.

The newcomers clustered in the cities because most of them were almost penniless when they stepped ashore, and those who had some money were liable to be fleeced within a day or so by fellow countrymen who met the "greenhorns" at the docks and offered to help them adjust to American life. New Immigrants did get inland, of course. Large concentrations of Greeks, Italians, and Poles could be found in Colorado coal-mining towns, to cite but one example. But the city of disembarkation, most often New York, was the farthest into America that most immigrants penetrated. The metropolis was the largest Irish and Jewish city in the world, and the second largest Polish city.

In fact, the big city was precisely where the two biggest contingents of the New Immigration intended to settle when they left their homes. Few Eastern European Jews had a farming background; they had been artisans and merchants in Europe, and if New York was not exactly a sleepy *shtetl*, it was where hand manufacture and a good deal of buying and selling took place. The Italians had been peasants but extremely hard-used ones, and they often blamed their Old-World woes on the land itself. Although Italian-American agricultural communities flourished in places like southern New Jersey and California, most Italian immigrants wanted no part of tilling the soil in America. They wanted cash wages, and the city was where the jobs were.

The rapid growth of Chicago in the late nineteenth century led to crowding and congestion, as this 1910 photograph illustrates.

1900, when William Penn's "green countrie towne" claimed 1.5 million people. New York, with thirty-three thousand people in 1790, and over 1 million in 1860, quadrupled its numbers until, by 1900, 4.8 million lived within its five "boroughs." New York was the second largest city in the world, smaller only than London.

Chicago's crazy rate of growth as the hub of the nation's railroad system amazed Americans and foreigners alike. With only a little more than one hundred thousand people in 1860, Chicago increased its size

twenty times in a generation, numbering 2.2 million inhabitants in 1900.

Before the 1870s, cities so vast were unimaginable. When the mass of a city's population moved around by foot, city growth was limited in area to a radius of a mile or two, as far as a worker could walk to work or a housekeeper could walk to market in an hour or so. To be sure, the well-to-do owned horses and carriages in the walking city and could, therefore, live a greater distance from their places of business and entertainment. But not too far. A horse moves only marginally

Urban and Rural Population: 1860–1900

| | 1860 | | 1900 | |
	Places	Population	Places	Population
Urban territory	392	6,217,000	1,737,000	30,160,000
Places of 500,000 or more	2	1,379,000	6,000	8,075,000
Places of 100,000–500,000	7	1,260,000	32,000	6,134,000
Places of 50,000–100,000	7	452,000	40,000	2,709,000
Rural territory	—	25,227,000	8,931,000	45,835,000

faster than a pedestrian and not a bit faster when the streets are choked with people making their way to and fro. Indeed, the most common layout of a mill town was a factory or two at the geographical center of the city and residential areas surrounding it in concentric circles or, more likely, because mills were generally located near rivers, in semicircles fronting the water. The workers clustered close by; with a twelve-hour day to work, there was little time for commuting. The small businessmen who owned the shops lived behind them. The millowners, their top supervisors, and professionals lived on the outskirts. They were not strangers to the crowding, noise, dirt, and turmoil, of the walking city, but when the opportunity to flee presented itself, they were quick to seize it.

Getting Around

The first means by which wealthy and middle-class people could put some distance between their residences and the workingpeople who swarmed in center city was the horsecar line. With charters from city hall, entrepreneurs strung light rails down major thoroughfares and ran horse-drawn carriages with seats open to the public. Cheap as the fares were, five cents and sometimes less, they were still too expensive for the workingpeople, who still walked. However, skilled artisans, white-collar workers, and small businessmen took advantage of the quick, cheap transportation to move away from their places of business—north on the island of Manhattan in New York, west across the Schuylkill River in Philadelphia, north and west in Chicago and in Boston, which absorbed once independent towns and villages.

Allowing even more distant residential neighborhoods was the steam-powered elevated train, or El, which ran at high speeds above the crowded streets on ponderous steel scaffolding. In 1870, New York completed the first El on Ninth Avenue, and the range of the trains, soon up to the northern tip of Manhattan, encouraged the middle classes to move even farther away from Wall Street and the once leafy, now crowded Bowery. Another effect of the Els was to push the very poorest city dwellers, who lived in ramshackle shanty towns on the outskirts of most cities, into the increasingly less desirable centers.

The utility of elevated trains was strictly limited, however. They were extremely expensive to construct;

An elevated train moves above street traffic in the 1895 painting by W. Louis Sontag, Jr.,
The Bowery at Night.

THE BIG RED CARS

Somewhat different from the streetcar lines within cities were the "Interurbans," the fast electric trains that connected one city or town with another. The most famous of these lines was the Pacific Electric, the "Big Red Cars" that tied together the many small agricultural towns of the Los Angeles basin. Built by Henry E. Huntington, nephew of railroader Collis P. Huntington, the Pacific Electric was, in the words of William H. Hutchinson, "one of the most efficient interurban transportation systems ever known." At its peak, the company ran thirty-seven hundred trains a day over twelve hundred miles of track.

The automobile killed the Big Red Cars. Many of the lines were actually bought out by oil companies in order to close them down. But the routes survive today as the famous freeway system of Los Angeles. The Pacific Electric opened the possibility for the unusual expansion of that city by tying surrounding towns to it.

only the richest cities, such as New York, Philadelphia, and Chicago, could afford to build them. Moreover, no sooner did they stimulate residential construction on the outskirts of cities, where they ran at ground level, than the noisy, dirty, and dangerous locomotives roused the ire of the very people who rode on them to work and recreation.

Consequently, it was the electric trolley car, pioneered by inventor-businessman Frank J. Sprague, that really turned the walking city into a memory and ensured the sprawl of the great metropolises. Economical, fast but easy to stop, clean, quiet, even melodious in their rattling and ringing of bells, the trolleys were the key to the growth of big cities and assets to smaller ones. Richmond was the first to build a system in 1887. By 1895, fully 850 lines crisscrossed American cities on 10,000 miles of track. They were as important to the urbanization of the United States as the railroads were to the settlement of the West.

Building Up

By enabling the construction of residential neighborhoods miles from city business districts, the streetcars also made it possible for many more people to congregate in city centers for work, business, and entertainment. This caused real-estate values to soar to near prohibitive heights.

The solution was obvious enough: multiply the square footage of midtown properties by building multistoried structures such as the electric-powered elevator theoretically made possible.

Elevator or not, there was still a catch in vertical construction. In order to support the weight of huge towering structures, the bearing walls of a building had to be so thick on the lower floors, virtually solid like the pyramids of Egypt, as to defeat the whole purpose of building up.

Once again, technology provided the solution in the form of extremely strong I-shaped steel girders. With these at their disposal, architects were able to abandon the very concept of weight-bearing walls and design skeletons of steel on which, in effect, they hung decorative siding of iron or of stone. The potential height of steel buildings seemed almost limitless. They could rise so high as to scrape the sky. Indeed, once the method was perfected, corporations competed to erect the tallest tower, as medieval cities had competed to build the tallest cathedral spire.

In time, New York was to become the greatest of the skyscraper cities; but Chicago architects pioneered in the design of "tall office buildings," as Louis H. Sullivan, the most thoughtful of architects, rather prosaically described his graceful structures. In an article in *Lippincott's* magazine in 1896, Sullivan explained how through the use of "proud and soaring" vertical sweeps, "a unit without a single dissenting line," the artistic form of the skyscraper reflected the essence of its con-

The Flatiron Building, an early skyscraper, photographed around 1905.

SUBWAYS

The electric-powered subway train was to nurture the sprawl of cities even more than did surface trolleys and Els. Underground trains moved faster than trolley cars in traffic but they did not, like the Els, make life intolerable along the line. The subway was a twentieth-century development in the United States. London had a line by 1886, but America's first, in Boston, did not open until 1897. In New York City, where the subway was to become supreme, the first line began operating in 1904.

struction. In the twentieth century, Sullivan's even more imaginative protégé, Frank Lloyd Wright, was to apply the principle of "form follows function" to a wide variety of structures.

Building Over

Another technological innovation that contributed to the expansion of cities was the suspension bridge, which erased wide rivers as barriers to urban growth. Its pioneer was a German immigrant, John A. Roebling, who came to the United States in 1831 as a canal engineer and set up the first American factory for twisting steel-wire cable. Roebling's associates scoffed at his contention that if a bridge were hung from strong cables instead of built up on massive pillars that had to stand in the water, much broader rivers could be spanned. Obsessed with the concept of a suspension bridge, Roebling devoted his life to perfecting a design, and before the Civil War, he had several to his credit, including one over the Niagara River near the Falls.

Roebling planned his masterpiece for the East River, which separated downtown New York, which was beginning to burst at the seams, from the independent and roomy seaport of Brooklyn on Long Island. While working on the site in 1869, he was injured, contracted a tetanus infection, and died. Without delay, his equally devoted son, Washington A. Roebling, carried on the work. Despite serious injuries of his own (he was crippled from the "bends," later associated with deep-sea divers, as a result of working too long below water level on the foundations of the towers), he saw the great structure, called the Brooklyn Bridge, completed

This 1877 engraving from Harper's Weekly *depicts construction of the Brooklyn Bridge.*

URBAN DEVELOPMENTS

1867   New York built the first elevated railroad.

1870   New York and Boston incorporated museums of fine art.

1873   San Francisco built its first cable car.

1878   New Haven, Connecticut, opened the first telephone exchange. By 1800, 85 cities had exchanges.

1879   Cleveland and San Francisco were the first cities to install electric street lighting.

1881   Andrew Carnegie donated a library to Pittsburgh, the first of many Carnegie libraries.

1883   The Brooklyn Bridge was completed.

1884   Chicago built a ten-story building, the first skyscraper.

1887   Richmond, Virginia, built the first electric trolley car line. By 1894, 850 such lines were in operation.

1892   Telephone connection was completed between New York and Chicago.

1897   Boston opened the first subway.

in 1883. It was admired for its beauty as well as its engineering.

In providing easy access to Manhattan—33 million people crossed it each year—the bridge ignited a residential real-estate boom in Brooklyn; within a few years, it was the fourth largest city in the United States. but the bridge eventually spelled the end of Brooklyn as an independent city. A satellite of New York in fact, Brooklyn was incorporated into the city by law in 1898.

The Brooklyn Bridge was dedicated with a mammoth celebration. President Chester A. Arthur proclaimed it "a monument to democracy"; sides of beef were roasted in the streets; oceans of beer and whiskey disappeared; brass bands competed in raising a din; races were run; prizes were awarded; dances were danced; and noses were punched. A fireworks display of unprecedented magnificence topped off the festivities, illuminating the looming silhouette from both sides of the East River. The Brooklyn Bridge was a celebration of the city.

It was also an indictment of the city. On the morning of the gala, one dissenting newspaper editor groused that the Brooklyn Bridge had "begun in fraud" and "continued in corruption." It was no secret to anyone that much of the $15 million that the project had cost had gone not into concrete, steel, and Roebling cable but into the pockets of crooked politicians.

The glories of the bridge were also marred by its cost in human lives. At least twenty workers were killed—others just vanished, probably falling unnoticed—and many more were maimed. Then, just a few days after the dedication, a woman stumbled while descending the stairs that led to the ground, and someone shouted, "The bridge is sinking!" In the stampede that followed, twelve people were trampled to death.

The Evils of City Life

City people died in numbers never before known in the United States. At a time when the national death rate was 20 per 1,000 (20 people in each 1,000 died annually), the death rate in New York City was 25. In the slums, it was 38, and for children under 5 years of age, 136 per 1,000. The figures were only slightly lower in the other big cities, and in parts of Chicago they were higher. In one Chicago slum as late as 1900, the infant mortality rate was 200; 1 child in 5 died within a year of birth. By way of comparison, the infant mortality rate in the United States today is less than 20 per 1,000, and the total death rate is less than 9.

Too Many People, Too Little Room

City people died primarily because of impossibly crowded living conditions, another consequence of high real-estate values. In Philadelphia and Baltimore,

Lewis W. Hine's photograph of a rear tenement bedroom on New York's Lower East Side shows the crowded conditions in which poor city dwellers lived.

the poor crowded into two- and three-story brick "row houses" that ran for two hundred yards before a cross street broke the block. In Boston and Chicago, typical housing for the New Immigrants was in old wooden structures that had been comfortable homes for one family; in the late nineteenth century, they were crowded by several families, plus boarders. In New York, the narrow confines of Manhattan Island made the crowding even worse. Former single-family residences were carved into tenements that housed a hundred and more people.

In 1866, the New York Board of Health found four hundred thousand people living in overcrowded tenements with no windows, and twenty thousand living in cellars below the water table. At high tide, their "homes" filled with water. The board closed the cellars and ordered forty-six thousand windows cut in airless rooms; but in 1900, people whose memories dated back to 1866 said that conditions were even worse than ever.

Jacob Riis estimated that 330,000 people lived in a square mile of slum; 986.4 people an acre. New York was more than twice as crowded as the London that had turned Charles Dickens's stomach, and parts of it were more populous than Bombay, the American's image of a living hell. On one tenement block in the Jewish section of the Lower East Side, just a little larger than an acre, twenty-eight hundred people lived. In one apartment of two tiny rooms there, Riis found a married couple, their twelve children, and six adult boarders.

When architect James E. Ware designed a new kind of building to house New York's poor, he worsened the situation. His "dumbbell" tenement, named for its shape, ostensibly provided twenty-four to thirty-two apartments, all with ventilation, on a standard New York building lot of twenty-five by one hundred feet.

However, when two dumbbells were constructed side by side, the windows of two-thirds of the living units opened on an air shaft, sometimes only two feet wide, that was soon filled with garbage, creating a threat to health worse than airlessness. Nevertheless, the dumbbells met city building standards, and by 1894, there were thirty-nine thousand of them in New York, housing about half the population of Manhattan.

Sanitation

Such crowding led to epidemic outbreaks of serious diseases like smallpox, cholera, measles, typhus, scarlet fever, and diphtheria. Quarantining of patients, the indispensable first step in dealing with highly contagious diseases in the nineteenth century, was out of the question in slums: where were the unafflicted people to go? Even less dangerous illnesses like chicken pox, mumps, whooping cough, croup, and the various influenzas were killers in the crowded cities. Common colds were feared as the first step to pneumonia.

The crowding itself was the chief cause of poor sanitation. Whereas free-roaming scavengers—chickens, hogs, dogs, and wild birds—quite handily cleaned up the garbage in small towns, and backyard latrines were adequate to disposing of human wastes, neither worked when more than a hundred people lived in a building and shared a single privy. All city governments provided for waste collection, but even when honestly administered (which was the exception), sanitation departments simply could not keep up.

Horses compounded the problem. They deposited tons of manure on city streets daily, and special squads could not begin to keep pace. Moreover, on extremely hot and cold days, horses keeled over by the hundreds; sometimes in New York the total topped one thousand. Although by law the owner of the dead beast was re-

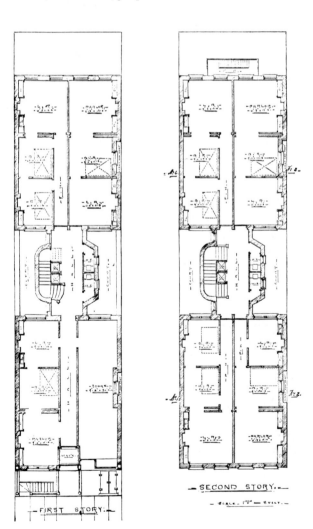

The plans for a "dumbbell" tenement.

Dead horses left to rot in the streets compounded New York's growing sanitation problems at the turn of the century.

quired to dispose of the carcass, this meant dumping it into the river at best. More often, because the task was so formidable, owners of faltering nags cut their horses out of harness and disappeared. In summer, the corpses would bloat and begin to putrefy within hours.

In the poorest tenements, piped water was available only in shared sinks in the hallways, which were typically filthy. Safe water had been so heavily dosed with chemicals that it was barely palatable. The well-to-do bought bottled "spring water" that had been trucked into the cities. Other people depended on wells in the streets that were inevitably fouled by runoff.

Tenement apartments did not have bathrooms. Children washed by romping in the water of open fire hydrants or by taking a swim in polluted waterways. If you did not come home tinged gray or brown, one survivor of New York's Lower East Side remembered, you had not washed. When a bath was necessary, adults went to public bathhouses where there was hot, clean water at a reasonable price. Many of these establishments were quite respectable. Others became known as dens of immorality.

Vice and Crime

As they always are, slums were breeding grounds of vice and crime. With fourteen thousand homeless people in New York in 1890, many of them children—"street Arabs"—and work difficult to get and uncertain at the best of times, many found the temptations of sneak thievery, pocket picking, purse snatching, and, for the bolder, violent robbery too much to resist. As early as the 1850s, police in New York were vying with (or taking bribes from) strong-arm gangs that were named after the neighborhoods where they held sway: the Five Points Gang, Mulberry Bend, Hell's Kitchen, Poverty Gap, the Whyo Gang. They occasionally struck outside their areas, robbing warehouses and the like, and preying on the middle- or upper-class fops who took to slumming in these neighborhoods. But the gangs' typical victims were slum dwellers struggling to survive and escape the slum: the workingman who paused for a beer before he took his pay envelope home, the small businessmen who were forced to make regular payments or risk physical violence. Whereas the homicide rate declined in German and British cities as they grew larger, it tripled in American cities during the 1880s. Although the prison population rose by 50 percent, the streets in some sections grew more dangerous.

By the end of the century, the more sophisticated gangs moved into vice, running illegal gambling operations, opium dens, and brothels. Prostitution flourished at every level in a society where sex was repressed, and there was a plentiful supply of impoverished girls and young women who had no other way to survive. The lucky ones set themselves up as mistresses or in fancy houses that catered to the wealthy. More common was the wretched slattern who plied her trade in the slums under the "protection" of a gang.

Coping with the City

No city in the country lacked laws that aimed to fight or at least alleviate these problems. Ordinances that regulated housing conditions were on the books. Idealists such as Frederick Law Olmsted designed and lobbied for parks so that, at least for a few hours on Sunday, poor people might get away from the milling throngs.

Police reformers established detective departments to fight organized gangs. Saloons were licensed, water supplies tested, fire inspectors sent out to examine buildings, sanitation departments increased in size. However, as all objective observers testified, conditions generally continued to deteriorate until the very end of the century.

One reason was the inadequacy of private charities to deal with problems of such immensity. Another was that city government remained, for the most part, under the control of a unique new breed of politician who did not look on government as a way to shape society but as a business.

The Response of the Churches

The first reaction of the Protestant churches to the deepening poverty of the cities was to flee it. Between 1868 and 1888, seventeen congregations in downtown New York packed up and followed the streetcar lines north. It was not just that the membership was moving uptown (or out of town in other cities). The people who were moving into the old neighborhoods wanted nothing to do with Episcopalians, Presbyterians, and Congregationalists. Overwhelmingly, the New Immigrants were Roman Catholic, Jewish, Eastern Orthodox, and even Islamic. The doctrinal and ritual gulf between them and old-stock American Protestants, as well as the cultural chasm, accounts for the fact that a

man who was considered the finest preacher of his time, Henry Ward Beecher, could make coarse, callous jokes (duly reported in the newspapers) about the misery of the urban poor from his pulpit—and win the response of gay laughter from his genteel congregation.

By the end of the century, ministers who preached the Social Gospel, the message that Christians bore a solemn obligation to help the less fortunate, would stimulate their listeners to contribute to charity and to dedicate themselves to actual work in the slums. The evangelical Protestants, who traditionally were more concerned with the poor than were better-fixed classes, were the first to go to the slums where, Baptist Walter Rauschenbusch wrote, "one could hear human virtue cracking all around."

Dwight Moody, theatrical and huge—he weighed three hundred pounds—took his traditional revivalist message to the worst neighborhoods of New York and Chicago. The Young Men's Christian Association, founded in 1851, came into its own after the Civil War, providing sanitary and moral residential and recreational facilities in city centers at a nominal cost. The Salvation Army, an evangelical group founded in England in 1880, brought its military uniforms, ranks, and brass bands to the United States the next year, offering decent meals to the city's disinherited in return for their attendance at religious services. The cynical laughed at the ritual of the "soup kitchen," but the Salvation Army undoubtedly saved many lives.

Sephardic and German Jewish families who were comfortably established in the United States founded the Hebrew Immigrant Aid Society to minister to the needs of the penniless Eastern European Jews who flocked into the cities. The Young Men's and Young Women's Hebrew Associations, dating back to 1854, expanded several times over during the last decade of the century.

Among the Catholic population, which grew from 6 million in 1880 to 10 million in 1900 (making it the country's largest single denomination), traditionally charitable religious orders such as the Franciscans and the Sisters of Mercy established hospitals and houses of refuge in the slums. The St. Vincent de Paul Society functioned much like the Salvation Army, but without the military trappings.

Curiously, a sort of ethnic prejudice helped to hamstring the older Jewish and older Catholic communities in responding to the needs of the New Immigrants. Sephardic and German Jews worried that the numbers, poverty, and provincialism of the Eastern European newcomers would arouse an anti-Semitic spirit among Christians that would be turned on them too. The American Catholic Church was dominated by Irish-

Americans who were no more cordial toward Italians, Poles, and other Catholic nationalities than were old-stock Protestants. Only after an encyclical of 1891, *Rerum Novarum,* in which the pope proclaimed a Catholic Social Gospel, did the Church hierarchy take much interest in the material well-being of its communicants.

Settlement Houses

The most important charitable response to urban problems came not from established institutions but from individuals who were shocked by what they saw around them and were determined to do something useful with their own lives.

Their creation was the settlement house, the first of which, Toynbee Hall, was founded in Whitechapel, a notorious slum in London.

During the 1880s, a number of middle-class Americans who were imbued with the New England conscience that dictated concern for others traveled to England to learn how Toynbee worked. They found that the house provided food and drink to the disinherited, as traditional charities had, but also child care for working mothers, recreational facilities, and courses of study in everything from household arts (which were not generally known among the very poor) to the English language and social skills needed for self-improvement. Most important of all, the young men and women who worked at Toynbee Hall told the Americans that they had been morally elevated by their sacrifices and exposure to a misery that they had not known in their own lives.

The first American settlement house was the Neighborhood Guild, set up in New York City in 1886. More famous, however, because of the intelligence and powerful personalities of their founders, were Jane Addams's Hull House in Chicago (1889), Robert A. Wood's South End House in Boston (1892), and Lillian Wald's Henry Street Settlement in New York (1893). From comfortable middle-class backgrounds, well educated, and finely mannered, Addams, Woods, and Wald were exemplars of the old-stock American middle class who were determined to fight the materialism of their time and keep traditional values alive. Their personal contributions were inestimable, but they found it very difficult to affect the way in which cities were governed.

The Political Machine

City government in America traditionally was town government writ large: a small elected Board of Aldermen or Supervisors and an elected mayor who made

Scenes like this one of homeless children sleeping on the street, photographed by Jacob Riis, prompted middle-class Americans to establish settlement houses in crowded cities.

day-to-day administrative decision. They were unable, as had been the case with New England towns, to turn to the entire electorate when major issues were to be decided. The electorate was, simply, too large and fragmented both by social class and by ethnic divisions to function as a community.

Moreover, just as wandering hogs and chickens could not dispose of the mountains of garbage in a large, crowded city, the traditional town governments were not capable of supervising the huge fire, police, and sanitation departments, tax-collection agencies, and education, housing, and health bureaucracies that were established in response to felt needs but with little thought as to how they would work.

Politics as Business

The *opportunities* that were presented by the fragmentation of cities and, particularly, the growth of urban tax revenues accounted for the evolution of the political machine. Essentially, ambitious men realized that if they could command the loyalty of a majority of voters in a neighborhood (ward) and could form alliances within a party (usually the Democratic party) with other ward "bosses" like themselves, they could take over municipal government and use it for their own mutual benefit.

That is, they could use politics and government as a way to get ahead that demanded no capital, technological discovery, or birth into a privileged class or an accepted ethnic group. All they needed was votes,

Boss Tweed, as seen by cartoonist Thomas Nast.

and they were in business. And business was how they looked at politics.

"You are always working for your pocket, are you not?" an investigator asked New York boss Richard Croker. "All the time, the same as you," he snapped back. On another occasion, Croker told reporter Lincoln Steffens, "Politics is business, and reporting—journalism, doctoring—all professions, arts, sports—everything is business."

The Profit Column

A political machine made money in a number of ways. There was outright corruption, of course. In return for regular cash payments, politicians who controlled law enforcement could wink at the operations of illegal businesses: unlicensed saloons, gambling houses, opium dens, brothels, even strong-arm gangs. "Bathhouse" John Coughlan and "Hinkey-Dink" Kenna, Chicago's "Gray Wolves," openly collected tribute from the kings and queens of Chicago vice at an annual ball.

There was influence peddling. For example, William Marcy Tweed of New York, the first of the great city bosses, was on Cornelius Vanderbilt's payroll as a "legal adviser" despite the fact that Tweed was no lawyer. What the Commodore was buying was the rulings of judges who belonged to Tweed's organization. In San Francisco after the turn of the century, Boss Abe Ruef would hold office hours on designated nights at an elegant French restaurant; purchasers of influence filed in and made their bargains.

In an age when expansion meant many city contracts, kickbacks on contracts awarded by city governments were especially lucrative to those in control of city hall. Along with the Brooklyn Bridge, Central Park was the occasion of rich profit. The most notorious swindle of all was the New York County Courthouse, a $600,000 building that cost taxpayers $13 million to erect. Plasterers, carpenters, plumbers, and others who worked on the building had standing orders to bill the city two and three and more times what they actually needed to make a reasonable profit and kick back the padding to Tammany Hall, the "men's club" that controlled the Democratic party in New York. For example, forty chairs and three tables cost the city $179,000. The most intriguing item was "Brooms, etc.," which cost $41,190.95.

Then it was possible to do business directly with the city at exorbitant prices. Boss Tweed was part owner of the stationery and printing companies that supplied and serviced the New York City government at ridiculous prices—$5 for each bottle of ink, for example.

Another technique for getting rich in public office was called "sandbagging." It worked particularly well in dealing with traction companies, the streetcar lines that needed city permission to lay tracks on public streets. It goes without saying that it took bribes to get such contracts in machine-run cities. Moreover, the most corrupt aldermen, such as Coughlan and Kenna in Chicago, would grant a line the rights to lay tracks on only a few blocks at a time; thus the "Traction

King" in that city, Charles T. Yerkes, would be back for a further franchise at an additional cost.

Another variety of sandbagging involved threatening an existing trolley line with competition on a nearby parallel street. Rather than have their traffic decline by half, traction companies coughed up the money to prevent new construction.

Honest Graft

It was not necessary to break the law in order to profit from public office. A well-established member of a political machine could expect to be on the city payroll for jobs that did not really exist. In one district of New York City where there were four water pumps for fighting fires, the city paid the salaries of twenty pump inspectors. Probably, none of them ever looked at the pumps. They were working to keep the political machine in power at taxpayer expense.

It was possible to hold several meaningless city jobs simultaneously. Cornelius Corson, who kept his ward safe for the New York Democratic party from an office in his saloon, was on the books as a court clerk at $10,000 a year, as chief of the Board of Elections at $5,000 a year, and as an employee of four other municipal agencies at $2,500 a year per job. Another ward boss, Michael Norton, held city jobs that paid him $50,000 a year.

George Washington Plunkitt, a turn-of-the-century ward boss, thought that politicians who stole were worse than immoral, they were stupid. He preferred what he called "honest graft." "My party's in power in the city," Plunkitt explained,

and it's goin' to undertake a lot of public improvements. Well, I'm tipped off, say, that they're going to lay out a new park at a certain place. I see my opportunity and I take it. I go to that place and I buy up all the land I can in that neighborhood. Then the board of this or that makes its plan public, and there is a rush to get my land, which nobody cared particularly for before. Ain't it perfectly honest to charge a good price and make a profit on my investment and foresight? Of course, it is. Well, that's honest graft.

Plunkitt was satisfied with a comfortable living. Other machine politicians had the monetary appetite of Rockefeller and did less well than he only by comparison. Altogether, the Tweed Ring, which controlled New York City for only a few years after the Civil War, looted the city treasury of as much as $200 million. (Nobody really knew for sure.) Tweed went to jail, but his chief henchman, Controller "Slippery" Dick Connolly, fled abroad with several million.

Richard Croker, head of Tammany Hall at the end of the century, retired to Ireland a millionaire. Timothy

"Big Tim" Sullivan also rose from extreme poverty to riches as well as adulation; when he died as the result of a streetcar accident, twenty-five thousand people attended his funeral.

Staying in Business

Big Tim's sendoff illustrates that despite their generally obvious profiteering, machine politicians stayed in office. Although few of them were above stuffing ballot boxes or marching gangs of "repeaters" from one polling place to the next, they won most elections fairly; the majority of city voters freely chose them over candidates who pledged to govern honestly.

The machines acted as very personalized social services among a hard-pressed people. During the bitter winter of 1870, Boss Tweed spent $50,000 on coal that was dumped by the dozens of tons at street corners in the poorest parts of the city. Tim Sullivan gave away five thousand turkeys every Christmas. It was the duty of every block captain to report when someone died, was born, was making a First Holy Communion in the Catholic Church, or was celebrating a Bar Mitzvah in the Jewish synagogue. The sensible ward boss had a gift delivered.

Ward bosses brought light into dismal lives by throwing parties. In 1871, Mike Norton treated his constituents to one hundred kegs of beer, fifty cases of champagne, twenty gallons of brandy, ten gallons of gin, two hundred gallons of chowder, fifty gallons of turtle soup, thirty-six hams, four thousand pounds of corned beef, and five thousand cigars.

Ward bosses fixed up minor (and sometimes major) scrapes with the law. In control of the municipal gov-

---

VOTE EARLY, VOTE OFTEN

Because voter-registration methods were quite lax in the nineteenth century, it was not difficult to march a group of men from one precinct house to the next, voting them in each one. When Tim Sullivan was a low-level worker in the New York machine, he used this system with his "repeaters,"—unemployed men who voted "early and often" for the price of a day's wages or a day's drinking money:

When you've voted 'em with their whiskers on, you take 'em to a barber shop and scrape off the chin fringe. Then you vote 'em again with the side lilacs and a mustache. Then to a barber again, off comes the sides and you vote 'em the third time with the mustache. If that ain't enough and the box can stand a few more ballots, clean off the mustache and vote 'em plain face.

ernment, the machines had jobs at their disposal, not only the phoney high-paying sinecures that the bosses carved up among themselves, but jobs that required real work and that unemployed men and women were grateful to have. Boss James McManes of Philadelphia had more than five thousand positions at his disposal; the New York machine controlled four times that number. When to the votes of these people were added those of their grateful relatives and friends, the machine had a very nice political base with which to fight an election.

Gratitude for such personal attention was the key to the success of the big-city politician. "There's one way to hold your district," said George Washington Plunkitt. "You must study human nature and act accordin'." Richard Croker expanded on the thought: "Gratitude is the finest word I know. . . . All there is in life is loyalty to one's own family and friends." To which Martin Lomasney of Boston added, "There's got to be in every ward somebody that any bloke can come to, no matter what he's done and get help. Help, you understand, none of your law and justice, but help!"

The Failure of the Goo-Goos

Not everyone was grateful. The property-owning middle classes, which paid the bills with their taxes, periodically raised campaigns for Good Government—the bosses called them "Goo-Goos"—and sometimes won elections. The Tweed Ring's fall led to the election of a reform organization, and in 1894, even the powerful Richard Croker was displaced. Chicago's "Gray Wolves" were thrown out of city hall, and a major wave of indignation swept Abe Ruef and Mayor Eugene Schmitz out of power in San Francisco in 1906. But until the turn of the century, reform governments were generally short lived. The machines came back.

One political weakness of the Goo-Goos was that they did not offer an alternative to the informal social services that the machine provided. They believed instead that honest government was synonymous with very inexpensive government. Faced with their great material problems and inclined from their European backgrounds to think of government as an institution that one used or was used by, the immigrants preferred the machines.

Indeed, Goo-Goos often combined their attacks on political corruption with attacks on the new ethnic groups, not a ploy that was calculated to win many friends among recent immigrants. In the persons of the successful machine politicians, however, the ethnics could take a vicarious pleasure in seeing at least some Irishmen, Jews, Italians, Poles, or blacks making good in an otherwise inhospitable society.

Ethnic Brokers

"The natural function of the Irishman," said a wit of the period, "is to administer the affairs of the American city." In fact, a few bosses had other lineages: Cox of Cincinnati and Crump of Memphis were WASPs; Tweed was of Scottish descent; Ruef was Jewish; and Schmitz was German. But a list of nineteenth-century machine politicians reads like a lineup of marchers in a St. Patrick's Day parade: Richard Connolly, "Honest" John Kelley, Richard Croker, George Plunkitt, Charles Murphy, and Tim Sullivan of New York; James McManes (unlike the others, a Republican) of Philadelphia; Christopher Magee and William Finn of Pittsburgh; Martin Lomasney of Boston.

The Irish were so successful in politics in part because they were the first of the large ethnic groups in the cities, and in part because they had been highly political in their homeland as a consequence of rule by Great Britain. Moreover, the Irish placed a high premium on eloquent oratory, which led naturally to politics, and, recent study has revealed, they were far less mobile than other groups and thus less likely to sacrifice their votes to residency laws.

The primacy of the Irish did not mean that the New Immigrants were shut out of politics. On the contrary, the political machine lacked ethnic prejudice. If a ward became Italian and an Italian ward boss delivered the votes, he was welcomed into the organization and granted a share of the spoils commensurate with his contribution on election day. In many cities, while the police forces retained an Irish complexion, sanitation departments and fire departments often were highly Italian. After the turn of the century, it became the unwritten law among New York Democrats that nominations for the three top elective offices in the city (mayor, president of the city council, and controller) be divided among New York's three largest ethnic groups—Irish, Italians, and Jews. Later, with the arrival of Puerto Ricans and of blacks from the South, certain public offices were assigned to their leaders—for example, president of the borough of Manhattan to a black and political leadership of the borough of the

---

CITIZENSHIP

The New York machine naturalized newly arrived immigrants almost as soon as they stepped off the boat. The record day was October 14, 1868, when a Tweed judge swore in 2,109 new citizens, 3 a minute. One James Goff attested to the "good moral character" of 669 applicants. Two days later, Goff was arrested for having stolen a gold watch and two diamond rings.

JANE ADDAMS (1860–1935)

Internationally known because she dedicated her life to the welfare of the poverty-stricken immigrants in the worst of Chicago's slums, Jane Addams did not decide to become a social worker because she was moved by the sufferings of the urban poor. On the contrary, she was a young middle-class lady whom society educated and then told to spend her life at home as a wife and mother. Addams rebelled against this convention and was searching for something useful that she might do when the opportunity presented by urban poverty was brought to her attention.

Jane Addams was the eighth child of John and Sarah Addams of Cedarville, Illinois. She never really knew her mother; Sarah Addams died in 1863. But she was fortunate in the woman whom her father wed five years later; Anna Hademan, a cultivated and strong-willed person, recognized a rare intelligence in Jane and encouraged her to cultivate it.

Addams completed a four-year classical education at Rockford Female Seminary, and when it was chartered a college in 1882, was awarded a degree. This and the tutoring she received at home from her father and step-mother made her very likely as well educated as anyone in the United States.

But what was she to do with her knowledge? It appears that she never considered marriage, but she was also uninterested in teaching, which was considered an appropriate profession for genteel young ladies. Another possibility, recently opened to women, was medicine, and Addams enrolled at the Woman's Medical College of Pennsylvania. Then she suffered a personal misfortune, illness from a congenital curvature of the spine that did not disfigure her, but periodically laid her up for long periods throughout her life. She withdrew from medical school, and while convalescing, learned of the death of her beloved father. After these personal blows, Addams spent two years as a virtual recluse in the home of a college friend, and some historians believe that her ailment was more psychological than physical.

In any case, a substantial bequest from John Addams enabled her in 1883 to take the "grand tour" of Europe, then fashionable for people of her class. She visited the requisite monuments and museums, and studied history and philosophy, proving particularly adept at languages. But she did not find meaning for her life in art or scholarship. In 1885, she returned to the United States, apparently still foundering and growing more impatient with the social uselessness that, as for so many women of the era, took form in religious piety.

In December 1887, came the turning point. Addams returned to England with a similarly frustrated friend,

Ellen Gates Starr. This time they forswore the cultural sights and, instead, lived at Toynbee Hall, a settlement house run by Samuel A. Barnett in London's squalid Whitechapel slum. Founded to teach young Church of England ministers that many people lived daily with misery and deprivation, Toynbee immediately appealed to Addams. This time when she returned to the United States, she knew what she was going to do. In 1889, she and Starr founded Hull House in the Chicago slum.

It was not the first American settlement house. The Neighborhood Guild in New York had been founded in 1886 by Stanton Coit. But Hull House soon became the best known of them, in no small measure because of Jane Addams's inexhaustible energy and extraordinary talents. Not the least of these was her ability to convince wealthy industrialists and other philanthropists that Hull House was no mere soup kitchen, but provided educational programs for the urban poor, mostly immigrants and their children. It was as sacred as gospel to millionaires such as Rockefeller and Carnegie that their money not simply be given away, but be used to create opportunities for the poor to improve themselves.

Hull House did offer meals and beds, and Addams provided a day-care center for the children of women who had to work (of which she never approved), a boys' club, a gymnasium, and a hall for dances and parties. But the heart of the settlement-house idea lay in the night classes that were offered in everything from economical cooking to English grammar and good citizenship.

So successful was Addams with these self-improvement programs that she was showered with money. By the end of the nineteenth century, Hull House consisted of thirteen buildings in Chicago and a summer camp at Lake Geneva, Wisconsin, where slum children could enjoy a week or two in the country.

Another index of her success is evident in the nature of the criticisms that were leveled at her, mostly by historians since her death. Some have faulted Addams and like-minded social workers for their devotion to the idea of "Americanization." Indeed, Addams did believe that the immigrants must ultimately become integrated into American life, but she was not intolerant or disdainful of their traditional ways. On the contrary, the colorful and lively cultural life of the ethnic ghettos fascinated her, and Hull House provided facilities that enabled the immigrants to pass on their folklore, teach dances to their children, make clothing such as they knew at home, and prepare traditional dishes.

Hull House was the training ground for a great many men and women who would make their mark in social work, journalism, and politics in the twentieth century; among them were Grace Abbott, Enella Benedict, Alice Hamilton, Florence Kelley, Julia Lathrop, Robert Morse Lovett, Mary McDowell, Eleanor Smith, and Gerard Swope. But Addams realized early in her career that private efforts were not enough to cope with the enormity of the social problems presented by American cities. "Private beneficence is totally inadequate to deal with the vast numbers of the city's disinherited," she said. By the late 1890s, not always to the pleasure of those philanthropists who gave money to her, she worked actively on behalf of social legislation at city, state, and federal levels.

Addams was a supporter of the woman-suffrage movement and also a pacifist. Her opposition to American intervention in the First World War cost her the friendship of many of her admirers, including Theodore Roosevelt. Nevertheless, she was justified in the end, winning the Nobel Peace Prize in 1931, an honor that, with considerably less justification, Roosevelt had won a generation before.

Bronx to a Puerto Rican. Other cities worked out similar arrangements.

In this way, the urban political machine served a beneficent purpose, acting as a brokerage house for ethnic groups and therefore speeding their entrance into full citizenship. When the big-city machines became vital to the success of the national parties, anti-ethnic feelings among national political leaders miraculously died or, at least, were no longer voiced.

For Further Reading

A. M. Schlesinger, *The Rise of the City, 1878–1898* (1933), is the pioneering work in American urban history and, though modified by later historians in some respects, is still a solid introduction. The most important updating is Blake McKelvey, *The Urbanization of America, 1860–1915* (1962). Two other insightful studies are Howard Chudakoff, *The Evolution of American Urban Society* (1975), and Sam B. Warner, *The Urban Wilderness: A History of the American City* (1972). Books about immigrants listed at the end of Chapter 31 generally treat of immigrant life in the cities.

On political machines, see A. B. Callow, Jr., *The Tweed Ring* (1966), and Seymour Mandelbaum, *Boss Tweed's New York* (1965). The American reaction to poverty is discussed by R. H. Bremner, *From the Depths: The Discovery of Poverty in the United States* (1956), and to the reformers, by John G. Sproat, *The Best Men: Liberal Reformers in the Gilded Age* (1968).

The characters of this period of American history speak very well for themselves. See Jane Addams, *Twenty Years at Hull House* (1910); Jacob Riis, *How the Other Half Lives* (1890); and Lincoln Steffens, *The Shame of the Cities* (1904).

Jane Addams, founder of Hull House, the best known of America's settlement houses.

33

Parties, Patronage, and Pork
Politics and Politicians, 1868–1896

The presidents of the late nineteenth century were not an inspiring lot. Their portraits arranged side by side—Grant, Hayes, Garfield, Arthur, Cleveland, Harrison, McKinley—they resemble nothing so much as a line of mourners at a funeral. They are dignified, to be sure, and grandly bewhiskered (except for McKinley). They are also competent (except perhaps for Grant), drab (except for Arthur), entirely unexciting.

Many twentieth-century historians, accustomed in their own lifetimes to vigorous chief executives who seized the initiative in domestic and foreign matters alike, have given up on these men of the nineteenth century. Finding more talented but no more attractive characters in Congress and the statehouses, they have generally concluded that what was vital in late-nineteenth-century America was the nation's economic life, the extraordinary expansion of

Political cartoonist Thomas Nast created the Republican elephant and the Democratic donkey, symbols that have been with the two parties for more than a century. The donkey cartoon here was drawn by Bernhard Gillam. The elephant was drawn by Nast in 1875 as an editorial comment on New York City's Tammany Hall.

what is now called the private sector. In this, they are quite correct.

Nevertheless, in the very cautious aversion to innovation in national politics during the final quarter of the nineteenth century—the final third in matters not related to Reconstruction—the national political system perfectly suited the American people of the time. Certainly they thought so. In no other period of American history did a higher percentage of eligible voters actually vote, more than 80 percent as compared with less than half that in a typical election of the late twentieth century.

How the System Worked

To some degree, national politics in the late nineteenth century worked just like municipal politics. While by no means pervasive, corrupt practices were common; party leaders accounted it a minor triumph when they could come up with a presidential candidate whose reputation for honesty was spotless.

Like the big-city political machine, neither of the national parties was built around an ideology, a distinctive set of principles according to which, members believed, the nation should be governed. On the contrary, Republicans and Democrats pretty much agreed on essentials. Indeed, there was more political conflict within the two major parties than between them—at least before 1896.

Also like the big-city machine, which brought together leaders of ethnic groups and neighborhoods for mutual benefit, the national parties were loose coalitions of regional, state, and city political organizations that got together in Washington as Republicans or Democrats for reasons of tradition or simple convenience.

Like the no-nonsense bosses of the cities, politicians on the national level thought of their calling as a business or, at best, as a profession that involved organizing majorities, winning public office, and using the power of government to bestow benefits on members of the party. Finally, since there were few substantive differences between the two major parties, both Republicans and Democrats fought election campaigns with symbols, slogans, and sentiments. Late-nineteenth-century politics was magnificent theater, and in a country that was preoccupied with its fabulous economic growth, a little diversion in the form of theater served very well.

The Politics of Memory

The Republican specialty was "waving the bloody shirt," reminding northern voters that Democrats had caused the Civil War. Lucius Fairchild, a Wisconsin politician who had lost an arm in battle, literally did flail the air with his empty sleeve during campaign speeches. With armless and legless veterans like Fairchild hobbling about every sizable town to remind voters of the bloodletting, it was an effective technique.

The Civil War loomed over the period. Between 1868 and 1901, every president but the Democrat Grover Cleveland had been an officer in the Union Army, and every one of them but William McKinley had been a general. When Grover Cleveland, believing that sectional bitterness was fading, issued an order to return captured Confederate battle flags to their states for display at museums and war monuments, an angry protest in the North forced him to back down and contributed to his failure to win reelection the next year.

The man who defeated Cleveland in 1888, Benjamin Harrison, was still waving the bloody shirt after twenty years and not apologizing for it. "I would a thousand times rather march under the bloody shirt, stained with the lifeblood of a Union soldier," Harrison told voters, "than march under the black flag of treason or the white flag of cowardly compromise." Dwelling on the past could not possibly be constructive, but it won elections.

Vote Yourself a Pension

In their pension policy, the Republicans converted the bloody shirt into dollars and cents. Soon after the war ended, Congress had provided for pensions to Union veterans who were disabled from wartime wounds and diseases. The law was strictly worded, excessively so. Many genuinely handicapped veterans did not qualify under its terms. Instead of changing the law, however, northern congressmen took to introducing *special* pension bills that provided monthly stipends for specifically named constituents who had persuaded them that their case was just.

By the 1880s, the procedure for awarding the special pension had become grossly abused. Congressmen took little interest in the truthfulness of the grievance of a petitioner. (One applicant for a pension had not served in the army because, he said, he had fallen off a horse on the way to enlist.) They simply introduced every bill that any constituent requested. When almost all Republicans and some northern Democrats had a few special pension bills in the hopper, the bills were rushed through collectively by voice vote. Instead of

U.S. GOVERNMENT
EXPENDITURES AND RECEIPTS
(in millions of dollars)

	Expenditures	Receipts	Debt
1860	63.1	56.1	64.8
1865	1,297.6	333.7	2,677.9
1870	309.7	411.3	2,436.5
1875	274.6	288.0	2,156.3
1880	267.6	333.5	2,090.9
1885	260.2	323.7	1,578.6
1890	318.0	403.1	1,122.4
1895	356.2	324.7	1,096.9
1900	520.0	567.2	1,263.4

declining as old veterans died, the cost of the pension climbed to $56 million in 1885 and $80 million in 1888. Pensions made up one of the largest line items in the federal budget, and a veterans' lobby, the Grand Army of the Republic (G.A.R.), came to serve effectively as a Republican political-action committee.

In 1888, Congress passed a new general pension bill that granted an income to every veteran who had served at least ninety days in the wartime army and was disabled for any reason whatsoever. An old soldier who fell off a stepladder in 1888 would be eligible under its terms.

President Cleveland vetoed the law and was sustained. The Republicans ran against him that year with the slogan "Vote Yourself a Pension" and won the election. The next year, the new president, Benjamin Harrison, signed an even more generous Dependent Pensions Act and appointed the head of the G.A.R., James "Corporal" Tanner, to distribute the money. "God help the surplus," Tanner said, referring to the money in the Treasury. He meant it. By the end of Harrison's term, Tanner had increased the annual expenditure on pensions to $160 million. Local wits took wry notice of young women who married doddering old Billy Yanks.

Northern Democrats posed as the party of principle in the controversies over the bloody shirt and pensions. In the South, however, Democrats played the Civil War game in reverse. State governments provided pensions for Confederate veterans, and candidates for public office reminded white voters that the Democratic party had rid Dixie of carpetbaggers and had destroyed the political power of the blacks.

The Democrats were more effective than the Republicans. Except in areas where blacks continued to vote, and in mountain regions where whites had been Unionists during the war, the Republican party simply disappeared in the South. With good reason, Democrats spoke of the "Solid South." Between 1876 and 1896, no former Confederate state voted Republican in a national election.

Patronage and Pork

Politics also meant concrete benefits for party activists as a result of a spoils system that vastly exceeded the patronage that Boss Tweed or Richard Croker had at their disposal. Most government jobs—50,000 in Grant's time, 250,000 at the end of the century—involved real work. There was a postmaster in every town and other postal employees in the cities. Indian agents administered the government's treaty obligations to the tribes. In some federal bureaucracies like the Customs Service, there was enough paperwork to bury thousands of clerks.

Who got these jobs? For the most part, they were filled by supporters of the party in power. Political activists who worked to get the vote out were rewarded with government employment. In return, their party assessed them a modest percentage of their income in election years to finance the campaign. The result was politics for its own sake.

The higher ranking of a party official, the more rewarding the job. Not only was corrupt income possible in some positions, but it was possible to grow quite rich legally in government service. The post of Collector of Customs in large ports was particularly lucrative. In addition to a handsome salary, the collector was paid a share of all import duties on goods reclaimed from smugglers who had been caught at their work. This curious incentive system made for a remarkably uncorrupt Customs Service; there was more to be made in catching violators than in taking bribes from them.

Thus, Collector of the Port of New York Chester A. Arthur earned an average $40,000 a year between 1871 and 1874, and in one big case he shared a bounty of $135,000 with two other officials. He was the best-paid government official in the country, earning more than even the president. And he was assessed a handsome sum for the privilege by the Republican party.

Other party supporters were rewarded with contracts for government work in "pork-barrel" bills. At the end of each congressional session, at the same time that the special pension bills were speeding through, congressional alliances pieced together bills to finance government construction projects in each member's district—a new post office here, a government pier there, the dredging of a river channel somewhere else. The idea was not so much to get needed work done, but to reward businessmen who supported the proper party.

Thus, the River and Harbor Bill of August 1886 provided for an expenditure of $15 million to begin one hundred new projects, although fifty-eight government projects that had been started two years before remained unfinished.

A Time for Professionals

The late nineteenth century produced few high-minded statesmen of the sort who are immortalized as statues. Instead, party leaders were professional organizers. They built up state organizations in much the same way as Mike Norton and George Washington Plunkitt built up their wards, and they bargained with other like-minded politicians as to how the patronage and pork would be carved up.

Republican state bosses such as Roscoe Conkling and, later, Thomas C. Platt in New York, Boss Matt Quay in Pennsylvania, and the "Bourbon" Democrats of the South (so-called because of their extreme conservatism, like that of the Bourbon dynasty in prerevolutionary France) were in business. Like conventional businessmen, they had little time for lofty principles. They were interested in holding office. In 1896, when

Campaign songs and songbooks were popular in the late nineteenth century, when election campaigns were fought with slogans and sentiments.

a crusading spirit swept over the Democratic party—with silver money taking on the symbolism of good, and gold becoming a symbol of evil—Richard Croker of New York exclaimed in disgust that he did not understand what the fuss was about. As far as he was concerned, both gold and silver were money, and he was for both.

Political Equilibrium

The two parties remained evenly matched between the end of the Civil War and the turn of the century. For only two years between 1869 and 1897 did either Republicans or Democrats control the presidency, Senate, and House of Representatives at the same time. In large part, this balance owed to unvarying voting patterns in New England and the South and among some social classes.

New England voted heavily Republican largely in response to the bloody shirt. In the region where abolitionism had been strongest, distaste for the solidly Democratic South was a potent political motivation.

The upper and middle classes throughout the North and Midwest were generally Republican. They thought of the G.O.P, the Grand Old Party, as a bastion of morality and respectability that was fighting against the former slave drivers become Ku Klux Klansmen and the corrupt big-city bosses who were backed by undesirable, sheeplike immigrants in the Democratic party. (Except for Philadelphia, big cities voted Democratic.) Blacks voted Republican for a somewhat different reason. To them, the G.O.P. was the party of Lincoln and emancipation; the Democrats whom they knew, whether white ethnics in the cities (with whom they competed for jobs) or white southerners, were white supremacists.

As a result of these steady voting patterns, the outcome of national elections turned on the vote in a handful of "swing" states, particularly Indiana, Ohio, and New York. In each of these states, with their large blocs of electoral votes, hard-core Republicans and Democrats were about equal in number; the decision was thus in the hands of independents who might swing either way depending on local issues, the personalities

---

ONE-PARTY POLITICS

When M. B. Gerry sentenced Alfred E. Packer to death for murdering and eating five companions during a blizzard in Colorado in 1873, he stated as the reason for his decision: "There were seven Democrats in Hinsdale County, but you, you voracious, man-eating son-of-a-bitch, you ate five of them."

Benjamin Harrison heads the Republican slate on this 1888 election ticket.

The Presidents, 1868–1872

The only big winner in the presidential sweepstakes of the period, Ulysses S. Grant, has been considered by some historians to have been the worst president. In 1868, the still potent Reconstruction issue carried Grant into the White House. In 1872, despite rumors of scandal in his administration that, along with their disillusionment with Reconstruction, drove the Liberal Republicans into an alliance with the Democrats, Grant was comfortably reelected.

Grant Sets Low Standards

Grant was a comparatively young president, only forty-seven years old when he took office in 1869. In appearance he remained as unimpressive as he had been whittling sticks on the battlefield. Stoop-shouldered and taciturn, Grant has a peculiar frightened look in his eye in most of the photographs of him, as though he knew that he had risen above his capabilities.

Grant's presidential campaign banners commemorated his march into Richmond, Virginia, during the Civil War.

of the candidates, or mere whim. Indeed, several presidential elections during the period were decided in New York State, where the result depended on how big a majority the New York City Democrats could turn in to counterbalance the Republican edge upstate.

Party leaders believed that the personal popularity of a candidate in the swing states could make the difference; thus a disproportionate number of late-nineteenth-century presidential and vice-presidential nominees came from Indiana, Ohio, and New York. Of the twenty-eight men who ran for these offices on major party tickets in the elections between 1876 and 1892, twenty-four (87 percent) came from three states. Neither party was interested in finding the best man for the job. They wanted to win, and to do so they had to carry the swing states.

More likely, that slightly panicked expression was the look of a man who knew that he was vulnerable to manipulation but could do nothing about it. For Grant unduly loved the perquisites that came with the White House. He took with relish to eating fine food and to sipping the best French cognac. The general whose uniform had looked like that of a slovenly sergeant developed as president a fondness for expensive, finely tailored clothing.

Indeed, the elegant broadcloth on his back was the emblem of Grant's undoing as president. Money and fame had come too suddenly to a man who had spent his life struggling to survive. Both he and his wife were overwhelmed by the adulation heaped on him. When towns and counties took his name, and when cities made gifts of valuable property and even cash— $100,000 from New York alone—Grant accepted them with a few mumbled words of thanks. He never fully understood that political gift givers were actually paying in advance for future favors. Or, if he did understand, he saw nothing wrong in returning kindness with the resources at his disposal. Among the lesser of his errors, he gave federal jobs to any of his and his wife's relations who asked.

Black Friday

Grant was hardly settled in the White House when he stumbled. Unlucky in business himself, he reveled in the flattery that was lavished on him by wealthy men and had struck up a friendship with Jay Gould and Jim Fisk, the rapscallion veterans of the Erie War. Delighted by their conquest, the two hatched an ingenious scheme to use their well-publicized intimacy with Grant to corner the nation's gold supply. And they very nearly succeeded.

After having won the assurance of Grant's brother-in-law that the president would not put government gold on the open market, Gould and Fisk bought as much gold and as many gold futures (commitments to buy gold on a given date at a low price) as their resources allowed. Then, they let it be known that the president would not increase the amount of gold in circulation.

With dozens of speculators obliged to get gold to sell to the pair, the price of the precious metal soared. It was not, however, only speculators who got stung. Businessmen who were not involved in speculation needed gold to pay their debts and their employees' wages. Banks needed gold to meet their commitments. Both had to buy from Gould and Fisk at an exorbitant price, which, in September 1869, reached $162 an ounce. The two scoundrels were on the verge of making a record killing when Grant finally realized that he was

being used. On Friday, September 24—"Black Friday"—the president dumped $4 million in gold on the New York Stock Exchange. The price collapsed, not soon enough to harm Gould and Fisk (although they did not make as much as they had hoped), but just in time to bankrupt hundreds of legitimate businesses, throw thousands of workingpeople out of jobs, and besmirch the reputation of a great military hero.

The Election of 1872

It was Black Friday, along with their unhappiness with Grant's Radical Reconstruction program, that led prominent, mostly eastern Republicans such as Charles Sumner and E. L. Godkin, editor of the influential *Nation* magazine, to break with Grant in 1872 and form the Liberal Republican party.

In a sense, the Liberals were a throwback to the period when, they believed, the people voted into office the "best men", refined and educated natural leaders who thought of public office as not only their birthright, but also a public trust. Their idealistic view of the past was not entirely accurate. There had been political bosses before William Marcy Tweed, relatives of presidents' wives on the federal payroll before Grant, instances of collusion between government officials and speculators before Black Friday. But the baldness of politics for self-benefit that the Liberals saw around them in the wake of the Civil War was something new.

Unfortunately, as is often the case with nostalgic political movements, the Liberal Republicans not only loathed the circumstances of the present, but were unwilling to compromise with the spirit of their time even in trivial matters of style. Their impracticality was most obvious in their choice of a presidential candidate.

Horace Greeley, the editor of the New York *Tribune*, was a lifelong eccentric. Throughout his sixty-one years, he had clambered aboard almost every reform wagon that had rattled down the road, from abolitionism and women's rights at one end of the spectrum to vegetarianism, spiritualism (communicating with the dead), and phrenology (reading a person's character in the bumps on his or her head) at the other.

Even in his appearance, Greeley invited ridicule. He looked like a crackpot with his round, pink face exaggerated by close-set, beady eyes and a wispy fringe of white chin whiskers. He wore an ankle-length overcoat on the hottest days, and carried a brightly colored umbrella on the driest. Sharp-eyed Republican cartoonists like Thomas Nast, who had just brought down Boss Tweed of New York with his caricatures, had an easy time mocking Greeley.

To make matters worse, Greeley needed the support of the Democrats to make a race of it against Grant, and he proposed to "clasp hands across the bloody chasm." This was asking too much of Republican party regulars. Voters who disapproved of Grant disapproved much more of southern Democrats.

Moreover, throughout his editorial career, Greeley had printed just about every printable vilification of the Democrats—particularly southerners—in the English language. The Democrats did give him their nomination. But southern whites found it difficult to support such a leader. A large black vote for Grant in seven southern states helped give the president a 286 to 66 victory in the electoral college.

Mugwumps, Half-Breeds, and Stalwarts

The Liberals sheepishly returned to the Republican party. For all their contempt for Grant, they found their flirtation with the Democrats humiliating. The Republican regulars took them back—votes were votes—but they jibed at the Liberals' self-proclaimed righteousness by dubbing them Mugwumps, from an Algonkian Indian word meaning "great men" or "big chiefs." The Mugwumps were never more than a fringe of the G.O.P., mostly middle- and upper-middle-class people of high social standing in the northeastern states. Nevertheless, they helped keep corruption in check by their vigilance and quickness to moralize. One more time they would leave the Republican party to support a Democrat, in 1884. Then they were more successful; they took just enough votes with them in New York State to help elect Grover Cleveland, the only Democratic president of the era.

The major part of the Republican party was divided into two factions called Half-Breeds and Stalwarts. In practical politics there was not much difference between them. Rather, they were competitors for patronage and claques devoted to the persons of their leaders.

James G. Blaine of Maine was the leader of the Half-Breeds. An intelligent and charming man, Blaine reputedly never forgot a name, one of those curious little

talents that are so useful in public life. Blaine believed in Radical Reconstruction; he waved the bloody shirt with as much gusto as any Grant man, and he coveted the patronage as avidly as any Tammany Democrat. But Blaine's ambition, which was enormous, several times brought him into conflict with Grant, and he urged the party, if not quite to stamp out corruption, then to reject the man who silently shrugged it off. The term *Half-Breed* was tacked on Blaine in order to convey what his Republican enemies considered to be his hypocrisy.

Blaine's chief rival and Grant's chief henchman was Stalwart Roscoe Conkling of New York. To this day, Conkling remains distinguished by, if nothing else, his total innocence of hypocrisy in political matters. "I do not know how to belong to a party a little," he said. What Conkling meant was that a politician should support the president, as the leader of his party, regardless of what mistakes he might have made.

Conkling had no apologies for doling out the patronage to party faithful. He was the designer of the system of senatorial courtesy, by which Republican senators (or congressmen) submitted lists of worthy party members and the jobs they wanted to the president, who then appointed them to office. Naturally, those people worked for the senator who had been their sponsor, and the senator, in turn, was loyal to the president. A party was a machine to Conkling; he called reformers who preached against it "man milliners," casting aspersions on their masculinity. He and Blaine hated each other.

More Scandals Do In Grant

Conkling wanted Grant to run for a third term in 1876. With three southern states still governed by Republicans, he believed that the party could stay in power if its great leader would head the ticket. He may have been right. But by 1876, Grant and many of his advisers were demoralized. Scandals that had been only rumors in 1872 had burst into the open during Grant's second term, and the president refused to run.

Actually, the biggest scandal of the era had occurred during the Johnson years, but it had involved some of Grant's supporters. This was the affair of the Crédit Mobilier, a dummy construction company set up by the directors of the Union Pacific Railroad that had charged the Union Pacific (and therefore the government) $5 million for work that actually had cost $3 million. This wholesale fraud escaped congressional attention because key members of Congress were cut in on the proceeds. Among the beneficiaries was Schuyler Colfax, a Conkling man from New York and Grant's vice president. Speaker of the House James A. Garfield also accepted a small payment.

THE PLUMED KNIGHT

Although in retrospect it is difficult to understand, James G. Blaine inspired a deep love among his supporters. Nominating him for the presidency in 1880, Robert G. Ingersoll quite unabashedly said of him: "Like an armed warrior, like a plumed knight, James G. Blaine marched down the halls of the American Congress and threw his shining lance full and fair against the brazen foreheads of the defamers of his country and the maligners of his honor."

Grant's Secretary of War, William W. Belknap, took bribes from companies that operated trading posts in Indian reservations under his authority. He and his subordinates shut their eyes while the companies defrauded the tribes of goods that they were due under the terms of federal treaties. Grant insisted that Belknap leave his post, but since Belknap was Grant's old crony, the president refused to punish him on behalf of cheated Indians.

Nor did Grant punish his Secretary of the Treasury, Benjamin Bristow, or his personal secretary, Orville E. Babcock, when he learned that they had sold excise stamps to whiskey distillers in St. Louis. Whenever the president came close to losing his patience (which was considerable), Roscoe Conkling or another Stalwart reminded him of the importance of party loyalty. Better a few scoundrels escape than party morale be damaged and the Democrats take over. As an old army man, Grant found these arguments persuasive.

Hayes and Integrity

Conkling was unable to have his way with the Republican nominating convention of 1876. Mugwump-like cries for reform were in the air, and both major parties nominated men who had reputations for honesty. The Democratic candidate, Samuel J. Tilden of New York, took credit for having crushed the Tweed Ring, although, in fact, he had cooperated closely with Boss Tweed until Thomas Nast and other Republicans had exposed the scale of larceny in New York.

The reputation for bold honesty of the Republican candidate, Rutherford B. Hayes, was only a little more substantial. He was an amiable man, a model of midwestern propriety. His wife, a staunch advocate of temperance, helped to enhance his image by her refusal, when she was first lady of Ohio, to serve alcoholic beverages at official functions, thus earning the nickname "Lemonade Lucy."

But Hayes was so amiable and obliging, it is difficult to avoid suspecting that he had earned his reputation largely because no one had ever forced dubious money on him. He was a Half-Breed in fact if not in name. As long as his subordinates were not overt profiteers, as so many of Grant's men had been, Hayes was content.

Once the disputed election of 1876 was resolved (see p. 410), Hayes moved into the White House and proceeded to please no one. Stalwarts were disappointed by his abandonment of southern black voters; Half-Breeds believed that Hayes did not provide them with as much of the patronage as they deserved. There never was a question of renominating him. Long before Hayes retired, James G. Blaine announced that he would seek the Republican nomination. Fearing that Blaine was

Rutherford B. Hayes was called "His Fraudulency" by political enemies.

too popular for any ordinary Stalwart candidate, Roscoe Conkling persuaded Grant, who had just returned from an around-the-world tour and was almost broke, to run against him.

Garfield: A Dark Horse

Neither Blaine nor Grant was able to win the support of the majority of the delegates to the Republican convention. They were frustrated by the ambitions of several "favorite-son" candidates who actively hoped for a deadlock between the front runners, which would force the tired delegates to turn to them as compromise candidates.

Finally, after thirty-four ballots, the Blaine men recognized that the cause of their hero—the "plumed knight" according to Robert G. Ingersoll in his nomination speech—was lost. But instead of turning to one of the favorite sons whom they held responsible for their disappointment, they switched their votes to a man whose name was not even in nomination, James A. Garfield of Ohio. On the thirty-sixth ballot, he became the Republican candidate.

Garfield was a Half-Breed, a Blaine supporter, but he

played on Conkling's vanity by traveling to New York to seek the boss's blessing and promise him a share of the patronage. Garfield went to the polls with a unified party behind him.

The Democrats, having failed to win with an antiwar Democrat in 1868 (Seymour), a Republican maverick in 1872 (Greeley), and a reformer in 1876 (Tilden), tried their luck with a Civil War general, Winfield Scott Hancock. An attractive if uninspiring man, he made the election extremely close. Garfield drew only ten thousand more votes than Hancock, just 48.3 percent of the total.

This close shave was typical of the period. Between 1876 and 1896, no winning presidential candidate won as much as 50 percent of the vote. In 1876, Hayes had fewer popular votes than Tilden. In 1884, Grover Cleveland won with 48.5 percent of the total. In 1888, Grover Cleveland outdrew Republican candidate Benjamin Harrison, but lost in the electoral college. In 1892, Cleveland won in a comeback bid, by 360,000 votes. That was a virtual landslide by the standards of the late nineteenth century; but even at that, Cleveland's total amounted to only 46 percent of the popular vote. A third party, the People's party, won more than 1 million votes in 1892, 8.5 percent of the total.

The Assassination of Garfield

It was not, however, the narrowness of his win that doomed Garfield, but the burden of distributing the federal patronage. During the few months that he was active as president, he devoted practically all his time to sorting out the claims of Republican campaign workers to rewards for their work in the form of government jobs. At one point he explained in disgust to Blaine, his Secretary of State who wanted very badly to be president, that he could not understand why men pursued the post, considering all its trivial tawdry concerns. Garfield tried to placate both wings of the party. But when he handed the choicest plum of all, the post of Collector of Customs of the port of New York, to a Blaine man, Roscoe Conkling openly broke with the president. He and his protégé in the state Republican machine, Thomas Platt, resigned their seats in the Senate. Their intention was to remind Garfield of their power in the New York Republican party by having the state legislature reelect them.

By the summer of 1881, it appeared that Conkling and Platt had lost their battle, for the Garfield–Blaine Half-Breeds had succeeded in blocking their reelection. But the issue was finally resolved by two gunshots in a Washington train station. On July 2, 1881, Charles Guiteau, a ne'er-do-well preacher and bill collector who had worked for the Stalwarts but had not

ORDINARY PEOPLE

Presidents were not so remote and sheltered from the people in the late nineteenth century, as Garfield's assassination shows. When he was shot, the president of the United States was waiting for a train on a public platform.

An incident that involved Rutherford B. Hayes after he left the White House illustrates the point more amusingly. While attending a G.A.R. encampment, Hayes was stopped by a policeman, who brusquely pulled him back to a park pathway, and gave him a finger-shaking lesson because he was walking on the grass. Likewise, President Grant, who never lost his love for fast horses, was written a ticket by a Washington officer for speeding.

been rewarded with a government job, walked up to Garfield as he was about to depart on a holiday and shot him twice in the small of the back. After living in extreme pain for eleven weeks, the second president to be murdered died on September 19.

"I am a Stalwart! Arthur is president!" Guiteau was alleged to have shouted when he fired the fatal shots. He meant that the new president was none other than Conkling's longtime ally, Chester A. Arthur. Indeed, the deranged Guiteau expected Arthur to free him from prison and reward him for his patriotic act.

Once in office, however, Chet Arthur, recently the prince of spoilsmen, proved to be an able and uncorrupt president who signed the first law to limit a party's use of government jobs for political purposes.

Civil-Service Reform

The Pendleton Act of 1883 established the Civil Service Commission, a three-man bureau that was empowered to draw up and administer examinations that applicants for some low-level government jobs were required to pass before they were hired. Once in these civil-service jobs, employees could not be fired simply because the political party to which they belonged lost the presidency.

At first, only 10 percent of 131,000 government workers were protected by civil service. But the Pendleton Act also empowered the president to add job classifications to the civil-service list at his discretion. Ironically, because the presidency changed party hands every four years between 1880 and 1896, each incumbent's desire to protect his own appointees in their jobs—a violation of the *spirit* of civil-service reform—led by the end of the century to a fairly comprehensive civil-service system.

After the Democrat Grover Cleveland was elected in November 1884, but before he took office in March 1885, outgoing President Chester Arthur protected a number of Republican government employees by adding their jobs to the civil-service list. Cleveland did the same thing for Democratic government workers in 1888, Benjamin Harrison for Republicans in 1892, and Cleveland again for Democrats in 1896. By 1900, 40 percent of the federal government's 256,000 employees held civil-service positions. About 30 percent of government clerks were women, an unlikely proportion at a time when jobs were given out in order to win votes.

Another provision of the Pendleton Act was the abolition of the assessment system. That is, the parties were forbidden to insist that those of their members who held government positions "donate" a percentage of their salaries for political campaign chests each election year. Until the presidency of Benjamin Harrison (1889–93), the professional politicians were at a loss as to how to replace these revenues. Harrison's Postmaster General, John Wanamaker, came up with the solution,

at least for the Republicans. He established a system of levying "contributions" on big businessmen who had an interest in Republican victory at the polls. This remained the chief means of financing political campaigns until the 1970s.

How Little Things Decide Great Elections

Chester A. Arthur did a good job in the White House, cutting an elegant figure in the fashionable clothing he favored, acting with good judgment and dignity as head of state, and attempting to placate both wings of his party. Twice he offered his old boss, Conkling, who was a brilliant lawyer, a seat on the Supreme Court. But he also tried to woo the Half-Breeds so that he might run for reelection in 1884 with their support. It was not to be. Frustrated in 1880, Blaine did not care how reasonable Arthur was. He resigned from the cabinet and, with Conkling's career in eclipse, easily won the Republican nomination in the summer of 1884.

Blaine expected to win the election as well. As usual, New York State seemed to be the key to victory, and Blaine believed that he would run more strongly there than most Republicans. The Mugwumps had deserted the party, announcing that the Democratic candidate, Grover Cleveland, was the more honest man. But Blaine expected to make up this defection and more by winning the Irish-American vote, which usually did not go Republican. He was popular in the Irish-American community because, in an era when Republican leaders frequently disdained the Catholic Church, Blaine had Catholic relatives. Moreover for reasons of his own, Blaine liked to "twist the lion's tail," taunt the British, the ancestral enemy in Irish eyes. Finally, news broke that seemed a bonus: it was revealed that Grover Cleveland had fathered an illegitimate child while a lawyer in Buffalo. The stringent sexual code of the period seemed to dictate that such a libertine should not be president.

But Cleveland nimbly neutralized the morality issue by publicly admitting the folly of his youth and explain-

Chester A. Arthur, Collector of the Port of New York from 1871 to 1874, and later, James A. Garfield's successor as president.

CONKLING THE IDEALIST

Although he is chiefly remembered for his cynical attitude toward the patronage and party loyalty, Roscoe Conkling remained truer to the Radical Republican ideals of his young manhood than did most members of his party. Until his death in 1888—he froze to death in a blizzard—Conkling's extremely successful law firm was instructed to take cases from blacks at nominal or no cost.

THE GREAT AGNOSTIC

Robert G. Ingersoll was a rare politician for the late nineteenth century. He sacrificed a career for the sake of a principle. Acknowledged as one of the greatest orators of his time and a man of immense talent, Ingersoll was an agnostic who preached his uncertainty about the existence of God at every opportunity and with every oratorical trick he knew. As a result, despite his considerable contributions to the Republican party, the only political office that Ingersoll ever held was the comparatively minor one of attorney general of Illinois, and then for only two years.

Grover Cleveland was elected to a second term as president after a bitter election campaign.

ing that he had tried to make amends by financially supporting the child. Indeed, the Democrats turned the scandal to their advantage when they argued that if Cleveland was indiscreet in private life, he had an exemplary record in public office, whereas Blaine, who was admirable as a husband and family man, had engaged in several dubious deals as a congressman from Maine. Put Cleveland into public office where he shined, they said, and return Blaine to the private life that he richly adorned.

Just a few days before the election, disaster struck the Blaine campaign. The confident candidate made the mistake of dining lavishly with a group of millionaires in Delmonico's, the most regal restaurant in New York City—not a good idea when he wanted the votes of many poor men. Before another group, he ignored the statement of a Presbyterian minister, Samuel Burchard, who denounced the Democrats as the party of "rum, romanism, and rebellion," that is, of the saloon, the Roman Catholic Church, and southern secession.

This was pretty ordinary stuff in the Republican oratory of the period, but Blaine was not fighting the campaign with an ordinary strategy. He was wooing Irish-American votes, and the Irish were sensitive about their Catholic religion. When Democratic newspapers plastered the insult "romanism" across their front pages, Blaine rushed to express his sincere distaste for this kind of bigotry and to explain that had he heard Burchard's words, he would have called him on them. But the damage was done. The Irish voters trundled back into the Democratic column, giving New York State and thus the presidency to Grover Cleveland.

In 1888, four years later, Cleveland was undone in his bid for reelection by a similarly trivial incident. A Republican newspaperman, pretending to be an Englishman who was a naturalized American citizen, wrote to the British ambassador in Washington asking which of the two candidates, Cleveland or Benjamin Harrison, would be the better president from the British point of view. Foolishly, the ambassador replied that Cleveland seemed to be better disposed toward British interests. The Republican press immediately labeled Cleveland the British candidate. Thousands of Irish Democrats in New York, who were reflexively hostile to anything or anyone the British favored, voted Republican and gave that swing state to Harrison.

This sort of fuss, and the color and excitement of political rallies, seemed to make the difference in an era when the two parties were so evenly balanced. Unlike late-twentieth-century Americans, who are flooded with entertainment from a dozen media and to whom elections are just one show among many, late-nineteenth-century Americans enjoyed politics as a major diversion. They flocked to rallies in numbers almost unknown today in order to hear brass bands, swig lemonade or beer, and listen to speeches that were as much bombastic show as statements of principle

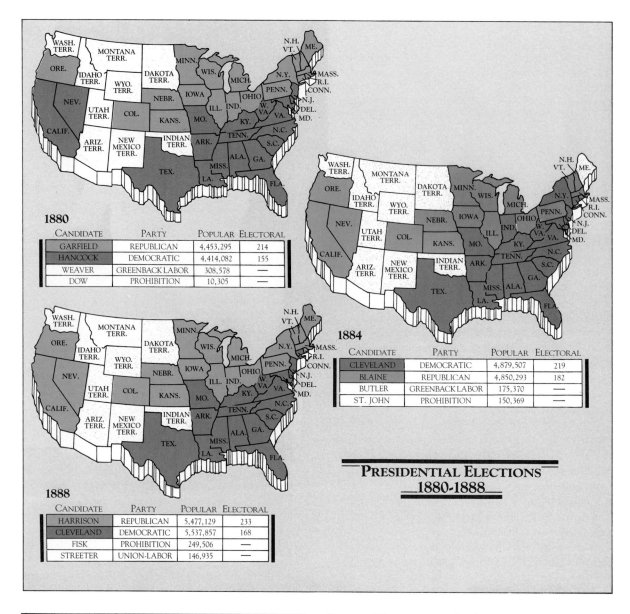

1880

CANDIDATE	PARTY	POPULAR	ELECTORAL
GARFIELD	REPUBLICAN	4,453,295	214
HANCOCK	DEMOCRATIC	4,414,082	155
WEAVER	GREENBACK LABOR	308,578	—
DOW	PROHIBITION	10,305	—

1884

CANDIDATE	PARTY	POPULAR	ELECTORAL
CLEVELAND	DEMOCRATIC	4,879,507	219
BLAINE	REPUBLICAN	4,850,293	182
BUTLER	GREENBACK LABOR	175,370	—
ST. JOHN	PROHIBITION	150,369	—

PRESIDENTIAL ELECTIONS 1880-1888

1888

CANDIDATE	PARTY	POPULAR	ELECTORAL
HARRISON	REPUBLICAN	5,477,129	233
CLEVELAND	DEMOCRATIC	5,537,857	168
FISK	PROHIBITION	249,506	—
STREETER	UNION-LABOR	146,935	—

The Issues of the Era

This is not to say that there were no issues of substance in late-nineteenth-century politics. There were. But until the 1890s, the lines of division were not so much between the parties as within them.

Foreign Affairs

Despite the propensity of politicians of both parties to twist the lion's tail, relations with Great Britain generally improved during the final decades of the century. In 1872, Grant's Secretary of State, Hamilton Fish concluded the Treaty of Washington with Great Britain. The treaty resolved a number of aggravating differences between the two English-speaking nations. Great Britain compensated American shipowners for damages that had been done to their ships by the British-built Confederate commerce-raider the *Alabama.* Squabbles between fishermen from New England and Canada over fishing rights in the North Atlantic were smoothed, and a minor but locally bothersome boundary dispute in the Strait of Juan de Fuca between Washington Territory and the province of British Columbia was ironed out—the last point of contention on the long Canadian-American border.

President Grant was less successful in his pet foreign scheme. Encouraged by American investors and a pro-American political faction in Santo Domingo, the

Spanish-speaking half of the island of Hispaniola (the Dominican Republic today), Grant tried to annex it to the United States. He came very close to success and was foiled only because of the opposition of the Liberal Republicans, particularly Senator Charles Sumner of Massachusetts, chairman of the Senate Foreign Relations Committee.

The great debate over imperialism—the control of colonies or economic dependencies abroad—which was to take place at the turn of the century, was also prefigured in the efforts of James Blaine, Secretary of State under both Garfield and Harrison, to assert American economic primacy in Latin America. After years of campaigning for closer relations between the United States and the Latin American republics, Blaine succeeded in 1889/90 in hosting a Pan-American Congress in Washington. Of all the Latin American nations, only Santo Domingo refused to attend. Primarily producers of raw materials, the Latin American countries were willing to listen to Blaine's case for tying their fates to the United States rather than to Great Britain, which then was the major supplier of manufactured goods in the Western Hemisphere.

The delegates agreed to the establishment of a permanent Pan American Union in Washington, a clearing house for diplomatic relations within the Americas. But they would not agree to Blaine's proposal for a customs union, that is, free trade within the Americas and tariff protection against the rest of the world. Blaine had to be satisfied with unilateral action. In the McKinley Tariff of 1890, Congress included a reciprocal-trade clause. The president was empowered to declare reduced duties on the goods of nations that lowered their own tariffs on American goods.

The Tariff

The tariff could be an emotional issue in the late nineteenth century. Most southern and western Democrats, who represented agricultural sections, and some Republicans from rural districts urged low import duties. With the exception of a few who grew specialized crops such as sugar cane, American farmers had no fear of foreign competition. So cheap were their products that they were able to undersell farmers almost everywhere in the world, if other countries did not levy taxes on American crops in response to high American duties on the goods that those countries shipped abroad. Moreover, low duties on imported manufactured goods meant lower prices on the commodities that consumers of manufactured goods, such as farmers, had to buy.

American manufacturers and most industrial workers insisted on protection, a high tariff. The size of their profits and wages, they believed, depended on keeping out foreign competition. The debate was a reprise of the tariff dispute before the Civil War, but somewhat more complicated. For example, railroaders and bankers often supported the low-tariff forces. As far as they were concerned, the more goods being shunted about the better, whether the goods bought, sold, and transported were foreign or domestic in origin. Railroaders had an added incentive to support a low tariff. They were huge consumers of steel, which was one of the commodities that received the most protection.

Increasingly in the late nineteenth century, high-tariff interests had their way. After bobbing up and down from a low of 40 percent (by no means a "low" tariff) to a high of 47 percent, rates were increased to 50 percent in the McKinley Tariff of 1890. That is, on the average, an imported item was slapped with a tax that was equivalent to half of its value.

When a depression followed quickly on the act, however, Grover Cleveland and the Democrats campaigned against the McKinley rates in 1892 and won the election. But the tariff that Congress prepared, the Wilson-Gorman Act, lowered duties by only 10.1 percent—to 39.9 percent. Cleveland knew that this rate was not low enough to satisfy many of his supporters, so he killed the bill with a pocket veto.

The Money Question

Another issue that generated a great deal of heat during the final third of the nineteenth century was the money question: what should be the basis of the nation's medium of exchange? Should it continue to be gold, with every piece of paper money backed by gold in a vault and redeemable in the precious metal, or should the money supply be regulated by the government in such a way as to determine the level of income of workers and, particularly, farmers?

Like the tariff issue, the monetary question predated the Civil War, but the form it took in the early 1880s was a result of a wartime policy.

In order to help finance the war effort, the federal government had issued about $450 million in paper money that was *not* redeemable in gold. The greenbacks, so called because they were printed in green ink instead of gold on the obverse, were accepted at face value by the federal government. That is, their value in payment of taxes was a matter of law.

As long as the word of the government was of dubious value, and as long as anxious moments continued during the war, individuals involved in private transactions insisted on discounting the greenbacks, redeeming them at something less than face value. Bankers were particularly suspicious of any paper money that

JAMES ABRAM GARFIELD (1831–1881)

Perhaps if he had lived longer, he would be better understood. As it is, James A. Garfield of Cuyahoga County, Ohio, is one of the most puzzling (and disappointing) personalities of the late nineteenth century. A man of exceptional intelligence and talent, he has gone down in history as just another lackluster politician in an age that was crowded with them. Perhaps it would have been different if he had made a mark as president. But he was fatally shot just four months after his inauguration in March 1881, the fourth president to die in office, and the second to be assassinated. And yet, even before his dark-horse nomination and election in 1880, Garfield had failed to distinguish himself from his run-of-the-mill colleagues. Perhaps, understanding the character of politics in his era, Garfield consciously strived to be a mediocrity.

James Abram Garfield was born in a log cabin, the last of the frontier presidents. Poverty stricken then, the family was devastated when Garfield's father died and young James had to shoulder the responsibility of supporting his mother. He worked on a canal boat, developing the powerful physique that, after he was shot in 1881, enabled him to survive for two months while infection festered painfully in his body.

Like Lincoln, Garfield educated himself, not merely to read and write but well enough to gain admission to Williams College. There he distinguished himself, mastering the demanding classical curriculum that was still the rule in colleges. Although he entertained friends by simultaneously writing in Latin with his right hand and Greek with his left, Garfield's erudition was not limited to tricks. His diaries reveal a man who was familiar with history (although not with literature, save the Bible) and who understood, as did very few of his politician contemporaries, the forces of industrialization and urbanization that were changing America.

After serving as an officer in the Civil War, brevetted as a general, Garfield entered Congress as a Radical Republican. He was a leader, becoming Speaker of the House, but also a straight party man who risked nothing with imaginative speeches and viewpoints, of which he seemed to have been capable. Indeed, while the details are vague, it appears that he accepted some money from the Crédit Mobilier company during Johnson's presidency.

In 1880, Garfield was elected to the Senate from Ohio and attended the Republican national convention as floor manager for presidential hopeful John Sherman. When the convention deadlocked and turned quickly to Garfield as its nominee, he remained silent. Sherman was convinced that he had been betrayed. In fact, Garfield allowed his opportunities to develop without either encouraging them or choking them off—again, standard operating procedure for a politician of the Gilded Age.

He was nominated and elected, but served only four months in good health. Ironically, this exceptional individual who forced himself to be a political hack was struck down at fifty years of age because of one of the most sordid aspects of that era's politics that Garfield tolerated—the patronage.

On July 2, 1881, the president was waiting for a train when Charles Guiteau, an insane man to whom Garfield had refused to give a government position, pumped two bullets into the small of his back. Had the wounds been inflicted in the late twentieth century, Garfield would have been up and around in a few days; the slugs would have been located by x-ray and easily removed, and the danger of infection eliminated with antibiotics. No vital organs were damaged; no bones were broken. But because one bullet was lodged against Garfield's spine, the doctors were afraid to operate. Instead, they treated the president by probing with metal rods and by "irrigating," flooding the worst wound with water. It did more harm than good. After living in excruciating pain for eleven weeks, Garfield died on September 19.

Garfield's single contribution to American political development occurred two years after his death, when Congress enacted the Pendleton Act, which instituted the civil service in the United States. Garfield was a martyr to the principle that lower-level government employees remain in their jobs no matter which party is in power. But would he have signed the bill had he

---

was not redeemable in gold, and after the war, Secretaries of the Treasury who shared the conservative views of the bankers adopted the policy of retiring the greenbacks. When the notes flowed into the Treasury, they were destroyed and were not replaced by new bills.

The result was deflation: a reduction in the amount of money in circulation and, therefore, an increase in the value of gold and of paper money that was redeemable in gold. Prices dipped; so did wages. It took less to buy a sack of flour or a side of bacon than it had when the greenbacks had flowed in profusion. And, of course, the farmer who grew the wheat and raised the hogs received less for his trouble.

Farmers, who were generally debtors, were hit hardest by deflation. They had borrowed heavily to increase their acreage and to purchase machinery when the greenbacks had been abundant and prices therefore high. After the Treasury began to retire the greenbacks, they found themselves obligated to repay these loans in money that was more valuable and more diffi-

been alive and well in the presidency at that time? As with almost everything about the man, it is impossible to say. On the one hand, he had lived happily with the spoils system during the two decades he had sat in Congress. On the other hand, when he was at the top, the tyranny of the patronage disgusted him. Referring to the fact that most of his time as president was spent dividing up the spoils among his supporters, Garfield exclaimed, "My God! What is there in this place that a man should ever want to get into it!"

James Garfield had served as president for only four months when he was shot and incapacitated.

cult to get. For example, one economist calculated that a $1,000 mortgage taken out on a farm during the 1860s represented twelve hundred bushels of grain. By the 1880s, when a farmer was still paying off his debt, $1,000 represented twenty-three hundred bushels.

The Greenback Labor Party

Protesting the retirement of the greenbacks as a policy that enriched banker-creditors at the expense of pro-ducer-debtors, farmers formed the Greenback Labor party in 1876. In an effort to convince industrial wage-workers that their interests lay in an abundant money supply, the party chose as its presidential candidate Peter Cooper, New York philanthropist and exemplary employer.

Cooper made a poor showing. But in the congressional race of 1878, the Greenbackers elected a dozen congressmen, and both Republicans and Democrats backed their inflationary policy. However, President Hayes's monetary policy was as conservative as Grant's had been, and in 1879, retirement of the greenbacks proceeded apace. In 1880, the Greenback Labor ticket, led by a Civil War general from Iowa, James B. Weaver, won 309,000 votes, denying Garfield a popular majority but, once again, failing to affect policy.

In 1884, Benjamin J. Butler led the Greenbackers one more time, but received only one-third of the votes that Weaver had won in 1880. The demand to inflate the currency was not dead. Indeed, within a decade the structure of American politics was turned upside down and inside out because of it. But the greenbacks were gone and soon forgotten. The new symbol of abundant money that farmers rallied around was silver, a precious metal that almost had been forgotten in the United States until huge stores of it were discovered during the extraordinary development of the American West.

For Further Reading

The most comprehensive study of politics during the late nineteenth century is H. Wayne Morgan, *From Hayes to McKinley: National Party Politics, 1877–1896* (1969). D. J. Rothman, *Politics and Power, The United States Senate, 1869–1901* (1966), focuses on the Senate, where the balance of power rested during this period. Two classics that are highly opinionated but much worth reading for their literary bent are Matthew Josephson, *The Politicos: 1865–1896* (1938), and William A. White, *Masks in a Pageant* (1928). On the Republicans, see R. O. Marcus, *Grand Old Party: Political Structure in the Gilded Age, 1880–1896* (1971), and on the Democrats, Horace S. Merrill, *Bourbon Democracy of the Middle West* (1953), and J. R. Hollingsworth, *The Whirligig of Politics: The Democracy of Cleveland and Bryan* (1963).

There are several excellent studies of specific administrations: Harry Barnard, *Rutherford B. Hayes and His America* (1954); R. G. Caldwell, *James A. Garfield, Party Chieftain* (1931); T. C. Reeves, *Gentleman Boss: The Life of Chester Alan Arthur* (1975); and Allan Nevins, *Grover Cleveland: A Study in Courage* (1932). At least as important as the presidents are James G. Blaine and Roscoe Conkling. See the classic by D. S. Muzzey, *James G. Blaine: A Political Idol of Other Days* (1934), and D. B. Chidsey, *The Gentleman from New York: A Life of Roscoe Conkling* (1935).

The Last Frontier

Winning the Rest of the West, 1865–1900

In long-settled parts of the world, the point where the territory of a sovereign nation comes to an end and that of another nation begins is a frontier. In Europe, for example, the crest of the Pyrenees marks the frontier between France and Spain; the Alps are the frontier between Switzerland and that country's many neighbors.

European frontiers have been moved about frequently enough as the result of wars and treaties. But redrawing a frontier in Europe means detaching from one country lands that are already occupied, usually quite densely, and attaching them to another.

In the United States, the word *frontier* came to mean something rather different. To Americans, the frontier was the vaguely demarcated zone where the nation's settled lands ended and its undeveloped region began. The frontier was thought to have no history, no law, no civilization—only land for the using. Because the course of American expansion had begun on the eastern rim of the continent, the frontier usually took the form of a line that ran from north to south and that was more or less constantly moving westward. On and beyond that line was the area that Americans called "the West."

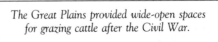

The Great Plains provided wide-open spaces for grazing cattle after the Civil War.

The Last Frontier

In the first half of the nineteenth century, the Census Bureau's definition of "settled land" was not very rigorous. If a square mile was home to 2.5 or more persons, that land was settled. Late-twentieth-century Americans would consider a square mile on which no more than 2 or 3 or 4 people lived as something on the order of howling wilderness. At the time of the Civil War, the part of the United States that was *unsettled* comprised roughly half the total area of the nation. With the exception of California, Oregon, and Washington Territory on the west coast, where 440,000 people lived; the Great Salt Lake basin, where the Mormon Zion had grown to be home to a population of 40,000; and New Mexico, which was the seat of a gracious culture and home to 94,000 mostly Spanish-speaking citizens, the American frontier was only 150 to 200 miles west of the Mississippi River. Settlement barely spilled over the far boundaries of Minnesota, Iowa, Missouri, and Arkansas. Half of the state of Texas was still not settled at the end of the Civil War.

An Uninviting Land

Rather more striking in view of what was to happen in the late nineteenth century, few Americans believed that this West would ever be settled. Pioneering meant bringing land under tillage, and, except for isolated pockets of fertile, well-watered soil, none of the three geographical regions of the West was suitable to agriculture. Quite as discouraging, those isolated pockets of good land were far away from the markets and the sources of supplies that any settlers would need in order to prosper.

In the middle of the West lay the majestic Rocky Mountains, which range from Alaska to northern Mexico. The snowy peaks of the Rockies were familiar to easterners from landscape paintings by artists who had accompanied the transcontinental wagon trains or military expeditions, or, learning of the natural glories of the American landscape, had traveled west on their own, easel and canvases rather than farm tools packed in their wagons. The very grandeur of the Rockies, however, told Americans that the mountains could not support a population living as people did in the older regions.

West of the Rockies and east of California's Sierra Nevada lay the high desert and the Great Basin—the mountainous and arid home of birds, snakes, rodents, coyotes, antelope, the grotesque Gila monster and comical armadillo, cactus, sagebrush, and tumbleweed. The soil was rocky, thin, and often alkaline. A few rivers found their way to the Pacific or the Gulf of California, while others, such as Nevada's Humboldt and California's Owens, lost heart as did so many overland emigrants and pooled up in the desert, sinking into the earth and evaporating in the sun. The Mormons had worked miracles in one of those sinks, the Great Salt Lake basin. But no part of the West seemed less inviting to Americans than this genuine desert.

East of the Rockies stretched the Great Plains, also a land of little rain and no trees. A short grass carpeted the country, and rivers like the Missouri and the Platte flowed through it, making the Great Plains less forbidding than the Great Basin. Nevertheless, there was simply not enough rainfall on the plains to support staple agriculture as Americans knew it.

The Native Peoples of the West

These regions were not bereft of human habitation. In addition to the Mormons and the people of the Mexican borderlands, Indians living according to traditional, sometimes ancient ways survived throughout the country. Even the most forbidding parts of the Great Basin supported a few thousand Ute, Paiute, and Shoshone who coped with the torrid summers by dividing into small wandering bands.

Farther south, in the seemingly more hostile environment of present-day Arizona and New Mexico, the

The terraced dwellings of a Hopi pueblo at Walpi, Arizona, 1879, photographed by John K. Hillers.

Pima, Zuñi, and Hopi had developed methods for farming the desert intensively. They lived in pueblos, communal houses or groups of houses, sometimes perched high on sheer cliffs, where a finely integrated urban culture evolved. The Navajo, more numerous than the other peoples in the desert south of the Grand Canyon (and comparative newcomers there) lived in family groups that were spread out over the country, but they too came together on special tribal occasions. They already were skilled weavers of cotton when the introduction of Spanish sheep provided them with the opportunity to raise their craft into a durable art. Both the Navajo and the Pueblo Indians feared the warriors of the Apache tribes, which lived farther south.

In what was then called Indian Territory, present-day Oklahoma, the "civilized tribes," which had been forced out of Georgia and Alabama decades earlier, had rebuilt their amalgam of native and European cultures: an intensive cash-crop agriculture, which until the Civil War was based on slave labor; a town life; a written language; a school system; and newspapers. Indian Territory came to loom large in the American imagination after the Civil War because, outside the pale of state and territorial law, it was an attractive sanctuary for some of the most famous "outlaws" and "badmen" of the era.

But the Indians who most intrigued Americans were, curiously, those who were most determined to resist the whites and their ways, the tribes of the Great Plains. Thanks to the writings of intrepid travelers such as historian Francis Parkman and painters Alfred J. Miller, Karl Bodmer, and George Catlin, the Comanche, Cheyenne, and Arapaho peoples of the central and southern plains, and the Mandan, Crow, Sioux, Nez Percé, and Blackfoot peoples of the northern half of the grasslands were a source of awe and admiration to easterners and of dread to those whites who came into their country to compete with them.

Plains Culture

Everything in the lives of the Plains Indians—economy, social structure, religion, diet, dress—revolved around two animals: the native bison and the Spanish horse. The bison not only provided food, but its hides were made into clothing, footwear, blankets, portable shelters (the conical tepees), bowstrings, and canvases on which artists recorded heroic legends, tribal histories, and genealogies. The bison's manure made a tolerable fuel for cooking and warmth in a treeless land where winters were harsh.

The Plains Indians were nomadic. Except for the Mandan, they grew no crops but trailed after the herds of bison on their horses—to southern grazing grounds in the winter, and back north to fresh grass in the summer. It was by no means an ancient way of life. Runaway horses from Mexican herds had been domesticated only about 150 years before the Plains Indians were confronted by Americans. Nevertheless, in that short time the Indians had developed their own way of riding, which was quite independent of Mexican example and awe-inspiring to American observers. "Almost as awkward as a monkey on the ground," wrote painter George Catlin in 1834, "the moment he lays his hand upon a horse, his face even becomes handsome, and he gracefully flies away like a different being."

The wandering ways of the Plains tribes brought them into frequent contact with one another and with Indians who had developed different cultures. While they traded and could communicate with remarkable subtlety through a common sign language, the tribes were just as likely to fight. Since the Indians had no concept of private ownership of land, their wars were not aimed at conquest, but at capturing horses, tools, and sometimes women, and at demonstrating bravery, the highest quality of which a Great Plains male could boast. The English word *brave*, as used to define Indian warriors, was not chosen on a whim.

With only about 225,000 Native Americans roaming the Great Plains in 1860, war was not massive in scale. But it was chronic. A permanent peace was foreign to the Indians' view of the world.

By 1860, every Plains tribe knew about the "pale-faces." They did not like the wagon trains that had traversed their homeland for two decades, and they occasionally skirmished with the white wayfarers. But the outsiders did move on and were welcome to the extent that they traded (or abandoned) horses, textiles, iron tools, and rifles, all of which improved the natives' standard of living.

The Destruction of the Bison

All this began to change as soon as Congress authorized the construction of a railroad to the Pacific. The crews

---

WHOSE LAND?

Bear Rib, chieftain of the Hunkpapa Sioux, during treaty talks at Pierre, South Dakota, in 1866: "To whom does this land belong? I believe it belongs to me. If you asked me for a piece of it I would not give it. I cannot spare it, and I like it very much. . . . I hope you will listen to me."

Sioux Indians, camouflaged by animal skins, stalk buffalo in this painting by George Catlin.

that laid the tracks of the Union Pacific and Kansas Pacific across the plains were not interested in staying. But unlike the California and Oregon emigrants, their presence led to the destruction of the bison, the basis of the native peoples' way of life.

The killing began harmlessly enough. In order to feed the big work crews cheaply, the Union Pacific Railroad hired hunters like William F. "Buffalo Bill" Cody to kill bison. The workers could hardly consume enough of the beeflike meat to affect the size of the herds, which numbered perhaps 15 million bison in 1860. When a few of the hides that were shipped back east caused a senation as fashionable "buffalo robes," however, wholesale slaughter began.

A team of marksmen, reloaders, and skinners could down and strip a thousand of the great beasts in a day. Living in huge herds, the animals were not startled by loud noises and stood grazing, pathetically easy targets, as long as they did not scent or see human beings. With dozens of such teams at work, the bison population declined quite rapidly.

The railroad companies encouraged the slaughter when it was discovered that merely by crossing over the flimsy iron tracks, a herd of bison could obliterate them. To apply the finishing touches, wealthy eastern and British sportsmen chartered special trains to take them to the plains where, sometimes without stepping to the ground, they could shoot trophies for their mansions and clubs. By the end of the century, when preservationists rushed in to save the species, only a few hundred buffalo remained alive. It was the most rapid extinction of a species in history, but no more rapid than the extinction of the culture of the people whose fate was tied to them.

The Indian Wars

The United States cavalry accompanied the railroad construction crews, ostensibly to enforce the Indians' treaty rights as well as to protect the workmen. (Many of these troops were black—former slaves who had enlisted and found army life preferable to hard-scrabble farming and menial jobs open to them at home.) Some soldiers and officers respected the tribes and their rights and tried to deal fairly with them. For example, General George Crook, who is remembered as the greatest of the army's Indian fighters, preferred being known for his respect for the tribes and his just dealings with them. Crook was, however, the exception. For the most part, the sympathies of the army were with the whites—the railroaders, miners, cattlemen, and eventually farmers who intruded on Indian lands. They believed that because the Indians used the land so ineffi-ciently, their claim to it was not equal to that of the newcomers. From 1862, when the first of the Indian wars began with a Sioux uprising in Minnesota, to 1890, when the power of the last untamed tribe was shattered at Wounded Knee, the United States cavalry joined with the buffalo hunters to destroy a way of life.

Indian war remained a war of small skirmishes and few pitched battles. Between 1869 and 1876, for example, the peak years of the fighting, the army recorded two hundred "incidents," a number that did not include many unopposed Indian raids and confrontations between civilians and the tribes. The army preferred to fight decisive battles. But the Indians generally clung to traditional hit-and-run attacks and exploited their mobility to escape fights in which, with their inferior arms and numbers, they were at a disadvantage. The result was frustration and a cruelty toward the enemy such as had not been seen in the Civil War. In 1871, Commissioner of Indian Affairs Francis Walker explained that "when dealing with savage men, as with savage beasts, no question of national honor can arise. Whether to fight, to run away, or to employ a ruse, is solely a question of expediency."

By 1876, the army's victory seemed complete. Little by little, they had hemmed in the wandering tribes and had whittled away at their ability to subsist. The typical state of a surrendering tribe was near-starvation, with a goodly proportion of the young men dead. But Indian resistance was not quite at an end.

In June of the centennial year, an audacious colonel of the Seventh Cavalry, George Armstrong Custer, led 265 men into a battle with the Sioux on Montana's Little Bighorn River. In a rare total victory for the Indians, every one of Custer's men was killed. Although a completely unexpected defeat, "Custer's Last Stand" thrilled Americans. Denied in life the advancement that he believed he deserved, "Yellow Hair," as the Sioux called him, became a romantic hero in death. A brewery commissioned an imaginative painting of the incident by Cassilly Adams and within a few years distributed 150,000 reproductions of it. Only in the next century would it be recognized that the Little Bighorn was most significant as the final victory of a doomed people.

An advertisement for buffalo robes, which were fashionable in the 1870s.

Good Intentions, Tragic Results

In 1881, a Colorado writer, Helen Hunt Jackson, published *A Century of Dishonor*, which became a best-selling book. In meticulous detail and with little distortion of fact, she detailed the cynical immorality with which the United States government had dealt with the Indians since independence. The broken treaties

A drawing of the battle of Little Bighorn by Red Horse, 1881.

were almost too numerous to be listed. Time and again, according to Jackson, "Christian" whites had cheated "savage" Indians of their land, had herded them onto reservations on lands judged to be the least useful, and even had chipped away at those.

By 1876, the government had ceased to make treaties with the Indians. Those Indians who did not resist American control were defined as wards of the federal government; they were not citizens but were under Washington's protection. After the publication of *A Century of Dishonor*, many easterners demanded that the government use wardship in a just manner.

In 1887, reformers were strong enough in Congress to pass the Dawes Severalty Act. Their intentions were of the best. Assuming that the traditional Indian life was no longer feasible, the supporters of the Dawes Act agreed that the Indian peoples must be Americanized; that is, they must become self-sustaining citizens through adoption of the ways of the larger society. Under the Dawes Act, the tribes were dissolved and the tribal lands were divided into 160-acre homesteads to be distributed to each household.

The easterners who pushed for the Dawes Severalty

Act overlooked several facts. First, few of the western Indians were farmers; traditionally they had been hunters, gatherers, and traders. Second, the reservation lands were rarely suited to agriculture; they had been allotted to the Indians precisely because they were unattractive to white farmers. Finally, no western tribe thought in terms of private ownership of land as vested

A CENTURY OF DISHONOR

"It makes little difference . . . where one opens the record of the history of the Indians; every page and every year has its dark stain. The story of one tribe is the story of all, varied only by differences of time and place; but neither time nor place makes any difference in the main facts. Colorado is as greedy and unjust in 1880 as was Georgia in 1830, and Ohio in 1795; and the United States Government breaks promises now as deftly as then, and with added ingenuity from long practice."

Helen Hunt Jackson,
A Century of Dishonor (1881)

Helen Hunt Jackson, author of Ramona *and* A Century of Dishonor.

in a family. The tribe, which the Dawes Act aimed to abolish, was the basic social unit.

Defeated, demoralized, and frequently debauched by idleness and alcohol, the Indians were now susceptible to being defrauded of what land was left to them. Because they owned it as individuals, they could sell it. When whites found Indian lands to be of value, for example, because there was oil deep beneath them, they generally had little difficulty in talking the owners into accepting cash.

Wounded Knee

Among these demoralized people appeared a religious reformer in the tradition of Tecumseh's brother, The Prophet. Wovoka, a Paiute who had lived with a white Christian family and had been fascinated by the religious doctrine of redemption, began to wander through the West and preach a religion that appealed to thousands of Indians. His message was that by performing a ritual dance, the Indians, who were God's chosen people, could prevail on the Great Spirit to make the white man disappear. This "Ghost Dance" would also bring back to life the buffalo herds and the many Indians who had been killed in the wars—and

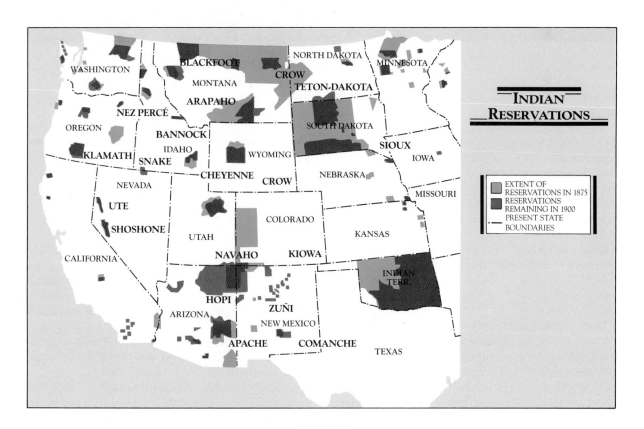

The Sioux camp near Pine Ridge, South Dakota, in 1891.

the old way of life, which, in the 1880s, many Indians remembered quite vividly.

Such beliefs, simultaneously edifying and pathetic, are common among peoples who have seen their world turned upside down. In parts of the Southwest that were untouched by Wovoka's religion, defeated Indians turned to peyote, a natural hallucinogenic drug, as a way to escape an intolerable reality. To understand the appeal of the Ghost Dance religion, it is necessary to recall just how rapidly the culture of the Plains Indians was destroyed. For example, the Dakota Sioux did not go to war with the whites until the end of the 1860s. Within another decade, the survivors had been herded on the Pine Ridge Reservation in South Dakota.

There, on Wounded Knee Creek, the Dakotas took avidly to the Ghost Dance religion. When the soldiers guarding them heard that there were guns in the camp, they grew nervous. In December 1890, after a shoving incident, they opened fire with rifles and artillery. About two hundred people, half of them women and

children, were killed. For the Indians there was no escape, even in religion.

The Cattle Kingdom

As the Indians lost the West, the Americans won it. Indeed, the final decades of the nineteenth century stand as the greatest era of economic expansion in American history.

In 1870, American forests yielded about 12.8 billion board feet of lumber. By 1900, this output had almost tripled to about 36 billion. Although this increase reflects in part the development of forest industries in the southern states, the region of greatest expansion was a new one, the Pacific Northwest.

In 1870, Americans were raising 23.8 million cattle. In 1900, 67.7 million head were fattening on grasslands, mostly in the West, and in feedlots.

Annual gold production continued only slightly below the fabulous levels of the gold-rush era, and by the end of the century, it was nearly double the totals of 1850. Annual silver production, only 2.4 million troy ounces in 1870, stood at 57.7 million in 1900.

Beginnings

Acre for acre, cattlemen won more of the West than did any other group of pioneers. They were motivated to bring the vastness of the Great Plains into the American economy by the appetite of the burgeoning cities for cheap meat, and they were encouraged in their venture by the disinterest in the rolling arid grasslands of anyone save the Indians. Their story thrills Americans (and other people) to this day, partly because it was romanticized, partly because the cattle kingdom was established so quickly and just as quickly destroyed.

The cowboy first rode into American legend just before the Civil War. In the late 1850s, several groups of enterprising Texans rounded up herds of the half-wild longhorns that ranged freely between the Nueces River and the Rio Grande and drove them north over a trail that had been blazed by Shawnee Indians to Sedalia, Missouri, a railroad town with connections to Chicago. Although the bosses were English-speaking, the actual workers were Mexican. They called themselves *vaqueros*.

Vaquero, which translates roughly as "cowboy," entered the English language as *buckaroo*. Indeed, while Anglo-Americans soon comprised the majority of this mobile work force, and former black slaves were a significant minority, much of what became part of American folklore and parlance about the buckaroos was of Mexican derivation. The cowboy's colorful costume was an adaptation of functional Mexican work dress. The bandana was a washcloth that, when tied over the cowboy's mouth, served as a dust screen, no small matter when a thousand cattle kicked up alkali grit. The broad-brimmed hat was not selected for its picturesque qualities but because it was a sun and rain shield. Made of first-quality beaver felt, the sombrero also served as a drinking pot and washbasin.

The pointed, high-heeled boots, awkward and even painful to walk in, were designed for riding in the saddle, where a *vaquero* spent his workday. The "western" saddle itself was of Spanish design, quite unlike the English tack that was used by Americans in the East. Chaps, leather leg coverings, got their name from chaparral, the low-growing brush of the plains against which they were designed to protect the cowboy.

Meat for Millions

The Civil War and Missouri laws against importing Texas cattle (because of hoof-and-mouth disease) stifled the first long-distance commerce in beef before it really got started. However, in 1866, when the transcontinental railroad reached Abilene, Kansas, a wheeler-dealer from Illinois, Joseph G. McCoy, saw

The typical crew of cattle-herding cowboys included black and Chicano cowboys.

the possibilities of underselling steers raised in the East with the half-wild longhorns of Texas. McCoy built a series of holding pens on the outskirts of the tiny Kansas town, arranged to ship his then-nonexistent cattle with the Kansas Pacific Railroad, and dispatched agents to southern Texas to induce Texans to round up longhorns and drive them north to Abilene on an old trading route called the Chisholm Trail.

In 1867, McCoy shipped thirty-five thousand "tall, bony, coarse-headed, flat-sided, thin-flanked" cattle to Chicago. In 1868, seventy-five thousand of the beasts, nearly worthless in Texas, passed through Abilene with Chicago packers crying for more. In 1871, six hundred thousand bawling "critters" left the pens of several Kansas railroad towns to end up on American dinner tables.

The profits were immense. A steer that cost $5 when raised on open public lands could be driven to Kansas at the cost of one cent a mile and sold for $25 or, occasionally, as much as $50. Investors from as far as England went west to establish ranches that were as comfortable as big-city gentlemen's clubs. The typical cattleman at the famous Cheyenne Club never touched a gun and rarely sat on a horse. Instead, he sank into plush easy chairs and discussed account books, very often in an English accent, with his fellow businessmen.

The railhead continued to move westward, and with it the destination of the cowboys, who were soon coming from the North as well as the South. After a few years, the citizens of towns like Abilene concluded that the money to be made as a cattle-trading center was not worth the damage done to their own ranches and farms by hundreds of thousands of cattle. The wild atmosphere given their towns by the rambunctious cowboys,

ready for a blowout after months on the trail, was even less conducive to respectable civic life. As a cow town grew, its "better element" demanded churches and schools in place of saloons and casinos, and the stage was set for the "taming" of a town, which is the theme of so many popular tales.

Never, though, did the cowboys lack a place to take their herds. There were always newer, smaller towns to the west to welcome them. In Kansas alone, Ellsworth, Newton, Wichita, Dodge City, and Hays had their "wide-open" period.

The Twin Disasters

The cattle kingdom lasted only a generation, ending suddenly as a result of greed with the assistance of two natural disasters.

The profits to be made in cattle were so great that cattlemen ignored the natural limits of the range in supporting huge herds. Vast as the plains were, they were overstocked by the mid-1880s. Clear-running springs were trampled into unpotable mud holes. Weeds never before noticed replaced the grasses that had invited overgrazing. Hills and buttes were scarred by cattle trails. Some species of migratory birds that once passed through twice a year simply disappeared; the beefsteaks on hoof had beaten them to their food.

On January 1, 1886, a great blizzard buried the eastern and southern plains. Within three days, three feet of snow with drifts of twenty and thirty feet suffocated the range. About three hundred cowboys could not reach shelter and were killed; the casualties among the Indians never were counted; between 50 and 85 percent of the livestock froze to death or died of hunger. When spring arrived, half the American plains reeked of death.

The summer of 1886 brought ruin to many cattlemen who had survived the snows. Grasses that had weathered summer droughts for millennia were unable to do so in their overgrazed condition; they withered and died, starving cattle already weakened by winter. Then, the next winter, the states that had escaped the worst of the blizzard of 1886 got sixteen inches of snow in sixteen hours and weeks more of intermittent fall.

The cattle industry eventually recovered, but only when more methodical businessmen took over the holdings of the speculators of the glory days. Cattle barons like Richard King of southern Texas foreswore risking all on the open range. Through clever manipulation of federal land laws, he built a ranch that was as large as the state of Rhode Island. If not quite so grandiose in their success, others imitated King's example in Texas, Wyoming, Montana, and eastern Colorado.

Even more important in ending the days of the long

THE GREAT LOCOMOTIVE CRASH

A bizarre illustration of just how fast the West was "developed" took place in Waco, Texas, on September 15, 1896. William Crush, general passenger agent of the Missouri, Kansas, and Texas Railroad (which was called the "Katy"), had two obsolete locomotives at his disposal. He decided to put on a show, which, among other things, sold a lot of tickets. One engine was painted red and the other, green, and they were parked facing each other at either end of a four-mile stretch of track. They were fired up and the throttles tied back. By the time they collided, they were each traveling at ninety miles per hour. Over fifty thousand people witnessed the spectacle. Several were killed and hundreds were injured by the flying steel.

drive and the cowboy as a romantic knight-errant was the expansion of the railroad network. When new east–west lines snaked into Texas and the states on the Canadian border, and the Union Pacific and Kansas Pacific sent feeder lines north and south into cow country, the cowboy became a ranch hand, a not so free-wheeling employee of large commercial operations.

The Cowboy's Life

Even in the days of the long drive, the world of the cowboy bore scant resemblance to the legends about him that survive today. Despite the white complexion of the cowboys in popular literature and in Westerns of the twentieth century, a large proportion of cowboys were Mexican or black. In some cases, these workers and the whites acted and mixed as equals. Just as often, however, they split along racial lines when they reached the end of the trail.

The appellation "boy" is more nearly accurate. Photographs that the buckaroos had taken in cow towns like Abilene and Dodge City as well as arrest records (usually for nothing more serious than drunk and disorderly conduct), show a very young group of men, few apparently much older than twenty. The life was too hard for anyone but youths—days in the saddle, nights sleeping on bare ground in all weather. Moreover, the cowboy who married could not afford to be absent from his own ranch or farm for as long as the cattle drives required.

The real buckaroos were not constantly engaged in shooting scrapes such as make the legends so exciting. Their skills were in horsemanship and with a rope, not with the Colt revolver that they carried to signal co-workers far away. Indeed, toting guns was forbidden in all the trail-head towns. With a drunken binge on every cowboy's itinerary, the sheriff or marshal in charge of keeping the peace did not tolerate shooting irons on every hip. Those who did not leave their revolvers in camp outside town checked them at the police station.

The Wild West in American Culture

The legend of the cowboy as a romantic, dashing, and quick-drawing knight of the wide-open spaces was not a creation of a later era. On the contrary, all the familiar themes of the Wild West were well formed when the cold, hard reality was still alive on the plains. Rather more notable, the myths of the Wild West were embraced not only by easterners in their idle reveries, but by the cowboys themselves.

The most important creator of the legendary Wild West was a shadowy character named E. Z. C. Judson. A former Know-Nothing who was dishonorably discharged from the Union Army, Judson took the pen name Ned Buntline, and between 1865 and 1886, churned out more than four hundred romantic, blood, guts, and chivalric novels about western heros; some of them he invented, and others were (highly fictionalized) real people. Called pulps after the cheap paper on which they were printed or dime novels after their price, the books by Judson and his many competitors were devoured chiefly but not exclusively by boys. Indeed, the mythical world appealed to those who knew much better. During the 1880s, while living as a rancher in North Dakota, future president Theodore Roosevelt helped capture two young cowboys who had robbed a grocery store. In their saddlebags, Roosevelt found several Ned Buntline novels that no doubt featured outlaws who were unjustly accused.

Legendary Characters

Americans discovered that the bank and train robbers Jesse and Frank James, and several cohorts from the Clanton family, were really modern-day Robin Hoods who gave the money they took to the poor. When Jesse was murdered, his mother made a tourist attraction of his grave, charging admission and explaining that her son had been a Bible-reading Christian.

Belle Starr (Myra Belle Shirley) was immortalized as "the bandit queen," as pure in heart as Jesse James was socially conscious. Billy the Kid (William Bonney), a Brooklyn-born homicidal maniac, was romanticized as a tragic hero who had been forced into a life of crime. James Butler "Wild Bill" Hickok, a gambler who killed perhaps six people before he was shot down in Deadwood Gulch, South Dakota, in 1876, was attributed with dozens of killings, all in the cause of making the West safe for women and children. Calamity Jane (Martha Cannary), later said to have been Wild Bill's paramour, wrote her own romantic autobiography in order to support a serious drinking problem.

Indeed, Calamity Jane and other "living legends" of the West personally contributed to the mythmaking by appearing in Wild West shows that traveled to eastern and European cities, where they dramatized great gun battles. The most famous of these shows was the creation of "Buffalo Bill" Cody, who had begun his career as a buffalo hunter for the Union Pacific. Among his featured players was Sitting Bull, the Hunkpapa Sioux chief who had overseen the defeat of George Custer. Reality and myth were impossibly confused. After a successful career in show business, Sitting Bull returned to the Rosebud Reservation where, during the Ghost Dance excitement, he was accidentally killed by two

Sitting Bull, a squaw, and three of his children pose with two white visitors to the Standing Rock reservation in 1882.

Gold and Silver Rushes

After the richest of the California gold fields played out, prospectors in search of "glory holes" fanned out over the mountains and deserts of the West. For more than a generation, they discovered new deposits almost annually and very rich ones every few years. In 1859, there were two great strikes. A find in the Pike's Peak area of Colorado led to a rush that was reminiscent of that of 1849. At about the same time, gold miners in northern Nevada discovered that a "blue mud" that had been fouling their operations was one of the richest silver ores ever discovered. This was the beginning of Virginia City and the Comstock Lode, which, before it pinched out in the twentieth century, yielded more than $400 million in silver and gold.

In 1862, Tombstone, Arizona, was founded on the site of a gold mine; in 1864, Helena, Montana, rose atop another. In 1876, rich placer deposits were discovered in the Black Hills of South Dakota (then forbidden to whites by Indian treaty). The next year, silver was found at Leadville, Colorado, almost two miles above sea level in the Rockies.

During the 1880s, the Coeur D'Alene in the Idaho panhandle drew thousands of miners, as did the copper deposits across the mountains in Butte. In 1891, the Cripple Creek district in Colorado began to outproduce every other mining town. As late as 1901, there was an old-fashioned rush when a desultory old prospector in a slouch hat, Jim Butler, drove his pick into a desolate mountain in southern Nevada and found it "practically made of silver." From the town of Tonopah, founded on its site, prospectors discovered rich deposits in Goldfield, a few miles away.

Indian policemen who were arresting him on suspicion of fomenting rebellion.

Some creators of the legendary West were conscientious realists; Frederic Remington, whose paintings and bronze statuettes of cowboys and Indians are studiously representative, is a fine example. Others, while romantics, were talented artists; Owen Wister, an aristocratic easterner, created the prototype of the western knight without armor in *The Virginian*, published in 1902. But for the most part, the Wild West was the invention of highly commercial merchandisers of popular entertainment.

The Mining Frontier

The folklore of the precious-metal mining frontier is second only to the legend of the cowboy in the American imagination. Deadwood Gulch, for example, where Wild Bill Hickok was gunned down and Calamity Jane spent much of her life, was no cow town but a gold-mining center.

Of Mining Camps and Cities

Readers of the dime novels of the time and film viewers since have avidly absorbed the images of boisterous, wide-open mining towns, complete with saloons rocking with the music of pianos and the shouts of bearded men. The live-for-today miner, the gambler, the prostitute with a heart of gold are permanent inhabitants of American folklore. Nor is the picture altogether imaginary. The speculative mining economy fostered a risk-all attitude toward life.

However, efficient exploitation of underground (hard rock) mining required a great deal of capital and technical expertise, both to finance the operation and to build the railroads that hauled ore out. Consequently, the mining camps that were home to five thousand and even ten thousand people within a year

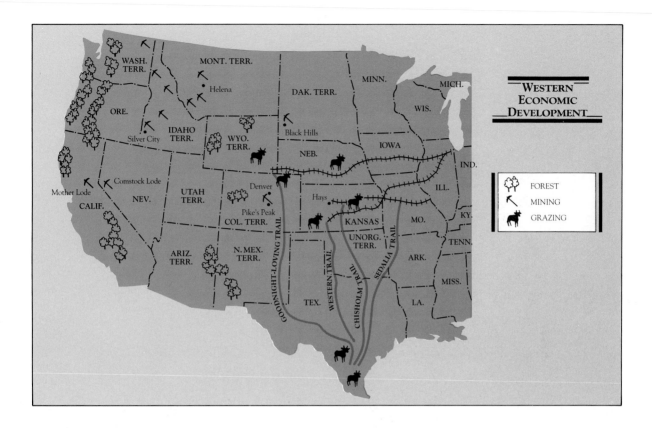

WESTERN
ECONOMIC
DEVELOPMENT

FOREST
MINING
GRAZING

of their founding were also cities with a variety of services and a social structure that were not unlike those in older industrial towns.

In 1877, only six years after gold was discovered on its site, Leadville, Colorado, boasted several miles of paved streets, gas lighting, a modern water system, thirteen schools, five churches, and three hospitals—hardly the tiny, false-front set that is used to represent mining towns in Hollywood films.

Towns like Virginia City in Nevada, Deadwood Gulch in South Dakota, and Tombstone in Arizona are best remembered as places where legendary characters like Wild Bill Hickok and Wyatt Earp fired their revolvers; but they were also the sites of huge stamping mills (to crush the ores) that towered over the landscape, and of busy exchanges where mining stocks were traded by agents of San Francisco, New York, and London bankers.

In Goldfield, the last of the wide-open mining towns, one of the most important men in the camp was the urbane Wall Street financier Bernard Baruch. The Anaconda Copper Company of Butte, Montana, was one of the nation's ranking corporate giants. The Guggenheim mining syndicate was supreme in the Colorado gold fields. Rockefeller's Standard Oil was a major owner of mines in the Coeur D'Alene. If it was wild, the mining West was no mere colorful diversion for readers of the dime novels, but an integral part of the national economy. In the case of the silver that was mined in increasing quantities during the final three decades of the century, the West also played a divisive part.

SOLID GOLD

Observing the centennial year (1976) of America's richest and longest-lived gold mine, the Homestake of Lead, South Dakota, historian T. H. Watkins calculated that if all the gold that the Homestake had produced "could somehow be gathered together, melted, and poured into a solid cube, that cube would measure only a little over twelve feet to a side. Yet that hypothetical cube, hardly large enough to fill an average bedroom, would weigh more than 1,093 tons, or 35 million ounces." At the time that Watkins wrote, this bauble was worth $4,725 million. According to the average price of gold in 1983, the price tag was $14 billion.

A shipment of silver ore is loaded into wagons at the Tonopah Mining Company in Nevada in 1901.

Background of the Silver Issue

Before 1849, paper money in the United States had value according to the amount of gold and silver that the issuing banks kept in their vaults. The two precious metals were not equal in value. Because the quantity of silver in the country was about sixteen times that of gold, the value of silver was pegged to that of gold at the ratio of sixteen to one; by law, one ounce of gold that was sold to the government brought the same price as sixteen ounces of silver. Because the government was the chief market for silver, the value of the metals were pegged to each other on the open market.

This system worked well enough until 1849; thereafter, despite the Comstock Lode, the rate of American gold production increased far more rapidly than the supply of silver. Indeed, by 1873, the miners on the Comstock appeared to have reached the bottom of their treasure trove; flooding and other problems prevented them from bringing out silver ore in any quan-

tity. The value of silver on the open market therefore rose. By 1873, sixteen ounces of silver could be sold privately for more than one ounce of gold. Silver dollars ceased to circulate because they brought more than one hundred cents if melted down and sold to jewelers, speculators, or foreign buyers. Recognizing this, Congress demonetized silver; the silver dollar was dropped from the coinage list. With the Civil War greenbacks in the process of retirement, gold was now the sole basis of American paper currency.

The Free-Silver Debate Begins

The timing was tragic. No sooner was the Demonetization Act of 1873 on the books than Nevada miners made rich new discoveries on the Comstock, and Leadville, Colorado, was founded on a mountain of the white metal. Silver flooded the market, and, with the government buying none, the price plunged. Greenbackers, fighting for inflation of the currency through the issuance of paper money, suddenly began to think conspiratorially when they realized that they would have had their cheaper, more abundant money if the new silver was being coined into dollars. In Congress, inflation-minded representatives of the Democratic, Republican, and Greenback Labor parties spoke of the "Crime of '73," as though the Demonetization Act had been deliberately designed by the nation's bankers to keep money scarce.

There was no "crime." Although silver production began its upswing in 1870, it was a gradual one and the price of the metal had not decreased. In 1873, no one could have predicted that the nation's silver production would increase from twenty-two thousand ounces in 1872 to sixty-four thousand in 1892, and the open-market price of the metal slide from $1.32 an ounce to eighty-seven cents (and to sixty-seven cents in 1896). Nevertheless, there was no denying that banking interests were delighted with the consequences of the act. They were staunchly opposed to the kind of inflation that would have resulted had the price of the newly abundant silver been pegged to that of gold.

Therefore, in 1878, when Richard "Silver Dick" Bland introduced a bill in the House of Representatives to remonetize silver—to peg the price by law at the old ratio of sixteen to one with gold—financial conservatives in the Senate forced a compromise. Under the Bland-Allison Act, the Secretary of the Treasury was required to purchase from $2 million to $4 million in silver each month, but at the market price. Although the government's silver would be minted into dollars, silver was not monetized. In effect, the silver dollars were tokens; they had value only in the same way that dollar bills had value, because they were backed by gold stored in the vaults of the banks and federal Treasury.

Inflationists, mostly from western farming states, were not happy. Nor were the owners of the silver mines and the men who worked them. Because the Treasury Department was controlled throughout the 1880s by financial conservatives, whether Republican or Democratic, the secretaries invariably bought the minimum amount of silver required by law, while production steadily increased.

The stage was set for a political eruption. It came to a head as the farmers of the West, suffering from an ever-deepening depression, increasingly attributed their problems to the manipulation of the currency by bankers. In 1889 and 1890, when six new agricultural or mining states were admitted to the Union, the eruption came.

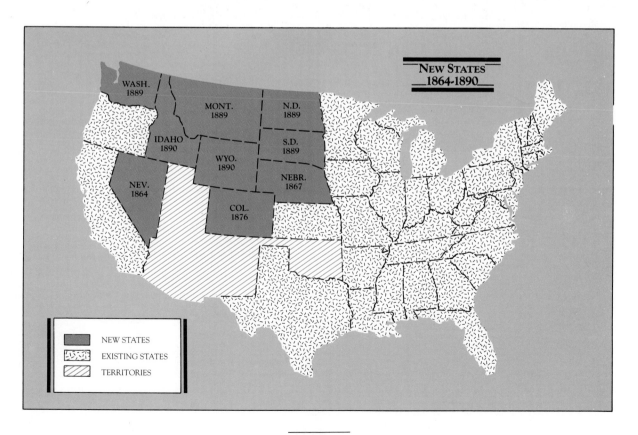

PUNCHING COWS

A cowboy chuck wagon, photographed by Erwin Smith.

It took three or four months to drive a herd of cattle from the environs of San Antonio, Texas, to a railhead town in Kansas. To be asked to join a trail crew was a coveted honor among the young men of the country. The wages were low, only $1 a day plus board and as good a bed as the sod of the Great Plains provided. But because a lot of money and many lives rested on every member of a crew, only those men who had impressed a trail boss with their skills and reliability would be invited along.

A trail crew consisted of the trail boss, usually the owner of the cattle; his *segundo*, or assistant; a cook; a wrangler, who was in charge of the *remuda*, or large herd of horses that accompanied the expedition; and a hand for each 250 to 300 cattle. Most herds were made up of between 2,500 and 3,000 cattle, so 10 to 12 cowpunchers, or buckaroos, was typical. (The "cows" were really steers, males that had been castrated at their first roundup; the "punchers" got their name because one of their jobs was to punch the cows into corrals and loading chutes—using poles.)

A herd moved about ten to fifteen miles a day, the animals grazing as they got the chance. The usual procedure for getting a herd along was for two men to ride "lead," or "point," one on either side of the milling beasts; two to ride "swing" and "flank," in pairs at regular intervals alongside the herd; and two or three to ride "drag," behind the herd to hurry up stragglers.

Each position had its peculiarities and was assigned in rotation or with an eye to a particular cowpuncher's abilities or his personal standing at the moment in the trail boss's graces. Riding point was the most dangerous in the event of a stampede, but it was also the most pleasant in terms of dust and odor (unless there was a powerful tailwind). Conversely, riding drag was the safest but also the least desirable job, not only because of the quality of the air that 3,000 animals left behind, but also because there was not a moment in which some independent-minded "dogies" were not determined to set off on their own.

The day's drive started at first light and ended as late toward dusk as the trail boss could find satisfactory grass and water, but the cowboy's work was not done. After a big dinner at the chuckwagon, the hands had to ride night. In two-hour shifts, pairs of riders circled the herd in opposite directions, looking out for predators and soothing the nervous steers. Some folklorists (and some old cowpunchers) say that the western singing and guitar-playing tradition developed as a means of keeping a herd calm; music soothed the generally docile as well as the savage beast. Indeed, night riding was as dangerous as it was detested. Almost all stampedes started at night, tripped by a bolt of lightning, a steer dodging a coyote, or, to human reckoning, no reason whatsoever. Except for river crossings—there were four major and numerous minor watercourses between Texas and Kansas—the stampede was the most frequent cause of death written on the wooden markers that dotted the Shawnee, Chisholm, and Goodnight-Loving trails. (Indians were not a serious threat to the cow puncher's life, only his cattle.)

There would be no strumming guitar in the pouring rain that came often enough. Then the night riders donned their yellow oilskin slickers that covered their whole saddle, and gently cursed, or slept. It was said that a cowpuncher who had a good night horse could sleep in the saddle, since his mount even knew to wake him at the end of the two-hour shift.

Cowboys on the long drive might bring along a horse or two of their own, but the boss supplied the tough, wiry work ponies. They were geldings, about seven to ten for each hand. (Stallions fought, and mares were considered too temperamental for the job.) Each had a unique identity and job. There were morning horses and afternoon horses. The night horse had singular qualities already noted. The cowboy used the strong rope horse to help pull a stray out of a bog or for some other problem involving a lasso. Perhaps the most important horse was the water horse, a good swimmer on which a cowboy could count to get him across as much as a mile of strong current with wild-eyed steers thrashing about on every side. But the most talented was the cutting horse, which knew exactly how a steer would act without the rider's instructions. Some of them had the agility of sheepdogs.

The cowboy's attachment to his horse, an easy target of parody as Hollywood films presented it, was nevertheless genuine. The cowpuncher was a horseman; he shunned any work that he had to do on his two feet. Everyone had stories of crews that quit rather than slop hogs or milk dairy cows.

If passionate in general, however, the cowboy's attachment to horses in the particular was fickle. He did not own the mounts on which he worked, and at the end of the trail they were sold off along with the cattle. Only a few hands returned home to Texas overland. After they had spent most of their money on liquor, women, and cards, cowboys climbed aboard an eastbound train, rode it to the Mississippi River, and struck south by river boat.

For Further Reading

Because the "winning of the West" is so central to American folklore, the writing about the experience is voluminous, sometimes not too reliable, but often congenial reading. The starting point of any reading program is indisputable: Frederick Jackson Turner, *The Frontier in American History* (1920), and by Turner's great student, Ray A. Billington, *Frederick Jackson Turner* (1973) and *Westward Expansion: A History of the American Frontier* (1967). Another student of Turner also wrote a comprehensive study: Frederick Merk, *History of the Westward Movement* (1978).

On Indians, there are three choices for an introduction: J. R. Swanson, *The Indian Tribes of North America* (1953); William T. Hagan, *American Indians* (1961); and Wilcomb E. Washburn, *The Indian in America* (1975). A comprehensive, up-to-date study of the cattleman's frontier is badly needed, but the standards remain quite good: E. S. Osgood, *The Day of the Cattleman* (1929), and E. E. Dale, *The Range Cattle Industry* (1930). For cowboys, see J. B. Frantz and J. E. Choate, *The American Cowboy: The Myth and the Reality* (1955). On mining, see Thomas H. Watkins, *Gold and Silver in the West* (1960) and Rodman W. Paul, *Mining Frontiers of the Far West, 1848–1880* (1963). Also see William S. Greever, *The Bonanza West: The Story of the Western Mining Rushes, 1848–1900* (1963).

The Revolt of the Farmers
The Struggle to Save Agrarian America

Ever since the first farmer poked a hole in the ground and inserted a seed, tillers of the soil have understood that they were engaged in a game of chance with nature. Farming involved gambling a year's living on such uncertainties as winter's final frost, summer's yield of sunshine and rain, and an autumn storm's driving winds and hailstones. Farmers accepted the fact that they were at the mercy of insects and birds whose behavior seemed capricious. They knew that illness at the wrong time, particularly when the harvest was begun, resulted in twelve months of privation.

But farmers also knew that they produced the necessities of life. Come what may, people must eat, and they must have fibers from which to make clothing. The farmer would always be society's most valuable citizen. Indeed, Thomas Jefferson and four generations of politicians had told American farmers that those who toiled on the earth were the "bone and sinew" of the republic.

In the final decades of the nineteenth century, the farmers of the West and South discovered that these century-old truisms were not necessarily so. The power of nature paled in comparison with the power of people whom the farmers considered to be far from valuable to society. Railroad barons, industrial millionaires, landlords, bankers (most of all), lawyers, newspaper editors, and politicians—all were parasites

A little girl scatters grain to chickens on a turn-of-the-century family farm.

who sucked a rich living from hard-working producers, contributing nothing in return but exploitation and arrogance.

The farmers learned that they were no longer the bone and sinew of the body politic, but just one interest group among many. And, in an urban and industrial America, they were not a particularly important one. Indeed, the new America was apt to view cultivators as somewhat ludicrous people, hayseeds and yokels to be mocked on the vaudeville stage and in joke books.

The Paradox of American Agriculture: Its Finest Hour Is Its Worst

Farmers rarely led the way on America's last frontier. They generally followed miners, loggers, cattlemen, and soldiers when these people were numerous enough in an area to provide a local market for foodstuffs. Large-scale commercial agriculture was not feasible until the railroad arrived to carry crops in quantity to hungry eastern and foreign cities.

Once settled, farmers often clashed with other westerners. The Grangers battled the railroads. In California, valley farmers demanded that the state legislature take action against hydraulic miners who, in washing down whole mountainsides to win their gold, polluted the rivers with mud so that the water was unfit for irrigation.

On the Great Plains, homesteaders, who were called "nesters" by open-range cattlemen, fenced in their holdings with barbed wire, which prevented some cattle from reaching streams and water holes. The cattlemen fought back by damming up streams before they reached the nesters' lands and by cutting fence wire. In

THE FARMER FEEDS THEM ALL

When the Lawyer hangs around and the Butcher cuts a pound,
Oh the farmer is the man who feeds them all.
And the preacher and the cook go a-strolling by the brook
And the farmer is the man who feeds them all.

Oh the farmer is the man, the farmer is the man,
Lives on credit 'till the fall.
Then they take him by the hand and they lead him from the land
And the middle man's the one that gets them all.
                                    Song of the 1890s

Johnson County, Wyoming, a shooting war erupted. However, as in the conflict between farmers and miners in California, most of these disputes were resolved in the legislatures and courts, and as long as the conflicts were local, the farmers usually had their way. On the national level, against other forces, the story had a different plot.

A Success Story

Never in the history of the world has there been anything to rival the expansion of agriculture in the final three decades of the nineteenth century. As of 1870, when the takeoff occurred, Americans had brought 408 million acres of land under cultivation, an average of 1.6 million acres of new farmland a year. Between 1870 and 1900, a single generation of farmers put 431 million acres of virgin soil to the plow, an average of 14.4 million acres each year.

Crop production increased just as sharply. By 1900, American farmers were producing up to 150 percent more of the staples—cotton, corn, wheat—than they had in 1870. Hogs, which may be considered a byproduct of corn, numbered 25 million in 1870 and 63 million in 1900.

The ravenous appetites of American and foreign city dwellers encouraged this amazing growth, and the expansion of the railroads made it possible for crops raised by a Great Plains farmer to feed the inhabitants of Chicago and New York, even London and Warsaw. Even at that, however, the pioneer farmers of the West had to overcome formidable difficulties to accomplish what they did.

New Methods for a New Country

Farming the land west of 98° longitude, with its paucity of rain, called for innovations in traditional farming methods. The absence of trees, except for scrub cottonwood and poplar on riverbanks, made the cost of fencing prohibitive. But because millions of cattle roamed the open range, protection of crops was more urgent than it was back east. The solution came in 1872 when Joseph Glidden of Illinois perfected a machine that mass-produced cheap barbed wire, the makings for an extremely efficient steel "hedge" that could be erected on the flimsiest of scavenged fenceposts.

Traditional wood-frame houses could be built only after a family had harvested a few crops and squirreled away enough money to buy lumber. In the meantime, pioneers lived in sod houses, which were constructed by piling uniformly cut blocks of the tough plains sod as though they were bricks. Sod houses were snug

*Wearing masks so they won't be recognized, settlers cut fifteen miles
of Brighton Ranch fence in 1885.*

enough in the winter, but dripped mud in the spring thaw and became hellholes of choking dust during the long arid summers.

The lack of water was the chief obstacle to farming on the Great Plains. In part, the pioneers overcame it with improved windmills that pumped water for irrigation from far below the surface. In part, however, "dry farming" depended on a grand self-serving delusion. The summers of the 1870s and 1880s, when much of the Great Plains was settled, were untypically wet. When normal conditions returned, a few experts warned in advance, the deep wells would run dry and crops would wither. The pioneers airily waved away these warnings. They believed that they had changed the rainfall patterns; when they broke the sod, moisture was liberated from the earth and would return indefinitely in the form of heavier rains.

Improvements in farm machinery furthered agricultural expansion. Equipped with chilled steel plows that sliced through the sod, disc harrows that cultivated wide swaths with each pass, and machines that planted seeds, shucked corn, threshed wheat, bound shocks, and shredded fodder to make food for livestock, farmers were able to cut down on waste, raise more animals, and tend to more acreage than earlier generations had dreamed possible.

The value of farm machinery in use in the United States increased from $271 million in 1870 to $750 million in 1900. The meaning of this statistic for an individual can be appreciated if it is translated into the number of hours that a hand had to devote in a season to produce wheat on an acre of land. By plowing and seeding by hand, harvesting with a sickle, and threshing the wheat by flailing it, a farmer had to spend between fifty and sixty hours to harvest about twenty bushels of wheat per acre. With a gang plow and a horse-drawn seeder, harrow, reaper, and thresher—all of which were in widespread use by 1890—a farmer produced a much larger crop after only eight to ten hours of work per acre. Potentially, a single man could

PLOWING AND HARVESTING BY STEAM
A SUCCESS.

I am now manufacturing the Celebrated **REMINGTON TRACTION ENGINE OR STEAM PLOW**, adapted to all kinds of heavy work usually done by mules or horses. A number of these Engines are now in use, giving entire satisfaction, for plowing and pulling Combined Harvesters. I have also patented and put into the field a successful **STEAM HARVESTER**, which the above cut represents, and can be seen on the ranch of Mr. J. H. Kester, St. Johns, Colusa county, harvesting 65 to 100 acres per day. Note what the owners say in testimonial:

St. Johns, Cala., August 1, 1889.

DANIEL BEST—*Dear Sir:* You ask us to report how we like the Traction Engine and Steam Harvester purchased of you this season. We can only say that we are delighted with the purchase, and it is giving entire satisfaction. In other words, the whole outfit is a success. We never had better work done with any machine than we are doing with the Steam Harvester. We are using our 25-foot Header, traveling three miles per hour, cutting and threshing 65 to 100 acres per day. You can put us down for another rig for next season. Very truly yours,
KESTER & PETERS.

If you are interested in Steam Plowing and Steam Harvesting, go and investigate for yourself and be convinced. The following parties are using my Traction Engines and Harvesters, who will take pleasure in showing them up: J. S. Butler, W. Fennell, Tehama, Tehama county; Henry Best, Yuba City, Sutter county; and Kester & Peters, St. Johns, Colusa county. These last parties are running a complete steam outfit, consisting of Traction Engine and Steam Harvester. For further description, prices, etc., address

Daniel Best Agricultural Works
SAN LEANDRO, CAL.

An 1889 advertisement for heavy farm machinery.

cultivate six times as much land in 1890 as his father had farmed before the Civil War. With wife, sons, and daughters in the fields, the potential was even greater.

Hard Times

Amidst these marvels and feats, many farmers suffered. Those who lived in the Northeast or in the Ohio and upper Mississippi watersheds stopped growing staples and began producing perishable crops such as dairy goods, poultry and eggs, and garden vegetables to supply nearby urban markets. For the most part they prospered. But the western raisers of wheat, corn, and livestock, and the southern growers of cotton, watched their incomes sag beginning about 1872, and collapse by the 1890s. A crop that in 1872 had brought a farmer $1,000 in real income (actual purchasing power) was worth only $500 in 1896. A man who was forty-eight years of age in 1896, still an active working farmer, had to produce precisely twice as many hogs or twice the tonnage of corn or wheat as he had produced as a young man of twenty-four just to enjoy the same standard of living that he had known in 1872.

With their machinery, many farmers were doing just that. But it was not comforting to know that a quarter century of backbreaking toil and openness to new methods yielded nothing but more struggle. By the 1890s, the price of corn was so low (eight cents a bushel) that farmers had to forgo buying coal and burn their grain for winter warmth.

Between 1889 and 1893, some eleven thousand Kansas farm families lost their homes, foreclosed by the

STOVEPIPING

In the autumn of 1893 there was so much rain in the wheatbelt of eastern Washington State that much of the year's crop was ruined. Some farmers tried to stave off disaster by means of a technique called "stovepiping." A length of stovepipe was inserted into an upright sack and filled with the rotten grain. Then the rest of the sack—top and sides—was filled with good wheat, and the stovepipe was removed. When the purchasing agent opened the sack, the grain looked good. But not for long. Buyers learned to use their own hollow tube to dig for samples deep within each sack.

banks for failure to make their mortgage payments. In some of the western counties of Kansas and Nebraska during the same period, nine out of every ten farm-steads changed hands; thousands lay vacant until after 1900, houses and barns decaying amidst thistles and dust. The number of farm tenant families—those who did not own the land they worked—doubled from 1 to 2 million between 1880 and 1900, most of the increase coming after 1890.

The South: Added Travails

Fortunately for cotton growers, southern winters were mild and firewood was abundant, for the price of cotton fell to six cents a pound during the 1890s (below five cents in 1893), and the staple of the South did not burn as well as corn. In every particular, southern farmers were worse off than farmers anywhere save in the wretched western counties of Kansas and Nebraska. Whereas landowners outnumbered tenants three to one in the North and West, owners and tenants were equal in the South, although among blacks, tenants and sharecroppers outnumbered landowners by almost five to one. Nothing better illustrates the benighted condition of southern farmers than the fact that pellagra, a fatal niacin-deficiency disease unknown even in slavery times, was endemic in the rural South by the turn of the century.

Just as in the West, these difficulties accompanied a success story. Southern agriculture made a remarkable recovery after the Civil War. The land survived, and the work force remained; few of the South's 4 million black people went north or west. Cotton production reached the 1860 level in 1870 and exceeded the pre-war record (1859) within a few more years. This was accomplished with a system of cultivation that was born of expediency and survived only by exploitation of the people on the bottom of southern society.

Tenants and Sharecroppers

The challenge facing southern agriculture after the Civil War lay in three interrelated facts: the blacks were free and would no longer work for nothing; the Radical Republicans missed an opportunity to make them independent farmers when, instead of dividing the old plantations into homesteads for former slaves, they left the land in the possession of its prewar owners; the landowners had no cash with which to pay wages to black (and white) farm laborers. Indeed, even if a gang-labor system based on wages had been financially possible, the blacks would have resisted it as being too much like the way they had lived under slavery.

The solution was the share-tenant or the share-

In southern agriculture, a system of sharecropping replaced slavery. Here, sharecroppers pick cotton in the 1890s.

cropper system. The owners of the old plantations partitioned their land into family-farm-size plots on which a cabin, usually quite rude, was constructed. In return for the use of the house and the land, share tenants, who provided their own daily bread, mule, plow, and seed, turned over to the landlord one-quarter to one-third of each year's crop. No money changed hands. Both tenant and landlord marketed their shares of the crop.

Sharecroppers, who were likely to be black, were tenants who were too poor to supply their own mule, plow, and seed. The landlord provided everything in return for one-half of the crop. In practice, the land-lord or sometimes an independent merchant took the rest, too. In order to live day by day, the sharecropper bought on credit from a general merchandiser, using as collateral a lien on the fall's harvest. All too often, with the price of cotton and corn declining steadily during the late nineteenth century, the sharecropper family found that it had no share left to sell when the books were balanced at the store. All the family had was an open line of credit, a lien on a crop that was not yet in the ground.

There was, of course, an element of security in this debt bondage; the cropper who owed money to the landlord was not likely to be evicted. But there had been an element of security in slavery too.

The Great Protest

Who or what was to blame for the agricultural depression? Most economists answered that the blame lay in the complex, invisible operation of the international marketplace. The weather in western China affected the price that a South Dakota wheat grower sold at in Rapid City; the decision of a British colonial administrator in Bombay influenced the quotations on the Mobile cotton exchange.

The beginning of the long slide in agricultural prices dated from the bankruptcy in 1873 of the prestigious Jay Cooke & Company, respected Philadelphia bank. When Cooke went broke, manufacturers who depended on his bank for credit shut their doors. Tens of thousands of workers lost their jobs. Unemployed, they cut their food expenditures, thus reducing demand and forcing down prices. During the depression of the 1870s the average wholesale price of agricultural products dropped almost 30 percent, more than enough to ruin a farmer who had mortgage payments to meet. A similar disaster far from the fields, the failure of the Reading Railroad, launched the worse depression of the 1890s.

The farmers knew that they were part of a complex international economy. They were prepared to accept the negative possibilities inherent in this finely integrated commerce as another condition of farming life. But, it seemed, only they bore the brunt of misfortunes in the end. When a New York banker stumbled in his office, it was the Iowa pig raiser or the Mississippi sharecropper who broke a leg.

Too Many Farmers? Too Much Crop?

The farmers suffered most, economists explained, because there were too many of them producing too much grain, livestock, and fiber. American agriculture had expanded too quickly, far beyond the capacity of society to consume the cornucopia. Supply was greater than demand; therefore, prices dropped.

Some leaders of the protesting farmers agreed.

Farm leader "Sockless" Jerry Simpson engaging in an outdoor debate in Kansas in 1892.

"Sockless" Jerry Simpson of Kansas (in reality a keenly intelligent and sophisticated man) urged the federal government to create new markets abroad. Others, including Mary Elizabeth Lease, Simpson's fellow Kansan and one of America's first woman lawyers, saw it differently. How could overproduction be blamed, Mother Lease asked, while American cities teemed with hungry people. "The makers of food are underclad," Lease said, "and the makers of clothes are underfed." The problem lay not with production but with distribution and exchange of foodstuffs for industrial goods.

Debt

Angry agitators such as Mother Lease almost always came back to bankers as "the sinister forces at work in the night" to cheat farmers and industrial workers. Both groups were defrauded by the artificially small amount of currency in circulation. To the worker, scarce currency meant low wages. The farmers suffered additionally because so many of them were debtors. They had taken out loans to develop new land or to buy machinery when money was abundant—thanks to the greenbacks and to freely coined silver—and now had to pay back their creditors in ever scarcer, even more valuable gold.

For example, if a Great Plains farmer borrowed money to buy machinery in 1882, calculating that he could devote 20 percent of his income (at 1882 prices)

Mary Elizabeth Lease, one of America's first women lawyers and a leader of protesting farmers.

to paying off the obligation, the deflation of the currency and the decline of wholesale prices in only four years forced him to carve out 30 percent of his income for the bank in 1886. If the farmer still owed on the loan in 1896, he had to devote almost 40 percent of his income to making mortgage payments.

Hayseeds

A more subtle blow to the farmers was the decline in their political power and status. Not only did the proportion of agriculturalists in the population go down annually, but the legislators whom they sent to Washington and the state capitals often seemed to forget about their constituents once they made the acquaintance of lobbyists for the railroading, industrial, and banking interests.

A newly confident urban culture depicted the man of the soil in popular fiction, songs, and melodramas as a thick-skulled yokel, a ridiculous figure in a tattered strawhat with a hayseed clenched between his teeth.

Serious writers such as Hamlin Garland understood the hardships of the agricultural life but also rejected them. In his popular book of 1891, *Main Travelled Roads,* Garland depicted farm life as dreary and stultifying. State insane asylum statistics bore out this dismal picture. In states that were both industrial and

---

POPULIST ANTI-SEMITISM?

The hatred of farmers for bankers sometimes took the form of anti-Semitism, hatred of Jewish bankers. One book that blamed Jews particularly for the ruination of the American farmer was Ignatius P. Donnelly's novel *Caesar's Column.* One character's explanation of why Jewish bankers were exploiting farmers is curious: past anti-Semitism with a Darwinian twist:

Christianity fell upon the Jews, originally a race of agriculturists and shepherds, and forced them, for many centuries, through the most terrible ordeal of persecution the history of mankind bears record of. Only the strong of body, the cunning of brain, the long-headed, the persistent, the men with capacity to live where the dog would starve, survived the awful trial. Like breeds like; and now the Christian world is paying, in tears and blood, for the sufferings inflicted by their bigoted and ignorant ancestors upon a noble race. When the time came for liberty and fair play the Jew was master in the contest with the Gentile. . . . They were as merciless to the Christians as the Christians had been to them.

---

agricultural, such as Ohio and Indiana, farm people were proportionately more numerous than city people in the institutions, and farm women (who lived a more isolated life than their husbands) outnumbered the men.

Tens of thousands of farmers' sons and daughters followed Garland in his flight to the city. In part, they despaired of ever making a living on the land. In part, they were lured by the social and cultural attractions of the city. "Who wants to smell new-mown hay," playwright Clyde Fitch wrote in 1909, "if he can breathe gasoline on Fifth Avenue instead?" With each son and daughter who opted for urban fumes, farmers who clung to the Jeffersonian image of themselves became further dejected and agitated.

The Farmers Organize

One of the greatest obstacles that farmers faced in attempting to defend their interests was their tardiness in organizing to fight their battles collectively. At the center of the agrarian mystique in the United States was the vision of Jefferson's independent yeoman. The American farmer stood on his own two feet, beholden to no one. In owning his own land, he was the lord of his fief. Only the compilation of evidence all around them—from corporation to labor, from temperance movement to woman-suffrage movement—that they lived in an organizing age, changed the farmers' ways.

The Co-Op Movement

The first type of organization to which the farmers turned was the cooperative. In consumer cooperatives, farmers banded together to purchase essential machinery in lots and therefore more cheaply.

Money pools, associations much like contemporary credit unions, sprouted all over the Midwest. Through these associations, which were capitalized by members and operated on a nonprofit basis, farmers hoped to eliminate their dependence on the hated banks. While many survived to serve the credit needs of their members for generations, money pools suffered from the opposition of the banks and the inexperience of amateur administrators. Distrusting professionalism almost as much as exploitation, farmers too often put friends rather than experts in charge of the money pools, and the rate of mismanagement and embezzlement was sadly high. Failed farmers who were suddenly entrusted with large sums of money frequently could not resist the temptation to steal and abscond.

Producer cooperatives were designed to counter the great power of the railroads. After the Supreme Court's decision in the case of *Wabash, St. Louis, & Pacific Railway Co.* v. *Illinois* (1886) effectively permitted railroads to set their own rates for storing and carrying grain, corn-belt farmers built their own grain elevators. Members of producer co-ops believed that with their own storage facilities, they could not only circumvent the high costs of holding their crops until the railroads were ready to move them, but also withhold their products from the market until they liked the selling price.

State and Regional Organization

To the extent that individual co-ops succeeded, they were of inestimable aid to their members. But their effect was limited. Because the farmers believed that control of the currency by bankers and control of the government generally by bankers, railroaders, industrialists, and other oligarchs was the ultimate cause of their problems, they moved by the late 1880s toward political organization.

At first, farmer organizations such as the Agricultural Wheel, the Texas State Alliance, and the Colored Farmers' National Alliance and Cooperative Union contented themselves, as had the Grangers before them, with endorsing politicians of any party who agreed to support their programs. But once many of these congressmen and state assemblymen began to be seduced by lobbyists for opposing interests, the state and regional organizations moved decisively toward the idea of independent political action.

By 1889, the various alliances and wheels had merged into three large associations—one representing mostly western farmers; another of southern white farmers, tenants, and sharecroppers; and the third of southern black farmers. In December 1890, delegates representing them gathered in Ocala, Florida, to draw up a list of grievances.

The Populists

Although the Ocala Conference was constructive, it took more than a year for the farmers to make the break with the Republican party (to which the blacks and most midwesterners belonged) and the Democratic party (traditionally the party of white southerners). At Omaha, Nebraska, in February 1892, they organized the People's party, or, as it was commonly known from the Latin word for "people" (*populus*), the Populist party. Once the new movement was proclaimed, a virtually religious enthusiasm swept over the delegates. Far from just a pressure group or a political organization, the Populists believed that they were engaged in a sacred cause. Not only would they capture the American government, but they would remake the republic of democratic virtue that the Founding Fathers had envisioned.

To symbolize that farmers from both North and South had overcome the sectional chasm that had separated them, the Populists nominated former Union general James B. Weaver for president and former Confederate general James G. Field for vice president.

A Far-Reaching Program

At Omaha, the Populists drafted a comprehensive platform that would have significantly altered American history had it been enacted. Overproduction was addressed only obliquely in a call for the prohibition of land ownership by aliens. Aliens were the only people who, constitutionally, could be denied the right to farm, and the anti-immigrant policy was expected to win support for the new party from the trade-union movement.

As a means of crippling the influence of the special interests with their insidious lobbies, the Populists demanded a series of political reforms. Senators, who were elected by state legislatures, should be chosen in popular elections. The Populists also endorsed the adoption of the secret "Australian" ballot. (In many states at that time, particularly in the South, a voter's choice was a matter of public record; the Populists believed that this practice led to intimidation by employers and landlords.)

The new party also introduced the concepts of the initiative, recall, and referendum. The initiative allows voters, through petition, to put measures on the ballot independent of action by legislatures and thus free of manipulation by powerful lobbies. The recall allows voters, also through petition, to force a public official to stand for election before his or her term is up. The Populists hoped that the recall would discourage politicians from backing down on campaign pledges. The referendum allows voters to vote directly on laws rather than indirectly through their representatives; it is the means by which initiative measures and recall petitions can be decided.

The most controversial Populist demands were for the abolition of national banks and for government ownership of railroads and the telegraph. The Populists were not socialists. Since so many of them were landowners, they could hardly advocate state ownership of all productive property. But they did believe that "natural monopolies," enterprises that could be run efficiently only under a single management, should not be in private hands. Decisions that affected the interests of all should be made democratically, not by combina-

THE *POLLOCK* CASE

In the Wilson-Gorman Tariff of 1894, provision was made for an income tax of 2 percent on all incomes of $4,000 or more, a pretty modest tax by today's standards. It was widely condemned by men of means, and in the case of *Pollock* v. *Farmers' Loan and Trust Co.* (1895), the Supreme Court ruled that because the tax was a direct tax that did not fall on all equally, it was unconstitutional. Only after the Sixteenth Amendment was adopted in 1913 was it constitutional to tax the wealthy at a higher rate than the poor.

tions of individuals who were interested only in their own enrichment. The "socialistic" parts of the Populist program were actually designed to protect the property of the common man and his opportunities to improve himself.

The party also called for a postal savings system, so that ordinary people might avoid depositing their money in the hated banks, and for a graduated income tax. In 1892, the federal income tax was 2 percent for all, and the Populists wanted the wealthy to pay a higher percentage of their income than the modest farmer or wageworker paid. Finally, the Populists addressed the currency problem. They demanded an increase in the money in circulation of $50 per capita. This inflation was to be accomplished through the free and unlimited coinage of silver valued at the old ratio with gold of sixteen to one.

The Movement Grows

The Populists did not expect to win their first election, and they did not. In 1892, Grover Cleveland swept back into office over the Republican incumbent, Benjamin Harrison. However, the Populist candidate, James B. Weaver, won a creditable 1 million votes (twenty-two electoral votes), and the Populists sent a dozen senators and representatives to Washington, including the majority of the Kansas delegation.

That was enough to set the enthusiastic movement working toward 1896. Flamboyant orators like Simpson, Lease, Weaver, Ignatius P. Donnelly of Minnesota, and William A. Peffer of Kansas crisscrossed the western states stirring up a zeal of religious intensity. The national leaders of the two major parties worried aloud at what sometimes looked like revolution. On the scene, conservative but by no means reactionary middle-class people like the journalist William Allen White of Emporia, Kansas, wondered

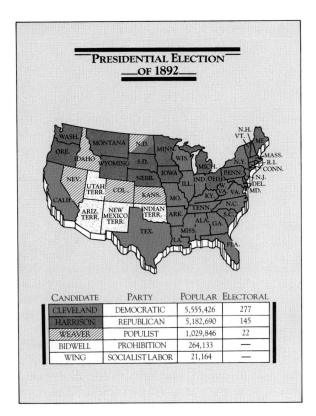

CANDIDATE	PARTY	POPULAR	ELECTORAL
CLEVELAND	DEMOCRATIC	5,555,426	277
HARRISON	REPUBLICAN	5,182,690	145
WEAVER	POPULIST	1,029,846	22
BIDWELL	PROHIBITION	264,133	—
WING	SOCIALIST LABOR	21,164	—

ings. You are made to hate each other because upon that hatred is rested the keystone of the arch of financial despotism which enslaves you both."

He had his successes. In 1890, Watson was elected to Congress in opposition to the Democratic party machine in Georgia and was defeated two years later only because the bosses of the state redrew the lines of his district and probably miscounted the votes. On another occasion, Watson rallied two thousand white Georgians to protect the home of a black Populist whose life had been threatened. Such scenes had never been played in the South, and would not be again for fifty years.

In the end, however, Watson failed, and in his failure, he helped to usher in the most tragic period of race relations in the South. He failed in part because most southern blacks who retained the right to vote into the 1890s refused to desert the Republican party. Within the Democratic party, at the same time, emerged a canny kind of politician who appealed to poor white farmers on the same class issues that Watson raised; but

what was the matter with the farm belt. Was a revolution brewing? White won the approval of conservatives throughout the nation when he wrote disdainfully (and fearfully) of the angry and, in his opinion, destructive rebellion of the hayseeds.

The Populists hoped to win a following in the cities. Urban reformers like Henry Demarest Lloyd joined the new party and tried to persuade union leaders and wageworkers to support it. Eugene V. Debs, the head of the American Railway Union, drifted toward Populism. Prominent Democrats such as Governor John Peter Altgeld of Illinois showed interest in the movement; in the end, Altgeld remained a Democrat.

Populism in the South

Populism most fundamentally threatened the established order in the South, where, particularly in Georgia, Populist leaders tried to form an alliance of poor farmers across racial lines. The leading advocate of the principle that social class was more important than race was Thomas E. Watson, the diminutive red-headed son of an impoverished Georgia planter who had trained himself in the law and had a knack for inflammatory journalism and oratory. "You are kept apart," Watson told audiences of black and white farmers, "that you may be separately fleeced of your earn-

Thomas E. Watson, a Populist candidate for vice president who ran with William Jennings Bryan in 1896.

instead of calling for an alliance with blacks, they attacked the minority race more viciously than ever had been done during Reconstruction.

Democrats like Benjamin "Pitchfork Ben" Tillman of South Carolina baited the corporations and promised to preserve white domination of the South by excluding blacks completely from political life and by forcing them to observe a strict and humiliating color line in every aspect of daily life.

The combination was sure-fire politics, and a tradition of racist demagoguery that was to curse southern politics for half a century was born. One of those to capitalize on it was Tom Watson. Embittered by his failed experiment in interracial cooperation, he became after the turn of the century one of Georgia's fiercest race baiters, actually encouraging lynchings in his *Weekly Jeffersonian*. Having been cheated of a seat in Congress when he championed the civil rights of blacks, Watson was elected to the United States Senate in 1920.

Free Silver

On the national level, the Populist party had a different fate. It foundered on neither class nor racial issues, but on the silver-coinage question.

When the party was founded in 1892, there was no sign that it would become obsessed with the silver issue. Since the enactment of the Sherman Silver Purchase Act of 1890, the silver question seemed to be settled. The Sherman Act, which had been pushed through Congress by an alliance of senators and congressmen from both farm and mining states, required the Secretary of the Treasury to buy what amounted to the entire output of the nation's mines.

However, the act did not peg the purchase price of silver to the value of gold; nor did it require the Treasury to treat silver as a basis of the currency. Because both the Harrison administration and the second Cleveland administration, which took office in March 1893, were determined to keep the United States on the gold standard, they refused to pay the government's obligations in silver. Cleveland was particularly inflexible. He called the free coinage of silver a "dangerous and reckless experiment," and in 1893, events seemed to prove him right. Government gold reserves slipped below the $100 million mark that economists regarded as safe, and by the end of the year, fell to $80 million. Although the causes of the crisis were complex, including a British financial crisis and a decrease in tax receipts because the high McKinley Tariff discouraged imports, Cleveland blamed the problem entirely on the Sherman Silver Purchase Act. In November 1893, he persuaded Congress to repeal it. The United States was

back on the gold standard in law as well as in fact.

Populists and the growing free-silver wing of the Democratic party were enraged, especially when they learned that Cleveland had to call on the banker J. P. Morgan to stop the run on government gold, In 1894, William H. Harvey of Chicago published *Coin's Financial School*, a book that argued in easily understood terms that the free coinage of silver was the key to restoring prosperity. Also in 1894, the silver-mine operators of the Mountain states launched a well-financed campaign demanding government purchase of silver. They had no interest in the far-reaching Populist reforms. Indeed, as wealthy capitalists they were hostile to most of them.

They therefore threw their influence and money behind prosilver Democrats like "Silver Dick" Bland, still going strong, and Congressman William Jennings Bryan of Nebraska. While these men sometimes sounded like Populists with their evangelical style of oratory, they were only mildly interested in most of the Populist demands and were actively opposed to others, such as the nationalization of the railroads and the telegraph.

Henry Demarest Lloyd called free silver "the cowbird of the reform movement." Like the cowbird, which lays her eggs in another bird's nest whence the hatchlings eat the food and eventually starve to death the birds

William Jennings Bryan carries a cross of gold in this cartoon by Grant Hamilton, who viewed Bryan as a despoiler of the Bible.

THE NEW SOUTH: THE PROPHET AND THE BUILDER

In speech after speech throughout the South, he told the story of a funeral that he had attended in rural Georgia. "They buried him in a New York coat and a Boston pair of shoes, and a pair of breeches from Chicago and a shirt from Cincinnati." The coffin, continued Henry W. Grady (1850–89), the charming, wisecracking editor of the *Atlanta Constitution*, was made from northern lumber and hammered together with northern-forged nails. "The South didn't furnish a thing on earth for that funeral but the corpse and the hole in the ground."

Grady's point, to which he devoted most of his short life, was that the South must abandon its reliance on agriculture and promote industrialization. The North's industry explained why the Confederacy had been defeated. Only by accepting the realities of the modern world would the South prosper and escape its status as the nation's backwater.

Although Grady lived to see few of his ideas come to fruition, during the very period that southern agrarians like Thomas E. Watson were vilifying urban, industrial America, southerners scored the kind of successes that Grady had called for. Beginning with a federal grant of almost 6 million acres of forest land in 1877, southern syndicates laid the basis of a thriving lumber and turpentine industry in the vast pine woods of the section. Birmingham became the "Pittsburgh of the South," the center of a booming steel industry, following the discovery of coal and iron in northern Alabama in the early 1870s. By 1890, Birmingham was making more pig iron than was Pittsburgh. ("Pigs" are iron ingots, intermediate products ready for further processing.)

The southern oil industry was largely a twentieth-century development; the great Texas gusher, Spindletop, came through in 1901. Likewise the southern textile industry. Most of the New England textile mills migrated to the South after 1900, although, even before Grady died in 1889, the trend of "bringing the factory to the fields" was to some degree under way.

The southerner who was most successful in bringing the factory to the fields was not a maker of cloth but a maker of cigarettes and bad habits. James Buchanan "Buck" Duke (1856–1925) started out as a tobacco grower, a good southern agrarian on the face of it. In 1881, he was shown a new machine that rolled cigarettes by the hundreds per minute, and his head began to spin in contemplation of its possibilities. All cigarettes were then rolled by the smoker. Like a chess player, Duke had to see several moves ahead. To make money from manufacturing cigarettes, it was necessary not only to mass-produce them cheaply, but also to change Americans' tobacco habits.

In the late nineteenth century, polite women did not smoke (at least in public), upper- and middle-class men

Newspaper editor Henry W. Grady.

smoked cigars or pipes, and workingmen and the lower classes in the South chewed tobacco. Cigarettes were around. The soldiers in the Civil War had taken to them because they could carry papers and a pouch of tobacco but not cigars. After the war, however, the white cylinders were considered to be effete, a boy's smoke behind the barn. Duke would have to change that image, and he did.

Buying the patent to the cigarette-rolling machine, he encouraged adolescents to cultivate the habit by selling a pack of twenty for only a nickel and by including inside each pack a "trading card" that featured pictures and brief biographies of military heroes and popular athletes, mostly boxers and baseball players. No one better understood the wisdom in putting together a long-term market than "Buck" Duke. All the while he created his consumers, he improved machinery and bought out competitors. By 1889, his company accounted for half the cigarettes sold in the United States, and Duke had only begun.

In 1890, he set up a trust along the lines laid out by John D. Rockefeller. Through it he gained control of his major competitors, R. J. Reynolds and P. J. Lorillard, and built an almost perfect monopoly. Indeed, through loose arrangements with British cigarette manufacturers, Duke had a major say in the tobacco-processing industry on two continents. Only federal antitrust action in 1911 forced him to disband his gigantic corporation. By that year, he controlled 150 factories, and, even at that, his reputation as the South's greatest home-grown business mogul was being challenged by the directors of the recently founded Coca-Cola Company of Atlanta.

Like the Yankee moguls whose methods he adopted, "Buck" Duke was a generous philanthropist. His most enduring monument is Duke University, which had been a small, local college before it received an endowment from Duke and changed its name; it is now an architecturally magnificent Gothic-style campus in Duke's hometown of Durham, North Carolina. Until the militant antismoking campaigns of the 1970s, Duke was one of the few universities in the United States where students and faculty could light up the "coffin nails" that had built the institution wherever and whenever they chose. That practice has been abandoned, but his statue, which stands in front of the university's cathedral-size chapel, portrays James Buchanan Duke gently tapping the ash from his cigar.

James Buchanan "Buck" Duke, the father of the modern cigarette industry and the philanthropist after whom Duke University is named.

that belong in the nest, free silver, by attracting all the attention after 1893, destroyed popular interest in the rest of the Populists' many-faceted program. The election of 1896 proved Lloyd right.

For Further Reading

For the problems from which American farmers suffered, see Fred A. Shannon, *The Farmer's Last Frontier: Agriculture, 1860–1897* (1945), and G. C. Fite, *The Farmer's Frontier, 1865–1900* (1966). Everett Dick, *The Sod-House Frontier, 1854–1890* (1937), deals with the settling of the plains, and for a "feel" of that unique experience, students might read three classic novels: Willa Cather, *O Pioneers!* (1913); O. E. Rölvaag, *Giants in the Earth* (1927), which was originally written in Norwegian: and Mari Sandoz, *Old Jules* (1935).

The Patrons of Husbandry are the subject of Solon J. Buck, *The Granger Movement* (1913), which has been updated only as part of a book, albeit an excellent one: Theodore Saloutos, *Farmer Movements in the South, 1865–1933* (1960). The Populists, the climax of the protest, have been belabored and dissected time and time again. A lively controversy has arisen on the meaning of the movement. Start with the old standby, John D. Hicks, *The Populist Revolt* (1931), and continue with W. T. K. Nugent, *The Tolerant Populists: Kansas Populism and Nativism* (1963), and R. F. Durden, *The Climax of Populism* (1965). On individual agrarian leaders, the most admired book is C. Vann Woodward, *Tom Watson: Agrarian Rebel* (1938). Martin Ridge, *Ignatius Donnelly* (1962), and F. B. Simkins, *Pitchfork Ben Tillman: South Carolinian* (1949), are also quite good.

36

Bryan, McKinley, and Empire
The United States Becomes a World Power, 1896–1903

Few presidential elections have been held amidst such anxiety as swaddled the election of 1896. If there had been nothing else, the election was novel because, for the first time in a generation, neither of the major party candidates looked to the Civil War as the central event of their lives. The Republican, William McKinley of Ohio, had served in Union blue, but only as a teenage private and young adult. His opponent, William Jennings Bryan of Nebraska, had been born in 1860. When the war ended, he was only five years of age.

But there was something else. Almost everyone who was involved in the contest recognized that 1896 was a watershed year. When the election was over, the old era would be dead and a new one under way. No one knew what the new era would be like. That depended on which candidate won the election. Thus the anxiety.

Taking It Easy During a Lull, *a photo of American troops in the Philippines taken around 1899 by Perley Freemont Rockett.*

The Election of 1896

The Republican convention was placid. The party's agrarians had long since defected to the Populists, so it was a meeting of like-minded men, for the most part conservatives who were at peace with the new industrial order. Viewing the unrest among farmers as a potential revolution that had stopped, they allowed themselves to be put through well-planned paces by a forceful coal and iron magnate from Ohio, Marcus Alonzo Hanna.

Mark Hanna and His Bill

Hanna was not himself a candidate. Nearly sixty years of age in 1896, he had only recently launched his political career. But Hanna had a candidate for the convention. For six years he had been quietly cornering Republican businessmen and politicians, assuring them that his close friend, former congressman and governor was presidential timber.

McKinley might never have persuaded the party of it himself. He was well known as a scholarly expert on

Industrialist Marcus Alonzo Hanna was an influential member of the Republican party.

the tariff, but that qualified him to be Secretary of the Treasury or Secretary of State at best. The trouble with congenial Bill McKinley was that he was too scholarly; he was not the sort of man whose presence impressed itself on a gathering of political professionals. The epitome of midwestern middle-class respectability—he refused to smoke cigars in public lest young men emulate his bad habit—McKinley was easy to overlook. Because Mark Hanna was the fellow who walked into an office, cigar blazing, and rested a hefty haunch on the desk of the person he wanted to see, Republicans and Democrats alike assumed that McKinley was his puppet.

Actually, while McKinley agonized over big decisions, he was quite capable of making them on his own. Nevertheless, when he agreed with Hanna that 1896 was the target year, he probably had no idea that the election would be as momentous as it was. When it turned out that 1896 was a crucial year, it was a lucky accident of fate that the Republicans had the solemn McKinley and the energetic Hanna to lead them.

Boy Bryan

The election was so gravely important because, in the opinion of conservatives, the Democratic party had been captured by dangerous, wild-eyed Populists. The opposite was true: the Democrats had co-opted and absorbed the Populists, declawing them by adopting one plank of the Populist platform, scuttling the rest,

THE CROSS OF GOLD

The following lines are the first and last from William Jennings Bryan's electrifying speech at the 1896 Democratic convention:

I would be presumptuous, indeed, to present myself against the distinguished gentlemen to whom you have listened if this were a mere measuring of abilities; but this is not a contest between persons. The humblest citizen in all the land, when clad in the armor of a righteous cause, is stronger than all the hosts of error. I come to speak to you in defense of a cause as holy as the cause of liberty—the cause of humanity. . . .

If they dare to come out in the open field and defend the gold standard as a good thing, we will fight them to the uttermost. Having behind us the producing masses of this nation and the world, supported by the commercial interests, the laboring interests, and the toilers everywhere, we will answer their demand for a gold standard by saying to them: you shall not press down upon the brow of labor this crown of thorns, you shall not crucify mankind upon a cross of gold.

William Jennings Bryan was famous for his impassioned oratory.

and winning the Populist endorsement of their candidate. Win or lose with the Democrats, the Populists were finished as an independent political force. Nevertheless, because of the Populist-like zeal and even the irresponsible youth of the Democratic nominee—Boy Bryan, as conservatives called him—conservatives felt every right to be alarmed.

William Jennings Bryan went to the Chicago convention already famous in Nebraska and neighboring states as a fiery advocate of the free coinage of silver. As an orator, he was electrically precise in his phrasing and timing. His "Cross of Gold" speech, which enlisted God in the cause of free silver and identified the gold standard with the crucifiers of Christ, was a masterpiece that synthesized everything that country people loved in an oration. Bryan had no difficulty in scheduling it to wind up the party's debate on the currency question.

It was a foregone conclusion that the Democrats would endorse free silver. Bryan's speech did not influence their decision. But he so aroused the delegates with his rhetoric and showmanship that, although a minor candidate, he easily won the party's nomination.

It was the speech that frightened the Republicans. While it was entirely on the subject of silver—Bryan had no sympathy for the "radical" and "socialistic" planks in the Populist platform—there was a troubling hint of fanaticism in the tone. Indeed, Bryan was a religious fundamentalist who tended to see disagreements in terms of good versus evil and political causes as crusades. Republicans who simply shrugged when a Democrat like Grover Cleveland was in the White House shuddered at the thought of Bryan residing there.

The Populists Join the Democrats

The nomination had quite another effect on the Populists. Highly evangelical in manner themselves, the majority of the midwestern Populists, for whom the Republican party was the political opposition, immediately called for the nomination of Bryan on the Populist ticket as well as the Democratic. Although Bryan had accepted only one plank of their platform, the Populists reasoned that he would almost certainly win if he had their support. But if Democrats and Populists split the free-silver vote, McKinley and the goldbugs were in for four more years.

Urban Populists like Henry Demarest Lloyd, who looked on free silver as an unimportant issue compared with the Populists' comprehensive reform program, argued that the party must think in long-range terms. Preserve the integrity of the platform by nominating a Populist who would run on the whole thing, accept the inevitable defeat in 1896, and plan for the future.

Some southern Populists, led by Tom Watson, also opposed fusion with the Democrats. In the South, it was the Democratic party, not the Republican, that was the enemy of the Populist. To ask southern Populists to support a Democrat was to ask them to commit political suicide. But the fusionists won the day. Bryan got the Populist nomination, and the stage was set for the momentous campaign of 1896.

The Campaign

Crusading was Bryan's forte. Handsome, boundlessly energetic, and at home among farm people—whether exhorting them or gobbling up potato salad and chow-chow after a speech—Bryan revolutionized the ways of presidential campaigning. Previously (with the possible exception of Stephen A. Douglas in 1860) presidential nominees had been quiet, as though it were an insult to the dignity of the office to court votes like a candidate for town councilman in an Appalachian hollow.

Not Bryan. His speaking tour took him more than thirteen thousand miles by train. He delivered six hundred speeches in twenty-nine states in only fourteen weeks (over six speeches a day). The roaring enthusiasm of the crowds that greeted him, at least in the West and South, convinced him that he was right and threw eastern bankers and industrialists into a panic.

This was exactly what Mark Hanna wanted to see. He pressured wealthy Republicans (and some Democrats) to make large contributions to McKinley's campaign. By the time of the election, Hanna had spent more on posters, buttons, rallies, picnics, advertisements, and a corps of speakers who dogged Bryan's steps than had been spent by both parties in all elections since the Civil War. Hanna was so successful that, before election day, he began to return surplus contributions.

Knowing that McKinley could not hope to rival the colorful Bryan on the stump, Hanna kept his candidate at his modest home in Canton, Ohio. Republican speakers pointedly compared McKinley's sense of self-respect with Bryan's hustling. A steady stream of Republican delegations traveled to Canton, where they marched through the town behind a brass band and gathered on McKinley's front lawn. McKinley delivered

Candidate William McKinley at home in Canton, Ohio.

a short speech from the porch, answered a few prearranged questions, and invited all his friends to join him for lemonade or beer, depending on the delegation's attitude toward alcohol (which had been discreetly ascertained by Hanna's agents when the visitors arrived at the railroad depot).

The Great Election

Although professional politicians thought that Bryan was well ahead in September, McKinley won handily—271 electoral votes to Bryan's 176. Bryan received more votes than any previous *winning* candidate, 6.5 million, but McKinley won more than 7 million. His vote was over 50 percent of the total; it was the first election in a quarter of a century in which any candidate won an absolute majority. In doing so, and in carrying large Republican congressional delegations into Congress, William McKinley (and Mark Hanna) blasted into history the political equilibrium of the late nineteenth century.

What happened? Basically, Bryan appealed to only the hard-pressed staple farmers of the South and West. McKinley easily won the Northeast, and also the largely agricultural states of North Dakota, Minnesota, Wisconsin, Iowa, Michigan, and Illinois. Many farmers whose situation was not desperate accepted the Republican contention that Bryan was a radical, never a useful tag in American elections. More important,

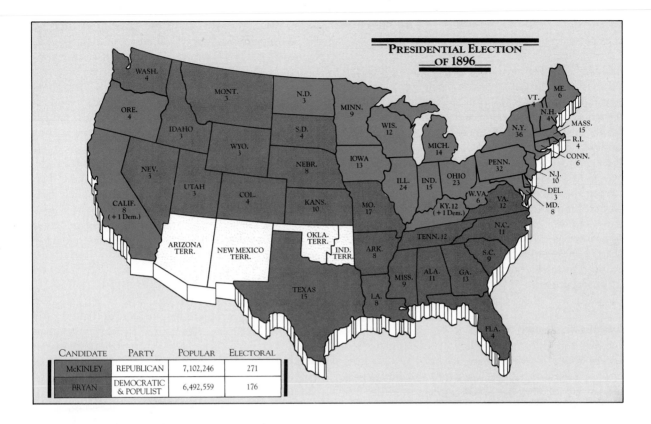

PRESIDENTIAL ELECTION OF 1896

CANDIDATE	PARTY	POPULAR	ELECTORAL
McKINLEY	REPUBLICAN	7,102,246	271
BRYAN	DEMOCRATIC & POPULIST	6,492,559	176

Bryan could not win the support of the industrial workers and city people who had good reason to vote for him. He hardly tried. Imbued with conventional rural prejudices against big cities and the "foreigners" who lived there, he made only one speaking tour in vital New York State and was quoted as having called New York City "the enemy's country," as though it were inhabited solely by bankers and grain speculators.

Some industrialists tried to intimidate their workers into voting for the Republican candidate. The Baldwin Piano Works posted notices on the eve of election day to the effect that if Bryan won, the plant would close for good the next day. But Bryan's weakness in the industrial districts was not due to such tactics. His single-issue free-silver campaign offered little to factory workers. They found more convincing the Republican claim that a high-tariff policy would protect jobs.

Finally, Mark Hanna shrewdly judged the instincts of a newly important element in American politics, the growing middle class of small businessmen, professional people, salaried town dwellers, and highly skilled, well-paid workingmen. Preoccupied with their respectability and considering themselves to be the new bone and sinew of the American republic, they were frightened by Bryan and the ragged, restive farmers whom he represented. These people committed themselves to the Republican party as "the party of de-

cency." For forty years after 1896, they helped to make it the majority party.

The End of Populism

As Watson and Lloyd had predicted, fusion with the Democrats sealed the fate of the Populists. Having sacrificed their reform program for the chance of winning free silver with Bryan, they had nothing left when the votes were counted against him. In the South, Populists who had worked to build a party based on interracial cooperation turned against the blacks (who voted Republican in 1896) and became the leading exponents of Democratic party rule and white supremacy. In the West, the party simply withered away, in part because of the electoral rebuke, and in part because, slowly under McKinley, the wholesale prices of farm products began to rise.

The agricultural depression lifted for a number of reasons. Rich new gold deposits that had been found in Canada and Alaska inflated the currency somewhat and helped raise prices. Several years of poor weather in Europe created a new demand for American farm products. Finally, farmers, like most of the American people, were distracted in 1898 by the McKinley administration's decision to win the United States a place among the empires of the world.

American Imperialism

McKinley hoped to have a presidency as restrained and decorous as his front-porch campaign had been. His personality was attracted to peace and quiet, and his implicit confidence in American business convinced him that prosperity was just around the corner. All he had to do was wait patiently.

He got his prosperity. Even before McKinley was inaugurated in March 1897, the economic indicators were on the upswing. But there would be little peace and quiet during his presidency. Little as the role suited him, McKinley led the American people into a series of overseas adventures that raised a furious debate and turned a nation that had been born in an anticolonial revolution into a country that possessed colonies in both hemispheres.

The Myth of Isolationism

Not that the United States had been an isolationist country before McKinley became president. Far from it. The American government maintained busy missions in all important capitals, and several wars had been fought to defend American interests. During the decade before McKinley was sworn in, the United States had come perilously close to war with Britain, Germany, and Chile. In 1889, only a typhoon that had sunk German and American warships in the Samoan harbor of Apia prevented a full-scale naval encounter in the South Pacific.

Trade made the United States an active participant in world affairs. American ships and sailors were a common sight in the world's most exotic ports. As early as 1844, the United States had signed a trade treaty with the Chinese Empire, as far off and foreign a place as Americans could imagine. In 1854, a naval squadron under Commodore Matthew Perry had anchored off Yokohama, Japan, and had threatened to bombard the city unless the Japanese agreed to abandon their country's genuine isolationism and begin to purchase American goods.

By 1870, American exports had totaled $320 million, mostly agricultural produce bound for Europe. By 1890, $857 million in goods was sold abroad, with American manufacturers competing with European industrialists in peddling steel, textiles, and other products in Pacific countries, Latin America, and Europe itself.

If Americans were not isolationists, neither were they imperialists. Neither the people nor most statesmen wanted anything to do with the scramble for colonies that engrossed Europe and newly powerful

Japan. With the exceptions of Alaska and the tiny Pacific island of Midway (both annexed in 1867), the United States possessed no territory that was not contiguous to the states.

Two deep convictions worked against the occasional proposals that the United States take such colonies. First, the country had been founded in a war against imperial control. Could the heirs of the first great anticolonial rebellion take over other peoples? Most Americans answered with a decisive no. Second, the vastness of the American continent provided a more than adequate outlet for American energies. There was plenty of work to be done at home. William McKinley took office imbued with these beliefs. In all sincerity, he said in his inaugural address that "we must avoid the temptation of territorial expansion."

The Nature of Imperialism

But the times were moving more quickly than was the easy-going McKinley. The United States was no longer a minor country that could sit on the international sidelines. By 1897, the nation was the single most important industrial power in the world. Consciousness of this new greatness stirred many people to believe that the United States should assume its rightful place among the great nations, and in the 1890s, the great nations were empires.

The European powers had partitioned Africa so that only two countries there maintained their independence, ancient Ethiopia and Liberia, a republic that had been founded by former American slaves. Indochina was a French colony. The Dutch flag flew over Indonesia. The Japanese had seized Korea and the Chinese island province of Taiwan, which they had renamed Formosa. Russia had designs on northern China. Germany and Italy, latecomers to the scramble, looked in Africa and Asia for areas to annex. India, the biggest prize of all, was British.

The primary motive of imperialist expansion was economic. Colonies were a source of raw materials and a market for the products of the mother country. Colonialism also generated an emotional justification of its own. Colonies were a source of pride. British imperialists took pleasure in seeing "all that red on the map." (Most mapmakers colored British possessions in red.) The Germans seized parts of Africa that had little economic value just for the sake of having colonies. In England and later in the United States, this bumptious chauvinism was known as "jingoism." To the jingoes, being strong enough to overcome less advanced peoples was reason enough to do so. "We do not want to fight," ran a patriotic British song of 1877. "But, by jingo, if we do. . . ."

Some young American politicians such as Henry Cabot Lodge of Massachusetts and Theodore Roosevelt of New York wanted to join the competition. They said openly that the United States must seize colonies before there were none to be taken. They worried publicly that, in their wealth and prosperity, Americans were becoming soft and flabby. The country needed war in order to toughen up. Roosevelt, a body-building enthusiast, often drew analogies between individuals and nations, and between boxing matches and wars.

Anglo-Saxons and Warships

Lodge, Roosevelt, and other expansionists were profoundly influenced by a theory of race that developed out of Darwinism. Whereas Herbert Spencer had applied his doctrine of "survival of the fittest" to relationships within a society, disciples such as Harvard historian John Fiske and Congregationalist minister Josiah Strong applied it to relationships *between* races and cultures. In separate publications of 1885, Fiske and Strong wrote that the Anglo-Saxons (British and Americans) were obviously more fit to govern than were other peoples. According to Strong's *Our Country*, the Anglo-Saxons were "divinely commissioned" to spread their institutions. It was not a betrayal of American ideals to take over other lands. There was a racial and religious duty to do so. Strong believed that inferior races eventually would die out. An influential political scientist at Columbia University, John W. Burgess, stated flatly in 1890 that the American commitment to self-government was irrelevant to dark-skinned people both at home and abroad. He wrote that "there is no human right to the status of barbarism."

Also in 1890, the expansionists found a highly rationalistic spokesman in naval captain Alfred Thayer Mahan. In his book *The Influence of Sea Power upon History*, Mahan argued that the great nations were always sea-faring nations that had powerful navies. He

A pro-expansion cartoon shows a sword-bearing Yankee Sam rolling up his sleeves for a fight.

chided Americans for having allowed their own fleet to fall into decay. (In 1891, jingoes who wanted war with Chile had to back down because the Chilean navy was superior to the American.) Mahan urged a massive program of ship construction, and Congress responded with large appropriations.

A modern steam-powered navy needed coaling stations at scattered points throughout the world. That in itself required taking colonies, even if they were only dots on the globe like Midway, or building bases in ostensibly independent countries like Hawaii, where in 1887, the United States established a port at Pearl Harbor on the main Hawaiian island of Oahu.

Fears for an America Without Frontiers

Another theory of history that fueled the expansionist movement was based on the announcement of the Director of the Census in 1890 that the frontier no longer existed. In 1889, Congress opened Oklahoma to white settlement; the last large territory that had been reserved for the sole use of Indians was occupied by whites literally overnight.

At the 1893 meeting of the American Historical Association, a young historian named Frederick Jackson Turner propounded a theory that the frontier had been the key to the vitality of American democracy, social stability, and prosperity. Turner was interested in the past. Nevertheless, the implication of his theory for the future was unmistakable. With the frontier gone, was the United States doomed to stagnation and social upheaval? To some who found Turner convincing, the only solution was to establish new frontiers abroad. Throughout the 1890s, American financiers pumped millions of dollars into China and Latin America because they felt investment opportunities within the United States to be shrinking.

All these forces combined to make the 1890s as uncertain a decade in foreign policy as in domestic politics. By 1898, America's attitude toward the world was delicately balanced. Pulling in one direction was the tradition of anticolonialism. Tugging the other way were jingoism, Anglo-Saxonism, and apprehensions for the future. All it took to decide the direction of the leap was a sudden shove. That was provided by a Cuban war for independence that began in 1895.

The Spanish-American War

On a map, Cuba looks like an appendage of Florida, a geographical curiosity that frequently aroused the interest of American expansionists. Cuba was also a historical curiosity because the rich sugar island and Puerto Rico alone of the old Spanish possessions remained under Spanish rule. Cuban rebels periodically had taken up arms, but weak as Spain was, the archaic monarchy was able to hold on to its last American jewel.

The uprising of 1895 was more serious. Smuggling in arms and munitions provided by Cuban exiles in the United States, the rebels for the first time won the support of a large number of ordinary Cubans, perhaps the majority. Until the 1890s, the island had been rather prosperous, exporting sugar to the United States, but the Wilson-Gorman Tariff of 1894 practically shut out Cuba's sole export and caused a deep economic crisis.

It was a classic guerrilla war. The Spanish army and navy controlled the cities of Havana and Santiago and most large towns. By day, Spanish soldiers moved with little trouble among a seemingly peaceful peasant population. By night, however, innocent peasants turned into fierce rebels and sorely punished the Spanish troops. As in most guerrilla wars, fighting was bitter and cruel. Both sides were guilty of atrocities, torture, and mutilation.

Americans were reflexively sympathetic to the Cubans. However, widespread interest in the conflict was aroused only when two competing newspaper chains decided that the rebellion could be used as ammunition in their circulation war.

The Yellow Press

William Randolph Hearst's New York *Journal* and Joseph Pulitzer's New York *World* were known as the "yellow press" because they relied on gimmicks rather than on straightforward news reporting to appeal to readers. The nickname came from one of those gimmicks: "The Yellow Kid," the first comic strip to appear in a newspaper.

The Hearst and Pulitzer chains also could squeeze the most lurid details out of celebrated murder and sex cases, and they pioneered the "invented" news story. In 1889, Pulitzer's *World* sent Elizabeth S. "Nellie" Bly around the world in an attempt to beat the record of the fictional hero of Jules Verne's *Around the World in Eighty Days*. (She did beat it, completing the trip in seventy-two days, six hours, and eleven minutes.)

It was easy to move from this kind of promotionalism to publicizing Spanish atrocities, many of which were genuine. The Spanish military commander in Cuba, Valeriano Weyler, was nicknamed "The Butcher" for his repressive policies, which include the establishment of the first concentration camps. Warring against a whole population, he tried to stifle the uprising by herding whole villages into camps; thus the people could be watched, and everyone who was found outside the camps could be defined as enemies to be shot on sight. This method was inevitably brutal, and Cubans died by the thousands from malnutrition, disease, and abuse.

But real atrocities were not enough for Hearst and Pulitzer. They transformed innocuous incidents into horror stories and actually invented atrocities. The yellow press wanted war. When Hearst artist Frederic Remington wired from Havana that everything was peaceful and he wanted to come home, Hearst ordered him to stay: "You furnish the pictures. I'll furnish the war."

McKinley's Dark Hour

While public outrage grew, McKinley tried to pursue a peaceful policy. His advisers in the business community had substantial investments in Cuba, about $50 million in railroads, mines, and sugar-cane plantations, and they feared the revolutionaries more than the Spanish. McKinley and his advisers wanted Spain to abandon its harsh policies and placate both Cubans and

The February 17, 1898, edition of William Randolph Hearst's New York Journal *reported the destruction of the U.S.S.* Maine *and suggested it was sunk by Spaniards.*

bellicose Americans by liberalizing government on the island.

Ironically, when the Spanish attempted to respond to this pressure, the war came anyway. In 1898, a new government in Madrid withdrew the hated Weyler and proposed autonomy for Cuba within the Spanish Empire. McKinley's administration was apparently satisfied but two events caused a complete change in policy.

On February 9, Hearst's New York *Journal* published a letter that had been written by the Spanish ambassador in Washington, Enrique Dupuy de Lôme. In it, Dupuy told a friend that McKinley was "weak, a bidder for the admiration of the crowd." It was by no means an unreal assessment of the president, but it was insulting. McKinley himself was riled, and war fever flared higher.

Six days later, on February 15, 1898, the battleship U.S.S. *Maine* exploded in Havana harbor with a loss of 260 sailors. To this day, the cause of the disaster is unknown. The explosion may have been caused by a fire in the bunker that spread to the magazine. A bomb may have been planted by Cuban rebels in an attempt to provoke the United States into declaring war on their behalf. Or it may have been the work of Spanish die-hards who opposed the new liberal policy in Cuba. So charged was the atmosphere that some people suggested that William Randolph Hearst had planted the bomb for the sake of a headline!

In any case, with the yellow press playing a big part, American public opinion accepted the least credible explanation: the Spanish government, which was trying to avoid war at all costs, had destroyed the *Maine*.

McKinley vacillated for a month and a half. He flooded Spain with demands for a change of policy. On April 9, in a last desperate attempt to avoid war, the Spanish government gave in on every count. In the meantime, fearing that to continue resisting the war fever would cost the Republicans control of Congress in the fall elections, McKinley caved in. With the Democratic party still led by William Jennings Bryan and the agrarians, the risk was not worth taking. On April 11, practically ignoring the Spanish capitulation, the president asked Congress for a declaration of war and got it.

The "Splendid Little War"

Declaring war was one thing. Fighting the Spanish was quite another. The United States army, which numbered only twenty-eight thousand men, most of whom were in the West supervising Indians, was not up to launching an invasion even just a hundred miles away.

The navy was ready, however. Much to almost everyone's surprise, it struck first not in Cuba but halfway around the world in Spain's last Pacific colony, the Philippines. On May 1, acting on the unauthorized instructions of Undersecretary of the Navy Theodore Roosevelt (the Secretary of the Navy was out of town for the day), Commodore George Dewey steamed a flotilla into Manila Bay and completely surprised the Spanish garrison. He destroyed most of the Spanish ships before they could weigh anchor.

But Dewey had no soldiers with which to launch an attack on land. For more than three months, he and his men sat outside Manila harbor, baking in their steel ships. In August, newly arrived troops finally took the capital. Although they did not know it, a peace treaty had been signed the previous day.

By that time, American troops had also conquered Cuba and Puerto Rico. Secretary of State John Hay called their campaign a "splendid little war" because so few Americans died in battle. In order to celebrate so gaily, however, he had to overlook the more than five thousand soldiers who died from typhoid, tropical diseases, and poisonous "embalmed beef," tainted meat that had been supplied to the soldiers because of corruption or simple inefficiency.

Although the Spanish army in Cuba outnumbered the Americans until the last, both commanders and men were paralyzed by defeatism. They might have

Theodore Roosevelt and his "Rough Riders" cavalry unit.

been overcome more easily than they were but for the ineptitude of the American commanders, General Nelson A. Miles and General William R. Shafter, who was so fat that he had to be helped into the saddle of an extremely large horse when it was time to move.

Despite shortages of food, clothing, transport vehicles, medical supplies, ammunition, and horses, an army of seventeen thousand was landed in Cuba in June and defeated the Spanish outside Santiago at the battles of El Caney and San Juan Hill.

The latter victory allowed Americans to forget the poor management of the war and gave them a popular hero. Theodore Roosevelt had resigned from the Navy Department to accept a colonelcy in a volunteer cavalry unit called the "Rough Riders." It was a highly unmilitary group, made up of cowboys from Roosevelt's North Dakota ranch, show-business people, upper-class polo players and other athletes, and even some ex-convicts. The Rough Riders had to fight on foot because the army had been unable to get their horses out of Tampa, Florida, but they fought bravely in the hottest action on San Juan Hill.

The Empire Confirmed

In August, the Spanish gave up. American troops occupied not only Manila in the Philippines and much of Cuba, but also the island of Puerto Rico, which had been seized without resistance. But what should be done with these possessions? Suddenly, the imperialism controversy was no longer an academic debate. It involved three far-flung island countries that were inhabited by millions of people who spoke Spanish, who clung to traditions very different from those of Americans, who were not Caucasian for the most part, and who did not want to become part of the United States.

To the chagrin of the imperialists, the independence of Cuba had been guaranteed before the war had begun. In order to get money from Congress to fight Spain, the administration had accepted a rider drafted by an anti-imperialist senator from Colorado, Henry Teller. The Teller Amendment forbade the United States to take over the sugar island. Therefore, the great debate over imperialism centered on Puerto Rico and, to a great extent, the Philippine Islands.

The Debate

The anti-imperialists were a disparate group, and their arguments were sometimes contradictory. In Congress, they included idealistic old Radical Republicans like George Frisbie Hoar of Massachusetts and former Liberal Republicans like Carl Schurz and much of the old Mugwump wing of the party. Some Republican regulars also opposed taking colonies; among them was Thomas B. Reed of Maine, the no-nonsense, dictatorial Speaker of the House who otherwise despised reformers. Finally, a substantial part of the Democratic party, led by William Jennings Bryan, opposed annexation of any former Spanish lands.

The anti-imperialists reminded Americans of their anticolonial heritage. "We insist," declared the American Anti-Imperialist League in October 1899, "that the subjugation of any people is 'criminal aggression' and open disloyalty to the distinctive principles of our government. We hold, with Abraham Lincoln, that no

man is good enough to govern another man without that man's consent."

Some of the anti-imperialists appealed to racist feelings. With many people unhappy about the nation's large black population, was it wise to bring millions more nonwhite people under the flag? When Congress finally decided to take the Philippines and pay Spain $20 million in compensation, House Speaker Reed resigned in disgust, grumbling about "ten million Malays at two dollars a head."

But racist feelings worked mostly in favor of the imperialist group. Brilliant propagandists like Roosevelt, who was now governor of New York; Henry Cabot Lodge; and the eloquent Albert J. Beveridge, senator from Indiana, preached that the white race had a duty and a right to govern inferior peoples. "God has not been preparing the English-speaking and Teutonic peoples for a thousand years for nothing but vain and idle self-contemplation and self-admiration," Beveridge told the Senate. "No! He has made us the master organizers of the world to establish system where chaos reigns."

Well-grounded fear that if the United States abandoned the Philippines, Japan or Germany would seize them motivated other politicians to support annexation. Such anxiety was especially significant in deciding McKinley's mind on the question. But most of all, the American people were in an emotional, expansive mood that had little relationship to reason. Coming at the end of the troubled, depressed, and divided 1890s, annexation of colonies seemed a way to unite the country.

This idea undoubtedly swayed McKinley, who, like it or not, was forced to take a stand. There is some reason to believe that two years before he came out for annexing the Philippines, McKinley could not have located the islands on a map. The ignorance with which he acted is evident in one of the reasons that he gave for supporting annexation. He said that the United States had a duty to Christianize the natives of the islands. McKinley was unaware that the majority of Filipinos had become Christian long before the first church bell had rung in his native state of Ohio.

Hawaii: The First Colony

McKinley found it relatively easy to support annexation of the Philippines and Puerto Rico because the United States already had taken its first real overseas colony. In July 1898, Congress had annexed the seven main islands and fourteen hundred minor ones that made up the mid-Pacific nation of Hawaii. Shortly thereafter, Guam, Wake, and Baker islands were added as coaling stations for the navy.

THE WHITE AMERICAN'S BURDEN

"The White Man's Burden," a poem by the British writer Rudyard Kipling, was often quoted by imperialists to justify governing nonwhite peoples as a duty. Kipling had subtitled the poem "The United States and the Philippines," and the final stanza was addressed specifically (and some think sarcastically) to the young American nation:

> Take up the White Man's Burden—
> Have done with childhood days—
> The lightly-proffered laurel,
> The easy, ungrudged praise.
> Comes now to search your manhood
> Through all the thankless years,
> Cold, edged with dear-bought wisdom,
> The judgement of your peers!

"The White Man's Burden" from the COLLECTED WORKS OF RUDYARD KIPLING. Reprinted by permission of Doubleday and Co., Inc.

Sanford B. Dole, a businessman and the first governor of the territory of Hawaii, seated next to Queen Liliuokalani, the last monarch of Hawaii.

The annexation of Hawaii was long in the making. The descendants of American missionary families in the islands had grown rich by exporting sugar to the United States, and they had won the confidence and support of the Hawaiian king, Kalakaua. Until 1890, they were more than content with their independent island paradise.

Then, the McKinley Tariff introduced a two cent per pound bounty on American-grown sugar. This encouraged enough mainland farmers to produce cane or sugar beets that Hawaiian imports declined sharply. Unable to affect American tariff policy from outside, the Hawaiian oligarchy concluded that it must join the islands to the United States and benefit from the bounty.

The plan was squelched before it got started. In 1891, Kalakaua died and was succeeded by his anti-American sister, Queen Liliuokalani. Weighing two hundred pounds with will power to match, "Queen Lil" announced that the theme of her reign would be "Hawaii for the Hawaiians." She introduced a number of reforms that were aimed at dismantling the whites' control of both the economy and the legislature.

Alarmed, the oligarchy acted quickly with help from the American ambassador in Honolulu. He declared that American lives and property were in danger and landed marines from the U.S.S. *Boston* who quickly took control of the peaceful islands. Back home, imperialists in the Senate introduced a treaty of annexation. But before they could push it through, Grover Cleveland was sworn in as president (March 4, 1893), and he withdrew the proposal.

Cleveland was not opposed to annexation on principle. But he wanted to know how the Hawaiian people felt, and he sent an investigator, James H. Blount, to the islands. Blount reported that very few nonwhite Hawaiians wanted to be part of the United States; they wanted independence and the restoration of Queen Liliuokalani. Cleveland ordered the marines to return to their ships and to the naval base at Pearl Harbor.

However, the Hawaiian whites had gone too far to chance restoring Queen Lil. They maintained control and declared Hawaii a republic. As long as Cleveland sat in the White House, they bided their time and quietly cultivated Republican senators. Annexation was probably inevitable under McKinley whatever happened with Spain. As it was, the thrill of overseas war was enough to push through the treaty on July 6, 1898.

Many Hawaiians continued to resent the takeover. But as the white population grew and the islands attracted Japanese and Chinese immigrants, the native Hawaiians declined into a weak minority. Like the American Indians, they became foreigners in their own homeland.

The Philippine Insurrection

The Filipinos, on the contrary, resisted annexation by the United States. If the war with Spain had been something like splendid, the war that followed was a great deal like ugly. Like the Cubans, the Philippine people were experienced in guerrilla warfare. Led by Emilio Aguinaldo, a well-educated patriot who was as comfortable in the jungle as he was in the library, the rebels withdrew from the American-occupied cities to the jungle and fought only when the odds favored them.

In response, the American army was expanded to sixty-five thousand men by early 1900, but made little progress outside the cities. The American commanders were unable to draw the *insurrectos* into a conventional battle in which superior fire power told the tale.

The war took a vicious turn. The Filipinos frequently decapitated their victims. The Americans, frustrated by their failures, the intense tropical heat, insects, and diseases, retaliated by slaughtering whole villages that were thought to be supporting the rebels. The army never did defeat the Filipinos. The rebellion ended only when, in March 1901, General Arthur Mac-Arthur succeeded in capturing Aguinaldo. Weary of the bloodshed, Aguinaldo took an oath of allegiance to the United States and ordered his followers to do the same. (He lived quietly and long enough to see Philippine independence established in 1946.) More than five thousand Americans died in the cause of suppressing a popular revolution, a queer twist in a war that had begun, three years before, in support of a popular revolution.

Roosevelt Affirms the Empire

In the same month that Aguinaldo was captured, William McKinley took the presidential oath for the second time. The preceding November, he had defeated Democratic candidate William Jennings Bryan by an even greater electoral margin than in 1896. Bryan's attempt to make the election a referendum on imperialism proved to be a fiasco. Most Americans either were happy with their overseas possessions or simply did not care. McKinley was able to side-step the issue and point to the prosperity of the country; indeed, the Republican campaign slogan was "Four More Years of the Full Dinner Pail." Several states that had voted for Bryan in 1896 slipped into the Republican column. The Great Commoner even lost his own state of Nebraska.

A new vice president stood at McKinley's side on Inauguration Day. Theodore Roosevelt had moved quickly from his exploits in Cuba to the governorship of New York. He immediately alienated the Republican boss of the state, Thomas C. Platt, by refusing to take orders and even attacking some corrupt members of Platt's machine.

In getting the vice-presidential nomination for Roosevelt, Platt believed that he was ending the Rough Rider's political career. Roosevelt sourly agreed. The vice presidency was a political burial ground, a powerless post that usually was assigned to political hacks who could help carry swing states. Just a few years later, Woodrow Wilson's vice president, Thomas Marshall, would liken election to the vice presidency to being lost at sea: one was never heard from again.

Only Mark Hanna had reservations about Roosevelt. What would happen to the country, Hanna asked McKinley, if something happened to him? The president was almost sixty at a time when that was a ripe old age.

DEWEY'S BLUNDER

Commodore George Dewey became a national hero by virtue of his victory at Manila Bay during the Spanish-American War. A group of conservative Democrats hoped to nominate him for the presidency in 1900 in order to head off William Jennings Bryan, who was still regarded as something of a radical. At first Dewey refused because he did not believe that he was qualified for the office. He later changed his mind, explaining that "since studying the subject, I am convinced that the office of the president is not such a very difficult one to fill." As a result of his candor, Dewey lost the support of virtually everyone, and Bryan was nominated once again.

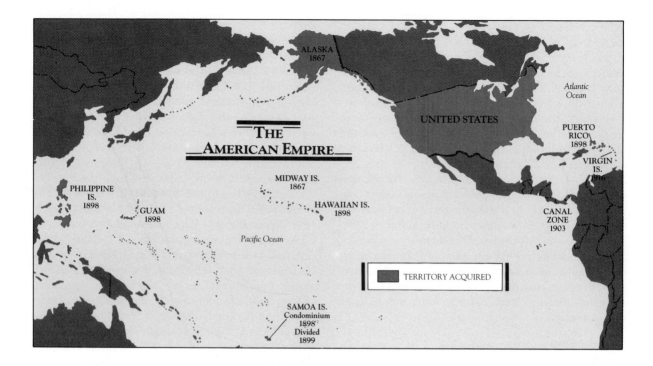

Something did happen to McKinley. On September 6, 1901, McKinley paid a ceremonial visit to the Pan-American Exposition in Buffalo. Greeting a long line of guests, he found himself faced by a man who extended a bandaged hand. The gauze swathed a large-bore pistol. Leon Czolgosz, an anarchist who "didn't believe one man should have so much service and another man should have none," shot the president several times in the chest and abdomen. Eight days later, McKinley died. "Now look," Hanna shook his head at the funeral, "that damned cowboy is president."

Roosevelt's Foreign Policy

Theodore Roosevelt, known affectionately as "Teddy," left an indelible mark on the presidency. Completely unlike his predecessors back as far as Lincoln, the exuberant young New Yorker (forty-three years old when he took office) knew only one way to do anything: take the lead. Nowhere was his assertive personality more pronounced than in his foreign policy, a peacetime extension of the zest that had taken him shouting up San Juan Hill.

Roosevelt's actions varied according to the part of the world with which he was dealing. With the European nations he insisted that the United States be accepted as an equal, active imperial power. Although friendship between Great Britain and the United States had been long in the making, Roosevelt sped it along by responding cordially to every British request for cooperation. Toward Latin America, however, he was arrogant. He told both Latin Americans and Europeans that the whole Western Hemisphere was an American sphere of influence. Toward Asia, Roosevelt continued a policy that had been designed during the McKinley administration by John Hay, who continued to serve as Secretary of State. It was called the "Open Door."

The Open Door Policy

China, the largest country in the world, had been left behind by modernization. Although there was a nominal emperor, powerful local chieftains ruled whole provinces as personal estates, and Japan and most of the imperialistic countries of Europe had carved out spheres of influence in which their own troops maintained order and their own laws governed their resident citizens' behavior. With Africa and the rest of Asia formally partitioned into colonies, it seemed inevitable that China would be carved up.

Great Britain opposed further colonization. More conscious than Japan, Russia, Germany, and Italy of the problems and expense of direct imperial rule, Britain also believed that it could dominate the market of an independent China on the basis of its competitive advantages in selling to the Chinese, its more efficient industry and its merchant marine.

British interests accorded with American policy, particularly because the United States had no clear sphere of influence in China. In 1899 and 1900, John Hay circulated a series of memoranda called the "Open Door" notes that pledged the imperial powers not to seize any Chinese territory. Germany and Japan were reluctant to acquiesce. However, faced with British and American support for maintaining the independence of China and for keeping a door open to the trade of all, they glumly agreed.

In 1900, international domination of China was put to the test by a rebellion encouraged by the empress dowager of the country. The rebels, called Boxers because the Chinese name of their secret religious, anti-imperialist, and antiforeign society meant "righteous

harmonious fist," besieged nine hundred foreigners in the British legation in Peking.

An international army made up of American, British, French, German, Austrian, Russian, Japanese, and Italian troops defeated the poorly armed rebels and wreaked havoc on the surrounding countryside. The victory encouraged racist belief in white superiority (despite the contribution of the Japanese) and ensured the continuation of the Open Door.

During Roosevelt's presidency, American capital poured into China. International consortia developed mines, built railways, and set up other profitable enterprises. In 1905, the president applied his policy of equilibrium in China by working through diplomatic chan-

European, Japanese, and American soldiers (photographed above at the Forbidden City in Peking) protected international domination of China during the Boxer Rebellion of 1900.

REMEMBERING THE *MAINE*:
SOLDIERS IN THE SPANISH-AMERICAN WAR

Secretary of State John Hay called it "a splendid little war." Undersecretary of the Navy Theodore Roosevelt resigned his post in order to fight in it. William Allen White remembered the glad excitement with which the declaration of war had been received in the Midwest: "Everywhere over this good, fair land, flags were flying, . . . crowds gathered to hurrah for the soldiers and to throw hats into the air." The celebrants' favorite cry was, "Remember the *Maine*; to hell with Spain." Americans regarded the occasion as an opportunity to prove the arrival of the United States as a world power and, at home, as a chance to seal the reunion of North and South by having northern and southern boys join together to fight Spain. While McKinley would not allow political rival William Jennings Bryan to go abroad and make a military reputation, he was delighted to appoint old Confederate officers like Fitzhugh Lee and General Joseph Wheeler to active command.

But, as historian Frank Freidel points out, for the soldiers in the ranks "it was as grim, dirty, and bloody as any war in history." He adds: "Only the incredible ineptitude of the Spaniards and the phenomenal luck of the Americans" kept the Spanish-American War small and short—splendid.

While the navy proved ready to fight on an instant's notice, the army was not ready for anything. In 1898, the army was only 28,000 strong, and those troops were scattered the length and breadth of the country. Congress had authorized increasing this force to 65,700 in wartime, but despite a rush of enlistments, the army never grew this large. The young men who rallied to arms in every state preferred to join the state militias or new units of volunteers, in which enlistments were for two years unless discharged earlier (as almost all would be).

In 1898, the militias numbered 140,000 men, but regular army officers justly suspected their training and equipment and generally preferred new volunteers units. Indeed, training was generally inadequate across the board because of the rush to get into action, and supplies were worse. Companies mustering, mostly in the southern states, were issued heavy woolen winter uniforms and Civil War-vintage Springfield rifles. Because of either corruption in the War Department or simple inefficiency, much meat that was provided the recruits was tainted and sanitary conditions in the crowded camps were such that filth-related diseases such as typhoid and dysentery ravaged them. When the dead were counted at the end of 1898, 379 men were listed as killed in combat, while 5,083 men were listed as dead of disease.

There was no difficulty in getting volunteers. While 274,000 eventually served in the army, probably an equal number were turned down. Among these rejects were Frank James, brother of the late train robber Jesse James, and William F. "Buffalo Bill" Cody, who annoyed the War Department by writing a magazine article entitled "How I Could Drive the Spaniards Out of Cuba with Thirty Thousand Indian Braves." Martha A. Chute of Colorado was discouraged in her offer to raise a troop of women, as was William Randolph Hearst in his suggestion to recruit a regiment of professional boxers and baseball players. "Think of a regiment composed of magnificent men of this ilk," the editor of the New York *Journal* wrote "They would overawe any Spanish regiment by their mere appearance." Nevertheless, the "Rough Riders," a motley collection of cowboys, athletes, and gentlemen like Colonel Theodore Roosevelt, was mustered. But because of shipping problems, the Riders had to leave their horses in Florida when they sailed for Cuba and fight on foot.

In fact, there were few battlegrounds in Cuba or in the Philippines that were suited to cavalry attack. Both are tropical countries, and most of the fighting was done in summer and much of it in jungle. The army tried to prepare for jungle warfare by authorizing the recruitment of up to 10,000 "immunes," young men who were thought to be immune to tropical diseases. However, medicine's comparative ignorance of the nature of tropical diseases combined with racism to make the immune regiments no more serviceable than any others. Whereas the original idea had been to fill these units with men who had grown up in marshy areas of the Deep South, within months recruiters were turning away white Louisianans from the bayous and accepting blacks from the upcountry South and even urban New Jersey. They were believed to possess a genetic immunity to malaria, yellow fever, and other afflictions of the tropics.

Blacks played a large part in both the Cuban and the Philippine campaigns. When the war broke out, there were four black regiments in the regular army: two infantry and two cavalry, the Ninth and the Tenth Horse Regiments. All four saw action. In fact, while Theodore Roosevelt was describing the capture of San Juan Hill as an accomplishment of the Rough Riders, less bumptious witnesses believed that the Rough Riders would have been devastated had it not been for the Tenth Negro Cavalry, which was immediately to their left during the charge. While the Rough Riders made a lot of noise, the Tenth simply did their job. In the words of the restrained report of their commander, later

Gay Nineties and Good Old Days
American Society in Transition, 1890–1917

All through December 1899, editors and writers of letters to the editor bickered in print about the significance of the New Year's Day that was rapidly approaching. One camp pronounced that New Year's Day 1900 would mark the beginning of a new century. Others replied that the end of the first century A.D. had come not with the conclusion of ninety-nine years but with the last day of A.D. 100. Thus the twentieth century would begin at the stroke of midnight on January 1, 1901, a year in the future.

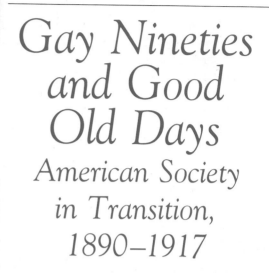

Men and women bicyclists riding at the turn of the century.

The Birth of Comfortable America

Those who said that the year 1900 would be the last year of the nineteenth century were correct, of course. Nevertheless, the others shrugged and announced that the novelty of writing such a portentously sounding date as 1900 on their next letter to the editor meant more to them than did the dictates of arithmetic. Americans would celebrate the new century on New Year's Eve 1899. However, the facts of life in the United States at the turn of the century were such that, in later years, people who looked back on the times had very diverse recollections.

George Bellows' painting, Cliff Dwellers, *shows an artist's view of a crowded slum in an American city.*

The Worst of Times?

For some, the 1890s clutched the memory as a decade of severe economic depression and social tension. They were the years of the Wounded Knee Massacre, of bloody clashes between workers and bosses at Homestead, Pullman, and in the Coeur D'Alene, of wandering tramps, and of various "armies" of the unemployed that marched to Washington to petition for work-relief laws (the most famous of which was Coxey's Army, which was led by an Ohio businessman named Jacob Coxey). It was the decade when millions of farmers in the grain and cotton belts spoke bitterly of revolution. It was a time when the lynching of blacks in the South became so routine that, in 1899, a mob in Palmetto, Georgia, announced in advance that a man would be burned alive so that thousands could flock aboard special excursion trains in time to see the show.

During the 1890s, 3.17 million impoverished immigrants warily stepped off steamships, most of them directly into squalid city slums. Life expectancy at birth for most white Americans was about forty-five years, lower for blacks and immigrants. Infant mortality in New York City was worse than it had ever been. Nationwide, people were six times more likely to die of influenza than they are today, sixty times more likely to die of syphilis, and more than eighty times more likely to die of tuberculosis. Diseases that are minor health problems in the late twentieth century—typhoid, scarlet fever, strep throat, diphtheria, whooping cough, measles—were common killers in the 1890s.

The first ten years or so of the twentieth century might accurately be described as equally troubled. It began with young soldiers fighting an ugly war of repression in the Philippines. In 1901, another president was assassinated, the third in a generation. The lynch-

ing of blacks continued at epidemic levels and was no more likely to be punished than during the 1890s.

The Indians were worse off than the blacks. Nearly forgotten by other Americans, they languished on the fringes of society, their numbers reduced sharply by disease and demoralization. Immigration of mostly destitute peasants and petty craftsmen reached flood levels, 8.8 million between 1900 and 1910.

It was a time so throttled by industrial violence that the president appointed a special commission to investigate the problem. In March 1911, Americans were stunned to read in their morning papers that 146 people, mostly young women and girls, had died in a fire at the Triangle Shirtwaist Company factory in New York City. Some jumped ten stories to their death. Others died in heaps at exit doors that had been locked to keep them from wandering from their scissors and sewing machines. And yet, for all the horror of crushed and charred bodies, the Triangle fire was merely the most notorious of avoidable industrial accidents that annually killed thousands of American workers.

The Best of Times?

It would not be surprising if memories of such things haunted American recollections of the end of the nineteenth century and the beginning of the twentieth century. But it was not so. Instead, the final decade of the nineteenth century has gone down in the popular consciousness as the "Gay Nineties," a decade of nickelodeon music and Coney Island, of a night of vaudeville and a week at the seaside, of beer gardens and ice cream parlors, of the bicycle craze and winsome Gibson Girls.

The years that preceded American intervention in the First World War have lived on in the national memory as the original "good old days." The prewar period is the slice of time to which popular novelists and filmmakers repair when they want to portray an America that is recognizable but unmistakably of a better time.

Life was less complex then. The summer sun was warmer; the hot dogs, tastier; the baseball, more exciting; the boys, more gallant; the girls, prettier; the songs, lilting and cheering the heart with melody and innocent lyrics. Even historians, who are trained to be skeptical of such images, have referred to the generation that lived before the First World War as the last to enjoy basking in an "age of American innocence."

The Golden Age of Middle America

The turn of the century has cast such an alluring glow through time because middle-class values and aspirations have dominated American culture in the twentieth century, and in the 1890s and early 1900s the modern middle class came into its own. The troubles of poor farmers, most industrial workers, blacks, Indians, and recent immigrants were real and tragic. But the class of people who, while not rich, did not have to struggle in order to survive reached unprecedented numbers at the turn of the century. The middle class became numerous enough to create and sustain a distinctive life style and to support a bustling consumer economy and technology devoted to physical comfort, convenience, individual self-improvement, and the enjoyment of leisure time.

Increasingly well educated, the new middle class quietly shelved the zealous, religious piety of their parents and grandparents. They embraced instead the material world and its pleasures. The people of the "good old

days" were by no means oblivious to social evils. But because war and revolution were not yet constant companions, and because the very idea that the world itself could be destroyed was preposterous fantasy, they could face their problems with confidence and optimism.

Teddy

The buoyant temper of the period was personified in the young New Yorker who, in September 1901, succeeded William McKinley as president. Theodore Roosevelt was climbing a mountain in the Adirondacks when he received the news of McKinley's death. He rushed to Buffalo, took the oath of office, and confided to a friend, "It is a dreadful thing to come into the presidency in this way. But it would be a far worse thing to be morbid about it." Roosevelt intended to enjoy the presidency, as his fellow Americans intended to make the most of life. And no other chief executive before or since has had such a "bully" time living at 1600 Pennsylvania Avenue.

Both critics and friends of the president poked fun at his personal motto: "Walk softly and carry a big stick." They said that they observed Roosevelt wildly waving sticks around often enough, but rarely knew him to

Horseback riding was one of Theodore Roosevelt's many athletic pursuits.

RETAIL PRICES: 1900–1910	
Junction City, Kansas—population 5,000	
Bacon (per pound)	$ 0.12
Beef (per pound)	.10
Butter (per pound)	.18
Eggs (per dozen)	.12
Ice cream soda	.10
Oranges (per dozen)	.20
Ladies' shoes (per pair)	1.50
Men's suit	9.00
Sewing machine	12.00

walk softly. Quite the contrary. Everything that Roosevelt did was accompanied by fanfare. He seemed to swagger and strut about like an exuberant adolescent, hogging center stage and good naturedly drowning out anyone who dared to compete for the spotlight.

Roosevelt shattered the image of solemn dignity that had been nurtured by every president since Rutherford B. Hayes. He stormed about the country far more than had any predecessor, delivering dramatic speeches, mixing gleefully with crowds of all descriptions, camping out, climbing mountains, and clambering astride horses and atop farm and industrial machines. When a motion-picture photographer asked him to move around for the ingenious new camera, Roosevelt picked up an ax and furiously chopped down a tree.

Of an old aristocratic Dutch family, Roosevelt had been sickly as a youth. He was hopelessly near sighted and suffered from asthma. But he had built up his body through a regimen of difficult exercise. He had fought on the Harvard boxing team, and had ridden with cowboys on his North Dakota ranch. As Police Commissioner of New York City, he had accompanied patrolmen on night beats as dangerous as any in the world. When the war with Spain had broken out, he had left his office job and joined the army. In dozens of articles and books, he wrote of the glories of "the strenuous life."

Roosevelt liked to show off his large, affectionate, and handsome family with himself at stage center, a stern but generous patriarch. He sported a modest paunch (fashionable at the turn of the century), a close-trimmed moustache, and thick pince-nez that dropped from his nose when he was excited, which was often. He had a peculiar set of teeth, all seemingly incisors of the same size and about twice as many as normal. He displayed them often in a broad grin that he shed only when he took off after enemies whom middle-class Americans also found it easy to dislike: Wall Street bankers, Socialists, impudent Latin Americans.

Unlike McKinley, Roosevelt had no compunctions about smoking cigars in public. What was the harm in a minor vice that brought a man pleasure? More than any other individual, he taught Americans to believe that their president should be a good fellow and part showman.

THE CENTER OF ATTENTION

"When father goes to a wedding," one of Theodore Roosevelt's sons explained, "he wants to be the bride. When he goes to a funeral, he wants to be the corpse."

The Symbol of an Age

Roosevelt had many critics. But most Americans, especially those of the vibrant new middle class, found him a grand fellow. They called him "Teddy" and named the lovable teddy bear after him. He was the first president to be routinely identified in newspapers by his initials, another signal of affection. Even Elihu Root, a stodgy eastern aristocrat who served as both Secretary of War and Secretary of State, waxed playful when he congratulated the president on his forty-sixth birthday in 1904. "You have made a very good start in life," Root said, "and your friends have great hopes for you when you grow up." The British ambassador quipped, "You must remember that the president is about six years old."

Kansas-bred journalist William Allen White, the archetype of the middle-class townsman, wrote that "Roosevelt bit me and I went mad." White remained a lifelong devotee of "the Colonel," as did Finley Peter Dunne, the urbane Chicagoan who captured the salty, cynical humor of the big-city Irish in his fictional commentator on current events, Mr. Dooley. Radical dissenters hated Roosevelt (who hated them back with interest). But they were at a loss as to how to counter his vast popularity. Labor leaders and Socialists stuck to the issues when they disagreed with him. There was no advantage in attacking Teddy Roosevelt personally.

Although Roosevelt was a staunch believer in Anglo-Saxon superiority, blacks liked him because he ignored the squeals of southern (Democratic) segregationists and invited Booker T. Washington to call on him in the White House. Woman suffragists, gearing up for the last phase of their long battle for votes, petitioned rather than attacked him. Elizabeth Cady Stanton addressed him from her deathbed in 1901 as "already celebrated for so many deeds and honorable utterances."

Much mischief was done during Theodore Roosevelt's nearly eight years in office. He committed the United States to a role as international policeman that damaged the nation's reputation in many small countries. He was inclined to define his critics in moral terms, a recurring and unfortunate characteristic of American politics since his time. Despite eloquent attacks on "malefactors of great wealth," he encouraged the big corporations to increase their power over the economy.

But the happy relationship between the boyish president and the majority of the American people may be the most important historical fact of the years spanning the turn of the century. Like the man who was their president between 1901 and 1909, the worldly middle class of the Gay Nineties was bumptious, self-confident, optimistic, and glad to be alive.

An Educated People

The foundation of middle-class vigor was wealth. America had grown so rich that millions of people could afford to indulge interests and pleasures that had been the exclusive property of tiny elites. Among these was education beyond "the three r's"—"readin', 'ritin', and 'rithmetic." During the final third of the nineteenth century, and especially after 1890, the American educational system expanded and changed to accommodate the numbers and inclinations of the new class.

There were no more than about three hundred secondary schools in the United States in 1860 (a country of 31.4 million people), and only about one hundred of them were free. While girls were admitted to most public elementary schools, very few attended beyond the first few grades.

Colleges and universities catered to an even more select social set. They offered the traditional course in the liberal arts (Latin, philosophy, mathematics, and history) that was designed to polish young gentlemen rather than to train people for a career. The handful of

A STATISTICAL PORTRAIT OF HIGHER EDUCATION: 1840–1902

Year	Number of institutions	Number of teachers	Number of students
1840	173	Not available	16,233
1850	234	1,651	27,159
1860	467	2,895	56,120
1871	426	4,125	53,130
1880	591	6,500	85,378
1902	530	10,700	101,064

"female seminaries" and colleges that admitted women before the Civil War also taught the ancient curriculum mixed with a strong dose of evangelical religion.

After 1865, and especially after 1890, educational facilities rapidly multiplied and changed character. By 1900, there were six thousand free public secondary schools in the United States, and by 1915, there were twelve thousand, educating 1.3 million pupils. Secondary schools no longer specialized in preparing a select few for university, but offered a wide range of

Stanford University, constructed by railroad baron Leland Stanford in memory of his son.

courses leading to jobs in industry and business, from engineering and accounting to agriculture and typing.

New Kinds of Universities

The Morrill Land Grant Act of 1862 and the philanthropy of millionaires combined to expand the opportunities for higher education. The Morrill Act provided federal land to the states for the purpose of serving the educational needs of "the industrial classes," particularly in "such branches of learning as are related to agriculture and mechanic arts." Thus it not only fostered the founding of technical schools in which middle-class youth might learn a profession, but put liberal-arts training within their reach. Many of the great state universities of the West owe their origins to the Morrill Act.

Gilded Age millionaires competed for esteem as patrons of learning by constructing buildings and by endowing scholarships and professorial chairs at older institutions. Some even founded completely new universities. The story was told that railroad king Leland Stanford and his wife traveled to Harvard with the notion of erecting a building in memory of their son, who had died. As President Charles W. Eliot was explaining how much it had cost to construct each of Harvard's magnificent stone buildings, Mrs. Stanford suddenly exclaimed, "Why, Leland, we can build our

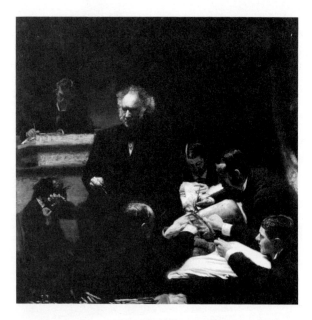

Thomas Eakins' The Gross Clinic, painted in 1875, shows young physicians learning their trade from more experienced colleagues.

own university!" And they did; Stanford University in Palo Alto, California, was founded in 1885.

Cornell (1865), Drew (1866), Johns Hopkins (1867), Tulane (1834), and Vanderbilt (1872) universities are other institutions that bear the names of the moguls who financed them. In Philadelphia, Success Gospel preacher Russell B. Conwell established Temple University in 1884 explicitly to educate poor boys who were ambitious to rise in social station. John D. Rockefeller pumped millions of dollars into the University of Chicago (1890), making it one of America's most distinguished centers of learning within a decade.

The midwestern and western state universities, beginning with Iowa in 1858, generally admitted women to at least some programs. In the East, however, separate women's colleges were founded, again with the support of wealthy benefactors. Barnard (1889), Bryn Mawr (1880), Mount Holyoke (1837), Radcliffe (1879), Smith (1871), Vassar (1861), and Wellesley (1870) offered demanding courses of study and, before long, diplomas that came to be larded with prestige.

Studying for Careers

The transformation of higher education was not simply a matter of more colleges, universities, and students. While some institutions, such as Yale, clung tenaciously to the traditional liberal-arts curriculum, the majority of schools adopted the "elective system" that was pioneered by the College of William and Mary and the University of Michigan and most effectively promoted by President Eliot of Harvard. Beginning in 1869, Eliot abandoned the rule that every student follow precisely the same sequence of courses. Instead, he allowed individuals to choose their field of study. "Majors" included traditional subjects but also new disciplines in the social sciences, engineering, and business administration. The new emphasis on university education as preparation for a career unmistakably revealed the interests of middle-class students who had not yet arrived financially and socially.

From Germany, educators borrowed the concept of the professional postgraduate school, Before the 1870s, young people who wished to learn a profession attached themselves to an established practitioner. A would-be lawyer agreed with an established attorney to do routine work in his office, sweeping floors and helping with deeds and wills, in return for the right to "read law" in the office and to observe and question his teacher. After a few years, the apprentice hung out his own shingle. Many physicians were trained the same way. Civil and mechanical engineers learned their professions "on the job" in factories. All too often, teachers received no training and were miserably paid, about $200 a year in rural states.

As late as 1867, there were only four hundred graduate students in the United States. In that year, Johns Hopkins University was founded in Baltimore with a postgraduate program that was as important as its four-year college. Following Hopkins's lead, many larger universities established graduate schools in the humanities, sciences, and social sciences as well as in medicine, law, and engineering. By 1900, there were five thousand graduate students in the United States.

Women, Minorities, and the New Education

Exceptional women who were dauntless enough to shake off the ridicule of their male classmates could be found in small numbers at every level of the new system. By the mid-1880s, the word *coeducational* and its breezy abbreviation, *coed,* had become part of the American language. The first female physician in the United States, Elizabeth Blackwell, was accredited only in 1849. In 1868, she established a medical school for women in New York City. By that date, the Woman's Medical College of Pennsylvania already was recognized, however grudgingly, as offering one of the nation's best programs.

Female lawyers were unusual at a time when women were not considered equal to men before the law. In 1873, the Supreme Court approved the refusal of the University of Illinois to admit women by declaring that "the paramount mission and destiny of women are to fulfill the noble and benign offices of wife and mother." But by the end of the century, dozens of women practiced law. Antoinette Blackwell, sister-in-law of Elizabeth, paved the way for the ordination of women ministers, and by the turn of the century, the more liberal Protestant denominations, such as the Unitarians and Congregationalists, had ordained some women.

Also in small numbers, well-to-do Jews and Catholics began to take advantage of the new educational opportunities. The Sephardic and German Jews were a

W. E. B. Du Bois, a founder of the National Association for the Advancement of Colored People.

secular people who had become assimilated into American society. They preferred to send their sons and a few daughters to established institutions.

The Catholic Church, the largest religious denomination in the United States but mainly a church of the lower classes, preferred to found its own colleges. Church policy was to prepare the sons and daughters of the Catholic middle class for active careers in business and the professions while simultaneously shoring up their loyalty to their faith by means of rigorous schooling in Church doctrine, history, and observance.

The most famous Catholic colleges dated from before the Civil War: Notre Dame had been founded in 1843; Holy Cross (1843) and Boston College (1863) had been explicitly designed as foils to aristocratic Harvard. Thomas Jefferson's dream of a national university was fulfilled by the Roman Catholic Church with the founding in 1889 of the Catholic University of America in Washington, D.C.

On a much smaller scale, educational opportunities for blacks also expanded. The traditional universities in New England and many of the sectarian colleges of the Ohio Valley continued to admit a small number of very well-qualified blacks. W. E. B. Du Bois, a founder of the National Association for the Advancement of Colored People, earned a Ph.D. at Harvard.

WOMEN IN GOVERNMENT

Just as the black cowboy virtually has been forgotten, few historians have noted that women played an important part in government long before they could vote. At the turn of the century, nearly one government worker in three was female. The federal bureaucracy was very much a woman's world.

In the North as well as the South, philanthropists and state governments founded institutions for blacks only. Beginning with Lincoln University in Pennsylvania (founded as the Ashmun Institute in 1854), idealistic benefactors supported schools to train a black elite such as Howard University in Washington (1867) and Fisk in Nashville (1866). After Booker T. Washington's Atlanta Compromise speech of 1895 and the Supreme Court's decision in *Plessy* v. *Ferguson* (1896) gave the go-ahead to segregation at all levels of education, southern state governments founded "agricultural and mechanical" schools patterned after Alabama's Tuskegee Institute (1881), at which blacks could train for manual occupations.

The accomplishments of these institutions should not be underestimated. Few scientific researchers of the time were more productive than Tuskegee Institute's great botanist, George Washington Carver. Nevertheless, the educational level of blacks lagged so far behind that of whites that in 1910, when only 7.7 percent of the American population was illiterate (the figure includes the millions of recent immigrants), one black in three above the age of ten could neither read nor write.

A Thriving Culture

Increasing numbers of white Americans could read, however, and they did. They continued to buy the books of European authors and the works of the older generation of American writers—Emerson, Longfellow, Whitman, Whittier—while supporting new ones. Nevertheless, the greatest poet of the late nineteenth century was virtually unknown until after her death. Emily Dickinson, who led a life of quiet gentility in Amherst, Massachusetts, published only two of her haunting verses before she died in 1886.

By way of contrast, the finest novelists of the period—some say in all American literary history—grew famous and some rich from the demand for their books. Samuel L. Clemens, or Mark Twain, was quintessentially and comprehensively American. A southerner by birth, he deserted the Confederate Army to go west to Nevada, and eventually settled in Hartford, Connecticut, when he became able to choose his style of life. Brilliantly capturing both the hardships and ribald humor of frontier life in *Roughing It* (1872), he earned an international reputation with *The Adventures*

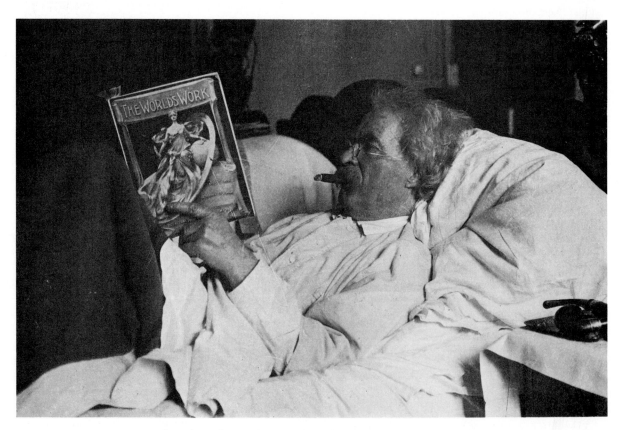

Samuel L. Clemens, known to his wide readership as Mark Twain.

of *Tom Sawyer* (1876) and *The Adventures of Huckle-berry Finn* (1884). American readers often missed the profound and subtle social criticism in Twain's work (as an old man, he grew deeply cynical and bitter), but they read him with pleasure for his rich wit and mastery of the American language.

Twain's favorite settings and themes were robustly western. The other great novelist of the period, Henry James, settled in England because he found American culture stultifying, and he set most of his novels in the Old World and peopled them with cultivated, cosmopolitan characters. But like Twain, he was obsessed with defining America. In *The American* (1877), *The Europeans* (1878), and *Daisy Miller* (1879), James dealt with the relationship of open, albeit less cultured American characters with a jaded and decadent European culture.

A Hunger for Words

A novelist in his own right, William Dean Howells presided over the American literary establishment as editor of the *Atlantic Monthly*. Like *Harper's*, *Forum*, and *The Arena*, the *Atlantic* published a mix of polite poetry, stories, and elegant essays that sometimes dealt with contemporary affairs but always at a fastidious distance. Impressed by the appeal of these magazines and most writers to a cultivated upper class, students of literature have called these years the era of "the genteel tradition."

Beginning in the 1890s, however, the magazines of the genteel tradition began to be challenged by upstarts that catered to the growing middle classes. The new magazines illustrate the interaction of industrial technology, the larger reading public, and the emergence of modern advertising that was first exploited in 1883 by Cyrus H. K. Curtis and his *Ladies' Home Journal*.

Improved methods of manufacturing paper, printing, and photoengraving, as well as the cheap mailing privileges that had been established by Congress in 1879, inspired Curtis to found a magazine for women who were hungry for a world beyond the kitchen and parlor but who found few opportunities in business and the professions. *Ladies' Home Journal* sold for only ten cents (compared with the thirty-five-cent *Atlantic* and *Harper's*) and emphasized women's interests. It was not a feminist publication. On the contrary, editor Edward Bok preached a conservatism that reassured homemakers that their conventional prejudices were proper and right. But it reached much further and much deeper than previous women's magazines, which were little more than fashion plates.

Somewhat more daring were the new general-interest magazines of the 1890s, such as *McClure's*, *Mun-*

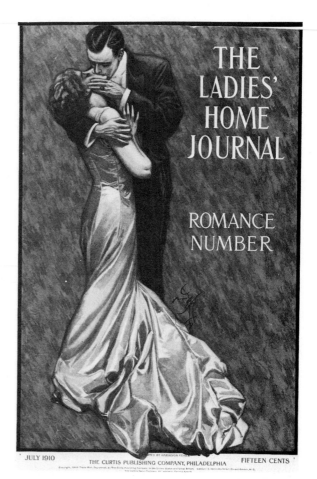

The cover of a 1910 copy of The Ladies' Home Journal.

sey's, and *Cosmopolitan*. They too cost a dime, thus putting them within reach of a massive middle-class readership. (*The Saturday Evening Post*, which Cyrus Curtis bought in 1897, sold for only a nickel.) Without stooping to sensationalism, they presented readers with a livelier writing style than the established journals and a lavish use of photographs and illustrations.

McClure's and *Munsey's* pioneered the curious but successful economics of selling their publications for less than it cost to print and mail them. They made their profit from building up big subscription lists and selling advertising to manufacturers of consumer goods wanting to reach people who had extra money to spend. The subscribership of *McClure's* increased from 8,000 in 1893 to 250,000 in 1895, and that of *Munsey's* grew from 40,000 to 500,000 during the same two years. By 1900, the combined circulation of the four largest magazines totaled 2.5 million per month, more than all American magazines combined only twenty years earlier.

BEST-SELLING NOVELS OF 1906

1. *Coniston*, by Winston Churchill.
2. *Lady Baltimore*, by Owen Wister.
3. *The Fighting Chance*, by Robert W. Chambers.
4. *The House of a Thousand Candles*, by Meredith Nicholson.
5. *Jane Cable*, by George Barr McCutcheon.
6. *The Jungle*, by Upton Sinclair.
7. *The Awakening of Helena Ritchie*, by Margaret Deland.
8. *The Spoilers*, by Rex Beach.
9. *The House of Mirth*, by Edith Wharton.
10. *The Wheel of Life*, by Ellen Glasgow.

Libraries and Lyceums

The cultural hunger of the middle class was also expressed in the construction of free public libraries. Again, men suddenly grown rich gave millions to build them. Enoch Pratt donated $1 million to Baltimore for its library. Wealthy lawyer and presidential candidate Samuel J. Tilden gave New York City $2 million, and William Newberry founded one of the nation's greatest collections of books and valuable manuscripts in Chicago with a munificent bequest of $4 million. Beginning in 1881, the self-taught Andrew Carnegie made libraries his principal philanthropy. Before his death in 1919, Carnegie helped found twenty-eight hundred free public libraries. In keeping with his belief in self-help, Carnegie insisted that the communities in which he built his ponderous gray structures buy the books to fill them and provide the money to keep them up.

The old lyceum idea of sending lecturers on tour to speak to people who lived far from big cities was revived in 1868 by James Redpath. Offering large fees, Redpath persuaded the most distinguished statesmen, ministers, and professors of the day to deliver highly moral and usually informative addresses in auditoriums and specially erected tents in hundreds of small cities and towns.

Chautauqua

The lyceum movement was a throwback to the antebellum period, when only the very wealthy traveled away from home and the middle class still held fast to the Calvinist beliefs that constant work was the human fate and idleness such as casual travel was a sin. The lyceum scheduled programs for the evening, when the day's toil was done.

The phenomenon that was born in 1874 at Lake Chautauqua in New York's scenic Allegheny Mountains was more characteristic of the new age. The "Chautauquas" originally were eight-week summer training programs for Sunday-school teachers. During the 1890s, however, cheap excursion fares on the trains made it easy for people who had little interest in active church work to make the trip for the sake of the cool mountain air and relaxation. To accommodate them, the Chautauqua organizers broadened their program to include lecturers on secular subjects. By the turn of the century, a middle-class family spending a few weeks at Lake Chautauqua could expect to hear lectures by men as prominent as William Jennings Bryan and to watch "magic-lantern" (slide) shows about the Holy Land, Persia, or China presented by professional world travelers. Distinguished professors (and more than a few quacks) expounded on their theories about human character, happy marriage, or childrearing; and German oom-pah bands, Hawaiian dancers, trained dogs, Italian acrobats, and Indian fire-eaters provided lighter entertainment.

Americans at Play

More than two hundred Chautauqua-type resorts were founded, some in the mountains, some at the seaside. Enough people could afford to take a holiday from work that a flourishing tourist economy based on leisure time soon grew up.

Nevertheless, old middle-class beliefs died hard. It was usually necessary for resort promoters to provide at least the appearance of "usefulness" for the vacations they offered. If the middle class trekked to Lake Chautauqua or Lake George in New York and to Long Beach or Atlantic City in New Jersey primarily for rest and relaxation, they could tell others and convince themselves of the cultural and educational aspects of their holiday. They were not just wasting time.

Taking the Cure

A similar conjunction of relaxation and constructive use of time underlay the resorts that were devoted to good health. Owners of mineral springs claimed miraculous powers for their waters. Baths in naturally heated mineral waters or in hot mud were described as nostrums for dozens of afflictions. "Hydropathy," a nineteenth-century medical fad, taught that virtually constant bathing and drinking water improved health. For decades, the wealthy had made prosperous summer resorts of places like Saratoga Springs in New York and White Sulphur Springs in Virginia where "taking the cure" could be done in pleasant natural surroundings among congenial people. Now thousands of middle-class people followed them, again rationalizing their desire for relaxation by extolling the health benefits of their holiday.

An advertisement for M. A. Lesem's Kneipp
Sanitarium in San Diego.

New York's Coney Island amusement park in 1896.

Leisure and the Working Class

Workingpeople could not afford to take off even a week
for the mountains or seaside. However, leisure came to
play a part in their lives, too. Great urban greens,
beginning with New York's magnificent Central Park,
provided free relief on weekends for the teeming masses
of the city's slums.

Just as important, workingpeople in all large cities
were able to enjoy themselves at the commercial
"amusement parks" that sprang up in order to solve à
serious business problem. Traction companies made a
profit only from those parts of their lines that traversed
the crowded parts of the cities and then only on work-
days. However, the expense of center-city real estate
required them to build their sprawling "car barns"
(storage and repair facilities) outside the city. If they
were not required by law to run trolleys on Saturday
and Sunday, they still wanted to make constant use of
their expensive equipment.

In order to encourage people to ride the trolleys beyond the city centers, the traction companies encouraged the construction of amusement parks "at the end
of the line" or, in many cases, built "playlands" themselves. Perhaps the most famous was New York's Coney
Island, located on the ocean in Brooklyn. The fare
from downtown New York was five cents with children
riding free. Once there, for a dollar or two, a large
family could ride the mechanical amusements, such as
George C. Tilyou's Bounding Billows, Barrel of Love,

and Human Roulette Wheel. They could imitate
Buffalo Bill at shooting galleries, visit side shows and
exotic "Somali Villages," or simply loll on the beach
with a picnic lunch or "a weird-looking sausage muffled
up in two halves of a roll."

These homely pleasures were as exciting to bedraggled workers as was a trip to Saratoga to the new middle
class. Most important, Coney Island, Philadelphia's
Willow Grove, Boston's Paragon Park, and Chicago's
Cheltenham Beach represented an organized industry.
Since the amusement parks manufactured and mer-
chandised leisure time, they marked a sharp break with
traditional forms of recreation.

Working-class leisure was more frankly devoted to
simple "fun" than were the middle-class Chautauquas.
Nevertheless, insistence that even a day at Coney
Island was educational and healthful demonstrated the
pervasiveness of traditional ideals. Side shows were
touted with moralistic spiels. Knocking over weighted
bottles for a prize of a Kewpie doll was defined as hon-
ing a valuable skill. Even suggestive dancing by
"hoochie-koochie girls" such as Fatima, the sensation
of the Chicago World's Fair of 1892 who toured the
country for a decade, were described as glimpses into
the culture of the Turkish Empire. A writer in prim
Harper's Weekly approved of the "trolley parks" because

they were "great breathing-places for millions of people in the city who get little fresh air at home." In a nation that was not yet free of its Calvinistic past, every hour must have a purpose.

Bicycles

Good health was also the rationale for a series of sporting manias that swept over the United States at the turn of the century. To some extent, the concern for bodily health was a contribution of German immigrants, whose *Turnvereins,* clubs devoted to calisthenics, were old-country carry-overs like democratic socialism and beer gardens. However, it was obvious as early as the mid-nineteenth century that the urban population walked less and got less exercise generally than had its farmer forebears. In the first issue of the *Atlantic Monthly* in 1858, Thomas Wentworth Higginson asked, "Who in this community really takes exercise? Even the mechanic confines himself to one set of muscles; the blacksmith acquires strength in his right arm, and the dancing teacher in his left leg. But the professional or businessman, what muscles has he at all?" Only a society with plenty of spare time could ask such a question.

Croquet, archery, and tennis, all imported from England, enjoyed a vogue in the 1870s. Roller-skating was even more popular. Great rinks like San Francisco's Olympian Club, with five thousand pairs of skates to rent and a sixty-nine thousand square foot floor, charged inexpensive fees that were within reach of all but the poorest people. But no sporting fad was so widespread as bicycling.

Briefly during the 1860s, French "dandy horses" were seen on American city streets. These crude wooden vehicles were powered by pushing along the ground. About 1876, the "bone crusher," with its six-foot-high front wheel, made its appearance; by 1881, when the League of American Wheelmen was founded, more than twenty-thousand intrepid young Americans were devoting their idle hours to pedaling furiously about parks and city streets.

While some praised bicycling as a "health-giving outdoor exercise," it was condemned by moralists for promoting easy, informal relations between young people of the opposite sex. While young men and ladies might leave home for a Sunday ride in proper groups of their own sex, they found it easy to strike up casual acquaintances in parks far from the eyes of parents and chaperones. More than one worried preacher thought that the bicycle was a first step toward moral chaos.

Indeed, it was on the pneumatic tires of the bicycle that emancipated young women of the 1890s escaped into a refreshing new freedom. The "safety bicycle," which had much the same design as bicycles today, took the risk of broken bones out of the sport. On Sundays, the streets were full of them, and a goodly number carried young women in colorful blouses, sporty broad-brimmed hats, and free-flowing skirts.

The Gibson Girl

The "new look" woman of the 1890s took the name of the "Gibson Girl" after a popular magazine illustrator, Charles Dana Gibson. His vision of ideal American womanoood charmed the nation from Newport high society to working-class suburbs. The Gibson Girl was by no means a feminist. She took little or no interest in woman suffrage or other political issues. Essentially she remained an object of adoration—fine-featured, trim, coy, seductive, and flirtatious.

Neither was the Gibson Girl a shrinking violet. She did not faint after the exertion of climbing a staircase. She played croquet, golf, and tennis. She rode a bicycle without chaperones. She was quite able to take care of herself; one of Gibson's favorite themes was the helplessness of young men in the hands of his self-assured young ladies.

Theodore Roosevelt's oldest daughter, Alice, who became a national sweetheart when the popular waltz "Alice Blue Gown" was named for her, might have been sculpted by Gibson, and middle-class women adopted her style. Photographs of mill girls leaving textile factories in Massachusetts and of stenographers in offices in New York reveal an air of Gibson Girl self-assurance. The new independence of women was also indicated by the fact that they were marrying later. In 1890, the average age for a woman on her wedding day was twenty-two, two or three years older than it had been in 1860.

Sports

The turn of the century was also a golden age of organized sport. Although football (with somewhat different rules from today) was almost exclusively a game played by university students, people of all social classes avidly followed the fortunes of the nearest "Ivy League" team. Basketball, which was invented in 1891 by Dr. James Naismith, a physical-education instructor who was looking for a sport that his students could play during the rigorous Massachusetts winter, was still in its infancy. The spectator sports that obsessed Americans were baseball and boxing. Both had evolved from traditional folk recreations, but by the end of the nineteenth century, both already were organized as money-making enterprises.

The National Pastime

Baseball developed out of two children's games, rounders and town ball, which had been brought to the United States by English immigrants. Abner Doubleday of Cooperstown, New York, is traditionally credited with having devised the rules of the modern American game in 1839, but, in reality, there was little agreement on a number of fine points until well after the Civil War, and Doubleday himself probably never invested a minute in thinking about the game.

While many towns organized teams to play neighbors on special occasions, the professional sport emerged from upper-class baseball "clubs" such as the New York Knickerbockers. Soon concerned more with defeating rivals than with enjoying an afternoon of exercise, the clubs began to hire (at first secretly and despite noisy protest) long-hitting and fast-pitching working-class boys to wear their colors. In 1869, however, the first openly professional team, the Cincinnati Red Stockings, went on tour and defeated all comers.

When thousands of people proved willing to pay admission fees to see well-played games, businessmen in most eastern and midwestern cities organized other professional teams, and in 1876, the National League was founded. (The American League, "the junior circuit," dates from 1901, and the first World Series was played in 1903.) Very profitable enterprises, the teams became focal points of civic pride. Important games often received more attention in the newspapers than did foreign wars. After Brooklyn became a borough of New York City in 1898, its baseball team, the Trolley Dodgers, became the former city's sole symbol of an independent identity.

Boxing and American Society

Watching a fight between two strong men was as ancient a recreation as playing rounders. In 1867, because boxing was becoming a "manly art" practiced by the upper class, an English lord and sportsman, the marquis

The Cinncinati Red Stockings baseball team in 1869.

SCOTT JOPLIN (1868–1917)

Ragtime composer Scott Joplin.

The music of the good old days at the turn of the twentieth century was ragtime, and its foremost practitioner and composer was a Texarkana-born black man named Scott Joplin. Many of the popular histories do not say that. They attribute the birth of the syncopated style of music that both delighted and enraged Americans to Irving Berlin and his "Alexander's Ragtime Band" of 1911. But Berlin was rather late in composing ragtime, and it was not even he who popularized it. Scott Joplin put the music into more than 1 million American parlors with the "Maple Leaf Rag," which was published by John Stark in Sedalia, Missouri, in 1899. "Maple Leaf Rag" sold over 1 million copies of sheet music, perhaps more than any other piece of purely instrumental music. (Joplin wrote words to the song only later.)

Both the Texas and Arkansas sides of the state-line town of Texarkana claim to be Joplin's birthplace. His father was an ex-slave who urged his children to learn a trade, which was about the only realistic means that a black person had of ensuring comfort and security in the South or the North in the late nineteenth century. It was the course of action that, during the 1890s, Booker T. Washington codified into a gospel.

By the 1890s, however, Scott Joplin's life had taken another turn, which he attributed to the fact that his mother, who had been born free in Kentucky, worked as a laundress for several white families in Texarkana.

It was through his mother that Scott's reputation as a musical prodigy became known among the city's whites. The Joplin family was musical; there were any number of cheap instruments around their house, and all the children learned to play at least one. Before he was seven years old, Scott had mastered the bugle and guitar. Then he discovered the piano, and within months he was the talk of his mother's employers. A German music teacher who heard him play was so impressed that he gave Scott lessons for free. It was through his teacher, Joplin said, that he was introduced to and instilled with love for the great European composers for piano, a professional expertise rare among blacks of the era.

By the time he was fourteen, Scott's single-minded dedication to music caused a violent rift between him and his father that may never have been healed. Rather than give up the piano and take up a trade, Scott left home. Thus began an obscure period of his life that, however, can be conjectured.

There was only one class of establishment in which a black musicmaker could make a living. Through the 1880s and early 1890s, Joplin was "the professor," as pianists were called, in saloons, gambling casinos, and brothels (then called honky-tonks) up and down the Mississippi Valley and as far west as Oklahoma City. He played in the fanciest and highest-priced houses, such as Lulu White's famous "high yellow house" in New Orleans and Mother Johnson's lavish brothel in St. Louis. He also remembered playing some wretched dives that were run by madams with names like Ready Money, Suicide Queen, and Scarface Mary. What was just a living for many "professors," however, was an education for Joplin. Already a capable classical pianist and familiar with the black musical tradition, he mastered the sentimental themes that were popular among whites and became acquainted with other southern regional forms from other black professors.

For a few years during the early 1890s, Joplin toured with a group that included two of his brothers and appeared as far east as Syracuse, New York, where he published one of several waltzes. Then, however, he went to Sedalia, Missouri, to attend the George R. Smith College for Negroes (probably to sharpen his knowledge of the classics, for such institutions regarded the folk music of the black people as beneath them). While a student, Joplin continued to play the honky-tonks, and it was after a Sedalia honky-tonk, the Maple Leaf Club, that he named the composition that made him financially independent.

Already by 1900, when Joplin and his publisher struck it rich and moved to St. Louis, ragtime was sweeping the nation, displacing the waltzes of the Gay Nineties. Only a few people realized, however, that the form was more than a novelty, particularly in the hands of Scott Joplin. With his formal training in the classics, Joplin did precisely what Mozart, Chopin, Brahms, and Dvořák had done. He applied his knowledge to the rhythms and structures of folk dances, especially the cakewalk and two-step favored by southern blacks.

English music critic Arnold Bennett understood Joplin's intent and acidly criticized his American colleagues for condemning ragtime as "nigger whorehouse music." The trouble, Bennett wrote, was that "the American dilettanti never did and never will look in the right quarters for vital art. A really original artist struggling under their very noses has small chance of being recognized by them, the reason being that they are imitative with no real opinion of their own." Indeed, the name *ragtime* (which Joplin did not particularly like) was originally pejorative, signifying music that had been carelessly stitched together.

While he continued to write rags, tangos, and waltzes, in order to support himself, Joplin was developing ideas with which to overcome the prejudices of American critics and make a lasting contribution to American music. In music critic Rudi Blech's words, Joplin was aiming at a musical form that was "respectful of but not subservient to European music, a racially balanced music."

In 1902, he wrote a folk ballet, *The Ragtime Dance*, which was performed once in Sedalia, and then forgotten. In 1913, he applied for a copyright for an opera, *A Guest of Honor*, but either because he never found a libretto that satisfied him or because he quarreled with his friend and publisher John Stark, the opera was never published and has been lost.

In 1916, when his second wife was forced to commit him to an insane asylum (Joplin had contracted syphilis, probably as a young man), he was said to have been working on a symphony that synthesized European form with melody and rhythm of African origin. If so, this symphony also has been lost. However, *Treemonisha*, another unfinished opera, did survive. Following the revival of interest in Joplin's music after the popular movie *The Sting* used another of his compositions as a theme, *Treemonisha* was produced in Atlanta. The unpolished opera excited many music critics with its bold attempt to use rag, barbershop-quartet harmonies, "country music," spirituals, and Negro work chants in an operatic setting. And yet, it was unfinished and unpolished. In the end, Joplin failed in his great mission.

Oddly, Joplin died just as the musical form that had supported him well, if not lavishly, was dying out. By the end of the First World War, ragtime had gone out of style in the United States. Essentially European musical comedy replaced it in eastern music halls, while driving New Orleans jazz, known today as "Dixieland," came into vogue among blacks, some whites, and venturesome "flaming youth" of the 1920s. Because New Orleans jazz was more sophisticated than ragtime, allowing considerably more room for creativity, it is impossible not to wonder what Joplin might have done had he not died at the young age of forty-nine.

of Queensberry, devised a code of rules that was quickly accepted throughout Europe and the United States. The Queensberry rules were hardly strict by contemporary standards. One read that "all attempts to inflict injury by gouging or tearing the flesh with the fingers or nails and biting shall be deemed foul."

As with baseball, the opportunities to make money from paid admissions encouraged promoters to search out popular heroes. The first to win a national reputation was a burly Boston Irishman named John L. Sullivan, who started out by traveling the country and offering $50 and later $1,000 to anyone who could last four rounds with him. Between 1882 and 1892, "the Boston Strong Boy" bloodied one challenger after another, personally collecting as much as $20,000 a fight and making much more for the entrepreneurs who organized his bouts.

The crowds that watched the great championship bouts included comparatively few workingpeople. However, they followed their heroes in the new sports pages of the newspapers, which, as with baseball, devoted column after column to important fights. Because Sullivan and his successor as heavyweight champion, Gentleman Jim Corbett, were Irish, they became objects of ethnic pride. So entangled in the culture did the sport become that when a black boxer rose to the top, he caused an anxiety that reached into the halls of Congress.

Jack Johnson

Jack Johnson won the heavyweight crown in 1908 and proceeded to batter every challenger who stepped forth. Such a feat by a black man rankled many white Americans. Johnson aggravated the hatred for him by gleefully insulting every "great white hope" who emerged. A tragically indiscreet man, he flaunted his white mistresses at a time when the color line was being clearly drawn in every American institution.

Southern states, which had been the most hospitable to professional prize fights, forbade Johnson to fight within their borders. Politicians raved at every Johnson victory and gaudy public appearance. Congress actually passed a law that prohibited the interstate shipment of a film of Johnson's victory over former champion Jim Jeffries in Reno in 1910. Finally, in 1912, racism defeated him not in the ring but through an indictment under the Mann Act, which forbade "transporting women" across state lines "for immoral purposes." (Johnson had taken his common-law wife to another state.)

Johnson fled to Europe, and then to the West Indies. But he was unhappy away from home and agreed to

Jim Jeffries (left) and Jack Johnson boxing in the ring.

fight the white boxer Jess Willard in Havana in 1915. He lost, and it was widely believed that he threw the match as part of a deal with the Justice Department by which he could reenter the United States without fear of arrest. A famous photograph of the knockout shows Johnson on his back, apparently relaxed and unhurt, and shielding his eyes from the Caribbean sun.

For Further Reading

Frederick Lewis Allen, *The Big Change* (1952), provides a good brief overview of American society as it evolved around the turn of the century. An earlier and much longer (six-volume) book that is well worth reading is by journalist Mark Sullivan, *Our Times* (1926–35). Henry F. May sees the period as *The End of American Innocence* (1959), an arguable idea because it is vague, but excellently put in this book. Van Wyck Brooks, *The Confident Years, 1885–1915* (1952), has a somewhat different perspective, and quite unlike May is Ray Ginger, *The Age of Excess* (1965). An extremely useful overview is Robert Wiebe, *The Search for Order, 1877–1920* (1967).

On specific subjects discussed in this chapter, see Foster Rhea Dulles, *America Learns to Play* (1940), and J. R. Krout, *Annals of American Sport* (1924). There is a huge, mostly recent, literature on the changing status of women. Perhaps the most important is Ann Douglas, *The Feminization of American Culture* (1977).

On Teddy Roosevelt as a cultural phenomenon, the best appreciation is Henry F. Pringle, *Theodore Roosevelt* (1931). Also see John M. Blum, *The Republican Roosevelt* (1954), and W. H. Harbaugh, *Power and Responsibility: The Life and Times of Theodore Roosevelt* (1961).

A Compulsion to Reform
The Emergence of the Progressives After 1900

In 1787, when many of his political cronies were launching the Constitution, in part because they feared social turmoil, Thomas Jefferson wrote several letters in which he advocated periodic revolution as essential to the health of a free society. "A little rebellion, now and then, is a good thing," he wrote to James Madison, "as necessary in the political world as storms in the physical." To another friend a few months later he added, "The tree of liberty must be refreshed from time to time with the blood of patriots and tyrants."

Was Jefferson correct? Some historians believe that he was. They argue that essential changes have been brought about in the course of American history only because of violent protest and riot by people with deep grievances or, at the least, because of the fear of disorder among those who held the reins of power.

Other historians discount the importance of riot and rebellion as significant forces in American development. They point out that the causes of social disturbance are as likely to be trivial or destructive as to represent a serious need for progressive change. These scholars emphasize the stability that has characterized the American experience during an epoch of world history that has been anything but stable. Only once in two centuries has there been a revolution in the United States, and it, the Civil

Members of the Women's Trade Union League demonstrating in New York.

War, was grandly unsuccessful. Historians attribute this to the fact that a mechanism of reform is built into the Constitution in the amendment process. In the United States, as in few other countries, strict and orthodox adherence to the instrument of government has resulted in peaceful change.

Just as important, for the Constitution is amended only in matters of fundamental law, Americans as a people periodically have felt the impulse to rid the country of political and social abuses. Sometimes by violent protest and sometimes by peaceful petition, they have worked to restore the principles of liberty, democracy, and equality, to which, they believed, the United States was consecrated. Indeed, so intense has been the fervor to reform that it may be called a *compulsion*.

The Progressive Era

The first decade and a half of the twentieth century, which has come to be known as the Progressive era, was just such an age of reform. The changes that the progressives demanded and, for the most part, put into effect were not original with the new century. The movement borrowed ideas from the Mugwumps, the preachers of the Social Gospel, woman suffragists, urban social workers, moralists, even the adherents of various socialistic theories of the preceding era. William Allen White oversimplified the ancestry of the twentieth-century reform movement he supported, but he made a point worth noticing when he wrote that the progressives "caught the Populists in swimming and stole all of their clothing except the frayed underdrawers of free silver."

Nevertheless, whereas the social protesters of the late nineteenth century reached only parts of the American population—small parts except in the case of the Populists—the reformers of the early twentieth century encouraged Americans at the polls to institute their programs for change.

Who Were the Progressives?

Few progressives came from the industrial and financial elite. Fewer still rose from the masses of laboring people and poor farmers. For the most part, the progressives were middle class. Those who took to the stump or typewriter and those who ran for public office were lawyers, physicians, ministers, teachers, journalists, social workers, small businessmen, and the wives and daughters of the middle classes whose first reform was personal: to break free of the nursery, parlor, and chapel in order to play a part in public life.

The progressives were acutely aware that they were "in between." Eternally knocking about in the back of the progressive mind were the assumptions that what was good about America was its middle class and that the middle class was threatened by both plutocrats from above and the potentially dangerous mob from below.

Thus, progressives objected to the immense power of the great corporations or, at least, to the way that power was used. They wanted the Rockefellers and the Morgans to be forced to behave in ways that were compatible with the good of society.

While the progressives were concerned with the material and moral welfare of those below them on the social ladder, they also feared them. In the cities, progressive reformers often voiced concern that the slums were tinderboxes of anger, ready to explode in destructive anarchy. In the Midwest and West, most progressive leaders had been staunch enemies of the Populists during the 1890s, having condemned them for social irresponsibility. William Allen White, a leader of the independent Progressive party between 1912 and 1916, had made his name as the author of a scathing piece of anti-Populist propaganda called "What's the Matter with Kansas?" Years later, a little sheepishly, White explained that he had been impelled to write it not because of an idea that had occurred to him in his study, but because he had been jostled on a street corner in Emporia, Kansas, by "lazy, greasy fizzles," impoverished farmers whose crudeness and vulgarity, fruits of their poverty, had offended him above all else.

Of Towns, WASPs, and Righteousness

The progressives' disdain for "hayseeds" also revealed their urban character. Progressivism was a movement

---

REFORM

What is reform? One dictionary defines it as "to change into a new and improved condition; removal of faults or abuses so as to restore to a former good state, or bring from bad to good." In the context of American history, *reform* has also come to mean peaceful, usually gradual change, as opposed to violent and sudden change, which Americans define as *revolution*.

TRAINING LOBSTERS

Finley Peter Dunne, who wrote a column in Irish dialect for a Chicago newspaper, was a friend to reform, but shared few of the illusions of the progressives that improvement was an easy matter of acting. According to his commentator, Mr. Dooley: "A man that'l expict to thrain lobsters to fly in a year is called a loonytic; but a man that thinks men can be tur-rned into angels by an iliction is called a rayformer, an' remains at large."

of the cities and towns, not of the countryside. It is no coincidence that the progressive president, Theodore Roosevelt, remains the only chief executive in American history to have been born in a large city, New York. Even those progressives who represented rural states, such as Robert M. La Follette of Wisconsin and George Norris of Nebraska, had grown up in small towns. As boys, they had rubbed elbows with farmers, but they had not walked behind plows or stood full of anxiety next to their wagons as agents weighed and graded the year's crop, the next year's standard of living.

A few progressives represented minority groups. Louis Brandeis, a Louisville, Kentucky, lawyer who helped design the Democratic party program, was Jewish. Alfred E. Smith and Robert F. Wagner, progressive politicians in New York State, were Irish and German respectively and devoted Roman Catholics. W. E. B. Du Bois, who supported most progressive reforms and helped to found the National Association for the Advancement of Colored People, was black. But they were exceptions. Most progressive leaders were old-stock Americans of northern European origin.

They were not a particularly broad-minded lot. The progressives inclined to be moralistic to the point of self-righteousness, ever searching for the absolute right and absolute wrong in every political disagreement—and finding them. California's Hiram Johnson irked even his strongest supporters with his clenched-teeth sanctimony. Robert M. La Follette did not know what a sense of humor was, let alone lay claim to one. To "Fighting Bob" and to many other progressives, life was a long holy crusade for what was right.

Theodore Roosevelt described the beginning of an election campaign in biblical terms: "We stand at Armageddon and do battle for the Lord." Lantern-jawed, unsmiling Woodrow Wilson, a seventeenth-century Calvinist in wing collar and pince-nez, eventually destroyed himself because he would not yield even a little on minor disagreements with his critics in order to save what he saw as the most important cause of his life.

Unity and Variety

Almost all progressives were statists. Unlike many earlier social critics, who considered strong government to be part of the problem, the progressives believed that an active, assertive state was the only force that could bring the corporations to heel and provide for the welfare of the weak and unfortunate. In *The Promise of American Life*, published in 1909, Herbert Croly explicitly called for serving "Jeffersonian ends," the good of the common people, by the use of "Hamiltonian means," the power of the state. What *business* was to the industrialists, *democracy* to the Jacksonians, and *liberty* to the Founding Fathers, *government* was to the progressives: the single word that summed up the central spirit of the age.

Beyond this general inclination, however, everything about progressivism was variety. Progressivism was a frame of mind rather than a single coherent program. Indeed, some progressives differed from other progressives as radically as they differed from their enemies, whom they generally called "conservatives" or the "Old Guard."

For example, while many progressives believed that labor unions had the right to exist and fight for the betterment of their members, others opposed unions for the same reason that they disliked powerful corporations: organized special-interest groups were at odds with American ideals. On one occasion, a few leaders of the National American Woman Suffrage Association said that women should serve as strikebreakers if by so doing, they could win jobs currently held by men.

The progressives sometimes disagreed about social action such as laws that regulated child labor. By 1907, about two-thirds of the states, governed or influenced by progressives, forbade the employment of children under fourteen years of age. However, when progressives in Congress passed a federal child-labor law in 1916, the progressive president, Woodrow Wilson, expressed grave doubts before signing it. Wilson wor-

PROGRESSIVES

It makes a difference whether the word *progressive* is written with a lower-case *p* or a capital *P*. In the lower case, *progressive* refers to the broad impulse that motivated all the many kinds of reformers during the first couple of decades of the twentieth century. A *Progressive*, however, was a member of the Progressive party, an offshoot of the Republican party, which was organized in 1912. Not every progressive, in a word, was a Progressive.

A white lynch mob prepares to kill its victim, a black man, in Paris, Texas, 1893.

ried that to forbid children to work infringed on their rights as citizens. This was essentially the same reasoning that was offered by the conservative Supreme Court in *Hammer v. Dagenhart* (1918), which struck down the law.

Many, perhaps most, progressives could not imagine blacks as full citizens. How, they asked, could a population that was 45 percent illiterate, as blacks were in 1900, contribute to an America that was based on educated citizenship? The increased oppression of blacks that began during the 1890s continued unabated during the Progressive era, sometimes furthered by white politicians who were otherwise committed to reform, such as Governor James K. Vardaman of Mississippi and Governor Jeff Davis of Arkansas.

Other progressives, regarding racial prejudice and discrimination as among the worst evils afflicting America, fought for equality. Journalist Ray Stannard Baker wrote a scathing and moving exposé of racial segregation in a series of articles entitled "Following the Color Line." In 1910, white progressives, including Jane Addams, joined with the black Niagara Movement to form the National Association for the Ad-

vancement of Colored People. Except for his race, W. E. B. Du Bois, the guiding spirit of the Niagara Movement, was an ideal progressive: genteel, middle class, university educated, and devoted to the ideas that an elite should govern and that this "talented tenth" would lead blacks to civil equality in the United States.

Some progressives were ultranationalists. Others clung to a humanism that embraced all people of all countries. Some progressives were expansionists in foreign policy. Senator Albert J. Beveridge of Indiana saw no conflict in calling for an expansion of democracy at home while urging the United States to rule colonies

---

LYNCH LAW

Progressive reforms made little difference in the lives of American blacks. Indeed, during the first five years of the twentieth century, lynch law reached its peak in the United States. For five years, blacks were lynched at a rate of almost one every other day.

abroad without regard to the will of their inhabitants. Theodore Roosevelt not only brought reform to the White House, but was more of a militarist than any president who preceded him, including those who had been career generals. Other progressives were anti-imperialists. Most were antimilitaristic. And a few, such as Jane Addams and William Jennings Bryan, were pacifists.

Forebears

Such a diverse movement had a diverse ancestry. From the Populists, the progressives adopted the demand for the direct election of senators; a graduated income tax that would hit the wealthy harder than the poor and middle classes; the initiative, referendum, and recall; regulation of big business; and government ownership of natural monopolies such as the railroads, the telegraph, and local public utilities such as water, gas, and electric companies.

The progressives also looked back to the other late-nineteenth-century reform movements. They emphasized "good government" quite as much as had the Liberal Republicans and Mugwumps. Indeed, in the progressives' intense moralism, their compulsion to stamp out personal sin as well as social and political evils, they sometimes sounded like the evangelical preachers of the early nineteenth century.

Finally, in exalting expertise and efficiency, and in their belief that a new social *order* must be devised to replace the social chaos of the late nineteenth century, the progressives owed a debt to people whom they usually considered their enemies. Marcus A. Hanna, described as a conservative when he died in 1904, had spent half his life preaching collaboration between capital and labor as an alternative to dangerous class conflict. This was a progressive ideal.

John D. Rockefeller, an archvillain to progressive propagandists, was the leading nineteenth-century spokesman for the rational, coordinated operation of industry. In her influential magazine articles on the "History of the Standard Oil Company," which were published in 1904, progressive journalist Ida M. Tarbell ruthlessly exposed Rockefeller's dubious business practices. But despite a deep personal antipathy for the billionaire (who had ruined her father), Tarbell could not help but admire the efficiency of his company.

Frederick W. Taylor, the inventor of "scientific management," was rarely described as a progressive and personally took little interest in politics. Nevertheless, in his conviction that the engineer's approach to solving problems could be fruitfully applied to human behavior, he was a forebear of the progressive movement. The progressives believed that society could be en-gineered as readily as Taylor engineered machine tools and the way a man wielded a shovel.

Most curious of all, many progressives praised the chancellor of Germany, Prince Otto von Bismarck, as an inspiration to them. Although a political reactionary, Bismarck sponsored a comprehensive program of social services in his nation such as the progressives hoped to imitate in the United States, and the German civil service was famous for its efficiency and honesty.

Progressives in Action

Progressivism began on the municipal level. Well before the turn of the century, as a result of widespread disgust with the corruption that had become endemic to American city government, a number of reform mayors were elected. They were not, as had been their predecessors, easily ousted after a year or two.

"Good Government"

One of the first of the successful city reformers was Hazen S. Pingree, a shoe manufacturer who was elected mayor of Detroit in 1890. He spent seven years battling

Progressive journalist Ida Tarbell. Standard Oil executives assumed she was a gullible female reporter, but learned otherwise after she effectively exposed Standard Oil founder John D. Rockefeller's unsavory business practices.

the corrupt alliance between the owners of the city's public utilities and Detroit councilmen.

More successful was Samuel M. Jones, a businessman in nearby Toledo, Ohio. Running for mayor of his city in 1897, Jones was mocked as an addle-brained and foolish eccentric. In addition to waging a long campaign against business support of crooked politicians, he ran his factory on the basis of fair treatment and profit sharing with his employees. Other capitalists laughed at "Golden Rule" Jones, a nickname that stuck. But it did him no harm at the polls. He won the election and proved to be a skillful administrator. Within two years, he rooted graft out of Toledo's city hall.

Another progressive mayor from Ohio was Cleveland's Thomas L. Johnson. A former single-tax advocate, Johnson was elected in 1901. Not only did he clean up a dirty government, but he actively supported woman suffrage, reformed the juvenile courts, took over public utilities from avaricious owners, and put democracy to work by presiding over open "town meetings" at which citizens could make known their grievances and suggestions.

Lincoln Steffens, a staff writer for *McClure's* magazine, called Cleveland "the best-governed city in the United States," and Steffens was the expert. In 1903, Steffens authored a sensational series of articles for *McClure's* called "The Shame of the Cities." Researching his subject carefully in the country's major cities, he named grafters, exposed corrupt connections between elected officials and dishonest businessmen, and demonstrated how ordinary people suffered from corrupt government in the quality of their daily lives.

Steffens's exposés hastened the movement for city reform. Joseph W. Folk of St. Louis, whose tips put Steffens onto the story, was able to indict more than thirty politicians and prominent Missouri businessmen for bribery and perjury as a result of the outcry that greeted "The Shame of the Cities." Hundreds of reform mayors elected after 1904 owed their success to the solemn, bearded journalist.

The Muckrakers

No single force was more important in spreading the gospel of progressivism than the mass-circulation magazines. Already well established by the turn of the century thanks to their cheap price and lively style, journals such as *McClure's, The Arena, Collier's, Cosmopolitan,* and *Everybody's* became even more successful when their editors discovered the popular appetite for the journalism of exposure.

The discovery was almost accidental. Samuel S. Mc-

Journalist Lincoln Steffens, pioneer of investigative journalism, exposed corrupt practices in America's big cities.

Clure himself had no particular interest in reform. He just wanted to sell more magazines so that he could woo more paying advertisers. He hired Ida M. Tarbell and Lincoln Steffens at generous salaries not because they were reformers, but because they wrote well. But when Tarbell's and Steffens's exposés caused circulation to soar, McClure and other editors were hooked.

The mass-circulation magazines were soon dominated by sensational revelations about corruption in government, chicanery in business, social evils like child labor and prostitution, and other subjects that lent themselves to indignant, excited treatment. In addition to his series on racial segregation, Ray Stannard Baker dissected the operations of the great railroads. John Spargo, an English-born Socialist, discussed child labor in "The Bitter Cry of the Children." David Graham Phillips, who was to become successful as a novelist dealing with social themes, exposed the domination of the Senate by millionaires.

Theodore Roosevelt called the new journalists "muckrakers" after a character in John Bunyan's religious classic, *Pilgrim's Progress.* The writers were so busy raking through the muck of American society, he said, that they failed to look up and see its glories in the stars.

He had a point, especially when after a few years the quality of exposure journalism deteriorated into sloppy research and wild, ill-founded accusations made for the sake of attracting attention. During the first decade of the century, no fewer than two thousand articles and books of exposure were published. Inevitably, the conscientious muckrakers ran out of solid material, and muckraking as a profession attracted incompetent hacks.

But the dirt could be real enough, and the early reform journalists were as determined to stick to the facts as to arouse their readers' indignation. Their work disseminated constructive progressive ideas from one end of the country to the other. The ten leading muckraking journals had a combined circulation of 3 million. No doubt the readership was many times larger.

In the Jungle with Upton Sinclair

The most successful of the muckrakers was novelist Upton Sinclair. His cometlike rise to fame and the rapid spread of the city-manager scheme of government and the "Oregon system" of political reform are good examples of just how suddenly progressivism seized on the American imagination.

Sinclair was a young, unknown Socialist when, in 1906, he wrote a novel about how ethnic prejudice and economic exploitation in Chicago turned an immigrant into a revolutionary who was determined to smash the capitalist system. *The Jungle* was too radical for the mass-circulation magazines, and Sinclair had to turn to a Socialist party weekly newspaper, the *Appeal to Reason,* to find an audience. Even the *Appeal* had a large subscription list. One issue sold over 1 million copies, and *The Jungle* was a mighty success, reaching even the desk of President Roosevelt. It sold one hundred thousand copies in book form, an extraordinary figure at the time.

Sinclair's book converted some of its readers to socialism. But the passages that made it a best seller were those that realistically and luridly described the conditions under which meat was processed in Chicago slaughterhouses. *The Jungle* publicized well-documented tales of rats ground up into sausage, workers with tuberculosis coughing on the meat they packed, and filth at every point along the disassembly line.

"I aimed at the nation's heart," Sinclair later said ruefully, "and hit it in the stomach." He meant that within months of the publication of *The Jungle,* a federal meat-inspection bill that had been languishing in Congress was rushed through under public pressure and promptly signed by President Roosevelt. It and a second Pure Food and Drug Act, which forbade food processors to use dangerous adulterants (the pet project of a chemist in the Agriculture Department, Dr. Harvey W. Wiley) expanded government power in a way that had been inconceivable just a few years earlier.

Reform in Government

The spread of the city-manager system of government was scarcely less dramatic. The first town to adopt the plan was Staunton, Virginia, in 1908. The small city abolished the office of mayor. The voters elected a city council, which then hired a nonpolitical, professionally trained administrator to serve as city manager. The progressives reasoned that democracy was protected by the people's control of the council; and because the daily operations of the city were supervised by an executive who was free of political influence, they would be carried out without regard to special interests.

It was an original notion, but did not prove universally successful. Nevertheless, by 1915, only seven years after Staunton's experiment, over four hundred mostly medium-size cities had adopted it.

The "Oregon system" was the brainchild of one of the first progressives to make an impact at the state level. William S. U'ren, a former Populist and single taxer, believed that the remedy for corruption in government was simple: more democracy. The trouble lay in the ability of efficient, well-organized, and wealthy special interests to thwart the good intentions of the people. Time after time, U'ren pointed out, elected officials handily forgot their campaign promises and worked closely with the corporations to pass bad laws or defeat good ones:

In 1902, U'ren persuaded the Oregon legislature to adopt the initiative, recall, and referendum, which returned government to the people. The Oregon system also included the first primary law. It took the power to nominate candidates for public office away from the bosses and gave it to the voters. Finally, U'ren led the national movement to choose United States senators by popular vote rather than in the state legislatures.

U'ren lived to the ripe old age of ninety, long enough to see twenty states adopt the initiative and thirty, the referendum. A number of progressive states also instituted primaries of one kind or another, but until the 1970s, the primary was a less popular idea. In the South, the "white primary," by which Democratic party candidates were chosen, was used in the interests of racism: since most whites were Democrats, the primary was the contest that counted; and because the primary was a "private" election, blacks could be legally excluded from it.

A careful diner cleans his food of contaminants in this cartoon from the British magazine, Puck.

"Fighting Bob" and the Wisconsin Idea

The career of Wisconsin's "Fighting Bob" La Follette is almost a history of progressivism in itself. Born in 1855, he studied law and served three terms in Congress before 1890. He showed few signs of the crusader's compulsion until he was approached by an agent of Wisconsin's millionaire Republican boss, Philetus Sawyer, and offered a bribe if he would fix the verdict in a trial. La Follette flew into a rage at the shameless audacity of the suggestion, and he never quite calmed down for the rest of his life.

In 1900, he defied the Republican organization and ran for governor, attacking the railroad and lumber interests that dominated the state and promising to devote the resources of the government to the service of the people. La Follette's timing was perfect. A state that recently had rebuffed the Populists was ready for reform, and he was elected.

As governor, La Follette pushed through a comprehensive system of regulatory laws that required every business that touched the public interest to conform to clear-cut rules and submit to close inspection of its operations. He went beyond the negative, or regulatory, powers of government to create agencies that provided positive services for the people. La Follette's "Wisconsin idea" held that in the complex modern world, people and government needed experts to work on their behalf. A railroad baron could not be kept on a leash unless the government had the support of knowledgeable specialists who were as canny as the railroad men. Insurance premiums could not be held at reasonable levels unless the state was able to determine what profit was just and what was rapacious. The government could not intervene to determine what was fair in a labor dispute unless it had the help of the labor experts and economists.

La Follette formed a close and mutually beneficial relationship with the University of Wisconsin. His organization generously supported the institution, making it one of the nation's great universities at a time when most state-supported schools were little more than agricultural colleges. In return, distinguished professors like Richard Ely, Selig Perlman, and John Rogers Commons put their expertise at La Follette's disposal. The law school helped build up the first legislative reference library in the United States so that assemblymen would no longer have to rely on lobbyists to draft their laws.

Nor did La Follette neglect farmers. The university's School of Agriculture not only taught future farmers, but carried out research programs that addressed problems faced daily in Wisconsin's fields. La Follette even made use of the football team. When enemies threatened him with violence if he spoke at a political rally,

Robert La Follette speaking to a crowd in Cumberland, Wisconsin, in 1897.

he showed up in the company of Wisconsin's burly linemen, who folded their arms and surrounded the platform. There was no trouble.

Perhaps La Follette's most important contribution to progressivism was his application of machine methods to the cause of reform. He was idealistic. But he was not naive. In order to ensure that his reforms would not be reversed, he built an organization that was as finely integrated as Boss Tweed's. Party workers in every precinct got out the vote, and if they did not violate La Follette's exacting demands for honesty in public office, they were rewarded with government patronage.

In 1906, La Follette took his crusade to Washington as a United States senator. He held that office until his death in 1925, and made several unsuccessful tries at winning the presidency. In Wisconsin and elsewhere he was loved as few politicians have been. He was "Fighting Bob," incorruptible and unyielding in what he regarded as right. La Follette's thick, neatly cropped head of brown hair combed straight back, which turned snow white with years, waved wildly during his passionate speeches. He looked like an Old Testament prophet, and, in a way, La Follette devoted his life to saving the soul of American society, as Jeremiah had done for Israel.

Progressives in Other States

In New York State, Charles Evans Hughes came to prominence as a result of his investigation into public utilities and insurance companies. Tall, erect, dignified, with a smartly trimmed beard such as was going out of fashion at the turn of the century, he lacked the charisma of La Follette and other progressives. If they were humorless in their intensity, Hughes was "a cold-blooded creature" (in the words of decidedly hot-blooded Theodore Roosevelt). But he was un-

shakably honest as governor of New York between 1906 and 1910.

William E. Borah was not elected to the Senate from Idaho in 1906 as a progressive. On the contrary, his career in politics to that date had been characterized by a close and compliant relationship with the mining and ranching interests that ran the state. In 1906, he made a national reputation as the prosecutor in the murder trial of the secretary-treasurer of the Western Federation of Miners, William D. "Big Bill" Haywood, a case that many thought was brought at the behest of the mine owners to destroy the radical union.

Once in the Senate, however, Borah usually voted with the growing progressive bloc. This record and his isolationism—like many westerners, Borah believed that the United States was corrupted by close association with foreign powers—guaranteed his reelection until he died in office in 1940. Only a generation later was it discovered that the old lion had accepted gifts of money from unlikely donors under rather dubious circumstances.

It is impossible to imagine Hiram Johnson of California accepting money other than in a spotlight so as to emphasize the perfect honesty of the transaction. He came to progressivism by much the same path as had La Follette. A prim, tight-lipped lawyer of no particular distinction, Johnson won notoriety after he took over the prosecution of the corrupt political machine of Abe Ruef in San Francisco.

At first it appeared to be an ordinary graft case such as was all too common at the time. Ruef and his ally, Mayor Eugene E. Schmitz, collected payoffs from brothels, gambling dens, and thieves in return for running a wide-open city. In the wake of the great San Francisco earthquake and fire of 1906, Ruef set up a system by which all those who wished to profit from the rebuilding had to clear their plans with him. Scarcely a street could be rebuilt or a cable-car line laid out until money changed hands. On one occasion, Ruef pocketed $250,000, of which he kept one-quarter, gave one-quarter to Schmitz, and distributed the remainder among the aldermen whose votes were needed to authorize public works. Like other city bosses, Ruef also bought and sold judges in lawsuits.

Johnson discovered that Ruef not only was associated with vice and petty graft, but was intimately allied with the most powerful corporation in the state, the Southern Pacific Railroad. The distinguished and ostensibly upright directors of the Southern Pacific, men whom Johnson had admired, were tangled in a web that stretched to include profiting from the misfortune of the wretched syphilitic whores on the city's notorious Barbary Coast.

ATTEMPTED MURDER?

In late May 1908, Robert La Follette led a filibuster against a financial bill of which he disapproved. He spoke for nearly seventeen hours before giving up. Through much of this time, La Follette sipped a tonic of milk and raw eggs prepared in the Senate dining room. After he had been taken violently ill on the floor, it was discovered that there was enough ptomaine in the mixture to kill a man. Because no one else suffered from eating in the Senate dining room that day, many assumed that La Follette's enemies had tried to kill him.

Johnson turned into "a volcano in perpetual eruption, belching fire and smoke." Never again would he assume that great wealth and a varnish of propriety indicated a decent man. His sense of personal rectitude was so great that it cost him a chance to be president. In 1920, Republican party bosses such as Johnson loathed asked him to run as vice-president in order to balance the conservative presidential nominee, Warren G. Harding. Johnson turned them down in a huff. As a result, when Harding died in office in 1923, he was succeeded by the passive Calvin Coolidge instead of the volcano from California. Coolidge adulated the big businessmen whom Johnson reflexively distrusted. If ever there were an example of an individual's decision profoundly affecting the course of history, Johnson's was it.

American Socialist Eugene V. Debs speaking in Canton, Ohio.

On the Fringe of Progressivism

Most progressives advocated municipal ownership of public utilities, but they were staunchly opposed to socialism. Indeed, progressive politicians like La Follette and Johnson warned that the reforms they proposed were necessary to preserve the institution of private property from a rising Red tide in American politics.

This message had a special urgency in the early years of the twentieth century because the Socialist party of America, founded in 1900, came very close to establishing itself as a major force in American politics. Pieced together by a number of local Socialist organizations, former Populists, and a group that broke with the older Socialist Labor party, the Socialist party nominated labor leader Eugene V. Debs for president in 1900, and he won 94,768 votes. In 1904, running again, Debs threw a scare into progressives and conservatives alike by polling 402,460.

The Socialists

Personally, Debs bore some resemblance to the progressive leaders. He was a fiery, flamboyant orator, a master of the theatrical and gymnastic style of public speaking that not only was necessary in an age when sound amplification was primitive, but was favored by Americans in their preachers and politicians. He was highly moralistic rather than intellectual, unlike most European Socialists. In fact, Debs freely admitted that he had little patience with the endless ideological hairsplitting with which Socialists were commonly associ-

ated. He wanted results and was willing to cooperate with anyone who shared his general commitment to use the means of production to serve the interests of ordinary workingpeople.

Debs was worshiped by his followers, as were progressives like La Follette, Borah, and Roosevelt. The adulation and loyalty accorded him made him a presidential candidate five times between 1900 and 1920. In 1912, he won almost 1 million votes, 6 percent of the total.

But Debs was not a progressive under a different name. He did not seek to smooth over the conflict between classes, but to exhort the working class to take charge. If he was more Christian than Marxist, he nevertheless agreed with Karl Marx that the class that produced wealth should decide how that wealth was to be distributed.

Victor Berger of Milwaukee represented a stronger link between socialism and progressivism. An Austrian middle-class immigrant, Berger forged an alliance among Milwaukee's large German-speaking population, the labor movement, and the city's reform-minded middle class. His Social Democratic party (a part of the Socialist party) soft-pedaled revolutionary goals and promised Milwaukee honest government and efficient city-owned public utilities. Once he and Debs were speaking to a newspaperman, and Debs said that capitalists would not be compensated when their factories were taken from them; their "property" had been stolen from workingpeople, and theft would not be rewarded. They would be compensated, Berger interrupted. Property might well be theft; he would not frighten Americans with the specter of wild confiscation.

In 1910, Berger's candidates for mayor and city council were swept into office, and he became the first Socialist to sit in Congress. To more radical members of the party, Berger's "sewer socialism," a reference to city-owned utilities, was nothing more than progressivism. Berger thought otherwise. He insisted that by demonstrating to the American people the Socialists' ability to govern a large city, the Socialist party would win their attention to the revolutionary part of its program.

Feminism and Progressivism

Another "-ism" that had an ambivalent relationship to the progressive movement was feminism. In 1900, the struggle on behalf of equal rights for women was more than fifty years old. Despite the tireless work of leaders like Elizabeth Cady Stanton and Susan B. Anthony, the victories had been few. In their twilight years at the beginning of the Progressive era, Stanton and Anthony could look back on liberalized divorce laws, women voters in six western states, a movement unified for the moment in the National American Woman Suffrage Association, and their training of a new generation of leaders including Carrie Chapman Catt and Anna Howard Shaw, a British-born physician.

But the coveted prize, a constitutional amendment that would guarantee women the right to vote, seemed as remote as it had at Seneca Falls in 1848. Most ar-

VOTES FOR WOMEN?
A WOMAN SOCIALIST SAYS: NOT IMPORTANT

"You ask for votes for women. What good can votes do when ten-elevenths of the land in Great Britain belongs to 200,000 and only one-eleventh to the rest of the 40,000,000 population? Have your men with their millions of votes freed themselves from this injustice?"

Helen Keller to a British suffragist, 1911

ticulate Americans, women as well as men, continued to believe that women's delicacy and fine moral sense made it best that they remain in a separate sphere from men. If women participated in public life, they would be sullied as men had been and lose their vital moral influence in the home.

In fact, when Anthony died in 1906, success was

Feminist Carrie Chapman Catt, leader of the National American Woman Suffrage Association.

VOTES FOR WOMEN?
T.R. SAYS: IT DOES NOT MATTER

"Personally, I believe in woman's suffrage, but I am not an enthusiastic advocate of it, because I do not regard it as a very important matter. I am unable to see that there has been any special improvement in the position of women in those states in the West that have adopted woman's suffrage, as compared to those states adjoining them that have not adopted it. I do not think that giving the women suffrage will produce any marked improvement in the condition of women. I do not believe that it will produce any of the evils feared, and I am very certain that when women as a whole take any special interest in the matter they will have suffrage if they desire it."

fewer than fifteen years away. The democratic principles of progressivism made it increasingly difficult for activists to deny the franchise to half the people. Even progressive leaders who had little enthusiasm for the idea of female voters publicly supported the cause.

Much more important in accounting for the victory of the suffrage movement was a fundamental shift in its appeal to the American people. Under the leadership of Carrie Chapman Catt, the National American Woman Suffrage Association came to terms with progressive prejudices and quietly shelved the comprehensive critique of women's status in American society that the early feminists had developed, including strong doubts about the institution of marriage. Moreover, the suffragists dropped the traditional argument that women should have the right to vote because they were equal to men in every way.

A few "social feminists" clung to the old principles. Charlotte Perkins Gilman, an independently minded New Englander, argued in *Women and Economics* (1898) that marriage was itself the cause of women's inequality. Alice Paul, a Quaker like many feminists before her, insisted that the suffrage alone was not enough to solve "the woman question."

But most of the middle-class suffragists argued that women should have the right to vote precisely because they were more moral than men. Their votes would purge society of its evils. Not only did the suffragists ingeniously turn the most compelling antisuffrage argument in their favor, but they told progressives that in allowing women to vote they would be gaining huge numbers of allies. In fact, women were in the forefront of two of the era's most important moral crusades, the struggle against prostitution and the prohibition movement.

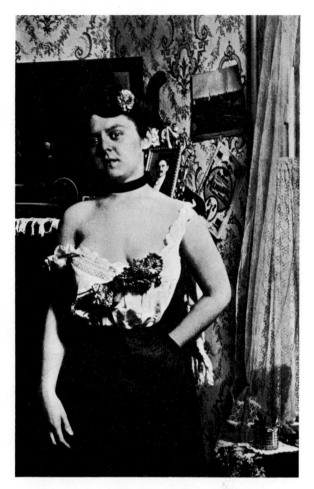

A prostitute poses for the camera. Ending prostitution became a goal of the progressives and members of the women's movement in the early 1900s.

White Slavery

To earlier generations, prostitution had been an inevitable evil that could be controlled and ignored by decent people, but not abolished. Most states, counties, and cities had laws against solicitation on the grounds that "hookers" were a public nuisance. Somewhat fewer governments declared the quiet sale of sex to be a crime. Even where prostitution was nominally illegal, it was common to tolerate "houses of ill repute" that were discreetly operated (and made contributions to the police).

Communities in which men vastly outnumbered women—cow towns, mining camps, seaports, migrant farm-worker and logging centers—typically tolerated red-light districts in a back corner of town. A stock figure of small-town folklore was the woman on the wrong side of the tracks who sold favors to those sly or bold enough to knock on her door. In the large cities, prostitution ran the gamut from lushly furnished and expensive brothels for high-society swells, such as Sally Stanford's in San Francisco, to "the cribs," tiny cubicles rented by whores who catered to the working class. Because their pay was so low, thousands of New York working women moonlighted as prostitutes at least part of the time. Novelists Stephen Crane (*Maggie: A Girl of the Streets*, 1892) and Upton Sinclair (*The Jungle*) both dealt with the theme of tacitly forced prostitution.

The world's oldest profession had affronted proper people long before the Progressive era. In most places, the middle class, was content to declare the trade illegal and then tolerate it out of their sight. Some

VICTOR L. BERGER (1860–1929)

Victor L. Berger tried to foster broad-based support for American socialism.

Victor L. Berger was born into a middle-class family in Nieder-Rehbach in the Austro-Hungarian Empire and educated at the universities of Vienna and Budapest. In 1878, he emigrated to the United States, settling briefly in Bridgeport, Connecticut. In 1881, he moved to Milwaukee, which had a large German-speaking population. A schoolteacher, Berger took an active role in the rich ethnic life of the German community, especially in the city's Old World oriented social democratic organizations. By the early 1890s, he was the most prominent Socialist in Milwaukee, and in 1897, he became editor of the *Wisconsin Vorwarts,* the movement's newspaper.

The German bloc was the core of the Milwaukee party, but Berger concluded that in order to succeed, the Socialists had to leave European preoccupations behind and attract old-stock Americans to the movement. In 1895, he converted Eugene V. Debs, the popular and quintessentially American labor leader, to socialism. In 1897, along with Debs and several other regional Socialist leaders, Berger founded the Social Democratic party of America, a broadly based alliance of Marxist, Populist, utopian, and Christian socialist groups. In 1901, Berger helped engineer the alliance with Morris Hillquit of New York that resulted in the formation of the Socialist party of America. In the same year, he also became editor of the *Social Democratic Herald,* the new English-language organ of his Milwaukee party that signaled his concerted campaign to win non-German support in his city.

Berger deeply admired liberal American political institutions, and he was convinced that socialism could triumph in the United States only when Socialists abandoned the notion of violent revolution and won majority support. In Milwaukee, he devised a strategy that became the model for the municipal socialist movement of the early twentieth century. The Milwaukee Social Democratic party deemphasized its ultimate revolutionary goal so as not to frighten off middle-class reformers. In an age of gross municipal corruption, the Berger Socialists offered scrupulously honest and efficient government. They attracted non-

Socialist members of the union movement by pledging prolabor legislation and support during strikes. The Socialists even won the support of many businessmen by promising stable labor relations. In one election campaign, Berger boasted that there would be fewer strikes when the Socialists came to power. Finally, by municipalizing public utilities (with generous compensation), Berger sought to demonstrate the workability of socialism as well as his party's competence to govern.

Following this formula, the Milwaukee party grew steadily through the first decade of the century. In 1910, it won a sweeping victory, sending Berger to Congress and electing the mayor and the majority of the city council. Other local parties, molded on Berger's design, won comparable victories in other cities—Butte, Schenectady, Berkeley—thus increasing Berger's prestige in Socialist party councils.

As a member of the party's National Executive Committee, however, Berger was not so flexible as he was in city politics. From the time the party was founded, he fought a running battle with the "revolutionist" left-wing Socialists on the issues of revolutionary militance and the party's relationship with the labor movement. The leftists scorned Berger's immediate program as "sewer socialism," and called for an unequivocally socialist plan. They argued that working for piecemeal reforms strengthened capitalism rather than hastening the day when the Socialists would take control, and they denounced Berger as nothing but a progressive. Berger, never slow to retaliate to criticism, said that the revolutionists' irresponsible rhetoric and policies held the party back.

Much more serious was the split between the two groups on the union question. The left wingers considered the AFL irretrievably committed to preserving capitalism and urged the party to support a truly socialist union that would organize the unskilled majority of the work force and work toward the overthrow of the system. After 1905, they advocated an informal alliance between the Socialist party and the Industrial Workers of the World, a revolutionary industrial union that, after 1909, fought and won several well-publicized strikes.

Berger opposed the I.W.W. from the beginning because he feared that it would damage the AFL, which, however antisocialist, was a genuine working-class organization. After 1909, he argued that the I.W.W. endorsement of revolution and sabotage alienated the very middle-class reformist elements to whom his faction was appealing with increasing success. In 1913, Berger took the lead in engineering a divorce of the two movements by successfully removing William D. "Big Bill"

Haywood from the National Executive Committee. Haywood was the chief spokesman for an alliance between party and union, and Berger forced him out on the grounds that Haywood advocated violent sabotage.

In the wake of Haywood's recall, party membership declined, and in the autumn of 1913, most of the Socialist party's electoral gains of the previous years were lost. In 1916, Berger's long-standing wish to replace Eugene V. Debs with a moderate Socialist as presidential candidate was realized with the nomination of Allen Benson. But despite an increased electorate, Benson won less than two-thirds of Debs's 1912 total.

The next year, the United States entered the world war, and the party revived in Milwaukee and nationally. The only national political body to stand unequivocally against the war, the Socialist party attracted many non-Socialist antiwar voters and thus increased its strength throughout the country. In 1918, Berger won back the congressional seat that he had lost in 1912.

By this time, however, the federal government had moved against the party for its opposition to the war. The *Milwaukee Leader* (a Socialist daily that had been founded by Berger in 1911) lost its cheap mailing privileges, and several editions were confiscated by the Post Office. Berger was convicted of having violated the Espionage Act of 1917, a law that declared practically all antiwar agitation to be illegal. By a vote of 309 to 1, Congress refused to seat him on this basis, and after Berger won a special election to fill the seat in 1919, again turned him down.

In 1921, the Supreme Court overturned Berger's conviction. In 1923, he finally took his place in Congress and served until 1928, when he was ousted in the Republican landslide of that year. With the 1920s, however, the Socialist party was in disarray. The success of the Bolsheviks in Russia had led to the growth of a largely foreign-born Communist faction in the Socialist party, which, after Berger and Morris Hillquit expelled them in 1919, formed two Communist parties. By 1923, both Communist parties and the now almost completely reformist Socialist party were tiny sects with a combined membership that was smaller than the socialists alone had claimed before 1919.

Anti-Communist himself by this time, Berger drifted slowly but steadily away from socialism. In 1928, he supported Alfred E. Smith for president solely because the Democratic nominee was opposed to Prohibition. On July 16, 1929, Berger was struck by a streetcar in Milwaukee, and he died of his injuries three weeks later.

cities restricted prostitution to neighborhoods far from middle-class residential areas, such as New Orleans's Storyville, San Francisco's Barbary Coast, and Chicago's South of the Loop.

The progressives, spearheaded by the women's movement, determined to wipe out the sin; they considered it an evil in itself and a threat to the family. During the first decade of the twentieth century, most states and innumerable communities passed strict laws against all prostitution and enforced them rigorously. In 1917, prodded by the army when it established a big training camp nearby, even wide-open Storyville, the birthplace of jazz, was officially closed. By 1920, all but a few states had an antiprostitution law on the books. Within a few more years, only Nevada, with its stubborn mining frontier outlook, continued to tolerate the institution in the law.

The Limits of Progressive Moralism

Action on the federal level was more complicated. Prostitution was clearly a matter for the police powers of the states and localities. However, progressives were so convinced that government held the key to social reform and must act at every level that, in 1910, they joined with some conservatives to put the interstate-commerce clause of the Constitution to work in the cause. Senator James R. Mann of Illinois sponsored a bill that struck against the probably exaggerated practice of procurers luring poor girls from one part of the country to become prostitutes elsewhere. The Mann Act forbade transporting women across state lines "for immoral purposes."

Of course, neither local, state, nor federal law abolished prostitution. The campaign may be the best example of the progressives' excessive faith in the powers of the government. Brothels continued to operate, albeit less openly and probably with more police graft than before. Streetwalkers, previously the most despised and degraded of whores, became the norm because they were less easily arrested. Wealthy men continued to maintain paid mistresses and created the "call girl," a prostitute who stayed at home until "called" by a hotel employee or pimp who worked the streets and hotel lobbies.

Prohibitionism

The impulse to overcome the evils of drink dated to the reform era of the early nineteenth century. Temper-ance advocates and outright prohibitionists had battled back and forth with the distillers of liquor and with ordinary people who simply enjoyed a cup of good cheer. By 1900, however, antialcohol crusaders were emphasizing social arguments over their moral distaste for drunkenness and, in so doing, won widespread progressive support.

The prohibitionists pointed out that the city saloon was often the local headquarters of the corrupt political machines. Close the saloons, and the bosses would be crippled. Moreover, generally overlooking the fact that poverty caused a widespread drinking problem among the working classes, the prohibitionists argued that the misery of the working classes was the result of husbands and fathers spending their wages on demon rum and John Barleycorn. Because the public bar was then an all-male institution, the temperance movement formed a close alliance with the women's suffrage movement of that time.

Carry Nation of Kansas was one woman who suffered her whole life with a drunken husband and poverty. Beginning in 1900, she launched a campaign of direct action, leading hatchet-wielding women into saloons where, before the bewildered eyes of saloonkeeper and customers, they methodically chopped the place to pieces.

Frances Willard, head of the Woman's Christian Temperance Union, opposed such tactics. She and her followers also entered saloons, but instead of breaking them up, they attempted to shame drinkers by kneeling to pray quietly in their midst. In addition, the W.C.T.U. turned to politics, supporting woman suffrage for its own sake as well as for the purpose of winning the final victory over liquor.

Increasing numbers of progressives adopted the reform. Only in the big cities, mostly in the eastern states, did socially minded politicians like Alfred E. Smith and Robert Wagner of New York actively fight the prohibitionists. The large Roman Catholic and Jewish populations of the cities had no religious tradition against alcohol; on the contrary they used wine as a part of religious observance. Elsewhere, libertarian progressives argued that the government had no right to interfere with the individual decision of whether or not to drink.

Nevertheless, the possibilities of moral improvement, of striking a blow against poverty, and of joining battle against the political manipulations of the big distillers and brewers converted many progressives to prohibition, and in the waning days of the movement (though they were not known to be waning at the time), they had their way.

For Further Reading

The historians' output on the Progressive era has declined somewhat during the last decade, but the subject was among the most controversial in American studies about twenty years ago. To study it will require an extensive reading program, the scope of which is less forbidding because the quality of the work is so high. The following books are only the highlights of the literature.

George Mowry, *The Era of Theodore Roosevelt* (1958) and *The California Progressives* (1951), discusses the early period of reform; Richard Hofstadter, *The Age of Reform* (1955), presents a picture much like Mowry's. A quite different point of view can be found in Gabriel Kolko, *The Triumph of Conservatism* (1963), and useful in balancing Kolko is Robert H.

Wiebe, *Businessmen and Reform* (1962).

In addition to the books on Theodore Roosevelt cited at the end of Chapter 37, see two books by G. W. Chessman, *Governor Theodore Roosevelt* (1965) and *Theodore Roosevelt and the Politics of Power* (1969). The chapter on T. R. in Richard Hofstadter, *The American Political Tradition* (1948), is indispensable. On "Fighting Bob" La Follette, see R. S. Maxwell, *La Follette and the Rise of Progressivism in Wisconsin* (1956).

On the muckrakers, see Louis Filler, *Crusaders for American Liberalism* (1939), and D. M. Chalmers, *The Social and Political Ideas of the Muckrakers* (1964).

39

Standing at Armageddon

The Progressives in Power, 1901–1916

By 1904, progressivism was more than a hodge-podge of single-issue and locally oriented reform groups. It was becoming a potent political movement that commanded the allegiance of a large bloc of senators and congressmen from both major parties and boasted as its leader none other than the chief executive himself, Theodore Roosevelt.

The irony that he, as a scion of the privileged classes, should lead a popular-protest movement was not lost on T.R. In a letter to his equally aristocratic and decidedly nonprogressive friend, Senator Chauncey Depew of the New York Central Railroad, Roosevelt wrote in mock weariness: "How I wish I wasn't a reformer, Oh Senator! But I suppose I must live up to my part, like the Negro minstrel who blackened himself all over!"

In fact, while the pedigreed Depew was acceptable company for dinner, Roosevelt found it easy to disdain the newly rich and powerful industrial capitalists who were the chief villains in progressive eyes. He recognized their energies and organizational skills as essential in a healthy, dynamic society, but as an heir to pre-industrial wealth and social station, Roosevelt was also inclined to consider them to be "male-factors of great wealth" who occasionally needed a brusque reminder that they had betters who enjoyed formidable popular backing. Moreover, despite the sigh of fatalism in his letter to Depew, Roosevelt loved to be in the thick of things, and during T.R.'s nearly eight years in the White House, reform was the bully, tangled thick.

Theodore Roosevelt speaking at Newcastle, Wyoming, in 1903.

T.R. Takes Over

Roosevelt moved cautiously at first. He was aware that the Republican bosses were suspicious of him as a "damned cowboy" and that through 1901, at least, they were more powerful than he. Indeed, Mark Hanna weighed the possibilities of opposing T.R. for the 1904 Republican nomination, but in February 1904, he suddenly died.

By that time, a challenge to T.R. was a fool's cause. Not only was the president's personal popularity immense, but Roosevelt quietly had replaced members of the Old Guard with his own men in middle-level government positions, eased out the McKinley–Hanna mediocrities in his cabinet, and won the loyalty of the able holdovers by reorganizing their departments in a way that gave them an authority and autonomy that they previously had not enjoyed. Among those whom he kept in office were Secretary of State John Hay; Secretary of War Elihu Root, who succeeded Hay in the State Department in 1905; Attorney General Philander C. Knox; Secretary of the Interior E. A. Hitchcock; and Secretary of Agriculture James Wilson.

The "Trust-Buster"

Roosevelt was delighted to leave day-by-day administration in the hands of others because there was no doubt in the public mind about who was in charge. In April 1902, he conspicuously directed Attorney General Knox, a former corporation lawyer, to take on the most powerful corporate organizers in the United States. His target, the Northern Securities Company, had been designed by J. P. Morgan and railroaders Edward H. Harriman and James J. Hill to end struggles for control of the railroads in the northern quarter of the country. Funded by the nation's two richest banks, Northern Securities was a holding company that was patterned after Morgan's United States Steel Corporation.

Morgan was shocked. Under McKinley (and pre-Roosevelt Knox) the Sherman Antitrust Act had nearly died from disuse. In a pained and revealing moment, the great financier wrote to Roosevelt, "If we have done anything wrong, send your man to my man and we can fix it up." In other words, let the president of the United States do his job while holding hands in a quiet room with big business.

Roosevelt blithely ignored the proposition and pushed on in the courts. In 1904, he won. The Supreme Court ordered the Northern Securities Com-

Theodore Roosevelt aggressively enforced antitrust laws. In this cartoon he is depicted as a powerful lion tamer whipping the trusts into shape.

pany to dissolve, and progressives cheered. When Roosevelt instituted other antitrust suits, forty in all, of which he won twenty-five, progressives nicknamed him the "trust-buster."

It was an overstatement. Roosevelt made it clear that he did not believe that bigness was itself the evil, and he continued to socialize with business leaders. In 1907, he allowed Morgan's United States Steel to gobble up a major regional competitor, Tennessee Coal and Iron, in an informal agreement. His criteria for determining what made one trust "good" and another "bad" were vague. Essentially, Roosevelt wanted to show big business and the American people that he and the United States government were boss. In order to take over Tennessee Coal and Iron, Morgan had to send his man to see T.R.'s man and not vice versa.

The Workingman's Friend

Much more startling than trust-busting was Roosevelt's personal intervention in the autumn of 1902 in a strike by 140,000 anthracite miners. The men's demands were moderate. They asked for a 20 percent increase in pay, an eight-hour day, and recognition of their union, the United Mine Workers, as their bargaining agent (their voice in all negotiations with employers).

But the mine owners refused to yield. Theirs was an unstable industry. The price of coal fluctuated so radically and suddenly that they feared long-term contracts with their employees. Moreover, most of them were entrepreneurs of the old hard-nosed school. Their property was their property. They would brook no interference in their use of it, least of all by employees. George F. Baer, a leader of the operators, stirred up a furious public reaction when he told a newspaper reporter that he would never deal with the UMW because God had entrusted him and the other owners with control of the mines of Pennsylvania.

By way of contrast, union leader John Mitchell was

a modest likable man, and Roosevelt knew that he was constantly fighting Socialists in his union. In October, the president let it be known that if the strike dragged on through the winter with no settlement, he might use federal troops to dispossess the owners and run the mines. Believing that the Rough Rider was quite capable of so rash an action, J. P. Morgan pressured the mine owners to go to Washington to work out a settlement.

The result was a compromise. The miners got a 10 percent raise and a nine-hour day, but the owners did not recognize the legal status of the UMW. (They even refused to meet face to face with Mitchell.) The miners were elated anyway. So were people who counted on coal to ward off winter's cold. But the big winner, as in most of his chosen battles, was Theodore Roosevelt. He had reversed the tradition of using federal troops to

Striking miners, members of the United Mine Workers, parade silently in their Sunday best during the 1902 coal strike.

help employers break strikes and had forced powerful industrialists to bow to his will on behalf of a "square deal" for workingmen.

As with his reputation as a "trust-buster," Roosevelt's image as the workingman's friend was a distorted oversimplification. Amity did not, for example, extend to socialist unionists, no matter how just their side in an issue. In 1905, Charles Moyer and William D. "Big Bill" Haywood, respectively president and secretary-treasurer of the socialistic Western Federation of Miners, were arrested in Colorado for the murder of a former governor of Idaho and illegally spirited to Boise for a trial. Roosevelt not only refused to intervene in what was little better than a kidnapping, but described the defendants as "undesirable citizens," virtually inviting the jury to convict them. (They were acquitted.)

In 1906, the Western Federation of Miners and the Industrial Workers of the World called a peaceful strike among miners and town workers in Goldfield, Nevada. The owners of the mines asked Roosevelt for troops to break the two radical unions, and he obliged.

Teddy's Great Victory

By that time, T.R. was basking in the warmth of idolization. He was unanimously renominated by the Republicans in 1904 and presented with a huge campaign chest. The Democrats, hoping to capitalize on conservative grumbling over the president's stinging remarks about business, did a complete about-face from the party's agrarianism of 1896 and 1900 and named a Wall Street lawyer, Judge Alton B. Parker, to oppose him.

Parker was a stodgy sort, but even the second most colorful politician in the country would have looked like a cardboard cutout next to T.R. Even the conservative big businessmen supported him. If they disliked T.R.'s antitrust adventures, they recognized that Roosevelt hewed to conservative lines in advocating an anti-inflationary money policy and a high tariff, which were of far greater importance to business interests than was anything else. J. P. Morgan, recently stung in the Northern Securities case, donated $150,000 to Roosevelt's campaign.

The president won a lopsided 57.4 percent of the vote, more than any candidate since popular totals had begun to be recorded. His 336 to 140 electoral sweep was the largest since Grant's in 1872, and he did it without the help of the southern states. Never was it more clear that the Republicans were the majority party. Building on the coalition of money and respectability that had been put together by McKinley and Hanna in 1896, T.R. proved equally popular with conservatives and progressives.

The President as Reformer

The only sour note in a giddy election week for the Republicans was the news that Socialist party candidate Eugene V. Debs did so well. His four hundred thousand votes amounted to only 3 percent of the total, but represented an astonishing fourfold increase over what he had won in 1900. Roosevelt did not like it. Armed with his mandate, he unleashed a whirlwind of reform during his second term that was aimed in part at blowing away the socialist menace that he and many other political leaders regarded as genuine and fearful.

The Railroads Derailed

As they had been for thirty years, the railroads remained a focus of popular resentment. The freewheeling arrogance of their directors and the vital role of transportation in the national economy preoccupied progressives at every level of government. Prodded by eloquent regional leaders, most notably Senator Robert La Follette, Roosevelt dove into a long, bitter struggle with the railroad companies. In 1906, he won passage of the Hepburn Act. The new law authorized the Interstate Commerce Commission to set maximum rates that railroads might charge their customers, and forbade them to pay rebates to big shippers, a prohibition that had been enacted before but had not been effectively enforced. The Hepburn Act gave the I.C.C. some teeth. More than any of T.R.'s previous actions, it blasted the railroaders' traditional immunity from government interference.

Also in 1906, Congress passed an act that held railroads liable to employees who suffered injuries on the job. By European standards, it was a mild compensation law, but in the United States, it marked a sharp break with precedent.

Pure Food and Drugs

Several Pure Food and Drug Acts crippled the patent-medicine industry, which marketed dangerous and addictive opiates as "feel-good" nostrums; struck at the adulteration of foods with sometimes toxic preservatives and fillers; and provided for federal inspection of meat-packing plants and other food-processing industries.

While such wholesale federal interference annoyed some big businessmen, others quietly supported it. They realized that strict sanitary standards could work to their benefit at the expense of smaller competitors, for with their greater resources, they were better able to comply. For example, as early as 1902, the gigantic Coca-Cola Company of Atlanta, striving for a monopoly of soft-drink production, had come up with a substitute for cocaine as the "kick" in its beverage. With its vast national apparatus and huge purchasing capacity, Coca-Cola had been able to contract with drug manufacturers for the residue from processed coca leaves (what was left *after* drug companies had extracted cocaine) and to incorporate caffeine, an acceptable stimulant, into its secret recipe. Small cola companies that attempted to compete with "coke" found it difficult to match the big company's advanced technology and to conform to federal standards.

Although it had been the giant meat packers that Upton Sinclair had attacked in *The Jungle,* only the smaller abattoirs found federal inspection to be an impossible burden. Swift, Armour, Wilson, and other large packers quickly came to terms with the ubiquitous government officials and their notebooks. They even made advertising hay of the inspection stamps on their products: the government approved of them. Local slaughterhouses, however, could not comply and survive; it was too expensive. The only alternative was to restrict their sales of meat to the states in which they were located. (Like all national reforms, federal meat inspection applied only to firms involved in interstate commerce.) But the opportunity to challenge the big packers was forever closed. Roosevelt the trust-buster did not object to the consolidation that the Meat Inspection Act tacitly encouraged. It was not bigness itself to which he objected, but irresponsibility in business.

The Need to Conserve Resources

No progressive reform gave Roosevelt more personal satisfaction than the movement to conserve natural resources. As a lifelong devotee of the outdoors, he loved camping, riding, hiking, climbing, and hunting. As a historian, he was more sensitive than most of his contemporaries to the role of the wilderness in forming the American character. He sought and gained the friendship of John Muir, the adopted Californian and Alaskan who had founded the Sierra Club in 1892. Muir's interest in nature was aesthetic, cultural, and spiritual. He wanted to protect from destructive development such magnificent areas of untouched wilderness as Yosemite Valley, which he had helped to establish as a national park in 1890.

Somewhat different were the motives of progressive conservationists such as T.R.'s tennis partner and America's first trained forester, Gifford A. Pinchot of Pennsylvania. While by no means oblivious to the

Theodore Roosevelt and Sierra Club founder John Muir in Yosemite National Park.

noneconomic values in keeping natural resources out of the hands of rapacious developers, Pinchot and like-minded conservationists primarily wanted to ensure that future generations of Americans would have their share of nonrenewable natural resources such as minerals, coal, and oil to draw on and the use of renewable resources like forests, grasslands, and water for drinking and generating power.

They had good reason to worry on both counts. Concerned with nothing but short-term profits, lumbermen mowed down forests, moved on, and left the land behind them to bloom in useless and unsightly scrub. Western cattlemen overgrazed delicate grasslands, thus destroying them. Coal- and phosphate-mining companies and drillers for oil thought in terms of the account books that were open and were not concerned that in a century or less the United States might run out of these vital resources. All over the country, abuse of the land in the pursuit of wealth was destroying its very capacity to produce food because of soil erosion. Americans had always been reckless with the land; none were worse than pioneers. But there was a big difference between what a few frontiersmen could do to it with axes and horse-drawn plows and the potential for destruction of irresponsible million-dollar corporations.

A Revolution in Conservation Policy

The National Forest Reserve, today's national forests, dates from 1891, when Congress had empowered the president to withhold forests in the public domain from private use. Over the first ten years of the law, Presidents Harrison, Cleveland, and McKinley had declared 46 million acres of virgin woodland off limits to loggers without government permission.

Enforcement was desultory until, prodded by Pinchot, Roosevelt began to prosecute "timber pirates" who raided public lands and cattlemen who abused government-owned grasslands. Within a few years, Roosevelt also added 125 million acres to the national forests, as well as 68 million acres of coal deposits, almost 5 million acres of phosphate beds (vital to production of munitions), a number of oil fields, and 2,565 sites suitable for the construction of dams for irrigation and generation of electrical power.

Such defiance of business interests (as short-sighted businessmen saw them) gratified progressives. The concept of "multiple use" of national forests—recreation and preservation as well as conservation for the future—won the adulation of groups like the Sierra Club and other naturalists. The principle of "sustained yield"—managing forests to ensure an adequate supply of lumber into the indefinite future—appealed to heavily capitalized lumbermen and encouraged them to employ foresters on their own lands.

In the West, however, an angry opposition developed. Cattlemen, clear-cut loggers, and private power companies banded together in an anticonservation movement that succeeded, in 1907, in attaching a rider to an appropriations bill that passed Congress. It forbade the president to create any additional national forests in six western states.

Roosevelt had no choice but to sign the bill; the Department of Agriculture could not have functioned otherwise. But he had one last go at what he called the "predatory interests." Before he wrote his name on the bill, he reserved 17 million acres of forest land in the interdicted states.

Theodore Roosevelt's conservation campaign remains one of the single most important contributions of his presidency. Nevertheless, his policies could hurt ordinary people as well as special interests. For example, he and Pinchot helped Los Angeles, the burgeoning metropolis of southern California, to grab with dubious legality the whole Owens River, three hundred miles to the north, for its water supply. The president regarded the mammoth construction project, now known as the Los Angeles Aqueduct, as a showpiece of resource development and public control of electrical power. In the process, however, he helped to destroy the fertile Owens Valley. Then a land of prosperous, self-reliant small farmers, it would become by 1930 an arid, desolate region of sagebrush, dust storms, and tarantulas.

Had Roosevelt lived to see its results, he might well have regretted his action. Although the only American president born in a big city, he was a devotee of the family farm as one of the essential American institutions. He established the Country Life Commission, which lamented the steady disappearance of this way of life and submitted to Congress a number of recommendations designed to help family farmers. Conservative congressmen who had soured on their progressive president refused even to publish the report.

The Reformer Retires

Congress side-stepped most of Roosevelt's legislative proposals for 1908. In two major speeches he called for

A 1905 caricature of the ample figure of
William Howard Taft.

a comprehensive, even radical, program that included federal investigation of major labor disputes and close regulation of both the stock market and businesses that were involved in interstate commerce.

But Roosevelt was in the unfamiliar and uncomfortable position of "lame duck." It was a presidential election year. Four years earlier, celebrating the great victory of 1904, T.R. had publicly declared that "a wise custom which limits the President to two terms regards the substance and not the form, and under no circumstances will I be a candidate for or accept another nomination." Having served three and a half years of McKinley's term, Roosevelt had defined himself as a two-term president.

In 1908, he probably regretted his impulsive statement. Roosevelt did not want to quit. He loved his job as no other president has. He had been a marvelous success in it. Just as important, despite simmering problems with his party's conservatives, he was as popular as ever in 1908 with the voters. Roosevelt undoubtedly would have won reelection in 1908 had he been willing to forget his pledge of 1904.

But he kept his word and settled for hand-picking his successor, which no president had been able to do since Andrew Jackson in 1836. That William Howard Taft, then Secretary of War, was not the man whom either conservative or progressive Republicans would have chosen indicates just how powerful Roosevelt was.

Big Bill Taft, A Conservative President in a Progressive Era

Taft never would have been nominated without Roosevelt's blessing. He never would have dreamed of running for president. Regularly in his correspondence he dashed off the exclamation "I hate politics!" and meant it. He was a lifelong functionary, not a politician. His only elective post prior to 1908 was as a judge in Ohio. Taft remembered that job as the most congenial he ever had held, and, indeed, his temperament was judicial. Sober, cautious, reflective, dignified, even shy before a crowd, he was an excellent administrator, but no showman.

Even physically, Taft was ill fit to follow the gymnastics of the athletic Roosevelt. He weighed over three hundred pounds, and was truly at ease only when he settled into a swivel chair behind a desk or sank into an overstuffed couch with other easygoing men. His single form of exercise, golf, did not help his image; batting a little white ball around an oversize lawn was considered a sissy's game in the early twentieth century.

Taft was no reactionary. He had loyally supported Roosevelt's reforms, and T.R. calculated that he, more than anyone else, would carry out the Square Deal. So did other progressives. They supported him, as did the conservative wing of the Republican party. Anyone was preferable to the man whom they had begun to refer to privately as "the mad messiah."

The Election of 1908

The election was an anticlimax. The Democrats returned to William Jennings Bryan as their candidate. But the thrill was gone. The Boy Orator of the Platte was no longer young; almost fifty, he was shopworn beyond his years and growing a paunch as a consequence of a lifelong habit of gluttony. Moreover, his loyal supporters, the staple farmers of the Midwest, were no longer struggling to survive and no longer jostling prosperous townspeople such as William Allen White. They were beginning to dress well and to build substantial homes. Even the issue of 1900, imperialism, was dead. Rather, Taft, who had served as American governor of the Philippines, could claim credit for having transformed the anti-American Filipinos, whom he called his "little brown brothers," into a placid and apparently content colonial population. A lethargic Bryan won a smaller percentage of the popular vote than in either of his previous tries, although several western states returned to the Democratic column.

The Socialist party was even more disappointed in the results. Optimistic at the start of the campaign, they chartered a private train, the "Red Special," on which candidate Debs crisscrossed the country. His crowds were big and enthusiastic. But Debs's vote was only sixteen thousand higher than in 1904 and represented a smaller percentage of the total. It appeared that Roosevelt's tactic of undercutting the socialist threat with a comprehensive reform program had worked.

Taft Blunders

Unfortunately, President Taft lacked both the political skills and the zeal to keep reform rolling. For example, even though he initiated ninety antitrust suits during his four years as president, twice as many as Roosevelt had launched in seven and a half years, no one complimented him as a trust-buster. Taft had alienated the progressives immediately after taking office when he stumbled over the obstacle that T.R. had danced around so nimbly—the tariff.

In 1909, duties on foreign goods were high, set at an average 46.5 percent of the value of imports by the

Dingley Tariff of 1897. Republican conservatives insisted that this prohibitive rate was necessary in order to protect the jobs of American factory workers and to encourage industrial investment by capitalists. Midwestern progressives disagreed. They believed that American industry was strong enough to stand up to European competition. The high tariff was purely and simply a subsidy of excessive corporate profits because it allowed manufacturers to set their prices inordinately high. Moreover, farmers were twice stung because the European nations, except Great Britain, retaliated against the Dingley Tariff by levying high duties on American agricultural products.

Roosevelt had let the conservatives have their way on the tariff, placating progressives by moving on other reforms. By 1908, that was no longer possible, and Taft pledged during the campaign to call Congress into special session for the purpose of revision. He did so in March 1909, and the House of Representatives drafted a reasonable reduction of rates in the Payne bill. In the Senate, however, Nelson Aldrich of Rhode Island, a close ally of industrial capitalists, engineered eight hundred amendments to what became the Payne-Aldrich Act. On most important commodities, the final rate was higher than under the Dingley Tariff.

Taft was in a bind. Politically, he was committed to lower rates. Personally, however, he was more comfortable with the aristocratic Aldrich and the five corporation lawyers in his cabinet, and he disliked most of the Republican low-tariff men in the Senate, including the crusading La Follette, bombastic Albert Beveridge of Indiana, and Jonathan Dolliver of Iowa. After equivocating, Taft worked out what he thought was a compromise in the Roosevelt tradition. The conservatives got their high tariff but agreed to a 2 percent corporate income tax and a constitutional amendment that legalized a personal income tax. (It was ratified in 1913 as the Sixteenth Amendment.) Instead of emphasizing the progressive aspects of his arrangement, as T.R. surely would have done, Taft described the Payne-Aldrich Act as "the best tariff that the Republican party ever passed."

The Insurgents and a Wounded Pinchot

The statement infuriated the midwestern Republican progressives, especially after Taft came out in favor of a trade treaty with Canada that threatened to dump Canadian crops on the American market. But they broke with the new president only when he backed the reactionary Speaker of the House of Representatives, Joseph G. Cannon of Illinois, against them.

Illinois congressman "Uncle Joe" Cannon, a hard-bitten Republican conservative.

"Uncle Joe" Cannon offended the progressive Republicans on several counts. He was so blatantly a spokesman for big business as to be a ludicrous stereotype. As Speaker of the House and chairman of the House Rules Committee, he put progressives on unimportant committees and loaded the meaningful ones with his stooges. Moreover, while the progressives inclined to be highly moralistic, even priggish in manner, Uncle Joe was a crusty tobacco chewer, a hard drinker who was not infrequently drunk, and a foul-mouth.

The proper Taft also found Cannon's company unpleasant. However, the president believed in party loyalty, and when a number of midwestern Republican progressives, calling themselves Insurgents, voted with Democrats to strip Cannon of his near-dictatorial power under House rules, Taft joined with the Speaker to deny the Insurgents access to party money and patronage in the midterm election of 1910.

It is impossible to say how Theodore Roosevelt would have handled the quarrel between Cannon and the Insurgents. But he assuredly would not have done what Taft did in a dispute between Secretary of the Interior Richard A. Ballinger and Chief Forester Gifford A. Pinchot.

When Ballinger released to private developers a number of hydroelectric sites that Pinchot had persuaded Roosevelt to reserve, Pinchot protested to Taft and presented him with evidence that Ballinger was in secret collusion with the very business interests that his decision favored. Taft was unimpressed with the evidence and ruled in favor of Ballinger. However, little as he liked the intense, crusading Pinchot, who was so much like the Insurgents in manner, Taft asked his chief forester to stay on.

Pinchot did. But, still seething, he leaked his evidence against Ballinger to *Collier's* magazine, which was still in the muckraking business. For this inexcusable offense, Taft fired him, which was exactly what Pinchot wanted. Almost immediately he booked passage to Italy, where his friend and patron, former president Roosevelt, was vacationing. Pinchot brought with him an indictment of Big Bill Taft as a traitor to the cause of reform.

Enter Stage Left the Conquering Hero

Roosevelt was having a grand time on his extended world tour. He had left the country shortly after Taft's inauguration to give his successor an opportunity to function outside his predecessor's aura. First Roosevelt traveled to East Africa, where he shot a bloody swath through the still abundant big game of Kenya and Tanganyika (Tanzania). He bagged over three thousand animals, many of which he had stuffed for the trophy room of his home at Oyster Bay, Long Island.

Then he went to Europe to bask in an adulation that was scarcely less fierce than he enjoyed at home. He hobnobbed with royalty and powerful politicians, who thought of him as the ultimate American, much as Benjamin Franklin had been considered in eighteenth-century France. Roosevelt topped off his year-long junket by representing the United States at the funeral of King Edward VII, successfully shining in the greatest collection of royal personages ever assembled.

And yet, something was missing. Roosevelt longed for the hurly-burly of American politics, and he was all too willing to believe Pinchot's accusations. When he returned to the United States in June 1910, he exchanged only the curtest greetings with the president. He spoke widely on behalf of Republican congressional candidates, at first playing down the split between regulars (conservatives) and Insurgents (progressives). Then, at Osawatomie, Kansas, in September 1910, Roosevelt proclaimed what he labeled the "New Nationalism," a comprehensive program for further reform. To Republican conservatives, it was frighteningly radical.

Among other proposals, Roosevelt called for woman suffrage, a federal minimum wage for women workers, abolition of child labor, strict limitations on the power of courts to issue injunctions in labor disputes, and a national social-insurance scheme that resembled present-day Social Security. He struck directly at Taft's policies by demanding a commission that would set tariff rates "scientifically" rather than according to political pressures. He supported the progressive initiative, recall, and referendum, including a new twist, a referendum on judicial decisions. This was enough in itself to anger the legalistic Taft, but in demanding a national presidential-primary law under which the people, and not professional politicians, would make party nominations, Roosevelt also hinted that he was interested in running for the presidency again.

The Republicans Split

Taft was not the only politician who worried about Roosevelt's presidential plans. Robert La Follette believed that he had a chance to win the Republican nomination from Taft *if* Roosevelt did not run. He had friends ask Roosevelt his intentions, and the Colonel responded that he was not interested in the White House, tacitly encouraging La Follette. In January 1911, the Wisconsin senator organized the Progressive Republican League as the vehicle of his campaign.

Most progressive Republicans supported La Follette, including Roosevelt backers who not so secretly hoped that their real hero would change his mind. Indeed, Roosevelt was itching to run. In March 1912, La Follette collapsed from exhaustion during a speech, and Roosevelt announced, "my hat is in the ring."

La Follette was not seriously ill, and he never forgave T.R. for having used him as a stalking-horse. But he was no match for the old master when it came to stirring up people, and his campaign fell apart. Roosevelt swept the thirteen states that held primary elections, winning 278 delegates to Taft's 48 and La Follette's 36. However, if La Follette was beaten, the suddenly aroused Taft was not, and he had an important weapon.

Taft may have lacked Roosevelt's popularity with grass-roots Republicans, but he still controlled the party organization. As president, he appointed people to thousands of government jobs, wedding their careers to his own success. In the Republican party, this power of the patronage was particularly important in the southern states, where the party consisted of little more than professional officeholders, including many blacks, who made their living as postmasters, customs collectors, agricultural agents, and the like. While the Republicans won few congressional seats and fewer electoral votes in the South, a substantial bloc of delegates at conventions represented the southern states. These people were in Taft's pocket.

Consequently, when the convention voted on whether Taft or Roosevelt would be awarded 254 disputed seats, Taft delegates won 235 of them. Roosevelt and his supporters shouted "Fraud!" and walked out. They formed a third party, the Progressive party, or, as it was nicknamed for the battle with the Republican elephant and the Democratic donkey, the Bull Moose party. (In a backhanded reference to La Follette's allegedly poor health and Taft's obesity, Roosevelt said that he was "as strong as a bull moose.")

Democratic Party Progressivism

The Republican party was no longer the majority party after it had been split into two, and the Democrats smelled victory. Consequently, when the convention assembled in Baltimore, there was an abundance of

THE LATEST ARRIVAL AT THE POLITICAL ZOO

DRAWN BY E. W. KEMBLE

A Harper's Weekly *cartoon depicting Theodore Roosevelt as a bull moose that relies on a trust for survival.*

would-be nominees. As at the Republican convention, but for a rather different reason, the key to winning the party's presidential nomination lay in the southern state delegations.

Because the South was "solid" in delivering electoral votes to the Democratic column, it held a virtual veto power over the nomination as a result of the two-thirds rule. In order to be nominated, a Democrat needed the votes of two-thirds of the delegates; no one could win two-thirds if the South solidly opposed him. The trouble in 1912, however, was that none of the four leading candidates was offensive to the South, and each had his southern supporters; thus the usual southern bloc was split.

The Democratic Hopefuls

William Jennings Bryan was still popular in the South, but as a three-time loser, he was not an attractive candidate. Although he hoped to be selected as a compromise candidate in case of a deadlock, few Democrats wanted to risk sure victory for the sake of old times.

Oscar Underwood of Alabama was another minor hopeful; he commanded the support of the southern "Bourbon" conservatives, but for that reason he was unacceptable to southern progressives, who might more accurately be described as Populists who preached racism along with attacks on big business. Some progressives backed Champ Clark, the "Old Hound Dawg" of Missouri, which was as much a southern as a western state. In fact, Clark went into the convention confident of winning. The man who left it a winner, however, was New Jersey governor Woodrow Wilson, who was nominated on the forty-sixth ballot when Bryan threw his influence behind him.

Wilson was actually a southerner; he had been born in Virginia and had practiced law in Georgia as a young man. He had abandoned the law, however, earned a Ph.D. degree, and ended up as a professor of political science at Princeton University. In 1902, he had been named president of Princeton, the first nonminister to hold that post at the still strongly Presbyterian school.

And yet, Wilson had more than a little of the Presbyterian clergyman in him. His father and both grandfathers were parsons. So was his first wife's father. He had been raised to observe an unbending Calvinist morality, and his stern sensitivity to the struggle between good and evil in the world was reflected in an ascetic, lean figure and a sharply chiseled, thin-lipped face. In dealing with everyone but a few intimate friends, Wilson was formal, even icy. A less talented man with such a personality would never have risen half so high as Wilson did.

Indeed, his meteoric rise in politics was almost acci-

*Woodrow Wilson was the president of Princeton University before
entering political life.*

dental. In 1910, he was merely an honored educator, the president of Princeton University. He had transformed the college from an intellectually lazy finishing school where rich young men made social contacts into a nationally respected university. (Reflecting his southern prejudices, he also tried to establish segregation in the picturesque little town where Princeton is located.) But Wilson's self-righteous stubbornness caught up with him. Clashing repeatedly with trustees and alumni, he quit academic life.

There was no loss of face involved. He had been offered the Democratic nomination for governor of New Jersey, and in winning in the traditionally Republican state, Wilson became a national figure overnight. He was more an honest-government progressive than a

social reformer, and, like Theodore Roosevelt in New York a decade before, he proved to be a nuisance to some of New Jersey's political bosses. They were delighted when he decided to seek the presidency. Ironically, in terms of what followed, he first offered himself as a safe and sane conservative alternative to William Jennings Bryan.

The Campaign of 1912

In fact, Wilson's "New Freedom," as he called his platform, was a decidedly less ambitious blueprint for reform than was Roosevelt's "New Nationalism." Wilson emphasized states' rights to the extent that he opposed the Progressive party's comprehensive social program as strongly as Taft did. He considered Roosevelt's proposals to be a dangerous expansion of government powers.

The two men differed even more sharply on the question of the trusts. Whereas T.R. concluded that consolidation, even monopoly, was inevitable in an industrial society, and that the federal government should supervise the operations of the big corporations in the public interest, Wilson condemned this vision as "a partnership between the government and the trusts." Wilson believed that competition in business was still possible in modern America. In his view, the government's task was to ensure free competition by breaking up the trusts and then letting the economy function without direction. In 1912, he wanted no huge, permanent government apparatus such as Roosevelt suggested.

With the Republican organization in tatters and Taft practically dropping out of the race, it would have been difficult for Wilson to have lost the election. Nevertheless, he campaigned tirelessly and skillfully. Articulate, as a college professor is supposed to be, Wilson was also an electrifying orator, as few are. Lifelong dreams of winning public office flowered in eloquent speeches that left no doubt that the Presbyterian schoolmaster was a leader.

Wilson won only 41.9 percent of the popular vote but a landslide in the electoral college, 435 votes to Roosevelt's 88 and Taft's 8. Eugene V. Debs, making his fourth race as the Socialist party nominee, won 1 million votes, 3 percent of the total. The big jump after four years of a conservative president seemed to indicate that it was necessary to reform in order to stifle the socialist challenge. The Socialists even elected their second congressman, Meyer London of New York, although Victor Berger lost his bid for reelection, the victim of a multiparty alliance against him. (He returned to Washington in 1918.) The message appeared to be that the American people wanted reform; Taft, the only conservative candidate, won only 23.2 percent of the vote.

Tariff and Taxes

T.R. had governed by outflanking Congress, interpreting the president's constitutional powers in the broadest possible terms. Taft had deferred to congressional leaders, ultimately collapsing before the most persuasive of them. Wilson's style was to act as a prime minister. He was not a member of Congress, as the British prime minister is a member of the House of Commons, but he could and did address Congress per-

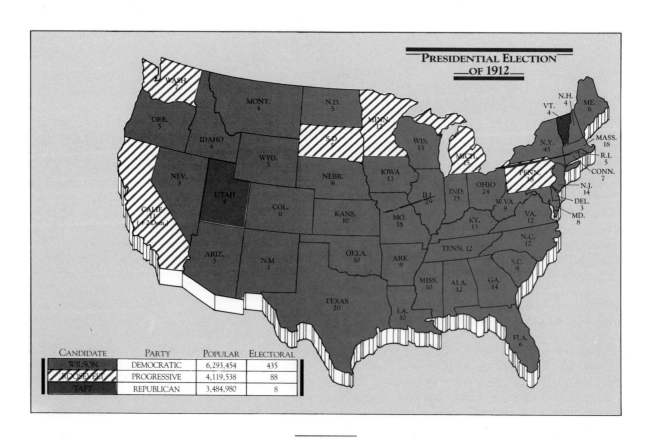

sonally as though he were. When soon after his inauguration he asked the House and Senate for sharp reductions in the tariff, he was the first president to appear on Capitol Hill since John Adams. Adams's successor, Thomas Jefferson, had suffered from a stammer and had set the precedent of communicating with Congress only through written messages.

Wilson's short but dramatic address was aimed less at persuading congressmen than at inspiring their constituents to put pressure on them, and it worked. A number of Democratic senators who had been dragging their feet on tariff revision fell into line. The Underwood-Simmons Tariff reduced the Payne-Aldrich rates by 15 percent and put on the free list several commodities that were controlled by trusts—iron, steel, woolens, and farm machinery—thus lowering prices on them.

The lower tariff reduced revenue for the government. To make up the losses, Wilson enacted both a corporate and a personal income tax. It was not high by late-twentieth-century standards. People who earned less than $4,000 a year paid no tax. On annual incomes between $4,000 and $20,000, a tidy sum in 1913, the rate was only 1 percent. People in the highest bracket, $500,000 and up, paid only 6 percent, a fraction of the low brackets today. Nevertheless, by forcing the rich to pay proportionately more toward supporting the government, the tax provisions of the Clayton Act represented a triumph of progressivism.

Wilson's Cabinet

Wilson designed his cabinet in order to unite the Democratic party behind him. The president never had liked William Jennings Bryan, but he named him Secretary of State because Bryan was the widely loved elder statesman of the party. Moreover, Bryan had been instrumental in nominating Wilson.

Most other appointments rewarded key components of the party, especially the South and, through Secretary of Labor William B. Wilson, the labor movement, whose support the president needed. The most valu-

able member of the cabinet was William G. McAdoo of Georgia (later of California). As Secretary of the Treasury, he provided the president with shrewd advice on banking policy. When McAdoo married Wilson's daughter, he became a kind of heir apparent.

Wilson's three confidants did not sit in the cabinet. Joseph Tumulty, a canny Irish politician, served as private secretary and reminded the president of the often sordid realities involved in keeping together a political machine. Colonel Edward M. House, a Texas businessman, was a shadowy, but not sinister figure. Self-effacing and utterly devoted to the president, House neither desired nor accepted any official position. Instead, he traveled discreetly throughout the United States and abroad, conveying the president's views and wants to businessmen and heads of state.

Louis D. Brandeis, a corporation lawyer become antitrust progressive, provided Wilson with both economic principles and a social conscience. The father of the New Freedom, Brandeis turned Wilson away from the limitations of the program after 1914 and toward a broader progressivism. In 1916, Wilson rewarded him by naming him to the Supreme Court, on which Brandeis served as one of the great liberal justices of the twentieth century.

The New Freedom in Action

Two laws that reflected Brandeis's influence were the Federal Reserve Act of 1913 and the Clayton Antitrust Act of 1914. The first was designed both to bring order to the national banking system and to hobble the vast power of Wall Street. The law established twelve regional Federal Reserve Banks, which dealt not directly with people but with other banks. The Federal Reserve System was owned by private bankers who were required to deposit 6 percent of their capital in it. However, the president appointed the majority of the directors, who sat in Washington, theoretically putting the government in control of the money supply.

The greatest power of the Federal Reserve System was (and is) its control of the prime interest rate, the level of interest at which money is lent to other banks for lending to private investors and buyers. By lowering the prime rate, the Federal Reserve could stimulate investment and economic expansion in slow times. By raising the prime rate, the Federal Reserve could cool down an overactive economy that threatened to blow up in inflation, financial panic, and depression.

The Federal Reserve Act did bring some order to the national banking system. But it did not, as many progressives hoped, tame the great bankers. Indeed, because representatives of the private banks sat on the

---

SONG AND DANCE MAN

Rigid and dignified in public, Woodrow Wilson could be quite informal in private. After his wedding night with his second wife, Edith Bolling, whom he married while president, Wilson broke out in a chorus of the then popular song "Oh, You Beautiful Doll."

THE CASUAL WORKERS

"Home, a permanent place of abode, respect of others, the decencies of right living, have neither meaning nor attraction for them," wrote the editor of the *Record,* a newspaper in the small northern California farm town of Chico. He was talking about people who were familiar to everyone who lived west of the Mississippi in 1910, and to many easterners as well—the hobos, otherwise known as migrant workers or casual laborers.

Although a few women road the rails with them, most of these wandering workers were men who had no homes, families, or ties to the sort of proprieties to which the editor of the *Record* referred. They were essential to the economic life of the western states. They brought in the wheat from the Mississippi to Oregon; picked the fruit in the Pacific states from Washington to the Mexican border; and manned the construction crews on projects far from any town, such as the aqueduct that rerouted the Owens River three hundred miles across the Mojave Desert to the thirsty metropolis of Los Angeles in southern California. They worked in canneries and lumber mills, and those with the skills were the lumberjacks in the great redwood, spruce, and Douglas fir forests of the Northwest.

Almost all this work was seasonal or, at best, temporary; a mammoth construction job like the aqueduct took years to complete, but the day came when hands were no longer needed. Therefore, the kind of worker who made his way to a job at his own expense and disappeared when the job was done was precisely the kind of worker who was called for.

Of course, the casual worker did not disappear into thin air. When there was no work, as in winter, or when he did not feel like working, the casual laborer headed for a town in which he could expect to find a "main stem" or "skid row" on which were located cheap restaurants, cheap saloons, cheap hotels, pawnshops, second-hand clothing stores, brothels, and "missions" run by evangelical religious groups.

Here was a big part of their problem. On the main stem, the hobos rubbed elbows with derelicts, and it took a practiced eye to distinguish them. The casual workers knew the difference. Whereas "tramps" wandered but did not work and "bums" did little but drink, hobos were self-sufficient workers. They did not beg for handouts or even accept them. They held tough jobs, albeit only as long as they chose to work, and when they were down on their luck, they chopped wood, hauled water, or mowed a lawn in return for a meal. Hobos explained to dozens of investigators that they could usually be identified by the bedroll of "bindle" that they carried. Most of the jobs they took required them to furnish their own bedding, whereas tramps and bums had little use for it. One of the terms used to describe casual workers was "bindle-stiff."

Nevertheless, the hobos looked much the same as tramps and bums. When they were traveling by freight train (which was illegal but generally tolerated), they were dirty, in clothing just a few notches above rags, unshaven, and ripe to the nose. And they patently did not live as the "respectable classes" believed people should live. The "hobo jungle" on the outskirts of every railroad town, a camp where casual workers gathered to eat and sleep while waiting for a train, was a dangerous and forbidden place in the imagination of children and many adults as well.

Indeed, as University of Washington sociologist Carlton Parker discovered after a thorough study of the casual laborer, the hobos had a higher rate of alcoholism and venereal disease than did the population at large. Nevertheless, Parker cautioned that essentially these people were homeless men.

The hobos themselves had a rather more positive self-image. They believed that they were the builders of the West. "It is we," one of their songs had it, who

> Dug the mines and built the workshops, endless miles of railroad laid.
> Now we stand outcast and starving, 'mid the wonders we have made. . . .

A hobo poem caught the same sense of resentment that society should scorn them:

> He built the road,
> With others of his class, he built the road,
> Now o'er it many a mile he packs his load,
> Chasing a job, spurred on by hunger's goad,
> He walks and walks, and wonders why
> In Hell he built the road.

The casual worker considered himself to be the last frontiersman—freewheeling, independent, not "afraid of his job" but quick to quit when something about it displeased him. In other words, he was the kind of American who, already by the turn of the century, was enshrined in nostalgic myth as the best kind of American.

At the very least they were not afraid to stand up for their rights when they believed that those rights were threatened. In 1894, when Jacob Coxey led his march of the unemployed from Ohio to Washington, the "petition in boots" demanding federal action to create jobs during the depression, a contingent of western casual laborers called "Kelley's Army" set off from Oakland, traveling to Washington by freight trains that they virtually commandeered.

After the turn of the century, western migrant workers turned in large numbers to the Industrial Workers of the World to voice their grievances. Between 1909 and

1914, they fought a number of "free-speech fights" in such western towns as Missoula, Spokane, and San Diego. These actions, directed against laws that forbade street speaking on the main stem, anticipated the protest tactic of nonviolent civil disobedience that later was employed by Mohandas Gandhi in India and Martin Luther King, Jr., in the United States. By deliberately disobeying the obnoxious laws but peacefully submitting to arrest, the free speechers put the burden of law enforcement on the shoulders of the authorities. They were happy to be arrested. As long as they were in jail, the city governments had big bills to feed them, and the judicial calendars were clogged because every free speecher demanded a separate jury trial. Most of the cities in which free-speech fights were joined found it preferable to repeal the ordinances.

What happened to the army of casual workers? The virtual completion of the western railroad system eliminated many jobs. Mechanization of harvesting wheat or even picking fruit destroyed other jobs that had been filled by hobos. So did the practice of good forestry: by farming trees and harvesting a forest in order to have a steady supply of timber ("sustained yield"), lumbermen could maintain a permanent, more reliable work force rather than send out the call for migrant workers.

Perhaps as important as anything else was the advent of the cheap automobile by the 1920s. The used Model T Ford, which almost everyone could afford, led to the family's becoming the chief unit of the migrant work force. A family of five or six, including children, was cheaper to hire than were the homeless men who rode the rails. Moreover, with children to feed, the family was more stable as employees than was the vagabond adventurer who was not "afraid of his job."

By the 1930s, when the Great Depression caused a big jump in the number of people who were tramping the country, the working hobo was already a vanishing figure. Indeed, the work of harvesting fruit and vegetables on the west coast was becoming increasingly dependent on Mexicans who, coming from extreme poverty, could be hired even more cheaply than the solitary hobo.

Seasonal workers and hobos used trains as a free form of transportation.

President Woodrow Wilson conferring with aides.

Federal Reserve Board, the long-term effects of the law were to provide Wall Street with an even more efficient, albeit more accountable, control of national finance.

In 1914, Wilson pushed his antitrust policy through Congress. The Clayton Antitrust Act stipulated that corporations would be fined for unfair practices that threatened competition, forbade interlocking directorates (the same men sitting on the boards of "competing" companies and thereby coordinating policies), and declared that officers of corporations would be held personally responsible for offenses committed by their companies. Another bill that was passed at the same time created the Federal Trade Commission to supervise the activities of the trusts. This agency was more along the lines of the New Nationalism than the New Freedom.

Wilson Changes Direction

After the congressional elections of 1914, Wilson shifted far more sharply toward the reforms that Teddy Roosevelt had promoted. Although the Democrats retained control of both houses, many progressives returned to their Republican voting habits in 1914 and cut the Democratic margin. It was obvious to both the president and Democratic congressmen that if they were to survive the election of 1916 against a reunified Republican party, they would have to woo these progressive voters.

Consequently, Wilson agreed to support social legislation that he had opposed through 1914. He did not like laws that favored any special interest, farmers any more than bankers, but in order to shore up support in the West, he agreed to the Federal Farm Loan Act of 1916, which provided low-cost credit to farmers. Early in his administration, Wilson had opposed a child-labor law on constitutional grounds. In 1916, he supported the Keating-Owen Act, which severely restricted the employment of children in most jobs.

The Adamson Act required the interstate railroads to put their workers on an eight-hour day without a reduction in pay. Wilson even moderated his antiblack sentiments, although Washington definitely took on the character of a segregated southern city during his tenure. Despite a lifelong opposition to woman suffrage, the president began to encourage states to enfranchise women and to hint that he supported a constitutional amendment that would guarantee the right nationwide.

By the summer of 1916, Wilson could say with considerable justice that he had pushed progressive reformism farther than had any of his predecessors. He enacted or supported much of Theodore Roosevelt's program of 1912, as well as his own. By 1916, however, Americans' votes reflected more than their views on domestic issues. They were troubled about their nation's role in a suddenly complicated world. Simultaneous with Wilson's enactment of progressive reforms, Europe had tumbled into the greatest war in history.

For Further Reading

Since this chapter is a continuation of the subject of Chapter 38, consult the books that are listed at the end of that chapter. In addition, a number of good books deal with the Taft and Wilson administrations. An excellent sympathetic study of the unhappy Taft is D. F. Anderson, *William Howard Taft: A Conservative's Conception of the Presidency* (1973). P. E. Coletta focuses on the events of the Taft years in *The Presidency of William Howard Taft* (1973). Woodrow Wilson's progressive career is dealt with in the monumental biography, still in progress, by Arthur S. Link, *Wilson* (1947–). Link is also the author of a one-volume study, *Woodrow Wilson and the Progressive Era* (1954). Two other books that are well worth reading are John M. Blum, *Woodrow Wilson and the Politics of Morality* (1956), and John A. Garraty, *Woodrow Wilson* (1956).

America Discovers Europe
The Path to World War, 1914–1918

A few days before his inauguration, Woodrow Wilson was reminded of some difficulties in American relations with Mexico. Briefly he thought about the problem and set it aside, remarking offhand, "It would be the irony of fate if my administration had to deal chiefly with foreign affairs."

Wilson did not fear such a challenge. He was a pillar of confidence in whatever he did. But his academic and political careers had been devoted to domestic concerns. He had paid scant attention to the thorny snarls of relations among nations, and never had been particularly interested in them. When Wilson considered the rest of the world, it was on the basis of reflexes, assumptions, and sentiments rather than on that of a coherent policy.

Soldiers in battle during the Meuse-Argonne offensive of 1918.

Wilson, America, and the World

Like most Americans, the president was proud that because of its population and industrial might, the United States ranked with only a handful of nations as a great world power. Also like other Americans, he believed that the United States was unique among great and lesser powers alike. Built on an idea rather than on inheritance of a common culture and territory, the United States acted toward other countries in accordance with principles rather than with a narrow self-interest. Protected from Europe by a broad ocean, the United States required no huge armies to defend its security but, instead, expended its resources in constructive ways.

As a moralist, Wilson had roundly criticized Teddy Roosevelt's gunboat diplomacy. To bully small nations was to betray the American ideal of self-government. He proclaimed that his administration would deal with the weak and turbulent Latin American countries "upon terms of equality and honor." As a progressive who was suspicious of Wall Street, Wilson also disapproved of Taft's dollar diplomacy. Shortly after he took office, Wilson canceled federal support of an investment scheme in China because it implied an obligation to intervene in the event that Wall Street's profits were threatened.

Wilson was influenced by the Christian pacifism toward which Secretary of State William Jennings Bryan also leaned. Bryan believed that war was justified only in self-defense. If nations would act cautiously and discuss their problems, they would not have to spill blood. With Wilson's approval, Bryan negotiated conciliation treaties with thirty nations. The signatories pledged that in the event of a dispute, they would negotiate for one year before declaring war. Bryan believed that during this "cooling-off" period, virtually every dispute between nations would be recognized as relatively minor and capable of being easily resolved without the use of force.

High ideals. But once in the cockpit, Wilson found that applying them consistently was more difficult than flying the recently invented airplane. In part this was because he was also impelled by assumptions that conflicted with his moral and progressive ideals. Raised to believe in the superiority of the white race, he found it difficult in practice to act as an equal in dealing with the Japanese and the racially mixed Latin Americans. His commitment to diplomacy by good example was complicated by a missionary's impulse to dictate proper behavior. When weaker nations did not freely emulate American ways of doing things, Wilson became arrogant, patronizing, and demanding. If other peoples did not realize what was good for them, Wilson would teach them.

So he raised no objections to a California state law that insulted racially sensitive Japan by restricting the right of Japanese-Americans to own land. In 1915, he ordered the marines into black Haiti when chaotic conditions there threatened American investments, and the next year, he landed troops in the Dominican Republic under similar circumstances. These actions angered Latin Americans, but they were minor irritants compared with Wilson's prolonged and blundering interference in Mexican affairs.

¡Viva Madero! ¡Viva Carranza!

In 1911, the Mexican dictator for thirty-five years, Porfirio Díaz, was overthrown following a revolution supported by practically every Mexican social group save the tiny elite that Díaz had favored. Foreign investors, who had reaped rich rewards by cooperating with the dictator, waited and fretted, none more so than the British and Americans. The leader of the revolution spoke of returning control of Mexican wealth to Mexicans, and Americans alone owned $2 billion in property in Mexico, more of the country's railroads, mines, and oil wells than Mexicans controlled.

Francisco Madero was the reflective idealist who headed the revolution. He and Wilson would have disagreed, but they might also have gotten along. Madero was cultivated, educated, and moderate, not given to acting rashly. Moreover, he shared Wilson's liberal political philosophy and admired American institutions.

They never had the chance to talk. Quietly encouraged by the Taft administration, a group of Díaz's generals led by Victoriano Huerta staged a coup. Apparently making their plans in the American embassy, the rebels struck shortly before Wilson was inaugurated, murdered Madero, and seized control of the federal government.

It was the murder that offended Wilson. He said that he would not deal with "a government of butchers," and he pressured England to withdraw its hasty recognition of the Huerta government. When peasant rebellions broke out in scattered parts of Mexico and a Constitutionalist army took shape behind a somber, long-bearded aristocrat, Venustiano Carranza, Wilson openly approved.

In April 1914, the United States intervened directly. Seven American sailors on shore leave in Tampico were arrested by one of Huerta's colonels. They were freed almost immediately, but Huerta refused the demand of Admiral Henry T. Mayo for a twenty-one gun salute as an appropriate apology. Claiming that American honor had been insulted (and seeking to head off a German ship that was bringing arms to Huerta), Wilson ordered troops into the important port of Vera Cruz.

Somewhat to Wilson's surprise, ordinary Mexicans joined the fight against the Americans, and street fighting in Vera Cruz claimed more than four hundred lives. Wilson failed to understand that while they had little love for their military dictator, the Mexican people resented gringo interference more intensely. Even Carranza, in control of the north of Mexico, condemned the American landing. Somewhat alarmed, Wilson agreed to an offer by Argentina, Brazil, and Chile to mediate the crisis.

Pancho Villa Versus the United States

Before anything could be settled, Carranza ousted Huerta. However, he then quarreled with one of his own generals, a charismatic figure who was born Doroteo Arango, but was universally known as Pancho Villa. Alternately jovial and vicious, half bandit and half social revolutionary, Villa was romanticized by young journalist John Reed as "The Robin Hood of Mexico." For a time even Wilson was convinced that Villa represented democracy in Mexico, and would be friendlier to American interests than was Carranza.

But Wilson wanted stability most of all. When Carranza took Mexico City in October 1915, Wilson recognized his de facto control of the government, stinging Villa and prompting him to show his seamier side. Calculating that if he provoked American intervention he could unsettle Mexico again and make a play for power, Villa stopped a train, ordered off seventeen American passengers, and shot all but one. Early in 1916, he led a raid across the border into the dusty little desert town of Columbus, New Mexico, where his men killed nineteen people.

Instead of allowing Carranza to root out and punish Villa, as was proper with neighbors who were equals,

Bandit and revolutionary Pancho Villa (center) with the leader of agrarian revolt in Mexico, Emiliano Zapata (right).

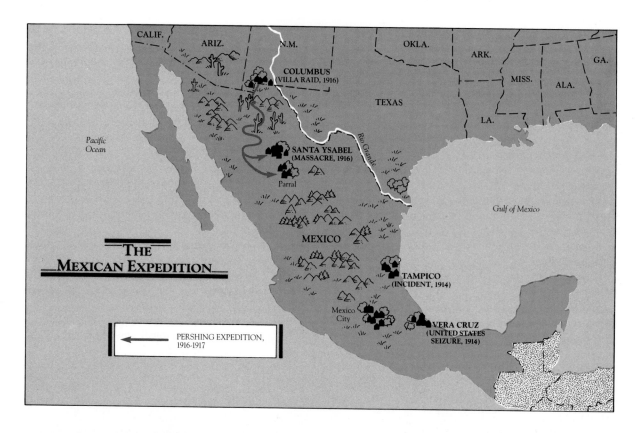

CALIF. ARIZ. N.M. OKLA. ARK. GA.

COLUMBUS
(VILLA RAID, 1916)

MISS. ALA.

TEXAS

LA.

Pacific
Ocean

Rio Grande

SANTA YSABEL
(MASSACRE, 1916)

Parral

Gulf of Mexico

THE
MEXICAN EXPEDITION

MEXICO

TAMPICO
(INCIDENT, 1914)

Mexico
City

VERA CRUZ
(UNITED STATES
SEIZURE, 1914)

PERSHING EXPEDITION,
1916-1917

Wilson ordered General John J. Pershing and six thousand troops, including the Tenth Cavalry, one of the last black regiments, to capture the bandit guerrilla. They were humiliated. In the arid mountainous country that was his home, the clever Villa easily evaded the Americans, leading them on three hundred miles of a zigzag route during which time they never gained sight of Villa's main force. Pershing's men did, however, exchange shots several times with Carranza's troops. In one skirmish, forty died. While accomplishing nothing, Wilson had succeeded in alienating every political faction in Mexico.

In January 1917, he finally gave up and ordered "Black Jack" Pershing to return home. Only because Americans were faced by a more formidable enemy, the German emperor, were they able to make light of their humiliation at the hands of a man whom they considered an illiterate *bandido*.

Europe's Tragic War

By early 1917, Europe had been at war for two and a half years. In June 1914, a Serbian (Yugoslavian) nationalist, Gavrilo Princip, had assassinated the archduke of Austria. As he doubtless had hoped to do, Princip had set rolling a series of actions made almost

inevitable by the secret treaties, international jealousies, and reckless arms race in which the great powers had been engaged for a generation.

Serbia was an ally of Russia, which backed the little country in defying Austria. Austria-Hungary, a decaying empire, looked to powerful Germany for encouragement, and got it. France became involved because of French fears of German industrial might, which had led to secret agreements promising mutual support to Russia. England, traditionally aloof from European wrangles, had been frightened by Germany's construction of a worldwide navy (larger than America's and second only to Britain's) and, in 1907, had signed mutual-assistance treaties with both France and Russia. Many of the smaller nations of Europe were associated with either the Central Powers (Germany, Austria-Hungary, Bulgaria, Turkey) or the Allied Powers (England, France, Russia, eventually Italy). By September 1914, the Continent was at war.

Americans React

The American people reacted to the explosion with a mixture of disbelief and disgust. For a generation, European rulers had filled the air with the sounds of saber rattling. Americans were used to that; their own Teddy Roosevelt was a master of noisy bluff. But T.R. always understood the difference between a bully show and a catastrophe, and until 1914, so had the Europeans. Even Kaiser Wilhelm II of Germany, a somewhat ridiculous figure with his extravagant military uniforms, comic-opera waxed moustache, and penchant for bombast, had acted prudently in the crunch. Like most Europeans, Americans concluded that the constant talk about war without going to war would continue indefinitely. They did not really believe that powerful, civilized countries would turn their terrifying technology for killing on one another.

Once European nations had done just that, Americans convinced themselves that their nation, at least, remained above such savagery. Politicians, preachers, and editors quoted and praised the wisdom of George Washington's warning against "entangling alliances." They blamed Europe's tragedy on the corrupt Old-World empires, kings and princes, religious intolerance, national hatreds, and insane stockpiling of armaments that were superfluous if they were not used, suicidal if they were.

Never had American political and social institutions looked so superior. Never had Americans been more grateful to have turned their backs on Europe's ways. As reports of hideous carnage on the battlefield began to hum over the Atlantic Cable, Americans shuddered and counted their blessings. No prominent person

raised an objection when President Wilson proclaimed absolute American neutrality. However, when the president also called on Americans to be "neutral in fact as well as in name, . . . impartial in thought as well as in action," he was, as he was wont to do, demanding too much of human nature.

Divided Sympathies

A large proportion of Americans looked to England as their ancestral as well as cultural motherland, and they were naturally sympathetic to Britain's cause. Wilson himself was an unstinting Anglophile. Before he had become president, he had vacationed regularly in England, and in his first year in office, he had resolved the last minor points of difference between England and the United States: a border dispute in British Columbia, a quarrel between Canadian and American fishermen off Newfoundland, and British objections to discriminatory tolls on the Panama Canal.

Hardly noticeable at first, but ominous in the long run, American and British capitalists were closely allied. British investments in the United States were vast, and when the cost of purchasing everything from wheat to munitions required that these holdings be sold to Americans, often at bargain rates, the relationship grew warmer. Banking houses like the House of Mor-

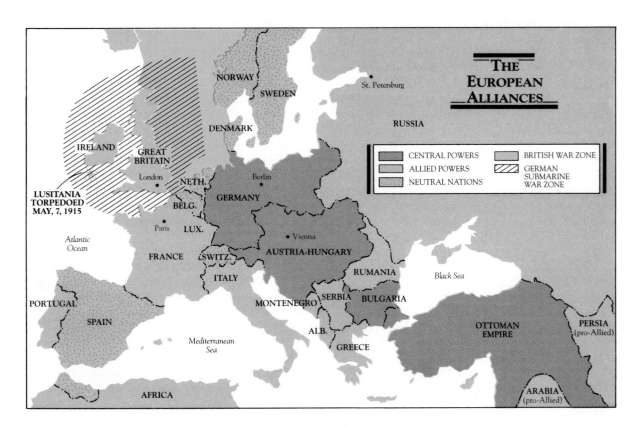

gan lent money to the English, at first with Wilson's disapproval, and acted as agents for Allied bond sales. By 1917, Great Britain owed American lenders $2.3 billion. It was a strong tie, when compared with the meager $27 million that the Germans managed to borrow in the United States. Wall Street had good reason to favor an English victory or, at least, to pale at the thought of an English defeat.

Old-stock Americans were also sympathetic to France. The land of Lafayette was America's "oldest friend," the indispensable ally of the Revolution. Americans never had formally gone to war with the French. And France was, except for the United States, the only republic among the world's great powers, constitutionally pledged to civil equality and representative institutions.

But Americans were by no means unanimously in favor of the Allies. One American in three was either foreign-born or a first-generation citizen, many of them with strong Old-World sentiments that made them pro-German or unfriendly toward the Allied Powers. As many as 8 million Americans traced their roots to Germany or Austria-Hungary. They had come to the United States for its economic opportunities. But many of them clung to their old culture. Few German-, Austrian-, or Hungarian-Americans seriously believed or suggested that their adopted country take the side of the fatherland. But they did hope for American neutrality, and in heavily German areas like Wisconsin, they loudly said so.

Many of the 4.5 million Irish-Americans hated England as the oppressor of their homeland for six hundred years. They wished England ill in every venture, and when Germany aided Irish rebels in 1916, and England summarily crushed the "Easter Rising," many Irish-Americans expressed strong pro-German loyalties.

Similarly, many Russian and Polish Jews, who had suffered brutal persecution under the czars, supported Germany. They thought of Germany as a country where Jews enjoyed nearly equal citizenship. Socialists, who were an important minority within the Jewish community in New York, hated Russia above all other countries because of the cruelty of the czar's secret police.

With such a diverse population and tangle of conflicting loyalties, Wilson's policy of neutrality not only was idealistic, but was the only practical alternative, especially for a Democratic party politician who depended on ethnic voters. And it might have worked if Europe's "Great War," as the First World War was called until the second broke out in 1939, had been fought for clearly stated and limited goals, and had

been concluded with a decisive and early victory by one side or the other, as previous wars had been.

Stalemate on Land

That was not to be. In the first campaign, the German General Staff threw away a chance to score a limited victory that might have satisfied Kaiser Wilhelm II. At a critical moment, the generals withdrew troops from the assault on France and shipped them east to fight the Russians. This departure from plan allowed the French to regroup and the English to land a large army on the Continent. Then the war bogged down into two parallel lines of entrenchments, hundreds of miles long, with a desolate no man's land in between.

Due to a revolution in military technology that the generals failed to understand, winning a mere five hundred yards of territory was costly in both money and men. For example, the newly perfected machine gun made the old-fashioned mass infantry charge, such as had dominated battle during the American Civil War, an exercise in suicide. When one army charged "over the top," out of its own trenches, enemy machine guns filled the air with a hurricane of lead that mowed down soldiers by the thousands. On the first day of the Battle of the Somme in July 1916, 60,000 young Britons were slaughtered or wounded, the majority of them within the first half hour. By the time the campaign sputtered to a meaningless end, British losses totaled 400,000; French, 200,000; and German, 500,000. On the Ypres sector of the lines in April 1917, 160,000 British soldiers were killed in only five days in order to advance the front four miles.

The new warfare overwhelmingly favored the defenders. Neither side developed an effective technology of attack. Massive shelling before an assault was designed to wipe out the enemy's machine guns, but did little damage because defenders burrowed deep into the ground and waited for the crazing noise, smoke, and explosions to cease. Both Allies and Central Powers experimented with poison gases as a means of weakening defensive positions. But they soon learned that a slight shift in the wind blew the deadly, maiming fumes back on their own men.

The airplane saw its first military use in the First World War, but it was of little importance in battle. (Ordinary soldiers considered pilots to be pampered playboys.) Even reconnaissance meant little when nearly impregnable entrenchments made attack so difficult. The British developed the tank as a means of neutralizing German machine guns. Armored vehicles could drive unharmed directly into gun emplacements. But the generals never used their edge intelligently.

Soldiers relied in part on trenches for protection in France during World War I.

They attached the tanks to infantry units, thus slowing them to a walk, rather than sending groups of the steel monsters in advance of the foot soldiers.

Incompetence at the top of every army contributed substantially to the bloodshed. Petty personal jealousies among generals of the Allies, especially between the English and the French, resulted in decisions that had nothing to do with the welfare of the common soldier or even the winning of the war.

The War at Sea

Americans were sickened by the news from Europe, but it was the war at sea that directly touched American interests. As in the past, naval war was economic war; it was aimed at destroying the enemy's commerce and,

therefore, its ability to carry on the fight. Its naval superiority allowed Great Britain to strike first, proclaiming a blockade of Germany.

According to the "rules of war," all enemy merchant ships were fair game for seizing or sinking, although tradition required that crews and passengers be rescued. The ships of neutral nations, however, retained the right to trade with any nation as long as they were not carrying contraband (at first defined as war materiel).

The laws of blockade were more complicated and allowed for several interpretations; blockades had caused friction between England and the United States before. In 1914, England introduced several new wrinkles that created a potentially more serious situation. The British mined some parts of the North Sea. Ships, including those of neutrals, would risk being destroyed merely by attempting to trade with Germany. The Royal Navy stopped many American ships on the high seas and took them to English ports for search. England redefined *contraband* to mean almost all trade goods, including some foodstuffs. And when neutral Holland, Denmark, and Sweden began to import goods for secret resale to Germany (pastoral Denmark, which never purchased American lard, imported eleven thousand tons of it in the first months of the war), England slapped strict regulations on trade with those countries.

American objections were mild. The German market never had been important to American shippers, and wartime sales to England and France rose so dramatically that few exporters needed the business. Trade with the Allies climbed from $825 million in 1914 to $3.2 billion in 1916, a fourfold increase in two years.

At first the Germans were indifferent to the British blockade. Their plan had been to win a quick victory on land, which rendered economic warfare moot. When the war stalemated, however, the German General Staff recognized the necessity of choking England's import economy. Germany's tool for doing this was another creation of the new military technology, the *Unterseeboot* (undersea boat, or U-boat), or submarine.

Submarine Warfare

Ironically, the modern submarine was the invention of two Americans, John Holland and Simon Lake. When the navy rejected their device as frivolous, however, they took their plans to Europe. The Germans recognized the submarine's potential and launched a large-scale construction program. By February 1915, Germany had a large enough flotilla of the twenty-thousand-ton vessels, each armed with nineteen torpedoes, to declare the waters surrounding the British Isles to be a "war zone." All enemy merchant ships within those waters were liable to be sunk, and the safety of neutral ships could not be absolutely guaranteed. Within days, several British vessels went to the bottom, and President Wilson warned the kaiser of Germany's "strict accountability" for American lives and property lost to U-boats.

Because submarines were so fragile, the kind of warfare that they engaged in appeared to be particularly inhumane. On the surface, the submarine was helpless; a light six-inch gun mounted inconspicuously on the bow of a freighter was enough to blow a U-boat to bits. Because submarines could dive only slowly, British merchant vessels were instructed to ram them. There-

With a large flotilla of submarines, Germany turned British waters into a war zone during World War I.

fore, German submarines had to strike without warning, giving crew and passengers no opportunity to escape. And since submarines were small, their crews were cramped, and there was no room to take aboard those who abandoned ship. Survivors of torpedoed boats were on their own in the midst of the ocean.

Many Americans grumbled that if the English blockade was illegal, the German submarine campaign was immoral. The English were thieves, but the Germans were murderers. They drowned seamen by the score. And more than seamen. The issue came to a head on May 7, 1915, when the English luxury liner *Lusitania* was torpedoed off the coast of Ireland, and 1,195 people were killed, including 128 Americans. What kind of war was this, Americans asked, that killed innocent travelers? The *New York Times* described the Germans as "savages drenched with blood."

Wilson Wins a Victory

The Germans replied that they had warned Americans against traveling on the *Lusitania* through advertisements in major New York and Washington newspapers. They pointed out, moreover, that the *Lusitania* had not been merely a passenger ship. It had been carrying forty-two hundred cases of small arms purchased in the United States and some high explosives. So many people had drowned because the *Lusitania* had gone down in only eighteen minutes, blown wide open not by the torpedo but by a secondary explosion. The British had been using innocent passengers as hostages for the safe conduct of war materiel.

Wilson was well aware of this and did not hold the British blameless in the tragedy. Nevertheless, Germany's military right to use the new weapon was less important to him than the sacred principle of freedom of the seas for those not at war. He sent a series of strongly worded notes to Germany. The second was so bellicose that the pacifistic Bryan feared it meant war. He resigned rather than sign it, and Wilson replaced him in the State Department with Robert Lansing, an international lawyer.

While making no formal promises to Wilson, the Germans stopped attacking passenger vessels, and the uproar faded. Then, early in 1916, the Allies announced that they were arming all merchant ships, and Germany responded that the U-boats would sink all enemy vessels without warning. On March 24, 1916, a French channel steamer, the *Sussex,* went down with an American among the casualties. Wilson threatened to break diplomatic relations with Germany, the last step before a declaration of war, if "unrestricted submarine warfare" were continued.

The German General Staff did not want the United States to enter the war. Plans for a major offensive on all fronts were afoot, and the German navy did not have enough U-boats to launch a full-scale attack on British shipping. In the Sussex Pledge of May 4, 1916, the German foreign office promised to observe the rules of visit and search before attacking enemy ships.

America Goes to War

Wilson had won a spectacular diplomatic victory at the beginning of his campaign for reelection. He was nominated without opposition at the Democratic convention, and his campaign was given a theme that did not entirely please him. The keynote speaker designed his speech around the slogan "He Kept Us Out of War."

He Kept Us Out of War—While Preparing for It

Wilson did not like the slogan because, as he confided to an aide, "I can't keep the country out of war. Any little German lieutenant can put us into war at any time by some calculated outrage." He meant that a submarine commander, acting on his own, could bark out the order that would torpedo the Sussex Pledge. Like many national leaders before and since, Wilson had trapped himself in a position where control over a momentous decision was out of his hands, and he knew it.

Wilson began to prepare for the possibility of war as early as November 1915, when he asked Congress to beef up the army to four hundred thousand men and fund a huge expansion of the navy. He was pushed into this "preparedness" campaign by his political enemy Theodore Roosevelt, who jabbed and poked at the fact

> ### WHAT'S IN A NAME?
>
> The British called it the European War, and Americans were inclined to use that term until the United States intervened in April 1917. Then, a few idealistic but awkward tags were tried: War for the Freedom of Europe, War for the Overthrow of Militarism, War for Civilization, and—best known—Woodrow Wilson's War to Make the World Safe for Democracy. Only after 1918 did the Great War and the World War become standard—until 1939 when the outbreak of another great worldwide war made it World War I.

The New York Times.

EXTRA
5:30 A. M.

Weather Today and Sunday. Fair.

VOL. LXIV...NO. 20,923. NEW YORK, SATURDAY, MAY 8, 1915.—TWENTY-FOUR PAGES. ONE CENT In Greater New York, Jersey City and Newark. Elsewhere TWO CENTS.

LUSITANIA SUNK BY A SUBMARINE, PROBABLY 1,260 DEAD; TWICE TORPEDOED OFF IRISH COAST; SINKS IN 15 MINUTES; CAPT. TURNER SAVED, FROHMAN AND VANDERBILT MISSING; WASHINGTON BELIEVES THAT A GRAVE CRISIS IS AT HAND

SHOCKS THE PRESIDENT

Washington Deeply Stirred by the Loss of American Lives.

BULLETINS AT WHITE HOUSE

Wilson Reads Them Closely, but Is Silent on the Nation's Course.

HINTS OF CONGRESS CALL

Loss of Lusitania Recalls Firm Tone of Our First Warning to Germany.

CAPITAL FULL OF RUMORS

Reports That Liner Was to be Sunk Were Heard Before Actual News Came.

The Lost Cunard Steamship Lusitania
X Where the First Torpedo Struck. XX Where the Second Torpedo Struck.

SOME DEAD TAKEN ASHORE

Several Hundred Survivors at Queenstown and Kinsale.

STEWARD TELLS OF DISASTER

One Torpedo Crashes Into the Doomed Liner's Bow, Another Into the Engine Room.

SHIP LISTS OVER TO PORT

Makes It Impossible to Lower Many Boats, So Hundreds Must Have Gone Down.

ATTACKED IN BROAD DAY

Passengers at Luncheon—Warning Had Been Given by Germans Before the Ship Left New York.

Only 650 Were Saved, Few Cabin Passengers

QUEENSTOWN, Saturday, May 8, 4:28 A. M.— Survivors of the Lusitania who have arrived here estimate that only about 650 of those aboard the steamer were saved, and say only a small proportion of those rescued were saloon passengers.

Cunard Office Here Besieged for News; Fate of 1,918 on Lusitania Long in Doubt

Nothing Heard from the Well-Known Passengers on Board—Story of Disaster Long Unconfirmed While Anxious Crowds Seek Details.

List of Saved Includes Capt. Turner; Vanderbilt and Frohman Reported Lost

Saw the Submarine 100 Yards Off and Watched Torpedo as It Struck Ship

Ernest Cowper, a Toronto Newspaper Man, Describes Attack, Seen from Ship's Rail—Poison Gas Used in Torpedoes, Say Other Passengers.

The front page of the New York Times on May 8, 1915, announcing the sinking of the Lusitania, an English luxury liner.

that American forces totaled fewer than one hundred thousand; that the Quartermaster Corps (entrusted with supply) had only recently begun using trucks; that at one point in 1915 the American artillery had only enough ammunition for two days' fighting with cannon that were a generation obsolete.

Wilson had to contend with an antipreparedness Congress led by Representative Claude Kitchin of North Carolina. With widespread backing among the western and southern progressives, on whom Wilson depended for support, the antipreparedness forces pointed out that it had been "preparedness" that had led to Europe going to war in the first place. If the United States had the means to fight, they argued, it was all the more likely that the United States *would* fight. Wilson had to settle for a compromise.

The Election of 1916

While Wilson wrestled with the preparedness issue, the Republicans patched up their split of 1912. Most leading Progressives wanted to maintain their independent party, and they held a convention that renominated Theodore Roosevelt. But the Colonel decided that ousting Wilson from the White House was more important than the slim chance of his own election. He turned down the nomination and urged the Progressives to support the Republican candidate, Supreme Court Justice Charles Evans Hughes.

On the face of it, Hughes was an excellent choice. As governor of New York between 1907 and 1910, he had been a progressive. However, as a Supreme Court judge during the party split of 1912, he had taken no part in the battle and was therefore acceptable to conservatives.

Hughes's integrity was unimpeachable. In dignity and presidential bearing, he was more than a match for Wilson. His distinguished gray beard was a reminder of the simpler days before the Great War. He spoke in high-sounding phrases. But Hughes was also a dull fellow on the speaker's platform, and he lacked Wilson's moral toughness. His views on the war issue actually differed little from the president's. He wanted to avoid war if he could. But thanks to Theodore Roosevelt, who stormed about the country sounding as militaristic as the German emperor, the Republican choice came to be known as the war candidate.

This undeserved reputation cost Hughes just enough votes to give the election to Wilson. It was very close. Hughes carried every northeastern state but New Hampshire and every midwestern state but Ohio. He went to bed on election night believing that he was president. Wilson, thinking he had lost, sketched out plans to name Hughes Secretary of State and resign along with Vice President Thomas R. Marshall, thus allowing Hughes to deal with the foreign crisis immediately.

But then one antiwar western state after another turned in majorities for Wilson. When he carried California by a paper-thin margin, he was elected, 277 electoral votes to 254. The election was on Tuesday. Not until Friday did the American people know for certain who would lead them for the next four years.

Trying and Failing to Keep the Peace

Elated but still nervous about the "little German lieutenant" who could plunge the United States into war, Wilson tried to act as a mediator. Only by ending the war in Europe could he be sure of keeping the United States out. During the winter of 1916/17, he believed that he was making progress, at least with the Germans. To Wilson, the British were the major obstacle to peace.

But it was all an illusion. He and the American people were in for a rude awakening. On January 22, 1917, Wilson outlined his peace plan to Congress. Only a "peace without victory," a "peace among equals" with neither winners nor losers, could solve the problem. The progressive idealist did not call for a mere cessation of hostilities. He proposed to pledge the war-ring powers to uphold the principles of national self-determination and absolute freedom of the seas, and to establish some kind of international mechanism for resolving future disputes.

This proposal was not even half-digested when, a week later, the German ambassador informed Wilson that on February 1, German submarines would begin sinking neutral as well as enemy ships in the war zone around Great Britain. With a fleet of one hundred submarines, the German military planners had concluded that they could knock Great Britain out of the war within a few months. They knew that breaking the Sussex Pledge meant almost certain American intervention. But because the United States was unprepared, the German leaders calculated that the war would be over before more than a token American force could be landed in Europe.

Wilson was crestfallen, then irate. He broke off diplomatic relations with Germany, as he had threatened to do, and asked Congress for authority to arm American merchant ships. When former progressive allies such as La Follette and Borah filibustered to prevent this, he denounced them as "a little group of willful men, representing no opinion but their own." For the first time, the president was the leader of the war party. Nevertheless, Wilson did not abandon all hope of staying out until German submarines sent three American freighters to the bottom. On the evening of April 2, mourning that "it is a fearful thing to lead this great peaceful people into war," a solemn Wilson asked Congress for a formal declaration.

For four days a bitter debate shook the Capitol. Six senators and about fifty representatives fought to the end, blaming Wilson for having failed to be truly neutral and claiming that the United States was going to spill its young men's blood in order to bail out Wall Street's loans to England and to enrich the munitions manufacturers, the "merchants of death." In one of the most moving speeches, freshman Senator George Norris of Nebraska said, "We are going into war upon the command of gold. . . . We are about to put the dollar sign on the American flag."

Why America Went to War

In later years, many historians would say that Norris had been correct. With varying emphases, they agreed that special interests had methodically maneuvered the United States into a war that did not concern the country. To the extent that Wall Street favored a British victory for the sake of its own profits and that the "merchants of death" fed off the blood of soldiers, they were correct.

A banner headline on the New York American *reported the beginning of war between the United States and Germany, April 6, 1917.*

But to say that certain interest groups wanted the war does not explain the dramatic shift of public opinion from 1914 and even 1915, when virtually no American dreamed of declaring war, to the spring of 1917, when the majority did. The reasons for this about-face lie in the growing popular belief that Germany represented a force for evil in the world and the skillful propaganda of the British and pro-British Americans in encouraging this perception.

The depiction of Germans as savage "Huns" began even before the submarine campaign of 1915. Germany's first military action was the invasion of France through neutral Belgium. The military occupation of the little country was harsh but generally no more brutal than, for example, the wartime controls that the British slapped on the Irish. However, as finely attuned to American sympathies as they were, the British skillfully wove reports of rape and beatings in Belgium into a tapestry of daily horror. The wall poster reached its fullest artistic development during the First World War, and the typical representation of Belgium showed the broken body of a young girl at the mercy of a bloated, beastlike German soldier in a spiked helmet. Sometimes she was impaled on a bayonet.

German insistence that these allegations were ridiculous were undermined in October 1915, when the German army executed Edith Cavell, the British head of the Berkendael Medical Institute in Brussels. Although Cavell was admittedly guilty of acts that are considered espionage in international law (she helped a number of British prisoners escape), the execution of a woman for charitable acts was profoundly stupid in an age when women were only rarely executed for murder.

The submarine war further angered Americans. Not everyone agreed with Wilson that the rights of neutrals during modern war could be absolute. But repeated incidents of unarmed merchant seamen and innocent passengers drowning in the dark, cold waters of the North Atlantic touched a delicate nerve. Artists brilliantly aroused basic human fear in posters that showed seamen fighting vainly to swim while their ship sank in the moonlit background.

German saboteurs were probably not so active in the United States as British and pro-British propagandists claimed. Nevertheless, several German diplomats were caught red-handed in 1915 when an agent left incriminating papers on a train, and in 1916, the huge Black Tom munitions plant in New Jersey was completely destroyed in a suspicious "accident."

But the real blockbuster was a mere piece of paper. On February 25, 1917, while Wilson was searching for a last chance to avoid war, the British communicated to him a message that the German foreign minister, Arthur Zimmermann, had sent to the Mexican government. In the event that the United States declared war on Germany, Zimmermann had proposed, Germany would finance a Mexican attack on the United States. Assuming Germany won, Mexico would be rewarded after the war with the return of some of the territory that it had lost in the Mexican War half a century before, specifically the "lost provinces" of New Mexico and Arizona.

Mexico was still wracked by civil turmoil, and was in no condition to make war on the United States. It was a foolish proposal. Nevertheless, with the American people already angered, the Zimmermann Telegram persuaded many that the unprincipled Hun must be stopped.

The American Contribution

The Germans provoked the American intervention on a gamble. The German leaders bet that their all-out U-boat attack would starve England into surrender before the Americans could contribute to the war effort. For three frightening months, it appeared as though they had guessed right. In February and March 1917, German submarines sank 570,000 tons of shipping bound to and from England. In April, the total ran to almost 900,000 tons. A quarter of the British merchant fleet lay at the bottom of the sea. At one point, England had enough food on hand to feed the island nation for only three weeks. Starving people cannot fight a war.

HALT ᵀʰᵉ HUN
SUBMARINE

CLEAR ᵗʰᵉ ROAD ᵗᵒ FRANCE

Join the Navy,
Naval Reserve
or Coast Guard

One Service, One Call

A Navy recruitment poster from World War I played on American outrage over the submarine war.

But the Germans lost their wager. The major American contribution to the war was precisely in keeping England and the other Allies supplied. At the insistence of Admiral William S. Sims, merchantmen ceased to travel alone. Guarded by naval vessels, particularly the small, fast, and heavily armed destroyers (the nemesis of the U-boats), merchant ships crossed the Atlantic in huge convoys.

Over the objections of the Royal Navy (but with the support of Prime Minister David Lloyd George), Sims succeeded in building his "bridge of ships." As early as May 1917, U-boat kills dropped drastically, far below what the German navy claimed it could do. By July, the American navy took over most defense operations in the Western Hemisphere and sent thirty-four destroyers to Queenstown (present-day Cóbh), Ireland, to assist the British. So successful was the well-guarded convoy system that not one of the 2 million American soldiers sent to France in 1917 and 1918 was drowned on the way. In the meantime, by commandeering more than one hundred German ships that were in American ports at the time war was declared (including the behemoth *Vaterland,* renamed the *Leviathan*) and by launching a massive shipbuilding program, the Americans were soon producing two ships for every one that the Germans sank. Into their holds poured so much food, clothing, munitions, airplanes, vehicles, and other vital material that in 1918 the Allies were better supplied than they had been in the first months of the war.

The Fighting Over There

Soldiers went too. General John Pershing arrived in Paris on July 4, 1917, with the first units of the American Expeditionary Force, the First Infantry Division. This was primarily a symbolic gesture. Because Pershing refused to send poorly trained men to the front, the Germans were proved right in gambling that American reinforcements could not in themselves turn the tide. The first Americans to see action, near Verdun in October, were used merely to beef up decimated French, British, and Canadian units.

The autumn of 1917 went poorly for the Allies. The Germans and Austrians defeated the Italians in the south and, in November, knocked Russia out of the war. A liberal democratic government that had deposed the czar in March 1917 proved unable to keep a mutinous Russian army supplied, and a group of revolutionary Communists, the Bolsheviks, led by Vladmir Ilyich Lenin, seized power on the basis of promises of "Peace and Bread." The Treaty of Brest-Litovsk, which

"THEY DROPPED LIKE FLIES": THE GREAT FLU EPIDEMIC OF 1918

About 10 million people died as a result of battle during the four years of the First World War. Small wonder that the event staggered the confidence and morale of the European nations.

But the war was a modest killer compared with the "Spanish flu." During only *four months* late in 1918 and early in 1919, a worldwide flu epidemic, or pandemic, killed 21 million people. The American army in Europe lost 49,000 men in battle and 64,000 to disease, the majority of them to the flu. At home, fully 548,452 American civilians died, 10 times as many as soldiers felled in battle.

The disease first appeared in March 1918, at Fort Riley, Kansas. After a dust storm, 107 soldiers checked into the infirmary complaining of headaches, fever and chills, difficulty in breathing, and miscellaneous aches and pains. Most curious to them, the illness had befallen them in an instant; one moment they were feeling fine and fit, the next they could barely stand. Within a week, Fort Riley had 522 cases, and in a little more than a month, when the affliction abruptly disappeared, 8,000 cases. Almost 50 of the sick men died, not too disturbing a rate in an age when any number of contagious diseases forgotten today were considered deadly. Some doctors noted that these flu victims were in the prime of life and, presumably after basic training, in excellent condition. Moreover, most of them were strapping farm boys, who usually shook off such ailments as though they were colds.

It was wartime, however, and the soldiers from Fort Riley were shipped to Europe in May. The flu made a brief appearance in the cities of the eastern seaboard, but did not rival any of a number of epidemics, including a serious one in the United States in 1889 and 1890.

In Europe, the disease was far more deadly. In Switzerland alone, 58,000 died of it in July. The deaths in the trenches on both sides of the line were enough, according to the German general Erich von Ludendorff, to curtail a major campaign. By June, the flu was sweeping Africa and India, where the mortality was "without parallel in the history of disease." That could be attributed to the wretched poverty of the subcontinent. But what of Western Samoa, where 7,500 of the island's 38,000 people died?

The total figures had not been calculated when the flu began a second and even more destructive tour of the world. The war had created ideal conditions for such a pandemic. People moved about in unprecedented numbers; 200,000 to 300,000 crossed the Atlantic to Europe each month, and many were carrying the unidentifiable germ. Moreover, war crowded people together so that conditions were also perfect for the successful mutation of viruses. With so many handy hosts to support propagation, the emergence of new strains was all the more likely.

That is apparently what happened in August, in western Africa, France, or Spain, which got the blame. A much deadlier variation of the original swept over the world, and this time the effects in the United States were cataclysmic.

In Boston, where it struck first, doubtless carried in by returning soldiers, 202 people died on October 1. New York City reported 3,100 cases in one day; 300 victims died. Later in the month, 851 New Yorkers died in one day, far and away the record. Philadelphia, which was particularly hard hit, lost 289 people on October 6; within one week, 5,270 were reported dead. The death rate for the month was 700 times its usual rate. Similar figures came in from every large city in the country. Just as worrisome, the disease found its way to the most obscure corners of the country. A winter logging camp in Michigan, cut off from the rest of humanity, was afflicted. Oregon officials reported finding sheepherders dead by their flocks.

Most public officials responded about as well as could be expected during a catastrophe that no one understood. Congress, many of its members laid low, appropriated money to hire physicians and nurses and set up clinics. Many cities closed theaters, bars, schools, and churches, and prohibited public gatherings such as parades and sporting events. Others, notably Kansas City, where the political boss frankly said that the economy was more important, carried on as usual. Mystifying moralists, Kansas City was no harder hit than were cities that took extreme precautions. (Nationwide and worldwide, about one-fifth of the population caught the Spanish flu, and the death rate was 3 percent.)

Several city governments required the wearing of gauze masks and punished violators with fines of up to $100. Many photographs that were taken during the autumn of 1918 have a surreal quality because of the masks. San Franciscans, their epidemic at a peak on Armistice Day, November 11, celebrated wearing gauze. Some wretched poet wrote the lines:

> Obey the laws
> And wear the gauze
> Protect your jaws
> From septic paws

Philadelphia gathered its dead in carts, as had been done during the bubonic plague epidemics of the Middle Ages. The city's A. F. Brill Company, a maker of trolley cars, turned over its woodshop to coffinmakers. The city of Buffalo set up its own coffin factory. Authorities in Washington, D.C., seized a trainload of coffins headed for Pittsburgh.

Then, once again, the disease disappeared. There was a less lethal wave (perhaps another mutation) in the spring of 1919, with President Wilson one of the victims; and the leading historian of the phenomenon, Alfred W. Crosby, suggests that another minor epidemic in 1920 may have been a fourth wave. But the worst was over by about the time that the First World War ended, leaving physicians to reflect on the character of the disease and to wonder what they could do if it recurred.

There were some things to reflect on. The first has already been noted: the Spanish flu struck very suddenly, offering individuals no way to fight it except to lie down and wait.

Second, the disease went fairly easy on those people who are usually most vulnerable to respiratory diseases, the elderly; and it was hardest on those who usually shake off such afflictions, young people. In the United States, the death rate for white males between the ages of 25 and 34 was, during the 1910s, about 80 per 100,000. During the flu epidemic it was 2,000 per 100,000. In a San Francisco maternity ward in Octo-

ber, 19 out of 42 women died. In Washington, a college student telephoned a clinic to report that 2 of her 3 roommates were dead in bed and the third was seriously ill. The report of the police officer who was sent to investigate was "Four girls dead in apartment." Old people died of the flu, of course, but the death rate among the elderly did not rise a point during the epidemic!

Third, people who had grown up in tough, poor, big-city neighborhoods were less likely to get the disease and, if they got it, less likely to die of it than were people who had grown up in healthier environments.

These facts eventually led scientists to conclude that the Spanish flu was a mutation of a common virus that caused a flu that was nothing more than an inconvenience. It was postulated, although never proved, that the deadly germ was the issue of an unholy liaison between a virus that affected humans and another that affected hogs. Spanish flu became "swine flu."

Thus, poor city people, who were more likely to suffer a plethora of minor diseases, had developed an immunity to the virus that farm people had not. Because old people were spared in 1918 and 1919, it has been said that the Spanish or swine flu virus was related to the less fatal virus that had caused the epidemic of 1889 to 1890. Having been affected by it, the elderly had relative immunity to its descendant.

An office worker wears a facemask to protect herself during the deadly flu epidemic of 1918.

WORLD WAR I CASUALTIES

	Total mobilized forces	Killed or died	Wounded	Prisoners & missing	Total casualties
United States	4,791,000	117,000	204,000	5,000	326,000
Russia	12,000,000	1,700,000	4,950,000	2,500,000	9,150,000
France	8,410,000	1,358,000	4,266,000	537,000	6,161,000
British Commonwealth	8,904,000	908,000	2,090,000	192,000	3,190,000
Italy	5,615,000	650,000	947,000	600,000	2,197,000
Germany	11,000,000	1,774,000	4,216,000	1,153,000	7,143,000
Austria–Hungary	7,800,000	1,200,000	3,620,000	2,220,000	7,020,000
TOTAL	58,520,000	7,707,000	20,293,000	7,187,000	35,187,000

the Germans forced on the Russians, was vindictive and harsh. News of it convinced many Americans that they had done well in going to war to stop the Hun's hunger for world conquest. By closing down the eastern front, the Germans were able to throw a bigger army than ever into France.

In May 1918, Germany launched a do-or-die offensive. The Allies fell back to the Marne River, close enough to Paris that the shelling could be heard on the Champs Élysées. But by this time there were 250,000 fresh American troops in France, including about 27,000 at Château-Thierry, near the hottest

American soldiers move supplies during the Argonne offensive, the last large battle involving Americans before World War I came to an end.

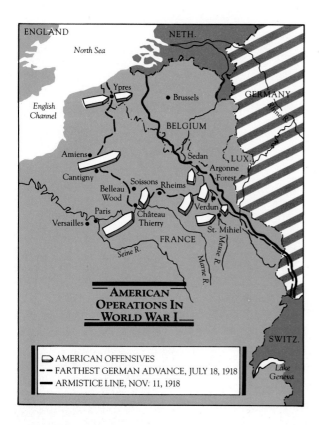

AMERICAN OPERATIONS IN WORLD WAR I

□ AMERICAN OFFENSIVES
- - FARTHEST GERMAN ADVANCE, JULY 18, 1918
— ARMISTICE LINE, NOV. 11, 1918

1 million "doughboys" were sitting when, on November 11, 1918, the Germans surrendered.

Armistice

In the trenches and back home, Americans celebrated deliriously. Millions of people gathered in city centers throughout the country, dancing and whooping. They believed that the Yanks had won the war. After all, the Germans had stalemated the French and British until the boys had gone "over there," in the words of a popular song of the time. Then, just a year after the Americans had begun to fight, it was over.

The American intervention was essential to the Allied victory, but the unmitigated joy in the United States was possible only because the American sacrifice was a comparatively minor one. Over 100,000 Americans were dead, more than half of them from disease (particularly the influenza that swept the world in 1917) rather than from bullets. By comparison, 1.4 million French and almost 1 million British soldiers died. Three-quarters of all the Frenchmen who served in the armed forces were casualties. Never again would France really qualify as a great power, and Great Britain was also badly maimed. Germany and Russia were defeated. If it was not strictly true that the United States had "won the war," it was certainly true that the United States was the only nation whose people could feel like victors.

of the fighting. By the middle of July, when the Germans attempted one last drive toward the capital, about 85,000 Americans helped hurl them back at Belleau Wood.

The Supreme Allied Commander, Field Marshal Ferdinand Foch, wanted to incorporate American troops into exhausted British and French units. Pershing stubbornly insisted that the Yanks fight as a unit. This was important to him not only for reasons of morale, but because Wilson had made it clear that the United States was not an "ally" of Britain and France but merely their "associate." In order to ensure his "peace without victory," Wilson was determined to play an independent role at the peace conference that would follow the war. Foch had no choice but to give in and grumble.

By the summer of 1918, the Americans in France represented the margin of victory over the Germans. In July, the Americans took over the attack on a bulge in the German lines called the St. Mihiel Salient, and succeeded in clearing it out. The final great American battle was along a twenty-four-mile line in the Argonne Forest, a naturally rugged country just short of the border between France and Germany that had been transformed into a ghostly wasteland by four years of digging and shelling. It was in that position that over

---

For Further Reading

The studies of Woodrow Wilson cited at the end of Chapter 39 deal with the events leading up to the First World War, but add to the list Arthur S. Link, *Wilson the Diplomatist* (1957), and N. G. Levin, Jr., *Woodrow Wilson and World Politics: America's Response to War and Revolution* (1968). R. E. Quirk, *An Affair of Honor: Woodrow Wilson and the Occupation of Vera Cruz* (1962), helps explain Wilson's reaction to the larger events of 1914 to 1917.

Ernest R. May, *The World War and American Isolation, 1914–1917* (1959), and E. H. Buehrig, *Woodrow Wilson and the Balance of Power* (1955), offer a sympathetic view of Wilson's reaction to the European crisis. They are contradicted in C. C. Tansill, *America Goes to War* (1938), and Walter Millis, *The Road to War* (1935). See also William A. Williams, *The Tragedy of American Diplomacy* (1959).

On American participation, see Lawrence Stallings, *The Doughboys* (1963). A. E. Barbeau and F. Henri, *The Unknown Soldiers* (1974), tells the story of the blacks who fought in the First World War.

41

Over Here
The First World War at Home, 1917–1920

Truth, an old saying has it, is the first casualty in every war. That is, in order for a nation to wage war effectively, that nation must be ruthless. Strict adherence to high moral principles has no place in a conflict involving the life and death of a nation as well as thousands of people. When the warring nation is a democracy, pledged to responding to the will of the people and *reporting to them*, waging war means lies. President Wilson knew this. On one hand, he called the First World War a war to make the world safe for democracy. On the other hand, he told a newspaper reporter in April 1917, "Once lead this people into war, and they'll forget there ever was such a thing as tolerance. To fight you must be ruthless and brutal, and the spirit of ruthless brutality will enter into the very fiber of our national life." It was to be one of the tragic ironies of Wilson's career that he, a lifelong liberal, was to initiate many of the policies that made his prophecy come true.

Movie hero Douglas Fairbanks, megaphone in hand, raises patriotic fervor at a liberty loan rally in April, 1918.

The Progressive War

Equally tragic and ironic, the First World War was simultaneously the apogee of progressivism, when reformers had a free hand in turning their beliefs into policy, and the undoing of the progressive movement. Within two years of the conclusion of the war, there was no progressive movement, only a few isolated voices crying in the wilderness of a congressional minority and getting no replies but echoes.

The Movement Splits

The war split the progressives. A few of them itched to get into the fight. The most famous was Theodore Roosevelt, a pathetic shrill figure in his waning years. When the United States finally intervened, T.R. asked for a command in Europe. Wisely, Wilson ignored him, but in doing so permanently embittered many of Roosevelt's friends.

Other Republican progressives, mostly westerners such as La Follette, Norris, Borah, and Hiram Johnson, held out to the bitter end for American neutrality. After the declaration of war, they toned down their rhetoric in the interests of national unity. (And in order to save their careers: some newspaper cartoonists depicted them accepting medals from the German kaiser.) But they never changed their opinion that going to war was a tragic blunder that had been foisted on the country by munitions makers and bankers. They prolonged the debate on the Conscription Act of 1917 for six weeks, finally forcing Congress to exempt men under twenty-one from the draft. Any warmth they felt toward Wilson before April 1917 quickly dissipated thereafter.

Not so with most progressives. In Congress and out, the majority of them wholeheartedly supported the war. Like Wilson, they had come to believe that imperial Germany represented a deadly threat to free institutions all over the world. Defeating the Hun was a noble cause in itself. Moreover, in the task of mobilizing resources in order to fight the war, and in the wave of patriotic commitment that swept the country, the progressives saw a golden opportunity to put their ideas about economic and social reform to work.

They were right on one count. It was impossible to wage modern total war and cling to the nineteenth-century commitment to a free, unregulated economy. Armies that numbered millions of men could not be supplied with food, clothing, shelter, medicine, and arms by companies that were free to do as their owners

An American soldier says goodbye to his weeping sweetheart as he leaves to fight in the First World War in Europe.

chose. France and England had clamped tight controls on their factories and farms. American progressives believed that the United States would have to do the same.

The progressives were not disappointed. Suggestions for regulation of business that had been rejected as too radical proved, in the emergency of wartime, to be not nearly enough. The federal government virtually took over the direction of the economy.

The Planned Economy

Some five thousand government agencies were set up during the twenty months that the United States was at war, a statistical average of more than eight new agencies a day! Some were useless, wasteful bureaucracies that were established without careful thought and served no purpose but to provide desks, chairs, paper clips, and salaries for the functionaries who ran them. A few were failures. The Aircraft Production Board was commissioned to construct twenty-two thousand airplanes in a year. That figure was unrealistic (and unnecessary). But the twelve hundred craft and fifty-four hundred replacement motors that the board actually delivered to France were far fewer than might have been expected.

Other agencies were more successful. The Shipping Board, actually founded in 1916 before the declaration of war, produced vessels twice as fast as the Germans could sink them. Privately run shipbuilding companies were not up to that herculean task.

The United States Railway Administration, headed by Wilson's son-in-law and Secretary of the Treasury, William G. McAdoo, was created early in 1918 when the owners of the nation's railroads proved incapable of moving the volume of freight needed for shipment to Europe. The government paid the stockholders a rent equal to their earnings in the prosperous prewar years and simply took over. McAdoo untangled a dangerous management mess within a few weeks, and reorganized the railroads into an efficient system such as the nation had never known. About 150,000 freight cars short of what was needed to do the job in 1917, American railroads enjoyed a surplus of 300,000 by the end of the war.

The various war production boards were coordinated by a superagency, the War Industries Board, which was headed by a Wall Street millionaire, Bernard Baruch. His presence at the top of the planning pyramid indicated that the progressives had not won their campaign for a directed economy without paying a price. American industry and agriculture were regulated, indeed regimented, as never before. But democratically elected officials and public-spirited experts with no stake in the profits were not in the driver's seat. Businessmen were.

Herbert Hoover:
The Administrator as War Hero

The task given to Food Administrator Herbert C. Hoover was even more difficult than McAdoo's, and his success was more spectacular. He was assigned to organize food production, distribution, and consumption so that America's farms could feed the United States, supply the huge Allied armies, and help maintain many European civilians.

Only forty-three years old when he took the job, Hoover already was known as a "boy wonder." Beginning life as a penniless orphan in Iowa, he became a millionaire as a mining engineer. Working in London when Europe went to war, he was asked to take over the problem of getting food to devastated Belgium. He jumped at the challenge, liquidated his business, and undoubtedly saved tens of thousands, if not hundreds of thousands, of lives.

He did it without charm or personal flash. Hoover was an intense, humorless, businesslike man. His method was to apply engineering principles to the solution of human problems. Progressives admired just such expertise, and the cool, methodical Hoover was a refreshing contrast to other humanitarians who moved about in a cloud of pious self-congratulation.

Hoover preferred voluntary programs to coercion. Food was not rationed during the First World War, as it would be during the Second. Instead, Hoover sponsored colorful publicity campaigns that urged American

A National War Gardens Commission poster encouraged citizens to plant home vegetable gardens, thus freeing commercial producers to concentrate on providing goods for the war effort.

families to observe Wheatless Mondays, Meatless Tuesdays, Porkless Thursdays, and so on. Hoover was devoted to public service as an ideal in itself and believed that other people only needed encouragement. Moreover, his campaign was shrewd psychology. Making do without a vital commodity one day a week was a simple sacrifice that made civilians feel as though they were part of the fighting machine. When observed by millions, the savings were enormous.

Hoover also encouraged city dwellers to plant "Victory gardens" in their tiny yards. Every tomato that was raised at home freed commerically produced food for the front. His agency promoted classes in economizing in the kitchen and distributed cookbooks on how to prepare leftovers. The impact was so great that, half-seriously, Americans began to use the word *hooverize* to mean "economize." Chicago proudly reported that the housewives in that city had hooverized the monthly production of garbage down by a third.

Hoover increased farm production through a combination of patriotic boosting and cash incentives. He helped increase wheat acreage from 45 million in 1917 to 75 million in 1919. American exports of foodstuffs to the Allies tripled over already high prewar levels. Hoover was called "the Miracle Man," and another young Washington administrator, Undersecretary of the Navy Franklin D. Roosevelt, wanted the Democratic party to nominate him for president in 1920. No other person, not even Wilson or General Pershing, was so much the hero of the war as was this young engineer.

Managing People

People were mobilized too: workers and ordinary citizens as well as soldiers. In May 1917, Congress passed the Selective Service Act, the first draft law since the Civil War. Registration was compulsory for all men between the ages of twenty-one and forty-five. (In 1918, the minimum age was lowered to eighteen.) From the 10 million who registered within a month of passage (24 million by the end of the war), local draft boards selected able-bodied recruits according to quotas assigned them. Some occupational groups were deferred, but no one was allowed to buy his way out, as had been done during the Civil War. Indeed, authority to make final selections was given to local draft boards in order to silence critics who said that conscription had no place in a democracy. About 3 million young men were inducted through selective service in addition to the 2 million who volunteered.

About twenty-one thousand draftees claimed to be conscientious objectors on religious grounds, although,

in the end, only four thousand insisted on being assigned to noncombatant duty, as medics or in the Quartermaster Corps. Approximately five hundred men refused to cooperate with the military in any way (some for political rather than religious reasons). Under the terms of the Selective Service Act, they were imprisoned and, generally, treated poorly. Camp Leonard Wood in Missouri had an especially bad reputation. In Washington State, a man who claimed that Jesus had forbidden him to take up arms was sentenced to death; he was not executed. But the last conscientious objector was not freed from prison until 1933, long after most Americans had come to agree with him that the war had been a mistake.

In order to keep the factories humming, Wilson made concessions to the labor movement that would have been unthinkable a few years earlier. He appointed Samuel Gompers, the patriotic president of the American Federation of Labor, to sit on Baruch's War Industries Board. In return for this recognition, Gompers pledged the AFL unions to a no-strike policy for the duration of the conflict.

Because wages steadily rose during the war, there were comparatively few work stoppages. Business boomed, and employers who became dizzy with bonanza profits did not care to jeopardize them by resisting moderate demands by their employees. Most important, the National War Labor Board, on which five AFL nominees sat, mediated industrial disputes before they disrupted production and, in many cases, found in favor of the workers.

The quiet incorporation of organized labor into the decision-making process made the AFL "respectable," as it never had been before. From 2.7 million members in 1914, the union movement (including independent unions) grew to 4.2 million in 1919.

Blacks in Wartime

Like Gompers, leaders of American blacks hoped that through proving their patriotism in time of crisis, blacks would win an improved status. About four hundred thousand young black men enlisted or responded to the draft; proportionately, more blacks than whites donned khaki.

It was difficult to ignore the contradiction between Wilson's ringing declaration that the purpose of the war was to defend democracy and liberty and the second-class citizenship suffered by black people. W. E. B. Du Bois, the leader of the NAACP, pointedly reminded the president of the dichotomy, and Wilson did go so far as to issue a strong condemnation of lynching. Nevertheless, it was a time when racism was

Members of the 369th Infantry, a black regiment, returned to the United States in 1919 wearing medals given to them by the French government commending them for gallantry in battle.

a part of mainstream American life. Black soldiers were assigned to segregated units and usually put to menial tasks such as digging trenches and loading trucks behind the lines. Only a few black units saw combat, although one that did was awarded the Croix de Guerre by the French goverment for gallantry in battle.

Military segregation had its advantages for some blacks. In order to command the black units, the army trained and commissioned more than twelve hundred officers. This was particularly gratifying to Du Bois, who staked his hopes for the future on the creation of a black elite. Curiously, however, he sounded much like his old nemesis Booker T. Washington when he said that blacks should bear with discrimination and prove their worth as loyal soldiers.

More important in the long run than service in the army was the massive movement of blacks from the rural and strictly segregated South to the industrial centers of the North. Before 1914, only about ten thousand blacks a year drifted from the South to cities like New York, Philadelphia, Detroit, and Chicago. After 1914, when naval war choked off immigration from abroad while factories filling war orders continued to offer jobs, one hundred thousand a year made the trek. It was not so great a leap in miles as the European immigration, but it was just as wrenching socially. From a Mississippi delta cabin to a Detroit factory and slum was a big change in life.

Those who served in the army, and most of those who moved north, were young people. They represented the first generation of American blacks who had not experienced slavery personally. Consequently, they were less inclined to accept the daily humiliations that accompanied being black in white America. This was particularly true of the men in uniform, who believed that their service entitled them to respect.

The result was that 1917 was a year of racial conflict, with a frightening race riot in industrial East St. Louis, Illinois. In Houston, white civilians fought a pitched battle with black soldiers, and twelve people were killed. Although both sides shared the blame for the riot, thirteen black soldiers were hanged and fourteen were imprisoned for life. Du Bois and the NAACP were only partly correct in their analysis of how the war would affect blacks. Society made economic concessions to blacks in the interests of winning the war, but it did not grant civil equality.

Women's War, Women's Victory

The woman-suffrage movement, on the contrary, skillfully parlayed wartime idealism and fears into final victory for the long-fought cause. Imitating British and French examples, the armed forces inducted female volunteers, mostly as nurses and clerical workers. More important was the same labor shortage that created

This welder was just one of thousands of American women who entered the industrial work force to fill slots vacated when men left to join the wartime military.

opportunities in industry for blacks. Working-class women began doing factory work and other jobs that had been closed to them. Women operated trolley cars, drove delivery trucks, cleaned streets, directed traffic, and filled jobs in every industry from aircraft construction to zinc galvanization. Middle-class women took the lead in organizing support groups. They rolled bandages, held patriotic rallies, and filled whole ships with knitted sweaters and socks and home-baked cookies for the boys in France. With women's contributions to waging the war so obvious, it was increasingly difficult for patriotic politicians to oppose suffrage with the argument that women belonged in the nursery minding infants.

By 1917, the feminist movement had split once again into radical and conservative wings. Curiously, while they were hostile toward each other, their different approaches both contributed to final victory. Thus, when the aggressive Women's Party led by Alice Paul demonstrated noisily in Washington, burning a copy of Wilson's idealistic Fourteen Points and chaining themselves to the fence in front of the White House, many politicians went scurrying for reassurance to the more polite National American Woman Suffrage Association.

Led by Carrie Chapman Catt, the association shrewdly obliged them. Not only did most American women oppose such irresponsible behavior, Catt argued, but social stability and conservative government could be ensured only by granting women the vote. Their numbers would counterbalance the increasing influence of radicals and foreigners at the polls, not to mention the blacks who were showing signs of demanding their rights.

The suffrage movement was too long in the field and too large to be denied. Even Wilson, who instinctively disliked the idea of women voting, announced his support. On June 4, 1919, a few months after the Armistice, Congress sent the Nineteenth Amendment to the states. On August 18, 1920, ratification by Tennessee put it into the Constitution. "The right of citizens . . . to vote," it read, "shall not be denied or abridged by the United States or by any State on account of sex." Carrie Chapman Catt had no doubt about what had put it over. It was the war, the former pacifist said, that liberated American women.

The Moral War

Another long progressive campaign already had been brought to a victorious end. Like the suffragists, the prohibitionists appeared to be stalled permanently on the eve of the war. In 1914, only one-quarter of the states had prohibition laws on the books, and many of those were casually enforced. With American intervention in the war, however, the antidrinking forces added a new and decisive argument to their armory: the distilling of liquor consumed vast quantities of grain that were needed as food. Shortly after the declaration of war, Congress passed the Lever Act, a section of which forbade the sale of grain to distilleries.

Because many breweries were run by German-Americans, they were doubly handicapped in fighting the prohibitionists. Although Americans had developed a taste for cold lager beer, the beverage was still associated with Germans. Moralism, hooverizing, and the popular insistence on 100 percent Americanism all combined to bring about, in December 1917, the passage of the Eighteenth Amendment, which prohibited "the manufacture, sale, or transportation of intoxicating liquors" in the United States. It was ratified in 1919 and put into effect by the Volstead Act.

War usually leads to relaxation of sexual morality, as young men are removed from the social restraints of family and custom. The First World War proved to be no exception. However, well-meaning moralists in Wilson's administration hoped to take advantage of the mobilization of millions in order to instill high moral standards in the young men under their control. Josephus Daniels, the deeply religious Secretary of the Navy, thought of his ships as "floating universities" of moral reform. He gave orders to clear out the red-light districts that were a fixture in every naval port, and the army did the same in cities near its bases.

Prostitution was not eliminated by these orders any more than whiskey- and beer drinking were abolished by the Eighteenth Amendment. But the short-term victories encouraged reformers in their belief that, among the horrors, the First World War was a blessing on reformers.

Conformity and Repression

It was not a blessing on civil libertarians. As Wilson had predicted, white-hot patriotism scorched the traditions of free political expression and tolerance of disparate ways of life. Not that free speech, religious expression, and ethnic variety had not been assaulted before the First World War. But never had violation of the Bill of Rights been so widespread as during the war, and never had the federal government so stridently supported, even initiated, repression.

The Campaign Against the Socialists

The Socialist party of America was the only national political institution to oppose American intervention in the war. In April 1917, in the wake of the declaration of war, the party met in emergency convention in St. Louis and proclaimed "unalterable opposition" to a conflict that killed workingpeople and paid dividends to capitalists. Rather than hurting the party at the polls, its stance earned an increase in votes as many non-Socialists cast ballots for the Socialist party as the only way to express their dissent on the issue.

The government moved quickly to head off the possibility of an antiwar bandwagon. The state legislature of New York expelled seven Socialist assemblymen simply because they objected to the war. Not until after the war did courts overrule the unconstitutional action. Victor Berger was elected to Congress from Milwaukee, but denied his seat. When he also beat the candidate supported by both the Democratic and Republican parties in the special election to fill the vacancy, Congress again refused to seat Berger. The seat remained empty until after the Armistice. In the meantime, Berger's *Social Democratic Herald* and a number of other Socialist papers were denied cheap mailing privileges by Postmaster General Albert S. Burleson. Most of them never recovered from the blow.

The most celebrated attack on the Socialists was the indictment and trial of longtime leader Eugene V. Debs for a speech opposing conscription. In sending Debs to prison, the Wilson administration was taking a chance. The four-time presidential candidate was loved and respected by many non-Socialists for his sincere dedication to his ideals. At his trial in September 1918, Debs's eloquence lived up to his reputation. "While there is a lower class I am in it; while there is a criminal element I am of it; while there is a soul in prison, I am not free," he told the jury. But in prosecuting and jailing him and other prominent Socialists such as Kate Richards O'Hare, the government also made it clear that dissent on the war issue would not be tolerated.

The Destruction of the Industrial Workers of the World

The suppression of the I.W.W. was more violent. There was a paradox in this because while the radical union officially opposed the war, Secretary-Treasurer "Big Bill" Haywood tried to play down the issue. For the first time since its founding in 1905, the I.W.W. was enrolling members by the tens of thousands every month, and Haywood hoped to ride out the patriotic hysteria and emerge from the war with a powerful organization.

But the government did not move against the I.W.W. because of its position on the war. Most of the union's members were concentrated in three sectors of the economy that were vital to the war effort: among

WOBBLIES

Members of the I.W.W. were called Wobblies by both friends and enemies. There are several explanations of the origin of their name; according to one, they were so strike prone that they were "wobbly" workers. The story the I.W.W. favored told of a Chinese restaurant operator in the Pacific Northwest who would give credit only to Wobblies because they could be depended on. When someone asked for a meal on credit, the restaurant owner, unable to pronounce the name of the letter W, asked, "I-Wobbly-Wobbly?"

SHOUTING "FIRE!" IN A THEATER

Charles Schenck was a Philadelphia Socialist who was imprisoned for having violated the Espionage Act of 1917. He had circulated fifteen thousand pamphlets that attacked the government for going to war and criticized the draft. Schenck appealed his conviction to the Supreme Court but lost his case. In the words of the court's leading liberal, Oliver Wendell Holmes, Jr., his attack constituted "a clear and present danger" to the nation. Schenck was no more entitled to his freedom of expression in wartime than a person falsely shouting "Fire!" in a crowded theater was entitled to that expression.

While acknowledging the validity of the "clear and present danger" principle, Harvard law professor Zechariah Chafee said that it did not apply to Schenck. His act had been more along the lines of someone informing the manager of the theater between the acts that there were not enough fire exits.

the harvest workers who brought in the nation's wheat; among loggers in the Pacific Northwest; and in copper-mining towns like Globe and Bisbee in Arizona and Butte in Montana. And the "Wobblies" refused to abide by the AFL's no-strike pledge. It was a labor organization that the government attacked.

The I.W.W. was crushed by a combination of vigilante terrorism and government action. In July 1917, a thousand "deputies" wearing white armbands in order to identify one another rounded up twelve hundred strikers in Bisbee, loaded them on a specially chartered train, and dumped them in the Mexican desert, where they were without food for thirty-six hours. The next month, I.W.W. organizer Frank Little was lynched in Butte, probably by police officers in disguise. In neither case was any attempt made to bring the vigilantes to justice. In fact, President Wilson ignored Haywood's protest of the Bisbee deportation and his demand for action in the case of Little's murder.

In the grain belt, sheriffs and farmers had a free hand in dealing with suspected Wobblies. In the Sitka spruce forests of Washington and Oregon (spruce was the principal wood used in aircraft construction), the army organized the Loyal Legion of Loggers and Lumbermen to counter the popularity of the I.W.W. There, at least, conditions were improved as the union was repressed, but attacks on the I. W. W. were consistently vicious. Local police and federal agents winked at and even participated in everyday violations of civil rights and violence against Wobblies and their sympathizers.

Civil Liberties Suspended

The fatal blow fell in the autumn of 1917, when the Justice Department raided I.W.W. headquarters in several cities, rounded up the union's leaders, and indicted about two hundred under the Espionage Act of 1917. Along with the Sedition Act of 1918, the Espionage Act outlawed not only overt treasonable acts, but

made it a crime to "utter, print, write, or publish any disloyal, profane, scurrilous, or abusive language" about the government, the flag, or the uniform of a soldier or sailor. A casual snide remark was enough to warrant bringing charges, and a few cases were based on little more than that.

In *Schenck v. the United States* (1919), the Supreme Court unanimously upheld this broad, vague law. Oliver Wendell Holmes, Jr., the most liberal minded and humane man on the Court, wrote the opinion, which established the principle that when "a clear and present danger" existed, such as the war, Congress had the power to pass laws that would not be acceptable in normal times.

Even at that, the government did not prove that the I.W.W. was guilty of sedition. In effect, the individuals who were sentenced to up to twenty years in prison were punished because of their membership in an unpopular organization. Many liberals who had no taste for I.W.W. doctrine but who were shocked at the government's cynical policy of repression fought the cases. In 1920, led by Roger Baldwin, they organized the American Civil Liberties Union to guard against a repetition of what almost all historians regard as a shameful chapter in the evolution of American law.

Manipulating Public Opinion

The attack on the Socialists and the Wobblies was only one fulfillment of Wilson's prediction that the spirit of ruthless brutality would enter the fiber of American life. Americans in general were stirred to believe that they were engaged in a holy crusade, "a war to end war" against a diabolical foe. Violent acts against German-Americans and the very idea of German culture were commonplace.

Some of the innumerable incidents of intolerance that marred the wartime years were spontaneous; for example, a midwestern mob dragged a German-American shopkeeper from his home, threw him to his knees, forced him to kiss the American flag, and made him spend his life savings on war bonds. But the fire of intolerance that burned from coast to coast was also instigated and abetted by the national government.

The agency that was entrusted with mobilizing public opinion was the Committee on Public Information. It was headed by George Creel, a progressive newspaperman who had devoted his career to fighting the very intolerance and social injustice he now encouraged. In 1913, Creel had worked closely with "Big Bill" Haywood and the I.W.W. in exposing poor working conditions before a presidential commission.

With the same energy, Creel now devoted himself to a twofold task. First, to avoid demoralization, the CPI censored the news from Europe. The CPI dispatches emphasized victories and suppressed or played down stories of setbacks. With most editors and publishers solidly behind the war, Creel had little difficulty in convincing them to censor their own correspondents.

Kultur

Second, and far more ominously, the CPI took up the task of molding public opinion so that the slightest deviation from full support of the war was considered disloyal. Obviously, all German-Americans could not be imprisoned. (Only sixty-three hundred were actually interned compared with forty-five thousand of Great Britain's much smaller German community.) However, the CPI could and did launch a massive propaganda campaign that depicted German culture (*Kultur*) as intrinsically vile.

The government employed pamphlets, editorials, posters, massive rallies, parades, a corps of seventy-five thousand "Four-Minute Men" who delivered patri-

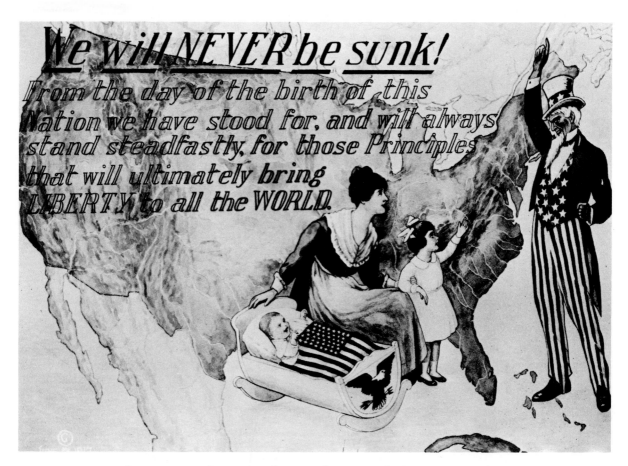

A wartime poster that was one of many used to encourage Americans to support their government's involvement in World War I.

otic speeches of that length at movie theaters during intermission, and, for the first time, the infant film industry itself.

The new but sophisticated techniques of advertising could be used to sell attitudes as well as corn flakes and Coca-Cola. Brilliantly painted CPI posters depicted a powerful and sinister network of German spies in the United States and urged loyal patriots to be vigilant. After a Hollywood film company was prosecuted in 1917 for having released a film about the American Revolution that depicted British troops unfavorably, Hollywood got the point and churned out movies with titles like *The Barbarous Hun*. Film stars such as Douglas Fairbanks, Charlie Chaplin, and Mary Pickford ("America's Sweetheart") appeared at Liberty Bond rallies and spoke anti-German lines written by the CPI.

The anti-German hysteria could take ludicrous form. Restaurants revised their menus so that sauerkraut became "liberty cabbage," hamburgers became "Salisbury steak" (after a liberal British lord), and frankfurters and wiener sausages, named after German and Austrian cities, became widely known as "hot dogs."

The real dog, the dachshund, had to be transformed into a "liberty hound." Towns with names of German origin chose more patriotic designations. German measles, then a common childhood disease, became "patri-

otic measles." Hundreds of schools and some colleges dropped the German language from their course offerings. Dozens of symphony orchestras refused to play the works of German composers, which left rather gaping holes in the repertoire. Prominent German-Americans who wished to save their careers found it advisable to imitate the opera singer Ernestine Schumann-Heinck. She was a fixture at patriotic rallies, her ample figure draped with a large American flag and her magnificent voice singing "The Star-Spangled Banner" and "America the Beautiful."

But the firing of Germans from their jobs, discriminating against German farmers, burning of German books, and beating and occasional lynching of German-Americans were not so humorous. Nor was the treatment of conscientious objectors by organizations of self-appointed guardians of the national interest with names like "Sedition Slammers," "Terrible Threateners," and even "Boy Spies of America." The members of such organizations stopped men on the streets and demanded to see their draft cards. The largest of these groups, which were responsible for hundreds of illegal acts, was the American Protective League. At one time it numbered 250,000 members, many of whom probably had signed up simply to avoid having their loyalty questioned.

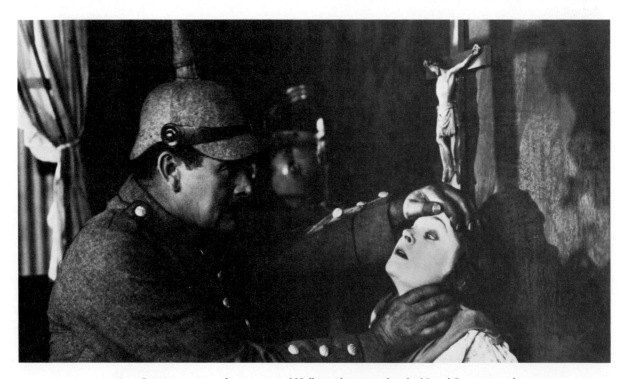

Anti-German sentiment became part of Hollywood movies after the United States entered World War I. In the film Stake Uncle Sam to Play Your Hand, *actress Mae Marsh was shown under the threatening grasp of an evil German soldier, played by A. C. Gibbons.*

Wilson and the League of Nations

Why did Woodrow Wilson, a lifelong libertarian, tolerate and even encourage such behavior? The answer seems to lie in the fact that the president's dream of building a new and just world order became a virtual obsession with him. Like no president before him, like several since, he lost interest in domestic events except insofar as they related to all-consuming foreign concerns. Repression of dissenters, even unjust and illegal repression, appeared to hasten the defeat of the kaiser, so Wilson abandoned values that had guided his life.

The President's Obsession

In January 1918, Wilson presented to Congress his blueprint for the postwar world. It consisted of "Fourteen Points," which, Wilson insisted, were to be incorporated into the eventual treaty. Mostly, they dealt with specific European territorial problems to be resolved, but several general principles were woven through the plan.

First, Germany must be treated fairly and generously in order to avoid the deep resentments that could lead to another war. In practical terms this meant that Germany must not be saddled with huge reparations payments—"fines" as punishment for the war—such as British and French leaders already had told their people would be paid.

THE FOURTEEN POINTS

1. "Open covenants of peace, openly arrived at." No secret treaties.
2. Freedom of the seas.
3. Removal of barriers (tariffs) to international trade.
4. Reduction of armaments.
5. Question of colonies to be settled in a "free, open-minded, and absolutely impartial" manner.
6. Russia to be treated justly.
7. Belgian independence to be restored.
8. France to regain control of all French-speaking areas of Europe.
9. Italian boundary to be set along linguistic lines.
10. Austro-Hungarian Empire to be broken up into nation-states.
11. Balkan countries to be established along linguistic lines.
12. Turkish Empire to be broken up according to national groups; free passage for all nations through the Dardanelles.
13. An independent Poland to be established.
14. The League of Nations.

Second, the boundaries of European countries must conform to nationality as defined by language. Like many other people, Wilson believed that the aspirations of people to govern themselves had been a major cause of the war. No such concessions were to be made to the nonwhite peoples in Europe's colonies. However, Wilson called for Germany's colonies to be disposed of on some basis other than as spoils of war divided among the victors.

Third, Wilson demanded "absolute freedom upon the seas, . . . alike in peace and in war." This was a reference to the German submarine campaign that Wilson blamed for American intervention, but it also challenged Britain's primacy on the waves. Fourth, Wilson called for disarmament. It was obvious to all parties that the arms race of the two decades preceding the war had not been a deterrent but a major cause of the tragedy.

Most important toward avoiding a repetition of the Great War, Wilson insisted on the establishment of "a general assembly of nations," a kind of congress of countries, to replace the old system of alliances and secret treaties. More than any other aspect of his program, the dream of a League of Nations came to obsess the president.

Wilson Fools Himself

As ultimate victory was ensured by the Allied advance during the summer of 1918, Wilson turned virtually all his energies to planning for the peace conference in Paris. He announced that he would personally head the American delegation, the first president to do such a thing and only the second to leave the United States during his term of office. (Theodore Roosevelt had traveled to Panama to see his canal.)

But Wilson mistook his own enthusiasm for the mood of the American people. In the congressional elections of 1918, voters returned Republican majorities of 240 to 190 to the House and of 49 to 47 to the Senate, but Wilson ignored the unmistakable signal that Americans wanted to cool off. The new Congress not only was Republican, but had a decidedly unidealistic tinge. Old bosses and professional politicians who had struggled against the reformers for a decade were returning to power. They were not all hidebound reactionaries by any means. They were the kind of men who were willing to make deals. But Wilson did not even appeal to them by including a prominent Republican among the delegates with whom he sailed to Europe on December 4.

Wilson's reception in England, France, and Italy increased his blindness to political realities. Everywhere he went he was greeted with blizzards of flowers thrown

Woodrow Wilson with (right to left) France's Georges Clemenceau, Britain's David Lloyd-George, and Italy's Vittorio Orlando at Versailles in 1919 where they established terms for settlement of World War I.

by adoring crowds who thought of him as the savior of Europe. They were welcoming a conqueror. However, Wilson believed that they were expressing their support for "a peace without victory" and the principles of his Fourteen Points.

The Peace Conference

He could not have been more mistaken. The men with whom Wilson negotiated in Paris had a much more realistic view of what the four dreadful years of war had meant to Europe. People wanted to forget the bitterness of sacrifice by tasting the sweetness of victory. The other three members of the "Big Four," paid lip service to Wilson's ideals, but once behind the closed doors of

the conference room, they put their national political interests first.

Georges Clemenceau, the prime minister of France, was a cagey, tough, and bitter infighter who was determined to hang the blame for the war on Germany and to ensure that France would never again be attacked. He was committed to stripping Germany of valuable territory and saddling the conquered nation with huge reparations payments. "God gave us the Ten Commandments and we broke them," he quipped in private. "Wilson gives us the Fourteen Points. We shall see."

David Lloyd George of Great Britain was personally more cordial to Wilson. But he was a chronic backroom manipulator given to inconstancy, and he too had political demands to meet. His country had suffered dreadfully from the bloodletting and wanted reparations. Moreover, Britain had no intention of giving up its dominance on the high seas.

Vittorio Orlando of Italy had little interest in any of the larger questions. He went to Versailles to make sure that Italy was rewarded with Austrian territory, including several regions of the Alps that were home to two hundred thousand German-speaking people, and the port of Fiume on the Adriatic, a city that was largely Serbian in population. His goals directly contradicted Wilson's Point Nine. The Japanese delegate, Count Nobuaki Makino, was determined to retain the German colonies in the Pacific that Japan had seized.

Bit by bit the Allies whittled away at Wilson's program. When the president revealed how all-important the League was to him by insisting that its Covenant (constitution) be acted on early in the proceedings, they knew that he would give in on other questions in order to save it. He did. The terms of the Treaty of Versailles, which Wilson brought home in July 1919, bore little resemblance to the Fourteen Points.

Article 10

Europe's rejection of Wilson's idealistic call for national self-determination in Europe and just treatment of Germany did not much concern the senators who had the constitutional power to approve or reject the treaty. On the contrary, twelve of the forty-nine Republican senators, mostly the western progressives who had opposed going to war in 1917, announced themselves to be "irreconcilable" in their opposition to the pact that ended it. They wanted the United States to withdraw into a state of isolation from Europe that they believed the country never should have abandoned.

In March 1919, before Wilson returned from Versailles, the other thirty-seven Republican senators signed a round robin declaring themselves to be "reservationists" on the issue. While they considered the Treaty of Versailles as it stood to be unacceptable, they put the president on notice that they would vote to ratify if Wilson made some changes in it or agreed to their reservations. What worried them most was Article 10 of the League Covenant, which pledged all member states to "preserve against external aggression the territorial integrity and . . . political independence of all members." Article 10 seemed to commit the United States to go to war if any other member were attacked.

Wilson replied that Article 10 was merely a moral obligation on the part of members, and, long after his day, he would be proved correct; throughout its his-

ROUND ROBIN

A round robin is a petition or statement that is signed by several people with no one of them identified as the leader or instigator. All sign around the text of the document in order to disguise the order of signing. The intent of the round robin is precisely the opposite of that of John Hancock in signing his name so prominently to the Declaration of Independence.

tory, the League was unable to enforce its rulings. Nevertheless, having said that the article had little concrete meaning, Wilson refused to make a single concession to the worried senators. In his stubbornness, he created an opportunity for the chairman of the Senate Foreign Relations Committee, an old friend of Theodore Roosevelt who despised everything about the president.

The Fight for the League

Henry Cabot Lodge was a dapper, aristocratic, and ill-tempered senator from Massachusetts who was not very popular with his colleagues. As intolerant a man as Wilson, he proved in the battle over the League to be much shrewder. Perceiving that Wilson was growing less flexible, Lodge became open and cooperative with senators who disliked the League less avidly than he did. Understanding that the longer the debate dragged on, the less the American people would be interested in the League, Lodge played for time and welcomed every one of Wilson's refusals to compromise. He read the entire 264 pages of the treaty into the record of his committee's hearings, even though it already had been published and placed on every senator's desk.

Lodge guessed right, and Wilson, reacting impulsively rather than rationally, guessed wrong. Whereas the majority of Americans doubtless favored the League in the first months of 1919, their interest waned slowly but perceptibly as the months passed.

The climax came in September. With the treaty about to come before the Senate, Wilson undertook an exhausting eight-thousand-mile speaking tour. He believed that by rallying the people behind him, he could pressure wavering senators to support the treaty. By September 25, when he moved into Colorado, the crowds seemed to be with him. At Pueblo, however, his speech was slurred, and he openly wept. Wilson either suffered a mild stroke at that time or was on the verge of a nervous breakdown. His physician hastily canceled the remainder of the tour and rushed him

A weakened Woodrow Wilson relied on a cane and the aid of an escort following a massive stroke.

back to Washington. A few days later he crumpled to the floor of his bedroom, felled by a cerebral thrombosis, a blood clot in the brain.

Historians are still not positive about the extent of Wilson's incapacity over the next several months. For six weeks he was isolated completely by his protective and strong-willed wife. She screened all papers sent to him and brought them back with shaky signatures. When suspicious advisers insisted on seeing him, they discovered that his left side was paralyzed and his speech was halting. However, he appeared to be in control of his wits.

Wilson did not meet officially with his cabinet for six months, and photographs of that occasion show a haggard old man with a look of fear in his eyes that cannot be found in any earlier picture. The quality of his thinking undoubtedly was affected. But since Wilson in the best of health had refused to consider compromising with Lodge, the president's removal from the scene probably had little effect on the final outcome of the battle.

That outcome was defeat. In November, on Wilson's instructions, the Democratic senators voted with the irreconcilables to kill the treaty with the Lodge reservations by a vote of fifty-five to thirty-nine. When the treaty was introduced without the reservations, the reservationists and the irreconcilables defeated it against the Democrats. In March, over Wilson's protest, twenty-one Democrats worked out a compromise with the reservationist Republicans and again voted on the treaty. The twenty-three Democrats who went along with Wilson's insistence that he get the original treaty or no treaty at all made the difference. They and the irreconcilables defeated it.

The Election of 1920

Wilson believed that he could win the Treaty of Versailles and the League of Nations in the presidential election of 1920. Incredibly, considering his shaky health and the tradition against a third term, he also wanted to be the Democratic party's nominee. That was too much for even the most faithful Democrats to swallow. They chose Governor James M. Cox of Ohio, a competent if lackluster party regular. For vice president the Democrats nominated a staunch young Wilsonian, the athletic and aristocratic Undersecretary of the Navy, Franklin D. Roosevelt. The Democrats were pessimistic. But perhaps the Roosevelt name on the Democratic ticket would win enough progressive votes to put the party across.

The Republicans expected to win. The congressional elections of 1918 had seemed to show that despite six years of Democratic government, the Republicans remained the majority party. As is common when parties are optimisitc, there was a fight for the nomination between General Leonard Wood, an old comrade of Theodore Roosevelt (but no progressive) and Illinois governor Frank O. Lowden, who had a reputation as an innovative scientific farmer. Both arrived in Chicago with large blocs of votes, but neither had a majority.

Early in the proceedings, a group of reporters cornered a political wheeler-dealer from Ohio named Harry M. Daugherty and asked him who he thought would be nominated. Daugherty replied genially:

Well boys, I'll tell you what I think. The convention will be deadlocked. After the other candidates have failed, we'll get together in some hotel room, oh, about 2:11 in the morning, and some 15 men, bleary-eyed with lack of sleep, will sit down around a big table and when that time comes Senator Harding will be selected.

Senator Harding was Warren G. Harding. A Daugherty crony, Harding was a handsome, likable man who was considered one of the least competent figures in Congress, but, perhaps because of that, was acceptable to almost everyone. Because Harding had been a "mild reservationist" on the treaty issue, as usual taking an innocuous stand, Henry Cabot Lodge (in whose "smoke-filled room" at the Blackstone Hotel the nomination took place) undoubtedly believed that he could control him.

During the campaign, Harding waffled on the treaty, sometimes appearing to favor it with reservations and at other times hinting that he would let the issue quietly die. If there was a theme to his campaign, it was the need for the country to cool off after almost two decades of experimental reform and white-hot wartime crusading. "America's need," Harding told an audience in Boston in September, "is not heroism but healing, not nostrums but normalcy, not agitation but adjustment, not surgery but serenity, not the dramatic but the dispassionate, not experiment but equipoise, not submergence in internationality but sustainment in triumphant nationality."

The acerbic journalist H. L. Mencken said that Harding's speech reminded him of "stale bean soup, of college yells, of dogs barking idiotically through endless nights." But he added that "it is so bad that a sort of grandeur creeps through it." A Democratic politician remarked that the speech "left the impression of an army of pompous phrases moving over the landscape in search of an idea."

But Harding did have an idea. He sensed that no specific issue, including the League of Nations, was as important to the American people in 1920 as "a return to normalcy," and he was right. He won 61 percent of the vote, more than any man who preceded him in the White House since popular votes were recorded and the landslide record until 1964.

Wilson lived on quietly in Washington until 1924, a semi-invalid specter out of the past, frustrated and bitter. Unlike the pedestrian Harding, he was a giant who loomed over an age. His intelligence, dignity, steadfastness, and sense of rectitude overshadowed even the ebullient Theodore Roosevelt. His end was therefore more tragic than that of any other president, including those who were assassinated. For Wilson, like the tragic heroes of great drama, was murdered by his own virtues.

SAMUEL GOMPERS (1850–1924)

American Federation of Labor head Samuel Gompers receives a Red Cross button from a child in 1924, a short time before his death.

Born in London in 1850, the son of Dutch Jewish cigarmakers, Samuel Gompers emigrated to the United States as a teenager. On the Lower East Side of Manhattan, he took up his parents' work.

A disproportionate number of cigarmakers became labor leaders in the nineteenth century. One reason was that the trade provided an attentive person with a first-rate education. Cigars were made in tenement apartments. It was handwork, so there was no noisy machinery involved. It was also "mouthwork," however; cigarmakers were constantly moistening the tobacco with their tongues, and so they could not talk much. In order to allay the monotony, they hired one of the crew to read them novels as well as heady works of history and economics. Gompers had a good voice. He read often and thus became an excellent orator as well as a rather well-educated man.

By the age of thirteen, Gompers already was a formidable participant in the tempestuous intellectual life of melting-pot New York. At fourteen, he was elected president of the Cigarmakers Local No. 15, the English-speaking branch of the union. During these years he attended night classes at the Cooper Union, an educational institution that had been founded to help ambitious poor boys get ahead. But the intellectual mentor he remembered was Ferdinand Laurrell, a Danish cigarmaker who convinced Gompers that the anticapitalist ideology espoused by many of their associates was a waste of time. What workingpeople should fight for, Laurrell believed, was not some dreamlike perfect future but better wages, hours, and working conditions in the present. This remained the touchstone of Gompers's views on trade unionism. He was always suspicious of Socialists, and toward the end of his life was their sworn enemy.

In 1881, Gompers joined with Adolph Strasser, the head of the German-speaking cigarmakers, to spearhead the formation of the American Federation of Labor, a loose association of unions of skilled workers. Gompers was elected the AFL's first president, and was reelected every year but one until his death in 1924.

The position of AFL president had little direct power. The member unions remained in control of their own affairs. As a mediator in disputes among them and through the force of his personality, however, Gompers was the undeniable head of organized labor in the United States. In that capacity, he impressed three lasting principles on the AFL.

First, the AFL was strongly antisocialist. From the beginning, the mainstream of the American labor movement was procapitalist, quite unlike the union movements in other countries.

Second, Gompers trained the AFL to fight against any unions that were not associated with them. The Brotherhoods of Locomotive Engineers, Firemen, Brakemen, and Conductors were exempt from this campaign against "dual unionism" because they were also conservative and quite powerful. However, Gompers zestfully led attacks on every attempt to establish a union movement dedicated to socialism. His greatest battle was against the Industrial Workers of the World (I.W.W.), which was founded in 1905.

Third, Gompers believed that only skilled workers could organize into effective unions. So committed was Gompers to this principle that even when he was proved wrong, when unions like the I.W.W. and the AFL's own United Mine Workers successfully organized unskilled workers, he refused to grant so much as the possibility that he might be wrong.

When the United States went to war in 1917, Gompers saw an opportunity to carve out a place for the AFL in the Establishment. He helped the Justice Department destroy the I.W.W.; it was a pleasure. He also acted as an adviser to President Wilson's War Industries Board, swore the AFL to no strikes for the duration of the conflict, and in 1919 went to the Versailles Peace Conference and sat on the Commission on International Labor Legislation.

During the final years of his life, Gompers served as unofficial American ambassador to Mexico. Indeed, he was in Mexico when stricken with his final illness and urged his companions to rush him across the border so that he could die on American soil. They made it to San Antonio, where Gompers died on December 3, 1924.

In appearance Gompers was not an impressive figure. He kept his personal life intensely private. Little is known of his first wife, Sophia Julian, except that she was a working-class girl of sixteen when they married in 1866. (Gompers was also sixteen.) After his wife's death in 1921, Gompers married Gertrude Gleaves Neuscheler, who survived him. So private a man was Gompers that biographers do not know how many children he had. But of twelve who have been identified, only five lived to maturity, an illustration of the kind of social conditions that Gompers dedicated his life to fighting.

For Further Reading

The home front recently has been accorded masterful portrayal in David M. Kennedy, *Over Here: The First World War and American Society* (1980). Older but still useful studies of the same topic are Preston Slosson, *The Great Crusade and After* (1930), and Frederick L. Paxson, *American Democracy and the World War* (1948).

Zechariah Chafee, *Free Speech in the United States* (1941), deals with civil-liberties questions. On the same subject, see the early chapters of Robert K. Murray, *The Red Scare* (1955); William Preston, Jr., *Aliens and Dissenters: Federal Suppression of Radicals, 1903–1933* (1963); and William E. Leuchtenburg, *The Perils of Prosperity, 1914–1932* (1958).

The tragic diplomatic aftermath is treated in the various Wilson biographies. Also see Harold Nicolson, *Peacemaking 1919* (1939), and two books by Thomas A. Bailey, *Woodrow Wilson and the Lost Peace* (1944) and *Woodrow Wilson and the Great Betrayal* (1945). Ralph Stone, *The Irreconcilables: The Fight Against the League of Nations:* (1970), also discusses the rejection of the treaty.

42

The Age of Harding
Troubled Years of Transition, 1919–1923

The ten years between 1919 and 1929 have come down to us with a ready-made personality, a nickname that seems to capture the flavor of a decade. In the popular imagination, the 1920s are and always will be the "Roaring Twenties." Exhausted by the prolonged fervor of progressivism and disillusioned by a righteous war to save humanity from itself, the American people set out to have a little fun, and ended up by having a lot.

Images of the Roaring Twenties, lovingly re-created in novels, stories, films, and television programs, easily flood the mind: speakeasies (illegal saloons), college boys and flapper girls defying traditional morality during breaks between dancing to the exciting new jazz music; bootleggers and gangsters, somehow menacing and engaging at the same time.

The 1920s were the golden age of sport: Babe Ruth's Yankees, Connie Mack's A's, and John McGraw's Giants were the superteams of baseball; Harold "Red" Grange was the saint of the regional religion of football; Jack Dempsey and Gene Tunney were prizefighters as mythic as Odysseus and Hercules.

Radio made its debut with the decade; the first commercial broadcast told of Warren G. Harding's landslide victory in the presidential

---

The cover of Life magazine on February 18, 1926, captured the spirit of the Roaring Twenties in caricature.

election of 1920. The movies became a part of almost every American's life during these years. So did the automobile, the modern world's idol of individual freedom, from the homely, accessible Model T Ford to the Stutz Bearcat, Dusenberg, and Cord, still among the most glorious creations of the auto maker's technology and craft.

The list can go on and on, but at any length it will be a distortion. Only a small proportion of the American population—the wealthy and the well-to-do middle classes who lived in cities and sizable towns—enjoyed even a semblance of the roaring good times of legend. And the banner years were not ten, but five or six in number, beginning only after Calvin Coolidge became president in 1923.

The Worst President

During the four years that preceded the reign of "Silent Cal," American life was beset more by contradictions, uncertainties, and fears than by diverting good times. In fact, during the two years immediately before and the two immediately after the inauguration of President Harding in March 1921, American society was on edge, and so was the man whom many historians consider to have been the worst president.

Warren Harding, a newspaperman who entered politics as a United States senator and later became president.

Warren G. Harding

A newspaperman, Warren Gamaliel Harding worked his way up in politics on the basis of a friendly smile, a firm handshake, the reliable support of the Republican party line in his newspaper (the *Marion Star*), and the happy discovery by Ohio's political bosses that whenever they asked favors, and whatever favors they asked, Warren G. Harding said yes.

He loved the Senate, where voters sent him in 1914; the job suited his temperament. Being a senator called for making the occasional speech—Harding was good at that—but as only one senator among ninety-six, he was not expected to take the lead in anything.

No one objected that Harding helped old cronies find government jobs that they were unfit to perform, and the affable Ohioan had plenty of time to enjoy the all-night poker and bourbon parties with his pals that were his second most favorite recreation. Because newspaper reporters were more restrained in dealing with the private lives of public officials than they are today, Harding could carry on his favorite recreation

with a minimum of discretion. He had a series of mistresses and even fathered an illegitimate daughter by one, Nan Britton, without scandal.

A Decent Man

Harding had no illusions about his intelligence or his moral capacity for leadership. However, after the sour experience with the brilliant and imperious Wilson, neither he nor the American people regarded an ordinary mind as a handicap in a president. Harding was genuinely kind and decent. If he could not hope to be "the best president," he could, in his own words, try to be "the best liked," a distinction that was beyond the reach of the icy Wilson.

He displayed his humanity when, at Christmas 1921, he pardoned Eugene V. Debs and other Socialists who had opposed the war. (Vindictively, Wilson had refused to do so.) Harding personally pressured the directors of United States Steel to reduce the workday in their mills to eight hours. Most striking was Harding's reaction when political enemies whispered that he was part black. In an era when most white people thought in at least mildly racist terms, that kind of talk could ruin a career. Other politicians would have responded with a lawsuit or an indignant racist diatribe that outdid their accusers for spleen. But Harding merely shrugged, an extraordinary response in that era.

Hoover and Hughes

Unfortunately, the presidency called for more than personal decency. Because Harding simply did not understand many of the problems that were suddenly thrust on him, he left policy making to his cabinet and to other appointees. No harm was done in the cases of Secretary of Commerce Herbert C. Hoover and Secretary of State Charles Evans Hughes. They were able men of integrity and some vision whose policies shine all the more because the Harding administration's record is otherwise so murky.

As he had done during the First World War, Hoover worked quietly, encouraging the formation of private trade associations in industry and agriculture. His hope was that these organizations would eliminate waste, develop uniform standards of production, and end "destructive competition." His success was limited, but to a large extent, Hoover anticipated the corporate liberal system that Americans would adopt for half a century as their preference in government policy.

Charles Evans Hughes first terminated the state of war with Germany that still formally existed because the United States had not ratified the Treaty of Versailles. At his behest, Congress merely resolved that the war was over. Then the Secretary of State presented his alternative to the League of Nations as a means of keeping the peace, calling an international conference in Washington to discuss naval disarmament. The delegates, who expected the usual round of receptions and meaningless pieties that most such conferences involved, were shocked when Hughes proposed that all the great powers scrap their capital ships (battleships and cruisers) and cancel plans for future naval construction.

Because every diplomat agreed that the arms race had been instrumental in bringing on the First World War, the delegates in Washington had no choice but to listen, particularly when Hughes reminded them that by limiting the size of their navies, the powers could save millions: the construction of even a single capital ship was a major line item in a national budget.

In the Treaty of Washington of 1921, the five major naval powers agreed to limit their fleets according to a ratio that reflected their interests and defensive needs. For each five tons that Great Britain and the United States floated in capital ships, Japan would have three, and France and Italy would have somewhat smaller fleets. Each nation gave up ships, but each benefited too. Great Britain maintained naval equality with the United States, a primacy that American plans for ship construction would have destroyed. (The United States scrapped thirty battleships and cruisers that were under construction or planned.) The American government cut the budget, its principal interest at the time. Japan, which needed only a one-ocean navy whereas Britain and the United States had worldwide interests, got parity (or even superiority) in the Pacific. Italy and France, still reeling from the war, were spared the strain of an arms race, but retained naval strength in the Mediterranean.

The Harding Scandals

Unfortunately, the work of Hoover and Hughes just about sums up the accomplishments of the Harding years. The other men in the administration were either servants of narrow special interests or blatant crooks. Secretary of the Treasury Andrew Mellon pursued tax policies that extravagantly favored the rich and helped bring on the disastrous depression that ended the Roaring Twenties. More dismaying in the short run were those old cronies whom Harding appointed to office. No sooner were they settled in their jobs in Washington than they set about filling their pockets and ruining their generous friend.

Attorney General Harry Daugherty winked at violations of the law by political allies. Probably with Daugherty's connivance, Jesse L. Smith, a close friend

A cartoon showing a teapot that looks suspiciously like an embarrassed elephant illustrated the Republican Party's uncomfortable involvement in the Teapot Dome scandal.

of the president, sold favorable decisions and public offices for cold cash. Charles R. Forbes, the head of the Veterans Administration, pocketed money intended for hospital construction. Grandest of all, Secretary of the Interior Albert B. Fall leased the navy's petroleum reserves at Teapot Dome, Wyoming, and Elk Hills, California, to two freewheeling oilmen, Harry Sinclair and Edward L. Doheny. In return, Fall accepted "loans" of about $300,000 from the two. Fall also tarred Harding with his corruption because, some time earlier, he had persuaded the president to transfer the oil reserves from the navy's authority to that of the Interior Department.

By the summer of 1923, Harding realized that his administration was shot through with thievery. When he set out on a vacation trip to Alaska, he knew that it was only a matter of time before the scandals hit the newspapers and destroyed his name. His health was already suffering; the famous handsome face is haggard and gray in the last photographs.

Nevertheless, a weak and obliging man to the end, Harding allowed his friend Forbes to flee abroad, and he took no action against the others. Jesse Smith killed himself. Mercifully, perhaps, Harding died too, before he got back to Washington. Only later did Americans learn of the secrets that plagued him, from the corruption in his administration to the irregularities in his personal life, which Nan Britton described in her book, *The President's Daughter*. So tangled were the affairs of the Harding administration that scandalmongers suggested that Harding's wife had poisoned him, and they were widely believed. Actually, the president suffered a massive heart attack, possibly brought on by the realization that he had failed on so colossal a scale.

Social Tensions: Labor, Radicals, Immigrants

If Harding's poignant tale is symbolic of his time, the social tensions that strained and snapped while he was in the White House ran far deeper than the personality of an unhappy man from Marion, Ohio. Had Harding been a pillar of moral strength and probity, the years he presided over would have been much the same as they were. Indeed, the troubled half of the 1920s began two years before Harding was inaugurated. As far as most Americans were concerned, the social conflicts that first broke into the open then were quite closely related: labor, political radicalism, and the presence of so many immigrants in an idyllic America that had never really existed.

The Great Strikes: Seattle and Steel

During the First World War, the conservative trade unions of the American Federation of Labor seemed to become part of the federal power structure. In return for Wilson's recognition of their respectability, most unions agreed not to strike for the duration of hostilities. Unfortunately, while wages rose slowly during 1917 and 1918, the prices of consumer goods, including necessities, increased quickly and then soared during a runaway postwar inflation. The end of the war also led to the cancellation of government contracts; tens of thousands were thrown out of work, and the inevitable occurred: thirty-six hundred strikes during 1919 involving 4 million workers.

Striker grievances were generally valid, but, to the surprise of many workers, few Americans outside the labor movement were sympathetic. When employers described the strikes of 1919 as revolutions, aimed at destroying middle-class decency as well as themselves, much of America agreed. In Seattle, a dispute that began on the docks of the busy Pacific port turned into a general strike involving almost all the city's sixty-thousand workers. Most of them were interested in nothing more than better pay. However, the concept of the general strike was associated in the popular mind with class war and revolution. Mayor Ole Hanson was able to depict the dispute as an uprising that had been inspired by dangerous foreign "Bolsheviks" like those who had taken over Russia during the war. With the help of the marines, he crushed the strike.

Steel-industry magnates used similar methods to fight a walkout in September by 350,000 workers, largely in the Great Lakes region. The men had good reason to strike. The majority of them worked a twelve-hour day and a seven-day week. It was not unusual for individuals to put in thirty-six hours at a stretch. That is, if a man's relief failed to show up, he was told to stay on the job or lose it. When the extra shift ended, his own began again.

For this kind of life, steelworkers took home subsistence wages. For some Slavic immigrants in the industry, that home was not even a bed to themselves. They contracted with a landlord to rent half a bed. After their wearying shift and a quick, cheap meal, they rolled under blankets still warm and damp from the body of a fellow worker who had just trudged off to the mill.

These wretched conditions were well known. And yet, the heads of the industry, Elbert Gary and Charles Schwab of United States Steel, easily persuaded the public that the strike was the work of revolutionary agitators like William Z. Foster. Because Foster had a radical past (and future as the leader of the American

POPULATION OF TEN LARGEST CITIES—1920

New York	5,620,000
Chicago	2,702,000
Philadelphia	1,824,000
Detroit	994,000
Cleveland	797,000
St. Louis	773,000
Boston	748,000
Baltimore	734,000
Pittsburgh	588,000
Los Angeles	577,000

Communist party) and because many steelworkers had ethnic roots in Eastern Europe, the home of Bolshevism, the strikers were almost universally condemned.

The Boston Police Strike

The Boston police strike of 1919 frightened Americans more than any of the other conflicts. While the shutdown of even a basic industry like steel did not immediately affect daily life, the absence of police officers from the streets caused a jump in crime as professional hoodlums and desperately poor people took advantage of the situation.

Boston's policemen, mostly Irish-Americans, were underpaid. They earned prewar wages, not enough to support their families decently in a city where many prices had tripled. Nevertheless, they too commanded little public support. On the contrary, when Massachusetts governor Calvin Coolidge declared that "there is no right to strike against the public safety by anybody, anywhere, anytime," and ordered the National Guard into Boston to break the strike, he became a national hero. It was his unimaginative hard-line policy that won him the Republican vice-presidential nomination in 1920.

Some strikes ended in victory. But the defeat of most of them ushered in a decade of decline for the labor movement. The membership of unions stood at over 5 million in 1919, but at only 3.6 million in 1929, despite the expansion of the nonagricultural working class during the same years.

Red Scare

Public reaction to the strikes of 1919 revealed widespread hostility toward recent immigrants and second-generation Americans. This xenophobia took more virulent form in the Red scare of 1919. Even before the Armistice was signed, a new stereotype had replaced the "bloodthirsty Hun" as the villain whom Americans had most reason to fear: the seedy, bearded, and wild-eyed Bolshevik. American newspapers exaggerated the many real atrocities that took place during the civil war that followed the Russian Revolution and invented tales of mass executions, torture, children turned against their parents, and women declared the common property of all men. Already in an uneasy mood, Americans were prepared to believe the worst about a part of the world from which so many immigrants recently had come.

It was widely believed that foreign-born Communists were a threat to the United States. In March 1919, the Soviets organized the Third International, or "Comintern," an organization that was explicitly dedicated to fomenting revolution around the world. So it seemed to be no accident when, in April, the Post Office discovered thirty-eight bombs in the mail addressed to prominent capitalists and government officials. In June, several bombs reached their targets. One bomber who was identified—he blew himself up—was a foreigner, an Italian. And in September, two American Communist parties were founded in Chicago, and the press emphasized the immigrant element in the membership. Many Americans concluded that the Red threat was closely related to the large number of immigrants and their children within the United States.

In reality, very few ethnic Americans were radicals, and most prominent Socialists and Communists boasted impeccable WASP origins. Max Eastman, the editor of the radical wartime magazine *The Masses,* was of old New England stock. John Reed, whose *Ten Days That Shook the World* remained for many years the classic English-language account of the Russian Revolution, Debs, Haywood, and William Z. Foster had no strong ethnic ties. Moreover, neither they nor the foreign-born radicals posed a real threat to established institutions. Within a few years, the combined membership of the two Communist parties and the Socialist party numbered only in the thousands.

But popular dread of Communists was real, and the temptation to exploit it for political gain was overwhelming. Wilson's Attorney General, A. Mitchell Palmer, tried to ride the Red scare into a presidential nomination by ordering a series of well-publicized raids on Communist headquarters.

Although an investigation found that only 39 of those whom he had arrested could be deported according to the law, Palmer put 249 people on a steamship dubbed "the Soviet Ark" and sent them to Russia via Finland. On New Year's Day 1920, Palmer's agents again swooped down on hundreds of locations, arresting 6,000 people. Some of them, such as a Western

Union delivery boy, merely had the bad luck to be in the wrong place at the wrong time. Others were arrested while merely peering into the windows of Communist storefront offices. Nevertheless, all were imprisoned for at least a short time.

Palmer's popularity fizzled in the spring of 1920. He predicted that there would be mass demonstrations on May Day, the international Communist holiday, and nothing happened. By midsummer, the great scare was over, but antiforeign feeling continued to affect both government policy and popular attitudes throughout the 1920s.

Sacco and Vanzetti

The two most celebrated victims of the wedding of antiradicalism to xenophobia were Nicola Sacco and Bartolomeo Vanzetti. In 1920, the two Italian immigrants were arrested for an armed robbery in South Braintree, Massachusetts, in which a guard and a pay-master were killed. They were found guilty of murder, and sentenced to die in the electric chair.

Before they could be executed, the American Civil Liberties Union, Italian-American groups, and labor organizations publicized the fact that the hard evidence against Sacco and Vanzetti was scanty and, at least in part, invented by the prosecution. Judge Webster Thayer was obviously prejudiced because the defendants were radicals (anarchists). He was overheard speaking of them as "damned dagos."

At the same time, Sacco and Vanzetti won admiration by acting with dignity during their trial, steadfastly maintaining their innocence but refusing to compromise their political beliefs. "I am suffering," Vanzetti said in court,

because I am a radical and indeed I am a radical; I have suffered because I was an Italian, and indeed I am an Italian . . . but I am so convinced to be right that if you could execute me two times, and if I could be reborn two other times, I would live again to do what I have done already.

Nicola Sacco and Bartolomeo Vanzetti, immigrants and anarchists whose case became an international cause in the 1920s.

Despite a movement to save them that reached international proportions, Sacco and Vanzetti were finally executed in 1927. Although recent research has indicated that at least Sacco was guilty, that question was irrelevant during the 1920s. The two simply were not proved guilty, and many American intellectuals accused the state of Massachusetts of judicial murder by bowing to popular prejudice against foreigners. The same prejudice also ended the great age of immigration.

Shutting the Golden Door

In 1883, the American poet Emma Lazarus had written, "Send these, the homeless, tempest-tost to me, I lift my lamp beside the golden door." Immigration continued at high levels until 1915, when all-out naval war made the Atlantic too dangerous for large numbers of people to cross. By 1918, immigration into the United States was down to 110,000.

With peace came newcomers whose numbers approached prewar levels. In 1921, 805,000 people, mostly southern and Eastern Europeans, passed through the golden door. Congress was alarmed and, encouraged by antiforeign sentiment, passed a bill that stipulated that 350,000 people could enter the United States each year. However, each European nation was allowed to send only 3 percent of the number of its nationals who had been residents of the United States in the base year of 1910. In 1924, an amendment reduced the quota to 2 percent and changed the base year to 1890. Because most southern and Eastern Europeans had begun to emigrate to the United States after 1890, the quotas of such poor countries as Poland, Czechoslovakia, Hungary, Rumania, Yugoslavia, Bulgaria, Greece, and Italy were very low. For example, the annual quota for Italy was a minuscule 6,000, and was inevitably filled within the first few months of each year.

By way of contrast, the quotas for the comparatively prosperous countries of northern and Western Europe, the nations of the Old Immigration, were generous and rarely filled. The annual quota for Great Britain was 65,000, one-fifth of the total. During the 1930s, however, an average of only 2,500 Britons emigrated to the United States each year.

Social Tensions: Race, Moral Codes, Religion

The 1920s were also a time of anxiety and tension in relations between the two major races, between people who held fast to traditional moral codes and those who rejected them, and (closely allied to the moral issue) between rural people and urban people.

Black Scare

Having supported the war effort at the behest of organizations like the NAACP, blacks looked forward to a greater measure of equality after the Armistice. The two hundred thousand young black men who had served in the army in Europe had been exposed to a white society in which their color was not a major handicap. Although they had been segregated within the American armed forces, they had found that the French people looked on them as Yanks of a different color, nothing more or less, and had been grateful for their help against Germany. At home, blacks who moved to northern cities experienced a less repressive life than they had known in the rural South and felt freer to express themselves.

But white America had not changed its mind about race. In 1919, of the seventy-eight blacks who were lynched, ten were veterans; several were hanged while dressed in their uniforms. Race riots broke out in twenty-five cities with a death toll of more than one hundred. The worst was in Chicago, where a petty argument on a Lake Michigan beach mushroomed into vicious racial war. White and black gangs with guns roamed the streets shooting at anyone of the wrong color whom they stumbled across.

ANTI-SEMITISM

The hatred of Jews that was to acquire nightmarish proportions in Germany had its counterpart in the United States, albeit never so vicious or significant as it was under Adolf Hitler. For a time during the 1920s, automobile millionaire Henry Ford sponsored a newspaper, the *Dearborn Independent,* that insisted, as Hitler did, that Jews in general were party to an "international conspiracy" to destroy Western and particularly Christian civilization. The most astonishing aspect of this kind of anti-Semitism was that it posited an alliance between wealthy, conservative Jewish bankers like the Rothschild family of Europe and their worst enemies, Jewish Socialists and Communists.

If not too preposterous for Germans, these allegations never were taken very seriously in the United States. However, anti-Semitism was acceptable and even respectable when it took the form of keeping Jews out of some businesses (banking, ironically) and social clubs. Moreover, a number of universities applied Jewish "quotas" when they admitted students. Jews were admitted, but only up to a certain percentage of each class.

A black man lies wounded at the base of a staircase, the victim of an attack by whites during the Chicago race riot of 1919.

Black Nationalism

In this charged atmosphere emerged a remarkable but doomed black leader. Born in the British colony of Jamaica, Marcus Garvey came to the United States in 1917. He concluded that whites would never accept blacks as equals, and, filled with a glowing pride in his own race, he rejected integration. Garvey's alternative to the violent racial conflict of 1919 was the joining together of blacks throughout the world to organize a powerful black nation in Africa.

Garvey's Universal Negro Improvement Association (UNIA) was based on pride in race, the strong organizing point of all racial-separatist movements. Although itself racist, of course, it was a positive, assertive gospel for an oppressed group. "When Europe was inhabited by a race of cannibals, a race of savages, naked men, heathens, and pagans," Garvey told cheering throngs in New York's Harlem, cleverly turning white stereotypes of blacks upside down, "Africa was peopled by a race of cultured black men who were masters in art, science, and literature."

He made little headway in the South, but in the North, urban blacks who already were uprooted found his call for a return to Africa appealing, at least in the abstract. Estimates of UNIA membership as high as 4 million were probably exaggerated, but many more blacks than that listened to Garvey's message with open minds and enjoyed the pageantry of nationhood with which he surrounded himself.

Garvey decked himself in ornate, regal uniforms and commissioned paramilitary orders with exotic names such as "The Dukes of the Niger" and the "Black Eagle Flying Corps." Even veterans in the fight for racial equality were influenced by Garvey's magic. W. E. B. Du Bois wrote, "The spell of Africa is upon me. The ancient witchery of her medicine is burning in my drowsy, dreamy blood."

The popularity of black nationalism unnerved whites who were accustomed to a passive black population. When Garvey ran afoul of the law with one of his dozens of business enterprises, the authorities moved against him with an enthusiasm that cannot be ex-

Wearing ornate uniforms and commissioning paramilitary orders, Marcus Garvey led a large black nationalist movement that was born in response to the violent racial conflict that scarred America in 1919.

plained by the character of his offense. Whether because of mismanagement or deliberate fraud, Garvey's Black Star Line, a steamship company, had sold worthless shares through the mails at a mere $5 a share. Although the operation had been small time by any criterion, beginning in 1922 and dragging on for five years, the government pressed its case, draining the resources of the UNIA.

Garvey went to prison. When he was pardoned in 1927, he immediately was deported to Jamaica as an "undesirable alien." His dream of black equality through racial separation survived only in small religious (often Islamic) sects in urban ghettos.

The Ku Klux Klan

Marcus Garvey's use of ritual, costume, and ceremony was paralleled in a white racist organization of the same era, the Ku Klux Klan. The twentieth-century KKK was founded in 1915 by William Simmons, a Methodist minister. After viewing *Birth of a Nation*, a film that glorified the antiblack movement of the post-Civil War period, Simmons began organizing, first in the South but, by 1919, in the North and West as well.

Under Hiram Wesley Evans, the KKK gave local units and officials exotic names such as Klavern, Kleagle, Grand Dragon, and Exalted Cyclops. Evans was a shrewder businessman than Garvey. The Klan's central office retained a monopoly of "official" bed-sheet uniforms that all members were required to buy. The Klan provided a cash incentive for local organizers by giving

Ku Klux Klan members concealed their identities under white sheets, which made them resemble ghosts from another world. Here a group of klansmen waits in cars parked in Washington, D.C., in 1925.

them a percentage of all money that they collected, a kind of franchised bigotry. By the mid-1920s, membership may have risen as high as 4.5 million.

In the South, the KKK was primarily an antiblack organization. Elsewhere, however, KKK leaders exploited whatever hatreds, fears, and resentments were most likely to win members. In the Northeast, where Catholics and Jews were numerous, Klan leaders inveighed against their religions. Immigrants generally were a target.

In the Owens Valley of California, a region of small farmers whose water was drained southward to feed the growth of Los Angeles, the big city was the enemy. In the Midwest, some Klaverns concentrated their attacks on saloonkeepers who ignored Prohibition and "lovers' lanes" where teenagers flaunted traditional morality on weekend nights. Stripped of the hocus-pocus and the mercenary motives of the central office, the Klan represented the belief of generally poor, Protestant, and small-town people that the America they knew was under attack by immigrants, cities, and modern immorality.

Klan power peaked in 1924. In that year, the organization boasted numerous state legislators, congressmen, senators, and even governors in Oregon, Ohio, Tennessee, and Texas. In Indiana, state Klan leader David Stephenson was a virtual dictator. At the Democratic national convention of 1924, the Klan was strong enough to prevent the party from adopting a plank that was critical of its bigotry.

The KKK declined as rapidly as the UNIA. In 1925, Grand Dragon Stephenson was found guilty of second-degree murder in the death of a young woman whom he had kidnapped and taken to Chicago. In an attempt to win a light sentence, he turned over evidence showing that virtually the whole administration of the KKK was involved in thievery and that Indiana Klan politicians were thoroughly corrupt. By 1930, the KKK had dwindled to ten thousand members.

Wets and Drys

To a large extent, the Klan was a manifestation of hostility between cities and country and small towns. This social conflict was also evident in the split that developed as soon as the Eighteenth Amendment was ratified in 1919. Violation of the Prohibition law was nearly universal. While some bootleggers smuggled liquor into the country from Mexico, the West Indies, and Canada, liquor distillers in isolated corners of rural America continued to practice their ancient crafts, distilling "white lightning" and "moonshine" and battling government agents with guns as well as stealth.

Nevertheless, there was a clear geographical and social dimension to the political battle between "drys," people who supported Prohibition, and "wets," those who opposed it. The drys were strongest in the South and in rural areas generally, where the population was largely composed of old-stock Americans who clung to fundamentalist Protestant religions. The wets drew

This model T and its cache of illegal alcohol were seized in a Marfa, Texas, raid.

their support from the big cities, where ethnic groups of Roman Catholic and Jewish faith were powerful forces and often in control of local government.

Wet mayors and city councils often refused to help federal officials enforce Prohibition. Democratic Mayor James J. Walker of New York openly frequented fashionable speakeasies. Republican "Big Bill" Thompson of Chicago ran for office on a "wide-open-town" platform and won. As a result, smuggling, illegal distilleries and breweries, and theft of industrial and medicinal alcohol were commonplace and provided the basis for an extremely lucrative, if illegal, business. In Chicago by 1927, the Alphonse "Al" Capone bootleg ring grossed $60 million by supplying liquor and beer to the Windy City's speakeasies. (Capone also made $25 million that year from gambling and $10 million from prostitution.)

Gangsters as Symbols

As far as Capone was concerned, he was a businessman. He supplied ten thousand drinking houses and employed seven hundred people. He and other gangsters needed the administrative acumen of a corporation executive to run their affairs and the same kind of political influence that conventional businessmen courted. "What's Al Capone done?" he told a reporter. "He's supplied a legitimate demand. . . . Some call it racketeering. I call it a business. They say I violate the prohibition law. Who doesn't?"

With incredible profits at stake, however, rival gangs engaged in open, bloody warfare for control of the trade. More than four hundred "gangland slayings" made the name of Chicago synonymous with mob violence, although other cities had only scarcely better records.

Very few innocent bystanders were killed. Capone and his ilk tried to keep their violence on a professional level. But Americans were appalled by the carnage, and they did not overlook the fact that most prominent gangsters were "foreigners." Capone and his predecessors in Chicago, Johnny Torrio and Big Jim Colosimo, were Italians. Dion O'Bannion (Capone's rival), "Bugsy" Moran, and Owney Madden were Irish. Arthur "Dutch Schultz" Flegensheimer of New York was German. "Polack Joe" Saltis came from Chicago's Polish West Side. Maxie Hoff of Philadelphia, Solly Weissman of Kansas City, and "Little Hymie" Weiss of Chicago were Jews.

Ethnic domination of organized crime is easily explained. "Illegal business" attracted members of groups on the bottom of the social ladder because success in it required no social status or family connections, no education, and, to get started, little money. With less to

Al Capone, a gangster who supplied thousands of drinking houses with illegal liquor, regarded himself as a businessman fulfilling a public demand.

lose than respectable established people who patronized the speakeasies, ethnics had fewer compunctions about the high risks involved. But the majority of Americans were not inclined to take a sociological view of the matter. To them, organized crime was violent, and "foreigners" were the source of it.

Hollywood as Symbol

Show business was also a low-status enterprise that presented no competitive advantages to wealthy and established groups. The film industry, which was booming by 1919, had been largely dominated from the beginning by Jewish studio bosses such as Samuel Goldwyn and Louis B. Mayer, graduates of the rich Yiddish-language theater tradition of New York City. Consequently, when protest against nudity and loose moral standards in Hollywood films boiled over, it took

AIMEE SEMPLE MCPHERSON (1890–1944)

Evangelist Aimee Semple McPherson.

Aimee Elizabeth Kennedy was born in a small town in Ontario, Canada, in 1890. Little is known of her youth except that she underwent an intense religious experience and was "born again" while a young woman after hearing an impassioned sermon by an illiterate but eloquent preacher named Robert Semple. She married Semple—the dates are uncertain—and went with him to China where they intended to devote their lives to missionary work. In less than a year, however, Aimee's husband died, and she returned home.

She married again, to Harold McPherson, but the marriage appears to have been unhappy from the start; Aimee was an ambitious person with an effervescent personality, and McPherson was shy, perhaps dull. After separating from her husband, she was apparently destitute except in ideas. A handsome woman, extroverted with a theatrical bent at a time when women were leading more public lives, Aimee's religiosity made her a natural as a preacher. Her model was Billy Sunday, a major-league baseball player turned revivalist who combined an appeal for simple, emotional fundamentalism with vaudeville entertainment. Sunday leaped around the speaker's platform, used colorful, sometimes almost salacious illustrations for his lessons, and condemned cities, Roman Catholics, Jews, alcohol, smoking, and dancing—save for that done in the pulpit in the name of Jesus. He also knew how to fill a collection basket. More than a few theatrical producers gladly would have exhanged their receipts for Billy's offerings.

Aimee never quite outdid him, but she came close. With her practical-minded mother acting as business manager, she started out on the "sawdust trail," traveling up and down the east coast in what she called her "gospel automobile." It was a difficult life with modest returns. Aimee preached to whatever congregation would allow her in the pulpit in exchange for a share of the collection. Her audiences were poor, rural people or recent emigrants to the cities. They could not afford to contribute much to what, for them, was religion, fellowship, relief from hardship, and entertainment combined.

In 1918, Aimee made the same decision that a great many people were making at that time—she decided to move to southern California—and it changed her life.

Los Angeles, just a dusty pueblo a generation earlier, had boomed and boomed again as the city fathers had brought water into what was a natural desert and successfully touted the pleasures of the southern California climate to people who were tired of struggling "back East" but who had enough money to put a down payment on a home lot. Everyone in Los Angeles had arrived only recently. No one had roots there, and the extraordinary growth of the city (the population doubled every few years) made for a sense of insecurity that sent people searching desperately for something unchanging to grab. "Old-time religion" was a perfect response, as Aimee Semple McPherson understood before anyone else.

Aimee and Los Angeles suited each other. She was as good a showman, alternately poignant and clownish, as Charlie Chaplin and Buster Keaton. She dressed in flowing, low-cut white robes, surrounded herself with choirs of angels, dropped rose petals from the ceiling of her Angelus Temple (which seated more than five thousand people), released balloons and pigeons at climactic moments in her sermons, pounded the Bible, broke down in tears, exploded in ecstatic exultation, and dependably healed several people of fatal diseases and impairments at every meeting. On one occasion she set the congregation to cheering by entering the temple on a motorcycle, roaring up the aisle. Before another meeting in San Diego, she bombarded the city with tracts from an airplane.

The anomaly of Aimee Semple McPherson and her less successful imitators was the fact that they exploited the technology, novelties, and social trends of the New Era at the same time that they inveighed against the evils of them. Aimee condemned sinful radio, but she owned a station. She railed against the immorality of Hollywood movies, but missed no opportunity to be filmed in her highly sexual and suggestive act. "To visit Angelus Temple," one cynic wrote, "is to go on a sensuous debauch served up in the name of religion." She called herself "Everybody's Sister," but encouraged the racism and violence of the Ku Klux Klan.

And the formula worked. Not only did she fill the Angelus Temple, but on a month-long visit to Denver, she spoke to twelve thousand people nightly. She founded a college, owned a publishing house, opened branch churches of her "Foursquare Gospel Religion" every month during the 1920s, and sent money to overseas missions (or at least she said she did).

But it would be presumptuous to say that she and other revivalists were simply cynics, parting generally poor people from their money. Novelist Sinclair Lewis recognized the difficulty of sorting out sincere religious commitment and humbug for profit in his book about fundamentalism during the 1920s, *Elmer Gantry* (in which a major character is patterned on Aimee).

A pall was thrown over Aimee's reputation in the summer of 1926. On May 18, after an excursion to the beach, Aimee failed to show up for a meeting at the Angelus Temple. For weeks the papers were filled with sensational speculations about what had happened to her. On June 24, just when the press was losing interest in the case, Aimee stumbled into a desert town in Arizona. From a hospital bed in Douglas, she told of having been kidnapped, tortured by men who burned her with cigars, and held in an isolated desert dwelling.

Skeptical reporters noted that Aimee's wrists were bruised, but there were no other signs of mistreatment. A physician who examined her noted wryly that she was neither sunburned, dehydrated, nor especially dirty, which was remarkable considering that she had fled across a parched wasteland in order to get to Douglas.

Rumors flew furiously. Aimee had been enjoying a month-long tryst with a radio operator from the Angelus Temple who also had been missing (and showed up in Los Angeles about the same time that Amy stumbled into Douglas). Others said that there had been a Mexican abortion. Yet others wrote off the incident as a plain and simple publicity stunt to distract people from dissension within Aimee's organization and to fill those five thousand seats at the temple. Sister Aimee did not quell that tale when she reenacted the kidnapping for photographers from the Los Angeles *Examiner*, a newspaper that fully exploited the event and indignantly defended the evangelist. (Publisher William Randolph Hearst, who knew how to put on a show, also appreciated one.) In any case, while there never was any positive evidence that an abduction had taken place, Aimee was quickly acquitted when she stood trial for fraud.

Aimee lost her celebrity status in the years that followed the abduction and had to fight a series of civil suits to protect her share in the property of the Foursquare Gospel Church. But the organization survived her, and today has more than two hundred thousand members in almost one thousand congregations.

HOORAY FOR HOLLYWOOD

The first filmmakers set up shop wherever they happened to be. By the 1920s, however, the movie industry had become concentrated in Hollywood, one of the myriad communities that make up Los Angeles. The official explanation of the choice of location was the weather; southern California is one of the sunniest parts of the nation, and early filmmakers depended on natural light. But there was another reason for choosing Hollywood. Like the organizers of many infant industries, filmmakers took considerable liberties with business law, particularly copyright and contract law. Everyone, it seemed, was engaged in a dozen lawsuits at all times. Hollywood was only a hundred miles from the Mexican border. If a case seemed to be getting serious, the filmmakers could make a quick dash out of the country.

by fast-changing times and urged on by such influential leaders as William Jennings Bryan, the fundamentalists tried to prohibit the teaching of evolution in the public schools; in Tennessee, they succeeded in passing a law to that effect.

In the little Appalachian town of Dayton in the spring of 1925, a group of friends who had been arguing about evolution decided to test the new law in the courts by having one of their number, a high-school biology teacher named John Scopes, deliberately break it. In front of adult witnesses, Scopes would explain Darwin's theory, submit to arrest, and stand trial. The motives of the men were mixed. Dayton businessmen thought of a celebrated trial as a way to put their town on the map and to make money when spectators, including reporters for newspapers and radio stations, would flock to Dayton in search of lodging, meals, and other services.

on an ethnic flavor. Preachers who demanded that controls be slapped on filmmakers were not above attributing immorality on the screen to "non-Christian" influences that aimed to subvert Protestant America.

By 1922, Hollywood's nabobs feared that city and state governments would ban the showing of their films. They banded together to censor themselves and, sensitive to ethnic prejudice, hired a man who was the epitome of the small-town midwestern Protestant to be chief censor and film-industry spokesman. Will H. Hays of Indiana, Postmaster General under Harding, quickly drafted a code that forbade movies that allowed adultery to go unpunished or that depicted divorced people in a sympathetic light. The Hays Code went so far as to prohibit showing a married couple in bed together or, indeed, a double bed in the background of bedroom scenes. In the movies, couples slept in twin beds, and so powerful was the medium that separate beds became fashionable in the real society.

The Evolution Controversy

The clash between traditional values and the worldly outlook of the twentieth century was clearest cut in the controversy that surrounded the theory of the evolution of species as propounded half a century before by the English biologist Charles Darwin. Although many scientists insisted that there was no contradiction between the biblical account of the creation of the world (if interpreted as literary) and Darwin's contention that species changed character over the eons, fundamentalist Protestants who insisted on the literal truth of every word of the Bible disagreed. Feeling threatened

The "Monkey Trial"

Dayton's boosters succeeded beyond their dreams. The "Monkey Trial," so-called because evolution was popularly interpreted as meaning that human beings were "descended" from apes, attracted sensation-hungry broadcasters and reporters by the hundred; among them was the nation's leading iconoclast, Henry L. Mencken, who came to poke fun at the "rubes" of the Bible belt. Number-one rube in Mencken's book was William Jennings Bryan himself, aged now—he died shortly after the trial ended—who agreed to go to Dayton to advise the prosecution.

Bryan's advice was ignored. He wanted to fight the case on the strictly legal principle that, in a democracy, the people had the right to dictate what might and what might not be taught in tax-supported schools. Unfortunately, their heads spinning from the crowds and the carnival atmosphere of the town, the Daytonians wanted to debate religion versus science.

The defense, which had been put together and funded by the American Civil Liberties Union, also intended to fight the case on the basis of two significant principles. Led by the distinguished lawyer and libertarian Arthur Garfield Hays, the attorneys planned to argue that the biblical account of creation was a religious doctrine and therefore could not take precedence over science (evolution) because of the constitutional separation of church and state. The defense also insisted that freedom of intellectual inquiry, including a teacher's right to speak his or her mind in the classroom, was essential to the health of a democracy.

Hays was assisted by the era's leading criminal lawyer, Clarence Darrow, who loved the drama of court-

A courtroom scene from the Scopes "Monkey Trial," which addressed the question of evolution and its instruction in classrooms.

room confrontation more than legal niceties. Darrow regarded the trial as an opportunity to discredit fundamentalists by making their leader, Bryan, look like a superstitious old fool. Against his better judgment, Bryan allowed Darrow to put him on the stand as an expert witness on the Bible. Under the trees—the judged feared that the tiny courthouse would collapse under the crowd—Darrow and Bryan talked religion and science. Was the world created in six days of twenty-four hours each? Was Jonah literally swallowed by a whale?

Supporters of Darrow rested content that Bryan himself looked like a monkey, but they lost the case; Scopes was found guilty and given a nominal penalty. However, this was small consolation to the antievolutionists, who were crestfallen when Bryan admitted that some parts of the Bible may have been meant figuratively. In fact, the only winners in the Monkey Trial were Dayton's businessmen, who raked in dollars for almost a month, and the people in the business of ballyhoo. This was appropriate in itself, for by 1925, the second full year of Calvin Coolidge's "New Era," raking in money and ballyhoo were what America seemed to be all about.

For Further Reading

The books cited at the end of Chapter 41 are also relevant to this chapter. Also see Wesley Bagby, *The Road to Normalcy* (1962), and Robert K. Murray, *The Harding Era* (1969). Murray's *The Politics of Normalcy* (1973) is also excellent, and an entertaining brief biography of Harding is Andrew Sinclair, *The Available Man* (1965).

On the labor upheavals of the postwar years, see David Brody, *Labor in Crisis: The Steel Strike of 1919* (1965); Robert L. Friedheim, *The Seattle General Strike* (1965); and the early chapters of the standard labor history of the period, Irving Bernstein, *The Lean Years* (1960).

Good general overviews are George Soule, *Prosperity Decade: From War to Depression, 1917–1929* (1947), and J. W. Prothro, *The Dollar Decade: Business Ideas in the 1920s* (1954). Excellent social histories include Frederick Lewis Allen, *Only Yesterday* (1931), and Isabel Leighton, *The Aspirin Age* (1949). On Prohibition, the most enjoyable book is Andrew Sinclair, *Prohibition: The Era of Excess* (1962). Perhaps the only recent sympathetic study of Prohibition is N. H. Clark, *Deliver Us From Evil* (1976). D. M. Chalmers, *Hooded Americanism* (1965); is on the Ku Klux Klan, and Ray Ginger, *Six Days or Forever?* (1958), is the best short book on the evolution controversy. John Higham, *Strangers in the Land* (1955), deals with nativism.

The Coolidge Years
When the Business of America Was Business, 1923–1929

Vice President Calvin Coolidge was visiting his father, a justice of the peace in rural Vermont, when he got the news of Harding's death. Instead of rushing to Washington to be sworn in by the Chief Justice of the Supreme Court, Coolidge walked downstairs to the darkened farmhouse parlor, where his father administered the presidential oath by the light of a kerosene lamp. To the very pinnacle of his political career, he was the image of simplicity and homely rectitude or, as some historians have suggested, of sloth and bewilderment.

Members of an organization of "boosters," the Minneapolis Commercial Club, gather for a meeting.

Coolidge and the New Era

Coolidge was not a bit like his predecessor. Far from strapping and handsome, he was physically slight and had a pinched face that, even when he smiled, seemed to say that he wished he were somewhere else. Alice Roosevelt Longworth, the acidulous daughter of Theodore Roosevelt, said Coolidge looked as though he had been weaned on a pickle.

Whereas Harding lived a tawdry secret life, Coolidge was a man of impeccable, priggish, even dreary personal habits. His idea of a good time was a long nap. He spent twelve to fourteen hours out of twenty-four in bed except on slow days, when he was able to doze a little longer. When writer Dorothy Parker heard that Coolidge had died in 1933, she asked, "How could they tell?"

Coolidge might have appreciated that. He was no dull wit himself, as a woman who sat next to "Silent Cal" at a banquet learned to her discomfort. In an attempt to break the ice pleasantly, she told the president of a friend who had bet her that the untalkative president would not say three words all evening. "You lose," Coolidge replied, and returned to his appetizer, resuming the blank stare that was his trademark. Coolidge also took a curious pleasure in posing for photographers in costumes that were ludicrous on him: wearing a ten-gallon hat or a Sioux Indian war bonnet; strapped into skis on the White House lawn; dressed as a hard-working farmer at the haying, in patent-leather shoes with a Pierce Arrow in the background.

Perhaps the photos were Coolidge's way of saying that he was at one with the American people of the 1920s in enjoying novelties and pranks. However that may be, he was assuredly at one with them in abdicating political and cultural leadership to the business community. Coolidge worshiped financial success and believed without reservation that millionaires knew what was best for the country. "The man who builds a factory builds a temple," he said. On another occasion, he put his faith with sublime simplicity: "The business of America is business."

An old hand at grabbing publicity, Calvin Coolidge posed in an Indian headdress for photographers.

Coolidge Confirmed in 1924

And so, while Coolidge quickly rid the cabinet of the political hacks whom he had inherited from Harding, he retained Harding's appointees from the business world, most notably Herbert Hoover and Secretary of the Treasury Andrew Mellon. He then sat back to preside over the most business-minded administration to his time, and, in return, business praised his administration higher than they built skyscrapers. The Republicans crowed about "Coolidge prosperity," which revived the erratic postwar economy beginning in 1923, and, thanks to the president's unblemished record for honesty, the G.O.P. never suffered a voter backlash as a result of the Harding scandals.

On the contrary, the biggest of the scandals, Teapot Dome, hurt progressive Democrats. The Wilsonian, William G. McAdoo, a leading contender for the Democratic nomination in 1924, had been an attorney for the oilman Edward L. Doheny. Although McAdoo knew no more of the crooked transaction than did Coolidge, people associated him more closely with the wrongdoers than they did the Republicans. Montana Senators Thomas J. Walsh and Burton Wheeler, who had led the investigation into the oil leases, were stymied by the Republican slogan "Keep Cool With Coolidge." The president's supporters chastised them for ranting and raving about past crimes that Coolidge had quietly remedied.

Then the Democrats tore themselves apart. Their 1924 convention deadlocked between Alfred E. Smith of New York, the leader of their eastern urban wing, and McAdoo, who represented the rural South and West. After more than a hundred ballots, the convention turned to a compromise candidate who was, as remarkable as it seems, as dull a character as Coolidge. But Wall Street lawyer John W. Davis was not away from his lucrative practice for long, winning only 29 percent of the vote to Coolidge's 54 percent. Aged Robert La Follette tried to revive the Progressive party in 1924. But he captured only 17 percent of the popular vote and carried no state but his native Wisconsin.

For four more years, Calvin Coolidge napped through good times. It was eight months after he left office, in October 1929, that what business called the "New Era" came crashing to an end. Ironically, in view of the impending Great Depression, Coolidge retired from office with great reluctance. It was whispered that when the Republican convention of 1928 took his enigmatic statement, "I do not choose to run," as a refusal to run, and nominated Herbert Hoover to succeed him, Coolidge threw himself on his familiar bed and wept.

Mellon's Tax Policies

The keystone of New Era government was the taxation policy worked out by the most powerful figure in the Coolidge cabinet, Andrew Mellon of Pittsburgh. Mellon looked less like the political cartoonist's stereotype of a big businessman—a bloated, fleshy moneybags— than like a sporting duke, but a moneybags he was. Trim, with chiseled aristocratic features, and dressed in deftly tailored suits and tiny pointed shoes that shone like a newly minted coin, Mellon was one of the three or four richest men in the world, a banker closely tied to the steel industry.

Believing that economic prosperity depended on the extent to which capitalists reinvested their profits in business, Mellon favored the rich by slashing taxes that fell most heavily on them. He reduced the personal income tax for people who made more than $60,000 a year, and by 1929, the Treasury was actually shoveling refunds back to large corporations. United States Steel, the company with which Mellon had made his fortune, was paid $15 million.

To compensate in part for the loss in government revenues, Mellon worked constantly to cut government expenditures. The costs of government that he conceded were indispensable were to be paid for by raising the tariff on imported products—a double benefit for industrial capitalists—and by increasing those kinds of taxes that were disproportionately paid by the middle and lower classes.

In the Fordney-McCumber Tariff of 1922, import duties reached levels that had been unheard-of for a

Andrew Mellon, a powerful businessman and a member of the Coolidge cabinet.

generation. Mellon also sponsored increases for some kinds of postal services, the excise, and a new federal tax on automobiles. To those who complained that these measures penalized the middling and poor, Mellon answered that the burden was small and that his overall scheme helped ordinary people as well as the rich.

Mellon's program was based on his belief that when businessmen reinvested their government-sponsored windfalls, they created jobs and the means of a better standard of living for all. The share of the middle and lower classes in Coolidge prosperity would "trickle down" to them. Moreover, the inducement to get rich, enhanced by government policy, would reinvigorate the spirit of enterprise among all Americans.

For six years, from late 1923 to late 1929, it appeared as though Mellon was indeed the greatest Secretary of the Treasury since Alexander Hamilton, as he was so considered by his friends in the business community. Just how much damage he did to the national economy would not be known until after the collapse of the New

Era in 1929. As early as 1924, however, the policy of subordinating everything to the short-term interests of big business and banking was helping to make a shambles of the international economy.

The Legacy of the Treaty of Versailles

The fundamental weakness of the international economy during the 1920s owed to the demands of Britain and France that Germany pay them $13 billion in reparations.

At the same time, the former Allies owed the United States $10 billion for loans that had been made to them during the war. In short, international payments would flow from Germany to Britain and France (and other smaller countries) and from there to the United States. The trouble was that the flow drained too much wealth out of Germany for the economy of that important industrial nation to remain healthy. Insane inflation ravaged the German mark—bundles of paper money were need to buy food—and experts warned that to continue to bleed Germany was to promote political extremism (including Adolf Hitler's Nazi party) and to threaten the economies of all nations.

The British and French governments acknowledged the point but insisted that as long as they were obligated to make huge debt payments to the United States, they had no choice but to insist on German payments to them, lest their own economies founder.

New Era Foreign Policy

There were several ways out of the morass. First, the United States, the world's wealthiest nation, could invigorate European industry by importing European products. The Fordney-McCumber Tariff, a vital part of Mellon's fiscal policy, shut the door on that idea. Second, the United States could forgive Britain and France their debts, in return for which they would cancel reparations payments from Germany. The international economy would, so to speak, have a fresh start. Unfortunately, an administration that was closely allied with banking interests would not do that. "They hired the money, didn't they?" Coolidge said of the French and British war debts, as though he were talking about a household grocery bill.

In the Dawes Plan of 1924 (named for Budget Director Charles G. Dawes) and the Young Plan of 1929 (named for Owen D. Young), the United States agreed to a rescheduling of reparations payments, but not to a reduction of the total burden. Instead, American bankers helped German industry and governments with the money that they made as a result of Mellon's tax policies. On the surface, money flowed in a circle: Ameri-

can bankers loaned it to Germany; Germany paid about $2.5 billion in reparations to Britain and France between 1923 and 1929; Britain and France paid $2.6 billion to American creditors. In reality, the European economy was steadily, if slowly, sapped, and the American economy was indirectly damaged: capital that was supposed to be reinvested at home to "trickle down" was devoted to a nonproductive balancing of international books.

Isolationism

After the Treaty of Washington, the Harding and Coolidge (and Hoover) administrations refused to make meaningful cooperative cause with other nations; the foreign policy of the 1920s thus is described as "isolationist." The name is helpful in the sense that the United States remained isolated from the League of Nations, which had been its own invention. The nation did continue to pay lip service to the idea of maintaining the peace through international cooperation, and in 1928, Secretary of State Frank B. Kellogg joined with French Foreign Minister Aristide Briand in writing a treaty that "outlawed" war as an instrument of national policy. Eventually, sixty-two nations signed the Kellogg-Briand Pact, a clear indication that, as a broad and pious statement of unenforceable sentiment, the agreement was meaningless.

Moreover, the United States did not abstain from significant relations with non-European powers. In Latin America, American business investments climbed from about $800 million in 1914 to $5.4 billion in 1929. The United States replaced Great Britain as the chief economic force in South America, particularly in the nations of the Caribbean.

The poorer Latin American nations sorely needed capital, and to that extent every dollar invested there was potentially a boon—if the population of the host countries as a whole benefited from it. Unfortunately, American businessmen had little interest in how the Latin American countries were governed until their profits were threatened by political instability. Then they supported those in the "banana republics" who promised law and order, usually military dictators who cared nothing for the welfare of their subjects.

When even these "gorillas," as reformers and revolutionaries called them, were unable to contain popular resentments, American investors turned to Washington for protection of their profits. By 1924, American officials directly or indirectly administered the finances of ten Latin American nations. For at least part of the decade, the marines occupied Nicaragua, Honduras, Cuba, Haiti, and the Dominican Republic. The business of the entire Western Hemisphere was business.

Prosperity and Business Culture

It is one thing for a government to defer openly to powerful special interests. It is quite another for a substantial majority of voters, of whom few are businessmen, to support such a government. But that is exactly what Americans did during the 1920s, overwhelmingly so. In 1924, Coolidge won 54 percent of the popular vote and a landslide in the electoral college. In 1928, as Coolidge's successor, Herbert Hoover won 58 percent of the vote over his Democratic opponent, Alfred E. Smith of New York.

More important, every Congress between 1920 and 1930 had comfortable Republican majorities. The Democrats were in the minority everywhere except the South, some thinly populated western states, and those big cities where old-fashioned political machines held fast to city hall.

Even if the Democrats had won national elections during the 1920s, policy would have been much the same. The leading national Democrats of the period, William G. McAdoo, John W. Davis, and Alfred E. Smith, were all closely tied to large corporations. Elder statesman William Jennings Bryan, who had said that no man could honestly earn a million dollars, became a millionaire as a publicity man for Florida real-estate companies, which were less observant of ethics and self-serving proprieties than was any other enterprise in the nation. Business reigned supreme in politics because of the general prosperity of the New Era and because a great many Americans were sincerely convinced that businessmen were the new messiahs Woodrow Wilson had tried so hard to be.

A BUSINESSMAN'S PRAYER

The following is not a parody, but a "prayer" that was quite seriously recommended to those in business during the 1920s:

God of business men, I thank Thee for the fellowship of red-blooded men with songs in their hearts and handclasps that are sincere;

I thank thee for telephones and telegrams that link me with home and office, no matter where I am.

I thank thee for the joy of battle in the business arena, the thrill of victory and the courage to take defeat like a good sport.

I thank thee for children, friendships, books, fishing, the game of golf, my pipe, and the open fire on a chilly evening.

AMEN.

The Shape of Prosperity

Industrial and agricultural productivity soared during the 1920s, even though there was not much increase in the size of the industrial work force and there was an actual decline in the number of agricultural workers. Wages did not keep up with the contribution that the more efficient workers were making to the economy. While dividends on stock rose 65 percent between 1920 and 1929, wages increased only 24 percent.

Nevertheless, the increase in wages was quite enough to satisfy many workingpeople, particularly because consumer goods were relatively cheap and business promoted an alluring new way for a family to live beyond its means—consumer credit.

Businessmen and farmers traditionally borrowed money, but their loans were invested in ways that were designed to increase their income, thus providing the means to retire their debts. In the 1920s, large numbers of Americans began to borrow in order to live more comfortably and more enjoyably; they borrowed not in order to produce but to consume.

An advertisement for Crane bathroom fixtures encouraged consumers to buy on credit, a new marketing concept in the 1920s.

Buy Now, Pay Later

A refrigerator that sold for $87.50 could be ensconced in a corner of the kitchen for a down payment of $5 and monthly payments of $10. Even a comparatively low-cost item like a vacuum cleaner ($28.95) could be had for $2 down and "E-Z payments" of $4 a month. During the New Era, 60 percent of all automobiles were bought on time; 70 percent of furniture; 80 percent of refrigerators, radios, and vacuum cleaners; and 90 percent of pianos, sewing machines, and washing machines. With 13.8 million people owning radios by 1930 (up from virtually none in 1920) and 27 million autos on the road, the Americans who shared in Coolidge prosperity were also up to their necks in debt.

Some moralists pointed out that borrowing in order to consume marked a sharp break with American ideals of frugality—the axioms of Benjamin Franklin—but few listened. Businesses that catered to consumption grew almost as dramatically as the radio, automobile, and electrical industries. Chains of retail stores expanded. By 1928, 860 grocery chains competed for the dollars of a population that was eating better. Among the biggest success stories between 1920 and 1929 were the first supermarkets: Piggly-Wiggly (from 515 to 2,500 stores), Safeway (from 766 to 2,660 stores), and A & P (Atlantic and Pacific Tea Company, from 4,621 to 15,418 stores). Chains also came to dominate the sundries trade (F. W. Woolworth and J. C. Penney), auto parts (Western Auto), and, of course, the retailing of gasoline.

Indeed, everything related to automobiles, from highway construction to that new feature of the landscape, the roadside motor hotel, or "motel," prospered during the New Era. The same went for movies. During the 1920s, 40 million people paid admission to movie theaters each week. The money that they saved by buying consumer goods on time could be spent on an evening's entertainment.

The Limits of Prosperity

A few economists joined the moralistic critics of runaway consumption, pointing out that the time would come when everyone who could afford a car, a washing machine, and other consumer durables would have them. They would no longer be buying, and the consumer industries would be in trouble. One of the major weaknesses of the economy was that significant numbers of Americans did not share in the good times and were shut out completely from the buying spree. The seven hundred thousand to eight hundred thousand coal miners and four hundred thousand textile workers and their dependents suffered depressed conditions and wages throughout the decade; they were not buying many cars and radios. Staple farmers struggled to survive. Even those who did well usually lived in places where there was no electricity; they were buying no appliances that had to be plugged in.

The southern states generally lagged far behind the rest of the country in income and standard of living.

LET'S HAVE A LOOK UNDER THE HOOD

Americans and Britons speak a different language when they talk about their cars. What Americans call the hood, the British call the bonnet. Some other differences:

American English	British English
clunker or junker	banger
gas	petrol
generator	dynamo
headlight	headlamp
muffler	silencer
station wagon	estate wagon
trunk	boot
windshield	windscreen

The different vocabularies provide a little case study in how languages develop. The automobile roared into history long after the United States and Great Britain had gone their separate political and cultural ways, but before instantaneous electronic communication allowed words coined on one side of the Atlantic to become immediately familiar on the other.

Because the early automobile was largely a French development, many American automotive terms were taken from the French language: *automobile* itself, *cabriolet* (later shortened to *cab*), *chassis, chauffeur, coupe, garage, limousine,* and *sedan.*

THE TIN LIZZIE

Although Americans did not invent the automobile, they democratized it by putting cars within the reach of almost everyone. By striving for simplicity (shunning all "extras," including a choice of color), by adapting the assembly line to the manufacture of cars, and by refusing to change his design, Henry Ford managed to whittle the price of a brand-new Model T to $260 in 1925. That is more than $2,000 in today's dollars, but still considerably less than the cheapest new car on the market. By 1927, Ford had sold 15 million tin lizzies, as Model T Fords were affectionately known, more than all other auto makers combined.

Rows of parked automobiles lining a main street became a common sight in American cities in the 1920s.

Blacks, Indians, Hispanics, and other minority groups tasted Coolidge prosperity only in odd bites.

Business Culture

But economically deprived groups usually are not politically articulate when the mainstream society is at ease in its world, and in the 1920s, mainstream America was. Business leaders hastened to take the credit for good times.

On a local level, businessmen's clubs such as the Rotary, Kiwanis, Lions, and Junior Chambers of Commerce seized community leadership and preached *boosterism:* "if you can't boost, don't knock." Successful manufacturers like Henry Ford were looked to for wisdom on every imaginable question. Any man who made $25,000 a day, as Ford did during most of the 1920s, must be an oracle on whatever subject he chose to speak about. Even that once most hated man in America, John D. Rockefeller, now in his eighties and retired to Florida, became a figure of respect and affection, thanks to Coolidge prosperity and the skillful image building of the Rockefeller family's public-relations expert, Ivy Lee.

The career of an advertising man, Bruce Barton,

showed just how thoroughly the business culture dominated the way Americans thought. In 1925, Barton published a book called *The Man Nobody Knows.* It depicted Jesus as a businessman, an entrepreneur and advertising genius whose religion was like a successful company. Instead of finding Barton's vision blasphemous or laughable, Americans bought *The Man Nobody Knows* by the thousands of copies. It was a best seller for two years.

John Jacob Raskob of General Motors promoted the worship of business in popular magazines such as *The Saturday Evening Post.* Because the value of many kinds

---

MANUFACTURED HEROES

"Shakespeare, in the familiar lines, divided great men into three classes: those born great, those who achieve greatness, and those who have greatness thrust upon them. It never occurred to him to mention those who hire public relations experts and press secretaries to make themselves look great."

Daniel Boorstin,
The Image (1962)

During the 1920s, Americans became accustomed to advertisements like this one appealing to middle-class America to follow the lead of "many people who can afford to pay far more."

of property was rising throughout the 1920s under the stewardship of business, Raskob said that it was a simple matter for workingmen to save a little money and invest it, thus becoming capitalists themselves. To an astonishing degree, middle-class Americans who had a small nest egg in the bank believed him. They plunged their savings into one get-rich-quick scheme after another, feeding but at the same time dooming the speculative economy.

Get Rich Quick

The most colorful get-rich-quick craze of the decade centered on Florida, previously a backward and isolated agricultural state. Improved train connections with eastern and midwestern population centers, retirement in Florida by celebrities such as Rockefeller and Bryan, and the lively nationwide ballyhoo of shrewd promoters such as Wilson Mizner soon aroused people to the Sunshine State's possibilities as a vacation and retirement paradise.

The Florida Land Boom

The development of cities like Orlando, Fort Lauderdale, and Miami Beach would take months or even years. The way to make money from their growth was to buy orange groves and sandy wasteland at bargain prices and hold the land for resale to the actual builders of vacation hotels and retirement homes. In 1925, however, enough people believed that they could make a fortune in Florida that the speculative fever began to feed on itself. As had happened in the early-nineteenth-century American West, prices of land rose as speculator bought from speculator, each convinced that someone else (a "greater fool") would soon buy from him at an even higher price. Some lots in Miami Beach changed hands dozens of times within a few months, the price climbing with every sale. At the height of the craze, one issue of a Miami newspaper ran more than five hundred pages of advertisements of land for sale. At that time, there were over two thousand real-estate offices in the little city.

Since the price of every acre in Florida seemed to be skyrocketing, many northerners were willing to buy sight unseen, and frauds were inevitable. More than a few snowbound speculators bought patches of alligator-infested swampland from fast-talking salesmen who assured them that they were purchasing the downtown of a major resort. Others purchased "beachfront lots" that were closer to the ocean than they counted on—underneath ten feet of it at high tide. But the major fuel of the mania was not fraud. It was a foolishness born of a culture that exalted business and money-making above all else.

As with all speculative crazes, the day inevitably arrived when there were no more buyers, no one willing to bet on higher prices in the future. Then came the "crash." The speculators who were caught holding overpriced property were hurt; the banks that had lent them money to speculate failed; and the people who had trusted those banks to invest their savings sensibly lost those very savings.

The Florida crash was triggered by a hurricane that hit Miami and showed, as Frederick Lewis Allen put it, what a soothing tropical wind could do to a vacation paradise when it got a running start from the West Indies. The price of Florida land plunged within weeks to dollars per acre. Many citrus farmers who had cursed themselves for having sold their groves so cheaply at the beginning of the boom discovered that, thanks to

a chain of defaults, they were back in possession of their land, only a little worse for the wear of speculators having tromped through it. Wilson Mizner, one of the architects of the boom and a big loser in the bust, was good humored about it. "Always be pleasant to the people you meet on the way up," he said, "because they are always the very same people you meet on the way down."

Playing the Market

Middle-class America was almost as nonchalant as Mizner. Even before Florida busted, they began to fuel another speculative mania, driving up the prices of shares on the New York Stock Exchange.

Speculation in stocks always had been a game for a few very rich people. However, the prosperity of the 1920s created enough savings accounts that within three years after Calvin Coolidge entered the White House, about 1.5 million Americans were "playing the market."

Beginning in 1927, prices began to soar beyond all reason. During the summer of 1929, values went crazy. American Telephone and Telegraph climbed from $209 a share to $303; General Motors went from $268 to $391, hitting $452 on September 3. Some obscure issues enjoyed even more dizzying rises. Each tale of a fortune made overnight, related with great satisfaction at a club or a social gathering, encouraged more people to carry their savings to the stockbroker.

Empty Values

The value of a share in a corporation theoretically represented the earning capacity of the company. The money that a corporation realized by selling shares was expended, again theoretically, improving the company's plant and equipment. Thus, when the price of stock in General Motors or Radio Corporation of America rose during the late 1920s, it represented to some extent the extraordinary expansion of the automobile and radio industries.

During the speculative "Coolidge bull market," however, the prices of shares also reflected nothing more than the willingness of people to pay them because "greater fools" would buy from them in the belief that the prices would rise indefinitely. It was immaterial that the companies they owned did not pay dividends or even use their capital to improve productive capacity. In fact, as in the Florida land boom, the rising prices of stocks fed on themselves. It became more profitable for companies to put their money into further stock speculation than into production. The face value of shares was inflated.

ALL SOLD OUT!

DAVIS ISLANDS
TAMPA   IN THE BAY

$18,138,000
In Sales in 31 Hours

$8,250,000
OVERSUBSCRIBED

More and Greater Records in the
Spectacular History of

DAVIS ISLANDS

D. P. DAVIS PROPERTIES
TAMPA, FLORIDA

An advertisement typical of those prompting a Florida land boom among real estate speculators in the 1920s.

THE LONE EAGLE: CHARLES A. LINDBERGH (1902–1974)

Charles Lindbergh standing beside his plane, the Spirit of St. Louis.

Raymond Orteig was a wealthy French restaurateur living in New York whose two enthusiasms were Franco-American friendship and aviation. He believed that airplanes had a much brighter future than, in 1926, seemed likely. During the 1920s, the fragile but ever improved crafts served as toys for rich hobbyists, as showpieces at state and county fairs where nomadic "barnstormers" did aerial tricks such as walking on the wing of a plane in flight, and, here and there in the United States, as vehicles to deliver "air mail," which the Post Office regarded as an experiment.

Even the prospects of military aviation were dim. Despite the publicity that had been given aerial dogfights during the First World War, planes had been more show than substance, playing no significant role in any action. In 1921 and 1923, General William

Mitchell of the Air Service, a branch of the army, had proved in a series of tests that bombs dropped from planes could sink a capital ship (a captured German vessel); but in order to prove his point, Mitchell had disobeyed orders and won the enmity of his superiors. He was court-martialed, and his vision momentarily discredited.

But Orteig believed in the commercial potential, if not in the military uses, of airplanes. Partly to demonstrate the feasibility of long-distance trips, the only kind of transportation in which flying made sense, and partly because he enjoyed ballyhoo as well as most people in the 1920s, Orteig offered a $25,000 prize to the first plane to cross the Atlantic nonstop between France and the United States.

By the spring of 1927, a number of pilots, including First World War flying ace René Fonck, and polar explorer Admiral Richard A. Byrd, using huge biplanes powered by three motors, had tried and failed. Both survived their accidents, but in other attempts, including an east–west flight by two Frenchmen who almost made it to North America, six were dead and two were seriously injured.

In the meantime, in San Diego, California, another challenger for the prize had been making news. Charles A. "Slim" Lindbergh, Jr., a shy twenty-five-year-old mail pilot from the Midwest, had a different approach to the problem. He had persuaded a group of St. Louis businessmen to finance the construction of a plane that would be capable of flying the Atlantic, and he had found a company, Ryan aircraft of San Diego, to build it. Instead of pinning his hopes on a massive machine powered by three large (and heavy) engines and flown by a crew (more weight), Lindbergh believed that the way to get to France was with a plane of the utmost simplicity, a machine designed to carry little more than gasoline and a single pilot.

Far from being the rickety wing and a prayer, as the press had described the *Spirit of St. Louis*, it was the creation of careful calculation and engineering expertise that had no commercial value, but was designed down to the last rivet to do one thing: get off the ground with a maximum load of fuel. In effect, the *Spirit* was a flying gas tank. The press would dub the young pilot "Lucky Lindbergh" when he succeeded in his mission, but most of the luck involved in the venture was in the ease with which he persuaded his backers of his idea and found a builder who shared his confidence. Indeed, in getting the *Spirit* from San Diego to the airfield on Long Island from which he would depart, Lindbergh broke two aviation records: he made the longest nonstop solo flight to date (San Diego–St. Louis) and the fastest transcontinental crossing. It was no reckless experiment.

But that was how the press of the 1920s played it. Lindbergh was mobbed wherever he went in New York, and was depicted as the simple, plucky, American frontiersman sort of hero. He was not allowed to examine his plane without the presence of thousands of well-wishers, sensation-seekers, and even hysterics who wanted to touch him as though he were a saint. Historians have compared the fuss made over him with the adoration that Americans of the 1920s lavished on movie stars and boxing champions; but it seems more accurate to describe the preflight hoopla in terms of Daniel Boorstin's definition of a celebrity: a person who is well known for being well known.

On May 16, 1927, conditions for a takeoff were less than ideal. The airstrip was muddy from rains, which meant additional drag on the plane, and by the time that Lindbergh was ready to go, he was taking off with a tailwind, not recommended procedure even when the craft is not loaded to the utmost of its theoretical limitations. (At the last minute, Lindbergh called for an additional fifty gallons of gasoline in the tanks.)

But Richard A. Byrd's plane was sitting at the same field, mechanically ready to go but stalled by legal complications; and another challenger was almost ready. Impatient, emotionally geared for the moment, perhaps influenced by the press notices of his singularity, Lindbergh packed five sandwiches into the tiny cockpit and took off. Once he was airborne, the riskiest part of the venture was behind him. Unless he fell asleep. That, and occasional threats of ice on the wings, which would add weight to the plane, were the worries he later recalled as most serious. At ten o'clock at night, two days after his departure, he landed amidst a screaming mob of one hundred thousand people at Le Bourget Field, Paris.

Americans were popular in Europe during the 1920s, and Lindbergh was exalted as the greatest of them. Back home it was the same thing: ticker-tape parades, thousands of invitations merely to appear in towns and cities. For a while, the soft-spoken hero luxuriated in the fame and money that came to him. In 1929, he married Anne Morrow, the daughter of the American ambassador to Mexico (Lindbergh was himself the son of a congressman), and as a team they continued to tour on behalf of the government and commercial aviation. The couple's infant son was kidnapped from their New Jersey home and, despite the payment of ransom, murdered. Police (and the Lindberghs) believed that the frenzied publicity surrounding the event contributed to the death of the child by frightening the abductor. After the trial, conviction, and execution of a carpenter, Bruno Hauptmann, which were criticized because of the relentless press coverage, the Lindberghs moved to Europe, where, they believed, they could escape the spotlight.

There, Lindbergh was impressed by the new German air force built up by Adolf Hitler and Hermann Goering, and he accepted a medal from the German dictator. After 1939, when he returned to the United States to lecture on behalf of the isolationist America First Committee, Lindbergh was criticized as being pro-Nazi. He was not, but he was an Anglophobe, and he believed that Germany would win the war that broke out in September 1939. Therefore, he opposed those who wanted to go to war before England fell.

Like most of the America Firsters, Lindbergh ceased his opposition to the war once the United States had entered it. He worked as a technical expert to aircraft companies, and, although over forty, he flew several missions in the Pacific theater. In the end, Lindbergh's accomplishment of 1927 overshadowed his politics of 1939 to 1941, and he was commissioned a general in the air force.

This is what accounted for much of the 300 percent rise in stock values between 1925 and 1929. Speculators bought in the belief that someone else would buy from them at a higher price. Banks and corporations put their capital into speculation. Politicians, either unable to understand what was happening or afraid to appear pessimistic in a time of buoyant optimism, reassured their constituents that there was nothing wrong. When a few concerned economists warned that the bubble eventually had to burst, with disastrous consequences, others scolded them. President Coolidge told people that he thought stock prices were cheap.

The Inevitable

Joseph P. Kennedy, a Boston millionaire (and father of President John F. Kennedy), said in later years that he had sold all of his stocks during the summer of 1929 after the man who shined his shoes had mentioned that he was playing the market. Kennedy reasoned that if such a poorly paid person was buying stock, there was no one left to bid prices higher. The inevitable crash was coming soon.

Kennedy was right. On September 3, 1929, the average price of shares on the New York Stock Exchange peaked and then dipped sharply. For a month, prices spurted up and down. Then on "Black Thursday," October 24, a record 13 million shares changed hands, and values collapsed. General Electric fell forty-seven and a half points on that one day; other stocks dropped almost as much.

On Tuesday, October 29, the wreckage was worse. In a panic now, speculators dumped 16 million shares on the market. Clerical workers on Wall Street had to work through the night just to sort out the avalanche of paperwork. When the dust settled early the next morning, more than $30 billion in paper value had been wiped out.

Businessmen crowd Wall Street on October 24, 1929, the day the stock market began to crash, sending America into economic depression.

It was phony value, representing little more than the irrational belief that prices could rise indefinitely. Nevertheless, the eradication of so many dollars profoundly shattered the confidence of businessmen and belief in the business culture of the 1920s. The Great Crash eventually contributed to the hardship of millions of people who did not even know what a share in a company looked like.

Crash and Depression

The Great Crash of 1929 did not cause the Great Depression of the 1930s. That was the result of fundamental weaknesses in the economy that had little to do with the mania for speculation. But the crash helped to trigger the decline in the American economy that was well under way by New Year's Day 1930. Middle-class families who had played the market lost their savings. Banks that had recklessly lent money to speculators went broke. When they closed their doors, they wiped out the savings accounts of frugal people.

Corporations whose cash assets were decimated shut down operations or curtailed production, thus throwing people out of work or cutting their wages. Those who had taken mortgages during the heady high-interest days of 1928 and 1929 were unable to meet payments and lost their homes; farmers lost the means by which they made a living. This contributed to additional bank failures.

Virtually everyone had to cut consumption, thus reducing the sales of manufacturers and farmers and stimulating another turn in the downward spiral: curtailed production to increased unemployment to another reduction in consumption by those newly thrown out of work.

For Further Reading

Most of the books cited at the end of Chapter 42 also deal with the subjects of this chapter. On Calvin Coolidge, William Allen White, *A Puritan in Babylon* (1938), still seems the best, although D. R. McCoy, *Calvin Coolidge: The Quiet President* (1967), may be more objective. The farm problem is the subject of Theodore Saloutos and John D. Hicks, *Twentieth Century Populism: Agricultural Discontent in the Middle West, 1900–1939* (1951). David Burner, *The Politics of Provincialism: The Democratic Party in Transition* (1968), deals with the minority party of the 1920s, while John D. Hicks, *Republican Ascendancy, 1921–1933* (1960), focuses on the party that held power.

J. H. Wilson, *Herbert Hoover: Forgotten Progressive* (1975), presents a rather different picture of the president who is best remembered for having presided over the Great Crash and Great Depression. His opponent in 1928 has, oddly, attracted more sympathetic treatment. See Oscar Handlin, *Al Smith and His America* (1958), and E. A. Moore, *A Catholic Runs for President* (1956).

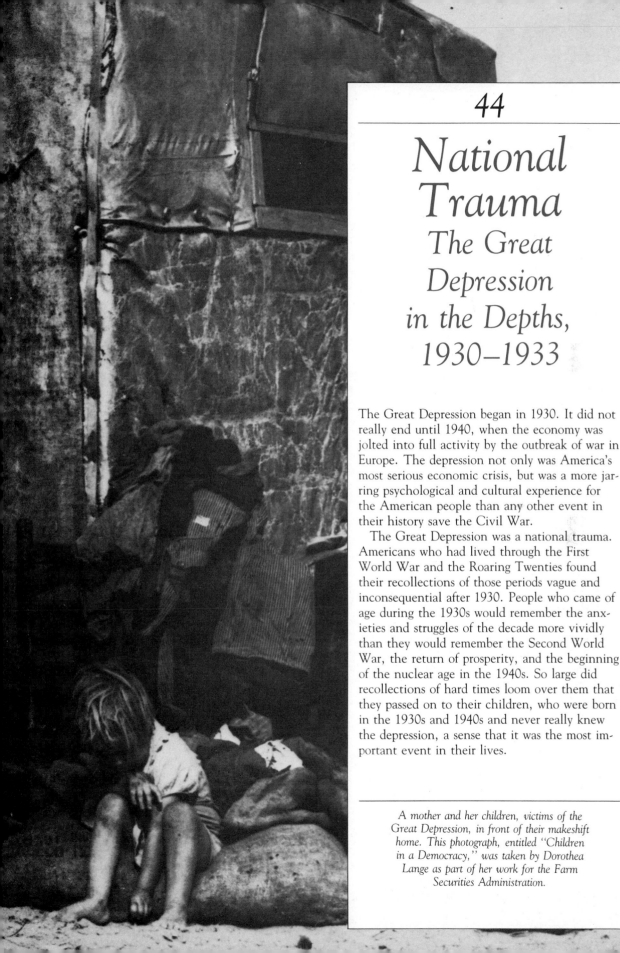

44

National Trauma
The Great Depression in the Depths, 1930–1933

The Great Depression began in 1930. It did not really end until 1940, when the economy was jolted into full activity by the outbreak of war in Europe. The depression not only was America's most serious economic crisis, but was a more jarring psychological and cultural experience for the American people than any other event in their history save the Civil War.

The Great Depression was a national trauma. Americans who had lived through the First World War and the Roaring Twenties found their recollections of those periods vague and inconsequential after 1930. People who came of age during the 1930s would remember the anxieties and struggles of the decade more vividly than they would remember the Second World War, the return of prosperity, and the beginning of the nuclear age in the 1940s. So large did recollections of hard times loom over them that they passed on to their children, who were born in the 1930s and 1940s and never really knew the depression, a sense that it was the most important event in their lives.

A mother and her children, victims of the Great Depression, in front of their makeshift home. This photograph, entitled "Children in a Democracy," was taken by Dorothea Lange as part of her work for the Farm Securities Administration.

The Face of Catastrophe

Not every memory of the 1930s was doleful. On the contrary, many people were proud that when times had been worst, they nevertheless had survived and, what is more, had carried on vital cultural, social, and personal lives. Negative or positive, however, the depression generation was the last American generation to date (until, perhaps the present) whose character and values were forged in an era of economic hardship, a fact of profound importance to the history of the United States in the middle and later twentieth century.

The Statistical Depression

During the first year after the crash of the stock market, 4 million workers lost their jobs. By 1931, one hundred thousand people were being fired each week. By 1932, 25 percent of the work force was unemployed, 13 million people with about 30 million dependents. Black workers, "the last hired and the first fired," suffered a higher unemployment rate than whites, 35 percent. In Chicago, 40 percent of those people who wanted work could not find it. In Toledo, 80 percent were unemployed. In coal-mining towns like Donora, Pennsylvania, virtually no one had work.

Employees who held on to their jobs took cuts in pay. Between 1929 and 1933, the average weekly earnings of manufacturing workers fell from $25 to less than $17. The income of farmers plummeted from a low starting point. By the winter of 1933, some corn growers were burning their crop for heat because they could not sell it at a profit. Growers of wheat estimated that it took five bushels to earn the price of a cheap pair of shoes. The wholesale price of cotton dropped to five cents a pound, laughably low if the consequences were not so tragic.

Banks failed at a rate of two hundred a month during 1932, wiping out $3.2 billion in savings accounts. When New York's Bank of the United States went under in December 1930, four hundred thousand people lost their deposits. Much of the money was in small accounts that had been squirreled away by working-people as a hedge against economic misfortune. When, understandably frightened, they withdrew their emergency funds, the downward spiral continued.

Hundreds of thousands of people lost their homes between 1929 and 1933 because they could not meet mortgage payments. One farm family in four had been pushed off the land by 1933, mainly in the cotton, grain, and pork belts of the South and Midwest. With their customers unable to buy, more than one hundred thousand small businesses went bankrupt, thirty-two thousand in 1932 alone (eighty-eight a day). Doctors, lawyers, and other professionals reported huge drops in income. Where schools were not closed for lack of money, teachers took sharp cuts or worked without pay. Some teachers in Chicago were not compensated for ten years. Others never were.

What Depression Looked Like

Even people who were not personally affected saw reminders of the depression everywhere. More than five thousand people lined up outside a New York employment agency each week to apply for five hundred menial jobs. When Birmingham, Alabama, called for about eight hundred workers to put in an eleven-hour day for $2, twelve thousand applicants showed up. In 1931, a Soviet agency, Amtorg, announced openings for six thousand skilled technicians who were willing to move to Russia; one hundred thousand Americans said

On a Washington, D.C., sidewalk, a man sells apples to support himself while unemployed.

they would go. Once-prosperous workers and small businessmen sold apples or set up shoeshine stands on street corners, claiming that they preferred any kind of work to accepting charity.

Charitable organizations were not up to the flood of impoverished people anyway. Philadelphia's social workers managed to reach only one-fifth of the city's unemployed in order to provide $4.23 to a family for a week, not enough to buy food, let alone pay for clothing, rent, and fuel. Soup kitchens set up by both religious and secular groups offered little more than a crust of bread and a bowl of thin stew, but for three years, they were regularly mobbed by people who waited in lines that strung out for blocks.

On the outskirts of most large cities (and right in the middle of New York's Central Park), homeless men and women built shantytowns out of scavenged lumber, scraps of sheet metal, flimsy packing crates, and cardboard boxes. The number of people who simply wandered the land brought the face of catastrophe to rural America. Because it was impossible to stay the flood, railroads gave up trying to keep people off the freight trains. About 14,000 people hopped freights on the Missouri Pacific in 1928; in 1931 186,000 rode the same rails. Rough estimates indicate that 1.5 million people were moving about in search of casual work, and others were simply moving about; railroad officials noted ever increasing numbers of children in the trek.

This revelation plus increased desertion of their families by unemployed men, a rise in the divorce rate, and a decline in the birth rate—from more than 3 million births in 1921 to 2.4 million in 1932—convinced some moralists and sociologists that the depression was destroying the American family. But others responded that hardship also caused families to pull together.

This was true of the tragic odyssey of the "Okies" and "Arkies." In 1936 and 1937, the hardships of depression were compounded by a natural disaster in the arid states of Oklahoma, Texas, and Arkansas: dust storms

---

NO ONE HAS STARVED

At the worst of times early in the Great Depression, it was common to say that "no one has starved." But some came close, as these two excerpts from the *New York Times* indicate:

MIDDLETOWN, N.Y., December 24, 1931.—Attracted by smoke from the chimney of a supposedly abandoned summer cottage near Anwana Lake in Sullivan County, Constable Simon Glaser found a young couple starving. Three days without food, the wife, who is 23 years old, was hardly able to walk.
DANBURY, Connecticut, September 6, 1932.—Found starving under a rude canvas shelter in a patch of woods on Flatboard Ridge, where they had lived for five days on wild berries and apples, a woman and her 16-year old daughter were fed and clothed today by the police and placed in the city almshouse.

---

literally stripped the topsoil from the land and blacked out the sun. Whole counties lost half their population as people fled across the desert to California, typically in decrepit Model T Fords piled with ragged possessions. Novelist John Steinbeck captured the desperation of their lives in *The Grapes of Wrath*, which was published in 1939.

The Failure of the Old Order

Will Rogers, himself an "Okie" and the nation's most popular humorist, quipped that the United States would be the first country to go to the poorhouse in an automobile. He was trying to restore a sense of proportion to the way people thought about the Great Depression. No one was starving, President Hoover added in one of his many unsuccessful attempts to ease tension.

In the broadest sense, both men were right. The troubling paradox of America's greatest depression was that deprivation was widespread in a country that was blessed with plenty. American factories remained as capable as ever of producing goods, but they stood silent or working at a fraction of capacity because no one could afford to buy manufactured goods. Farms were pouring forth food in cornucopian abundance, but hungry people could not afford to consume it. One of the most striking images of the early 1930s transformed a mild, white-haired California physician into an angry crusader. Early one Sunday morning, Dr. Francis E. Townsend looked out his window to see old women picking through the garbage pails of a store that was heaped high with foodstuffs.

SOUP LINE

A reporter for *The New Republic* described the soup line at the Municipal Lodging House in New York City in 1930:

There is a line of men, three or sometimes four abreast, a block long, and wedged tightly together—so tightly that no passer-by can break through. For this compactness there is a reason: those at the head of the grey-black human snake will eat tonight; those farther back probably won't.

Farm equipment lies buried under dust in Dallas, South Dakota, May 13, 1936.

The Tragedy of Herbert Hoover

Business and the Republican party had reaped credit for prosperity. Now they took the blame for depression, and the recriminations were aimed particularly at the titular head of the party, Herbert Clark Hoover. The shantytowns where homeless thousands dwelled were usually called Hoovervilles; newspapers used as blankets by men who were forced to sleep on park benches were Hoover blankets; a pocket turned inside out was a Hoover flag; a freight car was a Hoover Pullman.

Still remembered as a great humanitarian when he entered the White House in 1929, Hoover was the callous national villain a year later. Celebrated for his energy and efficiency as Secretary of Commerce, Hoover as president was thought to be incompetent, paralyzed by the economic crisis. When Hoover made one of his rare public appearances, a motorcade

through the hard-hit industrial city of Detroit, sidewalk crowds greeted him with dead silence and sullen stares. The president could not even take a brief vacation without arousing scorn. "Look here, Mr. Hoover, see what you've done," an Appalachian song had it. "You went a-fishing, let the country go to ruin."

In truth, Hoover's self-confidence decayed rapidly during his four years in the presidency. Beaming, dapper, and confident, if never a warm man, Hoover became subdued, withdrawn, and embittered in the White House. Sitting down to talk with him, an adviser remembered, was like sitting in a bath of ink.

Hoover was unjustly accused when critics called him uncaring, a do-nothing president, a stooge for the Mellons and other big businessmen. Hoover was moved by the suffering in the country. He gave much of his income to charity and urged others to do the same. Far from paralyzed, he worked harder at his job than had any president since James K. Polk. Nor was he a Coolidge, letting business do as it pleased; Hoover led government to greater intervention in the economy than had any preceding president. It would soon be forgotten, but the man who replaced Hoover in the White House, Franklin D. Roosevelt, several times criticized Hoover for improperly expanding the powers of government. It would be forgotten because Roosevelt would recognize, as Hoover never did, that the Republican had not gone far enough.

A CHICKEN IN EVERY POT

The Republican party slogan in the election campaign of 1928 had been "A Chicken in Every Pot and Two Cars in Every Garage." In 1932, the advertising man who had coined it was out of work and reduced to begging in order to support his family.

Beliefs and Policies

An orphan in Iowa, Hoover went to California, where he worked his way through Stanford University. A mining engineer, he traveled the world and was a millionaire and quite satisfied with his business career when, during the First World War, he entered public service. His dour personality made him few friends—Coolidge was always uneasy with his brilliant Secretary of Commerce—but his efficiency in everything he attempted got results. As a member of the Harding and Coolidge cabinets, Hoover encouraged and helped organize more than six thousand local and regional business associations that were designed to cut down waste and inefficiency.

As a president faced with a collapsing economy, Hoover went much further. In an attempt to create jobs, he spent $500 million a year on public works, government programs to build or improve government properties. The most famous was the great dam on the Colorado River, which was begun in 1931 and now is called Hoover Dam.

He cut Mellon's consumer taxes in order to encourage purchasing and, therefore, production. In the Reconstruction Finance Corporation (RFC), established by Congress in 1932, he created an agency to help banks, railroads, and other key economic institutions stay in business. The RFC lent money to companies that were basically sound but were hamstrung by the shortage of operating capital.

The trouble was that more was needed—massive relief to get the very poor over the crisis, and massive federal intervention in the economy to get it moving again. This Hoover would not do. A self-made man himself, he was committed to the ideal of self-reliance. He believed that rugged individuals who looked to no one but themselves were the secret of American cul-

Suffering from unemployment and poverty, these men constructed homes from scrap lumber at West Houston and Mercer Streets in New York. They were photographed by Berenice Abbott on October 25, 1935.

Herbert Hoover entered the presidency with a reputation for humanitarianism.

The Depression Goes International

For a few months, in 1931, Hoover's prediction that "prosperity was just around the corner" seemed to be coming true. Most economic indicators made modest gains. Then the entire industrialized world followed the United States into the economic pit. In May, a major European bank, the *Kreditanstalt* of Vienna, went bankrupt, badly shaking other European banks that had supported it and toppling many. In September, Great Britain abandoned the gold standard. That is, the Bank of England ceased to redeem its paper money in bullion. Worried that all paper money would lose its value, international investors withdrew $1.5 billion in gold from American banks, further weakening the financial structure and stimulating the new wave of local failures.

But the worst consequence of the European collapse was what it did to Hoover's state of mind. It persuaded him that America's depression was not the fault of domestic problems that he might remedy, but of foreigners over whom he had no power. The result was that by 1932 his administration was genuinely paralyzed. The country merely drifted, and conditions worsened by the month.

tural vitality. For the federal government to stimulate that trait of the national character was one thing; for the government to sponsor huge handouts was quite another. Federal relief measures were not, in Hoover's opinion, the first step in defeating the depression, but were the first step in emasculating the American spirit. There was indeed a difference between helping deprived Belgians and helping deprived Americans.

Hoover also clung to certain assumptions that prevented him from realizing just how much federal guidance was needed. Failing to recognize that state boundaries had no economic significance, he wanted the states to take the lead in fighting the depression. Viewing government as much like a business, he was particularly inflexible when it came to the ideal of a balanced budget and the government's power to manipulate the value of the currency.

Government, Hoover insisted, must spend no more money than it collected; the books must balance. As for money questions, Hoover knew that during every depression since the Civil War, only Greenbackers, Populists, and others who were defined as radicals had proposed increasing the supply of money (deliberately inflating prices) in order to stimulate the economy. Each time they had been defeated, and each time the country had emerged from hard times more prosperous than before. Hoover was positive that this cycle would be repeated if the old faith were kept: if the budget were balanced and the dollar remained rooted in gold.

Americans React to the Crisis

If Hoover's failure represented the inability of conservatives to cope with the depression, radicals were no more successful. Critics of capitalism believed that the crisis represented the death throes of the system and that they would soon be in power. They waited, and to some extent Americans responded to them.

The Not-So-Red Decade

After polling only 267,000 votes in prosperous 1928, Socialist party presidential candidate Norman Thomas won 882,000 in 1932. Communist candidate William Z. Foster doubled his vote in those four years, from 49,000 to 103,000. But the combined anticapitalist vote of less than 1 million was minuscule compared with the 23 million cast for the Democrats in that year and even the 16 million won by the discredited Hoover. Thomas's total in 1932 was less than the Socialists had won twenty years before, when the electorate was much smaller.

Later in the 1930s, American Communists made some gains among intellectuals and in the leadership of the labor movement. Former muckraker Lincoln Steffens traveled to the Soviet Union and returned to announce, "I have been over into the future and it works." Distinguished writers such as Mary McCarthy, Edmund Wilson, and Granville Hicks joined the Communist party. Even F. Scott Fitzgerald, the chronicler of "flaming youth" during the 1920s, flirted with Marxist ideas that he did not really understand. Theodore Dreiser, the dean of American novelists, wanted to join the Communist party but was told by party leaders that he could do more good for them outside than in.

The love of conspiracy and manipulation that this decision illustrated drove intellectuals out of the party as quickly as they had joined. It also prevented the Communists from establishing a base in the labor movement despite their indispensable contributions to its success. Wyndham Mortimer of the United Automobile Workers, labor journalist Len De Caux, lawyer Lee Pressman, and many other Communists and "fellow travelers" (sympathizers who were not members of the party) devoted their lives to building up the union movement. However, most Communist organizers either denied or thickly camouflaged their affiliation with the party. The result was that few rank-and-file union members were exposed to, let alone converted to, Communist ideas. When anti-Communist leaders took the offensive, they found it easy to oust party members from the unions.

A Curious Response

Americans simply did not interpret the Great Depression as evidence that capitalism had failed. During prosperous times, Americans had believed that individual success was primarily due to individual initiative, and not to general social conditions. So their initial response to the depression was to blame themselves for the hardships that beset them. Sociologists and journalists reported on homeless hitchhikers who apologized for their shabby clothing. A walk through a big-city park revealed unsuccessful job seekers slumped on benches, heads in hands, elbows on knees, collars drawn up, wondering where they, not the system, had failed.

The Gillette Company, a manufacturer of razor blades, exploited the feeling of personal failure by running an advertisement that showed a husband reporting shamefully to his wife that he still had not found a job. The message was that employers had turned him down because he cut a poor appearance with his badly shaved whiskers. A maker of underwear put the responsibility for the unemployment of a bedridden man squarely on his own shoulders. He was out of work not because 13 million others were, but because he wore an inferior brand of undershirt and so caught a cold that he well deserved.

Unemployed men gathered in city parks after unsuccessful searches for work.

Long after the depression ended, it was the proud boast of many families that however bad things had gotten, they never had gone "on the county," never had taken handouts from public-welfare agencies. The unmistakable message was that coping with hard times was a personal responsibility.

Episodes of Violence

There was violence. Hungry, angry people rioted in St. Paul and other cities, storming food markets and clearing the shelves. Wisconsin dairy farmers stopped milk trucks and dumped the milk into ditches, partly in rage at the low prices paid by processors, partly to dramatize their need for help. In Iowa, the National Farmers' Holiday Association told hog raisers to withhold their products from the market—to take a holiday—and attracted attention by blockading highways. Eat your own products, Holiday Association leader Milo Reno told the Iowans, and let the money men eat their gold.

But these incidents were isolated and exceptional. For the most part, Americans coped with the depression peacefully and without a thought for revolution. In fact, the most violent episode of the early depression was launched not by stricken people but by the authorities. This was the demonstration and destruction of the "Bonus Expeditionary Force" in Washington during the summer of 1932.

The Bonus Boys were twenty thousand veterans of the First World War who massed in Washington to demand that Congress vote them a promised bonus for their wartime service as a relief measure. When Congress adjourned in July without having done so, all but about two thousand men and women left the capital. Those who remained set up a Hooverville on Anacostia Flats on the outskirts of the city, policed themselves, cooperated with authorities, and were generally peaceful.

But Hoover, thoroughly frustrated by the failure of his policies, persuaded himself that they were led by Communist agitators. (Actually, the most influential organization among the Bonus Boys was the American Legion.) He sent General Douglas MacArthur, who arrayed himself in his best dress uniform and ceremonial sword, to disperse them. Using armored vehicles and tear gas, MacArthur made short work of the protesters. However, when an infant died from asphyxiation and Americans mulled over the spectacle of young soldiers attacking old soldiers on presidential orders, Hoover's reputation sank even lower.

Midwestern Robin Hoods

Americans displayed their disenchantment with traditional sources of leadership in other, less direct ways. Businessmen, who had been almost universally lionized just a few years before, became objects of ridicule in films, on radio programs, and in the columns and comic strips of daily newspapers. Perhaps the most curious example of the rebellion against traditional values was the admiration lavished on one kind of criminal, the midwestern bank robber.

The combination of hard times, automobiles, good roads, wide-open spaces, and a sensationalist press created John Dillinger, "Pretty Boy" Floyd, "Machine Gun" Kelly, Bonnie Parker and Clyde Barrow, and "Ma" Barker and her family-centered gang. They were primarily bank robbers who operated in the nation's heartland, where paved but lightly traveled roads allowed for rapid escape.

Unlike the businessmen-gangsters of the big cities, they were small-time, guerrilla operators who botched

The Bonus Marchers' encampment on Anacostia Flats was destroyed by troops led by Douglas MacArthur and sent by a frustrated President Hoover.

as many holdups as they pulled off. They were also reckless with their guns, killing bank guards and even innocent bystanders in their attempt to create an atmosphere of terror to cover their escape. But because they robbed the banks whose irresponsibility had ruined many poor people and because they came from poor rural (and WASP) backgrounds themselves, the outlaws elicited a kind of admiration among midwesterners.

The gangsters themselves cultivated the image of Robin Hood. John Dillinger (who killed ten men) made it a point to be personally generous. "Pretty Boy" Floyd, who operated chiefly in Oklahoma, never had trouble finding people who would hide him from the authorities. Bonnie Parker actually sent doggerel epics that celebrated the exploits of "Bonnie and Clyde" to newspapers, which greedily published them.

The Movies: The Depression-Proof Business

The film industry exploited this widespread envy of a few who "beat the system" by making movies that slyly glamorized lawbreakers. Still fearful of censorship, the studios always wrote a moral end to their gangster films: the wrongdoer paid for his crimes in a hail of bullets or seated in the electric chair. But the message was clear: criminals played by George Raft, Edward G. Robinson, and James Cagney were pushed into their careers by poverty and often had redeeming qualities.

The film industry did not decline during the depression. Movies flourished during the worst years, occupying the central position in American entertainment that they would hold until the perfection of television. Admission prices were cheap. Each week, 85 million people paid an average of 25 cents (10 cents for children) to see Marie Dressler, Janet Gaynor, Shirley Temple, Mickey Rooney, and Clark Gable in a dizzying array of adventures and fantasies.

The favorite themes were escapist. During the mid-1930s, Shirley Temple, an angelic, saccharine little blonde girl who sang and danced, led the list of money-makers. Her annual salary was $300,000, and her films made $5 million a year for Fox Pictures. Royalties from Shirley Temple dolls and other paraphernalia made her a millionaire. Choreographer Busby Berkeley made millions for Warner Brothers with his dance-sequence tableaux of dozens of beautiful starlets (transformed by mirrors and trick photography into hundreds). People bought tickets to Berkeley films to escape the gray rigors of depression life. For the same reason, they supported the production of hundreds of low-budget Westerns each year. The cowboy was still a figure of individual freedom in a world in which public events

> ### THE DEPTHS OF DECLINE
>
> During the 1920s, the American Locomotive Company had produced six hundred steam locomotives each year. In 1932, only one rolled out of the mammoth factory.

and private lives had become all too complexly interrelated.

The Election of 1932

In later years, Americans would look back on the decade of the Great Depression as almost a "Western" adventure in itself. Once they had weathered the hardships, people waxed nostalgic about their accomplishment. In the summer of 1932, however, when the economy hit bottom, few people took the situation with a light heart. The country's mood during the presidential election campaign of that year was somber and anxious.

A Democratic victory was a foregone conclusion, and the Republicans quietly renominated Herbert Hoover to bear the brunt of the reaction against the New Era. The leading Democrats fought a tough fight. The chief candidates were John Nance Garner of Texas, who inherited the McAdoo Democrats from the South and West; Al Smith, the standard-bearer in 1928, now closer to big business than to the streets and sidewalks of New York; and Governor Franklin D. Roosevelt of New York, Smith's former protégé.

When the beginnings of a convention deadlock brought back memories of 1924, a large number of Garner supporters switched to Roosevelt and gave him the nomination. With a nose for the dramatic, Roosevelt broke with tradition, according to which a nominee waited at his home to be informed of the convention's decision. He flew to Chicago (conveying a sense of urgency) and told the cheering Democrats that he meant to provide a "New Deal" for the American people. In so saying, Roosevelt simultaneously slapped at Republican policies during the 1920s and reminded people of both major parties that he was a distant cousin of the energetic president of the Square Deal, Theodore Roosevelt.

Hoover's campaign was dispirited. He was in the impossible position of having to defend policies that obviously had failed. Roosevelt, on the contrary, like any candidate who expects to win, avoided taking controversial stands. Any strong position on any specific question could only cost him votes. At times, indeed,

WEEKNIGHTS AT EIGHT

A couple in Hidalgo, Texas, listening to the radio in 1939.

Although commercial radio broadcasting began in 1920 and the first radio network, the National Broadcasting Company, was founded in 1926, it was during the Great Depression of the 1930s that the new medium of communication and entertainment found a place in the lives of almost all Americans. Radio receivers were ensconced in about 12 million American households in 1930. By 1940, they were in 28 million. Fully 86 percent of the American people had easy daily access to a radio set.

Hard times themselves were a big reason for the dramatic expansion of radio. During the 1920s, the average price of a receiver was $75, far out of reach of most families. During the 1930s, a serviceable set could be bought for $10 or $20, an amount that, with sacrifices, all but the utterly destitute could scrape up.

The New Deal also played a part in the radio boom. While most cities and towns were electrified before 1933, very little of the countryside was. Private power companies were not interested in the small return to be had from stringing wire into the hinterlands. By putting the advantages of electrification for country people above profits, Roosevelt's Rural Electrification Administration brought isolated farm families into the mainstream of society. With more than 57 million people defined as living in "rural territory" in 1940, the significance of radio to American culture may be said to have owed largely to New Deal reforms. Indeed, country people depended more on the crackling broadcasts

of news, music, and dramatic programs for brightening their lives than did city dwellers.

Manufacturers that produced consumer goods rushed to advertise on the three networks: the Columbia Broadcasting System; the Mutual; and the National Broadcasting Company with its two chains, the red and the blue networks. (When antitrust proceedings forced NBC to dispose of one of its networks, the American Broadcasting Company was born.) In 1935, the first year for which there are reliable statistics, networks and local stations raked in $113 million from advertisers with operating expenses at an estimated $80 million. In 1940, expenses were up to $114 million, but advertising revenues had almost doubled to $216 million.

The manufacturers of Pepsodent toothpaste got the best bargain of all. In 1928, they contracted with two white minstrel-show performers who had a program in black dialect on Chicago station WGN. "Sam 'n' Henry" agreed to pick two new names and do their show nationally on the NBC network. The new show was called "Amos 'n' Andy," and from the start it won a popularity that, comparatively speaking, has probably never been duplicated in the history of the entertainment industry.

Basically, "Amos 'n' Andy" was a blackface minstrel show set in Harlem instead of on a southern plantation. One of the two performers, Freeman Gosden of Richmond, said that he based the character of Amos Jones on a black boyhood friend. Amos was the honest, hard-working proprietor and sole driver of the Fresh Air Taxi Company—his cab had no windshield. Neither during the program's thirty-two years on radio nor after it had moved to television was Gosden's character offensive. However, Amos came to play a comparatively small part in the series as the program evolved. The chief protagonist was George (Kingfish) Stevens, a fast-talking con man who usually bungled his stings and ended up outsmarting himself. During the 1950s black groups began to protest that the Kingfish, who was rather stupid underneath his pretensions and self-estimation, was an insulting stereotype.

The character of the Kingfish's usual mark, Andrew "Andy" H. Brown, also caused trouble. Andy was an infinitely gullible character whom even the Kingfish easily swindled. He depended for survival on the con man's own ineptitude or on Amos's intervention.

Everyone in America, it sometimes seemed, listened to the program, which ran on weeknights at eight o'clock. Particularly interesting plots were discussed each day. Few needed to be told what Amos, Andy, and the Kingfish were like, or even the minor characters (also played by Gosden and his partner, Charles Correll): Lightnin', who swept up the hall of the Mystic Knights of the Sea; the shyster lawyer Algonquin J. Calhoun; Ruby Jones; and Sapphire Stevens, who made life as miserable for George as he made it for Andy.

In November 1960, "Amos 'n' Andy" went from radio to television in a weekly half-hour format featuring black actors who mimicked the voices that had been created by Gosden and Correll. Already, however, the program was an anachronism. The civil-rights movement was in full swing by 1960, pushing toward victory in the long campaign to establish full equality for blacks. The National Association for the Advancement of Colored People and other black organizations denounced "Amos 'n' Andy" as "a gross libel on the Negro."

The show's sponsors believed that blacks enjoyed the program as much as whites (which appears to have been so until the 1950s), and Gosden insisted that "both Charlie and I have deep respect for black men" and felt that the show "helped characterize Negroes as interesting and dignified human beings." Today, it is easy to see their point. Even the most ridiculous characters on "Amos 'n' Andy" were examples of stock comic figures, and there was nothing derogatory in the depiction of Amos and Ruby Jones. Nevertheless, the NAACP had a point too. The social effects of ridiculing members of an oppressed group are mischievous at best. It is easy to shrug off ridicule when it does not relate to reality or ignore stereotypes when the stereotyped group is well established. But in the fight in which blacks were engaged in the early 1960s, such ridicule and stereotypes stood in the way of justice. After one hundred episodes, "Amos 'n' Andy" went off the air.

he seemed to be calling for the same conservative approach to the crisis that Hoover already had applied; he warned against an unbalanced budget and reassured voters that he was no radical.

The only obvious difference between the president and his opponent was Hoover's gloomy personality and Roosevelt's buoyant charm. He smiled constantly. He impressed everyone who saw him as he whisked around the country as a man who knew how to take charge, liked to take charge, and was perfectly confident in his ability to lead the country out of its crisis. The theme song of Roosevelt's campaign, which was blared by brass bands or played over loudspeakers at every whistle stop and rally, was the cheery "Happy Days Are Here Again."

Only after his lopsided victory—472 electoral votes to Hoover's 59—did it become clear that Roosevelt had spelled out no program for recovery. Because Inauguration Day came a full four months after the election, there was one more long winter of depression under Herbert Hoover. The repudiated president, now practically a recluse in the White House, recognized that a void existed and attempted to persuade Roosevelt to endorse the actions he had taken.

Roosevelt nimbly avoided making any commitments either in favor of or opposed to Hoover's policies. He took a quiet working vacation. He issued no statements of substance, but he was not idle. During the interregnum, Roosevelt met for long hours with experts on agriculture, industry, finance, and relief. It was the calm before the storm.

For Further Reading

Frederick Lewis Allen, *Since Yesterday* (1940), is not so engrossing as his *Only Yesterday* (1931), but it still is an entertaining and informative look at the social history of the Great Depression. Probably the first book to read on the subject is Arthur M. Schlesinger, Jr., *The Crisis of the Old Order* (1957), which deals judiciously with political history as well. However, because of his New Deal liberal's point of view, Schlesinger's vision of Herbert Hoover is probably unbalanced. For another point of view on Hoover, whose reputation hit both extremes during his lifetime, see Joan Hoff Wilson, *Herbert Hoover: Forgotten Progressive* (1975), and H. G. Warren, *Herbert Hoover and the Great Depression* (1956). Also a must for the first years of the national trauma is Jordan A. Schwarz, *The Interregnum of Despair: Hoover, Congress, and the Depression* (1970).

On the emergence of Franklin D. Roosevelt, see Schlesinger, *The Coming of the New Deal* (1959), which succeeds *The Crisis of the Old Order* in his multivolume study, *The Age of Roosevelt*. Also relevant are the first chapters of the books listed at the end of chapter 45.

Making Modern America

Franklin D. Roosevelt and the New Deal, 1933–1938

A few days before his inauguration, Franklin D. Roosevelt made a public appearance in Miami. From the crowd that surged around him, an unemployed and demented worker named Joe Zangara stepped up and emptied a revolver at Roosevelt and Anton Cermak, the mayor of Chicago. Cermak died. But the president-elect was lucky. He escaped without a scratch.

From the episode, the American people learned that they had chosen a leader who was cool in a crisis: Roosevelt barely flinched during the shooting. But what else did they know about him? Not a great deal, and that little was not altogether reassuring.

Franklin Roosevelt is sworn into office as president, March 4, 1933.

The Pleasant Man Who Changed America

Walter Lippmann, the distinguished political commentator, called Roosevelt "a pleasant man who, without any important qualifications, would very much like to be president." Others wondered if a person who had lived so pampered and sheltered a life as Roosevelt had was capable of appreciating what real suffering was.

Writer Gore Vidal later described him as an "aristo-sissy." He was born into an old, rich, and privileged New York family. Boyhood vacations were spent in Europe and at elegant yachting resorts in Maine and Nova Scotia. He attended only the most exclusive private schools and was sheltered to the point of suffocation by an adoring mother. When Roosevelt matriculated at Harvard, Sara Roosevelt packed up, followed him, and rented a house near the university so that she could take care of her boy. F.D.R.'s wife, Eleanor Roosevelt, was from the same narrow social set. Indeed, she was his distant cousin.

Even the vaunted charm with which Roosevelt ran his campaign, the jaunty air, toothsome smile, and smooth ability to put people at their ease with cheery small talk, was very much a quality of the fluffy socialite who was a popular satirical target in films and popular fiction.

Franklin Roosevelt's cheery grin and ever-present cigarette holder became his trademarks.

Roosevelt's Contribution

And yet, from the moment he delivered his ringing inaugural address—"the only thing we have to fear is fear itself!"—the clouds over Washington parting on cue to let the March sun through, it was obvious that F.D.R. was a natural leader. Within a few months, Roosevelt took over center stage, as Theodore Roosevelt had done thirty years earlier. Poor sharecroppers and slum dwellers tacked his photograph on the walls of their homes. Within a few years, he was so intensely hated by many rich people that they could not bear to pronounce his name. Much to the amused satisfaction of Roosevelt's supporters, they referred to him through clenched teeth as "that man in the White House." Long before he died in office in 1945, after having been elected four times, Roosevelt was ranked by historians as one of the greatest of the chief executives, the equal of Washington, Jackson, Lincoln, and Wilson (his one-time political idol).

Roosevelt's unbounded self-confidence was itself a major contribution to the battle against the depression. His optimism was infectious. People believed in him. The change of mood he brought to Washington and the country was astonishing, and shortly after assuming office he exploited his charisma by launching a series of radio-broadcast Fireside Chats. In an informal living-room manner he explained to the American people what he was trying to accomplish and what he expected of them.

Roosevelt was also a man of action. The day after he was sworn in, he called Congress into special session for the purpose of enacting crisis legislation, and he declared a "bank holiday." Calling on emergency presidential powers that are rarely used, he ordered all banks to close their doors temporarily in order to forestall additional failures. Although the immediate effect of the bank holiday was to tie up people's savings, the drama and decisiveness of his action won wide approval.

Roosevelt was by no means brilliant. He never fully understood the complex economic and social processes with which his administration had to grapple. But he recognized his limitations and sought the advice of experts. This corps of advisers was called the "brain

AMERICAN ARISTOCRAT

Franklin D. Roosevelt was descended from or related by marriage to eleven presidents of the United States who had preceded him. Curiously, only one of them, Martin Van Buren, had been a Democrat.

F.D.R. THE PRAGMATIST

In a conversation with Secretary of Commerce Daniel Roper, Roosevelt made clear his practical policy-making: "Let's concentrate upon one thing. Save the people and the nation and if we have to change our minds twice a day to accomplish that end, we should do it."

trust." It was largely made up of professors from prestigious eastern universities and was supervised by a pipe-smoking political scientist, Raymond Moley.

Roosevelt was open to everyone's suggestions. But because he never doubted his abilities and responsibilities as the elected "chief," he was able to maintain his authority over his stable of headstrong intellectuals, who themselves were often prima donnas. He soothed their vanities, played one brain truster against another, and retained the personal loyalty of even some of those whose advice he rejected. Faces changed. Moley himself became a critic of the New Deal. But Roosevelt never lacked talented advisers.

In the end, Roosevelt's greatest strength was his flexibility. "The country needs bold, persistent experimentation," he said. "It is common sense to take a method and try it. If it fails, admit it frankly and try another." Roosevelt's pragmatic approach to problems not only suited the American temperament, but contrasted boldly with Hoover's insistence on making policies conform to abstract principles.

A Real First Lady

Not the least of F.D.R.'s assets was his remarkable wife, Eleanor. Only in later years did Americans learn that the personal relationship between the two had been cold and strained due to F.D.R.'s ongoing love affair with Eleanor's personal secretary, Lucy Mercer. At the time, the homely, shrill-voiced First Lady was thought of by friend and foe alike as a virtual vice president, the alter ego of "that man in the White House."

Politically, she was. F.D.R. was a cripple, paralyzed by polio in 1921 and unable to walk more than a few steps in his heavy steel leg braces, but Eleanor Roosevelt was a dynamo of motion. With no interest in being a social hostess, she raced about the country, both a political force in her own right and her husband's legs and eyes. She picked through squalid tenements and descended into murky coal mines. Whereas F.D.R. was in reality a cool, detached, and calculating politician whom few ever got to know well, Eleanor was compassionate, deeply moved by the misery and injustices

As first lady, Eleanor Roosevelt traveled around the country meeting average Americans and investigating social problems.

suffered by the "forgotten" people on the bottom of society.

She interceded with her husband to appoint more women to government positions. She supported organized labor when F.D.R. tried to waffle on the question. She made the grievous problems of black Americans a particular interest. Much of the affection that redounded to F.D.R.'s benefit in the form of votes was actually earned by his wife.

The Hundred Days

Never before or since has the United States experienced such an avalanche of laws as Congress passed and the president signed during the spring of 1933. Usually a cautious and deliberate body, Congress was jolted by the crisis and by Roosevelt's decisive leadership to pass most of his proposals without serious debate, a few without even reading the bills through. During what came to be known as the Hundred Days, Franklin D. Roosevelt and his brain trusters were virtually unopposed. The most conservative congressmen simply shut up, cowed by the New Deal machine and their own failure.

Saving Banks, Farms, and People

The most pressing problems were the imminent collapse of the nation's financial system, the massive foreclosures on farm and home mortgages that were throwing people out on the streets and roads, and the distress of the millions of unemployed.

The Emergency Banking Act wiped out weaker banks merely by identifying them. Well-managed banks that might have failed were saved when the Federal Reserve System was empowered to issue loans to them. Just as important, when the government permitted banks to reopen, people concluded that they were safe. They ceased to withdraw their deposits, and others returned funds that they already had withdrawn and thereby taken out of circulation. Roosevelt also stopped the drain on the nation's gold by forbidding its

In an effort to stave off panicky customers, President Roosevelt ordered banks to close their doors for emergency "holidays."

export and, in April, by taking the nation off the gold standard. No longer could paper money be redeemed in gold coin. Instead, the value of money was based on the government's word, and the price of gold was frozen by law at $35 an ounce.

The New Deal attempted to end the dispossessing of farmers through the establishment of the Farm Credit Administration. This agency refinanced mortgages for farmers who had missed payments. Another agency, the Home Owners' Loan Corporation, provided money for town and city dwellers who were in danger of losing their homes.

Nothing better illustrates the contrast between Hoover and Roosevelt than the establishment of the Federal Emergency Relief Administration. Whereas Hoover had fought relief measures, the FERA quickly distributed $500 million to states so that they could save or revive their exhausted relief programs. The agency was headed by Harry Hopkins, a New York social worker who disliked the idea of handouts. Hopkins thought it better that people work for their relief, even if the jobs they did were not particularly useful. His point was that government-paid jobs not only would get money into the hands of people who needed it, but would give those people a sense of personal worth. Nevertheless, Hopkins recognized that the crisis of 1933 called for quick handouts, and he won F.D.R.'s confidence through his administration of the FERA.

Alphabet Soup: CCC, CWA, WPA

The Civilian Conservation Corps (CCC) was a New Deal measure that was more to Hopkins's liking. With an initial appropriation of $500 million, the CCC employed 250,000 young men between the ages of eighteen and twenty-five and about 50,000 First World War veterans. Working in gangs, they reforested land that had been abused by lumbermen and took on other conservation projects in national parks and forests. Ultimately, 500,000 people worked for the CCC, and it became one of the New Dealers' favorite programs. The CCC not only relieved distress (employees were obligated to send part of their paychecks to their families), but accomplished many sorely needed conservation measures, and got city people into the fresh air of the woods, a moral tonic in which Americans have always placed great faith.

Critics of the CCC disliked the strict military discipline with which the army ran the program, but the idea of relief through jobs rather than through charity remained a mainstay of the New Deal. The Civil Works Administration (CWA), which Harry Hopkins

headed after November 1933, put 4 million unemployed people to work within a few months. They built roads, constructed public buildings—post offices, city halls, recreational facilities—and taught in bankrupt school systems.

When the CWA spent more than $1 billion in five months, F.D.R. shuddered and called a halt to the program. But private investors would not or could not take up the slack, and unemployment threatened to soar once again. In May 1935, the president turned back to Hopkins and Congress to establish the Works Progress Administration (WPA).

The WPA actually broadened the CWA approach. It hired artists to paint murals in public buildings, and writers to prepare state guidebooks that remain masterpieces of their kind and, in the South, to collect reminiscences of old people who remembered having been slaves. The WPA even organized actors into troupes that brought serious theater to people who never had seen a play. By 1943, when the agency was liquidated, it had spent more than $11 billion and had employed 8.5 million people. The National Youth Administration, part of the WPA, provided jobs for 2 million high-school and college students.

Perhaps Roosevelt's support of the Twenty-first Amendment, the repeal of Prohibition, should be listed as one of the New Deal's relief measures. On March 13, F.D.R. called for the legalization of weak beer, and when the amendment was ratified, most states quickly legalized stronger drink. Certainly many people looked on the possibility of buying a legal drink as relief. An Appalachian song praising Roosevelt pointed to repeal of Prohibition as his most important act:

> Since Roosevelt's been elected
> Moonshine liquor's been corrected.
> We've got legal wine, whiskey, beer, and gin.

The Blue Eagle

The New Deal's relief programs were a great success. Although direct benefits reached only a fraction of the people who were hit by the depression, they were a godsend to the worst off, and the government's willingness to act in the crisis encouraged millions of other people. Nevertheless, relief was just a stopgap. F.D.R. and the New Dealers were also concerned with the problem of actual economic recovery, and in this area their accomplishments were more dubious.

The National Industrial Recovery Act, which created the National Recovery Administration (NRA), was a bold and controversial attempt to bring order and

WPA workers widen a road in 1935.

prosperity to the shattered economy. Headed by General Hugh Johnson, a bluff and blustering believer in cooperation and discipline, the NRA supervised the writing of codes for each of the nation's basic industries and, before long, some nonbasic ones.

These codes were designed to cover just about every aspect of doing business within an industry. Standards of quality for products were set; production quotas and limits (the share of the market) were assigned to individual companies; fair prices for goods were specified; and wages, hours, and conditions for workers were defined. The NRA was designed to eliminate waste, inefficiency, destructive competition, and exploitation within an industry through cooperation among competitors and between labor and capital. The federal government acted as referee in this new order.

The NRA was a direct outgrowth of Teddy Roosevelt's New Nationalism of 1912, the mobilization of the economy during the First World War, and Herbert Hoover's trade associations. The difference was that the NRA codes were compulsory. A business was bound to its industry's code not by the moral suasion that Hoover had preferred, but by the force of law. Noncompliance led to prosecution by the government.

Critics of the NRA, including some within the New

CHRISTMAS SEASON

In 1939, in order to give retailers an extra week of Christmas shopping season, President Roosevelt moved Thanksgiving Day one week earlier than had been the custom.

THE REGULATED SOCIETY

Regulatory agencies are established by Congress and given authority to act as watchdogs over specific aspects of American life. For example, the Interstate Commerce Commission (I.C.C.) regulates the movement of goods and people across state lines, assigning rights over certain routes to trucking companies, setting rates, settling disputes, and so on. The Federal Communications (F.C.C.) keeps an eye on the practices of radio and television broadcasters.

The first regulatory agency is only a century old. The Civil Service Commission was founded in 1883. Today, fifty-five major regulatory commissions in the United States government turn out seventy-seven thousand pages of decisions and rules each year.

Deal administration, likened it to the Fascist system that had been set up in Italy in 1922 by Benito Mussolini, and to the Nazi economy that had been instituted in Germany in 1933 under Adolf Hitler. But the initial response of the American people was enthusiastic. More than two hundred thousand people marched in an NRA parade in New York, carrying banners emblazoned with the NRA motto, "We Do Our Part." The symbol of the NRA, a stylized blue eagle clutching industrial machinery and thunderbolts, was painted on factory walls, pasted on shop windows, and adopted as a motif by university marching bands.

For a brief time, Hugh Johnson seemed as popular as Roosevelt himself. He was certainly more conspicuous. Johnson stormed noisily about the country, publicly castigating as "chiselers" those businessmen who did

Eight thousand children form an eagle at a National Recovery Administration rally in San Francisco.

not fall into line. He apparently inherited his bullying personality from his mother, who at an NRA rally in Tulsa said that "people had better obey the NRA because my son will enforce it like lightning, and you can never tell when lightning will strike."

The New Deal Threatened

The excitement did not last. Industrialists disliked Section 7(a) of the law because it gave labor unions the right to represent employees in companies that signed NRA codes. It was the first time the federal government actually seemed to encourage union organization. Small businessmen worried because the codes that were handed to them were drafted by the biggest corporations and favored the giants of each industry over struggling small competitors. The more rigorous the standards of product quality and working conditions, the more likely only big companies could meet them, thus driving small competitors out of business.

Hugh Johnson's bombastic personality soon became wearying, and Roosevelt forced his resignation in September 1934. But the most damaging blow to the Blue Eagle among ordinary Americans was the lengths to which NRA functionaries would go in forcing codes on businesses that were not very vital.

It was in a minor industry that the NRA met its doom. The Schechter Poultry Corporation was a small family business in New York that slaughtered and processed chickens according to rituals observed by religious Jews. Resenting NRA sanitary standards that threatened to destroy their company, the four Schechter brothers claimed that the NRA was unconstitutional because the codes regulated intrastate commerce (business carried out entirely *within* one state), which Congress was not empowered to regulate, and because in the codes, the executive branch was exercising a legislative function. In the "sick chicken" case of 1935, the Supreme Court agreed and destroyed the NRA.

Farm Policy

Roosevelt may have been relieved to be rid of the Blue Eagle. He was not happy with its excesses. But he was not at all pleased when the Supreme Court struck down a number of other New Deal laws during 1935 and 1936. The most important of these casualties was the Agricultural Adjustment Act, which had established the Agricultural Adjustment Administration (AAA). Also passed during the Hundred Days, the act embodied the principle of "parity," for which farmers'

organizations had fought throughout the 1920s. Parity was a system of increasing farm income to the ratio that it had borne to the prices of nonfarm products during the prosperous years of 1909 to 1914, a kind of golden age of agriculture as farmers looked back on it. The AAA accomplished this by restricting farm production. Growers of wheat, corn, cotton, tobacco, rice, and hogs were paid subsidies to keep some of their land out of production. The costs of this expensive program ($100 million was paid to cotton farmers alone in one year) was borne by a tax on processors—millers, refiners, butchers, packagers—which was then passed on to consumers in higher food, clothing, and tobacco prices.

Because the 1933 crops were already growing when the AAA was established in May 1933, it was necessary to destroy some of them. "Kill every third pig and plow every third row under," Secretary of Agriculture Henry A. Wallace said. The results were mixed. Many people were repelled by the slaughter of 6 million small pigs and 220,000 pregnant sows. Others not so sensitive, wondered why food was being destroyed when millions were hungry. (In fact, 100 million pounds of pork was diverted to relief agencies and inedible waste was used as fertilizer.) Nevertheless, the income of hog growers began to rise immediately.

Fully a quarter of the 1933 cotton crop was plowed under, the fields left fallow. Within two years, cotton (and wheat and corn) prices rose by over 50 percent. However, because cotton growers cultivated what was left of the crop more intensely, production actually rose in 1933.

A less desirable side effect of AAA restrictions on production was the throwing of people off the land. Landowners dispossessed tenant farmers in order to get the subsidies that fallow land would earn. Between 1932 and 1935, 3 million American farmers lost their livelihood. Most of them were very poor black and white tenants who already were struggling to survive.

The Fight Against the Court and Big Business

Despite its weaknesses, the loss of the Agricultural Adjustment Act in a Supreme Court ruling in January 1936 was a serious blow. The New Dealers fought back by salvaging what they could of the unconstitutional law. In the Soil Conservation and Domestic Allotment Act, parity and the limitation of production were saved under the guise of conserving soil. A similar strategy was followed in passing the Wagner Labor Relations Act of 1935; in it, the government granted to labor unions the right to bargain with employers that they enjoyed under the NRA.

But many New Dealers worried that they would be

unable to respond if the Supreme Court overturned the Rural Electrification Act and the bill that had set up the Tennessee Valley Authority (TVA). The Rural Electrification Administration (REA) brought electricity to isolated farm regions that had been of no interest to private utility companies, and it was vulnerable to Court action because it put the government into the business of generating power, indirectly competing with private enterprise.

The TVA was farther reaching yet. It was the brainchild of Senator George Norris of Nebraska, who was a longtime advocate of economic planning and regional development engineered by the government. Almost every year, the wild Tennessee River flooded its banks and brought additional hardship to southern Appalachia, one of the nation's poorest areas. Norris proposed that the government construct a system of dams both to control floods and to generate electricity and manufacture fertilizers. The mammoth facility would be owned and managed by the government. By getting so completely into the power business, Norris argued, the government would be able to determine the fairness of prices that were charged for electricity by private companies elsewhere in the country.

His dream had been impossible during the pro-business administrations of Coolidge and Hoover. However, with the turnaround in Washington in 1933, the TVA became a reality and a major cause of the split between big business and the New Dealers. By 1934, no longer reeling from their failure in 1929, big businessmen founded the American Liberty League, which accused Roosevelt of having destroyed free enterprise, instituted a socialist system, and set up an anti-democratic dictatorship through his reforms. Among those public figures who spoke for the American Liberty League were the Democratic presidential nominees of 1924 and 1928, John W. Davis and Alfred E. Smith.

Roosevelt had little trouble with the opposition of those whom he called "economic royalists." Most Americans remained distrustful of big businessmen. But Roosevelt sincerely feared the power of the Supreme Court, and in 1937, he proposed a scheme by which he would "pack" the Court with additional justices who would endorse the New Deal.

A dam under construction by the Tennessee Valley Authority.

Reaction in both Congress and the nation was hostile. Fortunately, the crisis passed when the Court endorsed several reforms (the anti-New Deal votes generally had been close) and when a series of retirements and deaths allowed Roosevelt to appoint New Dealers to the bench without tampering with tradition.

The Spellbinders

A much more serious threat to Roosevelt's program than either the American Liberty League or the Supreme Court were three popular demagogues who appealed to the same underprivileged people on whom Roosevelt and his political adviser, Postmaster General James A. Farley, based the future of the New Deal.

With the coming of depression, Charles E. Coughlin, a Canadian-born Roman Catholic priest, had transformed a religious radio program into a platform for his political beliefs. At first, Coughlin enlisted his mellow, baritone voice in support of Roosevelt. "The New Deal is Christ's Deal," he said in 1933. A year later, however, he became convinced that the key to solving the depression was a complete overhaul of the national monetary system, including the abolition of the Federal Reserve System. Despite his reputation among the rich as a radical, Roosevelt had no patience for such extreme proposals. But because Coughlin had a huge and devoted following—perhaps 10 million listeners to some programs—his scathing attacks were a source of worry to Farley and other tacticians.

Dr. Francis E. Townsend, a California physician, was also a threat. Himself sixty-six years old in 1933, Townsend was appalled by the plight of the nation's aged citizens. He proposed that the federal government pay a monthly pension of $200 to all people over sixty years of age, with two conditions. First, pensioners would be forbidden to work. Second, they would spend every cent of their pension within the month. His "Townsend Plan" not only would provide security for the nation's elderly, the kindly doctor told audiences all over the country, but would reinvigorate the economy by creating jobs for young men and women.

By 1936, seven thousand Townsend Clubs claimed a membership of 1.5 million. When Roosevelt rejected the plan as unworkable, Townsend went into the opposition and laid tentative plans to join his movement with those of Father Coughlin and of Roosevelt's most serious political rival, Senator Huey P. Long of Louisiana.

The Kingfish

Huey Long remains one of the most fascinating figures of the Great Depression decade. He rose from the poor farming people of northern Louisiana to educate himself as a lawyer. He never forgot the poor. He built a successful political career as a colorful and often profane orator who baited the railroad and oil industry elite that ran the state. Unlike most southern demagogues, however, Long did not also attack black people. Indeed, he had the support of those blacks, mostly in New Orleans, who had held on to their right to vote.

As governor of Louisiana between 1928 and 1932, Long built roads and hospitals, provided inexpensive or free textbooks and lunches for school children, social benefits that were almost unknown in the South and were not universal in the North and West. Long was an ambitious and egotistic showman. He called himself the Kingfish after a clownish character on the popular radio program "Amos 'n' Andy." He was the Kingfish, and all the other politicians were little fishes. He led cheers at Louisiana State University football games. He made the university the best in the South. Once, when a circus announced that it would open in Baton Rouge on the date of an important LSU game, Long killed the competition by closing down the show on the grounds that lion tamers were cruel to animals.

Louisiana politician Huey Long demonstrates his flair for theatrical oratory.

The New Deal Supreme

People loved Huey Long, not only in Louisiana, which he continued to run even after entering the Senate in 1933, but all over the South and Midwest. He based his national ambitions on a plan called "Share the Wealth," which called for a heavy tax on big incomes and no personal incomes of more than $1 million a year. To people struggling for the necessities, it was an appealing program.

Because Long was the virtual dictator of the Pelican State ("I'm the Constitution around here," he said with a smile), Roosevelt considered him a threat to democracy as well as to his own reelection in 1936. In the end, however, he overcame him and Townsend and Coughlin by a combination of cooptation and good luck. Roosevelt undercut Coughlin's financial program through his own moderate monetary reforms. To steal Townsend's thunder, he supported the Social Security Act of 1935. Its pensions were tiny compared with the $200 a month for which Townsend called. Nevertheless, it was a revolutionary law; for the first time, the United States government assumed responsibility for the welfare of people who were disabled or too old to work. Also in 1935, Roosevelt supported a revision of the income tax law that did not abolish huge incomes but taxed people in the upper brackets much more heavily than those in the lower.

In every case, the New Deal reforms were half a loaf. In no case was the program of the critics adopted. But so great was Roosevelt's personal popularity that his would-be rivals lost support and, eventually, lost heart. Townsend's clubs declined slowly, as did Coughlin's radio audience. In the end, the "radio priest" discredited himself by turning to a vicious Nazi-like anti-Semitism and praising Adolf Hitler. Long was assassinated in 1935 (the motive was personal, not political).

Thus in the election of 1936, Roosevelt had to face only the congenial and moderate Republican governor of Kansas, Alfred M. Landon. Offering no real alternative to the New Deal, Landon was swamped, carrying only Maine and Vermont. Emboldened by his victory and resentful of what he considered betrayal by big business, Roosevelt then turned to programs aimed at reforming American society in quite a different way from the programs of 1933.

The Legacy of the New Deal

Historians write of the reforms that were sponsored by Roosevelt after his reelection as the *Second* New Deal. Whereas the president had seemed to be seeking a way to reconcile all social classes and interest groups before 1936, after the election year he faced up to the fact that big business and other privileged groups would oppose him no matter what he did and that almost all his political support would come from workingpeople: union members and blue-collar ethnics in the cities, poor farmers, and blacks, who had been Republicans since the ratification of the Fifteenth Amendment. In responding to the needs of "the masses" in opposition to the interests of "the classes," Roosevelt and the New Dealers remade many of the basic institutions of American society, some by transforming directly and others by creating a legacy for liberal reform groups in the generations to come.

The Roosevelts and the Blacks

Roosevelt emphasized the economic problems of disadvantaged groups almost to the exclusion of other problems. On the question of civil rights for blacks, for example, F.D.R. was nearly silent. The Democratic party depended on its southern bloc for support, and southern politicians were committed to white supremacy and racial segregation. In deference to them, Roosevelt refused to support a federal antilynching bill, and he allowed the racial segregation of work gangs on government-supported building projects such as the TVA.

Under constant pressure from the NAACP (National Association for the Advancement of Colored people), from Eleanor Roosevelt, and from such individual black leaders as Mary McLeod Bethune, the New Dealers made sure that blacks shared in relief programs. As a result, the 1930s saw a revolution in black voting patterns. In 1932, about 75 percent of

AS MAINE GOES

Until the 1930s, people in the state of Maine voted in September, almost two months before voters in the other states. The saying "As Maine goes, so goes the nation" reflected the significance that was attributed to the results there. In the twenty-eight presidential elections in which Maine voters participated, the state's record in picking the winner was twenty-two to six, good but not foolproof, as Herbert Hoover learned in 1932: he won Maine, but few other states.

In 1936, Maine again voted Republican. Democratic party campaign manager James Farley quipped, "As Maine goes, so goes Vermont." He was right on the button. F.D.R. won every state that year except Maine and Vermont!

American black voters were Republicans. They still thought of the G.O.P. as the party of Lincoln and emancipation. By 1936, however, more than 75 percent of registered blacks were voting Democratic, and this proportion increased steadily for thirty years. The Democratic party might not have been the friend of the blacks, but it was the friend of the poor, and most blacks were poor.

The Growth of the Unions

Roosevelt also won the organized-labor movement to the Democratic party. Left to his own prejudices, he would have remained neutral in disputes between unions and employers. However, when militant unionists such as John L. Lewis of the coal miners and Sidney Hillman and David Dubinsky of the large needle-trades unions made it clear that they would throw their influence behind the president only in return for administration support, Roosevelt gave in. Lewis raised a donation of $1 million to the president's campaign for reelection in 1936. In return, Roosevelt had to be photographed accepting the check, smiling with approval on the burly, bushy-browed Lewis.

"The President wants you to join the union," the Committee on Industrial Organization told workers in basic industries. At first a faction within the American Federation of Labor, the committee left the AFL in 1937 to become the Congress of Industrial Organizations (CIO). Massive, colorful campaigns won recruits in unprecedented numbers. The Steel Workers' Organizing Committee, parent organization of the United Steel Workers, was founded in 1936. By May 1937, it had 325,000 members. The United States Steel Corporation, the nerve center of antiunionism in the industry, recognized the union as bargaining agent without a strike.

United Mine Workers Union president John L. Lewis.

The United Automobile Workers enlisted 370,000 members in a little more than a year. The story was the same among workers in other basic industries: rubber, glass, lumber, aluminum, electrical products, coal mining, the needle trades, even textiles. "The Union" came to have a mystical significance in the lives of many workers. Workers fought for the right to wear union buttons on the job. The union card became a certificate of honor. Old hymns were reworded to promote the cause. Professional singers like Woody Guthrie, Pete Seeger, and Burl Ives lent their talents to organizing campaigns.

The sit-down strike was a particularly dramatic manifestation of worker militance. Beginning with automobile workers in the Fisher Body Plant of Flint, Michigan, in early 1937, workers shut down factories not by picketing outside the gates, but by occupying the premises and refusing to leave.

Not every employer responded so peacefully as United States Steel. Tom Girdler of Republic Steel called the CIO "irresponsible, racketeering, violent, communistic" and threatened to fight the union with armed force. In this heated atmosphere occurred the Memorial Day Massacre of 1937, so called because Chicago police attacked a crowd of union members,

UNION MEMBERSHIP	
(Includes Canadian members of U.S. unions)	
1900	791,000
1905	1,918,000
1910	2,116,000
1915	2,560,000
1920	5,034,000
1925	3,566,000
1930	3,632,000
1935	3,728,000
1940	8,944,000
1945	14,796,000

killing ten and seriously injuring about one hundred.

Although he eventually came to terms with the United Automobile Workers, Henry Ford at first responded to the new unionism as did Girdler. He employed an army of toughs from the underworld and fortified his factories with tear gas, machine guns, and grenades. At the "Battle of the Overpass" in Detroit, Ford "goons" (as antiunion strong-arm forces were called) beat organizer Walter Reuther and other UAW officials until they were insensible. Violence was so common in the coal fields of Harlan County, Kentucky, that the area became known in the press as "Bloody Harlan."

But such incidents, well documented in photographs and newsreel films, redounded to the benefit of the union movement, and by the end of the depression decade, organized labor was a major force in American life. In 1932, there were 3.2 million union members. In 1940, there were 9 million, and by 1944, more than 13 million.

The Results

The greatest positive accomplishment of the New Deal was to ease the economic hardships suffered by millions of Americans and, in so doing, to preserve their confidence in American institutions. In its relief measures, particularly those agencies that put jobless people to

Police attack a crowd of union members during the "Memorial Day Massacre" in Chicago, 1937.

POPULATION OF TEN LARGEST AMERICAN CITIES—1940

New York	7,455,000
Chicago	3,397,000
Philadelphia	1,931,000
Detroit	1,623,000
Los Angeles	1,504,000
Cleveland	878,000
Baltimore	859,000
St. Louis	816,000
Boston	771,000
Pittsburgh	672,000

work, Roosevelt's administration was a resounding success.

As a formula for economic recovery, however, the New Deal failed. When unemployment dropped to 7.5 million early in 1937 and other economic indicators brightened, Roosevelt began to dismantle many expensive government programs. The result was renewed collapse, a depression within a depression. The recession of 1937 was not so serious as that of 1930 to 1933. But it provided painful evidence that for all their flexibility and willingness to experiment and spend, the New Dealers had not unlocked the secrets of maintaining prosperity during peacetime. Only when preparations for another world war led to massive purchases of American goods from abroad (and to rearmament at home) did the Great Depression end. By 1939, the economy was clearly on the upswing. By 1940, with Europe already at war, the Great Depression was a memory.

Through such programs as support for agricultural prices, rural electrification, Social Security, insurance of bank deposits, protection of labor unions, and strict controls over the economy, the federal government came to play a part in people's daily lives such as had been inconceivable before 1933. In the TVA, the government became an actual producer of electrical power and commodities such as fertilizers. It was not "socialism," as conservative critics of the New Deal cried, but in an American context it was something of a revolution.

Perhaps the most dubious side effect of the new system was the extraordinary growth in the size of government. Extensive government programs required huge bureaucracies to carry them out. The number of federal employees rose from six hundred thousand in 1930 to 1 million in 1940, a total that would rise even more radically during the Second World War. To the extent that every bureaucracy is concerned above all with its

HOW THE WEALTHY COPED

The Union Cigar Company was by no means an industrial giant, but the collapse of its stock in the Great Crash of 1929 nevertheless made history. When the price of Union shares plummeted from $113.50 to $4 in one day's trading, the president of the company jumped to his death from a hotel room that he apparently had rented for that purpose. The incident helped fuel a popular belief that rich men shouting "Ruined!" were hurling themselves wholesale from high buildings during late 1929 and early 1930. Cartoonists in newspapers and magazines had a field day with the theme. But it was only wishful thinking. When a historian researched the matter, he discovered that the suicide rate was higher in the months just preceding the crash than it was thereafter.

While many, perhaps most, middle-class investors and speculators were "ruined" in the collapse, the very rich suffered little more than a loss in paper wealth (relative richness) and not poverty. Still, the moneyed classes, which had been so at home during the age of Coolidge, very confident of their right and duty to govern the country, were stunned and even paralyzed by their failure. "I'm afraid," said Charles Schwab, chairman of the United States Steel Corporation, "that every man is afraid." Franklin D. Roosevelt, celestially noncommittal during his campaign for the presidency, may have had as much support from the nation's financial elite as did Hoover. Certainly the attitude of Wall Street and corporate board room alike was to give him a chance.

It did not last. By 1936, Roosevelt was being called "a traitor to his class" in society circles. Some of the jokes told about him and his wife, Eleanor, were vicious and ugly. Others were simply lame, as was this attack on Roosevelt's programs for putting people to work as welfare in disguise:

Q. Why is a WPA worker like King Solomon?
A. Because he takes his pick and goes to bed.

By 1937, while most people were still wrestling with depression, the very wealthy were living comfortably again. Stock prices were up—although far below 1929 levels—and a new kind of social whirl made its appearance. Unlike the society of Mrs. Astor, J. P. Morgan, and Bradley Martin, with its regal ballrooms, private railroad cars, club parlors, and yachts, the café society of the late 1930s centered in Prohibition era speakeasies that had come above ground with repeal as restaurants and as clubs in which to sit and to dance all night, to see and to be seen. In New York City, the undisputed capital of café society, the chief seats were El Morocco, the Stork Club, and the "21" Club, which reveled in its cryptic speakeasy designation.

The young always had played an important part in the social whirl. Marrying daughters to European noblemen had been a way to display wealth during the late nineteenth century; youth had set the pace of fashion during the 1920s. In café society, however, the "rich, young, and beautiful" became the center of the piece.

What was more remarkable about café society was the interest that ordinary Americans took in its doings.

Wealthy customers lounge at a cafe.

Whom Alfred Gwynne Vanderbilt was dating was breathlessly reported in syndicated "society columns" by hangers-on such as Walter Winchell and "Cholly Knickerbocker." It was a news item if the heiress of an industrial fortune dropped in at El Morocco several times a week in order to dance the rhumba with her "agile husband." Naughtier gossip made reference to blond hubbies having been with willowy debutantes.

Debutantes (or debs), young women who were "coming out" into society, when in fact they had been lounging around night clubs since they were fifteen or sixteen, were the queens of café society. The leading deb of 1937 was Gloria "Mimi" Baker, whose mother replied to someone who called her a decadent aristocrat: "Why Mimi is the most democratic person, bar none, I've ever known." Indeed, café society was "democratic" in ways that earlier high societies had not been. Because status depended on beauty, on what passed for wit and talent, and on simply being well known and rich, the café set admitted movie stars, athletes, and even impoverished but sauvely mannered nobles from Europe. They, in turn, were delighted to rub shoulders and dance the rhumba with the very rich.

Indeed, international "playboys" jumped at the opportunity to do more than be photographed at night clubs and race tracks they could not afford, and therein lay the great morality play of the 1930s and, possibly, part of the explanation for the fascination of many Americans with the doings of café society. Like people who attended high-speed automobile races, they were interested in the collisions as much as in the running.

Barbara Hutton, who had to stick to spartan diets in order to keep her weight down, was sole heiress to $45 million made in the five-and-tens of F. W. Woolworth. In 1933, she married Alexis Mdivani, who claimed to be a dispossessed Russian prince. Almost immediately after the marriage, the debonair Mdivani began to make her miserable, railing particularly at her weight problem. Using the $1 million that Barbara's father had given him as a wedding present, the prince spent much of his time in the company of other women. In 1935, Barbara won Mdivani's consent for a divorce by giving him $2 million.

Almost immediately, she married a Danish count, Kurt von Haugwitz-Reventlow. Hutton showered him with gifts, including a $4.5 million mansion in London, but divorced him in 1937. The same photographers who snapped pictures of laughing, dancing debutantes at the Stork Club rushed about to get shots of tearful Barbara Hutton, the "poor little rich girl."

Some of the people who pored over them were sympathetic. "She's made mistakes," wrote columnist Adela Rogers St. Johns, "been a silly, wild, foolish girl, given in to temptations—but she's still our own . . . an American girl fighting alone across the sea." Others took pleasure in her repeated comeuppances. "Why do they hate me?" Barbara asked. "There are other girls as rich, richer, almost as rich."

own survival and expansion, leading to wasteful use of tax moneys and to annoying operations, the New Deal represented a worrisome turn in American development.

A Political Revolution

Politically, F.D.R.'s presidency shattered the secure Republican majority of the 1920s and replaced it with a Democratic party domination of national politics that lasted for half a century, longer than any other distinct political era in United States history. During the fifty years between 1930 and 1980, Republicans occupied the White House for sixteen years, but those presidents (Eisenhower, Nixon, and Ford) were moderates who had made their peace with New Deal institutions. Until 1980, no strongly anti-New Deal politician achieved more than a brief ascendancy on the national scene, and in 1980, Republican Ronald Reagan repeatedly quoted F.D.R. as though he were carrying on his work.

In Congress, the Democratic majority was even more obvious. During the same fifty years, Republicans held majorities in the Senate for only six years and in the House of Representatives for only four. The Republican party controlled presidency, Senate, and House at the same time for a mere two years (1953 to 1955). The alliance of Solid South, liberals, blue-collar workers (particularly white ethnics), and black voters that had been forged by Roosevelt and Jim Farley was almost impregnable.

For Further Reading

On the difference that Franklin D. Roosevelt meant for the United States, there is a wealth of literature. See Arthur M. Schlesinger, Jr., *The Coming of the New Deal* (1959) and *The Politics of Upheaval* (1960), for the comprehensive work of an unstinting admirer. More reserved is William E. Leuchtenburg, *Franklin D. Roosevelt and the New Deal, 1932–1940* (1963). Paul Conkin, *The New Deal* (1975), and E. E. Robinson, *The Roosevelt Leadership* (1955), are critical assessments.

Students will enjoy the skillful social history of the New Deal years that have been woven out of personal recollections in Studs Terkel, *Hard Times* (1970). On special subjects, see Irving Bernstein, *Turbulent Years: A History of the American Worker, 1933–1941* (1970); Frank Freidel, *F.D.R. and the South* (1965); Roy Lubove, *The Struggle for Social Security, 1900–1935* (1968); Thomas K. McCraw, *TVA and the Power Fight, 1933–1939* (1971); D. R. McCoy, *Angry Voices: Left of Center Politics in the New Deal Era* (1958); C. J. Tull, *Father Coughlin and the New Deal* (1965); Abraham Holtzman, *The Townsend Movement* (1963); and T. Harry Williams, *Huey Long* (1969).

46

Headed for War Again
Foreign Relations, 1933–1942

In 1933, the year Franklin D. Roosevelt became president, Germany also got a new leader. Adolf Hitler, the head of the extreme right-wing National Socialist, or "Nazi," party, was named chancellor of the Weimar Republic.

The two paid little attention to each other during their first years in office. F.D.R. had his hands full fighting the Great Depression. Hitler was also preoccupied with the home front, feeling his way toward the day he could seize absolute power. Both men were virtuosos in using the radio and other modern forms of communication as a means to persuade. Roosevelt was at his best as a soothing voice in his Fireside Chats, quietly reassuring Americans that through reform they could preserve what was of value in their way of life. Hitler was at his best ranting through loudspeakers, whipping up Germans to a hatred of the democracy of the Weimar Republic, the foreigners who had humiliated Germans in the Versailles Treaty, and people whom he defined as enemies within: Socialists, Communists, and Jews.

Roosevelt and Hitler would eventually confront each other and clash, but only after Americans had experimented with a foreign policy designed to avoid another foreign war, and had failed.

Thousands of German soldiers listen to Adolf Hitler speak at the Nuremberg Rally, 1936.

New Deal Foreign Policy

At first Roosevelt seemed to be as casual as Woodrow Wilson about foreign policy. Like Wilson, he passed over diplomats in naming his Secretary of State and made a political appointment, the courtly Tennesseean Cordell Hull, whose elegant manner and bearing belied log-cabin origins.

Hull and Roosevelt were generally content to follow the guidelines that had been charted by Hoover and his Secretary of State, Henry L. Stimson. Where they departed from blueprint, their purpose was to support the New Deal program for economic recovery at home.

The Good Neighbor

Roosevelt and Hull even adopted Hoover's phrase "good neighbor" to describe the role that Roosevelt meant the United States to play in Central and South America. Following through on Hoover's plans, Roosevelt withdrew marines from Nicaragua, the Dominican Republic, and Haiti. Like Hoover, he refused to intervene in Cuba despite the chronic civil war that plagued the island republic and America's legal right, under the Platt Amendment, to send in troops.

In 1934, when peace returned to Cuba under a pro-American president who later became dictator, Cordell Hull formally renounced the Platt Amendment. No longer would the "Colossus of the North" be a bully, using its overwhelming power to force its way in the Caribbean. As a result of the about-face, no president was ever so well liked in Central and South America as was Roosevelt. Even when, in 1938, Mexico seized the properties of American oil companies and offered very little compensation to the former owners, Roosevelt kept cool and took a conciliatory stand. A few years later, he worked out a friendly settlement. By then, the Good Neighbor Policy was reaping concrete benefits for the United States. The Second World War had begun, but despite German efforts to win a foothold in the Western Hemisphere, most Latin American nations backed the United States, and the few neutrals were very cautious.

The Stimson Doctrine

Toward Asia, New Deal diplomacy also moved along paths that had been staked out during the Hoover administration. The problem in the East, as policymakers saw it, was to maintain American trading rights in China—the Open Door Policy—in the face of an ambitious and expansion-minded Japan. China was disorganized, inefficient, and increasingly corrupt, despite the efforts of Chiang Kai-shek to unify the country. Late in 1931, taking advantage of this chaos, Japanese military men detached the province of Manchuria from China and set up a puppet state that they called Manchukuo. Hoover considered but rejected Stimson's proposal that the United States retaliate against Japan by imposing severe economic sanctions, denying Japan the vital American exports it needed, particularly oil. Instead, Hoover announced that the United States would not recognize the legality of any territorial changes resulting from the use of force. Curiously, this policy was known as the Stimson Doctrine.

The Stimson Doctrine was little more than a rap on the knuckles, a painless moral statement of disapproval like the Kellogg-Briand Pact. Japanese militarists, imbued with a compelling sense of national destiny, shrugged it off. In 1932, they launched an air attack on Shanghai, which was considered the worst example of warring on civilians to that day. Nevertheless, Roosevelt went no further than Hoover. Both he and the

A young Chinese survivor of the Japanese air attack on Shanghai, 1932.

League of Nations responded to Japanese aggression with words alone. With economic problems so serious, no Western country would consider risking war in China.

New Directions

Where the Roosevelt administration parted ways with Hoover and Stimson, the cause was that all-pervasive reality, the depression at home. For example, in May 1933 Roosevelt scuttled an international conference that was meeting in London for the purpose of stabilizing world currencies. Delegates of sixty-four nations had gathered with Hoover's approval and, so they thought, with Roosevelt's as well. Before discussions actually began, however, Roosevelt announced that he would not agree to any decisions that ran contrary to his domestic recovery program, specifically his decision to abandon the gold standard. The conference collapsed.

In November 1933, Roosevelt formally recognized the Soviet government, which four presidents had refused to do. In part this was a realistic decision that was long overdue. For good or ill, the dictatorship of Joseph Stalin was fully in control of the Soviet Union and its traditional territories. But Roosevelt was also swayed by the argument that the Soviet Union would provide a large and profitable market for ailing American manufacturers. This was an illusion. Soviet Russia was too poor to buy much of anything from the United States. Still, it was the hope of stimulating economic recovery at home that made possible the end of a pointless sixteen-year policy of nonrecognition.

Increased trade was also the motive behind Secretary of State Cordell Hull's strategy of reducing tariff barriers through reciprocity. With his southern Democratic distaste for high tariffs, Hull negotiated reciprocal-trade agreements with twenty-nine countries. The high Republican rates were slashed by as much as half in return for other nations' agreements to lower their barriers against American exports.

Isolationism Supreme

Roosevelt probably would have liked his administration to take a more active part in the affairs of nations than the United States did. He admired his cousin Theodore Roosevelt's forcefulness, and he was an old Wilsonian, as was Hull. He had staunchly supported the League of Nations when it was first proposed and, while recovering from his polio attack during the early 1920s, had studied and written about foreign policy.

But F.D.R. was also a politician. He knew that it was political suicide for an elected official to wander too far from pouplar prejudices in any matter, and according to an authoritative public-opinion poll of 1935, 95 percent of all Americans were isolationists. They believed that the United States had no vital interests to protect in either Europe or Asia and wanted their government to act accordingly.

Suspicion of Europe was reinforced by the theory that the economic collapse of the Old World was responsible for the American depression. This feeling intensified in 1934, when Senator Gerald Nye of North Dakota began a series of investigations into the political machinations of the munitions industry. Nye insisted that the United States had been maneuvered into the First World War by "merchants of death" such as the giant Du Pont Corporation and other companies, which had been only too willing to see young men slaughtered for the sake of bigger sales. Nye's beliefs were popularized in a best-selling book of 1935, *The Road to War* by Walter Millis, and many academic historians took a similarly jaundiced view of the reasons why, in 1917, Americans had gone "over there" with such disappointing results.

Neutrality Policy

In a series of Neutrality Acts passed between 1935 and 1937, Congress said "never again." Taken together, the three laws warned American citizens against traveling on ships flying the flags of nations at war (no *Lusitanias* this time) and required belligerent nations to pay cash for all American goods they purchased and to carry them in their own ships. There would be no United States flagships sunk even by accident, and no American property lost because of a war among Europeans. Finally, belligerent nations were forbidden to buy arms in the United States and to borrow money from American banks. This law was designed to prevent the emergence of an active lobby of munitions makers and bankers with a vested interest in the victory of one side in any conflict.

Critics of the Neutrality Acts argued that they worked to the disadvantage of countries that were the innocent victims of aggression. Such nations would be unprepared for war, whereas aggressor nations would equip themselves in advance. This was certainly the message of Fascist Italy's invasion of Ethiopia in 1935 and of Japan's huge purchases of American scrap iron. But until 1938, Americans were interested only in avoiding a repetition of the events that had taken them into war in 1917. The majority wanted no part of trying to influence international behavior if it meant American involvement.

The World Goes to War

Each year brought new evidence that the world was drifting into another blood bath. In 1934, the Nazi government of Adolf Hitler began rearming Germany. In 1935, Hitler introduced universal military training and Italy invaded Ethiopia, one of the few independent countries of Africa. In 1936, Francisco Franco, a reactionary Spanish general, started a rebellion against the unstable democratic government of Spain and received massive support from both Italy and Germany, including combat troops who treated the Spanish Civil War as a rehearsal for bigger things.

In July 1937, Japan sent land forces into China and quickly took the northern capital, then called Peiping, and most of the coastal provinces. In March 1938, Hitler forced the political union of Austria to Germany in the Anschluss (union), increasing the resources of what Hitler called the Third Reich. In September, claiming that he wanted only to unite all Germans under one flag, Hitler demanded that Czechoslovakia surrender the Sudetenland to him.

The Sudetenland was largely populated by people who spoke German. But it was also the mountainous natural defense line for Czechoslovakia, the only dem-

ocratic state in central Europe. Nevertheless, in the hope that they could win peace by appeasing Hitler, England and France agreed to the takeover; Hitler mocked their good intentions only a few months later. In March 1939, he seized the rest of Czechoslovakia, where the people were Slavic in language and culture and were generally fearful of or hostile to Germans.

The Aggressor Nations

In some respects, the three aggressor nations of the 1930s were very different. Japan was motivated to expand into China primarily for economic reasons. A modern industrial nation, Japan was poor in basic natural resources like coal and iron. China was rich in these raw materials, and Japanese leaders hoped to displace the United States and Great Britain as the dominant imperial power on the Asian mainland.

Until the summer of 1941, Japanese policymakers were undecided about whether they could best serve their country's purposes by negotiating with the United States or by going to war. American trade was important to Japan; indeed, the Asian nation was the third largest customer of the United States. Japan imported vast quantities of American cotton, copper, scrap iron, and oil.

Italy under the Fascists, however, seemed locked

Adolf Hitler and Francisco Franco giving the fascist salute.

into chronic poverty. Dictator Benito Mussolini, something of a buffoon in his public posing, made do with the appearance of wealth and power. Ethiopia was an easy victim, a destitute and backward country that had to resist the invaders with antiquated muskets and even spears. Mussolini's own army was poorly trained and poorly armed. Tanks, which were designed for showy parades rather than for war, were sometimes made of sheet metal that could be dented with a rock or even a swift kick. By itself, Mussolini's Italy represented no real threat to world peace, and Americans either applauded what progress the Italian economy made under Fascist rule or laughed at Mussolini's comic-opera antics.

There was nothing comical about the Nazi dictator of Germany beyond his Charlie Chaplin moustache. Adolf Hitler's strutting was all too serious because it took place in a potentially rich and powerful nation. Moreover, Hitler was far more cunning, ruthless, and deliberate than Mussolini. He knew what he wanted and had said as much in an autobiography entitled *Mein Kampf*, or *My Struggle*. German domination of the continent of Europe was his goal, and while his

Japanese soldiers believed that Emperor Hirohito was divine and swore to fight to the death serving him.

strategy was not without flaws, Hitler had a brilliant grasp of just how much he could get away with in his dealing with the other European powers and the United States.

Perverted Nationalism

In other ways, the three aggressor nations were much alike. Japanese militarists, Italian Fascists, and German Nazis were all bitterly antidemocratic. They sneered at

Benito Mussolini loved military displays, but most of the Italian army was in fact poorly trained and armed.

TWO DIFFERENT WORLDS

In December 1940, Adolf Hitler told Germans that there could be no reconciliation between Germany, on the one hand, and Great Britain *and the United States*, on the other. They were "different worlds."

The next month, President Roosevelt accepted Hitler's dichotomy and said that his world was devoted to the Four Freedoms, "freedom of speech and expression, freedom of worship, freedom from want, freedom from fear."

Nazi repression included destroying ideas as well as people. Here, students burn "subversive" books in front of the Berlin Opera House, May 10, 1933.

the ideals of popular rule and individual liberties, regarding them as the sources of the world's economic and social problems. In the place of humanistic principles, they exalted the totalitarian state as mystically personified in a single person: Hirohito, the divine emperor of Japan; Mussolini, the Italian *Duce;* and Hitler, the German *Führer.*

The aggressor nations were militaristic. They worshiped armed force as the best means of serving their national purposes. If militarism could be less than ominous when practiced by a poor and disunited country like Italy, it was frightening when combined with fanatical Japanese nationalism and Nazi racism. The Japanese considered other Asians to be their inferiors. Westerners who had for a century looked down on the Japanese found it intolerable that they now dominated the economy of the Far East. Japanese soldiers were sworn to solemn oaths to die serving emperor and homeland.

Nazi racism was criminal from its inception. Calling on ancient Germanic mythology and nineteenth-century pseudoscience, it taught that "non-Aryans" were subhuman degenerates who had no claims to decent treatment by the master race. After disposing of the German Communists and Socialists, Nazi paramilitary organizations routinely brutalized German Jews. Hitler's government stripped them of their civil rights and eventually, during the war, murdered them in extermination camps along with millions of Jews from conquered lands, gypsies, handicapped persons, political dissidents, and resistance fighters.

And the War Came

There was no coming to terms with Germany when Hitler invaded Poland in September 1939. The German dictator had neutralized the Soviet Union by signing a "nonaggression pact" with the Communist leader Stalin. There was little Britain and France could do to help Poland when Hitler's legions moved swiftly and efficiently to cut off the country's access to the sea. Within two days, both countries declared war on the Third Reich. However, attacked from both east and west, Poland's fate was sealed.

An uneasy quiet fell on Europe during the winter of 1939/40. Journalists spoke of a "phony war" in which neither side attacked the other with force. Whatever the French and British had in mind, the Germans were planning a blitzkrieg (lightning war): massive land, sea, and air attacks with which, in the spring, the crack German armed forces overran Denmark, Norway, Luxembourg, Belgium, and the Netherlands. In June 1940, France collapsed, and the British managed to evacuate their troops from the little port of Dunkirk only by mobilizing virtually every ship and boat that was capable of crossing the English Channel. The motley fleet returned three hundred thousand demoralized men to England to await a German invasion.

"We shall fight on the beaches, we shall fight on the landing grounds, we shall fight in the fields and in the streets, we shall fight in the hills; we shall never surrender," said the new British prime minister, Winston Churchill, and his eloquence inspired Americans as well as Britons. But few were truly confident that the British alone could withstand a German onslaught.

Instead of invading Great Britain with land forces, however, Hitler ordered relentless aerial bombardment of the country while Germany expanded its power to the south. Mussolini's Italy had joined the war against France (forming with Germany the Rome–Berlin Axis) and faced British and Anzac (Australian and New Zealand Army Corps) troops in Libya in North Africa. Then in June 1941, the *Führer* made what is

Winston Churchill stands amid the ruins of the bombed-out House of Commons, 1940.

widely regarded as his greatest blunder. He invaded the Soviet Union.

At first, the German army met little resistance. Armored units rolled unimpeded into the Russian heartland, almost surrounding Leningrad in the north, threatening Moscow in the center, and capturing much of Stalingrad in the south. There the advance stalled. The Germans still held the upper hand. But while reeling, the Red Army was a huge, formidable armed force. Just as important, England no longer stood alone. By the end of 1941, the United States was to all intents and purposes, already fighting against Hitler.

The United States and the War in Europe

The fall of France and the heroic resistance of Britain changed American attitudes toward neutrality. Those two nations were the last democracies in Europe. France was America's oldest friend, and Britain, if the nation's oldest enemy, was still the cultural motherland. Moreover, ugly pro-Axis and racist rhetoric in the United States by small but noisy Nazi organizations such as William Dudley Pelley's Silver Shirts and Fritz Kuhn's German-American Bund, as well as German machinations in Latin America, persuaded Americans that Hitler had no intention of stopping in Europe. During the "phony war" in March 1940, only 43 percent of Americans thought that a German victory in Europe would threaten them in any way. By July, almost 80 percent thought so. They viewed Hitler as a madman who wanted to conquer the world.

Roosevelt Leads the Way

Franklin D. Roosevelt played no small part in shaping this change of opinion. As early as 1938, when few Americans could conceive of getting involved in a foreign war, and the French and British governments were appeasing Hitler in the belief that he wanted peace, Roosevelt concluded that only a show of force—or the use of it—would stop the *Führer*. In this opinion he was one with Winston Churchill, then a bellicose gadfly in Parliament, later the wartime prime minister and F.D.R.'s close personal friend.

But whereas Churchill was in opposition and could snipe at Britain's policy of appeasement, waiting for events to rally public opinion behind him, Roosevelt was president. He could not afford to get too far ahead of the country, least of all in calling for preparation for war. His technique was to float trial balloons by delivering militant anti-Nazi speeches. If the reaction was hostile, he backed down; if friendly, he moved ahead.

By the summer of 1940, F.D.R. was able to do more than talk. With a large majority of Americans worried about how a Nazi victory would affect them, he announced that he was trading fifty old destroyers the British needed to counter German submarines for naval bases in Bermuda, Newfoundland, and British colonies in the Caribbean. Roosevelt described the deal as a defensive measure and not involvement in the war, which, strictly speaking, was true. Preparedness was also the justification for the Burke-Wadsworth Act of September 1940, which instituted the first peacetime draft law in American history and appropriated $37 billion to build up the navy and army air corps.

It was comparatively easy to win support for these measures. Nevertheless, when Roosevelt decided to break with tradition in 1940 and run for a third term as president, he felt it necessary to assure the American people that "your boys are not going to be sent into any foreign wars."

The Third Term

Despite the shift in public opinion in favor of fighting Hitler, Roosevelt feared that an antiwar Republican candidate might eke out a victory against him. He remembered very well that his idol, Woodrow Wilson, had won reelection in 1916 only by claiming the antiwar position for himself. In 1940, however, the war versus peace debate never materialized. The Republicans chose a man who did not disagree with Roosevelt on any essentials. Indeed, utilities magnate Wendell Willkie had been a Democrat most of his life. An attractive and personable Indianian who had relocated to Wall Street, Willkie made it clear that he differed only in degree from the popular incumbent.

Thus, Willkie attacked the undisputed waste of many New Deal programs without calling for their abolition. He assailed the vast presidential powers that Roosevelt had assumed as bordering on dictatorship, but he did not propose to dismantle the huge executive apparatus that the New Deal had created. Willkie claimed that he was the better bet to keep the United States out of war, but he did not oppose either arming for defense or aiding Great Britain. In short, he offered Americans the kind of choice that was better resolved by sticking to the leader who was already tested.

Willkie ran well. He captured Maine, Vermont, and eight midwestern states and 45 percent of the popular vote. But Roosevelt's popularity was too great to overcome. The president ran an incumbent's campaign. He did his job while the exuberant challenger barnstormed the country. His landmark third-term reelection, which broke the tradition established by Washington and Jefferson and challenged by only Grant and Theodore Roosevelt, was an anticlimax, and it did not interrupt the nation's drift toward war.

Undeclared War on Germany

A few weeks after the election, Roosevelt responded to Winston Churchill's plea for additional aid by sending the lend-lease bill to Congress. As passed, the Lend-Lease Act provided that the United States would serve as the "arsenal of democracy," turning out arms of all sorts to be lent to Britain. Eventually, with lend-lease extended to the Soviet Union, such aid totaled $54 billion.

Because no amount of aid in materiel could help the British defend their shipping against "wolf packs" of German submarines, Roosevelt proclaimed a neutral zone that extended from North American waters to Iceland. He sent troops to Greenland, a possession of conquered Denmark, and ordered American destroyers to patrol the sea lanes, warning British ships of enemies beneath the waves. This permitted the British to concentrate their navy in the waters around their home islands.

The United States was at war in everything but name. Indeed, in August 1941, Roosevelt met with Churchill on a ship off the coast of Newfoundland and adopted what amounted to mutual war aims patterned after Wilson's Fourteen Points. The Atlantic Charter provided for self-determination of nations after the war; free trade and freedom of the seas; the disarmament of aggressor nations; and some new means of

---

LEND-LEASE

Britain could not afford to pay for the destroyers that Winston Churchill requested at the end of 1940. Britain had spent $4.5 billion in the United States for arms, and in December 1940 had only $2 billion in reserve. Roosevelt explained the "loan" of the ships to Britain with the following parable:

Suppose my neighbor's house catches fire, and I have a length of garden hose. If he can take my garden hose and connect it up with his hydrant, I may help him to put out the fire.

Now what do I do? I don't say to him before that operation, "Neighbor, my garden hose cost me $15; you have to pay me $15 for it." What is the transaction that goes on? I don't want $15—I want my garden hose back after the fire is over.

Winston Churchill welcomes Franklin Roosevelt to the Atlantic Charter Conference, which took place on a ship off the Newfoundland Coast, August 1941.

collective world security, a provision that would evolve into the United Nations.

It was only a matter of time before guns were fired. After a few ambivalent incidents involving German submarines and American destroyers, the U.S.S. *Reuben James* was sunk in October 1941 with a loss of one hundred sailors. Prowar sentiment flamed higher.

A Bitter Debate

Roosevelt still did not ask Congress for a formal declaration of war. He hoped that Britain and the Soviet Union could defeat Germany without the expenditure of American lives, a commodity with which every American president had been cautious. More important, Roosevelt did not want to go to war without a unified nation behind him. By the autumn of 1941, he had his majority. Most Americans had concluded, without enthusiasm, that Hitler must be stopped at any cost. Even the American Communist party, which had been opposed to fighting until Hitler invaded the Soviet Union, was now in the prowar camp, and much of the eastern big-business establishment had concluded that Hitler represented a threat to American commercial primacy in the world.

There was, however, an opposition. Roosevelt did not worry about the antiwar agitation of extremist Hitler supporters such as Father Coughlin and members of the Bund and Silver Shirts. But he was concerned

about the old-fashioned isolationists who formed the well-financed and active America First Committee. Former president Herbert Hoover, ex-New Dealer Hugh Johnson, and progressive intellectuals such as Charles A. Beard despised Hitlerism. Whatever hostility toward Great Britain they harbored was aimed at British imperialism; they feared that the United States would go to war to protect the British Empire, an unworthy goal. Their priority in supporting the America First Committee was to avoid making the mistake of 1917 as they saw it—pulling British chestnuts out of the fire.

The America First Committee's case was weakened because most of its members agreed that the United States should arm for defense. Roosevelt and the rival Committee to Defend America by Aiding the Allies described every contribution to the British cause in just such terms, and this justification confounded the isolationists. Nevertheless, Roosevelt hesitated. He confided to Winston Churchill that he would not ask for war until some dramatic incident—in other words, a direct attack on the United States—rallied the America Firsters to his cause.

As it turned out, the bitter debate over intervention missed the point. Both sides in the argument trained their eyes on Europe and the Atlantic as the crisis area. Neither side paid much attention to Asia and the

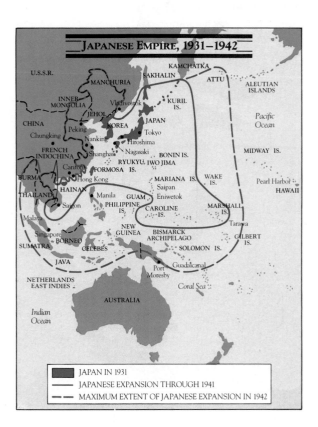

Pacific, where Japan moved into the former French colonies of Indochina and continued its war against the indecisive government of Chiang Kai-shek. War in Asia was an old story. It seemed reasonable to conclude that it would go on indefinitely without a decisive turn in either direction. If Roosevelt took a tougher line toward Japan after the occupation of Indochina, negotiations with Tokyo continued too, into the summer and autumn of 1941.

America Goes to War

Nevertheless, it was in the Pacific that the United States felt the sting of the Second World War. All the while the Japanese continued to negotiate during the summer of 1941, the prowar faction of the imperial government, headed by General Hideki Tojo, increased its power at the expense of the peace party. As premier, Tojo gave the negotiators until early November to come up with a formula for peace that the United States would accept. But the minimum Japanese demand that Japan be recognized as the dominant economic power in China could not be reconciled with the Open Door Policy, to which the United States was committed.

Pearl Harbor

Curiously, the Japanese and American governments concluded on the same day that there could be no peaceful resolution of their differences. Talks continued, but Secretary of State Hull put the matter of Japanese-American relations under the authority of the War Department, and military commanders in the

Destruction of the American fleet at Pearl Harbor, December 7, 1941.

Pacific were warned that hostilities could begin at any time. Indeed, the Japanese had initiated preparations for attack that could not easily be reversed.

On December 7, 1941, it was launched. Admiral Isoroku Yamamoto, a tragic figure who admired the United States and feared the result of a war he did not want, engineered a tactically brilliant aerial attack on Pearl Harbor, the huge American naval base on Oahu in the Hawaiian Islands. His planes sank or badly damaged 8 battleships, 7 other vessels, and 188 airplanes, and killed or wounded 3,435 servicemen. Yamamoto did not fully join in the celebrations that swept over his fleet and the people of Japan. The three American aircraft carriers that he believed would be at Pearl Harbor were at sea when the assault force arrived and thus escaped unscathed.

Yamamoto understood that air power was the key to war in the broad Pacific, and, in this area, the United States retained superiority over Japan. As a one-time resident of the United States, he also appreciated better than did the Tojo group how great American industrial might was compared with Japan's. "I fear we have only awakened a sleeping giant," he told his officers, "and his reaction will be terrible."

The Reaction

The wounded giant awakened immediately. Pearl Harbor was attacked on Sunday. The next day, Roosevelt went before Congress and described December 7, 1941, as "a day that will live in infamy." He got his unanimous vote, or very nearly so. In both houses of Congress, only Representative Jeanette Rankin of Montana, a pacifist who had voted against entry into the First World War, refused to declare war.

In every city in the nation during the next several weeks, the army's and navy's enlistment offices were jammed with stunned and angry young men. Pearl Harbor was so traumatic an event in the lives of Americans that practically every individual remembered exactly what he or she had been doing when news of the attack was announced.

Quietly at the time, more publicly later, Roosevelt's critics accused him and other top officials of having plotted to keep Pearl Harbor and nearby Hickham

Field, an air base, completely unprepared for the attack. It was said that Washington knew the assault was coming but withheld vital intelligence from Hawaii, sacrificing thousands of American lives for the political purpose of getting the United States into the war.

In truth, the lack of preparation at Pearl Harbor was stupid and shameful. Numerous indications that something was brewing either were ignored or reached the appropriate commanders after unjustifiable delays. At Hickham Field, fighter planes were drawn up wing tip to wing tip so that they could be protected against sabotage on the ground. This made destruction from the air all the simpler, and, even after the attack began, it was difficult to get the fighters into the air. But to say that there was a deliberate conspiracy among the highest ranking officials in the United States government was absurd, an example of the paranoia that periodically curses American politics. The blunders of the military in Hawaii were just another example of the chronic incompetence in all large organizations, and the key to the stunning Japanese victory was the brilliant planning behind it.

Nevertheless, there is no doubt that Roosevelt was relieved to get officially into the conflict with a united people behind him. He was totally convinced by December 1941 that the survival of democracy, freedom, and American influence in the world depended on the total defeat of the aggressor nations, which only American might could ensure.

Getting the Job Done

Of all the nations that went to war, only Japan, whose participation in the First World War had been nominal, celebrated at the start of it. In Europe and the United States, there was very little of the exuberance with which people had greeted the first days of the fighting in the First World War. Among Americans, the attitude was that there was a job to be done.

The popular songs of the period were concerned with getting home again. There was a melancholy tenor to "I'll Be Seeing You" and "I'll Never Smile Again." The lyrics told of the sadness of separation, however necessary it might be. Few people were attracted by the foot-stomping patriotism of George M. Cohan's "Over There," the American anthem during the First World War.

Once in the service, soldiers and sailors referred to the conflict as "W-W-2," a sardonically mechanical description of a war that was reminiscent of the name of a New Deal works project. Indeed, because the country had been through it before, and because the New Deal reforms had introduced the idea of government-supervised order to the national economy, mobilization of resources and people was far more orderly and effective than it had been twenty-five years earlier.

Organizing for Victory

The mobilization of fighting capacity began before Pearl Harbor. By December 1941, more than 1.5 million men were in uniform, most of them well trained. By the end of the war, the total number of soldiers, sailors, and airmen, and women in auxiliary corps in every service climbed to 15 million.

The draft accounted for the majority of these "GI's," a name that referred to the "government issued" designation of uniforms and other equipage. Boards made up of local civic leaders worked efficiently and with comparatively few irregularities to fill the armed forces. The "Friends and Neighbors" who informed young men of their fate with the salutation "Greetings" exempted only the physically disabled and those with work skills designated as essential to the war effort, including farmers and agricultural workers. As time passed, another sad category of those exempted was adopted: "sole surviving sons," men of draft age whose brothers had been killed in action.

Money was mobilized too. When the war began, the government was spending $2 billion a month on the military. During the first half of 1942, the expenditure rose to $15 billion a month. By the time Japan surrendered in August 1945, the costs of the war totaled more than $300 billion. In less than four years, the American government spent more money than it had spent during the previous 150 years of national existence. The national debt, already considered high in 1941 at $48 billion, doubled and redoubled to $247 billion in 1945.

A few businessmen continued to oppose government policy, particularly the wartime labor laws. One of the most graceless was Sewell L. Avery, head of the huge retail chain store Montgomery Ward. Roosevelt's policies had saved his company from bankruptcy, and during the war, full employment in the work force resulted in bonanza profits for his firm. But Avery had to be carried bodily to jail for refusing to obey a law that guaranteed his employees the right to join a union.

He was not typical. Most big businessmen, including former opponents of the administration, grew silent and rushed to Washington to assist the government. They were responding in part to the need for national unity. Corporation executives also recognized that wartime expenditures meant prosperity. General Motors, for example, received 8 percent of all federal expenditures between 1941 and 1945, literally *$1 of every $12.50* that the government spent. Few criticisms came from the General Motors board room. Indeed, General Motors president William S. Knudsen was one of the most prominent "dollar-a-year men," business executives who worked for Roosevelt in effect without pay. He headed the War Resources Board (WRB), which had been established in August 1939 to plan for the conversion of factories for military production in the event of war.

New Alphabet Agencies

After the congressional elections of 1942, which brought many conservative Republicans to Washington, Roosevelt announced that "Dr. New Deal" had been dismissed from the country's case and "Dr. Win-the-War" had been engaged. He explained that since there was now full employment, social programs were no longer necessary.

However, the New Dealers' practice of establishing government agencies to oversee public affairs was vastly expanded. In addition to Knudsen's WRB, the Supplies Priorities and Allocation Board (SPAB), under Donald M. Nelson of Sears Roebuck and Company, was commissioned to ensure that raw materials, particularly the scarce and critical ones, were diverted

UNITED STATES EXPENDITURES AND RECEIPTS

(millions of dollars)

	Expenditures	Receipts	Debts
1900	521	567	1,263
1905	567	544	1,132
1910	694	676	1,147
1915	761	698	1,191
1920	6,403	6,695	24,299
1925	3,063	3,780	20,516
1930	3,440	4,178	16,185
1935	6,521	3,730	28,701
1940	9,062	5,144	42,968
1945	98,416	44,475	258,682

to military industries. The Office of Price Administration (OPA) had the task of controlling consumer prices so that the combination of high wages and scarce goods did not lead to runaway inflation.

After Pearl Harbor, a National War Labor Board (NWLB) was set up to mediate industrial disputes. Its principal purposes were to guarantee that production was not interrupted and that wage increases were kept within government-set limits. This offended many of Roosevelt's former supporters in the labor movement, none of them more important than John L. Lewis of the United Mine Workers, who returned to the Republican party. But the NWLB also worked to ensure that employees were not gouged by avaricious employers. The board was reasonably successful. There were strikes, including a serious one led by Lewis in 1943. But labor relations were generally good, and union membership continued to rise.

The Office of War Mobilization (OWM) was the most important of the new alphabet agencies. Theoretically, it oversaw all aspects of the mobilized economy, as Bernard Baruch had done during the First World War. It was considered to be sufficiently important that James F. Byrnes of South Carolina resigned from the Supreme Court to head it as a kind of "assistant president." Many believed that Byrnes's contribution to the war effort earned him the right to a presidential nomination.

Success

In essentials, Dr. Win-the-War's treatment was an overwhelming success. The size of the federal government swelled at a dizzying rate, from 1.1 million civilian employees in 1940 to 3.3 million in 1945. (State governments grew at almost the same rate.) Inevitably there was waste (agencies doing the same thing), inefficiency (agencies fighting at cross-purposes with one another), and corruption (many unessential jobs). But with national unity and military victory constantly touted as essential, the few critics of wartime problems, such as Senator Robert A. Taft of Ohio, were unable to carry the day. The most effective check on waste, inefficiency, and corruption, the Senate War Investigating Committee, was headed by a Democratic New Dealer, Senator Harry S Truman of Missouri.

The lessons learned during the First World War and the administrative skills of dollar-a-year businessmen and bureaucrats trained in the New Deal worked wonders on production. New factories and those formerly given to the manufacture of America's automobiles canceled civilian production and churned out trucks, tanks, the versatile jeeps, and amphibious vehicles in

incredible numbers. In 1944 alone, 96,000 airplanes (260 per day) rolled out of American factories. Industrialist Henry J. Kaiser perfected an assembly line for producing simple but serviceable freighters, the so-called Liberty ships. By 1943, his mammoth yards were christening a new one every day. Altogether, American shipbuilders sent 10 million tons of shipping down the ways between 1941 and 1945.

Such statistics would have been regarded as pipe dreams before the war. But they were duplicated in every basic industry, including steel, rubber, glass, aluminum, and electronics.

Workingpeople

Unemployment vanished as a social problem. Instead, factories running at capacity had difficulty finding people to fill jobs. There was a significant shift of population to the west coast as the demands of the Pacific war led to the concentration of defense industries in such ports as Seattle, Oakland, and Long Beach. Among the new Californians (the population of the Golden State rose from 6.9 million in 1940 to 10.5 million in 1950) were hundreds of thousands of blacks. Finding well-paid factory jobs that previously had been closed to them, blacks also won a sense of security, which had been unknown to earlier generations, because of the generally antiracist policies of the young CIO unions.

Economic equality for blacks remained a long way in the future. Everywhere they went they found resentments and discrimination, and serious race riots in 1943. Nevertheless, prodded by Eleanor Roosevelt and pressured by influential black leaders such as A. Philip Randolph of the Brotherhood of Sleeping Car Porters, F.D.R. issued an executive order forbidding racial discrimination in companies that benefited from government contracts.

Women, including many of middle age who never had worked for wages, entered the work force in large numbers. The symbol of the woman performing "unwomanly" work was "Rosie the Riveter," assembling airplanes and tanks with heavy riveting guns. Indeed, women did perform just about every kind of job in the industrial economy. Rosie dressed in slacks, tied up her hair in a bandanna, and left her children with her mother. But off the job, she remained reassuringly feminine by the standards of the time.

Curiously, these genuinely independent women did not turn to traditional feminism. Comparatively little was heard of demands for equality during the war. On the contrary, woman after woman told newspaper reporters that she looked forward to the end of the war, when they could quit their jobs to return home as wives

EDWARD R. MURROW (1908–1965)

While President Roosevelt sparred with congressional isolationists and with the America First Committee in 1940 over the extent to which the United States should become involved in the European crisis, a young radio broadcaster stationed in London was helping to tip the scales in favor of intervention. Edward R. Murrow did not in so many words call for America to come to the aid of England. But he demonstrated even more skillfully than did F.D.R. (and Adolf Hitler) how very effective a persuader radio could be in the hands of someone who understood it. Murrow *was* in favor of American intervention. And he won the hearts of many Americans to this cause in his news broadcasts, which began with the byline "This—is London." During one blitzkrieg attack on the city, for example, Murrow set his microphone on a street, where it picked up the sounds of air-raid sirens, exploding bombs, the steps of Londoners running for underground shelters, and wailing children.

Edward Roscoe Murrow was born in Greensboro, North Carolina. At the age of twelve, he moved west with his family. He attended the State College of Washington in Pullman, one of the few schools in the United States that offered courses in radio journalism. Already liberal in his politics, Murrow was a leader on the campus, and, on graduating in 1930, became head of the National Student Federation. This job led him in 1932 to the directorship of the Institute of International Education, but it appears that he already was intrigued by the educational capabilities of radio.

So was Secretary of Commerce Herbert Hoover, who, in 1927, had established the Federal Radio Commission, now the Federal Communications Commis-

Edward R. Murrow kept Americans informed about World War II with his radio broadcasts from Europe.

sion. It was inconceivable, Hoover said, that the new medium should be "drowned in advertising chatter." But that was precisely how radio could be described in 1935, when Murrow went to work for the Columbia

and mothers within the traditional family system. There were exceptions, of course. Many women enjoyed the economic and social freedom. For the most most part, however, the female wartime workers were an ideal wartime work force: intelligent, educated, energetic, impelled by patriotism, and generally uninterested in competing with the soldiers who eventually would come back and take their jobs.

Prosperity at a Price

Labor shortages inevitably produced a demand for higher wages. The unions grew stronger; membership rose from 10.5 million to 14.7 million. With a few

exceptions, however, strikes were short and did not disrupt production. The NWLB mediated disputes, generally keeping raises within the limit of 15 percent over prewar levels that the government had set as an acceptable standard. This made the task of the OPA all the easier.

The success of the OPA was remarkable. Coveted consumer goods—coffee, butter, sugar, some canned foods, meat, shoes, liquor, silk, rayon, and nylon—were scarce or even unavailable because of rationing, and high wages gave workers the money to spend on them (real wages rose 50 percent during the war). But the black market, or illegal sale of goods, never got out

Broadcasting System as "Director of Talks." President Roosevelt had shown the political power of the medium in his cozy Fireside Chats, but there were few newscasts on any of the three networks. When CBS sent Murrow to London in 1937—he was the first full-time foreign correspondent on the airwaves—he was told to build programs around such themes as "the song of a nightingale from Kent." His immediate supervisor in New York told him that "broadcasting has no role in international politics."

Murrow did "nightingale" programs, but acting on a rumor in March 1938, he risked his job by chartering a plane to fly to Vienna. There he covered the Nazi takeover of Austria. The exclusive broadcasts were followed so avidly that CBS authorized Murrow to put together a network of broadcasters all over Europe. Among them were William L. Shirer in Berlin, Edgar Ansel Mowrer in Paris, Howard K. Smith, and Eric Sevareid. By 1940, there were twenty news broadcasts a day from Europe, most of them from CBS.

A CBS newsman independent of Morrow's team was H. V. Kaltenborn. During the crisis surrounding Hitler's demands on Czechoslovakia in September 1938, Kaltenborn was on the air almost constantly for eighteen days, presenting eighty-five special broadcasts. Americans were better informed about the attempt of Britain and France to win peace by appeasing Hitler than were the British and French. The American appetite for news was firmly fixed, but the capacity of radio for advertisement was not affected in any way. Following a Kaltenborn broadcast on Germany's invasion of Poland in September 1939, which touched off the Second World War, CBS in New York signed off with

We should like to express our appreciation again at this time to the makers of Oxydol, sponsors of "The Goldbergs," the makers of Ivory Soap, sponsors of "Life Can Be Beautiful," the makers of Chipso, sponsors of "Road of Life."

Murrow remained in London for the duration of the war, and then returned to the United States to pioneer two television programs, "See It Now" and "Person to Person." He remained liberal in his politics and, quite courageously at a time when most institutions in America were cowering before Senator Joseph McCarthy, fiercely attacked the senator's Red baiting. But Murrow never liked television as much as radio; he regarded it as less flexible and, in newscasting, too much concerned with what reporters looked like. He may have had in mind the ability of pioneers such as he and Kaltenborn to extemporize. Well read and intelligent, they could analyze and discuss news events. Of Kaltenborn, for example, it was said that someone could wake him "at four o'clock in the morning and just say 'Czechoslovakia' and he could talk for 30 minutes on Czechoslovakia." Already by the time Murrow left CBS in 1961, local news programs were being built around handsome "anchormen" and pretty "anchorwomen" who were lost without a script.

Murrow left CBS to accept John F. Kennedy's appointment as director of the United States Information Agency. Suffering from lung cancer—he was a chain smoker—Murrow resigned from the government in 1964 and died the next year. The men and women who had been trained in news broadcasting during the 1940s dominated the profession until the 1980s, on both radio and television and on all the networks.

of control, and prices rose only moderately between 1942 and 1945. Instead of consuming, Americans pumped their wages into savings accounts, including $15 billion in loans to the government in the form of war bonds. It became a point of patriotic pride with some women to paint the seam of a silk or nylon stocking on the calf of a naked leg (although a pair of stockings remained a kind of treasure).

There was a kind of good-humored innocence about the way Americans fought the Second World War. If they did not believe that a world free of problems would follow victory, which few doubted lay ahead, Americans were confident that they and their allies were in

the right. By the time the fighting was over, 290,000 Americans were dead. But shocking as that figure is at first glance, and bloody as some individual battles were, American suffering was insignificant compared with that of other nations. Indeed, keeping the casualty list short was one of Roosevelt's priorities throughout the conflict, and he succeeded. If Winston Churchill was right in describing the year 1940, when the British stood alone against Nazism, as "their finest hour," the Second World War was an hour of confidence and pride for Americans too, particularly in view of the difficult depression era that had preceded the war and the age of anxiety that was to follow.

Female workers manufacture noses of fighter planes at the Douglas Aircraft Plant in Long Beach, California.

For Further Reading

On the men who headed the State Department during the 1930s, see Eltin E. Morison, *Turmoil and Tradition: A Study of the Life and Times of Henry L. Stimson* (1960); Richard N. Current, *Secretary Stimson: A Study in Statecraft* (1954); and J. W. Pratt, *Cordell Hull* (1964).

A good overview of the diplomatic history of the period is R. H. Ferrell, *American Diplomacy in the Great Depression: Hoover–Stimson Foreign Policy, 1929–1933* (1957). Bryce Wood, *The Making of the Good Neighbor Policy* (1961), is an excellent discussion of the change in relations between the United States and Latin America during the 1930s. The debate between "isolationists" and "interventionists" is dealt with in Manfred Jonas, *Isolationism in America, 1935–1941* (1966); W. S. Cole, *America First: The Battle Against Inter-* vention (1953); Walter Johnson, *The Battle Against Isolationism* (1944); and Robert A. Divine, *The Illusion of Neutrality* (1962).

For a great historian's highly negative depiction of President Roosevelt's actions during the years leading up to the Second World War, see Charles A. Beard, *American Foreign Policy in the Making, 1932–1940* (1946) and *President Roosevelt and the Coming of War, 1941* (1948). An altogether different picture is painted in Basil Rauch, *Roosevelt: From Munich to Pearl Harbor* (1950). For the controversies surrounding America's defeat at Pearl Harbor, see Herbert Feis, *The Road to Pearl Harbor* (1950), and Roberta Wohlsetter, *Pearl Harbor: Warning and Decision* (1962).

47

America's Great War

The United States at the Pinnacle of Power, 1942–1945

In the histories of Europe, the First World War is the "Great War," The ferocious bloodletting of 1914 to 1918 badly shook a people who believed that their advanced civilization was incapable of such savagery. Even before the First World War ended, artists and intellectuals voiced the fear that the beginning of the end was upon the Old World. In 1922, the German philosopher Oswald Spengler published *The Decline of the West:* European civilization would never make a moral recovery from its great sin. After more than sixty years, it is easy to agree that, at the least, the First World War signaled the decline of Western Europe's domination of world politics and economy.

For Americans, on the contrary, the First World War was a jarring experience but by no means shattering. Casualties were few compared with those the Europeans suffered. The American material investment in the war stimulated rather than damaged the national economy. In view of the fact that the United States emerged from the conflict comparatively unscathed and indisputably the world's richest and most powerful nation, the expense was inconsequential. Even the social divisions and tensions that the war brought into the open seemed to evaporate in the crisis of the Great Depression.

American troops on a Pacific beachhead during World War II.

Stopping and Holding Japan

America's great war was the Second World War. Even so, the nation was not a battlefield, and casualties were fewer than those suffered by other combatant nations. But Americans knew that they were in a fight between December 1941 and August 1945. During those years, almost every adult remembered where he or she had been on the day Pearl Harbor was attacked, on D-Day when the invasion of Nazi-dominated Europe began, on the day Franklin D. Roosevelt died, on the days when Germany and Japan surrendered. Housewives saved tin cans for conversion into weaponry, and children saved tin foil and participated in scrap drives, collecting waste iron and steel for resmelting.

The national contribution in material and men was decisive in the outcome. Lend-lease kept the American allies—Great Britain, the Soviet Union, and China—afloat. American strategists designed the winning formula. American military administrators oversaw the huge and intricate apparatus of a modern military operation. American field commanders became heroes. American troops played an important part on the western front in Europe, and the Pacific war was practically their show alone. Without the United States, Germany and imperial Japan could not have been totally conquered.

American soldiers surrender to the Japanese on the Philippine island of Corregidor in one of the bitterest military defeats in U.S. history.

It Began in Defeat

The first months of the war brought nothing but depressing news. Immediately after paralyzing the American Pacific Fleet by the stunning blow at Pearl Harbor, the Japanese advanced easily into Malaya, Hong Kong, the Philippines, Java, Guam, and the two most distant islands of the Aleutians in Alaska. Within a few weeks, the dramatic Japanese battle flag, rays emanating from the rising sun, flew above Singapore, Burma, and present-day Indonesia.

There was heroism in the defeat. On the island of Luzon, twenty thousand crusty GI's under General Douglas MacArthur and their Filipino allies fought valiantly on the Bataan Peninsula and on the rocky island of Corregidor in Manila Bay. At first they thought they would be relieved or evacuated. Slowly the sickening truth sank in: they were alone, isolated, doomed, "the battling bastards of Bataan." Nevertheless, they grimly accepted their assignment of delaying the Japanese.

Roosevelt ordered MacArthur to flee to Australia. The general was an arrogant man, in fact an egomaniac who was given to posturing like Wellington and Napoleon, and F.D.R. did not like him. But MacArthur was one of the army's true professionals, and a superb commander. The country needed him to organize the long, difficult war ahead, and he promoted his mystique with his parting words to the Filipinos: "I shall return."

On May 6, the last ragged defenders of Corregidor surrendered. Humiliation in the worst military defeat in the nation's history gave way to furious anger when reports trickled into the United States of Japanese cruelty toward the prisoners on the infamous Bataan Death March. Of ten thousand men forced to walk to a prison camp in the interior, one thousand died on the way. (Another five thousand died in the camps before the war was over.)

Japanese Strategy

In the meantime, the poorly equipped but well-commanded Japanese moved on. Admiral Isoroku Yamamoto's plan was to establish a defense perimeter distant enough from Japan that the Americans could not bomb the homeland or force a decisive battle in their favor. By early May 1942, Japanese soldiers occupied the Solomon Islands, swarmed over most of New Guinea, and threatened Port Moresby on Australia's doorstep. There, however, the flood was dammed.

On May 6 and 7, 1942, the Japanese and American fleets fought a stand-off battle in the Coral Sea off Australia's northeastern shores. It was a unique naval encounter. The ships of the opposing forces never came within sight of one another; carrier-based aircraft did the attacking. Yamamoto claimed victory in terms of ships sunk and planes lost. But he had to abandon his plan to cut the supply lines between Hawaii and Australia and steam instead into the central Pacific. Japan's defense perimeter would not extend to the subcontinent "down under," but Yamamoto still hoped to capture the island of Midway, located about one thousand miles northwest of Hawaii.

There, on June 3 to 6, 1942, the Japanese suffered a decisive defeat. The American fleet under Admirals Raymond A. Spruance and Frank J. Fletcher lost the carrier *Yorktown* to the cheap but excellent Japanese fighter planes, the "Zeroes," but the Americans clung to strategic Midway and destroyed four large Japanese carriers.

It was more than a one-for-four trade. Unlike the United States, Japan lacked the wealth and industrial capacity to replace the fabulously expensive warships. After Midway, Japan's offensive capability was smashed. Much earlier than he planned to do, and somewhat closer to Japan than he hoped, Yamamoto had to shift to defending what had been won. The great commander did not live to see the disastrous end of the war. In 1943, having cracked the Japanese naval code, Americans learned that Yamamoto would be flying over Bougainville in the Solomon Islands. They shot down his plane, and Yamamoto was killed.

Concentration Camps at Home

Not even the most ambitious Japanese leaders entertained the possibility of invading the United States or Hawaii. Japan's goal was to force a negotiated Asian settlement on favorable terms. Nevertheless, the Japanese victories of early 1942 and the success of a few submarines in torpedoing ships off the beaches of Oregon and California caused ripples of invasion hysteria to wash over the Hawaiian Islands and the Pacific states. Newspaper magnate William Randolph Hearst hurriedly moved out of San Simeon, his fabulous castle on the isolated oceanfront north of Los Angeles. He had baited the Japanese with racial insults, calling them the "yellow peril," for fifty years and deluded himself into believing that his person was a prime Japanese target. Humbler but equally nervous citizens

organized patrols to keep an eye on the surf from the Canadian border to San Diego.

Fear of attack declined after Midway, but by that time Japanese-Americans already had suffered the single worst violation of civil rights in American history. On the west coast, the shock of Pearl Harbor, which was regarded more as an act of treachery than of war, coalesced with a longstanding resentment of Japanese-American prosperity and clannishness to result in a military directive (the Justice Department would not do it) to intern more than one hundred thousand people without regard to their political sentiments or citizenship. In a matter of weeks in February 1942, most Americans of Japanese descent were relocated in concentration camps in seven states. Government officials never proved the disloyalty of more than a handful of people, and in making ancestry and race the sole criterion for internment, the government clearly violated the Constitution. But tempers were so high that few people protested. In *Korematsu v. United States* (1944), a liberal Supreme Court upheld the action. At one point, Governor Earl Warren of California proposed excluding Japanese from his state permanently.

In many cases, the internees lost their property (in all, $350 million was lost) as well as their freedom. Things were equally harsh for Japanese-Americans outside the camps, who were often the subjects of attacks by racist thugs. In California and Oregon, Americans of Chinese and Korean descent took to

This girl was one of thousands of Japanese-Americans who were forced into concentration camps in 1942 without trial or substantial evidence of their danger to national security.

wearing buttons identifying their origins in order to avert such attacks.

In Hawaii, however, where about one-third of the population was of Japanese ancestry, the Nisei (American-born Japanese) were treated brusquely but not abused. A few thousand known sympathizers with Japan were arrested, but, as a vital part of the islands' work force, Hawaiian Japanese had to cope with only informal prejudice and the inconvenience of martial law. After repeated requests for a chance to prove their loyalty, seventeen thousand Hawaiian Nisei and some from the mainland fought against the Germans in Italy and turned in one of the war's best unit records for bravery.

The War in Europe

Treatment of conscientious objectors and the few people who opposed the war on political grounds was exemplary in comparison with the treatment of Japanese-Americans. Never did it approach the ugliness of the First World War. While some seventeen hundred known Nazis and Fascists were arrested, German-Americans and Italian-Americans were not persecuted as a people. In retrospect, this might appear to be surprising since the war against Japan was essentially a war for economic domination of Asia, whereas Nazi Germany was palpably a criminal state that—it was

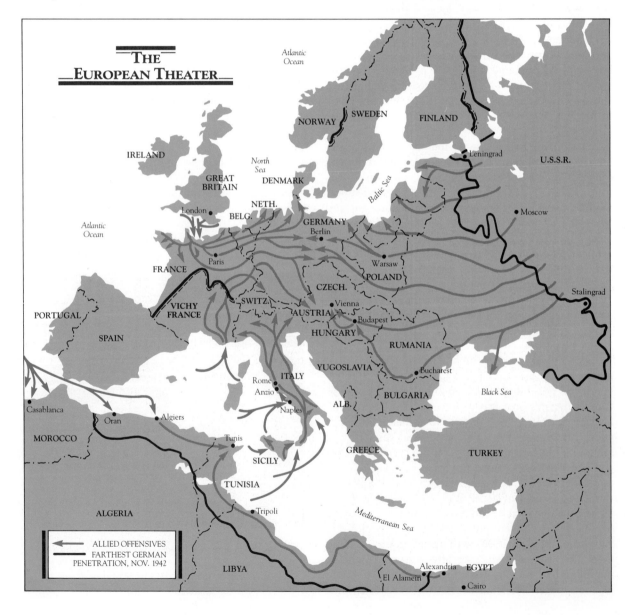

clear by 1943—was practicing genocide against Europe's Jews.

But the Japanese were of a different race from most Americans and had a vastly different cultural attitude toward war. Surrender was always a disgrace to the Japanese soldier, and the Japanese army treated American prisoners of war with contempt and cruelty. Americans thus found it easier to hate the enemy in Asia.

Defeating Germany First

Nevertheless, President Roosevelt and his advisers were committed to defeating Germany first, and with good reason. Germany threatened the Western Hemisphere; Japan did not. If either Russia or England collapsed, or if Hitler were allowed too much time to entrench himself on the continent of Europe, it would be almost impossible to destroy Nazism. Strategists realized that Japan must eventually buckle under superior American power, particularly after Germany was defeated and the British and Russian allies were able to join the United States in the Pacific.

SABOTEURS

The Germans attempted to put several teams of saboteurs in the United States from submarines, and there may have been some successful attempts at sabotage at defense plants. However, of 19,649 reported cases, the FBI was unable to trace a single one to enemy action. Between 1938 and 1945, the FBI arrested about 4,000 people, mostly German aliens, who were accused of espionage activities. Only 94 were convicted.

The first priority was to stop Hitler from increasing his control of the territory that Germany already occupied. To strike at German industry and the morale of the people, the United States army air corps (only later the air force) joined the British in constant day and night bombing raids over Germany. Eventually, 2.7 million tons of bombs would level German cities.

But Soviet Premier Joseph Stalin wanted action on the ground. His Red Army was barely hanging on along

The ruins of Dresden, Germany, following bombing raids by the Royal Air Force during February 1945.

a one-thousand-mile front in the east, and he demanded the British and Americans to open a second front in Western Europe so that Germany would have to withdraw divisions from the Soviet Union.

The Second Front

Both Churchill and Roosevelt agreed that Soviet Russia must be relieved. However, neither believed that a successful second front was possible without long, extensive preparation, and they differed about where their joint assault should be made. In order to allay Russian suspicions that he and Churchill hoped to see Germany bleed the Soviet Union to death, Roosevelt dispatched huge shipments of war material to Russia. Nevertheless, he had to cancel his provisional promise to Stalin to launch an attack on Fortress Europe in 1942.

From the beginning, American strategists wanted to open the second front in France, using England as the staging area. The British disagreed. Because the crack German *Afrika Korps* was threatening the Suez Canal, the vital link that held the British Empire together, the British wanted an assault in North Africa followed by a thrust into what Churchill called "the soft underbelly of Europe." Even more anxious to placate his British ally than to accommodate Stalin, Roosevelt agreed.

In June 1942, British Field Marshal Bernard Montgomery turned back a combined German and Italian advance at El Alamein in Egypt. In November, Americans under General Dwight D. Eisenhower landed far to the west in French North Africa, made a deal with French forces who, under pressure, had previously cooperated with the Germans, and moved eastward to join "Monty."

At Kasserine Pass in Tunisia in February 1943, American tanks fought a brutal battle with Field Marshal Erwin Rommel's seasoned *Afrika Korps*. They appeared to be stalemated when the "Desert Fox" was recalled to Germany. Then his army collapsed. American soldiers had participated in a signal victory.

About the same time, deep within the Soviet Union, the Russians had won a far more important victory, surrounding and capturing 250,000 seasoned German soldiers at Stalingrad. There seemed little doubt in any Allied capital that the course of the war had been turned against the Germans. Stalin's Red Army began to drive slowly toward Germany. However, he stepped up his pleas and demands for a second front. Roosevelt joined him in arguing with Churchill: "Uncle Joe," as Roosevelt called Stalin, "is killing more Germans and destroying more equipment than you and I put together."

Catch-22

In July 1943, an American, British, and Anzac force invaded Sicily. After initial reverses, they conquered the island in six weeks. Americans got a new hero to crow about: the eccentric General George Patton, who rallied his troops in coarse "blood and guts" language and was a personally brave, even reckless commander of tanks.

The fall of Sicily knocked Italy out of the war. Mussolini's enemies among Socialists and Communists were joined by the conservative Field Marshal Pietro Badoglio, who, disturbed that his country had become Hitler's pawn, ousted *Il Duce* and made peace with the Allies.

Nevertheless, the victories in Italy were far from decisive. Hitler rescued Mussolini from his captors and established him as the puppet head of the "Republic of Salo" in northern Italy. To take the place of the Italian troops who had gone over to the Allies, he rushed German units to easily defended strongholds south of Rome. It was mountainous country, and only after eight months of bloody, almost constant battle did the Americans reach the capital. The "soft underbelly" had proved as hard as Apennine granite; the second front was a failure.

A generation later, novelist Joseph Heller wrote a black-comic novel about the war in Italy called *Catch-22*. Its message was that a mentally disturbed soldier who wanted out of the horrible campaign was thereby demonstrating his sanity and could not qualify for a mental discharge. Grotesque as it was, Heller's image was by no means absurd. Germany itself would fall before the Allies made much headway up the boot. Nevertheless, the American fighting man proved his mettle in the frustrating campaign. Cartoonist Bill Mauldin immortalized him in a strip that recounted the adventures of Willie and Joe, two GI's in Italy who

---

IKE'S CONTINGENCY PLAN

Knowing that he would be busy on D-Day, General Eisenhower scribbled out the following note to be dispatched to Washington in the event that the invasion of Europe was a failure:

Our landings in the Cherbourg-Havre area have failed to gain a satisfactory foothold and I have withdrawn the troops. My decision to attack at this time and place was based upon the best information available. The troops, the air corps and the navy did all that bravery and devotion to duty could do. If any blame or fault attaches to the attempt it is mine alone.

wearily slogged on, no heroes, just ordinary men getting a job done.

Ike and D-Day

Because the Germans foiled the drive through Italy without withdrawing toops from the Soviet Union, the Red Army continued to suffer, and Stalin stepped up his insistence on a second front. By the beginning of 1944, General Eisenhower, headquartered in London, had the operation under way. "Ike" had put in a solid but undramatic military career. He was not a colorful man. A plodding administrator rather than a glamorous figure like MacArthur or a daring combat commander like Patton, he was affable, even tempered, and able to soothe sensitive egos and smooth over differences among headstrong associates.

They were these qualities that Army Chief of Staff George C. Marshall had in mind when he jumped Eisenhower over a number of senior officers to command the Allied forces in Europe. Marshall appreciated field officers. But he knew that modern warfare required the organizational and administrative talents of a corporation president.

Eisenhower was the perfect choice. He not only won the confidence of Churchill, a notoriously irascible character with whom to work, but usually could handle Montgomery, a prima donna who burned with envy of any superior. Ike dealt as well as could be expected with the proud leader of the Free French, Charles de Gaulle, and he made a fast personal friend of Soviet Marshal Georgi Zhukov. Eisenhower also was able to discipline Patton, without losing his services in combat, to the satisfaction of critics after that erratic general slapped a shell-shocked soldier.

Most important, Eisenhower supervised Operation Overlord, the extremely complex and largest amphibious attack ever ventured in war. The task involved mobilizing four thousand vessels, eleven thousand aircraft, tens of thousands of motor vehicles of various

General Dwight D. Eisenhower briefs a group of paratroopers about to leave for the coast of France where they would be among 1 million Allied troops who began liberating that country from Nazi control, June 6, 1944.

sorts, and weapons, as well as billeting and training more than 2 million soldiers. Such a massive operation did not go unnoticed by the Germans, of course, but the British and Americans successfully kept secret the date and, more important, the place of the invasion.

The date was June 6, 1944, and the place was Normandy in northwestern France. Eisenhower's caution and meticulous planning of every detail paid off. The Allied troops—1 million men—marched across France and into Paris on August 25. Immediately thereafter they entered Belgium. By September, they were across the German border, farther than the Allies had penetrated during all of the First World War.

Politics and Strategy

The British and Americans disagreed about how to finish off Germany. Montgomery wanted to concentrate power in one thrust into the heart of Germany, a traditional strategy that had much to recommend it. Tactfully, Eisenhower overruled him. In part his decision was military, reflecting his innate cautiousness and perhaps his study of the American Civil War. He feared that extending supply lines too quickly would tempt the Germans into a massive counterattack that might lead to disaster. He preferred to exploit the overwhelming Allied superiority in arms and men by proceeding cautiously. The western Allies would advance slowly on a broad front that extended from the North Sea to the border of Switzerland, strangling Germany as Grant had strangled the Confederacy.

Diplomatic considerations entered into Eisenhower's decision. Still absorbing tremendous casualties as they slowly pushed the Germans westward, the Russians remained suspicious of American and British motives. Stalin jumped at every rumor that his allies were considering a separate peace. Some American diplomats feared that too rapid an American and British thrust would only arouse Stalin's suspicions. On an earthier level, Eisenhower worried about spontaneous trouble between his soldiers and the Red Army if an orderly rendezvous were not arranged in advance.

The Bulge

For a while in 1944, it appeared that Eisenhower's strategy of advancing slowly was a mistake. In the summer, V-2 rockets from sanctuaries inside Germany began to rain down on London, killing eight thousand people. The V-2's were not decisive weapons from a military point of view, but with the end of the war apparently in sight, their psychological effect was disheartening to civilians. There was no warning, as there was in conventional aerial attack—only a whine high in the air, a few seconds of silence, and an explosion.

Much more demoralizing was a German military counteroffensive in Belgium in a bitter cold and snowy December. In the Battle of the Bulge, German troops pushed the Americans back, forcing a "bulge" in the German front lines and threatening to break the Allied forces in two. But an isolated army under General Anthony McAuliffe at Bastogne refused to surrender ("Nuts!" McAuliffe replied to the German commander), creating a weak point in the German offensive; after two weeks, the Americans advanced again. Delayed by about six weeks, the Eisenhower plan resumed. One by one German defenses collapsed. Along with his oldest and closest Nazi party associates, a Hitler close to breakdown withdrew to a bunker under the streets of Berlin where he presided over the premature destruction of his "Thousand-Year Empire." To the end, he thought in terms of the perverted romanticism of his ideology. He was involved in Götterdämmerung, the mythical final battle of the gods. On April 30, 1945, he committed suicide after having named Admiral Karl Doenitz his successor as *Führer*. A few days later, Doenitz surrendered.

Wartime Diplomacy

Eisenhower's sensitivity to Russian suspicions reflected President Roosevelt's policy. At a personal meeting with Premier Stalin at Teheran in Iran late in 1943, and again at Yalta in the Crimea in February 1945, F.D.R. did his best to assuage the Russian's fears by agreeing to most of Stalin's proposals for the organization of postwar Europe.

In after years, when the Soviet Union was the Cold War enemy and Americans lamented Russian domination of Eastern Europe, *Yalta* became a byword for diplomatic blunder and even, to a few extremists, treasonous "sellout." It was at Yalta that Roosevelt and Churchill consented to Stalin's requests that they recognize Soviet Russia's "special interests" in Eastern Europe, that is, governments friendly to the Soviet Union.

Right-wing extremists later said that Roosevelt sold out the Poles, Czechs, Hungarians, Rumanians, and Bulgarians at Yalta because he was himself sympathetic to Communism. Other more rational analysts ridiculed such conspiracy theories, but thought that the president's weariness and illness, obvious in the haggard face and sagging jaw of the official photographs, caused him to reason poorly in dealing with the shrewd Stalin.

Whatever effect Roosevelt's failing health had on his

Winston Churchill, Franklin D. Roosevelt, and Joseph Stalin pose for photographers at Yalta, February 1945.

mental processes, there was nothing unreasonable about his concessions to Russia. The recognition of special Soviet interests in Eastern Europe was simple realism. Roosevelt and Churchill did not give Stalin anything that he did not already have. In February 1945, the Red Army was racing over and occupying the very countries that Stalin envisioned as buffer states against renewed German aggression or other threats from the West.

The Twilight of Japan, the Nuclear Dawn

Also influencing Roosevelt at Yalta was his desire to enlist the Soviet Union in the war against Japan in order to save American lives in the final battles. While agreeing that the Red Army would attack Japanese forces in China, Stalin insisted on delaying action until the Soviet Union felt secure in Europe.

Pacific Strategy

After Midway in June 1942, American strategy in the war against Japan involved three distinct campaigns. First, just as the United States pumped material into Russia, supplies were flown into China from India, "over the hump" of the Himalayas, in order to keep the Chinese in the war. Unfortunately, Chiang Kai-shek was no Stalin, and his Kuomintang troops were no Red Army.

Chiang hated and feared his Chinese Communist allies as much as he hated the Japanese. He diverted thousands of troops to battling them, and never forced the kind of battle against Japan that the Americans needed in order to tie down the Japanese army on the mainland. In addition, inefficiency and corruption in Chiang's government resulted in misuse of American supplies.

General Joseph W. "Vinegar Joe" Stilwell, the gritty American commander on the mainland, despised Chiang. He poured out an avalanche of warnings to

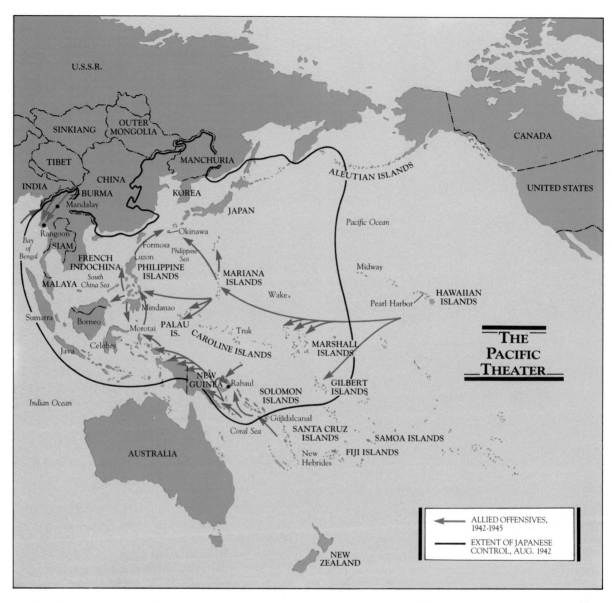

THE
PACIFIC
THEATER

ALLIED OFFENSIVES,
1942-1945

EXTENT OF JAPANESE
CONTROL, AUG. 1942

Washington about "the monkey," as he called the general. But when Stilwell tried to get command of the Chinese army for himself, Roosevelt recalled him. Somewhat to Churchill's amazement, Roosevelt was convinced that China under Chiang was a valuable ally.

The second and third prongs of the attack on Japan were more successful, but extremely bloody. After driving the Japanese out of the Solomons in order to ensure Australia's security, one force under MacArthur began to push toward the Japanese homeland via New Guinea and the Philippines, while another commanded by Admiral Chester A. Nimitz struck through the central Pacific, capturing islands from which aircraft could reach and bomb Japan.

Island Warfare

To soldiers slogging in the mud and frigid cold of Italy and France, the troops in the Pacific were on a picnic, basking in a lovely climate and only periodically meeting the enemy in battle. Ernie Pyle, the great war correspondent, made this comparison in his celebration of the American fighting man in Europe. (Ironically, Pyle was killed by Japanese machine-gun fire on Iwo Jima in the closing months of the war.)

Life behind the lines in the Pacific was pleasant, if not quite idyllic. But capturing islands that were specks on the map meant battles more vicious than those in Europe. The Japanese soldier was a formidable fighter. He was indoctrinated with a fanatical sense of duty and taught that it was a betrayal of national and personal

An apprehensive Marine photographed during battle against the Japanese on Peleliu Island, Palau, May 1945.

WORLD WAR II CASUALTIES

	Total mobilized	Killed or died	Wounded
United States	16,113,000	407,000	672,000
China	17,251,000	1,325,000	1,762,000
Germany	20,000,000	3,250,000	7,250,000
Italy	3,100,000	136,000	225,000
Japan	9,700,000	1,270,000	140,000
U.S.S.R.	—	6,115,000	14,012,000
United Kingdom	5,896,000	357,000	369,000
TOTAL	72,060,000	12,860,000	24,430,000

honor to surrender, even when his army was obviously defeated. Japanese soldiers were expected to fight to the death, taking down as many of the enemy as they could.

To an astonishing degree, this was how they fought. It took the Americans six months to win control of Guadalcanal in the Solomons after August 1942, even though the defenders had not had time to construct fortifications as strong as they had hoped to build.

In New Guinea and along the route through the Gilbert, Marshall, and Marianas islands that Nimitz was to follow, the concrete bunkers and gun emplacements were stronger than in the Solomons, and the resistance of the Japanese was chillingly effective. Marines discovered at places like Tarawa in the Gilberts in November 1943 that when a battle was over, they had few prisoners. They had to kill almost every Japanese on the island at high cost to themselves.

As MacArthur and Nimitz moved closer to Japan, the fighting grew tougher. Attacking the Marianas and the Philippines in 1944, both American forces were hit hard. But MacArthur's dramatic return to Luzon boosted morale, and Nimitz's capture of the Marianas enabled larger land-based American planes to bomb the Japanese homeland at will. The wooden cities of Japan went up like tinder when hit by incendiary devices. A single raid on Tokyo on March 9, 1945, killed 85,000 people and destroyed 250,000 buildings.

Fighting to the Last Man

By the spring of 1945, Japan's situation was hopeless. Germany was defeated, thus freeing hundreds of thousands of battle-hardened soldiers for combat in the Pacific. Although Stalin was procrastinating, the Japanese leaders believed that the Soviet Union was on the verge of declaring war. After the huge Battle of Leyte Gulf in October 1944, the Japanese navy had ceased to exist as a fighting force, while the Americans cruised the seas with four thousand ships. United States submarines, which were more effective than German U-boats ever had been, destroyed half of the island nation's vital merchant fleet within a few months.

And yet, the Japanese high command frustrated every attempt by civilians in the government to make peace. They were themselves victims of the extreme nationalistic fervor they instilled in their men, and they had 5 million in uniform. There were 2 million in Japan itself, and about the same number in China, where Chiang's half-hearted warmaking had been just enough to make them first-rate soldiers without inflicting heavy casualties.

With so many soldiers fighting to the death, the taking of islands close to Japan resulted in hundreds of thousands of casualties. Iwo Jima, a desolate tiny volcano needed for a landing strip, cost four thousand lives. The invasion of Okinawa, considered part of Japan, killed or wounded eighty thousand Americans. In the same fighting, more than one hundred thousand Japanese died, and only eight thousand surrendered. Saipan was even bloodier. Planners said that the invasion of Japan itself, scheduled for November 1, 1945, would cost 1 million casualties, three times more than the United States had suffered in over three years of fighting in both Europe and the Pacific.

A Birth and a Death

This chilling prediction helped to make the atomic bomb so appealing to policymakers. The Manhattan

THE LETTER THAT LED TO THE BOMB

In his own hand, to emphasize the importance of his message, Albert Einstein wrote to President Roosevelt in 1939:

Some recent work by E. Fermi and L. Szilard, which has been communicated to me in manuscript, leads me to expect that the element uranium may be turned into a new and important source of energy in the immediate future. Certain aspects of the situation seem to call for watchfulness and, if necessary, quick action on the part of the Administration.

Project, code name of the group that built the bomb, dated from 1939, when the great physicist Albert Einstein wrote to President Roosevelt that it was possible to unleash inconceivable amounts of energy by nuclear fission, splitting an atom. Einstein hated war. But he was also a refugee from Nazism who knew that German science was capable of producing a nuclear bomb. Such a device in Hitler's hands was an appalling prospect.

Einstein was too prestigious to ignore. The government secretly allotted $2 billion to the Manhattan Project. Under the direction of J. Robert Oppenheimer, scientists working on Long Island, underneath a football stadium in Chicago, and at isolated Los Alamos in New Mexico progressed steadily and, by April 1945, told Washington that they were four months away from testing a bomb.

The decision whether or not to use it did not fall to President Roosevelt. Easily reelected to a fourth term in 1944 over Thomas E. Dewey, the unexciting governor of New York, Roosevelt died of a massive stroke on April 12, 1945. He was at Warm Springs, Georgia, sitting for a portrait painter when he said, "I have a terrific headache," slumped in his chair, and died.

The outpouring of grief that swept the nation at the loss of the man who had been in office longer than any other president was real and profound. Silent crowds lined the tracks to watch the train that brought F.D.R. back to Washington for the last time. People wept in the streets of every city. But in Washington, the sorrow was overshadowed by apprehensions that his successor, Harry S Truman, was not up to being president.

Truman, Little Boy, and Fat Man

Truman was an honest politician who had risen as spokesman for the Kansas City machine of Boss Thomas J. Pendergast. He proved his abilities as chairman of an important Senate committee during the war,

but impressed few as the kind of person to head a nation. Unprepossessing in appearance and manner, bespectacled, something of a midwestern dandy (he once operated a haberdashery), and given to salty language, Truman had been nominated as vice president in 1944 as a compromise candidate. Democratic conservatives wanted left-liberal Henry A. Wallace out of the number-two spot, but could not force conservative James J. Byrnes on the liberals. They settled on Truman despite whispers about President Roosevelt's health.

Truman was as shocked by his accession as anyone else. "I don't know whether you fellows ever had a load of hay or a bull fall on you," he told reporters on his first full day in office, "but last night the moon, the stars, and all the planets fell on me." After a shaky start, however, Truman proved to be up to making difficult decisions and never doubted his responsibility to lead. A plaque on his desk read "The Buck Stops Here"; as the president of the United States, he would not "pass the buck."

Truman met with Churchill and Stalin at Potsdam in July 1945, informing them of the existence of the

It took the personal intervention of Emperor Hirohito to persuade the Japanese military to surrender to the United States. The official surrender took place aboard the battleship Missouri *on August 15, 1945.*

bomb. When it was made clear to him that the alternative to using it was a conventional invasion of Japan and 1 million casualties, he opted as Roosevelt always had, to avoid massive carnage. On August 6, an atomic bomb nicknamed "Little Boy" was dropped on Hiroshima, killing one hundred thousand people in an instant and dooming another one hundred thousand to death from injury and radiation poisoning. Two days later, when the Japanese leadership showed no signs of buckling under, "Fat Man" was exploded over Nagasaki.

Incredibly, the Japanese high command still wanted to fight on. But Emperor Hirohito stepped in and agreed to surrender if he were allowed to keep his throne. Because the Americans valued him as a symbol of social stability in Japan, they agreed. The war ended officially on the decks of the battleship *Missouri* on August 15, 1945.

Was the Bomb Necessary?

At first there was only wonder at a weapon that could destroy a whole city, and joy that the war was over. Within a few years, however, many Americans began to debate the wisdom and morality of having used the atomic bomb. When novelist John Hersey's *Hiroshima* detailed the destruction of the ancient city in vivid, human terms, some of Truman's critics stated that he was guilty of a war crime worse than any the Japanese had perpetrated and exceeded only by the Nazi murder of 6 million European Jews. Truman and his defenders

THE COSTS OF WAR

The Second World War was the most expensive war that the United States ever fought:

Revolutionary War	$149 million
War of 1812	124 million
Mexican War	107 million
Civil War (Union only)	8 billion
Spanish-American War	2.5 billion
First World War	66 billion
Second World War	560 billion
Korean War	70 billion
Vietnam War	121.5 billion

A view of Hiroshima after it was flattened by an atomic bomb, August 6, 1945.

RATIONING AND SCRAP DRIVES

A group of children, signaling a ''V'' for victory, display a pile of scrap metal collected for the war effort.

German submarines set a pair of four-man saboteur teams ashore in Florida and on Long Island. (They were immediately captured.) Japanese subs ran a few torpedoes up on California beaches, and several paper bombs, explosives held aloft and pushed by winds, detonated over Texas. Otherwise, the continental United States was untouched by the war that devastated most of Europe, half of China, and the cities of Japan. Considering the colossal scale of the American material contribution to the war, it is a remarkable testament to the nation's wealth that people on the home front experienced the war only in the form of shortages in consumer commodities and then not to a degree that could be called sacrifice.

Because the Japanese quickly gained control of 97 percent of the world's rubber-tree plantations in Malaya, automobile tires were the first consumer goods to be taken off the market. Washington froze the sale of new tires and forbade recapping early in 1942; the armed forces badly needed tires, and the national stockpile of rubber was only 660,000 tons, or just about what civilians consumed in a year. Huge quantities were collected in a scrap drive. One Seattle shoemaker contributed 6 tons of worn rubber heels that he had saved, and a Los Angeles tire dealer provided 5,000 tones of trade-ins. People cleared closets of old overshoes, and the Secretary of the Interior took to picking up rubber doormats in federal office buildings. Unfortunately, reclaimed rubber was not suitable to tire manufacture, and doormats were usually made of previously reclaimed rubber, so they were not very suitable even for new doormats.

It was fear of a rubber rather than a gasoline shortage that accounted for the first controls on driving, although, on the east coast, which was dependent on tanker imports, gasoline was also short by the summer of 1942. The president proclaimed a nationwide speed limit of thirty-five miles per hour, and all pleasure driving was banned. (Zealous officials of the Office of Price Administration jotted down license numbers at picnics, race tracks, concert halls, and athletic events.) In addition, the total miles a car could be driven was limited by the category of sticker issued to each owner. Ordinary motorists received "A" cards, entitling them to four gallons of gasoline a week, later three, and for a short time only two. A "B" card added a few gallons; these were issued to workers in defense plants for whom driving to work was necessary. Physicians and others whose driving was essential got "C" cards, a few more gallons. Truckers ("T") got unlimited gas, as did a few others, including political bigwigs who got "X" cards (a source of resentment). Counterfeiting and selling of gas cards (usually "C" category) was common, as was theft from government warehouses. The OPA discovered that 20 million gallons' worth of cards were stolen in Washington alone.

Surplus gasoline could not be collected, but just about every other commodity that was vital to the war effort could be saved, and was. Community organizations like the Boy Scouts sponsored scrap drives through 1942 and 1943, collecting iron, steel, brass, bronze, tin, nylon stockings (for powder bags), bacon grease (for munitions manufacture), and waste paper. Many of these campaigns were more trouble than they were worth, but not those that collected iron, steel, tin, and paper. Scrap iron and steel made a significant contribution to the national output, and about half of the tin and paper products came not from mines and forests but from neighborhood drives. So assiduous were the Boy Scouts in their scrap-paper drive of 1942 that in June the government had to call a halt to it; the nation's paper mills simply could not keep up with the supply of "raw materials."

The tin shortage was responsible for the rationing of canned goods. In order to buy a can of corn or sardines, as well as coffee, butter, cheese, meat, and many other food items, a consumer had to hand the grocer ration stamps as well as money. These stamps were issued regularly in books, and in effect they served as a second, parallel currency. In order to buy a pound of hamburger, a shopper needed stamps worth 7 "points" as well as the purchase price. A pound of butter cost 16 points; a pound of cheese, 8 points; and so on. The tiny stamps—which were color-coded red (meat, butter), blue (processed food), green, and brown—were a tremendous bother. More than 3.5 billion of them changed hands every month. In order to restock shelves, a grocer had to turn in the stamps to a wholesaler, who, in turn, had to deposit them with a bank in order to make additional purchases.

Everyone had a complaint of one sort or another, although, except for butter, the allotments were not stringent. For example, the weekly sugar ration was 8 ounces a person, about as much as a dentist would wish on a patient in the best of times. In 1943, the standard of living was 16 percent higher than it had been in 1939, and by 1945, despite rationing, Americans were eating more food and spending more money on it than ever before. Among the major foods, only butter consumption dropped appreciably, from seventeen to eleven pounds per capita per year, and some home economists believed that because of butter rationing, a larger proportion of the population was eating it.

In fact, the OPA noticed a curious fact about consumer habits in the cases of coffee and cigarettes. Coffee was rationed because of the shortage of ships available to carry it from South America. When rationing began in November 1942 (one pound a person per five weeks), people began to hoard it. At restaurants, some diners would trade their dessert for an extra cup. When rationing of coffee was dropped in July 1943, sales of coffee dropped! Then, in the autumn of 1943, when a coffee stamp was inadvertently included in ration books, Americans anticipated that coffee would be rationed again and stripped the market shelves bare. When the OPA announced that there would be no coffee ration, sales dropped again.

Cigarettes were rationed because 30 percent of the industry's production was reserved for the armed forces, which comprised only 10 percent of the population. The government was, in effect, subsidizing the smoking habit among the men and women in the service. At home, the operation of the principle that scarcity equals status may also have caused an increase in the habit.

A much more salutary consequence of wartime shortages was the popularity of gardening. There was no shortage of fresh vegetables, and they were never rationed. But because canned vegetables were and because truck and train space was invaluable, the government encouraged the planting of Victory gardens. Some 20.5 million individuals and families planted them, and by 1945, consumers were raising between 30 and 40 percent of all the vegetables grown in the United States. Nutritionists recognized that this was paying dividends in the national diet, but when the war was over, Americans quickly shed the habit. By 1950, they had returned to canned vegetables and to the frozen products of Clarence Birdseye.

replied that the nuclear assaults on Hiroshima and Nagasaki were humane acts since millions of Japanese as well as Americans would have been killed had Japan been invaded.

When other critics said that the Japanese surrender could have been forced by a demonstration of the bomb on an uninhabited island, as Secretary of War Stimson had suggested in 1945, defenders pointed out that no one was positive that the device would actually work. An announced demonstration that fizzled would have encouraged the Japanese die-hards to fight all the harder.

Much later, a group of historians who were called "revisionists" suggested that Little Boy and Fat Man were dropped not to end the war with Japan but to inaugurate the Cold War with the Soviet Union. Truman was showing the Russians that the United States held the trump card in any postwar dispute. Because history is not a science, capable of absolute proof, the debate over the use of the bomb will continue indefinitely. Only two things are certain: the atomic bomb did end the Second World War decisively and ahead of schedule, and it ushered in a new and dangerous epoch in world affairs, the nuclear age.

For Further Reading

The standard military history of the Second World War is A. R. Buchanan, *The United States and World War II* (1962), a huge and successful undertaking. A briefer survey is Fletcher Pratt, *War for the World* (1950), and a more extensive and, of course, somewhat weighted one is Winston Churchill's six-volume *The Second World War* (1948–53). A frankly personal account is Dwight D. Eisenhower, *Crusade in Europe* (1948). Neither Douglas MacArthur nor any of the commanders of the Pacific Fleet wrote a comparable account of the war against Japan, but Samuel Eliot Morison deals with it in detail (as well as with the war in the North Atlantic) in *The Two-Ocean War: A Short History of the United States Navy in the Second World War* (1963). Any good library will have a plethora of first-hand accounts of the experiences of soldiers and sailors.

Jack Goodman, *While You Were Gone: A Report on Wartime Life in the United States* (1946), while written as a chronicle of "current events," is still rewarding and illuminating reading. See also Richard Polenberg, *War and Society: The United States, 1941–1945* (1972). A number of insightful books on the Japanese-American internees have appeared in recent years. See Roger Daniels, *Concentration Camps USA* (1971), and Michi Weglyn, *Years of Infamy: The Untold Story of America's Concentration Camps* (1976).

48

America in the Early Nuclear Age
A Time of Anxieties, 1946–1952

Rarely had a war ended so abruptly as the atomic bomb ended the Second World War. Never had a new historical era been so unmistakably proclaimed as by the fireballs over Hiroshima and Nagasaki. During the final months of 1945, people sensed that the world had undergone a vital change, that the old rules and guidelines would not necessarily help them to negotiate the future.

But they had not left the past behind. History is legacy. The consequences of past actions live on whether or not people study the past. Three great legacies of the Second World War were so profound that they fostered anxieties that loom menacingly over the United States and the world to this day.

A radioactive mushroom cloud covers Bikini Atoll following a test of the atomic bomb, July 25, 1946.

The Shadow of Cold War

The first legacy of the Second World War was the atomic bomb that had ended it. Nuclear weapons made it technologically possible for man to destroy the world, an utterly novel circumstance in history.

The second legacy of the war was the discovery in the summer of 1945 that reports of genocide in German Europe had not been exaggerated. The Nazis had systematically exterminated 6 million Jews and probably 1 million other people in factories called "camps" that had been specifically designed for the killing and disposing of the bodies of the dead on a mass scale. The photographs and films of the walking skeletons of Da-chau, Auschwitz, and Buchenwald; the "shower baths" where the victims were gassed; the cremation ovens; the human garbage dumps, arms and legs protruding obscenely from heaps of corpses like discarded furniture: these shocking spectacles mocked human pretensions to enlightenment and decency such as no previous atrocity could do.

The capacity of humans for cruelty was nothing new. But the Hitler regime had gone beyond cruelty in coolly and deliberately applying modern technology and business methods to the destruction of human beings. The death camps were mass-production in reverse. Never again would it be possible to assume, as most of Western civilization had assumed for more than a century, that through reason, science, technology, and efficiency the human race was progressing toward a utopian future. If the atomic bomb showed that it was

Prisoners in a Nazi concentration camp await their release in this 1945 photo by Margaret Bourke-White.

technologically feasible to destroy the world, the death camps proved that governments and peoples were morally capable of doing so.

The third legacy of the war was that only two genuine victors emerged from it, and those two powers had little in common save for a now-accomplished desire to crush Nazi Germany. The United States and the Soviet Union faced each other across devastated Europe and East Asia, their other allies reeling almost as weakly as Germany and Japan. For about two years after the war, Russian and American leaders maintained the pretense of friendship and tried to some degree to come to an understanding that would govern postwar relations. By 1947, however, the two great powers were in a state of "cold war," belligerence without violent confrontation. At first, Americans were annoyed rather than frightened by what they believed was Soviet ingratitude and treachery. Their nation held the trump card, the atomic bomb. Then, in September 1949, the Soviets successfully tested a nuclear device. The total destruction of which humanity was capable seemed as likely to be unleashed sooner or later as not.

Background

The roots of the Cold War reached back even further than the Second World War, to the incompatibility of American determination to maintain an "open door" for trade and investment everywhere in the world, with the Communist determination to prevent capitalist economic penetration and free institutions on the Western model in Communist-controlled countries.

With such contradictory principles, the Soviet Union and the United States could form only a marriage of necessity. Both sides found themselves with a common enemy during the Second World War, and that was all that bound them together. At no time, despite good personal relations between Roosevelt and Stalin, did American or Russian policymakers believe that this conflict of interests had disappeared. People high in the American government continued to believe that Communism was a noxious ideology and that the lack of political democracy and individual freedom in the Soviet Union was an affront to common decency. The Russians, on the other side, remained suspicious of the intentions of the United States and Great Britain. Since 1917, the Western nations had isolated and threatened to destroy the revolution that the Bolsheviks had made.

During the war, personal friendships among the three leaders grew, but the old suspicions never died. Stalin was infuriated when Roosevelt and Churchill were slow to establish a second front in Europe. The Americans and the British worried that, after the war, Communist Russia would be a great power for the first time, in a position to enforce its will on its neighbors. Indeed, power may have been more important than ideology. Had Russia not been a Communist state, but had nevertheless emerged from the war as powerful as it was, there would most likely have been a similar Cold War—a conflict between two superpowers with interests throughout the world.

An Insoluble Problem

Roosevelt was confident that he could handle Stalin's frequently expressed determination that the nations bordering Russia be friendly to it. Although it is difficult to imagine what he had in mind, Roosevelt apparently believed that he could ensure that Poland, Czechoslovakia, eastern Germany, and the Balkan countries would be democratic, open to cooperation with the United States and merely friendly to the Soviet Union, not under Russian control as "satellites."

This was naïve at best. Political democracy, as it was defined in Roosevelt's and Churchill's Atlantic Charter, was alien to Eastern European history and culture. Moreover, some Eastern European countries, particularly Poland, had a long tradition of suspicion and hostility toward Russia. If the Western Allies suppressed the memory that the Soviet Union had joined Nazi Germany in invading Poland in 1939, the Poles did not. Indeed, Polish hatred for the Russians was given new life in 1943, when the Germans released evidence that the Red Army had secretly massacred five thousand captured Polish officers at Katyn in 1939.

In 1945, with Russian troops advancing rapidly toward Warsaw, the Polish government-in-exile in London called for an uprising behind the German lines. At this point, Stalin abruptly halted the Russian advance, and the relieved Germans were able to butcher the poorly armed rebels. Red Army soldiers were as brutal toward Polish civilians as they were toward Germans. A democratic Poland could not be subordinate to Russia in the sense that Stalin demanded Poland be. A Poland that was subordinate to Russia could not be democratically governed.

Roosevelt's confidence that he could solve this riddle on the basis of personal friendship with Stalin also required that he defy his own mortality, to which he should have been very sensitive in early 1945 as his health rapidly deteriorated. Nevertheless, he continued to treat diplomacy as a personal monopoly. When he died before the war was over, he left an inexperienced and uninformed Harry S Truman to make a settlement with Stalin.

Truman Draws the Line

Truman was not the sly manipulator Roosevelt had been. His virtues as a man and as president were his frankness, bluntness, and willingness to make and stick by a decision. Soviet suspicions that the new administration threatened Russian security festered and swelled after Truman had been tough with Stalin at Potsdam and, a little later, had scolded Soviet Ambassador V. M. Molotov so harshly that Molotov exclaimed, "I have never been talked to like that in my life!"

By March 1946, it was obvious that the Russians were not going to permit free elections in Poland. While Truman remained cautious in his official pronouncements on the subject, he gave full approval to Winston Churchill's speech that month in Fulton, Missouri. An "iron curtain" had descended across Europe, the former prime minister said, and it was time for the Western democracies to call a halt to the expansion of atheistic Communism.

In September 1946, Truman moved more directly. He fired Secretary of Commerce Henry A. Wallace, the one member of his cabinet who called openly for accommodating the anxieties of the Soviet Union. In early 1947, when the Soviets seemed to be stepping up their support of Communist guerrillas in Greece and Communist parties in Italy and France, Truman acted again. On March 12, he asked Congress to appropriate $400 million in military assistance to the pro-Western governments of Greece and Turkey. This principle of supporting anti-Communist regimes with massive aid, even when they were less than democratic themselves, came to be known as the Truman Doctrine.

On June 5, 1947, Secretary of State George C. Marshall proposed a much more ambitious program, which came to be called the Marshall Plan. The United States would invest vast amounts of money in the economic reconstruction of Europe. Not only would the former Western European Allies be invited to apply for American assistance, but defeated Germany (divided into two hostile zones), the Soviet Union, and the nations behind Churchill's iron curtain were also eligible.

Marshall and Truman calculated that Russia and its satellite states would reject the offer. By late 1947, Stalin's troops were firmly in control of the countries of Eastern Europe, including the one nation there with a strong democratic tradition, Czechoslovakia. Already in June 1946, Stalin had made it clear that he would brook no Western interference in areas under his sway. He turned down a proposal by elder statesman Bernard Baruch to outlaw nuclear weapons because the plan involved enforcement on the scene by the United Nations, which had been formed in 1945 under a charter that had evolved from the agreements of the various wartime Allied conferences.

The Americans had calculated correctly: the Soviets condemned the Marshall Plan. Massive American aid was pumped only into those countries where a political purpose could be served by overcoming the economic and social chaos in which Communism flourished.

Containment Policy

The policy of "containing" Soviet power was given coherent form by George F. Kennan, a Soviet expert in the State Department. First in a series of confidential memoranda, and then in an article signed by "Mister X" in the influential journal *Foreign Affairs*, Kennan argued that because of the ancient Russian compulsion to expand to the west and the deep Soviet fear of the capitalist nations, it would be impossible to come to a quick, amicable settlement with Stalin. American policy must therefore be to contain Russian expansionism by drawing clear limits as to where the United States would tolerate Russian domination—namely, those parts of Europe that already were under Russian control, and no more.

In Kennan's view, the Soviets would test American resolve, but very carefully. The Soviet Union did not want war any more than did the United States; it did want only as much control as it could exercise without war. In time, probably a long time, when the Russians felt secure, it would become possible to deal diplomatically with them and establish a true peace. In the meantime, the Cold War was preferable to bloodletting and the possibility of world destruction.

The containment policy worked in Europe. Neither Greece and Turkey nor Italy and France fell to pro-Russian guerrillas or Communist parties. The policy received its most severe test in June 1948, when Stalin blockaded West Berlin, deep within Communist East Germany. Unable to provision the city of 2 million by overland routes, the United States could have given up Berlin or invaded East Germany. Instead, a massive airlift was organized. For a year, huge C-47's and C-54's flew in the necessities and a few of the luxuries that the West Berliners needed in order to hold out. By this action, the Truman administration made it clear that the United States did not want war, but neither would it tolerate further Soviet expansion.

The Soviets responded as Kennan had predicted. Instead of invading West Berlin or shooting down the airlift planes, they watched. Once they had determined that the United States would not give in, the Soviets canceled the blockade in May 1949.

By that time, the Cold War had entered a new

A plane carrying supplies flies into West Berlin following a move by Joseph Stalin in June 1948 to block overland routes to that city from West Germany.

phase. In April 1949, with Canada and nine European nations, the United States signed a treaty that established the North Atlantic Treaty Organization (NATO), the first peacetime military alliance in American history. The NATO countries promised to consider an attack against any of them as grounds for going to war together. The Soviets responded by writing the Warsaw Pact, an alliance of the nations of Eastern Europe. In September 1949, the Soviet Union exploded its first atomic bomb, and soon thereafter the United States perfected the hydrogen bomb, a much more destructive weapon. The nuclear-arms race was under way.

Domestic Politics Under Truman

All the while Harry S Truman was designing and effecting a decisive foreign policy, he was struggling with little success to cope with postwar domestic problems. These were considerable: rapid inflation, a serious shortage of housing and a series of bitter industrial

disputes. At first he seemed to flounder. Professional politicians and ordinary voters alike began to suspect his competence. In his predecessor's regal shadow, Truman cut a second-rate figure. Compared with dynamic Eleanor Roosevelt, who was even more active in liberal causes after her husband's death, Bess Truman was a plain, frumpy homebody. The deadly serious nuclear age seemed to have caught the United States without leadership up to its challenges.

The Republican Comeback of 1946

Capitalizing on American anxieties about Truman, the Republicans ran their congressional election campaign of 1946 on a simple but effective two-word slogan, "Had Enough?" Apparently the voters had. They elected Republican majorities in both houses of Congress for the first time since 1930. One freshman Democratic senator who bucked the landslide, J. William Fulbright of Arkansas, suggested that Truman resign in favor of a Republican president. The Republicans did not take this proposal seriously, but, positive that they would elect their nominee in 1948, they sat back to wait out Truman's term.

Unfortunately for them, waiting involved doing nothing but try to reverse New Deal reforms and vote down Truman's proposals. Moreover, the election results shocked Truman, and made a new man of him. In contrast to his first two years in office, he emerged as a crusading liberal in 1947. If enemies mocked his homey manners and common appearance, he would turn the tables on them by becoming the common man, denouncing the Republicans as stooges of the rich and privileged. Behind his own slogan, Fair Deal, he vetoed eighty Republican attacks on New Deal reforms and sent to Capitol Hill proposal after proposal that expanded social services. Among his programs was a national health-insurance plan such as most European nations had adopted.

Civil Rights

The Truman health plan failed, as did the president's demand that Congress act to end discrimination against American blacks. In 1947, the Presidential Committee on Civil Rights reported to Truman on racial discrimination in the United States, particularly as it related to employment practices and the continued condoning of the lynching of blacks in the South. Truman sent its far-reaching recommendations to Congress, where an alliance of complacent Republicans and southern Democrats killed them. Truman responded with an executive order that banned racial discrimination in the army and navy, in the civil service, and in companies that did business with the federal government.

Truman's civil-rights program was moderate. He did not strike at the system of strict segregation that provided for separate public facilities for the white and black races in the southern and border states, including Truman's home state of Missouri. But he went further than Roosevelt had dared, and his program was politically very shrewd. Hundreds of thousands of blacks had moved out of the South, where they were politically powerless, into big cities in northern and western states with large electoral votes. For a Democratic president to continue to support segregation, as Roosevelt had done, was to risk throwing these big states to the Republicans, especially because none of the Republican party leaders had antiblack records and New York governor Thomas E. Dewey, the 1944 presidential candidate, was known to be friendly to black interests.

Give 'Em Hell, Harry

By the spring of 1948, Truman's popularity was on the upswing. Americans were getting accustomed to, even fond of, the president's hard-hitting style. Nevertheless, no political expert gave Truman a chance to survive the presidential election in November. The Democrats had been in power longer than any party since the Virginia Dynasty of Jefferson, Madison, and Monroe. The inefficiency of many government bureaucracies was undeniable, and the rumors of corruption were persistent. To make things worse, the party split. Henry A. Wallace led left-wing liberals into the newly formed Progressive party. He claimed to be the true heir of New Deal liberalism and insisted that there was no reason to abandon the nation's wartime friendship with the Soviet Union.

Democrats from the Deep South, angry at Truman's civil-rights reforms and an even stronger plank in the party platform written by the young mayor of Minneapolis, Hubert H. Humphrey, formed the States' Rights, or "Dixiecrat," party. They named Strom Thurmond of South Carolina as their candidate. Thurmond had no more chance of winning than did Wallace. His purpose was to deny Truman the election and thus impress on the Democratic party the necessity of sticking with their traditional support of racial segregation in the South.

Presented with what looked like a gift victory, the Republicans chose the safe Dewey over the controversial anti-New Deal conservative Robert A. Taft, and Dewey did just as the rules of electioneering said he should. As F.D.R. had done 1932, he ran a low-key,

THE 52-20 CLUB

Members of the 52-20 Club of 1945 and 1946 were demobilized soldiers and sailors who were allowed $20 a week for fifty-two weeks or until such time as they found a job. Although many were accused of avoiding work because of this payment, the average length of membership in the club was only three months.

PLANNING AHEAD

So confident were the Republicans that they were going to win the election of 1948 that the Republican Congress made a record appropriation for the inauguration festivities on January 20. The benefactor of the lavish parade, of course, was the Democratic president whom the Republicans despised, Harry S Truman.

Following his narrow victory in 1948, Harry Truman gleefully displays a newspaper that relied on early returns to predict his defeat to Republican presidential candidate Thomas Dewey.

noncommittal campaign. He would not jeopardize a sure win by saying anything that would alienate any group of voters.

Truman, faced with certain defeat, had nothing to lose by speaking out; "Give 'em hell!" a supporter shouted. During the summer of 1948, a corps of assistants led by Clark Clifford sent bill after bill to the Republican Congress. As Congress voted down his proposals, Truman toured the country, blaming the nation's problems on the "no-good, do-nothing" Congress. Did Americans want four more years of that sort of thing under a lackluster Thomas E. Dewey?

On election night, several complacent editors of Republican newspapers glanced at the early returns, which favored Dewey, and put out editions that declared the New Yorker to be the new president. The next day, Harry Truman took great pleasure in posing for photographs while pointing to their headlines. For Dewey had not won. Truman narrowly squeaked out victories in almost all the large industrial states and the majority of farm states. His popular vote was under 50 percent, and he lost a few Gulf states to Thurmond.

But he was president by a whopping 303 to 189 electoral-vote margin.

Containment in Asia

The Fair Deal did not fare so well as its author did. Like many presidents who had other things in mind, Truman found himself preoccupied with such serious problems abroad that domestic reforms seemed insignificant by comparison. Also like other presidents who became diplomats above all else, Truman discovered that he was not chief executive in world affairs, but only one player in a game in which the rules defied the power at his disposal and even his own understanding of them.

In Asia, only the Philippines and Japan developed as firm American allies. Given independence in 1946, the Philippines remained beholden to American financial aid and responded with friendship. In Japan, a prosperous capitalist democracy developed as a consequence of the absence of Soviet influence and interest, massive Marshall Plan-type assistance, and enlightened military occupation under Douglas MacArthur. Understanding the Japanese better than he understood Americans, MacArthur acted as shogun, or unofficial dictator, a familiar figure in Japanese history.

In China, however, containment policy failed. The principle derived from Kennan's theory—that Soviet expansionism and Communist infiltration lay at the bottom of all unrest abroad—simply did not apply to the civil war that broke out in China after the end of the Second World War. Kennan understood the difference between Europe and China and tried to point it out. Truman, the State Department, and the American public did not listen.

The Choice in China Policy

During the Second World War and after, two "governments" claimed to represent the will of the Chinese people: the Kuomintang, or Nationalist, regime of Chiang Kai-shek, and the powerful Communist party and military force behind Mao Tse-tung. Some Americans who were familiar with China urged Washington not to oppose Mao but to come to terms with him. During the war, General Joseph W. Stilwell repeatedly warned Roosevelt that the people around Chiang were

Chinese Communist party leader Mao Tse-tung (right) and a comrade in Yunan, 1938.

hopelessly corrupt and unpopular, while Mao commanded the loyalty of China's largest social class, the peasantry. From a realistic point of view, the United States should be friendly to Mao.

After the war, ambassador to China and later Secretary of State George C. Marshall suggested that the Chinese Communists were not necessarily tools of the Soviets but could be encouraged to chart an independent course through cooperation and friendship. Mao was bent on revolutionary change at home, particularly in regard to land, which was in the hands of a tiny elite allied to Chiang. Marshall, like many others who were familiar with the Nationalists, did not find Mao's program unattractive since the Kuomintang party included butchers of peasants and thieves who misappropriated American material aid for their own profit.

The "China Lobby"

Supporting Chiang's case was a "China Lobby" headed by his brilliant wife, Madame Chiang, who spent much of her time in the United States. This group drew support from conservative congressmen; influential church leaders such as the Catholic archbishop of New York, Francis Cardinal Spellman; and much of the press, most importantly Henry L. Luce, the publisher of *Time* magazine, and Clare Boothe Luce, a persuasive writer and speaker.

Through 1949, the China Lobby bombarded Americans with false information: most Chinese supported Chiang; Chiang was defeating Mao's forces on the battlefield; and Mao was a Soviet stooge. So effective was the China Lobby campaign that Americans were shocked when Chiang suddenly fled the mainland for the island province of Taiwan (then better known by its Japanese name of Formosa) at the end of 1949. They thought that Chiang had been winning the war. Instead of admitting that they had been wrong, at least in regard to the power of the Nationalists, the China Lobby insisted that Chiang had not been repudiated but merely betrayed by inadequate American support. They urged that he be "unleashed" for an assault on the mainland.

Truman and his new Secretary of State, Dean Acheson, knew better than to "unleash" Chiang Kai-shek. To have done so would have meant either humiliation when he was defeated or involvement in a war on the mainland of Asia, which every military strategist, from Douglas MacArthur on down, warned against. Whether Truman and Acheson ever rued the fact that they had ignored Stilwell's and Marshall's advice cannot be known. Whether American friendship would have significantly changed the course of Chinese history under Mao Tse-tung is also beyond certain knowl-

Madame Chiang Kai-shek lobbied influential conservative leaders in the United States to support her husband's effort to control mainland China.

edge. What is known is that China as a foe was dangerous and unpredictable.

Containment Policy Falters

Truman and Acheson were in the process of applying the principle of containment to East Asia when events left them behind. No one, including themselves, was quite certain about where the United States would accept Communist control and where the line of containment was to be drawn. Japan was off limits, of course, and so was Taiwan, as Truman immediately made clear. But what of Quemoy and Matsu, two tiny islands off the coast of China that were also occupied by Chiang's Nationalists? Dean Acheson was vague. And what of the Republic of Korea, set up by the United States in the southern half of the former Japanese colony of Chosen? Was the little country, bordered on the north by the thirty-eighth parallel (38° north latitude), to be protected like the nations of Western Europe?

The fact that American military strategists were on record as opposed to fighting a war on the Asian continent seemed to invite mischief. However, feeling the sting of the Communist victory in China, Truman was apt to think otherwise.

As it turned out, the decision about going to war in Korea was in the hands of neither the United States, China, nor the Soviet Union. Throughout the first months of 1950, the Communist government of North Korea and the government of Syngman Rhee in South

Korea exchanged ever more serious threats of war. In June, responding to South Korean troop movements, the North Korean army swept across the thirty-eighth parallel and quickly drove Rhee's ROK (Republic of Korea) troops to the toe of the peninsula.

The Korean War

Truman already had stationed an American fleet in Korean waters, and he responded immediately and forcibly. Easily persuading the United Nations to support his decision, he gave General MacArthur command of a "police action" against the invaders.

In a daring maneuver that might have served as the capstone of a brilliant military career, MacArthur engineered an amphibious landing at Inchon, behind North Korean lines, cutting off and capturing one hundred thousand enemy troops. The Americans and ROKs then surged rapidly northward, crossing the thirty-eighth parallel in September 1950. By October 26, they had occupied virtually the whole peninsula. American soldiers stood on the banks of the Yalu River, which divides Korea from Chinese Manchuria. Both Truman and the United Nations had approved this conquest of North Korea when the victories came easily and MacArthur assured them that the Chinese Communists would not intervene.

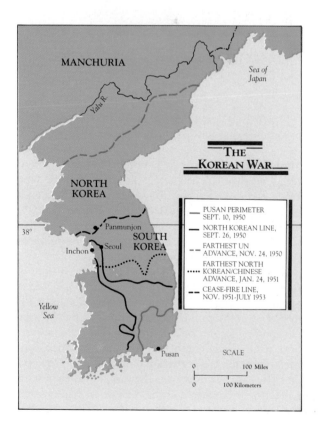

General Douglas MacArthur giving orders at the battle of Inchon, South Korea, in 1950.

MacArthur was wrong. Fearing the prospect of a powerful enemy army on the borders of a valuable province (the Japanese had invaded China from Korea), Mao Tse-tung threw two hundred thousand "volunteers" at the Americans. By the end of 1950, the battle-hardened veterans drove MacArthur back to a line that zigzagged across the thirty-eighth parallel. There, whether because the Chinese were willing to settle for a "draw" or because American troops found their footing and dug in, stalemate ensued. For two years, the Americans, ROKs, and token delegations of troops from other United Nations countries slugged it out to little effect with the North Koreans and Chinese. Both sides sustained high casualties for the sake of capturing forlorn hills and ridges that did not even have names, only numbers. Even after armistice talks began in a truce zone at Panmunjom, the war dragged on. The Chinese had won their goal, which was to protect their borders, and the Americans had ensured the independence of the Republic of Korea. Neither

side seriously attempted to end the war. Some days at Panmunjom, the negotiators simply sat at the table facing one another and saying nothing.

The Fall of MacArthur

With good reason, the American people were frustrated. The war put 5.7 million young men in uniform, killed fifty-four thousand, and wounded one hundred thousand. Defense expenditures soared from $40 billion in 1950 to $71 billion in 1952. Truman and Acheson had said that the goal was containment, but having accomplished that goal, they were unable to conclude hostilities. What was wrong?

In the spring of 1951, General MacArthur offered an answer. Forgetting his own warning against a war with the Chinese in China, and perhaps bruised in the ego by the stalemate, he complained to reporters that the only reason he had not won the war was that Truman would not permit him to bomb the enemy's supply depots in Manchuria. In April, MacArthur went further; he sent a letter to Republican congressman Joseph W. Martin in which he wrote that "there is no substitute for victory" and directly assailed the commander-in-chief for accepting a stalemate.

This violation of civilian command of the army appalled Truman's military advisers, and on April 11, with their support, he fired MacArthur. The American people, remembering the general's accomplishments in the Second World War and concluding that his war policy was the only sensible one, overwhelmingly cheered the old warrior upon his return to the United States. He was feted with ticker-tape parades in every city he visited, and addressed Congress in a broadcast speech that was listened to by more people than had tuned in to Truman's inaugural address in 1948.

MacArthur concluded his congressional appearance with a line from an old barracks song, "old soldiers never die; they just fade away," but he had no intention of fading anywhere. Establishing residence and a kind of command headquarters at New York's Waldorf-Astoria Hotel, he continued to issue political proclamations. He wanted and expected to win the Republican nomination for the presidency in 1952; then he would battle Truman's containment policy with his promises of victory in the Cold War.

STATISTICS: KOREAN WAR, 1950–53

Numbers engaged	5,720,000
Battle deaths	33,629
Wounds not mortal	103,284
Total casualties	157,530

But the great general was a poor politician. He had spent most of his life outside the country, and he was handicapped by a messianic vision of himself: the people would come to him. They did not. As the very able politician Harry S Truman had calculated when he had dismissed the general, enthusiasm for MacArthur faded within a few months. MacArthur was left to spend his final years in obscurity. In the meantime, the Korean War dragged on, chewing up lives like a machine.

The Anxiety Years

Historian Richard Hofstadter and others have pointed out that periodically in American history, during times of great stress, many people turn to "conspiracy theories" to account for their anxieties. The era of the Korean War was just such a time. Truman seemed to adopt a "no-win" policy; substantial numbers of Americans came to believe that the failure to achieve any security in the years following the Second World War was the result of widespread treason and subversion within the United States.

Twenty Years of Treason

The view that at Yalta, President Roosevelt had sold out Eastern Europe to Stalin was an early expression of this "paranoid streak," belief in a sinister conspiracy at work to destroy America from within. Then, in March 1947, President Truman inadvertently fueled anxieties by ordering all government employees to sign loyalty oaths, statements that they did not belong to the Communist party or to other groups suspected of disloyalty. Eventually, thirty states followed this example, requiring an oath even of people who waxed the floors of state university basketball courts.

Truman also promoted the belief that there was treason in government by allowing his supporters to "Red bait" Henry Wallace in the 1948 presidential campaign. Wallace was an eccentric (he had a weakness for bizarre religious ideas), and he may well have been mistaken in his analysis of Soviet intentions. But he was no Communist party stooge, as many Democratic speechmakers accused him of being. Moreover, if the Democrats could exploit fear of "the enemy within" in 1948, they created a political tactic that, in the end, could only work against them. If there were traitors in high places, the Democratic party was responsible, for, as of 1952, they had been running the country for twenty years.

Indeed, long before the campaign of 1952 was under way, frustrated right-wing Republicans such as John Bricker of Ohio, William F. Knowland of California, and Karl Mundt of North Dakota raised the specter of "twenty years of treason." The two chief beneficiaries of the scare were Richard M. Nixon, a young first-term congressman from southern California, and Joseph McCarthy, the junior senator from Wisconsin.

The Rosenbergs

The Soviet acquisition of the atomic bomb shocked Americans just as the fall of China did. They had been told that it would take Russian scientists a decade or more to catch up with the United States. A series of sensational arrests of Soviet spies in England and Canada seemed to provide the explanation for the rapid development of Russian science: the Soviets had stolen American nuclear technology with the help of American traitors.

The first and longest fought of the espionage cases involved two middle-class Communists from New York City, Julius and Ethel Rosenberg. According to Ethel Rosenberg's brother, who had worked as a machinist on the Manhattan Project, the couple had acted as a conduit for sending atomic secrets to the Soviet Union.

The Rosenberg case divided the nation. To many liberals and Wallace Progressives, the Rosenbergs were not convicted and sentenced to death for any proven acts (they both denied their guilt to the end), but for their Communist political affiliation. Civil-liberties groups believed that the Rosenbergs were the victims of an irrational hysteria. Administration liberals, however, prodded by conservative Red baiters, pushed through their conviction, and the two were executed on June 19, 1953.

Alger Hiss and Richard Nixon

The Rosenbergs were hardly powerful people. But Alger Hiss appeared to be just that. A bright, young Ivy Leaguer during the 1930s, when he had gone to Washington to work in the New Deal Agriculture Department, Hiss had risen to be a middle-level aide to Roosevelt at the time of the Yalta Conference. He was aloof and fastidious in his manner, and was a militant liberal.

RED SCARE

The police department of Columbus, Ohio, did its part in the fight against Communist spies by warning teenagers to be wary of "any new members of a group whose background is not an open book."

In 1948, a journalist named Whittaker Chambers, who confessed to having been a Communist during the 1930s, accused Hiss of having helped him funnel classified American documents to the Soviets. At first his testimony aroused little fuss. Chambers had a reputation for erratic behavior and dishonesty. From a legal point of view, there seemed scant reason to pursue the matter; all the acts of which Hiss was accused had transpired too long in the past to be prosecuted, and he was no longer in government services. It was Hiss who forced the issue to a reckoning. He indignantly swore under oath that everything Chambers said was false. Indeed, Hiss insisted, he did not even know Chambers.

To liberals, the well-spoken Hiss, with his exemplary record in public service, was obviously telling the truth. The seedy Chambers, with his background in Henry L. Luce's *Time* magazine, was a liar. But many ordinary Americans, especially working-class ethnics and citizens of western farming states, were not so sure. With his nasal aristocratic accent and elegant tailored clothing, Hiss represented the eastern Establishment, which they traditionally disliked, and the New Deal administrators, whom they were beginning to suspect. Congressman Richard M. Nixon shared these feelings and, following a hunch, pursued the Hiss case

Congressman Richard Nixon inspects microfilm of retyped classified documents found on Whittaker Chambers' farm that he used in his case against Alger Hiss.

when other Republicans lost interest. Nixon persuaded Chambers to produce microfilms that seemed to show that Hiss had indeed retyped classified documents for some reason, and, in cross-examination at congressional hearings, poked hole after hole in Hiss's defense. Largely because of Nixon's efforts, Hiss was convicted of perjury. Additional thousands of Americans wondered how many other bright New Dealers were spies. More than one Republican pointed out that Hiss had been a friend of none other than the "no-win" Secretary of State Dean Acheson and that the men resembled each other in their manners and appearance. Indeed, Acheson's style grated even more harshly than Hiss's. He favored London-made woolen tweeds and sported a bristling waxed moustache.

Joseph McCarthy

Acheson's loyalty was unimpeachable, and under his affectations, he was one of the most intelligent men in Washington. So great was the anxiety of the early 1950s, however, that he and even George C. Marshall were called traitors by a preposterous character who parlayed wild, groundless accusations into brief but vast political power.

This was Senator Joseph McCarthy of Wisconsin. In 1950, McCarthy told a Republican audience at Wheeling, West Virginia, that he possessed a list of 205 Communists who were working in the State Department with the full knowledge of Secretary of State Acheson. In other words, Acheson himself, as well as other high-ranking government officials, actively abetted Communist subversion.

McCarthy had no such list, of course. Only two days later, he could not remember if he had said the names totaled 205 or 57. He never released a single name, and never fingered a single Communist in government. Because he was so reckless, interested in nothing but publicity for himself, McCarthy probably was headed for a fall from the moment he stepped into the limelight. But the tumultuous response that met his use of the "big-lie" technique—making a complete lie so fabulous that people believe that it must be true—was an alarming symptom of just how anxious American society had become.

When a few senators publicly denounced him, McCarthy showed just how powerful he was. Senator Millard Tydings of Maryland was a conservative whose family name gave him practically a proprietary interest in a Senate seat in that state. McCarthy threw his support behind Tydings's unknown opponent in 1950, forged a photograph showing Tydings shaking hands with American Communist party leader Earl Browder, and the senator went down to defeat.

McCarthyism

Following Tydings's defeat, civil libertarians outside politics worried because senators who opposed McCarthy's smear tactics were afraid to speak up lest they suffer the same fate. By 1952, McCarthy was so powerful that Republican presidential candidate Dwight D. Eisenhower, who worshipped his former commander George C. Marshall and detested the vulgar McCarthy, refrained from praising Marshall in Wisconsin because the former Secretary of State was one of McCarthy's "traitors."

In the meantime, liberal Democrats in Congress rushed to prove their loyalty by voting for unnecessary and dubious laws such as the McCarran Internal Security Act, which effectively outlawed the Communist party, by defining dozens of liberal lobby groups as "Communist fronts," and even by providing for the establishment of concentration camps in the event of a national emergency. The Supreme Court fell into line with its decision in *Dennis et al.* v. *United States* (1951).

By a vote of six to two, the Court agreed that it was a crime to advocate the forcible overthrow of the government, a position that Communists were defined as holding by virtue of their membership in the party.

At the peak of McCarthy's power, only a very few opinion makers outside politics, such as cartoonist Herbert Block and television commentator Edward R. Murrow, and a few universities, including the University of Wisconsin in McCarthy's home state, refused to be intimidated by the senator's bullying. Not until 1954, however, did McCarthy's career come to an end. Failing to get preferential treatment for a draftee friend of his chief aide, Roy Cohn, McCarthy accused the United States army of being infiltrated by Communists. This recklessness emboldened the Senate to move against him. He was censured in December 1954 by a vote of sixty-seven to twenty-two. It was only the third time in American history that the nation's "most exclusive club" had turned on one of its own members, and McCarthy died in obscurity two years later.

Joseph McCarthy (right) and Joseph Welsh at the Army-McCarthy hearings.

ALGER HISS AND THE ROSENBERGS

Few events aggravated the anxieties of the late 1940s and early 1950s more than a series of spy trials, the most famous of which are still controversial. The first, the Alger Hiss case, was not properly a trial for espionage, but for perjury (lying under oath). The affair began in August 1953, when the House Un-American Activities Committee (HUAC) heard testimony from a *Time* magazine editor named Whittaker Chambers. It was not an important hearing, and was poorly attended, even by reporters.

However, Chambers got headlines when he accused Alger Hiss (b. 1904) of having been, himself, a member of the Communist party during the 1930s. This was sensational news because Hiss not only had been a high official in the administration of Franklin D. Roosevelt, but was acquainted with a number of even higher officials, including the Secretary of State at the time, Dean Acheson. Indeed, while not wealthy, Hiss looked the part of a cultured eastern aristocrat. He was somewhat snobbish in deportment, and had graduated from an excellent university (Johns Hopkins), and—many Americans thought—believed he had a right to a comfortable living. At the time Chambers dropped his bombshell, Hiss was the director of the Carnegie Endowment for International Peace, a liberal private foundation that was dedicated to finding ways to avert war.

Hiss had been forewarned of Chambers's testimony and immediately demanded that he be given a chance to deny his allegations under oath. So persuasive was he that despite the antiliberal predilections of every member of HUAC, they believed him. Not only did Hiss deny any Communist connections during the 1930s or at any other time, but he said that he did not have the slightest idea who Chambers was.

Although he too found Hiss impressive, freshman Congressman Richard M. Nixon of California was disturbed by the contradictory testimony of the two men. There was no possibility of honest error or misunderstanding; either Hiss or Chambers was a colossal liar. If the liar were Chambers, Hiss had a genuine grievance; his reputation as a public servant had been smeared, and he could not even sue Chambers because testimony before a congressional committee is privileged (immune from slander suits). If the liar were Hiss, it might well be that questions of national security were involved because, although he had been in the Department of Agriculture in the 1930s, Hiss had worked for the State Department during the Second World War and had attended the Yalta Conference.

In order to follow up the matter quietly, Nixon persuaded the chairman of HUAC, Karl Mundt of North Dakota, to allow him to question Chambers privately. During this hearing, Chambers revealed so much about Hiss's personal life that Nixon was convinced that Hiss was the liar.

Alger Hiss prepares to defend himself before the House Un-American Activities Committee in 1953.

In a series of face-to-face confrontations—readymade for dramatic presentation to the public—Hiss began to stumble and retreat. He admitted that he had known Chambers under a different name, had been friendly with him, and even had let Chambers live in his apartment and had given him an automobile. However, Hiss continued to deny the Communist connection and dared Chambers to make his accusation outside of the committee room, where he would be legally responsible for anything he said. If Hiss was bluffing, Chambers called it. On a national radio program, "Meet the Press," he repeated his accusation; after a delay that should have cautioned his defenders, Hiss sued for slander.

During this trial and a later one, in which Hiss was the defendant, Chambers produced a number of written documents that fairly conclusively proved that Hiss not only had lied repeatedly about his political past but had turned over government documents to the Soviets.

Hiss served several years in prison, but neither then nor later conceded that he was guilty of Chambers's accusations. This is not surprising. Once convicted of perjury, Hiss could gain nothing by saying otherwise. If, however, he was guilty—and the evidence is compelling—a question arises: Why did he bother to answer Chambers under oath and challenge him to a duel in which only he could be hurt? His reputation was excellent; Chambers's was not. Until the trials,

Hiss had solid support from liberals; it is unlikely that on the basis of the first Chambers testimony, which is all he planned to offer, HUAC would have pursued the matter, considering Hiss's reputation.

Because Hiss is an intelligent man, his actions have convinced some historians that he was indeed innocent of Chambers's charges and the victim of a cruel and convoluted plot. Others, however, have concluded that Hiss became panicked by the reference to past political associations and, much like other accused Communists during the era, mired himself more deeply in the ooze of deception. Ironically, the man who found him out, Richard M. Nixon, was to do the same thing a quarter of a century later during the Watergate investigation.

Hiss was convicted in January 1950, just a few months after the Soviet Union exploded its first nuclear device. Most of the nuclear physicists who had developed the bomb had repeatedly told the government that any number of scientists in other countries were capable of doing the same; they were not surprised by the news. But because Americans generally held Soviet science in low esteem, the conviction was widespread that espionage alone could account for the end of their nation's nuclear monopoly.

In February 1950, their suspicions seemed to be justified when the British arrested Klaus Fuchs, a Swiss-born scientist who had worked on the American bomb, and accused him of having turned over vital information to the Soviets. In May 1950, American authorities arrested Harry Gold, a chemist who had worked under Fuchs, and, shortly thereafter, a Brooklyn machinist named David Greenglass who, while in the army, had worked at the Los Alamos, New Mexico, site where the weapon had been perfected.

All of them eventually received long prison terms, but two more people identified as part of the ring, Julius Rosenberg (1918–53) and his wife, Ethel Rosenberg (1915–53), were put to death for treason.

Like Hiss, the Rosenbergs maintained their innocence until the end. Unlike Hiss, who never offered a reason for the accusations made against him, the Rosenbergs claimed that they were being persecuted because they held left-wing political sentiments and were, indeed, members of the Communist party.

"We are the first victims of American fascism," Ethel wrote in her last letter before her execution. Other critics of the trial, in which the evidence was not overwhelming, said that the two were the victims of anti-Semitism. Although American-born, both Ethel and Julius moved in an almost entirely Jewish world. They were not religious, but they spoke Yiddish as much as English and virtually all their friends were Jews.

Neither explanation of the Rosenberg case quite holds water. Had the trial been a means of prosecuting Communists, the government would have fastened on party leaders, not on the Rosenbergs. And although many anti-Semitic remarks made the rounds during the Rosenberg trial, the government was careful to appoint both a Jewish judge and a Jewish prosecutor to try the case. Moreover, all the important testimony against the pair was made by Jews who admitted to having been their confederates.

The underlying reason for exacting the ultimate penalty from these sad people may well have been their very refusal to confess. Gold and Greenglass, whose alleged crimes were identical to that of the Rosenbergs but who did turn state's evidence, were let go with prison terms. The late 1940s and early 1950s were not generally harsh on those people who, like reformed sinners, penitently owned up to left-wing sympathies in their pasts. Most of the victims of the House Un-American Activities Committee and of Senator Joseph McCarthy were those who, whether leftists or not in earlier years, refused to cooperate because of their insistence that their constitutional right to free political expression be guaranteed.

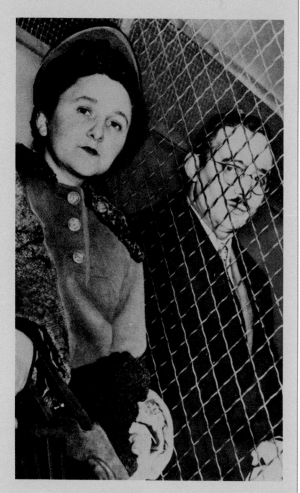

Ethel and Julius Rosenberg were convicted of treason and put to death in 1953.

Almost Everybody Likes Ike

Nixon and McCarthy built their careers on exploiting anxieties. To a certain extent, the personally dull leader of the congressional Republicans, Senator Robert A. Taft of Ohio, did the same. Taft encouraged his party's hell-raisers as a way of chipping at the Democrats. But the American people turned to no such political mover and shaker to take them through the 1950s. Instead, they chose a man with no political record whose strength was a warm personality and whose talent was the ability to smooth over conflict.

The name of General Dwight David Eisenhower was mentioned as a presidential possibility as early as 1948, when Truman told Ike that if he would accept the Democratic nomination, Truman would gladly step aside. Eisenhower was not interested. (He turned down the Republicans, too.) He was a career military man who, unlike MacArthur, believed that soldiers should stay out of politics. It is not certain that Eisenhower ever voted before 1948, and he identified with neither party.

After Truman's reelection and the Korean stalemate, Ike became increasingly distressed by the revelations of petty corruption among Truman aides, security problems, and the administration's apparent inability to end the Korean War. Moreover, Eisenhower naturally drifted into close professional and personal association with the wealthy eastern businessmen who dominated

Newly elected president Dwight D. Eisenhower and Vice President Richard Nixon wave to their supporters on election night, 1952.

the moderate wing of the Republican party and placed no ideology above the goal of defeating the Democrats in a national election. They showered Ike with gifts and financial advice. As an administrator himself, something of a businessman in uniform, Eisenhower found it easy to absorb their political attitudes.

Unlike Taft and his conservative midwestern backers, Eisenhower and the moderate wing of the Republican party did not intend to dismantle the government apparatus that had been created during the years of the New Deal, the Second World War, and the Fair Deal. They had come to terms with the America that Franklin D. Roosevelt had made. What disturbed them was corruption in government and particularly the excessive government expenditures and waste that led to high taxes. What impressed them most was that Eisenhower would almost certainly defeat any Democrat. His chief Republican rival, Senator Taft, probably could not.

Many conservative Republicans also supported Eisenhower over Taft. They were more interested in their party's victory than in honoring their veteran leader. Much as they admired Taft, they agreed with the Eisenhower moderates that the senator's uncompromising and frequently old-fashioned conservative statements would lose the votes of people who had benefited from the New Deal, but who were otherwise weary of the long Democratic era. Eisenhower's lack of a political record was an advantage. Even more attractive, he was immensely popular as a person. Almost everybody liked him ("I Like Ike" became his campaign slogan) because of his homey lack of pretension, his charming boyish smile, and his superb self-control that exuded both confidence and authority. He did not excite people; he reassured them. That was precisely what the nation craved in 1952, and the Republicans wanted to win an election.

The Election of 1952

Eisenhower's Democratic opponent was the comparatively obscure governor of Illinois, Adlai E. Stevenson. He was a liberal, but had taken no part in the increasingly unpopular Truman government. For a few weeks in the summer of 1952, it appeared as though Stevenson were catching up to Eisenhower. He was a personable, witty, and eloquent speaker, while Eisenhower, who functioned best in small groups, was bumbling on the podium.

But Stevenson labored under too many handicaps, and Eisenhower's shrewd campaign managers made the most of them. Stevenson was, after all, a Democrat and had to defend the Truman record or lose the president's support. Moreover, the Eisenhower forces turned Ste-

venson's intelligence and speaking skills against him. Ike and his supporters pointed out that "eggheads," or intellectuals, were responsible for "the mess in Washington." Finally, in October, Eisenhower ensured his victory by promising a way out of the Korean mess: if he were elected, he would "go to Korea" and end the now aimless war.

Stevenson won nine southern states. Although a supporter of civil rights for blacks, he brought the Dixiecrats back into the Democratic party by naming an Alabama segregationist, John Sparkman, as his running mate. Otherwise, Eisenhower swept the nation, winning 55 percent of the poplar vote and 442 electoral votes to Stevenson's 89. In December, he kept his promise. Eisenhower donned military gear, and was filmed talking and sipping coffee with soldiers in Korea. By recognizing that an all-out conventional offensive was foolish and by threatening to use the atomic bomb, he brought the hostilities to a close in July 1953. Eisenhower had not actually modified the concept of fighting a limited war that had been supported by Truman and Acheson. The Korean War ended with the acceptance of stalemate and satisfaction with containment rather than with the victory that MacArthur had demanded. With the termination of the war and the death in March 1953 of Soviet dictator Joseph Stalin, the 1950s promised to be a decade of normalcy.

For Further Reading

No single book about the conclusion of the Second World War and the inauguration of the Cold War is accepted as uncontroversial and definitive since the issues involved are still so heavily weighted with political partisanship. On the background of the problem, see Gaddis Smith, *American Diplomacy During the Second World War* (1965); J. L. Snell, *Illusion and Necessity: The Diplomacy of Global War* (1963); W. R. Deane, *The Strange Alliance* (1947); and H. W. Baldwin, *Great Mistakes of the War* (1950). Herbert Feis, *Churchill, Roosevelt, and Stalin* (1967), offers a judicious view. Gar Alperovitz, *Atomic Diplomacy: Hiroshima and Potsdam* (1965), has been extremely influential in recent debates among historians. Influential at the time and still a minor masterpiece is John Hersey, *Hiroshima* (1946).

On the Truman administration, see R. F. Haynes, *The Awesome Power: Harry S Truman as Commander in Chief* (1973), and Truman's own trenchant *Memoirs* (1955–56). Carl Berger, *The Korea Knot: A Military-Political History* (1957), and G. D. Paige, *The Korean Decision, June 24–30, 1950* (1968), add some information to the standard study of the subject, David Rees, *Korea: The Limited War* (1964).

On Senator Joseph McCarthy, the oldest book remains the most authoritative, Richard H. Rovere, *Senator Joe McCarthy* (1959).

49

Eisenhower's America
Life in the 1950s

The voters of 1952 wanted no upheaval. They wanted a change of pace. Almost all Americans accepted the Cold War with Communism as a national necessity, but they wanted an end to the stalemate in Korea. Most Americans approved of the social changes that the Roosevelt and Truman administrations had carried out; they did not want to return to the days of Coolidge and Hoover. But after a generation of Democratic party government, they were ready for new faces in Washington.

Most of all, Americans wanted to cool off. They wanted no more excitement, the intense moral demands of reform and war. There is a sense of 1920 about the election of 1952, of people opting for a reassuring America in which they could enjoy the rewards of living in the world's richest nation.

The suburban communities that sprung up across the United States during the 1950s were characterized by rows of nearly identical single-family houses.

Leadership

This reassurance is what Dwight D. Eisenhower gave them. The grinning, amiable Ike was the perfect leader for the times. He ended the Korean War and kept the peace through two full terms in office. He replaced the jaded political pros, earnest intellectuals, and reform-minded liberals of the Democratic years with administrators like himself, and with the wealthy businessmen who had become his friends.

They were neither colorful nor exciting. "Eight millionaires and a plumber," a scornful Democrat sniffed about Eisenhower's cabinet, and Secretary of Labor Martin Durkin, the leader of the AFL plumbers union, resigned within a year of his appointment to be replaced by another rich businessman. When Congress created the cabinet-level Department of Health, Education, and Welfare, Eisenhower's choice to head it was not a social worker with a cause to serve, but Oveta Culp Hobby, head of the Women's Army Corps during the Second World War, a military bureaucrat like himself.

Ike's Style and Its Critics

Eisenhower's style was calculated to soothe. Rather than leaping into political cat fights with claws flashing, which had been Truman's way, Ike sidled away from disputes and left the shouting to subordinates. His special assistant, Sherman Adams of New Hampshire, screened every person who applied to see the president. Adams turned away anyone who might involve Ike in a controversy, or trick him into making an embarrassing statement, which Eisenhower was inclined to do. Adams also studied every document that crossed the president's desk, weeding out those he thought trivial and summarizing the rest. Eisenhower disliked reading more than a page on any subject, a "brief" such as he had dealt with in the army.

Critics claimed that Adams was more powerful than an appointed official should be. They said that he made many presidential-level decisions himself, and he probably did. But there was never any doubt that the thin-lipped New Englander had Eisenhower's complete confidence. In 1958, when it was learned that Adams had rigged some government decisions in favor of a long-time friend, businessman Bernard Goldfine, and he was forced to resign his post, Eisenhower bitterly resented the loss of his right-hand man.

The president also delegated considerable power to the members of his cabinet. They were expected to study the details of issues, report to him, and if they disagreed among themselves, debate. Ike listened and handed down the final decision. Whenever possible, he preferred compromise to backing one adviser against another. That was how he had worked in the army. That was how, he believed, an administration should function.

Liberal Democrats and intellectuals, outsiders in Washington during the 1950s, poked fun at Eisenhower's losing battle with the English language. Not a reflective man and never comfortable before a large audience, Eisenhower lapsed into gobbledygook under pressure. His critics also accused Eisenhower of not leading America. The nation was merely drifting, while Ike relaxed on his model farm on the battlefield at Gettysburg, and took too many vacations in sunny climates where he could play golf.

The majority of Americans, however, did not object to a president who enjoyed himself. They were enjoying themselves too, and were delighted with the easygoing pace of the White House. In 1956, when Ike ran for reelection against Adlai Stevenson, a year after suffering a serious heart attack and just a few months after undergoing major abdominal surgery, the voters reelected him by an even larger margin than in 1952. Better Ike in questionable health than Stevenson, who was inculcated with New Deal ideas about reform and might unsettle a tranquil decade.

We're in the Money

For a majority of Americans, the 1950s were good times, an age of unprecedented prosperity. There had not been a shift in the distribution of wealth. The poor remained about as numerous as they had been for decades. The lowest-paid 20 percent of the population earned the same 3 to 4 percent of the national income that they had earned during the 1920s. The very rich held on to their big slice of the economic pie: the wealthiest 20 percent of the population continued to enjoy 44 to 45 percent of the national income. Proportionately, therefore, the middle 60 percent of the population were no better off than before.

What made the difference was the size of the pie in which all were sharing. America was vastly richer as a result of the extraordinary economic growth of the Second World War decade. Thanks to New Deal tax reforms and the powerful labor unions that protected one worker in three, Americans in the middle found themselves with a great deal of "discretionary income," money that was not needed to provide the immediate necessities of life. In 1950, discretionary income totaled $100 billion compared with $40 billion in 1940. This sum increased steadily throughout the decade.

Traditional values of thrift and frugality dictated that such extra money be saved or invested. However, with a generation of daily denial behind them—the hard times of the Great Depression and the sacrifices demanded by the Second World War—newly affluent Americans itched to spend their riches on goods and services that made life more comfortable, varied, and stimulating. A host of new consumer-oriented industries cropped up to urge them on.

Enjoy Yourself

"Enjoy yourself," a popular song went. "It's later than you think." Americans did. They lavished their extra money on a cornucopia of goods and services—some trivial, some momentous in their consequences, and most designed to amuse and entertain people in their spare time. The middle classes upgraded their diets, eating more meat and vegetables and fewer of the bulk starchy foods (bread and potatoes) that had nourished their parents. Mass-produced convenience foods such as frozen vegetables became staples of middle-class diet. They could be cooked in five or ten minutes, freeing people to enjoy additional leisure time.

Fashion in dress, buying clothing in order to be "in style," became a diversion in which tens of millions rather than just a handful of very rich people could indulge. Mass-producers of clothing imitated the creations of Paris couturiers with affordable department-store versions of "the latest," and the designers encouraged the impulse to be a step ahead of neighbors by changing styles almost annually. More people were able to identify the name of Christian Dior (a French clothing designer) than the members of Eisenhower's cabinet.

The 1950s were a time of fads, frivolous behavior in which people participated for no better reason than they could afford to do so or because others were. In late 1954, a Walt Disney television program about the nineteenth-century frontiersman and politician Davy Crockett inspired a mania for coonskin caps (usually made from rabbit or synthetic fur), lunch boxes decorated with pictures of Davy shooting bears, and plastic "long rifles" and bowie knives for use in backyard Alamos. Virtually any homely object with the magic name printed on it became a best seller. Within six months, Americans spent more than $100 million in memory of the Tennessee adventurer.

In 1958, a toy manufacturer brought out a plastic version of an Australian exercise device, a hoop that was twirled about the hips through hulalike gyrations. Almost overnight, 30 million "hula hoops" were sold for $1.98 (and, after the fad declined, for as little as fifty cents).

To some extent, the numerous manias of the 1950s were instigated and promoted by the advertising industry. For example, chlorophyll became the rage of the early 1950s when manufacturers of more than ninety products, ranging from chewing gum through soap and dog food, said that the organic green chemical improved the odor of the breath and body of those who chewed, ate, shampooed, or bathed in it. Americans responded by spending $135 million on chlorophyll products. The boom may have busted when the American Medical Association pointed out that goats, notoriously ill smelling, ate chlorophyll all day, every day. More likely, like all fads, chlorophyll disappeared when it simply ran its course.

Other fads profited no one but the newspaper and magazines that reported them. College students competed to see how many of them could squeeze into a telephone booth or a minuscule Volkswagen automobile, challenging others to top their record. Such behavior worried social critics. They concluded that inane faddism revealed the emptiness of lives based on material consumption: people defined themselves in terms of what they could buy. Others were distressed by the conformism of which fads were only the most bizarre example. The American people, it seemed, would do anything and think anything that they were told to do and think, or that others were doing and thinking. But they were afraid of the eccentric, the unpopular, and the adventurous.

The Tube

The most significant new consumer bauble of the 1950s, which became one of the greatest forces for conformism, was the home television receiver. Developed in workable form as early as 1927, "radio with a picture" remained a toy of electronics hobbyists and the very wealthy until after the Second World War. In 1946, there were only eight thousand privately owned receivers in the United States, about one for every eighteen thousand people.

Then, gambling that Americans were ready to spend their extra money on a new kind of entertainment, the

TELEVISION IN AMERICA		
	Number of TV Households	Percentage of American Homes with TV
1950	3,880,000	9.0
1955	30,700,000	64.5
1960	45,750,000	87.1
1970	59,550,000	95.2
1978	72,900,000	98.0

*Children born in the 1950s were the first generation of Americans
to grow up with television.*

radio networks plunged into television, making more extensive programming available. By 1950, almost 4 million sets had been sold, one for every thirty-two people in the country. By 1970, more American households were equipped with a television set than had refrigerators, bathtubs, or indoor toilets. Never in history did a whole society fall so suddenly and hopelessly in love with a device.

The social and cultural consequences of America's marriage to "the tube" are still not fully appreciated.

TELEVISION AND THE MOVIES

In 1946, 82 million Americans went to the movies each week. Ten years later, only about half that many did. The others were at home watching television.

In the short run, television seemed to destroy older kinds of popular entertainment such as the movies, social dancing, and radio. Hollywood studios that specialized in churning out low-budget films for neighborhood theaters went bankrupt when empty neighborhood theaters closed their doors and decayed. However, prestigious movie companies such as Metro-Goldwyn-Mayer, Columbia Pictures, and Warner Brothers survived and prospered by concentrating on expensive, grandiose epics that could not be duplicated on the small black-and-white home screen; by experimenting with themes that were thought unsuitable for showing in homes; and, in the 1960s, by producing shows for home television.

The "big bands" that had toured the country playing for local dances since the 1930s broke up when deserted dance halls closed. But the recorded music industry survived and prospered in the age of television by emphasizing individual ballad singers, such as Perry Como, Jo Stafford, Patti Page, and Frankie Laine, who promoted sales of their recordings on television. Radio stations adapted to the big change by scrapping the dramatic and comedy shows that television could do with pictures and offering instead a format of music, news, and weather aimed at people who were driving their cars or working and could not, during those hours, watch television.

Curiously, the "one-eyed monster" did not much change the reading habits of older Americans. Americans were soon staring into the flickering blue light for three hours a day. However, the time they devoted to magazines and newspapers declined very little, and purchases of books, particularly the cheap paperback editions, rose 53 percent over what they had been during the 1940s.

Social Consequences of Television

What older Americans cut out in order to watch television was socializing with one another. Instead of chatting with neighbors or with other members of their families, Americans watched "Mr. Television," Milton Berle, a burlesque comic who became a national sensation; situation comedies about white middle-class families supposedly like themselves; and particularly Westerns. The networks tried out forty dramas set in the Wild West as Americans liked to imagine it. One of the first, "Gunsmoke," ran through 635 half-hour episodes; it was estimated that one-quarter of the world's population saw at least one program in which Marshall Matt Dillon made Dodge City, Kansas, safe for decent law-abiding citizens. A less popular show, "Death Valley Days," revived the career of Ronald Reagan, and set him off on a trail that led to the White House.

Even movies and dances, social critics pointed out, had gotten people out of the house and talking to one another. Now they seemed to barricade themselves in, hushing up or resenting all interruptions. The frozen-food industry invented the "TV dinner," a complete meal that could be put in and taken out of the oven during commercials or station breaks and eaten in silence in front of the set on a "TV table," a metal tray on folding legs, one for each member of the family.

Fears for the Future

Early hopes for the educational potential of the new communications medium were dashed when people expressed a preference for frothy entertainment that demanded nothing but that a person watch. More worrisome to educators was the passive enthusiasm with which children born in the television age were en-

slaved to the tube. Networks and local stations filled late-afternoon hours and much of Saturday and Sunday mornings with programs that were aimed at children (sponsored by toymakers and manufacturers of breakfast cereals and sweets). If adults who had grown up before the advent of television continued to read, children did not. In 1955, a book by Rudolf Fleisch called *Why Johnny Can't Read* presented Americans with disturbing evidence that they were raising a generation of functional illiterates.

Nevertheless, and regardless of class, race, occupation, or region, Americans took television to their hearts. For good or ill, they were exposed at the same moment to the same entertainment, commercials, and even speech patterns. National businesses discovered that they could compete with local merchants thanks to the hypnotic influence of television advertising.

During the 1960s, American towns began to look alike with the growth of chain supermarkets and national franchise companies that drove family-owned businesses into bankruptcy.

Because the network and even local news programs preferred announcers who spoke "standard American English," regional variations in speech declined. City people and country people, who had been sharply divided by hostile world views in the previous generation, came to look, speak, and think alike. However, neither country folk nor city folk set the cultural tone of the age of Eisenhower. The people who did were pioneers of a new kind of American community, the middle-class suburb.

Suburbia and Its Values

The essence of the good life, to Americans of the 1950s, was to escape from the cities (and the country) and set up housekeeping in single-home dwellings in the suburbs. In part, this massive movement of population in the late 1940s and 1950s was an expression of an antiurban bias that dates back to the nation's rural beginnings. As a people, Americans never have been quite comfortable with city life.

Flight from the Cities

In part, young couples of the postwar period had little choice as to where they would live. The Second World War had forced millions of them to delay marrying and starting a family for up to four years. In 1945 and 1946, they rushed into marriage, childbearing, and searching for a place to live. But because of the stagnation of domestic construction during the depression and the war, when young couples looked for housing in the cities, they found impossibly high rents and real-estate prices. To demolish old neighborhoods as a first step in construction meant temporarily worsening an already critical housing shortage. The solution was the rapid construction of whole new "tracts" or "developments" on the outskirts of cities, far enough from the centers that the price of land was reasonable, but close enough that breadwinners could get to their jobs. Of the 1 million housing starts in 1946 and the 2 million in 1950 (compared with 142,000 in 1944), the vast majority was in the suburbs.

The first of the great suburban developments was Levittown, New York, the brainchild of a family company that adapted the assembly line to home building. In order to keep selling prices low, the Levitt brothers used cheap materials and only a few different blueprints. The houses of suburbia were identical, constructed all at once and very quickly. Armies of workers swarmed over the tract, grading thousands of acres at a sweep, and laying out miles of gently curving streets within a few days. Practically before they were done, batallions of men laid down water, gas, sewer, and electrical lines, while teams of carpenters erected hundreds of simple, identical shells.

Then came waves of roofers, plumbers, electricians, carpet layers, painters, decorators, and other craftsmen, each finishing their specialized task on a given house within hours or even minutes. Buyers were so anxious to move in that they were happy to take care of the cleaning up and landscaping. Within four years, Levittown, New York, was transformed from a potato farm into a city of seventeen thousand homes. On the outskirts of most large cities, developers who imitated the Levitts worked similar miracles of construction. The population of suburbs, never more than a small fraction of the whole, soared. By 1960, as many Americans lived in suburbs as in large cities.

Conformists . . . ?

No sooner did suburbia take shape than it attracted social and cultural criticism. Novelists and sociologists pointed out that the population of the new communities was distressingly homogeneous: 95 percent white, young (twenty to thirty-five years old), married couples with infant children who made roughly the same income from similar skilled and white-collar jobs.

Not only did the flight from the center cities leave urban centers to the elderly, the poor, and the racial minorities—a poor tax base—but it segregated the suburbanites too, cutting them off from interaction with other ages, classes, and races of people. Homogeneous communities were narrow-minded communities, critics said; suburbia's values were timid, bland, and superficial.

In politics, people whose comforts and security were made possible by New Deal reforms were afraid to experiment. The suburbanites were staunch supporters of Eisenhower calm. They swelled the membership lists of churches and synagogues, but insisted on easy, undisturbing beliefs. Rabbi Joshua Liebman, Catholic Bishop Fulton J. Sheen, and Norman Vincent Peale told the people of the three major faiths that the purpose of religion was to make them feel good: they, and no supreme being or eternal values, were at the center of the universe. The Reverend Billy Graham established himself as the country's leading revivalist by shunning the fire and brimstone of earlier evangelists and promoting his good looks and beautiful smile. A survey of Christians showed that while 80 percent believed that the Bible was the revealed word of God, only 35 percent could name the authors of the four gospels and 50 percent could not name one. Among Jews, highly secular and social Reform Judaism displaced Conservative Judaism, and Orthodox Judaism declined to the status of an anachronistic sect.

Suburban life was isolated and fragmented, in part because of television, in part because the new communities were built with little thought for social services—schools, shops, parks, professional offices. When such traditional social centers were constructed, they were miles from residences; thus suburbanites had to drive some distance even to buy a quart of milk. As a result, the suburban single-family dwelling became a kind of fortress that residents left only to hop into a car and drive somewhere else and back again. The super-

---

INTEGRATED NEIGHBORHOODS

Independent political organizer Saul Alinsky described the pattern of racial segregation in American cities in *Reveille for Radicals* in 1946: "A racially integrated community is a chronological term timed from the entrance of the first black family to the exit of the last white family."

MEMBERSHIP IN AMERICAN CHURCHES:
1845–1970
(thousands)

	1845	1895	1925	1950	1970
Methodist	995	3,990	7,066	8,936	10,672
Southern Baptist	352	1,469	3,649	7,080	11,629
Presbyterian	172	903	1,829	2,364	3,096
Roman Catholic	—	9,078	18,654	27,766	47,872

markets encouraged weekly rather than daily shopping expeditions, thus eliminating another traditional occasion of social life.

. . . Or Social Pioneers?

Such criticisms made little impression on the people at whom they were aimed. Suburbanites wanted homes they could afford, and they found the physical roominess of life outside the cities well worth the social isolation and cultural blandness. If the houses were cheaply constructed and identical, they were far better than no houses. Moreover, the new suburbanites, thrown into brand new towns with no roots and traditions, were great creators of institutions. Lacking established social services and governments, they formed an intricate network of voluntary associations that were entirely supported by private funds and energies. There were the churches and synagogues built from scratch, thousands of new chapters of political parties, garden clubs, literary societies, and bowling leagues. Most important of all were programs that revolved around their children: dancing schools, Cub Scouts and Brownies, Little Leagues, community swimming pools.

Since everyone was a stranger in town, the informal cocktail party became an efficient means by which to introduce people to one another. Because guests milled around the stand-up parties at will, it was possible to invite the most casual supermarket or Little League grandstand acquaintances without worrying about their sense of ease. Alcohol lubricated easy conversation among strangers, and statisticians noticed a change in American drinking habits toward the consumption of neutral spirits such as gin and vodka, which could be disguised in sweet soda pop or fruit juices. The conclusion was that people who did not like to drink were drinking to make themselves more comfortable and because it was the thing to do.

Insolent Chariots

The suburb could not have developed without the family automobile. In turn, the growth of suburbia made the automobile king, a necessity of life and in some ways a tyrant. Each family needed a car because suburbanites worked at some distance from their homes and public transportation to many of the new communities did not exist. Because it was necessary for a

With their move to suburbia, Americans needed automobiles to commute to their jobs in the city. Cars were also a means to display status.

suburban housewife and mother to cover considerable distances each day, the two-car family became a common phenomenon: one suburban family in five owned two vehicles.

Sales of new cars rose from none during the Second World War to 6.7 million in 1950, and continued to maintain high levels throughout the 1950s. In 1945, there were 25.8 million automobiles registered in the United States. By 1960, with the population increased by 35 percent, car ownership more than doubled, to 61.7 million vehicles.

The automobile was the most important means by which people displayed their status. Unlike the size of paychecks and bank accounts, the family car *showed*; it sat in the driveway for all to see. Automobile manufacturers devised and encouraged finely graded images for their chariots. The family that was "moving up" was expected to continue "trading up" from a low-priced model to eventual ownership of a Chrysler, Lincoln, or Cadillac. Indeed, the easy availability of credit made it possible for people to "keep up with the Joneses" by buying beyond their means, going deeply into debt for the sake of appearances. From 1946 through 1970, short-term loans—money borrowed in order to buy consumer goods—increased from $8 billion to $127 billion! Credit-card companies made easy spending even easier.

The Automobile Economy

Virtually universal car ownership among the middle classes fueled the growth of businesses that were devoted to cars or dependent on them. Service stations (gasoline consumption doubled during the 1950s), parts stores, car washes, motels, drive-in restaurants, and drive-in movie theaters blossomed on the outskirts of residential suburbs. The suburban shopping mall displaced city and town centers as the middle-class American marketplace. In 1945, there were eight automobile-oriented shopping centers in the United States. In 1960, there were almost four thousand.

Automobiles demanded roads for use. In 1956, Washington responded with the Interstate Highway Act, under which the government began pumping a total of $1 billion a year into road construction. (By 1960, this expenditure rose to $2.9 billion a year.) Forty-one thousand miles of the new roads ran cross-country, but five thousand miles of freeway were urban, connecting suburbs to big cities.

Not only did this road network encourage further urban sprawl, but it made the cities less livable. Already sapped of their middle classes, once lively urban neighborhoods were carved into isolated residential islands that were walled off from one another by the massive concrete abutments of the freeways. Suburbanite cars roared in on them daily, clogging the streets, raising noise to unprecedented levels, and fouling the air for those who could not afford to move out. Progressively poorer without a middle-class tax base, cities deteriorated physically and suffered from neglected schools and hospitals and rising crime rates. During the 1960s, faced with these problems, the center-city department stores and light industries joined the suburban movement, relocating in shopping centers or on empty tracts near the residential suburbs. When they left, they took not only their tax contributions, but jobs previously available to city dwellers.

Baby Boom

During and immediately after the Second World War, the number of births in the United States took a gigantic leap. While about 2.5 million babies were born in each year of the 1930s, 3.4 million saw the light of day in 1946 and 3.8 million in 1947. Population experts expected this. The depression and war had forced young couples to put off starting families. After a few years of catching up, demographers said, the low birth rate typical of the first half of the century would reassert itself.

They were wrong. The annual number of births continued to increase until 1961 (4.2 million) and did not drop to low levels until the 1970s. The same young couples who were buying unprecedented numbers of new homes and automobiles were having larger families than their parents.

Although all social groups participated in the "baby boom," children were most noticeable in suburbia, where, because most adults were young, children were proportionately more important. Beginning about 1952, when the first boom babies started school, massive efforts were required to provide educational and recreational facilities for them. Businesses oriented toward children, from toymakers to diaper services, sprouted and bloomed.

As the boom babies matured, they attracted attention to the needs and demands of each age group they swelled. By the end of the 1950s, economists observed that middle-class teenagers were a significant consumer group in their own right. They had $10 billion of their own to spend each year, and all of it was discretionary because their necessities were provided by their parents.

Magazines that appealed to young people prospered, including *Seventeen* (clothing and cosmetics for girls) and *Hot Rod* (automobiles for boys). Film

Hip-swinging, guitar-strumming Elvis Presley popularized rock-'n'-roll during the 1950s.

COLLEGE ENROLLMENT OF WOMEN: 1870–1980

	(Percentage)
1870	21
1900	36
1930	44
1960	35
1970	41
1980	44

studios churned out movies about adolescents and their problems.

Beginning in the early 1950s, a new kind of popular music swept the country. Rock-'n'-roll was based on black rhythms, but was usually performed by whites, often teenagers themselves. On the one hand, it was rebellious. Elvis Presley, a truck driver from Memphis, scandalized the country with an act that included suggestive hip movements. On the other hand, it was juvenile. Whereas popular songs had dealt with themes that were obviously adult, the new music's subjects were senior proms at high schools and double-dating. A new kind of record, the compact, unbreakable, and cheap 45 rpm disk, became the medium of competition for teenage dollars.

What worried social critics was that older people, seemingly outnumbered by the young, adopted adolescent ideals and role models. By the end of the decade, one of television's most popular programs was "American Bandstand," an afternoon show on which teenagers rock-'n'-rolled to recorded music and discussed adolescent problems. Adolescents watched it of course, but so did people of all age groups, particularly housewives. The baby-boom generation seemed to be proclaiming the society's cultural standards.

A New Role for Women

Middle-class America's twin obsessions with enjoying life and catering to its children caused a significant, if temporary, shift in the status of women. Since the beginning of the century, women of all social classes had been moving into occupations and professions that previously had been considered masculine monopolies. Throughout the 1940s, increasing numbers of women finished high school, attended college, studied medicine, the law, and other professions, and took jobs that would have been unthinkable for women before 1900. The Second World War seemed to hasten this blurring of the lines between what the two sexes could do as women took the place of men in heavy and dirty industrial jobs.

When the war ended, however, women willingly left those jobs and enthusiastically embraced the tradi-

Middle-class America's vision of the perfect woman of the 1950s was of a wife and mother with no interest in having a career outside the home.

tional roles of wife, homemaker, and mother. By the 1950s, middle America once more assumed that woman's place was in the home. However, the new woman was not the shrinking violet of the nineteenth century. If she was not employed, the woman of the 1950s was constantly out and about, the backbone of an active social whirl. Because the moral code that had required that women be sequestered had long since died, the modern American girl, wife, and mother were expected to be active and attractive. Wives were considered partners in furthering their husbands' careers as sociable hostesses and companions. Women's magazines added that wives should be "sexy."

Against the Grain

There would be no significant challenge to the new domesticity until 1963, when Betty Friedan published *The Feminine Mystique*. In her best seller, Friedan pointed out that American women had actually lost ground in their fight for emancipation since 1945. She considered the home to be a prison and said that women should move out into the world of jobs, politics, and other realms that she defined as productive. Criticism of other aspects of the culture of the 1950s, however, was widespread even during the age of Eisenhower.

Dissenters

As early as 1942, Philip Wylie's *Generation of Vipers* told the country that indulgence of children, particularly by their mothers (so-called momism), was creating tyrannical monsters. When juvenile-delinquency rates soared during the 1950s, even in the wealthiest suburbs, other writers elaborated on Wylie. John Keats attacked the sterility of suburban life, especially the social irresponsibility of the developers that left new developments without vital social centers. Later, in *Insolent Chariots*, he turned his attention to the automobile as an economic tyrant and a socially destructive force.

In *The Organization Man* (1956), William H. Whyte, Jr., fastened on the work place, arguing that jobs in the huge corporations and government bureaucracies that dominated the American economy placed the highest premium on anonymity, lack of imagination and enterprise, and generally just fitting in. Sociologist David Riesman suggested in *The Lonely Crowd* (1950) that Americans were becoming "other-directed." They no longer took their values from their heritage or their parents, least of all from within themselves, but

thought and acted according to what was acceptable to those around them.

Sloan Wilson fictionalized the conformism and cultural aridity of suburban life in *The Man in the Gray Flannel Suit* (1955), a novel about a suburban commuter who works in the advertising industry. In *The Hidden Persuaders* (1957), Vance Packard added to the attack on advertising by pointing out that all Americans were manipulated by advertisements that played not on the virtues of the product for sale but on people's feelings and insecurities.

Beatniks and Squares

The beat generation, or "beatniks" as people called members of it, offered a less articulate critique of Eisenhower tranquillity. Originally a literary school centered around novelist Jack Kerouac and poet Allen Ginsberg, "beat" evolved into a bohemian life style with capitals in New York's Greenwich Village, San Francisco's North Beach, and Venice, California, near Los Angeles.

Beatniks rebelled against what they considered to be the intellectually and socially stultifying aspects of 1950s America. They shunned regular employment. They took no interest in politics and public life. They mocked the American enchantment with consumer goods by dressing in T-shirts and rumpled khaki trousers, the women innocent of cosmetics and the intricate hairstyles of suburbia. They made a great deal of the lack of furniture in their cheap walk-up apartments, calling their homes "pads" after the mattress on the floor.

The beatniks were highly intellectual. They prided themselves on discovering and discussing obscure writers and philosophers, particularly exponents of an abstruse form of Buddhism called Zen. They rejected the ostensibly strict sexual morality of the "squares" and lived together without benefit of marriage or embraced homosexuality. Their music was jazz as played by blacks, whom they regarded as free of the corruptions of white America.

Beats simultaneously repelled, amused, and fascinated conventional American society. Traditional moralists demanded that police raid beatnik coffee houses in search of marijuana (which beatniks introduced to white America) and amateur poets reading sexually explicit verse. Preachers in the traditional churches inveighed against the moral decay that the beatniks represented.

But sexual mores were changing in suburbia, too. To be divorced was no longer to be shunned as a moral pariah, and in books published in 1948 and 1953, a

Literary and artistic tastes were challenged and changed by members of the beat generation. One artist, Jackson Pollock, became known for his "action painting."

PERCENTAGE OF SCHOOL-AGE CHILDREN ACTUALLY IN SCHOOL: 1850–1970 (percentages)		
	White	Nonwhite
1850	56.2	1.8
1860	59.6	1.9
1870	54.4	9.9
1880	62.0	33.8
1890	57.9	32.9
1900	53.6	31.1
1910	61.3	44.8
1920	65.7	53.5
1930	71.2	60.3
1940	75.6	68.4
1950	79.3	74.8
1960	84.8	81.5
1970	88.3	85.3

researcher at the University of Indiana, Alfred Kinsey, revealed that the majority of Americans were sexually active before marriage and that the adultery rate was also high.

The high courts approved the publication of books formerly banned as obscene, with celebrated cases revolving around D. H. Lawrence's *Lady Chatterley's Lover* and Henry Miller's *Tropic of Cancer*. The furor over Ginsberg's long poem *Howl* (1955) made it a best seller. Suburbanites, the favorite targets of beat mockery, flocked to Greenwich Village and North Beach on weekends to dabble in beatnik life and fashions. Like all cultural rebels, the beatniks did not really challenge society's basic assumptions but merely provided another form of entertainment.

The Awakening of Black America

The protest against racial discrimination was an altogether different matter. Rather than sniping at trivialities such as life style, America's blacks during the 1950s demonstrated to whites that their prosperous society was built in part on the systematic denial of civil rights to 15 million people.

For more than half a century, black leaders such as W. E. B. Du Bois, Mary McLeod Bethune, A. Philip Randolph, and Bayard Rustin had fought a frustrating battle against racial prejudice. Their most important organization, the National Association for the Advancement of Colored People, had won some significant victories in the courts. Lynching, formerly a weekly occurrence in the South and rarely punished, had become rare by the 1950s. Under Truman, the armed forces were desegrated (black recruits were no longer placed in all-black units), and the Supreme Court ordered a number of southern states to admit blacks to state-supported professional schools because the segregated medical and legal training they offered blacks was not equal in quality to that provided for whites.

Nevertheless, when Eisenhower moved into the White House, all the former slave states and a few others retained laws on the books that segregated parks, movie theaters, waiting rooms, trains, buses, and schools. In the Deep South, public drinking fountains were labeled "white" and "colored," and some states actually provided different Bibles in court for the swearing in of witnesses. This strict color line had been legal since 1896, when, in the case of *Plessy* v. *Ferguson*, the Supreme Court had declared that racially separate public facilities were constitutional as long as they were equal in quality.

The Brown Case

In 1954, Thurgood Marshall, the NAACP's brilliant legal strategist, argued before the Supreme Court that

Throughout much of the United States, and particularly in the South, racial discrimination was evident in the segregation of schools, neighborhoods, bathroom facilities, and drinking fountains.

racially separate educational facilities were intrinsically unequal and therefore unconstitutional because segregation burdened blacks with a constant reminder of their inequality. In *Brown* v. *Board of Education of Topeka,* (1954), the Court unanimously agreed. Led by the new Chief Justice, Earl Warren of California, the Court declared that segregated school systems were to be integrated "with all deliberate speed."

In some parts of the South, school administrators complied quickly and without incident. However, in Little Rock, Arkansas, in September 1957, an angry mob of white adults greeted the first black pupils to enroll in Central High School with shouts, curses, and rocks. Claiming that he was protecting the peace, but actually seeking to win the political approval of white racists, Governor Orval Faubus called out the Arkansas National Guard to prevent the black children from enrolling.

Eisenhower blamed the turmoil on both Earl Warren and Orval Faubus. Sharing the belief of many Americans that there was no great harm done by segregation, Eisenhower regarded the *Brown* decision as a mistake. If nothing else, by arousing black Americans to protest, it disturbed the tranquillity that Ike coveted, and he did not believe that laws could change people's feelings. He later said that his appointment of Earl Warren to the Supreme Court was the worst decision that he had ever made.

Nevertheless, the Supreme Court had spoken. The Court's ruling had the force of federal law, and Faubus was defying it. Eisenhower superseded the governor's command of the National Guard and ordered the troops to enforce the integration of Central High. Overnight, the mission of the Arkansas National Guard was reversed.

From the Courts to the Streets

The battle to integrate the schools continued for a decade. Beginning in 1955, however, the civil-rights movement ceased to be a protest of lawyers and lawsuits and became a peaceful revolution by hundreds of thousands of blacks who were no longer willing to be second-class citizens.

The leader of the upheaval was Martin Luther King, Jr., a young preacher in Montgomery, Alabama. In December 1955, Rosa Parks, a black secretary, refused to give up her seat on a bus to a white man, as city law

Black students, escorted and protected by the National Guard, enter the all-white Central High School in Little Rock, Arkansas, in 1957.

required, and King became the spokesman for a black boycott of the Montgomery buses. When the city tried to defend the color line, the dispute attracted journalists and television reporters from all over the country.

King's house was bombed, and he explained his strategy for ending racial discrimination from the wreckage of his front porch. Nonviolent civil disobedience, King said, meant refusing to obey morally reprehensible laws such as those that sustained segregation, but without violence. When arrested, protestors should submit peacefully to authorities. Not only was this the moral course of action—King hated violence of all kinds—but it was politically effective. When decent people were confronted with the sight of southern police officers brutalizing peaceful blacks and their white supporters simply because they demanded their rights as citizens, they would, King believed, force politicians to support civil rights.

Although it led to considerable suffering by demonstrators and to several deaths, King's strategy worked.

A few important labor leaders such as Walter Reuther of the United Automobile Workers marched with the young minister and helped finance the Southern Christian Leadership Conference (SCLC), which King founded to spearhead the fight for equality. After 1960, when SCLC's youth organization, the Student Nonviolent Coordinating Committee (SNCC), peacefully violated laws that prohibited blacks from eating at lunch counters in the South, white university students in the North picketed branches of the offending chain stores in their hometowns. When white mobs burned a bus on which white and black "freedom riders" were defying segregation, the federal government sent marshals south to investigate and prosecute violent white racists.

Although King fell out of favor with some younger blacks in the late 1960s, he loomed over his age as did no other man or woman of either race. After his assassination in 1968, under circumstances that remain mysterious, several states made his birthday a holiday.

FASHION AND THE FIFTIES

In 1840, the British consul in Boston noted with distaste that Americans did not observe social propriety in the way they dressed. Instead of wearing clothes that were appropriate to their station in life, as an English gentleman thought should be done, Americans dressed more or less the same, and the democracy of dress did not mean a drabbest common denominator. On the contrary, servant girls were "strongly infected with the national bad taste for being over-dressed; they are, when walking the streets, scarcely to be distinguished from their employers." In other words, they were trying to be *fashionable.*

By the twentieth century, the democratization of fashion in the United States was complete. The wealthy had a monopoly of the latest from Paris for only as long as it took the American garment industry to copy designs and mass-produce cheap versions of expensive "originals." Indeed, the insistence of American women of almost every social class on their right to dress as the arbiters of fashion pleased accelerated the natural life cycle of a style. The only way the wealthy woman could conspicuously display her capability to spend freely was to move rapidly from one new look to another, always one frantic step ahead of the power shears and sewing machines of the New York garment district.

In 1940, very soon after the Great Depression, the American clothing industry was doing $3 billion in business annually. By the end of the 1950s, it was by some criteria the third largest industry in the United States. Also during those two decades, American dress designers established partial independence from Paris, the capital of fashion, but not from the social preoccupations and values that were neatly reflected in the garments they produced.

For example, the fashions of the years of the Second World War were a product of four forces: the isolation from French designers; the rationing of materials; the unprecedented prominence of the military in daily life; and the entry of women into the professions and jobs previously held by men.

Because they had been so dependent on Paris for ideas, American fashion designers were disoriented by the fall of France and able on their own to come up with only a variant on 1930s styles. One of the factors that forced some change was the government's restrictions on the amount of fabric that might go into clothing. Skirts could be no larger than seventy-two inches around. Belts more than two inches wide, more than one patch pocket on blouses, and generous hems were forbidden, as were frills, fringes, and flounces. The result was a severe look in women's dress, accentuated by the fact that with so many uniforms on the streets, civilian clothing took on a military look. It also took on a "masculine look," according to fashion historians; the silhouette of women's clothing was straight and angular, with padded shoulders that emulated the male physique.

In 1947, Christian Dior, a Paris designer, reestablished French primacy in the fashion world. His "New Look" celebrated the end of wartime shortages with long, full, and flowing skirts. More interesting, Dior proclaimed a new femininity in fashion. "Your bosoms, your shoulders and hips are round, your waist is tiny, your skirt's bulk suggests fragile feminine legs," an American fashion editor wrote. Dior blouses were left unbuttoned at the top, and more formal bodices were cut in a deep V or cut low to expose shoulders.

The Frenchman either was very lucky or was a very shrewd psychologist. In the United States, the chief market for fashion in the postwar years, women were opting in droves for the home over the office, factory, and public life. As Betty Friedan would later explain, the new domesticity of the 1950s led to a halt and even a drop in the numbers of women entering the professions and other spheres that were traditionally the preserve of men.

But the domesticity of the 1950s was not the domesticity of a hundred years earlier. Thanks to labor-saving home appliances and the money to buy them, a yen for recreation after the austere years of rationing, and the steady relaxation of moral codes, the 1950s housewife was able to be "fashionable" to a degree previously open only to the doyennes of high society.

Another consequence of the new domesticity of the postwar years was the great baby boom, which in turn affected women's fashion. Just as numerically dominant young people led juvenile themes in films and popular music, the two-thirds of the female population that was under thirty years of age affected the way women dressed. "For the first time in fashion," wrote Jane Dormer, the British student of the subject, "clothes that had originally been intended for children climbed up the ladder into the adult wardrobe." While Dior and the Parisian couturiers continued to decree what was worn on formal occasions, American teenagers set the standards for casual wear, not only for themselves but for women of almost all ages. The most conspicuous of these styles was that of the ingénue: "childlike circular skirts," crinolines, hoop skirts, frilled petticoats that were seen not only at junior high school dances but at cocktail parties on mothers of five. Girls and women began to wear their hair loose and flowing or in ponytails, both styles then closely associated with juveniles.

Hollywood both responded to and fed this kind of fashion by coming up with actresses such as Audrey Hepburn, Debbie Reynolds, and Sandra Dee, who specialized in innocent, naïve, little-girlish parts. Well into their thirties, these women clung to what clothing historian Anne Fogarty has called the "paper doll look." When pixie-like Audrey Hepburn played the part of a prostitute in one film, it was considered a sensation. Not until the 1960s, when women adopted new values, would this fashion, like all fashions to a later age, look ridiculous.

Full skirts and ponytails were a popular fashion during the 1950s for teenage girls and adult women alike.

But King and black Americans only began their fight for equality during the age of Eisenhower. It was the next decade, the troubled 1960s, which saw the end of civil discrimination on the basis of race.

For Further Reading

Eric Goldman, *The Crucial Decade—and After: America, 1945–1960* (1961), is political in focus but helps give a feel for Ike's America. Eisenhower's own *The White House Years* (1965) is also useful; see also C. C. Alexander, *Holding the Line: The Eisenhower Era, 1952–1961* (1975) and Marquis Childs, *Eisenhower: Captive Hero* (1958). The people's decision in Ike's favor is discussed in F. M. Shattuck, *The 1956 Presidential Election* (1956).

Influential books about the culture of the 1950s are William H. Whyte, Jr., *The Organization Man* (1956); Paul Goodman, *Growing Up Absurd* (1960); Kenneth Keniston, *The Uncommitted* (1965); and David Riesman et al., *The Lonely Crowd: A Study of the Changing American Character* (1950).

C. Taeuber, *The Changing Population of the United States* (1958), and Robert C. Woods, *Suburbia* (1959), deal with the most notable population movement of the time.

On the beginnings of the black upheaval, see James Baldwin, *The Fire Next Time* (1963); C. E. Silberman, *Crisis in Black and White* (1964); and Louis E. Lomax, *The Negro Revolt* (1963). There is not yet the biography that Martin Luther King, Jr., should have but see his own *Stride Toward Freedom* (1958).

50

Consensus Decade
The Eisenhower and Kennedy Administrations, 1953–1963

A full generation has elapsed since Dwight D. Eisenhower became president in 1953. Most of the leaders of that era are dead. Events that are still vivid in the memory of older Americans are remote and antiquated to the majority of the population. For the historian, trying to sift out the meaning of these years, the continuity between them and the present gets in the way of objectivity.

One fact, however, stands out clearly. Eisenhower and Kennedy enjoyed something that none of their successors did—a consensus, the *general* accord of the people that almost all was well in the American corner of the world. Certainly there were dissidents. But most Americans felt that however serious the problems facing the nation, they were in the hands of a leader who was both capable and well intentioned.

Not that their victories in elections were so overwhelming. In 1960, Kennedy barely scraped through. In 1964, Lyndon B. Johnson won a bigger majority than Ike ever did, and so did Richard M. Nixon in 1972. But even the results of those elections, a great swooping swing of

Supreme Court chief justice Earl Warren swears in John F. Kennedy as president in 1961. Outgoing president Dwight Eisenhower stands solemnly on the far left, while a future president, Lyndon Johnson, stands on the far right.

voters from the Democratic to the Republican party in only eight years, indicate the nature of the problem that has faced national leaders since 1963. Americans have been uneasy and uncertain about them.

It would be an error to think of the age of Eisenhower and Kennedy's Camelot as golden times. Many of the domestic tensions and foreign concerns that have unsettled and fragmented Americans since 1960 began to simmer when Eisenhower sat in the White House, and decisions that were taken by both his administration and Kennedy's contributed to their gravity. Nevertheless, because Americans grew conscious of most of them only since the assassination of Kennedy, the decade before 1963 appears to have been an easier time in which to live.

Ike's Domestic Compromise

In his heart and soul, Dwight D. Eisenhower was an old-fashioned conservative. As a career soldier, he was isolated from the mainstream of political development, and he thought of government in terms of his small-town childhood at the turn of the century and the gruff platitudes about free enterprise spouted by the rich businessmen who befriended him after the Second World War.

The tremendous expansion of federal power since the New Deal disturbed him. He shuddered at the size of the government's budget and at the very notion of annual deficits piling up into a mountain of national debt. He believed that businessmen in the private sector were better qualified to manage the economy than were the bureaucratic agencies that had been created under Roosevelt and Truman. He publicly denounced the Tennessee Valley Authority, the liberals' model of regional economic and social planning, as "creeping socialism" and suggested that its facilities be sold off to private power companies.

Best-Laid Plans

Some of Ike's advisers, such as Secretary of Agriculture Ezra Taft Benson of Utah, were downright reactionary in their hostility to government regulation, social-welfare programs, and the big bureaucracies that implemented them. Given his own way, Benson would have rampaged through the office buildings of Washington like an avenging angel.

Secretary of Defense Charles Wilson sounded like a ghost of the Coolidge era when he gave his opinion of the role that corporations should play in framing national policy. In what was only in part a slip of the tongue, Wilson told a Senate committee that what was good for General Motors was good for the United States. (Wilson came to government from the General Motors board of directors.)

When Jonas Salk, a research physician, perfected a vaccine that promised to wipe out polio, then a scourge of children, Secretary of Health, Education, and Welfare Oveta Culp Hobby warned that for the government to sponsor an immunization program would be socialistic.

Dynamic Conservatism

That was how Ike's advisers spoke and, no doubt, truly felt. When it came time to take action, however, the president was moderate, pragmatic, and realistic. He faced up to the facts that the America of his Kansas boyhood was gone forever and that the federal government had to take some responsibility for economic and social welfare in the complicated world of the mid-twentieth century. His government did sponsor a polio immunization program.

Eisenhower also discovered the risks in trusting too closely to his businessmen friends when he supported a private company, Dixon-Yates, in a dispute with the TVA over which of them would construct a new generating facility for the Atomic Energy Commission (AEC). Rather than the contest between "free enterprise" and "creeping socialism" that had been described to him, Ike discovered that Dixon-Yates executives were mired deeply in collusion with friendly AEC officials in what amounted to a raid on the Treasury—"socialism for the rich." He withdrew his support of Dixon-Yates and accepted a face-saving compromise in which the city of Memphis, in the public sector, built the plant.

Even Ezra Taft Benson had to swallow his distaste for the agricultural-subsidy programs that he wanted to abolish. The 1950s were years of distress in the farm belt, and the application of free-market principles would have transformed them into years of catastrophe. As agricultural productivity continued to increase but neither domestic consumption nor foreign demand kept pace, grain piled up in volcano-shaped cones in the streets of farm towns throughout the Midwest. Agricultural income dipped, and farmers left the land for city and town jobs in numbers not seen since the 1920s. Actually, food production never lagged; agribusiness corporations gobbled up and consolidated family farms, operating them like any other industry.

One reason they were able to profit better was that the Eisenhower administration expanded the subsidy programs against which Benson had railed.

The Soil Bank Act of 1956 authorized the payment of money to landowners for every acre they took out of cultivation in order to reduce production. Within ten years, $1 of every $6 that farmers and agricultural corporations pocketed at harvest time came not from sales but from the federal government—for crops that were never planted. Eisenhower also adopted New Deal-like policies when he introduced programs under which the federal government purchased surplus crops for school lunches and foreign-aid programs.

The clearest indication that "dynamic conservatism" (as Eisenhower called his political philosophy) included taking responsibility for the health of the economy came when the sharp reduction of military expenditures after the Korean War threatened to drop the country into a depression. Eisenhower responded by asking Congress to lower taxes, and he persuaded the Federal Reserve Board to loosen credit restrictions in order to put more money into the hands of consumers, that is, to make it easier for them to borrow and spend.

In 1957 and 1958, a worse recession threw 7 percent of the work force out of jobs. Ike launched several large public-works projects like the New Deal programs that he earlier had condemned. In the area of social welfare, over 10 million names were added to the lists of people who received Social Security payments during Eisenhower's presidency.

The Cold War Continues

The Cold War continued under Eisenhower. Indeed, every president after Harry S Truman had to design foreign policy around the overwhelming fact that the United States was locked into a competition with the Soviet Union that left very little room for maneuver.

The Nature of the Beast

Because the rivals were nuclear superpowers, the contest could not rationally be resolved by all-out war. Already by the age of Eisenhower, it was obvious that armed conflict between the United States and the Soviet Union would lead to vast physical devastation in both countries and the death of tens of millions of people. By 1961, when Ike retired, nuclear technology was advanced to the point where a world war would lead to the destruction of civilization and, conceivably, the earth's capacity to support human life. Every president from Ike to Jimmy Carter has understood and

---

AMERICA UNDERGROUND

For a time in the early 1950s, fear of Soviet nuclear attack spawned a minor building boom in "fallout shelters," covered pits in backyards to which, upon hearing the sirens, families would repair and thus survive the atomic bomb. Although magazines such as *Popular Science* and *Popular Mechanics* suggested fairly cheap do-it-yourself models, a professionally built shelter, carpeted and painted beige, cost $3,000 and even more for luxury models. Even if her family never used their shelter, a suburban Los Angeles woman said, it "will make a wonderful place for the children to play in." Other people pointed out that shelters were useful storage areas. In the theological journals, ministers and priests argued about a person's moral justification in shooting neighbors and relatives who had not built their own shelters and, in the moment of crisis, were trying to horn in.

---

clearly stated that there would be no winners in a nuclear war.

Therefore, until the United States and the Soviet Union trusted each other enough to agree on disarmament, policymakers had to live with the balance of terror and compete with their rivals under the threat of it. The history of American foreign relations after 1953 is the story of how a succession of presidents and Secretaries of State coped with these restraints.

More Bang for a Buck

Although Dwight D. Eisenhower spent much of his life in an army uniform, he wanted to be remembered as a man of peace. "I have seen enough war," he said, and as president he acted with moderation in crisis situations. By the time he left office, Eisenhower appeared to distrust the motives of his generals and the business leaders who supported him. In his farewell address of 1961, Ike told Americans to beware of the "military-industrial complex," the intimate and self-serving alliance of the Pentagon (the Defense Department) and the big corporations that made their money by selling weapons to the government. Along with like-minded intellectuals in the universities and "think tanks," with their ivory-tower theories of how to fight the Cold War, Ike said, the military establishment and arms industry were apt to be reckless in the use of armed force.

Eisenhower's fiscal conservatism also played a role in his defense policy. If he were to balance the federal budget—to spend no more money in a year than the Treasury collected in taxes—he had to cut military expenditures, the biggest single item in the budget.

FEDERAL GOVERNMENT EXPENDITURES

(in millions of dollars)

	Total	Defense	Defense (% of total)
1902	572	165	28.8
1940	10,061	1,590	15.8
1950	44,800	18,355	40.9
1960	97,284	48,922	50.2
1970	208,190	84,253	40.4

Because complete disarmament was out of the question, Eisenhower adopted a comparatively inexpensive plan for maintaining national security, the "more bang for a buck" policy. Encouraged by his penny-pinching Secretary of the Treasury, George Humphrey, the president cut spending on the conventional army and navy and concentrated on building up America's nuclear deterrent: atomic and hydrogen bombs and the sophisticated ships, planes, and missiles that are capable of delivering them to Soviet targets. This purely defensive policy threatened no one, Ike told the world. The United States would never start a nuclear war, but the Soviet Union, unless it were deterred by the threat of "massive retaliation," might very well do so.

Critics claimed that the policy meant all or nothing. The United States could destroy the world, but could the nation respond in proportion to minor Soviet provocations? Secretary Humphrey was not impressed. With the frustrations of the limited war in Korea fresh in his mind, he growled that the United States had "no business getting into little wars. . . . Let's intervene decisively with all we have got or stay out."

Other Eisenhower supporters said that the conventional army and navy were more than adequate to act in minor crises. In 1958, when Eisenhower suspected that the Communists intended to take over Lebanon, he was able to send marines into the Middle Eastern nation to stabilize a government friendly to the United States. It was only a long, expensive, and demoralizing conventional war for which he did not choose to prepare.

Peaceful Coexistence

The United States was directly involved in no wars of any note during Eisenhower's eight years in office. In part this was due to a significant change in the Soviet leadership. Joseph Stalin, suspicious to the point of mental imbalance late in life, died in 1953. After a few years of murky maneuvering in the Kremlin, Stalin was succeeded by an altogether different kind of strong man, a homely and clever Ukrainian named Nikita Khrushchev.

Khrushchev confused American Soviet watchers, which may have been his purpose. At times he seemed to be a coarse buffoon who habitually drank too much vodka and showed it. Visiting the United Nations, he stunned that assembly of dignitaries by taking off his shoe and banging it on the desk in front of him to protest a speaker whom he disliked. At other times he was witty and charming, almost slick.

The new premier could issue frightening warlike challenges to the United States. But he was also the man who denounced Stalinist totalitarianism at home (in 1956) and called for peaceful coexistence with American capitalism. Khrushchev claimed that the Cold War would be resolved by historical forces rather than by armed conflict. "We will bury you," he told American capitalists; the world will choose the Soviet way of life.

A comparison of American and Soviet societies did not seem to justify Khrushchev's boast. Despite Khrushchev's reforms, Soviet citizens remained under tight controls; the Soviet economy was sluggish; and daily life in Russia was drab. By way of contrast, and with the glaring exception of the inferior status of black people and other minorities, Americans were free, and their material comforts were the envy of the world. Vice President Richard Nixon understood this when, in 1959, he visited Moscow and engaged Khrushchev in a debate in front of a mock-up of an appliance-filled American kitchen. There was nothing like it in Russia, and Nixon was delighted to rest a comparison of the two societies on the contrast.

Khrushchev had one big edge in the salesmanship contest that he proposed. He was flexible and opportunistic, even cynical, while the chief foreign representative of the United States under Eisenhower, Secretary of State John Foster Dulles, was a man of antique principle, petrified mind, and little charm.

Dull, Duller, Dulles

On the basis of his credentials, Dulles should have been a grand success. He was related to two previous Secretaries of State, and he had begun his diplomatic career under Theodore Roosevelt, half a century earlier. During the years he was out of government, Dulles practiced international law and was considered the best in the business. At the top of that business in 1953, Dulles turned out to be handicapped by an impossible personality for a diplomat and a simplistic view of the

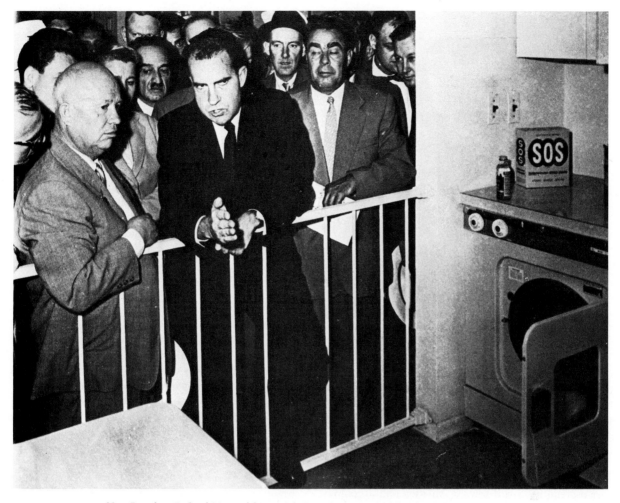

Vice President Richard Nixon debates with Russian premier Nikita Khrushchev in front of a mockup of a typical American kitchen in Moscow, 1959.

world. He was a pious Presbyterian of the old school, as self-righteous, intolerant, and humorless as any Puritan of old New England. "Dull, Duller, Dulles," the Democrats intoned.

He believed that all Communists were evil incarnate, veritable agents of Satan. He was unable to respond when Khrushchev hinted that he wanted to ease tensions, and he found it difficult to deal with neutral nations that maintained friendly relations with the Soviets. Photographs of Dulles with neutral national leaders like Jawaharlal Nehru of India reveal a man who fears he will be defiled if he sits too closely.

This kind of behavior made him unpopular not only in the Third World (unaligned countries), but among America's allies. To make matters worse, Dulles insisted on carrying out his policies in person. He flew five hundred thousand miles on the job, demoral-

izing American ambassadors by converting them into mere ceremonial figures who greeted his plane and then disappeared.

In his conception of the emerging nations of the Third World and of revolutionary movements in the republics of Latin America, Dulles's limitations were even more damaging. The old colonial empires of the European nations were falling apart during the 1950s, and new Asian and African countries were founded almost annually. Often committed to social reform, including socialist institutions, the leaders of these countries were rarely pro-Soviet. They needed American friendship and aid. In Latin America, revolutionary movements rose against the exploitative and repressive dictatorships that were practically the rule there. The leaders of these movements were committed to reducing American economic power in their coun-

John Foster Dulles, secretary of state under Eisenhower, was a staunch supporter of the Cold War.

tries, but they also recognized the advantage of having good relations with the world's richest nation.

Picking the Wrong Friends

At least at the beginning. Instead of exploiting the widespread good will toward America and accommodating the sensitive new leaders, Dulles divided the world into "us" and "them," with "us" defined as those nations that lined up behind the United States in every particular. He wrote off independently minded leaders and revolutionary movements as Communist inspired. Along with his brother, Allen Dulles, who headed the semisecret Central Intelligence Agency (CIA), he threw American influence behind compliant reactionary governments, including brutally undemocratic dictatorships in Portugal, Nicaragua, the Dominican Republic, and Cuba.

In 1953, the United States helped the unpopular shah of Iran overthrow a reform-minded prime minister, Mohammed Mossadegh, despite the fact that because Iran borders on the Soviet Union, the country cannot afford to be too friendly with Russia no matter who is in power. In 1954, the CIA took the lead in overthrowing a democratically chosen prime minister in Guatemala, Jacobo Arbenz, because he expropriated American-owned banana plantations.

Also in 1954, Dulles refused to sign the Geneva Accords, which ended a long and tragic war in Viet-nam between France and a Communist-led independence movement that was probably open to cooperation with the United States. Instead of courting the Vietnamese leader, Ho Chi Minh, the United States helped set up a petty dictator to oppose him in South Vietnam, Ngo Dinh Diem. In 1956, the CIA approved Diem's cancellation of democratic elections as required by the Geneva settlement.

In Dulles's hands, the Cold War with monolithic Communism took precedence over America's commitment to free institutions. What Dulles seemed to say was that the United States opposed social progress in those parts of the world where change was most sorely needed. This provided Khrushchev with the opportunity to play the friend of anticolonialism, freedom, and reform—a pretense that ill-suited the imperialist, dictatorial, and hidebound Soviet Union.

Brinksmanship

Dulles also demoralized America's allies by preaching a line that the prudent Eisenhower was unwilling to carry out. Instead of merely containing Communism, Dulles said, America would win the Cold War by going to the brink of hot war—"massive retaliation"—thus forcing the Communists to back down and, eventually, collapse. In 1953, Dulles hinted that he would support Chiang Kai-shek if the exiled Nationalist Chinese leader invaded the Communist People's Republic, and he led the peoples of Eastern Europe to believe that Americans would come to their aid if they rebelled against the Soviets.

However, when the Chinese Communists began to shell two tiny islands controlled by Chiang, Quemoy and Matsu, Ike and Dulles quickly backed off, stating that it was only Taiwan they would defend. The artillery exchanges between the two Chinas developed into a ludicrous ritual, a far more "limited war" than Korea. At one point, the Communists insisted only on the right to attack Quemoy and Matsu on alternate days of the month. The dispute was not resolved until after Eisenhower left office.

In Hungary in 1956, Dulles's talk of rolling back the iron curtain had more tragic consequences. Encouraged by him, anti-Soviet Hungarians rebelled and took control of Budapest. The Soviets hesitated, as though waiting to see what the Americans would do. They regarded Hungary as vital to their security, but feared nuclear war on the issue. When Eisenhower and Dulles did nothing, Soviet tanks and infantry rolled into Budapest, easily quashing the revolution. The net effect of the episode was to undercut confidence in Dulles's bold words throughout the world.

Also in 1956, Eisenhower and Dulles angered three important allies by first appearing to encourage them to take action against increasingly pro-Soviet Egypt and then refusing to back them. Britain, France, and Israel invaded Egypt to prevent the government of President Gamal Abdel Nasser from taking control of the Suez Canal. When Khrushchev threatened to send Russian "volunteers" to Egypt's aid, Eisenhower announced his opposition to the allied assault. Humiliated, the British, French, and Israelis withdrew. They could not carry on without American support.

Summitry and the U-2

When Dulles died in 1958 and Eisenhower took personal charge of foreign policy, American prospects brightened. Outdoing each other with statements of good will, Eisenhower and Khrushchev agreed to exchange friendly visits.

Khrushchev made his tour of the United States in 1959 and scored a rousing personal success. Many Americans were captivated by his unpretentious manner and interest in everyday things. Khrushchev made the nation laugh when after having been refused admission to Disneyland for security reasons, he explained that the real reason was that the amusement park was a disguise for rocket installations. (He seemed sincerely to have regretted missing his day there.) Eisenhower's visit to Russia was scheduled for May 1960. Because Eisenhower had been a hero in the Soviet Union during the Second World War, there was every reason to expect another amicable tour.

Then, on May 5, Khrushchev announced that the Russians had shot down an American plane in their air space. It was a U-2, a top-secret high-altitude craft designed for spying. Assuming that the pilot had been killed in the crash (or had committed suicide, as U-2 pilots were provided the means to do), Eisenhower said

Khrushchev holds up evidence of spying found in an American U-2 plane shot down by the Russians on May 1, 1960.

that it was a weather-monitoring plane that had flown off course.

Khrushchev pounced. He revealed that the U-2 pilot, Francis Gary Powers, was alive and had confessed to being a spy. Possibly because he hoped to salvage Eisenhower's forthcoming trip to Russia, Khrushchev left room in his announcement for Ike to lay the blame on subordinates.

Ike refused to do so. Smarting under Democratic party attacks that he was not really in charge of foreign policy, he acknowledged his personal approval of all U-2 flights. Khrushchev attacked Eisenhower as a warmonger and canceled his invitation to tour Russia. The Cold War was suddenly chillier than at any time since the truce in Korea.

1960: A Changing of the Guard

This perfectly suited the strategy of the Democratic presidential nominee in 1960, John Fitzgerald Kennedy, the forty-two-year-old senator from Massachusetts. His chief criticism of the Eisenhower administration was his contention that Eisenhower had let American defenses and deterrent power slip dangerously low. The Soviet Union was winning the Cold War.

Kennedy had to be careful about his campaign tactics. Ike's personal popularity was still high. If the Twenty-second Amendment, adopted in 1951, had not made a third term unconstitutional, Ike undoubtedly could have beaten Kennedy or any other Democrat in the election of 1960. Americans still liked Ike.

Times Change

The country also was a little tired of the 1950s. The American population was young and bumptious, restless under the cautious style of the dead decade. As prosperous as the age of Eisenhower was, it was a stale and boring time in the opinion of many Americans. The books of social critics such as Whyte and Packard had been best sellers, even in the suburbs. Although they were out of power, the Democratic liberals had loudly criticized Eisenhower lethargy in journals like *The Nation* and the *New Republic*. Liberal university professors were effective propagandists, spreading their views among young people. Although it was not a liberal majority, the Democrats had controlled both houses of Congress for six of Eisenhower's eight years in office.

As 1960 approached, the feeling that it was time "to get the country moving again" was in the air. In 1959, *Life*, the favorite magazine of the middle classes, published a series of articles by prominent Americans from Adlai Stevenson to Billy Graham on the subject of "the national purpose." Almost all the contributors conveyed the uneasy feeling that purpose was absent and needed.

John F. Kennedy

Kennedy was the politician who knew how to exploit this inchoate yen for change. As Eisenhower was tailor-made for the 1950s, Kennedy seemed to fit the spirit of the new decade. He was rich and attractive, breezy and witty. He had distinguished himself for bravery during the Second World War, had an elegant young wife who could have modeled for a fashion magazine, and was ambitious.

Kennedy was unbeatable in Massachusetts politics. He had won election to the House and the Senate in years that had not been kind to Democrats, and in 1956, he had made a bid for the Democratic party's vice-presidential nomination. Tennessee Senator Estes Kefauver had beaten him, but that turned out to be a blessing. Kennedy had not shared in the humiliation of the party's defeat that year, but by putting up an exciting fight on national television (the only one in a dull political year), he had made his name known in every corner of the country.

The avalanche of publicity in 1956 had done another favor for Kennedy by initiating discussion of his single political handicap, his religion. The senator was a Roman Catholic, and it was thought that too many people would vote against any Catholic for a member of that church to be elected to national office. The longer the question was examined, however, the less attractive the anti-Catholic position looked. Calmly and forthrightly, Kennedy addressed suspicious southern Baptist ministers in Texas, and the few who continued to oppose him were depicted as bigots by the national press. When Martin Luther King, Jr.'s, father (a Baptist minister) expressed his anti-Catholic prejudices, the civil-rights leader so hastily dissociated himself from them that he became, in the process, virtually committed to the Democratic nominee.

Kennedy and his team of advisers, which he started to assemble in 1957, understood the importance of manipulating the mass media, especially television, in creating a favorable image of their candidate. Thanks to his own father, an old-time Democratic glad hander, Kennedy already knew how to deal with Democratic party bosses. The campaign that he launched was calculated to convince younger Americans that he was more flexible, more open to change, than any of his rivals.

The Campaign of 1960

Kennedy's competition for the nomination included Adlai Stevenson, badly shopworn in an age that craved novelty, but hoping to be drafted; Lyndon B. Johnson of Texas, the efficient leader of the Senate Democrats; Hubert H. Humphrey of Minnesota, a leading liberal; and several minor candidates who were praying for a deadlocked convention.

Humphrey was the only one to challenge Kennedy head-on in the primary elections, and he was quickly eliminated. By edging him in Wisconsin, which neighbors Minnesota, Kennedy established himself as a national figure. Kennedy then won in West Virginia, a heavily Protestant "Bible belt" state where, experts said, anti-Catholic feeling was strong. Humphrey dropped out, and Kennedy's forces talked old-time political bosses like Governor Mike Di Salle of Ohio and Mayor Richard E. Daley of Chicago into supporting him as the most likely to win in November. By the time of the convention, Lyndon Johnson had been outraced, and Kennedy won on the first ballot.

Kennedy chose Johnson as his vice-presidential running-mate, which turned out to be the shrewdest move of a brilliantly run campaign. Although Johnson's syrupy Texas drawl occasioned ridicule in the Northeast, he was popular in the southern states where Kennedy was weak. Single-handedly, Johnson won Texas for the Democrats, a key to a close election. In the North, Kennedy's religion actually helped him by winning back many middle-class Catholics who had been drifting toward the Republicans as the party of respectability.

The Republican standard-bearer was Vice President Richard M. Nixon, who easily fought off a challenge by New York governor Nelson Rockefeller. Nixon had a difficult assignment. In order to keep the Republican organization behind him, he had to defend Eisenhower's policies. But he also had to appeal to the new spirit of youth and change.

A Modern Election

Nixon handled this juggling act remarkably well, but not without cost. Emphasizing his experience in the executive branch, he created an image of the responsible diplomat that did not mesh with his past reputation for free-swinging smears and dirty tricks.

John F. Kennedy and Richard Nixon grimly face each other in a television studio during the presidential campaign debates of 1960.

Reporters revived the nickname "Tricky Dicky" and the line, "Would you buy a used car from this man?" Kennedy wisecracked that Nixon played so many parts that no one knew who the real Nixon was, including the vice president himself.

Mistrust would dog Richard Nixon to the end of his career. Nevertheless, in 1960 he almost won the election. The totals gave Kennedy a wafer-thin margin of 118,574 votes out of the almost 70 million cast. His 303 to 219 electoral vote margin, apparently more comfortable, concealed narrow scrapes in several large states. Some analysts believed that Illinois went Democratic only because of fraudulent vote counts in Richard E. Daley's Chicago.

Other commentators said that Kennedy won because his wife was more glamorous than Pat Nixon, who disliked public life, or because the Massachusetts senator looked better in the first of four nationally televised debates with Nixon. Kennedy was tan, healthy, confident, and assertive, while Nixon was visibly nervous, and an inept make-up job failed to cover his five-o'clock shadow.

Aided by a handsome family that included photogenic toddler John-John, John Kennedy increased his popularity among the public as his term in office progressed.

It is impossible to know how much the appearances of the candidates affected the decisions of 70 million people. After 1960, however, many politicians and political scientists came to believe that a candidate's image, rather than issues, was the key to winning elections in the age of television. By 1984, few major political campaigns were run without the advice of high-priced advertising firms. Concerned observers wondered what it said for political democracy when a candidate's success depended on how skillfully he was packaged.

Camelot

As president, Kennedy remained a master at projecting an attractive image. Although no intellectual (his favorite writer was Ian Fleming, creator of the British superspy, James Bond), the new president won the hearts and talents of the intelligentsia to his cause; he invited the venerable poet Robert Frost to read his verses at the inauguration and cellist Pablo Casals to perform at the White House. Genuinely athletic and competitive, Kennedy appealed to young suburbanites by releasing photographs of his large family playing rough-and-tumble touch football at their Cape Cod vacation home.

There were plenty of Kennedy haters, but the vigor of his administration (*vigor* was a favorite Kennedy word) and his undeniable charm, wit, and self-deprecating humor captivated Americans. Inspired by the blockbuster musical of the early 1960s, *Camelot,* they spoke of the Kennedy White House as though it were an idyll, like King Arthur's reign in the mythical past. Indeed, John F. Kennedy is the last president to date whose popularity *increased* each month he held

office. Like Eisenhower, he seemed to be assembling a consensus. But just as in the Arthurian legend, Camelot was short lived.

The New Frontier

John F. Kennedy is more important as an inspiration for the reforms (and tragedies) of the 1960s than for what he actually accomplished. His inaugural address was eloquent and moving. "The torch has been passed to a new generation of Americans," he warned the world, and to Americans he said, "Ask not what your country can do for you; ask what you can do for your country." He sent Congress a pile of legislation that was more innovative than any presidential program between the time of F.D.R.'s Hundred Days and Ronald Reagan's conservative proposals of 1981.

A Peace Corps volunteer helps a worker in
Sierra Leone.

The New Frontier, as Kennedy called his program, included federal aid to education (both to institutions and in the form of low-interest student loans), assistance to chronically depressed Appalachia and the nation's decaying center cities, and help for the poor, the ill, and the aged. In 1962, Kennedy proposed a massive space research and development program, which set the goal of passing the Soviets and sending an American to the moon by 1970.

In Congress, however, despite comfortable Democratic majorities, the president found little but frustration. Not only did the Republicans oppose the New Frontier, but Kennedy was unable to swing the powerful bloc of southern Democrats behind his program. The southerners traditionally opposed big government spending on anything but defense and public-works projects located in the South, and were angered when the president and his brother, Attorney General Robert F. Kennedy, aligned themselves with the growing civil-rights movement. As a result, Kennedy was able to pass only a few of his proposals, such as the Peace Corps (volunteers working in underdeveloped countries in Latin America, Asia, and Africa) and the space program (which brought money to the South). Kennedy's other plans were either defeated or bottled up in congressional committees.

We Shall Overcome

Sensitive to the power of the southern congressmen, Kennedy wanted to go slow on civil rights. But America's blacks and their white allies, foiled for so long, would not be put off. In addition to King's Southern Christian Leadership Conference, the Student Nonviolent Coordinating Committee (SNCC) and the Congress of Racial Equality (CORE) struck out at racial discrimination on a dozen fronts, sponsoring demonstrations, protests, and nonviolent civil disobedience throughout the South.

White mobs and law officers turned high-pressure fire hoses on them, unleashed vicious attack dogs, and tortured demonstrators with electric cattle prods. Black churches, the typical meeting place of civil-rights workers, were firebombed and several children were killed. A bus carrying CORE "freedom riders" was burned to the ground. In April 1963, Medgar Evers, the moderate leader of the NAACP in Mississippi, was shot to death in the driveway of his home.

The Kennedys could not ignore such violence or the defiance of two southern governors, Ross Barnett of Mississippi and George Wallace of Alabama, who said that they would personally prevent the integration of their state universities and tacitly encouraged mobs to riot. Most of all, the government was pushed into action by the March on Washington in August 1963, which was organized and led by Martin Luther King, Jr. Believing that the time had come for decisive federal action, King led two hundred thousand supporters to the Lincoln Memorial in Washington, where he delivered the greatest sermon of his life.

"I have a dream today," he began.

I have a dream today that one day . . . little black boys and black girls will be able to join hands with little white boys and white girls and walk together as sisters and brothers. . . . When we let freedom ring, when we let it ring from every village and every hamlet, from every state and every city, we will be able to speed up that day when all of God's children, black men and white men, Jews and Gentiles, Protestants and Catholics, will be able to join hands and sing, in the words of that old Negro spiritual, "Free at last! Free at last! Thank God Almighty, we are free at last!"

Police dogs attack a civil rights demonstrator in Birmingham, Alabama, 1963.

Concluding that he had no choice but to choose between racist Democrats in the South and the large black vote in the North, which was strategically located in the cities of the states with the most electoral votes, Kennedy announced his support of a sweeping civil-rights bill to be debated in Congress in 1964.

The Assassination

How Kennedy would have fared in the contest is not known, for he was not the president who fought it. That president was Lyndon Baines Johnson, a very different kind of leader who had dramatically different strengths and limitations. Johnson became president just three months after Martin Luther King, Jr.'s, great march. Kennedy and Johnson were on a tour to shore up political support in Texas, when the president was assassinated by Lee Harvey Oswald, a ne'er-do-well warehouse worker.

The murder unleashed a raft of pent-up anxieties and conspiracy theories. Because Dallas, where Kennedy was killed, was a hotbed of right-wing political organizations inclined to paranoia, including the John Birch Society, which believed that Dwight D. Eisenhower was a conscious agent of international Communism, liberals were inclined to blame Kennedy's loss on such extremism. But Lee Harvey Oswald had been associated with left-wing organizations and had lived for a time in the Soviet Union. Right-wingers were confirmed in their theories that Communist agents were everywhere. Oswald was not around to clear things up. Two days after the assassination, he was murdered in the basement of the Dallas police headquarters by a distracted night-club operator named Jack Ruby.

EARL WARREN (1891–1974)

Chief Justice Earl Warren, front and center, with members of the Warren Court.

For sixteen years, Earl Warren of California was Chief Justice of the Supreme Court. Appointed by Eisenhower in 1953, he served long enough to inaugurate another Republican Californian, whom he did not much like, Richard Nixon. In the meantime, he led a Court that was more active in making decisions that shaped American historical development than any since the Marshall Court of the early nineteenth century, and Warren was the most controversial Chief Justice since Roger B. Taney and his divisive Dred Scott decision of 1857.

Earl Warren was born in Los Angeles in 1891, attended the University of California at Berkeley, and, when he graduated from law school, remained in northern California. After service in the army during the First World War, he made his home in Oakland and, in 1925, was elected district attorney of Alameda County.

He appeared to be satisfied with a career in county politics, remaining district attorney for fourteen years and virtually unknown elsewhere. However, a tough policy toward organized rackets brought him to the attention of the state's Republican bosses, and Warren was nominated for and elected California attorney general in 1939. The post traditionally was a stepping stone to the governorship in that state, and Warren's career took off. Fighting organized crime at the state

level enabled him to win the Republican nomination for governor in 1942 and, quite easily, the election. Warren was so popular that, in 1946, because statewide nominations were made in a popular primary, he won both the Republican and Democratic nominations for governor and received 92 percent of the popular vote. This victory caught the eye of the national leadership of the Republican party, and in 1948, Warren was tapped to run for vice president with Thomas E. Dewey of New York. The Republicans believed that they were winners in 1948, so Warren, just fifty-seven years old, seemed to be headed for the White House. Of course, Dewey was defeated in one of the great presidential upsets. Nevertheless, Warren was easily reelected to the California governorship in 1950.

As governor, Warren was aligned with neither the conservative nor the liberal wing of the Republican party. In fact, while clearly less shrill than William Knowland, the right-wing senator from California, Warren had been responsible for orders during the Second World War that allowed the seizure of property from Japanese-Americans who had been interned by the federal government. There was little in his career to anticipate what he would do after President Eisenhower named him Chief Justice in 1953.

What he did was to assume immediately the leadership of the Court liberals—most of the justices had been appointed by Franklin D. Roosevelt—and spearhead a rush of decisions that overturned long-entrenched policies and practices in racial segregation, apportionment of legislative districts, and police procedure.

He is best remembered for having written the unanimous decision that forbade racial segregation in the schools, *Brown* v. *Board of Education of Topeka* (1953). A series of similar decisions regarding segregation by race paved the way for congressional approval of the Civil Rights Acts of 1964 and 1965. They also made Warren the target of critics not only among segregationists but also among juridical conservatives who believed that the Warren Court had made its decision in the *Brown* case not on legal but on sociological grounds. (They had a point, but the Warren Court was not the first Supreme Court to do so.)

Warren won enemies among professional politicians as a result of a series of decisions on the issue of representation in elections to the House of Representatives and to state legislatures. It was common in states that were both urban and rural for rural voters to be "overrepresented"; because district lines had been drawn before cities had grown to house so many people, farm areas got to elect more legislators and congressmen than did city voters. In Virginia, for example, eighty-four rural voters had the same representation as one hundred city voters. In 1946, the Supreme Court had refused to intervene in this practice on the grounds that it was a political matter, which indeed it was: rural state assemblymen refused to give up their privileged position.

In *Baker* v. *Carr* (1962), however, the Warren Court ordered that states redraw the lines of congressional districts on the basis of "one man, one vote," all districts to contain approximately the same population. In *Westberry* v. *Sanders* (1964) and *Reynolds* v. *Sims* (1964), the Court went further. The justices ruled that "one man, one vote" also applied to state legislatures, and to *both houses*. Because the upper houses of most state legislatures were patterned on the United States Senate, with each member representing a county, these decisions revolutionized state government. Warren and a five to four majority of the Court said that whereas the Constitution provided for unequal representation in the Senate, state legislatures did not have the same mandate. In a sense, these decisions made the upper houses of state legislatures superfluous: they, like the lower houses, would be based on population.

The most controversial area in which the Warren court "legislated," as critics averred, was in police procedure. Three cases mark the development of what many people of the 1960s and 1970s regarded as Court insistence on coddling criminals. In *Mapp* v. *Ohio* (1961), the Court ruled that police could not use as a basis for criminal prosecution evidence that had been seized without a warrant. In the abstract, the decision was unexceptional, but in specific cases, it seemed to protect violators of the law. Mapp, for instance, was a woman whose house had been raided on suspicion that she dealt in drugs. No evidence to that effect was discovered, but police did discover obscene materials, which were used in court against her. The Court's decision in the matter seemed to rule out prosecutions in any cases when the evidence used was not the specific object of a warranted search.

In *Escobedo* v. *Illinois* (1964), the Court overturned a conviction. While the defendant, Danny Escobedo, was obviously guilty of the crime of which he had been convicted, he had been refused the right to see his lawyer when police were questioning him. Much more offensive to the growing anti-Warren forces who called for "law and order" was *Miranda* v. *Arizona* (1968), in which Warren himself wrote that a suspect in a crime must be informed immediately of his rights (particularly under the Fifth Amendment, which protects against self-incrimination), or any conviction secured could be in jeopardy. To many police officers and some civilians, the necessity of repeating a legally foolproof litany of constitutional rights in heated arrest situations was making the war against crime impossible and putting the rights of suspected criminals above those of victims. An "Impeach Earl Warren" movement sprang up during the 1960s, but never grew large enough to threaten the Chief Justice's job.

Immediately after President Kennedy's assassination in 1963, a reluctant Warren gave in to Lyndon Johnson's insistence that he head a commission to investigate the murder. He may have had a premonition that no possible findings would go unattacked. He was right. Despite the voluminous report (26 volumes of testimony from 552 witnesses, with an 888-page summation of evidence and conclusions), the Warren Commission was criticized for slipshod work and even of a "cover-up" in its conclusions that Lee Harvey Oswald was the sole killer and that the murder of Oswald by Jack Ruby was also unconnected to any conspiracy. Nevertheless, no conclusive evidence to the contrary has since been presented.

Warren tried to resign his post when Johnson was still president so that his successor would also be a liberal. However, when Johnson tried to give the Chief Justiceship to an old friend, Associate Justice Abe Fortas, enemies in the Senate dug up some irregularities in Fortas's record and prevented the appointment. Warren remained in office until 1969, when Richard Nixon replaced him with Warren Burger, a more conservative jurist whose revisions of the Warren Court decisions did not turn them around as much as many of Warren critics had hoped. Warren died in 1974.

*John Kennedy, Jr., salutes his father's coffin on November 25, 1963.
Behind him is his uncle, Robert Kennedy, who was assassinated during his
own presidential campaign in 1968.*

A blue-ribbon investigating commission headed by Chief Justice Earl Warren found that Oswald had acted on his own; he was neither associated with any political tendency nor assisted in his act. Simply put, he was a misfit. However, soft spots in one or another of the Warren Commission's conclusions continued to serve as grist for literally hundreds of articles and books that espoused theories about how the murder had taken place, the most common theme being that there was more than one gunman at the scene.

Beginning of an Era

multifarious and contradictory theories about how ~ly was killed were possible because of some dubi-

ous findings in the Warren Commission's report. There was, as one theorist called it, a "rush to judgment." However, the conspiracy theories won large followings because the temper of Americans changed after November 22, 1963. If Kennedy had not been particularly successful in terms of the legislation passed during his "Thousand Days" in office, he seemed to have been building a basis of political support such as had allowed Dwight D. Eisenhower to govern with authority.

Lyndon Johnson's mercurial character and his southwestern background were mistrusted by his fellow Americans. But it was in the area of foreign policy that Johnson was undone, although these policies had been established by his immediate predecessors, Kennedy and Eisenhower.

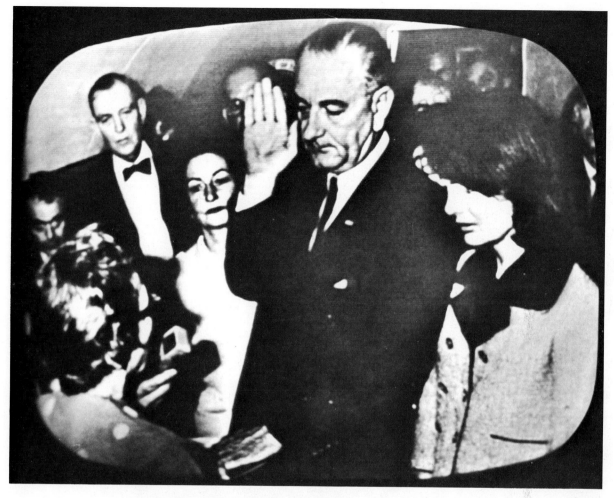

As a grief-stricken America watched on television, Lyndon B. Johnson, his wife to his right and Jacqueline Kennedy to his left, takes the oath of office aboard Air Force I, November 22, 1963.

For Further Reading

The works on Eisenhower that are cited at the end of Chapter 49 are appropriate here. See also Richard M. Nixon, *Six Crises* (1962), and J. T. Patterson, *Mr. Republican: A Biography of Robert A. Taft* (1972). John Foster Dulles is discussed in J. R. Neals, *John Foster Dulles* (1959), and T. Hoopes, *The Devil and John Foster Dulles* (1973). Ezra Taft Benson justified his service in *Crossfire: The Eight Years with Eisenhower* (1962). There will be other biographies of Adlai Stevenson; for now the most helpful is J. B. Martin, *Stevenson of Illinois* (1976).

H. G. Vatter, *The U. S. Economy in the 1950s* (1963), is the clearest discussion of its subject. For the forgotten poor of the population, the classic is Michael Harrington, *The Other America: Poverty in the United States* (1962).

Theodore H. White began a series of intensive studies of presidential elections in the 1960s, of which the best is *The Making of the President, 1960* (1962). For events of the Kennedy years, see L. J. Paper, *The Promise and the Performance: The Leadership of John F. Kennedy* (1975), and the memoirs of a distinguished historian who served in the Kennedy administration, Arthur M. Schlesinger, Jr., *A Thousand Days* (1965). The most comprehensive popular account of Kennedy's assassination is William Manchester, *Death of a President* (1967).

51

Tragic Presidency
The Turbulent Johnson Years, 1963–1968

In classical drama, the tragic hero overcomes great obstacles to rise to great heights. Then, at the height of attainment and glory, he is destroyed, not so much by enemies (although they are present to pick up the pieces), as by himself.

Lyndon Baines Johnson and Richard M. Nixon were tragic figures. Both rose to the presidency of the United States in the face of formidable handicaps, and both were confirmed in their position by huge majorities at the polls. Both enjoyed using the vast power given them, and both were immensely successful in the spheres in which they preferred to work: Johnson as a domestic reformer in the footsteps of his idol, Franklin D. Roosevelt; Nixon as a diplomat, an arranger of relations among nations, which he regarded as the twentieth-century president's principal responsibility.

And both were toppled, Johnson because he clung stubbornly to a cause both lost and discredited, and Nixon because of behavior that was not only unworthy of a great leader, but explicable only as a reflection of his character. Oddly, Johnson's undoing came about in foreign policy, which had never particularly interested him, and Nixon's on the domestic front, which he believed could take care of itself.

Marchers protest the Vietnam War in Washington, D.C., 1965.

Johnson and the Great Society

L yndon B. Johnson came out of what people call "the sticks," the Pedernales River country of rural Texas. He taught school for a year as a young man, but the hubbub and machinations of politics seem to have fascinated him from the start. In 1931, he went to Washington as a congressman's aide, became a spokesman for the New Deal, and returned to Congress in 1936 as a member of the House.

After losing a race for the Senate in 1941, Johnson won a controversial Democratic party primary for that post in 1948 by a handful of votes. In Texas, winning the Democratic primary was tantamount to winning the election, so Johnson went to the Senate in 1949 and quickly rose to be floor leader, then majority leader, of the Senate Democrats.

The Wheeler-Dealer

Johnson owed his speedy rise to the influence of his patron and fellow Texan, House Speaker Sam Rayburn, but he held on to it because he was good in the job. He was the master assembler of Senate majorities, many of them in support of President Eisenhower's bipartisan foreign policy. Johnson's method was a combination of folksy charm, bargaining with senators who were pursuing pet projects, arm-twisting, and, so it was said, a little blackmail. Rumor was that Johnson had something on every Democrat and most of the Republicans; he was not a man to be crossed when he was after something.

These extraordinary political talents enabled President Johnson to push through a comprehensive program of national reform that he called the Great Society and to effect a revolution in race relations that was more important in the long run than the Fourteenth and Fifteenth Amendments because it was Johnson, a century after their enactment, who put them to work.

L.B.J.

"Were there no outside world, . . . Lyndon Johnson might conceivably have gone down as the greatest of twentieth-century presidents."

Theodore H. White,
The Making of the President, 1968 (1969)

The Great Society

Johnson worshiped Franklin D. Roosevelt and wanted to be remembered in history as the president who completed what the New Deal had started. He envisioned an America

where no child will go unfed and no youngster will go unschooled; where every child has a good teacher and every teacher has good pay, and both have good classrooms; where every human being has dignity and every worker has a job; where education is blind to color and employment is unaware of race: where decency appeals and courage abounds.

His war on poverty program, which was directed by the new Office of Economic Opportunity, funded a Job Corps that retrained unemployed people for the new kinds of jobs available in high-technology industries. It recruited boys and girls from impoverished families for catch-up education in special Head Start schools and young men and women for placement in universities. Other programs provided financial help and tutoring in order to compensate for the economic and cultural handicaps of growing up in poverty. Volunteers in Service to America (VISTA) was a domestic Peace Corps, sending social workers and teachers into decaying inner cities and poor rural areas. Medicare provided government-funded health insurance for the elderly, chronically ill, and very poor.

Most of these acts were legislated after Johnson's lopsided victory in the election of 1964, when he won 61 percent of the popular vote and all but six states, and pulled into office on his coattails seventy first-term Democratic congressmen who faithfully voted for every proposal that he set before them. However, Johnson began his push for massive domestic reform within weeks of Kennedy's state funeral, taking advantage of the nation's grief at losing a young hero. Indeed, Johnson's single greatest accomplishment, because it overturned an institution that had been sanctioned for fifty years, was on the books before he went to the voters, the Civil Rights Act of 1964.

A Southerner Ends Segregation

Between 1955 and 1965, when blacks were fighting to overcome legal discrimination based on race, a few observers suggested that when segregation ended, as it had to do, white southerners would take a more human approach to race relations than would white northerners. These analysts argued that while legal segregation was a southern institution, personal interaction between blacks and whites was intimate in the South;

in the North, while there was no legal disability attached to being black, residential segregation isolated whites from blacks as people.

Civil-rights activists in the South found this difficult to believe, with southern police forces routinely beating them and white politicians proclaiming that they would fight to the death for white supremacy and segregation.

But events proved that there was more than a little truth in the speculation. It was a southerner, Lyndon B. Johnson, who pushed through the Civil Rights Act of 1964, effectively outlawing school segregation and the "white" and "colored" signs on public accommodations that had marked everyday life in the South for half a century. It was also Johnson who responded immediately to a challenge presented to him during the election campaign of 1964 that effectively rounded out the civil-rights revolution.

The Mississippi Freedom Democrats

Mississippi was the most stubborn of the segregated states. It took four hundred marshals, three hundred troops, $4 million, and a loss of two lives to enroll one black student at the state university at Oxford. Precisely because Mississippi was so tough, the Student Nonviolent Coordinating Committee chose it as the site of a campaign to register blacks to vote: if Mississippi could be cracked, the whole South would follow.

The campaign was not very successful at the grass roots. If anything, the arrival of hundreds of idealistic young black and white university students caused white extremists to step up harassment of outspoken local blacks. Most people who had to live and work in the state preferred not to take a public stand. The SNCC workers were terrorized. Three were kidnapped near Philadelphia, Mississippi, and murdered, probably with the connivance of law-enforcement officials.

A VISTA volunteer, one of thousands of recruits in the war on poverty, talks to a child in Alabama.

If it was a draw in Mississippi, however, national outrage encouraged activists in the state, led by the powerful and articulate Fannie Lou Hamer, to take a Mississippi Freedom Democratic party delegation to the Democratic party convention in Atlantic City, New Jersey. The Freedom Democrats, with much support from northern state delegates, demanded that they, and not the segregationists, be recognized by the party. (The symbol of the regular Mississippi Democrats was a white cock and the words "white supremacy.")

Working through longtime liberal Hubert Humphrey, whom he had selected to be his vice-presidential running mate, Johnson tried to work out a compromise, splitting Mississippi's convention votes between the rival groups. The Freedom Democrats were not happy with "half a loaf," but the segregationists were furious and walked out of the convention, announcing that they would vote Republican in November. It was a historic moment. Johnson and other Democratic policymakers concluded that it was futile to try to keep die-hard southern segregationists in the party, and they opted decisively to court black voters.

The Election of 1964

Senator Barry Goldwater of Arizona, the Republican who opposed Johnson, was the successor to Robert A. Taft as the leader of the party's conservative wing. A congenial and temperate man, Goldwater frightened Republican moderates because his supporters, quite unlike him, were carping, vindictive, fanatical, and filled with fears and hatreds that bordered on the unbalanced. The "radical right" never had repudiated Senator Joe McCarthy, and many were members of the John Birch Society.

Many of Goldwater's supporters were open racists, too, a position that was new to conservatism. Whereas Taft had been sympathetic to the demands of blacks for equality and Goldwater himself was without racial prejudice, many of the senator's supporters were former Democrats whose only goal was to stop the civil-rights revolution. To observers, it seemed as though Senator Goldwater had thrown in with them when in his speech accepting the nomination he said that "extremism in the defense of liberty is no vice."

Worst of all in an age of nuclear terror, Goldwater sounded like a lover of war when he spoke on foreign policy. He seemed to say that the Cold War with the Soviet Union was a matter of which country was ̇ ̇gher." Democratic strategists were able to depict ̇ ̇ ̇ a man who would rush for the red button in ̇ ̇ crisis. Johnson ran as the responsible peace candidate; ironically, he already was laying plans to expand the American military presence in the war in Southeast Asia.

The results in November 1964 were gratifying to liberals and moderates. Johnson won every state but a few in the Deep South where few blacks could vote and Goldwater's home state of Arizona. In 1965, the Great Society was legislated in great waves, and Johnson rounded out his revolution in civil rights.

The Voting Rights Act

The Voting Rights Act of 1965 put the federal power of enforcement behind the rights of blacks to vote. Secure in this right for the first time in almost a century, southern blacks rushed to register. In only ten years after Martin Luther King, Jr., had led his boycott against segregation on buses in Montgomery, the legal obstacles to black equality crumbled. Before long, southern white politicians who had built their careers on race baiting were showing up at black gatherings.

A former SNCC worker named Julian Bond, elected to the Georgia state assembly, was amused that businessmen who once called him a dangerous radical now wanted to take him out to lunch. In Alabama's guber-

A young black man urges an elder to register to vote in Edwards, Mississippi.

natorial election of 1982, George Wallace, the one-time leader of resistance to black equality, not only courted black votes, but owed his election to them: Alabama blacks found his Republican opponent by far the worse choice. Indeed, one of the two major consequences of Johnson's Voting Rights Act was to tie blacks closely to the Democratic party while sending southern whites who disapproved of civil-rights legislation scurrying to the Republicans.

The other major consequence was the election of many black leaders to political office. Newark, Gary, Detroit, and Atlanta elected black mayors. Edward Brooke (a Republican) was elected to the Senate from Massachusetts, the first black in that exclusive club since Reconstruction. President Johnson appointed Thurgood Marshall to the Supreme Court and Robert Weaver to his cabinet as Secretary of Housing and Urban Development. By the 1970s, black congressmen and congresswomen were numerous enough to form a caucus, and Los Angeles, the nation's third-largest city, elected a black mayor, former police officer Thomas Bradley.

Foreign Policy in the 1960s

Lyndon Johnson knew that the presidents whom history remembered were those who *acted*, and he wanted to be remembered. The reputation he hoped to earn was as a benefactor of America's poor and forgotten, and it may well be that future historians will center their attention on his Great Society.

During Johnson's five years in the White House, however, he and the country became increasingly obsessed with American military intervention in a Southeast Asian country of which, before 1964, few Americans had even heard. The policy decisions that Johnson made in Vietnam owed in large part to his determination to be decisive and to have his way abroad as well as at home. However, in order to understand fully the morass that, in time, almost everyone agreed Vietnam was, it is necessary to understand the foreign policy shifts of Johnson's predecessor, John F. Kennedy.

Flexible Response

Both Kennedy and Johnson accepted the fact of the Cold War with the Soviet Union; indeed, they had little choice to do otherwise. "Freedom and communism are in deadly embrace," Kennedy said, "the world cannot exist half slave and half free." Johnson concurred in that opinion. Acting on the claim of 1960

that a missile gap between the Soviet Union and the United States threatened American security, both presidents lavished money on research programs designed to improve the rockets with which, in case of war with Russia, nuclear weapons would be delivered.

Advised by intellectuals from universities and "think tanks," such as Walt W. Rostow, McGeorge Bundy, and Secretary of Defense Robert S. McNamara, Kennedy introduced the idea of "flexible response" to American foreign policy. Instead of threatening the use of nuclear weapons at every Soviet provocation, as Dulles had inadvertently proved was ridiculous, the United States would respond to foreign developments of which it disapproved in proportion to the threat. For example, if the Soviets were suspected of funding guerrilla movements in countries that were friendly to the United States, or of subverting elections, the United States would fund its own military forces to back and intervene clandestinely in the politics of other countries. Toward this end, Kennedy sponsored the development of elite antiguerrilla units in the army, such as the Green Berets, and increased funding of the spy network maintained by the Central Intelligence Agency.

Into the Third World

Unlike Eisenhower, who thought in traditional terms that wealthy Europe and Japan were the areas that counted in the Cold War competition, Kennedy stated that "the great battleground for the defense and expansion of freedom today is the whole southern half of the globe—Asia, Latin America, Africa, and the Middle East—the lands of the rising peoples."

He preferred to back democratic reform movements in the developing countries. Kennedy took the lead in organizing the Alliance for Progress in the Western Hemisphere, a program that offered economic aid to friendly Latin American nations in the hope that they would adopt free institutions.

However, the choice in the volatile Third World was rarely between liberal-minded reform movements and pro-Communist dictatorships. Envy of American riches, the long legacy of American support for repressive and exploitative dictators, and the easy flexibility of the Soviets meant that revolutionaries, particularly in Latin America, were at best suspicious of American imperialism and willing to look to the Russians for assistance.

Instead of trying to woo these groups with compromises, Kennedy and Johnson reverted to backing right-wing dictators. The immediate demands of the Cold War appeared to be more important to them than long-term friendships in "the lands of the rising peoples."

Setting the Stage for Crisis

At about the same time that Kennedy was inaugurated, Soviet leader Nikita Khrushchev reversed his movement toward détente with the United States. He may have been frightened by Kennedy's aggressive speeches (particularly the defiant inaugural address), may have been under pressure by hard-line Cold Warriors within his own government, or may have sensed that the youth and inexperience of the new president provided a rare opportunity for easy limited victories in the game of maneuver that Khrushchev loved so well. In any case, Kennedy's first year in office was a time of American setbacks in the international competition between

the superpowers and increasing recklessness on the part of the Soviet Union.

The first humiliation was Kennedy's doing. He had inherited from Eisenhower a well-advanced plan to upend the anti-American dictator of Cuba, Fidel Castro, who had come to power on New Year's Day 1960. Under Eisenhower, the CIA had trained two thousand anti-Castro Cubans and mercenary soldiers in Florida and Central America, and they were ready to invade Cuba when Kennedy took over. Castro was unpopular with the Cuban people, the CIA assured Kennedy, and at the sound of the first shot, rebellions against him would break out all over the island nation. On April

John Kennedy peers over the Berlin Wall into East Berlin during a Cold War era visit to West Berlin, June 26, 1963.

17, 1961, the shot was fired. The anti-Castro forces waded ashore at a place called the Bay of Pigs.

It was a disaster. There was no uprising, and Castro's crack troops, seasoned by a long revolution, made short work of the invaders. Castro's popularity soared at home for having resisted what he called imperialist aggression, and he moved closer to the Soviet Union. Kennedy was denounced all over Latin America, and, on national television, he assumed full responsibility for the fiasco.

At a summit meeting in Vienna in June, Kennedy was outwitted and upstaged by an arrogant Khrushchev. The Russian tongue-tied him in private and, when they were before reporters, treated him like a nice boy who only needed teaching. A man of perhaps too much self-confidence, Kennedy returned home seething with anger. Khrushchev, on the contrary, was encouraged to act more recklessly. The Soviets resumed nuclear testing in the atmosphere and ordered the sealing of the border between East and West Berlin.

The Communist East Germans had been plagued by the defection of their citizens, particularly highly trained technologists who could double and triple their incomes in West Germany's booming economy. This "brain drain" threatened to cripple East German industry, and the Communists winced at each defection as a Western propaganda victory, people "voting with their feet." To put an end to it, Khrushchev built a wall the length of the city that was as ugly in reality as it was symbolically.

Kennedy allowed the Berlin Wall to stand, and he was immediately attacked by critics who said that he could have bulldozed it without interference from the Russians. Although that was an arguable proposition, Kennedy was determined not to allow Khrushchev to win another round.

Drawing the Line

The crunch came in October 1962. A U-2 flight over Cuba had revealed that the Soviets were constructing installations for offensive nuclear missiles aimed at the United States. Kennedy rejected a proposal by Dean Acheson that bombers destroy them; instead, he proclaimed a naval blockade of the island and demanded that the sites be dismantled and the nuclear weapons removed.

For four days, Khrushchev refused to budge. Work on

the sites continued, and Soviet ships loaded with more missiles continued on their way to Cuba. Americans gathered solemnly around their television sets, apprehensive that the nuclear holocaust would begin any hour. Secretary of State Dean Rusk revealed that the White House was nervous too. "We're eyeball to eyeball," he said.

Rusk added, "I think the other fellow just blinked." The Cuba-bound freighters first stopped in mid-ocean and then turned around. On October 26, Khrushchev sent a long conciliatory letter to Kennedy in which he agreed to remove the missiles if the United States pledged never to invade Cuba. The next day, a second letter said that the Soviets would withdraw their nuclear weapons if the United States would remove its missiles from Turkey, which bordered the Soviet Union.

Before the Cuban missile crisis, Kennedy had considered dismantling the Turkish missile sites as a gesture of friendship. Calculating that the difference in the two Soviet offers indicated indecision in the Kremlin, he saw a chance for a prestigious victory. Kennedy ignored the second note and accepted the terms of the first. On October 28, Khrushchev accepted.

Relations Improve Again

Some historians consider Kennedy's accomplishment in the Cuban missile crisis to have been a great victory: he demonstrated to the Russians that he was not a soft touch. The president himself thought of it as the turning point of his presidency. He made commemorative gifts to everyone who had advised him during that tense October. Other historians credit Khrushchev with having saved the peace: in backing down, he showed he was more responsible than Kennedy.

Wherever the credit should go, both superpowers were shaken by their flirtation with disaster. A "hot line" was installed in both the White House and the Kremlin so that, in future crises, Russian and American leaders could communicate instantly with one another. Then, following a Kennedy speech, the Soviet Union joined the United States and every nuclear power except France and China in signing a treaty that banned nuclear testing in the atmosphere.

While relations between the superpowers were periodically strained over the next two decades, the threat of a nuclear holocaust was not repeated. Kennedy's successors from Johnson to Carter learned the lesson of October 1962, and worked to stop conflicts that could ~ome "eyeball to eyeball" nuclear confrontations be-
'hey did so.

~ shied away from the ultimate confrontation,
` Soviets, headed by Leonid Brezhnev after

1964, nor the Americans ceased to maneuver for little victories in the Third World. Through diplomacy, economic aid and technological assistance to developing nations, and clandestine operations (by the CIA on the American side), both superpowers continued to act as though the globe were a game board with two players and a hundred pieces to be moved and taken. Between 1962 and 1976, the United States was openly involved in Cold War actions in the Dominican Republic, the Congo, Angola, the Middle East, and Latin America. It was, however, in Indochina where the United States saw international politicking turn into a monster.

Vietnam! Vietnam!

By the middle of 1963, Kennedy had given up on the pro-American dictator of South Vietnam whom he had inherited from Eisenhower, Ngo Dinh Diem. Surrounded by corrupt relatives, the once liberal Diem had become a petty and unpopular dictator as a result of repressive policies, high taxes, and favoritism toward Roman Catholic Vietnamese. Capitalizing on Diem's failure, the National Liberation Front, then an alliance of many groups, including Communists, increased its power in the countryside; it governed many villages, hit others in guerrilla raids, and selectively assassinated Diem's officials. The Saigon government controlled little more than the capital, the major towns, and part of the fertile rice-growing Mekong River delta.

Buddhist monk Quang Duc immolates himself to protest the anti-Buddhist policies of South Vietnamese president Ngo Dinh Diem. The photo was taken by Malcolm Brown and was among the most shocking to come out of the Vietnam War.

In 1963, Diem was assassinated in a military coup, possibly with CIA connivance. There followed a period of comic-opera political instability and steady gains by the National Liberation Front. Kennedy apparently gave up on the possibility of military victory and ordered a reduction in the sixteen-thousand-man American contingent in the country. When some advisers told him that an increase in troops might win the war, he said that to get involved more deeply in the war was like "taking a drink. The effect wears off, and you have to take another."

This proved to be tragic prophecy when Lyndon Johnson determined that he was "not going to be the President who saw Southeast Asia go the way China went." His statement betrayed a failure of vision in which Kennedy may not have shared: the conviction that "liberation" movements in the Third World were not rooted in genuine grievances with which the United States might sympathize, but existed only because of support from outside powers, China or the Soviet Union or both. Therefore, it stood to reason, increased exertion of power by the United States on behalf of "our Vietnamese" could carry the day.

Escalation

In July 1964, in the Gulf of Tonkin, three North Vietnamese PT boats attacked an American destroyer that was providing cover for a South Vietnamese commando raid in North Vietnam. In August, Johnson asked Congress to pass a resolution that would give him authority to respond to such threats to American forces. With only two dissenting votes, from long-standing maverick senators Wayne Morse of Oregon and Ernest Gruening of Alaska, Congress complied. The Gulf of Tonkin resolution was, in effect, a blank check to wage war.

During the election year, Johnson did little. He was in the midst of the campaign against Goldwater, in which he characterized himself as the peace candidate. Once Goldwater was defeated, however, Johnson began the process of "escalation" that became the catchword of his presidency. On election day 1964, there were 23,000 American troops in Vietnam. By September 1965, there were 130,000, and by December 1965, 184,000. When Johnson left office in 1969, the total was 541,000, a massive military force.

Johnson also ordered an air war in both North and South Vietnam in which more bombs were dropped than on all America's enemies during the Second World War. By the time the war was concluded in 1973, it had cost $140 billion, 200,000 American casualties, 800,000 South Vietnamese dead and wounded, and probably about the same number of North Viet-

namese. During 1968, the most savage year of the war, 40 Americans were killed and 128 were wounded each day.

And yet, the Vietnam War never came close to succeeding. Each escalation brought a counterescalation from Communist North Vietnam and increased aid from both China and the Soviet Union. What had begun as a civil war among South Vietnamese, with minimal outside interference, became a Cold War battlefield on which both superpowers and China participated, but only Americans were killed. The experience frustrated, mystified, and divided the United States.

Troubled Years

No president ever craved consensus as did Lyndon B. Johnson. In making his plea for civil-rights legislation, he adopted the slogan of the movement, "We Shall Overcome." He meant that *all* Americans would overcome the blight of racial discrimination. Another favorite saying was a quotation from the biblical book of Isaiah, "Let us come together." Johnson did not want a majority, even a large one such as he won in 1964. He wanted an overwhelming unity of Americans behind him. What he got was a people divided.

A war protestor's sign hangs on the White House fence.

Black Separatism

Ironically, some of the fiercest anti-Johnson rhetoric came from the blacks, for whom the president believed he did so much. While the majority of black people supported the Great Society, many younger militants, particularly in the North, attacked the president's integrationist policies in the name of the "black-power" movement.

Black power meant many things. To realistic leaders such as the Reverend Jesse Jackson, and to intellectuals such as sociologist Charles Hamilton, it meant pressure politics, blacks demanding concessions for people of their race on the basis of the votes they could either deliver to or withhold from a political candidate. To a tiny group of black nationalists, it meant demanding a part of the United States for the formation of a separate nation for blacks only. To the great majority of advocates of black power, the slogan meant nothing more than fashion, dressing up in dashikis, wearing hair styles called "Afros," and cutting off casual social relationships with whites.

Black power was not a political program, but a cry of anguish and anger against the discrimination of the past and the discovery that legal equality did little to remedy the social and psychological burdens from which American blacks suffered: poverty, high unemployment, inferior educational opportunities, severe health problems unknown to whites, high crime rates in black neighborhoods, a sense of inadequacy bred over three centuries of oppression.

Malcolm X and Violence

Malcolm Little, or Malcolm X as he called himself, stating that a slaveowner had stolen his real African name, was the spellbinding preacher who inspired the black-power movement. A member of the Nation of Islam, or Black Muslims, Malcolm said that black people should reject Martin Luther King, Jr.'s, call to integrate into American society and, instead, separate from whites and glory in their blackness. Many young

In response to the vocal demonstrations of antiwar activists, supporters of the Vietnam War organized rallies at which they displayed their sentiment with slogans such as "America, Love It or Leave It."

The war in Vietnam was the chief source of Johnson's disappointment. Hundreds of thousands of Americans protested against it for a variety of reasons. Some believed that the enemy, which Americans called the Viet Cong, or Vietnamese Communists, more closely represented the will of the Vietnamese people than did the succession of governments that were set up in pro-American South Vietnam: the United States was on the wrong, undemocratic side.

Others believed that the United States was betraying its ideals by unleashing a destructive modern technology on an already poor nation: the war in Vietnam was a particularly brutal and inhumane war. There were pacifists in the antiwar movement. And some high-placed officials and even military men thought that the war was, simply, ill advised. The United States was draining its wealth and morale in a part of the world that did not matter in terms of American security.

If the antiwar movement was the protest that eventually toppled Johnson, it was not the only expression discontent in the Great Society. What is remarkable the troubles of the 1960s is that anti-Great Soci- came particularly from groups that most m the Johnson reforms.

BLACK POWER

The single most important individual in the emergence of the black-power movement was West Indian-born Stokely Carmichael. In 1966, he explained what he meant by black power: "If we are to proceed toward true liberation, we must cut ourselves off from white people. We must form our own institutions, credit unions, co-ops, political parties, write our own histories. . . ."

Malcolm X was a founder of the black-power movement of the 1960s.

by a white racist, James Earl Ray, in 1968, the smoke from burning set afire by rioters in Washington wafted into the White House itself.

The Student Movement

Just as troubling was discontent among another group that was favored by Johnson's Great Society reforms, university students. By 1963, it already was clear that the baby-boom generation was not so placid in its politics as the youth of the 1950s had been. Students demonstrated against capital punishment, protested against the violations of civil liberties by groups like the House Un-American Activities Committee, and worked in the civil-rights movement. In 1963, a new national youth organization, Students for a Democratic Society (SDS), issued the "Port Huron statement," a comprehensive critique of American society written by a graduate of the University of Michigan, Tom Hayden. The SDS called for young people to take the lead in drafting a program by which the United States

blacks, particularly in the North, were captivated by this message of defiance. One important convert was a West Indian immigrant, Stokely Carmichael, who expelled all whites from SNCC in 1966, effectively taking that group out of the civil-rights movement.

Malcolm's admonition to meet white racist violence with black violence appealed to former civil-rights workers who had been beaten by police and to teenage blacks in the urban ghettos. Carmichael's successor as the head of SNCC, Hubert Geroid "H. Rap" Brown, proclaimed as his motto, "Burn, Baby, Burn." In Oakland, California, two college students, Huey P. Newton and Bobby Seale, formed the Black Panther Party for Self-Defense. They were immediately involved in violent confrontations with police because of their insistence that they be allowed to patrol black neighborhoods with firearms.

Violence haunted black America during the 1960s. Malcolm X fell out of favor with the Black Muslims and was gunned down by assassins in 1965. Also in 1965, a riot in the Watts district of Los Angeles resulted in thirty-four deaths and $35 million in property damages. In 1966 and 1967, black riots raged in the ghettos of many cities. When Martin Luther King, Jr., was killed

A mule-drawn cart carries the body of civil rights leader Martin Luther King at his funeral in Atlanta, Georgia.

PROTEST IN AMERICA

Saul Alinsky, a well-known radical organizer, had little but contempt for the "New Left" of the 1960s. He regarded university student rebels as dilettantes and chided them for their claims that the United States was a repressive nation: "True, there is government harassment, but there still is that relative freedom to fight. I can attack my government, try to organize to change it. That's more than I can do in Moscow, Peking, or Havana."

thousands of teenagers gathered to establish what they called a "counterculture," a new way of living based on promiscuous sex, drugs (particularly marijuana and a synthetic hallucinogen, LSD), and extravagant colorful clothing. They called themselves "flower children," free of the pressures and preoccupations of American materialism. Other Americans called them "hippies" and alternately condemned them as lazy, immoral "long-haired kids" and were amused by them. In both New York and San Francisco, tour buses took curiosity seekers through hippie neighborhoods as though they were exotic foreign countries.

When commercialization seemed to be destroying the vitality of the Counterculture, numerous flower children retreated to communes in the California mountains and New Mexico desert. But because the self-fulfillment of individuals was the principal goal of the phenomenon, and because drugs played a large part in the culture, the communes were doomed from the start. The most fundamental matters of procuring the necessities of health and sanitation were neglected.

could be made genuinely democratic and a force for peace and justice.

Like the advocates of black power, the New Left, as SDS and other organizations came to be called, was not so much a political movement as an explosion of anger and frustration. Hayden and a few other youth leaders tried to channel student energies to concrete concerns like civil rights for blacks, the problems of the poor, and the power of large corporations in American society; but most of the campus riots of the late 1960s were unfocused, aimed at local grievances such as student participation in setting university rules, or directed against the war in Vietnam, a matter beyond the competence of university presidents and local merchants (chief targets of student rebellion) to solve.

Massive protest on campuses began at the University of California at Berkeley with the founding of the Free Speech Movement in 1964. By 1968, protest took a violent turn with students at Columbia University seizing several buildings and refusing to budge until they were forcibly removed by police.

The Counterculture

By 1966, many young people, high-school as well as college students, were dropping out of politics to pursue a personal rebellion. In the Haight-Ashbury district of San Francisco and in the East Village of New York,

The Antiwar Movement

Black-power militants, student activists, and ostensibly political rebels called "yippies" joined with pacifists and hundreds of thousands of troubled Americans in the single most important protest movement of the 1960s, the opposition to Lyndon Johnson's war in Vietnam. Each time the president escalated the American war effort, more and more people joined the angry opposition to it.

In the spring of 1965, organizers of a rally against the war in Washington made plans for two thousand protesters, and twenty-five thousand actually came. In October 1965, one hundred thousand people demonstrated in ninety cities. In April 1967, three hundred thousand people marched to protest the Vietnam War

BACHELOR'S DEGREES CONFERRED:
1870–1970

	Male	Female	Total
1870	7,993	1,378	9,371
1920	31,980	16,642	48,622
1940	109,546	79,954	186,500
1970	484,174	343,060	827,234

DEMONSTRATION DECADE

Between 1963 and 1968, according to the National Commission on the Causes and Prevention of Violence, there were

369 civil-rights demonstrations
239 black riots and disturbances
213 white terrorist attacks against civil-rights workers
104 antiwar demonstrations
 91 student protests on campus
 54 segregationist clashes with counter-demonstrators
 24 anti-integration demonstrations

Police confront antiwar demonstrators during the Democratic national convention in Chicago, August 28, 1968.

in New York and San Francisco. In Washington in the autumn of 1969, after Johnson had left office and the war continued, almost eight hundred thousand Americans rallied against the bloodletting.

By this time, a minority of the antiwar protesters turned to confrontation politics and even violence. A group called the Resistance urged those who opposed the war not to pay their taxes or, if they were young men, to refuse to serve in the armed forces. Protesters attempted to obstruct the induction process in Oakland, California. The greatest confrontation came in Chicago during the Democratic national convention in 1968, when several thousand young antiwar activists

battled with Chicago police in the streets of the city.

Although Lyndon Johnson had heard the shouts of many demonstrators, he was not in Chicago to hear the battle. If he had run again, in 1968, won, and served a full term, he would have been in office longer than any other president except F.D.R. But Johnson had dropped out of the race early in the year. He said it was because he did not expect to have a long life; indeed, he died at his Texas home in 1973 at the age of sixty-five. But Johnson was so quintessentially a politician that almost every political analyst agreed that he had quit because he thought the voters of 1968 would repudiate him.

BOB DYLAN (b. 1941)

Minstrel of the 1960s, Bob Dylan.

Bob Dylan was born Robert Zimmerman on May 24, 1941, in Duluth, Minnesota, and grew up in Hibbings, a drab and hard-working industrial town on the Mesabi Range, America's principal source of iron ore. Hibbings was a working-class town; the majority of its people were immigrants or the children or grandchildren of immigrants, particularly from Finland and the Slavic nations of Eastern Europe. This made Bob Zimmerman twice alienated, not quite at home. His family was Jewish, albeit highly secular, and was middle class, the proprietors of a furniture store.

The Zimmermans' fortunes were closely tied to employment in the iron mines. Later, as Bob Dylan, his stage name, Zimmerman said that his least favorite job at the store was repossessing furniture on which the purchasers could not make payments. It is possible that he was assigned that unpleasant task, although the repossession of sofas and chairs from frustrated, burly miners was not the kind of job on which one sent a skinny teenager. Indeed, much of what Bob Dylan said about himself as one of the most successful entertainers of the troubled 1960s was romantic contrivance. He told of living a vagabond's life and of struggling to make his voice heard. But his story was much more that of an instant sensation. He enjoyed a fairly ordinary, secure middle-class youth, and it was perhaps for

that reason that he was so important to the discontented middle-class youth who, in the 1960s, demonstrated their anger by protesting noisily and buying his recordings.

By 1965, half the American population was under the age of twenty-five, and, as marketing experts had calculated before the decade began, they were extremely affluent. Because they could spend their money on things that amused them, teenagers were responsible for 75 percent of the phonograph records sold in the United States.

Bob Dylan was one of the major beneficiaries of this phenomenon. Already as a teenager in Hibbings, he was rebelling. He adopted beatnik styles and took an interest in both past and contemporary critics of comfortable, materialistic, security-conscious, and conformist middle-class America.

He expressed his own criticisms through a guitar and harmonica bought for him when he was a teenager, learning to play both instruments simultaneously in the manner of the old "one-man band" comedy acts.

The songs that he wrote were far from comic. On the contrary, they were serious, if maudlin, romanticizations of the "common people" and sarcastic assaults on the America of the corporations, racial prejudice, war, and the timid middle classes. He disdained the slick, professional groups that were recording folk songs in the late 1950s, such as the Weavers, the Kingston Trio, and the Limeliters, and searched in the past for their predecessors. His hero was the Oklahoma balladeer Woody Guthrie, who had been a genuine vagabond and the author of perhaps hundreds of songs that celebrated the common people and condemned wealth and power.

Not only did Bob Dylan visit Guthrie, who was dying in a New Jersey hospital of a rare hereditary disease, but he updated the flavor of Guthrie's protest and imitated his rough-edged, grating singing style. Dylan could not sing very well; there must have been many better guitarists in the country; and the lyrics he wrote were trite. But he struck a chord in young people. He arrived in New York at the beginning of 1961, was a sensation in the coffeehouses of Greenwich Village within months, and had a contract with Columbia Records by fall.

His first album, released in February 1962, was an immediate hit. The curly-headed kid from Minnesota was the heir to such singing sensations of the 1950s as Bill Haley and the Comets, the first white musical group to record rock-'n'-roll, and Elvis Presley, the entertainment king of the decade. During the first half of the 1960s, only the Beatles, a quartet from England, made more money than Dylan in the recorded-music business.

There was something new about the entertainers of the 1960s, however. Bill Haley and Elvis Presley had been content to be show people, and troubadors such as Woody Guthrie and Pete Seeger, who sang about social issues, had only small followings. But songs of protest were at the center of the popular culture marketplace in the 1960s, and the stars of the decade were considered teachers and moral leaders by their fans.

They reacted in different ways. John Lennon, the most articulate of the Beatles, commented on the absurd implications of the mass worship of his group that the Beatles were better known than Jesus. (Instead of recognizing Lennon's barbed criticism of Beatlemania, religious leaders attacked *him* for being blasphemous.) Joan Baez, the leading woman protest singer, took her messianic role very seriously. Dylan, however, was overwhelmed and angered by it.

He refused to play the moral spokesman and, after a near-fatal automobile accident, retired to his country home in Woodstock, New York. Even when the central event of the counterculture of the 1960s was held within a few miles of his farm, Dylan refused to appear. He was, however, still taken very seriously. Professors of psychology, sociology, history, and political science wrote serious studies of his songs. In 1970, Princeton University awarded Dylan an honorary doctorate, which he accepted.

For Further Reading

On Lyndon B. Johnson, see Doris Kearns, *Lyndon Johnson and the American Dream* (1976); George Reedy, *The Twilight of the Presidency* (1970); Jack Valenti, *A Very Human President* (1975); and S. A. Levitan and Robert Taggart, *The Promise of Greatness* (1976).

Johnson's general foreign policy is treated in Theodore Draper, *Abuse of Power* (1967), and J. William Fulbright, *The Arrogance of Power* (1967). The titles indicate the authors' lack of sympathy for it. The subject catalog of any university library will list a vast number of books about Vietnam. Frances Fitzgerald, *Fire in the Lake* (1972), is essential reading. See also David Halberstam, *The Making of a Quagmire* (1956), which is sadly prophetic; M. G. Raskin and Bernard Fall, *The Vietnam Reader* (1965); and Arthur M. Schlesinger, Jr., *The Bitter Heritage: Vietnam and American Democracy* (1967).

On the black movement, writings by participants are still the best sources. See Malcolm X, *The Autobiography of Malcolm X* (1965), and Martin Luther King, Jr., *Where Do We Go From Here: Chaos or Community?* (1967). A good biography of King is David Lewis, *King: A Critical Biography* (1970). See Howard Zinn, *SNCC* (1965), for the pre-black power phase of that organization.

On the youth movement, see Kenneth Keniston, *Young Radicals* (1968), for a sympathetic view. Irwin Unger is dispassionate in *The Movement* (1974). Kirkpatrick Sale, *SDS* (1973), is the best history of the central organization of university-student protest in the era. On the counterculture, see Morris Dickstein, *Gates of Eden: American Culture in the Sixties* (1977); Theodore Roszak, *The Making of a Counter-Culture* (1969); and Charles Reich, *The Greening of America* (1970).

Less sympathetic toward cultural movements from the 1960s, albeit from different perspectives, are Ronald Berman, *America in the Sixties* (1968), and Joseph Conlin, *The Troubles: A Jaundiced Glance Back at the Movement of the 1960s* (1982). The best single overview is Godfrey Hodgson, *America in Our Time* (1976).

52

Repudiation and Resignation
The Presidency in Crisis, 1968–1974

Eugene McCarthy was in his second term as senator from Minnesota. He was a tall man, solemn, even glum in demeanor compared with a better-known Minnesota liberal, exuberant, talkative Vice President Hubert H. Humphrey. McCarthy's record was not stridently liberal; no one thought of him as a mover and shaker. Indeed, as would be learned after he became the mover and shaker of 1968, McCarthy was a poet, reflective and withdrawn by preference, a little out of sorts in the frenzied world that politics had become in the era of mass media.

Richard M. Nixon with transcripts of the Watergate tapes that implicated him in the criminal cover-up of a break-in at the Democratic party headquarters.

The Election of 1968

Anguished by what he considered the immorality of the war in Vietnam, McCarthy announced late in 1967 that he would be a candidate for the Democratic nomination for the presidency—in direct opposition to Lyndon Johnson. At first no political experts took him seriously. He was a mercurial, erratic character, and in an age when political campaigns were extremely costly, he had no money. Moreover, his only base of support was in the largely middle-class antiwar movement, not what professionals considered a reliable bloc.

McCarthy Ends Johnson's Career

So hungry was the burgeoning antiwar movement for a leader, particularly in the universities, that thousands of students dropped their studies and rushed to New Hampshire, site of the first presidential primary, to help the senator. If he did not have numbers, he had enthusiasm. The activists agreed to get "clean for Gene," to shear their long hair, shave, and don neckties and dresses in order not to alienate the people of New Hampshire from the antiwar position because of their appearance. Sleeping on the floors of campaign headquarters throughout the state, they stuffed envelopes and pushed most of the doorbells in New Hampshire to argue for their man. President Johnson was sufficiently alarmed that he kept his name off the ballot; the Democratic governor of New Hampshire ran as his proxy.

The vote was about evenly split, but such a rebuke of an incumbent president in a traditionally cautious and conservative state promised bigger McCarthy victories elsewhere. Johnson knew it. On national television, he announced that he would retire when his term expired.

The Democrats: Who Will End the War?

Johnson's announcement caught everyone by surprise. Vice President Humphrey, in Mexico on a good-will tour, rushed back to Washington to throw his hat in the ring. He had an immediate edge on McCarthy since the party professionals favored him and he was an old favorite of the labor movement and blacks, groups to whom he had devoted his career.

Antiwar feeling was not to be ignored, however, and Humphrey was closely associated with the Johnson policy. Throughout the campaign, Humphrey had to signal cryptically that his foreign policy would differ from the president's without going so far so to condemn the man under whom he still served.

The McCarthy backers expected Humphrey to run and welcomed the contest. What they could not foresee was that in the wake of Johnson's withdrawal, Senator Robert F. Kennedy of New York also would enter the race. Kennedy threatened both McCarthy and Humphrey. His antiwar record was almost as good as McCarthy's, and he maintained contacts with the party professionals and labor leaders on whom Humphrey was counting. Moreover, Kennedy was a personal friend and backer of Cesar Chavez, the leader of the Mexican-American farm workers; the Hispanic vote was as important in the key state of California as the black vote was in the eastern cities. When Martin Luther King, Jr., was assassinated on April 4, leading to anguished riots in the black sections of several cities, including Washington, Kennedy responded more sympathetically than did any other prominent leader. He clearly was the preferred candidate of the minorities.

Then, on the very night he won the California primary, Kennedy himself was murdered, shot in the head at point-blank range by Sirhan B. Sirhan, a Jordanian. The tragedy demoralized the antiwar Democrats and undoubtedly contributed to the week-long riots in Chicago that made a mockery of the Democratic national convention. Many Kennedy supporters found it impossible to swing behind McCarthy and backed Senator George McGovern of South Dakota instead. Humphrey won the Democratic nomination on the first ballot.

Nixon and Wallace

Richard M. Nixon easily won the Republican nomination at a placid convention in Miami Beach. Although the former vice president had retired from politics in 1962, after failing in an attempt to become governor of California, he had doggedly rebuilt his position in the G.O.P. He firmed up his support among eastern moderate Republicans and won over Republican conservatives by working hard for Goldwater in 1964. After 1964, Nixon attended every local Republican function to which he was invited, no matter how small the town, insignificant the occasion, or tawdry the candidate he was to endorse. By making himself so available to the party's grass-roots workers, Nixon built up energetic, active cadres of supporters, not entirely unlike the people who worked for McCarthy.

Because the Democrats were badly split, many in the antiwar wing announcing that they would vote for the pacifist pediatrician Benjamin Spock, Nixon was able to waffle on the war issue. He espoused a hawkish military policy at the same time that he reminded voters that a Republican president, Dwight D. Eisenhower, had ended the war in Korea.

Eugene McCarthy and youthful supporters during his campaign for the presidency in New Hampshire, 1968.

The threat to Nixon's candidacy came not from within his party but from outside. This was the American Independent party, founded by Governor George Wallace when he calculated that he had no chance to win the Democratic nomination. A diminutive, combative man—reporters called him a bantam fighting cock—Wallace barnstormed the country and attempted to forge an odd alliance of Republican right-wing extremists and blue-collar workingpeople who felt that the Democratic party had forgotten them in its anxiety to appeal to the blacks. This "white backlash" vote appeared to grow after Robert Kennedy was killed. Already indifferent to the aloof McCarthy, many workingpeople who had liked Kennedy found Wallace much more to their taste than civil-rights pioneer Hubert Humphrey.

A Close Call

It was soon obvious that Wallace could not win the election. His purpose was to take just enough electoral votes from both Humphrey and Nixon to throw the election into the House of Representatives. Because each state had one vote in selecting the president, anti-integration southern congressmen under his leadership could make a deal with Nixon: a reversal of Democratic party policies in return for their support.

Fearing this possibility, Humphrey called on Nixon to pledge with him that neither of them would deal with Wallace and his thinly veiled racism. Instead, Humphrey proposed, each would direct his supporters to vote for whoever of the two finished with the most votes.

Nixon evaded the challenge, and in the end it did

*Richard Nixon in the Oval Office with aides Robert Haldeman (left) and
John Erlichman (center, seated).*

not matter. Although Wallace did better than any third-party candidate since 1924, winning 13.5 percent of the popular vote and forty-six electoral votes, Nixon eked out a plurality of five hundred thousand votes and an absolute majority in the electoral college. It was close. A rush to Humphrey during the final week of the campaign indicated to some pollsters that he would have won had the election been held a week or two later. Indeed, the Democrats continued to hold a comfortable edge in both houses of Congress. The difference may well have been those antiwar Democrats who could not vote for Humphrey despite the alternative.

The Nixon Presidency

Richard M. Nixon is one of the most compelling and puzzling figures in twentieth-century politics. He lacked the qualities that are thought to be indispensable to political success in the late twentieth century: good looks, slick charm, social graces, wit, a camera presence. On the contrary, he was furtive in manner;

even after careful rehearsing, he looked grotesquely insincere in front of a crowd. Liberals hated him from his days as a young congressman when his political methods were, in their opinion, totally unscrupulous. And yet, right-wing Republicans did not love him for the enemies he had made. The only political passion Richard M. Nixon aroused was negative.

Through hard work and boundless tenacity he rose from a modest childhood in the sleepy citrus town of Whittier, California, to the highest office in the land. He was a real-life Horatio Alger hero. Whatever else may be said of Nixon, he earned everything he ever got.

Domestic Policy

Nixon was not very interested in domestic policy. He confessed to intimates that the issues bored him. He was able to gratify his conservative supporters by replacing liberal Supreme Court justices, including Earl Warren, with conservatives, but even that exercise of power was a nuisance. In filling one vacancy, Nixon had to withdraw the names of two nominees, one because he had a segregationist past, the other because he was clearly incompetent.

He left dialog with the nation on domestic issues to his vice president, Spiro T. Agnew, who delighted conservatives by baiting student protestors, "permissive" educators who tolerated their disruptive activities, liberal Supreme Court justices, defeatists, and the national news media. Agnew was best known for his fondness for alliteration in his speeches. His finest piece was "the nattering nabobs of negativism," which had been written out of a thesaurus.

The most troubling domestic problem of the Nixon years was inflation. The huge government expenditures of the Johnson years—financing the Great Society and the Vietnam War at the same time—caused prices to rise at an alarming rate, resulting in demands by workers for higher wages and a renewal of the spiral. In 1970, the Democratic Congress voted the president authority to freeze wages and prices, but Nixon refused to do so until the summer of 1971. By freezing wages and prices and by abandoning a promise to balance the budget, Nixon joined his liberal predecessors in saying that the federal government, particularly the president, was responsible for the health of the economy. Conservative Republicans such as Goldwater and Governor Ronald Reagan of California were disappointed, but

Nixon's shift helped him politically. While the economy was by no means robust in the election year of 1972, it was healthier than any other year of Nixon's first term and contributed to his reelection.

Nixon's Vietnam Policy

Nixon knew well that Johnson's political career had been snuffed out by the war in Vietnam. He was persuaded by his special assistant for national security, Henry A. Kissinger, that the war could never be won in the sense that Johnson, with his policy of escalation, had believed could be done. However, Nixon was just as determined as his predecessor not to be the first American president to capitulate to a battlefield enemy. To resolve the dilemma, he and Kissinger devised a policy to quiet the antiwar movement at home by reducing the long casualty lists while they searched for a formula by which the United States could get out of the war without winning but also without losing face.

Nixon's war policy had three parts. First, he stepped up the bombing of North Vietnam in order to hobble the enemy in South Vietnam (which was supplied from the north) and convince the North Vietnamese that they could not win a total victory. Second he beefed up programs to supply and train the never-efficient South Vietnamese army and, one by one, substituted South Vietnamese units for American detachments in high-casualty areas. Third, he gradually withdrew American troops, pointing to each reduction in the contingent (and the casualty lists) as proof that he was winding down the war.

The Defeat of the Antiwar Movement

From a high of 541,000 men in 1969, American troops in Vietnam were reduced to 239,000 in 1970, and 48,000 in 1972, the year Nixon ran for reelection. By that time, the president had successfully flanked the antiwar movement on every front. With each withdrawal of troops, Nixon, with temperate tone, and Agnew, with shrill sarcasm, depicted the antiwar protesters as irresponsible radicals who were encouraging the North Vietnamese to hold out, and thus impeding a conscientious president's efforts to make peace.

In fact, Nixon's political advisers were happy for the violent protests. They believed that each incident worked to the president's benefit because a majority of Americans disapproved of the turmoil. Antiwar protesters who called for peaceful demonstrations suspected that shouting and throwing incidents were actually engineered by the White House. In any case, the final spasm of 1960s-style protest was quite spontaneous. In May 1970, after Richard Nixon ordered troops

SOUTHEAST ASIA

Children hit by napalm flee in agony in Trangbang, South Vietnam, June 8, 1972.

into Cambodia, ostensibly to root out enemy sanctuaries, students on more than four hundred campuses shut down their universities, demonstrated noisily, and in many cases rioted.

At Kent State University in Ohio, National Guardsmen opened fire on demonstrating students, killing four. The incident was later condemned as avoidable and attributed by some critics to Agnew's inflammatory rhetoric. In any case, as if this were the first bloodshed during the decade of protest, the turmoil came to a halt. By the autumn of 1970, a hush had fallen over American universities. Two years later, Nixon won a resounding reelection against antiwar Senator George McGovern.

The antiwar movement was dead, and in the same month as Nixon's second inauguration, America's role in the Vietnam War was terminated too. In January 1973, Henry Kissinger and North Vietnamese negotiator Le Duc Tho signed an armistice in Paris. Ostensibly, South Vietnam would remain independent. But few informed people believed that the tragic war would end in any other way than it actually did in April 1975, after Nixon had left office. North and South Vietnamese never really stopped fighting one another, and in that month South Vietnam disintegrated. The army of militaristic North Vietnam occupied Saigon, and renamed the capital Ho Chi Minh City.

The Limits of Superpower

The most striking lesson of America's defeat in Vietnam was the curious limitations it revealed as being intrinsic to the possession of great military power. Short of destroying Vietnam, which the United States had the capacity to do, massive force and modern military technology were of little avail against guerrillas employing hit-and-run tactics and refusing to be drawn into a battle in which sophisticated weaponry made the difference. Whereas massive aerial bombardment could have devastating effect against a highly industrialized country because it was dependent on modern transportation and communications systems, the very primitiveness of the North Vietnamese economy rendered massive air attacks ineffective.

Vietnamese industry was decentralized, and the enemy moved its men and supplies by foot and bicycle along dirt tracks and across bamboo bridges that could be rebuilt almost overnight after a bombing. Walter Lippmann compared the United States to an elephant in a war against mosquitoes. There was no doubt which was the greater beast, but there was no way that the elephant could win. In the meantime, civilians inevitably suffered from massive bombing, and the reputation of the United States sank all over the world.

Nixon Triumphant, Nixon Destroyed

Even while the war in Vietnam continued, a diplomatic revolution was under way. While the Soviet Union and the People's Republic of China continued to aid North Vietnam in the fight against the United States, both countries signaled Nixon that they were prepared to establish détente, a recognition that in the nuclear age, regular diplomatic relations were preferable to sustained hostility and bickering that easily could lead to all-out war.

The first secret and then dramatically public invita-

Photos and roses left behind by visitors to the Vietnam War Memorial. Though the war ended in 1975, a memorial was not erected in Washington, D.C., until November 1982, an indication, perhaps, of the nation's unwillingness to confront the tragedy of Vietnam.

tions to détente were a result of the increasing hostility and, perhaps, military engagements on the long Soviet-Chinese border. Both great powers were sufficiently afraid of each other to wish to placate the United States. However, a constructive American response to the signals was possible only because Henry A. Kissinger, Nixon's chief foreign-policy adviser, was a man of imagination who wanted to be remembered in history as a great diplomat, and the president himself craved a lasting monument for his presidency.

The Diplomatic Revolution

In 1971, an American table-tennis team on a tour of Japan was startled to receive an invitation from China to play a series of exhibition games in the People's Republic before they returned home. Diplomats noted wryly that the Chinese had picked an area of competition in which they would shine (the Americans were soundly trounced), but Henry Kissinger recognized the implications of the trivial event. After negotiations that remain shrouded in mystery, he flew secretly to Peking in the wake of the table-tennis tournaments and arranged for a good-will tour by Nixon himself in February 1972.

The visit was a grand success. Nixon toasted world peace with Chairman Mao Tse-tung and, more important, for Mao was senile and fading, with Chou En-lai and Teng Hsiao-p'ing, the rising leaders of the populous nation. Few sights could have astounded Americans more. For twenty-five years, the United States had described the People's Republic as an outlaw nation, and China had vilified the United States as the fount of all the world's exploitation and injustice. Now, gradually but inexorably, the United States dropped its opposition to China's application for a seat in the United Nations, allowed the unseating of Taiwan (formerly recognized by the United States as the legitimate government of China), and exchanged ambassadors and consuls with the People's Republic. Indeed, American industrialists involved in everything from oil exploration to the bottling of soft drinks flew to China by the thousands, anxious to sell American technology and consumer goods in the market that always had symbolized the ultimate sales opportunity.

Consequences of the New China Policy

China did not turn out to be much of an importer of American know-how and products. The Chinese population was huge, but the country was not rich; there was neither money nor goods with which to pay for imports. Nor were the new leaders of China interested

*Nixon and Chinese leader Chou En-lai toast each other during Nixon's visit
to China in 1972.*

in resuming the status of a colonial market. Their principal motive in courting American amity was diplomatic, to win some edge of security in their conflict with the Soviet Union by forestalling a joint Soviet-American opposition.

From the American point of view, the rapprochement with China opened the way for détente with the Soviets. In June 1972, just months after his China trip, Nixon flew to the Soviet Union and signed the preliminary agreement in the opening series of Strategic Arms Limitation Talks (SALT), the first significant step toward a slowdown of the arms race since the Kennedy administration.

At home, the photos of Nixon clinking champagne glasses with the Chinese and Russians bewildered his conservative supporters. They knew the president as one of the most vociferous Cold Warriors for more than twenty years. Now he was cozying up to the two great

Communist powers as no Democratic liberal would have dared to do. Indeed, as Nixon and Kissinger understood, only a Republican with a Cold-Warrior past could afford to do what Nixon had done. Along with this and his New Deal-type price controls, however, Nixon appeared to betray everything that the conservatives stood for.

Henry A. Kissinger

The right-wing Republicans increasingly blamed Henry A. Kissinger for the Nixon policies. Kissinger's political background was liberal Republican—as foreign-policy adviser to Nelson A. Rockefeller—and he was from Harvard University, which conservatives considered to be a hothouse of un-American ideas. Kissinger's urbane charm, simultaneously arrogant and self-mocking, also infuriated the right wing. He was also a Jew, a refugee as a boy from Nazi Germany. Although American conservatives ostensibly had left anti-Semitism behind when they had backed Barry Goldwater, whose grandfather had been a Jewish merchant on the Arizona frontier, the prejudice could not help but revive in the suspicion of Kissinger.

They were right about one thing. Nixon became progressively more impressed with and dependent on Kissinger's brilliance, eloquence, and diplomatic skills. The president wanted a niche in history, and Kissinger was the man most likely to win it for him. In 1973, Nixon accepted the resignation of Secretary of State William P. Rogers, who already was just a figurehead, and gave the job to Kissinger.

Shuttle Diplomacy

Well into 1974, the diplomatic successes piled up. Kissinger's greatest triumph came in the Middle East. In 1973, Egypt and Syria attacked Israel on Yom Kippur, and fought the only reliable American ally in the area to a draw. It was the first time the Arab states had not been decisively defeated by Israel since the establishment of the Jewish state after the Second World War.

Fearing what a prolonged war in the strategically important and oil-rich Middle East would mean for the United States, Kissinger shuttled seemingly without sleep among Damascus, Cairo, and Tel Aviv, carrying proposal and counterproposal for a settlement. Unlike John Foster Dulles, who also had tried to represent American interests in person, Kissinger was a genius at the negotiating table. The terms he prevailed on all the warring powers to sign actually increased American influence in the area by winning the gratitude and friendship of Egyptian President Anwar el-Sadat, while not alienating Israel.

After 1974, however, Kissinger lost his magic touch

and reputation for infallibility. It became clear that he was less interested in ending the Cold War than in setting up spheres of influence dominated by the great powers while continuing the old rivalry in marginal areas. All the while right-wing Republicans stepped up their attacks on him, Kissinger practiced precisely the same kind of policy in the former Portuguese colony of Angola in Africa that had led to the Vietnam tragedy: fairly openly backing one faction in that land, while the Soviets backed another.

The most damaging mark on Kissinger's record as chief diplomat of a democratic country came with the discovery that, in September 1973, he had been aware of CIA activities in Chile that had led to a coup against democratically elected President Salvador Allende, his subsequent murder, and the establishment of a brutally repressive but pro-American regime.

By 1975, however, Kissinger was no longer serving Richard Nixon. The crisis of the presidency that had begun when Lyndon Johnson was repudiated took on a new dimension of gravity when Richard M. Nixon was forced to resign in disgrace.

The Election of 1972

Between 1968 and 1972, the Democrats reorganized the system by which they selected convention delegates, guaranteeing minimum representation of minority groups and women simply on the basis of ethnic origins and sex. The people who gathered in Miami in 1972 formed the youngest convention in political history and reflected the antiwar politics of their generation. They nominated war critic George McGovern of South Dakota to head their ticket.

A sincere and decent man who was deeply grieved by the ongoing war in Vietnam, McGovern ran a two-issue campaign: peace and his integrity compared with Nixon's longstanding reputation for deviousness and dirty tricks. The Republicans countered by depicting McGovern as a bumbling and indecisive radical. When McGovern first defended his running mate, Thomas Eagleton, who had undergone psychiatric treatment several years earlier, and then forced him to drop out, his race was doomed. Nixon won 60.8 percent of the popular vote and carried every state but Massachusetts and the District of Columbia. In only eight years, he had reversed the overwhelming Republican defeat of 1964.

There was one significant difference between 1964 and 1972, however. Even though Nixon trounced McGovern, the Democrats held on to their comfortable majorities in Congress, sometimes by runaway margins. The American people did not want George McGovern as president. But they did not want as lawmakers those Republicans who spoke of dismantling the reforms of the New Deal and the Great Society.

A President Resigns

On June 17, 1972, early in the presidential campaign, Washington police arrested five men who were trying to plant electronic listening devices in Democratic party headquarters in a Washington apartment and office complex called the Watergate. It was quickly learned that three of the suspects had White House contacts and were on the payroll of the Committee to Re-elect the President, which soon became unattractively abbreviated as CREEP.

McGovern tried to exploit this discovery, but the issue fizzled when Nixon and his campaign manager, Attorney General John Mitchell, denied any knowledge of the incident and condemned the burglary.

Nixon did not know about the burglary in advance, but he soon learned that the men had acted on orders from his aides. He instructed his staff to find money to hush up the burglars.

Unfortunately for the president, two of the burglars, James E. McCord and Howard Hunt, implicated government officials higher up. Robert Woodward and Carl Bernstein, two inquisitive reporters on the staff of the *Washington Post,* and a special Senate investigating committee headed by Sam Ervin of North Carolina picked away at the tangle from different directions and traced the Watergate break-in and other illegal actions to the White House. Judge John Sirica handed down several orders that crippled the cover-up, and Leon Jaworski, a Texas lawyer whom Nixon was forced to appoint as special prosecutor, proved to be an honest and relentless investigator.

Highly placed Nixon advisers abandoned ship one by one, each convinced that he was being set up as a scapegoat and naming others in the cover-up. A snarl of half-truths and lies descended on the president. Nixon already was reeling when it was revealed that Vice President Spiro Agnew had accepted bribes when he was governor of Maryland. Agnew was forced to plead no contest to charges of income-tax evasion and resign from the vice presidency in October 1973; he was replaced by Congressman Gerald Ford of Michigan.

Nixon might have survived except that he had kept tape recordings of numerous conversations in his Oval Office that clearly implicated him in the cover-up. Why he did not destroy them early in the Watergate investigation remains a mystery. Some historians

Nixon announcing on television on August 8, 1974, that he is resigning from the presidency.

have suggested that greed—the money that the electronic documents would bring after Nixon left the presidency—was responsible for his fatal error. As it turned out, the House Judiciary Committee, which was considering the impeachment of the president, was on the verge of beginning the trial when an obviously shattered Nixon resigned. Like Lyndon Johnson, he went from a landslide election victory to discredit within a few years.

A Ford, Not a Lincoln

Television news commentator Eric Sevareid began his nightly message: "A funny thing happened to Gerald Ford on the way to becoming Speaker of the House of Representatives, his greatest ambition." Ford put his ordinariness in another way. He told Americans that they had "a Ford, not a Lincoln" in the White House.

Gerald Ford lacked high intelligence as well as high ambition. He had accomplished little in Congress. He was best known for having led an abortive attempt to remove William O. Douglas from the Supreme Court in large part because the aged Douglas had married a twenty-year-old lawyer. Lyndon Johnson once told reporters that Ford's trouble was that he had played center on the University of Michigan football team without a helmet.

And yet his simplicity and forthrightness were a relief after Nixon's squirming and deception. There was an uproar and cries of "deal" when the first unelected president pardoned Nixon of all crimes, but by 1976, Ford's popularity was on the upswing.

The Mood of the 1970s

Within a year of the Kent State massacre, social pulse takers noticed a complete turnaround in the general attitudes of the American people, particularly those who had become the style setters by virtue of their numbers: the children of the baby boom. Whereas the young people of the 1960s had been socially conscious, concerned with pressing problems like racial injustice, poverty, dehumanization, and war, the young people of the 1970s turned inward. Historian Christopher Lasch wrote in his book *The Culture of Narcissism* (1979) that the American people had become obsessed with themselves as individuals. Writer Tom Wolfe was less classical in his image of his times: he called the 1970s the "Me decade."

Us

Part of the reason for the retreat into self was age. The movement of the 1960s had a motto, "You can't trust anyone over thirty." In the 1970s, the first contingent of boom babies celebrated their thirtieth birthdays. Their styles changed. It was not so much that the carefree life was in the past, but that the style setters of the era abandoned the mass demonstration as a means of self-gratification and turned to more personal outlets.

Because the 1970s generation was affluent, self-fulfillment took on commercial shape. One boom in consumer goods followed another, with the biggest

---

NARCISSUS

In Greek mythology, Narcissus was a handsome young man who one day leaned over a pond to take a drink, saw an image of himself, and fell madly in love. Christopher Lasch felt that this was an apt analogy for the fashionable young middle-class people of the 1970s.

---

profits made by companies that sold products that simultaneously provided fun and physical exercise. Successively, Americans spent billions of dollars on ski equipment, tennis paraphernalia, ten-speed bicycles, and backpacking gear. Research-and-development departments of sporting-goods companies worked overtime to devise new kinds of recreation that might have popular appeal, including hang gliders and parachutes for skydiving. Virtually no activity failed to gain some following, and some became national manias. For example, by 1980, one adult in five was jogging regularly.

A woman works out with weight equipment, a popular form of exercise during the 1970s.

CONSTITUTIONAL CONTRADICTION?

Gerald Ford was appointed to the vice presidency under the provisions of the Twenty-fifth Amendment, ratified in 1967, which stipulates that "whenever there is a vacancy in the office of the Vice President, the President shall nominate a Vice President. . . ." When he succeeded to the presidency, he appointed Nelson A. Rockefeller to the vice presidency. Neither the president nor the vice president held office by virtue of election. However, as some constitutional experts were quick to point out, Article II, Section 1 of the Constitution provides that the president and vice president are to "be elected."

In fact, the contradiction was always there, if never put to the test. At different times, the Constitution held that the Secretary of State and the Speaker of the House were next in line to the presidency after the vice president. A case could be made that the Speaker was elected, but not the Secretary of State.

EXPENDITURES OF AMERICAN TOURISTS ABROAD		
	Number of Travelers	Expenditures (in millions)
1920	302,000	$ 170
1930	538,000	655
1940	156,000	378
1950	676,000	1,022
1960	1,634,000	2,623
1970	5,260,000	6,173
1980	8,163,000	16,508

control of venereal disease, which was made possible by antibiotics, eliminated yet another fear.

The third source of liberalized sexual attitudes was the decision by the Supreme Court in a number of cases that frank, open, and even graphic discussion and depiction of sexual acts were protected by the constitutional right of free speech. While standards varied radically from state to state and city to city, sexually explicit books and films became freely available. Finally, the bohemian streak among style-setting young people of the 1960s insisted that repressive sexual codes as well as traditional social strictures be defied.

Self-Fulfillment

The affluent young of the 1970s became preoccupied with psychological as well as physical self-fulfillment. While Indian gurus had made their appearance in the 1960s, attracting acolytes from show business and the counterculture, they survived the end of the activist decade and multiplied. The Maharishi Mahesh Yogi, who became rich when the Beatles briefly adopted him in the mid 1960s, began to preach his transcendental meditation no longer as a way to reach spiritual fulfillment but as a means to make more money. Another guru took over a town in Oregon, encouraged free sexual expression, denounced material values, and bought fifteen Rolls Royce automobiles.

Any number of other paths to complete self-fulfillment flourished; most of them involved some form of immediate pleasure, but others, such as a school of massage called "rolfing," were downright painful. For the most part these serial fads were ridiculous, but some attracted hostile criticism. The Hare Krishnas and the followers of Sun Myung Moon, a Korean preacher who claimed to be divine, seemed to be easily manipulated young people who were, in effect, hypnotized to work for no wages in a variety of profitable enterprises. To critics it was a neat way to get around the Thirteenth Amendment, which forbids involuntary servitude, by appealing to the First, which guarantees freedom of religion.

Sources of the Sexual Revolution

The revolution in sexual morality that reached its apogee in the 1970s had its roots in the late nineteenth century and was accelerated in the 1960s from four different quarters. The sexual revolution owed first of all to the development of a reliable birth-control device—popularly called "the pill"—which eliminated the dread of pregnancy by single women. The

The Natural History of Swinging

In the 1970s, acceptance of liberated sexuality and even a preoccupation with sex became general among the middle classes, and then the working class. Bars for "singles" became fixtures in every big city and many towns. Landlords converted or constructed apartment

Betty Friedan, feminist author and founder of the National Organization for Women.

complexes that were designed to accommodate "swinging singles."

Married people could hardly have been unaffected, and the divorce rate soared, reaching 50 percent of all marriages in California and higher percentages in fashionable, affluent counties. The liberalization of sexual attitudes during the 1970s also extended to toleration of homosexuals, and, in sophisticated cities like San Francisco and New York, "gays" came "out of the closet" and made their predilections public.

Just as the control of venereal disease played a part in initiating the sexual revolution, a disease was a key element in its leveling off about 1980. A penicillin-resistant strain of gonorrhea made its appearance, and a mysterious, fatal disease—AIDS, or Acquired Immunity Deficiency Syndrome—began to afflict homosexuals. Herpes, an old and minor but bothersome venereal infection reached epidemic proportions among sexually active people, who began to have second thoughts at the aging singles bars.

Even before these shocks, however, one branch of the most significant political movement of the 1970s, the women's liberation movement, had condemned casual sexual relations as just one more way in which a male-dominated society exploited women.

Women's Liberation

After her book *The Feminine Mystique* (1963) received a rousing response, Betty Friedan was encouraged to form, in 1966, the National Organization for Women (NOW), a pressure group designed to secure legal and social equality for women.

At first, "women's lib" was widely ridiculed because of the activities of fringe "libbers," but the essence of the new feminism was too serious to be ignored. By the 1970s, NOW had established its leadership over the fringe groups and rapidly succeeded in striking down most state and federal laws and policies that explicitly discriminated against women.

Victories of the New Feminism

The victories were deceptively easy. Laws that prevented married women from borrowing money without the approval of their husbands were easily repealed. Only a little more difficult was NOW's campaign to win for women entrance to jobs that were restricted to men, particularly in manual and dangerous work such as construction and firefighting. The organization was also successful, although perhaps not permanently so, in de-sexing words like *fireman*. Almost instanta-

No longer confined to traditional female occupations, women became everything from lawyers to telephone line workers following the women's liberation movement of the late 1960s and early 1970s.

neously, businesses and government took to speaking of "mailcarriers" and "chairpersons" and addressing women as "Ms." rather than "Miss" or "Mrs." which, to the feminists, represented demeaning patronization.

Other gains were made in the matters of equal pay for women who did the same jobs as men and the adoption in government and business of "affirmative-action" policies. Universities and employers were obligated to admit or to hire women (and members of ethnic minority groups) in preference to white males if the applicants were as qualified as the males. Because, in practice, less qualified women, blacks, Hispanics, and others were often given preferential treatment, resulting in a quota system such as liberals had fought against when it had been used to discriminate against minorities, the Supreme Court dealt a major blow to affir-

MEXICAN-AMERICANS:
CHANGING TIMES, CHANGING VALUES

In 1971, a Chicano teaching fellow at Harvard Law School told a reporter for the *Boston Sunday Globe* that "my parents pushed me very hard in an Anglo direction. I rejected every Chicano value. For 29 years I have lived a life of total pretension. It has led to horrible complications in myself. I am just now learning who I am." Having expressed a deep-felt wish to be reconciled to Chicano culture, he referred to the handful of Mexican-American students at Harvard and observed, "None of us would be here if we hadn't tried to be Anglo." The implication was that Harvard Law School should also bestow its appointments and generous salaries on people who had clung to Chicano culture.

Agonizing about "identity" was a favorite activity in the 1970s among privileged members of minority groups. It was, among other things, a way to get ahead by playing on the sensitivity of the government, business, and academic establishments to their heritage of discrimination against minorities. It was difficult to sympathize with such identity crises when the vast majority of the members of minority groups such as Mexican-Americans struggled daily just to get by.

But such posing helped anthropologists and sociologists to focus on genuine clashes between traditional group values and the values that lead to success in the mainstream society. With Chicanos in the 1970s, as with immigrant groups of the early twentieth century, there was a wrenching cultural adjustment to be made in order to win a fair share of the benefits of American society. Old ways had to be abandoned, new ones adopted, and the process was more difficult for Chicanos because of the closeness of the mother country and the well-meaning but damaging policies of the Anglo establishment. (*Chicano* is a slangy contraction of *Mexicano* and connotes political activism; in Chicano usage, *Anglo* refers to all white Americans, not just those of English descent.)

Mexican-Americans were the second largest minority in the United States in the 1970s; only blacks were more numerous. They made up the single largest ethnic group in the southwestern states of California, Arizona, New Mexico, Texas, and Colorado. As recently as the 1950s, they had been a majority in New Mexico.

A word of caution is in order. Sociologically, no other American ethnic group has such a variety of backgrounds as the 7 million people who are lumped together by the Census Bureau as "Spanish surname." Setting aside Puerto Ricans, Cubans, and immigrants from other Spanish-speaking countries, seven categories of Mexican-Americans can be identified, of which four are not immigrants at all: (1) descendants of the *californios*, inhabitants of California before it was seized by the United States, most of whom were Indians or of mixed race; (2) the more quickly assimilated descendants of the upper-class Caucasian *californios*; (3) *tejanos*, descendants of the inhabitants of Texas before it became independent; (4) *nuevo mexicanos*, descendants of pre-Anglo New Mexicans, who were self-consciously more Spanish than Mexican because they were never much under the control of or particularly fond of the government of the Mexican Republic; (5) descendants of the refugees from the Mexican Revolution during the 1910s and 1920s, many of them well educated and affluent; (6) descendants of the *braceros*, imported farm laborers, of the 1930s and 1940s; and (7) immigrants of the 1960s and 1970s, who entered the United States (many illegally) in search of work.

A people of so many origins may be spoken of as an ethnic group only because of the development of the Chicano consciousness movement in the mid-1960s, which led to the first successful expressions of Mexican-American wishes through Cesar Chavez's United Farm Workers; *La Raza Unida*, a political party formed in Texas and similar to the blacks' Mississippi Freedom Democrats; and any number of university campus organizations. It is ironic that, as with those who spoke for other minorities, it was possible to represent Chicano interests effectively only to the extent that spokesmen had transcended the values of Mexican-American subculture.

Sociologist Fernando Peñalosa found examples of Mexican-Americans whose forebears had lived in Texas for two hundred years and yet "largely retained the language and culture." Such a phenomenon was possible only as long as Anglo prejudice shut such people out of the mainstream society and forced them to cling to traditional ways as solace. Despite their numbers in Texas, California, and New Mexico, communities of the sort Peñalosa discovered could not produce effective leaders so long as they were despised for being Mexican-Americans.

As a byproduct of the black struggle for civil equality in the 1960s, the external, legal obstacles that had prevented Chicanos from winning a place in American society were also struck down. However, long-established cultural habits could not be abolished with the signing of a law, and they continued to impede Mexican-American progress. Studies of Mexican-American social mobility in Albuquerque, Los Angeles, and San Antonio in the 1970s revealed what could have been predicted: a direct correlation between income and social station, and the degree to which the more successful had broken with old ways and adopted those of Anglo society. For example, in all three cities, Chicanos and Chicanas who had married Anglos already had moved out of the *barrio* and up the economic ladder.

In a 1972 study, B. S. Bradshaw and F. D. Bean divided a sample of 348 Mexican-American couples in Austin, Texas, into two groups according to their socioeconomic status. They found that 74 percent of those in the higher group lived outside the Austin *barrio*, but only 27 percent of the lower group did. The women in the higher group were more likely to work outside the home and to demand of their husbands an equal voice in household decisions. The higher group was more likely to have close Anglo friends, to speak English exclusively or more than they spoke Spanish, and generally to have middle-class values.

"Making good" in the United States by adopting American ways had been the experience of almost all immigrant groups, from the Irish and Germans of the mid-nineteenth century to the Jews, Greeks, Italians, Slavs, and other New Immigrants of the early twentieth century. However, the Mexican-Americans of the 1970s labored under two sociocultural burdens that these groups had not.

First, the closeness of Mexico and the steady influx of new immigrants from Mexico constantly reinvigorated the traditional values, including some that stood squarely in the way of social and economic advancement: valuing interpersonal relationships over competitiveness and acquisition of material wealth; emphasizing family welfare over individual advancement; recognizing male dominance (*machismo*) and female submissiveness; and producing extremely large families. In 1970, the Mexican-American annual fertility rate was higher than that of any other major ethnic group: 42.32 children per 1,000 women compared with 28.91 for Anglos and 34.89 for blacks.

Other ethnic groups had brought similar cultural baggage from Europe. But far from sentimentalizing the old ways and lamenting their loss, the leaders of Jews, Italians, Poles, and others browbeat their communities into recognizing that the United States was not Russia, Italy, or Poland and adjusting to that reality, however painful it might be to do so. Although the southern and Eastern European ethnic groups hardly approved of them, the immigration quota laws of 1921 and 1924 worked to their benefit by preventing the reinforcement of old-country ways by new arrivals.

Second, well-meaning state and federal policymakers in the 1970s did a disservice to Chicanos when they encouraged them to cling to traditional ways and particularly to the Spanish language by making it easy to do so. In California, for example, all state documents were published in Spanish (and Chinese) as well as in English. In many schools, catch-up classes in English

for Spanish-speaking children were neglected and even abolished in favor of classes in which the regular curriculum was taught in Spanish.

Unlike the children of other ethnic groups, who were forced to learn English in public schools and therefore were given access to the world beyond their neighborhoods, Mexican-American children were chained to the *barrios*, in other words, to chronic poverty. While it was easy at the end of the 1970s to get along in the *barrios* speaking only Spanish, and to read every California state publication in that language, Harvard Law School, which is in Massachusetts, had not instituted a program for the training of attorneys who remained loyal to this aspect of "Chicano consciousness".

Young Chicanos face a difficult choice between preserving their native language and traditional culture and adopting values that lead to success in American society.

mative action. In the *Bakke* case (1978), the Court forced the University of California medical school to admit a white male applicant whose qualifications were better than those of several affirmative-action applicants whom the school had accepted. Government, business, and universities entered the 1980s searching for ways to evade the charge of "reverse discrimination," but early in the decade, the feminists suffered a defeat that NOW regarded as much more important—the rejection of the Equal Rights Amendment (ERA).

ERA

Sent to the states from Congress in 1972, the ERA was a Fourteenth Amendment for women, forbidding any kind of legal or social discrimination on the basis of sex. Debate of the amendment seemed to reveal that it would do nothing more than guarantee rights that women were winning by statute and policy directive, and within a few years the amendment was ratified by all but a handful of the thirty-eight states needed to make it a part of the Constitution.

Then, seemingly from nowhere, emerged a ground swell of opposition to the ERA led by a longtime right-wing Republican writer, Phyllis Schlafly. Cautioning that ratification of the ERA would lead to the loss of certain privileges that women enjoyed, for example, exemption from military conscription, Schlafly encouraged hundreds of state legislators to oppose ratification. When the 1979 deadline for ratification was reached, the ERA was still three states short of approval.

The Senate immediately extended the deadline to 1982, a dubious changing of the rules to which three states responded by withdrawing their votes for ratification, a clear indication that the momentum was with Schlafly. NOW contested the right to revoke ratification, but the case was never tested because the ERA won no more states.

Changing Times

Why did the ERA fail? In part the failure was due to the efficient campaign mounted by Schlafly and the increasingly powerful Republican conservatives. More fundamentally, however, the ERA was not ratified because the 1970s were not political years. As a novelty early in the decade, the new feminism was popular among the middle classes. When the feminists did not win quick, decisive victories, however, their project was doomed.

NOW and women's liberation never did spark much enthusiasm among lower-class women. Equal pay for

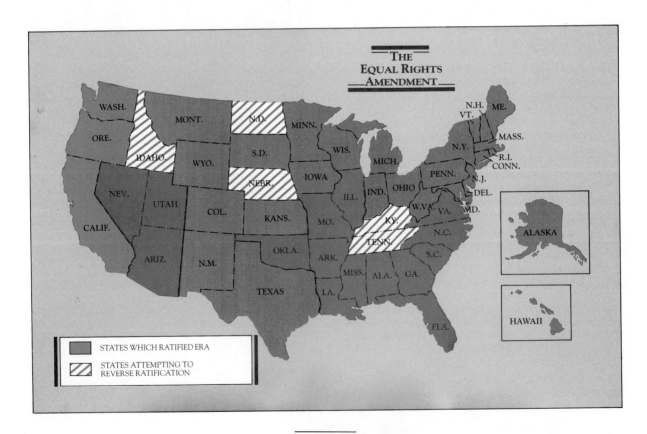

THE EQUAL RIGHTS AMENDMENT

STATES WHICH RATIFIED ERA

STATES ATTEMPTING TO REVERSE RATIFICATION

Opponents to the Equal Rights Amendment mounted an efficient campaign against the amendment.

equal work was important to them, but once that goal had been fairly well achieved, they turned to other economic problems that they shared with their fathers, husbands, and sons. In the 1980s, economic problems became paramount in the lives of the middle class as well. Throughout American history, financial concerns supersede interest in questions of status, rights, and privileges when this is so.

For Further Reading

Richard M. Nixon, *RN: The Memoirs of Richard Nixon* (1978), massive and self-justifying, nevertheless remains the starting point in reading about his presidency. Two other useful depictions are Garry Wills, *Nixon Agonistes* (1970), and Jules Witcover, *The Resurrection of Richard Nixon* (1970). Theodore H. White wrote a study of Nixon's elections in *The Making of the President, 1968, 1972* (1969, 1973). For the 1976 contest, see Jules Witcover, *Marathon* (1977).

Henry A. Kissinger, *White House Years* (1979), is the best reminiscence by an important political figure in the twentieth century. Needed for balance is the critical book by Roger Morris, *Uncertain Greatness: Henry Kissinger and American Foreign Policy* (1977). See also, A. E. Goodman, *The Lost Peace: America's Search for a Negotiated Settlement of the Vietnam War* (1978), and William Shawcross, *Sideshow: Kissinger, Nixon, and the Destruction of Cambodia* (1978).

Arthur M. Schlesinger, Jr., *The Imperial Presidency* (1973); Theodore H. White, *Breach of Faith* (1975); and Jonathan Schell, *The Time of Illusion* (1976), are necessary to understanding what happened to the presidency under Johnson and Nixon. For Watergate, the standard work is, of course, by the two *Washington Post* reporters who broke the story, Carl Bernstein and Robert Woodward, *All the President's Men* (1974).

53

The Third Century Begins
America Since 1976

"Break out the flag, strike up the band, light up the sky!" With those appealing old-fashioned words, President Gerald R. Ford proclaimed the nation's bicentennial celebration. The spirit of exultation had been in the air since the beginning of the year; but the American mood was also oddly ambivalent, and it is still not clear whether to put a positive or a negative construction on some aspects of the great birthday party.

For example, unlike in 1876, when Americans celebrated the centennial by going to a fair, by being spectators at a professional show, the people of 1976 were much more likely to *participate*, surely a healthy sign. In practically every community, Americans restored historic buildings, planted trees, marched in parades, mixed in huge picnics on the Fourth of July, participated in mammoth costume pageants that re-created historic events, and retraced by car, bicycle, horse and wagon, and foot the trails over which the American people had gone west.

But the only reason that there was no single mammoth exposition was because the people who lived near the proposed site on the northeastern edge of Philadelphia protested the proposal angrily, even violently. They did not want the traffic congestion, crowds, commercialization, and crime in their neighborhood. They did not want to play host to their compatriots. In

Tall ships sailed in New York harbor as part of America's bicentennial celebration, July 4, 1976.

the end, even the promoters of the event gave up. As 1976 approached, the steady rise in gasoline prices seemed to augur poor attendance and no profits.

The year's most glorious spectacle turned out to be the arrival in New York harbor of dozens of sailing ships and hundreds of sailboats, a vision of a past that has been gone for almost a century. The sight thrilled the entire nation. Once again, however, there was a worrisome contrast between the fleet of sailing ships as a symbol and the centerpiece of the Centennial Exposition of 1876. The ships were a nostalgic look backward; the gigantic Corliss steam engine had been a symbol of the future. Had Americans given up on the future in 1976?

They had not. But the end of America's second century and the beginning of its third did not occur in the best of times.

The Ford Interregnum

The period after a king dies, but before his successor is crowned, is called an interregnum, a period of waiting between reigns. Gerald Ford did not intend his presidency to be that, but it was his fate to preside over two years of neither success nor failure in grappling with inherited problems. The nation just waited for the election of 1976, when the people would either give Ford a chance as president in his own right or replace him.

In the meantime, the first of the problems that faced him was indeed grave, for it struck at one of the most firmly held assumptions of twentieth-century American life: the unlimited availability of cheap energy as a basis of both the economy and the comfortable, expansive, freewheeling American lifestyle.

President Gerald Ford and Secretary of State Henry Kissinger.

Running on Half-Empty

By the mid-1970s, 90 percent of the American economy was based on the burning of fossil fuels: coal, natural gas, and, most of all, petroleum. Fossil fuels are nonrenewable sources of energy. Unlike food crops, lumber, and water—or, for that matter, a horse and a pair of sturdy legs—they cannot be called on again once they have been used. There is only a limited amount of them in the earth. While experts disagreed about the extent of the world's reserves of coal, gas, and oil, no one challenged the obvious fact that one day there would be no more of them.

The United States was by far the biggest user of nonrenewable sources of energy. In 1973, while making up about 6 percent of the world's population, Americans consumed fully 33 percent of the world's annual production of oil. In the opinion of other nations and of numerous critics at home, much of this was wasted or frivolously burned: overheating and air conditioning houses; fueling a wide variety of purely recreational vehicles; clinging to the wasteful private automobile, instead of encouraging public mass-transit systems; packaging in throw-away containers, whether of glass, metal, paper, or petroleum-derived "plastics."

Nevertheless, individual use of oil was only part of the huge American consumption. The American economy itself was based on fossil fuels, 44 percent of which was oil. And with each year, regardless of warnings, American consumption increased.

OPEC and the Energy Crisis

About 61 percent of the oil that Americans consumed in 1973 was produced at home, and large reserves remained under native ground. Partly in order to conserve that oil, the nation imported huge quantities of crude, and in October 1973, Americans discovered just how little control they exercised over the 39 percent of their oil that was imported from abroad.

In that month, the newly formed Organization of Petroleum Exporting Countries (OPEC) levied a temporary embargo on oil exports and announced the first of a series of big jumps in the price of their product. Their justification for doing so was that irresponsible consumption habits of the advanced Western nations, particularly the United States, jeopardized their future. OPEC reasoned that if the oil-exporting nations continued to supply oil cheaply, consuming nations would continue to burn it promiscuously, thus hastening the day the wells ran dry. On that day, if the oil-exporting nations had not laid the basis for another kind of economy, they would be destitute. Particularly in the oil-rich Middle East, there were few other resources to exploit and fast-growing populations. Therefore, by raising prices even higher, the OPEC nations would earn capital with which to build for a future without oil while simultaneously encouraging the consuming nations to conserve, thus lengthening the period when oil would be available.

The weakness in this reasoning, as Saudi Arabia and a few other pro-Western OPEC nations soon realized, was that if the price went so high as to scuttle the economies of the United States and the other industrialized nations, oil-producing countries would go down too.

Americans were simply stunned. For several months, motorists had to wait in long lines in order to pay unprecedented prices for gasoline. In some big cities and Hawaii, gasoline for private cars was not to be had.

The price of gasoline never climbed to European levels (as much as $5 a gallon), but it was shock enough for a people who asked for "two dollars' worth" to discover that $2 bought a little more than a gallon. Moreover, the prices of goods that require oil in their production climbed too. Inflation, already a problem because of the size of the federal budget, worsened.

Whip Inflation Now!

During the period of wage and price controls before the election of 1972, inflation had slowed to 3 percent. Once in office again, however, Nixon dropped the program, and during 1973, inflation rose to 9 percent. During 1974, Ford's first year in the presidency, the rate jumped to 12 percent.

Opposed to controls, Ford announced a campaign called WIN!, for "Whip Inflation Now," a great voluntary effort by Americans to slow down inflation by refusing to buy exorbitantly priced goods and by ceasing to demand higher wages from their employers. The campaign was ridiculed from the start, and within a few weeks Ford quietly retired the WIN! button that he had been wearing on his lapel.

*The lines at a Los Angeles gas station stretched for blocks
during a gasoline shortage in 1979.*

Then Ford tightened the money supply in order to slow down the economy, which resulted in the most serious recession since the Second World War, with unemployment climbing to 9 percent. Ford was stymied by the same vicious circle that caught up his predecessor and successors: slowing inflation means throwing people out of work; fighting unemployment means inflation; trying to steer a middle course means "stagflation," mild recession plus inflation.

Ford's Image Problems

As a congressman, Ford had been a hawk on Vietnam. So when the North Vietnamese launched a major attack on South Vietnam early in 1975, Ford's first impulse was to intervene with American troops. Henry Kissinger, who had stayed on as Secretary of State, talked him out of this action. However, Ford displayed his determination to exercise American armed might in May 1975, when Cambodian Communists seized an American ship, the *Mayagüez*. Ford ordered in the marines, who successfully rescued the captives. Many people were so pleased at the news of a successful mil-

itary action that they tended to forget that in order to rescue thirty-nine seamen, thirty-eight marines died.

Kissinger savored the reports that the president hung breathlessly on his every word. This belief not only infuriated the anti-Kissinger conservative wing of the Republican party, previously Ford's political home, but made it easier for the Democrats to mock the president as being not intelligent enough to handle his job.

Polls showed Ford losing to most of the likely Democratic candidates, and Ronald Reagan, the sweetheart of the right-wing Republicans, made steady gains on the president.

An Unsuccessful President

Whether the perspective of time will attribute the failure of Jimmy Carter's presidency to his own unsuitability for the office or to the massiveness of the problems he faced, it is difficult to imagine future historians looking at the Carter years with other than doleful reactions.

An Unlikely Candidate

Since Eisenhower, every president had been identified primarily with Congress, the arena of national politics. The day of the governor candidate seemed to be in the past. Then James Earl Carter, Jr., came out of nowhere to win the Democratic nomination in 1976. His political career consisted of one term in the Georgia assembly and one term as governor. Indeed, it was his lack of a past in the federal government that helped him win the nomination and, by a slim margin, the presidency. Without a real animus for Gerald Ford, Americans still remembered the corruption of the professional politician Nixon and the stubbornness of the professional politician Johnson. They wanted an "outsider," which is how Carter presented himself. "Hello, my name is Jimmy Carter and I'm running for president," he told thousands of people face to face in the lilting accent of rural Georgia. Once he started winning primaries, the media did the rest. When television commentators said that there was a bandwagon effect favoring Carter, people responded by building and jumping on the bandwagon.

JIMMY CARTER AND THE SEGREGATIONISTS

Future president Jimmy Carter had an unusual record for a white southerner on the segregation issue. In the 1950s, as a successful businessman in Plains, Georgia, he had been asked to join the antiblack White Citizens' Councils, whose membership fee was only $5. Carter replied, "I've got $5 but I'd flush it down the toilet before I'd give it to you."

Drift in Domestic Policy

"Carter believes fifty things," one of his advisers said after leaving the administration, "but no one thing. He holds explicit, thorough positions on every issue under the sun, but he has no large view of relations between them." In this, Carter was not unlike most Americans. He had an "engineer," rather than an ideological, mentality, which is often described as the American way of thinking: as it arises, face each specific problem with a specific solution.

Jimmy Carter walks with his family from the capitol to the White House following his inauguration as president.

Such pragmatism had worked for Franklin D. Roosevelt, but it did not work for Jimmy Carter. In his hands, pragmatism took on the appearance of aimless drift. When Carter tried to get a grasp on what he called the national malaise by picking the minds of 130 prominent men and women from every sector of American life, he was able to conclude only that there was "a crisis of the American spirit."

Inflation reached new heights under Carter, almost 20 percent during 1980. By the end of the year, $1 was worth only 15 cents in 1940 values. That is, on the average, it took $1 in 1980 to purchase what in 1940 cost 15 cents. Indeed, the dollar had lost half its value during the 1970s.

Carter could not be faulted in any way for the energy crisis. After the crunch of 1974, Americans became energy conscious, replacing their huge "gas guzzlers" with more efficient smaller cars and forming car pools for commuting to work. But old habits proved stronger than impulsive conservationist resolutions. By 1979, oil consumption was higher than ever, and even more of it was being imported than in 1976! The oil refiners actually cut back on domestic production, which led many people to wonder if the crisis was genuine or was just a cover while the industry reaped windfall profits—which it did. As prices soared, all the refiners reported dividends of unprecedented size.

The price of electricity also rose, by 200 percent and more, because so much of it was generated by burning fossil fuels. The utility companies called for the construction of more nuclear-power plants in anticipation of even higher rate increases. But Americans became apprehensive about nuclear energy as an alternative to fossil fuels following an accident and near catastrophe at the Three Mile Island nuclear plant near Harrisburg, Pennsylvania; the release, at about the same time, of *The China Sydrome,* a film that portrayed a very similar accident; and the discovery that a California reactor that was about to open was crisscrossed with flaws.

Uncertain Foreign Policy

Carter named a career diplomat, Cyrus Vance, to be his Secretary of State. Then, however, just as Nixon had done with Kissinger, Carter installed in the White House a special assistant for national security, a Polish refugee from Communism, Zbigniew Brzezinski. Also like Nixon, he appeared to regard the Secretary of State as a figurehead and the special assistant as his adviser.

This policy had paid dividends to Nixon, but it did not help Carter. Whereas Kissinger had been flexible and pragmatic, Brzezinski's hatred of the Soviet Union

---

NO OLYMPICS

The 1980 Olympic Games were scheduled to be held in Moscow. After the invasion of Afghanistan, President Carter announced that in protest the United States would not send its athletes. Carter apparently assumed that because the Olympics were of great importance to the Soviets as a public-relations gesture, the Soviet Afghan policy might be revised. Although a few other nations followed Carter's example, the Soviet Union did not budge, and the games went on.

---

blinded him to every opportunity to improve relations between the nuclear superpowers. He simply did not want better relations. It was probably on Brzezinksi's counsel that in March 1977 Carter interrupted and set back the Strategic Arms Limitation Talks with completely new proposals. (The SALT-II treaty was postponed when, ignoring the lesson of Vietnam, the Soviet Union invaded rugged, primitive Afghanistan in December 1979.)

Moreover, whereas Kissinger was the ultimate charmer, Brzezinksi was tactless and often rude in a world in which protocol and manners can be as important as substance. The foreign ministers of several of America's allies discreetly informed the State Department that they would not deal with him personally under any circumstances. By the end of Carter's term of office, détente was dead, and relations between the United States and its allies were the poorest they had been in a generation.

With Third World nations, on the contrary, relations improved. This was the work of neither Vance nor Brzezinksi, but of Andrew Young, a former civil-rights fighter and a close friend of Carter in Georgia politics. Officially ambassador to the United Nations, Young also acted like a Secretary of State. A black man, Young was sympathetic to the national aspirations of the developing nations of sub-Saharan Africa, and he reversed a trend of suspicion of the United States in that part of the world.

Unfortunately, because the black African nations were generally sympathetic to the Palestine Liberation Organization (PLO), an anti-Israel group that the United States did not recognize, Young's friendship with them cost him his job. Without informing the State Department, he met secretly with a representative of the PLO, an amateurish and irresponsible act of which no professional diplomat would have been capable. When the story became public, Carter had no choice but to fire his old friend.

Anwar Sadat, Jimmy Carter, and Menachem Begin share a toast following the signing of the Camp David Accords in 1978.

Carter's Middle Eastern Breakthrough

Carter enjoyed his greatest success and suffered his greatest failure in the sensitive Middle East: oil rich, strategically located, and constantly poised on the edge of war. His success came in saving the rapprochement between Israel and Egypt that began in November 1977. After thirty years of intermittent warfare between the two countries, Egyptian President Anwar el-Sadat announced that he was willing to visit Israel and address the Knesset, the Israeli parliament, in an attempt to stabilize the Middle East. Israeli Prime Minister Menachem Begin, a former guerrilla fighter who had come into power by promising a tough policy toward PLO terrorists (and, by implication, Egypt), promptly invited Sadat.

It was a tremendous gamble on Sadat's part. For a generation, Egyptian governments had told their people that Israel must be fought until the Jewish state was extirpated. In the late 1970s, the other Arab nations were still doing so. They expelled Egypt from the Arab League, but Sadat had guessed right about the Egyptian people. They were tired of the constant threat of war

and rallied behind him, actually increasing his popularity and strengthening his grip on power.

When the campaign to iron out differences between the nations stalled in 1978, Carter called Sadat and Begin to meet with him at Camp David, the presidential retreat outside Washington. There, as was revealed only later in Carter's memoirs, Sadat grew so angry with Begin's refusal to make concessions that he actually packed his suitcases. Although Carter was unable to persuade Begin to agree that the West Bank of the Jordan River, which Israel had occupied in 1967, must eventually be returned to Arab rule, he did bring the two men together. In March 1979, Israel and Egypt signed a treaty.

In the United States, the political effect of this dramatic diplomatic turn was to swing American sympathies in the dispute in the direction of Sadat, who appeared to be more sincerely committed to making peace than was Begin. Begin was unpopular even among American Jews, who traditionally are staunch supporters of Israel. Jewish contributions to Israeli causes dropped sharply, and Carter himself betrayed impatience and annoyance with the Begin government and sympathy for the Palestinian refugees.

The Iranian Tragedy

Because of the steadily worsening economy, it is doubtful that Carter would have been reelected in 1980 under any circumstances. But it was a national tragedy in Iran that sealed his doom. Like Nixon and Ford, who similarly had been misinformed by the CIA, Carter believed that Reza Pahlavi, the pro-Western shah of Iran, was popular in his homeland. On one occasion, the president described Iran as an "island of stability" in the Middle East.

Nothing could have been farther from the truth. The shah was hated by every social group in the country save the military and the secular middle and upper classes of the cities. They were prosperous; their children studied abroad, many in the United States, funded by generous monthly checks from the shah's government. But liberal and leftist Iranians suffered brutal tortures at the hands of SAVAK, the shah's secret police. And the deeply religious peasantry was taught by reactionary Muslim religious teachers and scholars (mullahs and ayatollahs) that the shah was blasphemous.

In January 1979, after months of rebellion, the shah fled the country, and power was seized by the right wing of the broadly based revolution, led by the fanatical Ayatollah Ruholla Khomeini. In October, despite warnings from the embassy in Teheran that his action could lead to reprisals against Americans in Iran, Carter admitted the shah to the United States for medical treatment.

A few days later, probably with the ayatollah's consent, if not at his instigation, a group of Iranian students seized the American embassy compound and took fifty Americans hostage. For more than a year, they languished in confinement. A raid by commandos in 1980 failed to rescue the hostages, but cost Carter his Secretary of State, who had opposed the raid. When Vance resigned, Carter appointed Edmund Muskie to the post.

Muskie proved to be an able diplomat, and even succeeded in whittling away at Brzezinski's influence over the president. But he was no more successful at

Blindfolded American hostages at the United States embassy in Iran.

freeing the hostages than Vance. Not until January 20, 1981, the day Jimmy Carter left the White House, were they released.

Consequences of the Hostage Crisis

Many leftist American student groups joined Iranian students in the United States in celebrating the ayatollah's rise to power, and the seizure of the hostages did not greatly affect these sympathies. Only when the Khomeini regime began to institute wholesale executions of opponents on a scale that the shah never had dared did support for it evaporate. Many Iranian students in the United States continued to back the ayatollah, but as the hostage crisis wore on, their demonstrations grew quieter.

The crisis won Jimmy Carter renomination. Late in 1979, Senator Edward Kennedy announced that he would lead a liberal campaign against Carter, and all polls showed him easily defeating the president. Almost immediately, however, support for the president welled up, and Kennedy found himself soundly defeated by the time of the Democratic national con-

vention. Oddly, Carter's own ineffectiveness worked in his favor. The less capable he seemed to be in dealing with the Iranians, the higher his ratings rose. Even the disastrous commando attack increased his popularity.

For a while. By the end of the summer, Americans were abandoning him in droves. One benefactor was Congressman John Anderson of Illinois, who ran for the presidency as an independent. The big winner, however, was the Republican nominee, Ronald Reagan.

New Era? More of the Same?

When he was under contract as an actor with the Warner Brothers film company, Ronald Reagan was considered for the role of a state governor. "No, no," studio head Jack Warner said. "Jimmy Stewart for governor, Ronald Reagan for best friend." The other people at the meeting agreed. Reagan played likeable fellows tolerably well, but he could not convey the image of a man who was to be trusted with responsibility and power.

Newly inaugurated president Ronald Reagan and his wife Nancy greet a crowd during the inaugural parade.

Ronald Reagan

Very few people who knew Ronald Reagan could dislike him personally. He was cheerful, even tempered, tolerant, and optimistic. He was also an excellent raconteur who loved to tell hilarious stories from his long career in Hollywood.

But other people, including some who knew and worked for him, believed that Reagan lacked the intelligence and knowledge with which to make informed decisions and the substance with which to say no to his friends. Reagan's critics maintained that he never had ceased to be an actor. Others wrote the lines; he spoke them. His advisers were almost giddy with elation when he emerged unscathed from an unrehearsed situation.

The Moral Majority

The election of 1980 was not simply a repudiation of Carter or an expression of affection for the congenial Reagan. The final tally showed that little more than half of the eligible voters had cast ballots in the election, which continued a trend of decline in voter interest in the electoral process that had begun in the 1960s. If the election was a mirror of anything, it was that Americans were unsure of their power to influence their government.

Low turnout also allows militant, well-organized special-interest groups to affect the results of a poll, and the presidential election of 1980 was a prime illustration. An extremely well-organized alliance of single-issue, right-wing groups dubbed the Moral Majority not only contributed to Reagan's sweep, but turned out of office half a dozen liberal senators, including Senate Foreign Relations Committee chairman Frank Church of Idaho, Gaylord Nelson of Wisconsin, and George McGovern of South Dakota.

Ironically, the Moral Majority movement was able to exercise such muscle because of election reforms that had been proposed and adopted in the early 1970s by just such liberals. By limiting the amount of money that an individual or a corporation could contribute to the national party in an election campaign (seemingly a blow at special interests), the new laws, in effect, forced the diversion of such contributions to a number of political action committees, which could then choose which candidate they would financially back on the basis of his or her stance on a single issue. Thus, most of the defeated Senate liberals had supported civil-rights legislation and the ERA, and had opposed antiabortion proposals and prayer in public schools. Unlike the oldest political action committee, the labor movement's Committee on Political Education, the

Jerry Falwell, the prime mover behind the "Moral Majority," speaks to followers in Boise, Idaho.

Moral Majority committees tended to ignore or downplay the positions that their candidates would take on inflation, unemployment, and the other economic issues. But the candidates whom they indirectly assisted were invariably Reaganites, supporters of what came to be called "Reaganomics."

Reaganomics

Although Ronald Reagan frequently quoted Franklin D. Roosevelt, he never concealed his intention to overhaul the liberal economic and social policies that every president since Roosevelt either had espoused or had quietly accepted. Reagan repeatedly said during his campaign that his administration would not be a big brother to the American people; it would not assume responsibility for the economic and social security of individuals. Indeed, he blamed the troubled economy of the 1970s on big spending by government. Reagan confessed a personal admiration for Calvin Coolidge and moved Silent Cal's portrait to an honored place in the White House. And the economic program he set out in presidential actions and the bills he sent to Congress during the first two years of his administration more than casually resembled the Coolidge and Mellon theories of free enterprise and "trickle down."

Just six days after his inauguration, Reagan abolished all price and allocation controls on oil, and on March 6, he cut the federal payroll by thirty-seven thousand jobs. His tax-reform bill reduced the levy in every income bracket, but frankly favored the rich. Reagan, Secretary of the Treasury Donald Regan, and budget director David Stockman argued that whereas the poor would simply spend any tax savings, thus fueling the inflation that the Reagan administration was determined to slow down, the wealthy would invest their windfalls in new factories and industries, thus creating jobs.

Having reduced government revenues and federal control of the economy, as the Coolidge administration had done, Reagan did not follow Coolidge's example and cut gross government expenditures. Social services were slashed, but the increase in defense spending was so great that the Reagan budget was less balanced than even those of the Johnson years. Congress almost doubled the debt ceiling (the amount that the government can legally borrow) from $506 billion to $985 billion. In 1982, the ceiling was raised to more than $1 trillion. At the same time, President Reagan announced his support for a constitutional amendment that would require Congress to balance the budget!

Reagan's Critics: Crying in the Wilderness

The Democrats were not bashful about calling Reagan's budget-balancing schemes and pronouncements hypocritical. They also questioned the morality of cutting social benefits for the poor and the elderly in difficult times while, in an age of nuclear overkill, spending billions on weapons. Critics such as Senator Gary Hart of Colorado fastened on the apparent waste in the Reagan defense program, an intercontinental ballistic missile staging system called "densepack" (which Reagan allowed to die), and the refitting and recommissioning of several battleships that had been in mothballs for more than a decade. Experts in naval warfare pointed out that during the Falkland Islands conflict of 1982 between Great Britain and Argentina, one Argentine plane carrying a comparatively cheap missile was able to sink an extremely expensive and sophisticated British ship. The same could be done to

CRISIS IN AMERICAN MANAGEMENT

The steady loss of the domestic market in electronics and automobiles to Japanese companies was commonly blamed on American workers during the 1970s; they were paid too much, and their productivity was too low. By 1980, however, evidence indicated that management was at fault: too many executives who were making too much money were afraid to take chances. Thus, when workers purchased several factories in the Midwest from owners whose profits were failing and hired their own managers, the companies quickly reversed their downward spiral. When Japan's Sanyo Corporation bought Warwick Television from Sears Roebuck, three hundred middle-management jobs were eliminated, and the company turned in a profit within two years for the first time in a decade. (Workers were not fired, and wages were not lowered.)

The same thing happened in the Quasar Company, when Motorola sold it to Matsushita. Akio Morita, the chairman of Sony, a very successful manufacturer of electronics devices, said bluntly that "the problem in the United States is management"; he added that American workers were "excellent." American inventors repeatedly have expressed their disgust with American management. They have been forced to sell their patents to Japanese corporations because American business executives were afraid to make decisions.

an American battleship at the cost of $1 billion and thousands of lives.

Still, because the Republicans controlled the Senate and enough conservative, mostly southern Democrats supported Reaganomics, the president got just about everything he wanted until the congressional election of 1982.

By the autumn of 1982, the price of Reaganomics was obvious. In slowing down inflation to just a few percent, the president's policy created a higher unemployment rate than had been known since before the Second World War. Homeless people were camping permanently in state and national parks, and several hundred were said to be living under freeway viaducts in Los Angeles and in other cities with warm climates. In January 1983, an auto-frame manufacturer in Milwaukee advertised two hundred jobs, and fifteen thousand applicants showed up. A few days later, three thousand people stood in line to apply for thirty-five jobs at the Sun Oil refinery in Marcus Hook, Pennsylvania.

The president expected this, and urged Americans to "stay the course." With time, he said, investment would create jobs and prosperity without inflation. The

Job seekers line up at the Sun Oil Company in Marcus Hook, Pennsylvania, in 1983.

voters' response was unsure. While the Democrats gained two dozen seats in the House of Representatives, retiring many one-term Reagan supporters, the Republicans maintained control of the Senate. In February 1983, a Texas Democrat who had been stripped of his House Budget Committee seat for supporting Reagan won reelection as a Republican.

Hard Feelings with the Moral Majority

By 1983, the president was also dodging criticism from what seemed to be an unlikely quarter, the Moral Majority. In fact, the single-issue crusaders and the president always had been mismatched. Although Reagan had told an interviewer that he too was a "born-again Christian," he was not very comfortable with moral crusades. He had spent his adult life in Hollywood, a locale that was not to the liking of the Moral Majority, was divorced (the first president to be so), and had learned that the exigencies of presidential

politics made it unwise to hammer continually on the narrow issues that had been enough to defeat the liberal senators.

Reagan did not abandon the sentiments of the Moral Majority. He continued to oppose a federal handgun-control law even after having been shot by John W. Hinckley, the ne'er-do-well son of a Colorado oilman. He opposed the ERA, supported prayer in public schools, and backed a Health and Human Services Department directive that federally financed birth-control clinics inform the parents of teenage girls who request contraceptive devices.

But from the Moral Majority's viewpoint, the president was not *doing* enough. They could continue to raise funds only as long as they seemed to be influencing the administration of the president whom they claimed to have elected, and it was obvious that they were not doing so. Reagan appeared to be more responsive to the discovery by Republican party election strategists that he had fared very poorly among

Sandra Day O'Connor, the first woman to serve on the United States Supreme Court, poses with her new colleagues shortly after her appointment.

women voters, that if all eligible voters had voted in the proportions that women had, he might have lost the election. While he did not change his mind on the ERA, he appointed more women to high-level positions than had any previous president, including the first woman justice of the Supreme Court, Sandra Day O'Connor. By March 1983, two members of Reagan's cabinet were women.

The president's political strategists may well have taken heed of a deep-rooted trend in national politics, that when the economy remains poor over a period of years, voters lose interest in narrow moral causes such as sustained the Moral Majority, except as they seem directly related to hard times.

Labor, Mobsters, and Sagebrush Rebels

Reagan's most controversial high-level appointees were CIA director William Casey, Secretary of Labor Ray-mond Donovan, Secretary of the Interior James Watt, and director of the Environmental Protection Agency (EPA) Anne Burford. Casey, who was thought to be the shrewdest of the president's political advisers, was accused of financial irregularities in his past; but with Reagan's full support, he fought off a powerful drive to force his resignation.

Raymond Donovan also survived attacks by his critics. Soon after taking office, he was accused of being a crony of labor racketeers in his home state of New Jersey. Twice he had to appear before congressional investigating committees. Both times the hard evidence against him was found to be so negligible that even some liberals concluded that congressional Democrats were out to "get" him. In February 1983, Burford was attacked because during an investigation of her allegedly antienvironmental actions, several paper shredders were installed in EPA offices. After a month, she resigned to be replaced by William Ruckelshaus, a conservative with a reputation for fair dealing, even among liberals.

Conservationists and environmentalists did not disguise the fact that they were out to get Secretary of the Interior James Watt of Colorado. Watt was a leader of the "Sagebrush Rebels," a loose consortium of western businessmen who wanted what remained of the federally owned lands "returned" to the states in which they were located so that they might be exploited to their full economic worth by cattlemen, lumbermen, and mining companies.

Return was not the proper word, as was quickly pointed out by groups such as the Sierra Club and the Wilderness Society, which are pledged to protect the public lands. The lands in question had been owned by the federal government and therefore the people long before the states in question had come into existence. Therefore, with James Watt at the head of the Interior Department, which administered the national parks and the lands under the Bureau of Land Management, these groups were worried and stepped up their recruiting and lobbying efforts.

They fought all of Watt's attempts to open federal lands to private exploitation, and by 1983, the secretary and the protective societies were locked in a bitter draw. Watt's personality did not help his cause. His hatred of "posy-sniffers" was so unguarded that tens of thousands of people who never had belonged to environmental societies joined such groups.

Foreign Policy

Just as he had selected one of his Republican opponents, George Bush, to be his vice president, Reagan chose another, Alexander Haig, to be his Secretary of State. Haig was a former general and Nixon aide. The president and Secretary of State generally agreed that the United States had lost prestige and influence under Jimmy Carter, who had failed to demonstrate a willingness to use the nation's power and take a tough line with the Soviets. The SALT treaty, moribund under Carter, was allowed to die, and both Reagan and Haig regularly made fierce Cold-Warrior statements addressed at the Soviet Union.

More controversial was the open friendship shown by the Reagan administration toward the racist government of South Africa, and the militant opposition of the administration to leftist governments in Latin America, such as the Sandinistas in Nicaragua. Whereas these policies marked no sharp break from those of previous administrations, some Reagan aides such as ambassador to the United Nations Jeane Kirkpatrick openly praised "authoritarian" as opposed to "totalitarian" regimes. In practice, such words implied support for rightist dictatorships and opposition to leftist dictatorships.

While preferring moderates in El Salvador, where a guerrilla war raged into 1983, Reagan accepted rightists who had been elected in an open election. Curiously, the most successful antileftist government in Central America was that of Guatemala, where a "born-again" dictator crushed his opposition without American help and with arms purchased not from the United States but from Israel.

Haig and Reagan also agreed that the United States should support Great Britain in the Falkland Islands conflict of 1982, although Haig attempted a shuttle-diplomacy solution to the crisis, flying several times between London and Buenos Aires. They also concurred in the decision to exert stronger pressure on Israel to come to terms with its Arab neighbors and, ironically, with the left-wing Palestinian Liberation Organization. By the time the president became openly and harshly critical of Israel for having invaded Lebanon in late 1982 and having occupied half of that country, Haig was no longer with the administration.

The break had little to do with policy. Tension developed between the two men because of Haig's coup psychology. Haig had run the White House during the last months of the Nixon administration when the president had been deteriorating under the pressure (and a case of phlebitis, or inflammation of a vein, that almost killed him). When Reagan was shot and wounded in 1981, Haig announced that he was in control. He was reminded that the Constitution unambiguously stipulates that the vice president is to take charge in the event that the president is disabled. Haig had gone too far and his association with Reagan began to go downhill; in 1982, Reagan accepted Haig's resignation and replaced him with the more congenial George Schultz, a former executive with an internationally powerful corporation.

Peace or Public Relations?

In the final analysis, all political controversies and questions of public policy of the late twentieth century pale before the question of the world's survival. As every world leader must, President Reagan asserted that his primary objective was the permanent establishment of world peace. He insisted that his huge expenditures on weapons systems were the essential first step toward peace because the Soviet Union, the other nuclear superpower, responded only to force.

There was no shortage of evidence to support such a position, but reason dictated that it was to Soviet inter-

Concern about the arms race extends to both sides of the Atlantic. Here a contingent from Vermont marches across Manhattan during a 1982 antinuclear-arms demonstration that filled New York City's streets.

ests, quite as much as to American, to call a halt to the nuclear (and chemical) arms race that could have only one outcome. During 1982, Soviet leaders both answered Reagan's bellicose pronouncements and made peaceful overtures. Reagan regarded the Russian feelers as snares, and many American Kremlinologists said that since Soviet Communist party leader Leonid Brezhnev was seriously ill, no dependable agreements could be reached.

In November 1982, Brezhnev died, and his successor Yuri Andropov, launched a pronounced peace offen-

sive. When President Reagan shrugged off Andropov's concrete offers as "public relations," speakers at huge rallies in most of the big cities of Western Europe denounced the United States as the chief threat to peace in the world. In a dramatic about-face, Reagan abandoned the hard line and proposed a plan of his own design to denuclearize Europe, an essential first step to significant disarmament. Peace or public relations? That question is the future's and not the historian's to answer.

THE TYPICAL AMERICAN OF THE 1980S: A STATISTICAL PORTRAIT

*The typical American of the 1980s was a mother who
very likely had a job. However, because of economic
depression, her employment was precarious.*

The statistical American of the year 1980 was a Caucasian female, a little more than 30 years old, married to her first husband, with one child and about to have another. She was a shade over 5 feet 4 inches tall, and weighed 134 pounds. Statisticians are not sure of the color of her hair and eyes, but they were probably on the brownish side. Statisticians are sure that she had tried marijuana when she was younger, but no longer used it in 1980 (although some of her friends still did). She did not smoke cigarettes, but at least had tried them in the past; she still drank, just this side of moderately.

The statistical American adult female of 1980 considered herself middle class, and had attended college but had not necessarily graduated. She was likely to work outside the home, but economic conditions during the 1980s made her opportunities increasingly uncertain. Her household income was about $20,000 a year; she and her husband were watching their budget closely, which they were not accustomed to doing. It is a toss-up whether or not she voted in 1980 (or at all

during the 1970s), but if she did, it was probably for Jimmy Carter, at least in part because she supported the Equal Rights Amendment, as did Carter. She was not, however, very interested in feminism, and vaguely disapproved of some militant feminists. She was marginally more likely to be registered as a Democrat than as a Republican, but party affiliation meant less to her than did the merits of individual candidates for office.

More than half of the statistical American's female friends were married. Most of her friends who have been divorced have married again within three years. The statistical American of 1980 attached no stigma to divorce, and experienced only a slight sense of unease with people who lived with members of the opposite sex without benefit of marriage. But she found it difficult to agree that homosexuality is nothing more than an "alternate life style" on a moral parity with heterosexuality. She was both amused and repelled by the culture of the "gay" communities about which she read.

She almost certainly had sex with her husband before they married, and almost as likely with at least one other man. There is a fair chance that she had a brief fling since marriage, probably during a "trial separation." Within a few years of the 1980s, however, fear of venereal disease, particularly herpes, will add to other factors, including economic insecurity, to lessen the incidence of extramarital relationships.

The statistical American was more likely to be Protestant than Catholic. However, she was more likely to be Catholic than a member of any other *individual* denomination. If a Catholic, she practiced birth control, usually using the pill, in defiance of Church directives. Moreover, Catholic or Protestant, she attended church services far less frequently than had her mother.

The statistical American was in excellent health; she saw a dentist and a doctor more than once a year, and paid a little less than half of the cost of health care (state and federal government picked up about the same, private industry and philanthropy the rest). She had a life expectancy of almost seventy-eight years, and would outlive her husband by eight years, with the prospects that her dotage would be economically difficult.

The statistical American lived in a state with a population of about 3 million people—Colorado, Iowa, Oklahoma, Connecticut—and in a city of about one hundred thousand people—Roanoke, Virginia; Reno, Nevada; Durham, North Carolina.

Or perhaps, she lived at the population center of the United States, which in 1980 was west of the Mississippi River for the first time in American history. It was located "one mile west of the De Soto City Hall, Jefferson County, Missouri." An equal number of people in the continental United States lived east of that point as west, as many north of it as south.

As the question about her state and city of residence indicates, the statistical American is a somewhat absurd contrivance, distilled out of the majorities, means, and medians of the United States Census Bureau; the responses to surveys taken by a number of public-opinion experts; and, simply, the probabilities of the educated guess. On making judgments on the basis of what statistical Americans shake down to, it is well to remember the Ford Motor Company's Edsel automobile of the 1950s. The car was designed from scratch according to extensive, expensive surveys about the preferences of the statistical car buyer. The Edsel flopped and almost bankrupted Ford.

The virtue of the United States remains rooted in its diversity of people as well as of resources and in the survival of those people's right to change their minds as many times as they wish. And, as far as matters of public policy are concerned, to form majorities and effect their wishes. For a nation that has reached its third century, that is not so bad an accomplishment. In the star-crossed history of the human race, it has not been done anywhere else.

For Further Reading

On Ford and Carter, there are only two campaign autobiographies, both with ironic titles: Gerald R. Ford, *A Time to Heal: The Autobiography of Gerald Ford* (1979), and Jimmy Carter, *Why Not the Best?* (1975).

There can be no "classic" histories of the years most recently past, of course. The historian who fancies that he or she has a definitive grasp on what happened just yesterday has not paid attention to the difficulty of arriving at a confident view of remote events in which the writer has no involvement. Indeed, while the following are useful to a knowledge of the United States in the young new century, most of them were *projections* of what to expect rather than glances back.

On business and the corporation, see Raymond Vernon, *Storm over the Multinationals: The Real Issues* (1977); L. R. Brown, *Running on Empty: The Future of the Automobile in an Oil-Short World* (1979); John Kenneth Galbraith, *The New Industrial State* (1967); and V. I. Fuchs and I. F. Leveson, *The Service Economy,* (1968).

On minorities and women, see W. J. Wilson, *The Declining Significance of Race: Blacks and Changing Institutions* (1978); D. K. Newman, *Protest, Politics, and Prosperity: Black Americans and White Institutions* (1978); Albert Camarillo, *Chicanos in a Changing Society* (1979); S. A. Levitan and Barbara Hetrick, *Big Brother's Indian Programs* (1972); W. H. Chafe, *Women and Equality: Changing Patterns in American Culture* (1977); and G. G. Yates, *What Women Want: The Ideas of the Movement* (1975).

On what may or may not prove to be a significant political movement, see Peter Steinfels, *The Neoconservatives* (1979).

Appendixes

The Declaration of Independence*

The Unanimous Declaration of the Thirteen United States of America,

When in the Course of human events it becomes necessary for one people to dissolve the political bands which have connected them with another, and to assume among the Powers of the earth, the separate and equal station to which the Laws of Nature and of Nature's God entitle them, a decent respect to the opinions of mankind requires that they should declare the causes which impel them to the separation.

We hold these truths to be self-evident, that all men are created equal, that they are endowed by their Creator with certain unalienable Rights, that among these are Life, Liberty and the pursuit of Happiness. That to secure these rights, Governments are instituted among Men, deriving their just Powers from the consent of the governed. That whenever any Form of Government becomes destructive of these ends, it is the Right of the People to alter or to abolish it, and to institute new Government, laying its foundation on such principles and organizing its Powers in such form, as to them shall seem most likely to effect their Safety and Happiness. Prudence, indeed, will dictate that Governments long established should not be changed for light and transient causes; and accordingly all experience hath shewn, that mankind are more disposed to suffer, while evils are sufferable, than to right themselves by abolishing the forms to which they are accustomed. But when a long train of abuses and usurpations, pursuing invariably the same Object evinces a design to reduce them under absolute Despotism, it is their right, it is their duty to throw off such Government, and to provide new Guards for their future security. Such has been the patient sufferance of these Colonies; and such is now the necessity which constrains them to alter their former Systems of Government. The history of the present King of Great Britain is a history of repeated injuries and usurpations, all having in direct object the establishment of an absolute Tyranny over these States. To prove this, let Facts be submitted to a candid world.

He has refused his Assent to Laws, the most wholesome and necessary for the public good.

He has forbidden his Governors to pass Laws of immediate and pressing importance, unless suspended in their operation till his Assent should be obtained; and when so suspended, he has utterly neglected to attend to them.

He has refused to pass other Laws for the accommodation of large districts of people, unless those people would relinquish the right of Representation in the Legislature, a right inestimable to them and formidable to tyrants only.

He has called together legislative bodies at places unusual, uncomfortable, and distant from the depository of their Public Records, for the sole Purpose of fatiguing them into compliance with his measures.

He has dissolved Representative Houses repeatedly, for opposing with manly firmness his invasions on the rights of the People.

He has refused for a long time, after such dissolutions, to cause others to be elected; whereby the Legislative Powers, incapable of Annihilation, have returned to the People at large for their exercise; the State remaining in the mean time exposed to all the dangers of invasion from without, and convulsions within.

He has endeavoured to prevent the Population of these States; for that purpose obstructing the Laws for Naturalization of Foreigners; refusing to pass others to encourage their migrations hither, and raising the conditions of new Appropriations of Lands.

He has obstructed the Administration of Justice, by refusing his Assent to Laws for establishing Judiciary Powers.

He has made Judges dependent on his Will alone, for the tenure of their offices, and the amount and payment of their salaries.

He has erected a multitude of New Offices, and sent hither swarms of Officers to harass our People, and eat out their substance.

He has kept among us, in times of peace, Standing Armies without the consent of our legislatures.

He has affected to render the Military independent of and superior to the Civil Power.

He has combined with others to subject us to a jurisdiction foreign to our constitution, and unacknowledged by our laws; giving his Assent to their Acts of pretended Legislation:

*Reprinted from the facsimile of the engrossed copy in the National Archives. The original spelling, capitalization, and punctuation have been retained. Paragraphing has been added.

For Quartering large bodies of armed troops among us:

For protecting them, by a mock Trial, from Punishment for any Murders which they should commit on the Inhabitants of these States:

For cutting off our Trade with all parts of the world:

For imposing Taxes on us without our Consent:

For depriving us in many cases, of the benefits of Trial by Jury:

For transporting us beyond Seas to be tried for pretended offences:

For abolishing the free System of English Laws in a neighbouring Province, establishing therein an Arbitrary government, and enlarging its Boundaries so as to render it at once an example and fit instrument for introducing the same absolute rule into these Colonies:

For taking away our Charters, abolishing our most valuable Laws, and altering fundamentally the Forms of our Governments:

For suspending our own Legislatures, and declaring themselves invested with Power to legislate for us in all cases whatsoever.

He has abdicated Government here, by declaring us out of his Protection, and waging War against us.

He has plundered our seas, ravaged our Coasts, burnt our towns, and destroyed the lives of our people.

He is at this time transporting large Armies of foreign Mercenaries to compleat the works of death, desolation and tyranny, already begun with circumstances of Cruelty and perfidy scarcely paralleled in the most barbarous ages, and totally unworthy the Head of a civilized nation.

He has constrained our fellow Citizens taken Captive on the high Seas to bear Arms against their Country, to become the executioners of their friends and Brethren, or to fall themselves by their Hands.

He has excited domestic insurrections amongst us, and has endeavoured to bring on the inhabitants of our frontiers, the merciless Indian Savages, whose known rule of warfare, is an undistinguished destruction of all ages, sexes and conditions.

In every stage of these Oppressions We have Petitioned for Redress in the most humble terms: Our repeated Petitions have been answered only by repeated injury. A Prince, whose character is thus marked by every act which may define a Tyrant, is unfit to be the ruler of a free People.

Nor have We been wanting in attentions to our British brethren. We have warned them from time to time of attempts by their legislature to extend an unwarrantable jurisdiction over us. We have reminded them of the circumstances of our emigration and settlement here. We have appealed to their native justice and magnanimity, and we have conjured them by the ties of our common kindred to disavow these usurpations, which, would inevitably interrupt our connections and correspondence. They too have been deaf to the voice of justice and of consanguinity. We must, therefore, acquiesce in the necessity, which denounces our Separation, and hold them, as we hold the rest of mankind, Enemies in War, in Peace Friends.

We, therefore, the Representatives of the United States of America, in General Congress, Assembled, appealing to the Supreme Judge of the world for the rectitude of our intentions, do, in the Name, and by Authority of the good People of these Colonies, solemnly publish and declare, That these United Colonies are, and of Right ought to be FREE AND INDEPENDENT STATES; that they are Absolved from all Allegiance to the British Crown, and that all political connection between them and the State of Great Britain, is and ought to be totally dissolved; and that, as Free and Independent States, they have full Power to levy War, conclude Peace, contract Alliances, establish Commerce, and to do all other Acts and Things which Independent States may of right do. And for the support of this Declaration, with a firm reliance on the protection of divine Providence, we mutually pledge to each other our Lives, our Fortunes and our sacred Honor.

The Constitution of the United States of America*

We the People of the United States, in Order to form a more perfect Union, establish Justice, insure domestic Tranquility, provide for the common defence, promote the general Welfare, and secure the Blessings of Liberty to ourselves and our Posterity, do ordain and establish this Constitution for the United States of America.

Article. I.

Section. 1. All legislative Powers herein granted shall be vested in a Congress of the United States, which shall consist of a Senate and House of Representatives.

Section. 2. The House of Representatives shall be composed of Members chosen every second Year by the People of the several States, and the Electors in each State shall have the Qualifications requisite for Electors of the most numerous Branch of the State Legislature.

No Person shall be a Representative who shall not have attained to the Age of twenty five Years, and been seven Years a Citizen of the United States, and who shall not, when elected, be an Inhabitant of that State in which he shall be chosen.

Representatives and direct Taxes† shall be apportioned among the several States which may be included within this Union, according to their respective Numbers, which shall be determined by adding to the whole Number of free Persons, including those bound to Service for a Term of Years, and excluding Indians not taxed, three fifths of all other Persons.‡ The actual Enumeration shall be made within three Years after the first Meeting of the Congress of the United States, and within every subsequent Term of ten Years, in such Manner as they shall by Law direct. The Number of Representatives shall not exceed one for every thirty Thousand, but each State shall have at least one Representative; and until such enumeration shall be made, the State of New Hampshire shall be entitled to chuse three; Massachusetts eight; Rhode Island and Providence Plantations one; Connecticut five; New York six; New Jersey four; Pennsylvania eight; Delaware one; Maryland six; Virginia ten; North Carolina five; South Carolina five; and Georgia three.

When vacancies happen in the Representation from any State, the Executive Authority thereof shall issue Writs of Election to fill such Vacancies.

The House of Representatives shall chuse their Speaker and other Officers; and shall have the sole Power of Impeachment.

Section. 3. The Senate of the United States shall be composed of two Senators from each State, chosen by the Legislature thereof, for six Years; and each Senator shall have one Vote.*

Immediately after they shall be assembled in Consequence of the first Election, they shall be divided as equally as may be into three Classes. The Seats of the Senators of the first Class shall be vacated at the Expiration of the second Year, of the second Class at the Expiration of the fourth Year, and of the third Class at the Expiration of the sixth Year, so that one third may be chosen every second Year; and if Vacancies happen by Resignation, or otherwise, during the Recess of the Legislature of any State, the Executive thereof may make temporary Appointments until the next Meeting of the Legislature, which shall then fill such Vacancies.†

No Person shall be a Senator who shall not have attained to the Age of thirty Years, and been nine Years a Citizen of the United States, and who shall not, when elected, be an Inhabitant of that State for which he shall be chosen.

The Vice President of the United States shall be President of the Senate, but shall have no Vote, unless they be equally divided.

The Senate shall chuse their other Officers, and also a President pro tempore, in the Absence of the Vice President, or when he shall exercise the Office of President of the United States.

The Senate shall have the sole Power to try all Impeachments. When sitting for that Purpose, they shall be on Oath or Affirmation. When the President of the United States is tried, the Chief Justice shall preside: And no Person shall be convicted without the Concurrence of two thirds of the Members present.

Judgment in Cases of Impeachment shall not extend further than to removal from Office, and disqualification to hold and enjoy any Office of honor, Trust or Profit under the

---

*From the engrossed copy in the National Archives. Original spelling, capitalization, and punctuation have been retained.
†Modified by the Sixteenth Amendment.
‡Replaced by the Fourteenth Amendment.

*Superseded by the Seventeenth Amendment.
†Modified by the Seventeenth Amendment.

United States: but the Party convicted shall nevertheless be liable and subject to Indictment, Trial, Judgment and Punishment, according to Law.

Section. 4. The Times, Places and Manner of holding Elections for Senators and Representatives, shall be prescribed in each State by the Legislature thereof, but the Congress may at any time by Law make or alter such Regulation, except as to the Places of chusing Senators.

The Congress shall assemble at least once in every Year, and such Meeting shall be on the first Monday in December, unless they shall by Law appoint a different Day.*

Section. 5. Each House shall be the Judge of the Elections, Returns and Qualifications of its own Members, and a Majority of each shall constitute a Quorum to do Business; but a smaller Number may adjourn from day to day, and may be authorized to compel the Attendance of absent Members, in such manner, and under such Penalties as each House may provide.

Each House may determine the Rules of its Proceedings, punish its Members for disorderly Behaviour, and, with the Concurrence of two thirds, expel a Member.

Each House shall keep a Journal of its Proceedings, and from time to time publish the same, excepting such Parts as may in their Judgment require Secrecy; and the Yeas and Nays of the Members of either House on any question shall, at the Desire of one fifth of those Present, be entered on the Journal.

Neither House, during the Session of Congress, shall, without the Consent of the other, adjourn for more than three days, nor to any other Place than that in which the two Houses shall be sitting.

Section. 6. The Senators and Representatives shall receive a Compensation for their Services, to be ascertained by Law, and paid out of the Treasury of the United States. They shall in all Cases, except Treason, Felony and Breach of the Peace, be privileged from Arrest during their Attendance at the Session of their respective Houses, and in going to and returning from the same; and for any Speech or Debate in either House, they shall not be questioned in any other Place.

No Senator or Representative shall, during the Time for which he was elected, be appointed to any civil Office under the Authority of the United States, which shall have been created, or the Emoluments whereof shall have been encreased during such time; and no Person holding any Office under the United States, shall be a Member of either House during his Continuance in Office.

Section. 7. All Bills for raising Revenue shall originate in the House of Representatives; but the Senate may propose or concur with Amendments as on other bills.

Every Bill which shall have passed the House of Representatives and the Senate shall, before it become a Law, be presented to the President of the United States; If he approve he shall sign it, but if not he shall return it, with his Objections to that House in which it shall have originated, who shall enter the Objections at large on their Journal, and proceed to reconsider it. If after such Reconsideration two thirds of that House shall agree to pass the Bill, it shall be sent, together with the Objections, to the other House, by which it shall likewise be reconsidered, and if approved by two thirds of that House, it shall become a Law. But in all such Cases the Votes of both Houses shall be determined by yeas and Nays, and the Names of the Persons voting for and against the Bill shall be entered on the Journal of each House respectively. If any Bill shall not be returned by the President within ten Days (Sundays excepted) after it shall have been presented to him, the Same shall be a Law, in Manner as if he had signed it, unless the Congress by their Adjournment prevent its Return, in which Case it shall not be a Law.

Every Order, Resolution, or Vote to which the Concurrence of the Senate and House of Representatives may be necessary (except on a question of Adjournment) shall be presented to the President of the United States; and before the Same shall take Effect, shall be approved by him, or being disapproved by him shall be repassed by two thirds of the Senate and House of Representatives, according to the rules and Limitations prescribed in the Case of a Bill.

Section. 8. The Congress shall have Power To lay and collect Taxes, Duties, Imposts and Excises, to pay the Debts and provide for the common Defence and general Welfare of the United States; but all Duties, Imposts and Excises shall be uniform throughout the United States;

To borrow Money on the credit of the United States;

To regulate Commerce with foreign Nations, and among the several States, and with the Indian Tribes;

To establish an uniform Rule of Naturalization, and uniform Laws on the subject of Bankruptcies throughout the United States;

To coin Money, regulate the Value thereof, and of foreign Coin, and fix the Standard of Weights and Measures;

To provide for the Punishment of counterfeiting the Securities and current Coin of the United States;

To establish Post Offices and post Roads;

To promote the Progress of Science and useful Arts, by securing for limited Times to Authors and Inventors the exclusive Right to their respective Writings and Discoveries;

To constitute Tribunals inferior to the supreme Court;

To define and punish Piracies and Felonies committed on the high Seas, and Offences against the Law of Nations;

To declare War, grant Letters of Marque and Reprisal, and make Rules concerning Captures on Land and Water;

To raise and support Armies, but no Appropriation of

---

*Superseded by the Twentieth Amendment.

Money to that Use shall be for a longer Term than two Years;

To provide and maintain a Navy;

To make Rules for the government and Regulation of the land and naval Forces;

To provide for calling forth the Militia to execute the Laws of the Union, suppress Insurrections and repel Invasions;

To provide for organizing, arming, and disciplining, the Militia, and for governing such Part of them as may be employed in the Service of the United States, reserving to the States respectively, the Appointment of the Officers, and the Authority of training the Militia according to the discipline prescribed by Congress;

To exercise exclusive Legislation in all Cases whatsoever, over such District (not exceeding ten Miles square) as may, by Cession of particular States, and the Acceptance of Congress, become the Seat of the Government of the United States, and to exercise like Authority over all Places purchased by the consent of the Legislature of the State in which the Same shall be, for the Erection of Forts, Magazines, Arsenals, dock-Yards, and other needful Buildings;—And

To make all Laws which shall be necessary and proper for carrying into Execution the foregoing Powers, and all other Powers vested by this Constitution in the Government of the United States, or in any Department or Officer thereof.

Section. 9. The Migration or Importation of such Persons as any of the States now existing shall think proper to admit, shall not be prohibited by the Congress prior to the Year one thousand eight hundred and eight, but a Tax or Duty may be imposed on such Importation, not exceeding ten dollars for each Person.

The Privilege of the Writ of Habeas Corpus shall not be suspended, unless when in Cases of Rebellion or Invasion the public Safety may require it.

No Bill of Attainder or ex post facto Law shall be passed.

No Capitation, or other direct, Tax shall be laid, unless in Proportion to the Census or Enumeration herein before directed to be taken.

No Tax or Duty shall be laid on Articles exported from any State.

No Preference shall be given by any Regulation of Commerce or Revenue to the Ports of one State over those of another: nor shall Vessels bound to, or from, one State, be obliged to enter, clear, or pay Duties in another.

No Money shall be drawn from the Treasury, but in Consequence of Appropriations made by Law, and a regular Statement and Account of the Receipts and Expenditures of all public Money shall be published from time to time.

No Title of Nobility shall be granted by the United States: And no Person holding any Office of Profit or Trust under them, shall, without the Consent of the Congress, accept of any present, Emolument, Office, or Title, of any kind whatever, from any King, Prince, or foreign State.

Section. 10. No State shall enter into any Treaty, Alliance, or Confederation; grant Letters of Marque and Reprisal; coin Money; emit bills of Credit; make any Thing but gold and silver Coin a Tender in Payment of Debts; pass any Bill of Attainder, ex post facto Law, or Law impairing the Obligation of Contracts, or grant any Title of Nobility.

No State shall, without the Consent of the Congress, lay any Imposts or Duties on Imports or Exports, except what may be absolutely necessary for executing its inspection Laws: and the net Produce of all Duties and Imposts, laid by any State on Imports or Exports, shall be for the Use of the Treasury of the United States; and all such Laws shall be subject to the Revision and Controul of the Congress.

No State shall, without the Consent of Congress, lay any Duty of Tonnage, keep Troops or Ships of War in time of peace, enter into any Agreement or Compact with another State, or with a foreign Power, or engage in War, unless actually invaded, or in such imminent Danger as will not admit of delay.

Article. II.

Section. 1. The executive Power shall be vested in a President of the United States of America. He shall hold his Office during the Term of four Years, and, together with the Vice President, chosen for the same Term, be elected, as follows:

Each State shall appoint, in such Manner as the Legislature thereof may direct, a Number of Electors, equal to the whole Number of Senators and Representatives to which the State may be entitled in the Congress: but no Senator or Representative, or Person holding an Office of Trust or Profit under the United States, shall be appointed an Elector.

The Electors shall meet in their respective States, and vote by Ballot for two Persons, of whom one at least shall not be an Inhabitant of the same State with themselves. And they shall make a List of all the Persons voted for, and of the Number of Votes for each; which List they shall sign and certify, and transmit sealed to the Seat of the Government of the United States, directed to the President of the Senate. The President of the Senate shall, in the Presence of the Senate and House of Representatives, open all the Certificates, and the Votes shall then be counted. The Person having the greatest Number of Votes shall be the President, if such Number be a Majority of the whole Number of Electors appointed; and if there be more than one who have such Majority, and have an equal Number of Votes, then the House of Representatives shall immediately chuse by Ballot one of them for President; and if no Person have a Majority, then from the five highest on the List the said House shall in like Manner chuse the President. But in chusing the President, the Votes shall be taken by States, the Representation from each State having one Vote; A quorum for this Purpose shall consist of a Member or Members from two thirds of the States, and a Majority of all the States shall be necessary to a Choice. In every Case, after the Choice of the President, the Person having the greatest Number of Votes of the Electors shall be the Vice President. But if there should remain two or more who have equal Votes, the Senate shall chuse from them by Ballot the Vice President.*

The Congress may determine the Time of chusing the Electors, and the Day on which they shall give their Votes; which Day·shall be the same throughout the United States.

No Person except a natural born Citizen, or a Citizen of the United States, at the time of the Adoption of this Constitution, shall be eligible to the Office of President, neither shall any Person be eligible to that Office who shall not have attained to the Age of thirty five Years, and been fourteen Years a Resident within the United States.

In Case of the Removal of the President from Office, or of his Death, Resignation, or Inability to discharge the Powers and Duties of the said Office, the Same shall devolve on the Vice President, and the Congress may by Law provide for the Case of Removal, Death, Resignation or Inability, both of the President and Vice President, declaring what Officer shall then act as President, and such Officer shall act accordingly, until the Disability be removed, or a President shall be elected.†

The President shall, at stated Times, receive for his Services, a Compensation, which shall neither be encreased nor diminished during the Period for which he shall have been elected, and he shall not receive within that Period any other Emolument from the United States, or any of them.

Before he enter on the Execution of his Office, he shall take the following Oath or Affirmation:—"I do solemnly swear (or affirm) that I will faithfully execute the Office of President of the United States, and will to the best of my Ability, preserve, protect and defend the Constitution of the United States."

Section. 2. The President shall be Commander in Chief of the Army and Navy of the United States, and of the Militia of the several States, when called into the actual Service of the United States; he may require the Opinion, in writing, of the principal Officer in each of the executive Departments, upon any Subject relating to the Duties of their respective Offices, and he shall have Power to grant Reprieves and Pardons for Offences against the United States, except in cases of Impeachment.

He shall have Power, by and with the Advice and Consent of the Senate, to make Treaties, provided two thirds of the Senators present concur; and he shall nominate, and by and with the Advice and Consent of the Senate, shall appoint Ambassadors, other public Ministers and Consuls, Judges of the supreme Court, and all other Officers of the United States, whose Appointments are not herein otherwise provided for, and which shall be established by Law: but the Congress may by Law vest the Appointment of such inferior Officers, as they think proper, in the President alone, in the Courts of Law, or in the Heads of Departments.

The President shall have Power to fill up all Vacancies that may happen during the Recess of the Senate, by granting Commissions which shall expire at the End of their next Session.

Section. 3. He shall from time to time give to the Congress Information of the State of the Union, and recommend to their Consideration such Measures as he shall judge necessary and expedient; he may, on extraordinary Occasions, convene both Houses, or either of them, and in Case of Disagreement between them, with Respect to the Time of Adjournment, he may adjourn them to such Time as he shall think proper; he shall receive Ambassadors and other public Ministers; he shall take Care that the Laws be faithfully executed, and shall Commission all the Officers of the United States.

Section. 4. the President, Vice President and all civil Officers of the United States, shall be removed from Office on Impeachment for, and Conviction of, Treason, Bribery, or other high Crimes and Misdemeanors.

Article. III.

Section. 1. The judicial Power of the United States, shall be vested in one supreme Court, and in such inferior Courts as the Congress may from time to time ordain and establish. The Judges, both of the supreme and inferior Courts, shall hold their Offices during good Behaviour, and shall, at stated Times, receive for their Services, a Compensation, which shall not be diminished during their Continuance in Office.

Section. 2. The judicial Power shall extend to all Cases, in Law and Equity, arising under this Constitution, the Laws of the United States, and Treaties made, or which shall be made, under their Authority;—to all Cases affecting Ambassadors, other public Ministers and Consuls;—to all Cases of admiralty and maritime Jurisdiction;—to Controversies to which the United States shall be a Party;—to Controversies between two or more States;—between a State and Citizens of another State;*—between Citizens of different States,—between Citizens of the same State claiming Lands under Grants of different States, and between a State, or the Citizens thereof, and foreign States, Citizens or Subjects.

---

*Superseded by the Twelfth Amendment.
†Modified by the Twenty-fifth Amendment.

*Modified by the Eleventh Amendment.

In all Cases affecting Ambassadors, other public Ministers and Consuls, and those in which a State shall be Party, the supreme Court shall have original Jurisdiction. In all the other Cases before mentioned, the supreme Court shall have appellate Jurisdiction, both as to Law and Fact, with such Exceptions, and under such Regulations as the Congress shall make.

The Trial of all Crimes, except in Cases of Impeachment, shall be by Jury; and such Trial shall be held in the State where the said Crimes shall have been committed; but when not committed within any State, the trial shall be at such Place or Places as the Congress may by Law have directed. Section. 3. Treason against the United States, shall consist only in levying War against them, or in adhering to their Enemies, giving them Aid and Comfort. No Person shall be convicted of Treason unless on the Testimony of two Witnesses to the same overt Act, or on Confession in open Court.

The Congress shall have Power to declare the Punishment of Treason, but no Attainder of Treason shall work Corruption of Blood, or Forfeiture except during the Life of the Person attainted.

Article. IV.

Section. 1. Full Faith and Credit shall be given in each State to the public Acts, Records, and judicial Proceedings of every other State. And the Congress may by general Laws prescribe the Manner in which such Acts, Records and Proceedings shall be proved, and the Effect thereof.
Section. 2. The Citizens of each State shall be entitled to all Privileges and Immunities of Citizens in the several States.

A Person charged in any State with Treason, Felony, or other Crime, who shall flee from Justice, and be found in another State, shall on Demand of the executive Authority of the State from which he fled, be delivered up, to be removed to the State having Jurisdiction of the Crime.

No Person held to Service or Labour in one State, under the Laws thereof, escaping into another, shall, in Consequence of any Law or Regulation therein, be discharged from such Service or Labour, but shall be delivered up on Claim of the Party to whom such Service or Labour may be due.
Section. 3. New States may be admitted by the Congress into this Union; but no new State shall be formed or erected within the Jurisdiction of any other State, nor any State be formed by the Junction of two or more States, or Parts of States, without the Consent of the Legislatures of the States concerned as well as of the Congress.

The Congress shall have Power to dispose of and make all needful Rules and Regulations respecting the Territory or other Property belonging to the United States; and nothing in this Constitution shall be so construed as to Prejudice any Claims of the Untied States, or of any particular State.
Section. 4. The United States shall guarantee to every State in this Union a Republican Form of Government, and shall protect each of them against Invasion; and on Application of the Legislature, or of the Executive (when the Legislature cannot be convened) against domestic Violence.

Article. V.

The Congress, whenever two thirds of both Houses shall deem it necessary, shall propose Amendments to this Constitution, or, on the Application of the Legislatures of two thirds of the several States, shall call a Convention for proposing Amendments, which, in either Case, shall be valid to all Intents and Purposes, as Part of this Constitution, when ratified by the Legislatures of three fourths of the several States, or by Conventions in three fourths thereof, as the one or the other Mode of Ratification may be proposed by the Congress; Provided that no Amendment which may be made prior to the Year One thousand eight hundred and eight shall in any Manner affect the first and fourth Clauses in the Ninth Section of the first Article; and that no State, without its Consent, shall be deprived of its equal Suffrage in the Senate.

Article. VI.

All Debts contracted and Engagements entered into, before the Adoption of this Constitution, shall be as valid against the United States under this Constitution, as under the Confederation.

This Constitution, and the Laws of the United States which shall be made in Pursuance thereof; and all Treaties made, or which shall be made, under the Authority of the United States, shall be the supreme Law of the Land; and the Judges in every State shall be bound thereby, any Thing in the Constitution or Laws of any State to the Contrary notwithstanding.

The Senators and Representatives before mentioned, and the Members of the several State Legislatures, and all executive and judicial Officers, both of the United States and of the several States, shall be bound by Oath or Affirmation, to support this Constitution; but no religious Test shall ever be required as a Qualification to any Office or public Trust under the United States.

Article. VII.

The Ratification of the Conventions of nine States, shall be sufficient for the Establishment of this Constitution between the States so ratifying the Same.

done in Convention by the Unanimous Consent of the States present the Seventeenth Day of September in the Year of our Lord one thousand seven hundred and Eighty seven and of the Independence of the United States of America the Twelfth. *In witness* whereof We have hereunto subscribed our Names,

Articles in Addition to, and Amendment of, the Constitution of the United States of America, Proposed by Congress, and Ratified by the Legislatures of the Several States, Pursuant to the Fifth Article of the Original Constitution.

Amendment I*

Congress shall make no law respecting an establishment of religion, or prohibiting the free exercise thereof; or abridging the freedom of speech, or of the press; or the right of the people peaceably to assemble, and to petition the Government for a redress of grievances.

Amendment II

A well regulated Militia, being necessary to the security of a free State, the right of the people to keep and bear Arms shall not be infringed.

Amendment III

No Soldier shall, in time of peace, be quartered in any house, without the consent of the Owner, nor in time of war, but in a manner to be prescribed by law.

Amendment IV

The right of the people to be secure in their persons, houses, papers, and effects, against unreasonable searches and seizures, shall not be violated, and no Warrants shall

*The first ten amendments were passed by Congress September 25, 1789. They were ratified by three-fourths of the states December 15, 1791.

issue, but upon probable cause, supported by Oath or affirmation, and particularly describing the place to be searched, and the persons or things to be seized.

Amendment V

No person shall be held to answer for a capital or otherwise infamous crime, unless on a presentment or indictment of a Grand Jury, except in cases arising in the land or naval forces, or in the Militia, when in actual service in time of War or public danger; nor shall any person be subject for the same offence to be twice put in jeopardy of life or limb; nor shall be compelled in any criminal case to be a witness against himself, nor be deprived of life, liberty, or property, without due process of law; nor shall private property be taken for public use, without just compensation.

Amendment VI

In all criminal prosecutions, the accused shall enjoy the right to a speedy and public trial, by an impartial jury of the State and district wherein the crime shall have been committed, which district shall have been previously ascertained by law, and to be informed of the nature and cause of the accusation; to be confronted with the witnesses against him; to have compulsory process for obtaining witnesses in his favor, and to have the Assistance of Counsel for his defence.

Amendment VII

In suits at common law, where the value in controversy shall exceed twenty dollars, the right of trial by jury shall be preserved, and no fact tried by a jury, shall be otherwise reexamined in any Court of the United States, than according to the rules of the common law.

Amendment VIII

Excessive bail shall not be required, nor excessive fines imposed, nor cruel and unusual punishments inflicted.

Amendment IX

The enumeration in the Constitution, of certain rights, shall not be construed to deny or disparage others retained by the people.

Amendment X

The powers not delegated to the United States by the Constitution; nor prohibited by it to the States, are reserved to the States respectively, or to the people.

Amendment XI*

The Judicial power of the United States shall not be construed to extend to any suit in law or equity, commenced or prosecuted against one of the United States by Citizens of another State, or by Citizens or Subjects of any Foreign State.

Amendment XII†

The Electors shall meet in their respective States and vote by ballot for President and Vice-President, one of whom, at least, shall not be an inhabitant of the same State with themselves; they shall name in their ballots the person voted for as President, and in distinct ballots the person voted for as Vice-President, and they shall make distinct lists of all persons voted for as President, and of all persons voted for as Vice-President, and of the number of votes for each, which lists they shall sign and certify, and transmit sealed to the seat of the government of the United States, directed to the President of the Senate;—The President of the Senate shall, in the presence of the Senate and House of Representatives, open all the certificates and the votes shall then be counted;—The person having the greatest number of votes for President, shall be the President, if such number be a majority of the whole number of Electors appointed; and if no person have such majority, then from the persons having the highest numbers not exceeding three on the list of those voted for as President, the House of Representatives shall choose immediately, by ballot, the President. But in choosing the President, the votes shall be taken by states, the representation from each state having one vote; a quorum for this purpose shall consist of a member or members from two-thirds of the states, and a majority of all the states shall be necessary to a choice. And if the House of Representatives shall not choose a President whenever the right of choice shall devolve upon them, before the fourth day of March next following, then the Vice-President shall act as President, as in the case of the death or other constitutional disability of the President.—The person having the greatest number of

votes as Vice-President, shall be the Vice-President, if such number be a majority of the whole number of Electors appointed, and if no person have a majority, then from the two highest numbers on the list, the Senate shall choose the Vice-President; a quorum for the purpose shall consist of two-thirds of the whole number of Senators, and a majority of the whole number shall be necessary to a choice. But no person constitutionally ineligible to the office of President shall be eligible to that of Vice-President of the United States.

Amendment XIII*

Section. 1. Neither slavery nor involuntary servitude, except as a punishment for crime whereof the party shall have been duly convicted, shall exist within the United States, or any place subject to their jurisdiction.
Section. 2. Congress shall have power to enforce this article by appropriate legislation.

Amendment XIV†

Section. 1. All persons born or naturalized in the United States, and subject to the jurisdiction thereof, are citizens of the United States and of the State wherein they reside. No State shall make or enforce any law which shall abridge the privileges or immunities of citizens of the United States; nor shall any State deprive any person of life, liberty, or property, without due process of law; nor deny to any person within its jurisdiction the equal protection of the laws.
Section. 2. Representatives shall be apportioned among the several States according to their respective numbers, counting the whole number of persons in each State, excluding Indians not taxed. But when the right to vote at any election for the choice of electors for President and Vice-President of the United States, Representatives in Congress, the Executive and Judicial officers of a State, or the members of the Legislature thereof, is denied to any of the male inhabitants of such State, being twenty-one years of age, and citizens of the United States, or in any way abridged, except for participation in rebellion, or other crime, the basis of representation therein shall be reduced in the proportion which the number of such male citizens shall bear to the whole number of male citizens twenty-one years of age in such State.
Section. 3. No person shall be a Senator or Representative in Congress, or elector of President and Vice-President, or hold

*Passed March 4, 1794. Ratified January 23, 1795.
†Passed December 9, 1803. Ratified June 15, 1804.

*Passed January 31, 1865. Ratified December 6, 1865.
†Passed June 13, 1866. Ratified July 9, 1868.

any office, civil or military, under the United States, or under any State, who, having previously taken an oath, as a member of Congress, or as an officer of the United States, or as a member of any State legislature, or as an executive or judicial officer of any State, to support the Constitution of the United States, shall have engaged in insurrection or rebellion against the same, or given aid or comfort to the enemies thereof. But Congress may by a vote of two-thirds of each House, remove such disability.

Section. 4. The validity of the public debt of the United States, authorized by law, including debts incurred for payment of pensions and bounties for services in suppressing insurrection or rebellion, shall not be questioned. But neither the United States nor any State shall assume or pay any debt or obligation incurred in aid of insurrection or rebellion against the United States, or any claim for the loss or emancipation of any slave; but all such debts, obligations, and claims shall be held illegal and void.

Section. 5. The Congress shall have the power to enforce, by appropriate legislation, the provisions of this article.

Amendment XV*

Section. 1. The right of citizens of the United States to vote shall not be denied or abridged by the United States or by any State on account of race, color, or previous condition of servitude—

Section. 2. The Congress shall have power to enforce this article by appropriate legislation.

Amendment XVI†

The Congress shall have power to lay and collect taxes on incomes, from whatever source derived, without apportionment among the several States, and without regard to any census or enumeration.

Amendment XVII‡

The Senate of the United States shall be composed of two Senators from each State, elected by the people thereof, for six years; and each Senator shall have one vote. The electors in each State shall have the qualifications requisite for electors of the most numerous branch of the State legislatures.

When vacancies happen in the representation of any State in the Senate, the executive authority of such State shall issue writs of election to fill such vacancies: *Provided,* That the legislature of any State may empower the executive thereof to make temporary appointments until the people fill the vacancies by election as the legislature may direct.

This amendment shall not be so construed as to affect the election or term of any Senator chosen before it becomes valid as part of the Constitution.

Amendment XVIII*

Section. 1. After one year from the ratification of this article the manufacture, sale, or transportation of intoxicating liquors within, the importation thereof into, or the exportation thereof from the United States and all territory subject to the jurisdiction thereof for beverage purposes is hereby prohibited.

Section. 2. The Congress and the several States shall have concurrent power to enforce this article by appropriate legislation.

Section. 3. This article shall be inoperative unless it shall have been ratified as an amendment to the Constitution by the legislatures of the several States, as provided in the Constitution, within seven years from the date of the submission hereof to the States by the Congress.

Amendment XIX†

The right of citizens of the United States to vote shall not be denied or abridged by the United States or by any State on account of sex.

Congress shall have power to enforce this article by appropriate legislation.

Amendment XX‡

Section. 1. The terms of the President and Vice-President shall end at noon on the 20th day of January, and the terms of Senators and Representatives at noon on the 3d day of January, of the years in which such terms would have ended if this article had not been ratified; and the terms of their successors shall then begin.

Section. 2. The Congress shall assemble at least once in every year, and such meeting shall begin at noon on the 3d day of January, unless they shall by law appoint a different day.

*Passed February 26, 1869. Ratified February 2, 1870.
†Passed July 12, 1909. Ratified February 3, 1913.
‡Passed May 13, 1912. Ratified April 8, 1913.

*Passed December 18, 1917. Ratified January 16, 1919.
†Passed June 4, 1919. Ratified August 18, 1920.
‡Passed March 2, 1932. Ratified January 23, 1933.

Section. 3. If, at the time fixed for the beginning of the term of the President, the President elect shall have died, the Vice-President elect shall become President. If a President shall not have been chosen before the time fixed for the beginning of his term, or if the President elect shall have failed to qualify, then the Vice-President elect shall act as President until a President shall have qualified; and the Congress may by law provide for the case wherein neither a President elect nor a Vice-President elect shall have qualified, declaring who shall then act as President, or the manner in which one who is to act shall be selected, and such person shall act accordingly until a President or Vice-President shall have qualified.

Section. 4. The Congress may by law provide for the case of the death of any of the persons from whom the House of Representatives may choose a President whenever the right of choice shall have devolved upon them, and for the case of the death of any of the persons from whom the Senate may choose a Vice-President whenever the right of choice shall have devolved upon them.

Section. 5. Sections 1 and 2 shall take effect on the 15th day of October following the ratification of this article.

Section. 6. This article shall be inoperative unless it shall have been ratified as an amendment to the Constitution by the legislatures of three-fourths of the several States within seven years from the date of its submission.

Amendment XXI*

Section. 1. The eighteenth article of amendment to the Constitution of the United States is hereby repealed.

Section. 2. The transportation or importation into any State, Territory, or possession of the United States for delivery or use therein of intoxicating liquors, in violation of the laws thereof, is hereby prohibited.

Section. 3. This article shall be inoperative unless it shall have been ratified as an amendment of the Constitution by conventions in the several States, as provided in the Constitution, within seven years from the date of the submission hereof to the States by the Congress.

Amendment XXII†

No person shall be elected to the office of the President more than twice, and no person who has held the office of President, or acted as President, for more than two years of a term to which some other person was elected President shall be elected to the office of the President more than once.

But this Article shall not apply to any person holding the office of President when this Article was proposed by the Congress, and shall not prevent any person who may be holding the office of President, or acting as President, during the term within which this Article becomes operative from holding the office of President or acting as President during the remainder of such term.

Amendment XXIII*

Section. 1. The district constituting the seat of Government of the United States shall appoint in such manner as the Congress may direct:

A number of electors of President and Vice President equal to the whole number of Senators and Representatives in Congress to which the District would be entitled if it were a State, but in no event more than the least populous State; they shall be in addition to those appointed by the States, but they shall be considered, for the purposes of the election of President and Vice President, to be electors appointed by the State; and they shall meet in the District and perform such duties as provided by the twelfth article of amendment.

Section. 2. The Congress shall have power to enforce this article by appropriate legislation.

Amendment XXIV†

Section. 1. The right of citizens of the United States to vote in any primary or other election for President or Vice President, or for Senator or Representative in Congress, shall not be denied or abridged by the United States or any State by reason of failure to pay any poll tax or other tax.

Section. 2. The Congress shall have power to enforce this article by appropriate legislation.

Amendment XXV‡

Section. 1. In case of the removal of the President from office or of his death or resignation, the Vice President shall become President.

Section. 2. Whenever there is a vacancy in the office of the Vice President, the President shall nominate a Vice President who shall take office upon confirmation by a majority vote of both Houses of Congress.

Section. 3. Whenever the President transmits to the President pro tempore of the Senate and the Speaker of the House of Representatives his written declaration that he is unable to discharge the powers and duties of his office, and until he transmits to them a written declaration to the contrary, such powers and duties shall be discharged by the Vice President as Acting President.

Section. 4. Whenever the Vice President and a majority of either the principal officers of the executive department or of such other body as Congress may by law provide, transmit to the President pro tempore of the Senate and the Speaker of the House of Representatives their written declaration that the President is unable to discharge the powers and duties of his office, the Vice President shall immediately assume the powers and duties of the office of Acting President.

Thereafter, when the President transmits to the President pro tempore of the Senate and the Speaker of the House of Representatives his written declaration that no inability exists, he shall resume the powers and duties of his office unless the Vice President and a majority of either the principal officers of the executive department or of such other body as Congress may by law provide, transmit within four days to the President pro tempore of the Senate and the Speaker of the House of Representatives their written declaration that the President is unable to discharge the powers and duties of his office. Thereupon Congress shall decide the issue, assembling within forty-eight hours for that purpose if not in session. If the Congress, within twenty-one days after receipt of the latter written declaration, or, if Congress is not in session, within twenty-one days after Congress is required to assemble, determines by two-thirds vote of both Houses that the President is unable to discharge the powers and duties of his office, the Vice President shall continue to discharge the same as Acting President; otherwise, the President shall resume the powers and duties of his office.

Amendment XXVI*

Section. 1. The right of citizens of the United States, who are eighteen years of age or older, to vote shall not be denied or abridged by the United States or by any State on account of age.

Section. 2. The Congress shall have power to enforce this article by appropriate legislation.

*Passed March 23, 1971. Ratified July 5, 1971.

Admission of States

Order of Admission	State	Date of Admission	Order of Admission	State	Date of Admission
1	Delaware	December 7, 1787	26	Michigan	January 26, 1837
2	Pennsylvania	December 12, 1787	27	Florida	March 3, 1845
3	New Jersey	December 18, 1787	28	Texas	December 29, 1845
4	Georgia	January 2, 1788	29	Iowa	December 28, 1846
5	Connecticut	January 9, 1788	30	Wisconsin	May 29, 1848
6	Massachusetts	February 7, 1788	31	California	September 9, 1850
7	Maryland	April 28, 1788	32	Minnesota	May 11, 1858
8	South Carolina	May 23, 1788	33	Oregon	February 14, 1859
9	New Hampshire	June 21, 1788	34	Kansas	January 29, 1861
10	Virginia	June 25, 1788	35	West Virginia	June 20, 1863
11	New York	July 26, 1788	36	Nevada	October 31, 1864
12	North Carolina	November 21, 1789	37	Nebraska	March 1, 1867
13	Rhode Island	May 29, 1790	38	Colorado	August 1, 1876
14	Vermont	March 4, 1791	39	North Dakota	November 2, 1889
15	Kentucky	June 1, 1792	40	South Dakota	November 2, 1889
16	Tennessee	June 1, 1796	41	Montana	November 8, 1889
17	Ohio	March 1, 1803	42	Washington	November 11, 1889
18	Louisiana	April 30, 1812	43	Idaho	July 3, 1890
19	Indiana	December 11, 1816	44	Wyoming	July 10, 1890
20	Mississippi	December 10, 1817	45	Utah	January 4, 1896
21	Illinois	December 3, 1818	46	Oklahoma	November 16, 1907
22	Alabama	December 14, 1819	47	New Mexico	January 6, 1912
23	Maine	March 15, 1820	48	Arizona	February 14, 1912
24	Missouri	August 10, 1821	49	Alaska	January 3, 1959
25	Arkansas	June 15, 1836	50	Hawaii	August 21, 1959

Growth of U.S. Population and Area

Census	Population of United States	Increase over the Preceding Census Number	Percent	Land Area (Sq. Mi.)	Pop. per Sq. Mi.
1790	3,929,214			867,980	4.5
1800	5,308,483	1,379,269	35.1	867,980	6.1
1810	7,239,881	1,931,398	36.4	1,685,865	4.3
1820	9,638,453	2,398,572	33.1	1,753,588	5.5
1830	12,866,020	3,227,567	33.5	1,753,588	7.3
1840	17,069,453	4,203,433	32.7	1,753,588	9.7
1850	23,191,876	6,122,423	35.9	2,944,337	7.9
1860	31,433,321	8,251,445	35.6	2,973,965	10.6
1870	39,818,449	8,375,128	26.6	2,973,965	13.4
1880	50,155,783	10,337,334	26.0	2,973,965	16.9
1890	62,947,714	12,791,931	25.5	2,973,965	21.2
1900	75,994,575	13,046,861	20.7	2,974,159	25.6
1910	91,972,266	15,997,691	21.0	2,973,890	30.9
1920	105,710,620	13,738,354	14.9	2,973,776	35.5
1930	122,775,046	17,064,426	16.1	2,977,128	41.2
1940	131,669,275	8,894,229	7.2	2,977,128	44.2
1950	150,697,361	19,028,086	14.5	2,974,726*	50.7
1960 †	179,323,175	28,625,814	19.0	3,540,911	50.6
1970	203,235,298	23,912,123	13.3	3,536,855	57.5
1980	226,504,825	23,269,527	11.4	3,536,855	64.0

*As measured in 1940; shrinkage offset by increase in water area.
†First year for which figures include Alaska and Hawaii.

Political Party Affiliations in Congress and the Presidency, 1789–1983*

Congress	Year	House Majority Party	House Principal Minority Party	House Other except Vacancies	Senate Majority Party	Senate Principal Minority Party	Senate Other except Vacancies	President and Party
1st	1789–1791	Ad-38	Op-26	—	Ad-17	Op-9	—	F (Washington)
2d	1791–1793	F-37	DR-33	—	F-16	DR-13	—	F (Washington)
3d	1793–1795	DR-57	F-48	—	F-17	DR-13	—	F (Washington)
4th	1795–1797	F-54	DR-52	—	F-19	DR-13	—	F (Washington)
5th	1797–1799	F-58	DR-48	—	F-20	DR-12	—	F (John Adams)
6th	1799–1801	F-64	DR-42	—	F-19	DR-13	—	F (John Adams)
7th	1801–1803	DR-69	F-36	—	DR-18	F-13	—	DR (Jefferson)
8th	1803–1805	DR-102	F-39	—	DR-25	F-9	—	DR (Jefferson)
9th	1805–1807	DR-116	F-25	—	DR-27	F-7	—	DR (Jefferson)
10th	1807–1809	DR-118	F-24	—	DR-28	F-6	—	DR (Jefferson)
11th	1809–1811	DR-94	F-48	—	DR-28	F-6	—	DR (Madison)
12th	1811–1813	DR-108	F-36	—	DR-30	F-6	—	DR (Madison)
13th	1813–1815	DR-112	F-68	—	DR-27	F-9	—	DR (Madison)
14th	1815–1817	DR-117	F-65	—	DR-25	F-11	—	DR (Madison)
15th	1817–1819	DR-141	F-42	—	DR-34	F-10	—	DR (Monroe)
16th	1819–1821	DR-156	F-27	—	DR-35	F-7	—	DR (Monroe)
17th	1821–1823	DR-158	F-25	—	DR-44	F-4	—	DR (Monroe)
18th	1823–1825	DR-187	F-26	—	DR-44	F-4	—	DR (Monroe)
19th	1825–1827	Ad-105	J-97	—	Ad-26	J-20	—	C (J. Q. Adams)
20th	1827–1829	J-119	Ad-94	—	J-28	Ad-20	—	C (J. Q. Adams)
21st	1829–1831	D-139	NR-74	—	D-26	NR-22	—	D (Jackson)
22nd	1831–1833	D-141	NR-58	14	D-25	NR-21	2	D (Jackson)
23rd	1833–1835	D-147	AM-53	60	D-20	NR-20	8	D (Jackson)
24th	1835–1837	D-145	W-98	—	D-27	W-25	—	D (Jackson)
25th	1837–1839	D-108	W-107	24	D-30	W-18	4	D (Van Buren)
26th	1839–1841	D-124	W-118	—	D-28	W-22	—	D (Van Buren)
27th	1841–1843	W-133	D-102	6	W-28	D-22	2	W (Harrison) W (Tyler)
28th	1843–1845	D-142	W-79	1	W-28	D-25	1	W (Tyler)
29th	1845–1847	D-143	W-77	6	D-31	W-25	—	D (Polk)
30th	1847–1849	W-115	D-108	4	D-36	W-21	1	D (Polk)
31st	1849–1851	D-112	W-109	9	D-35	W-25	2	W (Taylor) W (Fillmore)
32d	1851–1853	D-140	W-88	5	D-35	W-24	3	W (Fillmore)
33d	1853–1855	D-159	W-71	4	D-38	W-22	2	D (Pierce)
34th	1855–1857	R-108	D-83	43	D-40	R-15	5	D (Pierce)
35th	1857–1859	D-118	R-92	26	D-36	R-20	8	D (Buchanan)
36th	1859–1861	R-114	D-92	31	D-36	R-26	4	D (Buchanan)
37th	1861–1863	R-105	D-43	30	R-31	D-10	8	R (Lincoln)
38th	1863–1865	R-102	D-75	9	R-36	D-9	5	R (Lincoln)
39th	1865–1867	U-149	D-42	—	U-42	D-10	—	R (Lincoln) R (Johnson)
40th	1867–1869	R-143	D-49	—	R-42	D-11	—	R (Johnson)
41st	1869–1871	R-149	D-63	—	R-56	D-11	—	R (Grant)
42d	1871–1873	R-134	D-104	5	R-52	D-17	5	R (Grant)
43d	1873–1875	R-194	D-92	14	R-49	D-19	5	R (Grant)
44th	1875–1877	D-169	R-109	14	R-45	D-29	2	R (Grant)
45th	1877–1879	D-153	R-140	—	R-39	D-36	1	R (Hayes)

*Letter symbols for political parties. Ad—Administration; AM—Anti-Masonic; C—Coalition; D—Democratic; DR—Democratic-Republican; F—Federalist; J—Jacksonian; NR—National-Republican; Op—Opposition; R—Republican; U—Unionist; W—Whig.

Table continued on page 878

Political Party Affiliations in Congress and the Presidency, 1789–1983* (continued)

Congress	Year	House Majority Party	House Principal Minority Party	House Other except Vacancies	Senate Majority Party	Senate Principal Minority Party	Senate Other except Vacancies	President and Party
46th	1879–1881	D-149	R-130	14	D-42	R-33	1	R (Hayes)
47th	1881–1883	R-147	D-135	11	R-37	D-37	1	R (Garfield)
								R (Arthur)
48th	1883–1885	D-197	R-118	10	R-38	D-36	2	R (Arthur)
49th	1885–1887	D-183	R-140	2	R-43	D-34	—	D (Cleveland)
50th	1887–1889	D-169	R-152	4	R-39	D-37	—	D (Cleveland)
51st	1889–1891	R-166	D-159	—	R-39	D-37	—	R (B. Harrison)
52d	1891–1893	D-235	R-88	9	R-47	D-39	2	R (B. Harrison)
53d	1893–1895	D-218	R-127	11	D-44	R-38	3	D (Cleveland)
54th	1895–1897	R-244	D-105	7	R-43	D-39	6	D (Cleveland)
55th	1897–1899	R-204	D-113	40	R-47	D-34	7	R (McKinley)
56th	1899–1901	R-185	D-163	9	R-53	D-26	8	R (McKinley)
57th	1901–1903	R-197	D-151	9	R-55	D-31	4	R (McKinley)
								R (T. Roosevelt)
58th	1903–1905	R-208	D-178	—	R-57	D-33	—	R (T. Roosevelt)
59th	1905–1907	R-250	D-136	—	R-57	D-33	—	R (T. Roosevelt)
60th	1907–1909	R-222	D-164	—	R-61	D-31	—	R (T. Roosevelt)
61st	1909–1911	R-219	D-172	—	R-61	D-32	—	R (Taft)
62d	1911–1913	D-228	R-161	1	R-51	D-41	—	R (Taft)
63d	1913–1915	D-291	R-127	17	D-51	R-44	1	D (Wilson)
64th	1915–1917	D-230	R-196	9	D-56	R-40	—	D (Wilson)
65th	1917–1919	D-216	R-210	6	D-53	R-42	—	D (Wilson)
66th	1919–1921	R-240	D-190	3	R-49	D-47	—	D (Wilson)
67th	1921–1923	R-301	D-131	1	R-59	D-37	—	R (Harding)
68th	1923–1925	R-225	D-205	5	R-51	D-43	2	R (Coolidge)
69th	1925–1927	R-247	D-183	4	R-56	D-39	1	R (Coolidge)
70th	1927–1929	R-237	D-195	3	R-49	D-46	1	R (Coolidge)
71st	1929–1931	R-267	D-167	1	R-56	D-39	1	R (Hoover)
72d	1931–1933	D-220	R-214	1	R-48	D-47	1	R (Hoover)
73d	1933–1935	D-310	R-117	5	D-60	R-35	1	D (F. Roosevelt)
74th	1935–1937	D-319	R-103	10	D-69	R-25	2	D (F. Roosevelt)
75th	1937–1939	D-331	R-89	13	D-76	R-16	4	D (F. Roosevelt)
76th	1939–1941	D-261	R-164	4	D-69	R-23	4	D (F. Roosevelt)
77th	1941–1943	D-268	R-162	5	D-66	R-28	2	D (F. Roosevelt)
78th	1943–1945	D-218	R-208	4	D-58	R-37	1	D (F. Roosevelt)
79th	1945–1947	D-242	R-190	2	D-56	R-38	1	D (Truman)
80th	1947–1949	R-245	D-188	1	R-51	D-45	—	D (Truman)
81st	1949–1951	D-263	R-171	1	D-54	R-42	—	D (Truman)
82d	1951–1953	D-243	R-199	1	D-49	R-47	—	D (Truman)
83d	1953–1955	R-221	D-211	1	R-48	D-47	1	R (Eisenhower)
84th	1955–1957	D-232	R-203	—	D-48	R-47	1	R (Eisenhower)
85th	1957–1959	D-233	R-200	—	D-49	R-47	—	R (Eisenhower)
86th	1959–1961	D-283	R-153	—	D-64	R-34	—	R (Eisenhower)
87th	1961–1963	D-263	R-174	—	D-65	R-35	—	D (Kennedy)
88th	1963–1965	D-258	R-177	—	D-67	R-33	—	D (Kennedy)
								D (Johnson)
89th	1965–1967	D-295	R-140	—	D-68	R-32	—	D (Johnson)
90th	1967–1969	D-247	R-187	1	D-64	R-36	—	D (Johnson)
91st	1969–1971	D-243	R-192	—	D-58	R-42	—	R (Nixon)
92nd	1971–1973	D-255	R-180	—	D-54	R-44	2	R (Nixon)
93rd	1973–1975	D-242	R-192	1	D-56	R-42	2	R (Nixon, Ford)
94th	1975–1977	D-291	R-144	—	D-61	R-37	2	R (Ford)
95th	1977–1979	D-292	R-143	—	D-61	R-38	1	D (Carter)
96th	1979–1981	D-277	R-158	—	D-58	R-41	1	D (Carter)
97th	1981–1983	D-242	R-192	—	R-54	D-45	1	R (Reagan)
98th	1983–	D-267	R-166	—	R-54	D-46	—	R (Reagan)

Source: U. S. Bureau of the Census, *Historical Statistics of the United States: Colonial Times to the Present*, Department of Commerce, Washington, D.C., 1957.

Presidential Elections, 1789–1980

Year	Voter Participation (Percentage)	Candidates	Parties	Popular Vote	Electoral Vote	Percentage of Popular Vote
1789		GEORGE WASHINGTON	No party designations		69	
		John Adams			34	
		Minor Candidates			35	
1792		GEORGE WASHINGTON	No party designations		132	
		John Adams			77	
		George Clinton			50	
		Minor Candidates			5	
1796		JOHN ADAMS	Federalist		71	
		Thomas Jefferson	Democratic-Republican		68	
		Thomas Pinckney	Federalist		59	
		Aaron Burr	Democratic-Republican		30	
		Minor Candidates			48	
1800		THOMAS JEFFERSON	Democratic-Republican		73	
		Aaron Burr	Democratic-Republican		73	
		John Adams	Federalist		65	
		Charles C. Pinckney	Federalist		64	
		John Jay	Federalist		1	
1804		THOMAS JEFFERSON	Democratic-Republican		162	
		Charles C. Pinckney	Federalist		14	
1808		JAMES MADISON	Democratic-Republican		122	
		Charles C. Pinckney	Federalist		47	
		George Clinton	Democratic-Republican		6	
1812		JAMES MADISON	Democratic Republican		128	
		DeWitt Clinton	Federalist		89	
1816		JAMES MONROE	Democratic-Republican		183	
		Rufus King	Federalist		34	
1820		JAMES MONROE	Democratic-Republican		231	
		John Quincy Adams	Independent Republican		1	
1824	26.9	JOHN QUINCY ADAMS	Democratic-Republican	108,740	84	30.5
		Andrew Jackson	Democratic-Republican	153,544	99	43.1
		William H. Crawford	Democratic-Republican	46,618	41	13.1
		Henry Clay	Democratic-Republican	47,136	37	13.2
1828	57.6	ANDREW JACKSON	Democratic	647,286	178	56.0
		John Quincy Adams	National Republican	508,064	83	44.0
1832	55.4	ANDREW JACKSON	Democratic	687,502	219	55.0
		Henry Clay	National Republican	530,189	49	42.4
		William Wirt	Anti-Masonic	33,108	7	2.6
		John Floyd	National Republican		11	
1836	57.8	MARTIN VAN BUREN	Democratic	765,483	170	50.9
		William H. Harrison	Whig		73	
		Hugh L. White	Whig	739,795	26	49.1
		Daniel Webster	Whig		14	
		W. P. Mangum	Whig		11	
1840	80.2	WILLIAM H. HARRISON	Whig	1,274,624	234	53.1
		Martin Van Buren	Democratic	1,127,781	60	46.9
1844	78.9	JAMES K. POLK	Democratic	1,338,464	170	49.6
		Henry Clay	Whig	1,300,097	105	48.1
		James G. Birney	Liberty	62,300		2.3
1848	72.7	ZACHARY TAYLOR	Whig	1,360,967	163	47.4
		Lewis Cass	Democratic	1,222,342	127	42.5
		Martin Van Buren	Free Soil	291,263		10.1
1852	69.6	FRANKLIN PIERCE	Democratic	1,601,117	254	50.9
		Winfield Scott	Whig	1,385,453	42	44.1
		John P. Hale	Free Soil	155,825		5.0

Candidates receiving less than 1 percent of the popular vote have been omitted. For that reason the percentage of popular vote given for any election year may not total 100 percent.

Before the passage of the Twelfth Amendment in 1804, the Electoral College voted for two presidential candidates; the runner-up became Vice President. Figures are from *Historical Statistics of the United States, Colonial Times to 1957* (1961), pp. 682–83; the U. S. Department of Justice.

Presidential Elections, 1789–1980 (continued)

Year	Voter Participation (Percentage)	Candidates	Parties	Popular Vote	Electoral Vote	Percentage of Popular Vote
1856	78.9	JAMES BUCHANAN	Democratic	1,832,955	174	45.3
		John C. Frémont	Republican	1,339,932	114	33.1
		Millard Fillmore	American	871,731	8	21.6
1860	81.2	ABRAHAM LINCOLN	Republican	1,865,593	180	39.8
		Stephen A. Douglas	Democratic	1,382,713	12	29.5
		John C. Breckinridge	Democratic	848,356	72	18.1
		John Bell	Constitutional Union	592,906	39	12.6
1864	73.8	ABRAHAM LINCOLN	Republican	2,206,938	212	55.0
		George B. McClellan	Democratic	1,803,787	21	45.0
1868	78.1	ULYSSES S. GRANT	Republican	3,013,421	214	52.7
		Horatio Seymour	Democratic	2,706,829	80	47.3
1872	71.3	ULYSSES S. GRANT	Republican	3,596,745	286	55.6
		Horace Greeley	Democratic	2,843,446	*	43.9
1876	81.8	RUTHERFORD B. HAYES	Republican	4,036,572	185	48.0
		Samuel J. Tilden	Democratic	4,284,020	184	51.0
1880	79.4	JAMES A. GARFIELD	Republican	4,453,295	214	48.5
		Winfield S. Hancock	Democratic	4,414,082	155	48.1
		James B. Weaver	Greenback-Labor	308,578		3.4
1884	77.5	GROVER CLEVELAND	Democratic	4,879,507	219	48.5
		James G. Blaine	Republican	4,850,293	182	48.2
		Benjamin F. Butler	Greenback-Labor	175,370		1.8
		John P. St. John	Prohibition	150,369		1.5
1888	79.3	BENJAMIN HARRISON	Republican	5,477,129	233	47.9
		Grover Cleveland	Democratic	5,537,857	168	48.6
		Clinton B. Fisk	Prohibition	249,506		2.2
		Anson J. Streeter	Union Labor	146,935		1.3
1892	74.7	GROVER CLEVELAND	Democratic	5,555,426	277	46.1
		Benjamin Harrison	Republican	5,182,690	145	43.0
		James B. Weaver	People's	1,029,846	22	8.5
		John Bidwell	Prohibition	264,133		2.2
1896	79.3	WILLIAM McKINLEY	Republican	7,102,246	271	51.1
		William J. Bryan	Democratic	6,492,559	176	47.7
1900	73.2	WILLIAM McKINLEY	Republican	7,218,491	292	51.7
		William J. Bryan	Democratic; Populist	6,356,734	155	45.5
		John C. Wooley	Prohibition	208,914		1.5
1904	65.2	THEODORE ROOSEVELT	Republican	7,628,461	336	57.4
		Alton B. Parker	Democratic	5,084,223	140	37.6
		Eugene V. Debs	Socialist	402,283		3.0
		Silas C. Swallow	Prohibition	258,536		1.9
1908	65.4	WILLIAM H. TAFT	Republican	7,675,320	321	51.6
		William J. Bryan	Democratic	6,412,294	162	43.1
		Eugene V. Debs	Socialist	420,793		2.8
		Eugene W. Chafin	Prohibition	253,840		1.7
1912	58.8	WOODROW WILSON	Democratic	6,296,547	435	41.9
		Theodore Roosevelt	Progressive	4,118,571	88	27.4
		William H. Taft	Republican	3,486,720	8	23.2
		Eugene V. Debs	Socialist	900,672		6.0
		Eugene W. Chafin	Prohibition	206,275		1.4

*Greeley died shortly after the election; the electors supporting him then divided their votes among minor candidates.

Candidates receiving less than 1 percent of the popular vote have been omitted. For that reason the percentage of popular vote given for any election year may not total 100 percent.

Presidential Elections, 1789–1980 (continued)

Year	Voter Participation (Percentage)	Candidates	Parties	Popular Vote	Electoral Vote	Percentage of Popular Vote
1916	61.6	WOODROW WILSON	Democratic	9,127,695	277	49.4
		Charles E. Hughes	Republican	8,533,507	254	46.2
		A. L. Benson	Socialist	585,113		3.2
		J. Frank Hanly	Prohibition	220,506		1.2
1920	49.2	WARREN G. HARDING	Republican	16,143,407	404	60.4
		James N. Cox	Democratic	9,130,328	127	34.2
		Eugene V. Debs	Socialist	919,799		3.4
		P. P. Christensen	Farmer-Labor	265,411		1.0
1924	48.9	CALVIN COOLIDGE	Republican	15,718,211	382	54.0
		John W. Davis	Democratic	8,385,283	136	28.8
		Robert M. La Follette	Progressive	4,831,289	13	16.6
1928	56.9	HERBERT C. HOOVER	Republican	21,391,993	444	58.2
		Alfred E. Smith	Democratic	15,016,169	87	40.9
1932	56.9	FRANKLIN D. ROOSEVELT	Democratic	22,809,638	472	57.4
		Herbert C. Hoover	Republican	15,758,901	59	39.7
		Norman Thomas	Socialist	881,951		2.2
1936	61.0	FRANKLIN D. ROOSEVELT	Democratic	27,752,869	523	60.8
		Alfred M. Landon	Republican	16,674,665	8	36.5
		William Lemke	Union	882,479		1.9
1940	62.5	FRANKLIN D. ROOSEVELT	Democratic	27,307,819	449	54.8
		Wendell L. Willkie	Republican	22,321,018	82	44.8
1944	55.9	FRANKLIN D. ROOSEVELT	Democratic	25,606,585	432	53.5
		Thomas E. Dewey	Republican	22,014,745	99	46.0
1948	53.0	HARRY S. TRUMAN	Democratic	24,105,812	303	49.5
		Thomas E. Dewey	Republican	21,970,065	189	45.1
		J. Strom Thurmond	States' Rights	1,169,063	39	2.4
		Henry A. Wallace	Progressive	1,157,172		2.4
1952	63.3	DWIGHT D. EISENHOWER	Republican	33,936,234	442	55.1
		Adlai E. Stevenson	Democratic	27,314,992	89	44.4
1956	60.6	DWIGHT D. EISENHOWER	Republican	35,590,472	457	57.6
		Adlai E. Stevenson	Democratic	26,022,752	73	42.1
1960	64.0	JOHN F. KENNEDY	Democratic	34,227,096	303	49.9
		Richard M. Nixon	Republican	34,108,546	219	49.6
1964	61.7	LYNDON B. JOHNSON	Democratic	43,126,506	486	61.1
		Barry M. Goldwater	Republican	27,176,799	52	38.5
1968	60.6	RICHARD M. NIXON	Republican	31,785,480	301	43.4
		Hubert H. Humphrey	Democratic	31,275,165	191	42.7
		George C. Wallace	American Independent	9,906,473	46	13.5
1972	55.5	RICHARD M. NIXON	Republican	47,169,911	520	60.7
		George S. McGovern	Democratic	29,170,383	17	37.5
1976	54.3	JIMMY CARTER	Democratic	40,827,394	297	50.0
		Gerald R. Ford	Republican	39,145,977	240	47.9
1980	53.2	RONALD W. REAGAN	Republican	43,899,248	489	50.8
		Jimmy Carter	Democratic	35,481,435	49	41.0
		John B. Anderson	Independent	5,719,437		6.6
		Ed Clark	Libertarian	920,859		1.0

Candidates receiving less than 1 percent of the popular vote have been omitted. For that reason the percentage of popular vote given for any election year may not total 100 percent.

Picture Credits

421 Southern Pacific Transportation Company
423 Great Northern Railway
424 Library of Congress
425 Steichen, Edward. *J. Pierpont Morgan*, 1906. Photogravure from *Camera Work*. 8⅛″ × 6¼″. Collection, Museum of Modern Art, New York. Gift of A. Conger Goodyear
426 United States Department of Agriculture

Chapter 28
428–429 HBJ Collection
430 Brown Brothers
431 Special Collections, University of Oregon Library
432 National Museum of American History, Smithsonian Institution
433 Ediphone Company
434 State Historical Society of Wisconsin
436 National Archives
437 Library of Congress
439 Brown Brothers
441 Ralph E. Becker Collection of Political Americana, Smithsonian Institution
443 Brown Brothers

Chapter 29
444–445 *Daughters of Edward Darley Boit* (detail) by John Singer Sargent, American, 1856–1925. Oil on canvas, 87″ × 87″. Gift of Mary Louisa Boit, Florence D. Boit, Jane Hubbard Boit and Julia Overing Boit in memory of their father. Courtesy, Museum of Fine Arts, Boston
446 The Breakers—Preservation Society of Newport County
447 Photo by Byron, March 28, 1903. Byron Collection, Museum of the City of New York
448 Brown Brothers
449 Culver Pictures
450 Photo by Gertrude Kasebier, c. 1903. International Museum of Photography at George Eastman House
451 The Granger Collection
452 Photo by Jacob A. Riis. Riis Collection, Museum of the City of New York
454 Culver Pictures
455 Culver Pictures
456 Museum of the City of New York

Chapter 30
458–459 Photo by Lewis W. Hine, 1909–1913. International Museum of Photography at George Eastman House
460 Photo by Lewis W. Hine, 1910. Library of Congress
461 Photo by Lewis W. Hine, 1909. Library of Congress
462 Brown Brothers
463 Photo by Lewis W. Hine. Library of Congress
464 Photo by Frances Benjamin Johnston, 1895. Brown Brothers
466 The Granger Collection
468 Library of Congress
469 Library of Congress
470 Photo by Jacob A. Riis. Riis Collection, Museum of the City of New York

Chapter 31
474–475 Museum of the City of New York
478 New York Public Library
481 (*left*) Mrs. J. R. Cade. Copy from the University of Texas Institute of Texan Cultures at San Antonio; (*right*) National Archives
483 Culver Pictures
484 Photo by R. F. Turnbull, 1900. Library of Congress
485 Photo by Arnold Genthe. Library of Congress
487 Photo by Byron, 1893. Byron Collection, Museum of the City of New York

488 Photo by Jacob A. Riis, c. 1890. Riis Collection, Museum of the City of New York

Chapter 32
490–491 Photo by Jacob A. Riis, 1888–1889. Riis Collection, Museum of the City of New York
492 Photo by Jacob A. Riis. Riis Collection, Museum of the City of New York
494 Chicago Historical Society
495 *The Bowery at Night* by W. Louis Sontag, Jr. Museum of the City of New York
496 Library of Congress
497 HBJ Collection
498 Photo by Lewis W. Hine, 1910. International Museum of Photography at George Eastman House
499 Science Technical Research Center, New York Public Library
500 Library of Congress
502 Photo by Jacob A. Riis. Riis Collection, Museum of the City of New York
503 Library of Congress
507 Sophia Smith Collection, (Women's History Archive), Smith College, Northampton, MA

Chapter 33
508–509 (*both*) Culver Pictures
512 New-York Historical Society
513 (*both*) Ralph E. Becker Collection of Political Americana, Smithsonian Institution
516 Ewing Galloway
518 Brown Brothers
519 Library of Congress
523 Library of Congress

Chapter 34
524–525 Photo by Erwin Smith, from *Treasures of The Library of Congress* by Charles A. Goodrum. Published, Harry N. Abrams, Inc.
526 Photo by John K. Hillers, 1879. National Archives
528 *Sioux Indians Hunting Buffalo* by George Catlin. Negative no. 325898. Courtesy, American Museum of Natural History
529 New-York Historical Society
530 Bureau of American Ethnology, Smithsonian Institution
531 Library of Congress
532 Library of Congress
533 Western History Collections, University of Oklahoma Library
536 National Archives
538 Nevada Historical Society
540 Photo by Erwin Smith, from *Treasures of The Library of Congress* by Charles A. Goodrum. Published, Harry N. Abrams, Inc.

Chapter 35
542–543 National Archives
545 Photo by Solomon D. Butcher, 1885. Solomon D. Butcher Collection, Nebraska State Historical Society
546 Caterpillar Tractor Company
547 Brown Brothers
548 Kansas State Historical Society
549 New York Public Library Picture Collection
552 Brown Brothers
553 The Granger Collection
554 Brown Brothers
555 Duke University Archives

Chapter 36
556–557 Photo by P. F. Rockett, c. 1899. Library of Congress
558 Library of Congress
559 Library of Congress
560 Library of Congress

563 Library of Congress
565 New-York Historical Society
566 Theodore Roosevelt Association
568 Hawaii State Archives
571 National Archives
573 Keystone Stereograph by B. L. Singley, 1898.
    Library of Congress

Chapter 37
576–577 Brown Brothers
578 *Cliff Dwellers*, 1913, by George Wesley Bellows,
    American, 1882–1925. Los Angeles County
    Museum of Art: Los Angeles County Funds
579 Library of Congress
581 Stanford University Archives
582 *The Gross Clinic* by Thomas Eakins, 1875. From the
    Jefferson Medical College of Thomas Jefferson
    University, Philadelphia
583 Culver Pictures
584 Brown Brothers
585 Culver Pictures
587 (*left*) San Diego Historical Society Title Insurance and
    Trust Collection; (*right*) Photo by Byron, 1896.
    Byron Collection, Museum of the City of
    New York
589 National Baseball Hall of Fame and Museum,
    Cooperstown, NY
590 The Bettmann Archive
592 The Bettmann Archive

Chapter 38
594–595 Brown Brothers
598 Library of Congress
599 Library of Congress
600 Library of Congress
602 HBJ Collection
603 State Historical Society of Wisconsin
605 Tamiment Institute Library, New York University
606 Sophia Smith Collection, (Women's History
    Archive), Smith College, Northhampton, MA
607 Providence Public Library
608 Brown Brothers

Chapter 39
612–613 Library of Congress
614 Culver Pictures
615 Brown Brothers
617 Culver Pictures
618 HBJ Collection
620 Culver Pictures
622 Culver Pictures
623 Brown Brothers
627 Pennsylvania Railroad photo
628 Culver Pictures

Chapter 40
630–631 National Archives
633 Culver Pictures
637 HBJ Collection
638 UPI
640 © 1915 by the New York Times Company. Reprinted
    by permission
642 New York Public Library
643 Navy Department/National Archives
645 Culver Pictures
646 National Archives

Chapter 41
648 National Archives
648–649 Brown Brothers
650 National Archives
651 Library of Congress
653 National Archives
654 National Archives
657 Library of Congress
658 National Archives

660 United States Army Signal Corps photo
662 Library of Congress
664 Tamiment Institute Library, New York University

Chapter 42
666 New-York Historical Society
668 Library of Congress
669 The Granger Collection
672 UPI
674 Chicago Historical Society
675 (*top*) UPI; (*bottom*) Culver Pictures
676 Smithers Collection, Humanities Research Center,
    University of Texas, Austin
677 UPI
678 UPI
681 Brown Brothers

Chapter 43
682–683 Minnesota Historical Society
684 Brown Brothers
685 Culver Pictures
687 Culver Pictures
689 Henry Ford Museum, The Edison Institute
690 Culver Pictures
691 Florida Photographic Collection, Florida State
    Archives
692 Culver Pictures
694 Wide World Photos

Chapter 44
694–697 Photo by Dorothea Lange, 1940. National Archives
698 UPI
700 Photo by Sloan, 1936. Records of the Soil Conser-
    vation Service/National Archives
701 Photo by Berenice Abbott, 1935. Museum of the City
    of New York
702 Wide World Photos
703 Photo by Fred G. Karth. Chicago Historical Society
704 United States Army Signal Corps/National Archives
706 Library of Congress

Chapter 45
708–709 UPI
710 UPI
711 The Bettmann Archive
712 UPI
714 The Bettmann Archive
715 UPI
717 Tennessee Valley Authority
718 FPG/Photo World
720 Culver Pictures
721 Photo by Carl Linde. Wide World Photos
722 Culver Pictures

Chapter 46
724–725 The Bettmann Archive
726 Photo by H. S. Wong. Wide World Photos
728 United States Army photograph
729 (*left*) The Bettmann Archive; (*right*) UPI
730 Culver Pictures
731 Courtesy, Western Mail and Echo Ltd. Wales, United
    Kingdom, TOPIX, London
733 By permission of the Trustees of the Imperial War
    Museum, London
734 United States Army photograph
738 By permission of CBS News
740 Office of War Information/National Archives

Chapter 47
742–743 Black Star
744 UPI
745 Records of the War Relocation Authority/National
    Archives
747 UPI
749 United States Army photograph
751 United States Army photograph

Index

t' Fort nieúw Amsterdam op de Manha